WELLINGTON

Wellington

THE PATH TO VICTORY
1769–1814

RORY MUIR

YALE UNIVERSITY PRESS
NEW HAVEN AND LONDON

Published with assistance from the Annie Burr Lewis Fund

For information about this and other Yale University Press publications, please contact:
U.S. Office: sales.press@yale.edu www.yalebooks.com
Europe Office: sales@yaleup.co.uk www.yalebooks.co.uk

Set in Minion Pro by IDSUK (DataConnection) Ltd
Printed in Great Britain by TJ International Ltd, Padstow, Cornwall

Library of Congress Cataloging-in-Publication Data

Muir, Rory, 1962-
  Wellington / Rory Muir.
    pages cm
    Includes bibliographical references and index.
    ISBN 978–0–300–18665–9 (v. 1: alk. paper) — ISBN 978–0–300–18786–1 (v. 2: alk.
      paper)
    1. Wellington, Arthur Wellesley, Duke of, 1769–1852. 2. Great Britain. Army—History.
    3. Great Britain—History, Military—1789–1820. 4. Generals—Great Britain—
    Biography. 5. Prime ministers—Great Britain—Biography. 6. Great Britain—Politics and
    government—19th century. I. Title.
    DA68.12.W4M85 2013
    941.07092—dc23
    [B]
                                                                                2013018606

A catalogue record for this book is available from the British Library.

10 9 8 7 6 5 4 3 2 1

CONTENTS

List of Illustrations   vii
List of Maps   x
Preface   xi

Prologue   1

Part I: Obscurity and Dependence   3
1 An Unsettled Childhood (1769–88)   5
2 Coming of Age in Ireland (1788–93)   12
3 Love and War (1792–96)   27

Part II: India and Independence   43
4 Arrival in India (1796–98)   45
5 Mornington and the Indian Scene   56
6 Seringapatam (1798–99)   65
7 The Mysore Years (1799–1802)   88
8 The Restoration of the Peshwa (1802–03)   106
9 The Maratha War (1803)   126
10 Farewell to India (1804–05)   150

Part III: War, Politics, Fame and Controversy   167
11 Return to England (September 1805–March 1807)   169
12 Chief Secretary for Ireland (1807)   189

13 Copenhagen (July–September 1807)   208

14 Dublin and Westminster (October 1807–July 1808)   221

15 Vimeiro and Cintra (July–September 1808)   234

16 The Cintra Inquiry (September–December 1808)   264

17 Politics, Scandal and Wellesley's Return to Portugal
(January–April 1809)   283

Part IV: Adversity and Triumph in the Peninsula   299

18 Oporto (April–May 1809)   301

19 Talavera (June–August 1809)   318

20 Misery on the Guadiana (August–December 1809)   345

21 Preparing for the Storm (December 1809–June 1810)   358

22 Busaco (July–September 1810)   377

23 Torres Vedras (October 1810–February 1811)   394

24 The Pursuit of Masséna (February–April 1811)   407

25 Fuentes de Oñoro (April–June 1811)   416

26 Ciudad Rodrigo (July 1811–January 1812)   436

27 Badajoz (February–April 1812)   446

28 Salamanca (April–July 1812)   458

29 Madrid and Burgos (July–November 1812)   478

30 Life at Headquarters   493

31 Vitoria (December 1812–June 1813)   517

32 The Pyrenees (July–September 1813)   537

33 Crossing the Frontier (September–December 1813)   553

34 Toulouse and the End of the War (January–April 1814)   566

Epilogue   590

Online Commentary   592

Digest and Chronology of Wellington's Life and Career to 1814   594

Endnotes   599

Bibliography   675

Index   712

LIST OF ILLUSTRATIONS

1 Silhouette of Arthur Wesley. Courtesy of the Trustees of the Stratfield Saye Preservation Trust.

2 Dangan Castle, Ireland, title page of *The Life and Times of the Late Duke of Wellington* . . . by William Freke Williams (*c.* 1850). Mary Evans Picture Library.

3 Benjamin Burnell (attrib.), *Anne, Countess of Mornington* (*c.* 1831). Courtesy of Brynkinalt Hall.

4 John Downman, *Richard Colley, Lord Mornington, afterwards Marquess Wellesley* (1785). © The Trustees of the British Museum.

5 Walter Robertson (attrib.), *Young Officer of the 76th* (*c.* 1787). Collection of Christopher Bryant.

6 Unknown artist, after Sir Thomas Lawrence, *Catherine Pakenham, Duchess of Wellington* (nineteenth century). Mary Evans Picture Library.

7 James Gillray, *Fatigues of the Campaign in Flanders* (1793). © The Trustees of the British Museum.

8 Arthur William Devis, detail of Lieutenant-General George Harris, in a group portrait of the Lushington and Harris families (*c.* 1802–03). Reproduced by kind permission of the Trustees of the Harris (Belmont) Charity.

9 John Hoppner, *Arthur Wesley, c.* 1795. Courtesy of the Trustees of the Stratfield Saye Preservation Trust.

10 Unknown artist, *Tipu Sultan, Ruler of Mysore* (1792). © The British Library Board.

11 Thomas Hickey, *Purniya, Chief Minister of Mysore* (*c.* 1801). Yale Center for British Art.

12 Laminet, colour aquatint after H. Singleton, *The Assault and Taking of Seringapatam* (1799). Courtesy of the Council of the National Army Museum, London.

13 Jonathan Engleheart, engraving after Abraham Cooper, *Colonel Maxwell's Last Charge at Assaye* (1839). McGill University Napoleon Collection.

14 Thomas Hickey, *Isabella Freese*. Courtesy of the Trustees of the Stratfield Saye Preservation Trust.

15 Henry Collen, after Henry Hoppner Meyer, *Charles Lennox, 4th Duke of Richmond* (1823). Private Collection / Photo © Christie's Images / The Bridgeman Art Library.

16 Robert Home, *Arthur Wellesley, 1st Duke of Wellington* (1804). © Crown copyright: UK Government Art Collection.

17 John Hoppner, *Portrait of Colonel Arthur Wellesley* (1806). Courtesy of the Trustees of the Stratfield Saye Preservation Trust.

18 Richard Cosway, miniature of Arthur Wellesley (1808). Victoria and Albert Museum, London.

19 C.W. Eckersberg, *The Bombardment of Copenhagen* (1807). © Københavns Museum.

20 Henri L'Evéque, *The Landing of the British Army at Mondego Bay, 1808* (*c.* 1808). Courtesy of the Council of the National Army Museum, London.

21 Léon Mauduison, *Jean-Andoche Junot* (c. 1845). Private collection.
22 Unknown artist, *Nicolas Jean-de-Dieu Soult* (1808). Hulton Archive / Stringer, Getty Images.
23 Antoine-Jean Gros, *Napoleon Accepting the Surrender of Madrid, 1808* (1809). akg-images / VISIOARS.
24 George Landmann, *Sir Arthur Wellesley's Quarters, Vimeiro, 21st & 22nd of August, 1808*, from *Historical, Military, and Picturesque Observations on Portugal* (1818), vol. 2, p. 228.
25 John Jackson, *Sir Hew Whitefoord Dalrymple, Lieutenant Governor of Guernsey* (c. 1800). © 2013 Guernsey Museums & Galleries (The States of Guernsey).
26 Unknown artist, after Sir William Beechey, *Frederick, Duke of York* (c. 1800–20). Royal Collection Trust / © Her Majesty Queen Elizabeth II 2013.
27 Charles Williams, *The last harvest or British Threshers makeing French crops* (1808). © The Trustees of the British Museum.
28 George Cruikshank, *Whitlock the second or another tarnish of British valor* (1808). © The Trustees of the British Museum.
29 Sir Thomas Lawrence, *William Wellesley-Pole, later 1st Baron Maryborough and 3rd Earl of Mornington* (c. 1815). Private collection.
30 Cooper, after Birch, *Miss Wilson* (c. 1808–09). Hulton Archive, Getty Images.
31 Edward Hodges Baily, after Joseph Nollekens, marble sculpture bust of the 1st Duke of Wellington (c. 1828–30). © Tate, London 2013.
32 Henry Edridge, drawing of Wellington's children. Courtesy of the Trustees of the Stratfield Saye Preservation Trust.
33 Henry Smith, *Oporto, with the Bridge of Boats* (1813). © The Trustees of the British Museum.
34 Unknown artist, *Fuga de Soult da cidade do Porto* (nineteenth century). Arquivo Histórico Militar, Portugal (PT/AHM/FE/10-A7-PQ-04).
35 Domenico Pellegrini, *Retrato de Lord Wellington* (1809). Museo Nacional de Arte Antiga, photograph by José Pessoa. Direção-Geral do Património Cultural / Arquivo de Documentação Fotográfica (DGPC/ADF).
36 T. Sutherland, aquatint after W. Heath, *The Battle of Talavera* (1815). Courtesy of the Council of the National Army Museum, London.
37 Sir Thomas Lawrence, *Robert Stewart, 2nd Marquess of Londonderry (Lord Castlereagh)* (1809–10). © National Portrait Gallery, London.
38 Sir Thomas Lawrence, *Charles William Vane-Stewart, 3rd Marquess of Londonderry* (1812). © National Portrait Gallery, London.
39 Sir William Beechey, *William Carr Beresford, Viscount Beresford* (1814–15). © National Portrait Gallery, London.
40 François-Pascal-Simon Gérard, *Lord Stuart de Rothesay* (1828–31). The Bettine, Lady Abingdon Collection. Bequeathed by Mrs T.R.P. Hole. Victoria and Albert Museum, London.
41 C. Turner, engraving after Thomas St Clair, *Troops Bevouack'd near the Village of Villa Velha, on the Evening of the 19th of May 1811. Shewing the various occupations of an Emcampment* (1812). Courtesy of the Council of the National Army Museum, London.
42 Denis Dighton, *Portuguese Army, 20th Infantry Regiment* (1812). Royal Collection Trust / © Her Majesty Queen Elizabeth II 2013.
43 Denis Dighton, *Portuguese Army, 4th Caçadores* (1812). Royal Collection Trust / © Her Majesty Queen Elizabeth II 2013.
44 C. Turner, aquatint after Thomas St Clair, *A View of the Sierra de Busaco at St. Antonio de Cantaro, showing the attack by Marshal Reigniers* (1812). Courtesy of the Council of the National Army Museum, London.
45 Sir William Beechey, *Lt. General Sir Thomas Picton* (c. 1815). © English Heritage.
46 Unknown artist, *General Robert Craufurd* (nineteenth century). Private Collection / Ken Welsh / The Bridgeman Art Library.

47 William Robinson, after Sir Thomas Lawrence, *General the Hon. Sir Galbraith Lowry Cole GCB* (1811). © National Trust / Bryan Rutledge.

48 Antoine-Jean Gros, *André Masséna, duc de Rivoli, prince d'Essling, maréchal de France* (1834). © Paris – Musée de l'Armée, Dist. RMN-Grand Palais / image musée de l'Armée.

49 Jean-Baptiste Paulin Guérin, *Auguste-Frédéric-Louis de Viesse de Marmont, duc de Raguse* (1834). © RMN-Grand Palais (Château de Versailles) / Gérard Blot.

50 Unknown artist, *British Light Infantry (95th Rifles)* (n.d.). Private collection.

51 Juan Bauzil, *Arthur Wellesley, 1st Duke of Wellington* (1812–16). © National Portrait Gallery, London.

52 G. Thompson, *A View of the Storming and Taking of Badajoz in Spain on April 6th 1812* (1812). Courtesy of the Council of the National Army Museum, London.

53 Francisco de Goya, *The Duke of Wellington* (1812–14). © The National Gallery, London.

54 Charles Williams, *See the Conquering Hero Comes, sound your trumpet, beat your drums* (1812). © The Trustees of the British Museum.

55 J.A. Atkinson, *Baggage Waggon* (1807). Courtesy of the Council of the National Army Museum, London.

56 J.C. Stadler, aquatint after Charles Hamilton Smith, *Battalion Infantry 6th Regiment and 23rd or Royal Welsh Fusiliers* (1812–15). Courtesy of the Council of the National Army Museum, London.

57 J.C. Stadler, aquatint after Charles Hamilton Smith, *Soldiers of the 1st Regiment of Foot Guards in Marching Order* (1812–15). Courtesy of the Council of the National Army Museum, London.

58 Wellington's dressing case. Apsley House, The Wellington Museum, London, UK / The Bridgeman Art Library.

59 *Pontoon Bridge over the Esla*, in J.H. Stocqueler, *The Life of Field Marshal the Duke of Wellington* (1852–53), vol. 1, p. 236.

60 Denis Dighton, *An Action during the Peninsular War, with riflemen of 95th (Rifle) Regiment acting as snipers* (c. 1810). Courtesy of the Council of the National Army Museum, London.

61 James Walker, after John Augustus Atkinson, *The Battle of Vittoria* (1820). © The Trustees of the British Museum.

62 Charles Williams, *Wellington and Glory, or the Victory of Vittoria* (1813). © The Trustees of the British Museum.

63 Thomas Jones Barker, *Wellington at Sorauren, 27 July 1813* (c. 1853). Courtesy of the Council of the National Army Museum, London.

64 John Heaviside Clark, *Storming the Town and Castle of St. Sebastian in Spain, Sepr. 1813* (1813). © The Trustees of the British Museum.

65 Thomas Heaphy, watercolour study of Wellington (1813). © National Portrait Gallery, London.

66 Anker Smith, engraving after Thomas Heaphy, *Field Marshal the Duke of Wellington Giving Orders to his Generals Previous to a General Action* (1822). © Crown copyright: UK Government Art Collection.

List of Maps

1 The Low Countries, 1794–95.   p. 32
2 India in 1798.   p. 58
3 Mysore in 1799.   p. 72
4 The siege of Seringapatam, April–May 1799.   p. 80
5 Southern and central India, 1803.   p. 115
6 The battle of Assaye, 23 September 1803.   p. 137
7 The Copenhagen expedition, August–September 1807.   p. 213
8 The Vimeiro campaign, August 1808.   p. 242
9 The combat of Roliça, 17 August 1808.   p. 246
10 The battle of Vimeiro, 21 August 1808.   p. 252
11 Spain, Portugal and southern France, 1807–14.   p. 304
12 The Oporto campaign, May 1809.   p. 309
13 The crossing of the Douro, 12 May 1809.   p. 312
14 The Talavera campaign, July 1809.   p. 324
15 The battle of Talavera, 27–28 July 1809.   p. 330
16 Masséna's invasion of Portugal, 1810–11.   p. 381
17 The battle of Busaco, 27 September 1810.   p. 386
18 The battle of Fuentes de Oñoro, 3–5 May 1811.   p. 420
19 The siege of Badajoz, 16 March–6 April 1812.   p. 449
20 Salamanca, Madrid and Burgos, June–November 1812.   p. 464
21 The battle of Salamanca, 22 July 1812.   p. 467
22 The Vitoria campaign, June 1813.   p. 521
23 The battle of Vitoria, 21 June 1813.   p. 525
24 The battles of the Pyrenees, July–August 1813.   p. 538
25 The Toulouse campaign, February–April 1814.   p. 569
26 The battle of Toulouse, 10 April 1814.   p. 579

PREFACE

THE DUKE OF Wellington is one of the most famous figures in British history. He was, arguably, the greatest and most successful of all British generals; and he went on to be a leading figure in British politics for a generation, twice serving as prime minister. Wellington made his name in India as a relatively junior officer, and then led British and allied armies to victory in Portugal and Spain in a succession of campaigns, overcoming not only an aggressive and battle-hardened enemy, but also opposition at home and the scepticism of many of his senior subordinates. Under his care the British army reached a peak of efficiency in 1813, when it was the finest fighting force for its size in the world, and his victories in the Peninsula played a crucial part in the defeat and exile of Napoleon in 1814. The crowning glory of Waterloo followed in 1815, putting a final end to Napoleon's career after his return from Elba. Wellington's triumph raised Britain's international prestige to unprecedented heights, giving her a unique place among the Great Powers, which she retained for the rest of the nineteenth century.

After Waterloo, Wellington used his influence to moderate the peace terms imposed upon France, and, as commander of the Army of Occupation, helped to reconcile France to her defeat. Over subsequent decades he promoted cooperation among the powers, endeavouring to preserve peace and stability and to prevent Europe splitting into rival, ideologically driven, camps. At home he defended the rights of the Crown and the old, balanced constitution in the face of challenges by Whigs and radicals who, under the pretext of broadening the political nation, substantially undermined long-standing checks on the power of the executive. He lost this struggle, and by the time of his death in 1852, his constitutional principles appeared outdated and irrelevant, although he was treasured both as a national hero and a link to a bygone, less enlightened age.

Wellington has not been well served by his biographers. None of the early biographies could match the brilliant achievement of William Napier's *History of the War in the Peninsula and the South of France.* But Napier, while an outstanding military historian, was a passionate radical who vehemently disagreed with Wellington's politics, and who poured unmerited scorn on the Tory governments that had supported him in the face of vigorous opposition from the Whigs and radicals. Sir Charles Oman and Sir John Fortescue, who built on and largely superseded Napier's work at the beginning of the twentieth century, were also military historians, and while they noted his political bias and made some effort to correct the record, they had little interest in the political dimension of Wellington's campaigns. Nor did political historians fill the gap; in the nineteenth century they were mostly concerned with celebrating the 'march of progress' and the triumph of liberalism, while in the twentieth century they generally shifted further to the left and concentrated on the enduring oppression of the proletariat. Even the minority of historians who had some sympathy for the Tory Party were more attracted to 'liberal', 'reforming' and 'progressive' Tories, such as Canning, Peel and Disraeli, than to conservative figures such as Wellington or Liverpool.

Biographers should have prevented this disregard by integrating the stories of the two aspects of Wellington's career: the triumphant general and the Tory politician; and by challenging the assumptions that underpinned the established accounts of domestic politics and foreign policy between 1815 and 1850. But instead, most Victorian biographers accepted the liberal consensus, drew heavily on Napier for the military history, skated quickly over the politics with an air of embarrassment, and concentrated their creative energies on the depiction of Wellington as the exemplar of a certain type of manly virtue: stern, upright, self-denying and imperturbable; cold, reserved and laconic, but – just to keep him human – delighting in the company of children. Later biographers were more realistic, presenting a rounded portrait that did not neglect the flaws in Wellington's character or his private life. But they also concentrated on trivia: the numerous anecdotes about the Duke, and the highly quotable remarks attributed to him, ranging all the way from 'That to be born in a stable does not make a man a horse' to 'Sparrowhawks, Ma'am'. Because this was not balanced by any serious engagement with Wellington's real achievements, as a soldier, an international statesman and a politician, the result was amusing but ultimately disparaging: the great man as comic turn.

The purpose of the present work is to undertake a thorough reassessment of Wellington's entire life, and particularly his public career, from the cradle to the grave. This volume covers the first forty-five years of his life, concluding with the end of the Peninsular War in 1814. A second volume will cover the remaining thirty-eight years until his death in 1852. Studying Wellington's life often means looking beyond the individual to understand the context in which he operated, for a soldier or a politician, however important, is but a single piece in a complex chessboard in which many pieces can be moving at one time. This has led to a biography in which three strands are constantly entwined: Wellington's own actions and perspective; the history of his military campaigns and the political debates in which he was engaged; and the way he was perceived by his contemporaries, or the history of his reputation, which was itself a significant influence on his life and actions.

One significant theme, which recurs in all three strands, is the connection between politics and the war, the army and Parliament. In the early nineteenth century, partly because of the long war with France, military and civil affairs were much more intermingled than they became later in Wellington's life, let alone today. Wellington was at home in both worlds and this undoubtedly contributed to his success, although its significance has been obscured in most later writing about him.

I have been researching subjects closely related to Wellington's life ever since 1984 (when I began work on my doctoral thesis), and I have been working full time on this biography, with a few interruptions, since 1999. Over these years I have received help and encouragement from a great many people, including many whom I have never met in person but who have responded to my queries with kindness and generosity. I must begin by thanking the University of Adelaide, where I have been a Visiting Research Fellow in the School of History and Politics since 1996; and the staff of the Barr Smith Library (and in particular Margaret Hosking), who have greatly facilitated my research. Back in 1990–91, a postdoctoral George Murray Scholarship from the University of Adelaide enabled me to spend a year in England, based at the University of Southampton, researching the period 1807–15 in the Wellington Papers and in other archives in Britain and Ireland. This research has proved immensely useful in writing the second half of the current volume. In 2000 I received a Hartley Fellowship from the Hartley Institute of the University of Southampton, which allowed me to spend a month working on the Wellington Papers for the period before 1807, and in particular the Indian years. I am deeply grateful for both these grants and for the less formal help and assistance I have received from both universities. My work on the Wellington Papers has been made much more enjoyable and rewarding by the pleasantness, efficiency and learning of the staff in the Special Collections of the Hartley Library, and without their painstaking work in making the papers available this book could hardly have been written. Professor Christopher Woolgar has been both a good friend and an unfailing source of advice and assistance, while his articles on Wellington's methods of business have opened new and rewarding approaches to the subject. Karen Robson's fine schol-arly work on patronage proved very helpful especially when I came to write the chapter on Wellington as Chief Secretary for Ireland, while her assistance on my visits to the archives, and with queries in between visits, has been greatly appreci-ated. I would also like to thank all the other staff at Southampton who have helped me in visits over many years especially Sarah Maspero, Pearl Romans, Mary Cockerill, Sabrina Harder, Emily Rawlings, Gwennyth McLay and Janet Giles.

The University of Southampton has also organised successive Wellington Congresses where I have heard a great many interesting and revealing papers and had many enjoyable discussions with others working in the field, including Andrew Lambert, Peter Jupp, Bruce Collins, Greg Roberts, Richard Gaunt, Mark Romans, Alan Forrest, Christine Wright, Mark Gerges, Nicholas Dunne-Lynch, Kathryn Beresford, Ruscombe Foster, Susan Jenkins and John Severn. It was at the Wellington Congress in 2006 that I met both Julia Page and Mark Thompson, and I have corresponded with them on many subjects connected with the Royal Engineers ever since, benefitting greatly from the generosity with which they have shared the results of their meticulous research as well as from their friendship.

I would like to thank the Trustees of the Wellington Estate for permission to use the Hoppner portrait of Wellington on the dust jacket of this book and several other illustrations from their collection. Jane Branfield, the archivist at Stratfield Saye, has very kindly answered my queries. A new and most welcome edition of the *Iconography* of the Duke of Wellington, entitled *Wellington Portrayed*, is to be published by Unicorn Press Ltd (www.unicornpress.org).

Christopher Bryant has most generously given me permission to reproduce his recent discovery: a *c.* 1787 miniature of an officer of the 76th which he persuasively argues is a portrait of the young Arthur Wesley.

The staff at many archives, libraries and other institutions have been immensely helpful, either when I visited in person or responding to letters and email messages. In particular I should like to thank Alastair Massie, of the National Army Museum; Susan Hood, Assistant Archivist at the RCB Library, Dublin, who verified the baptismal register showing the date of Wellington's christening; Colin Gibson of the Gwent Archives, who supplied me with a copy of Pole's letter to Arthur Wellesley of 22 August 1809 at short notice in 2012; Anne Mitchell and Andrew Mitchell from Woburn, for supplying me with copies of correspondence about Lord William Russell at Talavera, and Eimear Walsh, of the National Library of Ireland, who helped me pursue a supposed visit of Wellington to Ireland in the summer of 1806.

At a 2009 conference, 'Reworking the Regency', at the University of Melbourne I met Neil Ramsey, Karen Downing and Eleanor Morecroft: their conversation at the time, subsequent correspondence and their work has been rewarding and full of interest. Charles Fremantle and Gareth Glover were exceptionally generous in letting me see the typescript of their edition of the letters of John Fremantle (one of Wellington's ADCs) before it was published as *Wellington's Voice*. Anthony Gray has shared his research on the Portuguese side of the war, and particularly the invasion of 1810, as well as his enthusiasm for the subject; while John Brewster gave me a copy of his transcript of the 1809 diary and correspondence of Major-General John Randoll Mackenzie in Portugal and Spain. Robin Thomas kindly answered my queries about the 1794–95 campaign in the Low Countries, and Arthur Murchison was very helpful about his ancestor Roderick Murchison who landed at Mondego Bay on the same day as Wellington in 1808. I am also grateful to Tim Rooth for sending me a transcript of the unpublished journal of Henry Smith, 1809, located in the University of Kansas Library, and to Stephen Wood for a stimulating correspondence about Dalrymple's role in the Convention of Cintra which led me to look at this old question afresh. I had a most interesting correspondence with Dr C.I. Hamilton relating to his work on J.W. Croker and questions of patronage; John Cookson gave me helpful advice at an early stage of my research, and I have had much correspondence and a number of enjoyable meetings with Huw Davies which have been made all the more rewarding because our views of Wellington are not in complete alignment.

The online Napoleon Series, and especially its discussion forum, has proved an immensely useful resource and point of contact with other people who share an interest in the period, and in Wellington's campaigns. Like others, I owe a great debt to Bob Burnham for the endless hours of toil that lie behind the smooth functioning of the website, while I have also had much enjoyable correspondence with him directly. Among many others whom I met through the forum, I cannot help but mention Tom Holmberg, Caroline Miley, Steven Smith, John Cook, João Centeno, Paul Charnley, John Grodzinski, Robert Markley, Michael A. Taenzer, Jonathan North and Rod MacArthur. Unfortunately the urgent pressure to finish the present work and the progess of the narrative beyond the end of the war in 1815 have restricted my presence on the forum in recent years.

One of the pleasures of historical research is the exchange of information, news and opinion with others working in the same or related fields and, as well as those mentioned above, I would particularly like to acknowledge all the friendly help and encouragement I have received in this way from Giles Hunt, John Houlding, Ian Robertson, Neville Thompson, Conrad Kent, Philip Dwyer, Don Graves, Bernabé Saiz Martíen de Pisón, Christopher Bryant and Mark Urban. John Malcolm has frequently come to my assistance with details of the great and long-lasting friendship between Wellington and his ancestor and namesake, and on many other aspects of Wellington's years in India. David Elder talked knowledgeably to my parents about Colonel Light and his service under Wellington in the Peninsula when I was still a baby, and, when, quite coincidentally, my interest in the subject developed, he was full of enthusiasm and useful advice. And although I never met S.G.P. Ward, I had a most enjoyable and rewarding correspondence with him over a number of years, which gave me even more reason to admire the depth of his scholarship and the sharpness of his insight into the workings of the Peninsular army.

Although I had often thought of undertaking a life of Wellington the final impulse to do so came from a conversation with Dr Robert Baldock of Yale University Press in 1999. While the journey has been even longer and more arduous than I anticipated, I am nonetheless grateful to him, and for his unswerving faith in the project. Heather McCallum and Rachael Lonsdale have given painstaking attention to the manuscript, constantly striving to bring Wellington to the forefront of the narrative, and I am very grateful to Jonathan Asbury for the skill, tact and dedication he brought to the editing process. My agent, Bill Hamilton of A.M. Heath, has been an excellent source of advice whenever the project encountered difficulties. And although unconnected with Yale, this is also the appropriate place to thank Dr Penelope Eate of the University of Adelaide for her meticulous and efficient work on the manuscript which saved me many hours of labour and so made its completion possible.

Three good friends have watched over this project from its inception to the completion of this volume, answering my often unreasonable queries and listening to my discoveries and pet theories indulgently but not uncritically. I first met Charles Esdaile at Southampton in 1986 when we were both just beginning our lives as historians with a strong interest in Wellington, and in all the years since he has been unfailingly generous, knowledgeable and helpful. The other two I have never met in the flesh, but we have corresponded, sometimes daily, for many years and have even collaborated on a book of essays. Ron McGuigan's knowledge of biographical sources relating to officers of Wellington's army is astonishing, and his fascination with the way their careers intersected yields many rich and unexpected insights and information. Howie Muir's unwavering enthusiasm, reluctance to accept historical clichés and determination to go back to the original sources and build on them is inspiring, while his wit, good humour and zest have always enlivened our correspondence.

Finally I must thank three women whose influence on my life and work is boundless. My mother, Marcie Muir, died in late 2007 when the first draft of this volume had already been written. She inspired my love of history and commitment to scholarship, and thoroughly understood the unique mixture of pleasure and frustration that comes with research and writing. My sister, Kathie Muir, has been a constant source of support and encouragement over all the years this work has taken, and while our intellectual approach and fields differ widely, she has been a formative influence on my thinking. And so I come to thank, however inadequately, my beloved wife, Robin Muir, who met me when this book had already preoccupied me for a decade, and who has shared all the delights and disappointments that it has brought with it since then with love, patience, a fresh perspective and a great commitment to good writing and fine design. Unlike Arthur Wellesley I found my true companion, and I count myself fortunate indeed.

PROLOGUE

I T WAS A cold day a few weeks before Christmas 1808 and Sir Arthur Wellesley was walking through the grounds of Chelsea Hospital when he overheard a bystander say: 'What business has he to wear his sword!' The remark stung, but it did not come as a surprise. Ever since he had landed at Plymouth in early October he had been hissed at and abused by the crowd; newspapers of all political complexions had denounced him; *The Times* repeatedly questioned his honesty and his honour; and public meetings all across the country had called for an inquiry into his conduct, although many of the speakers had clearly already made up their minds. As usual the cartoonists had reflected and inflamed the public mood, with prints depicting him kneeling before a French general, or being hanged from a British gibbet. Yet only a few months before, in August, he had led a British army to victory over the French in two battles in less than a week at Roliça and Vimeiro in Portugal. News of these victories had made him the darling of the country and excited public expectations of more easy triumphs, the capture of Lisbon and the complete surrender of Junot's army. The disappointment was all the greater when news finally arrived of the Convention of Cintra by which Wellesley, and the two senior officers who had superseded him immediately after Vimeiro, not only agreed to let the French go home, but promised to send them there in British ships, complete with their weapons, and with no restriction on their resuming the war. It was this that triggered the outcry and forced the government to order an official inquiry, which was held at Chelsea in November and December 1808.

Sir Arthur Wellesley knew that his career was at stake. Earlier that year another unfortunate general, John Whitelocke, had been subjected to similar obloquy and had been cashiered from the army, destined to spend the rest of his life in provincial obscurity. If Wellesley's evidence failed to convince the Court of Inquiry, or if the ministers in the government lost faith in him, he might never be given a chance to redeem his reputation or take the field again.

But unlike Whitelocke, Wellesley was well known in Parliament as well as in the army, and while this added venom to some of the attacks on him, it also meant that many senior politicians, including important members of the Cabinet, knew him personally and admired his ability. So long as the Inquiry did not deliver a damning verdict they would not cast him aside, but would take a political gamble and give him another command. He was not, in the usual sense of the phrase, 'a political soldier', but both politics and the army were intimately entwined throughout his career, from the very beginning until the end. He was a Member of Parliament before he saw a shot fired in anger; held a senior political office even when he commanded the army at Vimeiro; and when he died he was both Commander-in-Chief of the army and an elder statesman of the Conservative Party in the House of Lords. The interplay between the two sides of his career was never simple; it hindered as well as helped his success, prejudicing many people against as well as in favour of him, both as a soldier and as a politician, but it was an essential part of his life.

Familiarity has made the story of Wellington's rise and triumphs appear too easy, almost inevitable, and has obscured the many moments at which his career was in jeopardy. We are too comfortable with the Victorian image of the 'Iron Duke'; the national hero 'retained for life' in the service of the Crown; the cold haughty aristocrat; and even the anecdote-encrusted, semi-comical figure of 'Atty, the long nosed bugger what beats the French'. There is a grain of truth in all of these, but they have become clichés, concealing more than they reveal and distracting us from the much richer, more complex and interesting figure of the man who eventually, after many vicissitudes and changes of fortune, became the Duke of Wellington.

PART I

OBSCURITY AND DEPENDENCE

CHAPTER ONE

AN UNSETTLED CHILDHOOD
(1769–88)

IN LATER LIFE the Duke of Wellington came to be regarded as the embodiment of aristocratic privilege, but this reflected his part in the politics of the 1830s rather than his own upbringing. As the younger son of an Irish peer he was clearly not among the under-privileged in eighteenth-century society, but even so his early life was marked more by obscurity and dependence than wealth and deference.

This obscurity extends even to his date of birth. His family always maintained that he had been born on 1 May 1769, his father giving this date to the Office of Arms as early as 1779. However two independent contemporary sources suggest that he was born a little earlier: the baptismal register of St Peter's Anglican Church, Dublin, records that he was baptised on 30 April, and a newspaper published a few days later states that he was born on 29 April. It seems unlikely that they are both mistaken.[1]

His family had been in Ireland since the reign of Queen Elizabeth, but had only begun to rise to prominence in 1728 when Richard Colley (his grandfather) had inherited considerable estates from his cousin and adopted their surname of Wesley (which was also spelt Wellesley). In 1746 Richard was elevated to the Irish peerage as Lord Mornington and spent vast sums creating a magnificent pleasure garden at Dangan Castle. When he died in 1758 his title and estates passed to his only surviving son, Garret Wesley, Wellington's father.[2] Garret Wesley was passionately fond of music, and was himself a composer and a talented performer on the violin and harpsichord. In 1764 he graduated as a doctor of music and shortly afterwards he was appointed first professor of music at the University of Dublin. He was also the leading spirit in organising aristocratic musical events, often on the pretext of raising money for charity. Possibly because of this, he preferred town to country life; he appears to have neglected the gardens at Dangan, and, in 1769, he leased an imposing mansion in Merrion Street – the most fashionable address in Dublin. He does not seem to have played any prominent part in politics, and yet, on 26 August 1760, he was elevated two steps in the peerage, becoming Viscount Wellesley of Dangan Castle and Earl of Mornington.[3] He had married, on 6 February 1759, Anne Hill, the daughter of Arthur Hill, who in 1766 was created first Viscount Dungannon. Anne's uncle was a prominent and successful politician who rose to become Marquess of Downshire and played an important part in Lord North's government. It is possible that Garret Wesley owed his elevation in the peerage to Downshire's influence.

Lord and Lady Mornington had nine children between 1760 and 1773, of whom two died young and a third as a young adult. Five sons and one daughter remained, and four of the five sons received peerages in their own right. The children were (using the later, more familiar, spelling of their surname):

Richard Colley Wellesley, born 20 June 1760, who bore the courtesy title of Viscount Wellesley from October 1760 until he inherited his father's titles in 1781;

Arthur Gerald Wellesley, named after his maternal grandfather, who died, aged six or seven, in 1768;

William Wellesley, born 20 May 1763, who was adopted as his heir by his cousin, William Pole, and inherited his estates in Queen's County in 1781, adding Pole to his name. Created Baron Maryborough, 17 July 1821;

Francis Wellesley, who died aged three on 10 March 1770;

Anne Wellesley, born 13 March 1768, who married the Hon. Henry Fitzroy (fourth son of Lord Southampton) on 4 January 1790. He died of consumption in Portugal in 1793 or early 1794, and on 9 August 1799 she married Charles Culling Smith, who served as under secretary at the Foreign Office when Lord Wellesley was Foreign Secretary (1809–12), but whose career was otherwise undistinguished;

Arthur Wellesley, born 1769, the future Duke of Wellington;

Gerald Valerian Wellesley, born 7 December 1770, who went into the Church, became Prebendary of Durham and would have risen higher if it had not been for the unhappy state of his marriage to Lady Emily Cadogan;

Mary, 1772–94;

Henry, born 20 January 1773, who became a diplomat and was created first Baron Cowley on 28 January 1828.

The Wesley children did not grow up together; Richard was sent to Eton when Arthur was only three, and before Henry was even born, and for much of their childhood they were widely dispersed, with Anne apparently spending much of her time with her maternal grandmother Lady Dungannon. Nonetheless, close bonds of loyalty and affection mixed with sibling rivalry bound them together. For more than thirty years Richard was the undisputed leader of the pack, seeking places and preferment for Arthur and his other brothers, and expecting loyalty, obedience and submission in return. Secure in his own superiority, he patronised them insufferably, and it was not for many years that they began to wonder if his assumption of superiority was really justified. Eventually the family ties loosened as the surviving brothers and sister made places for themselves in the world, married and established other connections. But throughout life it remained one of the most important networks in their lives; when friendships, affairs and working alliances faded or atrophied, brothers remained brothers, inescapable and infuriating though they were.

Surprisingly little is known about Wellington's childhood, mainly because he seldom talked about it in later life. Only his first seven years were spent in Ireland, for by 1776 Lord Mornington had moved his family to London. The young Arthur attended the Diocesan school at Trim, and in London he was sent to Brown's Seminary, King's Road, Chelsea. Nothing more is known of his early education, but there is some evidence that his health was poor, while G.R. Gleig (an early biographer who knew the Duke in later life) formed the impression that he was 'a dreamy, idle and shy lad'.[4]

On 22 May 1781 Lord Mornington died at Chelsea, aged only forty-five. We know nothing about Arthur's reaction to his father's death, but it must have contributed to the disruption of a childhood that was already unsettled and short of emotional support. Arthur's brother Richard, still a few weeks short of his twenty-first birthday, became head of the family, although Lady Mornington naturally retained the dominant voice in the affairs of her younger children. Lady Mornington was not yet forty, a strong-willed, rather hard woman who appears to have felt little affection for her son Arthur, although the evidence for this is necessarily fragmentary. Later, her correspondence with her younger children was far from intimate; in 1801, when Arthur had been out of England for five years, Henry apologised for opening a newly arrived letter from their mother to Arthur saying: 'If the enclosed letter had been from any person but my Mother I certainly should not have opened it, but I know that her letters never contain anything which might not be published at Charing Cross, & I was anxious to know something about her health.'[5]

A few months after his father died, Arthur Wesley, accompanied by his younger brother Gerald, was sent to Eton. Richard Wesley had shone there, establishing a reputation as a fine classical scholar and acquiring such an abiding love of the school that when he died in 1842 he was buried in the college's chapel. William Wesley also went to Eton and performed creditably although without rivalling Richard's triumph. Arthur failed miserably. He was a pupil there from 1781–84 and thereafter seldom returned, and never spoke of it with affection. He did not attribute the victory of Waterloo to its playing fields (that quip was invented by the French journalist and politician the Comte de Montalembert after Wellington's death), and on one occasion even refused to make a token contribution to its building fund.[6] He won a schoolboy fight with Robert 'Bobus' Smith, and is said to have been flogged for his share in a disturbance, while a contemporary recalled that he was 'not at all a Book boy, and rather dull'.[7] He was, almost certainly, miserable, displayed no academic aptitude, and made no lasting friends. Years later, in 1817, his mother related that Arthur 'was so poor a scholar, so inept and so unwilling, that the masters of Eton advised her (she had early been left a widow with the care of that numerous family) to take him from that school'.[8]

The only glimmer of light to emerge from these years concerns his holidays, which were partly spent with his grandmother Lady Dungannon at Brynkinalt in northern Wales. Here a fight with the son of the local blacksmith, Hughes by name, in which Arthur Wesley was soundly thrashed, established the basis of a friendship. In later years Hughes delighted in recalling 'that Master Wesley bore him not a pin's worth of ill will for the beating, but made him his companion in many wild a ramble'.[9] Few things in Wesley's childhood sound as attractive as wild rambles through the Welsh hills with a local friend.

Wesley was withdrawn from Eton at the end of the school year in 1784, and sent to study with a tutor, the Rev. Henry Michell, at Brighton for a few months. Evidently the experiment was a success, for years later Wesley employed Michell's grandson, the Rev. Henry Michell Wagner, as tutor to his own sons.[10] But, like so much else in Wesley's childhood, it was not to last; Lady Mornington decided to spend 1785 in Brussels, apparently for the sake of economy. Arthur accompanied her, together with John Armytage, the second son of a Yorkshire baronet who had been a friend of the late Lord Mornington, and who had also died recently. The two boys – Arthur turned sixteen that year, and Armytage was a few months older – studied under a French lawyer, M. Louis Foubert. According to G.R. Gleig, 'They were neither of them much given to hard work, but they mixed in the gaieties of the place', while Armytage's own account, on which Gleig draws, states that 'Arthur Wesley was extremely fond of music, and played well upon the fiddle, but he never gave indication of any other species of talent'.[11] In 1815 Wellington was delighted to find that M. Foubert was still alive, and placed a guard on his house to ensure that he was not disturbed by the soldiery. He appears to have met Armytage only once in later life, at the Doncaster races in 1827. After their year in Brussels, Armytage took up his commission as a cornet in the Royal Horse Guards, and stayed in the army for a few years until he married an heiress. This enabled him to live the life of a country gentleman near Northampton where he hunted, shot and patronised the turf. But his greatest pleasure was in driving the mail-coach from Northampton to Barnet and back again, almost every day. (He was not alone in this; many wealthy men acted as unofficial, amateur coachmen in these years, when the turnpikes had improved the roads and skill at driving 'four-in-hand' was something of which to boast.) He had no regrets, telling Wellington: 'Yours has been the more glorious career of the two, but mine I suspect has not been the least agreeable.'[12] He may well have been right, and perhaps, if life had treated the young Arthur Wesley equally generously, he too might have been happy to settle for a life of country sports and coach-driving. It seems unlikely, but his character was still unformed, and there was no sign as yet of the appetite for hard work and incessant activity that was to become so pronounced in him a few years later.

Lady Mornington later acknowledged that Arthur 'was always good-natured, frank [and] popular', but she was annoyed that at Brussels 'he continued incapable, from idleness and want of any disposition to apply, of redeeming his character in point of scholarship'.[13] Her daughter-in-law (William's wife Katherine) recalled her saying: 'I vow to God, I don't know what I shall do with my awkward son Arthur.' Her conclusion was that he was 'food for powder, and nothing more'; and so the decision was made to send Arthur Wesley into the army.[14] It was not his choice and, if John Armytage can be believed, 'his own wishes, if he had any, were in favour of a civilian's life'.[15] But as yet he had no control over his own destiny, and towards the end of 1785 his brother Richard, Lord Mornington, approached the Lord Lieutenant of Ireland, the Duke of Rutland, seeking a commission for Arthur.[16]

Richard Wesley was a success. His brilliant career at Eton had been followed by an equally brilliant career at Christ Church. He had won the Chancellor's Prize for a Latin ode on the death of Captain Cook, and he had made a number of friendships with rising young men, none closer or more important than that with William Grenville, brother of the Marquess of Buckingham and cousin of William Pitt the Younger. By 1785 Pitt was already Prime Minister (aged twenty-six, one year older than Mornington), and Grenville was a junior but influential minister. Mornington now counted both as close friends and was clearly marked as a coming man; he was a member of the British House of Commons, as well as the Irish House of Lords, and exuded talent and self-confidence. Securing a junior commission in an unfashionable regiment would usually have presented little difficulty to so well-connected a figure, but the American War had left a considerable backlog of deserving cases, while Mornington was never particularly good at turning his ability and connections into concrete advantages. Rutland evaded his repeated requests with practised dexterity, and Arthur Wesley remained a civilian for another sixteen months.[17]

Lady Mornington was returning to Britain after her year in Brussels, and saw little point taking Arthur home with her. With no place for him in the British army an alternative had to be found, and one soon presented itself: he would spend a year or two at the Royal Academy of Equitation at Angers in Anjou. There his manners and his French would be polished, and he would learn some of the basics of being an officer. There was nothing odd in a young Englishman (or Irishman, for that matter) completing his education at a French military school in 1786; there were a number of British students, and the Academy was by no means wholly military in character. According to the later recollections of another student, General Sir Alexander Mackenzie of Fairbairn, Arthur Wesley 'was ailing and sickly' while at Angers, 'too much so to take much part in the bodily exercises, riding, fencing, etc, which, I believe, were the principal part of the instructions at this school. He passed most of the time on a sofa, playing with a white terrier'. The dog's name was Vick, and it 'followed him everywhere', but unfortunately we know nothing more of it; not even whether Wesley was able to take it home with him when he left France.[18] However we do know that while Wesley may have neglected his studies, he was introduced into local society and attended dinners given by the Duc de Brissac – where he was scandalised to observe that the host was given better food and wine than his guests.[19] Despite this disillusioning experience, he developed a deep respect for the *ancien régime* in France which was to prove important in later life. He was well treated by the commandant of the Academy, the Duc de Sérent, and his wife; and in 1815, in Paris, greeted the Duchesse with reverence, telling Lady Shelley that it was in her 'society he had passed the happiest part of his life, and to whose matronly kindness he owed more gratitude than he could ever repay'.[20]

Arthur Wesley returned to England at the beginning of November 1787, when he was eighteen and a half years old. His mother was delighted with the transformation in his appearance and manner, although her praise was characteristically barbed: 'I do believe there is my ugly boy Arthur', for his hair was fashionably powdered and his cheeks bright. She told her mother's friends, the celebrated Ladies of Llangollen: 'He really is a charming young man, never did I see such a change for the better in anybody'.[21] By then his immediate future had been settled, and he had been an officer in the army for more than seven months. Mornington had obtained Wesley's first commission, as an ensign in the 73rd Foot, from Sir George Yonge, the Secretary at War, in the spring. The 73rd were then serving in India, and Mornington also obtained extended leave for his brother to pursue his studies at Angers.

Even before Arthur returned from France, Mornington was seeking to have him promoted and exchanged into another regiment, and on Christmas Day 1787 Arthur Wesley was gazetted lieutenant in the 76th Foot.[22] Less than a month later he transferred to the 41st Foot, and in June 1789 he became an officer of the 12th Light Dragoons. Having been an ensign, nominally at least, for nine months, he spent three and a half years as a lieutenant before becoming a captain (in the 58th Foot) on 30 June 1791, at the age of twenty-two. He was a captain for rather less than two years, and a major for only five months, but by then the war with France had broken out, and meteoric promotions were common as the army rapidly expanded.

Family influence ensured that Wesley's horizons were not limited to the confines of a regimental mess in peacetime. Mornington used his influence with the Marquess of Buckingham, the newly appointed Lord Lieutenant of Ireland, to make Arthur one of his numerous aides-de-camp. Lady Mornington now felt quite kindly towards Arthur, and told the Ladies of Llangollen: 'He is wonderfully lucky, in six months he has got two steps in the army and appointed Aid [*sic*] De Camp to Lord Buckingham which is ten shillings a day.' And, a few weeks later: 'I have so much to get settled for Arthur, that I am sure it will not be done in time. The King has given him leave to go to Ireland only upon condition of making an exchange into another regiment, as the one he is in is destined for the East Indies, and it cannot go without its full compliment [*sic*] of officers; this will cost some money and take some time to effect it; but at all events he will be the gainer.'[23] Early in the new year 1788, Arthur Wesley left London. He stayed for a few days with his grandmother in Wales, and paid a visit to her famous neighbours. Lady Eleanor Butler was delighted, describing him in her diary as: 'A charming young man. Handsome, fashioned tall and elegant. He stayed till two, then proceeded to Ireland.'[24]

CHAPTER TWO

COMING OF AGE IN IRELAND
(1788–93)

ARTHUR WESLEY SPENT eight years in Ireland from 1788 to 1796, dividing his time between regimental duty and serving as aide-de-camp to three successive Lords Lieutenant at Dublin Castle. In the early years the vice-regal court and the society that surrounded it were more attractive to the young man than garrison duty in the Irish provinces, but with the outbreak of war in 1793 and rapid promotion to command his own regiment, Wesley's attention shifted. He also became a member of the Irish Parliament and gained direct experience of electoral politics and parliamentary debates. The time at Dublin Castle completed Arthur's education, polished his manners and introduced him to court etiquette, politics and the ways in which patronage was bestowed and withheld. These were the years in which many of his contemporaries went to university, and although the life of an aide-de-camp was hardly conducive to study, Wesley made many friends and acquaintances, people who would reappear in his later military and political life, sometimes as patrons or allies, sometimes as rivals, and occasionally even as enemies. It was not a close network of support like that provided by his brothers, but it was a first small step in making an independent place for himself in the ranks of Britain's political, social and military elite.

One of the most durable connections that Wesley made was with his first Lord Lieutenant, the Marquess of Buckingham. The thirty-five-year-old Buckingham was head of one of the most powerful and durable factions in British politics. His father had been Prime Minister, while his brother, William Grenville, was in the process of becoming one of Pitt's most trusted ministers, and would himself become Prime Minister in 1806. Buckingham had already served as Lord Lieutenant of Ireland in 1782–83, and played a pivotal and controversial role in the defeat of the Fox–North coalition, which had paved the way for Pitt's accession to power. He was a major political figure who might have played an even greater role if he had been a less awkward colleague. 'The touchiest and most pompous nobleman in Britain' is how one historian has described him, and Buckingham's aristocratic hauteur and fondness for sine-cures, government places and other fruits of office made him and his family notorious.[1] On the other hand Buckingham had a reputation for being consid-erate to employees and servants, and his happy marriage created a warm atmosphere, which softened the prickly, often petulant side of his official char-acter. He treated Wesley with a kindness that won the young man's confidence and lasting gratitude.[2] As an aide-de-camp Wesley was part of the Lord Lieutenant's official family and the line between the official and private fami-lies was often blurred. Wesley would certainly have known Buckingham's twelve-year-old son, Earl Temple, and he revived the connection in later years, writing informative friendly letters to Temple from the Peninsula.

Buckingham resigned in a fit of pique in the late summer of 1789, mortified that he had not received the dukedom he craved or any other reward for his resolute support of Pitt during the Regency Crisis of 1788–89. His successor was the thirty-year-old John Fane, 10th Earl of Westmorland, who owed his appointment to the lasting friendship he had formed with Pitt at Cambridge. A few years later a well-disposed journalist wrote of Westmorland that, 'to all the advantages of a handsome and graceful person he unites a fluency of speech and an unembarrassed manner'.[3] Added to which he was one of the great landed proprietors of England and the head of an ancient family which, with Pitt's friendship, were qualifications enough to give him a lifetime in high office, including twenty years in Cabinet as Lord Privy Seal. His intellect and political acumen were not highly regarded – 'an insignificant trifler' is one of the kinder contemporary comments – and in Cabinet he was to acquire a repu-tation for asking foolish questions.[4] But there was more romance and drama in Westmorland's life than this suggests. In 1782 at the age of twenty-three he had eloped with Sarah Anne Child, the seventeen-year-old daughter, only child and heir of Robert Child, the fabulously wealthy banker of Osterley Park, just west of London. As the young couple dashed towards the Scottish border the outraged father set off in hot pursuit and managed to overtake them between Penrith and Carlisle. In the confrontation that followed Mr Child shot Westmorland's leading horse, but one of the Earl's servants disabled the pursuing carriage by cutting the leathers which held the body to the springs. The couple escaped and were married on 20 May 1782 at Gretna Green, and again, less hastily, at Westmorland's seat of Apethorpe on 7 June. Robert Child was not easily reconciled to his unwanted son-in-law and entailed his vast fortune on his female heirs, so that it would go first to Lady Westmorland and then to her eldest daughter. He died within a few years and his daughter, the Countess of Westmorland, did not long survive him, succumbing to a fever at the vice-regal lodge, Phoenix Park, Dublin, on 9 November 1793.[5]

Aides-de-camp were a purely personal appointment, and it was usual for most, though not all, the private staff to be replaced when one Lord Lieutenant made way for another. However Mornington intervened and used his influence to ensure that Arthur Wesley remained at Dublin Castle. Although Westmorland agreed to retain Wesley on his staff he initially treated the young man coldly, and in January 1791 Wesley visited England and went to see Buckingham, who reported to Grenville:

> Arthur Wesley came to me yesterday from Ireland, full of resentment to the Lord Lieutenant, who has not spoke one word to him since March last, and has refused to recommend him for any purchase out of his own regiment. You know the real cause of all this, but I think it probable that Wesley will soon fly out and resign his appointment. I have laboured to sooth[e] him upon it, but I rather think that it might be right for Mornington to call for some explanation for or some change in this marked line of disapprobation.[6]

Unfortunately we do not know what was 'the real cause of all this', although Buckingham's assumption that Grenville knew suggests a wider cause than a clash of personalities in Dublin Castle. Possibly Arthur Wesley was being punished for something Mornington had done that had annoyed Westmorland – pains as well as boons could be granted by proxy – but this is no more than a surmise.

Whatever the origins of the problem it seems to have been overcome; Wesley was promoted captain in the 58th Foot (from the 12th Light Dragoons) a few months later, and remained on Westmorland's staff. Years later Westmorland was a member of the Cabinet that sent him to Portugal in 1808 and which decided not to abandon him after the outcry over Cintra. And in 1809–10 Westmorland's son and heir, Lord Burghersh, served as a trusted aide-de-camp on Wellington's staff in the Peninsula, and then married his favourite niece, Priscilla Wellesley-Pole, in 1811. More strikingly, Wellington wished to bring Westmorland back into Cabinet in 1828 and was only dissuaded by the strong opposition of his colleagues.[7] This is not to suggest that Wellington and Westmorland were ever firm friends or close political allies, but the personal connection, forged so early in Arthur Wesley's career, was significant.

Although the Lord Lieutenant was the head of the Irish government, much of the executive work was done by the Chief Secretary, a post that Arthur Wesley would hold from 1807–09, including during the campaign that led to the Convention of Cintra. From 1789–93 this office was held by Robert Hobart, a friend and contemporary of Mornington's. Buckingham welcomed Hobart's appointment, praising his 'quickness, parts, and the most intimate knowledge of every man in Ireland'.[8] Wesley evidently liked and trusted him, for he begged Buckingham to consult Hobart when some accusations were made concerning Wesley's conduct when the Lord Lieutenant was in England in September 1789, and suggested that he had spent much time in his company.[9] Hobart went on to serve as governor of Madras (1794–98), Secretary of State for War and the Colonies in Addington's government (1801–04) and several other Cabinet positions.

Buckingham, Westmorland and even Hobart were senior figures, to be served and treated with respect, but for more familiar, relaxed society Arthur Wesley probably depended on his fellow aides-de-camp at Dublin Castle. In 1789 Wesley was one of nineteen ADCs to Lord Buckingham, so there was a choice of company. The senior aide was Lieutenant-Colonel George Nugent, a family connection (Lady Buckingham's half-brother's illegitimate son, to be precise) who benefitted greatly from Buckingham's influence and who was at the centre of several disputes over patronage as the King thwarted Buckingham's attempts to whisk him up the military ladder. Nugent was a serious and capable soldier who went on to serve as lieutenant-governor and Commander-in-Chief in Jamaica from 1801 to 1806. In 1808 he was one of the seven senior generals appointed to inquire into the Convention of Cintra, and in the following year he defended the Inquiry's findings and the Convention in Parliament. (He sat in the Commons for one of Lord Buckingham's seats, but seldom took part in the debates.) From 1811 to 1813 he served as Commander-in-Chief in India.[10]

Immediately below Nugent in the list published in the *Royal Kalendar for 1790* come two aides-de-camp 'in ordinary', Major J.F. Cradock and Lieutenant-Colonel R. St George; and then sixteen 'extraordinary' (that is, supernumerary) aides-de-camp, with Arthur Wesley listed third among the sixteen. Several of these men would cross paths with Wesley in the years to come. Born in 1762 Cradock was the son of John Cradock, Bishop of Kilmore and subsequently Archbishop of Dublin, a politically powerful prelate. Major Cradock was also one of the earliest and most intimate friends of the Prince of Wales, and one of Hobart's school friends. His nickname 'the Town Bull of Dublin' suggests a fondness for the pleasures of the flesh, and he may well have introduced Arthur Wesley to some of the fashionable vices. Certainly it seems that Cradock was a friend in these Dublin days, and when the two men met again in Madras in 1805 there was a reciprocal warmth in their welcome. The next meeting was more awkward, for Wesley superseded Cradock (his senior) in Portugal in the spring of 1809 and Cradock never really forgave him, although Wellington attempted to make amends by employing his son, John Hobart Cradock, as an aide-de-camp after Waterloo.[11]

Lieutenant-Colonel Richard St George was Cradock's half-brother. When St George married in 1786 Mornington lent him Dangan for his honeymoon. This was before Arthur Wesley returned from France, but Mrs St George knew him later, although not well: '[I] was acquainted with him . . . or rather I often received him as a guest, but was then so diffident and reserved, I do not believe I ever addressed five words to him. He was extremely good humoured, and the object of much attention from the female part of what was called "a very gay society", though it did not appear such to me.'[12] She was also bored by the parties given by Hobart in the grounds of Phoenix Park during which fashionable young men played cricket before dinner, followed by cards and dancing until supper, 'and then by the light of the waning moon or rising dawn, we parted to drive through the beautiful scenery of the park'.[13] The star on these occasions was Colonel Lennox who, as 4th Duke of Richmond, was to be Lord Lieutenant of Ireland from 1807–12, with Arthur Wesley as his first Chief Secretary. Lennox was a glamorous figure; he had fought a duel with the Duke of York (George III's son and second-in-line to the throne) which 'seemed to have something in it chivalrous, displaying a recklessness of all selfish considerations. We knew little of the particulars, but this mystery increased our respect'. Moreover he was handsome and good at sport, 'said to be the finest formed man in England, and his playing at cricket was praised as an exquisite display of grace, strength and skill'. No wonder that invitations to Hobart's parties were keenly sought![14]

Most of the other aides-de-camp were either family or political connections of Buckingham and the Grenvilles. The most important in Arthur's later career was Captain W.H. Fremantle, who was three years older than him, and who left the army and became the leader of Buckingham's MPs – an active and significant figure in the House of Commons. Despite being in opposition at the time, he spoke in favour of the Vote of Thanks to Sir Arthur Wellesley (as he had then become) for the victory of Vimeiro, although he subsequently voted against the government over Cintra. Memories of Dublin days twenty years earlier would not determine party tactics on an important political question, but they might affect the arguments employed and the tone of the debate, for it was much easier to pour scorn on an unknown soldier than on a friend of one's youth.[15] Despite political differences, Wellesley and Fremantle remained on good terms and corresponded intermittently over the years, mostly on matters of patronage. A month after voting against Cintra, Fremantle asked Wellesley to assist his nephew John who was serving in the army in Portugal, and the young man joined Wellesley's staff as an aide-de-camp, writing home revealing letters which have only recently been published.[16]

The other aides-de-camp were less notable, but mention may be made of Robert Williams, a Guards officer who was wounded before Dunkirk in August

1793. Westmorland dismissed him soon afterwards, and he retired from the army in 1795. Williams was later described as combining 'an eloquent and captivating person' with 'a pleasing and insinuating address'. He was a member of the British House of Commons for forty years, from 1790 until his death in 1830, most of the time representing Caernarvonshire. Yet he was notorious for his lax attendance and his dislike of business, preferring country sports – this despite the fact that he 'seldom failed to share a comfortable bed at a country inn with an attractive chambermaid on his way to and from Westminster'. Indeed his sexual adventuring became a matter of public ridicule at the time, while the graphic letters in which he described his exploits were regarded as unpublishable even in the 1960s.[17]

As these examples show, Wesley's fellow aides-de-camp were a diverse group – all well connected in one way or another, but by no means all wealthy or privileged – and while their manners may have been refined, their morals were distinctly raffish, as was fitting for an Irish court in an age of scandal. It was not an unpleasant environment for a young man to come of age, although it did little to encourage virtues such as frugality, sobriety, chastity or modesty. A more serious drawback, at least in Wesley's case, was the lack of any clear purpose in the life he was leading. If he had been on active service he might have devoted himself to mastering the practicalities of campaigning while learning how to handle his men and fellow officers. If he had been at university he might have chosen to study. And if he had been on the Grand Tour he might have gained an insight into Britain's European neighbours. But none of these would have given him as good a grounding in the working of the great world of British politics and high society, at least as they appeared in the cynical, slightly askew arena of eighteenth-century Dublin.

Few significant letters from Arthur Wesley survive from this early in his life, so we cannot tell what he made of the life he was leading, or even whether he was happy or miserable. Instead all we have are fragmentary glimpses of the young officer in the memoirs and reminiscences of his contemporaries. Some of these stories are so trifling as to be almost entirely inconsequential: Lady Aldborough, for example, whose affair with Westmorland was public knowledge, offered him a seat in her carriage on the occasion of a fête some miles out of Dublin, but found him so silent and dull that she left him to find his own way home with the fiddlers – and yet they became good friends in later years.[18] Lady Shelley says that his greatest friend in these years was Lady de la Zouche and that he later showed great kindness to her daughter, the widow of a general officer. Mr Ruxton 'of Black Castle' was impressed to see that the aide-de-camp had been reading Locke's *Essay Concerning Human Understanding*, but this is a flimsy basis on which to claim that he was engaged in a sustained course of self-education.[19] A fellow officer describes him as 'social in his habits ... but never given to excess ... his personal appearance and manners were extremely neat and elegant'.[20] William Napier, the historian of the Peninsular War, states that in Castleton society Wesley was 'generally considered a shallow, saucy stripling', but then ruins the story by claiming that his father, Colonel Napier, recognised 'the makings of a great general' in the young officer.[21] And Jonah Barrington describes him as 'ruddy-faced and juvenile in appearance, and popular enough among the young men of his station', but, as one of Wellington's early biographers comments, 'Sir Jonah Barrington is scarcely an authority which any historian or biographer would care to quote'.[22]

According to one female acquaintance Wesley was 'reserved, except to those who made the first advances', but he nonetheless received a good deal of attention from fashionable young ladies.[23] In July 1789 Cradock commented on his 'propensity to fall in love', and that he was 'now more in love with Mrs Stretford than I can describe, all his minor loves before are quite forgot', which makes him sound like a romantic twenty-year-old rather than a womaniser. A few weeks later he reacted angrily when teased by Fremantle: 'I know that there are people in Dublin ready enough to circulate reports to my or anybody's disadvantage, but I beg you will give them no credit until I tell you of them myself. I shall also be much obliged to you if you will tell me the name of the person whom you suppose I *burn* for.' And he went on to comment that no one could think him 'such an irresistible man as Williams'. Yet evidently he had something of a reputation, as Dean Butler declined to have him as a lodger because 'his wife & daughter were in the house'. Wesley was hurt rather than flattered by the suspicion, hinting to the Dean 'that I would not touch his wife, if she would let me', and would do all he could to prevent the daughter falling in love with him. What made the rejection particularly pointed was that Fremantle had previously rented the room without any difficulty.[24]

In 1790 Wesley and Fremantle were involved in an unsavoury incident that does something to justify the Dean's suspicions. The result was that the two officers were tried in the Court of the King's Bench the following July on a charge of 'riotously assembling together on the 21st of November last, and making a great affray before the house of Ann Maria Swettenham, and riotously and forcibly entering the same, and violently assaulting herself, her child, and her servant maid'. The jury convicted them without retiring to consider the verdict, and they were each fined £10. We do not know what lies behind the incident, but the mildness of the sentence suggests that there were at least some extenuating circumstances. There is also a story, presumably relating to the same affair, that the young Wesley was fined for thrashing a Frenchman in a Dublin bawdy-house; but it is unclear what, if any, weight should be placed on this as it is unsubstantiated.[25]

Less discreditable is the story that Wesley won a wager for as much as 150 guineas that he would walk from Cornelscourt outside Dublin to Leeson Street in an hour. It was about five miles, and the road was poor, but he made the journey in fifty-five minutes and won the bet. This was just as well, for he could not afford to lose 150 guineas, while even fifteen might have proved awkward.[26] Wesley's private income was negligible; he could not hope to live on his pay as an officer, even with the additional allowance he received as an aide-de-camp, for life at Dublin Castle and in society was expensive. Mornington might give some occasional assistance, but despite his vast inheritance, he never had much ready money and was frequently in financial difficulties of his own. Inevitably Wesley got into debt, borrowing money from several affluent Dublin tradesmen and from John Page, Mornington's estate agent. By the time he left Portsmouth in 1796 he owed Page £955 4s 8d, and probably a few hundred pounds elsewhere (there is a story of a bond for £100 borrowed from a friend of Page's brother which was not repaid until 1806).[27] On the whole it was a remarkably small amount to accumulate over eight years, but he disliked being in debt and felt keenly his lack of financial independence.

One of Wesley's creditors was Mr Dickson, a prosperous shoemaker on Lower Ormond Quay, who also provided him with lodgings. Nor was this all, for Wesley had an affair with Mrs Dickson, who bore him a son. The story emerges from a letter that Robert Peel wrote in 1814 when he was Chief Secretary for Ireland:

> When Lord Wellington was here as an aide-de-camp, he lodged at the house of a Mr Dickson, a shoemaker. Mrs Dickson had a son, who by some accident or other bore a much stronger resemblance to Lord Wellington than to Mr Dickson. In favour of this young man (who I believe is no doubt Ld W's son) he wrote to Lord Whitworth, on the latter's first arrival [as Lord Lieutenant] in this country, earnestly entreating the appointment of this young man, who was educated in Trinity College and is properly qualified for it, to some situation of about £200 a year, with a reasonable hope of further advancement according to his merits – 'to be put on the ladder' was his expression. A year has elapsed; of course Lord Whitworth has every good disposition towards him; but he has not put his foot on the first step yet.[28]

Unfortunately no trace can be found of young Mr Dickson's subsequent career, and his name does not appear among the surviving Wellington papers, but such accidents were by no means unusual in the life of a young man of the time.

Wesley seems to have spent most of his time with the vice-regal court in Dublin, but he was not entirely excused from regimental duties. He was with the 12th

Light Dragoons when they were inspected by Major-General C.W. Lyon at
Charleville on 16 June 1790, although six other officers, including the colonel,
were absent. Galbraith Lowry Cole, who went on to serve under Wesley with
distinction in the Peninsula, was a cornet in the same troop of the regiment,
but was on leave studying military science at the University of Stuttgart, and
the two men may have had little if any contact at this time.[29] An officer who did
know Wesley at this time was Thomas Brisbane, then serving in the 38th
stationed nearby, and who commanded a brigade at Vitoria in 1813. In his
reminiscences he recalled:

> At this time I became acquainted with the Duke of Wellington, who was then
> a lieutenant in a regiment of cavalry. Galway is a fine sporting country,
> abounding in all kinds of game, and affording us a wide range for all such
> occupations. We used frequently to go out sporting together, and to kill our
> five-and-twenty couple of woodcocks between breakfast and dinner time. We
> hunted on the demesne of the Earl of Clancarty, also at Mr Hancock's, now
> Lord Castlemaine, in the county of Westmeath. Both these noblemen were
> frequently of our party. Never have I seen a keener sportsman in hunting and
> shooting than the Duke then was.[30]

In June 1791 Wesley was promoted to captain in the 58th Foot, and sixteen
years later he warmly praised his commanding officer Colonel Browne. Most
of his time with the regiment seems to have been spent 'on recruiting duty' in
Dublin; but in 1814 the Duke of Clarence recalled with pride that 'I knew
Arthur Wellesley a Captain in the 58th regiment at Cork'.[31] The old story that
Wesley no sooner joined the army than he weighed a private with and without
his full kit is a nonsensical later invention.[32] But Wesley clearly mastered the
essentials of regimental soldiering. Brisbane praised his understanding of the
infantry drill regulations, and even claims to have seen him 'wheel a whole
division on the ground on which it stood, the left centre going to the right
about, both moving round, wheeling till the front was changed, and that in five
minutes'.[33] This would seem an unlikely accomplishment for a junior cavalry
officer; however, there is an explanation. From 1788 until the early 1790s the
Dublin garrison was used to test the new infantry drill that had been devised by
David Dundas (who was Quartermaster-General of the Irish army, 1778–89
and Adjutant-General, 1789–93). Buckingham was an enthusiastic supporter
of these experiments, and probably encouraged his aides to take part in them.
So Arthur Wesley had the opportunity to gain a thorough grounding in the
drill that the army would employ, with some modifications, in all his campaigns,
while it was still fresh, novel and as close to exciting as drill can be.[34]

Mornington found Arthur Wesley's presence in Ireland convenient, both as a source of news and to keep an eye on the family estates. The head of the family was steadily withdrawing from Ireland, selling Mornington House in Dublin in 1791 and the Dangan estate two years later. These sales enabled Mornington to reduce his inherited debts from £41,000 to £26,000, while leaving a surplus of £18,000 for his own use – or to pay off his own debts.[35] He remained a very substantial landowner, with 12,800 acres in County Meath, and another 1,000 acres in County Kildare, producing rents of some £6,000 per annum. These estates were not finally sold until 1816 when property values were still inflated by the wartime prosperity of agriculture, and they fetched about £150,000. Mornington was a wealthy man, although his mismanagement of his finances often left him embarrassed. His brother William, who inherited the Pole estates in Queen's County, was also affluent, but Arthur, Anne, Gerald and Henry inherited almost nothing.[36]

As late as 1794 when Arthur was on active service in the Low Countries Mornington passed on to him a difficulty with Burrowes over part of the Dangan estate. Arthur replied:

> Write to him & tell him that I shall be in Ireland in the course of the winter & that the question shall then be settled. My reason . . . is that I shall be a better judge of the circumstances when on the spot, shall be better able by a trial of the feelings of the neighbourhood upon the question to recommend an arbitrator to you, & I think it will be of advantage to you to have one of your family in the Country when the question is decided.
>
> This is *Irish* Language but not the less true of that Country of scoundrels.[37]

Mornington had decided, as early as October 1787,[38] that Arthur should replace William as member for the family seat of Trim in the Irish House of Commons, while William would move on to a seat at Westminster. Arthur therefore began to attend to local affairs at Trim. He subscribed five guineas to the local races, he became a freemason at the local lodge (no. 494), and he attended meetings of the local corporation.[39] At one of these he was ambushed by a motion to confer the freedom of the borough on Henry Grattan, the leading member of the Irish opposition. Before the question was put to the vote Arthur informed the family's supporters 'that it was a question of party, [and] that they must stick by me', and made a speech to the Corporation which showed determination, if little natural eloquence.[40] The motion was defeated and Wesley went on to announce his intention of standing at the forthcoming election. Inevitably the immediate response was for voters to besiege him with requests of all kinds in an effort to extract the maximum value for their vote. By his own account, Wesley reacted with prudent discretion:

[I] said I would have nothing to do with it, as in case of a General Election such a transaction would entirely vitiate my return . . . I was in the most difficult situation I ever experienced, and only got out of it by sticking manfully to what I first said. I must say that, although I was plagued with requests of all kinds and totally unable and disinclined to make any promise . . . they behaved as handsomely as people could do . . . They are all fine fellows.[41]

Unfortunately the election was held at the end of April, when Wesley was still only twenty years old and therefore, in the strictest terms, ineligible to stand. It was by no means unknown for candidates to be elected to the Irish (or, for that matter, the British) House of Commons while still minors although they did not normally attempt to vote or take their seat until they turned twenty-one. Arthur's brother William had been elected for Trim in 1783 while still only nineteen or twenty, so for Arthur to fall short by a mere day or two seems a venial sin.[42] Nonetheless petitions against Wesley's election as one of the two members for Trim were lodged on several grounds and eventually dismissed, but not before he had consulted the Irish Lord Chancellor and the Attorney-General about his defence.[43] None of this was particularly unusual by the standards of the day, let alone shocking or scandalous; and it is rather appropriate that such a stalwart defender of the old, unreformed constitution should have made his first entry into Parliament in slightly dubious circumstances.

It was prudent for a young Member of Parliament, unless he was very confident or very ambitious, to learn the ways of the House before he ventured to speak, especially if his election had been called into question. Arthur Wesley was therefore wise to remain silent throughout 1791; he made his maiden speech when he seconded the Address at the opening of Parliament on 10 January 1792. This was an opportunity often used to bring forward young members; they had a chance to prepare a speech defending the government's proposals, and were assured the attention of the House. Only the coolest and most insouciant young man could fail to find it an ordeal, but we have no record of the apprehensions Arthur Wesley must have felt as the dreaded hour approached. The surviving text of the speech is no more than a précis, and the content is suitable to the point of banality: the constitution must be defended against the subversive ideas spreading from Europe, and the proposed increase in the army was a necessary response to the threat of war on the Continent; the country had never known such prosperity, and the government's plan to grant concessions to the Catholics deserved universal support. 'I have no doubt of the loyalty of the Catholics of this country, and I trust that when the question shall be brought forward we shall lay aside animosities, and act with moderation and dignity, not with the fury and violence of partisans.'[44] As an aide-de-camp of the Lord Lieutenant, Wesley was expected to give unequivocal support to government measures especially on such a formal occasion as the debate on the Address, so we cannot assume that this speech reflected his private views, if indeed he had any settled views of his own.[45] Nonetheless it is interesting that his first speech in Parliament should touch on the Catholic Question, which was to run like a scarlet thread throughout his political career.

The civil wars and conflicts of the seventeenth century had led to the triumph of Protestantism throughout the British Isles. The Church of England was formally established in England and Wales; in Scotland the predominant place of the Presbyterian Church was equally secure; while in Ireland a small, overwhelmingly Anglican elite ruled over a mass of Catholic tenantry and a substantial intermediate class of Nonconformist (that is, not Anglican) Protestants. A series of severe penal laws restricting the rights of Catholics (and, in many cases, also Nonconformists) were introduced in the decades on either side of 1700, which were designed to entrench the power of the 'Protestant Ascendancy'. Many of these laws either soon fell into disuse, were successfully evaded, or were never enforced, but they nonetheless symbolised the triumph of the Anglican establishment. The first half of the eighteenth century saw little obvious change in this state of affairs, but this lull allowed memories of the horrors of the seventeenth century to fade, especially among the elite in Britain.[46]

By the middle of the eighteenth century the British government was beginning to feel confident in the loyalty of its Irish Catholic subjects. During the Seven Years' War (1756–63), for example, the official ban on Catholic recruits joining the army was increasingly ignored, and it was formally abolished in 1774.[47] The rise of the Protestant Irish Volunteer movement in the 1780s had far-reaching effects. On the one hand the Volunteers sought to win Catholic support by demanding – successfully – wide-ranging concessions that substantially undermined the whole structure of the penal laws. On the other, it destroyed the assumption at Westminster of a community of interests between Britain and the Irish Protestants.[48] With few personal religious prejudices, Pitt and Dundas came to see the Irish Protestants and Catholics as little more than rival factions, and were by no means sure that the former were more likely to prove more loyal or effective as allies. Indeed by the beginning of the 1790s, when Wesley embarked on his political career, the sympathies of the leading British ministers lay squarely with the Catholics. They regarded the remaining penal laws as absurd, archaic and unnecessary, and they were irritated by the importunity of the leading Irish Protestants, who always exacted a high price for their support at Westminster and who were far from dependable as allies. The spread of radical ideas from France in the first years of the Revolution led to concern in London and Dublin that it might lead to disaffection. Buckingham responded by advocating generous concessions to the Catholics in an attempt to remove the causes of discontent before they led to trouble. Pitt, Dundas and Grenville agreed, and proposed the virtual abolition of the remaining penal laws, retaining only a prohibition on Catholics sitting in Parliament and holding senior military and other specified positions. These measures were incorporated in an English Relief Act, which passed in 1791, but this did not apply in Ireland. Westmorland and Hobart strongly opposed these proposals, regarding them as little short of the complete abolition of the Protestant Ascendancy. For the moment they carried the day, and their own legislation, which was introduced in 1792 and which Arthur Wesley commended in his maiden speech, was only a ghost of those adopted in England.[49]

Half a loaf did nothing to satisfy the Irish Catholics whose expectations had been aroused by the English measures, and who fully understood that the policy pursued by Dublin Castle lacked support in London. During 1792 they adopted a much more assertive stance, demanding rather than asking for concessions, and hinting at unspecified trouble if they were not satisfied. Pitt and his colleagues were preoccupied by the growing probability of war with France, and, like many of their successors, heartily wished Ireland on the other side of the Atlantic. Westmorland and the leaders of the Irish Protestants knew that they could not rely on Pitt to support them in defence of laws that he privately opposed, and so, with deep reluctance, forebodings and considerable ill grace, they gave way. A new Catholic Relief Act was introduced into the Irish Parliament in 1793. Among the concessions it granted were the right of Catholics to sit on grand juries; the removal of the remaining bars for their entry into various trades and professions (including serving in the Royal Navy and as regimental officers in the army); and the right to bear arms. They were granted the franchise, but not the right to sit in Parliament. These measures have been described by one historian as 'scarcely other than revolutionary', and as 'proposing . . . a radical reconfiguration of the Irish political nation'.[50] Initially it looked as if the government party might collapse under the strain of being made to swallow such obnoxious measures, but in the end, helped by concessions and influenced by the war with France, the Act passed with many hostile speeches but few divisions.[51]

Arthur Wesley spoke in this debate, opposing a motion to allow Catholics to sit in Parliament, while defending the extension of the franchise to all forty-shilling freeholders:

With the Bill, as it stands, the Protestants are satisfied, and the Roman Catholics contented; why then agitate a question which may disturb both? A gentleman has said that admitting the 40 shilling freeholders of the Roman Catholic persuasion to vote at elections would annihilate the Protestant

Establishment in Ireland, and he has founded his assertion on the supposition that the Roman Catholics will, in voting, be directed by their priests. But have not Roman Catholics, like Protestants, various interests and various passions by which they are swayed – the influence of their landlords, their good and bad opinion of the candidates, and a thousand other motives? It appears to me that they will not vote in a body, as has been supposed, if the Bill should be passed in its present form; but if the motion of the gentleman shall be adopted, then indeed they would unite in support of Roman Catholic candidates.[52]

A sensible, reasonable speech and not a bad prophecy, but thirty-five years later the Catholic forty-shilling voters of County Clare united to elect Daniel O'Connell to Parliament, notwithstanding the fact that as a Catholic he was ineligible to take his seat. Their action precipitated the greatest political crisis Arthur Wesley, then Duke of Wellington, would face as Prime Minister, and the solution that he devised almost broke his party and fatally weakened his government.

Serving in the Irish Parliament gave Wesley the chance to play a small part in historic events, and, by his speeches, to give a hostage or two to fortune. It also introduced him to the cream of the Irish political world, and if he was too junior and insignificant a member to make much impression on Grattan or Curran, he at least made the acquaintance of some of the younger members. By far the most important of these for the future was his contemporary Robert Stewart, Viscount Castlereagh, the son of Lord Londonderry, who would be one of Wesley's greatest supporters in Cabinet in the first years of the Peninsular War, and, as Foreign Secretary, a loyal and sympathetic colleague from 1814 to 1822. At this early stage of his career, Castlereagh was an independent member, rather inclined to support the opposition. There is little evidence for the common assumption that Wesley and Castlereagh were close friends at this time; they knew each other as members of Parliament, and may have been drawn together by their shared love of music – Wesley played the violin and Castlereagh the cello – but it was only later, when they worked together after Wesley's return from India, that they developed their mutual respect and trust.[53]

The years Arthur Wesley spent in Ireland helped to shape his future career: they gave him a network of important connections, as much or more in the world of politics as in the army; they gave him a familiarity with the mores of high society so that he at least appeared at ease in it; and they ensured that his horizons were much broader than those of the regimental mess, and that he never acquired an ingrained awe of superior officers. To a casual observer he might have appeared a gilded youth: scion of a great landowning, aristocratic family, officer in the King's army, aide-de-camp to the Lord

Lieutenant, and a Member of Parliament, he must surely live a life of wealth and privilege. Yet this impression was misleading. For all the glitter and connections, Wesley did not have a sufficient income to support himself or any clear prospects; he had yet to establish a place in the world, or even to decide what line he would pursue; and if he failed, no one outside his family would notice or care. He still had very little control over his destiny and the goal of independence remained as remote as ever.

CHAPTER THREE

LOVE AND WAR
(1792–96)

T HE YEARS BETWEEN 1792 and 1796 were the most painful and humiliating in Wesley's long life, and they significantly influenced the development of his still-unformed character and the direction of his career. The troubles began in the most natural way; at the age of twenty-two he fell in love with a suitable young woman who warmly reciprocated his affections. Kitty Pakenham was the second child of Lord Longford, a staunch political ally of Lord Buckingham and the Irish government.[1] She was born in January 1772, making her a little less than three years younger than Arthur Wesley. We do not know when they first met. It is possible that they may have played together as children, for Dangan adjoined Summerhill, owned by Kitty's cousins; or he may have met her when she was presented at the vice-regal court, probably in 1789 or 1790; or when he visited Pakenham Hall when attending to business at Trim.[2] However they met, they were openly courting by the spring of 1792.

Kitty Pakenham was an intelligent and lively young woman; short and slight with grey eyes, a good complexion and a rather imperious manner. She was a close friend of Maria Edgeworth, four years her senior, with whom she shared some intellectual interests. She also enjoyed gossip, could be very indiscreet, and was vivacious, although grand society and fashion never had much appeal for her. She was certainly attractive, but not in a particularly obvious way, and it is interesting that she should have appealed so strongly to the young Arthur Wesley.

Before the spring of 1792 had turned to summer Arthur Wesley asked for her hand, and was refused. Kitty was willing, but her parents rejected the proposal. It is not hard to see why; Wesley was a captain in the 58th Foot with no obvious prospects, and could not live on his pay, let alone support a wife and family. But if their decision was reasonable, it was apparently expressed without tact. According to family tradition, Lord Longford used the occasion to deliver a stern homily to the young man, enumerating his many faults and suggesting that he correct them and embark on a useful career before thinking of marriage.

Specifically he commented that Arthur was a younger son in a large family and that his energies 'had seldom been displayed except in gaiety and music'.[3]

Illness or anxiety may have made Lord Longford unduly harsh, for he died soon afterwards, on 3 June 1792, at the age of only forty-nine. Propriety and consideration for Kitty's feelings prevented any immediate renewal of the proposal, but neither Arthur nor Kitty abandoned their hopes. In 1793 Kitty's elder sister Elizabeth married Henry Stewart, a rising young lawyer who was agent for the Pakenham estates – a connection that suggests the Pakenhams were neither snobbish nor absurd in their expectations. Meanwhile Arthur advanced from being a captain to a lieutenant-colonel, purchasing the promotions with money borrowed with Mornington's backing.[4] In 1794, two years after his first proposal, he again asked for Kitty's hand, this time directing his request to her twenty-year-old brother, who was, nominally at least, the head of the family. Again he was refused, although it was probably Kitty's mother rather than her brother who had the decisive say. This time the decision was final; Lady Longford forbade her daughter from having any further communication with Arthur Wesley.[5] In response he wrote to Kitty, refusing to accept defeat, but sounding very forlorn:

> If this letter should reach you, I hope you will impute my troubling you this second time to the fear I have that my first letter may have offended. It never was intended to offend, and if any expression it contained could at all tend to give offence, I hope that the determination I have just received is in your eyes a sufficient punishment for a crime of a much greater magnitude.
>
> As Lord Longford's determination is founded upon prudential motives and may be changed should my situation be altered before I return to Ireland, I hope you will believe that should anything occur which may induce you and him to change your minds, my mind will remain the same. In the meantime with the best wishes for your happiness believe me,
>   Your most attached and obedient servant,
>   A. Wesley[6]

He was undoubtedly sincere, and if he had come unexpectedly into a fortune in the next year or two he would surely have renewed his proposal and, in all probability, have been accepted. But he remained poor, and when he sailed for India in the summer of 1796, both he and Kitty regarded themselves as free agents, unbound by any engagement or tie, whatever the tenderness and regret they each still felt for the other.[7]

Wesley's courtship of Kitty coincided with the most dramatic stages of the French Revolution. In the spring of 1792 Austria, Prussia and assorted allies declared war on France, although Britain remained neutral, happy to leave the French to languish in their own troubles. A Prussian invasion of France was checked at Valmy on 20 September, and on the following day the National Convention suspended the monarchy. Dumouriez's victory of Jemappes early in November opened the way for a French invasion of Belgium. Pitt and his colleagues were already alarmed by the increasing radicalism of the Revolution and by the spread of similar ideas in Britain and Ireland; they also could not ignore the French advance into the Low Countries, which had always been an area of crucial strategic importance for British security. Reluctantly they began to prepare for war, which, by the end of 1792, appeared almost inevitable. On 21 January 1793 Louis XVI was sent to the guillotine, and the National Convention declared war on Britain on 1 February.

The outbreak of war and Lord Longford's harsh words encouraged Wesley to take his profession more seriously. He gave his violin away to a friend (rather than, as is often said, burning it), solemnly renouncing an indulgence which 'til then had proved his bane',[8] and he leapt at a chance of active service, even in the Caribbean. In the middle of 1793 orders arrived for the 33rd to detach its flank companies (the elite of the regiment) to take part in an expedition to the West Indies. Wesley wrote to Mornington begging him to use his influence to get him a command in this force.[9] Fortunately nothing came of this request. The expedition gained important strategic advantages and large sums in prize money, but the cost was terrible. A contemporary manuscript account of the services of the 33rd Regiment states baldly that the flank companies sent to the Caribbean 'were totally destroyed'.[10]

Saved from this fate Wesley instead took command of the 33rd gaining the lieutenant-colonelcy on 30 September 1793. He had reason to be proud of his new command, for it was a good regiment. An Inspection Report of August 1792 described it as: 'very well appointed, a good body of men, young, and well made. The interior economy well regulated and well attended to, upon the whole a fine regiment, and fit for service'.[11] The credit for this lay with Wesley's predecessor in command, Lieutenant-Colonel John Yorke, and with the regiment's colonel, Lord Cornwallis, whose reputation had survived his defeat in America, and who was serving as Governor-General of India. Two of the officers serving in the regiment at this time later rose to prominence. John Byng was a young ensign who joined the regiment on the day Wesley became its commander, and who went on to lead a brigade in the Second Division in the Peninsula from 1811, and to command the Guards brigade at Waterloo; he eventually rose to become a Field Marshal in 1855. More immediately important was Major John Coape Sherbrooke, Wesley's second-in-command, who would serve with distinction in India and the Peninsula. Sherbrooke was a capable and popular officer, but not without his foibles. Henry Bunbury, who served under him in Sicily in 1807, describes him as 'an original':

> A short, square hardy little man, with a countenance that told at once the determined fortitude of his nature. Without genius, without education, hot as pepper, and rough in his language, but with a warm heart and generous feelings; true, straight-forward, scorning finesse and craft and meanness, and giving vent to his detestation with boiling eagerness and in the plainest terms. As an officer, full of energy, rousing others to exertion, and indefatigable in his own person.[12]

He was five years older than Wesley but still yet to reach thirty in 1793. Despite his rough manners and lack of polish he ended his career as a highly successful Governor-General of Canada.

The 33rd spent the last months of 1793 and the beginning of 1794 busily recruiting to replace the lost flank companies; it was at its full strength of 1,060 NCOs and men when it embarked at Cork in May 1794. While the regiment passed these months quietly in Ireland the war on the Continent waxed and waned. The initial French invasion of Belgium (the Austrian Netherlands) was repulsed, and the French Republic was threatened on all sides and riven by royalist uprisings in the west in La Vendée and Brittany. The British government had an embarrassment of choice of tempting strategic opportunities, and with only limited forces ready for overseas service. There was already a small British army under the command of the Duke of York cooperating with the Austrians in Belgium. Sound strategic doctrine suggested that this receive the bulk of all reinforcements in order to concentrate British efforts in a single theatre. Yet even if this were done Britain's contribution would remain relatively slight, and was unlikely to be decisive. Supporters of the French royalists argued that a modest force sent to aid the insurgents in La Vendée would have a much greater effect, and might even enable the royalists to overthrow the Republic from within. This argument gained added weight in August 1793 when the great French naval base at Toulon rose against the Republic and invited the British navy to assist in its defence. Nor could the West Indies be ignored, for its trade was vital to British prosperity, and hence to funding the war effort, while a decisive success there might weaken the prestige of the new French government, undermine its finances, and actually reduce the number of troops needed to garrison the area once its conquest was complete. Pitt and his colleagues adapted to the demands of war with reluctance; they lacked an instinctive grasp of strategy and they made many mistakes. Their task, however, was not as easy as hindsight suggests, and some, though not all, of the criticism of them has been grossly unfair.[13]

Late in 1793 a substantial British force under Lord Moira was sent to aid the insurgents in La Vendée, but it arrived too late, after the royalists had suffered a serious defeat, and it returned to the Isle of Wight without landing. The government kept the force together through the winter and early spring, conscious of the value of a strategic reserve ready to take advantage of an unexpected opportunity or react to a sudden danger. In May 1794 an ambitious allied attack on the French in Flanders was defeated at Tourcoing, and the subsequent retreat threatened to expose the Channel ports of Ostend and Nieuport. Dundas had an acute, even exaggerated sense of the danger of invasion if these ports fell into French hands, and on 17 June Moira's force was ordered to defend them. Moira would come under the orders of the Duke of York, but it was intended that his command would be semi-independent and it was hoped that the commitment would only be temporary.[14]

Arthur Wesley's 33rd, which had sailed from Cork on 4 June 1794, was added to Moira's force and reached Ostend on 25 June, a day ahead of Moira and the bulk of the expedition. Moira initially believed that he had arrived just 'in time to have a chance of saving this important post', and expected to be attacked on 27 June. But the French did not press forward as quickly as he expected, and a more considered look convinced him that the town was indefensible – an opinion which was confirmed when news arrived that the French had won an important victory at Fleurus. On 29 June Moira and the bulk of his troops left Ostend to march overland to join the Duke of York. The 33rd remained behind, part of a rearguard commanded by Colonel Vyse, which would protect the reloading of stores, heavy equipment and the sick, and join the main army by ship. By evening the embarkation was almost complete and most of the troops were aboard, protected by the 33rd 'which lay that night on its arms on the sand hills to the west of the town'. The next morning it embarked without being attacked by the French, and on 11 July the rearguard had arrived safely at Antwerp. Wesley's first experience of active service had amounted to covering a retreat and evacuating his troops by sea before the enemy advanced. It was not an auspicious beginning, and it would soon get much worse.[15]

But first there was a lull in operations. The Duke of York, the commander of the British army in the Low Countries, wrote to his brother, the Prince of Wales: 'My situation during the last two months has been more unpleasant than can be described. My only comfort is that no part of the blame of this shamefull retreat can be thrown upon me, and that it is known that I have done everything in my power to prevent it.' Arthur Wesley was also feeling sorry for himself. He was sick, suffering from an unspecified illness similar to ague, brought on by fatigue and damp. He wrote to Dr Alexander Lindsay, who had previously treated him at home, and who now expressed considerable concern and prescribed a powerful laxative. Illness of one sort or another was not

1 The Low Countries, 1794–95.

uncommon, and the number of soldiers of the 33rd who were 'present and fit for duty' fell from more than 1,000 at the end of May to barely 700 two months later. The army's doctors were busy feuding among themselves, and Colonel Craig of the Adjutant-General's staff reported with dismay that the medical department 'is most extremely ill conducted'.[16]

Before the end of July the Austrians announced their intention of abandoning Belgium and withdrawing into Germany. This would make the British position near Antwerp untenable and it might have been better if the government had used the proximity of that great port to withdraw their army from the Continent. However a reluctance to admit failure and to abandon the Dutch led to an attempt to cover Holland – an attempt that could only have succeeded if the Dutch themselves had been more enthusiastic, or if the French had been completely distracted by fresh internal upheavals or defeats on other fronts. By the end of August York's army had moved some fifty miles north-east of Antwerp to Bois-le-Duc, well inside the Dutch border and just south of the River Maas.

On 14 September the French attacked and captured the British advanced post at Boxtel on the River Dommel. The Duke of York ordered General Abercromby to retake the position. Abercromby attacked at six o'clock the following morning but the French were stronger than he expected and his troops were driven back in confusion. The 33rd had not taken part in the initial attack and were now deployed to cover the withdrawal where the First Guards had been thrown into disorder when some friendly cavalry pushed through their ranks in a narrow road. According to a Guards officer: 'Fortunately the Thirty-Third regiment was formed in the rear, and opening to allow [the fugitives] to pass, wheeled up, and initially throwing a few cool and well-directed volleys into the enemy's squadrons obliged him to decamp precipitately, enabling Abercrombie [sic] to retire without further molestation.' It was Wesley's first action, and a highly creditable, if fairly inconsequential, baptism of fire. The Duke of York conveyed his thanks to the 33rd and its commander but nonetheless the position at Boxtel had not been retaken and on 16 September the army retreated across the River Maas.[17]

A short march brought the army to the River Waal, where it took up positions that still covered most of Holland, and here it remained for the rest of the year. The autumn and winter of 1794 were exceptionally cold and the troops suffered greatly. Dysentery and fever were common, and there was a shortage of greatcoats, shoes and other necessities. By the beginning of December there were 6,501 British soldiers reported sick, or more than 30 per cent of the rank and file, and the 'death rate was enormous'.[18] One senior officer thought that 'all the physicians in the army ought to be hanged' with only a single exception and believed that 'no distemper is as destructive or dangerous as the General Hospitals'.[19] The 33rd were comparatively well off; the men were 'very well clothed' and had 'new round tents' in which to sleep.[20] There was no great increase in the number of men sick in the regiment from the (admittedly high) level reached in August; but thirty men died in November and another forty-five in December and the regiment's strength was only maintained by the arrival of drafts from England.[21] The difficulties of these first few months in the field appear to have shaped Arthur Wesley's later conduct as a commander. As soon as he was in a position to exert more influence, he would place great value on logistics and, as far as possible, on the health of his men.

Arthur Wesley's own health had recovered, but he was disenchanted with the campaign and was eager to return home on leave. There seemed little prospect of action and his account of a night's vigilance shows a touch of unconscious, or deadpan, humour: 'All is quiet here; last night an empty boat floated down the river which is the only extraordinary circumstance. It was a very small one.'[22] A fortnight later he wrote to his cousin, Sir Chichester Fortescue:

> I intend to go to England in a few days, that is to say, if the French remain quiet, and if the regiment is relieved from the advanced post upon the river Waal, where it has been for above six weeks. At present the French keep us in a perpetual state of alarm; we turn out once, sometimes twice, every night; the officers and men are harassed to death, and if we are not relieved, I believe there will be very few of the latter remaining shortly. I have not had my clothes off my back for a long time, and generally spend the greatest part of the night upon the bank of the river, notwithstanding which I have entirely got rid of that disorder which was near killing me at the close of the summer campaign. Although the French annoy us much at night, they are very entertaining during the daytime; they are perpetually chattering with our officers and soldiers, and dance the *carmagnol* upon the opposite bank whenever we desire them; but occasionally the spectators on our side are interrupted in the middle of the dance by a cannon-ball from theirs.[23]

In later life Wesley was highly critical of the army's commanders at this time and makes it clear that he sought to act differently: 'I was on the Waal, I think, from October to January, and during all that time I only saw once one general from headquarters, which was old Sir David Dundas . . . We had letters from England, and I declare that those letters told us more of what was passing at headquarters than we learnt from the headquarters themselves . . . The real reason why I succeeded in my own campaigns is because I was always on the spot – I saw everything, and did everything for myself.'[24] And: ' "You can't conceive such a state of things," the Duke used to say long years afterwards. "If we happened to be at dinner and the wine was going round, it was considered wrong to interrupt us. I have seen a packet handed in from the Austrian head-quarters, and thrown aside unopened, with a remark, That will keep till tomorrow morning. It has always been a marvel to me how any one of us escaped." '[25]

Wellington's conversation is not always a reliable source of information and the picture he paints is probably exaggerated. Still, there was much contemporary criticism of the Duke of York's style of command, most vividly expressed in Gillray's savagely brilliant caricatures.[26] By the end of November Pitt had decided that York must be recalled, and the King, though hurt, had accepted the necessity. Face was saved by appointing the Duke Commander-in-Chief of the whole army, where his influence proved surprisingly beneficial, instilling order and regularity where there had been confusion and abuses; insisting that officers performed their duty; and ensuring that they served a specified time in each rank before they were eligible for promotion. Pitt hoped to secure the services of the Duke of Brunswick to command the army in Holland, but he declined, and the British forces were left under the command of Lieutenant-General Harcourt, while Count Wallmoden commanded the Hanoverians.[27]

Senior officers in the army may have been lax, but they were not unaware of the problems faced by the troops in the field. As early as 27 September Major-General David Dundas had recognised that the indiscipline and depredations of the troops had helped to alienate the Dutch and that this created a further danger if the army was forced to retreat.[28] Another officer put things much more dramatically: 'Despised by our enemies, without discipline, confidence, or exertion among ourselves, hated and more dreaded than the enemy, even by the well-disposed inhabitants of the country, every disgrace and misfortune is to be expected.'[29] The Dutch had never been united in their support for the war, and their resolution to continue was now visibly ebbing. If they surrendered or were overcome the British army would be in peril, far from any secure base from which it could be evacuated.[30]

On 27 December 1794 the French attacked across the frozen Waal, but were driven back by a counter-attack on the following day. Arthur Wesley played a small part in this fighting and the 33rd lost two men killed. A thaw gave the British security for a few days but on 3 January the French attacked again in intense cold. There was more fighting the next day with the 33rd heavily engaged as David Dundas reported to Harcourt:

About two in the afternoon of the 4th the enemy attacked our post at Meteren about a mile in front, where half of the 33rd with a Piquet of eighty cavalry and two curricle guns were posted. Their numbers and disposition to surround the post, soon made it necessary to fall back on the other part of the Regiment, which, [was] supported with two Howitzers, and in doing which they were hard pressed by a body of the Enemy's Hussars, that galloped along the road with great vivacity. – The troops having beforehand been in an alert situation, the village of Geldermalsen was soon covered by the 42nd and 78th. The 33rd took their place in the line of defence, and the other troops were in reserve on the opposite Dyke of the Linge, the River being completely frozen and passable everywhere. The enemy still persevering in their attack, advanced on the village both in Front and Flank. But, after a great deal of musquetry firing for above an hour, were everywhere repulsed by the steadiness of the Troops, and retired upon Meteren, thro' woody and inclosed country.[31]

This suggests that Wesley handled the 33rd with some skill in a dangerous situation, and the impression is confirmed by its few casualties: only one man killed and seven wounded.

Despite the local success at Geldermalsen the French had consolidated their position across the Waal and the British withdrew to the line of the River Lek. Once the retreat began the plight of the soldiers was much worse then it had been in their well-established winter quarters behind the Waal. The crumbling will of the Dutch to resist now gave way completely. Arthur Wesley may have witnessed one episode in this process. Soon after the army reached the Lek he was ordered to escort a Dutch officer to a meeting with the French commander, General Pichegru. 'I have often thought this Dutchman was in the French interest, and this had something to do with the betraying of Utrecht. I heard nothing they said, for I was only told to take the man to the rendezvous, allow him to converse with Pichegru, and bring him back. I heard afterwards that the ostensible reason was the recovery of some papers.'[32]

Without effective Dutch support the line of the Lek was indefensible, and the army was forced to fall back to the north-east to the River Yssel and from thence to the Ems and ultimately to Bremen on the Weser. This was one of the most disastrous retreats in British military history, and it is surprising that it is not as famous as the retreat to Coruña, which it resembles. The weather was atrocious and the medical, commissariat and transport services broke down. On 11 February 600 seriously ill patients had to be abandoned to the mercy of the French who, unlike the Dutch, treated them well.[33] Major William Harness wrote home to his wife: 'The difficulties our poor people have to contend with, by night marches, by cold, and by want of necessaries have been truly great, and have surpassed the strength of many a fine fellow, who sinking under them has been left frozen to death. Our stragglers are coming in every day. The miseries of the sick are too painful to write. Seven were found dead in one Waggon.' Sir John Fortescue, the historian of the British army, admits that 'marauders from the regiments of all nations swarmed round the columns; the drivers of the waggons freed themselves from all control, and the line of march was disorderly beyond all description'. Walmoden wrote to the Duke of York: 'Your army is destroyed; the officers, their carriages, and a large train are safe, but the men are destroyed.' Fortescue estimates that the retreat cost the British army some 6,000 men.[34]

The 33rd was one of the last regiments to cross the Ems on 11 February and the worst of the retreat was over. The men were quartered in a reasonable village, and although the flooding of the river caused some problems Wesley was able to secure bread for his soldiers.[35] As it seemed that the campaign was over, at least for the moment, Wesley renewed his application for leave and – rather surprisingly – this was granted on 25 February.[36] Ten days later he was back in England. The 33rd saw some further fighting, helping to repulse further French attacks across the frozen Ems on 6 and 8 March. At the end of March the army resumed its retreat, and by the second week of April it had crossed the Weser. The 33rd embarked on 13 April, and landed in Harwich in early May.

The ten-month campaign is said to have cost the regiment 6 men killed in action, 200 dead from disease and exposure, and 192 still in hospital. This amounted to just over one-third of its strength including the drafts it received during the campaign; although many of those still in hospital would recover and rejoin the ranks.[37]

For Arthur Wesley, it had been a harsh initiation into the realities of war, with no success and little fame or glory to soften the discomforts experienced and the horrors seen, both in the fighting and in the retreat. He could not avoid the fact that he might have died in the campaign, either from a chance bullet or, even less splendidly, from dysentery or some other foul disease, and his death would have passed almost unnoticed. He survived, but more than 200 men of his regiment – men whose lives were his responsibility – did not, and that was another initiation. He learnt many lessons from the campaign: that a Commander-in-Chief should not be too distant from his troops, but should see everything for himself, and let himself be seen by the ordinary soldiers and regimental officers who made up his army; that the commissariat and the medical department needed close attention if they were to perform well, and that they were essential to the efficiency of the army; and that good relations with the local civilian population were vital, and could only be maintained by strict discipline and by ensuring that the troops did not need to plunder in order to eat. Above all, he learnt that war was a serious business which should be undertaken in a thoroughly professional spirit or not at all. Having discovered what defeat was like, he gained a fierce determination to avoid it in future.

For six years Arthur Wesley had worn the King's uniform without seriously considering its implications. The decision to join the army had been made for him by his mother and brother, and he had acquiesced, possibly with reluctance, because there was no obvious alternative. Now, having seen war, his immediate reaction was to reconsider and to endeavour to find an opening to a civilian career. Another factor may have contributed to this decision; a well-paid civilian position with good prospects would enable him to renew his suit for Kitty Pakenham. He may also have felt despondent at his prospects of advancement in the army.[38]

The world of the army, no less than the political world, was dominated by interconnected, overlapping networks of patronage. Ambitious junior officers were given opportunities or staff positions by a senior officer and might follow him from one command to another, rising in his wake, and in turn employing his sons, nephews or protégés on their staff when they rose to high command. A cursory glance at the career of Sir John Moore or Sir Thomas Graham, for example, reveals a prominent Scottish connection, headed by Sir Ralph Abercromby, which also included Alexander and John Hope, Robert Anstruther and – although they were not Scottish – John Colborne and Charles Napier, among others.[39] The high quality and later success of these men makes the connection easy to trace, but there were similar networks around other important figures such as Lord Cornwallis and, pre-eminently, the Duke of York. In the campaign on the Continent Arthur Wesley had served under three important and influential superiors: Lord Moira, Ralph Abercromby and David Dundas. But his links to them were slight and soon severed; he was nothing more than the commander of a regiment in their force. His performance was competent but not outstanding, and he had no other military patron to help him to a good command. In contrast his political connections appeared more promising. Buckingham was well disposed towards him for his own sake, while Mornington remained close to Grenville and Pitt. Westmorland and Hobart were more doubtful champions, but they might add a good word if the need arose. Given this, it seemed possible that Wesley might do better to change his career before it was too late – he was still only twenty-five – and find some civil office where he could be usefully and profitably employed.

As soon as Arthur Wesley landed in England he went to London and saw Lord Camden, who had recently been appointed the new Lord Lieutenant of Ireland, and hinted at his hopes. Camden was courteous but noncommittal, making no promises, but encouraging Wesley to return to Ireland and to remain, nominally at least, one of the aides-de-camp at Dublin Castle. This was natural enough, for any new Lord Lieutenant or Chief Secretary of Ireland was deluged with hundreds of applications for places as soon as their appointment was rumoured, and their most necessary skill was that of the bland evasion. Camden was thirty-six years old, and had only recently succeeded to his father's title. He was a close friend of Pitt, 'very pleasing and gentlemanly in his manners', but without much obvious political energy or talent. His father, a former Lord Chancellor, had secured for him an extremely valuable sinecure, which may have lessened his ambition. Lord Charlemont, who, as a leading Irish politician, had seen many Lords Lieutenant come and go, described him as 'a plain unaffected, good humoured man, of pleasing conversation and conciliatory address, and though in understanding he be not exactly his father's son or his sister's brother, yet he does not seem to be in any way deficient'.[40]

Wesley made a more direct approach to Camden in Ireland before the end of April, buttressing it with a letter from Mornington. The post sought was probably that of Under-Secretary for Military Affairs in the Irish government.[41] Evidently this was aiming too high, or the position was already promised elsewhere, for Camden replied with a firm negative. In May, Wesley endeavoured to show his potential value to the Irish government in Parliament, when he sprang to the defence of Lord Westmorland's administration, which was being attacked by Curran and Grattan. His speech was competent, but only a great orator could make much impression with a single speech, and Parliament rose before he could repeat the performance or prove his usefulness by constant attendance and frequent interventions in debates.[42]

Towards the end of June, Wesley approached Camden again, writing with as much abject humility as he could summon, asking for a place on the boards of the Irish Revenue or Treasury. He made clear that Mornington supported his application, hoped that he was not attempting 'to place myself too high', and promised unwavering regard whatever Camden's decision.[43] No one would enjoy writing such a letter, but it is fair to conclude from what we know of Wesley's later character, that he would have found the task more painful than most – and it was all for nothing. Neither Arthur Wesley's own claims, nor Mornington's support, were sufficient to raise him above the ruck of other applicants eagerly pressing for positions in the Irish government.

Late in the summer or in the early autumn there were rumours of another suitable opening: the post of Surveyor-General to the Ordnance. Again Wesley wrote, again Mornington supported him, and again they failed, with the added mortification of offending the Pakenhams, for the incumbent Surveyor-General was Lord Longford's (and Kitty's) uncle, and the rumours of his resignation were unfounded. At this Wesley admitted defeat; the 33rd were under orders for the West Indies, and he told Camden that he would sail with the regiment. Camden's reply, while not unfriendly, contains more than a hint of relief mixed with implied reproof: 'I am very sorry that we are likely to lose you next winter, at the same time I cannot but approve of your determination to accompany your Regt to the West Indies, as I am convinced a profession once embraced should not be given up. I shall be very glad if I can make some arrangement satisfactory to you against you come back, but if a vacancy should happen, in the Revenue Board, I fear the Speaker's son must have the first.'[44]

The prospect of service in the West Indies in late 1795 was much less attractive than it had been two years earlier, for the considerable successes achieved by Sir Charles Grey and Sir John Jervis, and the enormous sums of prize money they had gained, had been overshadowed by the appalling mortality that fever had inflicted on their troops. Nonetheless Wesley joined the 33rd in England and turned his attention to preparations for embarkation. The regiment was in good condition; six months of quiet had allowed it to recover from the winter's ordeal, and its recruiting parties had been busy in Yorkshire, where it had a recruiting company permanently based at Halifax, and where it gained the nickname 'the Havercake Lads'. Wesley was ill again that autumn, either a recurrence of the fever picked up in Holland, or the effect of forcing himself to do something against his deepest inclination; he was to suffer from a similar attack on returning to southern India in late 1804 when his heart was set on going home, and on several other occasions.[45]

The expedition to the West Indies was commanded by Sir Ralph Abercromby, and had been planned on a generous scale; altogether more than 30,000 troops were sent out in the hope of bringing the war in the Caribbean to a rapid conclusion. Unfortunately the preparations to mount such a large expedition dragged through the late summer and autumn, and it was not until 16 November that Abercromby's force, escorted by a squadron under the command of Rear-Admiral Sir Hugh Christian, was ready to sail. Almost at once it was struck by a tremendous storm and was scattered. Five ships were thrown ashore on Chesil Beach with heavy loss of life and others were blown along the Channel as far as Dover. When the storm subsided the ships slowly returned to Portsmouth, made their repairs and refreshed their supplies. On 9 December the armada sailed again, and made good progress until 12 December when it was hit by another gale. This time Christian persisted but the storm was followed by yet another. Many ships were in poor condition and so much time was lost due to the storms and adverse winds that there was the threat of a shortage of drinking water. On Christmas Eve the Admiral gave up the attempt and on 29 December the convoy was back where it had started. Wesley and the 33rd disembarked and spent the rest of the winter ashore in relative comfort.[46]

Between Christmas 1795 and early January 1796 Kitty Pakenham was very ill, near death at one point, and it is not unreasonable to suppose that anxiety over the fate of the expedition, and of Arthur Wesley, contributed to her troubles, while possibly the news of his safe return hastened her recovery.[47] Wesley's own health was also poor, although far from life-threatening. He visited Dublin in the spring, partly to settle some business affairs relating to Trim, and partly to make yet another unsuccessful attempt to secure a civil position on the Irish Revenue Board. When this failed he resigned his post as one of Camden's aides-de-camp, although not until he was prompted to do so.[48] Even now he did not completely despair of turning his claims on the Irish government to account and, with Mornington's customary support, invited Camden to appoint him to 'some office in Ireland' worth £800 or so a year, which he could continue to hold while serving abroad. He can hardly have been surprised when this optimistic bid to solve his financial problems suffered the same fate as its many predecessors.[49]

He also visited London and it was probably at this time that he had his portrait painted by John Hoppner, RA. With Reynolds dead and Romney in decline, Hoppner was one of the leading portrait painters of the day, enjoying strong support from the court, and rivalled only by the precocious genius of Thomas Lawrence. His portrait of Wesley is pleasing, although so different from the familiar later images that it is disconcerting (see plate 9). This is partly because of the long, powdered hair, and partly because of the fuller face, which would be chiselled by exertion and fevers in India. The eyebrows are thick and the jaw strong, giving some hint of Wesley's character. The mouth is small – a family trait accentuated by the fashion of the day, which regarded a broad mouth as plebeian. Almost certainly the portrait was commissioned by Mornington who, more than forty years later, told his brother: 'It is admirable, much the best which exists of you; the likeness is perfect and conveys the true expression of your countenance.'[50] It was one of a series of portraits of the family which Hoppner painted in these years: Richard, William and Henry, all bearing a strong family likeness, which is increased by the powdered hair and similar poses; their sister Anne, with her two young daughters; and Richard's wife Hyacinthe, with their two eldest sons, born, like all their children, before their marriage in November 1794.[51]

Arthur's younger sister, Mary, died in 1794 at the age of twenty-two. His older sister, Anne, had married Henry Fitzroy in 1790, but his health was poor and they went to Portugal where he died of consumption. Henry Wesley was sent to escort her home, but their ship was captured by a French frigate and they were taken to Brest and then, after being harangued by the local Representative of the People, detained at an inland town. The fall of Robespierre in July 1794 may have saved their lives, and led to Anne's release; an American merchant vessel provided her with a passage home. At the same time Henry and a fellow detainee bribed their guards and escaped. They crossed the Channel in January 1795 in an open boat with a dozen British seamen also escaping. The weather was bad and the cold so intense that three of the sailors died of exposure and one was drowned; Henry's feet were frostbitten, and he took three months to recover from his ordeal.[52] Anne subsequently married Charles Culling-Smith in 1799, while Henry, who had already served briefly in the army and as secretary of legation and chargé d'affaires at Stockholm, became a précis writer at the Foreign Office.

Gerald Wesley, the brother younger than Arthur but older than Henry, had gone into the Church and, according to one of his parishioners, was 'very popular in society, and also in the pulpit'.[53] William, who was six years older than Arthur, had gone from Eton into the navy for four years as a midshipman, and then sat as MP for Trim in the Irish Parliament from 1783–90. In 1781 he had inherited the Queen's County estates of his cousin William Pole, and had changed his own name to William Wellesley-Pole. Unlike Arthur, he was financially secure and independent, and he married Katherine Forbes (daughter and co-heir of Admiral the Hon. John Forbes) in 1784. Many years later Lord Glenbervie wrote that she still surpassed her three admirable daughters 'in figure, sense and agreement'.[54] If any of the Wesleys made a happy marriage, it was William.

Richard's private affairs were a source of enjoyable scandal for London society; Hyacinthe Roland, the mistress whom he married in 1794, was French, from an obscure and probably disreputable background, but Richard was passionately devoted to her and to their children. The affair did not help his political career, although it was not a major obstacle. More serious, although still not critical, was the fact that his neglect of his constituents while MP for Windsor (1787–96) had made a bad impression on the King. Mornington had held minor government posts since 1786, but he had failed to make a substantial reputation in the House of Commons, and despite Pitt's promises and Grenville's support his lack of progress up the ladder of office was becoming noticeable. In the spring of 1796 there was nothing to distinguish the Wellesleys from any of the other families that made up the great mass of the ruling class in Britain – no hint of genius, or any suggestion that they would make any mark on history. Nor would any observer have guessed that Arthur, the rejected suitor and reluctant soldier, would become the most successful of them all.

PART II

INDIA AND INDEPENDENCE

CHAPTER FOUR

ARRIVAL IN INDIA
(1796–98)

IN FEBRUARY 1796 the British government decided to send substantial reinforcements to India and, as part of this plan, the destination of the 33rd was
changed from the West to the East Indies – a decision that would shape the rest
of Arthur Wesley's life. The regiment embarked in April, but Wesley did not sail
with them; he spent another two months at home recovering his health and
settling his affairs. On 3 May he received a promotion to colonel in the army,
while still retaining the rank of senior lieutenant-colonel and commanding
officer of the 33rd; a general officer (Lord Cornwallis) remained the regiment's
colonel, a sinecure with a loose role overseeing its internal affairs and an interest
in its finances.[1] By the middle of June Wesley was at Portsmouth preparing to
sail. A dozen East Indiamen were assembling at Portsmouth and the Isle of Wight
to carry two further regiments of infantry, the 12th and 86th Regiments, as well
as their usual cargoes, to India. The troops had been embarked on 8 June after an
inspection had weeded out fifty sickly men, but it was almost three weeks before
the convoy finally sailed. The Dutch fleet, now allied to France, was at sea, and
on the first stage of its voyage the convoy was escorted by Admiral Colpoys with
a powerful squadron of seven ships of the line. When Colpoys wished them *bon
voyage* at 'a certain latitude', HMS *Trusty* (fifty guns) and the frigate *Fox* continued
to protect the convoy until it reached the Cape of Good Hope. Wesley sailed
either on the Indiaman *Princess Charlotte*, or HMS *Fox* whose captain, Pulteney
Malcolm, was to be his host on several future voyages, and whose brother, John
Malcolm, was to become one of Wesley's most confidential friends in India.[2]

The voyage to the Cape appears to have been uneventful. The ships passed
within sight of Madeira, but did not stop, and saw the Peak of Tenerife and the
Cape Verde Islands in the distance. George Elers, one of the officers of the 12th
on the *Rockingham* (Indiaman) recalls an encounter with a small Portuguese
vessel that enabled them to buy 'some delicious oranges'. The days passed slowly,
walking the deck, reading, playing backgammon or chess and talking. Crossing

the equator they 'went through the wonted ceremony of receiving old Neptune, and paying the usual forfeit by those who passed it for the first time'. The ships were then becalmed for ten days or a fortnight while the passengers suffered from 'a most tormenting skin eruption called the prickly heat', but at last a breeze sprang up and Elers records his pleasure in the 'sublime' sunsets and 'delicious' moonlit nights.[3] Wesley had with him a formidable travelling library of some 200 volumes, half of which he had recently bought in London. The collection included much serious history and literature, books on India, military studies and a Persian dictionary and grammar. There were sets of Locke, Paley, Bolingbroke and Swift, together with Adam Smith's *Wealth of Nations* and Blackstone's *Commentaries on the Laws of England*. As a collection it suggests a desire for serious study and a plan of thorough self-education; but even the most dedicated scholar, in the most propitious circumstances, would have taken several years to master it completely. Throughout his life Wesley showed himself adept at absorbing information and drawing conclusions, while he wrote fluent, well-organised prose, but his bent was more practical than intellectual. No doubt he read some of the books, and was glad to have others when in India, but serious study was difficult at sea, as even Sir James Mackintosh, the Whig philosopher, found when he made the same voyage in 1804.[4]

The convoy reached the Cape, and Wesley joined the 33rd, in September. He mixed a good deal with the officers of the 12th, especially their commander, Colonel Henry Hervey Aston, who was a few years older than him. Aston had been a man of fashion, a companion of the Prince of Wales, and a noted duellist, until extravagance and debts forced him to seek to repair his fortune in India. According to George Elers, to whom he was very kind, his wardrobe included more than fifty pairs of boots and a couple of hundred coats. If Wesley had not already acquired a taste for fashion, Aston's influence may well have aroused his interest in clothes.[5] George Elers gives a good description of Wesley's appearance at this time:

> In height he was about 5 feet 7 inches, with a long, pale face, and a remarkably large acquiline nose, a clear blue eye, and the blackest beard I ever saw. He was remarkably clean in his person, and I have known him shave twice in one day, which I believe was his constant practice . . . He spoke at this time remarkably quickly, with, I think, a very, very slight lisp. He had very narrow jaw-bones, and there was a great peculiarity in his ear . . . the lobe of the ear uniting to the cheek. He had a peculiar way, when pleased, of pursing up his mouth.[6]

Elers adds that Wesley 'was all life and spirits', and that he was captivated by the seventeen-year-old Miss Henrietta Smith who, with her older sister, was travelling out to join her parents in Madras.[7]

After a pleasant interlude at the Cape, the troops re-embarked and sailed for India: the 12th to Madras, and the 33rd to Bengal. Wesley reached Calcutta 'after a most tedious passage' of more than three months on 17 February 1797.[8] On arrival, Wesley presented himself to Sir John Shore, the Governor-General, armed with a letter of introduction from Lord Cornwallis, who, as well as being colonel of the 33rd, had been Shore's predecessor and patron in India. The letter said very little more than that Wesley was 'a sensible man and a good officer', and certainly did not suggest any great warmth or personal interest, but it was sufficient for the occasion.[9] Shore would have welcomed Wesley even if he had come empty-handed. He was a colonel and commanding officer of one of the King's regiments – a recommendation that counted for much more in the small British society of late-eighteenth-century Bengal than it did in England or Ireland. And he was well born, the brother of a parliamentary supporter of the government, who was a friend of Grenville and Pitt, and a member of the Board of Control. Credentials that were insignificant in Dublin were impressive in Calcutta, especially as Shore himself had few strong political connections at home, and was at loggerheads with Lord Hobart, the governor of Madras. India gave a relatively junior officer, such as Arthur Wesley, opportunities that would have been far beyond his reach at home, and he seized them with remarkable and surprising confidence.

Shore was a modest, quiet, religious man, who had risen through the ranks of the East India Company while maintaining his integrity. He may have lacked warmth – he was described as being 'cold as a greyhound's nose'[10] – but his rare combination of efficiency and probity gained him the trust of Cornwallis. He was both hospitable and kind to Wesley, introducing him to his domestic circle and attending to his wishes on official matters. Shore's son, writing many years later, claimed that the Governor-General was much struck by Wesley's 'union of strong sense and boyish playfulness which he had never seen exemplified in any other individual'. He also records a family legend that Wesley was a great playfellow of Charlotte, Shore's eldest daughter, then still a child, 'whom he used to employ in intercepting the billets-doux which passed between a gallant Baronet, aide-de-camp of my father, and the lady to whom he was affianced, and of whom the [colonel] was enamoured'.[11]

But although Wesley was on such good terms with Shore and his family he did not become his partisan in the dispute with Lord Hobart. Mornington and Hobart were friends, and the governor of Madras had welcomed Wesley to India with an encouraging letter, promising to do all in his power to assist the colonel's career if, as he hoped and expected, he succeeded Shore in Bengal. Wesley privately told his brother that Shore was likely to take advantage of the success of some negotiations with one of the native powers to go home, rather than waiting for another storm to break. Yet within a few months Hobart had quarrelled violently with Wesley, sending him a letter 'in such terms as I suppose no Gentleman ever used to another: at all events in such as I have been unaccustomed to receive & never will submit to – I don't know what I did to offend him. I have never written to him since to ask the cause of his anger & am quite unconscious of having given him any'.[12] Unfortunately the letter does not survive, so we can only guess that rumour may have misled Hobart, or that Wesley was not being entirely frank with his brother. Given the tension between Hobart and Shore and the difficulties of communication between Bengal and Madras, the former seems more likely.

Colonel Wesley and the officers of the 33rd were a popular addition to British society in Bengal as a whole, not just to the Governor-General's family. It was a hard-drinking, masculine, raffish society, vividly portrayed in the *Memoirs* of William Hickey, a Calcutta lawyer and *bon vivant*. St Patrick's Day was celebrated 'with much hilarity', Colonel Wesley presiding at the dinner and 'doing the duties of the Chair with peculiar credit to himself'. Three days later a new figure arrived who outranked Wesley in both the social and military stakes: Major-General John St Leger who, like Colonel Aston, had come to India to repair the damage done to his finances by a close friendship with the heir to the throne, although betting and horses had also played their part in St Leger's ruin.[13] Such a man was little to the taste of the Governor-General, with whom he almost immediately quarrelled, but was welcomed with open arms by Hickey and his friends. Hickey's recollections of the resulting round of parties exude nostalgia, with the guests, the songs, the drinking and the splendour of it all recalled fondly: 'My first party besides General St Leger and family [i.e. his military staff], consisted of Colonel Wellesley, Mr Royds, Mr Simon Ewart . . . [and many others] so that we usually sat down a dozen at table when we pushed the claret about very freely'.[14] Wesley privately doubted St Leger's professional competence, but nonetheless joined the parties with enthusiasm and, among other guests, got to know the General's young aide-de-camp, Captain De Lancey, who, years later, was to hold important positions on his own staff, and to be mortally wounded at Waterloo. The climax of Hickey's entertainments came with the celebrations of the King's birthday on 4 June. Three days of horseracing delighted St Leger, who declared that it was almost as good as Newmarket. The races were followed by a dinner for sixteen for which Hickey procured 'a very fine turtle and half of a tolerably fat deer, engaging an eminent French cook from Calcutta' to prepare the dishes. Hickey sat at the head of the table with St Leger on his right and Wesley on his left and, with numerous toasts and songs from several of the company, the entertainment 'went off with the utmost hilarity and good humour'. The dinner began at three in the afternoon – still a fashionable hour – and 'we did not break up until between two and three o'clock in the morning, when my guests retired to their respective apartments'.[15]

Despite such excesses, Wesley's health was good and he found the climate less oppressive than he had been led to expect. Nonetheless, he regarded India as 'a miserable country to live in, and I now begin to think that a man well deserves some of the wealth which is sometimes brought home, for having spent his life here'. And he told his brother that:

The natives, as far as I have observed, are much misrepresented. They are the most mischievous deceitful race of people I have seen or read of. I have not yet met with a Hindoo who had one good quality, even for the state of society for his own country, and the Mussulmans are worse than they are. Their meekness and mildness do not exist. It is true that the feats which have been performed by Europeans have made them objects of fear; but wherever the disproportion of numbers is greater than usual, they uniformly destroy them if they can, and in their dealings and conduct among themselves they are the most atrociously cruel people I ever heard of . . .[16]

This was his opinion after a few months in Bengal. As time passed and he gained greater experience, particularly in Madras and southern India, he became much less sweeping and dismissive in his view of Indians, and learnt to work closely with native rulers and their ministers. In other words he soon discarded the second-hand prejudices he had picked up in Calcutta, and was as practical and pragmatic in his dealing with Indians as he was with Europeans. Unlike some British officers he did not fall in love with Indian culture, and his comments still tended to be caustic, but that would be true of him throughout his career, whether he was writing from India, Ireland, Portugal, France or Hampshire, for the milk of human kindness did not flow readily from his pen.

Fortunately for Wesley the prospect of action soon rescued him from Hickey's dangerous dinners. Spain had made peace with revolutionary France in 1795 and in the following year had joined her in war with Britain. The government in London responded by issuing orders for an attack on the Spanish colony in the Philippines to be mounted by a combined force from Bengal and Madras. The 33rd were to take part, and for a brief moment Wesley even had hopes that he might be given the overall command. As the opposition was expected to be minimal and success would bring a vast sum in prize money – of which the commander would receive the lion's share – it was a prospect to set the pulse racing. But such a plum was really too good for Wesley, and Hobart insisted that General Braithwaite (from Madras) command, with St Leger (from Bengal) as his second. The disappointment was keenly felt, and Wesley wrote some harsh things about the competence of both superior officers in his letters home, while criticising Hobart for his folly in imagining that capable staff officers could make up for poor commanders. This was understandable, but Wesley had no real grievance, for he had neither long service nor proven ability to justify a claim to the command, and when he thought that he might receive it, had admitted to his brother that he would have to rely on 'the known pusillanimity of the enemy and my exertions' to compensate 'for my want of experience'.[17]

Preparations for the expedition stretched over several months, and Wesley took a keen interest in all the practical details. He wrote with remarkable confidence to the Governor-General even on matters that were, strictly speaking, none of his business, such as the allowance to be paid to the captains of the East Indiamen for carrying troops. An order from St Leger, subordinating the officers and soldiers to the captain of their ship in the event of action at sea, produced a protest direct to Shore, and the order was hastily rescinded. The notable fact about this incident is not that Wesley was right – he usually was on such questions – but the peremptory tone in which he wrote to the most senior figure in British India, and the nervous, placatory manner with which Shore took responsibility for the mistake and promised to correct it. Clearly Colonel Wesley was not a man easily daunted, nor one who was likely to prove a comfortable subordinate.[18]

Not that Wesley had his way on everything. Before the expedition sailed he prepared a memorandum urging that a detachment from the main force be employed to capture the Dutch East Indies, or at least their main settlement at Batavia. However, Hobart had already considered and rejected this idea, arguing that it would weaken the expedition too much, and risk delays in an already lengthy operation.[19] Wesley was on safer ground in issuing detailed regulations for the shipboard routine of his soldiers. The object of these rules was to keep the troops clean, healthy and safe: 'The men should be made to wash their feet and legs every morning and evening, and occasionally water should be thrown over every man; every day if possible.' Smoking was only permitted in certain parts of the ship, to minimise the risk of fire, and the soldiers were to attend Divine Service every Sunday, dressed in their best clothes, which they were then to put neatly away. Fresh air was beneficial, so 'all men must be upon the deck from seven o'clock in the morning till sunset, unless obliged to go down by bad weather'. These regulations were closely modelled on guidelines issued by the War Office two years earlier to regiments (including the 33rd) bound for the West Indies, but Wesley added several new points, including twice-weekly musketry practice with live ammunition.[20]

The Bengal contingent of the expedition sailed for Penang on 9 August 1797. The 33rd had a new chaplain, Mr Blunt, a protégé of William Hickey, whom Wesley had agreed to take on trial, the position being vacant. Unfortunately after three days at sea, this 'incomprehensible young man', as Hickey calls him, 'got abominably drunk', stripped off his clothes, and ran stark naked among the soldiers and sailors, 'talking all sorts of bawdy and ribaldry, and singing scraps of the most blackguard and indecent songs, so as to render himself a common laughing stock'. The natural remorse of the following morning was strengthened by a paternal lecture from the ship's captain, who evidently did not mince his words. The young clergyman was 'quite overcome', declared that he was ruined beyond redemption, and shut himself in his cabin refusing to see anyone or join the mess at meals. The ship's officers tried to rally his spirits, but in vain, and in some alarm the captain sent for Colonel Wesley, whose ship was not far off. Wesley came at once and reassured Mr Blunt, 'that no one would think the worse of him for the little irregularities committed in a moment of forgetfulness, that the most correct and cautious men were liable to be led astray by convivial society, and no blame ought to attach to a cursory debauch'. It is a scene somewhat at odds with Wesley's reputation as a strict disciplinarian, but he was far from being a prude or a hypocrite, and Hickey's good cheer was still fresh in his mind. But not even the most sympathetic commanding officer could console Mr Blunt, who 'actually fretted himself to death', ten days after his moment of madness.[21]

After this absurd tragedy it must have been with relief that Wesley reached Penang. Evidently the troops from Bengal were the first to arrive, but they were soon joined by a division from Madras, including the 12th Regiment. According to George Elers, the men were not disembarked, but the officers spent time ashore and 'led a very quiet, stupid life'. Wesley used the interlude of enforced inactivity to compose a long memorandum advocating the permanent occupation of Penang and – either now, or at about this time – wrote another surveying the economy of Bengal.[22] These documents are more remarkable for the confidence with which Wesley tackled unfamiliar, and perhaps unappealing, subjects, ranging from Indian agriculture and the monsoons, to the sugar trade of the Caribbean, than for the depth of his knowledge. But they provide clear evidence of an unusually ambitious, intelligent and well-read officer who looked far beyond the horizons of his regiment, or even the immediate state of the war, and who was already comfortable assembling his thoughts into coherent arguments on paper.

Wesley never got further east than Penang. The expedition was first delayed when the second division of transports was late in reaching Madras, and then abandoned when news arrived that Austria, faced with Bonaparte's advance from northern Italy towards Vienna, had made peace. According to Admiral Rainier, this left the French free to turn 'their attention to the execution of their long projected plan of attack on the British Possessions in this Country in concert with Tippoo [Tipu] Sultan with whom they have had much friendly intercourse of late'.[23] Lord Hobart, who as governor of Madras was most directly threatened by Tipu, agreed, and ordered the troops to return from

Penang. Had the expedition gone ahead it might have made the principal officers wealthy and even given private soldiers and sailors some welcome prize money, but it would have done nothing to assist Britain's war effort. Subsequent reconnaissance showed that the Spanish ships in the Philippines were unseaworthy and so posed no threat to British trade with China. Once captured, Manila would have required a substantial garrison, depleting the disposable British force in India to no advantage. Crucially, the Spanish colony in the Philippines was not self-supporting, depending on large annual shipments of silver from Acapulco. When the British had captured Manila in 1762, the result had been a shortage of specie throughout the East, which had seriously disrupted trade.[24] Altogether the expedition of 1797 was ill conceived and its cancellation fortunate. As for Wesley, the capture of Manila might have made his fortune, but he might also have been appointed governor, or even lieutenant-governor, of the new conquest, and languished for years in obscurity.

By November, the 33rd was back in Bengal and William Hickey was again a frequent guest at the regimental mess. 'They lived inimitably well, always sending their guests away with a liberal quantity of the best claret. They generally entertained from five to ten guests daily at their table.' On one occasion Hickey was rather unwell and tried to avoid dinner with Wesley and other 'equally strong heads', but they overcame his scruples, and he recalls downing twenty-two formal toasts 'in glasses of considerable magnitude', before the guests were permitted to drink at their own pace. This was too much even for Hickey: 'The next day I was incapable of leaving my bed, from an excruciating headache, which I did not get rid of for eight-and-forty hours; indeed a more severe debauch I never was engaged in any part of the world.'[25]

Hard-drinking and hangovers were not the only problems to affect the officers of the 33rd. Captain Amos Norcott got into debt gambling and faced the prospect of having to sell his commission and leave the army. Wesley regarded him as an excellent officer and, rather than lose him and see his life ruined, borrowed £600 on his behalf to settle the debts, having first obtained a solemn promise that Norcott would never gamble again. As this suggests, Wesley's own finances – for so long a source of frustration and anxiety to him – were steadily improving; he told his Irish agent that 'I am richer now than I ever was' and would soon be able to remit two full years' interest on his debts.[26] Even so, he could not afford to give Norcott the money, and the young officer's connections at home proved rather reluctant to repay the debt. Norcott himself found the position awkward, and further complications arose with the suggestion that he purchase a promotion and transfer into another regiment – Wesley again lending him the necessary funds. This came to nothing, but not before some other officers, including Captain Keating, who had recently purchased his own promotion in the 33rd, showed their resentment at the apparent favouritism.[27] Yet in the end Wesley's judgement was vindicated; Norcott remained in the 33rd until 1802 when he transferred to the 95th Rifles. He had a distinguished career, serving at Coruña, Walcheren, Barrosa, and the closing campaigns of the Peninsular War, including the Nive and Orthez, before being severely wounded at Tarbes. He commanded the 2nd battalion, 95th Rifles in the Waterloo campaign and was again wounded on 18 June. When he died in 1838 he was Major-General Sir Amos Norcott CB, commanding the southern district in Ireland, whose honours included many British and foreign decorations. But if it had not been for the kindness and perception of his colonel forty years earlier, he would have been forced to throw up his commission and retire from the army.[28]

The standing orders that Wesley issued to the 33rd at this time have survived, and give an interesting insight into his priorities and style of command. They are quite lengthy, a dozen printed pages, and precisely detailed on matters that he regarded as important, but they leave considerable latitude on other questions. Compared to similar orders for other regiments there is remarkably little on dress, Wesley claiming that 'there is no subject of which I understand so little'. Given his later reputation for dressing smartly – one of his nicknames was 'the beau' – this is surprising and possibly disingenuous, an excuse not to harass the men unnecessarily, for he always cared far more for the true discipline and fighting quality of his men, than for their outward show. Not that appearances could be neglected, especially when it came to the men's weapons: 'It is expected from the Soldier that his arms and accoutrements are at all times in the highest order, that they be not only clean, but highly polished.' But his real concern was for the physical welfare of the troops – a legacy perhaps of his experience in the Low Countries – and he was stern in his demand that officers should not shirk their duty of ensuring that their men were comfortable and healthy. Fresh food was important; companies were to be divided into messes, 'and on each Market day a non-commissioned Officer is to go with a man of every mess to buy meat and vegetables'. Gambling of any kind was absolutely forbidden, but he a took a sensible, pragmatic attitude towards sex:

The Soldiers are not to bring into Barracks any Common Prostitute, if they do the Sergeant must turn them out and confine the man; however if any man wishes to keep a native woman and obtains his Captain's permission to do so, there is no objection to her being in the Barracks, and the Officer will be cautious not to give permission to any but well-behaved men.

Altogether the orders show a conscientious, humane and intelligent approach, suggesting that the 33rd was fortunate in its commander, although, of course, it was easier to draw up wise regulations than to ensure they were appropriately enforced.[29]

Wesley did not remain in Bengal for long; there was little chance of active service there, and regimental life soon palled. So, in January 1798, he set out on a private tour to Madras. If hostilities broke out in India they were most likely to involve war with Tipu, Sultan of Mysore, and be conducted primarily by the Madras army of the East India Company, with some support from the British forces in Bengal and Bombay. Few details of the two months Wesley spent in Madras have survived, but it is clear from the memoranda he drew up after his return that he had travelled extensively, making notes of the terrain and assessing its significance in a war with Mysore. He also met many of the leading British officers in the Madras army, including its commander Lieutenant-General George Harris, who became acting governor when Hobart sailed for home on 21 February. Not all were strangers, for Colonel Aston and the officers of the 12th entertained him hospitably, broaching a new shipment of wine from London, and finding it 'so bad as to be scarcely drinkable'.[30]

Wesley sailed from Madras on the *Endeavour* on 10 April 1798 and reached Calcutta on 3 May. Captain Eastwick, the ship's captain, later recalled:

When I became acquainted with [Colonel Wesley] he was a very spare man (as indeed he remained ever afterwards) most conversable and sociable, and without more pride than he ought to have. His behaviour towards ladies was exceedingly courteous. My second officer, Mr Ross, was married, and had his pretty young wife on board, and Colonel [Wesley] admired her very much, and constantly walked the deck in her company. One day I happened to show him a miniature of my wife, and his first exclamation was: 'Surely she is not so handsome as this!' His living was plain, and he drank but sparingly, and this at a time when hard drinking was considered fashionable. His wants were very few, and it is amazing what little sleep he required. Whenever I was on deck, late at night or early in the morning (and in those days I never slept more than two or three hours at a stretch), I always seemed to find him pacing the quarterdeck. There was one relaxation of which he was very fond, and that was a game of high whist, which he, the two Messrs Simpson (who were passengers on board) and myself played regularly every evening.[31]

Eastwick goes on to describe Wesley – increasingly characteristically – chafing at a delay when the tide was against them on the final stage of their journey upriver to Calcutta, and he needed to be at the Residency by morning to be entitled to his monthly field allowance. 'He said not a word, but he was essentially a prompt and determined man in his actions, and he could not brook anything approaching to opposition.' Eastwick managed to get him a paunchway – 'the commonest kind of craft on the river, and only used by the poorest natives' – and in this he completed his journey, and so arrived in time to claim his allowance.[32]

A fortnight later Wesley's prospects were transformed by the arrival of Shore's successor as Governor-General of Bengal. His name was Richard Wesley, Earl of Mornington.

CHAPTER FIVE

MORNINGTON AND THE INDIAN SCENE

ARTHUR WESLEY SPENT eight years in India, the last seven of them with his brother as Governor-General. They were crucial years in which he developed his skills as a commander of men, a tactician, a strategic planner and a civil governor. He considered great questions of war and peace, grand strategy and diplomacy, finance and how Indian affairs would be perceived by public opinion at home. He discovered his brother's strengths and weaknesses, and gained confidence in his own ability and judgement. He found his vocation and enjoyed great success – mixed with intense disappointment and some bitterness – and his mature character came into focus for the first time. However none of this can be properly understood without pausing to consider the strategic and political context in which he and Mornington operated and how it related to the wider war against France.

The British possessions in India were divided into three separate regions, or Presidencies, each with its own government based in Calcutta (Fort William), Bombay and Madras (Fort St George). The most important of these was Calcutta, which ruled the great province of Bengal where Wesley was stationed on his arrival in India. Bengal was populous and wealthy, able to assist the other territories when they were under attack. Bombay, the old centre of British trade, was now in decline and was chronically short of money. And Madras, around which Wesley conducted his private tour early in 1798, and which included the Northern Circars, exercised real, although indirect, control over the surrounding coastal territory of the Carnatic. Each of these Presidencies had its own government and army, while the extent of the Governor-General's supervisory authority was ill-defined and much influenced by the personality of the individuals in question.

Three significant Indian powers remained outside the British sphere and played an active role in the events of the next few years: Hyderabad, the Maratha

Confederation and Mysore. Hyderabad was a relic of the Mughal Empire surviving in southern India. By the 1790s it was ramshackle, ill-governed and edging towards chaos. Its ruler, the Nizam, was old and ill, doubtful of his ability to ensure the succession of his chosen heir in the face of revolts by his other sons. His faith in the British had been destroyed when Mornington's predecessor, Sir John Shore, would not intervene to assist him against a Maratha attack and his army was defeated at Kharda in 1795. He sought security by adding to his army a force of troops trained on European lines by European – mostly French – officers. However this was an expensive and uneasy solution, for the new troops absorbed much of Hyderabad's revenue and their loyalty was uncertain. Their presence also attracted the attention of Mornington and the government in London, who feared that they might assist any French attempt to intervene in India.

The Maratha Confederation was the largest single power in India, but it was deeply divided, with five great Maratha princes, each of them rulers of a virtually independent state, constantly jockeying for influence at the capital Poona. Britain generally maintained fairly good relations with the Marathas based not on friendship but on mutual respect and caution. When they had gone to war in 1775, the result had been indecisive and uncomfortable for both sides, and the seven-year conflict had ended with the conclusion of a formal alliance, the Treaty of Salbai (17 May 1782). In the early 1790s the Marathas joined the British in a war against Mysore, but their methods of campaigning were so different that cooperation proved difficult and frustrating.[1] The alliance remained nominally in place but it was marked more by wariness than by trust.

The third major Indian power was Mysore, a compact country in southern India ruled by Tipu Sultan from his fortress capital of Seringapatam (Srirangapattana). His father, Haider Ali, had been a brilliant soldier of fortune who had first served, and then usurped, the Hindu rajas of Mysore. Haider had established his government on secure foundations, and while Tipu lacked his father's shrewdness, he proved an effective, if autocratic and at times eccentric ruler. In the years before Mornington's appointment, Britain and Mysore had fought three wars, with Haider achieving considerable success in the first two, devastating the hinterland of Madras to within sight of the city and leaving a deep impression on the British inhabitants. European officers and men taken prisoner in these wars were kept in severe captivity for years, some of them in chains, and returned home with lurid tales of forced conversions to Islam and young English midshipmen transformed into dancing boys at the court of an Oriental despot.[2] Tipu was defeated by Cornwallis in the Third Mysore War (1790–92) but only after two long, difficult campaigns, the first of which had been abandoned beneath the walls of Seringapatam with the loss of the entire siege train and immense quantities of other equipment. The resulting peace

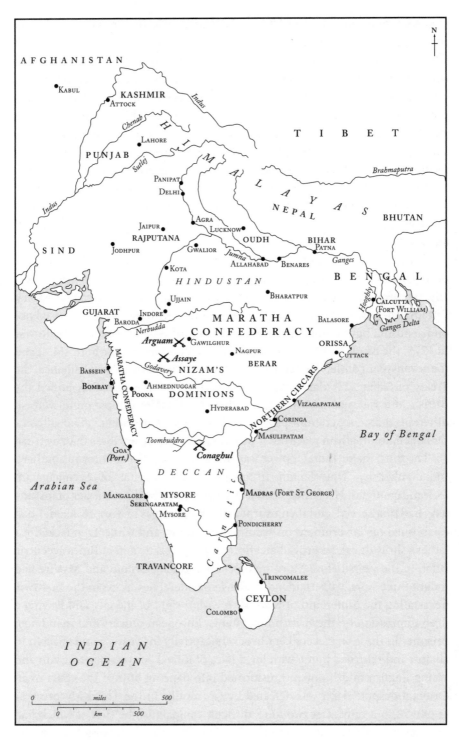

2 India in 1798.

had stripped Mysore of important territories and made it much more vulnerable to a fresh invasion, although neither Tipu nor the British appear to have
recognised just how far the scales had been tilted, for he continued to plot
revenge and the British – at least at Madras – continued to dread the prospect
of war with Mysore.

In deciding how to manage relations with Hyderabad, the Marathas and
Mysore, Mornington had to serve two masters: the British government and the
East India Company, which had been founded almost 200 years earlier to
conduct British trade in the region. So long as the Mughal Empire had flourished, European traders had been a minor element in Indian affairs, confined
to small enclaves on the coast, and militarily and politically insignificant,
although the trade they managed was mutually profitable. But the decline of
the Mughals in the first half of the eighteenth century created a power vacuum
which neither the Marathas nor the other local powers were able to fill. The
British and French seized the opportunity, driven more by rivalry and greed
than by a clear vision of empire and conquest. Clive's victory at Plassey in 1757
and much skilful diplomatic manoeuvring gave the Company effective control
of Bengal, and within a few years French power in southern India was broken.
The early years of the Company's rule in Bengal were marked by extraordinary
scenes of plunder, corruption and extortion far beyond the prevailing norms of
either India or Britain, even in an age when attitudes to financial probity were
comfortably relaxed.[3] These excesses soon triggered a reaction which led to a
marked improvement under Hastings and even more so under Cornwallis,
Shore and Mornington, but it was not until late in the eighteenth century that
wealth acquired in India began to lose its dubious reputation. (As late as 1810
a British journal would imply that there was something unsavoury behind the
modest fortune which Arthur Wesley had brought home from India, although
it quickly withdrew the insinuation when his brother William showed that it
was baseless in a statement to Parliament.)[4] After much controversy, and the
fall of the Fox–North coalition government in 1783, Pitt introduced an India
Bill in 1784 which left the Company with its patronage and trade, while the
government exercised effective control over the most senior appointments and
matters of policy.

Pitt's bill contained a solemn declaration that 'to pursue schemes of conquest
and extension of dominion in India, are measures repugnant to the wish, the
honour and the policy of this nation', and buttressed it with a prohibition on
treaties or alliances that were not strictly and narrowly defensive.[5] Subsequent
events make this appear sanctimonious and hypocritical, but at the time it was
sincere, accurately reflecting the revulsion against Indian conquests which was
the predominant mood of the moment. When Warren Hastings returned to
England in the following year he was not received as a national hero, but rather

faced concerted attacks from his old enemy Philip Francis, which led to his famous impeachment. The opening weeks of his trial in 1788 mark the climax of the phase of righteous rejection of empire, but the mood changed as the trial dragged on for months and then years, and the prosecution failed to make good its more spectacular allegations.[6]

The undoubted integrity of Cornwallis (who was appointed Governor-General in 1786) assisted this change of attitude, and his war with Tipu Sultan of Mysore (1790–92) was greeted with a patriotic outburst of support from which few dissented.[7] The Company's charter was renewed in 1793 with little opposition, and although the prohibition on wars of conquest was repeated, the feeling behind it had cooled. Sir John Shore may have taken it seriously, but Mornington cared little for the letter and less for the spirit of the law. The war with revolutionary France undoubtedly strengthened popular support for victories anywhere on the globe, although few ministers other than Henry Dundas (Pitt's lieutenant, whose responsibilities included India) felt much enthusiasm for colonial expansion for its own sake.

The war also absorbed the attention of the British government. Ministers, even Dundas, had little time to spare for India, and it seems highly unlikely that any member of the Cabinet ever read Mornington's enormously long despatches in full, let alone their interminable enclosures.[8] In any case close supervision was impossible, for it could easily take a full year from the composition of a despatch in Bengal to the receipt of the reply from London. The selection of Mornington for a position of such independence and responsibility is surprising, for at thirty-seven his career had not so much stalled as never properly started, and he had not held any major office at home. Originally he had been destined to succeed Hobart at Madras, but the directors of the East India Company had objected to the return of Cornwallis and, with no obvious alternative available, Pitt and Dundas elevated Mornington, hoping that his obvious ability and self-confidence would make up for his lack of experience.

Many years later, writing in old age, Mornington claimed that until he reached the Cape of Good Hope, part-way through his journey to India, he was not:

> imbued with a spirit of conquest, and an ambitious desire of extending our territorial possessions by violence or war. I arrived in the full hope and expectation of finding and of preserving not merely peace in India, but permanent security, and a general disposition to preserve tranquillity and good will among the native powers.[9]

But even if this is accepted at face value, the bias of Mornington's personality was towards action not inaction, and to shape events according to his will, not merely to react to them. He was an imperious, masterful man, intolerant of opposition and impatient when checked or thwarted. It seems unlikely that in any circumstances, far less those of 1798, he would have been the quiet custodian of Britain's Indian Empire, encouraging its trade, nursing its finances, and using tact and diplomacy to ensure peaceful relations with its neighbours. Still, it may equally be doubted whether Cornwallis or even Shore could have maintained the uneasy peace that existed in 1798, for like Mornington, the Indian princes were determined to pursue their own interests, and did not find the prospect of war repugnant.

Mornington landed at Cape Town on 28 January and spent six weeks ashore while his vessel was refitted. He was much influenced by Major William Kirkpatrick, the British envoy (or Resident) to Hyderabad, who was there on leave for the sake of his health. Kirkpatrick's firsthand account of Indian affairs made more of an impression than formal despatches read far away in London or on the high seas. In particular Kirkpatrick convinced Mornington of the danger posed by the Nizam's increasing reliance on troops trained and led by French mercenary officers. Mornington told Dundas that 'the chief officers are Frenchmen of the most virulent and notorious principles of Jacobinism; and the whole corps constitutes an armed French party of great zeal, diligence and activity'.[10] This was no mere fantasy, for we now know that the commander of the Nizam's troops, M. Raymond, had been in correspondence with the French government since 1787, and that in 1792 he had pledged his full cooperation whenever it was required, explaining that the corps was loyal to him not to the Nizam, and would readily join in a campaign against the British.[11]

Mornington was less concerned about the Marathas, partly because Kirkpatrick knew less about them, and partly because he believed that there was not such a strong French presence in their mercenary forces. This was not entirely true, but Mornington was inclined to pursue a cautious policy, at least at first, aiming to increase British influence in their affairs, but not inviting a confrontation.

If the attitude of the Marathas towards the British was uncertain, there was no doubt of Tipu Sultan's continuing hostility. Hatred of the British dominated his policies, and after his defeat by Cornwallis he rebuilt his army and scoured the world for allies.[12] He made overtures to both Hyderabad and the Marathas, and neither rejected him outright, although both remained a long way from joining his cause. Looking further afield, he sent a mission to Zeman Shah, the ruler of Afghanistan, who had been making annual invasions, or rather plundering expeditions, into northern India for several years.[13] And, although the British did not know it, Tipu made several overtures to the French during the 1790s. The first was immediately after his defeat in 1792, proposing an offensive-defensive alliance. By the time this approach reached Paris, however, the monarchy had been swept away by the Revolution, and the new government, at war with almost all of Europe, was too distracted to take it seriously. Tipu's second approach was made in the middle of 1796, just as Arthur Wesley was sailing across the Bay of Biscay. This was no mere gesture of friendship, but rather a plan of campaign, showing how a force of 10,000 French and 50,000 Mysorean troops, under Tipu's overall command, would sweep across India and drive the British into the sea. The proposal was warmly endorsed by the French officials in Mauritius, who forwarded it to Paris, but it is not clear if it ever even reached the French government, let alone how it was received.[14]

Mornington had no doubt of Tipu's hostility, and argued that the relative power of Mysore had increased greatly in recent years and needed to be checked. Tipu's intrigues with Zeman Shah were well known, and Mornington took them seriously, although he was aware that informed opinion in India was inclined to discount them. But if he overrated this danger, he totally dismissed Tipu's other potential ally, telling Dundas: 'It is true that [Tipu] must now have nearly lost all hope of assistance from France, or from any other European power.'[15]

Mornington sailed from the Cape on 10 March and reached Madras on 26 April, where he spent a fortnight in talks with General Harris and other officials, before sailing on to Bengal. He landed at Fort William on 17 May and took command of the government on the following day, 'at once bursting forth like a constellation in all his pomp and splendour amongst us', to quote Hickey's account.[16] Bengal had known no Englishman like him, for he believed that Shore's modest frugality and low social standing had diminished the dignity and authority of the Governor-General, and was determined to restore it by giving free rein to his innate love of magnificence and grandeur. He immediately and effortlessly dominated the Council, which was supposed to advise him, and did not hesitate to interfere in questions that the Commander-in-Chief in Bengal had always supposed to be within his sole jurisdiction.[17]

On 8 June, less than a month after Mornington had taken office, news arrived of a public proclamation made by M. Malartic, the French governor of Mauritius. It was an appeal for volunteers to assist Tipu, who, the governor told the world, 'only waits for the moment when the French shall come to his assistance to declare war on the English, whom he ardently wishes to expel from India'. Although Tipu had indeed sent envoys to consult M. Malartic, lured by intelligence that a French expedition was being prepared, he had done so with strict orders that their mission remain a secret. Worse still, there was no expedition and the governor's proclamation raised a mere ninety-nine volunteers, who landed at Mangalore on 28 April, two days after Mornington had reached Madras. Tipu might still, perhaps, have escaped his doom if he had immediately disowned the envoys, repudiated the governor's proclamation, and sent the volunteers home. But he was a proud man who had been lulled into a false sense of security by Sir John Shore's mild policies, and who still hoped that the French might prove valuable allies. He rewarded his envoys and welcomed the party, instructing his officials to satisfy their needs.[18]

Mornington was galvanised by the news, and for almost a month contemplated immediate war on Mysore. These plans horrified the soldiers and officials at Madras, who would be responsible for organising, supplying and leading the principal army in any advance on Seringapatam. Not unnaturally they had, as yet, little faith in Mornington, and believed that he was acting precipitately without understanding the immense practical difficulties of waging war in India. But before their objections could reach Bengal, Mornington had changed his mind; Tipu's offence was not forgotten or forgiven, but there would be no immediate war. The *volte-face* was due to advice from two soldiers in Bengal: one was Sir Alured Clarke, the Commander-in-Chief, who had previously held that position in Madras and so, presumably, understood the subject, although he did not make a favourable impression on Mornington; the other, and probably more influential soldier, was Arthur Wesley, who doubted the wisdom of war at all, and whose recent tour of Madras had convinced him that the government there could not act quickly, and would need careful handling and close supervision if it was to act effectively.[19]

Mornington bowed to their professional expertise and local knowledge and turned his attention back to the affairs of Hyderabad, for if he could dissolve Raymond's corps he would both remove a potential threat and improve the chances of effective cooperation in a war with Tipu. Fortune favoured him. Raymond had died on 25 March, and his successor Piron lacked his personal prestige and ability. Moreover the Nizam was growing increasingly uneasy at the power and arrogance of the foreign officers in the heart of his realm, while the pro-Tipu faction at court was steadily falling from favour. A close alliance with Britain had always been the Nizam's preferred policy, provided this offered real protection against Tipu and the Marathas, and as Mornington shared none of Shore's scruples on this point, an agreement was reached without difficulty. A force of four battalions of sepoys under Colonel Roberts was detached from the Madras army and sent to join the two battalions already at Hyderabad – although not without protests and some obstruction from officials at Madras, who resented Mornington's urgency and feared that the weakening of their army would leave them vulnerable to a sudden attack from Mysore.[20] Roberts reached Hyderabad on 11 October and an uneasy pause followed as the Nizam hesitated and secret overtures and intrigues were made in all directions. Fortunately Roberts received expert guidance from Captain James Kirkpatrick, who had succeeded his brother William as British Resident, and his Assistant

Resident, John Malcolm, who was to be an important figure in India for the next thirty years. Assurances were quietly given to Piron's officers that they would be well treated and sent home to Europe with their private fortunes, not regarded as prisoners of war. Other messages may have been sent to the private soldiers, for the troops soon rose in open mutiny demanding arrears of pay and promises for the future. The British force moved quickly to overawe the mutineers and 'rescue' the French officers, and the dissolution of the French corps was achieved without bloodshed, although the battalions, which remained in the Nizam's army under new officers, remained restive.[21]

It was a remarkable triumph. In one bold stroke Mornington had transformed Hyderabad from a constant source of worry into a useful ally. Sceptics at Madras (and Bengal) were forced to reconsider the new Governor-General, while in London Dundas was delighted. He had long been concerned at the growing number of French officers in India, and had alerted Mornington to the problem before the latter left London.[22] Now the most dangerous body of these officers had been removed in the most unobjectionable and economical manner. Tipu remained a menace, and the proof of his contacts with the French made war almost inevitable, but the balance of power in southern India had shifted decisively in Britain's favour.

Apart from Tipu's abortive attempt to form an alliance with the French, Indian affairs were largely insulated from the fluctuations of the war with revolutionary France. This changed on 19 May 1798 when a French armada set sail from Toulon, first to Malta and then to Alexandria. Bonaparte's principal objective was probably limited to the conquest of Egypt, which would be a valuable colony in its own right, and provide a base from which the French could dominate the eastern Mediterranean if the Ottoman Empire collapsed. But a permanent French presence in Egypt would certainly encourage Britain's Indian enemies such as Tipu and greatly facilitate future cooperation. It was also possible, although unlikely, that the French might attempt to push on to India immediately, either overland, in the footsteps of Alexander the Great, or by sea, if Tipu sent ships to meet them. The practical difficulties in the face of such a venture were immense, but it is not surprising that it caused alarm in London and Calcutta.[23] A naval squadron was despatched from Britain to blockade the Red Sea, several thousand British infantry were scraped together to reinforce the army in India, and the Company was pressured into sending out an additional £1 million in bullion.[24] News of Bonaparte's expedition also combined with Malartic's proclamation to dissolve any possible opposition in Britain to war with Tipu, and gave considerable plausibility to Mornington's warnings of the danger posed by French officers serving in the native armies. War was coming, and Arthur Wesley would play an important role in it.

CHAPTER SIX

SERINGAPATAM
(1798–99)

ARTHUR WESLEY HELPED to introduce his brother to the complexities of Indian affairs. After his visit to Madras in early 1798 he wrote a frank account of the problems Mornington was likely to have in dealing with its government, and of the personalities involved, which he either sent to Cape Town or left, sealed, for Mornington to read on his arrival.[1] Later, as we have seen, he argued successfully against an immediate war with Tipu, even doubting whether any war was likely to be worth the cost, given the difficulties facing Britain in Europe. Mornington may have felt that this was presumptuous – such broad questions of policy were the responsibility of the Governor-General, not of a mere colonel, however excellent – and the next few weeks saw Wesley write a series of memoranda on narrower, more technical subjects relating to the difficulties of moving forces through the border region between Madras and Mysore, and possible means of making the Marathas a more effective ally.[2]

The evidence for the personal relations between the two men at this time is scanty and ambiguous. Arthur had been delighted at Mornington's appointment and looked forward to his arrival, especially as he had felt rather cut off from England, and neglected by his family.[3] Yet the reunion brought a sharp reminder of his subordinate status. Before leaving Britain, Mornington had decided to change the spelling of the family name, reverting to the older form, Wellesley, and his brothers, including Arthur, had little choice but to follow his lead. Two days after Mornington's arrival Arthur added the required letters to his signature; the next change, eleven years later, would come when he was granted a peerage.[4]

For his part, Mornington evidently had a high opinion of his brother and, when he wrote his will before embarking, named Arthur as one of his executors and guardians of his children. But he was touchy and proud, and when Arthur took several hours to come aboard to greet him, he wrote home that he was 'disgusted', and that this neglect 'has caused a coldness between us which I am afraid will last all our lives'.[5] Fortunately Mornington was accompanied by Henry Wellesley, who was learning the art of diplomacy while acting as his brother's private secretary, and who proved adept at pouring oil on troubled waters.

Three months after Mornington landed in Bengal, Arthur Wellesley and the 33rd Regiment sailed for Madras. The two brothers were not to meet again for six years. They had not quarrelled, or rather, any petty quarrels there may have been were soon repaired, and they were to cooperate closely in the years to come. However, apart from these few months in 1798, and again briefly in 1804, Wellesley was not the Governor-General's principal military adviser, let alone his 'informal chief of staff'.[6] His role was less in the formation than in the execution of policy. Mornington employed him in a succession of prominent roles, which gave Arthur every opportunity of distinguishing himself and advancing his career. In part this was simple fraternal patronage and favouritism, and as such aroused considerable resentment and jealousy, even though it was the universal practice of the time. But brotherly love was not Mornington's only motive, for Wellesley performed each task he was set with admirable skill and efficiency, so that he could be selected for a difficult job with confidence that it would not go awry.

Wellesley and Mornington were both men of their time, and it was an age when patronage and personal recommendations were still the normal route to official employment, although the grosser abuses of the system were falling into disrepute. Mornington set himself high standards in this regard; he refused to make any promises to friends and connections in England before he sailed, and took no one with him but his brother Henry and his personal servants.[7] Once in India he demanded extremely hard work and considerable ability from his staff and those he employed in important positions. Naturally he was always ready to encourage a young man who arrived with a recommendation from an influential friend at home, but this alone was no passport to rapid promotion or wealth. Arthur Wellesley understood this well. When he had greeted the news of Mornington's appointment, he had hastened to add that the rules of the service would prevent Mornington from giving him any special treatment.[8] This was nonsense of course, but it helped to protect Wellesley's pride and prevent him from appearing to be an importunate younger brother clamouring for advancement. It simultaneously protected him from a snub and allowed Mornington's patronage to appear the more gracious for being freely given. As such it was probably unnecessarily defensive, but Wellesley was still sore from the personal and professional rebuffs he had received at home, and it was over a year since he had seen his brother. Later he became more confident and practical, recommending Captain Mitchell to Mornington as 'a good kind of man', whose sister, the wife of an officer of the 33rd, is 'a great friend of mine'.[9] And he earnestly entreated Mornington not to neglect a young man from Ireland whose influential patron in Trim must be conciliated if the family wanted to retain their hold on the borough.[10] Nor did he refrain from dropping a strong hint that if an expedition was going to be sent to seize Goa, he would like to take part.[11] None of this was unusual or, by the standards of the time, improper. After all, even that paragon of virtue Lord Cornwallis had ensured that the command of the naval squadron in the East Indies was given to his brother Admiral Cornwallis; and it had proved an excellent appointment.[12]

Arthur and the 33rd sailed to Madras in the middle of August as part of a larger reinforcement to strengthen the army for the war with Mysore that now appeared almost inevitable. On arrival, Wellesley found that the new governor, Lord Clive, son of the great Robert Clive, had just disembarked and taken up his post. The younger Clive was in complete contrast to his father, being a slow, heavy man, well intentioned but without a spark of genius or brilliance, although having some sense, including a recognition of his own limitations. His friends at home and many of those he worked with in India, were puzzled at his decision to come to India, for he was a wealthy man of frugal habits, his children were amply provided for, and he had never shown any signs of ambition. He was forty-four years old and had held only minor or predominantly ceremonial offices, the most important being that of Lord Lieutenant of Shropshire.[13] Wellesley's first impressions were perceptive, telling Mornington that Clive was: 'a mild, moderate man, remarkably reserved, having a bad delivery, and apparently a heavy understanding. He certainly has been unaccustomed to consider questions of the magnitude of that now before him, but I doubt whether he is so dull as he appears, or as people here imagine he is.' Wellesley felt that Clive's officials had alarmed him by exaggerating the risks and difficulties of any war, but that he could be guided into cheerful cooperation with Mornington's policies with a little care and encouragement.[14]

Wellesley had already met the Commander-in-Chief of the Madras army, Lieutenant-General George Harris, who had also acted as governor between Hobart's departure and Clive's arrival. A veteran of the American War of Independence and of Cornwallis's campaigns against Tipu, he gave Wellesley a warm welcome and suggested that they cooperate 'in keeping Lord Clive in the right road'.[15] This was pleasantly flattering coming from a much older man (Harris was fifty-two, Wellesley not yet thirty), as well as a more senior officer, but it was also rather misleading. Harris was by no means convinced of the wisdom of Mornington's policies, while Wellesley doubted his ability to command an army in the field, or even to make the military bureaucracy of Madras perform efficiently.[16] Still, he advised Mornington against the idea of bringing Sir Alured Clarke down from Bengal to take command; it would antagonise the whole Madras establishment for little gain, since Clarke was not noticeably more able than Harris. Moreover, Harris was more likely to listen to Wellesley's advice.[17]

However the real power at Madras lay less with Clive and Harris than with their leading subordinates, of whom the most important were Josiah Webbe and Colonel Barry Close. These men had served in Madras for many years; they had been the principal advisers of Lord Hobart in his quarrels with Sir John Shore; and they were disappointed that he had not been transferred to the governor-generalship, elevating them with him, so naturally they resented Mornington's appointment. They were strongly inclined to thwart Mornington's policies, and they made Wellesley's first months at Madras extremely uncomfortable. In October, writing partly in code, he told Henry: 'I cannot but consider myself, and I am afraid that if all were known others would consider me, as very little better than a spy.'[18] Yet Wellesley recognised that Webbe and Close were indispensable. They had the knowledge and ability to make the government of Madras work and its army fit to take the field, and no one else did. Nor were there any insuperable obstacles; Mornington's vigorous policies were not unlike those advocated by Hobart, while Close and Webbe were free of the taint of the corruption that was still common in the Madras Presidency. He therefore sought to win them over while removing the bad impression their opposition had made in Mornington's eyes. News had just arrived that the East India Company's Court of Directors had abolished various allowances paid to Close, Webbe and other important officials at Madras, and Wellesley recommended that the Governor-General seize the opportunity to be both just and generous by urging the directors to reconsider and by continuing the payments until their decision was known.[19] In a similar vein he counselled against the harsh letter of admonition that Mornington planned to write, arguing that such a letter would have to be answered, and that this would only entrench opposition. And he told Mornington that much of the hostility to his plans was due to ignorance of their ultimate object.[20]

Slowly Wellesley's approach bore fruit and the opposition weakened. Not that there was any sudden dramatic reconciliation (although the success in disarming the 'French corps' at Hyderabad was important), but the foundations were laid first for cooperation, and ultimately for mutual esteem and friendship. In the years to come Josiah Webbe and Barry Close were two of the most important and successful figures in the implementation of Mornington's policies, while they worked closely and harmoniously with Arthur Wellesley, championing his cause when he was in difficulty and delighting in his successes. Placed in an extremely awkward position, Wellesley had emerged with honour intact and with the goodwill and high opinion of some of the ablest men in Madras.

Meanwhile, preparations for war continued, although with a slowness that maddened Wellesley, for despite the growing support of Webbe and Close the military machinery of Madras was torpid and inefficient. Before the end of September Wellesley was urging Mornington to hasten the arrival of the three battalions of sepoy[21] volunteers from Bengal, by sea if possible. At the same time he urged the authorities in Madras to collect and store supplies of grain as far forward as possible, and to ready the heavy siege guns so that they could begin their slow journey towards the frontier before the season broke. A month later he wrote to Henry:

> What do you think of their having omitted to send away the battering train [i.e. the siege guns]? It was to have gone last Tuesday. The monsoon has not set in yet, and it would have been very nearly at Vellore at this time if it had been sent. Harris is really not equal to the management of that cursed institution, the Military Board . . . I did not hear of it till the day before yesterday, and have since been at work to get it sent immediately; whether I shall be successful or not, I can't tell. They begin to suspect me, and they keep everything secret. I hear nothing except from D. C. or H. and it is quite impossible to be always at the ear of one of them. Not being in office, I am obliged to proceed with great caution.[22]

The following day he was able to announce: 'a complete victory: the battering train is to go off to Vellore immediately. They are at this moment getting it out of the fort.' However, he was 'heartily sick of the business, and wish I was anywhere else', even enquiring if he might not be sent to Ceylon.[23]

A week later Wellesley's attention had moved on to the immense number of bullocks needed for an army to take the field in India; 12,000 had already been collected, but he calculated that no fewer than 40,000 would be wanted. This would be expensive: could Henry get Mornington to authorise the outlay? At the same time he was delighted to have persuaded Clive to appoint a commissary of stores and perhaps also a commissary of grain and provisions. 'Matters will then be brought into some shape, and we shall know what we are about, instead of trusting to the vague calculations of a parcel of blockheads, who know nothing, and have no data.'[24]

Wellesley was summoned from Madras to Vellore in the middle of December by the shocking news that Colonel Aston had been mortally wounded in a duel. Aston's death, on 23 December, deprived Wellesley of a good friend who would not easily be replaced. It also provided a salutary warning against duelling and allowing quarrels inside a regiment to get out of hand. With Wellesley and Sherbrooke both detached on other duties, the day-to-day running of the 33rd was left to the irascible Major Shee; but Wellesley kept a careful eye on its affairs, and sharply snubbed the major when he objected to his commander's interference.[25]

Two days after Christmas, Wellesley inspected the 25th Light Dragoons and was greatly impressed, telling Harris: 'I never saw a finer regiment in my life.'[26] Its commander was a handsome, rich cavalry officer, Lieutenant-Colonel Stapleton Cotton, four years Wellesley's junior, who was to command the British cavalry in Portugal and Spain a decade later. Like many officers in the light cavalry, Cotton was keenly interested in fashion, his taste was flamboyant, and he felt that while Wellesley tried to dress well, and was always remarkably neat, he was a little too plain in his attire. He also complained that the elder man was extremely reserved, though good-natured and cheerful. Mrs Floyd, the wife of General Floyd who commanded the army's cavalry, had just given birth to a daughter, Flavia, and Cotton and Wellesley were asked to become her godfathers. Unfortunately Flavia died of scarlet fever in 1802, but her slightly older sister Julia went on to marry Robert Peel, the future Prime Minister and Wellington's political ally in the 1830s and 1840s.[27]

Aston's death meant that Wellesley became the senior officer with the advanced part of the army camped near Vellore and, for a month, from late December to late January 1799, he was in command and kept busy with preparations for the campaign. These included training exercises and inspections for the troops, but the main emphasis was on supplies, for an advance on Seringapatam was more likely to fail due to logistical problems than to be defeated by Tipu's army. The rains had been poor, rice was scarce and famine not impossible even without the added strain of war.[28] This could be overcome by importing large quantities of rice and money from Bengal, but doing so would add to the burden on the army's transport, which was already its weakest link. Meanwhile Wellesley issued detailed regulations for the organisation of the bazaars, which accompanied the army and provided the troops with supplies beyond their basic rations.[29] He showed considerable tact in gently warning Lieutenant-Colonel Richardson, the superintendent of bazaars, that it was improper for him to have a financial interest in a contract for the supply of arrack to those bazaars.[30] And he dealt fairly with the inevitable quarrels between British and Indian soldiers, which in this case were caused mainly by British troops robbing the native servants and camp followers as they brought food up to their regiments.[31]

Despite all these preparations for war, Wellesley repeatedly urged Mornington to seek a diplomatic solution and remained pessimistic, doubting that it would be possible to capture Seringapatam in a single campaign. On 2 January he wrote to Henry Wellesley listing his concerns under five headings. First there was the shortage of grain; second the shortage of money; third came doubts that the Nizam's army from Hyderabad, including six battalions of the Company's sepoys that composed his subsidiary force, could join the main army in time; fourth, he did not believe that the Bombay army would be ready to cooperate by invading Mysore from the west coast of India; and last, he stated baldly, 'we have no general'. None of these arguments was new, and Wellesley admitted ruefully: 'I have repeated some of these objections to hostilities so frequently, that I am afraid I shall be accused of boring Mornington.'[32] These fears proved unfounded and Mornington's supreme confidence was vindicated by success. Neither man had any experience of planning and organising operations on such a scale, but, rather surprisingly, it was Mornington's judgement that proved the more realistic. Fortunately his self-assurance was not shaken by his brother's doubts, and he bore him no grudge, going out of his way to tell Dundas: 'The improvement of affairs [at Madras], ... and the advancement of the preparations, are to be attributed principally to my brother, Colonel Wellesley ... He is intimately acquainted with the affairs of this country, and [is] universally beloved.'[33]

Mornington's diplomatic campaign had begun on 4 November when he wrote to inform Tipu of Nelson's victory in the battle of the Nile, maintaining the pretence that Tipu was friendly to the British and would welcome the news. Four days later he wrote again demanding an explanation of Tipu's contacts with the French and proposing that Major Doveton should travel to Seringapatam to facilitate negotiations. Tipu responded with bland evasions and procrastination. He knew that he was in danger and that the French could do nothing to help him, but evidently believed that the British would not attack him without provocation, not realising that for Mornington and opinion in London, his refusal to disavow Malartic's proclamation already provided ample justification for war. Further letters were exchanged but no serious negotiations ever began; if they had, Mornington would have demanded the cession of Mangalore and all the territory of Mysore on the west coast of India, and the dismissal of Tipu's French officers and troops.[34] No prince was likely to yield to such demands unless he had already been defeated in war, but if Tipu had made a show of appearing conciliatory and protracted the negotiations he might have embarrassed the British, who had to open their campaign in early February if they were to hope to take Seringapatam before the monsoon broke in May. On 31 December Mornington arrived in Madras to supervise the negotiations – or the war – more closely, but it was not until early February that Tipu even agreed to receive Doveton, and by then it was far too late, for the British army was already on the move.[35]

General Harris left Madras on 26 January and took command of the army at Vellore on 29 January, and began the advance on 3 February. His plan of campaign was relatively simple; the army would advance from the Baramahal (the province ceded by Mysore to Madras in 1792), then up the Ghats, or range of low mountains which now marked the frontier, and then push on to Seringapatam itself. It was a march of about 270 miles, almost half of it before

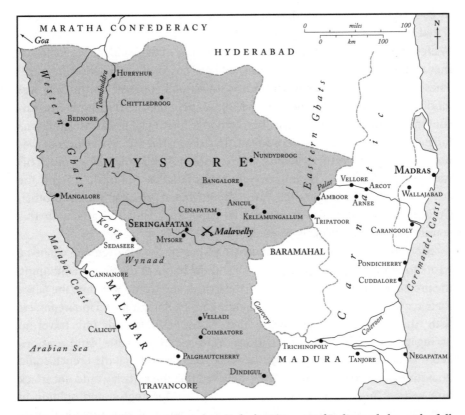

3 Mysore in 1799. (This map is based on Faden's 1793 map of India, and shows the full extent of Mysore territory under the terms of the peace of 1793; many modern maps omit Mangalore and its western coast, which Mysore only lost as a result of the war of 1799.)

entering Mysore. Two smaller British forces under Colonels Read and Brown would collect further supplies and escort them to join the main army once Seringapatam was besieged. The Nizam's army would be reinforced by a British battalion and would join the main force before it entered Mysore. And the Bombay army under General Stuart, acting with the support of the Raja of Koorg, would attack Mysore from the west beginning its advance from Cannanore. Harris was by no means confident of success. He had experienced the failure of Cornwallis's first campaign in 1791 and knew how quickly vast quantities of supplies could disappear and multitudes of bullocks could die. Knowing his limitations he had been reluctant to accept the command, but had succumbed to Mornington's flattery and encouragement, and he was wise enough to rely heavily on Barry Close, the army's Adjutant-General. Nonetheless, the ultimate responsibility rested with Harris, and it was not a light burden.[36]

Four days after joining the army Harris wrote to Mornington praising Wellesley's preparations, in particular 'the judicious and masterly arrangements in respect to supplies, which opened an abundant free market, and inspired confidence into dealers of every description', while the troops themselves showed 'a very handsome appearance and perfect discipline'.[37] However he did not make this praise public, allegedly to prevent jealousy, and the omission stung, for Wellesley felt that he had done exceptional work and was being denied the credit due to him.[38] This was not Wellesley's first complaint about the General; early in January he had told Henry Wellesley that the men Harris had sent to assist in organising the army were useless or corrupt, and added: 'There is no officer in the army excepting myself to whom he would dare to behave as he has done to me; and if I did not believe that he would be glad to seize an opportunity of sending me away from hence, and if I had not particular reasons for wishing not to appear to hang back upon the present occasion, I should desire to join my regiment'.[39] Relations between an under-confident Commander-in-Chief and an assertive, opinionated and extremely touchy subordinate, who was also the brother of the Governor-General, were never likely to be easy, unless the senior officer submitted entirely to the domination of his junior, and Harris avoided that fate at least. A remarkably unself-conscious letter from Wellesley to Mornington reveals the problem. He begins by explaining that the Commander-in-Chief in Madras lacks authority because officers in the army looked to the governor rather than him for promotion and patronage:

This want of respectability, which is to be attributed in a great measure to the General himself, is what I am most afraid of; however, I have lectured him well upon the subject, and I have urged publicly to the army, in which I flatter myself I have some influence, the necessity of supporting him, whether he be right or wrong. The ponderous machine is now nearly prepared, and all we have to do is to put and keep it in motion. The General has three or four people about him very capable of it, if he can only keep them well together. I have spoken to him about that, and I shall make it a particular object of my attention. He has confidence in me, and I don't fail to give him my opinion upon every subject.[40]

One cannot help but feel that if Harris lacked authority in the army, Wellesley's presence, with his lectures and scoldings, was hardly going to assist him. Still, Wellesley at least had the sense to discourage Mornington strongly, and successfully, from joining the army, and Mornington in turn prevented Clive from doing so.[41]

Towards the end of February the approach of the Hyderabad army provided the perfect solution for the problems caused by Wellesley's presence with the main army. Harris had already decided to add a battalion of British infantry to the six battalions of sepoys and assorted native troops that comprised this force. Arthur Wellesley had already indicated that he would like to command this detachment, while the appointment of the Governor-General's brother would be taken as a compliment by the Nizam.[42] Wellesley was delighted to be given the command of such a large force, and Harris was happy to have him distanced a little from the main army although acting in close cooperation with it. Only Major-General David Baird was unhappy. He was the fifth most senior officer in the army, twelve years older than Wellesley, and with much experience of service in India, including more than three years in captivity in Seringapatam after the defeat of Colonel Baillie's force in 1780. An irascible and pugnacious Scot, he complained forcefully to Harris that Wellesley was receiving unfair preferment and that he ought to have been given the position. He had a case, up to a point, but if seniority was the only consideration then the position would first have been offered to Major-Generals Floyd, Bridges and Popham, who were all superior to both Baird and Wellesley; while the very intemperance of Baird's protest shows how unsuitable he was for a semi-independent command requiring close cooperation with native forces. Indeed Baird's brutal assertion of his own interests makes Wellesley's behaviour appear a model of moderation and diffidence; but then, Baird had risen the hard way, and Wellesley was the Governor-General's brother.[43]

Arthur Wellesley and the 33rd joined the Nizam's army on 3 March 1799. Lieutenant-Colonel Dalrymple assumed the immediate command of the subsidiary battalions, although subordinated to Wellesley for the duration of the campaign. The rest of the army consisted of approximately 10,000 irregular cavalry and 6,000 infantry, some of which had previously been commanded by Raymond's French officers. These battalions were still unsettled, and an attempted mutiny was suppressed on 13–14 February, largely due to the coolness of John Malcolm. The overall command of the whole force was held by Meer Allum, the Nizam's leading General. Lieutenant Patrick Brown, serving in one of the subsidiary battalions of sepoys, told his father that the arrival of the 33rd greatly strengthened the force 'as the black people are very much afraid of European soldiers'.[44]

An army on the march in India at this time was a memorable sight, quite different from an army in Europe. Harris's main force consisted of rather more than 20,000 soldiers, but these were accompanied by at least three times as many camp followers, families, cooks, grooms, servants and traders selling grain, liquor, drugs and a vast variety of other luxuries and necessities. And the people were outnumbered by the animals; almost 100,000 bullocks accompanied the combined army, some pulling the heavy siege guns and innumerable carts loaded with ammunition and other supplies, but most laden with packs and panniers. There were more than 10,000 horses, with smaller numbers of elephants and camels. The whole formed a vast mass with the main army on one side, the Nizam's on the other, and the intervening space filled with animals and civilians. This cumbersome force could not move quickly, but would starve if it halted for long in one place unless foraging expeditions on a huge scale were organised.[45]

According to Ensign George Rowley, an assistant engineer with the Hyderabad force:

> The market of General Harris's army equals in extent, and in the variety of articles exposed for sale, that of a populous city. The followers of an army are so numerous, that on a moderate calculation they may be considered to exceed the number of fighting men in the proportion of five to one. The appearance of our army on the march from a neighbouring hill is truly surprising. It may be compared with the emigration of the Israelites from Egypt; the surrounding plains and downs appear to be in motion. Herds of cattle and flocks of sheep conceal the soil; the route of the troops is marked by the gleaming of their arms, and that of the battering train by a long slow-moving inky line. On a nearer view the scene is sometimes laughable: here a laden ill-bred bullock taking fright, scampers off, plunging and kicking and throwing a whole herd into confusion; twenty others follow his example, and broken pots and pans strew the plain.
>
> The drivers abuse their cattle, and each other; sometimes an alarm of the Looties' approach occasions a worse disorder; men, women and children scamper in all directions, and leave their unconcerned charge to its fate.[46]

The vast majority of faces in this multitude were brown; there were some 5,000 European soldiers in Harris's army, and less than 1,000 with Wellesley and the Nizam's contingent. All the rest were Indians: sepoys, allied infantry and cavalry, gun lascars, camp followers, servants and the rest. Britain conquered India with armies consisting predominantly of Indian troops, paid with money raised from Indians by taxes, trade, or loans eagerly subscribed to by wealthy Indian merchants and bankers, who understandably preferred the credit of the East India Company to that of any of the native princes.[47]

It took a month, from 3 February to 4 March, for the army to march the 120 miles from Vellore to the frontier. On 5 March Harris sent Tipu a letter from the Governor-General written on 22 February, which amounted to a declaration of war.[48] Harris commenced hostilities by seizing two nearby hill-forts and on 7 March the army advanced into Mysore. It met little resistance at first. Tipu used his central position to concentrate his initial effort on eliminating the lesser threat that faced him, by striking at the Bombay army. On 6 March he attacked its advanced guard under Lieutenant-Colonel Montresor at Sedaseer, but was repulsed after several hours of hard fighting. With Tipu and the main part of his army on the other side of the kingdom, Harris's army was able to advance steadily in the face of little opposition, although observed and sometimes harassed by small bodies of enemy light cavalry and the even more irregular looties. Lieutenant Patrick Brown describes them:

> Tippoo's [sic] Horse are the same as the Nizam's, without any discipline or uniform. Everyone arms himself and dresses as he chooses. They are generally armed with a sword and target, some have spears and others carbines, few have pistols, but all in general are well mounted and are excellent horsemen but the most part of them, great cowards, and in short are only formidable by their numbers.
>
> There are other horsemen called *Looties* who never give quarter but hover round the army in the march, kill all the stragglers they fall in with and plunder any baggage which they see unprotected.[49]

There was an unfortunate incident on 10 March when a company of the Nizam's army fell behind and was set upon, suffering sixty casualties before it could be rescued, but in general the Mysorean cavalry left formed bodies of troops alone. Nonetheless they impressed Arthur Wellesley, who told Mornington that Tipu's 'light cavalry, *looties*, and others, are the best of the kind in the world. They have hung upon us, night and day, from the moment we entered his country to this. Some of them have always had sight of us, and have been prepared to cut off any persons venturing out of the reach of our camp-guards'.[50] According to British estimates, Tipu had about 6,000 regular and 7,000 irregular cavalry in his army, 4,000 guards, and 30,000 regular infantry, as well as innumerable local levies, pikemen, and rocket-boys of little military value. 'Lally's French corps', which figures in some accounts, amounted to no more than 100 Europeans (10 officers and 90 privates) and 450 other privates.[51]

Harris believed that if Tipu had used his light cavalry and looties to devastate the Baramahal, he could have prevented the British from reaching Seringapatam, at least in a single campaign. Wellesley was inclined to agree: 'If Tippoo had had sense and spirit sufficient to use his cavalry and infantry as he might have done, I have no hesitation in saying that we should not now be here [Seringapatam], and probably should not now be out of the jungles near Bangalore.' Later critics also point to Tipu's decision, made years before, to demolish the fortifications of Hosur and Bangalore, fortresses which lay close to the route Harris was taking, and which he could not have ignored.[52] In other words, Tipu might have made the British task much harder, and perhaps protracted the war into a second season, but there is no doubt that the odds were heavily against him, and that even if he had shown more enterprise and skill he had only a slender hope of victory.

The British campaign appeared to go relatively smoothly, and to Tipu, Harris's advance must have appeared slow but inexorable. But beneath the surface there were problems. Wellesley later told Mornington: 'We have had much blundering and *puzzling*, and I have been present at many strong and violent discussions in the cabinet. However, all parties are apparently well together.'[53] Harris lacked the ability to plan the campaign himself, or the personal authority to quiet dissensus, but he was well liked by those close to him, and this helped to prevent the disputes from festering.

There were also inevitable problems with the cattle, which were suffering greatly from their heavy labour in unfamiliar conditions and from disease. 'After each day's march came a mournful catalogue of losses of stores, of shot (left with the dying cattle in the jungles and roads), and of rice, indispensable to the support of the fighting men of the army, and their fourfold, but unavoidable, number of followers.'[54] It was impossible to replace these losses and at one point General Harris was near despair, even wondering if his heavy siege guns could be dragged forward by the British infantry. But Wellesley, who had remained pessimistic right up to the middle of February, was now growing confident, and on 25 March he wrote to Mornington: 'There is not now a doubt but that we shall bring that monstrous equipment to Seringapatam, and, in that case, we shall certainly take the place . . . I write such good news that I don't put my letter in cypher . . . [P.S.] I am very well but not a little fagged.'[55]

Reports reaching the army stated that Tipu's troops were discontented at not being paid and 'would escape from him if they could with their families'.[56] On 25 March, Harris learnt of Stuart's victory at Sedaseer, while on the following day General Floyd with the advanced guard sent back word that Tipu was with his army near the village of Malavelly. Some of Harris's staff urged him to leave a strong guard on the siege train and stores and march with the bulk of the army at first light to attack Tipu. But to this, as Harris wrote in his private journal: 'I gave a decided negative. I told them my object was to set down before Seringapatam as speedily as possible; that the pains I had taken to be ready to fight Tippoo was entirely with the hope it would enable me to avoid it; that nothing but his stopping the high road should make me seek him.'[57] It was an unheroic policy, but sensible in the peculiar circumstances of the case. For in this campaign the enemy's field army was not the principal military object, because its defeat was not the most direct route to victory. Tipu's fate was tied inextricably to Seringapatam. Only its capture, or the chance of his death, would effect his defeat; anything else was a distraction.

On the next morning, 27 March, the army was roused at four o'clock as usual, assembled at five o'clock, and moved off at daylight; the marches always began very early in the day so that the troops would be in camp and resting before the midday heat. The country was more open than previously, although still rolling and broken with dry watercourses. Many pagodas and villages were in sight, some of the latter already in flames, but the general effect was still pleasing. By half past nine Tipu's army was plainly visible occupying a range of low hills behind Malavelly and to one side, rather than across, the army's line of advance. Tipu's heavy artillery opened fire on the cavalry leading the British advance, but the range was too long and the fire was ineffective. Harris now gave orders to prepare to camp, and was delighted with reports that the enemy was beginning to retreat. However, soon after, the outlying picquets of his army came under attack, and he reinforced them and ordered the whole army to form for battle. Wellesley, with the Nizam's army, was on the left, while the initial fighting was on the right. Hearing heavy firing he ordered his men forward; only the 33rd was already formed and it led the way, with the battalions of the subsidiary force behind and to its left, coming up as soon as they were ready, so that they formed a rather straggling, impromptu echelon. The 33rd ascended the heights rapidly with great spirit in the face of an irregular fire of musketry and the occasional rocket. The enemy's heavy guns had already been withdrawn, and the 33rd did not encounter much serious resistance, although the enemy cavalry attempted to turn their left flank, but were driven off by the steady fire of the battalion on that flank, supported by the cavalry.[58]

The fighting was a little heavier on the right, where Tipu's cavalry made a furious charge on Baird's brigade, but the final result was much the same; the Mysorean attack was repulsed despite some fleeting confusion in the British line, and they were driven from the field with losses which may or may not have been heavy. Ensign Rowley of the Madras Engineers recorded the affair with refreshing cynicism: 'Thus ended the *battle* of Malavelly, which appeared to those not in the secret to be a very confused sort of skirmish. The official account of it will appear as regular as those of Marlborough or Frederick, where every circumstance appears to have been foreseen, known, and provided for.'[59] Given that even so good a historian as Fortescue would have us believe that the 800 men of the 33rd were attacked by, and defeated, 'ten thousand infantry, supported by cavalry, [who] advanced boldly . . . and did not give way until the British bayonets were almost upon them', Rowley's sarcasm is not entirely misplaced.[60] But if Malavelly was considerably less than a great battle, it was still rather more than a mere skirmish. It is not clear what Tipu hoped to achieve, but the most likely explanation is that he had been misled by flattering reports into believing that he would be faced by only a detachment of Harris's army, which he could attack and destroy in isolation.[61] Seeing his mistake he ordered the withdrawal of his heavy artillery and either deliberately attacked in order to cover its retreat, or the fighting grew unintentionally from skirmishing between the picquets. In any case the failure of the engagement further undermined both his own confidence and the morale of his army. He would make no further attempt seriously to oppose Harris's advance in the open field, while his troops showed little resolution or enthusiasm in later fighting. In other words, Malavelly opened the road to Seringapatam and confirmed and increased the psychological advantage possessed by Harris's army.

Malavelly is only about twenty-five miles from Seringapatam as the crow flies, but Harris did not take the most direct route, turning south and crossing the River Cauvery at Sosily, thus avoiding country which Tipu's cavalry was busy devastating. Even so, the state of the army's cattle continued to cause him serious anxiety. 'The poor miserable starved bullocks,' Harris wrote in his diary, 'made out wonderfully, but some of the spare carriages were not in before nine o'clock in the evening.' Wellesley was not well; bad water had given him 'a bowel complaint', which did not confine him, 'but teased me much'.[62] The irritation this caused must have been increased by a blunder in Harris's headquarters, which meant that the line of march of the Nizam's army was crossed by the main army. As a result it took twelve hours to march three or four miles, and Meer Allum, who had been extremely cooperative, 'was exceedingly displeased at the extreme neglect with which he was evidently treated with today'.[63] The same thing almost happened on the following day, 2 April, as the army skirted round Seringapatam. The long march was now almost over, and the fabled capital of Mysore lay before the army.

Seringapatam was both a fortress and a city. It was built on an island in the River Cauvery, about three miles long and one wide, although the fortress occupied only its western end. At the height of Tipu's reign its population may have been around 150,000, crowded into narrow streets and mean houses. Dr Francis Buchanan, who visited it a few years later, declared that it had 'a most dreary, ugly appearance; for naked rock, and dirty mud walls are its predominant features'.[64] Officers who had taken part in the siege of 1792 were dismayed by the harshness of the scene, for many gardens and fertile spots devastated in the earlier siege had not been rebuilt. Colin Mackenzie, the senior Engineers officer attached to Wellesley's staff, described the prospect as frankly daunting:

Not an inhabitant to be seen as far as the eye can reach, one uninterrupted scene of *Brown horror*, and desolation, unenlivened by the smallest particle of verdure, or by any living Creature, excepting our own vast host, moving in Solemn silence in a Circular direction round our (I hope) destined prey; there was something very interesting in the march, and the minds of all seemed on the Stretch looking for something great and uncommon.[65]

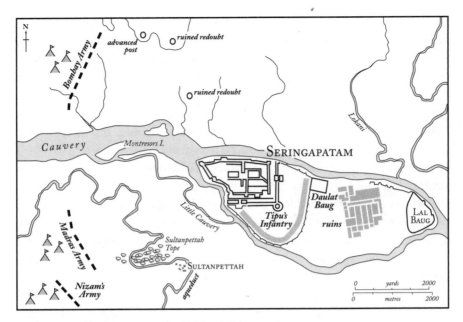

4 The siege of Seringapatam, April–May 1799.

Perhaps, but it seems more likely that most of the army was simply glad to have arrived. The more difficult half of the campaign was complete, but the fortress still had to be besieged and stormed before the season broke or the army exhausted its supplies. Harris expressed this mood with a General Order in which he congratulated the troops on the success of their advance and assured them that a 'continuance of the same exertions will shortly put an end to their labours, and place the British colours in triumph on its walls'. Arthur Wellesley was equally sanguine, telling Mornington in a confidential letter written on the following day, that the army's supplies were plentiful, that Seringapatam was strong only from its natural situation, that the weather would hold for at least forty days, and that once the siege guns were in place it would take only five days of battering to make a breach that Tipu's troops would not be able to defend.[66]

Harris's plan was to batter the western end of the fortress from both banks of the Cauvery; his own army would be south of the river, while Stuart's Bombay army, when it arrived in a few days, would be on the north bank. This meant that the storming troops would have to ford the southern arm of the Cauvery, but this should not be a problem providing the rains had not begun. From the outset, the campaign had been a race against time. But before the siege proper could begin, some patches of rough country between the army and the fortress had to be occupied, notably the ruined village of Sultanpettah and the adjacent palm and coconut plantations, or *tope* as they were called, which provided cover from which Tipu's 'rocket-boys' maintained a harassing fire on the army. The flank companies of Baird's brigade swept through the position on the night of 4 April, found it deserted, and returned to camp, for Harris had not ordered that it be held. Their operation nearly ended in disaster when they mistook their way in the dark, and were only saved from blundering into the outworks of the fortress itself by Lieutenant Lambton whose knowledge of the stars made him realise that they were headed in the wrong direction.[67]

Despite this salutary warning against night operations, Harris determined to repeat the attack on the following night. Colonel Shawe, with the 12th Regiment and two battalions of sepoys, would occupy a salient created by a dry irrigation canal, or *nullah*, to the north of the tope, while Wellesley and the 33rd would cross the canal and attack the tope itself. A letter survives from Wellesley, written on 5 April, asking Harris for more precise instructions and suggesting that they examine the position together. They did so about four o'clock that afternoon, although not very closely, so that in his account of the attack Captain Mackenzie states that 'no knowledge of the ground appeared to have been communicated, nor was anyone acquainted with the windings of the *Nulla* after we lost sight of it on the left of the *Tope*'. Given that Baird's troops had crossed the ground the previous night, this ignorance seems odd, but perhaps the lack of resistance they encountered led to overconfidence.[68]

Much has been written, both at the time and subsequently, about what happened that night in the Sultanpettah Tope, even though there was such confusion that none of the participants, let alone anyone else, could be certain of just what *did* happen. According to Captain John Chetwood of the 33rd the regiment advanced in silence about seven o'clock that night. When they approached the tope Wellesley halted half the regiment to act as a reserve and pushed forward with the other five companies, having instructed the troops not to load their muskets but to rely upon their bayonets. They quickly advanced along the bank of the nullah on the edge of the tope, not realising that a strong force of Tipu's men was waiting for them on the other side of the ditch concealed behind a thick aloe hedge. Other hostile infantry occupied some houses in front of the British advance, and on a signal the two bodies of Mysorean troops opened 'a warm but ill-directed fire of musketry'. The surprise led to confusion, but inspired by their officers, the men of the 33rd crossed the ditch, broke through the hedge, 'and drove the enemy before us'. However, once among the trees, all sense of order and direction was lost and Wellesley, with a few followers including Colin Mackenzie, became separated from the rest of the troops. The firing spread beyond the tope indicating that Colonel Shawe's men were engaged. Wellesley realised that he had little hope of regaining control over the men who had advanced into the tope, and moved back to bring up the five companies in reserve. However, he missed them in the dark and rode off to headquarters in search of reinforcements or fresh orders. Meanwhile most of the officers and men of the five leading companies gradually found their way back to the nullah and formed up under cover of the reserve, or made their way to join Colonel Shawe's men.[69]

From this it seems that Wellesley had fallen into something very like a trap. The operation was ill conceived and the principal responsibility for the failure rests with Harris, who ordered it. Wellesley's arrangements for the attack appear sensible; the retention of a strong reserve was particularly appropriate, although clearly there should have been more reconnaissance. Given the folly of a night attack over difficult, unknown terrain in the face of strong opposition, confusion and disorder were almost inevitable, and the 33rd was fortunate not to suffer even more heavily. As it was, one officer, Lieutenant Fitzgerald, and a few men, were killed; eight soldiers were taken prisoner and later executed on Tipu's orders; and between thirty and forty officers and men received wounds. Wellesley was hit on the knee, but was unhurt.[70]

The only aspect of Wellesley's behaviour that appears open to question was his decision to report to headquarters when he made his way out of the tope. We do not know enough of the circumstances to judge this with confidence, but it is clear that the fighting was not yet over, and Wellesley's responsibilities to his troops might suggest that he should have attempted to renew contact with the regiment, or, if this was impracticable (as seems likely), that he wait on the spot to rally and encourage the survivors when they emerged. Equally, it is surprising that Harris was not closer to the scene of the action.

Wellesley reached headquarters about midnight to find Harris anxiously waiting for news, and much concerned at the risk that the troops would fail to recognise each other in the dark and open fire on each other. According to Harris's journal, Wellesley arrived 'in a good deal of agitation, to say that he had not carried the *Tope*. It proved that the 33rd, with which he attacked, got into confusion, and could not be formed, which was a great pity, as it must have been particularly unpleasant to him'. Harris was a genuinely modest and sincerely religious man, yet it is hard to believe that he felt no glimmer of satisfaction at the mortification felt by his well-connected young subordinate. Certainly his private verdict on the failure of the attack, which he ordered, shows no recognition that he was in any way to blame: 'Altogether, circumstances considered, we got off very well'.[71]

Wellesley's discomfiture delighted many in the army who were jealous of his prominence or who simply enjoyed good gossip, and as the years passed and Wellesley's fame grew, the story became ever more delicious and ever more embroidered. Ensign Rowley, writing at the time, merely states: 'Wellesley is mad at this ill-success'. John Blakiston, who did not meet Wellesley until 1803, heard that when he reached headquarters Harris was asleep and the colonel 'threw himself on the table of the dining tent, and, being much fatigued with the night's labour, fell fast asleep'.[72] Richard Bayly, writing his memoirs many years later, was no friend of Wellesley, and does not hesitate to describe a scene straight from a third-rate melodrama:

> He soon reached the camp, and throwing himself on a table inside the Commander-in-Chief's dining marquee, burst into a violent passion of tears, exclaiming, 'Oh, I'm ruined for ever! I'm ruined for ever! My God, I'm ruined for ever! What shall I do? Where shall I go?' His actions were those of a madman, rolling backwards and forwards on a long table without intermission, uttering the most fearful and bitter invectives on the melancholy failure of his ill-fated attempt on the wood.[73]

However the effect is rather ruined when Bayly admits that he was not present at the scene, and heard the story from an unnamed staff officer.

Bayly's story is far from credible; Harris's diary and Wellesley's character both rule out such histrionics, although there is no reason to doubt the disappointment of the moment. More superficially plausible is the claim, made by George Elers and taken up by some modern writers, that Wellesley's career only survived the failure because of his connections.[74] Certainly an obscure officer might well have had his career damaged by this kind of gossip; but this misses the point that the failure of the attack on the Sultanpettah Tope only attracted the gossip because the figure at its centre was so well connected and later became so famous. In purely military terms the incident was insignificant. The post was occupied without difficulty on the following morning, and the initial failure had no impact on the course of the siege.[75] If Colonel Jones or Colonel Smith had led the attack instead of Colonel Wellesley the whole affair would have faded into obscurity within a week and been completely forgotten by the end of the siege. But Wellesley's very success in later life kept its interest alive, and gave it an importance that it does not deserve.

The next few days were spent assembling materials for the siege and organising the army's camp. Captain Malcolm was surprised by the lack of opposition at this time. 'The Fort has fired very little and it would be impossible to suppose or believe that we were besieging the Capital of a Powerful Prince from the extreme quiet the Army enjoys . . . Not a horseman is to be seen and the followers go out to forage and plunder to such a distance as is almost incredible – they are very successful both in plunder and forage.'[76] On 14 April the Bombay army joined, so that Seringapatam was besieged from both sides of the river. Two days later a sudden crisis arose when checks revealed a substantial shortfall in the amount of rice in the army's store. The cause was almost certainly theft and fraud; and it was solved, in part by fresh supplies arriving under the escort of Colonel Read, and in part by purchasing back the purloined grain at an inflated price. No wonder that Wellesley told his brother: 'I cannot write with common temper about our rice concerns ... [the shortage] is unpleasant and, considering the quantity of rice we brought with us, and the pains taken upon the subject, it is shameful.'[77]

The arrival of the Bombay army enabled Harris to press the siege forward with more energy and this in turn provoked Tipu into strenuous resistance. Harris hoped to capture the fortress before the end of April, but this proved too optimistic.[78] The engineers, believing that Tipu had a number of experienced French officers in his service, were determined to proceed with caution, and this inevitably took time. On 17 April troops from the Bombay army supported by the 74th Regiment from the main army occupied an old redoubt and village 900 yards from the north-west angle of the fortress, and that night established a battery which would enfilade Tipu's advanced positions south of the river. However, when dawn came it was discovered that the battery had been constructed in the wrong position (the engineers had relied on surveys made during the 1792 siege), and it had to be rebuilt farther to the left.[79] On the same night a smaller battery was established on the south bank but had to be abandoned temporarily due to heavy fire from the fortress. On 20 April Sherbrooke led a successful attack, which drove the defenders from their advanced positions on the south bank and enabled the engineers to establish a first parallel 780 yards from the fortress. The following night Tipu made a furious sortie on the Bombay army but was driven back with the loss, by British estimates, of some 600 or 700 casualties. At the same time a new battery was established in front of the first parallel with four 18-pounders and two howitzers being manhandled into position before daylight, and opening a destructive fire against the guns of the fortress. Two more 18-pounders were added to the battery the following night, while another battery was established on the southern bank. These two batteries supported each other and proved very effective.[80] Trenches were dug forward from the first parallel, although the work was much hampered by rain, which led to some concern, for the early arrival of the monsoon was almost the only thing that could now save Tipu.

The rain cleared and at sunset on 26 April Arthur Wellesley led an attack on a strongly-held line of entrenchments in front of the fortress. The attack succeeded and the 74th Regiment pressed on, spiking two guns guarding a bridge over the Cauvery and causing alarm and confusion in the fortress. The next morning, however, the defenders regained some of their positions and directed such a heavy fire on the advanced British posts that Sherbrooke suggested that they be withdrawn. Harris refused, ordering that the positions be held to the last extremity, and after a few hours the fire diminished. Nonetheless the fighting on 26 and 27 April cost the British some 300 casualties.[81] On the following day the first breaching battery was established, but the heavy siege guns could not be moved in until the next night. Several further batteries were established both for breaching the walls of the fortress and to enfilade the defences, while diversionary fire was maintained on a false line of attack to distract the defenders. Fire on the point actually selected for the main breach only began at sunrise on 2 May, and by the evening of 3 May a practicable breach had been made.[82]

Arthur Wellesley was again in command of the outposts that night and he sent officers forward to make a detailed reconnaissance both of the breach and of the fords of the Cauvery. But the honour of commanding the storm fell, appropriately, to Baird; not only had he spent years as a prisoner in close confinement in Seringapatam, but he was exactly the type of fire-eating soldier best suited to the job. In order to gain some element of surprise, it was decided to launch the attack at one o'clock on the afternoon of 4 May, even though this required the storming troops to take their places in the trenches before dawn, and spend hours tensely waiting in cramped discomfort and potentially under heavy fire. The risk paid off; the attack was a surprise and the initial onslaught carried the breach and then swept along the rampart in both directions. An inner wall led to a brief check, and there was some sharp fighting in which Tipu was killed.

Many tales are told of the wild scenes of plunder that followed, and they provide Wilkie Collins's novel *The Moonstone* with one of the most memorable opening scenes in English literature. The first-hand accounts by participants are scarcely less dramatic. Lieutenant Patrick Brown's battalion was ordered into the town during the afternoon to help restore order. Seringapatam, he told his father:

> presented a shocking sight scattered all over with dead black bodies cut and mangled in a dreadful manner and here and there lay an unfortunate European. During the storm (little over an hour) eight officers besides a number of brave men were killed.
>
> We stayed in the fort all night under arms where there was a terrible state of confusion, several of the houses on fire, and the soldiers running about through the streets with drawn sabres and lighted torches, dressed up in silk clothes etc which they had plundered and compelled the poor inhabitants to show them where their treasure was concealed. Some officers and many private Europeans made their fortunes that night but poor I, and many others who were but young hands, got nothing worth speaking of. I got a horse, some silver dishes and other small articles. The place was full of riches and I don't think there will ever be such a prize taken in India again.[83]

According to George Elers:

> The wealth captured was enormous, and consisted of all sorts of property from every Court in Europe. There was splendid china from the King of France, clocks, watches, shawls of immense value, trinkets, jewellery from all nations, pearls, rubies, diamonds and emeralds, and every other precious stone made up into ornaments – even solid wedges and bars of pure gold. A soldier offered me *one* for a bottle of brandy. Many of the officers received part of their prize-money in jewels at a fixed valuation. I saw an emerald in its rough and uncut state valued at £200. Many of our soldiers acquired by plunder what would have made them independent for life if properly managed. I heard that one of them soon after the storm staggered under as many pagodas as he could carry to the amount, it was said, of £10,000.[84]

Amid all the confusion no one knew what had happened to Tipu. Baird had secured the surrender of the inner fort and placed a guard on the palace to protect Tipu's sons and, less effectively, his treasury; but it was not until night was falling that a servant was found who had seen Tipu fall. Baird led a party, including Arthur Wellesley, who had commanded the reserve during the storm, to search for the body. The remains of the last Sultan of Mysore, Britain's most inveterate Indian enemy, were found in a gateway under a pile of corpses.

Harris's army had suffered a total of 1,531 casualties in the siege, including 367 in the assault; and although British troops amounted to only a small proportion of the whole force, they suffered slightly more than half the casualties, reflecting their employment in the positions of greatest danger.[85] The siege had taken a month, and the campaign as a whole barely three months, although the apparent ease of the victory conceals the extent of the logistical difficulties that had to be overcome. Harris bore the responsibility for the campaign and deserves the credit for its success, although Barry Close, the Adjutant-General, did much of the essential work. Arthur Wellesley's role in the fighting was unremarkable, but he had played an important, if secondary, part in the preparations for the campaign, and had been well placed to observe the difficulties of high command that Harris had faced. In the Low Countries he had experienced defeat and a miserable retreat in which the army's supply system had completely collapsed; now he took part in a victory based on immense preparations and constant care. He also gained valuable practical experience in cooperating with local allies, and had been included in discussions both of the policy behind the war and the strategy of the campaign. Harris was not a brilliant general but Wellesley learnt as much from watching his '*puzzling*' as he would have from a far abler commander.

On the evening of 4 May Baird sent Harris a message asking to be relieved. Whether he was exhausted or – as has been suggested[86] – wished to lessen his responsibility for the disorder that raged through the town, is not clear; but Harris took him at his word and appointed Wellesley to his place on the following morning. Harris always maintained that Wellesley was simply appointed as the next officer of the day on the regular roster; but Baird resented the choice, and his sense of grievance boiled over when, a few days later, Wellesley was made permanent governor of the city. This was understandable, but the decision was entirely reasonable. Baird was ideally suited to command the storm, but completely lacked the tact and sensitivity needed to conciliate the local population. Wellesley, on the other hand, had been destined for the position almost from the outset of the campaign, when he had been appointed to a committee that was to advise Harris on political questions relating to the ultimate fate of Mysore. His elevation to this position shows the difficulty of neatly separating patronage and merit into separate compartments, for of course no one could forget that he was Mornington's brother; but equally he had displayed skills in Madras and in his handling of Meer Allum and the Nizam's army that made him the logical choice for the post. And he was the only officer who properly understood Mornington's plans and possessed the full confidence of the Governor-General.[87]

Baird of course had no interest in such arguments. He genuinely felt cheated, but may also have realised that his grievance could, if given enough exposure, win him support and fresh patronage, if not in Mornington's India then at home. Few British officers of the period rose to prominence by modestly effacing themselves and quietly working at the task they had been set. Those who waited for their merit to be discovered usually waited in vain, while those who wished to succeed had first to overcome their natural modest reticence and sharpen their elbows.

Baird's complaints did not pass unnoticed at home, and there appears to be some foundation for the story told by George Elers, although its details may not be entirely accurate:

> Some two years afterwards, upon General Harris's return home, and on attending the Duke of York at one of his levees at the Horse Guards, Harris, who was not very quick in a difficulty, was asked quickly and suddenly by the Duke: 'Pray, General Harris, what reason had you for superseding General Baird in the command of Seringapatam and giving it to a junior officer?' Poor Harris stammered, and was at a loss for a reply, and the Duke turned his back upon him, and began a conversation with some officers.[88]

Mornington's patronage had opened many doors for Wellesley and given him the opportunity to display his ability to the world, but it had also aroused the jealousy of his rivals and attracted the adverse notice of the Commander-in-Chief of the British army.

CHAPTER SEVEN

THE MYSORE YEARS
(1799–1802)

LATE ON THE afternoon of 5 May 1799, the day after the fall of Seringapatam, Tipu, last Sultan of Mysore, was laid to rest with full ceremonial honours, in the mausoleum constructed by his father. The heavens acknowledged the funeral with a tremendous thunderstorm, and although this was far from unusual for the time and the season of the year, those who saw it as an omen were not disproved by subsequent events; Tipu's funeral marked the end of one era and the opening of another, both for the people of Mysore and in the life of Arthur Wellesley.[1]

Wellesley remained in command of Seringapatam from the morning of 5 May, although he was not formally appointed governor of the city for some days. He restored order, quelling the looting and mayhem by the summary execution of several soldiers and the flogging of others, caught by the provost in the act of committing their crimes. At the same time he urged Harris to keep the men of the army in camp by frequent roll calls, and to urge the officers to delay 'the gratification of their curiosity' and not to enter the city except on official business.[2] Innumerable lesser problems were dealt with: fires extinguished; treasure guarded; corpses buried; protection afforded to Tipu's family, the ladies of his *zenana* and his leading supporters; and attempts made to recapture the criminals released from the prisons in the confusion. As early as ten o'clock in the morning on 5 May Wellesley told Harris that Tipu's pet tigers were agitated: 'There is no food for them, and nobody to attend them, and they are getting violent.' He hoped that Meer Allum would send some experienced attendants to take charge of the beasts, but this did not happen, and a few days later the unfortunate animals had to be shot by soldiers from the 33rd.[3] On 7 May Wellesley took up residence in the Daulat Baug, Tipu's pavilion just outside the walls of the main city. This palace was decorated with elaborate frescoes depicting the destruction of Colonel Baillie's detachment in 1780 and Wellesley, showing surprising cultural sensitivity, ordered that these be protected and, where necessary, restored. As a result they can still be seen today.[4]

As normal life gradually returned to Seringapatam the prize agents, appointed to represent the officers and men of the army, set about cataloguing and valuing the victor's spoil which, by long-standing tradition, would be distributed in set proportions throughout the army. Wellesley felt that their zeal sometimes exceeded their discretion, objecting to their seizing Tipu's clothes, which he felt should be left to Tipu's sons, and to their attempt to remove even the doors of the palace, but otherwise he accepted their role.[5] He seems to have been pleased with his own share of the booty – just over £4,000, which gave him a first step towards financial independence – but other officers were disappointed. According to George Elers, Baird, who as a major-general received almost £11,000, said that he had expected 'at the very least £100,000'. And Harris, who as Commander-in-Chief received £130,000, told Mornington that he doubted that he could afford to accept a peerage.[6] (In the event the government ignored Mornington's recommendation and Harris did not get his peerage until 1815. He also spent six years in court resisting a determined, but ultimately unsuccessful, attempt by the East India Company to reduce his share of the prize money from one-eighth to one-sixteenth.) By contrast an ordinary sepoy received £4 16s and a European private £7 4s, figures that help to explain their preference for distributing the loot on the basis of 'first come, first served', rather than well organised, gentlemanly disproportion.[7]

The question of prize money nearly caused serious trouble between Mornington and the army, for the Governor-General was determined to assert his belief that the booty belonged by right to the government, which would decide what portion of it should be granted to the army.[8] As the army was absolutely convinced of the contrary principle, this dispute had the potential to test Mornington's authority to breaking point; however, when Mornington realised that Tipu's treasury was not quite so fabulously wealthy as rumour had reported, he defused the dispute while maintaining his stand on the principle.[9] He also paraded his personal integrity by declining the gift of Tipu's jewels, which the army proposed to bestow on him, while he brushed aside Wellesley's offer to repay the money which Mornington had lent him to purchase his lieutenant-colonelcy.[10]

Mornington believed that the capture of Seringapatam and the overthrow of Tipu would be celebrated at home as a great triumph, equal to any of the victories gained in the six years of war with revolutionary France, and surpassing Cornwallis's victory of 1792. But in fact, the news fell flat. Despite Bonaparte's expedition to Egypt, India seemed remote and irrelevant. The Second Coalition had made significant early gains in its campaigns against France, especially in Italy and Switzerland, and the Duke of York was about to

lead an Anglo-Russian expedition to Holland. Even the ministers gave the
triumph in India only a careless and perfunctory welcome, and inflicted the
greatest mortification Mornington was ever to receive by making him a
marquess, not in the peerage of Great Britain, but in that of Ireland. The slight
was all the more bitter for being the work of his closest friends and political
allies. Mornington revealed his feelings in a series of anguished letters which
did no good and which may well have harmed his reputation. For the rest of his
life he hoped that the appalling blunder would be corrected and that he would
be made a marquess, or, better still, a duke, in the British peerage, but it was not
to be, and to his dying day he remained the Marquess Wellesley.[11]

Fortunately this blow was yet to fall when the Governor-General determined the future shape and government of Mysore. Several possibilities were
open, each with advantages and drawbacks. The whole country could be
divided between the victorious allies, or one of Tipu's sons could be established
as the new ruler. Mornington considered these but in the end preferred to
establish the heir of the last Hindu Raja, while ceding some territory to Madras
and Hyderabad. The new state would be firmly under British control;
Seringapatam would be ceded to the East India Company, and a British
garrison, based there, would maintain security throughout Mysore. The new
Raja was only a child, and his government was conducted by Purneah, a capable
and experienced Brahmin, who had served Tipu, with Barry Close acting as
British Resident. This arrangement proved extremely successful, and soon
established the new state on secure foundations, while inaugurating a tradition
of good government, which lasted throughout most of the nineteenth century.[12]
Tipu's family was removed from Mysore and kept in comfortable retirement.
Several of his sons were implicated in the Vellore mutiny of 1806, which led to
closer supervision for a time, but this was gradually relaxed, and in later years
two of the younger sons visited England, one of them becoming a favourite of
Queen Victoria and a popular lion of London society until his death in 1872.[13]

With one great exception when he felt betrayed by his brother, the three and
a half years that Arthur Wellesley spent based at Seringapatam were among the
happiest of his life. He was in command, subject only to distant supervision
from Madras and ultimately Bengal. He had work to do, both in governing the
city and in pacifying Mysore, but there was also time to relax and to establish a
home such as he had not had in years. He told Mornington that his position
was 'the most respectable and the best situation for me that I could have in
India', and he forgot his earlier dislike of the country.[14]

At the outset of his time as governor of Seringapatam, Wellesley insisted
that his authority be clearly established, and warned Mornington that he would
not remain in Mysore if it was to be governed by civil servants from the Madras
establishment, 'for I know that the whole is a system of job and corruption

from beginning to end, of which I and my troops would be made the instruments'. He was eager for Harris and 'the plunderers of his army and that of the Nizam' to depart as soon as possible, although it was several months before Harris was satisfied that the conquest was secure.[15] In the meantime, Wellesley set to work repairing the damage caused to Seringapatam and its defences during the siege, converting public buildings into barracks for its new garrison, and proposing improvements including a new bridge over the Cauvery (which Harris vetoed as being too expensive).

Wellesley also relished the chance to play lawmaker, preparing a lengthy series of regulations which established the mechanisms by which both Hindu and Muslim courts should operate in Seringapatam. When a Bombay newspaper wrote that he had permitted Tipu's zenana to be searched for hidden treasure, he wrote immediately to Mornington explaining that he had strongly opposed the measure, but had been forced to give way by orders from Harris and that he had then taken 'every precaution to render the search as decent and as little injurious to the feelings of the ladies as possible'. Clearly he recognised that this was a subject that could easily inflame Muslim opinion throughout India, while greatly damaging his reputation at home. Later, when the Abbé Dubois sought the return of Christian women abducted by Tipu and forced against their will into the zenana (more often as servants than as concubines), Wellesley refused to interfere. He admitted that 'Justice and all our prejudices and passions are on the side of the Christians', but the government had taken Tipu's family under its protection and such interference would disgrace them 'in the eyes of the Indian world'. At the same time he acknowledged that if the government was forced to consider the question it would probably order that not just the Christians, but any woman who wished to leave the zenana, be permitted to do so.[16]

Military operations posed fewer dilemmas, and Wellesley had no qualms about ordering Captains Malcolm and Campbell, commanding flying columns, to destroy weapons and military stores wherever they found them, and to hang any rebels taken in arms. At the same time, however, he insisted that special care be taken to prevent the soldiers plundering or molesting the civilian inhabitants. This was to prove a consistent thread in his orders in all his operations in India, in the Peninsula and in France, and he made very clear to his subordinates that he would not tolerate practices such as the forcible impressment of civilians to act as coolies to carry officers' baggage.[17]

At the end of August 1799 Wellesley left Sherbrooke in command of Seringapatam and set off northwards to occupy a broad stretch of rough country bordering the Maratha Confederacy.[18] Following Tipu's defeat the Governor-General had offered this province to the Peshwa (one of the Maratha Princes) in exchange for a closer alliance, but the Marathas were alarmed by the growth of British power and preferred to keep their distance. Wellesley's advance faced only sporadic local opposition, but everywhere there were clear signs of devastation, for this had long been a debatable land, raided and plundered by the Marathas, and anarchy had reigned in the months since Tipu's fall. Wellesley was anxious not to risk provoking the Marathas and they proved equally wary of him, even returning some of the inhabitants they had driven off and part of the plunder they had taken. The contacts Wellesley established at this time with the southern Maratha lords, and the knowledge he gained of the border region, proved valuable in the years to come. The experience also turned his attention to Maratha affairs in general, where political intrigues at Poona and civil war appeared to presage the collapse of the Confederacy. Unlike some British observers, Wellesley did not welcome the prospect, for the chaos that would follow could not be confined within the Maratha frontiers, and, less perceptively, he believed the Confederacy provided a necessary counterweight to a resurgence in the Nizam's power.[19]

On 21 November Wellesley returned to Seringapatam and was delighted with what he found. 'You can have no conception', he wrote to Lieutenant-Colonel Agnew, 'how much this place is improved. The Toste Khanah is made into one of the best barracks for a complete regiment of Europeans that I have seen in India, and it has not cost the Company one shilling. The arsenal is in good order, and we shall have shortly a very fine parade.'[20] The first months of the year were the best season to sail for England, and both Sherbrooke and General Harris were going home. Sherbrooke's health had been poor ever since his arrival in India, and Wellesley had written to him in the middle of October a letter full of warm friendship and solicitude urging him to leave if he did not recover: 'I am now giving you an opinion contrary to my own interests; I know that if you go my troubles and anxieties will be twice greater than they are at present; but that consideration has no weight when the health of a man is at stake.'[21] As for Harris, his departure was natural after achieving fame and fortune beyond his dreams. And here too the prospect of separation made Wellesley uncommonly gracious, sweeping aside all recollection of past tensions and disagreements and writing as if Harris had been his greatest friend and mentor: 'I shall never forget the many marks of favour and kindness I have received from you, for which I again return my thanks. Wherever you go, I shall always be glad to hear of your happiness; of your success, there is no doubt.'[22]

Wellesley remained in Seringapatam until late March 1800 engaged in multifarious but not overly demanding tasks of administration and government. He wrote to Webbe asking that Lord Clive appoint a chaplain to the garrison, and paid a warm tribute to the ability of Surgeon Trevor of the 33rd.[23] He strongly urged the government at Madras to agree to the establishment of a permanent corps of bullocks and bullock drivers, which would overcome many of the problems experienced in the advance on Seringapatam, enabling the army to take the field at short notice and conduct the 'light and quick movements' which would be called for in any future war.[24] And he explained to the Adjutant-General that the high cost of European goods in Mysore made it impossible for an ensign, and very difficult for a lieutenant, to live upon his pay, and urged him to adopt 'such remedy as he may think proper'.[25]

In March there were some civil disturbances in the city arising from disputes between different groups or trades within one caste, and culminating in a riot on 17 March. Wellesley had to call out the garrison to restore order, and four civilians were killed and two wounded. The city then became quiet and Wellesley felt able to commute the death sentences passed on four rioters who had been tried by general court martial. Wellesley believed that the rioters were intent on testing the will of the new regime, for once it was clear that it would not be intimidated, there was no further trouble.[26] Despite the riot British rule was accepted relatively easily in Seringapatam, but unrest was endemic in many of the more distant provinces of Mysore, where the authority of any central government had always been contested. In the south-west, in Wynaad, the Pyche Raja had assumed that the overthrow of Tipu would restore the independence that he had lost only a few years before. Further north, the Raja of Bullum had similar aspirations, while in the north-east, towards the tract of territory that had been ceded to the Nizam as a reward for his part in Tipu's defeat, the local *polygars*, or petty chieftains, proved equally recalcitrant. In each case the result was a low-level insurgency, involving small forces scattered over a wide area and offering no quick or easy solution.

More urgent was a rapidly growing rebellion in the very north of Mysore, led by a hardened adventurer of considerable experience and skill called Dhoondiah Waugh. In the last decades of the eighteenth century Dhoondiah had served under the Raja of Kolhapur and several Maratha lords who found his boldness and enterprise very useful and who were willing to overlook his taste for plunder. Eventually he fell foul of Tipu Sultan, who caught and imprisoned him in the dungeons of Seringapatam. He escaped amid the confusion of the storm, fled north towards the Maratha frontier, and soon collected a considerable force under his banner. Harris sent troops after him in July 1799; Dhoondiah was defeated, his followers dispersed, and he fled as a fugitive, apparently finding refuge with one of his former employers. Early in 1800 he returned and soon had a large following made up of individual Marathas seeking their fortune, detached soldiers from Tipu's army, and desperate peasants whose holdings had already been devastated.[27]

By 20 April Wellesley was sufficiently alarmed to send three regiments of cavalry north and to undertake further preparations for a substantial campaign. Reports were arriving that Dhoondiah had up to 40,000 men under arms;

although figures such as these were probably much exaggerated, and should always be treated with great scepticism, it was clear that this was no mere band of brigands or freebooters. Like a traditional Maratha army, Dhoondiah's force lacked cohesion and discipline – it would dissolve in the face of adversity – but if it once got the upper hand and gained confidence it would become a formidable foe. Nor could any campaign against Dhoondiah hope to succeed without the cooperation of the Marathas, and permission to cross their frontier or into Hyderabad; otherwise Dhoondiah would simply withdraw in the face of a British advance and return as soon as they turned their backs.[28]

Webbe wrote to Wellesley on 24 May conveying Lord Clive's instructions to 'pursue Dhoondiah Waugh wherever you may find him, and to hang him on the first tree. For this purpose you will receive immediate authority to enter the Marhatta [sic] frontier'.[29] However, the same post brought an unexpected and distracting proposal from the Governor-General. An expedition to Batavia was being prepared and Lord Wellesley offered his brother the command of the troops, although the overall command would rest with Admiral Rainier. Little or no fighting was expected; the object was not to conquer the Dutch colony but rather to give its governor, who was understood to be discontented with the French domination of Holland, a pretext to surrender. Nonetheless, it was likely to be extremely lucrative and to bring considerable éclat to both the military and naval commanders. Wellesley would not need to give up his command in Mysore, and would only be away for four or five months.[30] No ambitious man could view such a prospect without a tremor of excitement, and it is clear that Wellesley was tempted. But his duty was equally clear; his immediate responsibility was to Mysore, and he was about to commence a campaign against an enemy who could not be ignored or given six months to establish himself merely to suit the convenience of a British officer. He left the final decision to Lord Clive, but had no doubt that the war against Dhoondiah must take priority; although if the admiral was forced to delay the expedition for a few months by a shortage of troops, he ought to be free then.[31]

The operation against Dhoondiah Waugh was Wellesley's first campaign as an independent commander responsible for its conception, planning and execution. In it he displayed all the characteristics of his subsequent campaigns in India, most notably a careful concern for logistics and unremitting aggression, as he drove at his enemy without wavering or hesitation. By early June Wellesley had concentrated a force of seven battalions of infantry (two British, five Indian) and five regiments of cavalry (two British, three Indian) at Chitteldroog in northern Mysore, while part of the Nizam's subsidiary force was ready to cooperate from Hyderabad. Despite the rains, swollen rivers and the inevitable problems with bullocks, Wellesley advanced rapidly, storming a succession of hill forts and thoroughly intimidating his enemy. The Marathas proved willing to cooperate, but Dhoondiah defeated Goklah, one of the southern Maratha lords, on 30 June, and so gained some breathing space. Nonetheless, the tide was now running against him, and large numbers of his followers deserted his cause and escaped as best they could. However, as his forts were captured and his army shrank he became more elusive, and Wellesley found it difficult to end the campaign. In the second week of July the British crossed the Toombuddra into Maratha territory, and for a moment it looked as if Dhoondiah was ready to give battle, but it proved a ruse, and he slipped away again.[32] Wellesley responded by publicly placing a reward of 30,000 rupees on his head, calculating that even if it were not taken up it would make Dhoondiah anxious and distrustful.[33] But still Dhoondiah eluded him. On 30 July Wellesley caught part of Dhoondiah's army and drove it into a river, but the chief escaped, and Wellesley's own army was now in need of rest and time to reorganise. A pause in operations followed, and Wellesley was rather despondent, writing to Barry Close: 'The war will literally have no object nor no end, if we are to follow a single man with a few horsemen to the end of the world'; and, nine days later: 'It is clear I shall never catch him.'[34]

This proved unduly pessimistic. Wellesley divided his forces and in the last days of August launched a concerted advance. Dhoondiah fled eastward into Hyderabad and there, on 10 September 1800, Wellesley caught him at Conaghul. The British had only four regiments of cavalry amounting to little over 1,000 men, whereas Dhoondiah is said to have had 5,000 or 6,000 men, although it is unlikely that this accurately reflects his true fighting strength. In any case the long pursuit had given the British immense confidence. Later that day a British officer wrote an account of what happened:

> Col. Wellesley with that alacrity and determination which he has shewn on all occasions gave immediate orders to charge, and after two rounds of Grape from each of the Gallopers [horse artillery], the 19th [Light Dragoons] & 1st Regiment [Native Cavalry] charged their front, while the 25th [Light Dragoons] & 2nd [Native Cavalry] followed as a reserve. The regular manner in which our Cavalry moved down soon threw them into confusion, & Dhoondiah falling in the first onset they fled in all directions. We pursued the largest Body for about four miles, and did not give quarter to anyone – We also charged through his Camp, & the Carnage was dreadful – not less than three or four thousand of the Enemy were killed, while the loss on our part was only 1 Private (25th Dragoons) killed, & 12 wounded – & 19th Dragoons, 1 wounded, & two or three of the N[ative] Cavalry, & in the whole about 20 horses killed & wounded. Dhoondiah received one cut in the sword arm, and several in various parts of his Body & two Pistol shots through him. We have just buried him in front of the Standard Guard of the 19th Dragoons – He was a very stout handsome man . . .[35]

The victory was complete and brought the campaign to a decisive conclusion. Dhoondiah's young son was found in the camp and Wellesley, whether from kindness or policy, took responsibility for the boy, Salabut Khan, paying for his education and establishment out of his own pocket. Although Dhoondiah's troops were, as Wellesley himself wrote, 'a despicable enemy', the achievement of hunting him down was considerable.[36] Wellesley learnt a great deal from the campaign, and showed himself to be flexible and quick to adjust to unfamiliar problems. Simply keeping his troops in the field and mobile was a far more demanding task than defeating Dhoondiah when he was at last brought to bay, while Wellesley had also proved adept at maintaining good relations with both the Marathas and the Nizam's government. Clearly the Governor-General's brother was a man of some ability, although there was, as yet, little reason for those who had not worked closely with him to appreciate the full extent of his talents.

Wellesley remained in an advanced position until the middle of November, partly to settle the country, and partly because there was a chance that he might be ordered to intervene directly in Maratha politics. But the moment passed and he received orders to withdraw the army into Mysore, and then to proceed to Trincomalee in Ceylon to consult with Admiral Rainier. Wellesley was a little annoyed at these orders at first, for they meant that he would have only a few days in Seringapatam after being in the field for six months, and they conflicted with his own plans for a campaign against the Pyche Raja. But a 'Private and Secret' despatch dated 5 November revealed that Lord Wellesley had an important and tempting role in mind for his brother: to command a strategic reserve based at Trincomalee that could be used to support operations from home against the French army in Egypt, or against Batavia, or the French possession of Mauritius. It was the last of these possibilities that particularly appealed to Lord Wellesley, for his enthusiasm had been fired by a Mr Stokes, a sailor who had recently arrived in Bengal with tales of discontent in the islands and a cunning plan to take the garrison by surprise.[37]

Arthur Wellesley arrived at Madras on 13 December and was soon immersed in details of troops, shipping and supplies. His initial scepticism faded as he studied the papers his brother had sent from Calcutta, and he grew increasingly confident that the operation could succeed, provided that the weather held and that the element of surprise was not compromised by unnecessary delays. He reached Trincomalee on Christmas Eve; some of the troops were there already, and Admiral Rainier with the rest of the expedition was expected from Bengal any day, so that with luck they would sail before the end of the year. But the admiral did not come. Days of waiting stretched into weeks; supplies ran short and the health of the troops was imperilled.

Lord Wellesley had blundered, forgetting that the British admiral, unlike the generals, was not subject to his authority, and failing to discover that Admiral Rainier did not share his faith in Mr Stokes, and had no enthusiasm for the projected attack on Mauritius.[38] To make matters worse, Lord Wellesley now came under great pressure from senior generals to give the command of the force at Trincomalee to one of them. Summoning the courage that had carried him through the breach at Seringapatam, Baird went to see the Governor-General to protest. And, to everyone's astonishment, the most imperious viceroy British India would ever know gave way.[39] The result was a nightmare for Arthur Wellesley. Eighteen months earlier, in June 1799 he had told his brother that it would be 'particularly unpleasant' for him to have to serve under Baird, and that he did not think that anyone (he meant General Harris) would be so tactless as to ask him to do so.[40] And now this very thing was being suggested, not by Harris or Braithwaite, or some other insensitive superior, but by the brother he had always looked to as his most dependable patron and friend.

A fortnight before this painful news broke upon him, Arthur Wellesley received a copy of secret instructions from the government in London, announcing that an expedition was being sent to the Mediterranean to attack the French in Egypt, and ordering that a force of at least 3,000 men be sent from India to the Red Sea to cooperate with it. As haste was essential, copies of the despatch were sent overland directly to Madras and Bombay as well as Calcutta, and these governments were ordered to act upon it without waiting for further instructions from Calcutta. The expedition should try to reach the Red Sea before the end of February, and Bombay was pointed out as its base.[41]

Faced with these orders there was little doubt what Arthur Wellesley should do. He had almost 3,000 men ready onboard ship, and one of the reasons they had originally been assembled was to answer just such a requisition. He decided to sail at once for the Red Sea, stopping on the way at Bombay to replenish his supplies and receive any fresh orders. He was a little anxious about the halt at Bombay, particularly as Frederick North, the governor of Ceylon, strongly urged him to bypass it and trust that supplies would follow. But Wellesley knew that logistics were the secret of operations whether in India or Egypt, and he would not blindly rely on the notoriously slow and inefficient government of Bombay for his subsistence. In any case, Captain Pulteney Malcolm, the senior naval officer present, assured him that calling at Bombay would not significantly delay the expedition.[42]

Unfortunately it proved a slow passage to Bombay. Wellesley, having set sail on 15 February, did not arrive until about 23 March, learning of Baird's appointment en route, and having plenty of time to speculate on how the hot-tempered Scot would react when he arrived at Trincomalee to find that Wellesley had sailed without him. At Bombay Wellesley pressed preparations forward with all speed, hoping to sail by 26 March, for the end of the season in which sailing ships could make their way up the Red Sea was approaching, and he had resolved not to wait even a single day for Baird. This was pushing his discretion to the limit, yet any other decision would clearly have been wrong.[43]

But before the ships were ready to sail Wellesley was struck down by a severe intermittent fever and Baird arrived. Relations between the two men were understandably strained at first, but Baird was disarmed by Wellesley's illness and proved surprisingly magnanimous, although Wellesley remained unhappy that some of his staff were replaced by Baird's men. Within a few days Baird and the expedition had sailed, leaving Wellesley behind. His fever had been followed by an unpleasant ailment known as 'Malabar itch', with his whole body covered with eruptions 'somewhat of the same kind as venereal blotches', and for which the prescribed treatment was a course of baths in diluted nitric acid. This prevented his 'laudable but highly disagreeable intention' of following the expedition.[44] The Mediterranean army under Sir Ralph Abercromby defeated the French at Alexandria in March, although its commander, the ablest senior general in the British army, was mortally wounded. Baird's force reached Kosseir on the Red Sea, but was too late to attempt to sail up the Gulf of Suez. Refusing to be thwarted, Baird led his men on an epic hundred-mile march across the desert to the Nile Valley near Luxor, which impressed his superiors and proved his determination and ability as a leader of men.[45]

Few events in Arthur Wellesley's life mortified him as much as his loss of the command of this expedition to David Baird. And for this he blamed not Baird, but the Governor-General who had summoned him from happy independence in Mysore, subjected him to weeks of tedium and frustration at Trincomalee, and then betrayed him by placing him under the command of an avowed enemy – a position he would never have voluntarily accepted, but from which he could not honourably resign as the expedition was about to take the field. Left in Bombay, ill, tired and full of despair, he let loose all the reproaches he had previously held back in a string of letters to his brothers in Calcutta. Why had he been superseded? Had he been grossly incompetent or 'guilty of robbery or murder'? No, it was because the Governor-General had been too weak to resist the predictable protests of Baird and the other senior generals. Worse still, people would assume that the Governor-General must have had good reason to sacrifice his own brother:

> I was at the top of the tree in this country; the governments of Fort St George and Bombay, which I had served, placed unlimited confidence in me, and I had received from both strong and repeated marks of their approbation ... But this supersession has ruined my prospects, founded on any service that I may have rendered.[46]

Most of these complaints were sent to Henry Wellesley, who did his best to soothe his brother with assurances that his reputation had not suffered; but at least one letter went direct to the Governor-General who was neither amused, nor inclined to apologise. As a result, Henry was soon writing: 'I cannot help urging you to write a conciliatory letter to Mornington [*sic*] who is really much annoyed by your letter of the 18th April.'[47] This was the last straw, for Arthur Wellesley was not a man to apologise for being wronged, even to his own brother, and a breach opened between them that never fully healed. Arthur's old confidence that in a pinch Richard could be relied upon to protect his interests was gone forever. They continued to be allies, to cooperate and to respect and admire each other's abilities, but they grew apart and for many months they even stopped corresponding, Arthur sending his letters to Henry, or to the Governor-General's private secretary.

The spring tides brought a recurrence of Wellesley's fever and he sailed from Bombay soon afterwards, still far from well. He landed at Cannanore on 27 April and reached Seringapatam on 7 May, delighted to be back in familiar surroundings after a year on the move. He had several more attacks of fever, and George Elers, who stayed with him for several months at this time, noted that the illness had taken its toll and that although Wellesley had only just turned thirty-two, some grey hairs were mixed with the light brown around his temples.[48] His return was warmly welcomed by Clive, Webbe and Close, none of whom had ever thought highly of the expedition to Mauritius or the Red Sea.

Wellesley was delighted to observe Mysore's recovery from the war and Tipu's misrule, telling his brother Henry:

> The Rajah's government is in the most prosperous state: the country is become a garden where it is inhabited, and the inhabitants are returning fast to those parts which the last savage [i.e. Tipu] had forced them to quit . . . Mysore is become a large and handsome Native town, full of inhabitants: the whole country is settled and in perfect tranquillity. I believe the Rajah's treasury is rich, as he pays his kisks with regularity; but Purneah, who has an eye to the future prosperity and revenue of the country, has repaired numberless tanks [reservoirs], particularly that large one near Milcottah; has rebuilt many towns and forts; and, I understand, encourages the inhabitants of the country in all parts by advances of money and remissions whenever they require them.[49]

Some of the credit for this success belonged to Barry Close, as well as Purneah, and Wellesley was concerned to find that he too had been ill, with recurrent attacks of fever and ague. In his letter to Henry, Arthur Wellesley went on to describe his relations with Close:

It is impossible for two men to go on better than he and I, notwithstanding
that his temper is not of the best, and his mode of enforcing his reasonings
not the most agreeable. But he is able and zealous to a degree in the public
cause, and it is always pleasant to act with such a man whatever his temper.[50]

The warm welcome and the flourishing state of Mysore gave Wellesley some
much-needed encouragement, for his spirits remained at a very low ebb. He
even toyed with the idea of leaving India and going home, reflecting that
'Between my prize money and my allowances I have as much money as would
keep me decently in England till something else would turn up'.[51] Nothing
came of this notion, and he suffered a further disappointment when he was not
among the colonels promoted to the rank of Major-General at the beginning of
1801. (This was not a reflection on his individual merit, for the promotion was
based on seniority – all colonels above a point in the *Army List* being elevated
together in a 'general brevet', and retaining their place relative to each
other – but it would have made it much easier for him to be given important
commands.) According to George Elers, he was much disappointed, saying
sorrowfully: '*My highest ambition* is to be a *Major-General* in His Majesty's
service.' However it seems unlikely that he would really have confided his
hopes to a young acquaintance like Elers, even if he had clearly formulated
them to himself.[52]

   Life in Seringapatam in 1801 offered few great opportunities or challenges,
but Wellesley was content to enjoy an interlude of relative tranquillity and quiet
domesticity, while recovering his health and spirits. He devoted a good deal of
time to humdrum questions of municipal government; a General Order on
measures to deal with the problem of mad dogs running loose through the
streets of the town is not untypical. He dealt sternly with a case of corruption
involving military stores in Seringapatam, court-martialling three officers of the
Company's artillery. And he continued to take vigorous measures to protect
the civilian population from military abuses, publicly warning British officers
that they had no more right to strike Indians than they had to strike Englishmen
at home, and that if they did so they would be prosecuted. Nor was this an
empty threat, for Wellesley had already ensured that an assistant-surgeon was
court-martialled when complaints were received of his misconduct, and
quashed an attempt by the court to minimise his offence.[53]

   In April 1802 Wellesley was finally promoted Major-General and placed on
the staff in India. This ended his active connection with the 33rd for a time, but
he had the satisfaction of leaving the regiment in good hands. The egregious
Major Shee had tendered his resignation after a quarrel with a brother officer
in the mess, and Wellesley would not let him retract it, although he relented
sufficiently to allow Shee to go home on health grounds and there sell his

commission.[54] Wellesley was pleased that this left Major Walter Elliot, 'a very good man, a Relation of Mrs Dallas, lately come from England', in temporary command of the regiment. When Sherbrooke realised that his health would prohibit a return to India, he left the regiment, exchanging with Lieutenant-Colonel Arthur Gore, whose family had contributed many officers to the regiment and who proved an excellent commander of the 33rd.[55]

Meanwhile there was much work to be done. Colin Mackenzie was busily engaged in an ambitious survey of the resources and geography of Mysore, but this did not prevent Wellesley from also supporting William Lambton's idea for another survey with a different objective: to measure the curvature of the earth and lay the foundation for the Great Trigonometrical Survey of India.[56] And there were still campaigns to be fought against the Pyche Raja, the Raja of Bullum and the Polygars, who still refused to submit to the new government of Mysore. Wellesley had some success in these operations (the Raja of Bullum was captured and executed in February 1802), and he admired the new country he saw, but on the whole he disliked the task. 'These Polygar wars are terrible,' he told Colonel Robertson in June 1801. 'We lose in them our best men and officers, and, by the existence of the contest, our credit, and neither the public nor individuals derive from them the smallest advantage.'[57] Such insurgencies could not be ignored once they existed, but every effort should be made to prevent them breaking out in the first place. This was one reason, although not the only one, why Arthur Wellesley was determined to promote the good government of Mysore and to protect its inhabitants from military exactions.

But Wellesley spent most of 1801–02 in Seringapatam, and George Elers gives us some vivid glimpses of his life there:

We used to get up early in the morning and attend the garrison parade, and Colonel Wellesley used, of course, to be saluted by the Guards as they marched off. His dress at this time consisted of a *long coat*, the uniform of the 33rd Regiment, a *cocked hat*, white pantaloons, Hessian boots and spurs, and a large sabre, the handle solid silver, and the mounting of the scabbard the same metal, but all gilt. He never wore powder, though it was at that time the regulation to do so. His hair was cropped close. I have heard him say that he was convinced the wearing of hair powder was very prejudicial to health as impeding the perspiration, and he was doubtless right.

[At dinner Wellesley] sat in the centre of the table, his A.D.C., Captain West, at the top of the table, and Captain Barclay, the Deputy Adjutant-General, at the bottom. This comprised the family, but there were always other officers, guests, altogether from eight to a dozen every day. Colonel Wellesley kept a plain but good table. He had a very good appetite, and his favourite dish was a roast saddle of mutton and salad. This dish was placed

opposite to him, and he generally made his dinner off it. He was very abstemious with wine; drank four or five glasses with people at dinner, and about
a pint of claret after. He was very even in his temper, laughing and joking with
those he liked, speaking in his quick way, and dwelling particularly upon the
few (*at that time*) situations he had been placed in before the enemy, the
arrangements he had made, and their fortunate results, all of which were
applauded by his staff, who had shared in the glory and the peril. This generally formed the topic of conversation after dinner. He was particularly severe
upon any neglect of the commissariat department, and openly declared that,
if he had commanded an army, he should not hesitate to hang a Commissary
for any dereliction of his duty.[58]

Half-jocular threats to hang commissaries were to recur in several popular
anecdotes of the Peninsular War, but it is rather dismaying to find that Wellesley
had already begun to entertain his dinner guests with accounts of his own
triumphs. Elers's definition of 'abstemious' will surprise modern readers, but
most accounts of drinking in this era mention quantities that defy belief or
suggest that wine was either very weak or well diluted by the servants. Wellesley
himself told his brother Henry:

I know but one receipt for good health in this country, and that is to live
moderately, to drink little or no wine, to use exercise, to keep the mind
employed, and, if possible, to keep in good humour with the world. The last
is the most difficult, for, as you have often observed, there is scarcely a good-
tempered man in India.[59]

As recreations, Elers mentions billiards (he beat Wellesley in two games, but
more often played Francis West, the ADC) and hunting, using Tipu's cheetahs
to hunt antelopes.[60] Fortunately Wellesley had a dog again, a terrier named
Jack, 'a very great pet and favourite', which accompanied him in his travels
around Mysore, and on one occasion found its own way home to Seringapatam
having been lost at Chitteldroog, more than 100 miles to the north.[61]

It was at this time that Wellesley had an affair with Isabella Freese, the 'very
young and rather pretty'[62] wife of an artillery officer, Captain John William
Freese, who had been appointed Commissary of Stores at Seringapatam.
Captain Freese turned a blind eye, but the liaison offended Francis West who
presumed to interfere and who was sharply snubbed for his pains. On 7 July
1802 Mrs Freese gave birth to a son, who was quite possibly Wellesley's, and
who was christened Arthur, with Wellesley being made his godfather. A few
years later, in 1807, the young Arthur Freese was sent home to England to be
brought up by an aunt, but the aunt died before he could arrive and, in an

arrangement that would not have been uncommon for an illegitimate child in this period, Arthur Wellesley gave him a home until he was old enough to go to Charterhouse, and greatly assisted his subsequent career in India.[63] The affair evidently ended well with warm feelings on both sides. Wellesley wrote a long, friendly letter from St Helena, while Mrs Freese did not hesitate to use her 'great influence with the Gen[eral]' in support of her cousin, John Orrok, when he wished to be made paymaster of the 33rd in 1806. And despite his marriage, Wellesley kept a portrait of Mrs Freese, and saw no reason to hide it away.[64]

There may well have been other affairs during Wellesley's years in India. He always enjoyed the company of intelligent, lively, attractive women, and he regarded himself as a free agent untied by engagement to Kitty Pakenham or anyone else. But if there were other liaisons they were either kept secret or were brief and unimportant. None left traces similar to those of his affair with Mrs Freese, and, as that shows, he was not unduly anxious to be discreet, for the social conventions of the day were relatively relaxed. Byron was not the first to discover that:

What men call gallantry, and gods adultery,
Is much more common where the climate's sultry.[65]

News from England and Europe arrived only intermittently, and was generally disheartening. The Second Coalition had collapsed in disarray with much recrimination. Russia had withdrawn and revived the Armed Neutrality of the northern powers against Britain only for this to be broken by Nelson's victory at Copenhagen, the assassination of the Emperor Paul and the accession of his son Alexander. In France, General Bonaparte had consolidated his position as First Consul of the Republic and was busy negotiating peace terms with Austria following French victories at Marengo and Hohenlinden. And in Britain, Pitt's government resigned after forcing through the Act of Union with Ireland. This was the news that shocked Arthur Wellesley the most; defeats in the war had become all too familiar, but Pitt had been in power for half Wellesley's life and seemed to provide a rock of stability on which the nation depended. A new government was to be formed, not from the Opposition, which was too weak and discredited by its support for the French Revolution to provide a credible alternative, but by the lesser lights of the old ministry. Wellesley was both dismayed and puzzled by the news:

If . . . Mr Pitt is no longer in office, I fear that our country is in but a bad way at this moment. It is impossible that any party formed by the remnants of his administration can have strength, or indeed abilities, to keep down the factions in England and at the same time to carry on the war in the manner in which it ought to be carried on; and this, after a nine years struggle, we shall be ruined by our own folly.[66]

As Pitt and Dundas provided the principal support for Lord Wellesley in London, their resignation had serious implications for his position in Bengal. The new prime minister was Henry Addington, who had been Speaker of the Commons and was a good friend of Lord Wellesley. But his ministry lacked the strength to provide a reliable defence against Wellesley's many enemies in the East India Company, who objected to the cost of his campaigns and the extravagance of some of his other projects, believing that he should instead give priority to paying off the vast debts the Company had already accumulated. Arthur Wellesley felt that the new ministry had 'too much moderation and candour for these bad times', and was unlikely to survive for long.[67] He also disapproved of the peace that Addington had negotiated with France in October 1801, believing that it 'establishes the French power over Europe, and when we shall be disarmed we shall have no security excepting in our own abjectness'.[68] Far from home, Wellesley failed to appreciate the depth of discontent in Britain compounded of war-weariness, despair and the effects of a bad harvest; or the rather desperate hope that the new regime in France might make good its promises of peace and stability. The peace failed in less than two years, but it was nonetheless reasonable that the attempt had been made, for the interlude helped reunite Britain and prepare her (psychologically, if not materially) for a renewed and even more demanding war.

Although Lord Wellesley's enemies in Leadenhall Street were unable to secure his recall, they did much to harass and annoy him, criticising his policies and vetoing some of his pet plans such as the College of Fort William to train young recruits for the Company's service. They attacked his appointment of Henry Wellesley to an important position in Oudh, and reduced Arthur Wellesley's allowance of 'table money' from 600 to 400 pagodas per month.[69] They also ordered the dismissal of Josiah Webbe from his position at Madras and made many other changes that tended to punish the supporters of Lord Wellesley and promote his opponents. Webbe's loss would have been an irreparable blow both to Lord Clive personally and to the whole system of government that Lord Wellesley had created. After some anxious cogitation a way round was hit upon; Webbe was appointed to replace Close at Mysore, but told to remain at Madras, for Purneah's government no longer needed constant supervision.

Close's position was vacant because he had been appointed British resident at Poona, the Peshwa's capital. Arthur Wellesley regretted his departure 'exceedingly' while acknowledging: 'There is no doubt whatever but that he is the ablest man in the diplomatic line in India, and that his knowledge of the languages is so extraordinary and superior to that of any other European in India, that that alone renders him the most fit for a diplomatic situation.' He was surprised that Close thought Poona could offer anything as interesting or rewarding as the steady improvement of Mysore, but here his partiality for the country blinded him, and Close showed superior judgement, for there could be no doubt that Poona was now the critical point in India, and that Maratha affairs would determine whether the Wellesley brothers would find themselves engaged in another major war.[70]

CHAPTER EIGHT

THE RESTORATION OF THE PESHWA
(1802–03)

TOWARDS THE END of 1802 a crisis in the internal affairs of the Maratha Confederacy brought Arthur Wellesley's quiet life at Seringapatam to an end. His remaining years in India were to be dominated by the intricate complexities of Maratha politics. He learnt to act on a large stage where the stakes were high, and where he had to rely upon his own judgement, not just on military questions, but also on issues of broader diplomatic and political consequence.

The Maratha Confederation was the largest single power in India, but it was deeply divided, with five major and innumerable lesser rulers, each giving only occasional and reluctant obedience to any central authority. In theory, it was governed by the Raja of Satara, but his power was now purely nominal and he was little more than a trophy to be secured along with the other ceremonial regalia. Real power was exercised by five great Maratha princes, each virtually independent, but whose territories were often intermixed. Of the five, the Peshwa, or hereditary prime minister, had a claim to seniority and even to make policy for the confederation as a whole, although in practice this was highly debatable. In the 1790s the Peshwa's power was in decline, while the house of Sindia was in the ascendant, based on its great territories in Hindustan and on its large army of well-disciplined infantry under European officers organised and led with great skill by a famous mercenary, Benoit de Boigne. As Sindia's fortunes rose those of the rival house of Holkar declined and for a time were completely eclipsed. The Bhonsle Raja of Berar, the fourth of the princes, had his capital at Nagpur, some 400 miles north-east of Poona. He was a conscientious and effective ruler, whose dominions flourished while he avoided being dragged into the devastating conflict between Sindia and Holkar. The least important of the princes was Anud Rao, the Gaikwar of Baroda, whose lands mostly lay in the north-west, beyond Bombay. He was a weak ruler, overwhelmed by family quarrels and unable to control his troops.

In July 1802 he signed a subsidiary alliance with the Company, which effectively detached him from the Confederation.[1]

Maratha politics were unstable and often violent, and the rise of the house of Sindia made matters worse. Sindia's force of sepoys was expensive to maintain: many jagirdars, or feudatory lords, in Hindustan had been dispossessed in order to pay for it, and they and their followers were ready to join any revolt against his authority. The head of the house was Daulat Rao Sindia, who had succeeded his uncle in 1794 when he was only thirteen. After a protracted power struggle, Sindia installed his nominee Baji Rao II as Peshwa – a success which was followed by scenes of terror and extortion as Sindia's enemies and rivals were executed and money seized to pay the troops.[2] Sindia's aunts (the widows of his uncle) had already taken up arms against him, and were now joined by Amrit Rao, the adopted brother of Baji Rao. Their revolt failed, but could not be completely suppressed and civil strife and insurrection became endemic throughout Sindia's territories.[3] At the same time Sindia gained control over the Holkar lands and wealth, holding prisoner Kashirao, the eldest son of the previous Holkar prince, and crushing a revolt led by Kashirao's brothers, of whom one was killed and two others went into exile. Sindia's pre-eminence was complete but it was obvious that both he and Baji Rao lacked the ability and the underlying conditions to consolidate his power. The wild instability of Maratha politics in these years was both a symptom and a cause of the growing crisis in the Confederacy. Neither Daulat Rao Sindia nor Baji Rao were capable of providing the state with the leadership it needed, or of checking the rising tide of anarchy that was engulfing their lands.

Few if any of these problems were caused by the British who, under Sir John Shore, maintained a distant and guarded alliance with the Marathas, but wanted nothing to do with their internal affairs. Mornington's arrival in India resulted in a change of policy, but one which had little immediate effect. His aim was a close alliance which would effectively subordinate the Marathas to the British, but there was no reason for the Maratha princes to accept such terms, and his proposals were politely declined. Tipu's rapid defeat was viewed with dismay at Poona, even though the Marathas remained officially on friendly terms with British India. They recognised that the best chance of preserving their independence was to steer a careful middle path avoiding both war with Britain and the proposed subsidiary alliance; and Sindia was conscious that the many British mercenaries serving as officers in his army did so on condition that they not be asked to fight against their country.[4]

In 1800, following the death of Nana Phadnavis, a Maratha elder statesman who had exerted some restraint on Sindia and Baji Rao, Sindia took full control over the Peshwa's government. Many old servants of the state were executed, some fired from the mouths of cannon, some after having their noses and ears cut off, while one unfortunate had rockets tied around his body and 'he was blown up like a kite in flight'.[5] Baji Rao was Sindia's eager accomplice in all this, but after a time he began to fear for his own safety, for Sindia's troops controlled the city and even the Peshwa's own palace. In his alarm, Baji Rao turned to Colonel William Palmer, the British resident, saying that he could no longer endure Sindia's domination and feared being deposed by him.[6]

This appeal was well timed, for Arthur Wellesley, at the head of a British army, was already in southern Maharashtra conducting his campaign against Dhoondiah Waugh.[7] Lord Wellesley responded to the Peshwa's appeal by ordering his brother to remain in Maharashtra after Dhoondiah was defeated so that he could quickly intervene in Poona if the Peshwa signed a treaty of alliance with Britain, or if he fled his capital, or was placed under physical constraint by Sindia. In other words, Lord Wellesley would only intervene directly if he was explicitly invited to do so by the Peshwa, or if the Peshwa were personally ill-treated.[8]

Arthur Wellesley and his army remained in camp in southern Maharashtra for almost two months (early September to early November 1800) waiting for a call to action which never came. Deep in plans for a march on Poona, and full of thoughts on how to deal with expected opposition, Wellesley told Barry Close: 'My fingers itch to begin'.[9] But despite this he was not an advocate of intervention or expansion, telling Thomas Munro:

> In my opinion, the extension of our territory and influence has been greater than our means. Besides, we have added to the number and description of our enemies, by depriving of employment those who heretofore found it in the service of Tippoo, and of the Nizam. Wherever we spread ourselves, particularly if we aggrandise ourselves at the expense of the Marhattas, we increase this evil. We throw out of employment, and of means of subsistence, all who have hitherto managed the revenue, commanded or served in the armies, or have plundered the country. These people become additional enemies . . . I am in general inclined to decide that we have enough; as much, at least, if not more, than we can defend.[10]

Such views were not common among influential British figures in southern India in 1800. Tom Sydenham and James Kirkpatrick, both writing from Hyderabad where Kirkpatrick was the Resident, urged forceful intervention at Poona in order to achieve 'the speedy Determination of this most important question' – which, in effect, meant the establishment of British predominance in Maratha affairs as it already existed at Hyderabad. Neither man felt the least concern at the prospect of war with the Marathas, arguing that their power was much diminished, while that even under the most favourable circumstances, at the Battle of Kharda, their army 'did not exceed 175,000 men'.[11] Even Barry Close, who was a much better judge of policy than either Sydenham or Kirkpatrick, felt that the British government could not afford to 'be a passive witness of the approach of a political calamity like that of the reunion of the Maratha Empire'. Close went on to argue that Wellesley's army ought to be used to establish British paramountcy at Poona.[12]

Arthur Wellesley responded on two levels. The first was largely pragmatic. The Peshwa's weakness, indecision and duplicity were notorious, and if Wellesley intervened to rescue him from Sindia without an unequivocal request he would probably:

> fly off and . . . declare that I had no authority from him, that I was an enemy, and was to be treated as such, government or I would be in a scrape, from which it would be difficult to extricate either of us. In truth, if the Peshwa is not in confinement, he has the power to call for our assistance; and if he does not call for it, we have no right to force it upon him. By the same reasoning, if, as long as he has the power, he omits to conclude with us that treaty, so advantageous to him, and so often offered, we ought to respect his sincerity, and ought not to interfere in his affairs till the last extremity. For all these reasons then, in my opinion, I ought not to move till the crisis is certain.[13]

But he had a deeper objection, grounded on political principles and abstract justice – topics which were less common in his correspondence than bullocks and supplies, but not less important. On 12 November 1800 he told Close:

> I have lately received a letter from Captain Kirkpatrick, and another from Tom Sydenham. They breathe nothing but war, and appear to have adopted some French principles upon that subject. They seem to think that because the Mahrattas do not choose to ally themselves with us more closely, because they may at some time or other connect themselves with the French, and because they are now in some degree divided among one another, it is perfectly justifiable and proper that we should go to war with them. The only question at Hyderabad is the prospect of ultimate success, upon which these gentlemen have no doubt, as they say that the Mahrattas in the last war with the Nizam, which ended with the peace at Kurdlah, had in the field only 175,000 men!!! N.B. The Nizam has not now got 5,000 horse, as I am informed, of any kind whatever.[14]

And to Kirkpatrick he raised the question of Pitt's Act prohibiting wars of aggression in India:

The refusal of the Mahrattas to accede to our terms of closer alliance cannot be deemed an attack, and I have not heard of any circumstances in their late conduct which can be deemed one. Hostility then on our part might be thought a breach of the laws for the government of this empire.

But not only might it be considered in that light, but as an act of great political injustice. In fact, one country has no right to commence a war upon another because at some time or other that other may form an alliance with its enemy prejudicial to its interests, and because it refuses to draw closer the terms of its alliance with the country which proposes it. The question of peace or war is not, and cannot be, only the probability of success, but must depend upon other circumstances, and in this country must depend upon the prospect of being attacked by the power with which it is proposed to go to war.[15]

By the time these letters were written the prospect of immediate intervention had passed. The Peshwa and Sindia had been reconciled, and Sindia talked of leaving Poona in order to attend to his affairs in Hindustan. Wellesley withdrew his army and, after a brief pause at Seringapatam, went on to Madras, Trincomalee and his supersession at Bombay. It was not until late 1802 that Maratha affairs would again fill his thoughts.

These two years saw no improvement in the Maratha Confederacy as misgovernment became worse and the endemic civil war grew more serious. In December 1800 Sindia finally departed from Poona, although he left some troops there to maintain his influence with the Peshwa, who had few resources of his own. A new rebellion now threatened Sindia and Baji Rao, led by two princes of the house of Holkar, who had been forced into exile by Sindia following the death of their father in 1797. The first was Jaswant Rao Holkar, who served as a rallying point for the old servants and jagirdars of the Holkars. He suffered some defeats, in one losing the sight in an eye, but on the whole his campaign flourished, benefitting from the instability of the times, which left many men desperate and ready to follow any leader. At the same time, but further south, his brother Vitoji Holkar had also gone to war against Sindia and the Peshwa, and was carrying fire and sword through Maharashtra almost to the walls of Poona. But Vitoji was defeated and captured by Goklah, one of the Peshwa's southern jagirdars. Baji Rao, determined to make an example of his prisoner, ordered that Vitoji be flogged, then chained to the feet of an elephant, he and Vitoji watched with delight while was trampled to death on 16 April 1801.[16]

The death of his brother only strengthened Jaswant Rao Holkar. Between June and October 1801 he fought a series of bloody but indecisive battles against Sindia's brigades along the River Nerbudda, which devastated the entire country around Indore and Ujjain (the traditional capitals of the houses of Holkar and Sindia respectively). Sindia finally tried to negotiate a settlement, but the talks failed, and Jaswant Rao Holkar began to move slowly south with his army, pillaging the country as he went. He entered the dominions of the Peshwa, whom he continued to recognise as his overlord, petitioning him for justice against Sindia, but ignoring his orders to halt and return to the traditional Holkar lands. Baji Rao responded by formally confiscating all the estates of the Holkars, and treating Jaswant Rao's emissaries with disdain. But as Jaswant Rao's advance continued, the Peshwa grew nervous, arrested many leading figures in Poona, and looked around for aid. Sindia and the Raja of Berar, the only Maratha leaders who could hope to stop Holkar's advance, sent assurances; Holkar could not move during the monsoon, and as soon as it was over they would combine against him. Baji Rao was not fully reassured by this, and again began tentative talks with Barry Close, who had replaced Colonel Palmer as British Resident in December 1801. The Peshwa still did not want to sign an alliance with the British, and knew that Sindia and the Raja of Berar were opposed to his doing so, but it offered a last resort in the face of Holkar's advance.[17]

As the months passed the Peshwa's desperation increased, for Holkar's advance continued, albeit slowly, while there was no sign of the promised aid from Sindia or Berar. Holkar took and plundered the city and fort of Ahmednuggar and destroyed the glorious palaces of Shrigonda and Jambgaon, built by Sindia's uncle, and then he turned his advance towards Poona itself.[18] He continued to proclaim his allegiance to the Peshwa, urging that he sought nothing but justice against Sindia, and begging Baji Rao not to flee. But the memory of Vitoji Holkar's execution was too fresh for the Peshwa to believe him. Still Sindia did not come, but on 22 October, as Holkar was drawing towards Poona, a contingent of Sindia's army reached the city. Three days later these men, together with the troops Sindia had left in the capital and the Peshwa's own forces, prepared to give battle. On that morning, 25 October 1802, Baji Rao sent Close preliminary terms for a treaty of alliance that conceded all the main points that Lord Wellesley wanted. No doubt if Holkar had been defeated in the battle before Poona the Peshwa would have abandoned the treaty, but Holkar's army won a crushing victory, known as the battle of Hadapsur, and Baji Rao fled.[19]

Holkar entered Poona, but although he sent out flying parties in all directions, he failed to capture the Peshwa.[20] Faced with this dilemma he summoned Amrit Rao who, with some reluctance, came and agreed to allow his young son Vinayakrao to be proclaimed the new Peshwa. But the position of the new regime was very uncertain: Sindia and the Raja of Berar remained hostile, as did the Peshwa's own jagirdars to the south; Holkar's troops were pressing to be paid or permitted to plunder the rich capital; and the attitude of the British was uncertain. Barry Close had not accompanied Baji Rao in his flight, and Holkar, while treating him with great courtesy, did not permit him to leave Poona until the end of November. Like most observers, Close felt considerable personal respect and liking for Amrit Rao, regarding him as the ablest and the most reasonable of the Maratha leaders. But Close realised that it was not for him to decide the British response to the crisis and he skilfully left Lord Wellesley's hands free. In case Lord Wellesley chose to act, Close sent a preliminary warning to the governments of Madras and Bombay advising them of what had happened and recommending that they mobilise their forces and take up position on the Maratha frontier, pending orders from Calcutta.[21]

Baji Rao escaped Holkar's pursuit and found refuge on the coast. At one time it was thought that he might go to Bombay, but in the end he remained in a small enclave of Maratha territory at Bassein, where the proximity of British troops ensured his safety. Barry Close joined him as soon as he was permitted to leave Poona. This interlude gave Lord Wellesley time to learn of the crisis and give his initial response. In essence, Wellesley decided to use the opportunity to achieve his long-standing goals. If the Peshwa would now sign a definitive treaty of alliance, Britain would intervene to ensure his restoration, and the permanent presence of a powerful British subsidiary force at Poona would help to ensure stability, peace and prosperity for the entire Maratha nation. Or, to put it another way, the Peshwa could have his throne back if he surrendered a large part of his sovereignty to Britain. The Peshwa was still reluctant, for his dislike of the British had not diminished, but he hated Holkar and Amrit Rao much more, and he had no faith in Sindia and the Raja of Berar. Thus, on 31 December 1802 he signed the Treaty of Bassein, by which it became not merely the right, but the duty, of the British to intervene in the affairs of their ally, the Maratha Confederacy.[22]

Preparations for British intervention began well before the Treaty of Bassein was signed. Close's account of the battle of Hadapsur and the flight of the Peshwa reached Madras on 9 November and orders were given at once to mobilise the army and begin collecting supplies. Webbe wrote to Arthur Wellesley telling him to suspend minor operations in remote parts of Mysore and to collect his forces so as to be ready to act if Lord Wellesley gave the word.[23] Reading Arthur Wellesley's correspondence over the next couple of months, two points emerge clearly: he had no say in the formation of the Governor-General's policy, indeed he only heard most of the important news indirectly, through Webbe and others; and he was surprisingly unsure what role, if any, he would be given in the proposed operations. On 12 November he wrote to Webbe detailing the logistical preparations he had set in train and added:

> You have not told me what part I am to act in this business, I think I can be more useful in it than anybody else. Independent of the experience I have of the country, the principal *Sirdars* are acquainted with me, and I have kept up a communication with them ever since I was there before. This will be of great consequence in our operations. It will not be inconvenient that I should quit Mysore, as I have been so long accustomed to the business and have so perfect a knowledge of the country that I could conduct the details of the service even though at a great distance from it; and, in fact, no inconvenience was experienced when I was in the Marhatta country before.
>
> I wish you would do me the favour to mention this subject to the General and Lord Clive, and offer my services: at all events, however, they may depend upon my doing everything in my power to forward the object in view.[24]

This might be seen as no more than a courteous offer of his services, pleasantly lacking in presumption, if not exactly modest. But if so, Wellesley would have been satisfied by Webbe's immediate reply, warmly assuring him that his talents were fully appreciated by Lord Clive, General James Stuart (who had moved from Bombay to be Commander-in-Chief of the Madras army), and by Webbe himself. Webbe wrote that although it was too soon to be specific, they intended to make extensive use of Arthur Wellesley in any operation.[25] But despite this, and despite a steady flow of letters from Stuart that implicitly and explicitly acknowledged his special expertise in everything relating to operations in the Maratha country, Wellesley remained uneasy.

On 24 November Webbe passed on the news of Wellesley's promotion to Major-General, and announced his immediate appointment to the staff of the Madras army, although this would require confirmation from home. Still Wellesley was not satisfied, and on 1 December he wrote directly to Stuart pressing his claim to be employed in the coming operation.[26] The question was complicated by a misunderstanding, Wellesley convincing himself that Stuart believed that he should resign his command in Mysore if he was to join the expedition. Webbe and Stuart both replied on 7 December soothing, flattering and reassuring their champion. Stuart had the highest opinion of Wellesley and believed that his participation in the campaign was essential to its success. There was never any question of his giving up the Mysore command, where his services were immensely useful; the only issue was a slight reduction in his staff to prevent jealousy from the other generals. Wellesley at last allowed himself to be convinced although he was typically sharp in his private comments on the staff question. But the episode as a whole shows a surprising hesitancy, which was probably a legacy of the humiliation he felt that he had suffered at Bombay.[27]

There was, in fact, no doubt of Wellesley's special expertise when it came to planning operations in Maharashtra. The experience of the campaign against Dhoondiah Waugh, the contacts that he had made then and subsequently maintained with the southern Maratha lords, and his highly intelligent approach to soldiering in general, made him an invaluable asset. It was wholly characteristic that more than a year before the current crisis he had written a lengthy memorandum on the subject, which he had subsequently brought up to date.[28] Equally, when the call to mobilise came, it found the forces in Mysore, and more especially their bullock trains, brinjarries and other logistical serv- ices, in prime condition and ready to take the field, while the long-established equivalents in Madras were slow and inefficient.[29] Thus when Wellesley received a letter from Stuart requesting him to organise the dooley men, who carried the palanquins on which sick or wounded soldiers were transported, he was able to reply at once, assuring the Commander-in-Chief that the men would be ready when needed, commenting on their character, their pay, and the effect of their absence on the local economy. He added with a note of pride and an implied warning: 'I have always had these people with me, and they appear to be much attached to Mr Anderson, who takes care that they are not ill treated. They have never deserted.'[30] And then he moved on to give his views on the best way of organising the bazaars that fed the army, of regulating the brinjarries who supplied the bazaars, and of filling the vacancies among the surgeons of the army, naming a number of suitable candidates. The range and command of detail is remarkable, as is the relish with which it is employed. Logistics is too often regarded as the handmaiden to strategy and tactics – an important, but dull and undemanding branch of military science – but Arthur Wellesley knew that it lay at the very heart of warfare in India, and he embraced it with genuine understanding and enthusiasm.

On 27 November, in response to a request from Stuart, Wellesley prepared an outline of his ideas for the campaign. He assumed that whatever the Governor-General's ultimate aims, the immediate objective must be the defeat and dissolution of Holkar's army. But Holkar was likely to try to avoid battle and his army was much lighter and more mobile than that of the British. There was no easy solution to this difficulty, but two points flowed from it: one was the importance of keeping open the army's supply lines; the other was main- taining good relations with the southern Maratha lords or jagirdars who owed their allegiance to the Peshwa. The link between the two was obvious: if the jagirdars were friendly they would protect the supply lines; if they were hostile, they would plunder them. Moreover, if they were sufficiently well disposed to cooperate actively with the British army they would provide just the type of

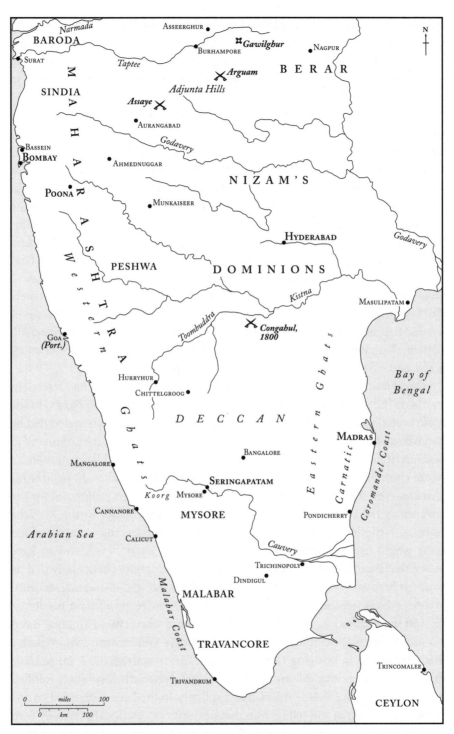

5 Southern and central India at the time of the restoration of the Peshwa and the Maratha War, 1803.

light troops needed to offset Holkar's greatest strength. If these issues could be managed successfully 'we shall always supply ourselves; the enemy may protract his defeat, but sooner or later it must happen'. Throughout all the changes of plan and circumstances that followed, these points remained central in Wellesley's mind.[31]

Stuart accepted the importance of the southern jagirdars and asked Wellesley to try to determine their sentiments without committing the British government. On the whole the news was good, but there was an immediate complication. Goklah, one of the most important of the jagirdars, feared that Holkar would seek revenge for his part in the capture of Vitoji Holkar, and asked refuge, with his many followers, inside the British frontier. Although Goklah gave the strongest assurances that he would control his men and prevent them plundering the countryside, no British officer could view the arrival of a Maratha army in his district with equanimity. Besides there were wider political implications, so the question was referred up the chain of command, from Wellesley to Stuart, to Lord Clive and ultimately to Lord Wellesley himself. Fortunately Goklah's fears proved premature and were overtaken by events, so he never needed to press Arthur Wellesley for an immediate decision, while his goodwill remained undiminished – in the subsequent operations he provided more active and effective cooperation than any of his peers.[32]

David Baird created an awkward problem of another kind. He had arrived in southern India towards the end of October, transferring from the Bengal to the Madras staff in the hope of seeing more active service. Webbe suspected that he had heard rumours that Arthur Wellesley would be giving up the command at Seringapatam and hoped to succeed him at last; although Webbe's comment, 'a worse choice could not be made than of Genl. Baird', did not bode well for his chances, even if there had been a vacancy.[33] As preparations progressed for the advance of the troops from Madras into Mysore, and thence to the Maratha frontier, Wellesley became extremely anxious that the leading elements of the army would be commanded by Baird rather than Stuart. He seems to have feared that Baird might disrupt his arrangements, but more particularly that he would ride roughshod over the government of Mysore and ill-treat its servants. Webbe, whose nominal position of Resident at Mysore gave him a particular interest in the question, agreed and spoke to Stuart, who assured him that Baird would be kept on a tight leash. This did not satisfy Webbe, who told Wellesley that it 'may end in bringing Genl. Baird to a Court Martial; but I am sensible that it will not prevent the immediate mischief'.[34] Nonetheless Stuart fulfilled his promise, giving Baird orders that explicitly limited his command to the troops from Madras and telling him that he must not interfere in any way with the Mysore government. A copy of these orders was sent to Arthur Wellesley, who wrote to Baird with the same superficial appearance of friendship that he had shown since their meeting in Bombay. Neither man liked the other; they were rivals and, more importantly, their style of command and attitude to the local population differed greatly; but they might still have to work together, and maintaining a civilised veneer which made cooperation possible mattered more than the frank expression of dislike.[35]

Slowly the Madras army and the Mysore contingent marched north towards the River Toombuddra, the Maratha frontier, where they would meet. Generally the march went smoothly, and Wellesley's logistical arrangements proved their worth, despite the inevitable setbacks. However Wellesley was somewhat alarmed at the amount of baggage the Madras army carried, and tried to persuade Stuart to lighten the load in order to make his army more mobile.[36] Behind the scenes more serious doubts were emerging. Lord Wellesley's despatches were more cautious than had been anticipated in Madras. He approved the preparations for military intervention, but hoped that the Peshwa could be restored without resorting to actual hostilities, and favoured a delay in the hope that Sindia could also be persuaded to sign a subsidiary alliance. This alarmed Webbe, who felt that Britain should intervene on a grand scale or not at all, and believed that half-measures were dangerous in the face of a potential enemy like the Marathas.[37]

Then, in the middle of February, fresh orders reached Madras from Lord Wellesley, which changed everything. Despite the Treaty of Bassein, Lord Wellesley would not attempt to impose a ruler on the Marathas if they did not want him. If Baji Rao retained support among his people, Britain would assist in his restoration, but not with the expectation that this would lead to war. Sending the whole Madras army, together with supporting contingents from Mysore, Hyderabad and Bombay to Poona would be too provocative and warlike. Instead a detachment, amounting to about half the force that was in the process of assembling on the Toombuddra, should go forward and link up with the Hyderabad contingent later on if necessary. Even this reduced force would be sufficient, in the Governor-General's opinion, to defeat Holkar, or Sindia, or both together.[38]

Plainly there was more to this decision than appeared on the surface and no explanation for it is completely satisfactory; but the most likely underlying reason is Wellesley's appreciation of his growing vulnerability in London. Addington's government was too weak to risk confrontation with the East India Company and neither the ministers nor the directors of the Company had any appetite for fresh wars in India. Already there had been unsuccessful moves to recall Wellesley, and the news that he had sent the Madras army into Maharashtra without provocation or obvious need would be bound to raise an outcry, which might easily result in immediate, peremptory recall. On the other hand, if he could announce that he had signed a subsidiary treaty with the Peshwa, which brought the Marathas into the British orbit; that he had ended the Maratha civil war, restored Baji Rao to Poona and forced Holkar to accept British arbitration; and that he had done all this without war, merely through skilful negotiations and the employment of a small military force to maintain order, then even his greatest enemies would have to acknowledge his achievement. Another factor which may have influenced Lord Wellesley's decision was the peace with France, which included provisions for the return of the old French colony at Pondicherry. This made it most undesirable that the entire disposable British force in southern India be committed to the Maratha problem, although it seems unlikely that this was the decisive consideration. After all, the possibility of French intervention in India increased the importance of settling Maratha affairs as decisively and as quickly as possible. Whatever his motives, the Governor-General had made his decision, and lesser mortals had to adjust their plans accordingly.[39]

Arthur Wellesley responded to the new plan in a letter to Stuart written on 3 March 1803. He did not comment on his brother's underlying policy, but expressed his opinion that the proposed detachment was probably adequate, although it was not quite as strong as the army he had led against Dhoondiah. His fear of being left behind had revived and he added:

If you should take the command of it yourself, I hope you will do me the favour to allow me to accompany you in any capacity whatever. All that is known of that country and its inhabitants, in a military point of view, was learned when I was in it; and I shall do everything in my power to make myself useful to you. If you should not think proper to take the command of this detachment yourself, and, in consideration of the information which I have had the opportunities of gaining of that country and its inhabitants, and the communications I have constantly held with its chiefs, you should be pleased to entrust it to me, I shall be infinitely gratified, and shall do everything in my power to forward your views.[40]

On the very day that this was written, Stuart received instructions from Lord Clive in Madras, which stated unequivocally that a detachment of 7,000 men was to be sent forward, and that it was to be commanded by Arthur Wellesley.[41] This was a remarkable order. The Commander-in-Chief of the Madras army was instructed, with no explanation or apology, to divide his force into two, and to entrust the active half to a junior officer who would use it to undertake a difficult and potentially dangerous operation, while his chief and the rest of the army cooled their heels on the banks of the Toombuddra. It was a humiliation far exceeding Wellesley's supersession – by a superior officer – at Bombay. Moreover, Stuart was an experienced, able officer. He was almost thirty years

older than Wellesley and had served widely, including in the American War of
Independence, before coming to India and commanding the Bombay army
with some distinction in the 1799 war against Tipu. He was one of the few, if
not the only senior officer in India who commanded the respect of both
Richard and Arthur Wellesley, the latter describing him as 'the heart and soul'
of the government of Madras, without whom it would 'fall to pieces, and a
scene of confusion will follow'.[42] Why then deprive him of his natural right to
decide whether to command the advanced corps in person, or to delegate it to
Wellesley? We can only surmise, for no explanation appears among the sources.
It may be that Clive and Webbe, who presumably took an active part in the
decision, did not fully share the high opinion of Stuart, or at least felt that his
abilities were not perfectly suited to the difficult task ahead. Or they may have
presumed (rightly or wrongly) that he would not wish to command the
advanced corps, and acted to ensure that he did not give the command to Baird
or Dugald Campbell – officers junior to him but senior to Wellesley. It is even
possible that they received a private hint from Lord Wellesley, or acted in anticipation of what they believed to be his wishes, although this is unlikely, for their
mutual respect was by now too well established for such crude measures. On
the whole, the most likely explanation is also the simplest: they believed that
Arthur Wellesley was ideally suited to the task and leapt at the chance to give it
to him, possibly without even realising the blow they were striking Stuart in the
process.

Certainly Stuart was deeply hurt, and it is infinitely to his credit that he did
not blame Arthur Wellesley, and exerted himself to support Wellesley's operations. Nonetheless he informed the Madras government and the Court of
Directors that he would resign the command of its army as soon as the current
service was completed.[43] Nor was he the only general to feel aggrieved. David
Baird had not transferred to Madras in order to go camping on the banks of the
Toombuddra, and he no sooner heard the news than he resigned in disgust and
prepared to go home, finally recognising that India was too small a continent
to share with Arthur Wellesley. To Baird, of course, there could be no doubt
that Wellesley's advancement was solely due to his brother's patronage. It was
simple, obvious and deeply consoling, for it meant that he was the injured party
and he need not concede any particular merit to his rival. But the truth was
never quite that simple and in this instance Wellesley was indisputably the best
man for the job.[44]

The army entrusted to Wellesley's command amounted to rather more than
10,000 troops (the official returns totalled 10,617 officers and men), plus the
usual train of families, camp followers, servants, bullock-drivers and brinjarries. More than three-quarters of the fighting men were Indians. There was one
regiment of British cavalry (the 19th Light Dragoons) and three of Indian

cavalry from the Madras army (the 4th, 5th and 7th Native Cavalry), amounting to around 1,700 men in all. The infantry were divided into two brigades, each containing one British and three Indian battalions, all strong units, averaging almost 1,000 men each. (They were the 94th Regiment or Scotch Brigade, and the 1/2nd, 2/3rd and 2/12th Native Infantry in the brigade commanded by Lieutenant-Colonel William Harness; and the 74th Regiment and the 1/3rd, 1/8th and 2/18th Native Infantry in Lieutenant-Colonel William Wallace's brigade.) There were some 300 artillerymen and gun lascars, and 700 pioneers. To Wellesley's regret the 33rd was not part of the force – only five companies had taken part in the march to the Toombuddra, the remainder being left near Vellore where they had been sent to regain their health.[45] Accompanying the army was a contingent of around 2,500 irregular Indian cavalry in the service of the Raja of Mysore, commanded by Bistnapah Pundit, an officer who had gained much experience under Haider Ali and Tipu Sultan, and who was to win high praise from Wellesley for his efficiency and discretion.[46]

In handing over command of the army Stuart told Wellesley to act according to the instructions already received from the Governor-General and Lord Clive. Nonetheless, he very properly added his own detailed instructions, for, formally at least, Wellesley was still his subordinate. Most of the points were familiar, and many reflected Arthur Wellesley's own advice, but it was both necessary and useful that they be officially spelled out in writing. Stuart stressed the importance of conciliating the southern Maratha jagirdars and encouraging their loyalty to the Peshwa. The advance should be as rapid as possible, and Wellesley was to link up with the Hyderabad contingent without delay, and to send the 94th (Scotch Brigade) to join it for the remainder of the campaign. With this reinforcement the Hyderabad force ought to be capable of acting independently and holding its own against Holkar or Sindia, but the two corps needed to cooperate closely. Wellesley had overall command, and must have been pleased that the commander of the Hyderabad contingent was his old friend, Colonel Stevenson, who had served under him in Mysore.[47]

Stuart instructed Wellesley to avoid hostilities if possible, and Webbe, writing from Madras, added some interesting comments on the broader picture. Webbe admitted that he had initially been dismayed by the Governor-General's instructions, but on reflection, and after discussing the matter fully with Malcolm, who was on a special mission from Lord Wellesley, he had become convinced that there was a good chance of success without any actual hostilities. He doubted that Sindia and Holkar could settle their differences to form a united front against the British advance. 'I think our natural policy is to adjust Holkar's claims if possible by accommodation; in order that the Holkar family may be preserved as a rival & counterpoise to Sindia in the northern parts of the Empire.' And if Holkar could be convinced that the British viewed him in this light, the chances of him combining with Sindia or opposing Wellesley's army would be much reduced.[48]

Wellesley crossed the Maratha frontier on 12 March 1803. On the previous day he had issued a General Order:

> The troops will enter the Marhatta territory tomorrow morning, but they are not to consider it as an enemy's country. The strictest order and discipline must be observed, and everything that is required from the country must be paid for. Major-Gen. Wellesley will certainly punish any person who may be found guilty of a breach of this order.[49]

This was the characteristic style in which he addressed his army, and would continue to do so for the rest of his career. Plain, dry and practical, deliberately avoiding the high-flown rhetoric of some of his contemporaries, Wellesley spoke to his troops without one eye on the drawing-rooms of London or the salons of Paris. His style did not fire the enthusiasm of those of his officers who were susceptible to the romantic, emotional spirit of the age; but then he cared less for men's enthusiasm than for their willingness to attend to their duty. And where Napoleon promised his men the rich plunder of the fertile plains of northern Italy, Wellesley insisted that the burden and misery of war for the civilian population be kept as light as possible.

The army's advance went smoothly; there was no opposition, although the troops suffered greatly from the heat, which several officers report as being well over 100 degrees Fahrenheit.[50] The country appeared poor and forage proved scarce, but the army was well supplied. Lieutenant-Colonel William Harness, the commander of one of the infantry brigades, wrote home to his wife on 23 March:

> Fortunately every Maratha we have seen is a friend, they came in every day offering to serve with 500 to 1000 Horse. They conceive we are invincible, and are ready to give in to whatever General Wellesley dictates. The respect paid to persons and property is as great as if we had an English jury to decide on all our acts.[51]

As usual, the soldiers began their march very early in the day, and were normally in camp before midday.

Years later, Wellesley himself described some of the other arrangements required for conducting the advance:

The soldiers were in messes of six or eight; each mess had its own native cook and a bullock which carried the men's knapsacks and their cooking materials, etc. The native soldiers, however, at that time carried their knapsacks on their backs, but I believe they no longer do so. An army in good order in India would march very nearly three miles an hour. Everything depended on finding halting stations at convenient distances, 16 or 18 miles, where there was water. Generally the villages were at the bank of what in winter was a river, but in summer was to all outward appearance perfectly dry, and a mere bed of sand. The water, however, though unseen, was always flowing at a depth of from one to three feet below this bed of sand. Scouts were always sent forward to look for these dry rivers, and on the arrival of the army a great number of small wells were excavated the first thing. A few days afterwards the sand would blow into these holes, and after a short time no vestige of wells or excavations would remain.[52]

John Blakiston adds the pleasing detail that, despite the heat, many officers kept their greyhounds ready while on the march, and if a fox was spotted the dogs would be unleashed and the chase began. 'The General himself often partook of the sport, which he appeared to enjoy much.'[53]

Wellesley was pleased with the early marches made by the army, but recognised that 'this expedition of mine partakes as much of politics as it does of military operations'.[54] The southern Maratha lords were friendly; they accepted that he was acting in the Peshwa's cause, and many promised active cooperation, although little of this was actually forthcoming, except from Goklah, who had his own particular reasons for welcoming the British. Before the end of March, Wellesley had taken 3,000 pindaris, or irregular light cavalry similar to Tipu's looties, into his pay, and was soon subsidising Goklah's force as well.[55] Like the Mysore cavalry, these troops were potentially useful, not in battle, but in protecting the army's march and in keeping the equivalent forces of the enemy at a distance, so that the main body was not constantly harassed; but their presence had political as well as military advantages, by lessening the appearance of an alien invasion of the Maratha lands.

As early as the middle of March, Barry Close was reporting that Sindia and the Raja of Berar were both displeased by the British advance, and rumours soon began to circulate of a reconciliation between Sindia and Holkar.[56] On 19 March Wellesley was joined by John Malcolm and greeted him warmly. The differences between them, which had arisen in the Seringapatam campaign, had long been forgotten, and the two worked well together – Wellesley said that they spent almost all that first day talking.[57] Malcolm provided valuable political and diplomatic advice, and a friend on the spot who could be consulted, but Wellesley remained firmly in control. Wellesley, Malcolm and Barry Close were now the central figures in determining how Lord Wellesley's policy should be implemented. They were assisted by occasional contributions, varying in subject and quality, from Stuart with the main or – as it may now be called – the reserve army; from Webbe at Madras; from Kirkpatrick at Hyderabad (who was constantly predicting an immediate junction between Holkar and Sindia); and from Colonel John Collins who, as Resident at Sindia's court, faced the task of trying to persuade that chief to welcome British intervention, and even to sign his own subsidiary treaty.[58]

At the beginning of April news arrived that Holkar had quit Poona with his army much diminished by desertion. However Amrit Rao and some troops remained in the capital, while Holkar, far from being in full retreat, was soon threatening to invade Hyderabad. This might be the first step in a full-scale war, but Wellesley thought it was more likely that Holkar was simply intent on gaining some plunder for his troops in lieu of pay before withdrawing further, and would not advance beyond the border marches of Hyderabad, which the Marathas had long been accustomed to pillage. But he told Stevenson: 'It will not answer to expose the Nizam's country to invasion on my political specula-tion; and we must therefore immediately turn our minds to taking measures for its defence.'[59] These precautions inevitably delayed the junction of the two British forces, but no great harm was done, and Wellesley's assessment of Holkar's intentions proved accurate.

Meanwhile Barry Close had particular difficulties of his own, for the Peshwa was proving to be a difficult ally. Arthur Wellesley had urged the value of even a token overture to Holkar and Amrit Rao, but Baji Rao had signed his pact with the British devils not to be reconciled with his enemies but to see them destroyed. Nor did he do much to encourage the southern jagirdars to cooperate with Wellesley, while he proved infuriatingly dilatory in his preparations to begin his journey back to Poona, preferring to pester Close with applications for money.[60]

Nonetheless, Wellesley and Close both remained confident that they could succeed in restoring the Peshwa without war. They understood that Sindia and Holkar could not settle their differences without a great deal of effort, and believed that both Sindia and the Raja of Berar recognised that war with the British would end in disaster. They took into account the weaknesses of their own position – notably the personal unpopularity of the Peshwa among his own jagirdars, and the resentment aroused by the mere presence of the British – but they also felt that there was a good deal of bluff in the talk of war. Two letters from Arthur Wellesley convey the gist of the argument:

> There can be no doubt but that the establishment of our influence at Poonah will be highly disagreeable to the majority of the Marhatta chiefs, and that it will interfere materially with the interests of some and the objects of ambition of all.[61]

And, more colloquially:

> We have taken into our hands the bone for which they have been contending
> for some years, not one of them is very well pleased; and each gives out that
> the whole will combine against us. But there are many considerations which
> must be maturely weighed, by at least two of the parties, Scindiah and the
> Rajah of Berar, before they will venture upon a war with the English, particu-
> larly when we are prepared, and they are not.
>
> It may be asked, why they give out that they intend to combine? I answer,
> because they know that some of us are, like other men, to be frightened by
> their threats; that, particularly they have their effect at the Nizam's *durbar*.[62]

Amid all the talk, Wellesley's army pressed on. Reports arrived that Amrit Rao
had left Poona after plundering it 'to the last rag', and that Mir Khan had been
left near the city with orders from Holkar to burn it to the ground before the
British arrived. At this, Wellesley made a dash for the capital with his cavalry
and a single battalion, travelling over forty miles in little more than twenty-
four hours.[63] He arrived to find the city safe and Holkar's troops gone. The
threat had probably always been empty, but such interludes, between the
departure of one army and the arrival of another, are always dangerous, and the
destruction of Poona would have cast a shadow over the whole policy of intervention in Maratha affairs.

Wellesley reached Poona on 20 April and even on the following day was
able to report to Stuart that life was rapidly returning to normal, the bazaars
were open, and the populace appeared confident and well disposed.[64] Clearly
the reports of looting and disorder by Holkar's men had grown in the telling.
Wellesley was already in correspondence with Amrit Rao, and the preservation
of the city made it easy to suggest a formal rapprochement. As a highly
respected and talented individual, and a plausible alternative to the Peshwa,
Amrit Rao could be a dangerous opponent or a valuable ally. If he could be
persuaded to submit to the Peshwa's authority, and if he was treated generously,
many other waverers might follow. For his part, Amrit Rao was quite ready to
come to terms; he had joined Holkar reluctantly and saw little prospect of
success once the British took an active part in the game. After some delicate
negotiations and some last-minute hesitations on the part of Amrit Rao, a
tentative arrangement was made. However the Peshwa's refusal to be reconciled with his adopted brother, or to show any signs of magnanimity, lessened
the value of the achievement as an example for others, and left Close and
Wellesley cursing the perversity of their ally – not for the first time. Amrit Rao
separated himself from Holkar and took no part against the British, but he
did not fully commit himself to supporting their cause, or join them in the

field, until November when the result of the hostilities was no longer in any doubt.[65]

The Peshwa's personal standing with his saviours was falling precipitately. Wellesley had been shocked at the level of antipathy towards him among the southern jagirdars, and he and Close were driven to distraction by the delays and difficulties that beset Baji Rao's return journey. Close told Wellesley, only half-jokingly, that the task of marching an army through 400 miles of poor, potentially hostile country, was simple compared to moving this single Maratha prince and his entourage one-quarter the distance.[66] While the Peshwa delayed, Wellesley had to keep his army near Poona, even though there was little forage in the district and he was anxious to link up with Stevenson to deter Holkar from threatening Hyderabad. On the other hand, Baji Rao was beginning to feel the price he had paid for his alliance with the British. He was safe, no longer a refugee, and was able to return to Poona; but the British had not, as he had hoped and expected, destroyed his enemies, and instead were proposing that he forgive Amrit Rao and even make terms with Holkar. Worse was to come. On 7 May Neil Edmonstone, one of Lord Wellesley's inner circle, wrote to Close, and began his letter by saying that the Governor-General had no intention of interfering in the Peshwa's government. Inevitably the rest of the letter flagrantly contradicted this assertion, laying down the policy the Peshwa should follow towards his vassals, his enemies and his friends, and on almost every point Lord Wellesley's policy was the opposite of Baji Rao's own preference.[67]

On 13 May Baji Rao II, Peshwa of the Maratha Confederacy, entered Poona and was restored to the *musnud*. That he was no longer master in his own house was true, but not unprecedented; Sindia had kept him a virtual prisoner and treated him as a puppet only a few years before. Only time would show whether it would be possible to escape from the overwhelming and objectionable embrace of the British without falling into the even worse hands of Holkar, but Baji Rao had seen too many reversals of fortune to despair easily. He was back in Poona and had no reason to think that the game was over.

CHAPTER NINE

THE MARATHA WAR
(1803)

THE PESHWA HAD been restored and not a shot had been fired; so far Lord Wellesley's policy – and his brother's part in its execution – had been a complete success. But the position remained unstable, with the other Maratha princes showing little sign of accepting British pre-eminence. Holkar had withdrawn before the British advance and, after plundering the Hyderabad borderlands, was preparing to retreat further north towards his family's traditional fiefdom. As Baji Rao refused to make any overture to him, it was not surprising that he remained unfriendly, but it did not seem likely that he would embark on active hostilities. By June 1803 Arthur Wellesley and his colleagues were more concerned with Sindia and the Raja of Berar than with Holkar. At one level, the two princes were pleased to see their ally, Baji Rao, restored to Poona, and their enemy, Holkar, discomforted; but not if this meant the loss of Maratha independence and the subordination of the Confederacy to British domination. They faced an appalling choice: either they could accept the British presence at Poona and all that it implied, perhaps even signing their own subsidiary treaties, or they could fight against the British, knowing that they had little hope of victory. Only a few years before, Sindia had been the effective ruler of most of Hindustan and the Deccan, arguably the most powerful man in all India; was he now to submit tamely to the British and go home and tend his garden? He was only twenty-three years old, a little young to retire. Raghuji Bhonsle, the Raja of Berar, was a generation older and much more careful than Sindia. Of all the Maratha princes, he was the only one who cared much for the welfare of his people, and his skill had preserved his dominions from the devastation caused by the wars of the previous decade. However he was not without ambition and looked to be either kingmaker at Poona, reconciling all the Maratha factions, or possibly even to take the place of the Peshwa himself. The presence of the British disrupted these hopes and offended his pride; and so, at the beginning of June, he collected his army and joined Sindia.[1]

Much to Wellesley's frustration, June and July passed in a protracted confrontation as the British endeavoured to force Sindia or Berar to commit themselves one way or the other. The Maratha leaders procrastinated, evaded and successfully sought to prolong the crisis.[2] They hoped for a reconciliation with Holkar, which would make war less desperate, but Holkar, though sincerely hostile to the British, could not bring himself to trust Sindia. He was probably right, for Sindia would have been delighted to see Holkar and the British destroy each other. Another reason why Sindia and Berar played for time was that it was the rainy season, and while campaigning in the wet was miserable for everyone, it deprived the Marathas of the strategic mobility their armies would need if they were to harass the British without being brought to battle (not so much through the rain and mud directly, but because the rains made the rivers impassable).[3] But above all they delayed because neither war nor peace offered salvation, and they hoped that some fresh element would change the equation. This was a desperate, but not an absurd, hope; the Nizam of Hyderabad was dying, and his death might trigger a succession struggle in Britain's ally. The British themselves were also unpredictable, swayed by influences of which the Maratha chiefs knew little; Lord Wellesley might well be recalled and the British army withdrawn.

Almost everyone, British and Maratha, recognised that if it came to war the odds heavily favoured the British. Sindia's lands had been impoverished and his army weakened by a decade of civil war, while he would be attacked not only by Wellesley's army in the Deccan, but also in Hindustan by General Lake with the Bengal army based in Oudh. Lake, moreover, could expect to be welcomed by many of Sindia's tributaries among the small Rajput states. Berar was also vulnerable on two sides: the Deccan and Cuttack, where a British force was assembled, ready to strike. The strength of Sindia's army lay in its battalions of sepoy infantry, trained and disciplined along European lines by European mercenary officers. But many of these officers were British, and it was understood that they would not serve against their country, so if war broke out, the army would be disrupted immediately by their departure, with a serious effect on the morale and confidence of the troops. Nor was it believed that Sindia's sepoys were as good as those of the British. The difference did not lie in technology or armament, but rather in organisation, training, discipline, pay, number and quality of officers, *esprit de corps*, and other intangibles. And this perception magnified the actual advantage, giving the British sepoys a confidence which counted for as much as all their other advantages combined.[4] Just as the British sepoys were, or felt themselves to be, superior to Sindia's sepoys, so the King's regiments of troops from Britain felt themselves to be superior to the Company's sepoys, and for much the same reasons. To offset this difference in quality the Marathas had only numbers, and most of the wars of the last hundred years in India had shown that numbers alone were not enough. The bulk of their army still consisted of irregular light cavalry – *pindaris* – who were virtually useless in battle but very effective in harassing an enemy army on campaign, or converting a retreat into a rout. Their performance depended enormously on confidence, and their greatest successes were always achieved against a timid, cautious or already half-beaten enemy. If these light cavalry are excluded, and one counts only the regular infantry and artillery, the forces of Sindia and the Raja of Berar in the Deccan were actually outnumbered by the armies of Wellesley and Stevenson. Even if one counts the irregular cavalry (and the similar Mysore, Maratha and Hyderabad troops operating with the British), the advantage was not great: rather more than 50,000 Marathas under Sindia and the Raja of Berar, compared to almost 40,000 men under Wellesley and Stevenson.[5]

As the weeks passed and June and then July slipped by, Wellesley and Barry Close grew increasingly impatient but, in fact, they gained some significant advantages from the delay. Holkar's continued march north made it obvious that he was not cooperating with Sindia, while his withdrawal from the theatre of operations reduced the risk that he would be dragged into the war by chance or the impulse to strike a blow when an opportunity offered. This greatly simplified Wellesley's task of planning his campaign. Wellesley also had time to solve a major logistical crisis, caused by very heavy deaths among his bullocks when the rains began. Never one to bear adversity without complaint, Wellesley wrote wildly of the need to reconsider the whole operation, avoiding war at almost any cost, and transforming the alliance with the Peshwa, if more bullocks could not be found. The crisis was resolved within a few weeks and he recovered his nerve, but the episode is interesting, revealing an unexpected quirk in his character, for this would not be the last occasion on which he over-dramatised a crisis involving transport and supplies, and used dangerously exaggerated language.[6]

The strain of these two months showed in other ways as well. Arthur Wellesley and Barry Close continued to work together extremely well, and John Malcolm was trusted with most, if not all, their secrets; but outside this charmed circle their tolerance grew thin. Naturally the Peshwa was an object of particular ire, for he continued to do everything he could to frustrate their plans without committing himself to outright opposition. His sympathy for Sindia was palpable, so that Wellesley and Close were soon wishing that Amrit Rao was in his place, and Malcolm contemplated the possibility of Baji Rao denouncing the alliance and fleeing Poona almost with longing. But there could be no open rupture; Baji Rao would not break with the British unless he could be certain that they would be defeated, and the British could not break with him, for his alliance provided the sole justification for their involvement in Maratha affairs and their presence in Poona. Not even Lord Wellesley's closest allies in London would be willing to defend the policy of intervening in Maratha politics in order to restore the Peshwa, only to then remove this same Peshwa and replace him with another.[7]

If Baji Rao was Arthur Wellesley's chief irritant, he was closely followed by Colonel Collins, the Resident at Sindia's court, who proved quite unable to force Sindia to commit himself one way or the other, and who allowed the confrontation to drag on without engaging in serious negotiations or bringing about a rupture. Wellesley had written to the Governor-General in early May, implicitly criticising Collins, and asking that someone be given over-riding powers to coordinate military and diplomatic policy. He repeated the point a month later, and in the middle of July he received sweeping powers from Lord Wellesley. It was a necessary and proper appointment; Arthur Wellesley, though careful not to spell it out explicitly in his letters, was the obvious man for the job, superior in rank to Barry Close, who was the only other person on the spot with sufficient knowledge. Nonetheless there had been some opposition to it in Bengal, and there would be more in London, where Lord Wellesley's enemies raised the tired cry of constitutional impro-priety as well as nepotism.[8]

Armed with his new powers, Arthur Wellesley moved at once to bring the confrontation with Sindia and the Raja of Berar to a head. Even so, it took another fortnight before Collins left Sindia's camp and military operations commenced. Wellesley attempted to place the whole blame for the outbreak of war on Sindia, writing to him: 'I offered you peace on terms of equality, and honourable to all parties; you have chosen war, and are responsible for all consequences.'[9] This was plainly untrue, but the outbreak of war is not an occa-sion that often inspires strict historical impartiality among the participants. Neither was the converse true, for although Arthur Wellesley determined when the hostilities commenced, he did not create the circumstances that made war, if not inevitable, at least the most likely outcome. Lord Wellesley's policies played a much larger part in causing the war, and it cannot be denied that from the moment of his arrival in India he had endeavoured to gain a dominant influence over the Maratha Confederacy. Yet despite this underlying purpose, Lord Wellesley had declined opportunities for intervening in Maratha affairs until Baji Rao's flight and appeal gave the British impeccable grounds for acting. The Marathas were well aware of Lord Wellesley's ambitions, but nonetheless gave him the opportunity of intervention because they allowed their internal power struggle to get out of hand. As for the final rupture, Sindia and the Raja of Berar had been threatening war for months. They had assembled their armies on the border of Hyderabad, and had been given ample warning of the consequences if they did not withdraw. By choosing not to do so they had risked war, and one can have little sympathy for statesmen who indulge in brinkmanship and then make a misjudgement.

Bad weather and other delays meant that active campaigning did not begin until the end of the first week of August 1803. After the restoration of the Peshwa, Wellesley had moved his army east-north-east from Poona towards the Nizam's frontier. When the war began he was camped only a few miles south of the important city and fortress of Ahmednuggar, which was held by Sindia's troops, although far to the south of the rest of Sindia's army. There had been a few changes to the army that Wellesley had led across the Toombuddra five months before. The 94th (Scotch Brigade) had been sent to join Stevenson and had been replaced by the 78th Regiment, from the Bombay force, which had escorted the Peshwa back to Poona. So Wellesley still had two battalions of British infantry, although they were not as strong as in March, amounting to only about 1,500 officers and men. The 2/3rd Madras Native Infantry had been left as a garrison in Poona together with a battalion from Bombay. During the campaign some further changes would occur as Wellesley detached 1/3rd and 2/18th but gained the 1/4th and 1/10th, which both arrived escorting convoys of grain. The net effect of these changes was that Wellesley's army was one battalion weaker than it had been when it crossed the Toombuddra, although it still numbered between 9,000 and 10,000 regular troops (officers and men). In addition, there were the 2,400 light cavalry supplied by Purneah on behalf of the Raja of Mysore, which Wellesley described as 'excellent', and 3,000 irregular Maratha cavalry belonging to the southern jagirdars including Goklah, who were considerably less reliable. The grand total was therefore close to 15,000 fighting men, plus the inevitable train of camp followers of various sorts.[10]

Stevenson's army was somewhat smaller: two regiments of Madras Native Cavalry (3rd and 6th); one British infantry regiment (94th, or Scotch Brigade); six battalions of Madras Native Infantry (2/2nd, 1/6th, 2/7th, 2/9th, 1/11th and 2/11th); artillery, gun lascars and pioneers, amounting to about 9,000 officers and men. This received some support from the army of Hyderabad, which was officially stated to comprise some 16,000 infantry and cavalry, although this figure is inflated, and the military value of the force was slight.[11] But even without this assistance, Wellesley was convinced that Stevenson's army was quite capable of defeating the combined forces of Sindia and the Raja of Berar by itself. Naturally he would prefer that the two British forces unite before the decisive battle, or that if they fought separately, his army, which was both larger and of higher quality, should take the lead; however, his whole campaign was based on the premise that both armies were strong enough to act independently.[12] There were several advantages in not combining the two forces into one grand army. The object of the campaign was to bring the Marathas to battle as quickly as possible without allowing them to mount an invasion of Hyderabad or strike at Poona; and it was much easier to outmanoeuvre them with two separate armies than with one. Equally, a single army would be cumbersome and unwieldy; including the camp followers, servants, brinjarries and other non-combatants it would amount to a host of at least 100,000 people, plus tens of thousands of animals.

According to a report from Colonel Collins, Sindia's army consisted of about 18,000 cavalry (almost all irregular light cavalry), eleven battalions of sepoys, amounting to almost 8,000 men, and a powerful train of artillery: 35 heavy guns and 170 field pieces. The Raja of Berar had about 20,000 cavalry, 6,000 infantry, 1,000 irregular infantry (rocket boys and the like) and 35 pieces of field artillery. Some of these figures are probably exaggerated, particularly the number of irregular cavalry, but even if they are taken at face value, they give a grand total of just under 60,000 men, of whom only 14,000 were regular infantry.[13]

These were the principal field forces in the Deccan, but there was an equally important theatre of operations far to the north in Hindustan where Wellesley's superior, General Lake, prepared to attack Sindia's main force of sepoys. A subsidiary operation was being prepared in Gujarat where a force of nearly 2,000 men would attack Baroach. Arthur Wellesley gave the command of this force to Lieutenant-Colonel John Murray in September; it proved an unhappy choice, and many quarrels arose between Murray and the government of Bombay. On the other side of India a small British force under Lieutenant-Colonel Harcourt was preparing to invade Cuttack, thus striking at the rear of the Raja of Berar. Meanwhile part of the Madras army remained in camp far to the south on the Toombuddra. This had been reduced as troops were withdrawn for other duties, but three battalions of sepoys, five companies of British infantry and a strong force of artillery remained. Wellesley was convinced that this force was of great importance in preventing trouble with the southern jagirdars and keeping open his immensely long supply lines. But it was dull duty and Stuart left the army under the command of Major-General Campbell, giving him clear orders not to accompany the troops if it was necessary to send them forward, for Campbell was senior to Wellesley, and would supersede him if he entered the same theatre of operations.[14]

Wellesley's plan of campaign was relatively simple. He would capture Ahmednuggar as quickly as possible, for he hoped that it would contain valuable supplies and prove a useful base of operations, while acting as a check on any Maratha advance on Poona. Then he would advance towards Stevenson and they would cooperate in bringing the Marathas to battle. He was very conscious of the importance of gaining the initiative and of intimidating his opponents. He told the Governor-General that the first trial of strength would determine the attitude of the southern jagirdars, Amrit Rao and other waverers, while it was equally important in enhancing the confidence of his own army and undermining that of the enemy. In this he displayed the same unremitting aggression he had shown in his operation against Dhoondiah Waugh.[15]

Wellesley began his advance on 8 August 1803. On the previous day he issued a proclamation to the population in which, after announcing the outbreak of hostilities, he said, using the third person pronoun, that:

> He does not, however, intend to make war upon the inhabitants; and, accord-ingly, all *amildars* and others are required to remain quietly in their stations, and obey the orders they will receive; and if they do no injury to the British armies, none will be done to them. But notice is hereby given, that if any of the inhabitants of the country either abandon their dwellings, or do any injury to the British armies or their followers, they will be treated as enemies, and suffer accordingly.[16]

Both the promise and the threat were meant seriously. As always, Wellesley took great pains to protect the civilian population from military abuses, and to keep the ravages of war to a minimum. But equally, he showed no mercy towards civilians who took matters into their own hands. A young officer, Jasper Nicolls, recorded in his journal:

> One of the camp followers was hanged yesterday for stealing a cow from a village, and this evening two villagers were executed in the same manner for binding a *sepoy* and carrying him off, with an intent to rob if not to murder him . . . The proceedings on these occasions are very summary; the fact and the person ascertained, punishment follows in a few hours. Many affect to think this a very arbitrary exercise of illegal power, but these are persons who are not daily subject to the deprivations occasioned by camp robbery; yet it cannot be questioned that such a mode of proceeding is in the end the mildest, best adapted to the people of the country, and the camp followers, and, as above mentioned, impartially applied to both.[17]

A short advance brought the army to Ahmednuggar on 8 August. Wellesley summoned it to surrender but was refused and at once stormed the *pettah*, or town. The attack was made in several places at once, but ran into difficulties when the storming troops were surprised to find that the curtain wall had no inner walkway or stairs which they could use to descend. This meant that some of the storming parties, particularly those from the 78th Highlanders, suffered quite heavily; the 78th are said to have suffered 55 casualties in fifteen minutes.[18] Despite the cost, Wellesley's approach had the wider effect that he intended. Captain James Welsh of the 3rd Madras Native Infantry commented:

Had we waited an hour or two longer, and battered a curtain [i.e. a breach in the curtain wall], our loss would, in all human probability have been little or nothing, but the apparent contempt for danger evinced in our mode of procedure, while it astonished the defenders, struck a terror into the garrison of the fort, and all the surrounding country, which amply compensated for our loss.[19]

The fort of Ahmednuggar was quite separate and detached from the pettah, and it continued to resist for a few days until Wellesley established a battery of four iron 12-pounders within 400 yards of the walls. The fire of the battery soon persuaded the governor, or *killadar*, of the fort to accept the generous terms Wellesley offered (the garrison were permitted to go free, taking their private property with them), and by the afternoon of 12 August Wellesley had untroubled possession of Ahmednuggar. The whole operation had cost fewer than 150 casualties, and had opened the campaign with just the rapid, decisive success Wellesley wanted.

Although the fort capitulated peacefully and was not stormed, the troops occupying it got out of hand and began plundering. Wellesley placed guards to protect Sindia's palace inside the fort, but their discipline succumbed in the face of temptation, and they joined the looters. Order was only restored when two sepoys were hanged, on the general's orders, one on each side of the gateway. John Blakiston admitted that this caused some disgust in the army at the time, but felt that it was a necessary warning at the commencement of a difficult campaign.[20]

Ahmednuggar was the occasion for a notable addition to Wellesley's small staff. In watching the 78th Regiment attempt to storm the town wall on 8 August, Wellesley was much struck by the bravery of one officer in particular. This was twenty-seven-year-old Lieutenant Colin Campbell, who had only recently joined his regiment at Poona, although he had already seen a good deal of the world. At the age of sixteen he had run away to sea and had eventually been found by his brother Patrick in the fruit market in Kingston, Jamaica. At this, his parents arranged for him to be made a midshipman in an East Indiaman, but life at sea soon palled and in 1795 he became a lieutenant in the Breadalbane Fencibles, commanded by his uncle. Finding military life agreeable he gained a commission in a West India Regiment and in 1800 was acting brigade-major on the island of St Vincent. Promotion to lieutenant brought him to India, where several of his brothers, a cousin and an uncle (a colonel) were already serving. Wellesley appointed Campbell his brigade-major, and he remained on the general's staff until Wellesley left India, subsequently rejoining him in Europe and holding comparable positions right up to the disbandment of the Army of Occupation of France in 1818. In later years his unpolished manners and execrable French formed a marked contrast to the aristocratic youths serving as Wellington's aides-de-camp; but Wellington valued him highly, and fought hard to keep him when, in 1810, the Horse Guards appointed him to a staff position in Malta.[21]

Another change to Wellesley's staff was caused by the illness of John Malcolm, who was forced to leave the army and return to Poona. In his place came a twenty-three-year-old civilian, Mountstuart Elphinstone, who had been Barry Close's assistant at the Poona Residency. Elphinstone came from an old Scottish family and was the nephew of Admiral Lord Keith; he was also a lifelong Whig, with liberal, even radical views at this time, and was a great admirer of Charles James Fox.[22] Wellesley did not know him well and treated him with some reserve at first, but relations soon warmed and before the end of the year Elphinstone was a trusted assistant, especially in diplomatic nego- tiations. He was blessed with a fresh eye and a lively pen, and some of the best first-hand descriptions of Wellesley and the campaign come from his journal and his letters to colleagues back in Poona.

Here is a camp day. General at half-past four. Tent-pins rattle, and I rise and dress while they are striking my tent. Go to the front, and to the Quartermaster-General's tent, and drink a cup of tea. Talk with the *état-major*, who collect there till it grows light. The assembly beats and the General comes out. We go to his breakfast table in front of his tent and breakfast; talk all the time. It is bitter cold, and we have our greatcoats on. At half after six, or earlier, or later, mount and ride, or, when there is no hunt, we do not mind one another. The General generally rides on the dusty flank, and so nobody stays with him. Now we always join Colonel Wallace, and have such coursing a mile or so out on the flank, and when we get to our ground from ten to twelve we all sit, if our chairs have come up, or lie on the ground. The General mostly lies down. When the tent is pitched we move in, and he lies on the carpet, and we all talk, &c., till breakfast is ready. Then we breakfast off fried mutton, mutton chops, curries, &c., and from eleven to two get to our tents, and I arrange my *hircarras* [scouts or couriers], write my journals, read Puffendorf, Lysias, and write to you and Adam, and sometimes translate, and sometimes talk politics and other privitie with the General; and then at two or three I eat a loaf and drink two glasses of port and water; and when it grows dark, unless I am writing, as I am now, I get shaved and walk about head-quarters line till it is pitch dark, and then dress, go to dinner, and we all talk about the march, &c., and they about their former wars, and about this war, and Indian Courts, and politics, &c. At nine we break up, and the Quartermaster-General and Major of Brigade and I hold a committee and settle whether we march next day, and then I go to palankeen. All this is extremely pleasant. I have enjoyed, I mean relished, society, and study, and business, and action, and adventure, all according to their several natures.[23]

This was written in the middle of November when Elphinstone had settled into life on campaign and recovered from some ill health that affected him at first. But the daily routine in August or September would have been much the same, except that the mornings would not have been so cold.[24]

Wellesley spent only a few days in Ahmednuggar, collecting supplies, restoring order, repairing its defences and establishing a garrison, before heading north towards Stevenson. By 22 August the army was across the River Godavery and a week later it had reached Aurungabad. Here Wellesley met Collins, who gave him the latest news of the Maratha armies and is said to have warned him that Sindia's infantry and artillery were far from contemptible. If such a warning was given, later events show that Wellesley did not give it due weight; however, there is no record of it in the letters written at the time, and the story smacks of hindsight.[25] Meanwhile the Marathas had advanced south through the Adjunta pass with their cavalry – but no infantry or artillery – and appeared ready to invade Hyderabad. The Nizam had died on 6 August, but his favourite son had succeeded without trouble or disturbance. Sindia seems not to have had any clear plan of campaign, although he certainly wished to avoid a pitched battle with either Wellesley or Stevenson. Wellesley's own plan was best summarised in his repeated advice to Stevenson: 'The best thing you can do is . . . dash at the first party that comes into your neighbourhood . . . A long defensive war would ruin us.' And: 'Dash at the first fellows that make their appearance, and the campaign will be our own.'[26] Yet this proved less easy than it sounded, and some weeks of frustrating manoeuvres followed as the armies crossed and recrossed the exhausted tract of country between the Adjunta hills and the Godavery. Wellesley and Stevenson prevented the Marathas from breaking out towards Hyderabad or Poona, but could not bring them to fight. Sindia responded by calling forward his infantry and artillery, which strengthened his army but reduced its mobility and increased the chances of a decisive battle.

On 21 September the two British armies camped within a mile of each other at Budnapore, and Wellesley and Stevenson discussed their plans. They knew that the Maratha army was not far away, and hoped to bring it to battle within a few days. Wellesley decided that the two armies should march on different roads, one on each side of a range of low hills, and unite again on the morning of 24 September at Borkadon, where he hoped to find the Marathas. This decision to 'divide' the army has sometimes been criticised, but the practical difficulties of advancing both armies, with all their camp followers and impedimenta, along a single road, beset by obstacles and defiles, were probably insuperable. Besides, Wellesley's whole campaign was based on the assumption that either British force was capable of defeating the combined Maratha army, and that the difficulty lay in catching, not in beating, them.[27]

At around eleven o'clock on the morning of 23 September 1803 Wellesley's army was preparing to make camp after a fourteen-mile march, when a cavalry patrol received word of the enemy. According to some captured brinjarries, the Maratha army was much closer than Wellesley realised, only a few miles away, but it was preparing to retreat; indeed some of the cavalry had already left and the remainder, and the infantry, would soon follow. Wellesley at once decided to advance, to reconnoitre the enemy and, if possible, to attack them. He left the rearguard and the 1/2nd Native Infantry to guard the baggage, and set the rest of the army in motion, riding ahead with the cavalry. After a few miles he reached the top of some rising ground and saw the Maratha camp stretched before him. Part of the news from the brinjarries was true – the enemy were close – but the other part was false, for this was the entire Maratha host, the combined armies of Sindia and the Raja of Berar, infantry, cavalry, artillery, camp-followers and all, amounting to some 50,000 soldiers and perhaps as many as 200,000 people altogether. Three distinct camps could be seen: Sindia's cavalry to the west, the Berar army in the centre, and the sepoy brigades to the east near the village of Assaye. The Marathas were in a strong position with their front protected by the River Kaitna, although it was made awkward by the River Juah, which ran close to their rear before joining the Kaitna a couple of miles east of Assaye.[28]

Wellesley admits that he hesitated at the sight of the Maratha army and wondered if it was not too late to withdraw to his original campsite and leave the attack until the following day when he could expect Stevenson's coopera-tion. But he decided that going back would be just as dangerous as going forward, for it would surrender the initiative to the enemy, he would lose the benefit of surprise, and the Maratha pindaris, emboldened by his withdrawal, would harass the army and attempt to plunder its baggage.[29] Displaying cool courage, and true to his earlier advice to Stevenson, Wellesley chose to 'dash' at his opponents.

The army Wellesley led forward amounted to some 7,000 regular troops, after deducting those left behind to guard the baggage.[30] In addition, he had about 5,000 irregular Mysore and Maratha cavalry, which, although it did not take any part in the actual fighting, played a useful role in preventing the pindaris from harassing the main body. Wellesley made his plans while waiting for the infantry to arrive. His object was to attack and destroy the Maratha infantry and capture their artillery, for they were the real fighting strength of the Maratha army, while the irregular cavalry would evade any direct attack. A frontal assault across the Kaitna would be difficult and costly, so he decided to ford the river a little further east, but still before it joined the Juah. By doing so he could turn the flank of the Maratha army and advance with one river protecting each flank. If he was defeated, his position would be extremely awkward, but any defeat in the face of a Maratha army was almost certain to end in disaster.

Wellesley's sudden appearance and immediate attack caught the Marathas by surprise. Their army was already discontented by lack of pay or plunder, and

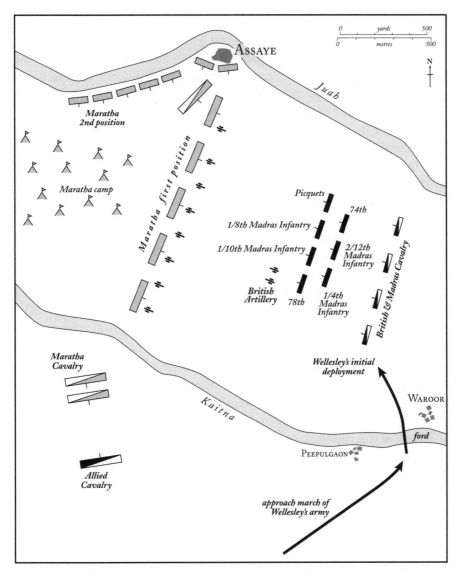

6 The battle of Assaye, 23 September 1803. (This plan is based on a sketch drawn by Mountstuart Elphinstone and sent to a friend just four days after the battle.)

had no clear command structure. Many of the bullocks that drew their artillery had been sent out to pasture, and not all could be brought back in time.[31] Above all, Wellesley's evident confidence and aggression in seizing the initiative left the Marathas reacting to his manoeuvres, rather than dictating terms of their own. Nonetheless, the Maratha infantry and artillery showed unexpected fighting qualities, and the battle that followed was far from one-sided.

As Wellesley's infantry appeared and began its diagonal march down to the river, Sindia's cavalry crossed the Kaitna and moved towards the British flank, but did not press its advance when faced with Wellesley's own Maratha and Mysore cavalry. The Maratha artillery behind the river opened fire at long range. When his secretary asked if this was 'a hot fire', Wellesley is said to have replied: 'Well! They are making a great noise but I do not see anyone hit.'[32] The fire became much heavier as the army forded the Kaitna; Colin Campbell was slightly wounded and one of Wellesley's orderly dragoons had his head carried off by a cannon ball. As the British troops took up their place in a line running north-south between the two rivers (and facing west), the Marathas redeployed their infantry and artillery to face them, and did so with greater speed and skill than Wellesley had expected. Their artillery was now much more effective. 'They had got our range completely', Colin Campbell wrote soon after the battle, 'and opened a most tremendous fire on us which galled us much.'[33]

The fire forced Wellesley to begin his advance before all his men were in line, for it was too heavy to be endured passively and some British gun teams had already been knocked out of action.[34] The British line advanced with the 78th Regiment on the left, then two battalions of sepoys, and the combined picquets of the day formed into a battalion of their own on the right. The picquets were commanded by Lieutenant-Colonel William Orrok, and Wellesley ordered him to make space as he advanced to allow two further battalions of sepoys to take their place to his left, while the 74th should deploy to his right at the exposed end of the line. This required a cool head and considerable care if these additional units were to be introduced into the line without confusion, and, as a further complication, Wellesley ordered Orrok to steer well clear of the village of Assaye on the Juah which appeared to be strongly held. Unfortunately Orrok was not the man for the task. According to Wellesley, 'habits of dissipation and idleness' rendered him 'incapable of giving attention to an order to find out its meaning'; although this was said after the battle and probably with some bitterness.[35]

Orrok badly misjudged his movements and led the picquets directly towards Assaye; a gap opened on his left between him and the centre, while on his right the unfortunate 74th came under devastating fire from the Maratha artillery around the village. According to the regimental history of the 74th:

Every officer and all but a bare hundred of the rank and file were down. At this moment the Quartermaster, James Grant, who had been following up with some coolies carrying ammunition, rations and medical supplies, ran forward fumbling with his sword hilt and followed by a few men of the baggage guard, clerks, orderlies and sick. They would not stand by idle and watch their Regiment cut down before their eyes.[36]

The 74th suffered terribly: according to the casualty return 13 officers were killed or mortally wounded; another 5 suffered lesser wounds; while 145 men were killed or died of their wounds and 250 were wounded – a total of 413 casualties from 498 officers and men present. Among the dead officers Colin Campbell numbered a brother and cousin.[37]

Seeing the 74th torn apart and the picquets wavering, the Maratha cavalry charged forward. If they had succeeded they might have gone on to roll up the whole British line and shake the power of British India to its foundations, but Lieutenant-Colonel Patrick Maxwell recognised the danger and launched a counter-attack with his 19th Light Dragoons supported by the 4th Native Cavalry. Maxwell's charge broke the Maratha horse and drove them in great confusion across the Juah. Here they mixed with some fleeing Maratha infantry and the British cavalry pursued them for some distance, inflicting heavy losses, before halting and reforming its ranks.[38]

The British advance was more successful in the centre and on the left, where the Maratha artillery fire, although heavy, was not as severe as on the right. The line halted for a moment when it was discovered that the picquets were going astray, but this check encouraged the Maratha gunners who redoubled their fire. Wellesley, realising that the troops would lose their forward momentum and begin to waver if they were expected to remain stationary under such fire, rode up to one of the battalions of sepoys and, waving his hat, cheered them on, repeating the command: 'March!' The troops resumed their advance in good order. According to Colin Campbell: 'The line moved forward rapidly (I may say without firing two rounds) and took possession of the first line of guns, where many of the enemy were killed.' Blakiston suggests that it was not quite so easy, with the sepoy battalions in the centre crowding against the 78th as they winced away from the heaviest concentration of Maratha artillery in the centre, and many individual soldiers taking cover and refusing to move forward despite every effort by their officers. Nonetheless he confirms that 'the main body of the infantry continued to advance rapidly and in good order, and were not long in coming in contact with the enemy's right wing, which they forced through without difficulty, their infantry standing no longer than the guns fired, which, however, they did to the last, many of the *golumdauze* [artillerymen] having been bayoneted in the act of loading their pieces'.[39]

The second line of Maratha infantry was formed facing south, with their backs to the Juah and the eastern end of their line protected by the village. But these troops had been disordered by fugitives from the first line and were unnerved by Maxwell's cavalry who were now in their rear; they did not make much resistance. 'Elated by their success, the *sepoys* now began to disperse in pursuit of the enemy; but happily the 78th stood their ground firmly', for the Maratha army was not yet completely broken.[40] A large body of cavalry and infantry remained a little to the west, from where it threatened the open flank of Wellesley's line, while some Maratha gunners, who had hidden or shammed dead, returned to their guns in the first line and opened fire again.

Wellesley personally led back the 78th and 7th Native Cavalry, recaptured the guns and secured the army's rear. In the process he lost his horse for the second time that day. One, a bay, was shot; the other, the grey arab, Diomed, 'who has carried me in so many campaigns', was piked and left for dead. But Diomed survived, and was eventually restored to his owner six months later. He was all the more valuable for having previously been owned by Wellesley's old friend Colonel Aston.[41] At the same time Lieutenant-Colonel Maxwell led his tired men in an attack on the remaining Maratha cavalry and infantry to the west of the British line. The charge failed, and Maxwell was killed, but the Marathas made no attempt to exploit the temporary advantage this gave them, and instead began a retreat, which rapidly became disordered. There was no pursuit, for most of Wellesley's army was exhausted and the Mysore and friendly Maratha cavalry, who were fresh, would not act by themselves.

Victory brought no immediate elation; the losses had been too heavy and the day too exhausting. According to one source Wellesley 'was so overcome by his great and gallant exertions throughout the day, so overpowered both in mind and body, that during the greater part or whole of the following night he sat on the ground with his head bent down between his knees, and said not a word to anyone'.[42] Elphinstone said that Wellesley spent the night in Assaye, 'not in "the pride, pomp and circumstance of glorious war", but on the ground, close to an officer whose leg was shot off, and within five yards of a dead officer'.[43] Samuel Rogers records Wellesley himself saying in 1824 that:

Strange impressions come now and then after a battle; and such came to me after the battle of Assaye in India. I slept in a farm yard; and whenever I awaked, it struck me that I had lost all my friends, so many had I lost in that battle. Again and again, as often as I awaked, did it disturb me. In the morning I inquired anxiously after one and another; nor was I convinced that they were living till I saw them.[44]

Wellesley had not lost all his friends, but his army had suffered heavily: 1,584 casualties, or between 20–30 per cent of the troops actually engaged in the battle. More than one-quarter of all these casualties were in the unfortunate 74th. The 78th suffered 109 casualties, including 28 killed, while the 19th Light Dragoons had 57 human casualties and 125 horses killed, wounded or missing.[45] These losses were comparable, proportionally, with the most costly of Wellesley's later victories in the Peninsula, and were much heavier than the British were accustomed to suffer in India. They were certainly more severe than anything Wellesley had previously experienced as a commander. It is clear that, in common with most other British officers and policy makers, he had seriously underestimated the Maratha army, and in particular Sindia's infantry and artillery. A few days after the battle he acknowledged as much in a letter to Malcolm:

> Their infantry is the best I have ever seen in India, excepting our own; and they and their equipments far surpass Tippoo's. I assure you that their fire was so heavy that I much doubted at one time whether I should be able to prevail upon our troops to advance; and all agree that the battle was the fiercest that has ever been seen in India. Our troops behaved admirably; the *sepoys* astonished me.
>
> These circumstances, and the vast loss which I sustained, make it clear that we ought not to attack them again, unless we have something nearer an equality of numbers.[46]

He concluded that his army and Stevenson's must act more closely together and try to avoid giving battle separately.

By his own admission, Wellesley's campaign had been based on an underestimation of the enemy, and he was probably fortunate that it was not Stevenson's force that had been engaged. But all war involves some risk, and he had succeeded in his main object of bringing the Maratha army to battle and defeating it. In the end, the victory had been decisive. Estimates of Maratha casualties vary widely and are not particularly important; what matters much more is that almost all Sindia's artillery was captured, his infantry was broken and dispersed, and his whole army demoralised. The Raja of Berar's army had escaped more lightly – it is not even clear whether his infantry was present at the battle – but it was never regarded as such a serious opponent. Wellesley's caution in contemplating future actions was based less on the fear that the troops defeated at Assaye might rally, than that Sindia might be able to bring fresh brigades down from Hindustan.[47] The trophies of victory included more than a hundred cannon and seven stands of colours. According to Blakiston, these 'latter were chiefly picked up by the pioneers when burying the dead. Not seeing any intrinsic value in them they had given them to their wives to make petticoats of; from which ignoble purpose they were rescued to hang as memorials of British prowess in the church of Fort St George, and perhaps from the dome of St Paul's'.[48]

Assaye was Wellesley's first great victory and, while it was not his finest in technical terms, he emerges from it with great credit. The immediate decision to seize the initiative and attack at once with the advantage of surprise was almost certainly correct; Stevenson could not join him that day or even, with certainty, on the following morning, and to wait twenty-four hours was to invite the Marathas to retreat if they wished, or take the initiative themselves. Wellesley quickly conceived an excellent plan of attack, which enabled him to concentrate his force against the key part of the enemy's army, while protecting his flanks and rear from their light cavalry. The execution was less successful, and Wellesley can fairly be criticised for not remaining on the right and personally supervising the execution of his orders to Lieutenant-Colonel Orrok. Still, he could not be everywhere, and his presence in the centre and on the left enabled him to lead them forward when the advance hesitated in the face of the Maratha artillery fire. Those who were with him in the battle give unreserved praise for his leadership. Colin Campbell wrote:

The General was in the thick of the action the whole time, and had a horse killed under him. No man could have shown a better example to the troops than he did. I never saw a man so cool and collected as he was the whole time, though I can assure you, till our troops got orders to advance, the fate of the day seemed doubtful; and if the numerous cavalry of the enemy had done their duty, I hardly think it possible that we could have succeeded.[49]

And Elphinstone agreed:

The General will doubtless get great credit for this; I am sure he deserves it. It is nothing to say of him that he exposed himself on all occasions, and behaved with perfect indifference in the hottest fire, for I did not see a European do otherwise (nor do I believe people ever do); but in the most anxious and important moments he gave his orders as coolly and as clearly as if he had been inspecting a corps, or manoeuvring at a review. I am afraid to say how well I like the General, for though I have known him for some time, I have only been with him six weeks, and I may change my mind; but all that can be said in six weeks' acquaintance I would have said before this action which has not lowered my opinion of him.[50]

Things did not go perfectly according to plan at Assaye. Mistakes were made and not all the troops behaved well: John Blakiston saw some sepoys in the centre take cover from the Maratha artillery fire and refuse to advance;[51] some reports suggest that the picquets and the 74th were broken and fleeing from the Maratha cavalry before Maxwell intervened; and it is clear that at least one, and probably two, of the regiments of regular Madras Native Cavalry refused orders to advance. Indeed, according to Elphinstone: 'Major Huddlestone is said to have been seen riding about, calling "Where is my regiment? Has anybody seen my regiment?" It must be observed that he was where he ought to have been, and where he would have seen his regiment if it had behaved as well as he.'[52] Such incidents were entirely normal in any hard-fought battle, although they are seldom recorded in official accounts or in the despatches written by victorious commanders. Not all men are heroes, and many men of proven bravery find their courage lacking on a particular day or in particularly difficult circumstances. Others, such as Orrok, show remarkable bravery, but lack judgement. It is this unpredictable human element that makes controlling a battle so difficult, and ensures that almost all battles go 'wrong' to a greater or lesser extent. In this sense, Assaye can fairly be compared to Marengo or Jena, and they were two of Napoleon's finest victories.

After the battle the Maratha army retreated in disorder towards the Adjunta hills. Sindia and the Raja of Berar were said to be stupefied by their defeat, while the army's baggage train and bazaar were pillaged by its own pindaris. There was a clean break between the armies. Wellesley's force was too battered and exhausted by its victory to give chase, and Stevenson did not reach the battlefield until late on 24 September or early the next morning, and then paused to rest his troops and assist the wounded. The few surgeons with the army were overwhelmed by the number of casualties; the last of the wounded were not treated until almost a week after the battle. Wellesley paid the wounded great personal attention, visiting them frequently and ensuring that they had every comfort available, drawing on his personal cellar to provide them with wine.[53]

After a few days operations resumed, although the campaign lacked a clear direction. In the middle of October Stevenson captured Burhampore and Asseerghur, Sindia's last important possessions in the Deccan. The fall of Asseerghur was particularly important; it was a strong fortress and Stevenson doubted that he could take it by *coup de main*, while he lacked the resources for a formal siege. However he learnt that the troops in the garrison were discontented, not having been paid for months, and when he offered them generous terms to surrender – free departure with their private property and their back pay – they accepted with alacrity. Neither Sindia nor the Raja of Berar could devise a practicable plan of campaign to retrieve their losses. They quarrelled and ultimately separated.[54] Nor did the news from other fronts offer them any hope, for Lake had gained a decisive victory at Delhi on 10 September which broke Sindia's power in Hindustan. This led him to make a tentative peace overture in early November, sending a high ranking *vakil*, or envoy, to Wellesley's camp. Wellesley received the ambassador 'in a liberal and delicate manner' and on 22 November concluded a suspension of arms, which did not include the Raja of Berar. He suspected that the Governor-General would disapprove of this armistice in principle, but argued that he was powerless to inflict any more damage on Sindia, who had no regular troops or territory left in the Deccan, while Sindia's irregular cavalry could still annoy Wellesley's army. In the event, Sindia did not abide by the terms of the truce, but this did no harm, and put him at a disadvantage in the subsequent negotiations.[55]

Wellesley now directed his campaign towards Gawilghur, a great mountain fortress where the Raja of Berar was supposed to have placed his treasure and other precious possessions. For reasons that are not clear, Wellesley seems to have felt a considerable personal animus towards the Raja, which contrasts with his relatively indulgent attitude towards Sindia. The army, on the other hand, was much struck with the flourishing state of Berar after the devastation and poverty to which it had grown accustomed ever since it had first approached Poona.[56]

On 29 November Wellesley's army united with Stevenson's at Paterly some fifty miles south-west of Gawilghur. Wellesley intended that Stevenson should undertake the siege, while Wellesley's own army provided the covering force, which would prevent interference from the Marathas. However, at the end of the day's march the British discovered that the Raja's army, supported by Sindia's cavalry, was deployed a few miles away at Argaum. Wellesley's first, rather uncharacteristic, inclination was to ignore them, for the troops were tired after a long march, but when some Maratha cavalry began to harass his outposts, he decided to attack.[57] The troops marched forward without fully realising that they were about to go into battle, for the country, though open, was covered in tall grain, growing higher than a man's head. Stevenson's army was on the left, its commander so ill that he was carried into battle in a litter on an elephant.[58] As the leading troops of Wellesley's army advanced through the village of Sirsoney and prepared to deploy, they came under heavy fire from the Maratha artillery: almost fifty guns. Although this fire was not nearly as heavy as that which these same troops had braved at Assaye, they were taken by surprise, and broke and fled. Fortunately Wellesley was nearby, giving orders to his brigadiers. He stepped forward and tried to quell the panic, but the men were not yet ready to rally, and rushed past, ignoring him. John Blakiston describes the sequel:

[Wellesley] mounted his horse, and rode up to the retreating battalions; when, instead of losing his temper, upbraiding them, and endeavouring to force them back to the spot from which they had fled, as most people would have done, he quietly ordered the officers to lead their men under cover of the village; and then to rally them and get them into order as quickly as possible. This being done, he put the column into motion, and leading these very same runaways round the other side of the village, formed them on the very spot he originally intended them to occupy.[59]

Blakiston was enormously impressed by Wellesley's 'intuitive knowledge of human nature', which allowed the troops to pretend that they had made an intentional counter-march and, by saving their pride, restored their confidence. As each battalion came into line, Wellesley ordered the men to lie down while they waited for the moment to advance. Lying down not only made them a small target for the enemy's fire, it also greatly reduced the temptation to run away.[60]

Waiting under fire was always difficult and time passed slowly, but at last the army was fully deployed and the advance began. The troops were formed very simply: the infantry in a single line with the cavalry of each army on its respective flank. There was no reserve. Wellesley rode at the head of the cavalry on the right until they were about 600 yards from the enemy cavalry. Then he ordered his men to halt and open fire with their horse artillery and, leaving orders to charge 'the moment the guns seemed to produce an effect', returned to the infantry.[61] When the infantry were only about 60 yards from the enemy line, they were attacked by a force of between 1,000 and 2,000 men, described by Welsh as 'Arabs' and by Blakiston as 'Persians', who were evidently the elite of the Berar army. These troops fired a volley then threw aside their muskets and 'charged with sword and buckler, somewhat in the style of the Highlanders of old', in Blakiston's words. But they were met with firmness and their charge repulsed with heavy loss. At this, the rest of the Raja's infantry began to give way, slowly at first but soon in a complete rout. The British cavalry now charged forward, the Maratha horse took to its heels, and the battle was over.[62]

The relative ease of the victory at Argaum compared to Assaye is clear from the casualty returns as well as from first-hand accounts. The British suffered only 46 men killed, 308 wounded and 5 missing: 359 in all.[63] The reason is simple: the Raja's army had never been as good as the veteran sepoys of Sindia's brigades, and it had been demoralised by Assaye and the whole campaign. It fought with no hope and little desperation against an Anglo-Indian army, which, despite the early panic, was full of confidence. Many standards, thirty-eight guns and most of the Maratha baggage were captured: 'Elephants laden with treasure fell into our hands. One elephant with a casket of jewels of great value was known to have been taken. Who was the fortunate captor of the casket was never ascertained; but suspicion fell upon an officer of cavalry, who from that day lived in a degree of splendour to which his rank and appointments would have given him no pretensions.'[64]

After Argaum the two British armies advanced on Gawilghur, as Wellesley looked to strike the final blow. This was an immensely strong fortress, a whole mountain, almost entirely inaccessible, defended with strong walls and held by a numerous garrison. The nearby plain was about 1,780 feet above sea level, while the fortress rose to 3,499 feet.[65] The approach to the southern side of the fortress was steep, but relatively simple. Wellesley's army took this route and mounted a diversionary attack on the southern gate. A breaching battery was established, but without any real hope of success, for the slope was so steep that the round-shot bounced harmlessly off the walls and rolled right back to the battery.[66]

The real attack would be mounted by Stevenson's army from the north. This required a long march through extremely difficult country. The route would not have been easy even for a small group of unencumbered troops, but was much worse for a whole army weighed down not only with its own normal baggage but by a heavy siege train and all its accompanying equipment. It took four days for Stevenson's army to get into position, but by 12 December he had established two batteries and on the following day he opened fire. By the night of 14 December a practicable breach had been made in the walls on the northern side. Wellesley was very active throughout the siege, making the rough trip from south to north repeatedly, reconnoitring in person, and doing much of Stevenson's work as well as his own, for Stevenson's health had continued to deteriorate.[67]

On the morning of 15 December the garrison tried to parley but were unwilling to commit themselves to an immediate surrender, and appeared undecided, or else playing for time. Faced with this prevarication, Stevenson's storming party moved forward at ten o'clock. They met only feeble, sporadic resistance, although they had to find their way over or through several separate walls before they reached the heart of the citadel. Many of the garrison panicked and fled, some opening the southern gate and seeking shelter with Wellesley's army. Inside the fortress there were horrific scenes of plunder, rape, murder and destruction. John Blakiston gives the fullest account, although other witnesses provide ample confirmation of its truth:

> The troops composing the storming party, particularly the Europeans, behaved with great bravery on this occasion. But, while I say this, truth obliges me to declare, that their moderation after victory was not equal to their valour in achieving it. I saw a party of the Scotch brigade bring out some of the enemy, whom they had found concealed in a house, saying that they would

give the rascals a chance. Then, taking them out one by one like basket-hares, they called to them in Hindostanee, to run, and, when they got to the distance of about thirty yards, they levelled and brought them down. It was with difficulty that they could be persuaded to give up this cruel diversion. Whether it is owing to the arrack they drink, or some other cause, I know not; but certainly the European soldiers in India became very blood-thirsty and ferocious. On this occasion I almost fell victim myself to this disposition; for, being attracted by a great noise in one of the houses, I went in, and found several of our soldiers in the act of plundering and ill-using the inhabitants. On remonstrating with them on their brutal conduct, and on their breach of orders (for all plundering was positively forbidden by the General in the orders issued previously to the assault), I was told to 'get about my business for a meddling young rascal, or they would put their bayonets into me; and that, having entered the place by storm, the devil himself should not hinder them from having their right of plunder'; which salutation was accompanied by such an evident determination to put their threats into execution, that I was glad to make my escape in a whole skin.[68]

The slaughter of the garrison and their families was immense, and troops under Wellesley's command seldom, if ever, behaved worse than on this occasion. Eventually order was restored and the amount of treasure taken was found to be much less than expected; it was thought that some may have been carried out of the fortress during the siege, for it was impossible to establish a complete cordon around the fortress or guard every mountain path.[69] The siege and storm had not been costly: only 14 besiegers had been killed and 112 wounded, so anger at their losses provides no justification for the barbarities committed by the soldiers. It was a valuable lesson for Wellesley; the looting at Seringapatam and the mass killing at Gawilghur showed him just how badly even good troops could behave when the restraint imposed by their discipline was cast aside.

The fall of Gawilghur effectively marked the end of the war. News arrived of fresh successes by Lake in Hindustan, and neither Sindia nor the Raja of Berar had any will to continue the struggle. On 16 December John Malcolm returned to headquarters, so Wellesley had his advice and assistance as well as Elphinstone's in the negotiations that followed. In each case, Wellesley effectively dictated the terms of peace, but was willing to make some concessions on points of detail. Some British demands caused no difficulty: for example, the Raja of Berar was able to say that he had never employed European officers in his army, while Sindia stated that he 'had not the smallest wish ever to see a Frenchman again', so neither objected to the proposed prohibition on European officers. But other demands were naturally more painful, particularly the sweeping territorial concessions required by Wellesley. Sindia was to lose most of his territory in Hindustan, his control of the old Mughal emperor, and all his lands in the Deccan, leaving him with little more than the traditional family fiefdom around Ujjein. As a special concession he was allowed to keep a few small pockets of territory around Ahmednuggar, where he had been born, but that city and fortress would remain in British hands. He was also expected to honour his promise to return all the Holkar estates to Jaswant Rao Holkar, even though this promise had only been made in an effort to persuade Holkar to join in the war against the British. But the war had broken Sindia's power and he was in no position to resist Holkar; indeed his *vakils* strongly hinted that he was afraid of Holkar and would be willing to enter a subsidiary alliance if this would offer protection from his great rival.[70]

The Raja of Berar was forced to yield large tracts of territory on both sides of his realm: Cuttack, in the east, to the British, and in the west, all the land between Gawilghur and the Godavery River, although the fortress itself would be returned to him. What made this concession particularly bitter was that this territory would be surrendered to the Nizam of Hyderabad, whom the Marathas continued to hold in contempt, and with whose government Wellesley himself was thoroughly disillusioned. But the Nizam, like the Peshwa, was an ally, however ineffectual and untrustworthy, and had to have his reward.[71]

The principal obstacle in these negotiations was not the intransigence of either side, but lack of information from other theatres of war. One of the guiding principles of the peace was that the Maratha princes should accept the fact that many of their vassals in Hindustan and Cuttack had come to terms with the British and changed their allegiance. But neither Wellesley nor the Maratha vakils had a complete list of these vassals; indeed some continued to change sides during, and even after, the negotiations, and the Marathas were understandably reluctant to sign a blank cheque. Wellesley himself was later to be highly critical of the British authorities in Cuttack who continued to persuade vassals to change sides after they received details of the peace – behaviour that he believed violated Britain's good faith.[72] In the course of the negotiations he refused a large bribe (five lakhs of rupees, or about £50,000) to reduce his demands on the Raja of Berar. What made this particularly remarkable was that the offer was made through Raja Mohiput Ram, a senior figure in the Nizam's service, although the Nizam would have been the loser if the bribe had been taken.[73]

In general Wellesley based his demands in the negotiations on instructions he had received from Lord Wellesley and members of his staff. However he was confident enough to exercise his discretion on a number of minor and some more important points. For example, the Governor-General had said that as well as yielding territory, the Raja of Berar should be forced to pay an indemnity of 'a crore or two of rupees if he possesses so much' (approximately £1.2 million). But after the capture of Gawilghur, Arthur Wellesley believed that the Raja was 'as poor as the other Marhatta chieftains', and dropped completely the demand for an indemnity.[74] He also pursued a more moderate policy towards Sindia than the Governor-General, encouraged by Lake's conquests, now had in mind. In part this was due to the slow communications from Hindustan; Wellesley was not aware how far Lake had advanced. In part it was due to a lack of background information, especially in the case over the claims to independence for the Rana of Gohud and the fate of the important fortress of Gwalior, which was to cause much heart-burning. But there was also a different emphasis in policy. Arthur Wellesley was less eager for conquests than his brother and he did not want to cripple Sindia completely. He hoped that with fair treatment Sindia might be reconciled to the British and become a useful ally; and he thought that it was important that Sindia be strong enough to act as a check upon Holkar, whom the war had left as the strongest of the Maratha princes. Moreover he saw, as Lord Wellesley did not, the growing anarchy throughout the Maratha lands and believed that it was essential to establish some stable government as quickly as possible. The Peshwa's authority was so weak that it scarcely extended to the gates of Poona; Sindia and the Raja of Berar had lost their armies, their treasure and most of the land; Holkar was a born rebel; and the government of Hyderabad was notoriously weak, corrupt and ineffectual. Throughout northern and central India tens of thousands of fighting men were being cast aside by their employers with little prospect of finding a fresh service to enter. To Wellesley's mind, there was a risk that all the hard work of the last year might be lost if chaos and anarchy spread across the land.[75]

Peace with the Raja of Berar was signed on 17 December, and with Sindia on 30 December, the day before the first anniversary of the Treaty of Bassein. Britain was now clearly acknowledged as the dominant power in Maratha affairs, and the predominant power in all India. To this extent Lord Wellesley's policy had succeeded. But the settlement achieved in 1803 was inherently unstable. The vanquished foes, and Baji Rao, that reluctant ally, were weak but not reconciled to their fate, and in the background lurked Holkar, who had kept out of the war, but who had no love of the British. Time, good fortune and exceptional diplomatic skill would be needed if the settlement was to survive and a fresh war was to be avoided. This was not due to any flaw in the victory or in the peace terms negotiated by Arthur Wellesley; rather, it was inherent in the scope of his brother's ambition. The Maratha Confederacy was too large a morsel to be consumed at a single meal.

CHAPTER TEN

FAREWELL TO INDIA
(1804–05)

T HE FIRST WEEKS of 1804 passed quietly as Sindia and the Raja of Berar came to terms with their defeat, and Arthur Wellesley waited to see if his brother, the Governor-General, would approve the peace treaties he had signed. The army marched south by easy stages; there was no reason to hurry, and it was important not to withdraw the British presence until it was quite clear that the peace would hold. The country was still very unsettled, with tens of thousands of leaderless men, ex-soldiers, pindaris and simple robbers preying on the peasants whose own plight was growing increasingly desperate as war, combined with a poor harvest, led to a shortage of food and raised the spectre of famine. The marauders lacked any organisation or, as yet, any real leadership, but if they were left unchecked they had the potential to become a serious problem just as Dhoondiah Waugh had been a few years earlier. Wellesley pursued and dispersed one large band (said to number 50,000 men, although this was surely an exaggeration) at Munkaiseer on 5 February with hard marching but little fighting.[1]

Subsequent operations convinced him that the Nizam's government had greatly contributed to the growing anarchy by foolishly discharging most of its soldiers and relying on the British subsidiary force for its defence. And he was so disgusted with the rapacity shown by the Nizam's officials in their occupation of the prosperous lands that the Raja of Berar had been forced to cede to Hyderabad, that he protested in an official letter to the Governor-General. The experience added to his reservations about the subsidiary system, which left allied states with few resources to maintain an army of their own. He argued strongly that it was not the role of British or Company troops to enforce the petty tyrannies and 'little dirty amildary exactions' practised by the Nizam's government. Their task ought to be restricted to opposing foreign invaders or 'great rebels', and using them to enforce the unjust demands of a corrupt government demeaned the British character and led to great resentment.[2]

These views influenced the instructions Arthur Wellesley gave to Malcolm, who was sent as Resident to Sindia early in the new year of 1804 to negotiate an alliance. In general the proposed alliance would follow the Hyderabad model, with Sindia yielding his ability to conduct an independent foreign policy in return for a contingent of Company troops (six battalions of sepoys) which he would pay for, and which would protect him from his enemies: in this case, Holkar. The most important variation was that Wellesley did not insist on stationing the subsidiary force in Sindia's territory. He argued that it was not in Britain's interests to extinguish Sindia's military power completely, and that if he disbanded his army the men would either become a menace to the surrounding country or take service with Holkar. Nor did Wellesley believe that a force of six battalions, unsupported by Europeans or cavalry, would be secure at Ougein (Sindia's capital) if Holkar decided to launch a sudden attack upon them, 'which, from the ferocious and superstitious nature of his disposition, must be expected'.[3]

Malcolm reached Sindia's camp on 12 January 1804 and was shocked at the near-famine that he found there. Sindia was ill and the troops were verging on mutiny over lack of pay. Negotiations proceeded slowly and were soon overtaken by disputes over the interpretation of the peace treaty, but a Treaty of Alliance was eventually concluded on 27 February 1804.[4] A few days after giving Malcolm his instructions, Arthur Wellesley received the first hint that the peace he had signed with Sindia might not be well received by his brother, the Governor-General. This came in the form of some papers written to guide him in the negotiations, but which had been overtaken by events. On looking through them he was disconcerted by the importance that they placed on securing the independence of the petty Rajput and Jat states in Hindustan; and he was alarmed by their acquisitive, uncompromising tone.[5]

Over the next few weeks his satisfaction in the victories he had gained and the treaties he had signed curdled as he discovered that solemn undertakings would be reinterpreted to satisfy the Governor-General's wishes. As early as 24 January he wrote to Malcolm, who shared his views: 'I tremble for the whole Treaty. They are wild in Bengal.' Five days later: 'The moderation of the British government in India has a strong resemblance to the ambition of other governments.'[6] On 11 February he ended some bitter complaints about the way the peace was being implemented in Cuttack with a wider lament:

In fact, my dear Malcolm, I see very clearly that I have made 2 very good treaties of peace, but I have not the influence to carry them into execution in any of their stipulations; and there is no person about the Governor-General to take an enlarged view of the state of affairs, and to resist the importunities of the local authorities to force on the treaties a construction which will tend to the increase of their own petty power and authority.[7]

Wellesley felt that his own good faith, and that of the British government, was called into doubt by the sharp practice of exploiting any loophole in the treaty provisions to gain the maximum possible advantage.

> I would sacrifice Gwalior, or any other frontier of India, ten times over, in order to preserve our credit for scrupulous good faith, and the advantages and honor we gained by the late war and the peace; and we must not fritter them away in arguments, drawn from overstrained principles of the laws of nations, which are not understood in this country.[8]

The idea that Britain in general had a reputation for 'scrupulous good faith' in India in 1804 seems implausible – little in the previous half-century of war, diplomacy and conquest justifies it – but it was Arthur Wellesley's own reputation that was at stake, and he was justly proud of it. To see it besmirched by the very knavery and double-dealing which he had always scorned and, wherever possible, stamped out, was a bitter pill; but worse was the fact that the blow was inflicted not by some of the notoriously corrupt officials of the Madras establishment, but by his own brother, whom he had always admired. On 13 April he told Malcolm: 'I am disgusted beyond measure with the whole concern; and I would give a large sum to have had nothing to do with the treaties of peace, and if I could now get rid of all anxiety upon the subject. All parties were delighted with the peace, but the demon of ambition appears now to have pervaded all; and each endeavours, by forcing constructions, to gain as much as he can.'[9]

The view from Bengal was very different. Lord Wellesley and his immediate circle of confidential advisers were determined to break the power of Sindia in Hindustan, and assert British paramountcy through a series of alliances with the small rajas, who had previously acknowledged Sindia as their overlord. The difference centred on the fate of the Rana of Gohud and the fortress of Gwalior. Lord Wellesley had listed these among the objectives to be included in any peace as early as 27 June 1803.[10] But Arthur Wellesley had not understood that the Gohud state had been annexed by Sindia, so that rather than being an existing state, which had changed allegiance, it was an old state, which needed to be revived. Lord Wellesley refused to accept either that his brother had made a mistake or that the treaty left Sindia in possession of Gwalior. Merrick Shawe later told Arthur Wellesley that when the treaty reached Bengal there were 'long and repeated discussions with Sir George Barlow & Mr Edmonstone', two of Lord Wellesley's closest advisers, but that the Governor-General himself had quickly concluded 'that it was calculated ultimately to secure every object he had in view'. Shawe went on to explain that if Sindia retained Gwalior, Hindustan was considered open to him. The Governor-General saw a solution to the problem in an article in the treaty, which confirmed the agreement signed between General Lake and Sindia's commander in Hindustan, and which, by a strained interpretation, could be said to award possession of Gwalior and Gohud to the British government. Writing to Malcolm, Shawe was brutally frank: if Gwalior and Gohud remained in Sindia's possession the peace would be regarded as unsatisfactory in Bengal because it would have failed to achieve one of the main aims of the war, the exclusion of the Marathas from Hindustan, and the blame for this failure would rest squarely on the shoulders of Arthur Wellesley.[11]

In the end, Lord Wellesley got his way. Sindia may not have been much surprised – he probably did not expect a scrupulously fair interpretation of the peace treaty – but any chance which may have existed of breathing life into the alliance with him, was lost. That policy may well have been hopeless from the outset; Sindia was too proud to relish the role of teacher's pet, but Lord Wellesley's faith in the petty Rajput states was to prove equally misguided. John Malcolm's repeated protests against the Governor-General's policy brought him into severe though temporary disfavour. Arthur Wellesley was much more restrained in the letters he sent to Bengal than in his private letters to Malcolm, and the Governor-General may never have understood the strength of his brother's feelings. Nonetheless the anger and disgust were real and they mark a significant moment in relations between the two men. The disillusionment was less personal than the sense of betrayal caused by the supersession at Bombay, but, as on that occasion, there was a diminution in the confidence and respect felt by the younger for the elder brother and his policies. Arthur Wellesley began to feel that he had been in India long enough.

Brotherly relations were further complicated in the early months of 1804, when Lord Wellesley was shaken by three letters from Henry Wellesley in London. Writing in late August and early September 1803, Henry warned that while Addington and Castlereagh (the President of the Board of Control) were personally well-disposed towards the Governor-General, the ministry was too weak to defend him against the inveterate hostility of the directors of the East India Company. Addington's private advice was that Lord Wellesley should return home as soon as possible, and Henry Wellesley sweetened this by confidently asserting that a brilliant career awaited in England. However Lord Wellesley had no wish to leave India immediately and argued that it would take some months to settle Maratha affairs and discharge all the routine business that had accumulated in his office. He wrote to Arthur on 6 January 1804 asking his advice in terms that reveal a deep reluctance to concede anything to his enemies at home.[12]

Arthur Wellesley replied to this letter on the last day of January 1804, with clear, unhesitating advice. Whatever Addington and Castlereagh said, it was plain that they did not appreciate Lord Wellesley's achievements and that they would not fight to defend him. Staying on would risk the humiliation of being recalled, which in turn would probably lead to a complete change of policy by his successor and the unravelling of the hard-won gains he had made. Obviously Wellesley would not be ready to sail by March, but if he announced his determination to sail at the next possible opportunity in October, he should be safe from recall and would have plenty of time to wind up the business of his office.[13]

This was not the advice that Lord Wellesley wanted, and over the next few months it became clear that he would not take it. By the middle of March, encouraged by rather more hopeful letters from London, he had decided to remain until at least the end of the year, and the departure date was subsequently pushed well into 1805, until it was eventually overtaken by events.[14] The cloud hanging over his future influenced the Governor-General's conduct in the dispute over Gohud and Gwalior. He was made angrier with Malcolm for maintaining that the treaty assigned the territories to Sindia since, as Shawe explained, this 'will give his enemies in Leadenhall-street room to found an accusation against Lord Wellesley of injustice and rapacity in insisting upon retaining these possessions contrary to the opinion of the Resident'.[15] But equally, it made him more determined to get his way in order to complete and round off his achievement in excluding the Marathas from Hindustan.

Arthur Wellesley's own attitude to the directors of the East India Company and to the British government had been rather jaundiced for some time. As early as April 1802 he told Malcolm (then attending on Lord Wellesley in Bengal) that he thought the Governor-General should resign:

> if the ministers do not give him security that he shall not be again liable to the corrupt and vulgar interference of Leadenhall street in the operations of his government . . . he cannot remain in the government, and no *gentleman* can succeed to him, if means are not taken to prevent them in future.[16]

A few months later he was surprised at Lord Wellesley's inclination to trust Addington's government, declaring that he felt 'very little confidence in them'.[17] And in March 1804 he roundly declared that:

> neither the Court of Directors nor the King's Ministers are capable of taking an enlarged view of the present state of affairs in India. Everything has been so much altered within these last five years that I doubt very much whether there is any man in England who understands our present situation. I am certain Lord Castlereagh does not, and, as proof of it, I enclose a copy of a letter which I have got from Mr Duncan in confidence.[18]

There is an odd mixture of impatience, disdain and willingness to throw in his hand and quit in all this. Of course, Arthur Wellesley was not dealing directly with the ministers, he knew little of their problems, and was free to write what he liked, for it was most improbable that Lord Wellesley would take his advice unless it coincided with his own inclinations. But the views he formed in India would influence his conduct later, in the Peninsula, when his relations with the government were a matter of much greater importance.

He was also annoyed that the ministers had not taken the opportunity of a necessary increase in the size of the British army to make it easier for experienced officers in the Company's service (men like his friend Colonel Stevenson) to transfer into the King's forces without loss of pension or seniority. And he felt hurt and slighted that he had still not been formally appointed to the staff of the Madras army eighteen months after the recommendation had been sent home. This was the principal reason he gave to General Lake when, on 23 April, he asked permission to resign his command and return to Europe.[19]

In fact, this grievance was undercut almost immediately when news arrived that the long-delayed appointment had finally been made, but Wellesley did not withdraw his resignation. He explained his motives in a letter addressed to Merrick Shawe, but intended equally for the Governor-General:

> My principal reason for wishing to go is, that I think I have served as long in India as any man ought, who can serve anywhere else; and I think that there appears a prospect of service in Europe, in which I should be more likely to get forward. Another reason is, that I have been a good deal annoyed by the rheumatism in my back, for which living in a tent during another monsoon is not a very good remedy; and a third is, that I do not think that I have been very well treated by the King's government.[20]

There is an element of polite fiction in these reasons, for it can hardly be doubted that the dispute over the implementation of the peace treaty played a large part in Wellesley's decision. And beyond this lay another motive: Wellesley had now been in India for more than seven years, he had made the most of his opportunities and achieved more than had ever seemed possible. To remain would be to invite the anticlimax of a descent into routine business. It was time to move on and to find a larger field in which to act, or he would be fixed forever as belonging solely to India, with no claims or aspirations beyond.

Shawe told Arthur Wellesley: 'I cannot describe to you the degree of alarm which the bare idea of your departure from India excited in Lord Wellesley's mind.' The Governor-General hoped that his brother would not persist in his intention, but he approved of Arthur's decision to resign his command in the Deccan and come to Bengal; indeed he had been urging this step since the beginning of the year.[21] For his part, Arthur Wellesley was happy to leave the Deccan and visit Bengal and see his brother again. He had come to believe that the Peshwa hated him personally and was led to oppose sensible measures simply because he advocated them. So bad were relations and so deep his contempt for Baji Rao, that Wellesley advised Shawe that the best way to secure the Peshwa's consent to the proposed partition of conquered territories was a succession of small bribes, for he 'is callous to everything but money and revenge'.[22]

At the end of February the officers of the army of the Deccan met in Colonel Wallace's tent and resolved to give their commander a handsome gold vase worth 2,000 guineas in commemoration of the battle of Assaye.[23] A few days later Arthur Wellesley left the army for Bombay where he stayed for two months, from the middle of March to the middle of May. The time seems to have passed pleasantly, with a mixture of celebrations, festivities, socialising and, of course, business, for he remained at the hub of a network of correspondents stretching across central and southern India. Wellesley always enjoyed appreciation and applause, and being fêted as a conquering hero must have eased his disappointment over the peace, while it helped to lay to rest the memory of the humiliation he had felt in Bombay two years before.[24]

Wellesley's plans to leave southern India for Bengal were disrupted early in May by the outbreak of war with Holkar. This was a strange business, for neither side was likely to benefit. The news was bound to strengthen the hand of Lord Wellesley's opponents in London, who had always criticised his expansionist policies and the cost of the wars he had undertaken. Even an easy victory over Holkar would do more harm than good, as it would undercut the Governor-General's claim that the defeat of Sindia and the Raja of Berar had led to a stable settlement of the Maratha question, and fuel the suspicion that his ambition would never be satisfied with peace and retrenchment. Holkar too had little to gain from war, for he could not hope to prevail where the combined forces of Sindia and Berar had been crushed with relative ease. At the beginning of the year Arthur Wellesley had written to Holkar congratulating him on his prudence in remaining aloof from the war, and assuring him 'that so long as you refrain from attacking the Hon. Company and their allies, the British government will not interfere with you'.[25] But Lord Wellesley was careless; preoccupied with other questions, he let General Lake handle the negotiations with Holkar, and Lake was either grossly heavy-handed or deliberately provocative. For his part Holkar was proud and fond of bombast; he hated the British and his large army could only be fed and paid with plunder. It is not clear whether Lake, Lord Wellesley or Holkar deliberately chose war, but none of them made the necessary effort to avoid it. Arthur Wellesley saw the disadvantages of a new conflict so clearly that he did not believe that it would occur, but he may have inadvertently played a small part in the drift to hostilities by encouraging his brother's overconfidence. At the end of January he told the Governor-General: 'It is difficult to say what line Holkar will take, or what ought to be done with him. He is evidently only a freebooter, and to crush him cannot be called a war in the present state of the Company's power.'[26]

There were as many strategic as political arguments for the British to avoid war with Holkar. The brunt of any fighting would have to be borne by Lake's army in Hindustan, but it had made few preparations for a possible campaign and there was little time before the heat and rains made active operations difficult, if not impossible. Sindia would need to be employed as an ally in any war with Holkar, but he was still angry and disaffected by the loss of Gohud and Gwalior, his army was in disarray, and the Governor-General had taken no steps to establish the subsidiary force that he had been promised under the treaty of alliance. Arthur Wellesley and the army of the Deccan could do little; Holkar's only possession within reach was the fortress of Chandore, and while that could be taken, it was not of great significance. The prevailing dearth of forage meant that there was no possibility of the army of the Deccan marching north to support Sindia until the rains had brought on fresh grass, and that was still some months away.[27] The British force in Gujarat under Colonel Murray might be able to take the field against Holkar and support Sindia, but its track record was poor. Arthur Wellesley had a loose, supervisory authority over this force, although he had tried to relinquish this responsibility in January.[28] He had appointed Murray to the command in the belief that he would work well with Jonathan Duncan, the governor of Bombay, but instead the two had quarrelled incessantly. Wellesley lost patience with both men and strongly urged Duncan to dismiss Murray, but this the governor refused to do. A magisterial letter of reproof from Bengal did nothing to improve matters, and in his efforts to soothe ruffled feathers and get everyone working together again Arthur Wellesley was driven to write letters that went beyond the normal insincerity of professional relationships into downright hypocrisy.[29] Early in the year he had written to Stuart urging the need to reinforce the corps in Gujarat, and two battalions had been sent there by early April, but even so he could feel little confidence that it would achieve much in a campaign against Holkar.[30]

Despite these problems Arthur Wellesley believed that the war could be won with relative ease if Lake would take an active and energetic part.

> The General's intention not to quit Hindustan, and not to follow Holkar, will
> be fatal. He ought to leave a corps in Hindustan for its security, and move with
> a light body in pursuit of Holkar, whose force will fritter away daily, whether

he retreats after fighting or without fighting. If he should not pursue Holkar, the war will immediately become defensive on our part in the most important quarter, and by such operations we must lose.

Colonel Murray's offensive operations must be feeble in comparison with those of the Commander-in-Chief; indeed I don't think he can venture far from the Myhie . . .

If General Lake should not be sufficiently strong to carry on the war in this manner, he ought to delay its commencement till he can be reinforced, or till Scindiah's subsidiary force can be arranged.[31]

Lake did indeed take the field, and in the second half of April and early May he achieved considerable success, driving Holkar before him and receiving encouraging reports of desertion, disaffection in the Maratha camp, and predictions of the imminent break-up of Holkar's army. Wellesley wrote to congratulate the Commander-in-Chief and to urge him to carry on the pursuit remorselessly so that Holkar would have no chance to rally his men or plunder until 'the freebooter ends by having with him only a few adherents; and he is reduced to such a state as to be liable to be taken by any small body of country horse'.[32] This is just what Lake did not do. The season was becoming uncomfortably hot and his supplies were running low. Holkar was on the run and seemed to Lake to be already thoroughly beaten, so he suspended the campaign and withdrew his army into its cantonments in Hindustan, leaving a detachment under Colonel Monson to guard against a revival of Holkar's power and to support the Rajput states. Misled by Lake's inflated claims of success, Lord Wellesley concluded that the war was over and ordered widespread reductions in military spending, in effect putting the army on a 'peace-footing' in order to strengthen his defence against the accusation of extravagance made by his enemies in London.[33]

Arthur Wellesley left Bombay in the middle of May and rejoined the army on 22 May in camp at Panowullah outside Poona. At first he hoped to be able to take the field against Holkar relatively soon, when the early rains brought up some forage, but these hopes were dashed when the wet weather led to heavy losses among the army's cattle, and he saw for himself the reality of the famine that was gripping the Deccan.[34] Wellesley had already given orders to Major Graham, the officer commanding at Ahmednuggar, to provide work for victims of the famine so that they could buy food, and to give rations to those who were too weak or exhausted to work. Inevitably this meagre bounty attracted desperate people from neighbouring districts, and Wellesley was forced to order Graham to reduce the pay and rations to the barest minimum so that they would stretch to feed as many people as possible.[35] He had told his brother Henry, with some exaggeration:

There is at present a famine in the Deccan, which, in my opinion will destroy half of the inhabitants. It is occasioned in part by the operations of the Marhatta armies of the last ten years, particularly by those of Holkar in the year 1802; in part by the operations of the Marhatta armies in the war, and by the want of arrangement and energy in the government of the Peshwah.[36]

Even the army camped near Poona suffered, with the price of food in the bazaar soaring so high that Wellesley was forced to contemplate issuing rations to the camp-followers. At Ahmednuggar Graham was feeding 5,000 people and still witnessing fifty deaths a day.[37]

Far from the principal theatre of operations, and unable to move his army because of the famine, Wellesley was reduced to being little more than a spectator of the campaign against Holkar. He gave Murray some encouragement and advice:

You have now a great game in your hands, but all will depend upon your management of the Natives with whom you will have to co-operate. I have only to recommend to you to conciliate them as much as possible; to treat them with the greatest kindness and attention is the only mode of drawing from them any assistance. At the same time you must not lose sight of the fact that they are Marhattas; that there is not one of them who can be implicitly trusted; and that, most probably, all are in correspondence with the enemy's camp. You must not allow them to perceive that you distrust them. You will excuse me for saying this to you. I have acted successfully as I now recommend to you; and my conduct and this recommendation are the result of long experience.[38]

But Wellesley could not do much to influence events, and there seemed no reason for him to remain in the Deccan. The Governor-General, believing that the war with Holkar was over, had already come to the same conclusion, and summoned his brother to Bengal.

Arthur Wellesley resigned his command on 24 June 1804 and two days later set off on the long journey to Seringapatam, Madras and Bengal – the first stage on the even longer journey home. On the way he had talks with the southern jagirdars and arranged for British mediation between them and the Peshwa, although the mediation ultimately failed. He reached Seringapatam on 16 July and received a warm reception from the inhabitants. Here, if anywhere, he could believe that his years in India had done good, producing a sound, honest and efficient government. Six months earlier, in January, he had written to Shawe, urging the importance of keeping Mysore quite separate from Madras lest the Raja's government 'be destroyed by corruption'. In March of the following year, at sea and with India below the horizon behind him, he filled a long letter to Malcolm with a discussion of how to regulate the harvest of the teak forests of Mysore. In July 1804 he thanked the inhabitants for their welcome, caught up with some paperwork, and told Major Symons, who was in charge of the police, that it was unreasonable to punish someone merely for being in possession of a single base coin: 'The accident might happen to anybody, to you as well as to me.'[39]

After a few days at Seringapatam he was on the road again, reaching Madras before the end of July. Here he met the new governor, Lord William Bentinck, of whom he had already formed a poor, but not entirely inaccurate, opinion.[40] He also saw General Stuart and wrote several official letters to him as Commander-in-Chief of the Madras army. One concerned a native officer, Soubahdar Kawder Nawez Khan, whom he had employed on several confidential missions, who had lost a brother and son killed at Assaye, and who was now quite worn out and incapable of further service. Wellesley requested that the soubahdar receive his full pay as a pension for the rest of his life, with an additional allowance for a palanquin. 'As he has been an example of zeal, activity, intelligence, and bravery in the army, I am anxious to recommend that he should be made an example of the generosity of government, and of its desire to reward meritorious servants.' On the following day he wrote again, this time paying tribute to the exertions of the Public Bullock department, without which 'I should never have reached Poona', and asking that those members of the department who had served in the campaign be granted an extra month's pay as a bonus. Victorious generals leaving their command usually bestow some patronage on their favourites, but the choice of an obscure native officer and the Public Bullock department says a good deal about Wellesley's outlook and priorities.[41]

Arthur Wellesley sailed from Madras on HM's sloop *Victor* accompanied by Captain Barclay, who was still officially Assistant Adjutant-General in Mysore, Lieutenant H.J. Close, the general's aide-de-camp, and Captain Colin Campbell, his brigade-major. They arrived in Calcutta on 12 August to an elaborate ceremonial reception, including a salute of thirteen guns, and followed by a grand dinner at Government House.[42] Few details of the conversations between the two Wellesleys at this time survive in the written record, although we know that Arthur intended to press the Governor-General to provide more effective support to Webbe, who had replaced Malcolm as Resident at Sindia's *durbar*, and probably to make arrangements for the establishment of Sindia's subsidiary force.[43] On a lighter note, a well-meant hint from Malcolm led to trouble, as Arthur Wellesley told him:

When you give advice in future, you must enter into particulars. You desired
me to admire Windham's picture – but you did not say whether it was that in
crayons or in miniature. I admired that which I ought not, and got into a
worse scrape than that in which I should have been if I had not admired any
picture at all.[44]

Despite this blunder, the major-general took the opportunity of this visit to
Calcutta to have his own portrait painted by Robert Home, who, according to
William Hickey, was 'then deemed the best artist in Asia'. Home had already
painted a full-length portrait of the Governor-General in full ceremonial
regalia, every inch of which suggested a grand statesman who enjoyed the
pomp and circumstance of state served with a generous dose of flattery. Arthur
Wellesley's portrait – also full-length and life-size – was much plainer, with his
right hand tucked inside his scarlet regimental jacket and his left on the hilt of
his sword (see plate 15). In the background are a tent, a camp scene, and
soldiers hauling a gun. The effect is much less memorable; Wellesley's figure is
wooden, and the face has only a suggestion of his lively intelligence. Home
subsequently made more than a dozen copies and variations of this portrait –
some full-length, but most smaller – for Wellesley's friends; and it reached a
wider public when it was engraved in 1806.[45]

Arthur Wellesley had scarcely arrived in Calcutta when news came that
Colonel Monson had got into difficulty. Monson's task was essentially defensive: to keep watch on Holkar and ensure that he did not break out into
Hindustan while the main body of Lake's army spent the heat and rains in
cantonments. But he had also been instructed to maintain good relations with
the Rajput states, and to support them if they were attacked; this led him to
make a succession of ill-judged advances which left him far from his base,
without secure supplies and with Holkar's forces around him. Having got into
this predicament his best hope of survival lay in boldness, in continuing to
advance and in attacking Holkar if the Marathas were willing to offer battle
and, if not, to link up with Sindia or Murray. In other words he had already
gone so far that it was dangerous to go back. But Monson lacked the nerve for
this desperate remedy; he hesitated, felt acutely the peril he was in, and began
to retreat. This immediately made his position far worse: Holkar's troops were
greatly emboldened and began to pursue and harass him with redoubled
vigour; his own men were disheartened; and the Rajput princes who had
encouraged his advance lost confidence in him, some withdrawing their
cooperation and seeking to conciliate Holkar. The retreat soon became a nightmare, with constant attacks by Holkar's pindaris and the lack of supplies
exhausting the men. A swollen river blocked the march, and Holkar brought
up his infantry and artillery, inflicting severe losses before the tattered remnants

of Monson's force could escape. Even after having been joined by reinforcements, the unnerved colonel continued to withdraw, until all India was talking of the greatest disaster British arms had suffered in the subcontinent for a generation.[46]

The full extent of the defeat took some time to become apparent, but as early as 4 September Arthur Wellesley told Barry Close: 'Affairs in Malwa have gone very badly indeed, and a great effort is necessary to regain our character, and to place matters on the footing on which they should be. This effort will shortly be made . . .' He indicated that he intended to leave Calcutta soon and join either Murray in Gujarat or Colonel Wallace in the Deccan.[47] Wellesley felt little enthusiasm for the prospect of leaving Bengal to return to the Deccan or Gujarat to help repair the damage done by Monson's blunders; his heart was set on returning to England. A letter from John Malcolm, which suggested that he should stay for some years at least, produced an angry but confidential reply, such as is only written to a close friend:

> I don't exactly see the necessity that I should stay several years in India in order to settle affairs which, if I had been permitted, I should have settled long ago, or any reason for which I should involve myself in fresh troubles and difficulties with which I have hitherto had no concern. I look to England, and I conceive that my views in life will be advanced by returning there. I don't conceive that any man has a right to call upon me to remain in a subordinate station in this country, contrary to my inclination, only because it will suit his views, and will forward objects for which he has been labouring . . . I am positively determined that, whether the Governor-General goes or stays, I quit India as soon as Holkar will be defeated.[48]

Throughout his life Arthur Wellesley had an unusually strong sense of duty and a keen appetite for employment, but on this occasion he baulked at the traces and felt inclined to consider his own interests and needs as well as those of the public.

He remained in Bengal until the middle of November, acting as his brother's military adviser and writing many memoranda on a wide range of Indian subjects, which had little influence on events, but which preserved some of the lessons of his years of experience. On 9 November the Governor-General formally reappointed him to the command in the Deccan with all the military and diplomatic powers he had previously held. A few days later he sailed for Madras on board the frigate *Bombay* and arrived a week later, after 'the best passage I have ever had at sea'.[49] He was not happy at the state of affairs at Madras, and was shocked to learn that Webbe was dangerously ill at Sindia's court. He reached Seringapatam on 30 November and a few days later learnt that Webbe had died. This was a heavy blow, for after the initial awkwardness between them in 1798, Wellesley had come to like and admire Webbe more than any man in India, except his brothers, his staff, and possibly Barry Close and John Malcolm. His domestic servants now added to his misery by refusing to accompany him back to the Deccan, and he privately admitted 'if the prevalent reports are [well] founded, they are not in the wrong; the sickness of the army is terrible, and must sweep off many who escaped the famine'.[50] At this point Wellesley's own health gave way; he suffered from fever and ague, and although he threw off the attack after a few days, he did not regain his full health for as long as he remained in India. Early in February John Malcolm described him as suffering from a slow fever, and being fretful, anxious and undecided.[51]

Fortunately news now reached Seringapatam that Lake had gained the upper hand over Holkar. The war was still far from finished, and Lake's extraordinary series of unsuccessful assaults on the fortress of Bhurtpore meant that a decisive victory would not be achieved, but the immediate crisis was over.[52] Wellesley was confident that neither Sindia nor the Raja of Berar would join Holkar, and, with the famine still raging around Poona, there was little he could do if he joined the army of the Deccan. By 19 December his mind was made up, and he wrote to Major Shawe that he had decided to go home.[53] It is clear that this was what he had wanted to do for months, but despite, or even because of this, he was beset by doubts and regrets until seasickness finally removed the luxury of second thoughts.[54]

An old friend arrived in India at the end of 1804: Sir John Cradock, who had been a senior aide-de-camp when the young Arthur Wesley had first joined the Lord Lieutenant's staff in Dublin in 1788, and who was the new Commander-in-Chief of the Madras army in succession to Stuart. Wellesley welcomed him with real affection, while Cradock urged him to stay in India, for he had heard that the government was considering appointing Wellesley as Commander-in-Chief at Bombay with a seat on the Governor's Council. Lord Wellesley was quite taken with this idea, although he also thought that Arthur's presence in London would be invaluable in persuading the ministers to support him and his policies in India, so he graciously allowed his brother to make the final decision for himself. One of the Governor-General's assistants, Benjamin Sydenham, went further, suggesting that it was Lord Wellesley's hope that his brother might one day preside over the destiny of the whole Indian empire from Calcutta. Arthur Wellesley was unmoved by these prospects.[55] He told Cradock:

> You think about my staying in India like a man who has just come out, and I like one who has been here for seven years involved in perpetual troubles. I

acknowledge that I am anxious to a degree which I cannot express to see my friends again; and even if I were certain that I should not be employed in England at all, there is no situation in India which would induce me to stay here.

I am not rich in comparison with other people, but very much so in comparison with my former poverty, and quite sufficiently so for my own wants & desires. I got a great deal of prize money in the last war; which with what I got before, and a sum of money which the Court of Directors gave me for a service rendered to them in this country, and the accumulation of interest upon those sums, have rendered me independent of all office or employment.[56]

As for the hint of higher office, Arthur Wellesley would not have been human if he had not reflected that he was now almost the same age as that at which his brother had been appointed Governor-General of India; that he had unrivalled experience and knowledge of the subcontinent, whereas his brother had had none; and to resent the fact that he was expected to be flattered by an unconfirmed offer of the command of the Bombay army, and the distant, uncertain prospect that one day he might be regarded as worthy to fill his brother's shoes. Not that such disloyal thoughts found their way onto paper – or at least onto any paper that has survived.

In the middle of February news arrived from England that Lake had been granted a peerage, and Arthur Wellesley made a Knight of the Bath in recognition of their services in the Maratha War. Cradock, inspired by memories of Dublin frolics, got Wellesley's coat from his servant that night and pinned the red ribband onto it so that his friend should see the decoration when he woke in the morning. But although Wellesley did not share his brother's passion for honours and distinctions, he felt that this was making the award ridiculous, and the joke fell flat. Moreover, certain formalities had to be conducted, and by dispensing with them Cradock created a problem that could not be resolved without a good deal of correspondence and some embarrassment.[57]

Slowly Wellesley wound up his affairs with, now it came to the point, some hesitation and regret. He disposed of two elephants given to him by the Raja of Koorg, and three more which were already in his service. He bade farewell to the officers and men of the 33rd, assuring them 'that I shall never forget their services, and that I shall always be happy to forward their views'. He recommended his staff officers, particularly Colin Campbell and Lieutenant Close, to the Governor-General's protection. He wrote a fine letter of farewell to Purneah, praising the minister's personal kindness and public integrity, enclosing a copy of Home's portrait as a memento, and requesting that he would keep an eye on the young Salabut Khan, Dhoondiah Waugh's son, and advance him in the Mysore service if he proved worthy when he became a young man. And he wrote to Malcolm: 'I cannot express to you how much distressed I am at going away and parting with my friends in this country. I recommend Mrs Freese to your kindness and attentions, which, I am convinced, you will show her on my account.' On 10 March 1805 he sailed, an honoured passenger on board HMS *Trident*, the flagship of Admiral Rainier, who was also returning home.[58]

Eight years in India had given Arthur Wellesley an extraordinary range of experience. As a soldier, he had not merely seen action, but learnt to command an army on campaign and in battle. He had shown boldness, daring and courage, but also meticulous planning and preparation, and great care for the welfare and discipline of his troops. His correspondence displays strong common sense, attention to detail and a passion for mundane necessities as well as the more glamorous aspects of soldiering. But it would be a mistake to believe that a conscientious devotion to logistics and a command of paperwork are sufficient to explain his success. He had demonstrated the intelligence and breadth of vision to devise a plan of campaign that was sufficiently flexible to allow for myriad uncertainties, but which still helped shape events to his own advantage. He had the patience to cope with the difficulties created by bad weather and fickle allies, even when they drove him to the edge of distraction. He had, as all generals must have, the necessary ruthlessness to send men forward and watch them die to achieve his objectives. He had the quick eye and bold spirit to seize a fleeting opportunity and throw his army into a sudden attack; the cool head to adjust his plans in the midst of battle in the face of an unexpected setback; and the character and personality to inspire men to follow him, loyally and with confidence, into the cannon's mouth. A good general – and Wellesley was already a very good general – needed all these abilities, and they were not things that could be tested except amid the heat and dust of battle.

Wellesley had also shown an unusual and very practical desire to minimise the miseries of war for the local civilian population, refusing to turn a blind eye to abuses committed by the men or officers of his army. He had conducted negotiations and made peace, not perfectly, but with confidence, assurance and skill. His handling of ambiguous, difficult allies, such as the Peshwa and the Nizam, and of hostile neutrals like Holkar in 1803, had been adept. He had been less involved in the formulation of policy at the highest level, but his criticism of his brother's handling of the peace with Sindia, and of the drift to war with Holkar, was well founded. In his role as governor of Seringapatam he showed an unexpected taste for civil administration, an inclination not to impose foreign forms of government on the local population, and a determination to protect Mysore from the corruption of Madras. Very few officers of any rank in the British army had received such practical training, or were as well equipped to deal with the mixture of military, diplomatic, political and financial problems that would present themselves in commanding an army in an extended campaign in Europe.

Wellesley was certainly not free of vanity, but he could, on occasion, be unduly modest. During the negotiations for peace in 1803 Elphinstone records that, 'he said he was a very sensible man, but that he was very slow; that opportunities went by before he really understood them'. Yet Elphinstone rated him much more highly than this: 'The General is an excellent man to have a peace to make. I would pick him out of all India for it . . . he seems a sensible moderate unprejudiced man, and unprejudiced on subjects where you would expect to find him so.' Nonetheless it is clear that Wellesley prided himself on his common sense and hard work, rather than attributing his success to innate genius. For example, in September 1804 he told Malcolm, 'You generally see what is right and what is desirable, I what is practicable', adding a characteristic touch: 'In this instance I think I have taken a correct view of the subject.'[59]

When, in January 1805, he told Shawe, 'I am not very ambitious', the statement was both true and false. He cared little for money beyond the minimum needed to give him independence, and considerably less for his own comfort. Honours and titles mattered little, but he did expect that his services would be recognised properly, and greatly resented any shortfall. The applause of his peers was especially welcome, and he was extremely sensitive to criticism. Above all, he wanted to be actively employed, using his abilities to the full. He was a very difficult subordinate, because he was convinced that he could do the job better himself. In general, he took disappointments badly, and felt keenly the merest hint of humiliation. He was, on the whole, an excellent superior, protecting even Lieutenant-Colonel Orrok despite his blunder at Assaye. But he had a sharp tongue and a sharper pen, and was not always aware of the pain he inflicted. Nor would he tolerate corruption, dishonesty or the abuse of power. According to Elphinstone, he was 'a remarkably conscientious man, and has no idea of letting private favour interfere at all with public duty'.[60]

Arthur Wellesley was thirty-five years old when he sailed from India, a Major-General and a Knight of the Bath. His place in the world and his financial independence were both assured, at least in a modest way. He may already have achieved his early ambitions, but in India he had discovered that the army – and public service more broadly – was his vocation, not merely a means to an end; and for the rest of his life he would be assiduous in seeking out opportunities to put his skills to use. The next few months, however, were a time of enforced shipboard idleness. For the first week or so he was very seasick, but when that passed he found that his health benefitted from the voyage and the rheumatism and lumbago that had plagued him virtually disappeared. Four months after leaving Madras the *Trident* arrived at St Helena, halfway home, and his thoughts turned back to India. He wrote to Malcolm asking him to 'remember me most kindly to Purneah, Bistnapah, and all my friends, black, white and grey, at Seringapatam and elsewhere within your reach'. The Indian adventure was over.[61]

PART III

War, Politics, Fame and Controversy

CHAPTER ELEVEN

RETURN TO ENGLAND
(September 1805–March 1807)

A RTHUR WELLESLEY DID not come home to a hero's welcome. *The Times* did not even mention him in its report of the safe arrival of Admiral Rainier and the India fleet, although he had headed the complete list of passengers, which it had printed a month earlier.[1] His name was not unknown and the victory of Assaye had been celebrated in the press with considerable enthusiasm;[2] but that was eighteen months earlier, and in the interim Napoleon had crowned himself Emperor of France, Britain had been seriously threatened with invasion, a new war on the Continent had begun, and exaggerated reports of Monson's disaster had reached London.[3] Wellesley was yesterday's hero, while political support for his brother's aggressive policies in India had evaporated.

In professional circles, Arthur Wellesley's reputation was mixed. An enthusiastic friend assured him that: 'Your battles and campaigns have been discussed at every table and in every Military Society in England, and . . . your operations in the Deccan are considered to . . . reflect the highest honour upon any officer, in any service, or in any part of the world.' But others, including the Duke of York, felt that he had been unfairly favoured in receiving plum commands, or were still prejudiced by garbled accounts of the failure at Sultanpettah Tope in the siege of Seringapatam. And there was a widespread feeling that, as the King put it, 'military reputation was easily acquired in India.'[4] The Horse Guards[5] may not have known much about Wellesley, other than his obvious political connections, but they knew General Lake well, and Lake had been as successful as Wellesley in the campaign of 1803, so that despite Assaye and Argaum they had little reason to assume that Wellesley's abilities were unusual. George III, who greatly disliked Lord Wellesley, had consented with evident reluctance to Pitt's proposal to make Lake a peer and to give Arthur Wellesley the red ribband of the Order of the Bath (that is, his knighthood), stipulating that Major-General John Moore 'to whom our successes in Egypt are chiefly owing' and Commodore Samuel Hood receive the same honour 'and be senior to

Brigadier-General Welseley [*sic*]'.[6] It did not need the misspelling of Wellesley's name or the mistake over his rank (he had been a Major-General for two years, and the King was usually punctilious on such matters) to indicate that the wind of royal favour was unlikely to fill his sails.

Fortunately Arthur Wellesley was already highly esteemed by some of the leading politicians of the day. He reached England on 10 September 1805 and two days later was asked by Castlereagh to come to the Foreign Office so that he could advise the Cabinet on the situation in India. Castlereagh had just prepared some supplementary instructions for Sir David Baird, who had recently sailed in command of an expedition to the Cape of Good Hope (which had been returned to the Dutch under the Peace of Amiens). The news of Monson's failure led Castlereagh to warn Baird that if there were a crisis in India, Cornwallis (who had been nominated to succeed Lord Wellesley there) would have the authority to summon part or all of Baird's force to India. That Arthur Wellesley should thus be called upon to advise the Cabinet on the wisdom of depriving David Baird of his command suggests a malicious humour on the part of the gods, for it was plainly in his interest to resist the obvious temptation and assure the ministers that affairs in India were less alarming than they seemed, and that while the instructions were a wise precaution, there was little chance that they would be needed. To say anything else would be dishonest and would cast doubt on the success of his brother's policies and even on the success of his own campaigns.[7]

While waiting for the ministers to be ready to see him, Wellesley was kept company by a slightly-built naval officer, whom he could not fail to recognise as Lord Nelson. The conversation at first was rather unsatisfactory, for they were not introduced, and, as Wellesley later said, Nelson talked 'all about himself, and in, really, a style so vain and so silly as to surprise and almost disgust me'. Slipping a word in edgewise, Wellesley hinted that he was not insignificant himself, whereupon the admiral left the room briefly to ask the servant the name of his companion. When 'he came back he was altogether a different man, both in manner and matter. All that I had thought a charlatan style had vanished, and he talked of the state of this country and of the aspect and probabilities of affairs on the Continent with a good sense, and a knowledge of subjects both at home and abroad, that surprised me equally and more agreeably than the first part of our interview'. Three days later Nelson put to sea, and Trafalgar was fought less than six weeks later.[8]

Wellesley only stayed in London for a fortnight or so, renting a house at 18 Conduit Street. He went shopping, relishing the range of choice and up-to-the-minute fashions after his years of exile and, before that, of relative poverty. Good fortune has preserved a few of his bills, so we know that on 19 September he visited Robert Birchall's music shop in New Bond Street where he purchased the sheets for sonatas by Mozart, airs by Beethoven, duets and trios for piano and violin from popular light operas, and a number of romantic songs – the bill fills a whole page. On the following day he visited Flight and Barr's Worcester porcelain shop in Coventry Street and ordered a breakfast and dinner service, with extra muffin plates, in the Royal Lily pattern.[9] And he saw his family – or certainly his brothers and sister – again, for the first time in almost a decade.

Gerald Wellesley, Arthur's younger brother who had gone into the Church, was now Rector of St Luke's, Chelsea and a prebendary of Westminster Abbey. In June 1802 he had married Lady Emily Cadogan and two years later wrote to Lord Wellesley:

> I am going on in the old parsonic way, that is, [I] have a wife and one child, and am in daily expectation of another; am intolerably poor, but that excepted, as happy as possible. I long to introduce Lady Emily to you, and cannot help flattering myself that you will like her.[10]

The sight of Gerald's domestic felicity had made a deep impression on Henry Wellesley when he returned from India, and he soon proposed to, and was accepted by, Lady Emily's sister, Lady Charlotte Cadogan. His mother was not pleased, dismissing Charlotte as 'a good natured sort of person . . . but I can see no charm of either person or manner', and describing the connection with the Cadogans as 'odious'. The failure of the marriage a few years later may vindicate her opinion, but the Wellesleys showed little aptitude for domestic contentment.[11]

Anne Wellesley, the one surviving sister of the five brothers, was First Lady of the Bedchamber to the Duchess of York. She and her second husband, Charles Culling-Smith, were described as 'both very handsome and are fond of one another'. But according to contemporary gossip, the Duke of York returned to Oatlands unexpectedly one day, and 'actually surprised the Duchess and Mr Smith in the very fact. Violent fury on his part, and threats of an immediate divorce and public ignominy and disgrace. He immediately hastened to the King and told him the whole affair. The King said, "I am very sorry for it, Frederick. It is an infamous business, but it must be hushed up" – and it would seem that it is to be hushed up'.[12] There is no way of knowing if there is any truth in this story, but if it is true, it would not have endeared any of the Wellesleys to either the King or the Duke.

Of all the Wellesleys only William appears to have married happily. He was now well established as a Member of Parliament (for Queen's County, Ireland) and, since 1802, a junior member of the government (Clerk of the Ordnance). He seldom spoke in debate except to defend his brothers when their activities in India were attacked. His children were emerging from the schoolroom. His eldest son William, although only seventeen, had left England a few months before Arthur's return, accompanying Charles Arbuthnot on a diplomatic mission to Constantinople.[13] But the youngest of his three daughters, Priscilla, who would become Arthur's favourite niece, was still only twelve. Many years later Priscilla's daughter recorded the story: 'The joy in the family when "Arthur" arrived at their house on his return from India. It was late in the evening, and the . . . girls had gone to bed, but he was impatient to see them, so their mother woke them and brought them down in their nightgowns.' At first they mistook him for their uncle Gerald 'who he at that time was very like, and could not realise that he was the wonderful uncle from India of whom they had heard so much'.[14]

This warm welcome, and the sight of his brothers all comfortably settled with their wives and children (their marital troubles were still, mostly, in the future), must have strengthened Arthur Wellesley's own desire to marry. He had returned from India with clear intentions in this regard, for he knew that Kitty Pakenham was still unmarried, and had not forgotten him. Lady Pakenham's prohibition on correspondence had been scrupulously observed, but a few indirect messages had been conveyed through Kitty's friend Olivia Sparrow, who had occasionally written to Arthur in India. Later in life it suited Arthur Wellesley to blame Olivia Sparrow for the part she played, and to suggest that he had been induced to renew his proposals to Kitty from a sense of honourable obligation.[15] This was nonsense, designed to put the best possible gloss on what seemed – in hindsight – to have been an act of inexplicable folly. The exact nature of Wellesley's true feelings remains uncertain, but there is no doubt of the central fact: he renewed his proposal of his own free will, because he wished to marry Kitty, and she freely accepted him. They were both intelligent, capable adults and the responsibility for the decision rests squarely with them.

There was a certain amount of dishonesty on all sides. Arthur Wellesley had had his long affair with Mrs Freese, and possibly other less important dalliances. Kitty had been seriously courted by Galbraith Lowry Cole and had not discouraged his advances although, when it came to the point, she refused his offer. Later she had tried to renew the romance, but Cole did not respond. Olivia Sparrow and another friend, Colonel Marcus Beresford, concealed this in writing to Wellesley, just as they concealed the fact that Kitty's bloom had faded and exaggerated the retirement in which she lived.[16]

If Arthur had wished the affair forgotten he could easily have ended it by responding to Mrs Sparrow's letters with kindness, solicitude and the language of friendship. Instead he wrote of the disappointment he had suffered in being rejected by the Pakenhams, but added that 'I did not deserve such a woman and that I was treated exactly as I ought to have been'. And, even more significantly, that his 'Opinion and sentiments respecting the person in question are the same as they have ever been. They were the result of a long and intimate acquaintance, in the course of which I declare I do not recollect one action that I did not approve and that was not consistent with her character and the whole tenor of her life'.[17] This was in August 1804 when his thoughts were already turned towards home, and when he had just had an interview with Olivia Sparrow's sister, Lady William Bentinck, at Madras, in which she appears to have lectured him severely on his private life. That Wellesley would tolerate such a lecture from a woman he hardly knew, and with whose high-minded principles and hyperactive morals he had little sympathy, suggests that he was determined not to offend Kitty's friends or family.[18]

This was the last letter Wellesley sent to Mrs Sparrow from India, but it was quite enough to justify her expectation that when he returned home he would lose no time in renewing his proposal for Kitty's hand. Indeed it is remarkable that such a sensible man should commit himself so fully when he had not had direct contact with Kitty for fully ten years. Before he had been in London a week, Olivia wrote accusing him of 'neglecting' Kitty, but he was naturally unwilling to race headlong to Dublin without some assurance that his suit would be accepted. Nor, even now, would he break the family's ban and write directly to Kitty; he wrote instead to Olivia and asked her to renew his proposal. Not surprisingly, Kitty was thrown into confusion by this sudden offer, even though she had, of course, seen the contents of his letters to Olivia. She had expected to see him, to renew their old acquaintance and to be wooed, not to be confronted with a brisk demand, presented through a third party, in which she could detect no 'expression implying that "Yes" would gratify or that "No" would disappoint or occasion regret'.[19] In a way Kitty was as committed as Arthur was – she could hardly reject him now, and indeed had no wish to do so – but she had lost confidence in herself, and was desperately anxious to know that he was acting freely, from genuine feeling, not from a sense of obligation. 'I am very much changed and you know it', she told Olivia, 'so much so that I doubt whether it would be in my power to contribute to the comfort or happiness of anybody who has not been in the habit of loving me for years – like my brother or you or my mother ... I have been witness to all the happiness arising from affection where it was mutual and can feel what would have been the misery had that affection existed but on one side.'[20]

This was enough to convince Wellesley that he would have Kitty's consent, and he wrote at once to her and to her brother. The family was delighted, for Major-General Sir Arthur Wellesley KB, with a comfortable Indian fortune in his pocket, was quite a different suitor from Lieutenant-Colonel Arthur Wesley with no money and few prospects; and besides, Kitty's feelings could not be lightly disregarded after so many years. Kitty herself replied to his letter with a mixture of honesty, warmth and good sense, which does her great credit:

To express what I feel at this moment would be quite impossible. I will therefore only say that in making the acknowledgement of regard I now make for
you, I am conscious of a degree of happiness of which 'til now I had no idea.

It is indeed my earnest wish to see you, besides the pleasure it must give me
to meet again an early and truly valued friend, I do not think it fair to engage
you before you are quite positively certain that I am indeed the woman you
would have for a companion, a friend for life. In so many years I may be much
more changed than I am myself conscious of. If when we have met you can
tell me with the same sincerity which has ever distinguished you through life,
that you do not repent having written the letter I am now answering, I shall
be most happy. That I should ever have been the cause of your suffering
anything like mortification, distresses me. That it may be the last time I shall
ever give you pain is the earnest wish of C.D.P.[21]

Poor Kitty – the marriage was doomed from the start, for the different paths
she and Arthur had taken since 1793 had created a vast gulf between them. He
had succeeded in a hard world, gaining self-assurance, ambition and professional pride; public affairs had absorbed him almost entirely. She had lost her
youthful sparkle, gaiety and confidence, had come to fear rather than enjoy the
gossip of society, and hoped to find 'a companion, a friend for life' with whom
she could share domestic pleasures.

Kitty's hopes and fears are easy to understand, but Arthur Wellesley's
motives remain a puzzle. His letters suggest that the romantic passion, which
he had felt in 1793, had never completely died; but his actions raise doubts.
Instead of racing to Dublin to embrace his beloved, to keep her company and
build on the foundations of happy union with shared conversation and experience, he kept away for another six months, pursuing his career and other interests. He was genuinely busy – the eighteen months following his return from
India were some of the most varied and active in his life – but his reluctance to
make time for Kitty, even at the outset of the marriage, raises doubts about the
depth and nature of his feelings. Was it simply that after so many years in India
he had become thoroughly selfish, and took for granted that the demands of
his career should have absolute priority? Or did he marry Kitty because he
wanted to marry someone, because he knew and liked her, and trusted in her
good sense, equating this with a willingness to subordinate her interests to his?
Yet he was a man who admired and enjoyed the company of intelligent, strong-
minded women, who, while they might flatter him, would not do so uncritically. With his fame and fortune he could have come home and married a
fresh-faced beauty fifteen years his junior. Instead he chose to renew his suit
for a woman of his own age whom he remembered as cutting a figure in the
vice-regal court in Dublin while disdaining its frivolity, for being well-read as

well as gay, and for teasing him gently. The romantic story that when someone warned him that he would find her much altered he replied, 'he did not care; it was her mind he was in love with, and that could not alter', is not so improbable after all.[22] But alter it had, and so had his; she tried too hard to please him, and he did not try hard enough.

At the same time that Arthur Wellesley was clearing the path to his marriage, he was also moving to defend Lord Wellesley's reputation. In his first months home he discussed the Indian question with Castlereagh, Camden and Pitt, who praised Lord Wellesley's achievements 'in the strongest and handsomest terms', but doubted the wisdom of seeking a parliamentary vote explicitly approving the Maratha War. And he visited Lord Buckingham at Stowe, a visit that he described as a 'bore', but where he made a good impression on his old patron. Buckingham, Grenville and their connection had not followed Pitt when he returned to office in 1804, but had made an unlikely but durable alliance with Fox and the Whigs. Arthur and his brothers evidently inclined towards Pitt and the ministers in power, but they knew that Lord Wellesley's oldest friendship and strongest political ties were with Lord Grenville. They could not say which side Lord Wellesley would favour on his return from India, and it was probably best for him not to commit himself until the controversy over his conduct in India had been resolved. When Lord Wellesley returned to England in January 1806 he found that his connections both with Pitt's government and with the Buckingham–Grenville wing of the Opposition had been refreshed and revived by his brother Arthur's activity, while he remained free to choose which old friend he would support, and which he would disappoint.[23]

Arthur Wellesley's own political connections benefitted greatly from this work for his brother. Within a few months of his return from India he was personally known to at least four Cabinet ministers, including the Prime Minister and the Secretary of State for War and the Colonies: Pitt, Castlereagh, Camden and Westmorland. Old contacts from his youth in Ireland were renewed on a fresh basis which took account of his Indian experience and success. His brother William was a junior minister in the government, while he was also well known to Lord Hobart (now Earl of Buckinghamshire), to the Marquess of Buckingham, and, at least by repute, to Lord Grenville. Only the Foxite Whigs among the leading political groups were unrepresented among his political friends.

He could not boast such good connections in the army. Unlike many officers he did not have a father, grandfather or uncle who had served in the army and left a ready-made network of supporters. Cornwallis was back in India, and besides, was no great friend to any of the Wellesleys. General Harris had effectively retired and was engaged in a battle of his own with the East India Company over the Seringapatam prize money, which would lead to some political cooperation; but he had no influence in the Horse Guards, and Wellesley had in any case far surpassed his achievement. Wellesley had no connection with any of the leading soldiers or military cliques of the day. He was not one of Abercromby's circle; he was scarcely known to David Dundas; and he did not belong to the influential group of rising young officers who prided themselves on being 'scientific soldiers', and who were inclined to assume that he was an aristocratic amateur whose success was the result of political favour. The Duke of York saw him – once – and was civil, but asked him nothing about the military position in India.[24] Nonetheless the Horse Guards did not neglect him completely. On 27 November he was formally appointed Major-General on the staff in Great Britain (backdated to 30 October) with the right to employ one paid aide-de-camp.[25] He was given command of a brigade of three battalions, the 3rd, 8th and 36th Foot, stationed at Deal, and was viewed as a suitable officer to be employed on active operations.

An opportunity for foreign service appeared almost immediately when the government decided to send a large army to Hanover to support the allies against Napoleon. The first contingent of troops sailed before the end of October, but gales delayed others and Arthur Wellesley's brigade did not reach Bremerhaven on the Weser until after Christmas, after a very rough passage. They were met with the news that Napoleon had defeated the Austrian and Russian armies at Austerlitz on 2 December in the greatest of all his victories. Austria then sued for peace while the Russians withdrew the remnants of their army and the Prussians staged a hasty diplomatic *volte face*. There was clearly no role for the British army to play, and in February Wellesley's brigade was back in England.[26]

It must have felt strange to Wellesley to return to the banks of the Weser almost exactly eleven years since he had seen them at the end of his miserable first campaign, and to reflect that despite all that had happened since, he only appeared to be a few rungs higher on the ladder. He was now a Major-General commanding three battalions, rather than a lieutenant-colonel commanding one – and this as a thirty-six-year-old, not a youngster of twenty-five. It was enough to make a less ambitious man than Arthur Wellesley ponder. Fortunately for his morale on 30 January the Duke of York appointed him colonel of the 33rd, following the death of Lord Cornwallis in India. It was a well-earned and singularly appropriate compliment, for Wellesley retained a strong feeling for the regiment. He had felt rather aggrieved at not being given a regiment sooner, but the colonelcy of the 33rd meant much more than that of a regiment with which he had no personal association. And the money was welcome, for colonelcies were lucrative, and for the moment at least, Wellesley felt rich.[27]

On 7 January 1806, while Arthur Wellesley was still in Hanover, his brother Richard returned to England from India. Political observers had speculated about Lord Wellesley's return for months, with a common view being that Pitt would offer him the Foreign Office, although Lady Bessborough had suggested that he might find the vice-regal lodge in Dublin a suitable half-way house between his Indian magnificence and the mundane reality of life as a private citizen.[28] But by the time Wellesley reached London Pitt's health had deteriorated sharply; there was only time for an affecting final interview before Pitt died on 23 January. The surviving ministers, knowing the weakness of their position, refused the King's wish that they attempt to carry on, and George III had to bow to the inevitable. He summoned Lord Grenville and commissioned him to form a broadly-based ministry, knowing that this would include the Whigs and their leader, Charles James Fox, whom he had loathed for years. So Wellesley's oldest friend and political ally became prime minister, and Wellesley had no hesitation in offering his full support to save the country, and urging that the new government include some of the departing Pittites as well as representatives of all the other major political factions.[29] It is clear that Wellesley expected to be offered a senior post in Grenville's Cabinet, and would have accepted it eagerly; although given the long exclusion of the Whigs from office and the number of other influential claimants, he may have been disappointed.[30] But before this question could even be discussed, an obscure member of Parliament, James Paull, gave notice of a motion to call for papers on which to base an investigation of Lord Wellesley's government of India.

Grenville promised that he would use the full weight of his position as prime minister, and all his family's political influence, to defend Lord Wellesley, but he knew that he could not promise the support of the Whigs. They had played a leading role in the prosecution of Warren Hastings on his return from India twenty years earlier, and Fox had privately condemned Wellesley's 'abominable conduct'. It would be political suicide to begin a government with the Cabinet sharply divided over the conduct of one of its members, and the expected offer of a senior position never came. In return, many members of the government who might otherwise have encouraged Paull in his campaign held back.[31]

James Paull was a curiously inconsequential figure to cause such trouble. He had made a fortune at Lucknow by the time he was barely thirty, then returned home and gambled it away in the space of a few months. Undaunted, he returned to India, where he was well received by Lord Wellesley, who helped him re-establish himself at Lucknow. Paull made a second fortune in just a couple of years, but left in 1804 with a grievance against the Governor-General, who had put an end to private trading at Lucknow. According to Hickey, Paull was never 'held in much estimation or respect in the English community in Bengal', and Wellesley dismissed as beneath his notice the 'acts of so contemptible, insignificant and debased a character'.[32] He arrived back in England in February 1805 and by May was MP for Newtown in the Isle of Wight.

Although Paull was yet to make any specific allegations against Lord Wellesley, his attacks were dangerous for several reasons. He could appeal to all the old enemies of Hastings – men who generally had little sympathy with the directors of the East India Company, and would not have supported them in an attack on Wellesley. He could not be readily bought off or silenced, for his motivation was, and remains, unclear. And he could work upon a general feeling of unease about what Lord Wellesley had done in India: there had been too many wars, too many annexations; the expansion of the Company's territory, and its debt, had been too rapid; and Monson's defeat seemed to show that the critics had been right in forecasting disaster. This unease remained superficial; few Members of Parliament and even fewer ministers knew much about India or took a serious interest in it. For years this had worked in Wellesley's favour, giving him great freedom to pursue his policies, but now it counted against him, for he could not persuade people even to listen attentively to his arguments; and no wonder, for so much else of even greater importance was happening much closer to home. Even Arthur Wellesley, with his interest in India, did not have the time to read the enclosures his friend Malcolm sent him from India.[33]

Lord Wellesley realised that he could not depend entirely on Grenville for his defence and that the struggle would be on two fronts: in the Commons, and guarding his reputation in the eyes of the wider public. His supporters made an ostentatious show of their strength with a grand dinner for more than 200 guests held in his honour on 20 March 1806. The guests included many leading politicians: Buckingham, Sidmouth, Castlereagh, Camden, Bathurst and Charles Abbot, the Speaker of the Commons.[34] Wellesley also established an office in London staffed with clerks to handle the correspondence and business resulting from the campaign. Friends wrote pamphlets in his defence, which were distributed in large numbers free of charge by being given to Members of Parliament and scattered around the principal taverns and coffee-houses of London. Wellesley consulted his lawyer, William Garrow, about instituting proceedings against Paull, whose rhetorical attacks in the press had reached an extraordinary level of vituperation, accusing the former Governor-General of nothing less than rape, pillage and murder. But Garrow advised that a court case might drag on for years as witnesses were summoned from India, and would provide Paull with a perfect platform for his attacks. Instead Wellesley turned to the gutter himself and employed a disreputable hack, Henry Redhead Yorke, to retaliate directly to Paull's denunciations. Later in the year, Arthur Wellesley encouraged his brother to gain influence in a more respectable paper, the pro-Grenville *Oracle*, by lending a large sum of money to its editor, Peter Stuart. 'It appears that the Newspapers have at last made such progress in guiding what is called publick opinion in this Country, that no man who looks

to publick station can attain his objects without a connection with and assistance from some of the Editors. It is necessary therefore that you should form a
connection of this description.'[35] The *Oracle's* overriding commitment to the
Grenvilles was a disadvantage, but all the existing papers had some political
connection, and the risk and expense of gaining one that was wholly submis-
sive to Lord Wellesley's direction would be excessive. None of this
was cheap; Lord Wellesley later claimed, possibly with some exaggeration, to
have spent £30,000 on his defence. It was also an important education in the
arts of extra-parliamentary politics for his brother Arthur, who was active as
Wellesley's lieutenant in organising the campaign. It is hardly surprising that he
developed a cynical view of politics.[36]

Meanwhile in Parliament Paull had simply called for more and more papers
while hinting to the House that he would soon be ready to present a formal
accusation against Lord Wellesley. This placed Wellesley's friends in an
awkward position: they could not resist the call for papers without appearing
to be attempting a cover-up, but nor could they press for an immediate decision while the evidence was still being gathered. A dispute between the government and the East India Company over the nomination of Cornwallis's
successor led its directors to give their active support to Paull, while independent MPs, who were not necessarily hostile to Wellesley, were not yet ready
to declare in his favour.[37] The most active defenders of Lord Wellesley were
Buckingham's son Lord Temple, and Thomas Wallace, an independent Pittite
with a long-standing interest in Indian affairs. Fox remained evasive, vaguely
hostile, but noncommittal, squeezed between his loyalty to Grenville, his own
principles, the opinion of his followers, and his desire to see his old friend
Lauderdale become the new Governor-General.[38]

Lord Grenville, probably in response to a request from Lord Wellesley,
offered to use the government's influence to find a seat in Parliament for Arthur
Wellesley. Sir Arthur hesitated, for despite his brother's close friendship with
Lord Grenville and his own old connection with Buckingham, he felt closer to
the Pittites in opposition than to the government with its mixture of Grenvilles,
Sidmouths and Whigs. Only a few weeks before he had written to John
Malcolm, '*We* are not actually in opposition, but we have no power',[39] and now
he refused to accept Grenville's offer without first consulting Castlereagh.
Unfortunately Wellesley's letter does not appear to have survived, but the reply
came back at once: 'As far as I can venture, as an old and very sincere friend, to
express an opinion, I think you cannot permit yourself a moment to hesitate in
accepting Lord Grenville's proposal. Your presence in the House may be of the
utmost service to your brother, and you must feel that this consideration is and
ought to be conclusive.'[40] So Arthur Wellesley accepted. The Treasury found a
place as law clerk in the Home Office for Thomas Davis Lamb, one of the MPs

for Rye and son of the family that dominated the politics of that ancient borough. Lamb resigned from Parliament and, on 1 April 1806, Sir Arthur Wellesley, KB, was elected member for Rye at a cost of £367 17s, most of which was spent on an extravagant election dinner for the freemen, their wives and families, although the poor of the town also received a distribution of £50.[41]

There was nothing unusual in a serving soldier being elected to Parliament in 1806; Wellesley was one of many men for whom the worlds of war and politics were closely aligned. Both officers and MPs were first and foremost gentlemen, part of the mainstream of British society, not detached from it in a partially closed caste of their own. Roughly 2,000 men were members of Parliament between 1790 and 1820, and of these about 400 had been or were officers in the regular army, and another 100 were in the navy. In other words one-quarter of the Commons were, or had been, officers; and most of them were serving at the time of their election. Most of the British officers who distinguished themselves during the Revolutionary and Napoleonic Wars were also Members of Parliament including Sir Ralph Abercromby, Gerard Lake, Sir John Moore, Thomas Graham, Thomas Picton, Robert Craufurd, Brent Spencer, William Carr Beresford, Lord William Bentinck, William and Henry Clinton, Lowry Cole, Stapleton Cotton, Rowland Hill, Alexander, Charles and John Hope, Charles Stewart, Edward Paget and many more. (The list of distinguished officers who were *not* MPs would be considerably shorter, but would include Leith, Le Marchant, Sherbrooke, Edward Pakenham and, of course, the senior officers of the King's German Legion such as Charles and Victor Alten.)[42]

Officers served in Parliament for many reasons: some were wealthy landowners or sons of a family that had traditionally filled a seat in Parliament; some were no longer interested in active service and were primarily politicians, such as Pitt's friend Lord Mulgrave, who held a variety of Cabinet posts; but others entered Parliament in the hope of coming to the attention of ministers and receiving favour either in the form of a lucrative sinecure or of active employment. Many soldiers had important political connections: Robert Craufurd was the protégé of William Windham, Secretary for War and the Colonies in Grenville's government; Stapleton Cotton's interests were championed with more energy than discretion by his brother-in-law, the ultra-Tory Duke of Newcastle; Charles Stewart was Castlereagh's half-brother; and William Carr Beresford was the illegitimate son of the Marquess of Waterford, the head of a family whose determined pursuit of the fruits of Irish patronage made it 'notorious for arrogance, intolerance, and greed'.[43]

Arthur Wellesley went into Parliament to defend his brother and protect his family's reputation. He felt little enthusiasm for the task, describing it as 'a most difficult and unpleasant game ... in the extraordinary state of the parties'.[44] Nonetheless the move undoubtedly assisted his career. Looking back in 1813 from the foot of the Pyrenees he told John Malcolm: 'Although I had long been in habits of friendship with the public men of the day, and had some professional claims to public notice when I returned to England, I believe I should have been but little known, and should not be what I am, if I had not gone into Parliament.'[45] Not only did it give him a more prominent place in the minds of ministers, it also introduced him to potential enemies, often with beneficial results. For example, in 1808 when the outcry over the Convention of Cintra was at its height, J.W. Ward, then a maverick young Whig, wrote:

> I shall be amazingly glad if Wellesley really comes out of it quite clean. For the sake of the British name one wishes that the glory of the man who won the battle of Vimeira should not be tarnished. Besides, he is a person of such pleasing manners and gentlemanlike conduct that it is impossible to know him, however slightly, or even to have sat in the same assembly with him, without feeling interested in his favour.[46]

On the other hand, this added prominence meant that his role in any controversy would attract more attention than if he had been an obscure officer, while most of his brother's political enemies extended their hostility to him.

Before Wellesley took his seat in Parliament, he had a different ceremony to attend in Dublin. Since his return from Hanover plans for his marriage had progressed with scarcely a hitch. The legal business of the marriage settlement would not be finalised until August, but Wellesley was remarkably generous; he settled £20,000, half the fortune he brought back from India, on Kitty. She contributed £4,000 (with a further £2,000 to come on her mother's death). All this capital was held in trust to provide a secure income for Kitty and her children if Wellesley died or proved a wastrel. The trustees were Gerald Wellesley, Edward Pakenham and the family solicitors.[47]

Unfortunately time was more precious to Wellesley than money. He arrived in Dublin with Gerald on 8 April and saw Kitty for the first time in twelve years. (There is no good evidence for the story that he whispered to Gerald, 'She is grown d____ ugly, by Jove!'[48] any more than there is of Kitty's first reaction to the changes wrought by the years, and the Indian climate, on *his* appearance.) Two days later they were married by Gerald in the Longfords' drawing room, in Rutland Square, Dublin. Three days after that Arthur headed back to London by express coach, leaving Gerald to escort Kitty at a more sedate pace. It was, obviously, absurd. A separation of a dozen years could not be washed away in five weeks, let alone five days, and not one bride (or groom, if the circumstances were reversed) in a million would fail to resent the lack of attention and consideration in the proceedings.

Kitty had insisted that the engagement be kept secret with the result that when news of the marriage became known it caused a minor sensation. Not that Arthur Wellesley or Kitty Pakenham were figures of much consequence in London society, but their story seemed wonderfully romantic – how young love had triumphed over years of separation and disappointment and finally achieved a happy ending. Kitty was presented at Court soon after she reached London, and found Queen Charlotte full of curiosity: 'But did you really never write *one* letter to Sir Arthur Wellesley during his long absence?' 'No, never, Madam.' 'And did you never think of him?' 'Yes, Madam, very often.' The Wellesleys attended some of the grand parties that marked the height of the London season, but were unsettled, for the house Arthur had taken at 11 Harley Street was not ready, and before the end of May, less than two months after her marriage, Kitty suspected that she was pregnant.[49]

Wellesley took his seat in Parliament in April and threw himself at once into his brother's defence. His youthful experience in the Irish Parliament must have been a great help both in calming his nerves and in making him familiar with the procedure of the House. He made his maiden speech on 18 April and, like most of the several dozen which followed over the next three months, it was not a sustained, set-piece oration, but a short contribution to debate, in which he challenged his opponents to make good their charges, and used his personal experience of India to give weight to his arguments.[50] Lord Wellesley's friends continued to press Paull to bring forward his accusations as definite charges, so that judgment could be made and Lord Wellesley cleared. Late in April Paull obliged, outlining his first detailed charge: that Lord Wellesley had extorted money from the Nabobs of Oudh, Furrukabad and Arcot, and that he had unlawfully squandered the Company's money on his own luxury and ostentation. But no sooner had Paull done so than his attack broke down, for he had failed to follow the correct procedure and few of the papers he had already demanded were relevant to these particular accusations. A month of fruitless activity followed in which the accusations were given much publicity without being put to the test. On 28 May Paull renewed the charges in a new form, following the correct procedure, and including the sensational allegation that both Richard and Henry Wellesley were personally implicated in murder.[51] This probably did Paull's cause considerable harm – only a few radicals on the wilder fringes of the Whig party were willing to follow him down that road – but it at least ensured the attention of the House. A meeting of Wellesley's supporters agreed that they could not oppose the taking of evidence, although they determined to ensure that the inquiry would be made by the Commons and would be resolved quickly. Fortunately the directors of the East India Company were distancing themselves from Paull and were seeking a compromise with the government over the appointment of the new Governor-General. On the other hand, Fox remained noncommittal; Arthur Wellesley sensed that he would certainly prove adverse to Lord Wellesley, but could not predict exactly what line he would follow.[52]

On 18 June 1806 the House moved into committee and began taking evidence on Paull's charges. A succession of witnesses was called, beginning with Sir John Shore (now Lord Teignmouth) and including many other old hands from India, most of whom had felt the lash of Lord Wellesley's contempt at some time or other. With some exceptions the inquiry went well for Wellesley, and his supporters won votes on procedural questions by a comfortable majority. A crucial point came when Arthur Wellesley demanded that the House summon Captain Salmond, the former military auditor from Bengal. Paull, evidently taken by surprise, opposed the motion, but was defeated and Salmond coolly testified that Lord Wellesley's military administration was highly economical 'inasmuch as it was calculated to support the greatest number of men at the least possible expense'. That such evidence was accepted with a straight face was a clear sign that the mood of the House was swinging strongly in favour of the Wellesleys.[53]

On 4 July Lord Temple moved to bring on a vote on the question. This should have been the moment of Lord Wellesley's vindication and the permanent discrediting of Paull's accusations. However, something went wrong, although the full story is not clear. Spencer Perceval, a leading Pittite lawyer who had shown little interest in the case up until now, suddenly and inexplicably supported Paull's pleas for more time and further documents. And, more inexplicably still, when Temple tried to disregard Perceval and pressed for a vote, William Wellesley-Pole publicly disowned him. The result was chaos among Wellesley's supporters and great indignation on the part of Temple, who felt that he had been placed in a false position and humiliated by the very people he had been trying to help – although a sympathetic observer, George Canning, declared that Temple had mishandled the business. The opportunity for a resolution that session had been lost, and a cloud remained over Lord Wellesley. Nonetheless Paull's performance had made him few friends, the sting had gone out of the attack and the threat of impeachment had effectively disappeared.[54]

A few days later, on 10 July, Arthur Wellesley rose and delivered a long, carefully composed speech on the finances of the East India Company. His purpose was to show that the Company remained prosperous despite the enormous increase in its debt under Lord Wellesley's stewardship. It was late in the session, when attendances were traditionally thin, and the subject was doubly unappealing – the House had little taste for finance, or for India, let alone Indian finance – so it is probable that the audience for Wellesley's speech was

small and inattentive. Nonetheless he was evidently pleased by his performance (or determined not to waste the work he had put into its preparation) for
he published it as a pamphlet of fifty-six pages. One cannot imagine that many
copies were sold, or that many of those were actually read, but it was another
shot fired in Lord Wellesley's defence, while Arthur Wellesley's confidence in
handling a technical subject far removed from his professional expertise may
not have gone unnoticed.

With Parliament in recess, Major-General Wellesley took command of a
brigade of infantry quartered near Hastings. The task was undemanding, for
there was little prospect of Napoleon endeavouring to follow in William the
Conqueror's steps of 740 years previous. The Grande Armée was scattered
through southern Germany and the French emperor was turning his attention
towards Prussia, while keeping Britain and Russia engaged in fruitless peace
talks. According to Colonel Gurwood, who edited Wellesley's despatches in the
1830s, a friend asked at this time how he could endure being reduced to the
quiet command of a brigade of infantry when he had led armies of 40,000 men.
Wellesley is supposed to have replied:

> For this plain reason, I am *nimmukwallah*, as we say in the East; that is, I have
> eat[en] the King's salt, and, therefore, I conceive it to be my duty to serve with
> unhesitating zeal and cheerfulness, when and wherever the King or his
> government may think proper to employ me.[55]

Some of Wellesley's admirers have been tempted to take this statement as the
key to his character, and have constructed on its foundations the image of a
man dedicated to the stern, self-sacrificing pursuit of duty. This was certainly
an image he liked to project both at this time and, even more, in later life when
he was extremely conscious of the need to act as was becoming of the Duke of
Wellington. It represents his sense of how he *ought* to behave – the private
model or pattern to which he aspired, even if he did not always achieve it in
practice. For there are problems in reconciling this ideal with Wellesley's actual
conduct. On several occasions when he attempted to follow the call of duty
against his own inclination, the result was conflict, turmoil and then a collapse
in his health which resolved the dilemma: his return to the Deccan in late 1804
and his subordination to Baird at Bombay in 1802 being only the most obvious
examples. Nor is 'unhesitating zeal and cheerfulness' a good description of his
relationship with superiors at any time in his career, including his correspondence with his political masters when he was serving in the Peninsula. Yet he *did*
have an unusually strong sense of duty. This was an age when senior officers
would often decline a command without any sense of shame because it did not

suit their private comfort or convenience. Wellesley by contrast was almost invariably ready to serve anywhere, at any time. Two months after his marriage he wrote to the Duke of York's military secretary to deny emphatically a suggestion that he would be reluctant to return to India as Commander-in-Chief of the Madras army, and this was wholly in character.[56] Both ambition and a sense of duty contributed to this eagerness, but the strongest motive was probably the desire to be active, to employ his skills and to do the job properly, for he had acquired in India an inexhaustible confidence in his ability to accomplish anything to which he turned his hand.

There was little danger that Arthur Wellesley would be left languishing for long in obscurity at Hastings. Already in May he had been consulted by Windham and Grenville on the possibility of employing sepoys to help garrison the Cape of Good Hope, thus releasing some of the British troops employed there, and on the feasibility of an attack on Mauritius, which was still held by the French.[57] Then, on 13 September, remarkable news reached London. The adventurous Sir Home Popham RN had persuaded Baird to lend him some troops from the garrison of the Cape and had taken them across the Atlantic under the immediate command of Colonel Beresford and captured Buenos Aires. The ease of the victory and the enthusiastic welcome given to Beresford's men by most of the local population fired the imagination of a British public sickened by the endless war with France. Europe might be a lost cause, but might not an alternative be found in the vast untapped wealth and lucrative markets of Spanish America? Even habitually cautious ministers were caught up in the excitement of the moment as they saw a whole range of intractable problems dissolve, as if by a magic cure. Reinforcements were prepared as quickly as possible and a variety of plans produced to exploit the opportunity.

Grenville was eager to give the command of the force at Buenos Aires to Sir Arthur Wellesley, telling Windham: 'I have so very high opinion of his talents and military knowledge, and particularly of his powers of exciting spirit and confidence in his troops, which I have heard so very strongly stated by indifferent persons, that I am very desirous of his being employed there if the scale of our operations be large enough for him.'[58] And he asked Wellesley to comment on a scheme for an attack on Mexico which would require a detachment of the troops at Buenos Aires to circumnavigate the globe collecting reinforcements from the Cape of Good Hope and India (4,000 sepoys) before capturing Manila and sailing across the Pacific to land on the west coast of Mexico at the same time as an expedition from the Caribbean attacked it from the east.[59] Wellesley responded to this overambitious proposal with remarkable tact and good sense in a series of cool, clear memoranda, which used the same ingredients to produce a plan that stood a fair chance of success. He began by pointing out that the tropical seasons and prevailing winds made the attack on

Manila incompatible with that on Mexico. In any case, he argued, Manila would fall automatically if Mexico were captured, while it would be quite impossible to coordinate the two operations. Given this, he preferred to concentrate the British force in the attack from the east, and to regard the sepoys as a reinforcement to help garrison Mexico after it had been conquered. He also reduced the number of sepoys from 4,000 to 3,000, commenting that it was unlikely that more would volunteer or would be needed.[60] Additional memoranda written over the next few weeks later added more detail about the main attack, which Wellesley recommended should be delayed until December of the following year so as to minimise the risks of storms on the coast and ill-health to the troops once they landed. He immersed himself in the practical details of the proposed operation and consulted sea captains and read travellers' accounts to identify the most suitable points for a landing.[61]

Meanwhile war had broken out between France and Prussia, but before the British government could react, Napoleon had crushed the Prussian army at Jena-Auerstädt (14 October 1806) and taken Berlin. Fighting continued further east where the Prussians were joined by the Russians, but the ministers in London felt that they could do little and were inclined to despair of allies who had an insatiable appetite for subsidies yet were quite unable to face the French in the field. Latin America lost none of its allure by the comparison.

While Arthur Wellesley was working on his Mexican plans and Napoleon was overrunning Prussia, Lord Grenville struggled to reshape his ministry after the death of Fox on 13 September. There was again some speculation that Lord Wellesley might join the Cabinet, and he was eager to do so, but Grenville would not risk alienating the Whigs and preferred to promote his own brother Tom, and Fox's nephew and political heir Lord Holland, while giving the Foreign Office to the new Whig leader, Charles Grey, Lord Howick. He also decided to strengthen the position of the ministry by calling an election.[62]

The arrangement by which Arthur Wellesley sat for Rye only lasted until the dissolution of Parliament, so he needed to find another seat. Grenville suggested that he stand for Portarlington in Ireland, which the borough proprietor placed at the disposal of the government for 'the usual consideration'; but something went awry – according to the Irish Secretary 'more from trick than accident'.[63] The result was that Arthur Wellesley was left without a seat in the new Parliament, and Lord Wellesley wrote to Grenville 'in great alarm' fearing that the attack on him would be renewed 'from which it might be very injurious that he [Arthur] should be absent'. Grenville acted quickly and on 15 January 1807 Arthur Wellesley was returned for the seat of Mitchell in Cornwall, £4,000 being paid to the proprietor, Sir Christopher Hawkins, who controlled a string of seats and was thought to be aiming for a peerage.[64]

Lord Wellesley sought to use the general election to create a small faction of his own in Parliament. As well as Arthur and William (who was safe in his Queen's County seat, quite independent of his brother), Wellesley hoped to secure the return of Henry and half a dozen friends and connections from India. Most of these were soldiers who had returned home with comfortable fortunes and who now sought election partly from loyalty to Wellesley and partly to advance their social position. Arthur Wellesley played an active part in managing their campaign and must bear some responsibility for its almost total failure – although it is not clear whether the principal problem was lack of experience, insufficient money, or ineptitude. None of the Wellesley candidates (except William Wellesley-Pole) gained seats in the election, although several entered Parliament in the following few months.[65]

Lord Wellesley could draw some consolation for this failure in the defeat of James Paull, who had rashly stood as a radical candidate for Westminster, then one of the most open and hotly contested seats in the country. He petitioned Parliament against his defeat, and stood again in 1807, but was again defeated. He quarrelled with his radical supporters, lost heavily gambling, and committed suicide on 15 April 1808 leaving large debts behind him. Lord Wellesley is said to have remarked that Paull 'could not have died by a more ignoble hand'.[66]

Wellesley's brigade of infantry was ordered to Ireland in December, but he either did not accompany his men or returned at once to England. In January and again in February he was Lady Salisbury's guest at Hatfield, enjoying the hunting. He was there when, on 3 February 1807, Kitty gave birth to a son, who would be christened Arthur Richard.[67] He did not hurry home to see his wife and child, but, given the manners of the age, this was not particularly significant. The few letters that survive from Arthur to Kitty from this time are dry, businesslike and inconsequential, but this may be why they survived when more intimate letters, if they ever existed, were burnt after her death.[68] In other words it would be dangerous to make a bold assumption about his feelings for her at this time, although we can say that he certainly treated her with a lack of consideration, and made it quite clear that he would pursue his career in any corner of the globe without reference to her interests or wishes.

Later that February Wellesley's planned expedition to Mexico was threatened when Windham conceived the idea of using the troops in the meantime to capture Venezuela. Wellesley responded with a calm, careful memorandum, which argued that it would be impossible to launch such an attack before the rains began in May, and that the rains, and the sickness they brought with them, would last until November or December. This in itself would have been enough, but he proceeded to outline how an attack on Venezuela should be mounted, and the troops and equipment that would be needed, before casting doubt on the wisdom of any such operation (arguing that the country would require a substantial permanent garrison and any lasting increase in its prosperity depended on an extension of its agriculture, which in turn would require the importation of a large number of new slaves – but the government was on the point of outlawing the slave trade). It was typical of the breadth of his outlook which, from his first arrival in India, had extended far beyond the immediate requirements of military operations.[69]

Windham's idea was duly dropped, and the Mexican plan survived for the moment, but it remained vulnerable. Early in the new year reports had reached London that the inhabitants of Buenos Aires had risen up and forced Beresford and his men to capitulate. All other plans for operations in the Americas depended on reversing this misfortune and troops were collected from far and wide to be sent to Montevideo. Wellesley might have been given command of this army, but instead it was given to a more senior officer, Lieutenant-General John Whitelocke, apparently on the advice of the Duke of York.[70]

At the same time Wellesley was shocked by the news of a mutiny in the Madras army at Vellore. He discussed this with George Tierney, the Whig president of the Board of Control, with whom he got on well. They agreed that a clean sweep was needed at Madras, with both a new Commander-in-Chief and a new governor. Cradock's fate had been sealed for months – he had tendered his resignation in a huff after a series of disputes[71] – but now Lord William Bentinck would be recalled as well. Wellesley offered to replace both men, combining civil and military authority, or if this was deemed undesirable, to serve in either role. He was still keen on the Mexican scheme but 'every day affords a slighter hope that we shall be able to carry our plan into execution', and the situation in Madras required an urgent remedy. Although he had 'no particular desire to return to India, and no wish to stay there one moment longer than Government may think that I can be of service', he was confident that he was the right man for the job. He added that the Court of Directors would welcome his appointment and 'I am ready to set out at a day's notice'.[72]

Government did not move as quickly as Wellesley suggested, and it would be another month before detailed official reports describing what happened at Vellore would reach London. By then the ministry would be deep in a quite separate crisis of its own making, precipitated by its attempts to deceive the King over the extent of the concessions it proposed to extend to Catholic officers in the army. As a result, the government fell before the end of March and was replaced by a new, Pittite administration with the Duke of Portland at its head; and this new government had another, quite different, role in mind for Arthur Wellesley.

CHAPTER TWELVE

CHIEF SECRETARY FOR IRELAND
(1807)

O N 18 MARCH 1807 George III effectively dismissed Lord Grenville's government, and invited the members of Pitt's last administration to form a new ministry. Their leader was the Duke of Portland, a politician of vast experience, but who was worn out and ill in 1807, and who proved little more than a figurehead. The real strength of his government would lie in a generation of young ministers, including Canning, Castlereagh, Hawkesbury (the future Lord Liverpool) and Perceval. Their task would not be easy, for the Whigs were outraged at losing office so soon, and Parliament would need to be convinced that the inexperienced ministers were capable of governing the country without the leadership of a Pitt, a Fox or a Grenville.

The inclusion of Lord Wellesley in the Cabinet would have been particularly valuable, and on 21 March he was offered the Foreign Office; but after much hesitation he declined, unable to bring himself to break his old ties with Grenville. Within a few weeks he had repented of his folly and was hankering for office, but by then it was too late; the Cabinet could not be recast simply to suit his convenience.[1]

Wellesley's brothers – William, Henry and Arthur – were approached to join the government as ministers outside the Cabinet; they all accepted with little hesitation. Their inclusion signalled the support of the Wellesley family and its connections for the new administration, and reduced the risk of Lord Wellesley drifting into opposition, but they were also valued in their own right as capable men of business. William Wellesley-Pole took the onerous position of Secretary to the Admiralty, which in wartime involved an enormous amount of detailed administrative work. Grenville had considered offering him this position a few months before, describing him as 'eminently qualified . . . one of the most efficient men that ever filled the station he held at the Ordnance'.[2] His manner was unconciliatory and he was not generally popular, but Lord Mulgrave, the First Lord of the Admiralty whom he served, praised him highly when Pole was moved to another department in 1809: 'I make an immense Sacrifice to you in giving you Pole. His is the most quick, steady, intelligent, zealous & indefatigable Man of Business, I ever knew.'[3]

Henry Wellesley was appointed one of the two Secretaries to the Treasury. His colleague, William Huskisson, attended to the financial duties of the office, while Wellesley's role was that, later described as the 'patronage secretary', of attending to the interests of the government's supporters in the Commons, and ensuring that they were present in Parliament to give their vote on important questions. This task is now performed by the Whip's Office with much greater resources of both patronage and party discipline. A few years later a usually sharp-tongued diplomat described Henry Wellesley as 'one of the most amiable and gentlemanlike men I know',[4] and he soon became quite popular with Members of Parliament; but he disliked his duties, and the long hours of attendance when the House was sitting served to undermine his marriage. He made little contribution to debate and was not very successful in keeping the government's supporters up to the mark, resulting in disappointingly small majorities, which annoyed the senior ministers in the Commons. He talked of resignation in 1808 but remained unhappily in office until the spring of 1809, although it was now clear that diplomacy, not Parliament, was his forte.[5]

Arthur Wellesley was offered the position of Chief Secretary for Ireland on 26 March 1807. The Duke of Portland, writing to the King the previous evening, had declared that if he accepted, it would be 'a most fortunate event for the success of your Majesty's Administration', which was unusually strong language in a long letter that discussed many possible appointments.[6] The approach was made by Lord Hawkesbury who, as Home Secretary, would be the Cabinet minister responsible for Ireland in the new government. It is quite likely that Castlereagh had been singing Arthur Wellesley's praises behind the scenes, but there is no surviving evidence for this assumption, and besides, Wellesley was now well acquainted with several other members of the new ministry, including Canning and Perceval, as a result of the debates on Lord Wellesley's conduct in India.

Arthur Wellesley's only doubt in considering the office in Ireland was that this employment might prevent him being sent on active service; he saw the Duke of York and, having been reassured on this point, he accepted Hawkesbury's offer. The following day he wrote a letter to his brother explaining his reasons for taking office; he pointed to the hostility of the Whigs towards Lord Wellesley's policies in India to justify his support for the new ministry, and made it clear that he had been assured that, far from hampering his military career, his civil office would give him 'an additional claim to such employment'.[7] At first glance this suggests that Arthur Wellesley took office without consulting his elder brother, but this is most unlikely, and it is much more probable that this letter was written at Lord Wellesley's suggestion for him to show to Lord Grenville.[8] Neither brother wished to make an irrevocable break with the Grenville–Buckingham connection, and when the Marquess of Buckingham extended an olive branch later in the year, Arthur Wellesley responded with gratitude; his placatory letter mixes flattery with a justification of his acceptance of office that borders on the apologetic.[9] This was not without effect, for Buckingham retained warm feelings towards Arthur Wellesley, even when Lord Grenville became one of his sternest critics in both public and private.

In the years that followed, Arthur Wellesley continued to claim that he was 'no party man',[10] and to some extent this was true. He was primarily a soldier, and as a soldier was willing to serve a government of any complexion, while even as a politician he was not a particularly zealous partisan, being more interested in policy and good government than in scoring political points. But much the same could be said for many of his colleagues in the Portland government. The Pittites were essentially a party of government; they had no strong ideological glue to bind them together, and had been uncomfortable and disorientated in their brief period in opposition. On the contentious issues of the day Wellesley's views were those of a good Pittite, tending towards the conservative end of the broad spectrum included in the party, but underpinned by a strong sense of pragmatism and a willingness to compromise where necessary. There was nothing incongruous about his joining the Portland ministry in 1807, and his political allegiance, while always taking second place to his sense of a higher duty, would remain clear to all for the remaining forty-five years of his life.

Equally it seems probable that Wellesley accepted political office from a sense of duty and his pleasure in business and being actively employed, rather than from any secret political ambition. His distaste for the jobbery and corruption of Irish politics has been greatly exaggerated, but it is clear that he felt no eagerness to return to the land of his birth. In November 1805 he had written a letter to Olivia Sparrow, which reveals his attitude to the country:

You ask me whether I propose to be an Englishman or an Irishman. All countries are alike to me, who have been so much abroad and who have had as unsettled life as I have. But I acknowledge that I rather prefer England because my friends and relations reside there; because [Kitty's] reside there during a great part of the year; because you reside [t]here – and to tell you the truth, I must think that Ireland will not be a fit residence for any woman of this generation; and I acknowledge that if my profession should at any time call me away from her, which must be expected, I should feel the same kind of uneasiness about her, if she lived in Ireland, that I should at leaving her in a camp in the enemy's country.[11]

Wellesley's view was probably overly influenced by second-hand reports of the Irish Rebellion of 1798 and Emmet's conspiracy of 1803, but the experience of the next couple of years would do little to soften his opinion; when he drew up a will in July 1807 he expressed a wish that neither of his children should be brought up in Ireland or have any connection with it.[12]

As Chief Secretary for Ireland Arthur Wellesley served two masters simultaneously: the Home Secretary, Lord Hawkesbury, who was responsible for the government's policy towards Ireland, and the Lord Lieutenant of Ireland, who was considerably more than a vice-regal figurehead. The Act of Union had reduced the independence and power of the Irish government, but in 1807 the Lord Lieutenant and the Chief Secretary remained the principal players in Irish affairs, with the ministers in London determining the broad line of policy and playing a supervising and supporting role. Wellesley accepted the post of Chief Secretary before the new Lord Lieutenant was appointed. As head of Dublin society the Lord Lieutenant had to be a nobleman of some significance, and several were approached who declined, including Lord Clive. Finally Portland offered the position to the Duke of Richmond, who accepted it 'in the most becoming manner'.[13]

Richmond's appointment proved a happy chance for Arthur Wellesley. The two men were old acquaintances, perhaps even old friends, from Dublin days fifteen years before. They were both soldiers, although this was evidently coincidence rather than a deliberate policy (the other peers offered the Lord Lieutenancy were all civilians). Richmond was five years older than Wellesley and, as a fairly senior lieutenant-general, considerably his superior in the army, although he had seen little active service. He established a happy, productive alliance with Wellesley, which went far beyond professional cordiality into a warm friendship that included both their families. Given Wellesley's difficulties with military superiors throughout his career, this was no slight achievement, although it is unlikely that they could have operated so well on campaign unless Wellesley had first been made the senior officer.

It is important not to get the negotiations surrounding the accession of the Wellesleys to the government out of proportion; they were a significant family connection, but so were many others, and for a fortnight Portland and his colleagues were busy on a dozen similar fronts. Lord Harrowby and his brother Richard Ryder promised strong support, but would not take office. Lord Hardwicke favoured the opposition and his brother, Charles Yorke, lacked the courage to defy him. Canning prevented any overture being made to Lord Sidmouth, much to the regret of some of his colleagues, although others were quietly relieved. Lord Melville, somewhat to his chagrin, was not given the opportunity to decline office; nonetheless he rather grudgingly supported the government with all his immense influence in Scotland, and permitted his son,

Robert Dundas, to accept the position of President of the Board of Control, although not the seat in the Cabinet that was offered with it. Lord Lowther's wishes had to be considered, Lord Malmesbury consulted, and numerous former junior ministers had to be either encouraged or discouraged from buckling on their old harness. Lord Wellesley's refusal of office was one of several disappointments, but the new ministry that emerged was not short of talent and its members would dominate British politics for a generation.

Arthur Wellesley arrived in Dublin on 15 April after a rough passage from Holyhead. Richmond joined him four days later and they formally took over the reins of government, pleased to find that the country was relatively quiet. Wellesley's duties in his new post included defending the Irish government in the Imperial Parliament; steering Irish legislation through the Commons; and representing Irish interests and concerns to the British government, both when it was considering specifically Irish questions and when it considered general policies that had implications for Ireland. He oversaw the day-to-day administrative work of the Irish government, although fortunately much of this burden was borne by capable public servants, in particular the two under-secretaries, James Trail (head of the civil department) and Sir Edward Littlehales (head of the military department). He formulated policy on questions ranging from the defence of Ireland to paving the streets of Dublin, and had a part to play in the fashionable world of Dublin society. But by far the most time-consuming and demanding of his tasks was the distribution of government patronage.[14]

The first application came as early as 28 March, the day after Wellesley accepted the appointment. Mr Nevill wrote to express his 'great satisfaction' at the news (which he had heard from Castlereagh), to remind Wellesley of their old acquaintance, and to state his claim to be reinstated to the position of Teller of the Irish Exchequer from which he had been most unfairly dismissed by the previous government.[15] It was the first of a steady stream, which continued as long as Wellesley remained Chief Secretary, and then effortlessly diverted to his successor. Peers dusted off old promises dating back to the Act of Union (1801), and wrote to remind the new government of their claim to a higher title, or an honour, or that a brother should be made a bishop, or that the wants of some other relative or protégé be accommodated.[16] Respectable gentlemen wrote to ask that their son or nephew be given a commission in the army or navy, or, if this had already been done, that he be promoted, or given a better command, or transferred to a less unhealthy station. Ladies in distressed circumstances (or friends on their behalf) wrote asking for a small pension, sometimes as little as £20 a year, to alleviate their hardship and maintain their respectability. Clergymen wrote needing permission to exchange livings so as to be nearer family or friends, and enthusiasts wrote asking for support for their pet project, whether a school, an invention, a pamphlet or a play.[17]

Some of these requests could be dealt with easily. Wellesley wrote many letters to Lord Mulgrave at the Admiralty recommending young men (boys, really) as midshipmen, or drawing his attention to deserving officers who appeared overdue for promotion. Similarly, those wishing to join the army were recommended to Colonel J.W. Gordon, the Duke of York's military secretary, and if they did not mind serving in an unfashionable regiment or in a distant part of the world, they would become an ensign without needing to purchase their commission. But most requests were more difficult, for there were constraints on every side. Peerage promotions and honours were closely watched by the King, and besides, pleasing one such applicant would annoy two or three others who believed they had a superior claim. The large fund available for pensions was already almost wholly committed, leaving little available for even the most deserving new case, although Wellesley did ensure that his grandmother's impecunious old friends, the Ladies of Llangollen, were granted £50 per annum.[18] And, above all, there were not nearly enough government posts available to satisfy even half the well-supported applicants. The Union had significantly reduced the patronage available to the Irish government (especially the many valuable positions connected with the army such as commissaries, barrack masters, storekeepers and the like, which were now appointed from London), without in the least reducing the demand. After six months in Ireland Richmond declared: 'The patronage of Ireland is most extremely diminished. I can fairly say that there is hardly enough to carry on government.'[19] The problem was real, even though it is likely that, faced with insatiable demands, the Lord Lieutenant and Chief Secretary had always felt that their resources were totally inadequate.

The effective use of patronage lay at the heart of the government of Ireland in the early nineteenth century. Through it the ministers of the day rewarded the great landowners and gentry, and they in turn rewarded their dependents. It was Wellesley's task to decide whom to please and whom to disappoint given the significance of each grandee in a particular locality, and his attitude towards the government. He approached the task with clear-eyed, unsentimental realism; he had grown up watching the system at work as an aide-de-camp at Dublin Castle, and had felt the pain of repeated rejection when he had sought civil office in 1795–96. There is little reason to believe that he viewed the system with disdain or disgust, whatever he may have felt for the more audacious or outrageous applications he dealt with. He was not a radical, and probably viewed their denunciations of 'jobbery' and 'corruption' as so much cant, no better than Paull's attacks on Lord Wellesley's policies in India.

Before he left office in 1809 Wellesley drew up a long memorandum to guide his successors, which makes explicit the link between support for the ministry in Parliament and access to the government's patronage. Arranged alphabetically by the county they represented, the claims and connections of each Irish MP are dispassionately discussed. It begins:

> *Antrim Co: – Mr McNaghten*. Is brought in principally by the influence of Lord Hertford. Attends well and is a steady friend. Government are under an engagement to give him an office for life of £300 per annum, which was made at the period of the Union, and has been admitted by the Duke of Richmond. Lord Cornwallis was to have given him an office of this description and value, and had made an arrangement for it which was defeated by a trick of the late Lord Avonmore. Lord Castlereagh knows the whole story. Mr McNaghten has lately desired to have a pension for his life, of the value and instead of this office, but by Lord Hawkesbury's desire I have refused it.
>
> *The Hon. John O'Neill* [the other Member of Parliament for County Antrim] – is the brother of Lord O'Neill, supports Government and attends tolerably. I believe he is a Lieut-Colonel of Dragoons. The patronage of County Antrim should be distributed according to the recommendation of Lord Hertford and Lord O'Neill. It must be observed however that Lord Donegal will claim that of the town of Belfast.[20]

Antrim was fairly typical although the network of obligations was more complicated in some counties.

In cases where both members for a county supported the Opposition, Wellesley generally stated that its patronage was 'at the disposal of Government', although he would frequently add a rider that some particular supporter of the government in the district 'ought to be attended to in some degree in the disposal of it'. This left comparatively little patronage at the free and unhindered disposal of the Lord Lieutenant and his Chief Secretary, while every friend and relative they had naturally believed that some place or other could easily be found for their protégés, or their friends' protégés. Within a few months of taking office, Wellesley was approached by his mother, his wife's aunt, his sister and his eldest brother (twice), all recommending suitable candidates for undemanding positions. Lady Mornington, writing on 22 May, enclosed three letters that she had received with applications that she feared might bore him, but what else could she do but pass them on? This was tiresome but not altogether unreasonable. However, Wellesley's sister Anne was sharply snubbed when she urged the appointment of a Mr Marshall to the command of a Dublin packet. Arthur replied that not only was there no vacancy, but if one did occur 'I think it may be expected that the Duke of Richmond or I, who have been all over the world, have naval friends of merit, but not rich, to whom we may be desirous of giving such a provision'.[21]

Requests from William Wellesley-Pole were treated quite differently because they rested on his position as a large landowner and MP for Queen's County, and a member of the government, rather than upon fraternal affection. In his memorandum Arthur Wellesley had been unequivocal: 'Queen's Co ... The patronage of this county should be given to Mr Pole.'[22] An example of what this meant in practice came in early July when Lord Henry Moore asked to be given command of the Queen's County militia when Lord Castle Coote resigned. Wellesley advised Richmond that Moore had a good claim and that his appointment would please Lord Drogheda, 'but what passed at the last election shows clearly that Pole is the most powerful man in that county, and I should therefore recommend that this appointment may not be made without consulting his wishes, which I am sure will be in favour of Lord Henry Moore.'[23] Making clear to all concerned that Moore owed his appointment as much to Pole as to Drogheda was important in consolidating the influence of the former, confirming his newly dominant position in the county.

Both Richmond and Wellesley were highly conscious of the need to subordinate their private interests and friendships to the political needs of the government, but they did make a few exceptions to this rule.[24] Wellesley suggested that his brother Gerald be made a bishop of the Church of Ireland, but Hawkesbury vetoed this, expressing his determination to limit the influence of political considerations and personal favours on the composition of the Irish ecclesiastical bench.[25] This would not be the last time that Hawkesbury's scruples would deny Gerald Wellesley his mitre, and his attitude was part of a wider trend which, over the course of half a century (from, roughly, the 1780s to the 1830s) replaced the cheerful, unabashed opportunism and self-interest of the eighteenth century with Victorian morality and doctrines of merit and service. Arthur Wellesley's relationship to this transformation was curiously ambiguous, for he was simultaneously a product of the old approach (and generally comfortable with it, except when it led to inefficiency or dishonesty), and became, almost unwittingly, the archetype of the new, the very embodiment of incorruptible patriotism and subordination of personal desires to the stern dictates of duty.

Wellesley had little time to master the intricacies of Irish politics, for almost as soon as he arrived in Dublin, he was thrown into an election campaign. Portland's ministers had decided to go to the polls in May 1807 to strengthen their position in the Commons, and take advantage of the popular hostility provoked by Grenville's attempt to grant concessions to the Catholics. A second election in less than a year was unpopular with MPs who had to spend substantial sums indulging their voters even if their return was unopposed, while a severe contest in a large county such as Yorkshire might exhaust all but the greatest fortune. In Ireland the Chief Secretary's task in an election was openly partisan: to rally the government's supporters; to encourage uncertain patrons to support the ministry rather than the Opposition; to make promises and threats where necessary; and to watch the progress of all the doubtful contests. The work was highly detailed and personal, with little room for discussions of policy or questions of principle.[26] Wellesley was fairly confident in the beginning, but as the negotiations continued he began to lose heart and on 18 May warned Hawkesbury:

> We have a very difficult game to play in this country; and you must not be surprised if we should lose some of our elections. Notwithstanding that the objects to be attained by it are as numerous as ever, the patronage of the local government in Ireland has been very much diminished since the Union, and indeed I may say that at present it operates against the government in every instance. We have nothing to say to the army, the ordnance, the commissariat, the medical department, the barrack department, and the comptroller of army accounts; and the officers of the revenue, who by law ought not to interfere in elections, are against us in almost every instance.[27]

In the event, the hundred Irish members returned to the Commons included fifty-seven who generally supported the government, forty who belonged to the opposition, and three who were unpredictable; although it must be remembered that party ties were quite loose and many members wore their allegiance lightly. In the middle of 1808 Wellesley calculated that sixty-two of the Irish members now supported the government and only thirty-eight the Opposition. Only fourteen contests went to the ballot in 1807, although other tests of strength had been decided before voting began, and there were twenty-two new Members of Parliament. On the whole, this was not a bad result given the difficulties the government faced, and the speed with which Wellesley had to make his arrangements and master an unfamiliar subject.[28]

One of the new members was John Wilson Croker, a sharp-tongued Irish barrister and pamphleteer who had a knack for getting under the skin of his opponents, and who would play an important part in Conservative politics for most of the next half-century. Wellesley facilitated his election by arranging for him to receive £1,500 or £2,000 from the Privy Purse to cover part of his expenses. (Croker was not rich and had spent much of his own and his father's money on an unsuccessful contest in 1806.) It proved to be an excellent investment.[29]

Wellesley himself was returned as the government candidate for Tralee, but this was simply a temporary arrangement to keep the seat open, and he soon resigned it in favour of another government supporter. Henry Wellesley (who, as Secretary to the Treasury, was one of the election managers) arranged Arthur's election for an English seat: Newport on the Isle of Wight. An eighteen-month tenancy (until October 1808) was secured for which he would pay between £700 and £900; in the event he held the seat for almost two years, until April 1809. Newport had the advantage that his attendance at the poll was unnecessary; he was far too busy to leave Ireland, or he might have come in for Ipswich more cheaply, although not without a contest.[30] His fellow representative for Newport was the twenty-three-year-old Viscount Palmerston, who was entering Parliament for the first time, after two unsuccessful attempts to be elected one of the members for Cambridge University.

One notable aspect of the election in Ireland was the role played by the Catholic electors, and indeed by crowds of Catholics who lacked the vote. The ministers recognised this, and conceded that as a result some Irish MPs who would support them on most issues were bound to vote for any moves in favour of Catholic Emancipation.[31] More concerning was the case of Thomas Bligh, the member for County Meath who had told Castlereagh in London that he was inclined to support the government, but who, on returning to Ireland, was warned by Lord Fingall, the leader of the Catholics, that he would be vigorously opposed if he did not pledge himself to join the Opposition. Wellesley urged him to fight, but Bligh said that he could not afford a contest that he would be bound to lose. Wellesley then suggested that he decline to stand, publishing his reasons, but Bligh shrank from the controversy and asked to be absolved from his commitment to the government. Wellesley had the sense to give way with good grace and was rewarded, for Bligh, having been elected without fuss, proceeded to support the government, at least until the fall of the Portland ministry.[32]

Bligh's caution and the small number of other contests can be understood by the scenes being played out in Tipperary where John Bagwell, who had represented the county from 1801 to 1806, attempted to regain his seat. Bagwell was a protégé of Lord Westmorland, and his candidature had the blessing of the government. Wellesley did all he could to support him, despite having well-founded doubts of his chances of success. After the result, Wellesley told Hawkesbury:

> There never was anything equal to the violence of the priests and of the whole of the Roman Catholic body in the county of Tipperary. They have fomented serious riots to frighten Bagwell's freeholders and prevent them from going to the poll. The priests have inveighed against him from the altars, and have successfully endeavoured to prevail upon the Catholic tenantry to oppose the wishes of their landlords. Bagwell was supported by the whole property of the county; but in this contest property has no weight.[33]

Did he remember his speech in the Irish Parliament, fourteen years before, in which he had argued that Catholic voters would have a variety of interests like anyone else, and would not be directed how to vote by their priests? Now, as Chief Secretary, he was obliged to employ parties of dragoons to escort voters to the poll. Fortunately the Duke of York was not offended; instead the news appealed to his Hanoverian sense of humour as a fine example of the freedom of an Irish election.[34]

The hostility of the Catholic party in Ireland to the new government is not surprising. After all, Portland and his ministers had taken office to ensure that the King would not be forced to grant the Catholics concessions that he believed would violate his coronation oath. Yet the Cabinet included a broad range of opinion on the question, from Perceval's evangelical hostility to Catholicism, and the conservatism of Eldon and Hawkesbury, to Canning and Castlereagh who both followed Pitt's lead and favoured Catholic 'Emancipation', although not in the King's lifetime. This mixture of views and a preoccupation with other issues led the government to adopt a moderate policy in Ireland in the hope that the Catholics would remain reasonably quiet if not provoked. Soon after his arrival in Dublin, Wellesley took advantage of a meeting with Lord Fingall, one of the leaders of the Irish Catholics, to explain the ministry's intentions:

> I . . . told him that he was not to expect any farther concession; that the present government were determined not to recommend any to Parliament; but that the existing laws would be administered with mildness and good temper; and that the Roman Catholics would be considered by the government, in all arrangements in which the law allowed that they should be considered, in the same manner as the rest of His Majesty's subjects, according to their respective merits and claims.[35]

This policy proved relatively successful. The Irish Catholics and Whigs, while outraged at losing office so soon, were more inclined to squabble among themselves than unite against the new ministry. Endemic rural violence and disturbances continued (notably the 'Threshers') but did not worsen; and there was no rioting to greet Richmond's arrival as there had been the last time an openly pro-Catholic Lord Lieutenant had been displaced, twelve years earlier. But it shows how far even the defenders of the old Anglican confessional state had lost confidence that at the moment of their triumph they pursued a policy of moderation and conciliation in the hope of placating their enemies. No one seriously suggested a re-imposition of the penal laws or a repeal of the concessions granted to Catholics in 1793. Instead, the most that the champions of the Protestant Ascendancy could hope for was to hold the line against further

concessions and to enjoy the fruits of office a little longer. Opinion among the
political classes in Britain had turned, irrevocably as it proved, against sectari-
anism; and attempts to revive the Protestant cause through the Orange Order
and similar bodies proved counter-productive. During most of the eighteenth
century the Catholics won meagre concessions by proving their loyalty. In the
early 1790s they made far greater gains by threatening disloyalty. And even
after the 1798 uprising, London still insisted on forgiveness and clemency as
the only possible basis for a lasting settlement.

Wellesley appears to have accepted the government's policy completely and
to have been sincere in his assurances to Fingall. Certainly he shared the jaundiced English view of the more active Irish Protestants, describing them as
'those called "the loyal" in this country'.[36] He discouraged the Anglican clergy
of Dublin from organising an Address to congratulate the King on changing
his ministers, and the yeomanry from celebrating the anniversary of their
victory over the Irish rebels at Vinegar Hill in 1798.[37] Wellesley used his
meeting with Lord Fingall to ensure that his personal relations with his opponents were civil and free of rancour. He did not attempt, as some of his predecessors had done, to manipulate and control the Catholic party, preferring to
watch as an interested but detached observer the quarrels that engulfed it as a
younger and more radical generation challenged the aristocratic leadership of
Fingall and his friends.[38]

Not all Wellesley's efforts could be directed at quietening opposition; some
allies and followers had to receive their reward including a few 'red-hot'
Protestants such as John Giffard and Dr Duigenan (although not before Giffard
was warned to moderate his language in the Common Council of Dublin).[39]
Perceval also ensured that there was an inquiry into the size of the grant made
to Maynooth College for training Catholic priests, which duly led to a recommendation that a recent increase be partially reversed. These points all attracted
adverse notice in Parliament, confirming the impression that while the
Commons was not actually in favour of Catholic 'Emancipation', it was sympathetic to Catholic grievances.

Ireland's problems lay much deeper than the superficial jockeying between
Whigs and Catholics on one side and supporters of the Protestant Ascendancy
and the ministry on the other. The great mass of the population lived in rural
poverty and squalor, made worse by a pernicious system of land tenure and the
absenteeism of many great landowners. Yet peasants and agricultural labourers
were desperately poor in many parts of Europe and there is little reason to
believe that poverty in Ireland was worse than in regions of Spain, or Poland,
or even Sweden. Life in Ireland was made much harder by the population's
disaffection with the state and its rulers, and by a culture of violence with secret
societies, spies and betrayal following close in its wake. Some of the violence

had a religious or sectarian edge, some had political connotations, and historians can argue over its underlying cause, or the meaning of any particular outbreak; but the violence itself was chronic, dying down or being suppressed in one county only to spring up in another within months.

When Arthur Wellesley considered the defence of Ireland soon after his arrival in Dublin he was told by those who knew the country well that if the French should ever land a substantial force, 'the people in all parts of the country would rise in rebellion'. This was not a problem that could be easily overcome by conciliation: 'I am positively convinced', he told Hawkesbury, 'that no political measure which you could adopt would alter the temper of the people of this country. They are disaffected to the British government; they don't feel the benefits of their situation; attempts to render it better either do not reach their minds, or they are represented to them as additional injuries; and in fact we have no strength here but our army'.[40] Greater experience did nothing to alleviate Wellesley's pessimism. In 1813 Francis Seymour Larpent, the Judge Advocate with the army in the Peninsula, wrote that Wellesley had 'a strong notion that independence is what the Irish really aim at, and he is, therefore, for giving them no more, but proceeding upon King William's plan to keep them down by main force, for he thinks they have too much power already, and will only use more to obtain more, and at length separation'.[41] This was mere talk, although most indiscreet when coming from a former Chief Secretary. When, in 1829, the choice finally had to be made between concession and military rule, Wellesley, then Prime Minister, chose concession. But although his language was sometimes intemperate, his views on Ireland were not the product of ignorance or blind prejudice. One example from the many reports that he received while Chief Secretary helps to explain his pessimism, and sheds light on the state of Ireland in the summer of 1807. Mr Trail, the civil under-secretary, reported a long conversation he had just had with a Dublin gunsmith, a shrewd man who had taken part in the 1798 uprising and who kept in touch with the disaffected. According to Trail, the man was determined to take part in no further conspiracies, although he 'could not conceal a deep-rooted antipathy to Great Britain and to the English government in Ireland':

He says that the whole population of Ireland is decidedly hostile to the government and to the English connection; that the people, even the labouring poor, talk and think of nothing but Bonaparte's successes on the Continent, and rely with certainty on his invading this country and separating it from England. The poor say they cannot lose, and they believe they will gain by the change.

The antipathy to England pervades even the middling classes of shop-keepers and tradesmen: among them there are many intelligent people who speculate on the ruin of England without a conquest, by means of the loss of trade and the increase of the taxes; that the British trade must be excluded from the Continent, and the ruin of its finances, wealth, and power must soon be the inevitable consequence. Bonaparte will then be able to force England to acknowledge the independence of Ireland, as it has been obliged to do that of America.

... At the same time he declares there is no association or conspiracy now going on; nor will any measures be taken for assisting or joining a French army till it lands. The people are terrified from such attempts by what they suffered in 1798 ...

... The antipathy to England among the people is ancient, and has never varied. They consider themselves as oppressed. They are not protected or encouraged by their landlords, who are absent. It is the English tyranny that has prevented this country from prospering like England, and keeps the people in miserable houses and in rags, and ill fed. Some of the more intelligent are not sanguine in expecting much improvement from Bonaparte's government, but they hope this country may be made independent both of England and France. In speaking of the population I understood him to mean the Catholics.[42]

Wellesley sent this to Hawkesbury telling him that it provided 'a very accurate account of the state of Ireland at present, agreeing with every other account which we receive', and modern research does not disagree.[43]

The underlying problems of Ireland were too deep-rooted for the British government to solve. Nothing less than a wholesale transformation of society, such as that promised by the French Revolution or delivered by the Highland Clearances, would have had much effect, and it was in Britain's interests to avoid a revolutionising upheaval, while no one, in 1807, had the stomach for the reaction that would be provoked by any attempt to imitate the success of the Highland lairds. The existing pattern of society was preserved and the many improvements that were made could not keep pace with the growing population, until the Great Famine of 1845–51 swept it aside. Intelligent observers of Ireland in the early nineteenth century were well aware of its problems. Conscientious, attentive landlords (and there were many, of all political persuasions, just as there were many irresponsible absentees) spent fortunes searching for coal or trying to establish alternative forms of employment for their tenants and their tenants' children. It was obvious that Ireland was too dependent on agriculture, but most efforts to establish new industries proved unsuccessful, for Ireland lacked the combination of natural advantages which facilitated early industrialisation in the English midlands and parts of the Continent. The government, despite a general adherence to Adam Smith's doctrines of free trade, was inclined to help where it could; for decades it had fostered the growing of flax and the linen industry, and this had brought some valuable economic diversity to Ulster. It had also attempted to improve the transport infrastructure by subsidising the construction of canals, but the scheme was poorly managed and probably uneconomic from the outset. Nonetheless Wellesley, like many of his predecessors and successors as Chief Secretary, was beguiled by the arguments for the canals, and in April 1808 urged Hawkesbury to authorise the spending of a further £500,000 on them. He argued that private capital would not make the investment as the return on previous canals had been disappointing, but that the Irish economy as a whole would benefit from their construction:

> One of the greatest existing evils in Ireland is the want of employment for the overflowing population of the country. There is no resource but the land; every man within reach bids for a farm that becomes vacant; the consequence is that the rent of land is exorbitantly high, infinitely higher than the rent of land of the same fertility and equally well situated in Great Britain, and the wages of labour are much lower, because there is no demand for it. There are but few markets in Ireland, and the labouring poor almost universally subsist upon the produce of a small piece of ground, for which they pay the exorbitant rent of from £4 to £6 per acre, while they receive from 6d to 8d a day for their labour, and they are thus reduced to a state of misery which can scarcely be believed.[44]

But if the diagnosis was accurate, the proposed remedy was clearly inadequate – £500,000 spent on building canals would provide some additional employment but not nearly enough to make much difference – yet it was as much as the government, faced with the immense financial demands of the war, could possibly spare. As for Catholic 'Emancipation', or the right of a few wealthy educated Catholics to sit in Parliament and hold a handful of offices under the Crown, it was plainly irrelevant to the real problems of Ireland. For the Whigs and the leaders of the Irish Catholics it provided a safe, convenient, unthreatening cause, which enabled them, for an entire generation, to focus on the symbol and ignore the substance of Ireland's troubles. Not that this did much real harm, for even if all sides of British politics had concentrated their united efforts on Ireland, they could not magically alter its fundamental difficulties. Ironically, the greatest assistance the Irish economy received in these years came not from canal building or Whig orators, but from the war. The army, militia and yeomanry created a large and continuing demand for manpower, which eased the problem of unemployment. The presence of a substantial army in Ireland, and the construction of many defence works, injected money into the Irish economy.

The effect on trade was more uneven, with some painful disruptions, but by and large these were good years for agriculture, and the Irish economy was overwhelmingly agricultural.

The war would only benefit the Irish economy so long as it was fought elsewhere. A French landing or a repetition of the 1798 uprising would have brought untold misery to hundreds of thousands of ordinary people, whether it succeeded or not. The government had little fear of a popular rising except in conjunction with the arrival of a French army, but the French threat was taken very seriously indeed. When Wellesley took office in March 1807 Napoleon was still at war with Russia and the remnants of the Prussian army in Poland. The new government did not despair of the struggle and even hoped to persuade Austria to join the allies. Yet anything less than a complete victory would leave Napoleon dominating western Europe and controlling, directly or through his allies, the whole coastline from Hamburg to Cadiz with the sole exception of Portugal. Trafalgar may have averted the threat of a direct invasion of southern England, but Ireland was much more vulnerable. She could be approached from the north, the south or the west, and the French would only need to land a relatively small army (20,000 or 30,000) to have a real chance of success.

Wellesley did not treat the danger lightly. Early in May 1807, less than a month after he reached Dublin, he sent Hawkesbury a long, closely argued memorandum on the defence of Ireland. This was based on two unpalatable assumptions: that almost the entire coastline of Ireland was vulnerable, and that if the French did land they would receive the support of the population, while the British would have to operate as if 'in an enemy's country in which the hostility of the people would be most active'. He dismissed as impractical any attempt to defend the beaches by imitating the Martello towers and other works which had been built along the coasts of Kent and Sussex, but he did urge the establishment of a naval station at Bantry Bay, so that 'you would at all times have a fleet upon your most vulnerable point, and you would give to the coasts of this country the only general defence which they are capable of receiving'. If the French did succeed in landing, it was up to the army in Ireland to defeat them as quickly as possible, but the uncertainty of the direction the threat would come from made this very difficult. Wellesley foresaw that the army's movements could be facilitated by the establishment of a few strategically located, fortified centres, which might act as a base of operations and a depot for provisions and military stores. These did not need to be regular fortresses capable of withstanding a formal siege, but should be strong enough to be secure from Irish insurgents. In this discussion Wellesley was clearly drawing on the lessons he had learnt campaigning against the Marathas, while many of his comments anticipate the difficulties that the French would face in

Spain. He also stressed the vital importance of Dublin and Cork harbour. Even if all the rest of the country was overrun, it might be regained if these two vital links with Britain were maintained. Fortification could make them more secure. Wellesley also advocated the construction of permanent barracks outside the towns to house the troops, while keeping them concentrated and away from subversive elements.[45]

These ideas were all commendable, but they were also expensive and the government was unable to provide funds for all of them. Barracks for the troops were gradually built, and the defences of Cork and Dublin harbours strengthened, but little appears to have been done about some of the other proposals. On the other hand, Wellesley failed to persuade the ministers to approve the cheap but very effective measure of sending British regiments of militia to Ireland, and Irish regiments to Britain. The Irish militia was predominantly Catholic and was viewed with deep suspicion; far from adding to the security of the country it was seen as at best unreliable, and more probably as a potential danger. The removal of part of it and its replacement by the well-disciplined and undoubtedly loyal British militia regiments would produce a double benefit. Presumably the ministers refused from deference to popular prejudice in both England and Ireland, in the militia, and in wider society (English militia regiments might protest at being sent to Ireland, and English towns might object to having an Irish regiment stationed nearby, and vice versa), but when the measure was finally adopted in 1811 it proved most successful.[46]

The presence of a serving officer as Lord Lieutenant and another as Chief Secretary, both taking a keen interest in the defence of Ireland, might have caused some jealousy and ill feeling in the senior officers of the army in Ireland, whose chain of command was quite separate from these civil dignitaries. The Commander of the Forces in Ireland was Charles Stanhope, 3rd Earl of Harrington, who, in 1807, was fifty-four years old and a full general (making him a decade older than, and considerably senior to, Richmond, let alone Wellesley). Harrington had not seen active service since the American War, but he was highly regarded as an officer, and had been involved in the introduction of many reforms to the army since the 1780s. One account, dating from 1792, described him as 'beloved and respected by both officers and men' despite 'bordering on the martinet', while in 1808 Lieutenant-Colonel Richard Bourke, an intelligent Irish Whig, said that he 'is very much liked indeed, and I hear manages everything very well'.[47] Fortunately he and Wellesley were soon on excellent terms, cooperating without friction on official business and exchanging family news, gossip and chat. When Harrington's two youngest daughters fell ill with measles on a visit to England with their parents, Wellesley sent them a case of oranges and was delighted 'to find that my playfellows are getting well'. Wellesley was always good with children, but his correspondence with Harrington's military secretary, Lieutenant-Colonel H.M. Gordon, was equally pleasant and relaxed.[48] In November Wellesley asked the government to give him a provisional appointment to the Irish staff, to be used only in the event of a French landing or other active operations. This would enable him to command troops and serve under Harrington, for 'we are very badly off for want of intelligent general officers'. The Duke of York agreed to the unusual request without demur, which suggests that it had Harrington's support.[49]

In the middle of June Arthur Wellesley left Dublin to attend the first meeting of the new Parliament in London. Although the election had ensured that the government would have a secure majority, the first weeks of the session were important as each side sought to make a strong showing. Ireland was naturally the subject of some discussion, including a 'fierce debate' in the Commons on the evening of 26 June in which Grey and Whitbread, two of the leading Whigs, accused the Irish government of using improper influence to obtain votes. Wellesley made a stout defence and won the division 350 to 155 votes, but was sufficiently concerned to ask his under-secretary in Dublin if his recollection of events was correct.[50] But the government did not remain on the defensive for long. Early in July Wellesley introduced an Insurrection Bill, which gave more powers to the government to deal with the continuing unrest in the disturbed counties of Ireland. The ministers certainly believed that the powers were needed, but the political advantage of the bill was that it had been drawn up by the previous government. Publicising this would cause friction between the former ministers and their Irish supporters, while presenting the Opposition with a dilemma of whether to support or oppose the measure. It was not Wellesley who devised these tactics; he favoured modifications to the bill which, whatever their intrinsic merits, would have given the Opposition an easy escape route, but was overruled by Perceval and the other managers of government business.[51] Reluctantly, and with some ill grace, the vast majority of the Opposition supported the bill, taking comfort from following the lead of Henry Grattan. However, some of the younger members, such as Francis Horner, were shocked and disillusioned, and Sheridan, with characteristic irresponsibility, sought to exploit the moment by vociferous opposition. Wellesley crossed swords with the veteran orator in the debate and, at least by his own account, had the better of the exchange, getting the House to laugh *at*, not *with*, its most famous wit.[52]

Such triumphs would not be common; Wellesley's performance in Parliament was generally competent rather than brilliant or sparkling, but senior figures in the government could feel happy with their choice of him as Chief Secretary for Ireland. He had adjusted quickly to the demands of civil rather than military office; he handled delicate questions of patronage with admirable fairness and integrity; he worked well with Richmond and Harrington so that there was none of the rivalry and discord that marked many Irish governments; he minimised provocations to the Catholics at a time when their hopes had just been disappointed; and he showed a cool head in dealing with both the continuing disturbances within Ireland and the threat of a French invasion. The expectation that he would prove an efficient man of business had been fulfilled, and if he had chosen to abandon his military career he would probably have continued to hold high office and to have joined the Cabinet when the whirligig of ministerial politics moved him from Ireland to a more senior post. That was a choice he was determined not to make.

CHAPTER THIRTEEN

COPENHAGEN
(July–September 1807)

O N 1 JUNE 1807, before Arthur Wellesley left Dublin for London, he received a letter from Benjamin Sydenham, who remained one of Lord Wellesley's confidants. Sydenham wrote to warn Sir Arthur that a large military expedition was being prepared. Lord Wellesley had already been to see Castlereagh to remind him of Sir Arthur's claims to be employed and Castlereagh had replied 'that the expedition was so formed that even if Sir Arthur were on the staff in England, it would not fall to his turn to be employed; but that if Sir Arthur was extremely anxious on the subject they would rather add another brigade, expressly in order to afford an opening to him'. At the same time as making this remarkable offer, Castlereagh insisted that it would not be desirable for Sir Arthur to 'resign his present situation, in which he is of so much use to the country and to the government' in order to join an expedition whose fate depended upon events on the Continent.[1]

Arthur Wellesley's response to this letter was immediate. He wrote to Castlereagh to remind him of their previous conversations on the subject, and to insist that whether or not he was employed in the expedition he could not remain Chief Secretary for Ireland:

> It will be understood and said that I had avoided or had not sought for an opportunity for serving abroad in order to hold a large civil office.
>
> As I am determined not to give up the military profession, and as I know that I can be of no service in it unless I have the confidence and esteem of the officers and soldiers of the army, I must shape my course in such a manner as to avoid this imputation. If, therefore, you send the expedition, I wish you would urge Lord Hawkesbury to fix upon a successor for me, as I positively cannot stay here whether I am to be employed with it or not.[2]

Evidently there were limits to Wellesley's determination to serve with unhesitating zeal and cheerfulness wherever the King's government thought proper to
employ him, or else the King's salt he had eaten applied only to military and not
civil service.[3] The argument that his reputation would be seriously damaged if
he held civil office when an expedition was sent overseas was strained; after all,
there were scores of senior officers unemployed in Britain and only a handful
could be sent on any one expedition, and it is clear that he used it, and the
threat of resignation, to forward his own wish to go on the campaign. This was
not surprising or discreditable. Wellesley was an ambitious man whose ambitions were concentrated on his military career. He would never have succeeded
if he had not been willing to seek out and seize opportunities, rather than
passively doing what he was told and subordinating his wishes to the convenience of others. He had left India partly because he believed that there were
good prospects of service in Europe, and his claims had been recognised by his
employment in the Weser expedition. If he did not push himself forward in
1807 there was a risk that these claims would atrophy, while it was already
more than three years since he had seen any fighting.

Castlereagh was naturally concerned by Wellesley's threat to resign, and he
showed the letter to Hawkesbury and Portland. The three ministers agreed that
much as they valued Wellesley's presence in Ireland they could not expect him
to sacrifice his military career, and, with the Duke of York's agreement, they
devised a compromise that would satisfy both interests. Wellesley's lack of
seniority meant that he was not entitled to command more than a brigade in
the proposed expedition, and the Duke agreed to appoint him to one immediately with an acting brigadier as his second-in-command. The acting brigadier
would look after the troops until they were on the point of sailing while
Wellesley attended to his Irish business, and he would then join the expedition
and take up his command. This was a little hard on the acting brigadier, but
Wellesley had been careful to get the Duke's approval before accepting office in
the Portland government, and was entitled to some special treatment. Besides,
he had greatly impressed Castlereagh in their meetings since 1805; the minister
looked to him for professional advice on a wide range of military subjects and
was genuinely keen to advance Wellesley's career.[4]

The expedition was destined for the Baltic where, in conjunction with the
Swedes based at Stralsund, it would strike at the flank and rear of Napoleon's
army, assisting the Russians and Prussians, and – with luck – persuading the
Austrians to enter the war. The Portland government was committed to giving
vigorous support to Britain's continental allies, but when Castlereagh took
office he discovered that there were many practical difficulties to be overcome,
including a lack of suitable ships to carry the army to the Baltic. Nonetheless by
early June he had assembled a substantial force: the King's German Legion

(KGL) was already embarking for Stralsund, and it would be followed by some 12,000 British infantry and 4,000 cavalry, with Castlereagh hoping that he would ultimately be able to commit 30,000 men to the Continent. This was still only a fraction of the French or Russian armies, but it would have been the largest commitment of troops that Britain had made to the European mainland for more than twenty years.[5] Little wonder that Arthur Wellesley was so keen to be involved.

All these plans were ruined by Napoleon's great victory at Friedland on 14 June and his subsequent meeting with Alexander on the River Nieman at Tilsit, where the two emperors forged a warm alliance. News of Friedland reached London on 30 June, but for a while the ministers hoped that it might be exaggerated and that the war might be resumed. However they were also acutely aware of the danger to Britain if the Baltic powers led by Russia combined against them in support of Napoleon. Sweden was an ally and would be placed in peril by any alliance between France and Russia. Denmark was neutral, but since late 1806 she had been showing increasing signs of under-lying hostility and an inclination to side with France. By 10 July reports had reached London that the French were preparing to invade Denmark, while by 12 July there were rumours that Denmark would close the Sound and coop-erate with the French in an invasion of Ireland – rumours which were causing excitement in disaffected Irish circles, as Wellesley would have known.[6] On 14 July Lord Mulgrave, the First Lord of the Admiralty, proposed sending a strong naval squadron to Denmark to assist the Danes if they were attacked by France and to watch the Danish fleet. George III warmly approved. Fresh intelligence arrived almost every day, including confirmation of the alliance between Napoleon and Alexander, and reports that the Danish fleet was preparing for sea. (These reports later proved to be inaccurate, but they appeared well founded and convinced the ministers in London.) The troops that had already been sent to Stralsund would have to be withdrawn, and the ministers feared that if the French occupied Denmark (with or without Danish consent) they would use it as a base to attack Sweden. On 17 July Castlereagh advised the King that the navy should prevent the Danes from reinforcing their troops in Zealand, and that in the event of war Copenhagen should be attacked from the land. George III demurred, expressing strong reservations about an unpro-voked attack on a neutral country. Portland then sought an audience at which he persuaded the King to give his consent, although he remained unhappy with the policy. It was at this point that secret intelligence arrived from Tilsit: that Alexander was keen to commit Russia to a maritime war against Britain, and that the alliance with Napoleon was more than a way to escape from his mili-tary defeat. The significance of this news has been much exaggerated; it confirmed British fears and marks another step along the road to the decision to attack Denmark, but it was not uniquely important. Similarly, while Canning was evidently the prime mover behind the expedition, the other ministers had been closely involved from the outset and the responsibility rests with the Cabinet as a whole.[7]

By the end of July the policy was settled and the expedition had sailed. Its purpose was to lend weight to a diplomatic overture and, in the event of this failing, to take the Danish fleet by force. However, there was also the possibility, if Napoleon had already invaded Holstein, that the British troops might end up fighting alongside the Danes in defence of Zealand. Arthur Wellesley sailed from the Nore on 31 July aboard the fireship *Prometheus*. He was accompanied by the ever-reliable Colin Campbell as his brigade-major, and by the twenty-year-old Captain Fitzroy Stanhope, fourth son of Lord Harrington, as his aide-de-camp, together with some servants. According to Charles Chambers, the surgeon on the *Prometheus*, Wellesley and his staff made a good impression, and when they parted from the ship's captain and crew ten days later it was with mutual regret, Chambers describing them rather naïvely in his journal as 'pleasant gentlemanly characters'.[8]

Before he sailed Wellesley had apologised to the Duke of Richmond for abandoning the affairs of Ireland: 'I am convinced that, although you may feel some inconvenience . . . you would be the last man to desire or to wish that I should do anything with which I should not be satisfied myself. And I acknowledge that I should not be satisfied if I allowed any opportunity of service to pass by without offering myself.'[9] At this point it had not been finally settled whether or not Wellesley would return to his office in Ireland when the expedition was over, although Charles Long, a former Chief Secretary, agreed to handle the parliamentary business in his absence. In the event Wellesley kept the position, with Richmond and James Trail shouldering much of the additional burden in his absence. It was not a perfect arrangement, and Wellesley left himself open to criticism by continuing to accept his Irish salary while abroad, but he had made it clear that he was quite willing to resign, and it was Richmond and the ministers who decided that they would rather put up with the inconvenience of his absence than find a new Chief Secretary.[10]

The expedition had a good passage thanks to favourable winds and delightful weather, arriving in the Kattegat, between Denmark and Sweden, on 5 August. There was, as yet, no breach in diplomatic relations with Denmark, and Wellesley was able to go ashore at Helsingør on 7 August and look around the town. He was quite impressed by the Danish militia and seems not to have been embarrassed by the readiness of the Danes to supply the expedition with provisions.[11] On the whole the atmosphere on the expedition was surprisingly relaxed; some junior officers even obtained leave to go ashore at Helsingborg in Sweden to go to the theatre.[12] The commander of the expedition, Lord Cathcart, did not arrive from Stralsund until 12 August and in the interim his deputy, Sir Harry Burrard, was not inclined to take the initiative. (The awkwardness of having a commander arriving from a different direction from his troops, with Burrard attempting to fill the void, was to be repeated, with much more damaging results, in Portugal in the following year.) In the meantime the diplomatic overture was made and failed, and the Danes made some frantic last-minute preparations to defend themselves, but were prevented from reinforcing their troops in Zealand. The bulk of the Danish army was in Holstein preparing to defend the country from the French, while much of the navy was far from ready for sea.[13] British intelligence had been inaccurate, and the Danish attempt to preserve their neutrality had brought them to the verge of war with both Britain and France; but no manoeuvring, however skilful, could have enabled them to remain at peace in 1807.

Once it became clear that there was no chance of a negotiated settlement Cathcart's task was to seize, or at least destroy, the Danish fleet and naval stores in Copenhagen harbour. But the harbour was well guarded by both land and sea, and an attempt to emulate Nelson's daring attack of 1801 was likely to lead to disaster. Several other plans were discussed in meetings of senior officers on the admiral's flagship, with Cathcart providing little leadership and making his distaste for the operation rather too obvious. The Quartermaster-General, Lieutenant-Colonel George Murray, filled the void, proposing that Copenhagen be closely invested on all sides, the civilian population not allowed to leave, and the town then bombarded until the Danish government surrendered.[14] The ruthlessness of this proposal aroused much disquiet, and Wellesley believed that the necessity for it might be avoided if the British applied some psychological pressure by rapidly surrounding the city and cutting off all supplies of food and water; but if this was not done, he saw little alternative to Murray's plan.[15]

Cathcart adopted Murray's plan, and at four o'clock in the morning of 16 August the first troops landed at Vedbaek some twelve miles north of Copenhagen, and by the end of the long day, the bulk of the army was ashore. The initial landing had been made by Wellesley's brigade, which was rather misleadingly known as the 'Reserve', although there are also occasional references to it as 'the light brigade'. This was more appropriate, for it comprised the regiments that became the famous Light Brigade (later Light Division) in the Peninsular War, together with the Gordon Highlanders (1/43rd, 2/52nd, 1/92nd, five companies of 1/95th and five companies of 2/95th). They were strong battalions in excellent condition and must have made a favourable impression on Wellesley. In years to come he was to use them as the spearhead of his army, entrusting them with difficult and dangerous tasks not normally associated with light infantry, as well as employing them as a forward screen to conceal his other troops and protect them from harassment.

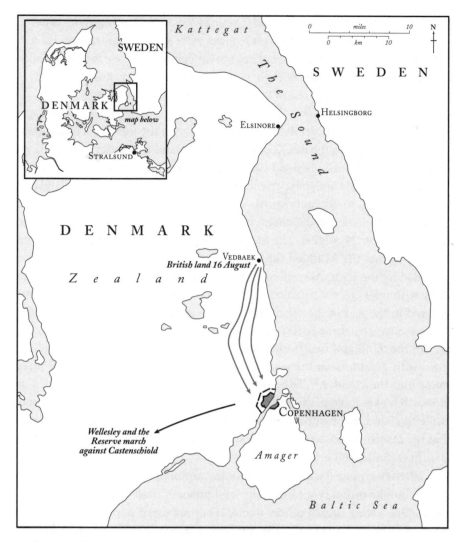

7 The Copenhagen expedition, August–September 1807.

On 17 August the British army advanced and loosely invested Copenhagen on the Zealand side. Over the following few days the blockade was gradually tightened while supplies and heavy artillery were landed from the fleet. However, Cathcart decided against occupying Amager, the island on the other side of the city, even though this greatly reduced the pressure on the Danes, and so meant that they were less likely to surrender without a bombardment. Wellesley privately deplored the decision, while Francis Jackson, a British diplomat who was observing the campaign, commented with characteristic acerbity, but not unfairly:

I believe Lord Cathcart understands making bows at the drawing-room better than commanding an army, which requires more spirit and enterprise. He is remarkably slow in all his operations, but his opponent, M. de Peumann [*sic* Peymann], a Hanoverian by birth, is an old man of seventy. It is well for his lordship that he has not one of Bonaparte's generals to do with.[16]

On 26 August Cathcart detached Wellesley with the Reserve, eight squadrons of KGL Hussars, the 6th KGL Line battalion and two batteries of artillery, to drive off the Danish General Castenschiold, who had collected 8,000 men (a mixture of militia and inexperienced regulars) in the interior of Zealand and was attempting to disrupt British operations. Wellesley advanced in two columns and encountered Castenschiold's force at Kioge at about ten o'clock in the morning on 29 August. The British attacked in echelon of battalions from the left, so that the 92nd led the way behind the usual screen of skirmishers provided by the 95th. According to Richard Howarth of the 95th: 'When we came within 50 yards of the enemy, our five companies, that were in front, were ordered to the rear of the other regiments to let them charge, but they would not go, so we gave three cheers and charged them ourselves, with three companies of the 92nd and two troops of light horse. We drove them all out of the town with great loss on the enemy's side. We pursued them for two or three miles into the country.'[17] The action was almost as simple and one-sided as Howarth makes it seem: the 95th lost only five men wounded and two missing, while the 92nd had two privates killed and one wounded. Wellesley reported that the Danish losses were 'very great, many have fallen, and there are nearly 60 officers and 1,100 prisoners'.[18]

Wellesley arranged with Cathcart for the captured officers to be released on parole, but the ordinary soldiers were held prisoner until Copenhagen surrendered. One young British officer wrote, 'They appeared poor raw troops, and we could not help smiling at the indifferent figure they cut',[19] while Francis Jackson told his mother:

The men are on board prison ships, and miserable wretches they are, fit for nothing but following the plough. They wear red and green striped woollen jackets, and wooden *sabots*. Their long lank hair hangs over their shoulders, and gives to their rugged features a wild expression. The knowing ones say that after the first fire they threw away their arms, hoping, without them, to escape the pursuit of our troops. In fact, the *battle* was not a very glorious one, but this you will keep to yourself.[20]

This impression became quite common in Britain, at least amongst those (especially the Whigs) who disliked the whole expedition, so that Wellesley received little credit with the public for his victory.[21] It was certainly not a difficult or dangerous operation, but it was well conceived and neatly executed.

Wellesley's campaign had been hindered by his inability to gain information from the countrymen, and he admitted to Hawkesbury: 'We are very unpopular in the country, and derive but little resource or assistance from it, and that little is procured with difficulty. The inhabitants have fled from their villages in many places; and in none have we yet succeeded in prevailing upon them to cut or bring in their harvest.'[22] That the British invaders were unpopular is hardly surprising, but the indiscipline and plundering of their troops made the situation much worse. Wellesley warned his command that while he 'regrets the necessity of resorting to measures of severity ... he is so fully convinced that soldiers guilty of marauding are unfit for any service, that he is determined to put a stop to their disgraceful practices'. Some of this 'marauding' was fairly innocuous and would have passed unremarked in a country and an army more used to war – one order refers to the theft of a goose and some fowls, which were retrieved and restored to their owners – but some was more serious. Lieutenant-Colonel Beckwith of the 95th had to admit to Wellesley that his men had stolen some silver plate belonging to a Danish princess. He was ashamed that any soldier of the Rifles should so misbehave; one offender had been caught and was being punished and almost all the goods had been recovered and would be returned. Wellesley apologised to the Princess and the affair ended quite happily, but many other incidents attracted less attention.[23]

The misconduct was not limited to Wellesley's command, and it added considerably to the discontent within the staff of the army at Cathcart's leadership. The Assistant Quartermaster-General John Pine Coffin, a highly intelligent soldier and one of the leading 'scientifics' in the army, told a friend (fellow 'scientific' Lieutenant-Colonel J.G. Le Marchant) a few months later:

At least you would imagine that the discipline of the army was preserved. No such thing. The villages around our lines give damning evidence to the contrary, and the outrages committed by our troops were worthy of a band of Cossacks. What were the steps taken to repress this spirit of indiscipline? Courts-martial were assembled, and instead of the culprits being executed in front of the Army as an example to the rest, the *tender feelings* of His Lordship would not permit him to approve a court-martial but they were all sent home to England, and there are now under the care of the Provost-Marshal two men for the rope, one for striking Lieut-General Lord Rosslyn in the attempt to secure him when in the act of plunder, and eleven artillerymen for robbing a house of near £10,000. In short, what will you think of an Army of 25,000 men, which for above a week after its landing had no provost-marshal appointed, or rather, I ought to say, what will you think of the man who commanded it.[24]

The experience must have confirmed Wellesley's belief that enforcing discipline firmly, and so preventing misconduct, would reduce the suffering of both soldiers and civilians, and that slackness and prevarication at headquarters would soon lower the morale and efficiency of the whole army. Fortunately the problems exacerbated by Cathcart's leniency were overcome when Copenhagen capitulated, and the British troops seem to have lived on surprisingly good terms with the local inhabitants once active operations ceased.[25]

Cathcart's performance throughout the siege attracted much well-informed criticism. Major John Macdonald who, as Cathcart's military secretary, bore the brunt of his chief's deficiencies, was most scathing:

> We have all been grievously disappointed in our man, and we are anxiously looking to a speedy termination of our present uncomfortable situation. For my own part I would not be obliged to do business again with Lord C. in the field for any consideration upon earth, and my colleagues about him are all of the same feeling. You can have no conception of the state of his temper or of the uncertainty and irregularity of doing business with him. The Navy are howling loudly about our slowness, and most of ourselves are doing the same.[26]

Pine Coffin agreed:

> However I might have heretofore disliked the conduct of Lord C. as a man, I had always given him credit for being one of the best officers in our service, but I am now convinced that there is scarcely *one* that is *worse*, and I believe I am correct in saying that there is hardly a general officer that has served with him on this expedition would consent to do so upon another.[27]

Despite Cathcart's failings the operation against Copenhagen succeeded. Several Danish sorties did little to slow the progress of the siege, and by the end of August the batteries were ready. On 1 September Cathcart summoned the Danes to surrender their fleet on the same terms Jackson had demanded before the first British troops landed. Peymann, the Danish commander, refused, and with evident reluctance Cathcart gave the order for the bombardment to commence.[28]

The firing began at half past seven in the evening on 2 September from forty-eight mortars and howitzers, twenty 24-pounders and several gunboats and bomb vessels. More than 2,000 shells were thrown into the city in the course of the night causing numerous casualties and fires to break out in many places. There was little resistance. Francis Jackson's brother George arrived at the fleet that evening and described the scene in a letter home:

We found the admiral and my brother in the stern gallery looking at the conflagration – for the city was on fire in three places. I never saw, nor can well conceive, a more awful, yet magnificent spectacle. It was the beginning of the bombardment *in forma*. We saw and heard it going on until daylight, as we lay in our cots; and as the work of destruction proceeded. I cannot describe to you the appalling effect it had on me. Our cabin was illuminated by an intensely red glow, then suddenly wrapped in deep gloom, as the flames rose and fell, while the vessel quivered and every plank in her was shaken by the loud reverberations of the cannon. Alas, poor Danes! I could not but feel for them.[29]

The bombardment was halted at eight o'clock in the morning on 3 September and the Danes gradually extinguished the fires in the town and treated the wounded, while the British gunners rested. Peymann gave no sign of surrender and that night the bombardment was resumed, although not quite so intensely. Again the guns stopped in the morning but at this time not all the fires could be extinguished and by late afternoon some appeared to be out of control. Still there was no surrender, so the artillery resumed its deadly work for a third night. 'Never, never have I lived through a more terrible night', wrote one Dane. 'The sky was full of smoke which seemed to ascend to Heaven, invoking a curse upon the barbarians who so ill-treated an innocent people.'[30] Shortly before dawn the spire of the Vor Frue Kirke, one of the landmarks of the city, crashed down amid the flames. By morning Peymann could endure no more; resistance was clearly futile, as indeed it had been from the outset. Rationally he would have prevented a great deal of useless suffering if he had capitulated on 1 September, but honour and basic human obstinacy would not permit such tame behaviour, however sensible. Even now he refused to take the full responsibility for surrender on his own shoulders, but summoned a council of war consisting of twenty leading officers and civil officials to approve his proposal. There was no opposition. Estimates of the casualties vary, with one report that about 2,000 Danish civilians, including women and children, had been killed in the bombardment and that some 400 houses and other buildings had been destroyed and many more damaged.[31] This was not a particularly high number by the standards of later wars, or even compared to other episodes in the Revolutionary and Napoleonic Wars, but Copenhagen was the capital of a nation that had genuinely tried to remain neutral, and the attack did nothing to make Britain more popular on the Continent, even among those who were not susceptible to Napoleon's propaganda. However the importance of popularity depends on circumstances, and for Britain in 1807 it mattered much less than denying Napoleon the use of the Danish fleet.

Sir Arthur Wellesley was one of the three British officers appointed by Cathcart and Gambier to negotiate the terms of the Danish surrender. (The others were Lieutenant-Colonel George Murray and Sir Home Popham of the navy.) The choice of Wellesley may simply have reflected the prominent part he had played in the campaign; Kioge may not have been much of a battle, but it was the most serious fighting there had been. Or Cathcart may have seen an advantage in implicating Wellesley in the capitulation; if the ministers approved, they would appreciate the compliment to their protégé, and if not, it might soften their criticism.

The negotiations took place on the night of 6 September and the capitulation was signed early the next morning. By his own account Wellesley was anxious to be as conciliatory as possible. He did not insist on occupying the Three Crowns battery, and agreed to the condition that the Danes were most anxious to secure: that few British troops be admitted to the town of Copenhagen other than those needed to occupy the citadel and the dockyards. But on the essential point he was firm, and Murray described how, when a Danish admiral attempted to haggle over the naval stores, Wellesley insisted: 'Now, Admiral! mind, every stick! every stick!'[32] On the day after the convention was signed, Wellesley told Hawkesbury that he might have demanded more, even the unconditional surrender of the whole town, but that he could see no advantage in so doing, while there was a risk that if pushed to extremities the Danes would refuse to surrender and defy the British to resume the bombardment. Instead he settled for certain and immediate possession of the Danish fleet and associated stores, and in return gave a commitment to evacuate the island within six weeks, arguing that 'this was all we wanted'.[33]

However the ministers in London were no longer sure that this *was* all they wanted. They were concerned for the safety of Sweden and intrigued by ambiguous messages from the Emperor Alexander, with the result that by early September they were seriously considering retaining a permanent garrison in Zealand. Wellesley was certain that this was pure folly and that any attempt to remain in Denmark over winter would end in disaster, and he cursed the convention and his involvement in it. 'Our friends in England will certainly be disappointed, whatever may be the ultimate result; & I am in some degree the cause of their disappointment.'[34] There was an uncomfortable echo here of the dispute with Lord Wellesley over the peace treaty he had signed with Sindia three years before; and the two experiences made Arthur Wellesley quick to doubt that his political masters would be ready to support him, or any general, if things went wrong, or circumstances changed, however blameless his actions. These doubts were to be amply confirmed by the controversy over the Convention of Cintra in the following year, and help to explain his attitude to the government throughout the rest of the war.

Wellesley applied to Cathcart for permission to return to Ireland: 'The *long nights* are approaching fast, and if I am to have any concern in the government of that country, it is desirable that I should be there.'[35] Cathcart was happy to agree, for if anyone could reconcile the ministers to the terms of the capitulation it would be Wellesley. He sailed on 18 September and after a rough passage reached Yarmouth ten days later. From there he went straight to see Castlereagh, who was staying at Sudborne Hall, Suffolk, and Canning in London, who was the minister most eager to retain Zealand. These discussions proved most useful, alerting them to the practical difficulties of the idea, and the strength of military and naval opinion against it, with the result that they allowed Cathcart and Gambier to honour the convention as it stood.[36]

Despite his fears, the issue did not damage Wellesley's reputation with the ministers, and, by bringing him into close contact with Canning on a military subject on which he could speak with confidence, it may actually have enhanced it. For although Canning pressed his views with passion and vigour, he respected and even admired those who disagreed with him if they did so plausibly and with ability. As for Castlereagh, he was already thinking of using Wellesley in operations directed at the defence of Lisbon or to attack the French naval squadron in the Scheldt.[37] Neither of these projects was destined to proceed at this time, but they make it clear that there was no question of leaving Wellesley to govern Ireland while other generals were sent to fight the French.

The general reaction in Britain to the campaign was tinged by party politics. Most Whigs criticised the expedition as immoral, and even some of the government's supporters were uncomfortable about it, although individual reactions could be surprising. George III privately declared the attack on Copenhagen 'a very immoral act'; William Wilberforce eventually gave it his approval, albeit with reservations; while Lady Bessborough, despite her impeccable Whig allegiances, was dismayed that London was not illuminated in celebration, and puzzled that 'the *Mob* do not seem to value it as they ought, considering what it saves us from'.[38] Even within the army the sense of triumph was muted by pity for the Danes. The whole campaign had cost the British fewer than 300 casualties, but this only emphasised the inequality of the struggle and the extent of Danish suffering. One young officer spoke for many: 'Believe me, my dear Brother, it requires all the assurance we . . . can muster to look the poor Danes in the face.'[39]

For the ministers the greatest advantage gained by the expedition was denying the Danish fleet to Napoleon, and they had no doubt that the point that would otherwise have been most threatened was Ireland. Even as the first troops went ashore Canning told Richmond: 'You will feel the Effects of our Success in Ireland; for in all the Reports of the Language and Expectations of the disaffected there, I see an Invasion by a Fleet from the Baltic is that which they reckon upon most confidently.'[40] And once the success was assured he was exultant: 'Nothing ever was more brilliant, more salutary, or more . . . [?] than the success. The invasion of Ireland prevented is the first good effect of it.'[41] Hawkesbury agreed, telling Richmond, 'Our left flank is now completely at liberty', while Sir Edward Littlehales, the military under-secretary in the Irish government, declared that the success 'will, in my opinion, contribute more to the defence of Ireland than any measure that could possibly have been undertaken'.[42] Taking part in military expeditions to the Continent was not normally one of the tasks performed by the Chief Secretary of Ireland, but in this case at least, it was not very far removed from his principal concerns.

CHAPTER FOURTEEN

DUBLIN AND WESTMINSTER
(October 1807–July 1808)

S IR ARTHUR WELLESLEY returned to Dublin and his family on Monday
12 October 1807. He had been married for eighteen months; his son,
Arthur Richard, was now eight months old, and Kitty was well advanced in her
second pregnancy although the new baby was not due until early 1808. It is
difficult to judge the state of the marriage at this time; none of Kitty's letters
have survived and Arthur's are mostly short and dry, giving little hint of his
feelings except, perhaps, in their lack of demonstrative affection. This may not
mean much, for even so devoted a husband as Castlereagh recoiled from
'committing the intolerable barbarism of writing a love letter to my wife'.[1]
Nonetheless there are some fragmentary signs of friction, or at least of misunderstanding, in the handful of letters which survive from July 1807 when
Arthur was in London and Kitty in Dublin. Apparently she left bills unpaid and
did not tell Arthur that she needed money, and when he found out he was
equally hurt and puzzled, wondering if she considered him 'to be a Brute, &
most particularly fond & avaricious of money'. His next letter points all too
clearly to the real problem: the gulf between his confidence, which frequently
made him brusque, and her nervous hesitancy. 'Once for all you require no
permission to talk to me upon any subject you please; all that I request is that a
piece of work may not be made about trifles, & things of ordinary occurrence,
& that you may not go into tears because I don't think them deserving of an
uncommon degree of attention.'[2]

The lack of mutual confidence is underlined by the absence of any discussion of public affairs from Arthur's letters. He did not confide his plans to her,
or even announce the likelihood that he would take part in the Copenhagen
expedition until it was finally settled. By early 1808 he was even concealing the
fact that he had been ill for a few days in London, writing to Richmond: 'Don't
tell Lady W. that I have been unwell, as it is only making a piece of work about
nothing.'[3] Still, Arthur's letters while on service in Denmark were frequent and

pleasant, if brief and fairly impersonal; the lack of discussion of politics and public affairs may have reflected Kitty's preference, while even the concealment may have arisen from a misguided anxiety for her health, for she was either pregnant or recovering from childbirth throughout 1807 and 1808.[4]

Their second son, Charles, was born on 16 January 1808, just as Arthur had to leave Dublin for London for the opening of Parliament. Kitty naturally remained behind and Arthur did not return to Ireland until the middle of April when he made a flying visit. He was engrossed in parliamentary business and military plans, and there are hints that Kitty felt excluded and neglected, and that she showed her feelings to her family. This was natural but unwise, for it simply drew attention to the fundamental incompatibility of the couple; Wellesley was essentially a public figure for whom private life was a minor, subsidiary diversion, while Kitty longed for private domestic felicity and neither shone in society nor took a serious interest in public affairs. There was evidently another, more specific trouble in the marriage at this time; we do not know the details, but just before Charles was born, Kitty did something that she was to regret for the rest of her life and for which Arthur never forgave her. There is a suggestion that she diverted money from the household accounts to pay debts incurred by her brother Henry, but this hardly seems to warrant the opening up of such a schism unless there were aggravating circumstances.[5]

Charles Wellesley was privately baptised on 12 February and there was a grander baptism for both boys by the Lord Bishop of Limerick on 27 June when Arthur was again briefly in Dublin. As well as the two baby boys, Kitty had several other children to look after, at least part of the time. She made a home for Arthur Freese, and divided responsibility with her mother for two young nephews and a niece whose mother (her sister Helen) had died in the middle of 1807.[6] The eldest of these orphan nephews, John Hamilton, recorded in his memoirs a little incident that occurred in November 1807 when he was seven and his brother Edward was five, which gives an appealing glimpse of their family life. Arthur Wellesley and Kitty's brother Henry took the two Hamilton boys with them as they walked through Phoenix Park talking over the events of the day. The sun began to set, the boys were tired and dinner-time approached so each man lifted a boy onto his shoulders and they set off for home. Soon their pace quickened as a spirit of rivalry and fun came to the fore. Henry Pakenham was only twenty and took an early lead in the race, but the thirty-eight-year-old Chief Secretary would not admit defeat and gradually closed the gap until the pair were neck-and-neck as they sprinted to the gates of the Lodge, their little jockeys whooping with laughter and excitement.[7]

Life in Ireland was not all business and Arthur Wellesley was not reluctant to relax with a day's shooting or a convivial evening. His financial position was comfortable, for the Chief Secretary's salary was some £6,500 p.a. He had an apartment in Dublin Castle and the Secretary's Lodge in Phoenix Park. This was a pleasant low two-storey house, built some thirty years before by a previous Chief Secretary. It faced south across a low sunken fence to the park beyond, while at the back there were fruit and flower gardens including peach trees grown under glass; and the cellar was well stocked. A few years later, when Robert Peel became Chief Secretary, he found that the drawing-room ceiling was sagging, the sanitation was old-fashioned and inadequate, and deer from the park continually broke into the gardens, all of which called for repairs and alterations costing some £1,600.[8] But Peel was English, of a younger generation, and had a rich father; it seems unlikely that either Arthur or Kitty were much troubled by these defects, if, indeed, they even noticed them.

Every morning Wellesley would ride across the park into Dublin and his office in the castle. Usually he would be joined in the ride by Richmond's daughters, then in their teens, for the two families were on most friendly terms. When Richmond was touring the country Wellesley would end his letters with family news and chit-chat to which the Lord Lieutenant responded with 'thanks for the news of the brats'.[9] Richmond was popular in Ireland and was noted for his good cheer and affability. Sometimes his hospitality proved too generous even for Wellesley, whose drinking had put Hickey to shame a decade before, and at Christmas 1807 Sir Arthur wrote to the Duke: 'The fact is that we have all drunk too hard lately, & have none of us been well.'[10] The warning had no lasting effect, but it was not resented, and the two men remained on excellent terms.

Wellesley's closest associate in the government of Ireland, apart from Richmond, was James Trail, the head of the civil department of the Chief Secretary's office. Trail was a Scottish lawyer in his early sixties, who was politically unaligned (he had connections with the Prince of Wales, the radical law reformer Samuel Romilly, and Lord Hertford). He had been appointed to his office under the previous Whig government, but was retained by Wellesley, who soon trusted him implicitly and praised his work highly. It was Trail's efficiency that enabled Wellesley to go off campaigning in Denmark without throwing the government of Ireland into disarray.[11] Trail's colleague at the head of the military department, which performed many of the same administrative functions as the War Office in England, was Sir Edward Littlehales. In July 1807 Littlehales had to inform Wellesley that many secret papers relating to the defence of Ireland had been illicitly removed from the office. One of the clerks was suspected of the theft but the case could not be proven, and the government was left uncertain just how seriously to take the affair.[12]

Wellesley was also assisted, especially when in London on business, by a confidential private secretary, Benjamin Dean Wyatt, the son of James Wyatt, the eminent architect. The young Wyatt had arrived in India in 1797 and had been employed in Lord Wellesley's secretariat; he returned to England in 1803 and it seems likely that Lord Wellesley employed him when mounting his defence against Paull's accusations, and that this was how he came into close contact with Arthur Wellesley. He appears to have been an efficient and trustworthy secretary, and in later years Wellesley would employ him in other, more responsible roles, although not always with happy results. He was, or at any rate became, a quarrelsome, discontented and even bitter man, although his artistic talents, when he followed in his father's footsteps, were considerable.[13]

The British success at Copenhagen had removed one danger to Ireland, but Napoleon had moved quickly in another direction, agreeing with Spain to partition Portugal, and despatching an army under his old friend General Junot to occupy Lisbon and seize the Portuguese fleet. The Portuguese government endeavoured to appease Napoleon, but when this proved useless the court, together with much of the ruling class and large quantities of treasure, embarked at the end of November for the long voyage across the Atlantic to Brazil. They sailed for barely a day before Junot's leading troops marched into the capital without having to fire a shot. Napoleon had failed to capture the Portuguese navy, but by a strange coincidence the Russian Mediterranean fleet under Admiral Siniavin arrived in Lisbon just days after Junot's army. Some alarmists in Britain saw this as evidence of Napoleon's genius at work, and imagined that Junot's men would scarcely break stride in boarding the Russian ships and would have landed in Ireland before any precautions could be taken. However the Royal Navy already had a powerful squadron off Lisbon, and the ministers were much more sanguine. Hawkesbury told Arthur Wellesley: 'Our apprehensions of any serious attack upon Ireland are considerably diminished in consequence of the fortunate issue of our affairs in Portugal. The capture of the Danish and the safety of the Portuguese fleet limit most essentially the powers of our enemies . . . The Russian fleet in the Tagus is, according to all accounts, in such a state as to be more fit for firewood than for any other purpose.'[14]

Wellesley did much work on his plans for the defence of Ireland in the last months of 1807, cooperating smoothly with Richmond, Harrington and the other soldiers in Ireland, and receiving support and encouragement from Castlereagh and Hawkesbury. But responsibility for artillery and for fortifications rested not with the army, but with the Ordnance, and Wellesley soon found that Lord Chatham, the Master-General of the Ordnance, was not disposed to listen to his suggestions and evidently resented his interference. Chatham was a man of great experience in high office, the elder brother of William Pitt, and favourite of the King. He may have had considerable natural ability, but he was notoriously lazy and dilatory, and Hawkesbury told Wellesley that he was very precise and pedantic about business, insisting that everything proceed according to its exact proper form.[15] He was also a soldier who had not renounced his military ambitions, and it is reasonable to suspect that he was jealous of Wellesley's growing reputation. Whatever the cause, Wellesley soon became aware that he could not expect much help from Chatham, and that it was best to raise Ordnance issues indirectly through other ministers. Worse was to come, for in January 1808 Wellesley became aware that Chatham had failed to include any sum for Irish fortifications in his department's estimates. If this was not rectified it would mean an entire year's delay in the construction of new works, but when Wellesley called on him to raise the matter, Chatham was out or unwilling to be disturbed. In the end, Wellesley referred the problem to Hawkesbury, but was left in no doubt of the disfavour with which he was viewed by one member of the Cabinet.[16]

When Wellesley returned to Ireland in October 1807 he brought with him authority to 'proclaim' the disturbed southern districts under the Insurrection Act – a measure that would give the government greater powers, as under a mild form of martial law. At the same time he knew that the ministers in London would prefer that this step was not taken, and that the troubles be dealt with by other means.[17] Rural violence was endemic in Ireland and outrages that would have been greeted with horrified fascination if they had occurred in England, were dismissed with a shrug when they were perpetrated in Tipperary, Limerick or Waterford. The causes of this violence may have been predominantly social and economic, but running through them was a strong element of disaffection, together with hopes and rumours of a French invasion. Wellesley's response was hindered by a rapid turnover of troops in the Irish garrison and by the chronic shortage of resident magistrates. He was reluctant to employ army officers as magistrates, telling Trail: 'I have great objections, founded possibly upon professional feelings, to throwing these duties upon officers and soldiers of the army: they are certainly unaccustomed and unacquainted with them, and yet, if they make a mistake we come upon them with a most heavy hand.'[18] Wellesley believed that the disturbances had little to do with the distinctions between Catholics and Protestants, and that their underlying cause was 'the restless disposition of the people' made worse by 'the oppression of their landlords, principally the resident gentry of the country, in demand of exorbitant rents for land, and in the payment of low wages for labour; although I believe that the complaints of these grievances are much exaggerated'. The disturbances slowly subsided in the early months of 1808.[19]

Parliament opened on 21 January 1808 and presumably Wellesley was there in good time, although his first letters from London are not dated until the following day. One of the first pieces of business of the new session was a Vote of Thanks to the army and navy for their services at Copenhagen, and on

1 February the Speaker of the Commons, Charles Abbot, addressed Major-Generals Finch, Grosvenor and Wellesley, who stood with their heads bare in their places as he praised their 'zeal, intrepidity and exertion'. Each officer then replied expressing his gratitude in suitably modest and vacuous terms. Abbot noted in his diary that 'none of them were in uniform; but in their morning dress'; and it is unlikely that Wellesley greatly enjoyed the occasion, for he was suffering from 'a very bad cold'.[20]

Before the session began Hawkesbury pressed Wellesley to ensure a good turnout of Irish MPs for the opening of Parliament, for he had heard that the Opposition intended to be very violent and a few early votes might establish, or shake, the government's authority for months to come. But Wellesley, like many an Irish secretary before and after, was reluctant to press his followers too hard at the outset. Most Irish MPs found life in the capital expensive and were reluctant to spend more than a few months each year in England. If they came in January they would be unwilling to stay beyond Easter, when the government might need their votes in a thin House. And every MP who was spurred into action sooner than he wished would feel that he had a claim on the government which would have to be satisfied in the summer.[21]

The Whigs conducted a vigorous and at times fractious campaign against the government during the session of 1808 in which Irish affairs figured prominently. By the end of February Wellesley was beginning to feel the pressure, complaining to Richmond:

We have hard work in Parliament. Every night a long debate, and as many as two and three divisions. The opposition most violent and persevering, and their adherents constant in their attendance, to the number of about seventy or eighty, every night. Our friends very naturally do not attend so well; but we must keep them to their work as well as we can. The business advances but slowly.[22]

A fortnight later he noted: 'In the last week no less than five late nights, and there will be as many in this. The House sat till six on Friday morning and till seven on Saturday.' The only hope he could see of any easing came from the weariness of the press, which was reducing its reports of debates to mere sketches, 'and as it is certain that there will be no debating if no persons were to be admitted to the gallery, it is to be hoped that the omitting to publish speeches for some time will have the effect of shortening them, or, at all events, of rendering the debates in Parliament less frequent'.[23]

In discussing Irish affairs the Opposition naturally ignored all the occasions on which the government had endeavoured to conciliate the Catholics or restrain the Protestants, and instead concentrated on cases that would feed the insatiable Irish appetite for grievances. There were debates over Dr Duigenan's appointment to the Irish Privy Council and the inquiry into the grant to the Maynooth seminary. The Opposition was encouraged to press their attack by the evident divisions in the government on both questions. Castlereagh absented himself from the Maynooth debate, and Canning from both, while writing privately to the Duke of Richmond that he felt that the combination gave the impression that the government was decidedly hostile to the Catholics. The government's majority fell, and Wellesley was left to defend the measures as best he could almost unaided. He was not pleased, telling Richmond: 'It is very extraordinary that they will not be convinced ... that the government weaken themselves much more here and consequently in Ireland by submitting to abuse, than they could do by the manly avowal and justification of any appointment which they might make.'[24]

Fortunately this was the nadir of the government's fortunes on Irish questions in the session. A fortnight later the Opposition overreached itself by proposing a motion for Catholic Emancipation. The debate began with an excellent, conciliatory speech by Grattan, which was privately praised by both Wellesley and Perceval. The remaining speeches were dull and when, at half past four in the morning, the Opposition proposed to adjourn the debate so that it could be resumed, they were defeated by 298 votes to 118. After some further delay the motion itself was rejected by 281 to 128. The result was never in doubt, and Canning and Castlereagh both spoke against the motion, arguing that the time was wrong and the result would be counter-productive.[25] The large majority on the question discouraged the Opposition and destroyed all the momentum they had gained in the earlier debates, while it triggered a dispute which left a legacy of discord between the Whigs and Catholics that undermined their campaign for years.

Although Arthur Wellesley's chief concern in Parliament was naturally Irish business, he was also keen to secure his brother's final vindication on the charges originally brought by James Paull. A handful of radicals including Lord Folkestone, Lord Archibald Hamilton and Thomas Creevey took up Paull's charges, but they had little support, for the Commons was weary of the affair. Between February and June 1808 a succession of debates and votes were held on questions relating to Lord Wellesley's conduct, all of which were won by his supporters with handsome majorities, for not even many Whigs were willing to support the vendetta any longer. The Oudh charges were dismissed after an all-night sitting, and a majority of 180 to 29 supported a motion declaring that Wellesley had acted for the best. Thin Houses later in the session reduced the numbers, but Wellesley was still securing majorities of near a hundred, compared to a bare score of votes against him. Finally on 17 June Thomas Wallace proposed a motion commending Wellesley, and even this passed with ease, 98 votes to 19.[26]

Arthur Wellesley was now quite comfortable in Parliament although he never particularly relished the cut and thrust of debate, and normally spoke only on subjects where he had either an official or personal connection. In February he defended the grant of an annuity to Lord Lake's family, and in June he opposed a radical motion against flogging in the army. In the course of this debate he employed the interesting argument that while the navy was the 'characteristic and constitutional force of Britain', the army was still 'to a certain extent, a new force . . . [which] has arisen out of the extraordinary exigencies of modern times, and must, I contend, upon every consideration of expediency, and from the necessity of the case, be left under the control of the Crown'.[27] This is a useful reminder of the latent suspicion of the army that remained an element of British political culture until well into the nineteenth century.

On 25 April 1808 Arthur Wellesley, together with more than two dozen other major-generals, was promoted to lieutenant-general. At the same time a large number (about sixty) new major-generals were created. Slowly Wellesley was rising up the military tree, but he remained relatively junior (there were still almost 200 generals senior to him) and he could not expect to be given an army of his own to command unless it was a relatively small force or sent on a distant service. But his reputation within the army was rising more rapidly than this suggests. George Murray had returned from Copenhagen full of praise for him, and he also greatly impressed Colonel Robert Anstruther, the Adjutant-General in Ireland, when they worked together on plans to restore order in Tipperary and Limerick. Anstruther was one of the leading 'scientific' soldiers in the army, a close friend of Murray and a long-standing admirer of Sir John Moore. Yet in October 1807 he astonished William Clinton, the Quartermaster-General in Ireland, who recorded the conversation in his diary, by telling him that despite Moore's excellent qualities, he ' "has one great failing, and that is his dread of responsibility, and you may rely on it," added he, "if he ever is placed at the head of an army *he will fail*".' Anstruther added these remarkable words: ' "No," said he, "the man upon whom I pin my faith as a military man, the man who must rise to the highest in his profession, is Sir Arthur Wellesley".' Clinton was unconvinced; he and his brother Henry would remain doubtful of Wellesley's talents and rather hostile towards him for years to come, and their attitude was shared by the Duke of York and the Horse Guards. But it is significant that Wellesley was winning the admiration of some of the most intelligent and professional officers in the army even before the first shot of the war in the Peninsula had been fired.[28]

The ministers were already convinced of Wellesley's ability and looked to him for informal advice on military questions. Robert Dundas, the President of the Board of Control, consulted him on the threat posed by a French embassy to Persia, and the possible danger of a combined Franco-Russian invasion of India. Wellesley, who was never reluctant to share his knowledge or to influence policy, responded with a detailed commentary on the defence of British India. In this he argued that the value of the River Indus as a barrier should not be overestimated, but that while precautions should be taken, preparations for a campaign should be kept low-key, to minimise both the expense and the risk of alarming the other Indian powers. And when Castlereagh wanted an intelligent officer to send to Sweden to prepare the way for a British expedition, he took Wellesley's advice and selected George Murray.[29] Wellesley's unusual confidence in marshalling evidence and setting out an argument in long, detailed memoranda – which had been evident ever since his early days in India a decade before – made him particularly useful as a military adviser. He not only had the experience and judgement to make sound decisions, he was also able and willing to explain the reasons behind his opinions in a way that civilian ministers could understand.

But Wellesley's principal role as a soldier in the first half of 1808 lay in advising the ministers on the rapidly changing position in Spain and her American colonies. The disastrous failure of Whitelocke's attempt to recapture Buenos Aires made the Cabinet wary of schemes for conquering Latin America, but the arrival of Francisco de Miranda in London in early 1808 led Castlereagh to embrace the idea of Britain intervening in support of local independence. Wellesley had a number of meetings with Miranda in January and early February and produced a slightly modified version of his earlier plan for an expedition to Mexico. He had little doubt that the scheme would work, although he foresaw that independent, neutral South American countries would not always be friendly, and would not appreciate the trade restrictions imposed by the Orders-in-Council. He may also have had some broader misgivings for he later said: 'I always had a horror of revolutionising any country for a political object. I always said, if they rise of themselves, well and good, but do not stir them up; it is a fearful responsibility.'[30]

Meanwhile Napoleon was sending more and more troops into northern Spain on the pretext of reinforcing Junot. Godoy, the Spanish chief minister, considered resistance and, if that failed, following the example of the Braganzas and taking refuge in the American colonies. However he was overthrown and the King was forced to abdicate by a series of riots at Aranjuez in March orchestrated by Prince Ferdinand, the heir to the throne. Ferdinand's accession was greeted with wild popular rejoicing and he returned to Madrid hoping to come to terms with the French, but the events at Aranjuez deprived the Bourbons of their legitimacy, which was the only asset they could offer Napoleon. Murat had already occupied Madrid and the Spanish royal family were now bullied and cajoled into meeting Napoleon at Bayonne where, amid mutual recriminations and threats from the emperor, they all abdicated and Joseph Bonaparte was elevated to the Spanish throne. Even before this last twist of the screw Madrid had erupted in a violent uprising against the French, which was suppressed with considerable bloodshed – the famous Dos de Mayo immortalised by Goya.

The British government watched all these events with great disquiet, rightly suspecting that one of Napoleon's motives was to gain control of Spain's American empire. In April the Cabinet and the King approved the idea of British intervention in Latin America in principle and Wellesley continued to work on the detail of his plans. Further talks with Miranda and the fear of being pre-empted by the French now led him to support an initial attack on Caracas in October before the main operation against Mexico in December. News of the Dos de Mayo and the abdication of the Spanish royal family led to another change of plan, with Wellesley urging that as large a force as possible should be sent to Gibraltar to encourage and assist any general Spanish uprising against the French. If the insurrection failed, its leaders should be urged to take refuge in the American colonies, where their presence would greatly facilitate British operations, although the colonies might be sufficiently moved by events in Spain to declare their independence without the need for active British intervention.[31] Castlereagh had similar ideas and at the beginning of June the government agreed to send 8,000 men from Cork to join the 5,000 men under Major-General Brent Spencer, who had been hovering off the Spanish coast since the beginning of the year. However the working assumption remained that any rising in Spain would probably fail and that the troops would ultimately be employed in the Americas.[32]

On 4 June Arthur Wellesley wrote to Richmond warning him that 'government have lately been talking to me about taking the command of the corps destined for Spain'. Nothing was yet settled, so he did not disturb Kitty with the news, but he felt that Richmond needed to be warned. Neither Richmond nor the ministers wanted to move Wellesley from a position in which he had given general satisfaction, and so it was decided that the precedent of Copenhagen would be followed and that Wellesley would remain Chief Secretary, although this clearly would have had to be reconsidered if he had crossed the Atlantic.[33]

In the last week of May uprisings against the French broke out all across Spain, and on 8 June two delegates from the ancient provincial Junta of Asturias arrived in London appealing for help. Their appearance sparked a fever of excitement in Britain, which grew steadily throughout the summer. On the very next day *The Times* called on the government to act with 'the utmost promptitude' to assist the Spanish patriots. 'We hope there will be no bartering about terms, no stipulation of retributive concessions or advantages to England . . . Let them but show a probability of our assistance being effected, and then let it be gratuitous, energetic, and unconditional.' The Whig *Morning Chronicle* was just as enthusiastic, claiming: 'At this moment the English people would cordially acquiesce in any effort, however expensive, that could assist the cause of that brave and noble nation.' And even Cobbett agreed, declaring: 'This is the *only* fair opportunity that has offered for checking the progress of Napoleon. It is the only cause to which the people of England have heartily wished success', and demanding action without hesitation or delay.[34]

The Spanish uprising appealed right across the British political spectrum. Whigs and radicals, who had always disliked coalitions with Continental autocracies, rejoiced in the popular nature of the Spanish risings and, misreading the lessons of the early 1790s, were confident that Napoleon's professional soldiers would be no match for the enthusiasm of a people in arms fighting for liberty. Conservatives preferred to concentrate on the loyalty to King Ferdinand proclaimed by the patriots, and lauded the role of Spanish priests and peasants in the uprising, while studiously ignoring any parallels with Ireland. And the public as a whole welcomed the news of a twist in the war that was fresh, novel and exciting. Spain was little known and for a time hopes ran ludicrously high.[35] Opposition politicians called on the government to act and Canning responded with the ringing declaration that 'we shall proceed upon the principle, that any nation of Europe that starts up with a determination to oppose . . . the common enemy of all nations . . . becomes instantly our essential ally'.[36] Canning's speech gave official expression to the ardent hopes and naive enthusiasm for the Spanish cause that swept through British society. Inevitably, as Arthur Wellesley would find to his cost, autumn and winter brought disappointment and disillusionment leading to a savage search for scapegoats and a great revulsion from all things Spanish, but in June 1808 the government was beset on all sides by clamour to do more for Spain.

The ministers honoured their promise. Vast quantities of arms, ammunition and money were despatched to assist the patriots. Spanish prisoners of war were released and, in a remarkable operation, the Royal Navy spirited away most of a corps of Spanish troops led by the Marquis de la Romana, which was serving under Napoleon in Denmark. The effect on Wellesley's expedition was less clear. Plainly the prospects of a sustainable insurrection in Spain were much brighter, and there was consequently less likelihood that the South American scheme would have to be acted upon, but beyond that, all was uncertain. Should Wellesley's army be sent to Asturias, or held back, or sent to Gibraltar so as to be ready to intervene in southern Spain, which had hitherto been the most promising region? Fortunately there was no need for an immediate decision, for the expedition was not yet ready to sail, but there could be no unnecessary delay, for everyone felt a sense of urgency that the opportunity of the Spanish rising must be seized as quickly as possible, or it risked being lost forever.

On 14 June Wellesley was formally appointed to command of the force assembled at Cork and given authority over Spencer's corps. He left London a couple of days later and reached Dublin on the afternoon of 20 June after a slow passage from Holyhead. Over the next fortnight practical preparations for the expedition continued apace. Anstruther sent Wellesley all the maps of southern Spain and other geographical information that he could find in the Adjutant-General's office in Dublin, commenting that while the maps were not very good, he believed they were the best that had been published. From London, Wellesley received the letter-books containing the papers relating to two British expeditions to Portugal, those of Sir Charles Stuart in 1797 and of Richard Stewart in 1803, as well as some other papers. Castlereagh had already sent three officers to the Asturias to gather intelligence, and now despatched Lieutenant-Colonel Samuel Browne to Oporto to report on the situation there – for, as well as the French troops under Junot and the Russian naval squadron, there were thousands of Spanish soldiers occupying Portugal and there had been rumours of an insurrection for some time. The Ladies of Llangollen gave Wellesley a Spanish translation of the English Prayer Book as a convenient and edifying way of studying the language, and Jonah Barrington entertained the general, recalling: 'I never saw him more cheerful or happy.'[37]

The news from Spain got better and better. On 26 June a delegation arrived in London from Galicia: the whole of northern Spain had risen against the French; the 8,000 Spanish troops at Oporto had imprisoned the French commandant and were marching to join the patriots; and risings had spread to Andalusia, Valencia and Catalonia. The Galicians were so confident that they declined the offer of British troops (though they were eager for arms, equipment and money), and instead urged that Wellesley's expedition be sent to Portugal where it could defeat Junot, whose presence posed a potential threat to their rear, and liberate the other Spanish troops, some 6,000 men, whom Junot had disarmed and imprisoned.[38]

The government was still very short of reliable intelligence from either Portugal or the south of Spain, but Castlereagh trusted Wellesley to use the broad discretion he was granted in his instructions. Essentially these were that if Wellesley felt that his force and Spencer's combined were powerful enough to defeat Junot and liberate Portugal he should do so; but that if intelligence revealed that reinforcements were needed he should wait at Coruña. A further force of 10,000 men was being prepared which should be ready to sail in about three weeks; and it was expected that Sir John Moore might soon return with the expedition that had been sent to Sweden in the spring.[39] In time a substantial British army of more than 30,000 men would be able to take the field to support the Spaniards, and this army would be commanded by Lord Chatham who, unlike Moore and Wellesley, had the seniority and royal favour needed for such a large command. This was not good news for Wellesley, who could expect no favours from Chatham, but it was probably not unexpected. Castlereagh added: 'I trust however you will have settled matters at Lisbon long before we shall have anything ready to follow you.'[40] No doubt Wellesley agreed.

On the very day these instructions were issued the government received despatches from Admiral Cotton off Lisbon, which reported that Junot had only 4,000 men in Lisbon and that the local population was 'highly enraged' against the French. In the admiral's opinion 5,000 or 6,000 British troops would have little difficulty in gaining possession of the Tagus forts and forcing the Russian ships to surrender.[41] Castlereagh at once sent the good news to Wellesley, varying his instructions only to urge him to act 'with the least possible delay', and to this end suggesting that he send a trusted officer to Coruña rather than go there in person. He also added two further regiments, the 36th and 45th, some 1,200 men, to Wellesley's force, but told him not to wait for them if their embarkation would delay his departure.[42]

Wellesley received Castlereagh's instructions on 4 July and left Dublin next morning, arriving in Cork on 6 July. He found that the expedition was still a couple of days from being ready to sail; there were some problems with the transport ships and the commissariat horses and men were still too crowded. He also decided that, contrary to Castlereagh's suggestion, he would go to Coruña in person, as it was unlikely to lead to any delay. By 9 July everything was ready to sail, but the wind was blowing strong from the south-west and seemed likely to last. It was not until 12 July that the expedition was able to get out of the harbour and into the open sea, but then the wind was fair, and gave them every prospect of a rapid passage. A new chapter was opening in Wellesley's life, one which might lead to Lisbon or Madrid, Mexico or Buenos Aires, to a dukedom or to public pillory and disgrace; but even so, he did not close the old chapter, for he remained Chief Secretary for Ireland, and his last letter from off the Irish coast was to James Trail, instructing him to forward Wellesley's official correspondence.

CHAPTER FIFTEEN

VIMEIRO AND CINTRA
(July–September 1808)

W HILE THE LAST-minute preparations for the expedition were being made, the regimental officers amused themselves in Cork with boating parties and dances. The news of the Spanish uprising caused great excitement, and Wellesley's appointment to command the expedition was met with approval; William Gomm, a young staff officer, was 'very glad' of it, and Captain William Warre told his mother: 'Sir A.W. is a very good officer, and much esteemed, and I trust we have neither a Whitelocke or Gower [the generals blamed for the defeat at Buenos Aires] amongst us.'[1] Still, not everyone was convinced, and William Clinton, the Quartermaster-General in Ireland, wrote in his diary on 3 July: 'Much mischief may be done to the cause by the landing of a corps under such a man as Sir A. Wellesley, who, though I believe is a very gallant man, has not hitherto shewn judgement in his military career in any instance and who, I fear, would not advert to the grand requisite of the strictest discipline being maintained by any troops of ours who should set foot on the Spanish shore.' The idea that Wellesley would neglect the discipline of his troops seems strangely wide of the mark, yet this is not the only mention of it at this time, for in 1809 Lady Hester Stanhope described him as 'famous for indulging his troops'. Lady Hester was, of course, a passionate admirer of Sir John Moore, whose shadow lies over many comments about Wellesley in these years.[2]

The expedition sailed from the Cove of Cork on 12 July with Wellesley aboard HMS *Donegal*, the 74-gun ship of the line commanded by Captain Pulteney Malcolm, the same officer who had carried him from Trincomalee to Bombay in 1801, and the brother of his friend John Malcolm. Wellesley's party included the dependable Colin Campbell, as well as Fitzroy Stanhope, Lord Harrington's son who had served with Wellesley at Copenhagen, and two new faces: Lord Fitzroy Somerset and Wellington's scapegrace nephew William Wellesley-Pole. Somerset was not yet twenty, and he would spend much of the rest of his life working closely with Wellesley, who valued 'his perfect manners, his good temper, [and] his ability to dispatch complicated business in the hurry and hubbub of active service'. Even William Napier who, as a regimental officer and fighting soldier *par excellence*, was inclined to despise the gilded youths of the staff, said of Somerset in 1812 that he was 'as good as he is clever, and nearly as clever as Lord Wellington himself; he will one day be a great man if he lives'.[3]

More senior and important than these aides-de-camp was Wellesley's military secretary, Lieutenant-Colonel Henry Torrens, a twenty-nine-year-old veteran who had served on Whitelocke's staff at Buenos Aires but emerged with his reputation unscathed, even enhanced by the manner in which he gave evidence at Whitelocke's trial.[4] Torrens was an immensely likeable man. At school 'the hilarity of his disposition' had led to him being called 'Happy Harry', while in 1813 Lady Anne Barnard wrote: 'He is a very sweet creature & a very friendly one & a very Handsome one too – & I like his wife's integrity & simplicity of manners very well, tho' he must be the first favourite.'[5] He worked very well with Wellesley and would have returned to Portugal with him in 1809 had he not been required to fill the post of military secretary to the Commander-in-Chief at the Horse Guards. He remained there until 1820 and did much to smooth the often-difficult relations between Wellesley and Sir David Dundas and the Duke of York.

As soon as the convoy was clear of the Irish coast on 13 July Wellesley transferred to the lighter, faster HMS *Crocodile* (22 guns) and sailed ahead to Coruña. He arrived on 20 July, the same day that Charles Stuart, a rising young diplomat, landed with £200,000 for the Galician Junta. They were received with an enthusiasm that proved almost overwhelming. The Spanish authorities were reassuring and cooperative. They told Wellesley that Junot had only about 15,000 French troops in Portugal and that he was isolated with the whole country in arms against him, and that 10,000 Portuguese troops were collected at Oporto. They urged him to land in northern Portugal to cooperate with these forces, and even offered to send some Spanish troops to assist his campaign. Their confidence was unshaken by the recent defeat of their army at the battle of Medina del Rio Seco (14 July) and they repeated that they had no need of British troops, only arms, equipment and money. Wellesley was impressed by their high spirits and the complete absence of any dissent or support for the French. His own confidence in the coming campaign was strengthened, so that he told Castlereagh: 'I should have no doubt of success, even without General Spencer's assistance, or that of the allies, if I were once ashore; but to effect a landing in front of an enemy is always difficult, and I shall be inclined to land at a distance from Lisbon.'[6]

Wellesley sailed from Coruña on the evening of 21 July, made contact with the main convoy off Cape Finisterre on the following day, and again sailed ahead to Oporto, which he reached on 24 July. Here too he was warmly welcomed, while the imposing sight of the convoy of more than eighty ships sailing south along the coast on the following morning eased the doubts and anxieties of the Portuguese, who had been much alarmed by the news of Rio Seco. As one British resident noted in her diary:

> It is now that the Portuguese have confidence in this contest proving successful. They could not persuade themselves the troops could come from England. On the conviction of their arrival the joy is excessive. They have such faith in the English that now they have no doubt but that victory will be reward of this effort for liberty.[7]

Wellesley found that although the whole of northern Portugal had risen against the French the patriots were short of arms, organisation and regular troops. There were thousands of peasants armed with scythes and pikes, but it would be suicidal to throw them into battle against a French army. Even the few thousand regular Portuguese troops who had been collected could not 'in any respect be deemed an efficient force'. The Bishop of Oporto, who led the uprising, promised Wellesley logistical support and the cooperation of the troops who were available.[8]

Wellesley ordered the convoy to wait off Mondego Bay, half-way between Oporto and Lisbon, which Admiral Cotton had suggested as a suitable place to disembark the army, while he sailed on to consult Cotton and look for Major-General Spencer and the subsidiary force. He reached Cotton off Lisbon on 26 July and found the admiral ready to further his plans in every way. But Spencer was not there; he had led his expedition back to southern Spain in case he should be needed to save Cadiz from the French. Worse still, he left a message for Wellesley in which he estimated, on the basis of reports from Hanoverian deserters, that Junot had some 20,000 men. Wellesley did not believe this estimate, which was much higher than the figures he had been given by the Spanish and Portuguese authorities, but he could not completely discount it, and he was annoyed that Spencer had not realised that it made his corps indispensable for Wellesley's operations. He at once wrote to Spencer ordering him to come to Portugal unless he was actually engaged in important operations. With luck it would take little more than a week for Spencer to return, and Wellesley felt that he could use the interval to disembark his army at Mondego Bay and collect the transport and supplies it would need before it could begin its advance on Lisbon.[9]

Wellesley did not get back to Mondego Bay until 30 July, and when he did, he received one of the most unpleasant surprises of his career. The ministers in London had been alarmed by Spencer's report and were hastening to reinforce Wellesley's army with every available man. This included two brigades of infantry under Anstruther and Acland that were almost ready to sail, and Moore's expedition, which had just returned from the Baltic and would soon be ready to sail on to Portugal. However Moore and his second-in-command Lieutenant-General John Hope were both superior to Wellesley, and an attempt by the ministers to detain them in England in order to leave the command in Wellesley's hands had been vetoed by the Duke of York and the King. The ministers had no faith in Moore who, they believed, had provoked unnecessary quarrels with Britain's allies in Sicily and Sweden and who was always making difficulties. Rather than leave the command with him they decided to appoint a more senior general, which pleased the King who thought that even Moore was too junior for such a large and important command. As Lord Chatham was unwilling to leave at such short notice they chose Lieutenant-General Sir Hew Dalrymple, the governor of Gibraltar, who was well aware of the unfolding events in Spain and who had reacted to them with considerable discretion and skill. It was unfortunate that he had seen little active service and none recently, but the ministers hoped that he would play a largely supervisory role and leave the fighting as much as possible to his subordinates. As second-in-command, Dalrymple was given Sir Harry Burrard who had played the same role to general satisfaction at Copenhagen. A number of other generals senior to Wellesley were appointed, and the staff included George Murray as the Quartermaster-General. Whether Dalrymple remained at the head or not, these officers were clearly intended not just for the immediate campaign in Portugal, but to lead the army on to its subsequent operations in Spain, and (again with the exception of Dalrymple and Burrard) they were a fair selection of the best talent in the British army.[10]

Castlereagh was well aware that the despatch of senior officers before Lisbon had fallen would be hard for Wellesley to accept. In his public letter he instructed Wellesley to carry on his operations 'with every expedition that circumstances will permit, without awaiting the arrival of the Lieut. General'. And privately he wrote to assure his friend: 'I have made every effort to keep in your hands the greatest number of men, and for the longest time that circumstances would permit. I shall rejoice if it shall have fallen to your lot to place the Tagus in our hands; if not, I have no fear that you will find many opportunities of doing yourself honour and your country service.'[11] He also recommended Wellesley to Dalrymple's attention with a warmth that was probably counter-productive:

Permit me to recommend to your particular confidence Lieut. Gen. Sir A. Wellesley. His high reputation in the service as an officer would in itself dispose you, I am persuaded, to select him for any service that required great prudence and temper, combined with much military experience.

The degree, however, to which he has been for a length of time past in the closest habits of communication with His Majesty's ministers . . . will, I am sure, point him out to you as an officer of whom it is desirable for you, on all accounts, to make the most prominent use which the rules of the service will permit.[12]

A hint as broad as this was likely to antagonise any self-respecting general (one need only imagine how, a few years later, Wellesley would have reacted), but Castlereagh was evidently feeling guilty.

Wellesley was understandably mortified by the news of his impending supersession, but he avoided the self-lacerating misery he had felt in Bombay seven years earlier. He was reassured not just by Castlereagh's explanation, but also by a private letter from William Wellesley-Pole, which confirmed that he retained the confidence of the Cabinet. This helped, but his main consolation was the hope that he might yet defeat Junot and conclude the campaign before any senior officer arrived. He was still very annoyed and hurt but managed to reply with conscious magnanimity, acknowledging Castlereagh's proven support and assuring him that 'whether I am to command the army or not, or am to quit it, I shall do my best to insure its success; and you may depend upon it that I shall not hurry the operations, or commence them one moment sooner than they ought to be commenced, in order that I may acquire the credit of the success'.[13]

In the midst of his disappointment, Wellesley also gave some thought to the wider war, and privately suggested to Castlereagh that Britain undertake 'to raise, organise, and pay an army in Portugal, consisting of 30,000 Portuguese troops, which might easily be raised at an early period'. This force, combined with a British army of 20,000 men 'including 4,000 or 5,000 cavalry' could play a decisive role in linking the Spanish armies based in Galicia and Andalusia. It 'would give Great Britain the preponderance in the conduct of the war in the Peninsula; and whatever might be the result of the Spanish exertions, Portugal would be saved from the French grasp'. And so, on the very day that the first British troops landed in Portugal, Wellesley formulated the idea that was to be the foundation stone of the strategy that Britain pursued in the Peninsula in years to come. Not that Wellesley's foresight was precisely accurate; he clearly underestimated the time and effort needed to make the Portuguese troops fit to take the field, and the proportions he proposed of British and Portuguese troops (2:3) needed to be reversed. The fundamental concept, however, was sound: that if Britain helped to rebuild the Portuguese army she would almost double the force she could bring into the field in the Peninsula; and that the Portuguese would be willing to give their whole-hearted cooperation to the plan, even though it would require considerable subordination to Britain (a price the Spaniards were less likely to be willing to pay). The idea lay dormant until the beginning of 1809, but it is remarkable evidence of Wellesley's insight that he saw the opportunity so early in the war.[14]

Wellesley's immediate concern however was to land his army and to begin the campaign against Junot. A more cautious officer might have contented himself with establishing a secure base and then waiting for the reinforcements and senior officers who were on their way. But Wellesley was a bold and ambitious soldier; his revised instructions not merely authorised but urged him to proceed expeditiously; and delay would bring disadvantages, both by discouraging the Portuguese and, more seriously, costing time that would be needed to position the British army to take part in the forthcoming campaign in Spain. Wellesley never forgot that the campaign in Portugal was no more than a preliminary operation, undertaken while waiting to see how the British army could be used most effectively in support of the Spanish patriots in their endeavours to drive the French back across the Pyrenees.

The landing began on 1 August and continued for five days. The weather was delightful – clear and still – and the sea was calm except where the powerful Atlantic swell rolled ashore on the beaches in a heavy surf, or where it met the outflow of the Mondego River. This was too dangerous and tricky for the ships' boats, and most of the troops were landed by Portuguese fishing boats and small coastal craft whose crews were familiar with the conditions. Remarkably the whole army seems to have landed without any lives being lost, except possibly one or two horses.[15]

Wellesley's own landing, on 1 August, was observed by the sixteen-year-old Roderick Murchison of the 36th Foot, who recalled it many years later:

It was a fine calm hot day, with little or no surf on the sterile and uninhabited shore, with its wide beach and hillocks of blown sand. The inhabitants of Figueira, on the opposite bank of the river, stood under their variously coloured umbrellas, and my boat being on the extreme left, I could scan the motley group, in which monks and women predominated. Just as I was gazing around, and as our boat touched the sand, the Commodore's barge rapidly passed with our bright-eyed little General. Perhaps I am the only person now (1854) living, who saw the future Wellington place for the first time his foot on Lusitania, followed by his aide-de-camp, Fitzroy Somerset, afterwards Lord Raglan. He certainly was not twenty paces from me, and the cheerful confident expression of his countenance at that moment has ever remained impressed on my mind.[16]

Once ashore, the troops marched a few miles inland to Lavos where they camped. According to Rifleman Harris: 'Next day the peasantry sent into our camp a great quantity of the good things of their country, so that our men regaled themselves upon oranges, grapes, melons, and figs, and we had an abundance of delicacies which many of us had never before tasted. Amongst other presents, a live calf was presented to the Rifles, so that altogether we feasted in our first entrance into Portugal like a company of aldermen.'[17] Before the landing began Wellesley had issued a stern General Order reminding his men that Portugal was an allied country, warning that any acts of outrage or plunder would be punished severely, and giving detailed instructions on how the troops should respect the Catholic Church (such as saluting the Host when it passed through the streets in procession).[18] This order, together with the practical precautions that accompanied it and the generous friendly reception given by the local population, ensured that the British army was on its best behaviour in its first days in Portugal, so that Wellesley could report with considerable satisfaction: 'The troops ... have conducted themselves remarkably well, and I have not heard one complaint of them since the army landed.'[19]

The last of Wellesley's troops disembarked on 5 August and that same night Major-General Spencer finally arrived, a few hours ahead of his corps. Spencer's men came ashore on the three following days (6–8 August), so that by 9 August Wellesley's whole army of some 15,000 men was ready to begin operations. The bulk of the army consisted of fifteen battalions of infantry, most of them excellent, powerful first battalions, between 800 and 1,000 men strong. Seven of them had been at Buenos Aires and others had served at Copenhagen, but they were far from veterans; well-trained, seasoned, but inexperienced, they were confident and eager for battle, although they still had much to learn about campaigning. For cavalry Wellesley had only the 20th Light Dragoons: 394 men with only 180 horses. It was an absurdly low proportion and resulted in the greatest weakness of the army. Presumably it reflected the original purpose of the expedition and a belief that horses could not maintain their condition on the long voyage across the Atlantic, but even so it reflects poorly on Castlereagh that he did not ensure that Wellesley receive at least a couple of regiments of cavalry, with their horses, by the time he sailed from Ireland. The artillery suffered even more grievously from lack of horses, for the Ordnance had provided none on the unhappy assumption that sufficient trained horses would be available locally wherever the expedition might be sent. Wellesley recognised the folly of this while still in London and did his best to overcome it by taking with him 300 horses and their drivers from the Irish Commissariat.[20] This proved sufficient for the three batteries of artillery in his own corps, but Spencer's guns had to be left behind for want of horses to draw them. Lieutenant-Colonel William Robe, the excellent and courageous commander of Wellesley's artillery, was so outraged by the problem that he wrote a series of letters to the

1 A silhouette portrait of Arthur Wesley as a child. Wesley's childhood was unsettled and he showed no signs of any great promise. The family moved from Ireland to England when he was seven and his father died soon after he turned twelve. He was over-shadowed by his eldest brother and did not do well at school, being removed from Eton and sent to a private tutor when he was fifteen.

2 Dangan Castle, County Meath, Ireland. Arthur Wesley's home before the family moved to England in 1776 when he was seven years old.

3 The Countess of Mornington, Wellington's mother. Lady Mornington did not have a high opinion of her son Arthur as a boy, but delighted in his later achievements, although she was never very close to him, or to any of her children, even Richard, her favourite.

4 Lord Mornington by John Downman, 1785. Wellington's eldest brother Richard inherited his father's title and estates in 1781 just before he turned twenty-one. In 1785 he was a fashionable young man with considerable political ambitions and excellent connections, being a close friend of Lord Grenville and the Prime Minister, William Pitt the Younger.

5 A miniature portrait of a young officer of the 76th Regiment in 1787 or 1788. This portrait was recently discovered by Christopher Bryant, and may be the earliest known painting of the future Duke of Wellington. Because the identification rests entirely on the similarity of features with later portraits (especially the lack of a distinct earlobe) it cannot be established beyond doubt, while it is not clear why the young Arthur Wesley would have had his portrait painted wearing the uniform of a regiment in which he only served for around a month. However, it is unlikely that there was another young officer in the same regiment at the same time who resembled later portraits of Wellesley this closely.

6 Kitty Pakenham in 1814 when she was Duchess of Wellington, after a chalk drawing by Sir Thomas Lawrence. Kitty disliked having her portrait painted and very few images of her survive.

7 *Fatigues of the Campaign in Flanders*, a print by Gillray published on 20 May 1793, which attacks the Duke of York for neglecting his troops while indulging himself. Gillray had actually visited the army with Loutherbourg to sketch portraits of the allied commanders for Loutherbourg's picture of the siege of Valenciennes. He was the son of a soldier who had lost an arm at Fontenoy and, as Dorothy George remarks, showed compassion for the hardships suffered by the ordinary soldiers in the army – in this case, the emaciated Guardsmen who wait on the Duke and his party.

8 Lieutenant-General George Harris, commander of the Madras army, later Lord Harris.

9 John Hoppner's portrait of the young Arthur Wesley.

10 and 11 Purneah (*right*), the chief minister, or Diwan, of Mysore, by Thomas Hickey. Purneah had served Tipu Sultan (*left*) and was employed by the British as the effective regent for the restored Raja of Mysore who was then a child. He won universal respect for his ability, hard work and integrity; Arthur Wellesley praised him highly and regarded him as a friend.

12 The Assault and Capture of Seringapatam on 4 May 1799 by Henry Singleton (c. 1800). A stylized depiction of fighting in the breach of the fortress as the storming party, under the command of Major-General David Baird attacked in broad daylight. Tipu was wounded and then killed in the fighting, although it took some time for his body to be discovered. His treasury and palace were thoroughly looted by British and Indian soldiers.

13 'Colonel Maxwell's last charge at Assaye' by Abraham Cooper painted in 1839 and engraved by Jonathan Engleheart for W. H. Maxwell's *Life of His Grace the Duke of Wellington.*

14 Isabella Freese by Thomas Hickey painted in 1804. Arthur Wellesley probably had an affair with Isabella Freese in Seringapatam in 1801-2, and kept at least one portrait of her. He also looked after his godson Arthur Freese (born July 1802) when he was sent home to England in 1807.

15 Charles Lennox, 4th Duke of Richmond, was Lord Lieutenant of Ireland when Wellesley was Chief Secretary, and the two soldiers worked happily and well together.

16 Major-General Sir Arthur Wellesley by Robert Home, painted in Calcutta in 1804. Lord Wellesley commissioned this portrait as a companion piece to Home's portrait of himself, intending both to be hung in Government House.

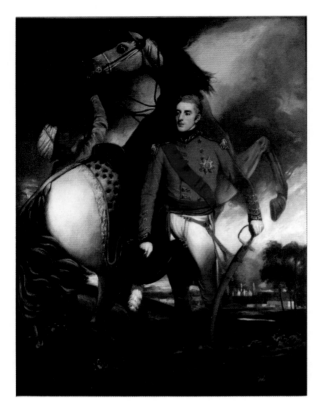

17 Major-General Sir Arthur Wellesley by John Hoppner, painted soon after his return from India in 1805 and exhibited at the Royal Academy in 1806. It is possible that this heroic image – or 'swagger portrait' – was painted as part of a deliberate campaign to remind the public of British victories in India, and so contribute to the defence of Lord Wellesley's policies which were then being attacked in Parliament and inside the East India Company. It was purchased by public subscription in 1808 for Government House, Madras.

18 Miniature of Sir Arthur Wellesley painted in 1808 by Richard Cosway, the most fashionable miniaturist of his day. Wellesley was Chief Secretary for Ireland at the time, but had not renounced his military career, serving in the Copenhagen Expedition in the previous year, and winning the first British victories of the Peninsular War at Roliça and Vimeiro in the year this portrait was painted. He was thirty-nine years old, and had been married for two years.

19 *The Bombardment of Copenhagen* by Christoffer W. Eckersberg depicts the plight of the civilian inhabitants of the city as they endeavoured to escape the buildings set ablaze by the British bombardment.

20 The disembarkation of the British army at Mondego Bay, August 1808, by Henri L'Evêque.

21 and **22** General Jean-Andoche Junot (*left*) was an old friend of Napoleon. He commanded the French army in Portugal in 1807–08, and served under Masséna in the campaign of 1810–11. Marshal Nicolas Jean-de-Dieu Soult (*right*) was one of Napoleon's ablest and most experienced marshals, winning glory at Austerlitz, and pursuing Moore's army to Coruña. He was defeated by Wellington at Oporto in 1809 and in the final campaigns of the war in 1813–14.

23 Napoleon accepting the Surrender of Madrid in 1808, by Antoine-Jean Gros.

24 Sir Arthur Wellesley's headquarters at Vimeiro where the Suspension of Arms which established the basis of the Convention of Cintra was signed on the day after the battle of Vimiero. This view was painted by Captain George Landmann, an engineer officer with the army.

25 Although he had been in his army since boyhood, Lieutenant-General Sir Hew Dalrymple had seen little action and had not relished his experiences in Flanders in 1793–94. However, he had displayed considerable ability as deputy governor of Guernsey in the late 1790s and as governor of Gibraltar in the uncertain months before and after the outbreak of the Spanish uprising.

26 The second son of George III, the Duke of York was Commander-in-Chief of the British Army from 1795 until 1809, when he was forced to resign after a scandal involving his mistress Mary Anne Clarke and allegations of corruption. He was reappointed in 1811 and remained at the Horse Guards until his death in 1827. He deserves considerable credit for the great improvement of the army between 1795 and 1808 which laid the foundations for Wellington's victories in the Peninsula.

27 *The last harvest or British Threshers makeing [sic] French crops*, a print by Charles Williams published in September 1808 celebrating the news of the British victory of Vimeiro (possibly even published before the news of Vimeiro arrived, for it is headed 'A Scene Expected to have happen'd near Lisbon'). This was Wellesley's first appearance in the popular prints and caricatures of the day, and a most flattering one, although the central figure shows no great resemblance to the man himself.

28 *Whitlock the second or another tarnish of British Valor*, a print by George Cruikshank showing three British soldiers abasing themselves before General Junot and hoping that he would be pleased to accept the terms of the Convention which they propose. The nearest of the three, although dressed as a soldier, represents Admiral Cotton; the furthest is Sir Arthur Wellesley. A Portuguese figure in a yellow coat protests that British valour is simply enabling the French to escape with their loot. This is one of many caricatures reflecting popular anger at the terms of the Convention of Cintra.

29 William Wellesley-Pole (1763-1845, created Baron Maryborough, 1821). William was six years older than Arthur, and inherited the estates of a cousin, William Pole, in 1781, making him a significant landowner in Queen's County, Ireland and financially secure. He served in both the Irish and British parliaments, holding a number of junior ministries and proving a capable and efficient man of business, but an unpopular speaker in the House. He also looked after his brother's interests while they were overseas, and kept Wellington well informed on political and family news when he was campaigning in the Peninsula.

30 Harriette Wilson, a courtesan with whom Arthur Wellesley had an affair, probably in 1808–09. In 1824 she published her memoirs attracting great interest and publicity, while ridiculing many of her old lovers, including Wellesley. Unfortunately there is no evidence that he ever scrawled 'Publish and be damned' across a blackmailing letter from her, or her publisher Joseph Stockdale.

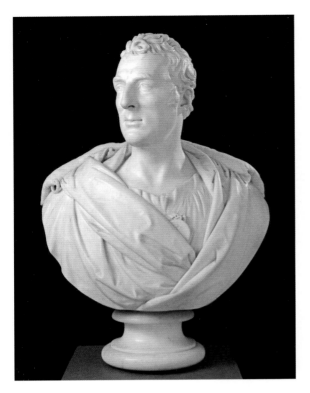

31 A copy of the bust of Sir Arthur Wellesley sculpted by Joseph Nollekens. In her diary entry for 17 July 1809 Kitty recorded, 'Wrote to Sir Arthur. Walked with Longford [her brother] to see Sir Arthur's bust at Nollekens's – it is indeed as like as possible'.

32 Watercolour of Wellesley's sons as infants by Henry Edridge, which Arthur Wellesley pasted to the lid of the dressing case he used on campaign in the Peninsula.

33 An 1813 watercolour by Henry Smith showing the view of Oporto from the River Douro with the bridge of boats which the French destroyed on the night of 11 May 1809. Arriving in front of Oporto on 12 May Wellesley seized the initiative and sent the British infantry across the river in three wine barges. The troops occupied the Bishop's Seminary upstream of the bridge of boats and, with the support of artillery fire from the heights on the southern bank, repelled French attacks.

34 The battle of Oporto, 12 May 1809. This Portuguese print was published a year later in May 1810 and gives an artistically naïve impression of the fighting, which forced Soult to flee Oporto leaving his hospitals and much of his heavy baggage behind. The print was probably intended to encourage patriotic spirits in 1810 faced with a renewed French invasion.

35 Viscount Wellington by Domenico Pellegrini. This portrait, which shows Wellington wearing Portuguese uniform with the ribbon and the star of the Bath, was painted at Lisbon in the autumn of 1809 when Wellington was making plans for the Lines of Torres Vedras and engaged in discussions with the Portuguese regency. An engraving was published in 1810 which extended the portrait to full length.

Board of Ordnance officially protesting at 'the impolicy of sending Artillery to a foreign country without horses. Even the horses we have now, old, blind and casts from the cavalry as they are, we find superior to what we can obtain from the country' – for which piece of impudence he was duly reprimanded.[21]

Wellesley organised his army into six small brigades, with two or three battalions and half a battery of artillery in each. Most of his generals in this campaign returned to the Peninsula later in the war. Major-General Brent Spencer, his second-in-command, was a good-hearted, brave and gallant officer, but nothing more. His role was poorly defined, for he did not command any of the brigades. This arrangement did not work well later in the war, and Wellesley ultimately wrote caustically of Spencer's limitations and foibles, but in 1808 the two men appear to have worked quite comfortably together. Of Wellesley's other subordinates the most significant and the most senior were Major-Generals Rowland Hill and Ronald Ferguson. Hill went on to become Wellesley's most dependable subordinate and was frequently entrusted with a semi-independent command. He was beloved by his troops for his courtesy, calm manner and care for their welfare, and he remained cool and unflustered in the hottest fighting. Ferguson seems also to have been a capable soldier, but he had the folly – or the courage – to attack the Duke of York in Parliament at the height of the Mary Anne Clarke affair in March 1809 (see Chapter 17). The Duke never forgave him, and this proved an obstacle, although not an insuperable one, to his subsequent career. Wellesley got on well with Ferguson, but he may not have greatly regretted the absence of such a vehement Whig from the army in his later campaigns.[22] The remaining brigades were commanded by more junior officers who held the temporary local rank of brigadier.

The advance guard began its march towards Lisbon on 9 August with the rest of the army following the next day. It was the first experience of campaigning for many in the army and Samuel Laing looked back on it with some nostalgia. 'It is not easy to give an idea of the cheerful, exhilarating life of a soldier in the field. Every hour has its novelty and its occupation. One has the same joyous feeling as at a fox chase.' Rifleman Harris and his comrades were equally enthusiastic: 'Being in a state of the utmost anxiety to come up with the French, neither the heat of the burning sun, long miles, or heavy knapsacks were able to diminish our ardour. Indeed, I often look back with wonder at the light hearted style, the jollity, and reckless indifference with which men who were destined in so short a time to fall, hurried onwards to the field of strife; seemingly without a thought of anything but the sheer love of meeting the foe and the excitement of battle.' The young Roderick Murchison, however, found the first few marches exhausting: 'Our whole kit, including three days' provisions, was on our backs, which, with a brace of pistols and the 36th regimental colours, loaded me absolutely to the utmost of my strength.'[23]

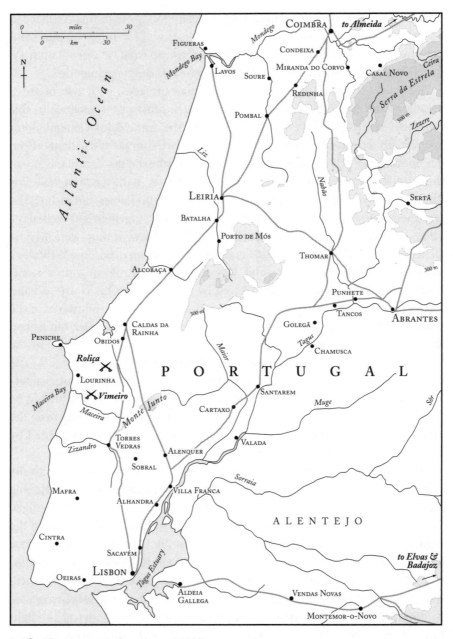

8 The Vimeiro campaign, August 1808.

On 11 August the army reached Leiria where it halted for a day, for the men were out of condition after weeks onboard ship. Here they were joined by the Portuguese army of some 5,000 men under General Bernadino Freire. Unfortunately Wellesley and Freire could not agree on a plan of operations. Freire urged that the army march south to reach the Tagus near Santarem and then advance down the river to Lisbon, whereas Wellesley was determined to stick to the coast road in order to maintain contact with the fleet. Freire believed that the country near the coast was too poor to provision the army, but was willing to march with Wellesley if the British would provide his men with bread from the fleet. Wellesley refused; he had barely enough transport to carry bread for his own men, and besides, he did not believe that Freire was sincere. Rightly or wrongly he formed the impression that Freire was afraid of the French, and of his own ill-disciplined troops, and expected the British to be defeated. He privately warned Castlereagh: 'If you should determine to form a Portuguese army, you must, if possible, have nothing to do with Gen. Freire.' This proved unnecessary, for Freire was murdered by his own men the following March, for not showing more confidence in the face of the French advance on Oporto, a circumstance which lends some indirect support to Wellesley's view of his behaviour in August 1808.[24]

In the end Wellesley and Freire both compromised, although not without considerable ill feeling. Freire lent Wellesley three line battalions, a battalion of caçadores (light infantry) and some 250 cavalry, all of whom would be fed by the British and commanded by Lieutenant-Colonel Nicholas Trant, a British officer in the Portuguese service. Nominally this amounted to some 2,300 men, or almost half of Freire's army, although its effective strength was probably much lower: between 1,600 and 2,000 men.[25] The Portuguese infantry were described by one British officer: 'The poor fellows had little or no uniform, but were merely in white jackets, and large broad-brimmed hats turned up at one side, some having feathers, and others none, so that they cut rather a grotesque appearance.'[26] The caçadores were mostly students from Coimbra University, enthusiastic but ill-disciplined, armed with a motley collection of fowling pieces and carbines and unready for the shock of war.[27] Roderick Murchison agreed that the 'Portuguese infantry was in a most wretched state of discipline', but he was favourably impressed by 'four squadrons of cavalry, good-looking, well-mounted dragoons, being the *garde de police* of Lisbon, who had made their escape from thence on hearing of our disembarkation'.[28]

As the army advanced it had its first contact with the French. Some deserters from the 4th Swiss Regiment, clad in long red coats, surrendered even before the army reached Leiria. Three French commissaries, taken prisoner by the Portuguese at Thomar on 12 August, were handed over to the British on 14 August and went aboard the fleet, lucky to be alive. There was much evidence of the French presence at Alcobaça that day; the town had been plundered and the corpse of a French soldier with all his accoutrements was found, drowned, in a large wine cask.[29] On 15 August near Obidos the first shots of the campaign were fired when the British advance guard encountered the outposts of a strong French force. Rather than giving the French time to withdraw peacefully the British pressed forward and suffered a sharp check when the French reached their main body several miles to the south. Lieutenant Ralph Bunbury of the 95th Rifles was killed, the first British officer to fall in the Peninsular War, and Wellesley's brother-in-law Captain Hercules Pakenham was slightly wounded.[30]

The skirmish at Obidos reflected a scarcely-contained exuberance in the army, which Wellesley himself shared. He was annoyed but not at all disheartened by the limited Portuguese assistance offered by Freire, and remained confident of victory if he could bring the campaign to a decision before the reinforcements and accompanying superior officers arrived. He had about 17,000 men under his command (including the Portuguese), and believed that Junot had scarcely this many in all Portugal. As the French had small garrisons at Almeida, Elvas, Peniche and Setubal, and would need to leave a significant force to hold Lisbon, he could expect to have the weight of numbers on his side if Junot offered battle.[31] But Wellesley's intelligence was mistaken, seriously underestimating the strength of Junot's army. The information provided by Spanish and Portuguese sources was extremely inaccurate, while even Spencer's estimate fell short of the mark, for there were more than 26,000 French troops in Portugal. Nonetheless Junot was in an extremely difficult position; he was completely cut off from the French forces in Spain and had no news, only discomfiting rumours of their fate. Apart from Elvas and Almeida (whose garrisons were much stronger than Wellesley believed: some 1,400 and 1,200 men respectively)[32] he had concentrated his whole army around Lisbon when the Portuguese insurrection spread throughout the country. Lisbon was the key to Portugal, but it was a great city and needed a large garrison if it was to be held securely. The task was made more difficult by the presence of 6,000 Spanish troops whom the French had disarmed and imprisoned in pontoons in the harbour when first news arrived of the Spanish uprising. Siniavin's naval squadron was a further complication, for the Russian admiral refused to provide any useful cooperation and Junot could not be sure of his intentions. Then there was the British fleet off the Tagus, which might at any time attempt to force its way into Lisbon harbour or land a force of troops near the city, encouraging the Portuguese populace to rise against the French.

On 25 July Junot sent Loison with 7,000 men to Elvas to discover what was happening in Spain and to open a line of communication with the other French armies. But when news that the British had begun landing reached Lisbon he recalled Loison and detached General Delaborde to observe, and if possible delay, Wellesley's advance. Loison's return march was impeded by the intense summer heat and he only reached Abrantes on 9 August, where he was forced to halt for two days to allow his men to rest. Even then his movements were slow and he was still a long day's march from Delaborde late on 16 August. Neither Wellesley nor Delaborde were sure of his exact location, although they knew that he was gradually approaching from the east.

Wellesley consolidated his position at Obidos on 16 August, distributing rations from the fleet, concentrating his army and reconnoitring the French position. According to Captain Landmann of the Engineers, the talk in the army ran on Junot's reported boast that 'he should make the pipe-clay fly out of us in good style as soon as we engaged his troops'. The British were confident and eager for battle but not all the officers were sure of Wellesley, with more than one remarking: ' "Oh, if Sir Arthur thinks he can beat the French troops as easily as he has been accustomed to conquer the Indians, we shall suffer severely".'[33]

Wellesley thought that Delaborde might withdraw during the night of 16 August, but dawn on 17 August found the French still in their position about Roliça and Loison still miles away.[34] Delaborde was far too weak to offer a serious threat to Wellesley's army (he was outnumbered four to one), but his aim was to gain time by forcing the British to deploy before withdrawing at the last minute, much as the rearguard of a retreating army would do. With this in mind he initially occupied a low hill to the north of the village of Roliça and well in advance of his main position. Wellesley determined to use his numerical strength to envelop the French, turning both their flanks and threatening Delaborde's line of retreat before engaging frontally. He therefore detached Trant with most of the Portuguese infantry to the west and Ferguson with two brigades to the east. The strength of Ferguson's force suggests that Wellesley wanted to be sure that it could defend itself if it encountered Loison's division. The rest of the army was in the centre and it advanced slowly, in good order, to give time for the flanking columns to gain ground.

Delaborde watched these manoeuvres with an appreciative eye, and at the last moment skilfully disengaged and retired to his main position. This was a line of steep hills or bluffs with narrow gullies splitting deep into their face. The hills rose some 300 feet above the surrounding country and were covered with pines. It was not a position to be attacked lightly and Wellesley intended that Ferguson and Trant would turn it and threaten the French retreat before the British centre attempted to scale the heights. But something went wrong. Exactly what happened and why is not clear, but it seems that Lieutenant-Colonel Browne persuaded or instructed Ferguson to abandon his flank march and that his column returned to the plain well short of the French position. There is not enough evidence to say whether Browne was acting on his own initiative, conveying orders from Spencer, or had mistaken some instructions from Wellesley, and each of these explanations presents problems, but no recriminations have survived in the written record. With Ferguson's column on the plain and the skirmishers already engaged, Wellesley decided that there was no time to renew the attempt to outflank the French position and gave orders for a frontal assault on the hills.[35]

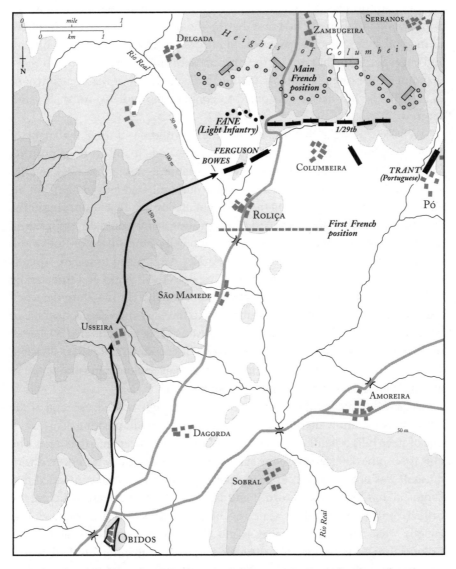

9 The combat of Roliça, 17 August 1808. (N.B. This map is oriented with south at the top. All troop positions approximate, many conjectural.)

The British light infantry had followed the French when they retired to their main position and were now pushing up the slope of the hill and trying to work their way round the French flanks. They made good use of the extensive cover, but found the heat of the day oppressive, and their progress appeared slow to the inexperienced troops in the centre. The grenadiers of the 29th Regiment grew impatient and called out to their commander: 'We can do as well as them, colonel.' But he replied: 'Never mind, my lads, Let the "light bobs" lather them first, we will shave them afterwards.'[36] Beneath the surface calm Lieutenant-Colonel the Honourable George Lake, the commander of the 29th, was probably just as impatient as his men. He was the son of Lord Lake and inherited his father's direct approach to military operations. His regiment was in splendid condition and he himself was a striking figure, wearing a sparkling new uniform and mounted on a handsome charger seventeen hands high.[37]

What happened next is controversial. Most secondary accounts of Roliça state that Lake's patience finally snapped and that, without Wellesley's authority, he ordered his men forward in an attack which led to heavy losses.[38] However, this does not seem to be quite correct. In a confidential letter written to his brother William two days after the battle (and not published until 1948, well after Oman and Fortescue had written their histories), Wellesley criticises Lake for attacking up the wrong gully, for hurrying his men and not giving time for the light infantry to clear the way, and for moving before other troops were in a position to support him, but not for flagrantly destroying orders or turning a demonstration into a serious attack contrary to his general's wishes. This is certainly more plausible; Lake may have been hot-headed and impetuous but he was too experienced a soldier to charge forward uncontrollably at the sight of the enemy.[39] And Wellesley would almost certainly have blamed him, at least privately, had he done so.

In an account that largely tallies with Wellesley's account of the action, Charles Leslie, a lieutenant of the 29th, describes how the regiment advanced up a steep gully so narrow that in places only two or three men could scramble side by side, under heavy fire from the French skirmishers. Halfway up the height the gully broadened into a small olive grove and the leading companies of the regiment paused as the men caught their breath and fell back into the ranks. Colonel Lake's fine horse was shot, and Major Way gave him his. The advance resumed up a narrow defile still under fire. The leading companies reached the summit and began to deploy when they came under even heavier fire from the main body of French infantry, which was sheltered behind a low bank or wall. The British could see the French officers unsuccessfully endeavouring to stop their men firing and charge instead. 'Colonel Lake called out, "Don't fire, men; don't fire; wait a little, we shall soon charge" (meaning when more companies should come up), adding "the bayonet is the true weapon for

British soldiers".' But at this moment he was killed and his men opened fire. Adding to the confusion, some Swiss soldiers serving the French now tried to surrender or change sides. Eventually, seeing that the regiment could not establish itself on the summit, Major Egerton ordered the men to fall back to the olive grove where they rallied on the left flank of the regiment and the 9th Foot, which had followed them up the gully.[40]

Although the 29th was repulsed for the moment it soon renewed the attack with the support of the 9th, which may have taken the lead – certainly both regiments were heavily engaged. At the same time the 5th Regiment found its way up a rock that the French had regarded as inaccessible and left unguarded, while the light infantry were pushing forward, gradually gaining the upper hand over the French voltigeurs. Delaborde had already engaged more heavily than he had intended; Wellesley's bold frontal attack had afforded him little time to withdraw and the precipitous enthusiasm of the British assault had taken away what little opportunity remained. He also had his own reasons for waiting, in the hope that he would be joined by Loison. It was now time for him to extricate his small force if it was to escape being crushed by superior numbers. The French managed their retreat with considerable skill, getting away in good order, although not without suffering quite heavy casualties.[41]

Wellesley's army suffered 479 casualties at Roliça including 70 dead and more than 70 missing, some of whom had been taken prisoner.[42] The 29th lost most heavily with 190 casualties including Lake, while both the 9th and 5/60th suffered more than 60 casualties, and Lieutenant-Colonel John Stewart of the 9th was also killed. French losses are more difficult to determine. Wellesley estimated them at 1,500, which was much too high; but even French sources suggest a total of around 600 casualties, and this is supported by Martinien's invaluable tables of French officer casualties.[43]

Wellesley gave his men unstinting praise, telling Castlereagh: 'I never saw such desperate fighting as in the attack of the pass by Lake, and in the three attacks by the French on our troops in the mountains. These attacks were made in their best style, and our troops defended themselves capitally.'[44] Some officers who were not present were inclined to be critical, with John Colborne writing home that 'the bull was taken by the horns and more bravery than generalship was shown'. But the general feeling in the army was one of triumph. At last they had come to blows with the French and emerged victorious despite the formidable position the enemy occupied. First-night nerves were overcome and the army's confidence in itself and in its general gained a new assurance. Samuel Laing wrote:

> The action was sharp and bloody. No other commander in the British Service at that period would have attacked troops so strongly posted. It was a presage of what Sir Arthur Wellesley, now Duke of Wellington, would attempt. It was

wisely done although contrary to military prudence and rule. Our men were fresh. They were naturally good at scaling heights, and men in their ignorance will do what experienced people would pronounce impossible. If they succeed at the beginning of a campaign in doing a difficult enterprise they take the lead and keep it. They gain confidence in themselves and the enemy is daunted by the unexpected result.[45]

On the morning after the engagement Wellesley received news that Anstruther's brigade had arrived off Peniche and that Acland's was expected at any moment. He therefore turned aside and marched south-west to Lourinha and Vimeiro, where he found a good position to cover the disembarkation of his reinforcements. The French still held Peniche but the 3,000 men of Anstruther's strong brigade were able to land near it late on 19 August. Acland had yet to arrive but Wellesley issued orders for the army to advance on Mafra on the following morning. Then on the afternoon of 20 August the ships carrying Acland's brigade were seen working their way up from the south and Sir Harry Burrard arrived in the *Brazen* sloop accompanied by George Murray, the Quartermaster-General, and Henry Clinton, the Adjutant-General. As soon as Wellesley heard of their arrival he hastened to greet his new commanding officer, explain the strategic position and outline the plans he had formed. He had already written to Burrard expressing his confident hope of defeating the French.[46] As the French were known to have concentrated their army (including Loison's force) near Torres Vedras only a few miles away there was every prospect that if the British advanced on 21 August they would bring on the battle that would decide the campaign. Wellesley relished the prospect and must have cursed the fair winds that had brought Burrard to Portugal at the critical moment.

In his innermost heart Burrard may have agreed. He had none of Wellesley's self-confidence and no relish for the task of taking over the command of a successful army in the middle of the campaign, also with the knowledge that he himself would be superseded at any moment when Dalrymple arrived from Gibraltar. He was a gallant soldier and not a fool, but he knew that his best role was as a second-in-command, and his preference was probably, as at Copenhagen, to do nothing until all the reinforcements had arrived and Dalrymple was able to take charge. He believed that Wellesley's advance had been over-adventurous and had no desire to bring the campaign to a crisis by sanctioning any further forward movement. Fortunately the arrival of Acland's brigade provided a good excuse for at least one day of inactivity; the army would halt on 21 August while it disembarked. If the French chose to bring on a battle by attacking, so be it; at least the army had a good position to defend. Yet having made this decision Burrard did not disembark and inspect the position or take command of the army on 20 August, and although this may be regarded as delicacy towards Wellesley, it is hard not to see in it a dread of responsibility and a preference towards inaction.

But despite his diffidence Burrard had already made a decision that had a profound effect on the whole campaign. When he arrived at Mondego Bay he received letters from Wellesley urging that Moore's corps be disembarked and sent to occupy Santarem where it might block any French retreat on either Almeida or Elvas. Burrard rejected this plan; he doubted that Moore's corps was strong enough to face the French alone, and believed that Wellesley might need to fall back on it if he were checked or defeated. Initially he still ordered Moore to disembark at Mondego but when he found that Anstruther and Acland were at hand he wrote to Moore ordering him to re-embark those of his men who had landed and sail south to join the main army, despite Wellesley's clear disapproval. Summoning Moore appeared the safe, prudent course of action but it proved a serious mistake, for there was little hope of forcing the French to surrender, even if they were defeated in battle, so long as they had a line of retreat open.[47]

Junot had left Lisbon on the night of 15 August with three battalions of infantry, some cavalry, ten guns, a large convoy of food and the army's military chest. He left a garrison of more than 6,500 men in and around Lisbon, which reduced his field force to barely 13,000 men. He has been much criticised for this, and certainly the field army proved inadequate, but it is not hard to see his dilemma.[48] Lisbon was the army's only base of operations, and its garrison not only had to overawe the inhabitants but also guard the Spanish prisoners, keep a wary eye on the Russian naval squadron and be strong enough to resist a possible landing from the British fleet which hovered off the mouth of the Tagus. A small garrison would risk the loss of Lisbon even before he could bring Wellesley's army to battle. This is not to say that Junot's judgement was correct; rather that the problem he faced was insoluble.

Having left Lisbon and united his field army of some 13,000 men near Torres Vedras, Junot had little hesitation in attacking the British. He probably did not know of the arrival of Anstruther and Acland or the approach of Moore when he made his plans, but he did not need those details to understand that time was not on his side. He had no prospect of reinforcement, but if he could defeat Wellesley's army he could hope to maintain his position in Portugal until Napoleon restored Spain to obedient tranquillity and reopened communication with France. Nor did the task appear too difficult; Delaborde had seen Wellesley's army deployed on 17 August and should have been able to tell Junot that it was scarcely bigger than his own field force, and that the numerical superiority was made up of Portuguese levies of little value. The arrival of Anstruther and then Acland, which his cavalry presumably reported during

20 August, was unfortunate; but it simply drew attention to the danger of delay and the importance of bringing on the decisive battle as soon as possible.

Junot began his advance on the evening of 20 August, getting his troops through the difficult ground north of Torres Vedras before they camped for the night. He resumed it on the morning of 21 August but halted out of sight well short of the British position to allow his men to eat their breakfast. In the British army the troops were kept in their ranks and on the alert longer than usual that dawn, but when full light brought no sign of the enemy the men were dismissed with orders to be ready to attend Divine Service at ten o'clock (it was a Sunday).[49] Many men went back to sleep but it was amid considerable bustle and activity. Rifleman Harris was woken and set to work repairing the shoes of the company, for he was a cobbler by trade. Other men washed their linen, cleaned their firelocks or collected firewood and water.[50] It was not until about eight o'clock that the alarm was sounded and the troops hurriedly fell in and took up their positions.

Wellesley had chosen his position for convenience rather than for defence, but it was a formidable one. A steep ridge ran east from the coast for about a mile and a half to the village of Vimeiro. Although much of the army was camped here it was never likely to be attacked, and this ridge was held throughout the battle by Hill's brigade, which scarcely fired a shot. Beyond the village, which was situated in a gap in the hills made by the Maceira stream, the ridge turned north-east and extended for several miles. It was less precipitous but a very steep gully at its foot on the French side made it a most awkward obstacle. (The two ridges may be thought of as the hands of a clock at about ten past nine.) The weak point in the line was clearly the narrow gap between the ridges, but this was covered first by the village (which lay a little in front, south of the gap) and beyond by a low gentle hill, not very different from the valley ground beyond, from which the French would advance. Wellesley occupied this rise, which is rather flattered by the name 'Vimeiro Hill', with the brigades of Fane and Anstruther, some six battalions, which also provided the outlying picquet of the army. They were strengthened during the night of 20 August by six guns: three 6-pounders and three 9-pounders.[51] To their rear, beyond the gap lay the army's cavalry, and all the Portuguese ox-carts, mules and other transport of the army. Most of the rest of the army spent the night on the ridge between Vimeiro and the sea.

Junot approached the British position from the south-east with his main body heading towards the village of Vimeiro. Despite the superiority of the French cavalry he had not made a thorough reconnaissance, and seems to have acted without a clear plan. He soon detached part of his cavalry and Brennier's brigade, which had fought so well at Roliça four days before, to try to turn the British flank to the east. However, Brennier, possibly due to the difficulty of

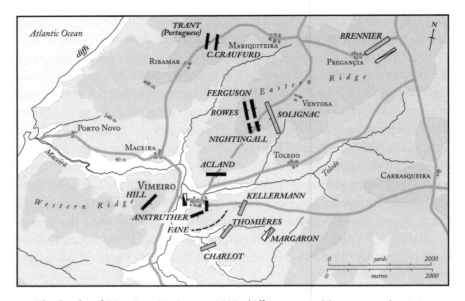

10 The battle of Vimeiro, 21 August 1808. (All troop positions approximate, many conjectural.)

getting his cavalry and guns over the gully at the foot of the ridge, took a circuitous route and lost contact with the rest of the army. Wellesley observed this detachment and realised that the French were likely to ignore his right wing (between Vimeiro and the sea) and began to shift his troops from right to left across the gap between the ridges and behind the screen formed by Anstruther and Fane. Junot followed suit, detaching Solignac's brigade of Loison's division to support Brennier, although Solignac could not find Brennier and acted independently. This significantly reduced the chances, always slim, of French victory, for it left Junot with barely half his infantry in the centre, where the decisive attack would need to be made.[52]

The French attack on Vimeiro Hill and village was made by eight battalions under Thomières, Charlot and Kellermann. It is not clear if these three brigades attacked simultaneously or in succession, but in either case the assault was not well managed. According to the account Anstruther wrote in his journal, the British artillery and light infantry inflicted heavy losses on the French in their advance. He then sent the 52nd to cover the withdrawal of the skirmishers and to turn the French flank, which 'they did very dexterously', while the 97th vigorously attacked the French in front, forcing them to give way. At the same time the 50th Foot in Fane's brigade had been very warmly engaged and had repulsed a determined French attack, while another French column had got into the village, but had then been driven out by the 43rd who charged them with the bayonet. The 20th Light Dragoons pursued the retreating French, but went too far and suffered heavily when they came too close to a wood held by the French reserves.[53]

The success in the centre was unequivocal and decisive. The 43rd suffered most heavily among the British regiments with 118 casualties, while the 50th lost 89 and the 20th Light Dragoons proportionately more with 55 casualties from 240 officers and men present.[54] The French would certainly have suffered more, but there are no reliable figures giving details of their losses. The two British brigades received a little assistance from Acland's brigade (which fired into the exposed right flank of the French troops attacking the village), but essentially they repulsed the attack without drawing on any of Wellesley's reserves except the cavalry. The British received some advantage from the terrain, and from the close support of their artillery, while their senior officers handled them with great skill; both Fane and Anstruther emerge with considerable credit. But underlying all this was the confidence and eagerness for action displayed by the troops, many of whom (Anstruther's brigade) had been ashore for less than two days, but who were far from intimidated or overawed by the occasion.

The French attacks on the British left seem to have been a little later than those in the centre.[55] Here Solignac's brigade came into action first for it had taken a more direct route across the gully and onto the ridge than Brennier's brigade, which was still making its wide detour. Having climbed the ridge onto the open ground beyond, Solignac swung round to his left (or south-west) and pushed forward parallel to the ridge through the village of Ventosa.[56] Wellesley had the three brigades of Ferguson, Nightingall and Bowes, or seven battalions, deployed in two lines to oppose Solignac's three battalions, making it a far-from-equal contest. Nor does this include Trant's Portuguese and the British brigades of Craufurd and Acland, which were also available if they had been needed.

Young Roderick Murchison, carrying the colours of the 36th in this, his first battle, describes this part of the fighting in a long letter to his uncle written only two days later:

> The fire of the enemy soon became very hot, and even though the 36th were lying on their breasts under the brow, our men were getting pretty much hit, whilst the regiment in our rear, the 82nd, which at that time could not fire a shot, suffered more than we did. General Spencer, who commanded the division . . . was hit by a ball in the hand, and I saw him wrap his handkerchief round it and heard him say 'It is only a scratch!' Soon after, the light infantry in our front closed files and fell in; our guns were pulled back, and then came the struggle. General Ferguson waving his hat, up we rose, old Burne (our Colonel) crying out, as he shook his yellow cane, that 'he would knock down any man who fired a shot'.

This made some merriment among the men, as tumbling over was the fashion without the application of their Colonel's cane. 'Charge!' was the word, and at once we went over the brow with a steady line of glittering steel, and with a hearty hurrah . . . not an instant did the enemy stand . . . Off they went, and all their guns were instantly taken, horses and all, and then left in our rear, whilst we went on chasing the runaways for a mile and a half, as hard as we could go . . .

The French attempted to rally several times, but the British kept pushing them back until at last they made a stand at a small hamlet. 'Here it was', Murchison continued:

that Sir Arthur Wellesley overtook us after a smart gallop. He had witnessed from a distance our steady and successful charge, and our capture of the guns, and he now saw how we were thrusting the French out of this hamlet. Through the sound of the musketry, and in the midst of much confusion, I heard a shrill voice calling out, 'Where are the colours of the 36th?' and I turned round (my brother ensign, poor Peter Bone, having just been knocked down), and looking up in Sir Arthur's bright and confident face, said, 'Here they are sir!' Then he shouted, 'Very well done, my boys: Halt, halt – quite enough!'[57]

There was a moment of danger for the British on this side of the battlefield when Brennier's brigade suddenly appeared in the flank and rear of the pursuing British infantry when they were disordered and vulnerable. The brunt of this new French attack seems to have fallen on the 71st and 29th while Murchison, in the 36th, was scarcely aware of it. Brennier's men recaptured the guns Solignac had lost only to lose them again when the British, recovering from their initial surprise, counter-attacked. Brennier's brigade, weakened by the casualties it had suffered at Roliça and possibly shaken by the sight of Solignac's flight, gave way without the British needing to call upon Bowes's brigade to assist the 71st and 29th. Brennier himself was wounded and captured by Corporal John Mackay of the 71st whose proud honesty in declining to take the French general's purse became the talk of the army and won him Wellesley's patronage.[58]

Many young men, including some who had been in the army for several years, had their baptism of fire at Vimeiro. Roderick Murchison admitted that he had felt and looked rather pale as the battle began and that Captain Hubbard, seeing his plight, gave him a good draught of Holland's gin from his canteen and patted him on the back, assuring him that he would never feel so uncertain again. 'And he was quite right; the first start over, and you are ever afterwards one of a united mass of brave men.'[59] Similarly, the even younger Colin

Campbell, the future Lord Clyde and hero of the Indian Mutiny, was led to the front of the regiment by his captain when it first came under distant fire and walked quietly up and down until his nerve steadied – treatment that Campbell described as 'the greatest kindness that could have been shown me at such a time'.[60] The anonymous memoirist from the ranks of the 71st had seen service at Buenos Aires, but he was still relatively inexperienced and he admits: 'In our first charge I felt my mind waver; a breathless sensation came over me. The silence was appalling. I looked alongst the line. It was enough to assure me. The steady, determined scowl of my companions assured my heart and gave me determination'.[61] Rifleman Harris takes the point further in one of the most explicit statements of the importance of the respect earnt by gallantry in action for all ranks: 'It is, indeed, singular, how a man loses or gains caste with his comrades from his behaviour, and how closely he is observed in the field. The officers, too, are commented upon and closely observed. The men are very proud of those who are brave in the field, and kind and considerate to the soldiers under them. An act of kindness done by an officer has often during the battle been the cause of his life being saved'.[62] These informal bonds of social pressure, self-respect and comradeship were vastly more important than the crude sanctions of formal discipline in supporting and sustaining courage in action. Very few men or officers were ever charged or punished with 'cowardice in the face of the enemy' in this period, but a reputation gained or lost on the battlefield would have immense implications for their standing in the regiment for years to come.[63] Even generals were not immune to this observation, and on the rare occasions that a senior officer became flustered or unhappy under fire, he could not hope to hide it, or to retain the confidence of his men. Wellesley's own courage was never in doubt, while his coolness and self-possession in action helped give confidence to all the officers and men under his command.

With Brennier's defeat the French army was almost completely broken. Junot had no reserves left except for some cavalry, his artillery and two battalions of infantry, which he had summoned from Lisbon the previous day and which arrived about midday, too late to take part in any of the attacks. By contrast the British army was in good order; not a single brigade had suffered so much that it could not be asked to do more, while at least half the army (the brigades of Hill, Craufurd, Bowes, Acland and Trant's Portuguese) had scarcely been brought into action. Wellesley had no doubt that the moment was ripe to transform the French defeat into a rout by ordering his men to advance. However the decision no longer rested with him. Burrard had disembarked and joined the army during the morning but had wisely allowed Wellesley to remain in charge during the fighting. Wellesley now approached him with the words: 'Sir Harry, now is your time to advance, the enemy is completely beaten, and we shall be in Lisbon in three days.'[64] But Burrard refused. He was worried

by the strength of the French cavalry and was not sure that Junot did not have
hidden reserves, and he may have been influenced by Henry Clinton, his
Adjutant-General. According to a much-repeated story, Wellesley turned away
in disgust and said to his staff: 'Well, then, we have nothing to do but to go and
shoot red-legged partridges' – although one veteran not present at the battle
improved this to the even more cutting: 'You may think about dinner, for there
is nothing more for soldiers to do this day.'[65] It proved a decisive moment, for
the opportunity Burrard squandered was not recovered. His decision the
previous evening to halt the army on 21 August can be defended; but his failure
to recognise that Junot's defeat had transformed the position was simply inexcusable. He commanded a victorious army that heavily outnumbered its
broken and disordered opponents; the French cavalry, which so concerned
him, numbered fewer than 2,000 men, some of whom were far to the flank
covering Brennier's flight. It is true that he had only just landed and was unfamiliar with the terrain and the army, but few generals can ever have been
presented with such an easy chance to strike a telling blow and gain lasting
fame, and his refusal showed that he was unworthy of the rank he held. Lack of
confidence was probably the explanation; he felt that Wellesley should be
content at having won a victory, and he would not do anything that risked its
reversal. Remarkably he was encouraged in his decision by Murray and Clinton,
his chief staff officers who maintained their arguments, and their desponding
attitude, of the previous day.[66] If Wellesley's approach echoed Nelson's ruthless
confidence and high expectations, Burrard's was not only similar to the timid
caution of Sir Robert Calder, but worse, for his force was clearly superior to
the French.

There was much surprise and discontent among the troops at the failure to
advance, but this was mixed with the usual occupations following a battle:
tending the wounded, discussing the events of the day, and looking for booty.
William Warre spent the afternoon 'collecting the wounded English and
French, and conducting them to a place of safety from the Portuguese cowards,
who won't fight a sixteenth of a Frenchman with arms, but plunder and murder
the wounded, poor wretches'.[67] But it was not only Portuguese peasants, soldiers'
wives and camp followers who prowled the battlefield; many a good soldier had
an eye to plunder. Rifleman Harris admits: 'After the battle I strolled about the
field in order to see if there was anything worth picking up amongst the dead.
The first thing I saw was a three-pronged silver fork . . .' He refused to take
some gold and silver crosses looted from a church from fear of 'incurring the
wrath of Heaven', but stripped the shoes off the body of an officer of the 50th
Foot who had already been thoroughly looted. He was fired upon by a lone
Frenchman, either one of the wounded or a fellow marauder, and killed him
before taking a long draught of wine from his calabash and searching the body

for money. A passing officer of the 5/60th, far from reprimanding him, advised him to search the lining of the Frenchman's coat, where Harris found a purse containing a few coins. The bugles of the 95th then sounded assembly and Harris fell in; Major Travers demanded to see what plunder Harris had found but again there was no rebuke, only sympathy that he had not done better.[68]

The British army suffered 721 casualties at Vimeiro: 135 killed, 535 wounded and 51 missing.[69] Wellesley privately estimated French losses at 'not short of 3,000 men'[70] but this was much too optimistic; few generals fail to see double when calculating enemy losses. Oman and Fortescue are both happy to accept Foy's statement that the French lost 1,800 men, including several hundred unwounded prisoners, and given the lack of pursuit this is a higher figure relative to the British than one would expect, although not implausibly high compared to the size of Junot's army.[71] (The infantry, the troops principally engaged, would have lost between 15 and 20 per cent of their strength – including prisoners – and this seems reasonable; one would not expect them to have been broken without suffering this much.) The French lost thirteen of the twenty-one guns they brought into action, a surprisingly high proportion, which reflects both the completeness of their defeat and the boldness with which the guns had been used to support their attacks.[72]

Wellesley's mood on the following morning was mixed. At one level he was still delighted with his victory, which he described in a confidential letter to William Wellesley-Pole as 'an unmerciful beating'; and he acknowledged his good fortune that the French had attacked while he was still in command of the army. He added, and this is confirmed by other sources, that 'the Army are delighted that they gained this second victory under the Command of their Old General'. But his supersession and Burrard's reluctance to follow his advice overshadowed everything and left Wellesley deeply unhappy. He told William that he was 'not pleased' with Burrard's decision on 20 August to prevent the army marching the next day, 'any more than I was with the manner in which it was made'. And he concluded: 'I am by no means satisfied with the way in which I see things will go on here; I should be glad to be called home to my Office, or anything else in which I could be useful'. It is significant that Wellesley was so despondent at this point, for he had yet to meet Dalrymple although the new commander's arrival had been signalled. If Dalrymple had favoured Wellesley, this *cri de coeur* might have caused unfortunate complications, but it was not uncharacteristic of Wellesley to slide precipitately into despair when thwarted.[73]

Dalrymple arrived on the morning of 22 August and Burrard probably breathed a sigh of relief that his brief authority was at an end. Dalrymple never concealed that he believed that Wellesley had undertaken a perilous campaign in which victory could bring no real advantage, and the slightest setback would lead to disaster.[74] Wellesley was soon made painfully aware of his new commander's lack of confidence in him. When he explained his plans for the army's advance Dalrymple listened coldly and was unconvinced until Colonel Murray 'took him aside, & settled in a few words that we should march'.[75] Wellesley strongly urged that Moore's corps be sent to Santarem where it might even now block the French line of retreat, and where it would draw its supplies from a fresh fertile area. But Dalrymple was, quite simply, afraid of the French, and felt that he could not have too many men in hand in case there was another battle.[76] Dalrymple was not in an easy position; he had no experience commanding an army in the field and had no time to learn, or even to grasp the strategic situation. But his position might have been worse: the army had just won a victory; it outnumbered the French field force by three to two; it had more than a week's supplies in camp; the troops were healthy and full of ardour; and numerous reinforcements were at hand. Wellesley might not have been an easy subordinate to manage but he had proved competent and he had a clear and reasonable plan to conclude the campaign; to reject this and show his distrust so openly was unwise.

Meanwhile in the French camp Junot and his generals contemplated the consequences of defeat. Their prospects were bleak. Although the British had not taken full advantage of their victory it would take some time to restore order and discipline in the army; stragglers were still coming in, and the loss of confidence was probably irreversible. At a Council of War Junot could not conceal his gloom. There appeared to be three options, none of them very promising. The French could fall back to the naturally strong position at Mafra and Montechique and attempt to hold it against British attack; they could attempt to retreat on Elvas, but they now knew that Joseph had evacuated Madrid and that there were no friendly troops closer than Burgos many hundreds of miles away; or they could attempt to negotiate with the British for the evacuation of Portugal. Not surprisingly the Council of War decided to investigate this last option first. It was possible, though not very likely, that the British would grant generous terms in order to conclude the campaign quickly and spare Lisbon any damage, while nothing would be lost if they refused. General Kellermann, who spoke some English, was deputed to undertake the negotiations; as he left he told another officer that he was being sent 'to see if he could get the army out of the mousetrap'.[77]

Kellermann's approach, escorted by two squadrons of cavalry, caused a brief flurry of alarm in the British army before it was realised that he had come to parley. The discussions took place in Wellesley's headquarters, as they were convenient; Dalrymple, Burrard and Wellesley all were present, and Clinton and Murray were consulted. Kellermann's proposals were optimistic, even audacious. The French army would agree to evacuate Portugal on certain conditions, including that the British transport it by sea back to France; that none of the officers or men be regarded as prisoners of war; that they take their weapons, equipment, ammunition and private property with them; that Siniavin's squadron be free to leave Lisbon as from a neutral port; that French residents in Portugal and Portuguese who had collaborated with the French be granted immunity and up to twelve months to depart the country; and that notice of forty-eight hours be given of any resumption of hostilities. All this was couched in language that eased French sensibilities while irritating those of the British – a reference to 'Sa Majesté Imperiale et Royale, Napoleon I' (His Imperial and Royal Majesty Napoleon I), a title which had never been recognised by the British government, being only the most obvious example. No doubt Kellermann hoped that if he pitched his initial demands high he would give the appearance of confidence, while leaving room to grant concessions and still obtain a satisfactory agreement. He must have been almost as surprised as delighted to find that the British were willing to accept these terms as the basis of negotiation, and only expressed firm reservations on a few points, notably the position of Siniavin's squadron and the definition of private property. The agreement was drawn up as a suspension of hostilities, a temporary truce that would last until a definitive convention was negotiated, and was signed by Kellermann and by Wellesley. Kellermann dined with the British generals and rode back to French headquarters in the comfortable knowledge that he had regained all that had been lost in the battle of 21 August, and perhaps a little more.[78]

Exactly what happened on the British side in the course of the negotiations became a matter of controversy, but the essential points are clear. Dalrymple was present throughout and made the decision to accept Kellermann's terms. He had taken command of the army and rejected Wellesley's plan of operations; the responsibility was his. Wellesley had no formal responsibility whatsoever. Less formally his advice may have had some influence, and he agreed with the central point that the French army should be assisted to evacuate Portugal. It is not hard to see why; he did not believe that any active operations would flourish under Dalrymple's command, and he was feeling jaundiced and sickened by the whole campaign. Any chance of rapidly forcing the French to surrender as prisoners of war had been lost when Burrard refused to send Moore's corps to Santarem and vetoed the pursuit of Junot's army when it was confused and broken after the battle. Wellesley objected to some of the details of the armistice, in particular to its indefinite duration and the provisions involving the Russian squadron, but was overruled by Dalrymple who told him that it would be useless 'to drive [the French] to the wall upon a point of form'.[79] The British generals agreed on demanding a strict definition of the 'private property' to be retained by the French to exclude at least some of the loot they had taken from the Portuguese; and made the provisions relating to Siniavin's squadron subject to Admiral Cotton's approval. It is clear that Wellesley expressed his views freely; but equally clear that he did not have the final say on any point. His signature on the armistice arose from a point of protocol; Dalrymple intended to sign it himself, but Kellermann objected that as he, a subordinate officer, would be signing for the French, a similar officer should sign on behalf of the British. Dalrymple then asked Wellesley to sign and he did so without demur.[80]

Wellesley himself was quick to set on record his role in the negotiations and his attitude to the result, writing to Castlereagh the next day: 'Although my name is affixed to this instrument, I beg that you will not believe that I negotiated it, that I approve of it, or that I had any hand in wording it . . . I object to an indefinite suspension of hostilities; it ought to have been for forty-eight hours only . . . [However] I approve of allowing the French to evacuate Portugal.'[81] And on 24 August he wrote to William Wellesley-Pole, outlining the same objections together with one more: 'I also think that some measures must be adopted to force the French Generals to disgorge some of the Church Plate which they have stolen.' Wellesley sent his brother a copy of his letter to Castlereagh and explicitly authorised him to reveal his reservations.[82] The attempt to distance himself from the suspension of arms was immediate and ruthless; but it was not unfair – he owed no particular loyalty to Dalrymple and the reservations he expressed on 23 and 24 August were the same as those he had expressed to Dalrymple on 22 August; if he explained himself more fully to Castlereagh and Pole that was because they had treated him with confidence and respect.

In these same letters Wellesley made clear that he felt that he could not continue to serve under Dalrymple, telling Castlereagh: 'I should prefer to go home to staying here. However, if you wish me to stay, I will; and I only beg that you will not blame me, if things do not go on as you and your friends in London wish they should.'[83] Beneath the veneer of calm he was feeling very sore, and he allowed his resentment and hurt pride to show through more clearly in his letter to his brother William:

I wish that I was away from this Army. Things will not flourish as we are situated and organized . . . There is no more confidence in me on the part of the Chiefs than if I had been unsuccessful . . . [they] ask my opinion about every thing and never act according to it . . . is this the confidence in the opinion of a Man who has conducted the Service successfully to the present moment, which is to make him responsible to his friends in the Govt. for the events which will occur here? . . . it is quite ridiculous; but there is not one of them capable of commanding the Army, & at this moment it rests with me; the Departments look to me alone . . .[84]

Wellesley's contempt for Dalrymple may have been coloured by pique, but it soon became obvious to all that the new commander was incapable of managing the army. Sir John Moore, who landed on 25 August, noted in his journal: 'I was sorry to find everything in the greatest confusion, and a very general discontent. Sir Hew, though announced to the army, had not as yet taken the direction of it; much was still done by Sir Arthur Wellesley, and what was not done by him was not done at all.' Moore was convinced that if Burrard had not interfered Wellesley 'would have been in Lisbon next day', and commented that both before and after the battle 'Sir Arthur's views . . . were extremely right'. He even agreed with Wellesley's reasoning on repatriating the French army, for 'it is evident that if any operation is to be carried on it will be miserably conducted'.[85]

Neither Wellesley's spirits nor Dalrymple's command of the army improved over the next few weeks as August gave way to September. The army was completely reorganised; brigades were broken up or given to new generals and Wellesley was relegated to the command of a mere six battalions. Many of the troops who had landed at Mondego Bay and fought at Roliça or Vimeiro were denied the chance of seeing Lisbon; while Wellesley's regulations for the discipline and routine of the army were cast aside as so much waste paper. Even the contracts that he had signed for the supply of fresh meat to the troops were dishonoured with the result that the army was soon forced back onto salt provisions from the fleet.[86] On 29 August Dalrymple called a meeting of the army's generals to show them the draft of the final Convention of Cintra, which Murray had negotiated on the basis of the initial suspension of arms. According to Wellesley this draft 'was so objectionable in many parts' that the generals pressed for many changes; he would have liked these alterations to have gone further, but concluded that 'the treaty will answer in its amended form'. However only a few of these alterations were included in the final Convention.[87]

Wellesley had now made up his mind to go home as soon as he could, but even this apparently simple wish presented serious difficulties. After all, the army was still on active service, and Wellesley had often proclaimed his willingness to serve anywhere in any capacity. Castlereagh and Wellesley-Pole both seem to have advised against an immediate return home, warning that it might appear that he had petulantly resigned rather than serving in a subordinate capacity. Wellesley responded by listing his grievances, pointing to his record of service and adding with defiance: 'I am aware that there is a party which will run me down for coming away; but I have never cared much for what people say of me without cause . . . in short I have determined to quit the Army if these gentlemen continue in the Command of it; & I never was more convinced of any thing than that I judge right in making the determination.' He would return to his office in Ireland, or, if the ministers did not want him, he would serve on the staff in England, 'or, if that is impossible, I'll do nothing, and amuse myself with hunting and shooting'.[88] Matters were desperate indeed for Wellesley to contemplate, however distantly, a life of idle hunting and shooting when the British army was about to embark on a campaign against the French on the mainland of Europe.

Wellesley's departure from the army was made easier by the news of the death of James Trail on 16 August 1808 after a short illness. This must have been a genuine shock and source of real sadness, for Wellesley had worked well with Trail and liked him. But it also left Richmond in sole charge of the Irish government without either Chief Secretary or Under-Secretary to share the work. One might cover for the absence of the other, but with Trail dead, Wellesley should either return or resign so that a new Chief Secretary could be appointed. On 17 September he wrote to Dalrymple for permission to go home.[89]

By this time Wellesley had become convinced, not only that Dalrymple needed to be replaced, but that the command should be given to Sir John Moore rather than Chatham or the Duke of York. He knew that the ministers were not predisposed to trust Moore, but Dalrymple's incompetence revealed the folly of entrusting the command to a novice, however senior. He wrote to Moore explaining his intention of speaking to Castlereagh on the subject as soon as he got back to London, and received a cautious but by no means unfriendly reply. In the event the ministers had already given the command to Moore before Wellesley reached London, so his intervention proved unnecessary; but his willingness to play the part of king-maker among his superiors is noteworthy.[90]

Wellesley sailed from Lisbon on the evening of 20 September along with General Ferguson and a number of junior officers. They landed at Plymouth on 4 October and found the whole country in an uproar over the Convention of Cintra. The campaign in Portugal had an important but ambiguous effect on Wellesley's reputation. On the one hand it plunged him into the midst of an intense political controversy that threatened to destroy his career (which will be discussed in the next chapter); on the other it gave him a chance to command an army in Europe against the French. Most of the officers and men who served under him, from Mondego Bay to Vimeiro, were greatly impressed by him. On 3 September the seven senior officers of his original army expressed their 'high respect and esteem . . . and unbounded confidence' in him by subscribing 1,000 guineas for a piece of plate to present to him, and the sum was soon augmented by contributions from Anstruther and Acland, and the junior officers of the army.[91]

There were some doubters amongst those who had not served under Wellesley. For example Lieutenant-General John Hope wrote home on 3 September that Wellesley had 'outstripped all common rules and even the most necessary measures of prudence', although he conceded that he was 'a man of ability and great energy, somewhat headlong and presumptuous, but on the whole certainly a very superior person'. But Moore's praise was less ambivalent and Lord Paget was persuaded, telling his father:

> He is, I really believe, an excellent officer. Every officer speaks well of him. He is very quick, and full of resources. He has lodged with me for two days, and I had during that time an opportunity of observing that he possesses much method and arrangement. He is, besides, the luckiest dog upon earth, for it is a sort of miracle, or rather by two or three combined, to detain Moore's corps ... I feel it to be a real misfortune to me, as a soldier that I am above him on the list, for I think there is a good chance of its cutting me off from all service.[92]

As Paget recognised, by September 1808 Wellesley was the most prominent and successful young general in the British army except for Sir John Moore. And his conduct of the campaign had set a standard that even Moore would find hard to match. Samuel Laing was one of many officers who, having served under Wellesley and then under Moore, made the comparison:

> My prejudices at the time were all in favour of Sir John Moore, but it was impossible not to see even on the first few days of the march that the Army was not victualled and quartered and kept in hand as it had been in the previous campaign by Sir Arthur Wellesley. In that campaign every Brigade saw the bullocks and provisions for its support in the rear or close at hand. Everything was close up. The troops within reach of any point without confusion or fatigue or hurry. Under his successors in command the troops in three days were victualled on salt rations landed from the transports. The Commissariat was ineffective the moment it was out of his command.[93]

Such things counted almost as much as winning battles in the eyes of an army, giving them confidence in their general; and Wellesley had twice led them into victory in battle as well.

CHAPTER SIXTEEN

THE CINTRA INQUIRY
(September–December 1808)

ARTHUR WELLESLEY LANDED at Plymouth on 4 October to find the whole country baying for his blood. According to a travelling companion 'hissings and hootings greeted him at every town and village . . . through which he had to pass on his way to the metropolis'.[1] This popular anger reflected the intense disappointment of shattered hopes and confident expectations, which had overwhelmed the public only a few weeks before. In the summer and autumn of 1808 the British public had become more engrossed in news of the war than at any time since the death of Nelson three years before. The Spanish uprising was novel and its almost miraculous early successes made a mockery of the pessimists who proclaimed French invincibility on land. The public was eager for its own troops to join the fray and had grown impatient even before Wellesley's expedition left Cork. But once the convoy carrying the army had sailed over the horizon, news of its progress came irregularly, by fits and starts, depending on the vagaries of wind and weather.

On 24 July news of the Spanish defeat at Rio Seco dampened spirits and caused some anxiety, even leading to fears that Bessières would advance into Portugal and unite with Junot;[2] but this turned to jubilation when, between 8 and 11 August, news arrived of Dupont's capitulation at Bailen, Bessières's retreat from Leon, and Joseph's flight from Madrid. Lord Hawkesbury felt that Wellesley's campaign would now be 'short and easy', while Edward Cooke (Castlereagh's under-secretary at the War Department) wrote that 'Dupont's Surrender has raised us to the Skies – we think that Junot will *now* try to make himself a golden Bridge, but don't let him carry away his Plunder'. Castlereagh was even more excited and allowed his imagination to soar far beyond the capture of Lisbon: 'How glorious to England it would be, after recovering Portugal, by her Command of the Sea, to meet the Enemy at the Foot of the Pyrenees, and to forbid his return to France.'[3] This optimism even spread to some leading members of the Opposition. Lord Auckland, Grenville's habitually gloomy friend, regarded success in Portugal as virtually a *fait accompli*, while Lord Grey was hearty in his enthusiasm for Wellesley's prospects and regarded Junot's escape as 'hardly possible', although he could not resist criticising the government for not giving Wellesley more men.[4]

Unconfirmed stories that Wellesley's army had landed safely circulated around London on 8 August, and on the following day the pro-Whig *Morning Chronicle* confidently but erroneously stated that the troops had disembarked at Peniche. Other newspapers were even more determined to achieve a scoop, going so far as to report Junot's complete surrender before a shot had, in fact, been fired. Genuine news of Wellesley's landing did not appear until the papers of 16 August and even then it was mixed with inaccurate stories of Spencer's movements.[5]

Another anxious pause followed until, on 1 September, Colin Campbell reached London with Wellesley's despatches describing both Roliça and Vimeiro. The reaction could hardly have been greater if Wellesley had defeated the entire Grande Armée led by Napoleon in person. Castlereagh was overjoyed, writing to Wellesley: 'You will easily believe that few events in my life – indeed, I may say none – have ever given me more gratification than the intelligence of your two splendid victories.' And Hawkesbury told Richmond: 'The Military reputation of our Friend Wellesley will stand now as high in Europe as it did in India.'[6]

It was natural for Wellesley's friends in the government to feel a sense of proprietorial delight in his success, but the celebrations spread across all classes of society and all shades of political opinion. Even the London radicals joined in the mood of the moment, with Cobbett declaring that Vimeiro, although 'not more glorious to the nation', was, in its consequences 'of far greater importance to us than the victory of Trafalgar'. Lord Granville Leveson Gower expressed the thoughts of many when he wrote to Lady Bessborough that, 'the Victory of Sir A. Wellesley is not only valuable as ensuring to us the possession of Lisbon and the Russian Fleet, but as an instance – in addition to those of Egypt and Maida – that the British Troops are at least equal, if not superior, to the French'. The Duke of York, who had presided over the reform of the British army which lay behind the victory, was 'delighted' at 'the glorious news'; even if privately still sore at not being given the command of the army sent to the Peninsula.[7]

The *Morning Chronicle* called for the British army to be sent on to liberate Italy as nothing remained for it to do on the Peninsula, while *The Times* confidently predicted 'the final dissolution of the Continental tyranny and the overthrow of the Tyrant'. And Wellesley made his first appearance in the popular caricatures of the day in a rather crude print by Charles Williams – *The last harvest or British Threshers makeing [sic] French crops* (see plate 27) – in which he is depicted as tall and handsome, in the foreground of a battle scene, in the act of cutting off Junot's long pigtail (a reference to the recent abolition of soldiers' queues).[8]

The Marquess Wellesley fully shared the enthusiasm for the victory, making clear that he regarded it as a triumph for the whole Wellesley family:

> Sir Arthur's most glorious and splendid success . . . is quite complete with regard to his fame, and nearly so with regard to its public result upon the state of Europe. The enthusiasm of the Country in his favour is not to be described; and the discovery is at length made, that some advantage is to be derived from the employment of those intriguing knaves, the Wellesleys, in the Public service.[9]

And when his estranged wife was unkind enough to suggest that Arthur's victories in Portugal eclipsed his own achievements in India, he replied with magnificent and wholly sincere egoism: 'Sir Arthur Wellesley has but followed on this occasion the lessons that I taught him . . . Arthur's glory has cast fresh splendour on that which I acquired in public life; and that which has come to pass under the auspices of my brother adds to my own reputation.'[10]

Lord Wellesley seized the moment and approached the prime minister suggesting that Arthur be granted a peerage. Portland had no objection, but the idea was put to one side when reports of the Convention arrived from Portugal.[11] Arthur Wellesley was not pleased by his brother's action and, before he knew that the proposal had failed, he told William Wellesley-Pole:

> In respect to rewards I have never allowed myself to think about them; much less to write to any body or make any application. I consider them valuable only as they are granted spontaneously, and from a conviction in the minds of those who have the power of granting them, and from the sense of the publick that they are deserved. In any other case they are favours which I feel no inclination to sollicit [sic]. . . . . I only beg that no friend of mine will ever even talk upon it with the Ministers, or those connected with them.[12]

Prouder than his brother, he would not risk refusal by asking for his due; besides he probably wished to be certain that any reward given was granted solely in recognition of his military achievements, and not with one eye on the political importance of the Wellesley family. His delicacy was unusual at a time when honours and rewards were quite openly sought and even haggled for, although the spirit of the age was moving in his direction, and ambition was increasingly inclined to wrap itself in a gauze of modesty, at least where there was a risk of being exposed to the public eye. Lying beneath Arthur Wellesley's attitude we can see, not just a disdain created by his experiences as Chief Secretary for Ireland, but also the memory of humiliations suffered in his search for Irish office before sailing to India a dozen years before. He felt no compunction at pressing his claims for military employment, but he would not stoop to ask for reward. Nor, after this episode, would he ever need to do so.

For more than a fortnight the public basked in the glow of success and the confident expectation of further good news. Even senior figures at the Horse Guards were convinced that the next despatches would announce Junot's unconditional surrender together with that of the Russian fleet.[13] But behind the scenes the complacency of the ministers had been rocked on 4 September when the Chevalier de Sousa, the Portuguese minister in London, had protested at the terms he claimed had been granted to the French. The news was kept within a tight circle of the Cabinet, the King, and a few trusted officers, and their reaction mixed dismay with incredulity. The King could 'hardly bring himself to believe that any British officers could . . . think of agreeing to such a Convention', and declared that he could never sanction such a proceeding if it were true. Portland did not know how to express his 'astonishment and perplexity', but concluded that it was 'impossible that any English officer could have sanctioned' such terms – let alone Sir Arthur Wellesley. Castlereagh wrote a letter to his half-brother, Charles Stewart, listing seven unbelievable advantages the French would derive from such an armistice and added, rather desperately: 'It must be a base forgery somewhere, and nothing can induce me to believe it genuine.' The general conclusion was that the report could not be true and that the terms, if not totally spurious, were those that the French had proposed at the beginning of the negotiation; but the anxiety for some definitive news was intense. Colonel J.W. Gordon told Sir John Moore: 'At the moment . . . we look upon it almost as a *Quiz* upon Sousa, but if it proves true, we shall have our faces as long as the Baggage train of a Regiment of Cavalry! In short we are in a desperate taking about it, and anxiously looking out for our Official Despatches.'[14]

Unfortunately Dalrymple had delayed writing home until the final Convention had been concluded and it was not until 15 September that his despatch of 3 September reached London, and the worst fears of the ministers were realised. By then Canning, Portland, Chatham and Hawkesbury had gone into the country, but the remaining ministers decided to try to put the best face on the news and celebrate it as a victory, in the hope that public opinion would follow their lead. The Park and Tower guns were fired and an *Extraordinary Gazette* published. The effect on the public was devastating. Expectations, already feverishly high and overwrought by the long delay, were raised further by the traditional signals of a triumph, only to be brought crashing to the ground when the terms of the Convention were seen. The condemnation was universal and heart-felt. Palmerston wrote to his sister Fanny:

What a pretty business this Portuguese Expedition has turned out! I think Dalrymple's capitulation by far the most disgraceful to the British army of any that were ever signed. Whitelocke's is *nothing* to it. Whitelocke was beat (by his own incapacity certainly) but still he treated with his conquerors – Dalrymple succeeds to the command of a victorious army, reinforced by half its original number of fresh troops, in a friendly country, opposed by an enemy defeated and without a chance of escape, whose utmost hope could be to make a protracted resistance but was sure of being ultimately overpowered, and then instead of forcing the Enemy to an unconditional surrender he grants them terms of which no more need or can be said than that they were agreed to unaltered as dictated . . . [by the] Duke of Abrantes [i.e. Junot].[15]

William Napier, who in later life included an influential defence of the Convention in his *History of the War in the Peninsula*, could see no advantages in it at the time and told his mother that 'somebody must be hanged'. At a ball in Carlisle, when the steward proposed a toast to Sir Arthur Wellesley, 'an officer rose and declared that he would not drink the health of a General who had disgraced England'. And Lord Auckland could not 'recollect any instance in which the feeling[s] of all parties were so strong and so warm as they are with respect to the French convention'.[16]

Naturally the press both reflected and increased the public outrage. According to Joseph Farington: 'Every newspaper contained expressions of the warmest kind condemning the act as most disgraceful to Great Britain, and unjust to the Allies – *The Sun, The Globe, The Pilot, The Traveller, The Star* – papers of all parties concurred in execrating the measure.' *The Times* made its position clear from the outset: 'We can hardly refrain from shedding tears . . . the common course has suffered most grievously by this expedition to the Tagus; it has been cruelly detrimental to our affairs, and, above all, to our character.'[17]

Unlike the King and the public, the ministers in London reacted with calm disappointment to Dalrymple's despatch; they were prepared for the blow by Sousa's report and while far from happy they saw no alternative but to make the best of it and move on as quickly as possible. But Canning, who was staying with his family at Hinckley in the Midlands, could not agree. He regarded the Convention unequivocally as a 'disgrace and [a] disaster', and, mixing hot anger with passionate disappointment, he expressed his feelings in a stream of letters to his colleagues as fresh objections kept occurring to him. He did not believe that the government could approve the Convention:

And if we do disapprove of it, I cannot foresee any circumstances which could reconcile me to our omitting to mark our disapprobation of it in the strongest manner . . . This Convention must be distinctly *ours*, or *our Commanders*. We must judge them, or the Public will judge *us*. And I confess, unless there are circumstances to come out, of which I can form no conjecture, I shall not be prepared to consent to take an atom of responsibility for this work upon our own shoulders.[18]

The vehemence of Canning's reaction shocked the ministers in London into reconsidering their response. Castlereagh told him: 'Your suggestion however of *breaking the Convention*, rather than suffer any plunder to Escape . . . goes much further than any opinion stated in Cabinet.'[19] Still the issue of plunder had worried other ministers, and Castlereagh amended his initial reply to Dalrymple to emphasise that the article guaranteeing the French their 'private property' must be interpreted so as to exclude loot. Then, as the public outcry against the Convention grew louder, he halted the letter before it had sailed so that the Cabinet could think again before finally committing itself.

The fact that Arthur Wellesley was inextricably connected with the Convention by his signature of the preliminary suspension of arms, was a cause of particular concern to almost all the ministers. Hawkesbury wrote that 'the treaty is moreover particularly painful as till explained it tarnishes the Reputation and glory of those whom we should most wish to uphold'. Portland told Canning: 'If we can save Sir Arthur and have full use of His Talents such . . . [amends?] may be made as will obviate, if not all, much of the mischief you apprehend.'[20] Even Canning was torn between his admiration for Wellesley and his anger at the Convention:

It is indeed a grievous consideration that Wellesley's name is mixed in this transaction. – He too I think must account for the armistice which he signed on the 22nd – and if he cannot do so satisfactorily he is available no longer for the high purposes for which he seemed destined. If he can – why should not *local* rank make him equal to any command, without regard to the technicalities of army etiquette?[21]

Castlereagh had no such doubts. He told Perceval: 'We ought well to weigh how we can best save, together with our own character and that of the country, *the instrument*, which of all others seems capable . . . of consoling us and the world for any faults which he himself or others have committed.'[22] Eight days later he wrote to Arthur Wellesley himself for the first time since the news broke, assuring him 'my first object is your reputation; my second is that the country should not be deprived of your services at the present critical juncture'. The whole letter was warm and sympathetic, and although Castlereagh referred to his disappointment he allowed himself no hint of criticism or blame for the

Convention, even though it had severely damaged his reputation as a war minister and placed him at the centre of a political storm. He even felt sorry for Dalrymple whose 'misfortune I cannot but feel, as having been the person to bring him from a situation in which he was respected and happy, to plunge him in his present embarrassment. But it is in vain to dwell longer on this distressing subject'.[23] Nonetheless, on 21 September the Cabinet decided to recall Dalrymple. The King approved, 'considering it very fair towards Sir Hew Dalrymple to give him an early opportunity of personally explaining his conduct'. Clearly there would have to be an official inquiry although its exact form was yet to be decided.[24]

Arthur Wellesley's brothers were horrified by the Convention, not doubting for a moment that he had made a terrible mistake that threatened to destroy his reputation. Lord Wellesley feared that the ministers would abandon Arthur, and toyed with fanciful ideas of an alliance with Buckingham and Grenville to drive the government from office and form a new administration in which he would play a prominent part.[25] In the meantime it was essential to limit the damage to Arthur's reputation, both privately and through the press. As early as 20 September Lord Wellesley felt able to assure Buckingham's son that he was 'satisfied that Sir Arthur Wellesley neither negotiated, nor approved, nor suffered to pass without remonstrance the articles signed with his name'.[26] This was the line advanced in a vigorous campaign pursued through the press connections that the family had developed when defending Lord Wellesley's conduct in India. William Wellesley-Pole met with William Dardis, a man much in the confidence of both the Wellesleys and the Buckingham connection and who seems also to have been involved with one of the newspapers. Pole read aloud extracts of Arthur Wellesley's letters to him and to Castlereagh written soon after the Convention was signed, and discussed the whole question at length. Curiously, Dardis's recollection of Arthur Wellesley's letters was inaccurate in several significant ways. He believed that Wellesley had written:

> I authorize you to make known in any manner you think proper, that I had no share whatever in consulting upon, negotiating, or drawing up the preliminary articles of the Convention. They were done by Kellermann, in the presence of Sir Hew Dalrymple and General Burrard, and adopted by them without any alteration whatever. And I was merely ordered to sign them, which I did, conceiving it my duty so to do, without being consulted in any single instance respecting any one of these articles whatever.

This was bad enough, but it was Wellesley-Pole's own comments that most wildly distorted the picture and introduced a red herring that would do Arthur Wellesley more harm than good:

The fact is, the case was so much altered after the French had ceased to be pushed, that my brother seeing there would be nothing but bungle go forward, thought it a wise thing to get the French out of Portugal, but distinctly protested against those terms which you have seen, but which you cannot abhor more than I do. And as to Arthur's signing them, I suppose he acted agreeably to the rules of his profession – at least his idea of them; but I tell you candidly, I would rather have thrust my right hand into this fire, than have put it to such an instrument.[27]

This is the genesis of the story of Arthur Wellesley's 'protest', which was to seize the imagination of the public over the next few weeks. There was no basis of fact for it; Dalrymple did not order Arthur Wellesley to sign the suspension of arms and although he requested him to do so, that request was not tantamount to an order. Arthur Wellesley did not protest, nor did he ever claim that he had protested. What he did say was: 'Sir Hew Dalrymple desired me to sign it. I object to the verbiage; I object to an indefinite suspension of hostilities . . . I approve of allowing the French to evacuate Portugal.'[28] But it is not clear whether the process that mutated these reflective objections into a formal protest was wishful thinking, cynical manipulation, genuine carelessness, or a journalist's desire to make two plus two equal five.

Once released the story spread with Wellesley's defenders pushing it hard. At the same time his friends in the Irish government were equally active. Sir Charles Saxton put pressure on newspapers in Dublin to moderate their criticism, while the Duke of Richmond told colourful stories, supposedly based on letters from Sir Arthur, which put all the blame on Burrard and Dalrymple.[29]

The campaign to defend Arthur Wellesley did little good, if it was not actually counter-productive. Even well-disposed observers were puzzled and unhappy with the story of the protest. The blatant determination of some newspapers to acquit Wellesley of any blame produced a fierce reaction from others, including many not generally aligned with the radicals, or even the Whigs, but who were happy to join a popular cause. The Times left readers in no doubt of its opinion:

It hardly now appears any longer to be worth our while to give consequence to the sneaking insinuations which are obtruded on the Public, in the way of apology for Sir Arthur Wellesley, by replying to them as if they were arguments. Sir Arthur is settled; and all the injudicious zeal of his friends can now do, is heap obloquy upon those who have supplied proofs of his guilt. When they find they cannot build a wall of defence around his person, they pelt his enemies with the stones which they had brought together.[30]

It was always inevitable that Wellesley's role in the Convention would attract disproportionate attention, and not just because of his signature on the suspension of arms. Dalrymple and Burrard were virtually unknown to the public while Wellesley had been prominent even before the campaign, and had briefly become a national hero. Perhaps if he had been an obscure, politically unconnected officer, the public might have taken his side, seeing in him true virtue and talent whose achievements had been squandered by incompetent superiors. But the very fact that he was well connected, a member of the government and of a politically powerful family, predisposed observers to assume that he was either incompetent or at the least that he, not Dalrymple or Burrard, wielded real power in the army.

Among the Whigs and radicals there were many who relished his discomfiture. Samuel Whitbread wrote to a friend, 'I grieve for the opportunity that has been lost of acquiring national glory, but am not sorry to see the Wellesley pride lowered a little', while William Cobbett wrote to Lord Folkestone, 'It is evident that *he* was the prime cause – the *only* cause – of all the mischief, and that from the motive of thwarting everything *after he was superseded*'.[31]

Arthur Wellesley reacted with defiance to the public hostility he encountered after he landed and the attacks on him in the press. He put on a brave face when visiting his mother, who reported – with unaccustomed warmth – that he was in 'good looks and health', and expressing herself 'delighted' at his 'high spirit' in refusing to serve any longer under superior officers who had 'so basely injured him, & thwarted all his Glorious enterprises for the welfare of his country'. And he wrote to Lord Wellesley from London: 'I arrived here this day, and don't know whether I am to be hanged, drawn and quartered; or roasted alive. However I shall not allow the Mob of London to deprive me of my temper or my spirits; or the satisfaction which I feel in the consciousness that I acted right'.[32] But behind the bravado he must have been shaken; only a few weeks before he had led the British army to two victories in a week. He did not believe that he had done anything wrong, but the public, without giving him a chance to defend himself, had condemned him *in absentia*. The injustice of the position and the ignorance of much of the criticism helped to harden his political cynicism and his low regard for the press and public opinion.

Once he was back in London, Wellesley lost no time in explaining in a formal letter to Castlereagh his role in the Convention, which was to be the cornerstone of his defence:

I beg leave to inform your Lordship that I did not negotiate that agreement; that it was negotiated and settled by his Excellency in person, with Gen. Kellermann, in the presence of Lieut. Gen. Sir. H. Burrard and myself, and that I signed it by his Excellency's desire. But I could not consider myself responsible in any degree for the terms in which it was framed, or for any of its provisions. At the same time, adverting to the situation I had held in Portugal previously to his Excellency's arrival, I think it but just to inform your Lordship, that I concurred with the Commander of the Forces in thinking it expedient, on the 22nd Aug, that the French army in Portugal should be allowed to evacuate that Kingdom, with their arms and baggage, and that every facility for this purpose should be offered to them.[33]

No protest, no order to sign, and full support for the central plank of the Convention – the contrast with the story told by Wellesley's friends over the preceding weeks could hardly have been more marked, and naturally made a bad impression, for those who had blamed Wellesley and scoffed at the claims of a protest felt vindicated, while his defenders found the wind taken from their sails when it was most needed.

Wellesley did not publish this letter but he circulated it widely as the authorised statement of his position, even sending a copy of it to Major Barclay with a request that he show it to all Wellesley's friends in India. He refused to enter into a press controversy and declined offers from some experienced polemicists, including J.W. Croker, who put their pens at his disposal.[34]

Soon after he reached London Wellesley went to see Canning, who had returned to the capital and was staying at Blackheath. There is no record of their conversation, but Canning's anger had had three weeks to cool, and it appears that Wellesley was able to satisfy the Foreign Secretary with his explanation. Certainly Canning's confidence in Wellesley's military abilities was fully restored and the two were to cooperate effectively and without discomfiture in 1809. In fact Wellesley was soon convinced that he had the support of all the cabinet 'excepting indeed Lord Chatham, who thought that I was responsible for signing the Armistice, for which act I ought to be tried'. Nonetheless he felt that over Cintra he stood alone and needed to make his defence independently of the government, which, with all good wishes, had its own interests to consider.[35]

Over the next few weeks it became clear that Arthur Wellesley's new line of defence had made little impact outside the government, even on those who were predisposed in his favour. The Marquess of Buckingham felt that he had 'completely marred his case by the different language he has held; and above all by his ill-judged letter to Lord Castlereagh'. Lord Grenville agreed: 'I return you Sir Arthur's letters – they make but an indifferent case for him, and I am sorry to see that public opinion runs more and more against him. There is something quite inexplicable about his protest. Are we to suppose it was all pure invention? And if so, whose?' And Buckingham's son, Lord Temple, was brutal in his dismissal, writing to his father: 'I send you, by the coach, a long letter I have received from Sir Arthur Wellesley. It is very bad, and we must take great care not to hang a millstone about our necks.'[36]

The Duke of York had never given much credence to the story of the protest and as early as 18 September felt that it was clear 'that Sir Arthur agreed to the general principle ... [and] only objected to some of the terms, particularly to that concerning the Russian Fleet. I therefore do not myself see how he can clear himself'. A month later he sent a packet of letters from the army in Portugal to the King: 'They prove perfectly to me at least that Sir Arthur Wellesley was the principal advisor of the Convention, and it is much to be regretted that he has stated the contrary as it must ... [count?] against him in everybody's opinion. Sir Hew Dalrymple's letter is certainly very fair and manly, and Sir Harry Burrard in my opinion fully explains and justifies his having refused to consent to the Troops advancing after the Affair of the 21st.' And, as if to underline the point: 'I have from the first always thought that Sir Arthur made much more of the Affair of the 21st [the battle of Vimeiro] than it really deserved.'[37]

Among the wider public, the flames of popular outrage were continually stoked by the press, by the caricatures that were sold by print shops, and by a series of county meetings called to protest against the Convention and petition the King. The caricatures began with a fine print by Williams, *Extraordinary News*, which commented on the high hopes raised by the firing of the Tower guns only to be dashed by details of the Convention. George Cruikshank followed this before the end of September with *Whitlock* [sic] *the second or another tarnish of British valor* (see plate 28), in which three British officers, Cotton, Dalrymple and Wellesley, abase themselves before Junot. Wellesley is made to say: 'May it please your Highness to Accept these Terms as a convention and should any of them seem to you Ungracefull, dictate according to your Noble Will: – and you shall be conveyed home (with all your Property *Moveable* and *Immoveable*) in a Bed of Cotton.' A Portuguese figure in the background laments: 'Why I thought you came as my friends ...' Some later prints concentrated their anger on Dalrymple, and there was even one attempt to defend the Convention, but these were rare exceptions, and the mood of the moment was best expressed by Gillray, who depicted the three British generals hanging from gibbets in the background of a print showing the triumph of the radicals.[38]

During the second half of October and the first week of November a series of county meetings gave the opponents of the government a perfect opportunity to condemn the Convention before sympathetic audiences. At Reading on 18 October the freeholders of Berkshire met to consider a motion calling for a full inquiry into 'the late disgraceful Convention in Portugal' and the 'punishment of the guilty person or persons in that disgraceful transaction'. Lord Folkestone led the charge and although he met some resistance from those who felt that it was improper to pre-empt the judgment of an inquiry, he carried the meeting by a large majority. Ten days later a large crowd of the freeholders of Essex met at Chelmsford where Earl St Vincent, one of the country's greatest living naval heroes, 'felt that so foul a stain had never been cast on the military character of the country, since the days of the tyrannical and detestable reign of the family of the Stuarts'. On 2 November Cobbett dominated a Hampshire meeting at Winchester with a sweeping attack which began with Sir Arthur and the Convention and moved on to the Wellesley family and thence to the government, the military establishment of the country and the Duke of York.[39]

While the storm raged, Sir Arthur Wellesley went about his business with at least an attempt at calm indifference. After ten days in London he left for Dublin where Richmond had been begging for a short visit to help ease Sir Charles Saxton into Trail's shoes. In fact Wellesley stayed for three weeks, and on 30 October gave a grand dinner to his friends at his house in the Park. He told Spencer, 'I have neither lost my temper nor my spirits', but this was no more than a front, and touches of bitterness slipped out whenever he relaxed his guard.[40]

His brothers were also showing signs of the strain. Lord Wellesley was so incensed by the *Morning Chronicle* of 4 October, which compared Napoleon's behaviour in Spain to his conduct in India and derided Arthur's military achievements, particularly Assaye, that he considered suing for libel; only to be warned, as he had been in 1806, that this would simply give his enemies a platform from which to attack him.[41] William sent jittery letters to Arthur in Dublin begging him to return at once as Sir Hew was endeavouring to put the whole blame for the Convention on Arthur's shoulders, and neither the Duke of York nor Castlereagh could be trusted to ensure that he got a chance to defend himself. Arthur responded calmly to this, and William was reassured by an interview with Castlereagh. Arthur's own nerves were frayed, and when he returned to London he despondently told Castlereagh:

> I have always been of opinion that I should not be able to convince the public of the goodness of my motives for signing the armistice; and the late discussions in Middlesex and elsewhere, and the paragraphs in the newspapers, which, after all, rule everything in this country, tend to convince me that it is determined that I shall not have the benefit of an acquittal; and that the newswriters and orators of the day are determined to listen to nothing in my justification.[42]

Disgrace and humiliation seemed far worse than death or injury in battle, and the campaign to clear his name and overcome the public vitriol required as much courage as any of his battles.

Wellesley remained eager to return to the army, even though he expected the Spaniards to suffer reverses. On 8 October he had told Moore that he looked forward to serving under him; while from Dublin on 21 October he expressed the hope that if an inquiry was established soon he could give his evidence and then go to Spain, or, if it was delayed, he could go to Spain and come back to give his evidence. This prompted the Duke of York to remark that 'Sir Arthur Wellesley does not appear yet to be perfectly aware of the situation in which he stands or of the opinion of the publick'. But of course Wellesley was aware that his reputation and his whole career were in jeopardy; talking of returning to the army was one way of defying the threat and showing that he would not yield or be browbeaten into accepting guilt, which he was certain he did not deserve.[43]

Meanwhile the government had been moving steadily to establish a formal Inquiry into the Convention. The Judge-Advocate, Richard Ryder, advised against a court martial of Dalrymple in the first instance, as this would require precise charges to be formulated which would narrow the focus of the Inquiry. Instead a Board of Inquiry was established with extremely broad terms of reference. It consisted of seven senior officers, selected by the Duke of York without consultation with the ministers. They were led by General Sir David Dundas, the author of the army's drill and one of the most senior and trusted officers in the army. The Duke of York evidently wished to pre-empt any doubts about the political impartiality of the Inquiry for he included two senior officers with close ties to the Opposition. The Earl of Moira had made his name as a dashing young officer in the American War, and at fifty-four was still a candidate for active service. His long-standing friendship with the Prince of Wales would lead him to the brink of financial ruin, but he was a major figure in both politics and the army, and was under no obligation to the existing government. Lieutenant-General Sir George Nugent had close family ties to the Marquess of Buckingham and had been a fellow ADC of Wellesley's at Dublin Castle twenty years earlier. Nugent was an MP and like the rest of the Buckingham connection generally opposed Portland's government, although his military duties made his attendance in the House irregular.[44] Lieutenant-General the Earl of Pembroke had not only distinguished himself in Flanders in 1793, but had more recently been entrusted by Canning with an important diplomatic mission to Austria in 1807. In January 1808 he married the daughter of a retired Russian ambassador to Britain, and in 1810 Perceval offered him the Ordnance, but he declined. He seems to have been generally regarded as able, if lazy; while in politics he was sympathetic to the government but neither very partisan nor very active.[45] Lieutenant-General Oliver Nicolls had seen some active and demanding service in the West Indies under Abercromby, and had been

Commander-in-Chief in Bombay from 1800 to 1807, which had given him a ringside view of the Assaye campaign. General Lord Heathfield was the son of the famous defender of Gibraltar, under whom General Peter Craig had served as a young officer. It was a fair selection of eminently respectable officers, and if none had had the opportunity to command an army in the field, that was hardly surprising, for such experience was rare in the British army in 1808.[46]

The Court of Inquiry opened its proceedings in the Great Hall of Chelsea Hospital on Monday 14 November 1808 in front of a large and fashionable audience. Attention was concentrated initially on the negotiations with Kellermann and the signature of the suspension of arms. Dalrymple maintained that Wellesley had played a prominent part in the discussions and Wellesley did not dispute this; he pointed out that his advice had been disregarded on several important points, but acknowledged that he supported the principle of the agreement. This was almost enough to convict him in the eyes of some of his critics, including *The Times*, which professed amusement at his vain endeavours to escape the odium of the Convention.[47]

The Court met four times in the week beginning 21 November and gradually its attention shifted to the wider campaign and the state of the armies on the morning after Vimeiro. Dalrymple argued that Wellesley's entire campaign was perilous, that his communication with the fleet was precarious, and that even a slight setback would inevitably have led to the total destruction of the army. He dismissed Roliça and Vimeiro, even claiming that the latter had done more harm than good because of the losses suffered by the handful of British cavalry present with the army. When he added that he had not intended to land at Maceira and take command of the army, but to sail on to Mondego Bay and wait for Moore's reinforcements, and that he had only changed his mind when he learnt that Wellesley had already been superseded by Burrard, the impression of a weak man out of his depth and afraid of responsibility was complete.[48]

Wellesley by contrast had no difficulty in defending the conduct of his campaign; this was perfect territory for him in which his mastery of detail, his concern for logistics, and his knowledge and understanding of the practical realities of waging war, were displayed to good effect. He also had the chance to explain at some length why he favoured allowing the French to evacuate Portugal rather than to continue the campaign. He did not need to say that no campaign was likely to prosper under Dalrymple's leadership, for Dalrymple's own evidence had already made that obvious. Rather he pointed out that the French had been given time to rally after their defeat, and that as Moore's corps had been summoned to join the army rather than being sent to Santarem, there was nothing to stop Junot retreating into Alentejo and making a protracted defence of Elvas and Almeida. This would enable the French to prolong the campaign until the end of the year, and force the British into operations in the most unhealthy season with immense problems of supply and transport. The British army would be unable to assist the Spaniards in the main struggle and in the end might still be glad to grant the French a capitulation on terms scarcely less generous than those conceded at Cintra.[49] It was a compelling display, and if it made no allowance for the difficulties facing the French, that was, in the circumstances, understandable; Wellesley's task was to shake the public conviction that the central element of the Convention was clearly and obviously wrong. He could not hope to do so overnight but the performance sowed seeds of doubt where previous attempts had failed.

Wellesley was encouraged by the progress of the Inquiry. On 23 November he told Richmond: 'The Court of Inquiry is going on as well as I could wish.' Dalrymple's hostility freed his hands so that he felt no obligation to gloss over the defects he saw in the Convention, and he noted with wry satisfaction that 'the papers have already changed their tone about the evacuation; and, excepting personal abuse of me and misrepresentation of what I said, they do what one would wish'. There would still be bad moments; one day, while walking in the Hospital gardens in a break in proceedings, he overheard a bystander say: 'What business has he to wear his sword!' And it stung. But he had been through the worst and gradually defiance would give way to renewed confidence and assurance.[50]

On 24 and 26 November the Court examined subordinate officers: Torrens, Ferguson, Acland, Spencer and Nightingall. None of them said anything very important, although they were asked many leading questions on the possibility of the French making a prolonged and destructive defence of Lisbon. All except Acland believed that if Moore's corps had been sent to Santarem it could have blocked a French retreat on Elvas or Almeida.[51] The Inquiry then adjourned for more than a fortnight while waiting for Sir Harry Burrard to return from Portugal and prepare his case.

The press was gradually shifting its ground. For example, *The Times* published a letter from 'A.B.' which, while still condemning the Convention as 'most impolitic, shameful and criminal', was more puzzled than angry about Wellesley – 'Why had he been so confident before his victory, but so timid afterwards?' – and reserved its scorn for Dalrymple whose arguments were shredded.[52] But attention was shifting from Cintra to the unfolding events in Spain. Moore had reached Salamanca with his advanced guard on 13 November but his army was widely dispersed and Napoleon had reinforced his armies on the Ebro and taken the offensive. One by one the Spanish armies were broken in a succession of unequal battles and soon Moore was anxious whether his army could unite before it was brought to battle or was forced to retreat. News of these disasters was slow to reach London, but it began to arrive in the last week of November, filling the newspapers and preoccupying the public and ministers.

The Inquiry resumed on Tuesday 13 December for two final days of evidence concentrating on Burrard's account of his actions. Burrard explained that he did not order Moore to Santarem as Wellesley suggested, because he doubted that Moore's corps was sufficiently strong to encounter the whole French army unaided, and because he feared that its march would be beset by logistical difficulties. Nonetheless he initially ordered Moore to land at Mondego so that his corps would be ashore and in a position to support Wellesley if the latter suffered a setback. Similar caution and lack of confidence lay behind his veto of Wellesley's proposed advance on the morning of 21 August and his order to Moore to re-embark and come south, and he mentioned that Murray and Clinton agreed with him on this, although he did not hide behind their opinions. As for the refusal to pursue a defeated French after the battle, he was concerned by the strength of the French cavalry; thought that some of their infantry might have had time to rally; was conscious of the number of wounded who needed treatment and prisoners who had to be guarded; believed that the British artillery and commissariat would have difficulty advancing; and thought that the soldiers might be tired and would like to have a rest and cook their dinner. In short, he advanced every possible reason as none could justify such a palpable error of judgement, and on this point he mentioned neither Clinton nor Murray.[53]

Wellesley responded to this quietly, although he did establish the fact that because the army had originally been ordered to advance on 21 August the men had already cooked that day's dinner and carried it in their haversacks. He also explained the advantages he believed would have been gained by the pursuit and outlined the subsequent operations he envisaged.[54] Spencer gave evidence on Burrard's behalf, suggesting that it was possible that the French had some undefeated reserves at the close of the fighting. When Wellesley privately taxed him about this later he became uncomfortable and replied: 'My dear Sir Arthur, he's a poor old man with a large family. I am sure you do not wish to ruin him.' Wellesley was not amused and never really forgave Spencer. Ferguson and Lord Burghersh both gave evidence supporting Wellesley's eagerness to advance both before and after the battle.[55]

The last two days of evidence had a decisive effect on Wellesley's reputation. After the first, *The Times* commented:

> It appears from the proceedings of the Board of Inquiry yesterday, that half the story told by the family and friends of Sir Arthur Wellesley, against his superiors in command, is true enough. It is proved that Sir Harry Burrard was strongly urged to allow the pursuit of the enemy after the battle of the 21st of August; but that he declined the proposition made to him in order to afford the troops time to refresh themselves, although he was perfectly aware that the enemy had been much longer under arms.[56]

And on the following day it went further, giving an account of the campaign which virtually exonerated Wellesley from any blame for the Convention by making it clear that if he had been left in command it would never have been necessary. The paper which, a few weeks earlier, had not thought it worth its time to demolish 'the sneaking insinuations' advanced in Wellesley's defence, now accepted his case almost without reservation, and praised his 'bold, enterprising and decisive' plan of campaign. On 24 December it reported that Wellesley would sail to join the army as soon as the Inquiry delivered its report – feeling that his vindication was self-evident – and, just to show that it was far from uncritical in its praise, went on to pick up Cobbett's cry and criticise him for retaining his Irish office while serving abroad.[57]

This proved premature in several respects. The Court presented a lengthy report on 22 December which blandly avoided outright criticism of anybody or making an explicit judgment of the Convention, although Wellesley's operations were praised as 'highly honourable and successful, and such as might be expected from a distinguished General at the head of a British army'. The Duke of York (or perhaps the King), would have none of it. Laying whitewash on that thickly only invited ridicule, and on Christmas Day the Duke of York wrote to Sir David Dundas requiring that the Court re-assemble and deliver an opinion on the subject it was established to examine, while any members dissenting from the majority view should also give their reasons.[58]

The seven members of the Court duly reassembled at the Judge Advocate General's office on 27 December. Six of the seven expressed their approval of the armistice, and four – Dundas, Craig, Heathfield and Nugent – approved the terms of the Convention. Oliver Nicholls approved of the Armistice because the opportunity to pursue the French when they were broken had been lost; but disapproved of the final Convention because the arrival of British reinforcements should have allowed Dalrymple to insist on more favourable terms. Lord Pembroke agreed and pointed also to the support of the local inhabitants as an advantage, which was not reflected in the final Convention, while he believed that the French would have yielded concessions if they had been pressed in the negotiations. Lord Moira approved neither the Armistice nor the Convention and expressed his reasons at some length. He thought that insufficient weight had been given to the problems facing the French and that it was unlikely that they would have been able to retreat across the Tagus and carry the war into Alentejo. Nor was he convinced that difficulties of supply or the insecurity of the army's communications with the fleet made an immediate end to the campaign essential. The main reason for sending the British army to Portugal was to fight and defeat the French rather than to liberate Portugal on any terms. By returning Junot's corps to France the Convention strengthened Napoleon's resources and damaged the reputation of British arms; while little advantage had been taken of the time gained to expedite the advance of the British army into Spain.[59]

Wellesley was disappointed with the report and was especially annoyed with Moira's opinion. He was anxious to know how the government would respond, evidently fearing that the controversy would be renewed in Parliament, and in the press, and that Moira's opinion would be used as the basis of further attacks.[60] But his fears proved groundless; the heat had gone out of the debate and most intelligent observers were left with a strong impression of Wellesley's ability, even if some continued to feel that pique at being superseded had distorted his judgement in the negotiations with Kellermann. The radicals and some Whigs remained hostile, convinced that he was incompetent and had only been saved from disgrace by the powerful political influence of his family, and this animus would continue even when his successes forced his opponents to acknowledge his ability. But it is not surprising that a general, closely allied to one political party, should be disliked and disparaged by politicians of strongly differing views.

The government, preoccupied with the war in Spain and other pressing questions, did not determine its response to the Inquiry's report until 17 January. On the following day it issued a formal declaration in the form of a letter to Sir Hew Dalrymple. This announced that no further official action would be taken over the Convention, but it expressed His Majesty's 'disapprobation of those articles, in which stipulations were made, directly affecting the interests or feelings of the Spanish or Portuguese nations', and it warned against generals including political provisions in military conventions. Dalrymple was also admonished for his long delay in sending home news of the armistice; but the merits of the substance of the Convention were not addressed, suggesting that Canning still could not bring himself to consent to its approval.[61]

Sir Hew Dalrymple and Sir Harry Burrard were never formally disgraced and both remained in the army. Burrard was given command of the Home District, but his life was clouded by the death of two of his three sons, one at Coruña, and the other at San Sebastian. He survived the second by only a few weeks, dying on 18 October 1813, aged fifty-eight. Dalrymple was more fortunate and evidently was not without some friends with influence, for in 1811 he was given the colonelcy of the 57th Foot, in 1815 he was made baronet and in 1818 he was appointed governor of Blackness Castle (an honourable, but not very lucrative, sinecure). He died in 1830. Nonetheless neither man ever had the chance to redeem themselves in the public eye. Their limitations had been cruelly exposed in a single brief scene; for a season they had been the object of public ridicule and contempt; and then they were cast aside while public, press and politicians moved on to the next subject that caught their fancy.

The effect of the Inquiry on Sir Arthur Wellesley was altogether different. In the summer and autumn of 1808 he became a national figure, known throughout the kingdom first as a popular hero and then as a villain, and finally as something betwixt the two. He would never again be out of the public eye, and he would remain a controversial figure with many more oscillations in his reputation as the populace alternately hissed and cheered at his name.

CHAPTER SEVENTEEN

POLITICS, SCANDAL AND WELLESLEY'S RETURN TO PORTUGAL
(January–April 1809)

A T THE BEGINNING of 1809, the allied cause in the Peninsula was in disarray. Napoleon had crushed the Spanish armies with contemptuous ease, occupied Madrid without significant popular resistance, and then turned upon Sir John Moore and forced the British army to embark on its epic retreat to Coruña and the safety of its ships. News of the battle of Coruña and Moore's death reached London a few days after the government issued its response to the Cintra Inquiry's report. With the British army driven from Spain, Arthur Wellesley had to accept that there was no immediate prospect of active service to distract him from the mundane duties of his Irish office, and the inevitable debates in Parliament over Cintra.

Wellesley reached London from Dublin on 21 January 1809, two days after the opening of the parliamentary session. On 23 January, Liverpool (as Hawkesbury had become on his father's death in December) moved a Vote of Thanks in the Lords to Wellesley and his army for the battle of Vimeiro. Moira protested at the exclusion of Burrard from the Thanks, and received some support from Erskine, but Harrowby, Sidmouth, Mulgrave and Buckinghamshire all opposed him, and the amendment was lost on the voices, although Moira then entered a formal protest in the Journals of the Lords.[1] Two days later Castlereagh moved Thanks in the Commons, pouring lavish praise on Wellesley and his victory. This provoked some opposition from the radicals (Folkestone and Whitbread both raised objections), which in turn prompted a number of members to speak in favour of the vote, including some, such as W.H. Fremantle, who did not generally support the ministers. Votes of Thanks were usually non-partisan and most members of the Opposition waited for a more suitable occasion to express their view on the campaign in Portugal, but the number of speakers keen to associate themselves with Wellesley's cause at the first parliamentary opportunity is striking, as is the warmth of their praise.[2]

A more critical note was struck on 2 February when Samuel Whitbread asked if Wellesley had continued to hold his Irish office, and receive its pay, while serving in Portugal. Wellesley admitted that this was so, while explaining that he had offered his resignation and only retained his position at the express wish of the Duke of Richmond.[3] A few days later Whitbread returned to the issue submitting a motion declaring 'that the Office of Chief Secretary for Ireland is an efficient office of the highest responsibility, which ought not to be held by any person absent from the realm, and that the emolument of it ought not to be paid to any person unable to perform the duties'. Whitbread was careful to soften the personal edge of his attack, declaring that 'no person possessed in a more eminent degree every qualification for the distinguished command to which he had been appointed' than Wellesley, while he was even willing 'to give him the greatest credit for the manner in which he executed, and the attention which he paid to the duties of his office of Chief Secretary for Ireland'. But he did not believe that anyone could simultaneously perform both roles effectively. Wellesley responded by informing the House that he had only accepted the position of Chief Secretary on the express understanding that it would not prevent his serving abroad, and that he had offered his resignation before sailing on both the expedition to Copenhagen and to Portugal. He defended his role in the government of Ireland and challenged Whitbread to produce any evidence of inefficiency or even delay caused by his absences; and he pointed to the high costs of the establishments needed by a Chief Secretary as the reason why he had continued to receive his salary. Nonetheless he virtually conceded the argument by assuring the House 'that he should in no future instance consent to hold his office in the event of his being appointed to a military command'. He then bowed to the chair and withdrew from the chamber. There was little further discussion – Castlereagh spoke in his defence and Lord Henry Petty and Whitbread both spoke briefly – but the opposition had secured its point and did not press the question to a division.[4]

After this preliminary skirmish Wellesley must have wondered what line the Opposition would take when the Convention of Cintra was debated in the Commons a fortnight later. But in the event the Opposition concentrated its attack on the ministers and, far from condemning Wellesley, its leading speakers went out of their way to praise him. Lord Henry Petty moved that the Convention had 'disappointed the hopes and expectations of the country', and that this was due 'in a great measure [to] the misconduct and neglect of his Majesty's Ministers'. Petty had no criticism to make of Wellesley's appointment: 'The gallant General's bravery, skill, and eminent military talents were so well known, that it was rather a source of satisfaction to everyone [that] Sir A. Wellesley was appointed.' Nor did he criticise the conduct of the campaign; on the contrary, Wellesley had no sooner landed than he 'commenced a bold system of operations, and with that gallantry and skill which so eminently characterize him', had gained the victories of Roliça and Vimeiro. Petty's fire was concentrated firmly on Castlereagh and Chatham, criticising the government for the lack of cavalry, the poor quality of the artillery horses, and above all for superseding Wellesley by Burrard and Dalrymple. It was not Dalrymple's fault that he arrived in the middle of the campaign, not knowing his army or the country in which it was operating, and his alarm at the superiority of the French cavalry was quite reasonable – indeed, even the intrepid Wellesley had been concerned about this. Petty then elaborated on the disadvantages of the Convention, concluding that 'blame must lie somewhere; and it was for the House to consider on whom that humiliation ought to fall'.[5]

Castlereagh's response to this attack was awkward, almost incoherent, suggesting that he had been taken by surprise by the Opposition's line. He was too heated and aggressive, as if conscious of defending a weak position, and this contrasted badly with the cool moderation of Petty's speech. He was followed by Sir George Nugent who, as the only member of the Court of Inquiry with a seat in the Commons, may have felt obliged to break his accustomed silence (he had been an MP for fourteen years and this was his first recorded speech). Nugent defended the Convention while blaming the poor equipment of the expedition for its necessity, thus reconciling his professional judgement and his political allegiances with surprising dexterity.[6]

General Banastre Tarleton, who had made his name as a dashing hero in the American War, ignored Petty's lead and entered into the details of the campaign, criticising Wellesley's conduct. Over the next few years he was to prove an inveterate critic, constantly predicting disasters that failed to eventuate, lauding the skill of the French commanders and disparaging Wellesley at every opportunity. He had briefly served in Portugal some years before, and may still have been listened to with some attention in early 1809, but he was not highly regarded even by his allies, and his credibility rapidly diminished.[7]

On this occasion Tarleton's attack provided the perfect entrance for Wellesley who proceeded to give a detailed account of the whole campaign from the time the expedition sailed from Cork. He acknowledged that the French army in Portugal was stronger than anyone expected, but rejected Tarleton's accusation of rashness, commenting that 'he would rather follow that Hon. General's example in the field, than his advice in the Senate'. If Burrard had followed his advice the campaign might have ended more happily, and he could not understand how the Court of Inquiry could approve his conduct of the campaign and also approve the refusal to pursue Junot's beaten army: 'It was too hard that the Government should be blamed for the Convention or Armistice.' Any deficiencies there might have been in the equipment of the expedition were quite irrelevant; once the French had been given the chance to rally, there was no alternative to a negotiated evacuation except protracted operations in Alentejo. It was a good speech covering thoroughly familiar ground, although W.H. Fremantle, reporting on the debate to Lord Grenville, claimed that 'the whole of Wellesley's argument and language, which was infinitely the best, was a condemnation of the Ministers'.[8]

Windham, and even Whitbread, continued the tactic of praising Wellesley as a way of attaching blame to the government, with the latter declaring that by superseding Sir Arthur, 'they nipped in the bud the blossoms of his military glory'. In response, Perceval could only ask how the government could be blamed for the failures of Burrard and Dalrymple, before moving to the more comfortable ground of attacking the record of the Talents. William Wellesley-Pole used the occasion to formally declare: 'that he gave no sanction to the reports that were first spread of Sir A. Wellesley's disapprobation of the Convention. He neither caused nor authorised the insertion of any paragraphs in newspapers to that effect. He thought it necessary for him to say so much, as he was the only relation of Sir Arthur's then in town.' This was simply preposterous and it is hard to know why Pole went out of his way to deny the undeniable, although it may have been in response to remarks not preserved in the surviving records of the debate.[9]

It was well after five in the morning on 22 February when the House divided, and the Opposition were delighted with the result: 153 in favour of Petty's motion, 203 supporting the government against it. But although this was a good result for the Whigs, it proved that the passionate disappointment aroused by the first news of Cintra had faded with time, while the debate itself revealed unexpectedly broad support for Wellesley.

The issue that dominated Parliament in early 1809 was not Cintra, or Moore's retreat, or the government's handling of the war, but allegations that the Duke of York's mistress, Mary Anne Clarke, had demanded and received bribes in return for securing commissions or promotions for junior officers, and that the Duke had connived at this corrupt practice. The emergence of these allegations followed a long subterranean campaign of rumour and innuendo against the Duke, which was said to have been inspired, or at least encouraged, by his brother the Duke of Kent, who had been denied an active command ever since his harshness provoked a mutiny at Gibraltar in 1802. But when Mary Anne Clarke came forward it was under the patronage of the radicals, in particular Gwyllym Wardle, a little-known MP who had only been elected to Parliament in 1807. Most Whigs, including even Whitbread, were reluctant to stir the question, believing that the evidence against the Duke would soon be discredited, but Wardle persisted, gaining support from Folkestone, Cobbett and their friends.[10]

The allegations were first raised in Parliament on 27 January on the same day that Wellesley received the Vote of Thanks. He spoke, expressing full confidence in the Duke's innocence, and praising his work at the head of the army. Privately Wellesley admitted to Richmond that he believed Mrs Clarke had received large sums of money and did exercise some influence over appointments, although he was 'positively certain' that the Duke was unaware of her activities.[11]

The government established a committee of the whole House to examine the allegations, but far from being intimidated Mrs Clarke soon had the House at her feet, with even Wilberforce admitting that she was 'elegantly dressed, consummately impudent, and very clever'.[12] It soon became clear that she was at the centre of a corrupt network of adventurers who demanded money for favours and promotions, and who did not limit their claims of influence to the Duke of York and the army. The Duke of Portland and Lord Eldon, the Lord Chancellor, both found that their names had been used to extract money from over-eager applicants for clerical patronage, and, on 11 February, similar allegations were made involving Arthur Wellesley. He explained what happened to Richmond:

There has appeared in the last two days a general system of swindling, applicable to all the offices of the state, in which Mrs Clarke has been most active, and a great gainer. My name was introduced by her in her examination of Saturday, as having been used by this gang of swindlers to impose upon the credulous. She said that Maltby, whom she represented as one of the swindlers, had told Lodovick, a gentleman of Essex, who had lodged money to obtain the place of assistant-commissary, that I was so busy with the Court of Inquiry that I could not attend to their applications in his, Lodovick's, favour. The House was in a roar when she mentioned my name; but I was happy to find that not a single man, not even Folkestone, imagined that I knew anything about the matter.[13]

Although the government succeeded in disproving most of the specific allegations against the Duke of York, their cumulative effect was damaging, and it was obvious that he had been extraordinarily unobservant in supposing that Mrs Clarke could maintain the lavish house in which she entertained him on the meagre allowance he gave her. Then she produced his letters which made a further sensation, both for their warmly affectionate wording, and because they showed that he had sometimes allowed her to discuss appointments with him, even arranging for one of her clerical protégés, Dr O'Meara, to preach before the Royal Family at Windsor. Public interest reached a frenzy; more than 120 prints on the subject were produced in a few months, while the war was almost totally forgotten. Mrs Clarke was cheered wherever she appeared in public and, when tossing a coin, the popular cry was not 'heads or tails' but 'Duke or Darling'.[14]

On 17 February Wellesley reported to Richmond: 'The *love-letters* have created a terrible impression . . . Last night there was a terrible case of a Mr Kennett, a bankrupt upholsterer, who had been in the pillory, for whom the Duke had endeavoured to obtain the office of Collector of the Customs at Surinam. Connected with this arrangement there was a negotiation for a loan of £70,000. I doubt whether this case was legally proved; but it has a bad appearance . . . The impression is strong against the Duke both in and out of the House. People are outrageous in the country on account of the immorality of his life, which makes no impression in town, and they have burnt him in effigy in Suffolk and in Yorkshire . . . In the meantime all other business is at a stand, and nobody talks or thinks of anything but Mrs Clarke.' There was no improvement over the next couple of days, and Wellesley became 'convinced that [the Duke] cannot continue to hold his office, and that if the present ministers endeavour to support him in it, they will be beat in Parliament'. He hoped that if the Duke was forced to resign Lord Harrington would be brought over from Ireland to replace him, with Richmond given command of the forces in Ireland, combining military and civil powers as Cornwallis had done a decade earlier.[15]

The Duke rejected hints from the ministers that he should resign and, after a fortnight's pause for consideration, the Opposition brought forward a succession of censure motions. Wardle's strongly worded condemnation was defeated quite easily (364 to 123) after an all-night sitting on 16 March, but a more moderate amendment proposed by the widely-respected independent Henry Bankes gained 199 votes to the government's 294; and a third critical motion was immediately introduced. The tide of feeling was running strongly against the ministers. At last, on 18 March, the Duke resigned. The King accepted the resignation with reluctance and in the same letter in which he communicated the news to the Prime Minister he also informed him of his decision to appoint Sir David Dundas 'to the chief temporary command'. Ministers were not consulted, and the choice clearly reflected the King's determination not to appoint someone like Harrington who might hold the office indefinitely, but instead a stop-gap who would loyally maintain the status quo, and whose age and failing powers would lead to his retirement within a few years, when the Duke of York could resume his office.[16]

Charles Williams Wynn, a generally moderate member of the Opposition, celebrated York's resignation as 'one of the greatest triumphs ever yet exhibited by the British Constitution'. He rejoiced that a little-known member of Parliament, unsupported by any great party or family connection, could force the King's favourite son from office after fourteen years at the head of 'an army of 12,000 Officers connected with every family in the kingdom': 'When this can be done things are not as corrupt or the voice of the people of as little effect as has been supposed.'[17] From this perspective, Williams Wynn's satisfaction was entirely justified; the case showed that the royal family was not immune from criticism and that the government was responsive to public clamour, although neither point was likely to surprise anyone not blinded by Whig rhetoric about the increasing power of the Crown.

But the Duke of York was not just the son of George III; he was also the man who had supervised the reform of the British army, replacing flagrant abuses of patronage and promotion with a well-regulated system, and laying the foundations for the success that it was to achieve in coming years. His personal role in these reforms may have been exaggerated by his admirers, but his patronage and support for the reformers in the Horse Guards was essential to their success. This does not mean that the charges against him were baseless; at the very least he had been careless and indiscreet, while it is possible that he had been wilfully blind to Mrs Clarke's activities without ever guessing their extent. But it was mortifying to think that such a substantial achievement should count for nothing compared to a cheap sensation drummed up by a discarded mistress, a few ambitious radical politicians and an irresponsible press. Still, that was how the British constitution would increasingly work in an age when 'the voice of the people' could not be ignored. Not everyone would share Charles Williams Wynn's enthusiasm.

Many Members of Parliament must have watched the unfolding of the Duke's scandal with a deep sense of unease, which only increased when it became clear that the public exposure of his affair with Mary Anne Clarke was in itself almost enough to force his resignation, even if he was acquitted on the claims of corruption. What was ruin for a royal Duke, might be equally damaging to less exalted figures. The late eighteenth and early nineteenth century was not an age when the British upper classes adhered to a particularly demanding code of sexual morality. The evangelical revival led by Wilberforce and the 'Saints' had made some progress – Perceval and Liverpool were both influenced by it – but it remained a minority taste, at least among Members of Parliament and the aristocracy. Many men kept mistresses; quite a few married ladies had lovers; and although divorce was difficult, embarrassing and very expensive, each year saw a handful of cases drag their way through the courts, with all the most salacious details being published at length in the newspapers.

By no standards was Arthur Wellesley a model husband. Since he left Dublin for London in early 1808, he seems to have spent no more than a few weeks under the same roof as his wife, during his brief visits to Dublin in June– July, October–November and December–January. While it is hard for us to be certain, it seems likely that the rift that divided them had already opened. Whether this was precipitated by some unspecified error on her part (see

Chapter 14) or from the recognition of the complete incompatibility of their
tastes and interests, cannot be finally determined. Nor does it much matter. He
treated her badly, being off-hand, neglectful and impatient; and she irritated
him by her lack of confidence and skill in society and by inept attempts to
please him. For, if he had fallen out of love with her, she had become even more
anxious and propitiatory and affectionate towards him. Quite simply, they
brought out the worst in each other.

Given this, it seems likely that Wellesley began his affair with Harriette
Wilson, a successful courtesan, in the early months of 1808. Her account
(published in 1824) is useless for dates – indeed, she lost a libel action by
misdating an affair of her sister by a decade – while many years later he told
Mrs Arbuthnot that the liaison occurred before his marriage. However the
evidence from that period makes this most unlikely, and although it is possible
that the affair began in late 1806 or early 1807, this raises other problems.
Unfortunately these doubts about the evidence pervade the whole question of
the affair (even the story of Wellesley's retort 'publish and be damned' proves
to be apocryphal). Other than Wellesley's brief confirmation to Mrs Arbuthnot
that he had indeed known Harriette Wilson, we have only the single source of
Wilson's own memoirs, which were written with one eye on entertaining the
public and the other on extracting money from her former lovers through
blackmail. Neither cause would be aided by too rigid adherence to the facts,
and her account, while wonderfully vivid and amusing, contains innumerable
contradictions and obvious errors. To take only the simplest example, Wellesley
is called 'the Duke of Wellington' throughout, and she makes much of his military fame and great eminence even at their first meeting. More seriously, he
departs and returns from 'Spain' far too often; this might be merely a mistake
for his visits to Ireland, but the impression is rather that she enjoyed trying out
different versions of the scene as she would have liked it to happen, and then
bundled them all into the *Memoirs*.

On the whole, the picture of Wellesley is most unflattering. Of course, it had
to be; he would hardly pay to suppress something that depicted him in glowing
colours, nor would the public be satisfied if, expecting to be astonished by revelations, they found that the private man bore a strong resemblance to the public
figure. Yet it is probably true that she found him rather dull – she was twenty-
three, he nudging forty – and years later he was to admit that he had 'no small
talk', while her interests did not extend to politics, the state of the war, the government of Ireland or military reform.[18] Nonetheless, he always enjoyed the society
of bright, vivacious women, and Harriette Wilson – 'although I have never been
called agreeable in my life' – was certainly entertaining. As for the famous scene
in which she has Wellesley hammering on her door but denied admittance
because the Duke of Argyll was with her, it *might* be true, but it reads very much

as the wishful thinking of a woman who had too often had to open her door to men whom she privately found distasteful. Nonetheless, this and other images of Wellesley ('her faithful lover', 'her modern Bluebeard') gained lasting currency, helping to deflate the public aura of the hero of the nation at a time (the 1820s) when he was actively engaged in partisan politics. Many a Whig or radical, and even some Tories, would have smiled quietly to themselves when, in the midst of some dull parliamentary debate or tedious ceremony, they recalled reading: 'Wellington was now my most constant visitor – a most unentertaining one, Heaven knows! and, in the evenings, when he wore his broad red ribbon, he looked very like a rat-catcher.'[19]

But in the spring of 1809 it was the private life of Arthur's brother Henry that amused the discerning British public. The previous year Henry's wife Charlotte had begun an affair with Lord Paget. Neither was in the first bloom of youthful folly: he turned forty on 17 May 1808 and was married with eight children; and Charlotte was twenty-seven and the mother of three, soon to be four, infants. Still, if they had limited themselves to a little discreet adultery they would not have violated the social code of the day – though they might still have made themselves and their families thoroughly unhappy. Henry was oblivious at first, being preoccupied with the demanding and to him unpleasant duties of a Secretary to the Treasury, maintaining the government's majority in the Commons. When Paget returned from Coruña he resumed the liaison with Charlotte. Henry now became suspicious and on the evening of 5 March confronted his wife. The next day Charlotte left her family and placed herself under Paget's protection. This, not adultery, was the decisive step in Regency society, for it amounted to an open acknowledgement of a transgression, which society would have preferred to ignore, but which it was thus forced – however hypocritically – to condemn. Neither Lady Charlotte, nor Paget, acted lightly or with joyous enthusiasm, but rather with a kind of desperate anguish, eyes wide open to the misery they would cause.

The aftermath of the affair was prolonged and complicated, involving attempts at mediation, tearful reunions and partings from children, a duel (between Paget and George Cadogan, Charlotte's brother, in which Paget deliberately fired wide) and finally two divorces. Henry Wellesley resigned from the Treasury and from Parliament; he felt that he had been publicly humiliated, although he was generally felt to have emerged quite creditably from the scandal. He sued Paget for damages – a common step at the time, although rather startling to a later point of view – and was awarded no less than £20,000. Paget and Charlotte were married by the end of 1810 and Paget's former wife Caroline soon married the Duke of Argyll (Harriette Wilson's old lover), telling her former brother-in-law that nothing in her previous life could be compared 'to the superlative degree of bliss which she was now enjoying'. Only Henry

Wellesley remained unmarried for long; it was not until 1816 that he again dared the experiment, although even that may have been due to the fact that he had spent most of the interim out of England in diplomatic postings.[20]

After the collapse of the Spanish armies and the retreat to Coruña there was widespread reluctance in Britain to commit any fresh forces to the Peninsula. Canning, the Foreign Secretary, shared the general disillusionment with Spain, but felt that Britain was obliged to make some effort to defend Portugal. There was already a small British force at Lisbon: the troops left behind when Moore had marched into Spain, which were now under the command of Sir John Cradock. Villiers, the British minister in Lisbon, wrote home at the end of 1808 urging that the force be increased to 10,000 infantry and 2,000 cavalry. He also warmly endorsed a Portuguese request for the loan of a British general to supervise the reconstruction of their army and to lead it in the field. Privately the Portuguese made clear that they hoped Wellesley might be appointed, and Villiers told Canning that Sir Arthur would be ideal because 'he is so venerated here'.[21]

However the British government now regarded Wellesley as too valuable to be employed on a secondary and probably hopeless task. The death of Moore and the disabling of Baird at Coruña had thinned the already meagre ranks of experienced and capable British generals, but even before this blow, Portland had told Canning that Wellesley was the only man he would trust in command of the nation's army in the field. So it is not surprising that the Foreign Secretary replied to Villiers in late January: 'Sir Arthur Wellesley is thought too good for the Portuguese.' The Duke of York doubted that any senior British officer would be keen to take the position and there was some delay before Major-General William Carr Beresford was given the command on 15 February. Beresford confided: 'The choice was not left to me, and the first thing that I was told was that it was not optional. From the probable state of affairs in the quarter I am bound to, it is not impossible that I shall have my voyage for my pains, and return immediately.'[22]

Beresford had served in Portugal and Madeira and had some knowledge of the language, which was probably what led to his selection. Wellesley had known him slightly in India and Portugal, but there is no evidence that he played a significant part in the appointment.[23] The Duke of York had already agreed that a number of British officers be employed to assist Beresford; as an incentive they were promoted one step in the British army and a second in the Portuguese, so that a captain almost overnight became a lieutenant-colonel. (Later, this was reduced to a single step in the Portuguese army for new appointments.) As a result the service soon attracted a number of bright, ambitious, energetic men whose prospects at home were limited by lack of money or connections. But their rapid promotion also caused resentment among their late comrades and led to some cases of serious friction in the Peninsular army.[24]

Beresford landed in Lisbon on 2 March, but it would take many months before his work could bear fruit and it was clear that without more direct help Portugal could not be defended. Throughout February Canning pressed his Cabinet colleagues to take further action and increase their commitment to Lisbon, arguing: 'If we think the trial worth making at all, we ought surely to make it in the most advantageous manner & with the best instruments that we can. All Portugal calls loudly for Sir Arthur Wellesley. And Sir A. Wellesley so far from declining or despising the command of the Armies of that Country, would most willingly undertake it.' Canning wanted to give Wellesley command of the British and Portuguese armies and to recall Cradock (who was senior to Wellesley) or transfer him to another command, probably Gibraltar. He also wished to strengthen the British force, although he was aware that there was considerable jealousy of Wellesley. But the Cabinet did not agree and Canning allowed his frustration to show in a private letter to Villiers a few days later: 'It is no want of urgency on my part, or of willingness on Sir A. Wellesley's – but, but, no matter what the impediments are, I will get over them if I can.' And: 'I am persuaded, as sincerely and as strongly as you could wish me to be, that Sir A. Wellesley at the head of a large combined force in Portugal, is the first neces-sary element of success to the Spanish cause.'[25]

The arguments used to oppose Canning in Cabinet are less clearly spelled out, but it seems that Castlereagh felt great reluctance to supersede Cradock with a junior officer when Cradock had done nothing wrong – had, indeed, been given no opportunity to distinguish himself. And Castlereagh had little confidence that Portugal could be saved, so he probably feared that Wellesley would arrive simply in time to supervise the evacuation, and that this would tarnish his reputation. Even worse, Wellesley's arrival might interrupt active operations leading to an absurd repetition of the farce of the previous year.[26] Yet it would probably be wrong to present this as a simple battle between Canning and Castlereagh; other ministers had powerful voices in the Cabinet, even if we do not know what line they took on this issue, or who supported and who opposed Canning on it.

No decision was taken at the end of February, but the position was changing. In January, even before Coruña, the government had sent Sherbrooke with 4,000 men to help save Cadiz from the French. Winter gales had greatly delayed this expedition and Sherbrooke did not reach Cadiz until March, when he found that there were no French troops within hundreds of miles and that the Spanish authorities would not let his men into the city. The British government then instructed him to sail back to Lisbon where, with the arrival of some stragglers from Moore's army and further reinforcements from England, he would take Cradock's force up to almost 20,000 men. Castlereagh declared that it was the government's intention to 'use every exertion to strengthen the defences of Portugal' and to remain 'for as long as possible'.[27]

Wellesley's role in the Cabinet debates over Portugal is far from clear. Canning told Villiers that he was quite willing to return to Portugal, and that he believed 20,000 British troops would be sufficient to defend the country. Charles Stewart, half-brother and under-secretary to Castlereagh, later accused him of having 'intrigued' for the command, but this was written in ill humour, and may be unfair.[28] Otherwise there is surprisingly little documentary evidence given Wellesley's habitual compulsion to put his thoughts on paper. This may be simply because he was in London, in frequent contact with the ministers, or it may reflect some embarrassment that he was acting in opposition to Castlereagh. It is even possible that he did not take a very active part at all – answering questions when put to him, but not advancing a line of his own – although that seems so out of character as to be inherently unlikely. The one exception is the famous 'Memorandum on the Defence of Portugal', which he submitted on 7 March. This is dry, prosaic and practical, while the ideas it contains are largely an elaboration of those in Wellesley's letter of 1 August 1808, written just before he landed at Mondego Bay. He argued that a British army of 30,000 men (including 4,000 cavalry) supported by 30,000 Portuguese regulars and 40,000 militia would be able to defend the country against anything less than 100,000 French even if all Spain were overrun. He warned that Portugal would require a very large subsidy and the British would have to interfere in all levels of the government and army to ensure their efficiency. The staff and the commissariat of the Portuguese army must be British and supplied on a generous scale, and he submitted a list of desirable reinforcements which, beginning modestly with a few companies of British riflemen, rapidly grew more ambitious including '3,000 British or German cavalry', and enough artillery and engineers for an army of 60,000 men. Horses for all the cavalry and artillery, reinforcements of infantry and '30,000 stands of arms, clothing, and shoes for the Portuguese army' completed the list.[29]

The memorandum produced no immediate change of policy. It may even have been counter-productive; by asking for more cavalry, artillery and equipment than were available, Wellesley probably allowed its opponents to argue that it was beyond Britain's capacity. And in fact the memorandum does *not* provide a blueprint for Britain's commitment to Portugal, except in broad outline. Some of the detailed proposals were never adopted, while others took years to achieve. But the most likely reason why it went unheeded was that the debates on the Duke of York's affair began on the day after it was presented, and while they lasted they completely absorbed the government's attention. When the Duke's resignation appeared inevitable, Wellesley hoped that this might ease his return to Portugal; if Harrington went to the Horse Guards, and Richmond became Commander of the Forces in Ireland, Cradock might be recalled to act as Richmond's deputy, a position which, while it offered little prospect of action, was sufficiently important and distinguished to remove any stigma from his recall.[30] The King's unilateral decision to appoint Dundas ruined this scheme, but even so the Duke's resignation may have removed an obstacle to Canning's ideas; there is no direct evidence, but it seems unlikely that the Duke would have favoured Wellesley at the expense of Cradock.

The Duke of York resigned on 18 March. On 21 March Canning told Portland: 'Portugal is a source of constant, daily, and nightly uneasiness to me.'[31] And on 26 March Castlereagh wrote to the King recommending that Cradock be appointed lieutenant-governor of Gibraltar and that Wellesley be given command of the forces in Portugal. A strong brigade of some 4,000 men under Major-General Hill was about to sail from Cork for Lisbon, and Castlereagh wanted to send out three regiments of cavalry as soon as they, and their transports, could be prepared, but there were no plans for any subsequent reinforcements. The King replied the following day, making clear that he disliked the decision:

> The King acquiesces in Lord Castlereagh's proposal that ... Lieut-Genl. Sir Arthur Wellesley should succeed to the command of the troops in Portugal. In agreeing however to so young a Lieut.-General holding so distinguished a command, while his seniors remain unemployed, his Majesty must desire that Lord Castlereagh will keep in view that if the corps in Portugal should be further increased hereafter, the claims of senior officers cannot with justice be set aside.[32]

Although the government had finally decided to send Wellesley to Portugal, its commitment to the wider war in the Peninsula was still hesitant. In the first draft of Castlereagh's instructions to Wellesley, dated 2 April, his primary objective was described as the defence of Portugal, but 'as the security of Portugal can only be effectually provided for in connexion with the defence of the Peninsula in the larger sense', he was permitted to use his discretion in concerting operations with Spanish forces and to advance into Spain. However, on the following day this was replaced by much more restrictive instructions, which prohibited operations in Spain without prior permission from the government, and required him to comply with any Spanish request for a garrison for Cadiz if it was threatened.[33] This alteration reflects the distrust created by Moore's campaign and continuing anxiety over the fate of Cadiz; but it also shows rather less faith in Wellesley's judgement than one would expect.

Wellesley wrote to Richmond breaking the news on 28 March. After the discussions in the press and Parliament there was no question of his again retaining his office while on active service, but it was with genuine regret that he parted from Richmond. Almost his last act as Chief Secretary was to help arrange for the election of a promising young Englishman to the Irish seat of Cashel. Robert Peel had only just turned twenty-one, but had a brilliant academic record and strong support from his wealthy father; his career and Wellesley's were to be closely intertwined, however unlikely that seemed in the spring of 1809 when they may never even have met.[34] At the same time Wellesley resigned his seat in Parliament. This was not really necessary (many soldiers retained their seat even while serving overseas for years at a time) but the patron of the seat wanted it back, and could no longer be put off with the excuse that Wellesley was a minister in the government. There is, however, no sense that Wellesley had renounced politics, or saw his departure as permanent; he probably expected to return to the Commons when he came home from Portugal.

The last days of March and the beginning of April were busy with preparations, for Wellesley wished to sail as soon as possible. Many of his staff from the 1808 campaign were eager to join him again, and influential figures approached him with requests that he find room for their protégés. Not all of these were welcome, but two young men who became part of his inner circle of trusted ADCs were introduced at this time: Charles Fox Canning, the cousin of the Foreign Secretary, and Alexander Gordon, nephew of Sir David Baird (under whom he had served in Spain) and brother of the Earl of Aberdeen. Neither of them was able to sail with Wellesley, but Canning followed soon after, and Gordon a few months later. Wellesley also took with him his brother-in-law, Lieutenant-Colonel Henry Cadogan, who was anxious to get away from the scandal surrounding his sister Charlotte's elopement. He was also able to get Richmond's nephew George Berkeley appointed to the staff as an Assistant Adjutant-General, although he complained that the new Commander-in-Chief was not very cooperative: 'Old David is so costive that it is difficult to get anything out of him, and I have not been able to get the assistance of many for whom I have asked.'[35]

On 11 April, while waiting to sail from Portsmouth, Wellesley was shaken by reports from Portugal that the French had taken Oporto and were advancing on Lisbon. It seemed almost certain that the campaign would be decided before he could arrive; either the British army would have embarked, or Cradock would have driven the French back, or at least be engaged in active operations. He asked for fresh instructions allowing him either to supersede Cradock or serve under him as circumstances suggested, and Castlereagh obliged, although he had already written a most embarrassed and uncomfortable letter to

Cradock announcing his supersession.[36] For three more days Portsmouth was battered by gales and Wellesley fretted. It was not until the early afternoon of 15 April that he sailed on the *Surveillante* frigate. There is a well-known story, told by at least one of Wellesley's party, that the ship was nearly lost that night off St Catherine's Head, Isle of Wight, and that the captain, Sir George Collier, urged Sir Arthur to dress and advised him – if the worst came to the worst – to stay close to the wreck and not attempt to swim ashore. However, neither the captain's nor the master's logs record anything more than 'fresh breezes' and 'squally rain', so it seems likely that the tale has grown in the telling.[37]

It was almost thirteen years since Wellesley had sailed from Portsmouth for India with the taste of failure in his mouth; and less than four since he had returned to England, successful and prosperous, but still relatively unknown. Now he sailed again, bearing on his shoulders, if not the hopes of the nation, at least those of the ministers who had come to believe that he was the best general in the British army and one of the few who could be trusted to face the French. Over the next few years he would vindicate their judgement and greatly surpass their most optimistic expectations.

PART IV

ADVERSITY AND TRIUMPH IN THE PENINSULA

CHAPTER EIGHTEEN

OPORTO
(April–May 1809)

LIEUTENANT-GENERAL SIR ARTHUR Wellesley arrived in Lisbon on 22 April 1809. He was greeted with rejoicing and the city was illuminated for three successive nights in his honour. Cintra had done little to damage Wellesley's reputation in Portugal. The shops were full of prints of Vimeiro, and the Portuguese government had privately asked for Wellesley's return months earlier when requesting the loan of a general to reform their army.[1] The news of Wellesley's appointment was greeted with equal delight in the British army. There was some sympathy for Cradock, but he had never gained the confidence of the officers or men, and the common feeling was expressed by one officer who wrote on 13 April:

> The Ministers, awakening from their reverie, seem willing to repay us for their past neglect, by removing a very gentlemanlike, but very inefficient man from the command, and putting one in his place who is known in this country, and known to be a fit man to face the cunning enemy we have to deal with. Sir Arthur Wellesley is not actually arrived, but we expect him every hour . . . This change will afford the greatest pleasure and give a great deal of animation to the Army which will now have every confidence in its leader. For my own part, I consider his arrival of as much value as a reinforcement of 10,000 men.[2]

Wellesley spent a week in Lisbon making plans and talking with the Portuguese government and with John Villiers, the British minister. Villiers was not a man to dominate the scene or overawe the Portuguese government, but he worked assiduously to support Wellesley and Beresford in Lisbon, and championed their cause with the British government, even pressing for reinforcements when Wellesley was reluctant to do so. He was not afraid to disagree with Wellesley occasionally over the best means of achieving their objectives, and his demands added to pressure on Canning, but both men approved of his performance and Wellesley was genuinely sorry when, in the autumn of 1809, he announced his desire to go home.[3]

While Villiers dealt with the government, the Portuguese army was commanded by William Carr Beresford, who had been given the local rank of Lieutenant-General in the British army and the Portuguese rank of Marshal, to ensure his authority over the existing Portuguese generals. Beresford had only arrived in Portugal on 2 March, and his great work reforming and revitalising the army had scarcely begun, but he was able to select the best units from the existing force and lead them with some success in Wellesley's first campaign. Less than a year older than Wellesley, Beresford was the illegitimate but acknowledged son of the Marquess of Waterford (possibly by his wife before their marriage, although this was naturally never confirmed). Twenty years later Thomas Creevey wrote a vivid sketch of him:

> I can safely say that in my life I never took so strong a prejudice against a man. Such a low looking ruffian in his air, with damned bad manners, or rather none at all, and a vulgarity in his expressions and pronunciation that made me at once believe he was as ignorant, stupid and illiterate as he was ill-looking. Yet somehow or other he almost wiped away all these notches before we parted. In the first place, it is with me an invaluable property in any man to have him call a spade a spade. The higher he is in station the more rare and more entertaining it is. Then I defy any human being to find out that he is either a marshal or a lord; but you *do* find out that he has been in every part of the world, and in all the interesting scenes of it for the last five and thirty years.[4]

Wellesley soon established an effective partnership with Beresford which proved the bedrock of the whole Anglo-Portuguese effort in the Peninsula over the next five years. There was no doubt that Wellesley was the dominant partner and this was officially confirmed by his appointment as Marshal-General of Portugal, so that even in the Portuguese service he outranked Beresford. But he was careful to foster Beresford's authority and seldom intervened in the internal workings of the Portuguese army, while taking every opportunity to praise Beresford's work in public and in private. Beresford for his part proved loyal and indefatigable, overcoming innumerable problems in the tedious, thankless task of reforming and training the Portuguese army.[5]

Including some reinforcements which arrived by the end of April, Wellesley's army amounted to around 27,000 British and German troops.[6] Sir John Moore had taken the cream of the British army to Coruña, and Wellesley's force included many sickly units and second battalions, some of which lacked the stamina for a sustained campaign. However there were also some good regiments including two strong battalions of the Guards and four of the King's German Legion. The army was also weak in cavalry and artillery – deficiencies that were not fully addressed for several years. Wellesley had particularly asked for the three regiments of light infantry (1/43rd, 1/52nd, 1/95th) which would win fame under his command as the Light Brigade (and later as the core of the Light Division). Castlereagh agreed, but found that even these elite units took weeks to be made ready for service, and then only after extensive exchanges between their first and second battalions. As a result they did not sail until the end of May and would fail to reach the army in time to fight at Talavera, despite a famous forced march.[7]

The army's generals included many familiar faces. The second-in-command was Wellesley's old deputy from the 33rd and Mysore, John Sherbrooke, now a major-general in the army with local rank of lieutenant-general in Portugal. The cavalry was initially commanded by Major-General Stapleton Cotton whom Wellesley had met in Madras a decade before, and who had written to Wellesley at the beginning of 1808 that 'there is nobody I am so anxious to serve under as yourself'.[8] Rowland Hill had served throughout the Coruña campaign and had only been allowed a few weeks at home before being ordered back out to Portugal with reinforcements; evidently Wellesley was not alone in recognising that the talents of this quiet, courteous soldier were far too valuable to be wasted. John Murray was another old hand from India, although his record there had been tarnished by his quarrels with the Bombay government and his peripheral role in Monson's disaster. Nonetheless Wellesley seems to have believed that he had ability, even telling Torrens in 1812 that 'Sir J. Murray is a very able officer'.[9] And finally there was Alexander Campbell whom Wellesley had known in India, where he had commanded the 74th Regiment against Tipu Sultan, and served Wellesley in the campaign against Dhoondiah Waugh. One of Campbell's sons had been killed at Assaye (the other was to fall in the Pyrenees); his nephew was Colin Campbell, Wellesley's ADC; and his daughter married Wellesley's friend John Malcolm. Wellesley showed the same marked favouritism towards Alexander Campbell that he did for his nephew, ensuring that he commanded a division in 1809 and again in 1810–11 at a time when more senior (though younger) officers commanded only brigades. This naturally aroused some resentment, but Wellesley's later critics, convinced of his strong preference for the aristocracy, have passed over his patronage of a Scottish family that lacked any great distinction of birth, wealth or social connection.[10]

Naturally there were also a number of officers in the army with whom Wellesley had not previously served. Major-General John Randoll Mackenzie was an Opposition MP, but this did not prevent Wellesley forming a high opinion of his talents and entrusting him with a semi-independent command and then a division. William Payne arrived soon after Wellesley and took overall command of the cavalry (with Cotton serving under him). Wellesley was pleased with his attention to the welfare of men and horses alike even when this led to disputes with the commissariat.[11] Edward Paget was the fourth son of the Earl of Uxbridge and the younger brother of Lord Paget. He was an excellent officer who had commanded the rearguard on the retreat to Coruña with great skill and fortitude.

When Wellesley reached Lisbon he was delighted to find that the reports of a French advance, which had so alarmed him at Portsmouth, were completely unfounded. Soult remained at Oporto which he had taken and sacked at the end of March; Victor remained at Medellin where he had been since defeating Cuesta on 29 March, and neither showed any disposition to advance on Lisbon. In fact the French armies in Spain had lost momentum, bogged down by logistical problems and the continuing insurrection across much of the country. Ney's corps was

11 Spain, Portugal and southern France, 1807–14.

fully occupied attempting to subdue Galicia; St Cyr was equally stretched in Catalonia; Suchet had just assumed the command in Aragon after the appalling siege of Saragossa; and Mortier had been ordered to disengage from active operations and assemble his corps in case Napoleon decided to withdraw it from the Peninsula. This left King Joseph at Madrid with only a small central reserve which was barely enough to maintain his authority in the neighbourhood of the capital. Nor could the French expect any significant reinforcement, for Napoleon's attention was concentrated on central Europe where Austria had taken the field on 9 April. The attempt to complete the subjugation of Spain and Portugal would have to wait until the Austrian war had been decided.

Wellesley quickly assessed the position and decided that his first objective must be to drive Soult from Oporto, so liberating Portugal's second city and its northern provinces. Victor's army was larger, but a campaign against him would require Spanish cooperation, which would take time to arrange; and besides, Wellesley's instructions clearly specified that the defence of Portugal was his primary task. But looking ahead Wellesley saw cooperation with Cuesta as the best way in which Britain could 'make another great effort for the relief of Spain', and certainly preferable to extending operations against Soult into the mountains of Galicia.[12] This was not what the British government had in mind when it sent Wellesley back to Portugal (ministers were thoroughly disillusioned with Spain and did not look beyond the defence of Portugal), but Wellesley was full of confidence and wrote to Castlereagh on 7 May asking that his instructions, drawn up only five weeks before, be amended to give him much broader discretion 'to continue my operations in Spain, if I should consider them important to the Spanish cause and consistent with the safety of Portugal'.[13]

In making his plans, Wellesley did not expect Soult to stand and fight at Oporto. He substantially underestimated the size of Soult's army and his chief concern was to ensure that the French retreated north into Galicia rather than east towards Zamora and Salamanca from where they would be able to threaten Portugal again when Wellesley turned south against Victor.[14] In the meantime the eastern frontier could not be left without some protection in case Victor stirred into action. Cuesta had succeeded in rallying his army and had been reinforced, and Wellesley wrote to him asking him to keep a close watch on Victor but not to risk a battle.[15] The job could not be left entirely to the Spaniards, however, and Wellesley detached Mackenzie with a force of about 4,500 men to Abrantes to protect his flank. The role was important, but Mackenzie would much rather have accompanied the main army into action and felt rather aggrieved.[16]

Before Wellesley left Lisbon he received an unexpected visit from an officer in Soult's army; this was Captain Argenton, adjutant of the 18e Dragoons, and one of a group of conspirators who hoped to capitalise on the discontent in the

French army to arrest Soult and those officers who remained loyal to him, and then lead their army back to France and attempt to overthrow Napoleon. Argenton and his friends were entirely serious, and he had risked his life making contact with the allied outposts and then coming to Lisbon. Wellesley was rather startled by the overture, but accepted Argenton's sincerity while privately doubting if the plot could succeed. Yet even an unsuccessful mutiny in the French army would be a great blow to Napoleon's prestige and create lasting mistrust and dissensus in the French officer corps; and if the revolt succeeded in Soult's corps it might spread and 'do more for Spain than Spain would ever do for itself'.[17] Nonetheless these were murky waters and Wellesley acted with care while referring the whole question to London. He gave Argenton some cautious encouragement but refused to enter into elaborate ruses for increasing the discontent in Soult's army or to reveal anything of his plans. If the conspiracy could not succeed without British help it was unlikely to succeed at all, but its existence was most encouraging, suggesting that French morale was much worse than might have been expected.

Wellesley was not ready to leave Lisbon until the afternoon of 28 April and he took a few days to ride the 140 miles to Coimbra where the army was assembling, for his horses had yet to recover their condition after their confinement at sea.[18] He turned forty during this ride, although there is no evidence that he celebrated the occasion. Still, he may well have thought back to his thirtieth birthday, spent before the walls of Seringapatam, reflected on all the triumphs and disappointments that had followed, and realised that his career still hung in the balance; he had earned the opportunity before him, but if he failed there was unlikely to be another chance.

The people of Coimbra gave Wellesley and the British army a rapturous reception. The church bells pealed with joy, rockets were fired into the sky, and from every window and balcony spectators cheered and sprinkled the procession with rose petals and holy water. So great were the crowds that Wellesley found it difficult to move through the streets; at night the city was illuminated, and these celebrations continued for several days.[19] The festivities coincided with a religious holiday (the feast of St John before the Latin Gate) and Wellesley allowed the Buffs (1st Battalion 3rd Regiment of Foot) to take part in the procession 'immediately in the rear of the image of St George, the titular Saint of England, who appeared mounted on a superb white charger'.[20] This was part of his continuing effort to conciliate local religious feeling, but it caused considerable unease to some ordinary soldiers in the British army for whom their Protestant faith was as central a part of the identity as being English. John Cooper was a private soldier in the 2/7th Royal Fusiliers, and was proud of his descent from John Wycliffe, the fourteenth-century reformer and translator of the Bible. 'Such a scene of babyism and buffoonery I never seen before nor since,' he wrote in his memoirs. 'A great number of bishops, priests, monks, friars, and boys were assembled in the cathedral to accompany the image of the beloved apostle along the streets, which were lined by nearly the whole population . . . While the procession passed, the natives kneeled, bowed, crossed and muttered. Where the Bible is prohibited, as in Spain and Portugal, paganism and idolatry never die.'[21] Cooper was unusual among ordinary soldiers in recording his reaction, but anti-Catholicism had been one of the central elements in British culture for most of the previous two centuries, and while it was much attenuated in the upper classes it remained potent among the wider population, a fact of some significance in Wellesley's later career.[22]

Like most though not all men of his class at the time, Wellesley combined loyal membership of the Church of England with a temperate and tolerant religious feeling which made it easy for him to respect the role of other churches, and indeed other religions, in foreign countries. In the course of his career he never had any difficulty in cooperating with Muslims, Hindus, Jews, Catholics or even Unitarians; but he believed that the establishment of the Anglican Church was essential to social and political stability in Britain and to British rule in Ireland. In other words, his support for the establishment of the Church was always based essentially on political rather than theological arguments, and he saw no inconsistency in insisting that his soldiers respect the Catholic Church in Portugal, just as he insisted that they respect Portuguese property and other customs.

On 6 May Wellesley held a grand review of his army at Coimbra. He had about 18,000 British and German troops after deducting the sick and those detached on other duties such as Mackenzie's force, and about 8,500 Portuguese, although many of the Portuguese were further north including the remnants of the army which had tried to defend Oporto.[23] He was not very impressed with the Portuguese regiments he saw, but still added four battalions of their infantry to his army, attaching them to otherwise weak brigades. The rest of the Portuguese troops would operate independently under Beresford's command.

The army was divided into a brigade of cavalry and eight brigades of infantry, one of which (commanded by John Murray) was really a double brigade, containing all four King's German Legion battalions. Sherbrooke, Payne and Paget were rather superfluous under this arrangement; Payne's command consisted solely of Cotton's brigade, and although Wellesley divided the army into right and left wings for Sherbrooke and Paget this proved a temporary and rather unsatisfactory arrangement. A far better organisation was made in June when the army was divided into five divisions, four of infantry and one of the cavalry.

The staff of the army was already falling into its enduring shape. George Murray was at the head of the Quartermaster-General's department, where his imperturbability and pleasant manners, his administrative efficiency and understanding of the importance of topography and logistics, made him a vital element in the smooth functioning of the army. Murray's counterpart as Adjutant-General was Charles Stewart, Castlereagh's half-brother and, until recently, Under-Secretary for War in the Portland government. With his strong political connections and divided loyalties Stewart was as awkward a subordinate as Wellesley himself had always been. Both Murray and Stewart wrote frequent letters home giving interesting and remarkably frank views on the operations as they were taking place, and their hopes and fears for the next stage of the campaign. Stewart drew heavily upon these letters when he wrote a history of the war in the 1820s. One of his ADCs, George Fitzclarence (the eldest illegitimate son of the Duke of Clarence, and grandson of George III) also published a useful and lively first-hand account of the early campaigns in the Peninsula.[24]

Wellesley's plan for the coming campaign was relatively simple. Beresford with all the Portuguese troops not attached to the main army, and Tilson's British brigade, would head north and east from Coimbra marching through Viseu to Lamego on the Douro, some fifty miles east of Oporto. He would collect some additional Portuguese forces on his march, and when he reached the Douro he would be able to unite with Silveira who had continued to harass the French flank even after the fall of Oporto and several defeats. Wellesley hoped that Beresford and Silveira would be able to block the road east from Oporto and so force Soult to retreat north into Galicia. When Wellesley made his plans Silveira was reported to be in a strong position holding the vital bridge on this road over the Tamega at Amarante, but news then arrived that the French had seized the bridge and driven Silveira's men back in disorder. This was disheartening, and Wellesley felt obliged to modify his plans, telling Beresford bluntly that while it 'would be a most important and decisive step' if he crossed the Douro and cut Soult's line of retreat, 'I should not like to see a British brigade, supported by 6,000 or 8,000 Portuguese troops, in *any but a very good post*, exposed to be attacked by the French army', especially as it might be several days before Wellesley could come to his assistance. The final decision was therefore left to Beresford's discretion, depending on the situation he found at Lamego.[25]

While Beresford moved to turn the French flank, Wellesley would march directly on Oporto some eighty miles north of Coimbra. He gave Beresford a day's start as the Portuguese force had further to go and on worse roads. On 7 May the main army began its march with high hopes. Charles Cocks, a promising young officer then serving on Cotton's staff, told his father: 'Sir Arthur Wellesley has taken command of the army and inspired fresh spirit into every breast.' And Ensign John Aitchison of the Scots Guards agreed: 'I feel more

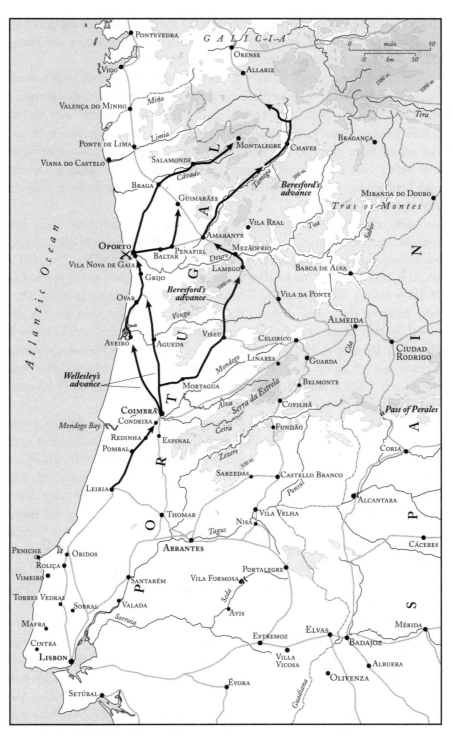

12 The Oporto campaign, May 1809.

confidence in the Commander-in-Chief than I should under any other officer in the service', although even so he cautioned that some reverses and heavy losses were to be expected before Oporto was captured.[26]

Soult's army of around 21,000 men was quite widely scattered. Soult himself was in Oporto with 8,500 men (the infantry of Delaborde and Merle's divisions and Caulaincourt's cavalry); Lorge's dragoons and a few infantry were well to the north near Braga; Loison with 6,500 men was at Amarante, which he had just seized from Silveira; and Franceschi with two brigades of cavalry and Mermet's division of infantry (almost 5,000 men in all) was south of Oporto with his outposts extending almost as far as the Vouga river halfway between Oporto and Coimbra.[27]

Franceschi slowly withdrew in the face of Wellesley's advance. There was some skirmishing on 10 May and more serious fighting the next day at Grijo, where both the Portuguese and KGL infantry behaved well. During the advance William Tomkinson of the 16th Light Dragoons was shocked to see the bodies of 'three priests the French had murdered for some cause or another. They were hanging on a tree, close to the roadside, and must have been a full month in that situation from their appearance'.[28] Such scenes would become dreadfully familiar as the campaign went on, testifying to the savage war of reprisal and counter-reprisal fought between the French army and the local population. Little wonder that the Portuguese welcomed the British with such enthusiasm.

Franceschi's men retreated to Oporto and at two o'clock the next morning Soult broke the bridge of boats across the Douro. He hoped that the great river would protect him for a few days while he organised the withdrawal of his army into Spain. Already he had prepared a large convoy of convalescents and heavy baggage which would begin its march east the following morning. Soult knew that Loison had succeeded at Amarante, and although he had not heard from him since, he had no doubt that he would clear the road through Tras os Montes, for his only opposition would come from the contemptible Portuguese led by Silveira. A greater worry was that Wellesley would use sea power to land a force north of the Douro turning the French position, and Soult deployed his troops with this danger in mind.[29]

The allied army resumed its advance early on the morning of 12 May. Wellesley sent John Murray with a small force to Avintes on the Douro four or five miles upstream from Oporto where there was a ferry and where he hoped to find some boats. The rest of the army marched to Vila Nova, the suburb of Oporto on the southern bank of the river, where 'the people expressed the loudest testimonies of joy and scattered flowers as we went'.[30] Wellesley was careful to keep his troops out of sight of the north bank while he reconnoitred. Few French were to be seen apart from some sentries on the quays who 'appeared quite at their ease, and not as if they were on the point of marching away'. Nonetheless the local inhabitants assured Wellesley that the bulk of Soult's army had already left the city and that no more than a rearguard remained. For a moment Wellesley toyed with the idea of pushing some troops across the river in small boats found at Vila Nova, but the risk was too great – even for a leader with his aggressive instincts – and he wisely preferred less direct methods.[31]

Staff officers were sent in all directions and Lieutenant-Colonel John Waters, a protégé of Charles Stewart now attached to the Portuguese army, met a barber who had crossed the river in a skiff that morning. The barber showed Waters four large wine barges left unguarded on the northern shore a little upstream from the city centre, where the curve of the river and its high banks concealed them from the quays. The barges were near the Bishop's Seminary, a large two-storey building in extensive grounds on the north shore just outside the city. Both banks of the Douro tower steeply above the river at this point, but the southern shore was higher and commanded the approaches to the seminary. Waters, guided by the barber and with the help of the Prior of Amarante and some other Portuguese, crossed the river in the skiff, made sure that the seminary was not occupied by the French, and brought the wine barges across to the southern bank. At the same time word arrived from Murray that the ferry boat at Avintes could be refloated. It was enough for Wellesley. He ordered Murray to cross the river as soon as he could; called his artillery up to the heights on the south bank from which he was viewing the scene; and gave the command for the leading regiment of Hill's brigade (the Buffs) to begin crossing in the barges Waters had retrieved.[32]

Each barge could carry twenty-five or thirty men, although they were unwieldy and their improvised crews unskilled. Nonetheless they made the crossing without mishap, and after several trips half the Buffs under the command of General Paget were ensconced in the seminary busily putting it in a state of defence. The French watch had been extraordinarily slack and it is a surprise to discover that the officer for guarding this stretch of the river was General Foy, who was usually a fine professional soldier.[33] When the alarm was eventually raised it took time to bring a single regiment (17e Léger, three battalions) up to try to drive the Buffs from the position. It is easy to imagine the fluster and alarm that accompanied this first attack as the men were suddenly and unexpectedly thrown into battle. As they advanced to the charge, their eyes on the walls of the seminary, they were raked by artillery fire from the British and Portuguese guns on the southern bank of the Douro which took them squarely in the flank. According to one British artillery officer the very first round fired – a shrapnel shell from a 5½-inch howitzer – killed or wounded every man and horse attached to a French gun that was unlimbering to support Foy's men. The French attack was broken, although the men rallied and

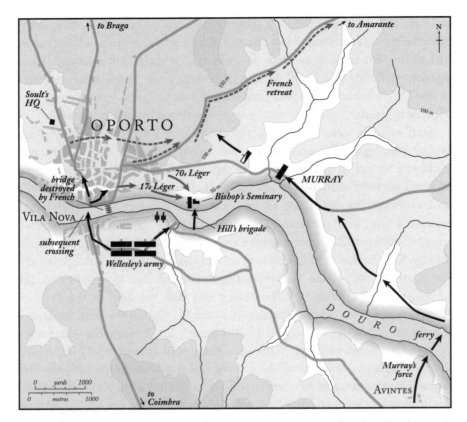

13 The crossing of the Douro, 12 May 1809. (All troop positions approximate, many conjectural.)

returned to the fray, approaching the seminary from the north, where they were less exposed to the British artillery, but were again driven back.[34]

After the initial French attacks on the seminary failed there was a lull while both sides brought up more troops. The Buffs were now all across the river and were being joined by the remaining battalions of Hill's brigade, the 2/48th and 2/66th. Hill was now in command as Paget had been wounded early in the action and his right arm had to be amputated. (He is said to have written home: 'Dear Mother – you will hear that I have lost *a fin*, but I am very well.')[35] General Delaborde had brought the 70e Ligne up to reinforce the 17e Léger and launched a much more serious and sustained attack on the seminary but without success. In the city Soult was making frantic preparations for an immediate evacuation, but there was no time to salvage anything that had not already been packed. The seminary lay to the east of the city, close to the road on which the army would march; if it could not be retaken, it had at least to be masked until the army had passed. But the only remaining troops available were those guarding the city and the quays, and as soon as they were withdrawn boats began crossing to and fro carrying the leading men of the rest of Wellesley's army. Caught in a hopeless position the French retreat became more and more disorderly. A final attack on the seminary was abandoned and Soult's army streamed east along the road to Amarante.[36]

As the French army fled it passed across the face of John Murray's force, which had succeeded in crossing the Douro at Avintes. Murray has been criticised for not attempting to harass the French, but he was probably wise to be cautious; he was vastly outnumbered, and although the French were disordered they might still have mauled the German infantry which, unlike the Buffs, had no seminary walls to protect them.[37] Charles Stewart arrived and led Murray's single squadron of the 14th Light Dragoons in an impetuous charge against the French rearguard, which added considerably to their confusion.

British casualties were remarkably light: 23 killed, 98 wounded and 2 missing: 123 in all.[38] French losses are much less certain, but it seems probable that they incurred at least 300 casualties in the fighting, and as many prisoners, as well as about 1,000 men left in the hospitals.[39]

It was a remarkable achievement; Wellesley had forced the passage of a great river in the face of veteran troops led by one of the finest soldiers in Europe, and he had done so without loss of time or suffering heavy casualties. He had recognised and seized a tiny opportunity where most generals would have seen only problems, and had thrown his men into battle with a boldness that could only be vindicated by success. By themselves the wine barges were useless; it was only their combination with the readily defensible seminary and effective supporting artillery fire from south of the Douro that made the operation feasible, and even then it required great nerve to take such liberties with a French army in 1809. Of course Wellesley benefitted from French mistakes, but that is the essence of the general's craft, and it enhances, not detracts, from the ability he showed on the occasion.

Wellesley allowed his army to rest on the following day while the wounded were treated, the dead buried, the streets cleared of debris, and an improvised bridge built over the Douro.[40] Only John Murray's brigade pushed east in the wake of the French. Soult's demoralised army camped on the night of 12 May at Baltar, some ten miles east of Oporto on the road to Spain. A little after midnight he received disastrous news: Loison had made an unsuccessful attack on Silveira at Mezãofrio near Lamego and then had inexplicably retreated, abandoning the vital bridge at Amarante. There was little hope of recapturing it with Wellesley's army closing in behind and Soult had little option but to give up the eastern route out of Portugal and head north, over the mountains, to Galicia. Twenty-four hours earlier the French could have taken the main road from Oporto to Braga, but now they were forced to leave all their heavy baggage, their artillery, their sick and their plunder by the roadside and take to mule tracks to cross two mountain ranges in two days before they reached Lanhoso in the valley of the Cavado, some eight miles north-east of Braga. From here they had a reasonable country road that led east and north-east to Chaves and Bragança. Yet even now they were not safe, for there was a risk that Beresford's force might occupy a strong position ahead of them near Chaves and block their retreat. Soult therefore turned off onto a back road to Montalegre and, brushing aside the Portuguese militia who attempted to defend two narrow bridges, made his escape, finally reaching the provincial town of Orense in Galicia on 19 May.[41]

Wellesley pursued him for a few days but gave up the chase even before Soult's tattered army had crossed the frontier into Spain. The British troops suffered a good deal in their pursuit, for the weather was very wet and miserable and they were less accustomed to the hardships of campaigning than the French. In any case Wellesley's thoughts were already turning south where there were reports of French activity near Alcantara. It was time to turn back and to move against Victor.[42]

Wellesley was disappointed not to have caught Soult, but was nonetheless delighted with the success of his campaign. It was only four weeks since he had landed in Lisbon, and he had driven the French army from Oporto and into Spain, turning the apparently inexorable advance of Napoleon's men into ignominious flight. The results of the campaign exceeded his hopes and he paid warm tribute to his men:

It is impossible to say too much of the exertions of the troops. The weather has been very bad indeed. Since of the 13th the rain has been constant; and the roads in this difficult country almost impracticable. But they have persevered in the pursuit to the last, and have been generally on their march from day-light in the morning till dark. The brigade of Guards were at the head of the column, and set a laudable example; and in the affair with the enemy's rear guard, on the evening of the 16th, they conducted themselves remarkably well.[43]

They generally reciprocated, with Captain Bowles of the Coldstream Guards summing up the change in mood in the few weeks since Wellesley had taken up the command:

The effect of the successful passage of the Douro on the minds of both the men and officers of our army has been most marked, and general confidence and goodwill has taken the place of a certain degree of gloominess and disposition to croak which was before prevalent, and we now began to consider whether it was not very possible to out-*manoeuvre* as well as *out fight* the French.[44]

And Brigadier Howorth, commander of the Royal Artillery in Portugal, wrote home that 'neither difficulty nor danger impedes Sir Arthur: he is all fire, and establishes confidence in the troops'.[45] Wellesley could not resist the obvious comparison: '[Soult] has lost everything, cannon, ammunition, baggage, military chest; and his retreat is, in every respect, even in weather, a *pendant* for the retreat to Coruña.'[46] The parallels were not exact – Soult's retreat was shorter, but over worse roads; his men were tougher, but less ready to fight – but they were surprisingly close; and there could be little doubt that the spring had brought a change of fortune in the war, when the same army that had chased Moore out of Spain was itself chased out of Portugal only four months later.

It has been calculated that Soult's army lost 6,000 men in the course of his campaign in Portugal, not including lightly wounded men who were able to remain with their units on the gruelling march into Galicia. Many of these losses, almost a third, occurred before Wellesley's army took the field, and many more were sick and convalescents captured when hospitals were overrun, but some 2,000 men were lost due to privation and exhaustion on the retreat between 13 and 19 May.[47] Wellesley concluded that Soult's army was 'so crippled that he can do no harm', and that he 'will be very little formidable to any body of troops for some time to come'.[48] This was a fair assumption; a British army would have taken months to recover in the comfort and security of home, with fresh clothing and plentiful rations. But the French army was different: not quite as effective on the battlefield, but much more resilient on campaign; less finely honed, but better suited to rough usage. Soult's men found few comforts waiting for them in Galicia, for the province was still in violent insurrection against the French. But within a few weeks they were ready to take the field again. Throughout the war in the Peninsula the French ability to recover rapidly from defeat would cause Wellesley many problems.

Rumours of Wellesley's victory and the capture of Oporto reached London on 23 May, but it was not until the following evening that Fitzroy Stanhope brought the official despatch. The Tower and Park guns were fired and some optimists dared to hope that Soult would be forced to surrender with all his men, but in general the public reaction was rather muted, reflecting the jaded atmosphere of the spring of 1809 after the feverish excitement and intense disappointment of the previous summer and autumn. Despite their praise for Wellesley in the Cintra debate, the Opposition had strongly disagreed with the government's renewed commitment to Portugal. Moira responded to Wellesley's appointment with telling incredulity: 'We are to endeavour to defend Portugal!!!' And Lord Auckland wrote to Grenville: 'I have not a doubt that Wellesley's expedition will end ultimately in waste and new mortifications; but it may possibly be of use to Ministers towards helping them to crawl through the session.'[49]

Underlying this disapproval was a genuine belief that the defence of Portugal was hopeless – a belief founded on deep pessimism about the war and awe of Napoleon's success, and which was much strengthened by the fact that Sir John Moore had declared that the Portuguese frontier was indefensible. (Moore did express this view, but in quite different circumstances, and there is no reason to suppose that he intended it as a universal truth. However, his quarrels with the ministers gave his views great weight in Opposition eyes.)[50] And finally there was Wellesley's close political connection to the Portland government, which made it only natural for the Opposition to view his military exploits with a jaundiced eye. The heated political atmosphere in the spring of 1809 was not conducive to bipartisanship.

All this was important, for it led the Opposition to adopt a carping, negative attitude to Wellesley's campaigns which, with some abatement from 1811, lasted for the rest of the war, and did it immense harm in the eyes of the country. Once adopted this stance soon became second nature. It is always tempting for a political opposition to exaggerate problems and predict disasters, and Grenville and Grey were natural pessimists, so they found it easy to believe that the country was on the brink of ruin and that the war could not be sustained for much longer. Wellesley's victories seldom brought them any joy and every flash of silver sent them in search of dark clouds. Grey set the tone perfectly when, in response to the news of Oporto, he told Grenville: 'Wellesley's success . . . appears to have been nothing more than the affair of a rear-guard, and is ridiculously magnified.'[51]

Much more surprising is Castlereagh's reaction, in which tepid praise for the victory was mixed with alarm at French movements elsewhere in Spain. This went far beyond a sensible attempt to dampen expectations of further successes, for it appears in Castlereagh's most confidential correspondence with his brother Charles Stewart and the King.[52] However, Castlereagh's response was active and positive. The Light Brigade was finally on the point of sailing, and Castlereagh now proposed that a further 5,000 infantry (all second battalions, unfortunately) be ordered to follow them. The Cabinet agreed and the King acquiesced, without mentioning his earlier stipulation that the command of the army be reconsidered if it was significantly reinforced. Plans were being made at this time to send a large amphibious expedition to Walcheren to strike at Napoleon's naval bases in the Scheldt, and this would give an opportunity for more senior officers to be employed in active service, so the question of their disadvantage was less pressing than it had been in April.[53]

Wellesley was annoyed by the lack of recognition for his success, and asked quite reasonably: 'What right had they to expect that I should do so much?'[54] He was also stung by reports that Whitbread had accused him of exaggerating his success, and wrote an extraordinary letter to their mutual friend General

Ferguson in which he equated exaggeration with '*lying*' and virtually demanded an apology. Fortunately both Ferguson and Whitbread responded calmly, with a placatory letter that soothed Wellesley's feelings and averted any further hint of a duel.[55]

It was a strange business and would have no sequel even though the next few years saw many attacks on Wellesley by the Opposition which went far beyond accusations of exaggeration. Wellesley was fortunate that Whitbread, whatever the faults of his judgement on questions of policy, was personally magnanimous, and pacifically minded; for an unresolved private quarrel between a leading Opposition politician and a general in the field would have been an encumbrance to both men. Subsequently Wellesley went out of his way to remain on civil, courteous terms with the leading Whigs and usually ignored their attacks. As a soldier he served his country, and if the Opposition came to power he would continue to serve unless recalled or driven to resign by differences over strategy. But it was not an easy line to follow when he was so closely associated with one political party, and his conduct was being criticised by the other.

CHAPTER NINETEEN

TALAVERA
(June–August 1809)

WELLESLEY'S CAMPAIGN IN Spain in the summer of 1809 was overshadowed by the outbreak of war in central Europe. The Austrians had been deeply alarmed by Napoleon's deposition of the Spanish Bourbons, and in the spring of 1809 – just two weeks before Wellesley arrived back in Portugal – they attacked the French in southern Germany. The Archduke Charles gained some initial successes, but lacked the confidence to exploit them, and a series of hard-fought actions turned the tide in favour of the French. Napoleon entered Vienna on 13 May, but the Austrian army was unbroken and they continued the war. A French attempt to cross the Danube was defeated at Aspern-Essling on 21–22 May with both sides suffering heavy casualties. It was the most serious setback Napoleon had ever suffered on the battlefield, but the odds were still greatly in his favour. For six weeks Europe held its breath while both sides strengthened their forces for the decisive battle. On the night of 4 July the French again crossed the Danube and over the next two days fought a dreadful battle of attrition at Wagram in which each army suffered about 40,000 casualties and prisoners. In the end the Austrians retreated and a few days later, on 12 July, signed an armistice at Znaim. The hopes of Napoleon's enemies were dashed, but never had the emperor paid such a price for his victory.

The British government did what it could to help the Austrians, delivering almost £1.2 million in specie (gold and silver coin) between April and July, at a time when the shortage of ready money was severely hampering Wellesley's military efforts in Portugal. It also decided to send an expedition to the Scheldt to attempt to destroy Napoleon's naval base at Antwerp. The ministers considered sending an army to northern Germany instead, but did not have the cash needed to pay for supplies in an extended campaign.[1] Unfortunately preparations for the expedition proceeded slowly, and it was not ready to sail until 28 July. The force consisted of some 45,000 men and more than 600 ships, with the army commanded by Lord Chatham. The operation proved a complete failure, dogged by bad weather and poor leadership. An unsuccessful initial landing at Cadsand and a fortnight spent besieging Flushing deprived it of any momentum, and it was not until 23 August that the army was ready to advance on Antwerp. The delay had given the French and Dutch plenty of time to collect troops and take other precautions, and Chatham decided that there was little prospect of success and abandoned the operation.

Unfortunately the withdrawal was even more protracted than the advance, and the last British troops did not embark until 9 December. This delay proved costly; only 106 British soldiers were killed in action in the campaign, but nearly 4,000 died of 'Walcheren fever' (probably malaria), while many more fell ill and were slow to recover (as late as 1 February 1810 there were still 11,000 men on the sick list). Even when the men did recover, their health had often been undermined and they quickly fell ill again when exposed to the demands and deprivations of active campaigning. The Walcheren expedition was a disaster for the British army, made all the worse because the army included a large number of the fine first battalions, which were just recovering from their experiences in the Coruña campaign. Regiments that might have been ready to return to the Peninsula in the second half of 1809 were decimated for a second time, and even when they were again fit for service, they had lost the confidence and condition they had in 1808 without gaining much in the way of useful experience of action. On the other hand, Walcheren convinced the British government to concentrate its efforts in the Peninsula and to reject the temptation of *coups de main*, and other diversions.[2]

News of Wellesley's victory at Oporto appeared in the London newspapers on the same day as reports of the surrender of Vienna.[3] When the Cabinet met, later that day, to consider Wellesley's request that his instructions be altered to permit him to extend his operations deep into Spain, the ministers had yet to commit themselves finally to the expedition to the Scheldt. A vigorous campaign in Spain might act as a diversion in favour of the Austrians, but this seems to have carried little weight with the Cabinet. The collapse of the Spanish army on the Ebro, and Moore's ruinous campaign, had left a deep distrust of Spain in Britain. On 19 April Canning privately told the British ambassador to Spain: 'There is a fixed determination not to hazard a British Army – (*the* British Army) again in Spain on anything like the same terms as before.' Yet the ministers trusted Wellesley as they trusted no other soldier. Canning had introduced him in the same letter with unqualified praise:

> In Wellesley . . . you will find everything that you can wish – frankness – temper – honesty – quickness – comprehensiveness – and military Ability – not only eminent beyond any other military commander that could be chosen – but perhaps possessed by him alone, of all our Commanders, in a degree that qualifies for great undertakings.[4]

Further, at the end of July Castlereagh told Charles Stewart:

> I am not disposed to consider Wellesley or any other Man as being without
> his drawbacks, or his faults if you please, but I do deliberately believe him to
> unite more of the Essential Qualities of an officer, than any Individual in the
> Service – he deserves to command great armies – we have already, under
> every difficulty, placed him in the most prominent Command the Service
> affords . . .[5]

This confidence seems to have been shared by all the Cabinet except Chatham,
and it led the ministers to grant Wellesley's request and to 'authorise you to
extend your operations in Spain beyond the provinces immediately adjacent to
the Portuguese frontier, provided you shall be of opinion that your doing so is
material, in a military point of view, to the success of your operations, and not
inconsistent with the safety of Portugal'.[6] The King, who shared all his ministers' doubts about Spain and little of their faith in Wellesley, gave his approval
reluctantly and with many forebodings.[7] If Wellesley chose to lead his army
into Spain it would be on his own responsibility, not in response to commands
from home.

There were more than 250,000 French troops in Spain at the beginning of
June 1809 – a far more powerful and effective army than the various Spanish,
British and Portuguese forces. Napoleon had taken the Imperial Guard with
him when he left Spain at the beginning of the year, but he had not withdrawn
any large bodies of troops in consequence of the Austrian war – although there
had been a sharp reduction in the normal flow of drafts of recruits and convalescents to regiments in Spain. Otherwise the French armies were little affected
by the fighting on the Danube, although at the beginning of April Napoleon
gave orders for Mortier's corps to disengage from active operations in case he
needed to summon it to Germany.[8]

Wellesley's eagerness to engage in a campaign in Spain arose not from any
misunderstanding of the overall strength of the French armies in the Peninsula,
but because he believed that their distribution created a strategic opportunity
that he could exploit. Of the seven French corps south of the Pyrenees, the
strongest was far away fighting an almost completely separate war against the
partisans and regular Spanish forces in Catalonia. Ney's corps was equally
occupied with the insurgency in Galicia, where it had just been joined by Soult's
demoralised and defeated army. Suchet had recently replaced Junot in
command of the Third Corps and had his hands full in Aragon covering the
gaps left by the withdrawal of Mortier's corps. Mortier was in Old Castile but
might be recalled to France at any moment, and Wellesley seems to have underestimated the strength of his corps. This left only two French corps south of

Madrid: Victor in Estremadura and Sebastiani in La Mancha, together with King Joseph's own small central reserve – about 50,000 men in all. The Spanish General Cuesta faced Victor with an army of rather more than 30,000 men, while Venegas had another 20,000 opposite Sebastiani. The Spanish armies were not equal to the French in quality, but Wellesley believed that the addition of his army of 25,000 excellent British troops could tip the balance decisively in favour of the allies, and force the French to evacuate Madrid and fall back to the Ebro. This would be a great blow to French prestige within the Peninsula and throughout Europe, but the sequel would largely depend on the state of the war on the Danube, for as the French withdrew into northern Spain they would concentrate their forces, and their underlying superiority would become more obvious. However, that was trying to look too far ahead; for the moment Wellesley was more concerned with planning his campaign against Victor, and he greeted the government's change to his instructions with pleasure, telling Villiers: 'The ball is now at my foot, and I hope I shall have strength enough to give it a good kick.'[9]

Wellesley's army spent the last week of May and the first two weeks of June moving south from Oporto to Abrantes. The troops marched in easy stages and were well supplied with food and other necessities, for Wellesley knew that the campaign against Soult had been exhausting and that his men needed a chance to recover before advancing into Spain, while many regiments were in urgent need of new shoes. Unfortunately the relaxation of tension led to a serious outbreak of indiscipline, with numerous instances of soldiers plundering the local population. Wellesley was furious and on 29 May issued a General Order condemning 'the conduct of the troops; not only have outrages been committed by whole corps, but there is no description of property of which the unfortunate inhabitants of Portugal have not been plundered by British soldiers, whom they have received into their houses, or by stragglers from the different regiments of the army'. He blamed a lack of discipline within regiments, and ordered that the soldiers within each company be divided into squads each of which would be led by a non-commissioned officer who would be responsible for their conduct. Officers were instructed to visit their men four times a day when not marching, including a visit at eight o'clock in the evening.[10]

Inexperience of life on campaign seems to have played a large part in creating the problem. Too many officers and NCOs were new to the demands of active service, while their soldiers were still discovering the distinction between tolerated 'foraging' and unacceptable 'plundering'. The Portuguese were unused to the presence of the British army, and were not quite sure what to expect or how best to defend their interests; and the commissariat and provosts were still learning how to perform their duties. The outbreak of indiscipline seems to have been brought under control when the army was encamped near Abrantes, but the problem of soldiers plundering the local civilian population would recur throughout the war, always arousing Wellesley's anger; unlike many generals he was never inclined to turn a blind eye to the misconduct of his troops.

Wellesley took advantage of the halt at Abrantes to reorganise his army. He decided to leave the Portuguese army behind to guard the north-eastern frontier near Almeida, and to train, gain discipline and *esprit de corps*, for despite its good service in the Oporto campaign it was far from ready to take part in an extended operation.[11] The British infantry were now divided into four divisions, each with some artillery permanently included, while the cavalry formed a separate division under William Payne. The First Division, commanded by Sherbrooke, was much the strongest, including the Guards, the King's German Legion, and Alan Cameron's line brigade – eight battalions in all, amounting to more than 6,000 men. The remaining three divisions each consisted of two British brigades under the command of the senior brigadier; Hill commanded the Second, Mackenzie the Third and Alexander Campbell the Fourth Division, with each division consisting of five or six battalions or 3,000–4,000 men. Several regiments joined the army at Abrantes or in the subsequent advance: 1/40th, 1/48th and 1/61st were welcome additions being strong battalions replacing some of the worst of the second battalions Castlereagh had sent out in March. The cavalry was also reinforced with the arrival of the 1st Hussars of the King's German Legion (an excellent regiment that proved invaluable throughout the war) and the 23rd Light Dragoons.

The army benefitted from the halt at Abrantes and the troops seem to have been quite comfortable. The total strength of the army at Abrantes was around 25,000 men, not including around 3,000 sick.[12] The proportion of sick was quite low – Wellesley thought 10 per cent a useful rule of thumb for an army on active service, although the figure in the Peninsula would generally be much higher than this, with an underlying upward trend throughout the war.[13] Reinforcements were on their way; the Light Brigade (1/43rd, 1/52nd and 1/95th) finally landed at Lisbon at the end of June after a slow and frustrating passage, and was soon followed by the 5,000 infantry Castlereagh had ordered out at the end of May. The Light Brigade (together with Hew Ross's troop of horse artillery) marched to join the army as soon as it could collect some transport; but Wellesley heard bad reports of the second wave of reinforcements and ordered them to remain in Lisbon until they were fit to take the field.[14]

Wellesley was in an ill humour during the halt at Abrantes, partly because of the indiscipline of the army on the march south, but mostly because his operations were being delayed by a shortage of cash. He would not advance into Spain without ready money to pay his soldiers and purchase supplies, and the military chest was almost empty. This was part of the wider shortage of

specie that hampered the British government at the time and had serious implications for the economy and everyday life in Britain. To Wellesley, the solution
was simple: the British government should send out large, regular shipments of
specie to finance the war (£300,000 at once followed by £200,000 per month);
but it was quite impossible for the Treasury to comply.[15] Yet Wellesley made no
allowance for the difficulties of others and complained in terms that were
grossly unfair and extremely indiscreet. As early as 31 May he told Villiers: 'I
suspect the Ministers in England are very indifferent to our operations in this
country.' And in July he again complained: 'It is not my fault if the British
government have undertaken in Spain and Portugal a larger concern than they
can find means to provide for.'[16] He did not really mean this – no one would
have been more horrified if the British army had been withdrawn from Portugal
simply because ready money could not be found to keep the soldiers pay up to
date; while it was Wellesley, not the British government, who wanted the new
campaign in Spain. But it was dangerous to put such views on paper at a time
when the Opposition at home was criticising the commitment to Portugal and
when letters went astray, sometimes being captured by French privateers and
being published in the *Moniteur*. It is not hard to imagine the storm that would
have erupted in England if the ministers' own favourite general, and former
colleague on the Treasury bench, was known to have written in these terms.
The Machiavellian interpretation of these letters is that Wellesley was seeking
political insurance in case the campaign went badly, but this is almost certainly
wrong. Throughout his life he indulged himself by giving way to the irritations
of the moment and expressing his annoyance in exaggerated caustic language,
regardless of possible consequences. And a logistical crisis, particularly at the
outset of the campaign, was exactly the sort of problem to produce the most
extreme reaction, as it had in the middle of 1803 before the Maratha War broke
out. Wellesley was extremely fortunate that this indulgence never involved him
in a fresh crisis of his own making.

The shortage of cash was relieved before the end of June when some money
was received from Cadiz, followed soon after by £230,000 in 'dollars, doubloons,
and Portuguese gold' sent out from London. The British government was
scraping the vaults of the Bank of England bare, and Castlereagh warned
Wellesley that while they might be able to collect another £100,000, that would
be all 'till dollars arrive from South America (the period of which is uncertain)'.[17] And so the problem was patched up rather than permanently solved,
and British operations in the Peninsula would be dogged by periodic crises
caused by lack of specie, each of which would provoke an intemperate response
from Wellesley. However as the war went on and merchants in Lisbon and
Cadiz gained confidence, more money was raised locally through the sale of
Bills on London, which the merchants used to purchase British goods that they

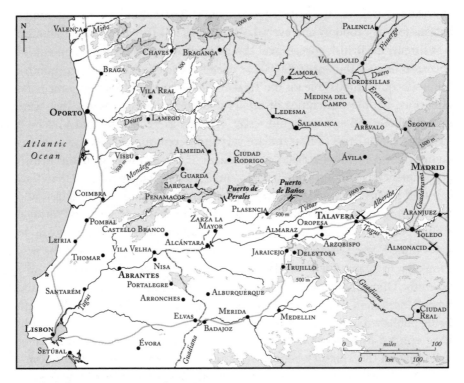

14 The Talavera campaign, July 1809.

then exported to the Peninsula or Latin America, so that their trade helped to finance the war.

Wellesley's temper was not helped by his negotiations with Cuesta over plans for the coming campaign. Initially it looked as if he might be able to advance behind Victor's flank and into his rear, but before the end of June the French marshal had abandoned his exposed position at Merida and withdrawn 150 miles north-east to Talavera de la Reina. His main reason was the shortage of food around Merida rather than fear of the allies, for the French had little idea of the location of Wellesley's army and no expectation that it was about to advance into Spain. Nonetheless Victor's retreat had brought him much closer to Madrid, and, by helping to concentrate French forces in central Spain, made them less vulnerable. Wellesley and Cuesta would need more effective cooperation from Venegas if Sebastiani was not to march to Victor's aid.[18]

The money finally reached the army at Abrantes on 25 June and Wellesley gave the order to march on 27 June, having brought the soldiers' pay up to date. The first week's march was through Portugal with Castello Branco being the main town on the route – the army was heading east and a little north, parallel to the Tagus but not attempting to follow the line of the river closely. The

Spanish frontier was passed at Zarza la Mayor on 3 July and on 8 July the army reached Plasencia where it halted for a few days. The weather was hot and the troops, who only six weeks earlier had been sodden and shivering in northern Portugal, now grumbled about thirst and the scorching sun. Their day began early, at first light, and the march was usually completed before noon when the soldiers would bivouac and cook their food. Many of the commissaries were still learning their trade, so although there was no real shortage of food there were often delays and unnecessary problems. Captain Hawker did not enjoy roughing it, complaining that at night he was beset by gnats 'and annoyed by every description of reptile, and by a *concert of toads and frogs*, which were by no means unlike *Portuguese women in a market*', while in the morning his blanket was so full of beetles and bugs that it would appall anyone other than Sir Joseph Banks.[19]

While the army halted at Plasencia, Wellesley rode ahead with a few staff to meet Cuesta and make detailed arrangements for the next stage of the campaign. He was disappointed to find Cuesta surly and uncooperative, while the officers in Wellesley's entourage were shocked that the Spanish general was elderly and so infirm that he needed to be held in his saddle by the ADC.[20] On the other side, Cuesta had reasons to view Wellesley with disfavour. He may have felt that Wellesley, who was a generation younger, much junior, and commanding a smaller allied army, ought to have shown him more deference rather than take the lead in the discussions. He also knew that John Hookham Frere, the British ambassador, had been working with his opponents in the Supreme Junta, and that there had been loose talk in Seville that he should be subordinated to the British general.[21]

Nonetheless the conference ended with an agreed plan of campaign and Wellesley formed a reasonably favourable impression of the Spanish army.[22] Venegas was sent detailed instructions to keep Sebastiani busy by advancing, or, if Sebastiani could not be prevented from moving to join Victor, Venegas was to threaten Madrid. However this plan was based on an underestimation of the strength of Sebastiani's army (which was close to 20,000 men, not 10,000 as Cuesta and Wellesley believed). This made Venegas understandably cautious, and as a result he failed to play his part in the campaign, neither containing Sebastiani nor creating a diversion at Madrid.

Wellesley and Cuesta did not anticipate any danger from Soult, Mortier or Ney. According to the latest reports, Ney was fully occupied trying to subdue Galicia, Soult's corps was still a wreck, and Mortier was too weak to act alone. However Cuesta agreed to detach a small force to occupy the Puerto de Baños on the main road from Salamanca to Plasencia to guard against a French raid on Wellesley's lines of communication.

The British army waited at Plasencia until 17 July to give time for Venegas to receive his orders, and to gather transport and supplies. In Portugal

Wellesley's army had relied on the local peasantry to carry supplies in their bullock carts, each going no more than a few days from home. But this hand-to-mouth system broke down in Spain, either because the Spanish peasantry were unwilling to cooperate and the authorities lacked the will or the power to compel them (which is what the British came to suspect), or because there simply were not the animals and vehicles available. In later campaigns the British relied heavily on Spanish muleteers and their great trains of pack animals, but that crucial alliance had yet to be forged, and Wellesley was faced with a serious, possibly insoluble problem. On 16 July he warned Cuesta that if the Spanish authorities failed to produce the transport they had promised he would withdraw from the campaign as soon as the first phase of operations was completed.[23]

The army marched from Plasencia on 17 July and crossed the River Tietar, which runs south-west from the mountains to the Tagus, on the following morning.[24] After a long march in intense heat on 19 July the army occupied Oropesa on 20 July, where it was joined a day later by the Spanish army. Captain William Stothert caught the mood of the moment when he wrote, describing the next day's march:

> This morning the combined army was in motion before day-break, and advanced along the extensive plain towards Talavera. Few officers had ever previously seen so large a body acting as if by one impulse, and marching as if in one direction. It was in truth a sublime and magnificent spectacle, and the occasion was calculated to excite the most exalted ideas in a soldier's bosom.[25]

Not even Wellesley had seen 50,000 fighting men marching together across a single plain, although he had seen larger hosts in India if all the camp followers and attendants are included in the count.

Victor's army occupied a strong position behind the River Alberche, which runs south-west into the Tagus three or four miles to the east of Talavera, but he had left a small force of infantry in the town. Guarding its approach from the west was Latour-Maubourg's division of cavalry. After some skirmishing between the cavalry of the two armies the French in the town withdrew. There were few casualties on either side, but the handful of French wounded left on the field were promptly murdered by the Spaniards. They had some excuse, for as the French withdrew they had plundered and destroyed all the detached houses and other buildings and set fire to the fields of corn.[26]

That evening it was clear that the French intended to hold the line of the Alberche, and Wellesley met with Cuesta to persuade him to agree to a dawn attack. Their talks continued for several hours until, around midnight,

Wellesley believed that Cuesta had agreed to his plan. This left little time for preparations, for only three hours later Wellesley was leading forward Sherbrooke's and Mackenzie's divisions and waiting for the French sentries to give the alarm. The Spaniards did not move. Either there had been a genuine miscommunication, or Cuesta had changed his mind. The attack was aborted and Wellesley was furious. In fact the wisdom of a dawn attack seems highly doubtful as the troops were tired, the ground rough and unfamiliar and the French on the alert. It would have been far simpler and better to allow the soldiers an uninterrupted night's sleep and to attack mid-morning when all the troops had been brought into position in daylight.[27]

The three armies spent 23 July in a state of uneasy passivity. That night Victor retreated; he had ridden his luck on the previous day and was too wise to tempt fate a second time, so he marched east, towards Toledo, forty miles away, where he might unite with Sebastiani and King Joseph. Cuesta was all energy and animation, and set off in hot pursuit of Victor, with the vision of a triumphal entry into Madrid quickening his pulse. But now it was Wellesley's turn to refuse to cooperate. His army was hungry and he was disgusted with his ally. Few of his men had received their full rations in the last few days and the promised transport had still not appeared. He had fulfilled his obligation by completing the first phase of the campaign, and now acted on his warning to Cuesta, given a week before, that if the logistical problems were not overcome he would abandon the campaign.[28]

At first sight this looks like a crude attempt to blackmail the Spanish authorities into supplying his needs. But it is possible that Wellesley had another motive for his dramatic decision. His exasperation with Cuesta had passed a critical point, and he told Frere: 'I find Gen. Cuesta more and more impracticable every day. It is impossible to do business with him, and very uncertain that any operation will succeed in which he has any concern.'[29] Eleven days earlier he had warned Frere that any attempt on the part of the Spanish government to dismiss Cuesta would do little good; but now he wrote that 'there has been a material change in the sentiments of the army respecting him; and I am told (although I cannot say I know it to be true) that if government were now to deprive him of the command, the army would allow that their order should be carried into execution.'[30] It is hard to read this other than as a strong hint that Wellesley would like to see Cuesta replaced, but Wellesley then continued: 'However, I think that the government, before they take this step, ought to have some cause for removing him, the justice of which would be obvious to everybody, or they ought to be more certain that their order would not be resisted by the army than I have it in my power to make them.'[31] That cause would probably not be long coming, for without the cooperation of the British army, Wellesley had little doubt that Cuesta 'will get himself into a scrape: any movement by me to his assistance is quite out of the question . . . If the enemy should discover that we are not with him, he will be beaten, or must retire'.[32] It is probably going a step too far to suggest that Wellesley deliberately set up a situation in which the Spanish army would be checked or defeated so that Cuesta would be removed from his command; but he certainly was aware that this was likely to be the consequence of his actions. The surly old man's suspicions of his young ally were not so unreasonable after all, and one can only wonder how Wellesley would have reacted if Cuesta had intrigued with the Whigs for the appointment of Lord Moira, or some other general, over his head.

The officers and men in Wellesley's army knew nothing of this, of course; they were hungry and frustrated over the aborted attack on 23 July (for both of which they blamed the Spanish), but their spirits were generally good, their confidence raised by their long advance and by the evident reluctance of the French army to face them in battle. They were troubled by the lack of food, but were not in the least intimidated by the prospect of fighting Napoleon's veterans. The prevailing opinion was that the French had retreated and would not be seen again at least until Madrid was near at hand, mixed with a conviction that if they could be brought to battle, it would end in a decisive victory. This refusal to countenance the possibility of defeat arose partly from training and tradition, and partly from Wellesley's capable leadership; and it was to play an important role in the events of the next few days.[33]

Victor halted his retreat at the River Guadarrama some ten miles west of Toledo on the evening of 25 July. Sebastiani had given Venegas the slip and arrived in Toledo that same day, while King Joseph, having left only a few thousand men to hold Madrid, had brought the rest of his reserve south and was now close at hand. The French had succeeded in concentrating all their disposable forces in central Spain (some 46,000 men), and were determined not to abandon Madrid without a fight. Their spirits were greatly helped by Napoleon's decision on 12 June, when he was in Vienna, to subordinate Ney and Mortier to Soult, whom he ordered to drive the British from Portugal. At first Soult intended to invade northern Portugal, but when he learnt of the British advance in the Tagus valley he reacted quickly, informing Joseph that he would bring his whole force south from Salamanca through the Puerto de Baños and into the British rear at Plasencia. Joseph and Jourdan calculated, rather too optimistically, that Soult's forces might reach Plasencia on 27 July and that this would force the British to abandon the campaign and withdraw south across the Tagus.[34]

Fortunately Cuesta learnt of the concentration of French forces at Toledo in good time, and withdrew towards Talavera on 26 July in fairly good order, even though Victor pressed his rearguard. That night the Spanish army camped on the eastern bank of the Alberche along with Sherbrooke's division. The following morning Cuesta's men fell back to Talavera, and Sherbrooke's division withdrew to the open ground north of the town, leaving Mackenzie's division as the most advanced allied infantry in the broken ground on the western bank of the Alberche. Wellesley was with them observing the farther bank of the Alberche from the tower of the Casa de Salinas, a large house in the trees, but even he failed to see the French advance and was caught by surprise. Around noon two French columns made a sudden attack on Mackenzie's men, catching them off-guard and creating considerable confusion. Wellesley had to scramble out of the house with his staff as quickly as he could, and for a moment there was some risk that his career might end with the humiliation of capture. Donkin's brigade (the 2/87th and 1/88th) fell back in considerable disorder, but the 2/31st and 1/45th from Mackenzie's own brigade and the 5/60th from Donkin's brigade were 'got in hand, and they covered the falling back of the other regiments in fine style from the wood into the plain. Here the cavalry were in readiness to support them; and from that moment a regular and well-conducted retreat began'.[35] It is impossible to determine the casualties suffered in the affair, as Donkin's brigade, which suffered most, was heavily engaged later in the day, but they were probably quite considerable.[36]

Mackenzie's division, now covered by the British cavalry, fell back three or four miles to the position Wellesley had already selected for the allies to occupy and offer battle. This ran in a line north from the town of Talavera to the steep hill of the Cerro de Medellin two-and-a-half miles from the Tagus. The right, or southern, end of the line was securely anchored in the town, whose ancient walls were useful, and beyond it the river. Around the town was a thick belt of olive groves and enclosures, which gave good cover to defending infantry. All this half of the line was occupied by the Spanish army, which was able to form in several lines. About a mile from the town was a low rise, the Pajar de Vegara, on which work had begun to build an artillery redoubt, although little progress had been made and neither the work nor the rise had any great tactical significance. This was the point of junction of the allied armies, with the British occupying the northern half of the position. First (moving south to north) was Alexander Campbell's division – at this point the front was still covered by olive groves and there was an embankment some sixty yards in front of the British line. On Campbell's left stood Sherbrooke's division, formed in a single two-deep line – the Guards brigade on the right, then Alan Cameron's two battalions, and then, on the lower slopes of the Cerro de Medellin, the two brigades of the King's German Legion. Sherbrooke's men had no cover; their position was flat and open and proved very exposed to French artillery massed on the Cerro de Cascajal, a lower, gentler hill opposite the Cerro de Medellin. The Portiña brook ran from north to south through a narrow gully in front of the British position. The gully was at its deepest where it squeezed between the Cerro de Medellin and the Cerro de Cascajal, but was still a significant obstacle,

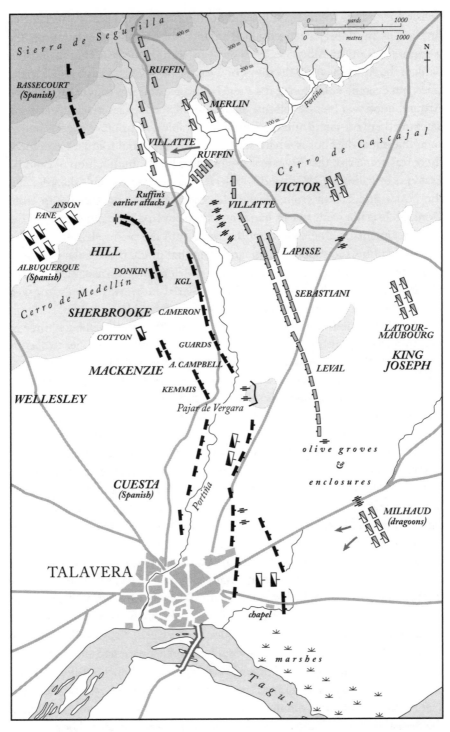

15 The battle of Talavera, 27–28 July 1809. (All troop positions approximate, many conjectural.)

especially to cavalry, opposite the Guards' position. The summit of the Cerro de Medellin was destined to be held by Hill's division. The height ran back to the west, gradually losing altitude, so that some of Hill's men could be formed facing north, protecting the left flank of the army. North of the Cerro de Medellin was half a mile of open ground, relatively flat but rising gently to the north, beyond which lay the rocky heights of the Sierra de Segurilla, but Wellesley's initial scheme of deployment did not extend beyond the Cerro de Medellin. As it was, the British army was stretched rather too thinly to cover the ground; the only reserves were the cavalry brigades of Fane, Cotton and Anson, and Mackenzie's division, which was now divided, Donkin's battered brigade joining the troops on the lower slopes of the Cerro de Medellin, whilst Mackenzie's three battalions formed well to the south behind the Guards.[37]

The British army had not yet properly taken up its position as Mackenzie's men withdrew towards it late on the afternoon of 27 July, and there was evidently a good deal of confusion. All of this suggests some surprising ineffi-ciency in the machinery – especially the staff work – of the British army, which may be attributed partly to inexperience, and partly to Wellesley's distraction, first with giving advice to Cuesta, and then to supervising the withdrawal of Sherbrooke and Mackenzie. Given that the army had been stationary for several days and that Wellesley had apparently selected the position it was to occupy before 27 July, there was clearly some uncharacteristic negligence in not taking more effective steps to ensure that the army was better prepared.

The leading French troops advanced hard on Mackenzie's heels and at once launched a probing attack on the Spanish position north of the town. The Spanish infantry were flustered, opened fire much too soon, and four raw battalions on the left broke and fled. This spread alarm behind, with the army joined in their panic by many camp-followers, commissaries, baggage-guards and other detached troops – British as well as Spanish – who did not know what was happening at the front and who naturally feared the worst.[38] Wellesley was close by when the Spanish infantry broke and the incident added a tinge of contempt to his disenchantment with his allies – a feeling that was now widespread in the British army. This was the most serious consequence of the event; the French made no attempt to exploit the opportunity and may not even have seen what had happened as the Spanish position was concealed by the trees.[39]

Victor's eyes were fixed further north, for in the fading light of a gathering dusk he saw the summit of Cerro de Medellin apparently unguarded; the German Legion had now arrived in their position, but Hill's division had yet to take up its ground on the height, having camped for several days near the town.[40] Victor was not a soldier to let such an opportunity go begging. As soon as he had the leading division of his corps in hand he threw it into a sudden – and completely unexpected – attack on the vital hill. Colonel Donkin described what happened in a letter written two days later: 'We had hardly time to get into our places in the Line, when the Enemy made a furious Attack on the Left, which was the Key of our Position. It fell at first on the left of the German Legion, about Dusk, which after a short resistance gave way.' Donkin advanced with the 88th, but the French 'broke thro' my Ranks, and the French Column advanced so fast that the 88th was driven with the Germans into the plain on my Right and in the rear of our centre'. He rode back up the hill and brought forward the 87th, but it too gave way before the furious French assault:

> after losing an immense number of Men and Officers . . . the Battle must have been lost as our flank would have been turned & the whole Line enfiladed from the Hill had not the 29th Regt. with Heroic Gallantry climbed up the Hill beyond my left sustained by the 48th and driven back the Enemy. This struggle lasted about an hour and a half – during the whole of it, our whole Line was cannonaded.[41]

The French attack was repulsed and the fighting died down. Only the three battalions of the 9e Léger, the leading regiment in Ruffin's division, seem to have been engaged, and they had broken or disordered five British battalions before finally being driven off. British losses were heavy: the 7th KGL lost 146 casualties including 77 missing, while the 2/87th lost almost 200 casualties (including its losses earlier in the day at Casa de Salinas). Altogether the British army lost over 800 casualties on 27 July, more than it suffered at Vimeiro or the battle of Coruña.[42] The French lost considerably fewer, although the figures are much less certain. The best estimate is that the 9e Léger suffered some 300 casualties in its attack on the Cerro de Medellin, and it was considerably shaken by its repulse. Other French units were scarcely engaged and would have lost only a handful of men.[43]

Victor's attack has been condemned as foolhardy and pointless,[44] but this seems unduly harsh. He saw an opportunity to gain a decisive advantage by a bold stroke and failed in the attempt, but the considerable measure of success he achieved suggests that the risk was worth taking. If the leading troops of the 9e Léger had been able to consolidate their hold on the summit of the Cerro de Medellin, Wellesley's whole position would have been rendered untenable, and the allies would probably have been forced into a perilous retreat on the following morning. This danger was averted by the confidence and indomitable fighting quality of the British infantry – particularly the 29th, but also the 48th and the Buffs who supported the counter-attack, and even the battalions that were broken, for they soon rallied without any permanent loss of nerve. George Fitzclarence, writing of the fighting at Casa de Salinas, makes a comment that applies to the whole of 27 July – and the whole of Wellesley's army – when he says: 'Though ever as gallant, we were by no means such good soldiers in those days as succeeding campaigns made us, and sufficient precautions had not been taken . . .'[45]

The troops spent a restless and uneasy night with frequent alarms and bursts of firing along the whole front, and, on the Cerro de Medellin, the cries of the wounded. Wellesley, surrounded by his staff, slept, wrapped in his cloak, on the open ground behind the centre of the British line, but his rest was disturbed and he repeatedly asked the time, making his staff feel that 'he looked for daylight with as much anxiety as the rest of us'.[46]

Before first light Wellesley and his staff mounted and rode slowly to the summit of the Cerro de Medellin.[47] From here they were soon able to observe the French army camped in front of them; Victor's leading infantry and artillery were barely half a mile to their east on the Cerro de Cascajal, with the other troops further back, south and east, as far as the Casa de Salinas where Joseph and Jourdan had spent the night. It was a formidable array: some 45,000 men including almost 5,000 cavalry and 80 guns. These troops were veterans of the Grande Armée; their memories of victories over Prussia and Russia were still fresh; they had been in Spain for less than a year, and so were acclimatised without yet being worn down by endless petty operations; and they had never previously faced the British in battle. It was the finest French army Wellesley would face during the entire war in the Peninsula. Opposing the French were about 22,000 British troops (3,000 cavalry, 5 batteries of artillery and almost 18,000 infantry), and a Spanish army of around 30,000 men (including at least 5,000 cavalry).[48] The Spanish troops were better than the needless panic of the previous evening suggested – the battalions that had fled were particularly raw – but they lacked the discipline and training to be able to manoeuvre safely in the face of the enemy. Both they and the British benefitted from being able to stand on the defensive, even though it enabled the French to concentrate their attack on a single part of the allied line.

As daylight spread across the field the French artillery opened a heavy fire on the British troops on the Cerro de Medellin and further south in the open plain. Victor had not given up hope of seizing the Cerro de Medellin in a limited operation, and he now threw Ruffin's whole division forward, although the 9e Léger, still shaken from its losses of a few hours before, seems to have played a secondary role in the attack, which was led by the six battalions of the 24e and 96e Ligne. The exact details of this attack are hard to establish, and it is not clear whether Wellesley was on the spot to direct the defence or not, but the fighting was fierce and often sustained, and a number of battalions on both sides were seriously engaged, although to regimental officers and men in the ranks it was obvious that their own unit played the decisive part at the critical point. According to a letter from George Murray, written three days later, a very strong French column pushed along the northern side of the hill, past the summit, and then swung south, advancing into the gap between the first and second British lines, formed by the two brigades of Hill's division. 'The progress of this formidable column was not checked until it got within a few yards of the summit of the hill, when our Men succeeded in driving it back in the utmost confusion.' Certainly both brigades of Hill's division were heavily engaged; Richard Stewart lost more than 500 casualties, or a quarter of his force, with all three of his battalions suffering; Tilson's losses were not quite so severe, 336 casualties during the day with the Buffs the worst hit with 142 casualties.[49]

While Hill's two brigades bore the brunt of the fighting, the German Legion and Donkin's brigades were also engaged. According to Donkin the Germans were again broken, 'but I had the good fortune to support them effectually from the Hill with my Brigade, and I took up a Line, a little in their front, with my Brigade & to their Left, and maintained it the whole day'.[50] However the history of the German Legion states that the 5th Line Battalion attacked a French column in front, while Major von Wurmb led his riflemen against its exposed left flank in a confused and deadly melee, which inflicted some 400 casualties on the French and sent them flying down the hill.[51] The losses of the German Legion are impossible to separate from those suffered later in the day, but there is no doubt that whether they were broken or succeeded in repelling the French, they regained their order and resumed their position in the lower slopes of the Cerro de Medellin.

Victor's second assault had been repulsed at a cost of about 1,200 casualties mostly in the 24e and 96e Ligne.[52] Hill's division probably suffered between 700 and 800 casualties, with Donkin and the German Legion adding some more. It is much harder to justify this attack than that of the previous evening, for there was little chance of catching the British off-guard and they had shown their determination to fight to preserve their hold on the hill. But Victor and his men were accustomed to success: the Russians had been doughty fighters and yet been beaten; even Cuesta's troops had performed well initially at Medellin before their resistance crumbled; and the French had little reason to believe that the British would not crack in a similar way if the pressure upon them was sustained.

The defeat of Victor's attack was followed by a lull in the fighting, which lasted several hours, and an informal truce soon sprang up as men from both armies looked for water in the pools of the Portiña brook. The British troops were not just thirsty; they were also very hungry and cast envious eyes at the French cooking fires. One private had the audacity to approach Wellesley and his staff and loudly declare: 'It was very hard that they had nothing to eat, and wished that they might be let to go down and fight, for when engaged they forget their hunger.' George Fitzclarence, who tells the story, adds that 'the poor fellow was, however, at last persuaded to retire', although he does not say if the 'persuasion' was accompanied by a loaf or a threat.[53] Despite the barriers of social distinction, military rank and formal discipline, Wellesley lived close to his men, not just on the battlefield but also on campaign. He did not permit much familiarity or seek popularity, but nor did he hide behind elaborate protocols or spend his time in a lavish headquarters far to the rear.

There was some debate among the French commanders over their next step, and they might easily have decided to hold their ground and not renew the attack if two fresh pieces of news had not arrived. The first was a despatch from the governor of Toledo; Venegas's army was skirmishing at his gates and there was little to stop it advancing on Madrid. And the second was a message from Soult; he had been delayed and could not reach Plasencia until 3 August at best, possibly not until the 5th or 6th. This was decisive; Venegas could not be ignored for a week or he would surely discover that almost nothing lay between him and Madrid, and the only troops that could be sent to drive him back were part of the army facing Cuesta and Wellesley. Time no longer favoured the French. And it clearly made more sense to fight an offensive battle against the allies with the whole French army, rather than be forced into a defensive action behind the Alberche with only 30,000 men, having detached the rest to drive Venegas back.[54]

Wellesley and Cuesta met at about ten o'clock near the junction of their two armies. Wellesley was concerned that the French might attempt to turn his left flank beyond the Cerro de Medellin. He had already decided to move two of his three brigades of cavalry (those of Anson and Fane) to counter this threat, but they would need some infantry to support them by occupying the rocky slopes of the Sierra de Segurilla, which rose beyond the open plain, not much more than half a mile north of the Cerro de Medellin. Cuesta responded generously, sending Bassecourt's whole division of infantry, some 5,000 men, across the rear of the British army to occupy the Sierra de Segurilla. He also supplied a battery of 12-pounders – heavier artillery than any in the British army. The exact distribution of these guns is unclear, but some were placed in the Pajar de Vegara and others sent to the Cerro de Medellin where their performance was much admired.[55]

It was the middle of the day, probably a little after noon, when the French artillery opened a very heavy bombardment along the whole line. Sherbrooke's division, occupying the lower slopes of the Cerro de Medellin and the open ground to the south, was particularly exposed, and though the men were ordered to lie down, they still incurred many casualties. More significant than the actual losses was the mental strain of waiting passively under fire with nothing to do to distract attention from the cries of the wounded and the imminence of danger. The soldiers hated this duty, but endured it with a stoicism and spirit that their officers found both admirable and surprising.[56]

Running from south to north the French attack would employ first Leval's division (nine battalions of German infantry from the Confederation of the Rhine) attacking the left of the Spanish line, the redoubt at Pajar de Vegara, and Alexander Campbell's division of British infantry. Next came Sebastiani's own division, the strongest in the whole French army, over 8,000 men in twelve good battalions of the French infantry. They would advance over the flat ground in the British centre, held by the Guards and Alan Cameron's brigade, some 4,000 men, with Mackenzie's brigade, some 2,400 strong, in their rear. On the lower slopes of the Cerro de Medellin stood the much-battered battalions of the King's German Legion and Donkin's brigade, originally some 4,500 men but now a good deal fewer. This was where Lapisse's division of Victor's corps, twelve battalions, or almost 7,000 men, would strike. Further north half of Villatte's division faced the summit of the hill, while the other half, together with Ruffin's exhausted division and Merlin's light cavalry, were ordered to turn the British flank. Latour-Maubourg's six regiments of dragoons (over 3,000 men) were ready to support the main attack in the centre.

Lieutenant John Carss, adjutant of the 2/53rd, described the attack on Alexander Campbell's division on the right of the British line:

> Their infantry kept advancing towards us in a thin wood. We never fired a shot until they cleared the wood and got over a small bank which was about 60 yards from our line, then we gave them a volley, then rushed on with the bayonet. They ran instantly when we charged, but before they could scale the bank again we killed near as many of them as our two regiments were composed of. During this charge their cannon had got close up to this bank which prevented the shot from hurting us, as they went over our heads. They were pulling down the part of the bank to get the guns up to our right for the purpose of raking our line, but when we ran our charge to the bank we commenced a very brisk fire and almost killed every man at their guns in half an hour, which guns fell into our hands, and the firing ceased immediately.[57]

Leval's attack extended south beyond Campbell's front of two or three battalions and the Pajar de Vegara to the northernmost part of the Spanish line. According to Spanish accounts the initial German attack was repulsed in disorder, but a second attack had some success before being defeated when Spanish troops further south wheeled round and attacked Leval's flank, and the Rey regiment of cavalry made a fine charge overrunning the French divisional battery and capturing four guns.[58]

The attack on Sherbrooke's division was much more fierce and determined than that on Campbell's, and here the whole battle came perilously close to being lost. Sebastiani and Lapisse appear to have employed only half their battalions in the initial assault (this still amounted to more than 7,000 men) while holding the other half back as a reserve. Captain William Stothert described the initial clash:

> At this awful moment all was silent, except a few guns of the enemy, answered by the British artillery on the hill. The French came on over the rough and broken ground in the valley, in the most imposing manner and with great resolution, and were met by the British with their usual undaunted firmness. As if with one accord the division advanced against the enemy, whose ranks were speedily broken, and thrown into confusion by a well-directed volley. The impetuosity of the soldiers were not to be repressed . . .[59]

But the British infantry, and in particular the Guards, got carried away in their enthusiasm and pursued the French over the Portiña, becoming increasingly disordered and vulnerable to a counter-attack by the French reserves. Sebastiani and Lapisse threw their remaining infantry into the fight, and the shaken British infantry fell back across the Portiña to their original position, and then further back, and Wellesley, watching events from the Cerro de Medellin, knew that this was the decisive moment of the day. Few British reserves were available to stem the tide. The three battalions of Mackenzie's brigade were well placed to cover the Guards, but further north there was only Cotton's brigade of light cavalry. Wellesley dared not weaken his grip on the Cerro de Medellin by detaching a whole brigade but he ordered the 1/48th from Richard Stewart's brigade down the hill. Unfortunately our sources for this crucial part of the battle are patchy and inadequate, but it is clear that a sustained and fierce fire-fight developed, which checked the French advance and gave the Guards time to rally. The 2/24th of Mackenzie's brigade suffered the most; it was a strong battalion that had begun the day with almost 900 officers and men, and it lost 343 casualties. Mackenzie himself was killed in the fighting and Charles Cocks commented that he was 'the man who did more than anyone towards our victory'.[60]

Many years later Sebastiani became French ambassador to London and, in discussing the battle, 'he stated that the English musketry was so deadly that in twenty minutes he had nearly 3,000 men "*hors de combat*". The troops, he said, were within thirty yards of each other, and he ascribed the fatal effect of [the] "Brown Bess" [musket] to its being so top-heavy that the men fired very low.'[61] This was flattering his hosts a little, but French losses in the centre were indeed very heavy. Of the 8,118 men of Sebastiani's division, 2,180 were killed, wounded or missing (27 per cent), while Lapisse's division suffered 1,767 casualties (26 per cent). On the British side the Guards had suffered 615 casualties (from more than 2,000 all ranks, 30 per cent); Cameron's brigade 548 (from about 1,600 all ranks, 34 per cent) and Langwerth's brigade of the German Legion 721 (from about 1,500, almost 50 per cent). Altogether the British in the centre lost over 2,500 casualties, and the French nearly 4,000.[62]

The fighting in the centre decided the battle. There was no third attack on the Cerro de Medellin, but the French did attempt to push forward on the open ground to the north of the hill, and this led to one of the most celebrated, if ultimately inconsequential, episodes in the battle: the charge of Anson's brigade of light cavalry. It is difficult to establish the timing of this attack relative to the fighting south of the Cerro de Medellin, although Wellesley's despatch suggests that it occurred fairly early in the afternoon. The French had pushed forward a strong force of infantry supported by cavalry into the open ground and were advancing to turn the flank of the British position on the hill. The allied artillery opened a heavy fire upon them but this did not check their advance, and Anson's brigade was sent forward. According to one account:

> The order for the charge being communicated to Lieutenant-General Payne, he led on the 23rd Dragoons and 1st Dragoons King's German Legion in line against the two columns of the enemy, who afterwards formed two solid squares. The distance was so great, and the ground so bad, that before the Dragoons arrived at the watercourse, marked in the plan, the whole line was in disorder, and the left squadron of the 23rd and 1st Regiment King's German Legion not being able to get over the watercourse without difficulty, and being exposed to a severe fire of musketry from the two squares of the enemy and grape from a battery, turned about and galloped off the field. The two squadrons of the 23rd Dragoons on the right, where the watercourse was not so formidable, proceeded to the charge . . .[63]

The unshaken French infantry had no difficulty repulsing the cavalry, which retired with heavy losses. The 23rd Light Dragoons lost 207 casualties (more than half of them missing, mostly taken prisoner) from a strength of about 500; while the KGL Light Dragoons (better known as the KGL Hussars) suffered only 37 casualties from a similar strength – their better horsemanship, and officers with more experience, possibly keeping their losses down. Many infantry battalions in the army suffered more casualties, and some even suffered proportionately more, but the slaughter of infantry in a firefight lacks the drama of an unsuccessful cavalry charge, and the misfortune of the 23rd Light Dragoons has always attracted disproportionate attention. The charge was a complete failure, but the French did not resume their advance and the potential threat to Wellesley's left flank never developed.

Apart from his meeting with Cuesta during the morning lull, Wellesley spent the battle on the Cerro de Medellin. It is impossible to reconstruct his movements, and most of his orders were oral, delivered either directly or through ADCs, and have generally disappeared without trace. However a few glimpses of him during the action survive, scattered among the sources. One records him ordering Captain von Rettberg's battery of King's German Legion artillery to fire shells into the French infantry north of the hill and being so pleased with the result that he clapped Bombardier Dierking on the back and said: 'Very well, my boy.' Colonel Donkin recalled finding Wellesley 'sitting on a low stone, his elbows resting on his knees, with his two hands flat on his face, each on one cheek, and his eyes looking out sharply beyond his two little fingers'. Charles Cocks wrote that 'he was the whole time in the most critical part of the action' and Captain Stothert commented upon 'his characteristic coolness and judgement'. Wellesley himself told his brother William: 'Never was there such a murderous Battle!!' And George Murray described it as 'the most interesting, most critical, and most costly [action] I think that I have ever witnessed'.[64]

Talavera was the bloodiest battle fought by the British army for at least fifty years, and possibly the greatest since the days of Marlborough. Total losses over the two days of fighting were 5,365 casualties (801 killed, 3,915 wounded, and 649 missing) or very nearly one-quarter of the army. Cuesta reported that his army had suffered 1,201 casualties – a surprisingly high figure, even if it included losses suffered in the retreat to the Alberche on 26 July, and men who had failed to return to the ranks after the panic on the evening of 27 July. French casualties were even higher than the combined total of the allies: 761 killed, 6,301 wounded, 206 missing, 7,263 in total, or almost one sixth of their army.[65] In both armies the infantry bore the brunt of the losses, while casualties in the cavalry and artillery were relatively light. The ferocity of the fighting clearly came as a surprise to both armies; the relative ease of Wellesley's victories over Junot and Soult may have led him to underestimate the French army, but at Talavera he saw it at its best – tough veterans full of confidence and accustomed to success. The British army carried the day, but Wellesley would be more cautious in future; such victories came at too high a price to be purchased often.

On the night of 28 July the French army withdrew behind the Alberche. It had been defeated but not broken; however, all ranks were much shaken by the severity of the fighting. French losses at Talavera were only a little lower than those at Austerlitz (about 8,300) and Friedland (8,000–10,000) where the armies had been much larger, although they were dwarfed by the

40,000 casualties from 188,000 men Napoleon had suffered at Wagram only a few weeks earlier. Next day Joseph and Jourdan marched with part of the army to endeavour to prevent Venegas advancing on Madrid, leaving Victor as a rearguard to face Wellesley and Cuesta.

The allied army was bolstered on 29 July by the arrival of the Light Brigade under Robert Craufurd, which made a forced march of some forty-two miles in a vain attempt to reach the army before the battle was over. Wellesley was not jubilant on 29 July – the battle had been too costly for much elation – but he looked forward with some confidence to an advance on Madrid and beyond, for he believed that he had defeated the only French army in central Spain strong enough to face him.[66] The ultimate success of the campaign remained uncertain, but it was not unrealistic to suppose that the French would be unable to collect and concentrate their forces until they had retired to the Ebro or beyond. He had already begun to receive reports of French troops moving south from Salamanca towards the Puerto de Baños, although the significance of this was not immediately obvious, for other intelligence still indicated that Soult was much too weak to make any serious move without assistance.

Soult's leading troops had begun their march on 27 July and carried the Puerto de Baños on 30 July, brushing aside the small Spanish force that was guarding it. They entered Plasencia on 1 August capturing over 300 British sick, who had been left in hospital there; other British detachments and most of the civilian population had withdrawn on the previous day. The French halted at Plasencia for a day to allow the main body to catch up, for the narrow pass inevitably elongated the French column and Ney's corps was still miles to the rear, but Soult had more than 30,000 in hand around Plasencia late on 2 August.[67]

Wellesley and Cuesta learnt of the fall of Plasencia early that morning but continued to underestimate Soult's force. Cuesta suggested that they should take the more mobile half of each allied army and march back to defeat Soult, while the other half held the position at Talavera. Wellesley would not agree to divide the British army, but offered to use it to fill either role, and Cuesta agreed, electing to remain at Talavera while Wellesley and the British cleared the French from Plasencia.[68] On the morning of 3 August the British troops began their westward march, reaching Oropesa around noon. Meanwhile Cuesta had received intercepted despatches from Soult to Joseph, which revealed the full strength of the force under Soult's command. Wellesley would be terribly outnumbered and Cuesta at once decided to march to his aid in the hope that together they could defeat Soult and then return to Talavera and resume the advance on Madrid. Accusations that the Spanish 'abandoned' the British wounded left at Talavera were misplaced, although understandable.[69]

However, when Wellesley finally understood the strength of Soult's force, he realised that there was little choice but to retreat. It was too much to ask his army to fight a second Talavera and again defeat twice its numbers of French veterans; and a battle against Soult would be even more difficult and dangerous than Talavera, for in the event of defeat the only retreat would be by a single narrow bridge across the Tagus, while at any moment Victor might appear in the rear and threaten even this tenuous line of retreat. Nothing but absolute necessity could justify such a risk, for nothing but a complete and over-whelming victory could lead to any real advantage; a partial victory, which left Soult still able to take the field, would leave the allies still trapped between two French armies, while making it harder to disengage and withdraw across the Tagus.

Wellesley and Cuesta had a heated meeting at Oropesa on the morning of 4 August which left the Spanish general angry and dismayed at his ally's refusal to fight; but the British army had borne the full weight of the fighting at Talavera, and would probably do so again in any subsequent operations. That morning the British army marched south to Arzobispo and crossed the Tagus before nightfall. Cuesta refused to follow at once and drove back Soult's advanced guard, but he finally bowed to the inevitable and withdrew across the Tagus on the night of 5 August, thus saving his army from almost certain defeat on the following morning. Much hardship and misery lay ahead for the British troops as they marched through the barren country south of the river with scanty supplies and a crushing sense of disappointment weighing them down.

Wellesley's advance into Spain was over, and it had failed. The glory garnered with such sacrifice at Talavera was barren. Madrid was, and for another three years remained, secure in the hands of the French. The failure was not due to any mistake by Wellesley, nor to any lack of Spanish coopera-tion. It was the result of a fortuitous chain of circumstances beginning with Napoleon's orders giving Soult command of the corps of Ney and Mortier; or, put more simply, it was just bad luck. Such risks are inherent in all military operations and over a long career Wellesley had no more than his share of ill fortune, but in the summer of 1809 it was decisive. It is not true that if Cuesta had sent a larger force to hold the Puerto de Baños the result of the campaign would have been different; Soult's army was too strong and determined to be halted in its tracks by a Spanish detachment in a mountain pass. Recognising the danger sooner would not have produced a solution, for the problem was inherent in the fundamental basis of the campaign; Wellesley advanced into Spain not because the French forces in the Peninsula were weak, but because they were poorly distributed with too many men in the remote, irrelevant north-west. However Soult and Ney abandoned Galicia and retired towards central Spain of their own accord before the British had even crossed the

Spanish frontier. This produced a kaleidoscope of moving pieces in which the result might still have favoured the allies, although the odds were gradually shifting against them. Perhaps if Wellesley had not been delayed at Abrantes by the shortage of specie the result may have been more favourable – certainly the campaign would have been very different – but greater initial success, even the capture of Madrid and an advance to the Ebro, might only have been the prelude to a longer and more dangerous retreat. The French in Spain in the summer of 1809 were simply too strong for the allies to secure a lasting triumph unless Napoleon got into serious difficulties in central Europe and were forced to withdraw men from the Peninsula. But this does not mean that Wellesley's campaign was unwise or unjustified; it was a risk, but probably a risk worth taking, for even a temporary success in capturing Madrid would have been a great blow to Napoleon's prestige in Europe and the authority of the French government in Spain. There was no other way that Britain could do so much for the allied cause in the wider war against Napoleon in 1809.

In Britain Wellesley's advance into Spain was generally overshadowed by other news including the war on the Danube, and by preparations for the Walcheren expedition which finally sailed the day the battle was fought. The Peninsula was rather *passé* – a tired story which, after the disappointments of the winter, didn't spark much enthusiasm. When news of Napoleon's victory at Wagram reached London, Castlereagh told Stewart: 'We have a *devil of a task* before us in the Peninsula now that Austria is disposed of – If any man alive can carry us through it Wellesley will, and whatever may be the issue – I am Confident he will personally rise with its difficulties.' This was written when the latest reports from the army were of Wellesley's first meeting with Cuesta when the British army was at Plasencia on 13 July, and Castlereagh concluded his letter with a postscript: '*Every step* Wellesley has taken since he landed appears to me to have been full of Judgment, and he has fulfill'd every wish I could have form'd.'[70]

With the advance on Talavera and the prospect of an imminent battle, the press and public began to show more interest in the campaign. News of the victory produced considerable enthusiasm. The young Lord Palmerston, who held a junior position in the government, regarded it as a 'Glorious Victory, gained in the good old English Style by one against two' and Lady Malmesbury described it as 'the most brilliant Exploit we have ... [ever?] had *by Land!*'[71]. The *Gentleman's Magazine* declared: 'Whatever may be the final issue of the context in the Peninsula, [Wellesley's despatch] will be read by every lover of his country, with mingled emotions of admiration and pride, as affording a decided proof of the unconquerable valor, discipline, and enthusiasm of the British army.'[72] And J.W. Croker wrote a long poem, modelled on Scott's *Marmion*, called *The Battle of Talavera*, which was a great success, running through eight editions by the following April and continuing to sell as late as 1815.[73] So William Wellesley-Pole had some reason for telling his brother that 'your action of Talavera has delighted and astonished the whole community . . . you would be gratified if you could see how People exult in your military glory, and how proud the nation is of possessing such a general'.[74]

The government marked the victory in the customary way: not only firing the Park and Tower guns, publishing an *Extraordinary Gazette*, and sending a message to the Lord Mayor of London, but also rewarding their successful commander. Wellesley was elevated to the peerage as 'Baron Douro of Wellesley, in the country of Somerset, and Viscount Wellington of Talavera, and of Wellington in the said country'. The titles were chosen by William Wellesley-Pole at short notice, and he was a little anxious about his brother's reaction: 'After ransacking the peerage and examining the map, I at last determined upon . . . [the title] – Wellington is a town not far from Welleslie . . . I trust you will not think that there is anything unpleasant or trifling in the name of Wellington.' But Sir Arthur, or rather Lord Wellington, was pleased: 'You have done exactly what you ought to have done; you could not take for me Lord Wellesley's title, you could not take Talavera, you were quite right in not taking Vimeiro; and in that situation I think you have chosen most fortunately, and I am very much obliged to you.'[75] The Wellesleys had been a Somerset family in the twelfth century before they went to Ireland, so the choice was not quite arbitrary. The title was supported by an annuity of £2,000 to Wellington and two successors, while the officers who commanded regiments at the battle were each to receive a gold medal.

However, not everyone joined in the chorus of celebration. The radicals criticised Wellington's peerage and pension, and the Whigs took a characteristically gloomy view of the state of the campaign. Tom Grenville's immediate reaction to the news was not untypical: 'We have just heard of Wellesley's victory, which the public papers are endeavouring to cry up . . . In truth it seems to me that though our Army has fought with distinguished valour, their situation is perilous in the extreme . . . I do not see what we can do except to endeavour to retreat.'[76] And this attitude went beyond the committed pessimists of the opposition. Mrs Calvert felt that 'a few such victories would soon annihilate our army', and disapproved of the peerage: 'I cannot say I think he has done anything to deserve such promotion.'[77] The Duke of York commented that 'the Battle seems to have been very severe and though it redounds much to the Honor of His Majesty's Arms, has certainly cost us dear', and the King himself 'deeply laments that success, however glorious, has been so dearly bought'.[78]

Even within the army the reaction was often hostile, reflecting considerable jealousy and resentment. Thomas Graham, who would later serve with distinction under Wellington, was a fine soldier, a moderate Whig and a protégé of

Sir John Moore, who might have been expected to praise Talavera; instead he wrote: 'The honors bestowed on Sir A.W. for the worst campaign ever made is too ludicrous and evinces a partiality the most disgraceful. He must be a *street* man if he is not ashamed of them.'[79] William Clinton was just as vehement:

> If the newly created Viscount saves his precious self it will be lucky for him, but if the French generals are not strangely altered in their way of managing things, I do not see how his Army can be saved from perdition, and this is the man who the country is to honour and ennoble and to call a hero ... Such, however, is the power of this Wellesley family that no one dares to animadvert upon such conduct, and thus John Bull is gulled.[80]

The withdrawal from Talavera appeared to vindicate the critics. Radicals accused Wellington of fighting a battle simply to gain a peerage, while the Common Council of the City of London called for an inquiry into Wellington's management of the campaign.[81] In some ways the government's supporters were even more disappointed, for their hopes had been higher and they did not have the perverse satisfaction of seeing prophecies of disaster fulfilled which cheered many an opposition pundit.

The year 1809 was still far from over, but the opportunities created by the Austrian War and the lopsided distribution of the French armies in Spain had passed, and the allies had lost the strategic initiative. The British government had now to consider the future of its commitment to the Peninsula: should it concentrate on the defence of Portugal or take an active part in the defence of Andalusia and, if that failed, the preservation of Cadiz? Senior ministers had never wanted the summer campaign in Spain, but they allowed themselves no hint of reproach in their correspondence with Wellington, and their faith in him was undiminished. The Opposition did not share this view however, and the Portland ministry was on the point of collapse. Over the next eighteen months British politics and Wellington's operations were to be intricately intertwined, with the final outcome impossible for contemporaries to foresee.

CHAPTER TWENTY

MISERY ON THE GUADIANA

(August–December 1809)

THE MONTHS FOLLOWING Talavera saw the British army sink to one of its lowest points of the entire Peninsular War, as bad as the miseries of Moore's march to Coruña earlier in the year and the retreat from Burgos in late 1812. In the first month the troops suffered severely from a shortage of food and long marches on bad roads through desolate country. From early September they were much better supplied, and were able to rest in relatively comfortable cantonments in the valley of the River Guadiana near Badajoz, but disease ran through their ranks sending one-third of the men to hospital and causing thousands of deaths. Adding to these material woes was intense disappointment that the glorious victory gained at such cost at Talavera had proved barren, leading to disillusionment with the Spanish cause and bitter contempt for the Spanish army. The sour mood was deepened by anxious forebodings as news of Napoleon's triumph over Austria reached the army; even the best of Wellington's subordinates came to regard the allied cause in the Peninsula as hopeless, and feared that an attempt to protract the struggle would lead to a dangerous retreat in the face of overwhelming odds and a chaotic, scrambling embarkation. In Britain, the Portland government collapsed just as it was considering the future of its commitment to the Peninsula, and the new ministry that emerged, led by Spencer Perceval, was so weak that its hold on office was precarious. Wellington alone was confident, and it was his clear vision and determination which decided the strategy that Britain would pursue in the Peninsula in 1810, while he sustained his authority in the army which, with all the mutterings of discontent, still generally trusted in his genius and its own fighting qualities.

The British army crossed to the southern bank of the Tagus at Arzobispo on 4 August and slowly withdrew to Jaraicejo where it stayed until 20 August. Wellington was concerned at first that Soult might cross the Tagus at Almaraz and threaten the British line of retreat, but King Joseph was content to remove the last threat to Madrid by defeating Venegas at Almonacid on 11 August. The country south of the Tagus was poor and thinly populated and supplies were scarce, so that the British troops, who had not been well fed since the middle of July, often went hungry. John Cooper of the Fusiliers recalled: 'Men looked like skeletons. Our clothing was in rags; shirts, shoes, and stockings were worn out; and there was no bread served out for six days. All we got was a pound of lean beef for each day. Happy was the soldier that had a little salt.'[1]

Wellington was well aware of the problem and on 9 August issued a General Order that the deduction from the soldiers' pay for their rations was to be reduced from six pence to three pence a day in recognition of the inadequacy of the rations issued; this was to be backdated to 23 July. At the same time he strongly condemned those soldiers plundering the local inhabitants, who were consequently deterred from bringing food to sell to the commissary. He explained to his brother: 'A starving army is actually worse than none. The soldiers lose their discipline and their spirit. They plunder even in the presence of their officers. The officers are discontented, and are almost as bad as the men; and with the army which a fortnight ago beat double their numbers, I should now hesitate to meet a French corps of half their strength.'[2]

Bad as conditions were for the men of the army, they were much worse for the sick and the wounded. Some 1,500 seriously-wounded men had been left in Talavera under the care of a few doctors when Cuesta withdrew from the town, becoming prisoners of war, though they were well treated by the French. However the majority of the sick and wounded, roughly 2,700 officers and men, accompanied the army in its retreat. About 2,000 of these unfortunates were carried on the rough carts of the country, and the rest were on foot. They found little comfort when they reached the general hospital a few miles beyond Deleytosa, for many of its buildings were in ruins, the others were overcrowded, and there was a great lack of food, bedding and medical supplies. The surgeons were themselves underfed and exhausted. Dr Guthrie, the surgeon of the 29th who later rose to great professional eminence, was shocked by what he saw at Deleytosa, and described it as the 'slaughterhouse . . . of the British army'.[3] On 9 August the wounded began to be moved from Deleytosa to Elvas in several divisions, travelling in better conditions and by relatively easy stages.

Wellington told Villiers on 12 August: 'We are starving, and are ill-treated by the Spaniards in every way . . . There is not a man in the army who does not wish to return to Portugal.'[4] It therefore seems rather surprising that the British army remained in its barren position south of the Tagus for more than a fort-night. However, Wellington needed time to move his wounded to safety at Elvas, and to make sure that the French did not intend to march south on Seville. He also knew that to abandon the campaign and retire to the Portuguese frontier would cause a serious rift in Anglo-Spanish relations and make future cooperation much more difficult. He may have doubted Spanish promises that ample supplies would be provided, but it was only fair to give them some time to be fulfilled. And there was a further complication; Lord Wellesley had landed at Cadiz on 1 August as the new British ambassador to Spain, and Sir Arthur was reluctant to sabotage his brother's mission when it had scarcely begun. As it was he greeted the new ambassador with a series of letters outlining the problems facing the army and the alliance, in terms that must have dismayed even Lord Wellesley's not inconsiderable self-confidence. 'You have under-taken a Herculean task; and God knows the chances of success are infinitely against you, particularly since the unfortunate turn which affairs have taken in Austria,' and 'if I remain in Spain, which I declare I believe to be almost impos-sible, notwithstanding that I see all the consequences of withdrawing', would have dampened any ebullience created by an enthusiastic popular reception the Marquess had received in Cadiz.[5]

On 19 August Wellington gave the order to withdraw into Portugal. Although threatened for so long, news of his decision caused great consterna-tion in Seville where ministers and the populace alike feared it would open the way for the French to overrun the whole of southern Spain. Faced with this clamour Lord Wellesley asked his brother if it might not be possible to halt his retreat on the south bank of the Guadiana between Badajoz and Merida, where the troops could be readily supplied with food, and where their presence would reassure the citizens of Seville that they were protected from imminent attack. The British general agreed to this with considerable reluctance. The Guadiana was not a good line to defend; he had no stomach for further operations in conjunction with the Spanish army; and he would be in just as good a position to threaten the flank of any advance on Seville in Portugal. With a little more persuasion he consented, although he would not commit himself to remaining there indefinitely.[6]

By early September the army had taken up its new position in cantonments along the Guadiana with headquarters at Badajoz, where it remained until December. Wellington's decision to halt his army inside Spain had been made in response to his brother's appeal from Seville, but another influence was also at work. On 23 August he had received a letter from Castlereagh asking him to outline his views on the future course of British operations in the Peninsula. This request had been prompted by news of Napoleon's victory over the Austrians at Wagram, and it was followed by a formal despatch from Canning to Lord Wellesley on which Wellington was invited to comment.[7] Canning wrote privately to Wellington: 'I still cling to the hope that . . . Spain may yet be saved, and you one of the main instruments of her salvation'; but to Lord Wellesley he admitted: 'I shall not be surprised, if the decision shall be, that there is no war to be carried on; that there is nothing to be done but to keep our army together, and bring forward the Portuguese.'[8]

Wellington replied to Castlereagh's letter on 25 August with a scathing denunciation of the Spanish government: 'They have attempted to govern the Kingdom in a state of revolution, by an adherence to old rules and systems, and with the aid of what is called enthusiasm; and this last is, in fact, no aid to accomplish anything, and is only an excuse for the irregularity with which everything is done, and for the want of discipline and subordination of the armies.'[9] And his conclusion was forthright: 'I feel no inclination to join in co-operation with them again, upon my own responsibility . . . and I do not recommend you have anything to do with them in their present state.' He would not now accept the command of the Spanish armies unless instructed to do so by the British government, and he warned that to do so would 'incur the risk of the loss of your army'.[10]

But Wellington also had doubts about Portugal. He told Castlereagh that he disapproved of the way Beresford was using his British officers to reform the Portuguese army, and he doubted the ability of the Portuguese government to enforce conscription to provide manpower for the army. He admitted that it would be 'very difficult' to hold the line of the frontier, while it 'is difficult, if not impossible, to bring the contest for the capital to extremities, and after-wards to embark the British army'. As if this was not enough to depress the ministers he predicted that when the French reinforcements arrived in the Peninsula 'their first and great[est] object will be to get the English out', and requested the return of the transports that had been withdrawn for the Walcheren expedition. Nonetheless it was obvious from the letter that he preferred to undertake the defence of Portugal than to join in further operations in Spain; and that he had hopes of devising means by which Portugal could be defended, even if the rest of the Peninsula was overrun by the French.[11]

By the time Sir Arthur's views reached London the Portland government had collapsed amid acrimony and intrigue. Castlereagh discovered that Canning had been pressing for months to have him moved from the War Department as part of a wider reconstruction of the government, and chal-lenged him to a duel which the two ministers fought at six in the morning on 21 September on Putney Heath. Portland had already resigned following a stroke, and the remaining ministers had little hesitation in choosing the modest, quietly determined Perceval as their new leader. But Perceval recog-nised that his ministry would be too weak to survive without reinforcements. He proposed that the Opposition join a broadly-based coalition, but Grenville and Grey dismissed this without even entering into negotiations. However Lord Wellesley accepted the Foreign Office under the impression that he, not

Perceval, whom he despised, would be the real power in the new government. William Wellesley-Pole became Chief Secretary for Ireland, and Liverpool replaced Castlereagh at the War Department.

News of the political crisis began to reach the Peninsula in early October when Wellington had been based at Badajoz for more than a month. His reaction was coloured by his personal ties to those involved; Castlereagh was an old friend and warm supporter, but Wellington had also worked well with Liverpool and Canning and knew the other members of the now divided government. His closest loyalty was to his three brothers, but he also viewed his own position as commander of an army in the field as at least partly detached from the cut and thrust of British domestic politics. Naturally he deplored the crisis, which threatened to bring down the government that had sustained his campaigns and provided some protection from Opposition criticism, but he would not tie his fortunes to any one political faction.

Wellington spelled out his own position in an important letter to William Wellesley-Pole:

> ... my wishes are in favour of Perceval & the cabinet, and as far as I shall take any part in politics I shall belong to them. But I don't conceive that I ought to embark in politics to such an extent as to preclude my serving the Country under any administration that may employ me. In fact I never felt any inclination to dive deeply into party Politics; I may be wrong but the conviction of my mind is that all the misfortunes of the present reign, the loss of America, the success of the French Revolution etc etc are to be attributed in great degree to the Spirit of Party in England; & the feeling I have for a decided party politician is rather that of Contempt than any other. I am very certain that his wishes & efforts for his party very frequently prevent him from doing that which is best for the Country; & induce him to take up the cause of foreign powers against Great Britain, because the cause of Great Britain is managed by his party opponent.
>
> ... my opinion is that the best result of the late confusion would be a Junction & confounding of all parties to support the Govt. against the Jacobins.[12]

This letter has sometimes been read as showing that Wellington stood above party politics, but this is to misunderstand the political language of the day. Pittites were essentially a party of government, hence their embarrassment and uncertainty on the rare occasions when they had been out of office. They had always denounced factious opposition and called on all good men to rally around the King, just as the Rockingham and Foxite Whigs had lauded party as an essential bulwark in preserving constitutional liberty in the face of an over-powerful executive. Wellington's criticism of party politicians who favoured foreign powers at the expense of Great Britain was an obvious swipe at the many Whigs who had welcomed the French Revolution, and the considerable number who, even in 1809, found much to admire in Napoleon. Similarly his call for a junction 'against the Jacobins', which in this context clearly referred to left-wing Whigs and radicals, men like Whitbread, Creevey, Folkestone and Cobbett, was anything but a proclamation of political neutrality. Not that his letter was a public manifesto; he was writing privately, in confidence, to the brother he trusted to represent him in his absence. Equally importantly, Wellington announced his intention of serving any ministry that would employ him in his professional capacity. There was an obvious constitutional propriety in separating personal political views and allegiances from the duty of serving the country, and Wellington's stand did not reflect any remarkable virtue or, conversely, any extraordinary ambition. By simultaneously declaring his private support for Perceval's ministry while detaching himself from their fate, he showed that he was well aware of the delicate path he had to tread.

Early in November Wellington was able to spend ten days with his brother in Seville and Cadiz giving them the opportunity to discuss fully the prospects of the war in the Peninsula and of British politics. He must have been pleased to find that Lord Wellesley had no hesitation in accepting Perceval's offer of the Foreign Office. Yet even with Lord Wellesley's help the new government would be hard pressed to survive. If it fell and the Opposition came to power Grenville would be prime minister, and his brother, the Marquess of Buckingham, Wellington's old chief from his youthful days in Dublin, would have considerable influence, even though he was unlikely to take office. Buckingham had written with congratulations upon Talavera, and in the middle of November Wellington replied mixing gentle flattery with a softly-worded justification of his campaign in Spain. He had always remained on good terms with Buckingham and his family, and the moment was propitious to refresh the old connection. Having presented his 'best respect' to 'Lady Buckingham, Lord and Lady Temple, and Lady Mary', Wellington signed not merely as Buckingham's 'faithful humble servant' but, less conventionally, his 'affectionate' one as well.[13]

In the meantime Wellington welcomed Castlereagh's successor to office. Liverpool could not have made the announcement in a more pleasing manner: 'I think I may be, perhaps, of more use to you in your command in Portugal than any other person who could be placed in the same situation. Let me know your wants and your wishes . . . and I will do my best for you, though I cannot promise I shall always succeed.'[14] It is possible that Wellington would have preferred Lord Wellesley to take the War Department, but if this misguided thought did cross his mind he concealed it and greeted Liverpool graciously:

I assure you that nothing can be more satisfactory to me than to renew my public communication with you. I am convinced that I shall always receive from you that fair protection, support and assistance to which an officer is entitled when he acts fairly by the public, and all the friendship and kindness which I have been accustomed to receive from you in another situation.[15]

Even before Liverpool formally took office on 1 November 1809, he picked up the interrupted discussion over the future of Britain's commitment to the Peninsula in the wake of the Austrian defeat and the experience gained in the Talavera campaign. He accepted Wellington's advice against attempting the defence of southern Spain, but was clearly uneasy about the risks involved in trying to defend Portugal against a French invasion. This was not surprising; Wellington's own letters showed no great confidence, and other military opinions were almost unanimously gloomy. On 1 November Liverpool told Wellington:

It must be our policy to remain in Portugal as long as we can remain there without risking our army. But we must secure the return of the army if a serious attack is made by the French upon the country. The delicate question will be as to the time of the embarkation, and this must be left in a great measure to the discretion of the officer commanding, who must decide it on the spot according to all circumstances which may be then known to him.[16]

This was a very pessimistic view, taking it almost for granted that Portugal could not be defended successfully; but while this was a common assumption at the time, both in London and in the army, it is most unlikely that Liverpool intended to convey a decided opinion on the subject, let alone express any lack of confidence in Wellington.

By the time this letter was written – let alone received – Wellington's ideas had changed. He had spent more than a fortnight in Lisbon (10–26 October) talking to Villiers, Beresford and Portuguese officers and officials, and inspecting parts of the country near the capital. He was received with great enthusiasm and crowds followed him about cheering at every opportunity.[17] The contrast with Spain could hardly have been more pointed, and he was much encouraged by his visit. It was at this time, on 20 October, that he issued orders for the construction of the famous Lines of Torres Vedras. This was only one element in his complete plan for the defence of Portugal, but it was particularly important at that moment for it allowed him to assure the government that even if the French attacked with overwhelming force, the British army could be safely evacuated.[18]

On 14 November Wellington wrote to Liverpool that he was confident that there was no danger of a successful attack on Portugal before the French received their reinforcements, and that even when these arrived 'the enemy will find it difficult, if not impossible, to obtain possession of Portugal'. He would need a British army with an effective strength of 30,000 men, which would require some 5,000 reinforcements. He estimated that the annual cost of this army would be £1,756,236 – claiming, a little misleadingly, that this was only £568,044 more than it would cost to keep it in England. To support the British army he would have the Portuguese army, theoretically some 45,000 men, and their militia. As the Portuguese government was impoverished it would be necessary to increase British aid to Portugal to just under £1 million per annum.[19] He gave no explanation of how he planned to defend Portugal, but at the end of November he wrote:

> You see that I agree entirely in opinion with you, not only that we cannot in good policy give up the Peninsula, but that we may be able to continue the contest in Portugal with success, and that we shall finally bring off our army. During the continuance of this contest, which must necessarily be defensive on our part, in which there may be no brilliant events, and in which, after all, I may fail, I shall be most confoundedly abused, and in the end I may lose the little character I have gained; but I should not act fairly by the government if I did not tell them my real opinion, which is, that they will betray the honor and interest of the country if they do not continue their efforts in the Peninsula, which, in my opinion, are by no means hopeless.[20]

This was enough for the British government, and in the middle of December Liverpool wrote again to Wellington formally renewing the government's commitment to the defence of Portugal and promising 5,000 reinforcements, and an increase in the Portuguese subsidy from £600,000 to £980,000.[21] Learning the lesson of Walcheren, Liverpool had presented his colleagues with a choice: they must either agree to support Wellington with all their resources and give up thoughts of other expeditions and diversions, or they should withdraw from Portugal. The ministers had agreed to stake their fortunes on Wellington and Portugal.[22]

The army in its cantonments along the Guadiana knew nothing of these high-level exchanges, and many officers were idle and bored in the autumn of 1809. The charm of good quarters and regular food soon palled on men who had been overstimulated by the constant activity of Wellington's first four months in the Peninsula. In subsequent years veteran officers came to expect and even welcome the quiet interludes between campaigns, but the army in 1809 was still inexperienced and rather at a loss how to employ its new-found leisure. There were the traditional pastimes of shooting and fishing, sight-seeing

(Roman ruins are mentioned in many memoirs), visiting friends and eating and drinking to excess, but these left many with a sense of wasted time. As one young officer wrote in similar circumstances a few years later: 'I feel myself so constantly engaged in the daily pursuits of infantry officers in England, viz: Watching fishes swim under the bridge, throwing stones at pigs, etc. I am ashamed of it, but have nothing else to do.'[23]

Young officers and new recruits in many (but not all) units were made to practise their drill under the eye of the adjutant, and a few poor units were given special attention. Routine training was enlivened by field days involving a whole brigade or even division, and inspections by Wellington.[24] Moyle Sherer, a twenty-year-old lieutenant in the 2/34th, describes one such occasion:

> On the fourth of October, our division, commanded by General Hill, was reviewed on the plain, near Montigo, by Lord Wellington. We had a league to march to the ground, and were kept under arms a considerable time before his lordship arrived. I was in the highest possible spirits, eager to behold the hero, and as he passed very slowly down the line, observing the men with a keen scrutinizing look, I had the fullest opportunity for indulging my curiosity. I was much struck with his countenance; and, in his quick-glancing eye, prominent nose, and pressed lips, saw, very distinctly marked, the ready presence of mind, and imperturbable decision of character, so essential in a leader . . .[25]

Less flattering was gossip about an attractive young woman at headquarters. One officer wrote home, in a letter that was published in the *Monthly Magazine* at the beginning of November, that Wellington must have been distracted to make so many mistakes in the Talavera campaign: 'Who lost Mark Antony the world? – A female (once, I believe, the mistress of Soult, captured at Oporto), accompanies the head-quarter establishment. She has not a handsome face, but a good figure, and sits astride on horseback as knowingly and neatly as Mister Buckle himself.'[26] Lady Sarah Lennox, mother of the Napier brothers, had already heard the story, for on 25 October she had written: 'You will know that a Comr-in-Chief, who publickly keeps a mistress at headquarters, does not give all the attention to the care of his army & disgusts his army, who lose all confidence in him.'[27] This was an overreaction – there is not the least evidence that the army felt jealous or neglected, let alone that Wellington's preoccupation with business ever suffered – but the circulation of such rumours could damage his reputation at home, even in the relaxed moral climate of the early nineteenth century. As for the truth of the story, the only reliable account comes from Charles Stewart who wrote to his mother Lady Londonderry at the end of 1811: 'When we first entered Spain, in 1809, a Spanish Girl was added to his establishment, in the second or Steward's Room. I believe the A.D.C.'s had more to do with his lady than the Chief. The occurrence, however, from one or two ridiculous Stories, was much talked of, and He had the good sense to send her packing, since which I really believe nothing but his Employment and Fox Hunting have occupied all his Affections and all his wants. This I can most conscientiously assert.'[28]

When Wellington visited Lisbon in October he sat for his portrait by Domenico Pellegrini which had been commissioned by Mr Villiers. The result – a half-length showing Wellington in Portuguese uniform and wearing the star of the Bath – is quite pleasing, although the face, especially the chin, appears a little heavy (see plate 35). There were several engravings of this portrait, some extended to whole-length, and prints of it were widely distributed.[29] Evidently Wellington liked the portrait for in later years he hung a print of it in the dining-room at Walmer Castle. According to Lord Ellesmere: 'The engraver inscribed under it the Latin word *invicto* [invincible]. Croker tells me that the Duke wrote under this in pencil "Don't cry till you are out of the wood" – a modest commentary which fortunately never became applicable.'[30]

These months saw some changes in the senior ranks of the army. Mackenzie had been killed at Talavera and Alexander Campbell, who had been wounded in the thigh by grapeshot, had gone home to recover. Their places were taken by Robert Craufurd and Lowry Cole. Craufurd had a high reputation as a dedicated professional soldier with special expertise in the command of light infantry. He also had good political connections with the Opposition, having been an MP from 1802 to 1806 and an unofficial adviser and protégé of William Windham, the Secretary for War in Lord Grenville's government. Wellington evidently thought highly of him, and gave him a plum command, but he was deeply unpopular in the Light Brigade due to his harsh discipline and abominable temper, which even led him to abuse his officers in front of their men – an almost unforgivable sin in any army. On 27 August 1809 Captain Jonathan Leach wrote in his diary:

> The Division paraded at six this evening when we got volleys of abuse and blasphemous language from that infernal scoundrel Brigadier Robert Craufurd, who, after flogging half a dozen men for some very frivolous offences committed on our late harassing marches, we were dismissed. Lay down to sleep at nine o'clock but not without offering hearty prayers for the discomfiture of our cursed commander.[31]

This hatred did not abate in the months ahead, but it was gradually supplemented by a grudging respect and a reluctant appreciation that, despite all his flaws, Craufurd was indeed a very capable commander.

Major-General Lowry Cole, who was given command of the Fourth Division at the end of October, was an Irishman, the second son of the Earl of Enniskillen, and three years younger than Wellington. He had proposed to Kitty Pakenham in 1802 and had been much hurt by her refusal; he did not marry until 1815. He had served in the West Indies, Egypt and at Maida and had been a Member of Parliament since 1803, and although often absent and never very active, he gave general support to the Portland government. He proved popular in the army; Lieutenant-Colonel George Bingham described him as 'a pleasant, sensible, agreeable man', while George Napier wrote later that 'he never would permit officer or *private soldier* to want anything that he had, or that it was in his power to procure for him; and though a hot-tempered man, he is as kind and generous as he is brave, and a more truly gallant, enterprising soldier never breathed'.[32] Even allowing for some exaggeration, the men of the Fourth Division were fortunate in their new commander, who led them for most of the rest of the war.

Throughout the autumn of 1809 the army was very sickly. Different accounts speak of malaria, typhus and various types of fever, so that it is uncertain if there was one principal cause or several, although it is clear that this was known to be an unhealthy time of the year, especially after the exertions and privations of the summer. A few days before Talavera the army had just over 4,000 rank and file sick from a strength of 26,000 (or not quite 16 per cent).[33] The large number of men wounded in the battle doubled this figure by the end of July, but rather than decreasing as the wounded men recovered (or were taken prisoner with the hospital at Talavera, or died), the figure remained stubbornly high as the sick replaced the wounded. On 15 October there were 8,660 sick from 32,667 men in the army (or 26.5 per cent); and on 1 November this had risen to 9,016 sick (or 28 per cent); while in the intervening fortnight 17 sergeants, 6 drummers and 655 rank and file men had died: the strength of a typical battalion dead in seventeen days.[34] In comparison, 801 British soldiers (including officers) had been killed at Talavera, and the whole army had been astonished at the severity of the fighting. This reflects the general truth that throughout the Napoleonic Wars many more soldiers died of disease and privations than in combat. Altogether 4,931 British soldiers died in the Peninsula from all causes between 31 March and 24 December 1809 (a figure that does not include artillerymen or engineers).[35]

So many men were sick that the medical services of the army were overwhelmed. General hospitals were established at Elvas, Olivenza and Estremoz and Villa Vicosa, but they were short of staff and equipment and were soon overcrowded and insanitary. John Cooper, who was a patient at several of the hospitals with a fever at this time, left an account of them:

The hospital at Olivenza was a long low room, with another at a right angle to it; crowded with fever patients; the ventilation bad; many deaths daily.

The hospital at Villa Vicosa was in a convent; about 150 patients in the four corridors; next to no ventilation; small windows; great barrels or tubs for all purposes; the stench horrible; logs of fir burning at the four corners of the building, to drive away the infection; smoke blinding.

The hospital at Elvas – a long bomb proof room; no ventilation, except by the door and chimney; twenty patients, of whom eighteen died. Convalescent room at Elvas; pavement bed for 1000 or 1500 men.[36]

Wellington did not have the authority to reorganise and reform the medical service of the British army, but he did what he could by paying personal attention to the state of the hospitals, encouraging capable doctors, and writing home repeatedly asking for more hospital mates and assistant surgeons – the junior doctors who did the most work – to be sent to join the army.[37] But although conditions in the Peninsula were bad, the medical disaster unfolding at Walcheren was far worse, and it naturally received priority. At least this led to sweeping changes in the medical department which, together with growing experience and expertise, led to a great improvement in British hospitals in the later years of the war.

Wellington was not greatly surprised by the sickness, which he regarded as inevitable at that season of the year, but he did not anticipate its severity or duration.[38] He himself was taken ill in the middle of August and was slow to recover, telling Villiers on 20 September: 'I have not been well for above a month, and have still hanging upon me a low fever which I cannot shake off.'[39] Fortunately he was remarkably tough and there is little sign that his illness interrupted his work, although it is said that he was obliged to travel in his carriage rather than on horseback for two days and it probably delayed his trip to Lisbon.[40]

The prevailing mood in the army in the autumn of 1809 was deeply unhappy. The high hopes raised by the success at Oporto and the advance to Talavera had come crashing down, and all the exertions and hardships of the summer were rendered futile. The sickness was a cause of misery and even fear, and over everything was the sense that the sacrifices being made were useless; that the war in the Peninsula was doomed to failure and that it was only a matter of time before the army would be withdrawn to England. William Warre, Beresford's ADC, told his mother on 18 August: 'There never was such folly as sending an army into Spain again.' And: 'We are very low in spirits at the bad accounts from Austria. A peace in that country will decide the fate of these most undoubtedly. We may prolong the war and sacrifice many lives, but I am convinced it will be to no purpose . . .' Charles Boutflower, the admirable surgeon of the 40th, admitted that 'there is certainly a general wish throughout the Army that we may soon be ordered to England, and I am sorry to observe that near nine out of ten of all the Officers I have conversed with on the subject would hail the News of Peace being concluded between Austria and France, provided it led to that event.[41]

Senior officers were, if anything, even more pessimistic than their subordinates, perhaps because they took a wider view of the war. Charles Stewart told Castlereagh: 'The question is then reduced to Portugal. After all that W. has said on the defence of it, I am sure if he has means he will fight it out to the last. He may make a long stand, but it must be with British troops alone, for whatever Beresford may say, be satisfied his Portuguese army are as little to be trusted as our Spanish friends.' George Murray wrote home that 'there are some people who seem to fancy we can defend Portugal but upon what solid grounds their expectations are founded I do not know'. And: 'I see Buonaparte promises to drive us out of the Peninsula, and I confess I am somewhat inclined under the present aspect of affairs to calculate upon seeing you sometime in the spring.' Rowland Hill agreed, telling his sister on 10 October: 'I am confident we can do no good by remaining. The Spanish & Portuguese Cause in my mind is hopeless, they will do nothing for themselves, and we can do no more than we have done. It appears to me that a storm is brewing and it behoves us to keep a good look out to take care of ourselves.' A month later, he wrote: 'I do not consider our prospects at all mended of late, consequently I entertain the same opinion I have always expressed respecting this Country. The cause in my mind is *hopeless* . . .'[42]

These views naturally influenced opinion in England, and the Opposition was quick to reflect them and to denounce the absurd folly of attempting to defend Portugal. The ministers trusted Wellington, but could not fail to be alarmed by the almost unanimous opinion of military experts at home and with the army. The full weight of responsibility for maintaining the British army in the Peninsula thus fell on Wellington's shoulders, for although the government took the final decision it rested entirely on his advice. This did not unduly perturb him, nor was he greatly disheartened by the doubts of his subordinates. Self-confidence is an essential requisite for a successful general and Wellington had it in abundance. He knew that he had studied the problem more carefully and in the light of more information than anyone else, and his successes in India and subsequently had taught him to trust his judgement even in the face of widespread scepticism. Nonetheless long months of holding the army on course by his will alone, doubted even by those officers he most respected, had an effect on his character, making him a harder man, less open to suggestion, more self-reliant and less tolerant, quick to dismiss others with biting sarcasm and equally quick to complain if he felt aggrieved. The change was one of degree, not kind, making existing characteristics more prominent rather than creating new ones, and in a sense it was the price of greatness, for a nicer man would surely have given way under the strain.

CHAPTER TWENTY-ONE

PREPARING FOR THE STORM
(December 1809–June 1810)

AFTER DEFEATING AUSTRIA Napoleon turned his attention to the Peninsula, intending to crush the Spanish resistance and force Wellington to evacuate his army and abandon Portugal. On 7 October 1809 he issued orders to prepare 100,000 reinforcements to join his armies in Spain, a figure that subsequently rose to almost 140,000, bringing the total French force to about 350,000 men. He initially planned to lead these armies in person, although he gave up the idea when he divorced Josephine in December and married the Austrian Archduchess Marie Louise in the following April. Few British observers saw much hope of riding out the storm that was brewing, but Wellington had confidence in his plans, which relied upon the whole-hearted cooperation of the Portuguese: the reform of their army, the devastation of the countryside in the path of the invader, and the construction of formidable defensive works across the Lisbon Peninsula. Even this might not be enough if the French advanced in overwhelming force, and Wellington would not jeopardise his army in a hopeless struggle; he studied the odds coolly and saw no reason to give up the struggle, but the strain of waiting took its toll.

Wellington urged the Spanish government to be prudent and husband its resources for the hard times that were coming, but the prestige of the Supreme Junta had been undermined by successive defeats, and it decided to mount one last great offensive before the French reinforcements arrived. The result was a complete failure, destroying the last substantial Spanish armies at Ocaña and Alba de Tormes in November. Unable to do anything to save Andalusia, Wellington withdrew from the frontier into the heart of Portugal, and the British army did not see any significant action until the second half of 1810. Despite the Spanish defeats, Wellington did not despair of their cause, and urged Liverpool to continue to send arms and equipment to the patriots.[1]

King Joseph waited until January to reap the fruits of his victories, but then the French armies swept through Andalusia meeting little resistance. Seville fell on 31 January, but Cadiz eluded their grasp and remained in Spanish hands throughout the war. British and Portuguese troops from Gibraltar, Lisbon and England soon arrived to bolster its garrison, and although the French maintained a siege, after the first few days the great port was never in any real danger of falling. The conquest of Andalusia was the high-water mark of French power in Spain, but the Spanish resistance continued. Small Spanish armies operated from Galicia, Valencia and even on the fringes of Andalusia, while the guerrilla war continued remorselessly in all the provinces the French had overrun. It required 70,000 French troops to keep Andalusia relatively quiet, and whenever Soult collected even a small field army together to face a Spanish force or the British and Portuguese in Estremadura, there was trouble in his rear. This was the pattern of the whole war in the Peninsula, with vast numbers of French troops constantly required to maintain a precarious hold on provinces nominally conquered. The momentum gained at Ocaña had been spent. Portugal, Galicia and Valencia remained outside the French grasp, and their conquest would have to wait for Napoleon's reinforcements to arrive. Whether even 350,000 French troops would be enough to conquer and hold the whole Peninsula remained to be seen.

The British army moved from the Spanish frontier to its new cantonments in central and northern Portugal, between Coimbra and Almeida, in December 1809 and January 1810. The march was well organised with plentiful supplies, and Wellington was pleased with the good behaviour of the troops. The officers and men were generally happy with the change of quarters, with one young officer noting: 'The civility which we have received in Portugal has formed a contrast to the brutal coldness of the Spaniards towards us. We are everywhere met with open arms . . .'[2] Yet British officers also frequently remarked on the poverty and dirt of Portuguese houses and towns compared to the cleanliness of those in Spain; and the Portuguese could be seen as *too* obliging, while Spanish pride inspired respect as well as resentment.

The army's health recovered during the winter and spring, and at the beginning of April Wellington noted with pleasure: 'The troops are becoming again very healthy and very strong, and the army is more efficient than it has ever been yet.' By the end of the month he had 28,000 rank and file fit for duty, while many of those still listed as sick were ready to return to their regiments. The benefits of the long months of inactivity and regular rations are reflected in the official figures with the number of sick falling from almost 30 per cent of the army's rank and file listed at the beginning of the year, to just under 12 per cent in early July, before the changing seasons and the resumption of active operations saw it rise back to almost 20 per cent in the last months of the year.[3]

The mood of the army also showed a modest improvement, although most officers continued to believe that they only waited for the French to advance before sailing for home. A natural anxiety at the prospect of the coming campaign was tempered by considerable confidence and faith in Wellington. John Carss of the 2/53rd wrote home: 'Lord Wellington will certainly be very careful how he goes to work again. He is a good soldier and very much beloved by the army. He gives no unnecessary trouble if people will conduct themselves as they ought, but otherwise he is very severe.' Lowry Cole told his sister, Lady Grantham: 'I never served under any chief I liked so much – Sir John Moore excepted – as Lord Wellington. He has treated me with much more confidence than I had a right or could have expected from anyone. Few, I believe, possess a firmer mind or have, so far as I have heard, more the confidence of the army.' Benjamin D'Urban was even more lavish in his praise: 'The firmness of mind which Lord Wellington has continued to preserve since the Battle of Talavera, in spite of the despondency of almost everyone about him, as well as of all the people at home, and the perseverance with which he has continued in forward position ready for offensive operations yet fully prepared for defensive ones, has saved Portugal, and may, and probably will, be the Salvation of Spain. This admirable firmness proves him a Hero, if he had done nothing else to deserve the name.'[4]

Wellington had given the defence of Portugal long and detailed consideration and laid his plans with care. The main French force would almost certainly come from the north-east, from Salamanca, through Ciudad Rodrigo and Almeida (the Spanish and Portuguese fortresses guarding the frontier) and then down the line of the River Mondego to Coimbra, and from thence south to Lisbon. Wellington hoped that the border fortresses would delay the French, but they could not hold out forever, and if the enemy army was as strong as he feared, he would not be able to come to their aid. The mountainous country between Almeida and Coimbra offered a choice of good defensive positions which he might hold against a superior enemy, but he dared not rely on these, for the French might simultaneously advance by one of the other routes into Portugal and so turn his flank. The best of these routes ran west from Spanish Estremadura into Portuguese Alentejo and then either crossed the Tagus at Abrantes or continued south of the river ending at the heights of Almada opposite Lisbon. It was guarded on the frontier by Badajoz and Elvas – both stronger fortresses than their northern counterparts – and Abrantes was also strongly held, but otherwise the country was generally open and there were few natural obstacles between the frontier and the Tagus. There were also several difficult roads between Ciudad Rodrigo and Badajoz crossing into central Portugal. Junot had followed one in 1807 at grievous cost to his army. Wellington ordered the destruction of another, the Estrada Nova, which was made completely impassable to wheeled vehicles. None of these roads could possibly carry the principal French army, but they might be used by a subsidiary corps to turn the allied flank. He therefore kept a close eye on this central region, roughly seventy miles of rugged country between Penamacor in the north and Portalegre in the south, with the fine town of Castello Branco in the centre. Finally Wellington had to consider the route Soult had taken in 1809 invading Portugal from the north. This was most unlikely; it was roundabout and would first require the reconquest of Galicia while the road itself was poor and crossed some large rivers. Yet the French made a move in this direction when they besieged Astorga in March. The Spanish town resisted bravely for a month and when it fell the French turned their attention from Galicia to Ciudad Rodrigo.

If the French advanced on more than one route it might give Wellington the chance to defeat them in detail, but he had also to guard against the danger of allowing any French force to get between him and Lisbon. This led him to conclude that he might be forced to fall back almost to Lisbon before making his main stand. The Tagus was unfordable, even in high summer, for some thirty miles north of Lisbon, and the country between the river and the sea was rugged and might be held against a superior enemy. Here, if anywhere, Wellington could offer battle with advantage. He calculated that the French army would lose strength and face increasing problems the farther it advanced into Portugal. Almost the whole population of Portugal would be arrayed against them. Able-bodied men who were not part of the army belonged either to the militia or to the ancient *ordenanza*, or home guard. The militia had some training and discipline, the ordenanza very little. Neither could hope to fight the French in open battle with any prospect of success unless they had an enormous numerical superiority; but they could harass the French rear, and force the invaders to detach large garrisons if they were to keep open their lines of communication with Spain.[5] The militia could also be used, with a mixture of regular troops to stiffen their resolve, to hold the frontier fortresses and other strong points. Portugal was a poor country and Wellington had expected that the French would find it difficult to feed their army, especially if its advance could be halted for any length of time in one of the more barren regions. There was already a Portuguese tradition of stripping the countryside in the face of an invader, and Wellington proposed to use this to heighten the logistical problems the French would face. Such a policy was unlikely to succeed without considerable popular support, but the horrors inflicted by the French in their earlier campaigns – especially Loison's tactics of terror, pillage and extortion in 1807–08 and Soult's sack of Oporto in 1809[6] – ensured willing cooperation from most of the population. But in the end Wellington expected that the fate of Portugal would be decided in a climactic battle, and he could not hope for victory if he was forced to rely entirely upon his British troops. The reform and rejuvenation of the Portuguese army had been central to his plans for the Peninsula ever since his letter to Castlereagh of 1 August 1808; its success would be crucial to his hopes of defending Portugal in 1810, and it would play a vital role in all his subsequent campaigns. The task of reviving the army had been entrusted to Beresford in February 1809 before the Cabinet had agreed to Wellington's return to the Peninsula, and it remained principally his work, although he was subordinated to Wellington in the Portuguese as well as the British service.

Beresford had arrived in Lisbon at the beginning of March 1809 and took up the command by the middle of the month after some negotiations with the Portuguese Regency. He had brought some British officers with him, and appointed them to important positions, but he was careful to balance them with Portuguese officers. Benjamin D'Urban was appointed Quartermaster-General of the army; but the Adjutant-General was Manoel de Brito Mosinho, who retained the position throughout the war and who bore the brunt of exacting obedience from Portuguese colonels and other senior officers who resented the new regime, with its incessant demands for accurate, punctual reports and compliance with many new and often onerous regulations. Similarly Beresford's military secretary, who handled innumerable delicate questions including applications for leave, promotion and transfers between units, was also Portuguese: Colonel Antonio de Lemo Pereira de Lacerda. These two men played an important role in lessening the natural feeling among Portuguese officers that their army had been taken over by the British, while assisting Beresford, whose knowledge of the language was still only rudimentary.[7]

When Beresford arrived there were already some foreign officers in the Portuguese army, and a number of British officers both from home and the army already in Portugal were permitted to join the Portuguese service. These officers were given an extra step in rank in the Portuguese army as a reward (or, in some cases, two steps) – an incentive that caused considerable ill feeling among the comrades whom they overtook. Many of these were junior officers who served as captains or majors in Portuguese regiments (see Chapter 14).

Beresford's first months in command of the Portuguese army were far from easy as he struggled to assert his authority. For generations the army had been dominated by men of good birth and independent means who frequently did not take soldiering very seriously. Despite the troubles that had befallen Portugal over the previous two years and the imminence of fresh dangers, many of these men found it hard to adjust to a world where they were expected to attend constantly to their duties, and to respect and obey a social inferior merely because he was a senior officer.

There were also far too many officers who, lacking connections, had grown old in the service. Examples included a seventy-eight-year-old lieutenant-colonel who commanded the 6th Regiment of the Line, and a sixty-seven-year-old lieutenant with forty-six years of service. Such men may well have been gallant, but they were unlikely to adapt easily to the rigours of active campaigning and were even less likely to embrace the spirit of reform. Beresford began by forcibly retiring six officers on 18 April and replacing them with promising young men. He weathered the inevitable storm that this occasioned and, with the precedent established, moved rapidly; over the next four months 200 officers were told that their services were no longer required and by the end of the year the number had risen to more than 350. Naturally such widespread dismissals led to further hostility and resentment, but they also opened the way for the introduction of much fresh blood – new Portuguese as well as British officers, and promotion for existing officers who showed themselves willing and able to adapt.[8]

Beresford and Wellington both recognised that their reform of the Portuguese officer corps would be hampered, perhaps fatally, by the very low pay that officers received. Because the army had been dominated by men of independent means, and because Portugal was a poor country, the pay of junior officers was totally inadequate. The fact that British officers serving in the Portuguese army continued to receive their higher British rate of pay highlighted the problem and added to the ill feeling with which they were regarded by their Portuguese colleagues. This was clearly unacceptable and Wellington pressed the British government which, despite being extremely short of money, promised an additional £130,000 per annum specifically to raise the pay of Portuguese officers. Beresford introduced new salary scales in early 1810; junior officers saw their pay double, while even senior officers had an increase of 60 per cent.[9]

While regenerating the officer corps Beresford also moved to enforce discipline in the ranks, which had often become very slack. As soon as he assumed command of the army Beresford began issuing stern warnings that the soldiers must obey their officers and that old abuses, such as selling their equipment, would no longer be tolerated. In April he ensured that a soldier who defied a direct order to march was sentenced to ten years in prison, and in June four deserters were executed. He gave these and other punishments wide publicity, and as a result acquired a reputation for harshness that was not entirely justified, but which probably helped in the restoration of discipline. Corporal punishment was retained but made less arbitrary, and it was much less severe than the flogging in the British army.[10]

Although the Portuguese army had performed well in the Oporto campaign, Beresford and Wellington both recognised that it needed a sustained period of inactivity for the reforms to take hold. By early September 1809 it had been withdrawn to Thomar in central Portugal and had begun a period of intensive training without the distraction of active operations. Wellington lent Beresford enough British sergeants to send two to each regiment of infantry and battalion of caçadores, and they drilled the Portuguese constantly. In November Beresford authorised the infantry to fire up to twenty rounds a day to practise their musketry, and to also increase their morale by giving point and purpose to their training.[11] But progress was not smooth and there were many stumbles along the way, especially at first. At the beginning of September Beresford learnt that the 9th Line had fallen apart, and would need to be 'entirely taken to pieces' and rebuilt if discipline was to be restored and it was ever to be fit for service. A few days later two of the most promising regiments, the 1st and 21st Line, erupted into large-scale riots sparked by a quarrel between two soldiers. Order was eventually restored, although not before Nicholas Trant, who commanded the brigade, had a narrow escape from his own men. Less dramatic but more widespread and insidious were the problems James Douglas faced in the 16th Line, where the senior Portuguese officers were hostile to his attempts at reform and tacitly encouraged the subalterns to be uncooperative, an attitude that soon spread to the men in the ranks.[12] In December Lieutenant-Colonel J.W. MacDonnel resigned in frustration because all his efforts to reform the 12th Line were being blocked by its elderly colonel, and many other British officers made similar complaints.[13] Their problems were exacerbated by the fact that, at least at first, few of them spoke fluent Portuguese, so that they were inevitably isolated inside their regiments. Beresford aimed to have five British officers in each regiment of infantry, and three in each cavalry regiment and battalion of caçadores, but he had less than half that number in October 1809 and was still well short of his target in May 1810.[14]

By December 1809 months of hard work were beginning to bear fruit. Beresford inspected part of the army and was well pleased with its appearance, while D'Urban, who accompanied him, could hardly contain his enthusiasm. After watching the 4th and 10th Line manoeuvre together D'Urban wrote in his journal: 'I have never seen an English Brigade with more steadiness and precision.' And, a few days later, having seen the 3rd Caçadores: 'The progress of Lt Col Elder in forming and training the 3rd is perfectly wonderful. Certainly no Regimental Officer has yet done so much in so short a time, since the British Officers began to act with the Portuguese Army.'[15] Beresford rewarded the men for their improvement with praise and by granting five men per company fifteen days leave – a most unusual concession at the time.[16]

Wellington joined Beresford for a second round of inspections at the end of the year and was impressed with what he saw. He told Liverpool that he had inspected fifteen Portuguese regiments and 'that the progress of all these troops in discipline is considerable; that some of the regiments are in very good order; and that I have no doubt that the whole will prove a useful acquisition to the country'. He praised the pains taken by Beresford and his officers and suggested that they receive some mark of official approbation. One of Wellington's ADCs, Alexander Gordon, who only a few weeks before had thought that the attempt to defend Portugal was doomed, now wrote home: 'I have a much better opinion of the cause ... from having seen the Portuguese Army ... I assure you their improvement has been very great & rapid. They will have in two months 20,000 effective men almost as well disciplined as any British troops and I have not a doubt incorporated with them they will fight ... General Beresford deserves the greatest credit for the manner in which he has already ... [improved] the Army of this Country.'[17] But most British officers, who did not get a chance to see the Portuguese troops, remained full of forebodings.

From the outset of his command Beresford had concentrated his attention on the Portuguese infantry; the artillery was already relatively efficient, while the cavalry would require even more sustained work than the infantry before it was reliable (it was also expensive and hampered by a severe shortage of horses). Inevitably, perhaps, the commissariat remained the weakest branch of the army, and in the campaigns that followed Portuguese soldiers would often go hungry or rely on the British to supply them with food. After the New Year inspections, Beresford concluded that sixteen of the twenty-four regiments of line infantry and five of the six battalions of caçadores were fit to cooperate in the field with the British army.[18]

The first operational deployment of the reformed army occurred in February when the 20th Line Regiment was sent to join the allied garrison of Cadiz. To Wellington's satisfaction the soldiers embarked cheerfully and without desertion, 'and excited much admiration' at Cadiz. They became a permanent part of the garrison and a constant reminder of what could be achieved through close cooperation with Britain.[19] On 22 February 1810 Wellington went a step further when he attached a Portuguese brigade (each of two line regiments) to the Third and Fourth Divisions of his army – a mixture that would prove immensely successful in the campaigns to come. At the same time two battalions of caçadores were added to the newly created Light Division.[20] Most of the Portuguese army remained in independent brigades (typically consisting of two line regiments and a battalion of caçadores), while some regiments were used to garrison important fortresses. However the Portuguese were not quite as advanced as the New Year inspections had suggested. The winter saw an increase in sickness due to a shortage of uniforms and problems with the regular supply of rations, which in turn led to outbreaks of insubordination and desertion. Close examination revealed deficiencies in training – some regiments had not mastered their arms drill, while others had neglected to practise route marching.[21] The two battalions of caçadores sent to the Light Division had to be withdrawn for further training. Throughout the winter, spring and early summer of 1810 Beresford and his officers, Portuguese and British alike, worked tirelessly to overcome these problems and to build on the foundations that had already been laid. New uniforms; increased pay for junior officers; the removal of those who were incompetent or uncooperative and the promotion of those who showed promise; endless drill; and the growing assurance that the British would stay and fight, not abandon the struggle: all these contributed to a steady improvement in the Portuguese army. By July Beresford had overcome some of the logistical problems so that uniforms, equipment and medicines were reaching the army smoothly. The commissariat was still unreliable but had considerably improved, while Wellington agreed to cover any deficiency when the campaign began.[22]

When the allied army finally took the field in July the Portuguese component exceeded even the optimistic calculations made at the beginning of the year. An entirely Portuguese division (the 2nd, 4th, 10th and 14th Line Regiments) commanded by Major-General John Hamilton was attached to Hill's force guarding the southern flank. Three Portuguese brigades formed an integral part of allied divisions, and the caçadores had returned to the Light Division (although Elder's 3rd Caçadores had replaced the 2nd). Three independent brigades served with the army, while a fourth was detached for separate operations. Portuguese batteries took their place alongside the British, and a brigade of cavalry was in the field although not with the main army. Other regiments garrisoned Almeida, Elvas and Abrantes – fortresses that would play an important part in the coming campaign. And the army was healthy and with its regiments brought close to full strength. As a result the Portuguese amounted to very nearly half Wellington's field army (over 25,000 Portuguese and just under 27,000 British at Busaco) and well over half his total force.[23]

The crucial unanswerable question was how the Portuguese army would perform when it came to be tested in action for the first time. Wellington was confident that it would do well; his whole strategy, not just for this campaign but for the continuing British involvement in the Peninsula, depended upon the success of the experiment, and if it failed, defeat, if not disaster, was inevitable. But few officers in the British army shared his confidence, and the responsibility rested heavily on his shoulders.

There were other, almost equally important, elements in Wellington's plan for the defence of Portugal. The most obvious was the creation of the famous Lines of Torres Vedras. The Lines were not a continuous barrier like Hadrian's Wall but rather a chain of separate but mutually supporting redoubts and field fortifications which ran all the way across the Lisbon Peninsula from the Tagus to the sea, taking full advantage of the naturally rugged, difficult country. A third much shorter line of defences enclosed a small bay beside Fort St Julian's near the mouth of the Tagus where, in the event of defeat, or if faced by an overwhelming force, the army could embark. The Lines were not impenetrable. A determined enemy could select his point of attack, bring up his artillery, and batter then storm the forts guarding a section of the Line. But such an attack would be slow, laborious and probably bloody, giving plenty of time for the defending army to concentrate in a good position to the rear of the threatened point. For the great advantage of the Lines was that they were occupied by second-tier troops (Portuguese militia and a few regular gunners), leaving the field army intact to their rear. To succeed the French would therefore have to fight their way through the first line, defeat Wellington's army in a position of his choice, and then repeat the process with the second line.

The idea for the Lines probably did not originate with Wellington. Major José Maria das Neves Costa had reconnoitred the country with something similar in mind in late 1808 and had prepared a series of maps and proposals which the Portuguese government passed on to Wellington. However in 1812 Wellington strongly denied the suggestion that Neves Costa deserved the credit, and a pension, for his ideas, complaining that his map and memoranda had been 'so inaccurate that I could place no reliance upon them'. This at least shows that Wellington was well aware of the major's proposals, and it seems likely that he used them as the starting point for his own plans, even if he then became irritated by their faults and came to regard them as too unreliable to be useful.[24]

When Wellington visited Lisbon in October 1809 he thoroughly reconnoitred the country between Villa Franca (where the Tagus becomes unfordable at any season of the year), and the coast some twenty-five miles to the west as the crow flies. As a result he prepared a detailed memorandum for Lieutenant-Colonel Richard Fletcher which contained twenty-one specific instructions, in some cases to prepare plans, in others to begin work. Experience led to many changes to these initial ideas, with clusters of small forts and redoubts taking the place of the entrenched camps that Wellington seems to have originally had in mind, but the broad outline had been provided and the impetus given for work to begin as quickly as possible.[25]

Within a few days of Wellington's memorandum almost all the engineer officers had received orders to leave the army and report to Fletcher; by early November the work had begun in earnest. It was not easy. Captain Mulcaster wrote to his good friend and fellow engineer John Burgoyne on 2 January 1810:

'My entrenchments are getting on, but not so rapidly as I had hoped, for I have met with a large proportion of rock and hard gravel, and have a month's work in store to finish completely and give myself a week over. I wish you could see my entrenchments. Unlucky dogs that ever have to attack them!'[26] Mulcaster kept to his schedule, for five weeks later D'Urban visited Torres Vedras and wrote in his journal: 'The works in front [are] in a great state of forwardness, wanting but a few days of their completion, and beautiful specimens of Field Fortification, doing infinite credit to Lt-Col Fletcher who traced, and Capt Mulcaster who executed them.'[27]

Fletcher not only laid out individual works and supervised the whole enterprise, he also had to manage all the administrative machinery which ensured that the large workforce was on-site and fed where it was needed. Wellington treated him with confidence (the initial memorandum ranged widely over strategic questions which Fletcher did not really need to know about), but there was a reserve and formality in Fletcher's reports on progress which may simply have reflected his personality, but which suggests that he was not entirely at ease with Wellington.

The hard physical labour of clearing the ground, excavating entrenchments and building the fortifications was carried out by about 6,000 Portuguese militia, ordenanza and peasants, with the assistance of some specialist artisans drawn from the British army.[28] The breadth, scale and thoroughness of the preparations were remarkable, and stand in stark contrast to the passive surrender which had been Portugal's response to Junot's invasion only three years before. Experience of French conquest had created an almost universal determination to resist; Wellington's guidance ensured that this will was harnessed to a useful plan, and Britain provided many of the resources that were needed.

By the beginning of July 1810 the main line was very nearly finished as were the defences at St Julian's. The principal line consisted of 59 redoubts and forts containing 232 guns and requiring garrisons totalling 17,500 men, and stretched over 22 miles of front.[29] Wellington permitted Fletcher and some of the other engineers to join the army, but after consulting Fletcher, he gave orders that the isolated strong points built well in advance of the main line be linked together by fresh works to make a new line. This work, which continued throughout the summer and early autumn, was supervised by Captain J.T. Jones and was not quite complete when the French arrived in October.[30] Even after the immediate crisis had passed work continued, maintaining and strengthening the Lines.

The strangest thing about the Lines of the Torres Vedras is that this enormous engineering project remained virtually a secret and ultimately came as an extremely unpleasant surprise to the French. Part of the explanation is that the British army was cantoned far to the north of the lines – officers and men might notice a few fortifications if they marched to or from Lisbon, but it was not something they saw every day. But there is a deeper reason: the purpose and function of the lines was not as obvious as hindsight suggests. Alexander Gordon wrote home on 14 February 1810 after accompanying Wellington in an inspection of the lines: 'Having seen all these places as well as the works already constructed, I can speak confidently with respect to their strength, but it is quite impossible with our force to hinder the Enemy from turning them, the roads are so numerous in every direction.' Even some of the engineer officers who constructed the redoubts that made up the Lines failed to grasp their strategic significance, and wrote home lamenting the waste of energy and resources on a futile project which 'will only serve to swell out a French Bulletin, and to expose us to the ridicule of both our friends and enemies'.[31]

Wellington was able to leave most of the day-to-day dealings with the Portuguese government to Beresford and the British envoy to Lisbon. Mr Villiers went home in February 1810, having already remained many months longer than he originally intended. Wellington regretted his departure, for he had worked well with Villiers and appreciated his strong support. Before he left office in the autumn of 1809 Canning had suggested Henry Wellesley for the Lisbon mission, but Lord Wellesley preferred to send Henry to Cadiz, and Charles Stuart to Lisbon. 'A man of wit, of fashion, and of learning', Stuart was a young diplomat whom Wellington had last encountered at Coruña in July 1808. He proved hard-working, shrewd and conscientious. Almost as soon as he arrived in Portugal he travelled to Thomar and spent a day with Wellington discussing the state of the alliance, and making clear that he saw his role as acting in accordance with Wellington's wishes, rather than pursuing an independent policy of his own. Remarkably he maintained this resolution through the years that followed, although he could not always avoid becoming embroiled in the factional rivalries of the Portuguese Regency Council.[32]

In February Wellington visited Lisbon and outlined his plans for the defence of Portugal to the Regency. He made it clear that it might be necessary to withdraw almost as far as Lisbon before the allied armies could be concentrated and give battle, but he also conveyed a strong sense of his own confidence that a French invasion would be defeated. The Regents endorsed his proposals, although it is not clear if they really understood that Wellington was not intending to attempt to defend the line of the frontier and expected the decisive battle to be fought in the heart of the kingdom.[33]

Throughout these months, between December 1809 and midsummer 1810, Wellington was troubled by the state of British politics and his relations with the British government. He had been dismayed by the criticism of the Talavera campaign led by the radical press, and reacted sharply when he heard that the Common Council of the City of London was calling for an inquiry into the campaign. Memories of the controversy over Cintra came flooding back, and he told his brother William: 'I see that the Common Council are determined to have me again *en Spectacle* at Chelsea at all events; but that shall not prevent me from endeavouring at least to give the French another beating.' And he melodramatically complained to Villiers: 'I act with a sword hanging over me, which will fall upon me whatever may be the result of affairs here; but they may do what they please, I shall not give up the game here as long as it can be played.'[34] It was more than half a century since Admiral Byng had been shot, the victim of political enmity as much as his own misconduct, but his fate had not been forgotten.

Wellington had no confidence that Perceval's government would survive, and even when it weathered its baptism of fire, he told Pole: 'I think that Govt and Country are going to the Devil as fast as possible; & I expect every day to hear the Mob of London are masters of the Country.'[35] But although the ministry remained weak, it survived a parliamentary inquiry into the Walcheren expedition (once Chatham, with characteristic tardiness, resigned), and three days of rioting when the radical politician Sir Francis Burdett was arrested for contempt of Parliament in April.

Lord Wellesley was discontented and alienated from his colleagues. He had taken office expecting to have the dominant voice, at least on questions related to the conduct of the war. He viewed his colleagues with ill-concealed contempt, and was astonished that they did not immediately defer to his judgement and even had the temerity to interfere in his conduct of the Foreign Office, ruining the beautifully rounded periods of his despatches by their alterations. He was not subtle in distancing himself from the other ministers in the debates over Walcheren, and he appeared all too well aware that if the ministry fell he was the obvious candidate to lead a new government that would be able to rally all shades of Pittites to its colours. But the salt in the wound was that he neglected his official business and seldom spoke in the Lords, being somewhat preoccupied – as all the world knew – by an infatuation with Moll Raffles, a well-known courtesan.[36]

Wellington commented to William Wellesley-Pole in true brotherly fashion:

I wish that Wellesley was *castrated*; or that he would like other people attend to his business and perform too. It is lamentable to see Talents & character & advantage such as he possesses thrown away upon Whoring. Then the ruin to his Private Fortune which at his time of life is irretrievable, is as certain as the loss of character, & the misuse of his Talents and the dereliction of his advantages; & the Injury which the Publick & his Party must suffer from this folly.[37]

Wellesley's inattention to business cost him the influence he might otherwise have had in Cabinet. He favoured a much more expansive war policy including a large increase in British aid to Spain as well as the annual subsidy to Portugal.[38] But Perceval had been alarmed by a long, strongly-worded memorandum from Huskisson, the leading financial expert in the Portland government, who had resigned with Canning. Huskisson argued that recent rapid increases in government spending, particularly on the war, were unsustainable, and that the government was testing the limits of the amount it could safely borrow. Compounding the problem was the chronic shortage of specie which was growing more severe. Coin was being replaced by paper money and the risk of inflation was obvious and – to a generation which had seen the fate of the French *assignats* – deeply troubling.[39] In late 1809 and early 1810 Perceval struggled to find the considerable savings Huskisson had demanded, but with very little success, finally concluding that 'we cannot without absolute reduction of Army, or Navy, make any such saving . . . a most terrible truth'.[40] He was therefore in no mood to contemplate large increases in spending and he had no difficulty in persuading his colleagues to reject Wellesley's proposals.

By the end of the session Wellesley was so frustrated and disillusioned that he intended to resign before the end of the year, possibly with the hope that if this brought down the government he might yet be called upon to form a new ministry. His presence in the Cabinet had been no help to Wellington; if anything it had created an awkwardness in Wellington's relations with the other ministers. Wellington had not written directly to his brother or attempted to use him to influence the government's policies, while he had great reservations about Lord Wellesley's ideas for an increased British involvement in Spain.[41] This difference, which subsequently widened, and Lord Wellesley's poor performance in office, loosened the residual loyalty Wellington felt for his elder brother. There was no open rift, but the ties between them were much weaker in June 1810 than they had been when they parted at Cadiz the previous November.

Three important debates during the Session of 1810 tested the strength of political support for the defence of Portugal. At the beginning of February there was heated debate although no division over the Vote of Thanks to Wellington and his army for Talavera. On 16 February the Commons considered the pension that accompanied Wellington's peerage; and on 9 March there was a debate over the subsidy to Portugal. On each occasion the Opposition vigorously attacked the government's policy and Wellington's operations, denying that Talavera was a victory and describing the defence of Portugal as hopeless. But on each occasion they clearly failed to gain the support of the House, losing the two votes 213 to 106 and 204 to 142, at a time when the government could not rely on scraping a majority together on other questions. Canning, Castlereagh, Sidmouth and the other Pittite splinters all voted with the ministers, and so did many independent members and even some who generally sided with the Opposition. But although this support was broad, it was fragile. If the campaign went badly, political support for Wellington, and for the government, would rapidly evaporate. Even an orderly evacuation of Portugal might bring down Perceval's ministry, while any hint of disaster would vindicate the radicals and provoke a witch hunt far greater than the controversy over Cintra. There was no salvation except through victory.[42]

Relations between Wellington and the ministers frayed under pressure in the first half of 1810 despite their mutual dependence. Wellington resented the government's emphasis on the need for economy. He was not a spendthrift like his brother, nor did he dismiss financial concerns with lordly disdain as beneath his notice; but he felt that he was already doing all that he, or anyone, could to keep the cost of the army to a minimum. 'If ever there was an officer at the head of an army interested (personally I may say) in keeping down the expenses of the army, it is myself.'[43] Liverpool's insistence that 'we are naturally anxious to know, with some certainty, that we have our money's worth for our money', jarred on him – as indeed it would with most generals on active service in any era.[44]

A recurrence of the specie shortage added greatly to this ill feeling, and led Wellington to make unreasonable demands on the government, and to complain in dangerously intemperate language when they were not met. For example, on 16 May Wellington wrote a long official despatch to Liverpool, which included the demand that the government regularly send out £150,000 in specie each month or run the risk of 'a failure in some important branch of the service at a critical moment'. A week later in a private letter he was even blunter: 'If you cannot supply us with money, you ought to withdraw us. We are reduced to the greatest distress . . .'[45] The scale of Wellington's demands was quite unrealistic and the implication that the government was sitting on large reserves of bullion that it would not dispense, was most unfair. But instead of rebuking Wellington, Liverpool searched high and low for fresh sources of specie, ranging from the Spanish government (which continued to receive large if irregular shipments of silver from Mexico and South America) to China. Most of these sources proved fruitless or disappointing, but some money was raised. More important was a steady improvement in the money markets in the Peninsula, which enabled Wellington's commissary general to purchase specie in Lisbon and Cadiz in exchange for Bills on London. Most of the cash received by the British army and the Portuguese government was quickly spent and once in circulation it would return to the merchants, for they were eager and ready to buy. The system was not perfect – civilians who could afford it liked to keep a ready supply of cash hidden for use in an emergency

– but it was the underlying mechanism that funded all Wellington's subsequent campaigns. For example, over the whole of 1810 the British government shipped £679,000 to the Peninsula in specie, while £5,382,000 was raised locally.[46]

Wellington was also alienated by the suspicion that the ministers lacked confidence in him and in his plans for the defence of Portugal. This was largely a problem of his own making, for at the end of January his nerve was briefly shaken by the speed of the French conquest of Andalusia, and he wrote home asking for fresh instructions, and specifically whether he should defend Portugal 'to the last' or make an orderly withdrawal as soon as he was convinced that the cause was hopeless.[47] Given that the ministers had undertaken the defence of Portugal on Wellington's advice and against the almost universal opinion of senior soldiers in Britain and his own army, it was natural that they were troubled by this moment of doubt. Wellington soon recovered his nerve and the ministers' faith in him was ruffled rather than seriously shaken. Liverpool wrote officially that the safety of the British army was their first concern, but that they would be reluctant to evacuate Portugal before it was absolutely necessary. A fortnight later he elaborated:

You would rather be excused for bringing away the army a little too soon than, by remaining in Portugal a little too long, exposing it to those risks from which no military operations can be wholly exempt. I do not mean by this observation that you would be justified in evacuating Portugal before the country was attacked in force by the enemy; but whenever this event shall occur, the chances of successful defence are considered here by all persons, military as well as civil, so improbable that I could not recommend any attempt at what may be called desperate resistance.[48]

This was well meant if rather tactless, but Wellington reacted with indignation, complaining that Liverpool was attempting to influence him with unofficial letters at variance from his official instructions. He complained to Pole: 'I don't think ... that Govt. have behaved very fairly by me.' And he told Liverpool: 'Whatever people may tell you, I am not so desirous, as they imagine, of fighting desperate battles: if I was, I might fight one any day I please.'[49]

Wellington was mortified at the strength and unanimity of opinion in Britain, which regarded the defence of Portugal as hopeless. He attributed this largely to the continuing influence of Sir John Moore's statement that the country was indefensible.[50] However while Moore's verdict may have predisposed some people in England to question whether Portugal could be defended when Spain was overrun, the real cause of the doubts, which affected all shades of 'informed opinion' in the early spring of 1810, were the letters coming from officers of all ranks in Wellington's own army. Men like Murray and Hill were highly respected at the Horse Guards, and their views were taken all the more seriously because they were known to be well disposed towards Wellington. Charles Stewart, Stapleton Cotton and several other senior officers returned home over the winter, naturally paying their respects to the Secretary of State and the Commander-in-Chief, and discussing the prospects for the coming campaign. And then there was the mass of second- and third-hand opinion coming from ordinary regimental officers writing to their family and friends at home who showed the letters to their social circle and repeated their opinions in conversation. Not all of these letters were gloomy – some officers were convinced that one Englishman was worth any number of Frenchmen when it came to a fight – but their general tenor was not optimistic. Ministers would have been even more concerned – and might even have ordered the army to evacuate Portugal as soon as the French advanced in strength – if the army, and especially its senior officers, had not also expressed great faith in Wellington. This confirmed their own view and so Liverpool responded to Wellington's challenge with the assurance 'that the fullest confidence is placed in your discretion in the important and delicate service in which you are engaged'.[51]

The fall of Andalusia added another complication to the relations between Wellington and the British government, for many reinforcements that had been destined for Portugal were diverted to Cadiz. Wellington was annoyed, and it took some months before he was mollified when it was made clear that his authority extended to the Cadiz garrison, which he could draw upon as he chose, provided a reasonable force was retained there.[52] In the end Wellington received the 5,000 reinforcements he had been promised and a few more besides. But if the campaign had begun in the spring or early summer he would have felt that the government's preoccupation with Cadiz had placed him at a disadvantage.

There was also much discussion between Wellington and the government in London over the question of his second-in-command, although this seems to have been quite harmonious. Sherbrooke's health was giving way, and he told Wellington that he wanted to go home before the summer of 1810. Wellington suggested Thomas Graham as Sherbrooke's replacement, but in the meantime Liverpool sent Graham to Cadiz where he became second-in-command in the Peninsula, and would have joined the army in Portugal if Wellington had been incapacitated. Sir Brent Spencer took Sherbrooke's place with the army and Payne came home, leaving the cavalry under Cotton's command.[53] Spencer's limitations would be revealed over the next fifteen months, but his reputation in the spring of 1810 stood high. Wellington had not forgotten his evidence to the Cintra Inquiry but approved the choice, although he soon found him a most unhelpful subordinate, later complaining that he 'has no mind and . . . is the centre of all the vulgar and foolish opinions of the day . . . I cannot depend upon him for a moment'.[54]

Major-General Thomas Picton arrived in Portugal at the end of January 1810 and Wellington gave him the command of the Third Division, with which he would be associated for the rest of the war. Picton was more than a decade older than Wellington (he turned fifty-two in August 1810), and was the son of a Welsh gentleman whose brother was a distinguished officer in the army. Wellington's verdict that Picton was 'a rough foul-mouthed devil as ever lived',[55] and the reputation of the 'Fighting' Third Division being always in the thick of the action, have suggested a misleading caricature of Picton as a crude, rumbustious fire-eater, always eager for the fray. But officers who served closely with him described him rather as stern, austere and cold, although subject to violent fits of fury, and he felt grievances keenly.[56] His language was often coarse, but he was an educated man and a gentleman, not a swaggering buffoon. He was capable of great kindness, whether to a young soldier who through carelessness had lost his pack on a long march, or in making himself agreeable at dinner to a nervous cornet who, years later, recalled that his 'sociable good humour rendered his hospitality still more agreeable'.[57] Most of his staff and subordinates admired and liked him – even the commissary attached to his division – and his reputation has suffered unduly by the hostility of memoirists from the Light Division and the 88th Foot who simultaneously settled old scores and enlivened their narratives with some highly coloured tales.[58] Picton was a thoroughly professional officer who kept his division in good order and maintained strict discipline.

Although pleased to be going on active service again, Picton felt little confidence or enthusiasm for the campaign in Portugal. His first impressions of the country were mixed: 'Cold rooms, hard beds, bad fare, but good civility and respect from all classes, and a most inveterate hatred of the French.' And it was encouraging to find that 'Lord W. is a great favourite with everyone, high and low, and they are all persuaded that he would certainly have destroyed the French army at Talavera had the Spaniards at all co-operated, and as far as I have been able to hear his Lordship would have gone far towards it with very little assistance'.[59] But like most British officers he had his doubts about the Portuguese army: 'I have seen several of the Marshall's Regiments, which are composed of good, active, nervous men, and tolerably well disciplined: but it was not possible to look into the interior and see how the *Heart* was situated.'[60] As late as the first weeks of May Picton regarded the campaign as hopeless and even thought the Portuguese were so miserable that French rule might prove beneficial. Nonetheless, he had no criticism of Wellington: 'I go on perfectly well with our Commander of the Forces, who appears to me, from what I have been able to Observe, to possess the Talents, decision and personal qualities necessary for his situation.'[61] It is a strange incongruity: to admire Wellington's judgement while fundamentally disagreeing with it; but not an uncommon one, for both views were widely held in the Peninsular army in the spring and summer of 1810.

Wellington's army was not seriously engaged with the French for almost a full year between Talavera at the end of July 1809 and the beginning of the campaign of 1810 in the middle of the following July. The long pause in active operations paid handsome dividends. The Portuguese army was drilled and marched into a state of competence and its officers became more skilful and assured. It would still need careful handling in action, but it was ready for the test of battle which alone could give it real confidence. The Lines of Torres Vedras could continue to be strengthened forever, but they only needed a few final preparations to be ready to withstand an onslaught. The British army had regained its health, received its reinforcements and the new subordinate generals had taken up their commands. The specie shortage had been weathered and the British government had survived the Parliamentary session and now appeared relatively secure in power. Wellington was still disgruntled with the ministers, but the worst of the distrust and misunderstanding generated in the spring had faded. Even the French conquest of Andalusia which at first seemed such a devastating blow, proved valuable as it became clear that the French would struggle to withdraw any of their troops from southern Spain for operations elsewhere. When Wellington contemplated the coming campaign in the summer of 1810 he could not be sure of victory, but he could be confident that the chances of success were very much better than they had been at the beginning of the year.

CHAPTER TWENTY-TWO

BUSACO
(July–September 1810)

NAPOLEON THOUGHT THAT the conquest of Portugal would help end the tiresome war in the Peninsula, which had already cost him far too many men and far too much money. He did not expect it to be difficult. His intelligence, largely gathered from reports in English newspapers, suggested that Wellington had an army of fewer than 30,000 British troops, and was only waiting for the French to advance to give him a decent pretext to evacuate the country. The same newspaper stories, commonly based on uncensored letters from British officers in Portugal, dismissed the Portuguese army as a negligible force and ignored the Lines of Torres Vedras. Nonetheless Napoleon did not take success for granted, and allocated 130,000 men to the Army of Portugal; one third of these would be required to hold its base area in Spain, the provinces around Salamanca, Valladolid and Leon, but this still left more than 80,000 men for the march on Lisbon.

Napoleon gave command of the army to one of his ablest and most experienced subordinates, Marshal André Masséna, who had won glory on many fields from the Italian Campaign of 1796–97 to the 1809 war with Austria. His principal subordinates were the hot-tempered Marshal Ney, and Napoleon's old companion General Junot (both of whom were inclined to resent Masséna's elevation over them), and General Reynier, who had recently arrived in Spain and taken command of II Corps, formerly under Soult.

Masséna's instructions were to proceed with care and deliberation, first taking the frontier fortresses of Ciudad Rodrigo and Almeida, and only advancing on Lisbon in September when the worst of the heat of the summer was over and the harvest had been gathered.[1] Masséna arrived at Valladolid on 10 May and on 2 June the French invested Ciudad Rodrigo, although the march of the siege guns from Salamanca was delayed by heavy rain and a shortage of draught animals.[2] Wellington watched the French operation closely, hoping for an opportunity to come to the aid of the garrison, but Ney and Masséna kept their forces together and it would have been foolish to risk the whole campaign at the outset when the odds still favoured the French. His inactivity, however, naturally provoked Spanish complaints of betrayal, especially as he had promised the governor, General Herasti, to do everything he could to relieve the fortress.[3]

The French found the siege difficult, both because the defence was determined, and because of a constant shortage of supplies. The surrounding country had already been stripped bare, and most of the supplies had to be carried forward by road from as far away as Salamanca. When Masséna's favourite aide-de-camp Major Pelet visited the siege lines he found that 'the conversation there was only about the lack of food. The shortage was so severe that we could not obtain bread, forage or lodging for our escort of five dragoons'.[4] It took more than a fortnight to establish the siege batteries, and even when they opened fire Herasti returned a defiant answer to a French summons. Sixteen days of bombardment followed which battered a breach forty yards wide in the walls, did immense damage to the town, and silenced the Spanish artillery. On 9 July, just as the French were preparing to storm the fortress, Herasti capitulated, thus sparing the town the horrors that would inevitably follow a successful assault. The garrison had lost 461 men killed and 994 wounded, together with several hundred civilian casualties, while the French had 182 killed and 1,043 wounded.[5]

When Ciudad Rodrigo fell, Wellington withdrew his outposts twenty miles to Almeida, the Portuguese frontier fortress. This left Craufurd and the Light Division on the eastern, or Spanish, side of the Coa, which ran through a rocky gorge and was crossed only by a single narrow bridge. Wellington gave Craufurd considerable discretion on how to manage the outposts, but on the evening of 22 July warned him that the French were showing signs of advancing and suggested that he withdraw to the western side of the river as 'I am not desirous of engaging in an affair beyond the Coa'.[6] But months of living in close proximity to the French had made Craufurd overconfident and he did not give orders to withdraw until it was too late to avoid a clash.

Ney attacked the Light Division at dawn on 24 July with overwhelming force: about 24,000 men compared to Craufurd's 4,000. The allies fought desperately, giving ground slowly to gain time for their cavalry and artillery to descend the tortuous road, file across the narrow bridge and ascend on the other side. One company of the 1/95th Rifles was cut to pieces by the French cavalry, and five companies of the 1/52nd seemed to be cut off, but were rescued by a gallant counter-attack. According to William Napier, who was in the thick of the fight, Craufurd 'was confused and agitated, and very wild in his appearance and manner', and it was generally agreed (not least by themselves) that the officers and men of the Light Division had won as much honour and credit in the affair as Craufurd had lost.[7] Despite the confusion and disorder, there was relatively little panic, and as soon as the troops crossed the Coa they took up positions on the rocky slopes on the further side. When the French sought to exploit their advantage and seize the bridge, they were met with a withering fire which drove them back. Ney then lost his temper and directed two further, futile and extremely costly assaults on the bridge, which took the gloss off his earlier success. In all, Craufurd suffered 333 casualties (36 killed, 214 wounded and 83 missing) and Ney 527, although the French could with justice claim it as a victory, if an unnecessarily costly one.[8]

Wellington was not present at the Coa and he was understandably annoyed at Craufurd's folly. He avoided any open blame, but made a point of praising the officers and men of the Light Division while passing in silence over Craufurd's role, an implied censure said to have been felt keenly by that officer, and noted with warm approval by the regiments under his command.[9] It might be argued that Wellington bore some responsibility for the affair by giving Craufurd the discretion to decide when to withdraw rather than ordering him to do so on 23 July; however this runs contrary to the more usual criticism that Wellington stifled the initiative of his subordinates by not allowing them to exercise their own judgement. Certainly Craufurd's mistake did not encourage Wellington to trust his subordinates to use their discretion in future.

Another aspect of the fighting at the Coa caused Wellington even more concern than Craufurd's poor judgement. First reports suggested that of the two battalions of Portuguese caçadores present 'the one ran away without hesitation, and the other is said to have behaved *in part tolerably* well'.[10] This was deeply alarming, for the caçadores, particularly Elder's 3rd Battalion, were among the best Portuguese troops in the army, and if they took to their heels under pressure, Wellington's whole strategy for the defence of Portugal would be in tatters. He therefore made discreet enquiries, and was greatly relieved to find that the stories of misconduct were greatly exaggerated. The 1st Caçadores had remained in position until ordered to withdraw; part of the battalion had then done so with precipitation and disorder, crossing the bridge mixed with the cavalry and artillery, thus creating an impression of panic and flight, but even these troops had rallied without hesitation once they had crossed the river and had received no orders to halt previously.[11] Reading between the lines it appears that some of the Portuguese troops were shaken, but that much of the blame for this rested with the lack of clear directions from Craufurd combined with the inexperience of their regimental officers. The 1st Caçadores suffered 16 casualties, and the 3rd Battalion 29, comparable with the 1/52nd, but much lighter than the 1/43rd or 1/95th who bore the brunt of the French attack.[12] The sceptics about the Portuguese army remained unconvinced, but at least their doubts had not been confirmed.

The French proceeded slowly and it was not until 26 August that their batteries were ready to open fire on Almeida. This was a well-designed fortress in good repair. It was garrisoned by 4,000 men, all Portuguese, including an entire regiment of line infantry and three regiments of militia, and there were plentiful supplies of food and ammunition. But now the French had their best – almost their only – stroke of luck of the whole campaign. About seven o'clock in the evening of 26 August, the day the French guns opened fire, a shell landed near the main magazine and ignited a trail of gunpowder that had spilled from a leaking barrel. The result was an appalling explosion, which devastated the entire town and killed some 500 men of the garrison. Further sustained defence was clearly impossible, and the governor, Brigadier William Cox, was left with no choice but to surrender on 27 August. Almost all the Portuguese regular troops, including their officers and some of the militia, then agreed – under some pressure – to serve the French. Cox, five other British officers and a handful of stubborn Portuguese were sent to France as prisoners of war, and the remaining militia were released on parole. The defection of such a large number of Portuguese troops raised serious doubts about the loyalty of the whole army, but these were quickly allayed as the Portuguese deserted the French by the hundred until Masséna sent the laggards back to France.[13]

The sudden fall of Almeida appeared to vindicate the pessimists in the army, while shaking, at least for a moment, the faith of even Wellington's greatest admirers. Charles Stewart declared that he was not surprised, and that it was a bad fortress with a bad garrison; while Alexander Gordon admitted that it was 'a most *unexpected* and a most *fatal blow*'. Letters such as these were widely circulated in influential circles at home and added to the apprehension over the outcome of the campaign, with even the friends of the government hardly daring to hope for a happy outcome. Lady Bessborough described the fall of Almeida as 'terrible', while Tierney evidently believed that treachery was involved.[14] In general the Opposition was quick to leap to the worst conclusions, although, because Parliament was not sitting and expectations were low, there was not much public debate or controversy. Lord Auckland told Grenville that he would have been happy to see the safe return of the British army from a conflict which, by his calculation, had wasted three years, and cost 30 million guineas and countless lives. At the Horse Guards, the influential Colonel J.W. Gordon told Lord Grey: 'The crisis appears to me to be very fast approaching, and I think Lord W will *now* be fortunate if he embarks half his army – yet the Government are sending out stores upon stores . . . if this ends well, I will break my [prophet's] wand and bury it 500 fathoms deep, and never consider more.' But the Home Secretary, Richard Ryder, was more optimistic, writing on 29 September that if Wellington 'should be able and willing to put off the battle till the 1st of October we calculate that he would have 36,000 British, as all his reinforcements or nearly all will have arrived ... with such an Army in such a country he may defy all the strength at this season that the French can bring against him'.[15]

Wellington had expected the French to advance much more rapidly, and while their slowness was advantageous, enabling the allies to complete their preparations, the strain of waiting took its toll. Charles Stewart reported that:

> Lord W's temper, especially when the prospect is gloomy, is more uneven than I had ever imagined or indeed witnessed until recently. One is obliged, therefore, to study him and no longer give way to the unreserved

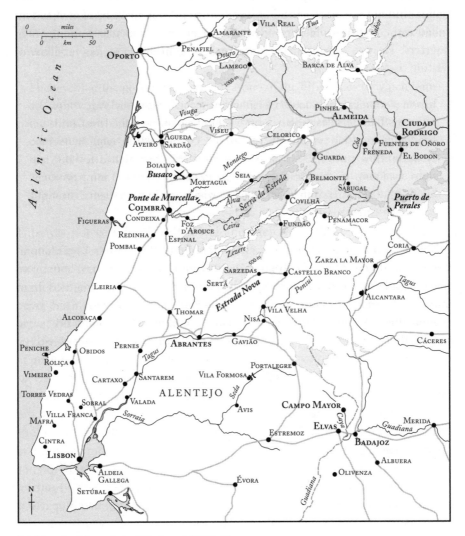

16 Masséna's invasion of Portugal, 1810–11.

communication that is so delightful, and of course, so interesting. As the clouds thicken Lord W grows more and more reserved and buried in himself. Neither Spencer nor Murray are confided [in] or communicated with more intimately than myself, so I have no grounds particularly to complain. I can tell you little of future intentions or resolutions, and nothing of the communications to or from the Government. We are all in the dark.[16]

It is not strictly true to say that Wellington had no one in whom to confide, for Alexander Gordon's letters show that he talked surprisingly freely to his immediate staff, but neither they, nor even Beresford, whose work was so vital to the success of the campaign, could share the weight of responsibility that their commander had to bear. Wellington's mood was not helped by what he called the 'croaking which prevails in the army, and particularly about headquarters'. He was clearly hurt by the lack of confidence in his judgement, writing that:

I have always been accustomed to have the confidence and support of the officers of the armies which I have commanded; but, for the first time, whether owing to the opposition in England, or whether the magnitude of the concern is too much for their nerves, or whether I am mistaken and they are right, I cannot tell; but there is a system of croaking in the army which is highly injurious to the public service, and which I must devise some means of putting an end to, or it will put an end to us.[17]

Nineteen days passed between the surrender of Almeida and the beginning of the French advance into Portugal. The army was so short of transport that Masséna was forced to reduce its artillery by one third (from twelve to eight guns per infantry division), and most of the reserve food, which had been accumulated with immense difficulty, had to be issued to the soldiers at once (giving them fourteen days' rations to carry as well as all their other equipment), with the inevitable result that much was wasted.

The advance began on 15 September. Masséna had summoned Reynier to join him, bringing the total strength of the army to 65,000 men, well short of the 80,000 who had theoretically been available at the beginning of the campaign. The French advanced on the road to Viseu, on the north bank of the Mondego, rather than the better, more direct road to Coimbra south of the river. Masséna's maps were poor and the Portuguese officers on his staff did not know this part of the country well, so it is possible that he chose this route by mistake; however he had also received reports that Wellington had prepared a strong defensive position at Ponte de Murcella where the direct road crossed the River Alva, which the northern route would avoid. He may also have hoped to replenish his supplies in the rich country around Viseu, but when the leading French troops entered the town on 19 September they found it almost totally deserted. Few supplies were available other than fresh fruit in the many orchards that surrounded the town, and some wine in the cellars. Masséna complained to Berthier: 'All our marches are across desert; not a soul to be seen anywhere; everything abandoned . . . We cannot find a guide anywhere.'[18]

On 4 August Wellington had issued a proclamation to the people of Portugal in the name of their Prince Regent in which he warned that the French had already ill-treated the inhabitants of villages near the frontier: 'The people of these devoted villages have suffered every evil which a cruel enemy could inflict. Their property has been plundered, their houses and furniture burnt, their women have been ravished . . .' And he pointed to the conclusion:

> The Portuguese now see that they have no remedy for the evil with which they are threatened but determined resistance. Resistance, and the determination to render the enemy's advance into their country as difficult as possible, by removing out of his way every thing that is valuable, or that can contribute to his subsistence, or frustrate his progress, are the only and the certain remedies for the evils with which they are threatened.[19]

To this end he declared that inhabitants who provided any assistance to the enemy would be considered traitors and punished accordingly. This was all part of the policy of stripping the countryside to deny the enemy resources, which had the strong support of the Portuguese government (at least while the campaign was fought in the poor, thinly populated frontier provinces), and was generally accepted by the population as a necessary evil. Indeed, it had been used before in this part of the country, most recently in 1762 when an invading Spanish army, faced with starvation, had withdrawn in despair. It is not clear if Wellington knew of this precedent or whether he originated the policy, but he may also have been inspired by the difficulties created by Tipu Sultan's devastation of the country in the face of the British advance in Seringapatam. There is a bitter paradox in the fact that Wellington, who, far more than most generals, sought to protect and insulate the civilian population from the disasters of war, should in 1810 have deliberately widened the nature of the campaign to include the whole of civil society, and thus prefigured the horrors that were to become routine in the twentieth century.

British officers were shocked at the human misery produced by the policy. Henry Mackinnon, one of the brigadiers in Picton's division, wrote: 'The consternation of the inhabitants of Pinhel, when they knew that we were about to abandon them, cannot be conceived: the whole population of the town took flight. Many respectable families were seen, with their servants carrying bundles on their heads, retiring in every direction, having no settled plan but that of avoiding the French . . . I have since heard that the town is completely abandoned.'[20] And Augustus Schaumann remembered: 'It was sad to behold the fugitives arriving in all directions. They marched wailing along in families, carrying bundles and packages; the children, the sick and the aged packed on donkeys and in bullock carts. They had no time to lose, for if they had been caught by the French, death and plunder could have been their lot.'[21] Meanwhile Masséna refused to recognise the legitimacy of the ordenanza, proclaiming that no quarter would be given to anyone caught carrying arms but not wearing a uniform. Wellington protested that the ordenanza was an ancient institution of the Kingdom of Portugal, that its members were entitled to the protection of the laws of war, and that Masséna had himself won much glory and renown in the armies of revolutionary France, which wore little in the way of uniforms. He also warned, without much effect, that such killing would inevitably lead to retaliation, and this seems to have occurred, with the war between the ordenanza and French stragglers and patrols quickly imitating the horrors of the guerrilla struggle in Spain.[22]

From Viseu, Masséna had the choice of advancing directly on Coimbra to the south-west, or taking the longer but rather better road that ran west to Aveiro on the coastal plain, and joining the main highway running south from Oporto to Coimbra and Lisbon. He preferred the more direct route even though it crossed the Serra do Busaco, a formidable ridge nine miles long. Either he did not think that Wellington would offer battle even in such a favour-able position, or he welcomed the prospect of fighting on almost any terms.

Wellington had been surprised by Masséna's decision to advance north of the Mondego, telling Charles Stuart: 'There are certainly many bad roads in Portugal, but the enemy has taken decidedly the worst in the whole kingdom.'[23] And he was delighted that they were attempting to advance via Busaco: 'We have an excellent position here,' he wrote from the convent on the summit of the ridge on the evening of 21 September, 'in which I am strongly tempted to give battle.'[24] His spirits and those of the whole army rose with the prospect of action. Charles Boutflower wrote in his journal for 22 September: 'Lord W is constantly on horseback reconnoitring, and if we may judge from his counte-nance and Spirits he anticipates a complete triumph over the enemy.' William Tomkinson observed: 'The army is in most beautiful order, and the Portuguese as fine-looking men and as steady under arms as any in the world. The only doubt rests with them; if they do their duty, and the business becoming general there can be no doubt of success.'[25]

Wellington gave battle at Busaco because the position was so strong that he could be almost certain of victory. It was unlikely that such a victory would halt the French invasion, for the allied army was too weak and inexperienced to follow up its success by counter-attacking the French, and if Masséna was only checked, he would surely find another way forward, even if it meant retracing his steps to Viseu and taking the road to Aveiro. But even if Wellington had to resume his retreat to the Lines after the battle, a victory would give the army – and particularly the Portuguese troops – confidence, and pacify the complaints of some members of the Portuguese government that he was abandoning too much of the country without a fight.[26]

The position at Busaco had one serious weakness: its left flank could be turned by an atrocious road through the hills, which eventually joined the Oporto–Coimbra highway. Wellington was well aware of this road and on the evening 19 September he asked Beresford to send Trant to hold its western end. But a brigade of Portuguese militia could not stop a whole French army, and Wellington continued to search for a solution to the problem long after the orders to Trant were issued, without discovering any alternative.[27]

By the evening of 26 September the entire allied army was camped on or close behind the Busaco ridge except for the cavalry, most of which had been withdrawn well to the rear. A little to the east of the foot of the hill the French army was camped, though its cavalry too was behind the line. The night was fine but very cold, and Wellington had ordered that no campfires be lit for he did not have enough men to occupy the whole length of the position, and fires would indicate the position of the troops to the French. Moyle Sherer of the 34th in Hill's division remembered: 'An evening passed in very interesting and animated conversation, though we had neither baggage nor fires, we lay down, rolled in our cloaks, and with the stony surface of the mountain for our bed, and the sky for our canopy, slept or thought away the night. Two hours before break of day, the line was under arms; but the two hours glided by rapidly and silently.'[28]

Hill's two divisions (one British, one Portuguese) were at the southern end of the line, close to the Mondego. Next came James Leith with the newly formed Fifth Division consisting of two Portuguese and one British brigade of infantry. Picton's Third Division was in the middle of the position, guarding the point where a country road crossed the ridge having first passed through the tiny hamlet of San Antonio de Contaro. Then came the First Division occupying the highest ground – an open plateau at this point some 1,800 feet above sea level and 300–400 yards across,[29] wide enough for Wellington to include a couple of squadrons of cavalry with Spencer's infantry. The grounds of a Carmelite convent began at the northern end of this plateau and were occupied by Pack's Portuguese brigade. The main road crossed the ridge in a pass immediately north of the convent close by the village of Sula. This position, the most obvious avenue of attack, was held by the Light Division with Coleman's Portuguese brigade in close support. To the north, occupying the left of the

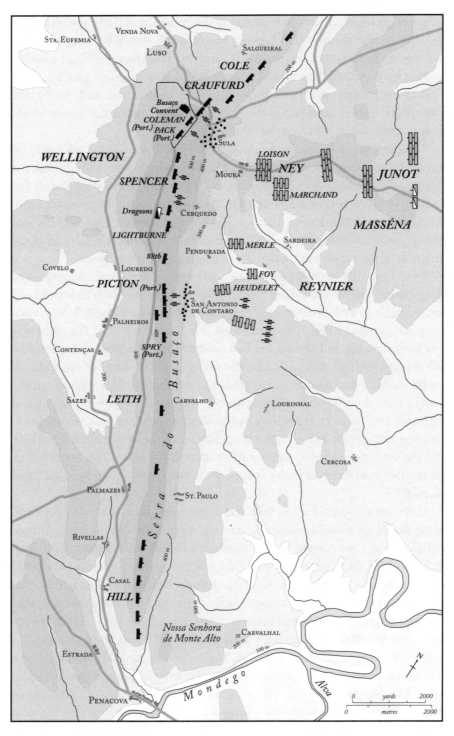

17 The battle of Busaco, 27 September 1810. (All troop positions approximate, many conjectural.)

line, was the Fourth Division under Lowry Cole. On the evening of 26 September Wellington shuffled his line a little to the north, probably because there were no French troops camped south of Picton's position. Leith was ordered to send Spry's brigade of Portuguese to join the Third Division, while Picton moved Lightburne's brigade to the southern end of the central plateau next to Spencer. Cole's division, which had been behind the convent, was moved north.[30]

The allied position was so strong that many British officers thought that the French would not dare to attack it, but Masséna had little hesitation in ordering an assault. Hindsight makes this look like folly, but at the time Masséna had no reason to regard the Portuguese troops as of any military value in open battle, and he probably believed that Wellington had been tempted to fight by the strength of the position, even though it was far too extensive to be held by 27,000 British troops. This gave him an unexpected opportunity to inflict a crushing defeat before the British could play their usual trick of escaping onto their ships. He boasted to his staff: 'Tomorrow we will finish the conquest of Portugal, and in a few days I will drown the leopard.'[31]

Masséna's orders were relatively simple. Reynier's corps would attack Picton at first light, advancing in one or two columns preceded by skirmishers and choosing the most accessible approach up the hill. Having defeated Picton's men it would swing north along the top of the ridge rolling up the British line until it reached the convent. Meanwhile Ney's corps would advance along the main road, but would delay its attack until Reynier had gained the summit, so that the allied troops near the convent would be threatened from front and flank at the same time. Junot's corps and the cavalry would remain in reserve. Given the circumstances there is little to object to in these orders, although it might have been better to direct Reynier's advance well to the south of Picton's position rather than risk a frontal attack, and to hold Ney more tightly in check.[32]

Although some details of the fighting are obscure it appears that Reynier's corps made three separate assaults on the ridge. Heudelet's division advanced directly along the road through San Antonio de Contaro; Merle's division went up the slope about a mile to the north where their reconnaissance had discovered a gap in the allied line; and Foy's brigade was thrown forward after Heudelet's attack had failed.

The pass where the road from San Antonio de Contaro crossed the ridge was held by the 74th Regiment. Wellington had inspected it when it joined the army a few months before and had asked Colonel Trench if there were many veterans of Assaye still in its ranks. 'But a bare handful m'Lord,' Trench had replied, 'but they are good lads, and your Lordship need have no apprehension but that they will do their duty.'[33] Heudelet's infantry advanced up the road under heavy fire from the Portuguese artillery and the allied skirmishers. Their march was checked by an *abatis*, or barricade, across the road, and the 74th counter-attacked, firing into the front and flanks of the leading French troops. The French attempted to deploy, but began to waver and soon turned and ran. Captain Lemonnier-Delafosse admits: 'All my attention was concerned with receiving a bullet in the back ... I was almost envious of the soldiers whose haversacks became a shield for the exposed portions of their bodies.'[34]

The second assault, by Merle's division, came much closer to success, advancing up the ridge into a gap between Picton's men at the pass and the 88th or Connaught Rangers, who were further north, closer to the plateau. The leading French infantry actually crowned the ridge and established themselves in some rocky outcrops before they were driven back by the 88th pushing south and Picton advancing north with the 1/45th and a battalion of the 8th Portuguese Line. Much of the fighting was quite confused and on a fairly narrow front, and it was decided more by the superior confidence and momentum of the British infantry than by firepower. Wellington was delighted and wrote home in his official despatch: 'I beg to assure your Lordship that I have never witnessed a more gallant attack than that made by the 88th, 45th and 8th Portuguese regiments on the enemy's division which had reached the edge of the Serra.'[35]

Reynier was a tough, experienced soldier. He was more angry than dismayed by the failure of these two attacks, and ordered Foy's brigade forward. If Picton's division had been unsupported, Foy's attack might have prospered, at least for a time, but Leith had begun to move his division north as soon as there was enough light for him to be sure that his own position was not going to be attacked. As Foy's leading French troops approached the top of the ridge they came under heavy fire from the 8th and 9th Portuguese, but pressed on and the Portuguese gave way before them in some disarray. Leith wheeled his leading battalion, the British 1/9th, into line coming under scattered fire from the leading French skirmishers as he did so. The other battalions of his first brigade formed up as best they could, and Leith led his men to the charge, driving Foy's men before him.[36] Reynier's corps was spent. Six of his seven infantry regiments had scrambled up the hill and run back down again, and he had suffered some 2,000 casualties and gained nothing.

At the same time that II Corps had been fighting to secure a foothold on the summit of the ridge against the allied Third and Fifth Divisions, Ney's corps had been making an even more difficult attack on the allied troops around the convent and the main pass over the ridge. The ground was much steeper here than further south and it was strongly held; there were no unoccupied stretches of open ridge which the French could hope to seize. Masséna had ordered Ney to delay his attack until Reynier had made some progress, but the hope that the allies opposing Ney would be distracted by a threat to their flank was disappointed. Even if Picton's men had been defeated, Wellington had five strong British brigades (the 8,000 infantry of the First Division and Lightburne's brigade) occupying the central plateau, and could have sent them against either French attack, though they were not needed against either.

Ney's attack was led by Loison's division which advanced up the main road through the little village of Sula to the pass, while Marchand's division attacked further south against the walls of the convent's park. Loison's men found that their progress was dearly bought. The allied skirmishing screen was very strong here: the whole of the 1/95th, and 3rd Caçadores, with the 1st Caçadores thrown into the struggle by Craufurd when the others began to tire. Taking advantage of ample cover, and supported by well-sited artillery higher up the slope, 2,000 skilled sharpshooters made a formidable opponent, but the French infantry were led with courage and determination, and they continued their advance, reinforcing their skirmishers, it is said, by several whole battalions from the main column. It seems the allies defended a succession of positions on the hillside, first the woods below Sula, then the village itself and finally a third line higher on the ridge, in each case holding it long enough to punish the French and then rapidly withdrawing upon supports further back. Unfortunately no first-hand accounts give a detailed description of this skirmishing, but French sources suggest that they found the allied fire fierce, while the allied light infantry suffered relatively little: 41 casualties in the 1/95th, 89 in the 3rd Caçadores and 23 in the 1st Caçadores – 153 in all, some of whom probably fell after Ney's main attack when there were several hours of desultory skirmishing.

Loison's men kept advancing although the steep slope left them breathless and disordered, and the heavy allied fire, from the artillery no less than the skirmishers, had shaken their morale and composure. Unlike the rest of Ney's corps, they were not veterans of the Grand Armée, but foreign troops from Hanover and Piedmont and 4th, 5th, 6th and even 7th battalions of French regiments. Some of them had served in Portugal before, under Junot at Roliça and Vimeiro, but their memories gave them little confidence. Still they pressed forward and Captain Jonathan Leach of the Rifles admitted: 'We must give the French their due and say that no man could come up in a more resolute manner.'[37] The allied light infantry gave way before them, and some of the allied guns were either overrun or abandoned as the French came closer to the summit, almost daring to believe that they had succeeded.

Robert Craufurd coolly watched them approach, showing none of the nerves and uncertainty that he had displayed at the Coa. Behind Craufurd on a shelf of level ground, out of sight of the French, 1,800 men of the 52nd and 43rd waited, deployed in line. When the leading French were only a few yards away, Craufurd turned to his men and called out: '"Now, 52nd, revenge the death of Sir John Moore! Charge! Charge! Huzza!" and waving his hat in the air he was answered by a shout that appalled the enemy.'[38] As the British companies in the centre of the line charged into the head of the French column, those on either flank swept around and poured a destructive fire into its sides. The French broke and fled; no infantry in Europe could have withstood the psychological shock of Craufurd's charge at the end of that gruelling ascent.

The totality of the French defeat is reflected in the casualties, for the 43rd and 52nd suffered only 24 casualties between them, while Loison's twelve battalions lost 1,253 casualties, two-thirds of them in the leading brigade. The unfortunate Legion du Midi, which may have found itself at the head of the column, lost over half its strength.[39]

At the same time, a little further south, Marchand's division was defeated by the Portuguese brigades of Pack and Coleman, and suffered almost as heavily as Loison. With this defeat the battle slowly died away, although some skirmishing continued in parts of the line. During the afternoon the French light infantry gained a footing in the village of Sula again, but were driven out by a company of the 43rd. At other times the armies fraternised peacefully and the French were unmolested as they removed their wounded from the lower slopes of the ridge.[40]

Many British officers have left glimpses of Wellington during the battle, although some of these may need to be taken with a pinch of salt. Moyle Sherer of the 2/34th in the Second Division, saw Wellington 'with a numerous staff' gallop up to Hill 'immediately in front of our corps; I therefore distinctly overheard him. "If they attempt this point again, Hill, you will give them a volley, and charge bayonets, but don't let your people follow them too far down the hill . . .".'[41] A Swiss officer on Cole's staff, Major de Roverea, was sent three times with messages to Wellington and noted the general's perfect calm and coolness, together with the extraordinary promptitude, precision and clarity with which he issued his orders. On the third visit, after the fighting had ended, Roverea found Wellington sleeping quietly![42] Schaumann, the German commissary with an eye for evocative details, wrote:

> Lord Wellington displayed extraordinary circumspection, calm, coolness and presence of mind. His orders were communicated in a loud voice, and were short and precise. In him there is nothing of the bombastic pomp of the Commander-In-Chief surrounded by his glittery staff. He wears no befeathered hat, no gold lace, no stars, no orders – simply a plain low hat, a white collar, a grey overcoat, and a light sword.[43]

Even the independently-minded Charles Cocks was satisfied: 'The way in which Lord Wellington took up that position was acknowledged by everyone to be the most masterly.'[44] Impressions such as these, shared by thousands of officers and men who left no record of them, reinforced the army's trust and confidence in its commander.

Masséna's army had been defeated, but it was far from broken. Junot's whole corps, the cavalry and Mermet's division of Ney's corps had scarcely been engaged, while only a few of the units that had been repulsed were so badly cut up as to be unreliable. In all, the French army had suffered almost 4,500 casualties or only about 7 per cent of its strength, although the figure was naturally much higher in those parts of the army that had been engaged.[45] The allied army lost 1,252 casualties and by an extraordinary and fitting coincidence exactly half of these were British and the other half Portuguese. This amounted to less than one man in forty of those present on the battlefield. It had been a remarkably easy and relatively bloodless victory.[46]

The general expectation in the allied army was that the French would renew their attack on the following day, but Masséna was not so foolish, and he allowed the morning of 28 September to pass quietly while sending out patrols to search for a means of turning the allied position. Inevitably they discovered the track that ran north-west from Mortagua through Boialvo to Sardão twenty-four miles away on the highway south from Oporto to Coimbra, and Masséna had little hesitation in deciding to use it.

Wellington observed the French gradually shift their forces to the rear on the afternoon of 28 September, and he received reports from reconnaissance officers, including George Scovell, who watched the French movements closely while keeping at a safe distance from their columns.[47] He had discovered no solution to the problem of this road, and even Trant's brigade was not in place due to the excessive caution of General Baccelar, his superior. Not that this mattered much; Trant might harass and perhaps slow the French advance, but he could not halt it.[48] Wellington therefore gave orders for the bulk of the army to begin its withdrawal on the evening of 28 September leaving only a rearguard to hold the Busaco ridge.

The battle of Busaco did not halt the French advance or decide the campaign. It did not even give the allied army any great strategic advantage; they retired on the Lines and the French advanced much as they would have done if it had never been fought. But Wellington gained enormous intangible advantages from his victory, and the greatest of these was confidence. For more than a year all his plans had depended on the answer to a single question: would the new Portuguese army fight or give way when tested in battle? The ambiguous evidence of the Coa and Almeida only sharpened the question and many officers in the British army, and many more at home, had no doubt that the answer would be negative. Busaco proved them wrong. With the exception of a single battalion of militia who really had no place in the front line, all the

Portuguese units engaged in the battle emerged with credit. Some, like the 9th Line and Douglas's battalion of the 8th, appear to have given way under pressure, but even they were willing to rally and return to the fray. Others, such as Pack's brigade and the *caçadore* battalions in the Light Division, did all that could be asked of any troops, so that the Portuguese army fully deserved an equal share in the honours of the victory. Well might Alexander Gordon write home: 'We are in high spirits at the Portuguese behaving so well', and Wellington tell Liverpool that 'they have proved that the trouble which has been taken with them has not been thrown away'.[49] Other British officers were equally impressed: 'The Portuguese astonished us by their coolness and bravery'; 'They behaved in a gallant manner, and full as well as the British'; and 'it has afforded proof that the Portuguese infantry are to be depended upon'.[50] This was important, for the British needed to be able to feel that they could trust the Portuguese if they were to fight happily alongside them. But even more important was the confidence that success gave the Portuguese themselves: they had had their baptism of fire and had performed well; they had seen the invincible French turn and run and were no longer intimidated by them; and they would go into their next action undaunted, believing in themselves and in their commander.

The victory spread a more optimistic spirit throughout the whole army, reviving martial ardour which had cooled during the long months of waiting, and reminding officers and men that Wellington knew what he was doing. After Busaco even the most confirmed pessimists began to hedge their bets, for it no longer seemed inevitable that the campaign would end in a tame withdrawal to the ships and the evacuation of Portugal. Charles Stewart told Castlereagh that he was now 'much more sanguine than I have been heretofore, and our campaign I think now may end brilliantly'.[51] He was not alone.

Nonetheless Wellington was nervous about how the news of Busaco and the subsequent retreat would be received in England. On 4 October he wrote to William Wellesley-Pole revealing how much he still smarted under the criticism of Talavera: 'The croakers about useless battles will attack me again on that of Busaco, notwithstanding that our loss was really trifling; but I should have been inexcusable if, knowing what I did, I had not endeavoured to stop the enemy there.'[52] However, his fears proved baseless, as public interest and expectations were both at a low ebb, and the news was greeted with none of the intense feeling of previous years.

Captain Burgh of Wellington's staff reached England with his official report of the battle in the middle of October. Lady Holland was delighted with 'the brilliant repulse of the French', but few other members of the Opposition had any good to say of it.[53] Lord Grey felt that it 'resembles in too many points the battle of Talavera. A vigorous repulse of the Enemy, a post unoccupied which exposed our flank and rear and the necessity of an immediate retreat.'[54] Tom

Grenville thought that the French had gained the advantage, while Lord Auckland believed that Masséna had 'out-generaled us, and turned our position, and forced our strong post and fortress, and forced us to retreat over the Mondego'. Auckland indeed went further than most of his colleagues in his criticism: 'There cannot be a doubt of Lord Wellington's bravery, and his troops seem to be attached to him; but history may perhaps doubt how far he has ever shown either quality as commander of an army or wisdom or truth as a writer of dispatches.'[55]

The ministers however were delighted. The pro-government *Courier* claimed that 'we gained a glorious victory, and established our invincible superiority, and . . . the French army was cut down like ridges of grass by the scythes of our mowers'.[56] Liverpool conveyed the government's thanks to Wellington and told him that, 'I never saw the King more entirely satisfied than he has been in the late operations of the army'.[57] And the cynical Edward Cooke declared, 'Ld Wellington will keep in Mr Perceval' – a view that may explain the jaundiced reaction of the opposition.[58] But for all Cooke's confidence the campaign had yet to be decided, and until it was, the fate of Britain's commitment to the Peninsula, the survival of Perceval's government, and Wellington's reputation, all hung in the balance.

CHAPTER TWENTY-THREE

TORRES VEDRAS
(October 1810–February 1811)

WELLINGTON WAITED UNTIL the afternoon of 28 September, the day after the battle of Busaco and then, when it was clear that the French were committed to the long march by Boialvo and Sardão, he gave the order for his army to withdraw. He did not again offer battle or attempt to delay the French advance until he reached the Lines of Torres Vedras, but the retreat was well managed, so that the troops retained the buoyant confidence they had gained at Busaco. The march was almost completed before the rains began at the beginning of the second week of October; however, the rapid movement gave little time for the Portuguese civilians to escape from the advancing French. Only a few of the richest and most prudent citizens of Coimbra had left before Busaco, most of them sailing from Figueras to Lisbon or Oporto. Now the remainder of the 40,000 inhabitants of Portugal's third largest city had to depart at short notice and generally on foot, carrying with them as many of their household goods as they could. Almost the entire population left the city, with a bare handful defying Wellington's proclamation and remaining to welcome the French.[1] Similar scenes took place all along the line of the retreat. One British officer wrote in his journal:

> To describe the confusion of the Day is utterly impossible. The Road was so thronged with Fugitives, that it was with the utmost difficulty we reached our destination before sunset. On passing through Condixe [Condeixa], a considerable Town, I observed Lord W at a window evidently affected at the Scenes of distress which were passing. It had never been apprehended that the Enemy would advance so rapidly, and therefore a great proportion of the Inhabitants had not left their Houses. In one mixed scene of confusion and misery were seen the old, the lame, and the blind, all hastening away as fast as their infirmities would allow.[2]

The hurry also meant that there was no time to strip the countryside. Farmers could flee with their families, their carts and most of their livestock, but the crops that had only recently been harvested remained in their granaries, or at best were hidden in underground stores. Wellington blamed the Portuguese government for not doing more to remove food supplies and so starve the French. But it was unrealistic to expect farmers who were only forty or fifty miles from Lisbon to destroy the harvest on which they depended, when the French were still far away beyond Coimbra in the remote uplands around Vizeu and Celorico. The population of central Portugal had much less experience of resisting invasions than that of the frontier provinces, and the French threat seemed a distant danger until it was too late. Some measures were taken: most if not all the mills were disabled by the removal of metal parts; large quantities of goods and many people were shipped across the Tagus; and all the boats on the river were effectively secured. Ideally more would have been done, and Wellington had been urging precautions for many months, but a tract of country forty miles wide and a hundred miles long, containing some of the most fertile land in the kingdom, could not be turned into a desert overnight, and not while there remained a chance that the French invasion might be halted north of the Mondego.[3]

Wellington halted the retreat at the first line of defences. This had originally been intended as a mere supplement to the main line, but over the summer and autumn it had been so improved that it was almost as formidable as the main works. Behind this line of closed redoubts and small forts occupied by the Portuguese militia and ordenanza and strengthened by escarpments and *abatis*, Wellington turned his army and prepared to fight the battle that would decide the fate of Portugal. Within a few days he was confident that he would be able to report Masséna's complete defeat. He told his brother Henry: 'My opinion is, that the French are in a scrape. They are not a sufficient army for their purpose, particularly since their late loss, and that the Portuguese army have behaved so well; and they will find their retreat from this country a most difficult and dangerous operation.' A few days later Alexander Gordon wrote home: 'Our Army is all assembled to be able to take up any position on which the battle will be fought at the shortest notice . . . Our army is in high spirits and no one fears the result of the approaching termination of the campaign. I really think that never before was Masséna in such a scrape. Nothing can equal the conduct of Lord Wellington, but I am sorry to say that he is not well supported & has to trust to himself alone.' And Charles Stewart reported that 'the crisis approaches nearer every day', and 'the fact is both parties are committed to a desperate game', but 'I feel very confident as to the result of our operations.'[4]

Masséna and his army had been greatly encouraged by the allied retreat after Busaco and soon began to hope that the campaign would end in an easy success. The French entered Coimbra on 1 October finding the city silent and empty: 'Not a soul was there and all the houses were closed. It had the solitude of a tomb.'[5] The troops thoroughly plundered the city, and Masséna established a large hospital for the 3,000 sick and wounded men with the army, but left only a token garrison (a single company of marines, fewer than 200 men) to guard it.

Pressing south, the French were confident that the British would embark at Lisbon, probably without any further resistance.[6] It was not until 7 October that they received the first vague reports that Wellington would make a stand at 'the Lines'. This caused little concern; it was a well-established axiom of military science that an army that extended itself attempting to hold any linear defences, even a river line, would be vulnerable to a sudden heavy blow at a single point. And so, as Masséna's ADC Colonel Pelet admits, 'the first announcement of the enormous English Lines did not make a very great impression on us'.[7] Much more upsetting was the news that Coimbra had fallen to the Portuguese. The shadow of the eagles had not kept Nicholas Trant and his militia at bay for long; they marched into Coimbra on 7 October and after some fighting the French surrendered. A few prisoners were killed by the Portuguese, but Trant kept his men in surprisingly good order and succeeded in conveying over 4,000 prisoners (those from Coimbra supplemented by several small detachments and probably also the wounded left at Busaco) to Oporto.[8] Even the toughest veterans of Masséna's army could not help being disheartened by the news, which heightened their isolation from the rest of the world, and hinted that even if Lisbon fell, Portugal would prove an uneasy and demanding conquest. And then the rains began.

The French advanced guard reached the Lines on the morning of 11 October and came to an abrupt halt. Over the next few days there was some quite heavy skirmishing at Sobral as the French probed the defences and recon-noitred to either side, looking for a way around or through the Lines. They did not find one, and it was obvious that the allied troops, Portuguese as well as British, were undaunted and eager for a fight.

Masséna was furious that none of the Portuguese officers in his suite, or the French generals who had served in Portugal in 1807–08, had warned him of the possibility of such defences. He had learnt the lesson of Busaco and did not again underestimate the ability of the allied infantry to defend a strong posi-tion. On 16 October he wrote to Ney: 'The enemy is dug in up to the teeth. He has three lines of works that cover Lisbon. If we seized the front line of redoubts, he would throw himself into the second line . . . I have already visited the line three times to the right and left and I see great works bristling with cannon.' And consequently: 'I do not believe this is the moment to attack the enemy. A check would destroy all our hopes and would overthrow the state of things; so we will indulge in temporizing.'[9] Although Junot affected to favour a headlong assault, Masséna's decision was strongly supported by Ney and Reynier who recognised that an attempt to storm the Lines would lead to almost certain defeat and very heavy casualties. On 21 October Wellington commented to his brother Henry: 'I have no idea what the French will, or rather what they can do. I think it is certain that they can do us no mischief, and that they will lose the greatest part of their army if they attack us. They will starve if they stay much longer; and they will experience great difficulty in their retreat.'[10]

But if Masséna would not attack, he had no intention of giving up the campaign and retreating from Portugal. From his point of view his duty was clear and simple: having encountered an unexpected obstacle he should maintain his position for as long as possible while referring the problem back to Napoleon. If he gave up and withdrew without even attempting to break the Lines, all the odium and responsibility for failure would fall on his shoulders. Colonel Pelet explained: 'The Prince was unable to take any other course than the one he adopted, as much for the honour of arms as for the good of the operation. Waiting for relief . . . he was obliged to remain in position before the enemy and maintain the ground we had seized under their cannon as long as subsistence permitted.'[11]

There was another reason why Masséna loitered in front of the Lines for a month: he hoped that Wellington would be tempted – or forced by pressure from the Portuguese government – to sally forth and attack him.[12] The balance of forces had shifted greatly since the morning of Busaco; the French had lost men in the battle, at Coimbra and from privations and hardships ever since, while the allied army had steadily grown, reinforced by British regiments arriving in Lisbon, the concentration of almost the entire Portuguese regular army, and by the Marquis de la Romana who had answered Wellington's call and brought the 8,000 men of his Army of Estremadura to assist in the decisive battle. The allies now had a clear and substantial numerical superiority, but Masséna was confident that his men would perform better in a battle in the open, and that even a partial victory might create sufficient confusion to open the road to Lisbon, while a defeat would at least provide an honourable reason to withdraw from a miserable campaign. Wellington conversely saw both the opportunity and the risk. There is no doubt that he was tempted. A decisive victory would force the French into a winter retreat through the mountains and barren wastes of Portugal where the militia and ordenanza were waiting to harass their every move; Masséna's army might be thoroughly wrecked by the time it reached Spain. A quick end to the campaign would please the Portuguese and the government in London, and make his name across Europe. But there would be a risk. His Portuguese troops were still very raw and a question mark must remain over their ability to advance and manoeuvre under heavy fire without becoming flustered or disordered. Even his British troops were not as good as they were to become a year or two later, while Wellington had great respect for Masséna and the French army. If he remained behind the Lines then Lisbon was safe, while if he ventured forth the whole cause might be lost. And the Whig and radical criticism of 'useless battles' lingered in his mind. He did not need to attack Masséna, and a costly victory might invite a repetition of the criticism of Talavera at a time when the government was too weak to provide certain protection. Looking out from the fort at Sobral over the French encampments he told Colonel James Stanhope: 'I could lick these fellows any day, but it would cost me 10,000 men, and, as this is the last army England has here, we must take care of it.' He evidently discussed the question at headquarters, not seeking advice but explaining his reasoning, and persuading even Charles Stewart that 'every *military* consideration of prudence, wisdom and ultimate success in our cause should induce us more rigidly than ever to persevere in the defensive *now*'. Wellington himself wrote to Liverpool that he would not risk a battle because the 'enemy can be relieved from the difficulties of their situation only by the occurrence of some misfortune to the allied army; and I shall forward their views by placing the fate of the campaign on the result of a general action, on ground chosen by them instead of that selected by me'. The arguments were all sound, but one is left with the impression of Wellington's inclination yielding reluctantly in the face of cool calculation.[13]

Spirits in the French camp sank rapidly. The land in front of the Lines had been stripped fairly thoroughly, and it was not long before hunger joined the rain to make life miserable for the French troops. Desertions soared in the last weeks of October as hopes of a comfortable winter in Lisbon faded into the distance. Many officers, despairing of taking Lisbon, began to murmur and suggest that the army might march north and winter at Oporto where there would be rich pickings.[14] But Masséna set his face against any confession of defeat and instead prepared to send a detailed account of his position to Napoleon. Previous couriers had been sent earlier in the campaign but none had reached their destination, and their messages kept Wellington, not Napoleon, informed of Masséna's plans.[15] Now he selected Brigadier-General Foy to carry letters and his own eye-witness impressions to the emperor, and gave him an escort of a whole battalion of infantry and 120 cavalry and covered his departure with a demonstration against Abrantes. Masséna reported to Marshal Berthier, Napoleon's chief of staff:

For twelve days I have been in front of the works of the Anglo-Portuguese army. It is behind three lines of entrenchments which have been in preparation for eighteen months . . . I am not able to attack fortifications supported by formidable artillery and an enemy twice as numerous as us. The lines have given them great advantage and I would have to compromise the safety of the army of his Majesty, the Emperor. I would not have the strength to give battle in open country and in the actual state of things, I limit myself to observing all his approaches ... Since our departure from Almeida, the army has declined by 7,000 to 8,000 – wounded, dead, and missing . . . We did not find any inhabitants in this entire country through which we passed.[16]

The ball was now in Napoleon's court, and he could decide whether to send reinforcements, or instructions to withdraw. In the meantime Masséna had to hold his position for as long as possible and preserve a deadlock which maintained at least the appearance of a French threat to Lisbon.

The abandonment of so much of central Portugal to the French placed great strain on the Portuguese government and on Anglo-Portuguese relations. Until August Wellington was able to leave Beresford and Charles Stuart to handle most of the business with the Regency in Lisbon, but once the French crossed the frontier and besieged Almeida he was forced into a more active role, even though he really needed all his time and energy for the conduct of the campaign. The sudden fall of Almeida created a sensation in Lisbon and brought to the surface popular fears that the British would simply withdraw from the country without a fight leaving the people at the mercy of the French. Two members of the Regency Council, 'Principal' Sousa and the Patriach of Lisbon (who had played a prominent role in the uprising of 1807–08 when he was Bishop of Oporto), gave leadership to these concerns. Both men were sincere patriots and warm supporters of the British alliance, but they were horrified by Wellington's abandonment of most of central Portugal. Sousa urged that Wellington be ordered to discuss his plans with the Council, and made it clear that he thought that the line of the frontier should be defended so as to spare the population from the ravages of war. The other members of the Council were not persuaded by this populist line of argument, and would not risk antagonising Wellington by interfering in strategic questions. Even so, Wellington was furious with Sousa and warned the Council (through Stuart) that he would recommend that the British army be withdrawn if the Portuguese government did not give him and Beresford its complete confidence.[17] He was convinced that if necessary he could force Sousa to resign, but did not think that it was worth the trouble, although he made his irritation plain in a letter to Liverpool in which he described Sousa as having an 'impatient, meddling and mischievous disposition', while conceding that he did not intend to do any harm.[18]

News of Busaco brought a brief moment of pride and celebration, but the loss of Coimbra and Wellington's rapid withdrawal revived fears that the British were about to abandon the country. There was remarkable ignorance about the

Lines; even Charles Stuart was under the misapprehension that they were some old fortifications on the outskirts of Lisbon.[19] On 10 October Admiral Berkeley wrote to Lord Bathurst: 'You can have no conception of the consternation which pervades this great city.' Most of the leading families were embarking on any vessel they could find, and taking with them all their plate, jewels and other portable wealth, while the majority of the population looked on resentfully. Yet order was maintained, there were no riots and by 14 October the Admiral could report: 'The people at Lisbon begin to pick up a little courage, and do not seem so much alarmed at having the enemy's army so near.'[20] Before the end of the month confidence had been fully restored, and fashionable parties of Portuguese ladies made excursions up the river to view the armies from a safe distance.[21]

There were no pleasure parties for the thousands of refugees, ordinary Portuguese peasants and townsfolk, who crowded into Lisbon that October, and the rain made their plight much more miserable. Still, their arrival was not unexpected and some preparations had been made to cater for them. As early as June Wellington had urged the Portuguese government to build up magazines of grain and flour at Lisbon, while Beresford pressed it to remove import duties on basic foods.[22] Soup kitchens and cheap, subsidised eating houses were established in Lisbon, and the allied army regularly fed those fugitives who preferred to stay with it rather than proceed to the capital.[23] By 10 October Charles Stuart believed that the population of Lisbon had swollen by 40,000 and that only a few stragglers were left on the roads.[24] Many of the refugees of course had relatives, friends or other connections who were able to give them some assistance once they reached the capital, so that their greatest hardship would usually have been in the journey south, not once they arrived. Wellington organised a subscription in the army to raise funds to assist the refugees, and suggested that Liverpool do the same in England.[25] In the spring of 1811 the British Parliament voted £100,000 to help relieve the suffering. During the winter there was a good deal of privation, but no general shortage of supplies and certainly no famine. This did not stop the British press reporting that not only the population of Lisbon but also the British army was threatened with starvation, with the result that Wellington was favoured with advice on how to make the most of his supposedly meagre supplies of grain and flour.[26]

Although his dealings with the Portuguese government added considerably to the pressure on Wellington during the autumn and winter of 1810–11, this should not obscure the fact that the alliance emerged triumphant from these months of intense strain. A large French army accompanied by several well-known Portuguese aristocrats had invaded the country and swept to within a few marches of Lisbon before its advance was checked; yet it received no support from the local population who made great sacrifices to impede its

progress. Wellington's plan of stripping the countryside was not fully imple-
mented, but nonetheless the great majority of the population fled from the
French taking all that they could with them. The ordenanza, ordinary
Portuguese civilians with a minimum of military training, played a vital role
manning parts of the Lines of Torres Vedras and cutting Masséna's lines of
communication, so that the French army was isolated from its bases in Spain.
More than anything else it was the hostility of the Portuguese that ensured
Lisbon did not become another Cadiz – an impregnable fortress contained and
blockaded by a superior French army which dominated the hinterland with
only occasional interruptions. It is remarkable that no pro-French peace party
emerged in Lisbon, but the experience of French occupation was still fresh.
Sousa and the Patriarch, who gave Wellington so much trouble, were as loyal
and committed to the cause as anyone, as Wellington freely admitted. Nor, for
all his threats of quitting the country if he did not get his own way, was
Wellington's own commitment to the defence of Lisbon ever seriously in question. Theoretically it was possible that the French might send such a vast army
against him that he would have no choice but to withdraw rather than be overwhelmed, but by the summer of 1810 that possibility had shrunk almost out of
sight, while by autumn his confidence was riding high.

Meanwhile in England, the public waited eagerly for news of the great battle
which was to decide the campaign. This state of suspense continued for many
days and then slowly faded. On 24 October *The Times* was still all eagerness,
assuring its readers: 'The Armies seemed all but engaged when we quitted
them, and the stakes for which they were to fight were the fate of a Kingdom
and their own safety.' But by 10 November Lord Harrowby was feeling a sense
of anticlimax; 'The long delay for news,' he told his wife, 'gives me the sickness
of hope deferred; and, tho' without the least reason, makes me grow less
sanguine than I was'. Two days later Harrowby consoled himself that 'the delay
of Masséna clearly shows that he is afraid of attacking us at present', but this
was no substitute for the expected triumph.[27]

   After Busaco the Opposition faltered in their predictions of a disaster, as
Richard Ryder explained: 'They have muttered about a victory being followed
by a retreat of 70 miles: but the tone of all the Communication from the Army
staggers them; and they do not know what line to hold.'[28] But by the beginning
of November old habits had reasserted themselves, and Grenville wrote to Grey:

We are still without news from Portugal. The friends of the Ministers are so
confident of triumph that they begin already to challenge any man to avow
now a disapprobation of our campaigning there. My own opinion remains
unaltered, nor shall I shrink from avowing it whatever be the result of this

battle. I think the project desperate and wicked; it puts to hazard our safety, failure may involve us in ruin, the utmost success cannot, I am confident, insure to us the least permanent advantage.[29]

By November the views of the Opposition had suddenly acquired much greater significance, for the King had fallen seriously ill with a recurrence of his 'madness' (mental derangement probably caused by porphyria), and Perceval's hold on office was again in jeopardy. Perceval followed closely the precedents Pitt had established in 1788–89 in moving to establish a regency while limiting some of the Regent's powers, despite the furious protests of the Whigs and the Prince. It was widely assumed that the Prince would dismiss Perceval and invite the Opposition to form a government as soon as he became Regent.[30]

Wellington and many other officers in the army took a close interest in the political crisis at home, suffering in their turn from the delays and uncertainties of the mail. On 11 December Wellington told Torrens: 'It is inconceivable how anxious we are all to receive accounts of the good King's health.'[31] He took a gloomy view of the government's prospects, and told his brother Henry that if the Opposition was called to office he would not resign, but would endeavour to work with the new ministers or let them take the initiative in dismissing him.[32] On 11 January, still believing that a change of government was imminent, he wrote to William Wellesley-Pole savagely attacking the government's handling of the war and Liverpool personally. He accused the ministers of starving the war, denying him reinforcements and never acting with him 'upon any broad or liberal system of confidence'.[33]

These criticisms were grossly unfair; Liverpool and his colleagues had been endlessly patient in the face of Wellington's grumbling. They had committed the government to the defence of Portugal, trusting his judgement against the almost unanimous views of senior officers both at home and with the army. They had supported the war even though its cost far exceeded Wellington's estimates, and in defiance of their leading financial experts who warned that they had embarked on a course of unsustainable borrowing that risked national ruin. And they continued to send reinforcements to Portugal even though the Commander-in-Chief had told Liverpool in June and again in December that recruiting was not replacing losses and that the home garrison had been stripped to the bone. By the end of November Wellington's army amounted to almost 50,000 British and German officers and men, although its fighting strength did not fully reflect this increase because the number of sick had risen sharply from just over 5,000 in July and August, to 9,405 (or 23 per cent of the rank and file) in late October. This was inevitable with the season of the year and the resumption of active operations, but it was hardly the fault of the government at home.[34]

Wellington's complaints were unreasonable, but they were not insincere; he was genuinely discontented with the government and alienated from Perceval and Liverpool in particular. There was less personal warmth in his relations with them than with Castlereagh, and despite his frustration with Lord Wellesley he probably felt some sympathy for his troubles in Cabinet. More significantly he was irritated by the constant harping on the need for economy, by the specie shortage, and by the despatch of more troops than he thought were necessary to aid in the defence of Cadiz. He blamed the ministers for failing to secure broader public support for the war, and resented their political weakness which meant that they would be unable to protect him in the event of failure. He may even have had moments when he felt that a change of government in London would improve his position, either by forcing the Whigs to take responsibility for the war, or by opening the door for a stronger Pittite government, possibly with Lord Wellesley at its head. This is mere speculation, but his letter of 11 January to William Wellesley-Pole makes clear that Wellington was happy to distance himself from Perceval's ministry.[35]

Portugal did not figure prominently in the discussions that accompanied the political crisis in England. It is unlikely that the Opposition leaders had decided any definite policy that they would pursue, although their dislike of the commitment to the Peninsula was clear. Fortunately for all concerned the issue was never put to the test. The Regency Bills completed their passage through Parliament on 29 January and received a fictional form of Royal Assent on 5 February. However by then the King's condition had so much improved that it appeared the regency would be brief. There would be little point for the Prince to dismiss his father's ministers, only for the King to restore them when he recovered a few weeks later. For several days the Prince hesitated before finally deciding that he would make no change so long as there was a fair chance that the King would soon recover.[36]

Wellington reacted to the news with a marked lack of enthusiasm and was clearly unconvinced by William Wellesley-Pole's assurances that his distrust of the ministers, and Liverpool in particular, was unjustified. The next few months proved testing for relations between Wellington and the government, even though Liverpool and his colleagues seem to have been oblivious to Wellington's discontent, and continued to treat him with unreserved confidence and frankness.

Masséna and his leading subordinates and staff were well aware of the political crisis in England thanks to newspapers which, like other luxuries, were smuggled through the Lines to them from Lisbon. Their understanding of British politics was not very sophisticated, but they were encouraged by the possibility of a change of government in London. However this was not the reason behind Masséna not retreating from Portugal in the autumn when he recognised that the Lines were too strong for him to storm; the check at Sobral preceded the first signs of George III's illness, and news of the political crisis in England did not reach Portugal until the second week of December, when both armies had gone into winter quarters.[37] There is little reason to believe that the campaign would have taken a different course even if there had been no political crisis in London.

Masséna's army remained camped in front of the Lines of Torres Vedras for a month, from the middle of October to the middle of November 1810. By the end of the first week of November the nearby country had been completely eaten out and hunger was becoming a serious problem. Bowing to the inevitable Masséna decided to withdraw his forces some thirty miles to the rich country near Santarem on the Tagus, where he hoped to remain until reinforcements or fresh orders arrived from Napoleon. This would be a far better position to hold through the winter, yet he took the decision with reluctance, fearing that even this modest withdrawal would encourage the Portuguese, both soldiers and civilians, enhance Wellington's reputation, and discourage his own troops.[38]

The French army now bunkered down to endure several months of inactivity and privation. There was little actual starvation, but life was hard and supplies short, so that many of the younger, less-experienced soldiers fell ill and died. Gradually the army's supplies dwindled; shoes, clothing, drugs and other medical necessities became increasingly scarce. Towards the end of January rations ceased to be distributed at headquarters and many of the army's staff were forced to send their servants and pack animals out with the foraging detachments. Masséna, however, kept back a private store for his own immediate household, and as Pelet notes: 'Until the end we had wine and rather good wheat bread in nearly sufficient quantity.'[39]

Without reinforcements even Masséna would have been forced to retreat before the end of winter. But in December General Drouet, Count d'Erlon, led a division of 8,000 or 9,000 men of IX Corps through Portugal and reached Masséna, bringing news from France and orders from Napoleon to maintain his position.[40] Significantly Napoleon did not promise to send another whole army of 50,000 or 100,000 men to Portugal, or to order Soult to abandon Andalusia and the siege of Cadiz and march through Alentejo to Masséna's aid, and without such dramatic measures there was no real hope that the French would capture Lisbon. Napoleon still had 350,000 men in the Peninsula at the beginning of 1811, but even this vast army was overstretched occupying the provinces it had overrun and mounting active operations on a dozen fronts from Lisbon and Cadiz to Catalonia and the Asturias. Napoleon's resources, both military and financial, were already fully committed and he was simply unable to raise another new army to send across the Pyrenees, as well as keeping his existing armies up to strength. At the same time his alliance with Russia was crumbling, and rumours of war swept Europe in January 1811. They came to nothing, but Napoleon had been taken by surprise and resolved that his forces in central Europe, not those in the Peninsula, should receive priority for reinforcements.[41]

While the French army withered the allies increased in strength over the winter. The number of sick British soldiers fell from over 9,400 at the end of October to only 5,600 in late February, and the number of fit rank and file rose from just under 29,000 to almost 35,000 in the same period. Wellington was delighted, telling Liverpool: 'I never saw an army so healthy as this', and describing the climate as 'delightful'.[42] Wellington was less happy with the number of senior officers who wished to go home over the winter to attend to 'private business'. He had nothing but kindness for those such as Rowland Hill who were really ill, but resented the self-indulgence of men like Craufurd and Cotton who went home merely to see their family and friends, ignoring the effect this had on the morale of ordinary regimental officers and soldiers who could not hope for similar leave. Wellington's constant presence near the front line drew the sting from any discontent, but it proved a perennial problem.[43] Fortunately the autumn and winter saw the arrival of some new senior officers, with Charles Colville (who initially commanded a brigade in the Third Division) proving the most capable, and Sir William Erskine ultimately the most disappointing. Wellington created a Sixth Division, which he gave to his old favourite Alexander Campbell, who had returned to the army in February 1810 having recovered from his Talavera wound, while Beresford took command of the detached forces in Alentejo in Hill's absence. Further substantial reinforcements arrived at the beginning of March: seven battalions and drafts for regiments already serving in Portugal. With them came Charles Alten, a relatively junior Major-General in the King's German Legion, and it is no small indication of his quiet competence and ability that within a year Wellington had entrusted him with the command of the Light Division, and that he gained the good opinion and affection of that demanding body of men.[44]

The two armies quietly faced each other near Santarem throughout January and February, without hostility and with a good deal of unofficial fraternisation between the outposts. The only military operations of significance at this time were 150 miles away on the Spanish-Portuguese frontier in Estremadura. Soult had, with considerable difficulty, collected a field force of 20,000 men, and marched against the Spanish army based at Badajoz. His force was much too weak to contemplate an invasion of Portugal, but he hoped to stage a diversion that might be of some use to Masséna, and at the same time gain a local advantage that would protect his flank. His campaign proved very successful. A short siege led to the capture of the antiquated fortress of Olivenza and the 4,000 men of its garrison, and this opened the way for the French to invest Badajoz on 26 January. The Spanish army occupied a strong position at Gebora on the north bank of the Guadiana, but on 19 February the French suddenly attacked and defeated them with an inferior force. This made it much harder for the allies to relieve the fortress, but the siege was not easy and Wellington's initial fears that the Spanish resistance would be feeble and short-lived were soon replaced by optimistic calculations that it might defy the besiegers until the arrival of reinforcements from England enabled him to detach a strong force to its aid. However the reinforcements were twice driven back by gales in the Bay of Biscay and did not reach Lisbon until early March.[45] By then the long winter had finally come to an end and with it the four-and-a-half months of deadlock; spring would come with a rush in 1811 with the sound of trumpets, the beating of drums and the tramp of marching feet. It was time to reap the winter harvest.

CHAPTER TWENTY-FOUR

THE PURSUIT OF MASSÉNA
(February–April 1811)

O N 1 MARCH 1811 Masséna issued carefully prepared orders for the army's retreat, although the troops holding the outposts facing the allies did not move until the night of 5 March. The first stage of the retreat was well organised and conducted, and although Wellington detected many signs that some movement was imminent, he was unsure whether the French were intending a desperate attack, an attempt to cross the Tagus, or a withdrawal.[1] It was not until five o'clock in the morning on 6 March that Wellington learnt that the French had marched in the night, leaving straw-filled dummies to maintain the illusion of outposts.[2] The nearest allied troops were at once put into motion, and as the word spread throughout the army, camps were struck with an air of eagerness and anticipation; it was time to take to the road again after months of inactivity, and this time they would be pursuing the French, not giving way before them.

The British were shocked at the scenes they discovered at Santarem and the other towns that the French had abandoned in their retreat. Surviving inhabitants were few and more than half-starved, while many others had been murdered, often after being raped or mutilated. Naturally the Portuguese retaliated upon the few French sick who had been left behind, too weak to be moved, although some were saved by the prompt intervention of British officers.[3] As the retreat went on the French routinely burnt every town and village they passed. Sometimes this destruction had a military purpose – it delayed pursuit and discouraged French stragglers from remaining behind – but even this poor justification did not always apply and it seems that the French often indulged in destruction for its own sake. There was an edge of hostility and contempt in French attitudes towards the Portuguese, evident in the two previous invasions as well as that of 1810–11, which is not easily explained. Wellington was disgusted by the extent of the destruction and wrote home on 14 March:

I am concerned to add to this account, that their [the French] conduct throughout this retreat has been marked by a barbarity seldom equalled, and never surpassed. Even in the towns of Torres Novas, Thomar, and Pernes, in which the headquarters of some of the corps had been for 4 months, and in which the inhabitants had been invited, by promises of good treatment, to remain, they were plundered, and many of their houses destroyed, on the night the enemy withdrew from their position.[4]

Wellington did not dwell upon the atrocities committed by the retreating French on these unfortunate civilians who fell into their hands, but many of his officers and men were less restrained. To give just one example, Robert Ballard Long wrote home to his brother on 17 March:

Every town they [the French] passed thro' was burned to the ground, and men, women, and little children were equally the objects of their insatiable cruelty. Their orgies in this particular out-rivalled those of the most savage Indian tribes, and will reflect eternal disgrace upon the Troops and the officers who connived at such an iniquitous proceedings. Mothers were hung up with the children by their sides, and fires lighted below them. Men and children, half-murdered, thrown upon the burning embers of the houses they had set on fire. In short murder and desolation mark their track in letters that ought never to be forgotten by the Portuguese for generations to come.[5]

The leading allied troops entered Thomar on 8 March and on the following day skirmished with the French rearguard. Over the next week a succession of small actions were fought at Pombal, Redinha, Condeixa, Casal Novo and Foz d'Arouce as the French gained time by forcing the allies to collect their troops and deploy, before giving way when the allies were ready to mount a serious attack. The allied troops, led by the Light Division, displayed great confidence and fighting spirit in all these actions, and gained an important psychological ascendancy over their opponents who were demoralised and disheartened. At Foz d'Arouce the French infantry panicked and stampeded across a narrow bridge resulting in a crush in which the 39e Ligne lost its Eagle and several hundred men were killed as they tried to ford the river.[6]

It is strange that Masséna did not detach a brigade at the outset of the retreat, to secure Coimbra and the passage of the Mondego. When Montbrun arrived on 11 March he found the bridge broken and Trant's militia ready to oppose a crossing. This should not have presented an insuperable obstacle, but Montbrun showed little initiative and lost time, while the pressure on the rearguard increased, until Masséna was forced to retreat on the southern side of the river.

After ten days of hard marching, maintaining the pressure on the French, Wellington allowed his men to rest on 16 March. Their rapid movement meant that they had outpaced their rations. The leading troops, including the Light Division, had been short of food for several days, and would have suffered more if it had not made the most of the supplies found in the cooking pots left behind by the French in their flight at Foz d'Arouce.[7] The British commissariat attempted to feed Portuguese troops serving in the same divisions as the British, but the independent Portuguese brigades relied on their own commissaries who failed dismally. Wellington reported on 16 March:

> It is literally true, that Gen. Pack's brigade, and Col. Ashworth's had nothing to eat for 4 days, although constantly marching or engaged with the enemy. I was obliged either to direct the British commissary Gen. to supply the Portuguese troops, or to see them perish for want; and the consequence is, that the supplies intended for the British troops are exhausted, and we must halt till more came up, which I hope will be this day.[8]

There was little immediate improvement. Wellington was obliged to leave Pack's brigade behind in the next stage of the advance, and on 31 March he reported angrily to Charles Stuart that the brigade had received only nine days' food over the previous twenty-four days, and that most of this had come from British sources.[9] The problems caused by the failure of the Portuguese commissariat became a major issue in allied relations, and were never entirely overcome. Still, its poor performance in the pursuit of Masséna is hardly surprising as even the much better resourced British commissaries were struggling.

Supplies could only be distributed to the troops if they were gathered locally or brought up from the rear. The country had suffered much from the ravages of war, and many of the inhabitants had fled, so food was never plentiful in early spring and the French had taken or destroyed all that they could. The army had only the supplies that had accompanied it all the way from Torres Vedras and Santarem, or those that the ingenuity of its commissaries, backed by promises of payment, could discover locally. One of them, George Head, describes how he frequently rode ten or twelve miles to the right or left of the line of march looking for supplies and would then have to catch up with his brigade, and supervise the distribution of his gleanings.[10] The efforts of hard-working commissaries such as Head did not go unnoticed, and Picton, a man not famous for the warmth of his praise, told a friend at the end of the campaign: 'The Commissary Genl., Mr Kennedy, has, however, done wonders; what we all thought impossible, in enabling us to do what we have done.'[11]

Not all commissaries were as able and conscientious as George Head, and the unofficial *Journal* of the Royal Dragoons gives a candid glimpse of one of the less efficient, Mr House:

Never existed a man so unfit for his place, so entirely ignorant of his duty ... Not that he was a villain. Rather, he was a good natured fellow, and wished the regiment well. But, as for exerting himself in the pen and ink way or in sending to the (ration) stations to make his arrangements, that was not his forte, as he would himself confess. When the regiment had been marching and fighting all day, and at nightfall had put up at a wet camp, Mr House would make his appearance, pitch his tent, and have his dinner cooking, and after it, in company with old Mason and Ryding, would drink hot rum and water until comfortable. But it was in vain that the poor officers and men looked to the rear and, at every jingling of the mule bells, thought that surely their rations had arrived at last. Alas, vain hopes! Mules would pass by with rum and corn and biscuit for Bull's artillery and the 14th. But nothing for the Royals! When spoken to on this subject, he would take off his hat, scratch his bald head, and assert that no man living was more sorry than he was. He had sent his mules across the Mondego, but they had returned empty, and he simply could not account for it. On one occasion the men went three days without even biscuit. So Radclyffe broke in on his store of portable soup, and Hulton more than once offered a dollar for biscuit in vain. One night, too, near Sabugal the men, driven to desperation, sent such a volley of stones at his tent that he (House) was lucky to escape with a whole skin.[12]

Wellington used the opportunity of the halt on 16 March to thank the army for its exertions and 'excellent conduct' in the campaign. He singled out the British regiments of the Light Division, the 43rd, 52nd and 95th for special praise asking the commanding officers of each regiment to nominate a sergeant for promotion to an ensigncy. The 1st Hussars of the King's German Legion at the same time received a similar if rather backhanded compliment. Private John Wagener of the regiment had been convicted by court martial of conspiracy to desert and sentenced to 800 lashes; Wellington however expressed himself 'unwilling, at this moment, to order the punishment of any soldier of the 1st Hussars' and ordered that Wagener be discharged from the army without further punishment.[13] This did not signal any wavering in Wellington's belief in the need for strict discipline. The very next day he reacted sharply to reports that soldiers from the 38th Regiment had taken a large quantity of corn from a nearby village, ordering that the regiment's roll be called every hour, with all the officers present at each roll call, and that the 'obedience of this order must be reported daily to headquarters'. Published in a General Order to the whole army this added humiliation to inconvenience and left little doubt that, as usual, Wellington blamed the misconduct of the men on the neglect and inattention of their officers.[14] Unwilling to rely purely on the power of example, the following day Wellington issued a fresh order to his divisional commanders, instructing them to place guards on all the villages near their camps 'to prevent the soldiers carrying off the furniture, the poles of the vines, and other property of the inhabitants'.[15] This did not mean that the army could not draw on available supplies for its sustenance, but, as a further General Order reminded the army on 20 March, that foraging parties should be accompanied by a commissary, quartermaster or regimental officer who could issue a receipt for any goods requisitioned. These receipts would eventually lead to payments by the Commissary General or could be sold at a discount to speculators who followed in the wake of the army. The system was not perfect, but at least the local inhabitants received some compensation for their property, and the presence of a figure of authority with each foraging party greatly reduced the prevalence of wanton plundering, violence and other crimes by the soldiers.[16]

On 14 March, two days before halting his advance at Foz d'Arouce, Wellington was dismayed to learn that Badajoz had fallen. The news came as a surprise, for all the recent reports from the fortress suggested that its resistance was undaunted and its defences little damaged. Wellington was angry and, as details of the surrender reached him, became convinced that General Imaz, the governor of the fortress, had either been bribed or betrayed his trust, although the suspicion seems to have been baseless. Imaz had taken over the command when his predecessor, the able and energetic General Menacho, was killed watching a sortie on 3 March. The new governor's conduct was certainly not very heroic, but there was now a practicable if not a good breach in the walls. Wellington had promised assistance, but had been promising assistance ever since the siege began, just as he had promised to assist Herasti at Ciudad Rodrigo in 1810, and had done nothing. Even if he honoured his promise it would take a week or more for his army to march from the Tagus, giving the French plenty of time to storm the fortress. The garrison had resisted for much longer than Wellington had initially expected, and while it was not one of the more desperate defences of the Peninsular War, there was nothing dishonourable about its capitulation.[17]

Wellington's promises of assistance had been genuine; he had prepared to detach Beresford with a strong force of three divisions of infantry and a brigade of heavy cavalry (about 20,000 men) as early as 8 March, although he held them back for a few more days when the clashes with Masséna's rearguard began. However the fortress surrendered on 10 March, long before Beresford could have come to its aid. Wellington now ordered him to continue his march, to protect Elvas and, if possible, to drive the French out of Estremadura and recover Badajoz before its defences could be repaired. At the same time Wellington gave up the full-scale pursuit of Masséna, believing that its benefits would be outweighed by the damage done to the army by repeated marches on empty stomachs. He therefore left the final phase of the chase to the cavalry and the Light Division, with the Third and Sixth Divisions advancing in support.

The French made several long, hard marches and put a considerable distance between them and their pursuers, so there was little fighting or even contact between the armies, although the British cavalry picked up hundreds of prisoners – men who had fallen out of the French ranks, unable to stand the pace. It was generally assumed that the French, having made their escape, would retire on Ciudad Rodrigo and Salamanca and lick their wounds. Wellington's thoughts were turning to Estremadura; he was anxious to join Beresford for a few days to see the situation for himself, but did not feel that he could leave the northern army under Spencer's command until the French had withdrawn a little further.[18] When the French paused on the frontier at the end of March Wellington collected his army and drove them across the Coa at Sabugal on 3 April, in an action in which the Light Division distinguished itself.

Not everything went according to plan at Sabugal or in the other actions in the pursuit, and Wellington was privately disturbed by the frequency with which even simple orders were not followed unless he could explain them in person. He had already complained to Liverpool that because so many of his leading subordinates (including Cotton and Craufurd) were still at home attending to their 'private business', 'I have been obliged to be General of cavalry, and of the advanced guard, and the leader to two or three columns, sometimes on the same day'.[19] All generals need a fair share of self-confidence, and Wellington was never unduly modest about his ability, but it was experience in the field, not vanity or self-importance that encouraged his growing belief that things tended to go awry whenever he was not present to supervise them personally, and that few of his subordinates could be trusted to act independently. It was not a particularly attractive attitude, but the events of the next couple of months would powerfully reinforce it.

The fighting at Sabugal marked the end of the campaign. The French now withdrew into Spain, leaving only a garrison in Almeida. Wellington did not follow them much beyond the frontier; Almeida was blockaded on 7 April but only a few outlying posts were established beyond Ciudad Rodrigo, and the allied army now settled into cantonments.

Some contemporary critics felt that Wellington's campaign should have been more aggressive and ambitious, risking more in the attempt to destroy Masséna's army.[20] It is true there was more of the sheepdog than the wolf in the allied pursuit – driving the French before them, preventing them halting and keeping them away from the rich pastures north of the Mondego, but not straining every nerve to bring on a full-scale action. However, Masséna's army was still a formidable force; it had not been broken in battle, and Wellington only ever had a narrow numerical superiority which disappeared entirely when he detached Beresford's force in the closing stage of the campaign. If an opportunity had arisen to trap and annihilate Masséna's army, Wellington ought to have taken it, but there was little point running any considerable risk simply to gain a partial victory over an opponent who was already in full retreat.

Stepping back and looking at the French invasion of Portugal as a whole, Alexander Gordon was emphatic in his sense of triumph: 'We have certainly made the most glorious campaign Gt. Britain ever made since the days of Marlborough, and France one of the most disgraceful.'[21] The best estimate is that Masséna's army lost some 25,000 men dead or taken prisoner – that is, soldiers permanently lost to the army – during the invasion of Portugal.[22] It was the greatest, most obvious and undeniable defeat suffered by French arms since the establishment of the empire seven years earlier.

The credit for the allied success, even more than with most military operations, belongs principally to Wellington. Without him the British army would almost certainly have been withdrawn from Portugal after offering only token resistance to the French advance. It was his foresight and inspiration that devised the plan that made the defence of Portugal possible, and his strength of character, self-confidence and determination that carried it through in the face of widespread doubt and scepticism. The burden of responsibility was heavy and it rested squarely on his shoulders, while the prolongation of the campaign far beyond his expectation placed a strain on his spirits from which they did not immediately recover. The French retreat which was his vindication and triumph also presented him with myriad practical problems to overcome, and he seems to have had little opportunity or inclination to relish his success. As a result his temper and spirits were not at their best at this time; nor were they helped by his nagging doubts over the support he could expect from the ministers, and Liverpool in particular, in London.

In that city, the news of Masséna's retreat was greeted with joy and delight. The long stalemate had dampened hopes, and on 3 March the radical weekly paper the *Examiner*, run by Leigh Hunt, poured cold water on 'extravagant expectations'. 'There seems,' it declared with great confidence, 'no reason for altering the opinion so often expressed by this paper, that happen what may partially, the ultimate loss of the Peninsula is as certain as it ever was, and that we are only delaying the catastrophe by needless proofs of a valour, which our enemies most probably admire more than our Allies.'[23] Not all intellectuals were so wrong-headed. A month later Walter Scott was celebrating the victory, which he attributed entirely to 'the coolness and generalship of Wellington manifested not in military [matters] only but in the firm and confidential feelings with which he has inspired our allies . . . It is astonishing with what unspeakable incredulity the opposition folks maintained this retreat to have been a mere colour'.[24]

The Opposition was deeply embarrassed by the news. They had prophesied disaster so long and so consistently that success was bound to cast doubt upon their judgement, and even to shed credit upon the ministry which had persisted in the campaign in Portugal in the face of their advice. As recently as 18 March George Ponsonby, the Whig leader in the Commons, had sarcastically remarked that 'our success consists in having lost almost the whole of Portugal, and that our army is now confined or hemmed in between Lisbon and Cartaxo'. He had gone on to ask: 'How long can this country support this expense?' and to declare 'that neither Spain nor in Portugal has anything happened that can give us reason to believe that the war there will terminate to our advantage, although I wish it sincerely'.[25]

The Opposition leaders handled the problem in the best way possible, by publicly admitting that they had been wrong. On 26 April 1811 when Liverpool moved a Vote of Thanks to Wellington and his army, Grey rose and seconded the motion. His praise for Wellington was generous: 'By the most patient perseverance under unfavourable circumstances, and at the moment of action by the most skilful combination of force and the most determined courage, a great success had been achieved.' He conceded that the result was very different from what he expected although he could not resist a touch of his habitual pessimism, in the form of a warning that the success might simply provoke Napoleon into a greater effort, while he could not see how ultimate success could be achieved unless the Spaniards took a greater part in the war.[26]

On the same day in the Commons a similar motion was proposed by Perceval, seconded by Canning, and supported by Tarleton, Lord George Grenville (Lord Grenville's nephew) and Ponsonby. The Whig leader now declared that he 'was of opinion that the campaign was judiciously planned, and ably executed; and that the result had not tended more to exalt the glory, than to insure the safety of the country'.[27] Even Whitbread, who was not in the House at the time, took an early opportunity to place on the record that 'he should have concurred most cheerfully and cordially in the vote [of Thanks]'.[28] Among the Opposition leaders only Lord Grenville did not publicly recant his views, a silence which did not go unnoticed, as his brother warned him: 'Your abstaining from the praise of Lord Wellington after the speeches of Grey and Ponsonby and Lord Lansdowne and Whitbread, is quoted *ad invidium*.'[29]

Wellington's success also helped convince the government to embrace a more active policy in the Peninsula. On 6 March, well before news of Masséna's retreat reached London, the Cabinet had agreed to double the subsidy to

Portugal to £2 million in 1811. But it still had to decide whether to limit its commitment to the defence of Portugal, and perhaps even to withdraw some troops in order to save money, or to increase their effort in order to take the war to the French in Spain. Liverpool asked Wellington to explain his plans for operations beyond the defeat of Masséna's army. In reply Wellington reiterated his view that Portugal was the keystone of British strategy in the Peninsula:

> Depend upon it that Portugal should be the foundation of all your operations in the Peninsula, of whatever nature they may be; upon which point I have never altered my opinion. If they are to be offensive, and Spain is to be the theatre of them, your commanders must be in a situation to be entirely independent of all Spanish authorities; by which means alone they will be enabled to draw some resources from the country, and some assistance from the Spanish armies.[30]

He argued that British resources should be concentrated in the main army under his command, rather than costly diversions like the garrison of Cadiz, and warned that any reduction of the army would lead to an immediate end of offensive operations.

By the time this letter reached England at the end of May the ministers had come to appreciate the full extent of Wellington's success. The Cabinet proceeded to renew unequivocally its commitment to Wellington's plans. Any idea of a reduction in the army in Portugal was abandoned and instead no fewer than 7,000 reinforcements including 1,300 cavalry were promised, while Wellington was reminded that he already possessed the authority to withdraw troops from the garrison of Cadiz and was encouraged to do so if he needed more men. Other problems, such as the chronic shortage of specie, remained, but the fever for economy had burnt itself out, and the ministers were clearly ready to embark on a steady expansion of their efforts in Portugal. The change in policy was formally established in new instructions issued to Wellington now that his operations seemed likely to take him beyond the Spanish frontier. In a private letter accompanying the instructions Liverpool told Wellington: 'You will see that a complete latitude has been given to your discretion by the Instructions sent out upon the present Occasion – You will feel yourself therefore fully at liberty to act in the manner which may appear to you to be most advantageous for the general Cause.'[31]

The terms had been set on which Wellington would conduct the rest of the war relying, as he always preferred, on his own judgement with the support, but without the interference, of his political masters. It would take time before his distrust of Liverpool would disappear completely, but the commitment made in May 1811 held fast through bad times as well as good and proved one of the foundations for his ultimate success.

CHAPTER TWENTY-FIVE

FUENTES DE OÑORO
(April–June 1811)

O N 18 APRIL 1811 Lieutenant-General Viscount Wellington rode into the
sleepy provincial town of Nisa in eastern Portugal at the head of his staff.
He was less than a fortnight short of his forty-second birthday, and he had
spent the night before at Castello Branco some thirty-one miles to the north,
on the other side the Tagus. It was a fair ride on mountain roads, and before he
went to bed that night he would write nine letters, five of them to the Secretary
of State, ranging from a broad survey of the strategic situation in the Peninsula
to forwarding a request from Major-General Alexander Campbell, as colonel
of the York Light Infantry, to send to England fifty French deserters who had
volunteered to serve in his regiment.[1] The following day he rode on, reaching
Elvas, some sixty miles to the south, in the middle of the afternoon of 20 April,
five days after he left the main army blockading Almeida. After four busy days
at Elvas, he turned around and rode back north, covering the 170 miles in only
four days, as he hurried on the last couple of days after learning that the French
army had again taken the field. Wellington did not regard these rides as at all
remarkable, but they are a reminder of the importance of his physical tough-
ness and stamina, and of the good health and resilience that underpinned his
constant activity through five years of war in the Peninsula. He was a light, lean
man, neither tall nor obviously strong, but very few of his subordinates, or even
the much younger men on his personal staff, had the endurance to keep pace
with him, month after month, without returning home or taking leave.

Wellington rode south to see why Beresford was making such slow progress
in his operations against Badajoz. It was a month since Wellington had detached
him with the Fourth, Second and Portuguese divisions, but little appeared to
have been accomplished. Beresford had suffered an embarrassing setback at
Campo Mayor on 25 March when he had failed to capitalise on the defeat of
some French cavalry and allowed a convoy of heavy guns to escape to Badajoz.
His engineers had also struggled to contrive a makeshift bridge over the

Guadiana with unsuitable materials, taking valuable time and ending with a result that was ingenious but not really adequate or reliable.[2]

Despite these problems Wellington was confident of success, telling Liverpool: 'I understand that the garrison is very weak, and I should hope that it will not hold out long. It does not appear that there is any chance of the place being relieved, unless the enemy should determine to raise the siege of Cadiz and quit Andalusia.' He also believed that it was only a matter of time before the garrison of Almeida was starved into surrender, and, looking ahead, he contemplated the possibility of either advancing against Soult in Andalusia and raising the siege of Cadiz, or turning his attention to Ciudad Rodrigo, 'and afterwards to push on our operations into the heart of Spain, and open the communication with Valencia. This latter plan, if practicable, would relieve Cadiz and the south of Spain as soon and as effectively as the first mentioned.'[3] It was unusual for Wellington to explain his hopes for future operations in this way, at least in letters home, but Liverpool had asked for an indication of his plans, and his confidence was high after the rapid advance through Portugal.

When Wellington reached Elvas on the afternoon of 20 April he found that Beresford had captured the old fortress of Olivenza and driven the French back to the mountains that marked the boundary between Estremadura and Andalusia. This was encouraging but reports soon arrived suggesting that Soult was collecting his forces to march to the relief of Badajoz, which made it 'urgent that not a moment should be lost' in undertaking the siege.[4] On 22 April Wellington and his staff reconnoitred the fortress and there was some fighting between his escort and a part of the garrison which sortied out to cover the withdrawal of a foraging party.

In besieging Badajoz the most obvious plan was to follow the precedent set by the French only a couple of months before and attack the southern face of the fortress. However the engineers calculated that they could not hope to achieve a practicable breach in the southern walls in less than twenty-two days after breaking ground, while Wellington estimated that they would only have sixteen days of open trenches before Soult would be able to disrupt the siege.[5] Faced with this constraint Colonel Richard Fletcher, the chief engineer, proposed an alternative line of attack, concentrating on the detached fort of San Cristobal on the northern side of the Guadiana and the eastern wall of the castle. This was attacking the fortress at its strongest point, but San Cristobal was on high ground overlooking the castle, and if the fort could be carried and the castle wall breached, the fortress as a whole would be untenable. It would be a difficult operation but it offered the prospect of success in the time available and both the engineers and Wellington were confident of success.[6]

However on the night of 23 April the Guadiana rose sharply, carrying away the improvised bridge at Jurumenha. It was ten days before the bridge could be re-established, and this loss of time virtually doomed the siege from the outset. Yet Wellington remained surprisingly optimistic. He rode north on 25 April leaving Beresford with detailed instructions for both the conduct of the siege and the covering operations. If Soult advanced to relieve the fortress Beresford would have to decide whether to withdraw across the Guadiana or stand and fight, depending on the strength of Soult's army. 'I authorize him to fight the action if he should think proper, or to retire if he should not.'[7] Spanish cooperation would be crucial for Castaños and Blake had almost as many men as Beresford, their presence would ensure that the allies would outnumber any force Soult would be able to put into the field. Fortunately Castaños was remarkably generous, waiving his claim, as the senior general, to command the whole allied force, and working effectively with Beresford for the common good.[8]

Over the course of the Peninsular War Wellington was repeatedly surprised by the speed with which the French army could recover from defeat, and there would be no more striking example of this remarkable resilience than the revival of the Army of Portugal in April 1811. Bedraggled, exhausted and thoroughly demoralised it had retired from Sabugal and gone into quarters beyond Salamanca. Masséna gave his men no more than a fortnight to rest and enjoy regular rations before beginning to collect them again for a fresh campaign, and they responded, not with enthusiasm, but with a weary professionalism that did them proud. It was an unhappy army that Masséna had collected at Ciudad Rodrigo; the men were far from fully recovered from their ordeal and had no faith in their general, but they were good soldiers and were willing to make one more effort to rescue their beleaguered comrades in Almeida. There was a strong imperative in the French army against abandoning a garrison if there was any chance of saving it, and over the years French generals would run great risks in their efforts to raise allied sieges. Masséna took the field with the hope of revictualling Almeida, and so maintaining possession of a foothold in Portugal, but if he could not achieve this, he intended at least to bring off its garrison. He had done his best to strengthen his army, and had been helped by finding thousands of convalescents and drafts waiting at Salamanca to join their regiments. With two small brigades of cavalry and thirty gun teams borrowed from the Army of the North, Masséna had a total force of about 48,000 men, including 42,000 infantry, 4,500 cavalry and 38 guns.[9]

Wellington had arrived back at headquarters on the evening of 28 April and Charles Stewart, who had recently returned from England, reported that: 'Lord W[ellingto]n is in high health and I never saw him in such good spirits or so confident.'[10] This was despite the fact that the allies were significantly outnumbered; Wellington had barely 40,000 men and from this he needed to deduct Pack's Portuguese brigade and the British 2nd Foot which maintained the blockade of Almeida. Not counting these he had only about 23,000 British and

11,000 Portuguese infantry, and fewer than 2,000 cavalry in all. Only in artillery, where they had forty-eight guns (four British and four Portuguese batteries), were the allies superior. Twelve months earlier Wellington would not have dreamt of accepting battle on such odds, so close to the frontier, and his readiness to do so in May 1811 is a sign of how much the Portuguese troops had improved in the interim, and the extent to which the French had lost their air of invincibility.

The allies occupied a strong position running south from the ruins of Fort Conception to the village of Fuentes de Oñoro eight miles away. The line was marked by a steep ridge with the Dos Casas stream running through a deep gully at its eastern foot. The village of Fuentes de Oñoro made a good outpost, but the country beyond, to the south, was open, so that Wellington's right flank was vulnerable. This was made more serious because the army's lines of communication, and the road by which it would retreat in the event of a defeat, lay on this flank, south-west of the main position, on the way to Sabugal.

Masséna advanced from Ciudad Rodrigo on 2 May and reached the allied position in the middle of the following day. He reconnoitred it and decided to attack the village of Fuentes, supported by a mere demonstration by Reynier's men further north. It was a remarkably crude plan, for the village was a natural stronghold being solidly built with many stone enclosures, while it was on a slope rising to the west so that the allied troops would always have the higher ground. Any such contest favoured the defence, and would inevitably continue so long as each side was willing to throw fresh troops into the fray. Unless Masséna believed that Wellington did not really intend to stand and fight, it is hard to see how he can have hoped that this attack would succeed.[11]

The French attack began in the late afternoon or early evening and was entrusted to Ferey's division, though at least part of Marchand's division also saw some heavy fighting. The French attacked with spirit and overran most of the village before Wellington threw in the 1/71st, the 1/79th and the 2/24th and regained possession. A private soldier in the 71st tells the story:

> We stood under arms until three o'clock, when a staff-officer rode up to our Colonel and gave orders for our advance. Colonel Cadogan put himself at our head, saying 'My lads, you have had no provision these two days; there is plenty in the hollow in front, let us down and divide it.' We advanced as quick as we could run and met the light companies retreating as fast as they could. We continued to advance, at double quick time, our firelocks at our trail, our bonnets in our hands. They called to us, 'Seventy-first, you will come back quicker than you advance.' We soon came full in front of the enemy. The Colonel cries, 'Here is food, my lads, cut away.' Thrice we waved our bonnets, and thrice we cheered; brought our firelocks to the charge, and forced them back through the town.

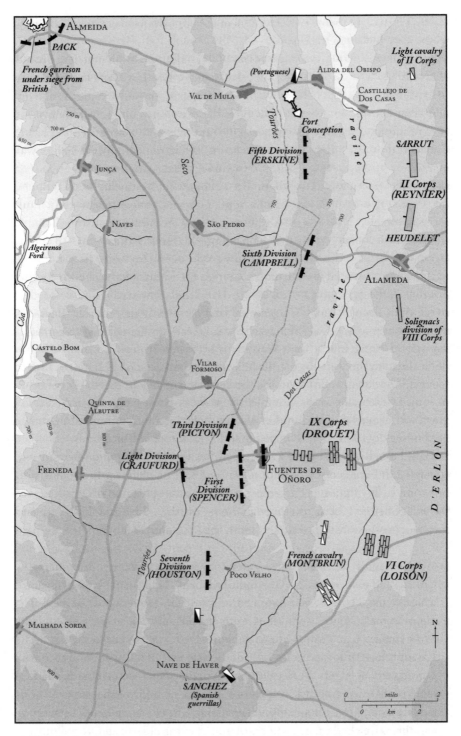

18 The battle of Fuentes de Oñoro, 3–5 May 1811. (All troop positions approximate, many conjectural.)

How different the duty of the French officers from ours. They, stimulating the men by their example, the men vociferating, each chaffing each until they appear in a fury, shouting, to points of our bayonets. After the first huzza the British officers, restraining their men, still as death, 'steady, lads, steady', is all you hear, and that in an undertone.

The French had lost a great number of men in the streets. We pursued them about a mile out of the town, trampling over the dead and wounded; but their cavalry bore down upon us and forced us back into the town, where we kept our ground, in spite of their utmost efforts.

In this affair my life was most wondrously preserved. In forcing the French through the town, during our first advance, a bayonet went through between my side and clothes, to my knapsack, which stopped its progress. The Frenchman to whom the bayonet belonged fell, pierced by a musket ball from my rear-rank man. Whilst freeing myself from the bayonet a ball took off part of my right shoulder wing, and killed my rear-rank man, who fell upon me. Narrow as this escape was, I felt no uneasiness; I was become so inured to danger and fatigue.

. . . After the firing had ceased we began to search through the town, and found plenty of flour, bacon and sausages, on which we feasted heartily, and lay down in our blankets, wearied to death. My shoulder was as black as a coal, from the recoil of my musket; for this day I had fired 107 round of ball cartridge. Sore as I was, I slept as sound as a top till I was awakened by the loud call of the bugle an hour before day.[12]

By nightfall, when the fighting was allowed to subside, the French had gained possession of no more than a few houses on the eastern side of the Dos Casas stream – and this small toehold had cost them more than 650 casualties. The allied defenders, being under cover, naturally suffered less: they had 259 casualties including 52 in the 1/71st.[13] To the surprise of the allies, daylight did not bring a renewed French attack. Instead an officer was sent in under a flag of truce requesting permission to remove the wounded and killed. This was agreed to and the soldiers fraternised cheerfully, shaking hands and sharing their food. Several French regimental bands played music and a carnival atmosphere reigned with the men dancing and playing football, while others enjoyed a leisurely meal.[14]

The truce lasted throughout 4 May and along the whole line, though there was little fraternisation or contact except at the village, and some reports mention skirmishing between the cavalry to the south of the village.[15] Masséna used the day to reconnoitre the allied position more closely. In the north he came rather too close to the Fifth Division, even within range of case shot, but Major-General Hay would not permit Bull's battery to open fire.[16] His main interest was in the open ground to the south where the allied flank appeared vulnerable. He decided to attempt to turn this flank with three divisions of infantry and almost all his cavalry. When this advance was seen to be making progress, he would renew the assault upon the village by Ferey's division and the two divisions of IX Corps. Reynier would not make a serious attack in the north unless the allies abandoned this part of their line.[17] The plan was certainly an improvement on the frontal assault mounted on the previous day, but Masséna's determination to storm Fuentes de Oñoro against the odds is rather puzzling, and he might have achieved greater results with less cost and no more risk by putting even more weight into the turning manoeuvre. Still, it is unwise for any modern critic, who inevitably cannot know all the circumstances and considerations influencing a general in Masséna's position, to be too assertive in their criticism.[18]

Wellington observed Masséna's reconnaissance and the steady shift of French infantry and cavalry to the south in the late afternoon, and drew his own conclusions. In the evening he ordered the Seventh Division from his central reserve to take up position around the village of Poco Velho, a couple of miles south of Fuentes de Oñoro, half-way to Nave de Haver. Julian Sanchez with his Spanish guerrillas already occupied Nave de Haver, and the allied cavalry covered the Seventh Division's right flank.[19] But a single division, supported by less than 2,000 cavalry and a few guerrillas, could not hold five miles of open ground against a serious attack. Wellington still had hard decisions to make.

Early on the morning of 5 May the French advanced, driving in the picquets of the Seventh Division and forcing the British 85th Foot and the Portuguese 2nd Caçadores from Poco Velho with considerable loss. Julian Sanchez hastily abandoned Nave de Haver before he was cut off from the rest of the allied army, and there was a good deal of fighting between the French and British cavalry. Wellington responded to the French attack by sending the Light Division south to reinforce the Seventh Division. It seems that his initial intention was to try to hold the line around Poco Velho, but he soon recognised that this would be impossible, or at least too dangerous, and ordered the whole of his right wing to withdraw and form a new line running west from Fuentes de Oñoro to Freneda, so that the allied position became a right angle with the village of Fuentes at the corner. The difficult retreat in the face of a superior and successful enemy was accomplished with remarkably light losses, but it meant that Wellington had surrendered his principal line of communication and retreat through Sabugal.

Cornet Francis Hall of the 14th Light Dragoons gives a glimpse of the confusion of this part of the battle:

Horses whose riders had been killed or overthrown ran wildly across the field, or lay panting in their blood. The general recontre was sub-divided into partial combats. Two heavy Dragoons were in the act of felling a Chasseur with their broad swords; his chaco [shako] resisted several blows, but he at length dropped. Another was hanging in the stirrup, while his horse was hurried off by a German Hussar, eager to plunder his valise. Some were driving two or three slashed prisoners to the rear: one wretch was dragged on foot between two Dragoons, but as he was unable to keep pace with their horses, and the enemy were now forming for a second charge, he was cut down.[20]

Although heavily outnumbered and often fighting at a disadvantage, the British cavalry succeeded in covering the retreat of the infantry of the Seventh and Light Divisions across several miles of open ground from Poco Velho to the new line running between Freneda and Fuentes de Oñoro. But the success of this dangerous movement was due at least as much to the steady discipline of the infantry themselves, who frequently had to present a bold face when the French cavalry threatened a charge. The infantry did not do much actual fighting in their withdrawal – although an effective volley from the Chasseurs Britanniques regiment was crucial in checking the French advance at the outset, and was warmly praised by Wellington in his official despatch.[21] The French infantry played little part in the pursuit while the cavalry concentrated most of their attention on the Light Division but were baffled by the coolness of Craufurd's men. The entire Seventh Division suffered only 237 casualties, most of them in the 85th and 2nd Caçadores. The Light Division suffered even less: only 67 casualties, while the British cavalry lost just 149 casualties.[22]

The one clear success achieved by the French cavalry occurred when they caught the picquets of the Guards brigade in open order and inflicted around 100 casualties in a few minutes. Despite this mishap Wellington had little difficulty in establishing his new line running east-west from Fuentes to Freneda, with the First Division to the east, the Seventh to the west, and the Light Division in reserve. Masséna made no serious attack on this line – there was some skirmishing in the gully of the Turone, and several batteries of artillery opened fire, but no real attempt was made to test the allied resolve. More surprisingly, Masséna made no effort to press the western end of the line, or to probe the gap between Freneda and the Coa. He had succeeded in turning the allied flank, but appeared unable to find any way of exploiting his advantage. He did not even detach a regiment of cavalry towards Sabugal to spread alarm among Wellington's rear echelons.[23] The preponderance of French cavalry, which had appeared so menacing in the early morning, achieved remarkably little. It is puzzling that 4,000 cavalry, supported by three divisions of infantry, should not have been allowed to play any further part in the battle. For rather than maintaining the pressure on the allied right, Masséna now resumed knocking his head against the granite walls of Fuentes de Oñoro, with predictable results.

The village was now a projecting buttress in the allied line, the hinge on which it turned, and in theory it was vulnerable to assault from the south as well as the east; in practice, it was as securely held as ever. Wellington had entrusted its defence to the 24th, 71st and 79th Regiments under the command of Lieutenant-Colonel Phillips Cameron of the 79th. As the French mounted one attack after another, Wellington reinforced the garrison with the combined light companies of the Third and First Divisions, the 6th Portuguese Caçadores, and the light companies of the Portuguese Line regiments in Ashworth's and Champalimaud's brigades. When even this was not enough to keep the French at bay, he threw in the 74th and 1/88th Regiments from the Third Division in a furious counter-attack which drove the French through the village and back to where they had begun. Altogether, in the two days of fighting, the allied army had suffered 1,804 casualties, including over 300 missing (mostly prisoners) and 241 killed. French losses were higher: 2,844 casualties in all, including 343 killed. The great majority of these casualties were incurred in the successive attacks on the village, although the French cavalry suffered rather more casualties (359) than might have been expected.[24]

Wellington made one of the few serious tactical errors of his career at Fuentes, for there is no doubt that the attempt to extend his line south of the village in an effort to cover the road to Sabugal was a mistake. He came close to acknowledging this himself, reportedly saying at dinner that he had never been in a worse scrape, and writing to his brother that, 'if Boney had been there, we should have been beaten'.[25] Yet it was the skill he displayed in recovering from the error that most impressed observers in both armies. George Scovell, who was never slow to criticise his chief, declared that 'the battle of Fuentes de Oñoro was to my mind one of the finest manoeuvres of Lord Wellington'.[26] George Simmons of the 95th told his parents proudly that: 'Lord Wellington is adored by his army; wherever he is, confidence of success is the result. The French own it that, next to Buonaparte, he is the first Captain in Europe. I wish his lordship had Buonaparte to contend with instead of Masséna; we should sooner settle the business.'[27] And Alexander Gordon, who had many opportunities to converse with French officers when sent to them under a flag of truce, confirms the point, telling his brother that Wellington 'remains the terror and admiration of the French army. They were all witness to his masterly change of position on the 5th, and which they were not able to prevent. You can have no idea what they think of him. They said the other day that their Emperor would not disdain to encounter him and that he was superior to the Archduke Charles'. Gordon's own verdict was simple: 'Lord W. was *perfect* throughout.'[28]

Fuentes de Oñoro was a clear victory – Wellington achieved his objective and Masséna failed to achieve his – but it was not the sort of victory that left the defeated army fleeing the battlefield in panic with the victors hot on their heels. Masséna's army was rebuffed but unbroken, and if he had chosen he could have renewed the action on the following day. Wellington might have taken the initiative himself and attacked the French on 6 May, but such a course would have been very risky (his army was still heavily outnumbered) and it offered no commensurate benefit. Even if he had completely defeated Masséna's army he was in no position to exploit the advantage, for he could not undertake the siege of Ciudad Rodrigo without a battering train, and his army was much too weak to undertake an advance on Salamanca. Conversely, even a small setback would be disproportionately costly, allowing the French to replenish Almeida, and denting the confidence of the allied army.

As the attempt to relieve Almeida had been defeated, the most that Masséna could now hope to achieve was to assist the garrison to escape. Three soldiers volunteered to attempt to carry a message to the governor, General Brennier. Two were caught and, as they were out of uniform, disguised as peasants, they were shot as spies. But the third, a private from the 6e Leger, succeeded, and Brennier acknowledged the receipt of his instructions by firing three heavy salvos at five minute intervals at ten o'clock that night.[29] On the following day, 8 May, the French army slowly withdrew towards Ciudad Rodrigo, but Reynier's II Corps maintained a strong outpost just behind the River Agueda at Barba de Puerco, the nearest crossing to Almeida. Wellington followed the French cautiously, and when convinced that their retreat was not a sham, he spread his army a little wider. On the afternoon of 10 May, he directed the Sixth Division to resume the blockade of Almeida, occupying the same positions as it had held before Masséna's advance.

That night (10/11 May) the French garrison slipped out of Almeida, leaving mines with slow fuses to explode and destroy the fortress behind them. The garrison formed two columns marching close together, with strict instructions not to halt on any pretext, or even to return fire. They avoided roads and paths, assuming that these would be well guarded, but maintained a clear sense of where they were going, and though they were followed and harassed the whole way by Denis Pack and the picquets, they had almost reached the bridge of Barba de Puerco before any sizeable body of British troops caught up with them. A scrambling fight ensued, but three-quarters of the garrison made its escape.

Wellington was mortified and furious. He told Liverpool: 'I have never been so much distressed by any military event as by the escape of even a man of them', while he described it to Beresford as 'the most disgraceful military event that has yet occurred to us'.[30] Letters from his staff suggest that his irritation was increased by the thought of how hostile critics at home might use the incident. Fitzroy Somerset told his brother: 'I fear the story which will be told in the *Moniteur* will weigh greatly with our Politicians, and give them a handle to abuse Lord Wellington.' And Alexander Gordon lamented 'the evil construction the enemies of Lord Wellington will put upon it'.[31]

Wellington did not publicly blame any officer for the escape of the garrison, although he used the occasion to reprimand Lieutenant-Colonel Basil Cochrane, of the 36th, for letting his men get out of hand in the pursuit, thereby suffering unnecessary casualties.[32] This was unfair, but Wellington evidently regarded this as part of a recurring problem caused by excessive impetuosity in both the infantry and the cavalry. Cochrane resented the slight and blamed Alexander Campbell, his divisional commander. The dispute simmered for weeks with Cochrane's sense of grievance growing as Campbell's patience wore thin. Finally Cochrane went too far, writing to Campbell in language that was clearly unacceptable to a superior officer. He was given the chance to withdraw his letter and apologise but refused, and was tried and convicted by general court martial on 24 August 1811. He was sentenced to a severe reprimand which, on Wellington's orders, was delivered not in private, but before the entire Sixth Division.[33] It was a further lesson, if one were needed, that Wellington would be as unsparing of his officers as he was of his men, and would not permit quarrels and feuds to fester until they became a serious threat to the army's efficiency. Soon afterwards Cochrane went home on sick leave and did not return to the Peninsula, although he remained in the army, and probably felt that he had been harshly treated.

Cochrane was not the only officer to feel aggrieved in the wake of the escape of the garrison of Almeida. Lieutenant-Colonel Charles Bevan of the 4th Foot felt that the whole weight of the blame rested on his shoulders, and, in the hope of clearing his name, he asked for an inquiry. When this was refused he blew his brains out on 8 July at Portalegre. His death caused a stir in the army, and some officers were inclined to blame Wellington. Major Thomas Downman of the artillery wrote in his diary: 'The feelings of our commander (Lord W.) will be as little troubled on this occasion, I imagine, as on most others. He has none. Ambition is his passion and carries him away, leaving those of very different sentiments to their own reflections.'[34] Although obviously hostile and certainly not typical of opinion in the army as a whole, this represents a persistent minority view, expressed on a number of occasions. In some respects it was plainly wrong. Wellington had not singled Bevan out for personal criticism,[35] and there was every reason for not reopening the affair by agreeing to an inquiry that would inevitably set one officer against another, adding to existing ill feelings. Bevan's complaint and sense of injustice had much less basis than Cochrane's, and pursuing the matter would simply reinforce the perception that he and his regiment had been the principal players in the escape of the French. But Bevan was evidently in no state of mind to keep the affair in perspective. He had long suffered from serious bouts of depression, which should probably have disqualified him from holding a position of such responsibility. Whether he committed suicide because he believed that he had been disgraced, or whether life simply proved too much for him to bear, is unclear; his last letter to his wife, written just a few days before his death, was warm, loving and positive, and makes no mention of Brennier, Almeida or Wellington's despatch.[36] The link, which was so glibly made by officers in the army, may have been well founded, but it remains unproven.

But Downman's view of Wellington raises broader questions which go well beyond the suicide of Charles Bevan and the escape of the garrison of Almeida. Was Wellington indeed as unfeeling and heartless as Downman believed, and what contributed to making this view of him, if not widespread, at least not uncommon? Part of the answer can be found in the terms of the rebuke to Colonel Cochrane mentioned above. In making his point vividly and with force Wellington wrote sharply, and there was at least a hint of sarcasm when he said that 'notwithstanding what has been printed in gazettes and newspapers, we have never seen small bodies, unsupported, successfully opposed to large; nor has the experience of any officer realised the stories, which all have read, of whole armies being driven by a handful of light infantry or dragoons.'[37] Officers would remember the lesson, but they would not warm to the teacher who addressed them thus, and Wellington was never reluctant to criticise the neglect or misconduct of his regimental officers. By doing so he immeasurably improved their performance and hence the lives of their men; he gave them good reason to feel proud of their accomplishments, and, contrary to some perceptions, he was not slow to praise them when they did well. But they craved something more, something to fire the imagination and warm the heart: devotion to a hero, belief in a cause, or the chimera of glory. Wellington never tried to appeal to the emotions of his officers as Nelson and Napoleon appealed to their followers. He despised gimcrack posturing, as he saw it,[38] and had no craving to be loved by his officers or men. This does not mean that he was indifferent to their opinion – he relished their approbation when it was spontaneously expressed – but he was too proud to seek to cultivate it. Nor, probably, did he have the necessary flair to do so, for his outlook and character were out of sympathy with the age of Romanticism, and if he had tried to act the heroic part he might have struck a false note from the outset.

Was he heartless? Was he the cold imperious upholder of military (and other) hierarchies, immune from the claims of humanity? Hardly, as a couple of instances from the spring of 1811 show. At the beginning of April, Major Henry Ridewood of the 2/52nd Foot wrote to Wellington complaining that his battalion had received insufficient credit in the public despatches describing recent actions. Wellington naturally refused to rewrite his despatches, already published, to please the major, but his reply was notable for its conciliatory tone:

> I received only yesterday your letter of the 1st April, and I am much concerned that any letter written by me should have given you a moment's uneasiness.
>
> It is impossible for me to enter into an explanation with any body on the contents of a public dispatch; but I am very certain that it is misunderstood by you, if you suppose that it contains any expression which can convey a notion that I was not convinced you had done your duty in the affair to which it relates, or that I was not satisfied with your conduct, or that any expression is omitted by which omission such meaning is conveyed.
>
> I have had more than one occasion to be satisfied with the whole Light division in the late affairs in which they have been engaged; and I have not failed to convey the expression of that satisfaction to the Prince Regent in the manner which I thought most suitable to the occasion, and I have certainly expressed dissatisfaction with none.[39]

And when Major-General Colville was disappointed at not being praised for his part in the second siege of Badajoz, Wellington invited him to dinner and paid him much attention ('I had a great deal of interesting and unreserved conversation with him') which helped soothe the feeling of neglect.[40] Then there are the letters he wrote to Major-General Alan Cameron, who had commanded a brigade in the Peninsula in 1808 and 1809–10, to tell him that his son, Lieutenant-Colonel Phillips Cameron, had been seriously wounded in the fighting at Fuentes, and subsequently that he had died of his wounds. Such letters are not easy to write well, but Wellington struck the right note on both occasions. In the first letter, when Cameron's wound, though dangerous, was not expected to prove mortal, he included a brief account of the battle, warmly praising the part played by the 79th (the regiment raised by the father and commanded by the son). And in the second, he gave the old warrior all the little comfort that could be given:

> You will always regret & lament his loss, I am convinced; but I hope that you will derive some consolation from the reflection that he fell in the perform-ance of his Duty at the Head of your brave Regt., loved and respected by all that knew him, in an action in which, if possible, the British Troops surpassed every thing they had ever done before & of which the result was most honour-able to his Majesty's Arms. At all events, if Providence had decreed to deprive you of your Son, I cannot conceive a string of circumstances more

honourable & glorious than those under which he lost his life in the Cause of his Country.

Believe me, however, that although I am fully alive to all these honourable circumstances attending his death, I most sincerely condole with you upon your loss.[41]

These letters were private and Wellington's critics knew nothing of them until many years later when his *Dispatches* were published. Nor should we overstate their significance; this was not the face that Wellington presented to the world most of the time. He could harry and bully officers whom he found incompetent, sometimes driving them to resign. He could, on a bad day, be harsh and unjust, and his deep-seated conviction that he was invariably in the right did not make mending fences easy. But he bore on his shoulders responsibilities that would have crushed a lesser man, and if the pressure led to the occasional venting of steam in which a bystander got scalded, it was a relatively small price compared to the number of lives that would be lost in a poorly handled battle. Not that most officers found Wellington difficult or unpleasant to deal with, and it is only fair to compare Downman's comments with those made at the same time by another gunner, Alexander Dickson, who wrote home: 'I have transacted business with many Generals, but never such a one as Lord Wellington, both for general knowledge, and attention to reason and suggestion.'[42]

On the morning of 16 May Wellington and his staff set off on the long ride south back to Estremadura, where things had not been prospering. At Badajoz trenches had been opened on both sides of the river on 8 May, but the garrison had made a large sortie two days later inflicting heavy casualties, and when the allied batteries opened fire on 11 and 12 May they were overwhelmed by the response from the guns of the fortress. News arrived on 12 May that Soult was advancing, and Beresford, judging that there was no hope of taking Badajoz in the next forty-eight hours, decided to lift the siege. Altogether the operation had cost some 533 British and 200 Portuguese casualties.

Beresford rather reluctantly gave battle at Albuera on 16 May. His army was much stronger than that of the French – roughly 35,000 allies (10,000 British, 10,000 Portuguese and 15,000 Spanish) compared to 24,000 French – but he lacked confidence in the Spanish troops and in himself. Soult turned the allied right flank but his advance was checked by the Spanish infantry, and a bloody firefight resulted. Beresford withdrew the Second Division from the centre and sent it to aid the Spaniards, but Colborne's British brigade was caught in the flank by French cavalry and three of its four battalions were destroyed in a matter of minutes. Nonetheless the other brigades of the Second Division took over the brunt of the fighting from the Spaniards, and both suffered and inflicted very heavy casualties in a fiercely contested battle of attrition. Beresford rode to the centre to try to bring up the Portuguese division, but in his absence Cole advanced with the Fourth Division, acting on his own responsibility. This decided the battle, although only after another bloody musketry duel. The French infantry gave way, but there was no pursuit, and both victors and vanquished were left equally stunned by the severity of the battle.

Both armies suffered very heavy losses at Albuera. Of 10,449 British soldiers present, 4,159 were killed, wounded or missing (882 killed, 2,733 wounded and 544 missing). The Spaniards lost 1,368 casualties and the Portuguese 389 so that the combined allied loss was only just fewer than 6,000 men. The French almost certainly lost more, although the official figures are unreliable and estimates vary, but it is likely that between one-third and one-quarter of Soult's entire army were rendered *hors de combat*. Beresford was completely unnerved by the burden of responsibility and by the cost of victory. Late in the battle he appears to have feared defeat and issued orders for a retreat, although the evidence is confused and it is just possible that this was a misunderstood part of his attempt to withdraw forces from the centre to reinforce the Second Division on the right.[43] The British infantry fought superbly but neither officers nor men had much confidence in their commander. The common view was expressed memorably by a soldier in the 7th Fusiliers: 'Turning to me Horsfall dryly said, "Whore's or Arthur?" meaning Wellington. I said, "I don't know, I don't see him." He rejoined, "Aw wish he was here." So did I.'[44]

Wellington reached Elvas on the afternoon of 19 May, three days after the battle. When he received Beresford's official despatch describing the battle, he was dismayed by its apologetic despondent tone, and instructed his staff to 'write me down a victory'. With Wellington lending a helping hand they recast the despatch keeping much of the original material but presenting it in a more positive form.[45] Wellington was equally anxious to console and reassure Beresford. He had already written, soon after reaching Elvas: 'You could not be successful in such an action without a large loss; and we must make up our minds to affairs of this kind sometimes, or give up the game.'[46] On 21 May he rode out to Albuera and went over the battlefield – his arrival being welcomed with intense relief by both the army and by Beresford. Despite Wellington's comfort Beresford could not regain his composure, and he was forced to retire to Lisbon where he spent several months in partial seclusion, before being able to slowly resume his duties. Wellington kept him at his side in 1812, but even then Beresford appeared nervous and inclined to counsel caution.

The combination of Albuera and the escape of the garrison of Almeida reinforced Wellington's conviction that he could not rely on his subordinates and that as far as possible he needed to supervise everything personally. After Brennier's escape he had told Liverpool: 'Possibly I have to reproach myself for not having been on the spot.' And: 'I certainly feel, every day, more and more the difficulty of the situation in which I am placed. I am obliged to be everywhere, and if absent from any operation, something goes wrong.'[47] He told his brother William: 'I begin to be of opinion, with you, that there is nothing on earth so stupid as a gallant officer.'[48] The opportune return of Rowland Hill from England at this time meant that Wellington could leave the southern wing of his army in safe hands if he returned to the north, but he had become less inclined than ever to delegate much power or discretion to his subordinates, just when the growing size of the army made this more necessary.[49]

On 23 May Wellington took stock of the strategic situation in the wake of Albuera. He knew that Drouet's IX Corps was being transferred from the Army of Portugal to join Soult in Andalusia, and he concluded that this would make the French too strong for an allied offensive in the south with the aim of raising the siege of Cadiz. For the moment he lowered his sights and looked no further than the capture of Badajoz and perhaps Ciudad Rodrigo. He knew that the relief of Cadiz was a matter of keen concern in England and wrote to Liverpool, asking that the public have patience 'and allow us to do our work gradually'.[50] On the whole he remained thoroughly optimistic. Portugal had been saved and he was much encouraged by reports of the scare that had swept Europe in the early months of 1811 following a sharp deterioration in relations between France and Russia. 'If there is a war in the north I think we shall make Boney's situation in Spain this year not a bed of roses; if there is not a war in the north this year, it is impossible that his fraudulent and disgusting tyranny can be endured much longer; and if Great Britain can only hold out I think we shall yet bring the affairs of the Peninsula to a satisfactory termination.'[51]

Wellington seldom expressed his view of Napoleon's regime during the war, but the phrase 'disgusting tyranny', which he repeats in several letters at this time, gives some idea of his attitude – the basis of which he apparently felt was too self-evident to need elaboration. A few weeks later, however, the capture of a letter from Joseph Bonaparte to Napoleon provoked the comment: 'It shows that this tyrant does not treat his relations or even his brothers, better than he does other people; and gives ground for hope that his tyrannical temper will at no distant period deprive him of the advantages which he would derive from the Austrian alliance.'[52]

The immediate task was to resume the siege of Badajoz. Hamilton's Portuguese division had reinvested the fortress on 19 May, and preparations had been made to bring back the siege guns and other equipment from Elvas. The British engineers were full of confidence, and on 30 May, hours before trenches were again opened, they boldly predicted that Badajoz would fall within a week. The plan of attack was essentially the same as in the first siege;

the easier line of attack from the southern side had again been discarded as being too slow, for Wellington was convinced that time was short: 'If we don't succeed in a few days, we shall not succeed at all.'[53]

On the morning of 3 June, four allied batteries mounting thirty-four guns opened fire against San Cristobal and the castle. Wellington was so hopeful of rapid progress that he drafted a summons to be sent in to the garrison that evening, if a breach had been made, or on the following morning.[54] Shortly before six o'clock in the evening Fletcher reported that good progress had been made, a large part of the wall had fallen, but that there was, as yet, no practicable breach. He recommended the construction of a more advanced battery, and his confidence was undiminished.[55] Following this, however, progress slowed to a crawl as each subsequent day's battering had surprisingly little effect and the garrison worked throughout the night to clear debris from the foot of the breaches. Each evening Fletcher renewed his assurances that the next day's battering would be decisive, and each day he was disappointed in the results. On the evening of 4 June Wellington decided that they should persist in the existing line of attack despite the slow progress and ominous signs that the garrison troops were constructing interior defences to prolong the siege even if the castle fell.[56] Fresh batteries were opened and on the night of 6 June an unsuccessful attempt was made to storm San Cristobal which cost almost 100 casualties. Time was now pressing. Wellington believed that if the fortress did not fall by 10 June he would have to raise the siege, for the French armies were certainly on the move. The Seventh Division made a second attempt to storm San Cristobal on the night of 9 June; if it had succeeded Wellington might have been tempted to press his luck and prolong the operation, but it failed with the loss of 55 killed, 81 wounded and 4 missing.[57] On the following day Wellington gave orders to raise the siege that night.

Wellington admitted to Liverpool that he was 'much annoyed' by the failure of the siege, although he was convinced that 'I could not have taken the place with the means we had of carrying on the operation.'[58] Alexander Gordon worried that 'there will be a good deal said in England about its failure I have no doubt' but he still thought that they had been right to make the attempt.[59] Rumours reported that Wellington blamed the failure on the engineers and declared that 'if he undertakes another siege, he will be his own engineer';[60] it is notable that his relations with his engineers and gunners were seldom so comfortable as with the rest of the army. But failure always breeds ill humour and whatever his private views Wellington had been careful to give generous praise to all the officers of the ordnance department in his official despatch, naming many of them with approbation and singling out Alexander Dickson – 'from whose activity, zeal and intelligence, the British service has derived great advantage in the different operations against Badajoz' – for special praise.[61]

36 *The Battle of Talavera, July 28th 1809* by William Heath. This stylised depiction of the battle was published a few years later. Wellesley is in the centre on a white horse directing the battle.

37 *Lord Castlereagh* by Thomas Lawrence, painted in 1809–10. A notoriously poor speaker in Parliament, Castlereagh's abilities were not properly recognised until he became Foreign Secretary in 1812, but as Secretary for War from 1807–09 he did much to advance Wellington's career. He was a tall, handsome man but had a cold aloof manner and was much more reserved than Wellington.

38 Sir Charles Stewart was Castlereagh's half-brother, and served as Under-Secretary for War from 1807–09 while retaining his military rank and serving in the Coruña, Oporto and Talavera campaigns. From 1809 to 1812 he served as Adjutant-General at Wellington's headquarters, but he disliked the paperwork and complained that Wellington did not confide in him.

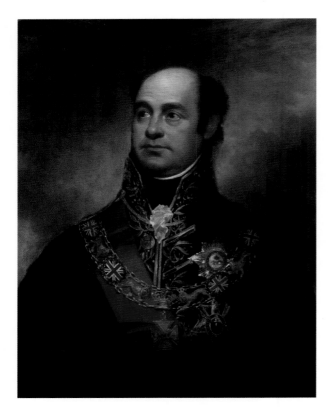

39 Field Marshal Lord Beresford by Sir William Beechey, painted in 1814. William Warre, Beresford's ADC, who had the chance to study him closely, wrote: 'There exists not a more honourable, firm man, or a more zealous Patriot. His failings are mere foibles of a temper naturally warm and hasty, and a great zeal to have everything right, without much patience.' Beresford did more than anyone to assist Wellington's work in the Peninsula, and his success in reviving the Portuguese army was crucial to all Wellington's campaigns from 1810 onwards.

40 As British minister in Lisbon, Sir Charles Stuart ably supported Wellington's operations and bore the brunt of day-to-day business with the Portuguese regency. Brougham, who had been a great friend of his when they were both students, described him to Creevey in 1814: 'He is a plain man, of some prejudices, caring little for politics and of very good practical sense. You will find none of his prejudices … at all of an aristocratic or disagreeable kind. He has no very violent passions or acute feelings about him.'

41 Troops bivouacked near Vila Velha, on the evening of 19 May 1811, by Thomas Staunton St Clair. St Clair was a British officer who served for much of the Peninsular War with the Portuguese, and his lively depictions of life on campaign, and of a number of battles, were engraved and published at the time.

42 and 43 A Portuguese infantryman of the 20th Line regiment (*left*) and a Portuguese caçador of the 4th Battalion (*right*). Portuguese troops, particularly their infantry, played an essential role in Wellington's army in all its campaigns from 1810 onwards. They endured harsh conditions, and were often hungry (their commissariat was less efficient than the British) but suffered less from disease. Wellington generally combined British and Portuguese brigades together to form an allied division, although some Portuguese brigades acted independently. The caçadores (Portuguese light infantry) strengthened the allied skirmish line and ensured that it was at least equal, and often superior, to the French. In the Pyrenees in 1813 Wellington described his Portuguese troops as 'the *fighting cocks* of the army'.

44 At the battle of Busaco, the British infantry counter-attack as the French reach the summit of the ridge. The illustration shows the repulse of Reynier's corps by Picton's division near the village of San Antonio de Contaro.

45 Sir Thomas Picton was one of the most colourful of Wellington's subordinates and was liked as well as admired by many of those who worked most closely with him. His reputation has suffered unduly from the hostility of the memoirists of the 88th and the Light Division. Still, there is no denying his furious disposition, coarse language and coldness to those who incurred his disfavour, but he was a capable divisional commander.

46 Wellington stretched the rules of seniority to keep Robert Craufurd in command of the Light Division while more senior officers commanded brigades in other divisions, evidently valuing his ability highly. Craufurd's harsh discipline made him bitterly unpopular with the officers and men of his command, although in time this came to be mixed with grudging respect. He mishandled the action at the Coa in July 1810, but recovered his nerve in time for the battle of Busaco. He was killed in the storming of Ciudad Rodrigo.

47 Sir Galbraith Lowry Cole by Sir Thomas Lawrence, painted in 1811. Cole commanded the Fourth Division from the autumn of 1809 to the end of the war, apart from when he was absent recovering from illnesses or wounds. He was a capable and popular divisional commander, 'a pleasant, sensible, agreeable man' according to Lieutenant-Colonel Bingham, who lived well on campaign and had a reputation for looking after his men.

48 Marshal Masséna was perhaps the most senior and distinguished of Napoleon's marshals. He had served in the Royal Army before the revolution, rising from the rank of private to become a senior non-commissioned officer, while under the empire Napoleon entrusted him with many important commands. Although he was known for being fond of money (whether obtained legitimately or not) and women, he was a thoroughly professional and capable soldier whose reputation suffered from being presented with an almost impossible task.

49 Marshal Marmont was an able, energetic general, full of self-confidence and keen to make the most of his opportunities. He instilled new life and vigour into the French Army of Portugal when he assumed the command in 1811, and forced Wellington to give up the second siege of Badajoz. But this early success encouraged his natural confidence and he was shocked to learn of the fall of Ciudad Rodrigo in January 1812 before he could do anything to intervene to save it. He was badly wounded at the outset of the battle of Salamanca in July 1812, but cannot escape responsibility for placing his army in a perilous position.

50 The green-clad riflemen of the 95th and the 5/60th were the elite skirmishers in the allied army, protecting the close-order infantry deployed in their rear from French skirmishers, and harassing French troops as they advanced. Deployed in open order these riflemen took advantage of natural cover and took their time to fire when a target presented itself. But success in many skirmishing actions depended as much on the careful control of reserves as the individual skill of the light infantrymen.

51 Watercolour portrait of Wellington, *c.* 1812–16, by Juan Bauzil (or Bauzit, or Bauziel). Bauzil also painted three miniatures of Wellington between 1812 and 1814, and many other miniatures for the Spanish court both before 1808 and after 1814.

52 *A View of the Storming and Taking of Badajoz in Spain on April 6th 1812.* Cheap topical prints such as these spread news of the progress of the war to a wide section of British society. In the foreground men of the Third Division climb scaling ladders into the Castle, while in the background can be seen the desperate but unsuccessful attempts to storm the breaches. The army lost 3,713 casualties in the storming of Badajoz, with officers suffering disproportionately heavily as they attempted to rally and lead forward their men in yet another attempt to overcome impossible obstacles. Wellington was moved to tears by the casualties and wrote home angrily denouncing the lack of specialist troops trained to undertake sieges.

53 Wellington sat for Goya while in Madrid in August 1812, but this portrait was not completed then, or some touches were added later, probably when Wellington visited Madrid again in 1814. The painting was purchased on behalf of the British nation in 1961, but was then stolen and remained missing for four years, allegedly as a protest at the use of public money for such a purpose when pensioners were struggling to pay their television license fee. The affair attracted considerable publicity at the time.

54 *See the Conquering Hero Comes*, a print published on 14 September 1812 celebrating Wellington's entry into Madrid following his triumph at Salamanca. In the background the French flee the city, chased out of it by women wielding brooms. The allied army was received in Madrid with wild enthusiasm and rejoicing, and many of the British troops were astonished by the warmth of their welcome.

55 Carts, mostly drawn by oxen rather than horses in the Peninsula, were the lifeblood of Wellington's army, carrying baggage for a regiment on the march (a practice he endeavoured to prohibit), as well as transporting sick and wounded men to hospital, and supplies from magazines at the furthest navigable point on the main rivers to forward depots where they would be carried forward by mule trains.

56 and **57** British infantry of the Peninsular War. On the left, two soldiers from the 6th and 23rd Regiments, both of which served with distinction under Wellington in the Peninsula, and on the right, soldiers of the 1st Regiment of Foot Guards in marching order. The latter illustration comes closer to depicting how soldiers would actually have looked on campaign, although even here the clothes and shoes are in better condition than most men would have had after a few weeks' rough wear in the Peninsula.

58 Wellington's dressing case with silver and ivory fittings. George Elers described Wellington in India as 'remarkably clean in his person' and commented with surprise that he sometimes shaved twice a day; while in the Peninsula, Mr Larpent remarked that he was 'remarkably neat, and most particular in his dress'. Officers in the Guards gave him the nickname 'the Beau', which he relished, although he generally dressed very plainly.

59 A pontoon bridge over the River Esla. Wellington's advance to Vitoria was a strategic triumph based on rapid marches through difficult country which gave the French no time to concentrate their superior forces against him.

60 Riflemen in the foreground act as snipers while staff officers observe a French attack which takes place in the background. Denis Dighton was a contemporary artist who specialised in military scenes and uniform plates, and for some years enjoyed the patronage of the Prince Regent.

61 A highly stylised depiction of the battle of Vitoria, with Wellington depicted in the centre of the action.

62 *Wellington and glory, or the victory of Vittoria – he came, he saw, he conquer'd*, a print published soon after the news of the battle reached London in July 1813. Wellington is depicted as a generic hero, complete with a white horse. A young officer proffers Marshal Jourdan's baton, which was captured in the battle, and summarises the news of the victory, while the officer on the far right says 'There goes King Joey!' Wellington intones, 'May this Trophy prove – our hope of future victory, and England once more restore Spain to her lawful Soveriegn [*sic*]!'

63 *Wellington at Sorauren*, 27 July 1813, by Thomas Jones Barker, and exhibited at the Royal Academy in 1853. This is a later, rather romanticised painting, noticeably different in style from contemporary images of Wellington.

64 In an attempt to avoid the strong landward defences, the British besiegers attacked San Sebastian across the tidal estuary of the River Urumea, but the difficulty of the approach and the strength and tenacity of the French resistance led to the failure of the first attempt to storm, and heavy losses in the second, successful attempt.

65 A watercolour study of Wellington's head by Thomas Heaphy, painted at headquarters in 1813. Heaphy was a talented and successful watercolour artist who visited the army in the autumn of 1813 on a private venture, finding no shortage of officers happy to sit for him. He made a large number of studies of faces and heads as preparation for the construction of a grand picture of Wellington, his staff and subordinates.

66 *Field Marshal the Duke of Wellington giving orders to his Generals previous to a General Action* by Thomas Heaphy, engraved by Anker Smith and published in 1822. The caption includes 'The Scene upon the Ground of the Battle of Nivelle' which identifies this as the 'General Action'. Heaphy's grand painting was complicated by many more officers desiring (and willing to pay) to be included, so that it became progressively more crowded. The current location of the original, if it survives, is unknown.

Wellington raised the siege because Marshal Marmont, who had replaced Masséna in command of the Army of Portugal, had marched south and joined Soult. Together they were able to put 60,000 men into the field, compared to Wellington's 54,000. In other circumstances Wellington might have considered giving battle despite being outnumbered, but three months of intense activity and much bloodshed had wearied the army, while there was little appetite for a third siege of Badajoz in the full heat of an Estremaduran summer. He therefore withdrew to a strong position behind the River Caya running north-east from Elvas through Campo Mayor. The French probed this position on 22 June, and there was some skirmishing but no serious fighting, and when the magazines of Badajoz had been fully replenished the armies retired into cantonments.

It was a flat end to a campaign that had promised so much, and Wellington must have been disappointed that the high hopes of April had come to so little. Almeida had been taken but its garrison had escaped and its defences had been destroyed. Two sieges of Badajoz had failed, while the half-hearted attempt to blockade Ciudad Rodrigo had been given up before it had really begun. Masséna's army had been defeated at Fuentes de Oñoro, and Soult's ground down in a bloody battle of attrition at Albuera, but this had not prevented them from taking the field again to relieve Badajoz a few weeks later. The glory garnered by such barren victories was of little interest to Wellington, although they did more firmly establish the psychological superiority of the allied troops, and showed that the Portuguese infantry could manoeuvre and fight with the coolness and aplomb of veterans.

Looked at in the context of the war as a whole the significance of these months becomes more clear: the retreat of Masséna's army from Portugal gave Wellington the initiative and by his operations against Almeida and Badajoz he retained it. His first attempts to use his advantage failed, but only because of the extraordinary resilience of the French armies, and some urgent scrambling and unusual cooperation among their commanders. When Soult and Marmont collected an army of 60,000 men on the Portuguese frontier in June their objective was wholly defensive: to preserve their existing conquests, not to make new ones. The tide of war had turned on the Peninsula and there seemed no prospect of the French regaining the ascendancy unless Napoleon could once more send huge reinforcements across the Pyrenees, or gave up whole provinces of Spain to free the troops that occupied them for active operations. For the moment Wellington had been contained on the Portuguese frontier and the illusion of French rule in Spain could be preserved, but there was nothing inherently stable about this stalemate, and all the pressure was building on the allied side of the dam's wall.

The operations of May and June were viewed with indulgence by the public in Britain. The enthusiasm aroused by Masséna's retreat had transformed the mood of the country and, except among a few diehard radicals such as Cobbett, there was little inclination to cast doubt on the value or purpose of a victory. *The Times* greeted the news of Fuentes de Oñoro without caution or equivocation: 'Lord Wellington has not only turned the rude intruder out of the abode in which he sought to establish himself, but has really afterwards chastised him for his presumption in front of the premises.' A week later early reports of Albuera and the escape of the garrison of Almeida reached London. Again, *The Times* judged the battle to have been 'at once splendid and sanguinary', and attributed the escape of the garrison of Almeida in part to Brennier's skill and more to good fortune. Neither affair attracted even a hint of blame or recrimination. Even the *Examiner* told its radical readers that Wellington 'will at no remote period rank with the proudest names in our military history'.[62] In this context the panegyrics of the pro-government *Courier* appear redundant, for even well-disposed readers might raise an eyebrow over the assertion that at Albuera 'Soult retired to tell the same tale as Masséna, and to assure his Master that the troops of France must yield the palm and place of honour to those of Great Britain'. Yet even this pales before an article headed 'Lord Wellington like the Sun' which begins: 'A few words more on the man, to the wisdom of whose plans, to whose steadiness and unremitted presence of mind in the execution of them, this country – O! even that is too little – Europe and Humanity itself, are indebted for the present bright dawn of their hopes.' Remarkably this fulsome tribute was written by Samuel Taylor Coleridge, but such gross flattery did Wellington's reputation no good, nauseating anyone even a shade less enthusiastic and perpetuating partisan attitudes that might otherwise have faded away.[63]

Nonetheless the Opposition showed no inclination to criticise Wellington's operations, or even to raise awkward questions about Albuera. The humiliation of having to recant their previous criticism of Wellington's campaign in Portugal was still too fresh for the Whigs to risk an appearance of backsliding, and so they followed the government's lead and treated both Fuentes and Albuera as unequivocal victories, and supported a Vote of Thanks for Beresford.[64] Yet in private their old doubts quickly resurfaced. Grey told Grenville on 4 June: 'The news from Portugal I think very bad. I have little doubt the French will claim the victory.' And on the following day Auckland declared the prospects in the Peninsula 'neither cheerful nor promising'.[65]

The news of Fuentes coincided with the Regent's decision to reappoint the Duke of York as Commander-in-Chief. The moment was politically opportune, but pressure for the move came also from the Horse Guards, where the failing mental powers of Sir David Dundas had become increasingly evident.[66] The Opposition leaders would not risk offending the Prince by criticising the reappointment, but a handful of younger Whigs and radicals could not resist the chance to make mischief and were lauded in the press which was violent on the subject. *The Times* was no less indignant than the *Examiner* that a man condemned to ridicule by the press should thus be rehabilitated.[67] Strangely the news attracted less comment in the army than in the press, although it seems to have been generally welcomed.[68] Wellington, who had never received any favours from the Duke, told Torrens: 'I rejoice most sincerely. The arrangement is not less a matter of justice to him than it is beneficial to the public interests . . . I would not allow the mail to go without telling you how well satisfied I am with this arrangement, and I beg you to take an opportunity at conveying my congratulations to His Royal Highness.'[69]

Wellington was surprised at the new enthusiasm for the war in Britain and relieved at the absence of the criticism he had expected, but he did not trust the mood to last, telling Liverpool: 'People in England appear to me to be as much elated by any success, and so much depressed by any temporary check, that I feel difficulty in describing the state of our affairs.'[70] Nonetheless the absence of any outcry over Albuera or the escape of Brennier's garrison showed Wellington that he was no longer a prime target for the Opposition's attacks, and this may have allowed him to sleep a little easier. The consensus of Westminster would probably not survive an outright defeat, but it was reassuring to find that he need not fear the political consequences of lesser setbacks and unduly costly successes, such as were bound to occur occasionally in any sustained series of campaigns.

CHAPTER TWENTY-SIX

CIUDAD RODRIGO
(July 1811–January 1812)

A FTER THE INTENSE activity of the spring and early summer, the rest of 1811 proved an anticlimax for the allied army in the Peninsula. Wellington accepted that a fresh attack on Badajoz would simply bring Soult and Marmont together for its relief, and instead turned his attention to Ciudad Rodrigo, establishing a blockade of the fortress on 10 August. However, Marmont combined with Dorsenne (who had replaced Bessières in command of the Army of the North) to advance to its relief in late September with 58,000 men. Wellington had left Hill with a substantial force near Elvas to guard the southern route into Portugal, so he had only 46,000 men in hand and had little choice but to lift the blockade. He assumed that the French would not advance beyond the fortress and was uncharacteristically careless, not concentrating the army or withdrawing to the strong position at Fuente Guinaldo a few miles to the rear. This left him in an uncomfortable position when Marmont and Dorsenne pressed forward on 25 September. The Third Division was most exposed and had a difficult retreat over more than four miles of open ground from El Bodon in the face of a powerful force of French cavalry.

Wellington was in the thick of the action and Charles Colville, who commanded one of Picton's brigades, wrote home: 'I must ever be thankful that he was at hand to direct, as he did, the general movements which his uncommon quickness and experience enables him to do with such happy effects, and by his presence authorizing such measures of defence and partial offence when without such authority retreat alone would have been justified.' Another officer commented that 'it is nothing less than miraculous how he escapes on these occasions, as he constantly exposes himself in the most unguarded manner'. Fortunately the French had no infantry at hand to support their cavalry, and the allied troops held their nerve just as they had done at Fuentes de Oñoro a few months before. The allies only lost 149 casualties in the action, fewer than the French, but if the infantry had shown any less discipline, or the cavalry less courage, the result could easily have been a small disaster.[1]

El Bodon was the only action of any significance fought by Wellington in the second half of 1811. Hill had a little triumph at the end of October when he made a long night march to catch Girard's division of Drouet's corps by surprise at Arroyo dos Molinos, scattering it to the winds and taking more than 1,300 prisoners, for the loss of less than 100 allied casualties. The action had little strategic significance, but was good for morale and enhanced Hill's reputation as the ablest, as well as one of the most popular, of Wellington's subordinates.

The French appeared to have found a way of containing the allies on the Portuguese frontier, and Wellington's high hopes of the spring were disappointed. The allied army was weakened by the large numbers of soldiers who were sick in hospital throughout the summer and autumn of 1811. The figures had been high even in April when there were 9,000 British rank and file sick and fewer than 35,000 present and fit for duty. Albuera and Fuentes de Oñoro led to a sharp increase (12,780 sick and fewer than 30,000 fit on 25 May) but there was no obvious improvement as those lightly wounded recovered and returned to their ranks; evidently their place in the hospitals was taken by victims of malaria, dysentery and other summer ailments. On 25 July there were still 12,277 sick and the figure never fell below this in the course of the year, reaching a peak of over 17,000 in October before falling sharply to 12,392 on 25 December.[2] According to Wellington, many of the sick were in newly arrived regiments that had served at Walcheren whose men, while apparently fit at first, quickly became ill in the Peninsula. Eating unripe fruit and drinking to excess often brought on their illness, but few died and most made a good recovery.[3] This may have been a little optimistic, for the official returns show that 3,404 soldiers of Wellington's army died between 1 July and 15 December 1811, a time when there was almost no action, compared to only 2,662 between 1 January and 15 June 1811, including all those killed at Albuera, Fuentes and during the pursuit of Masséna.[4] Even so, it is true that the great majority of soldiers who fell ill and went to hospital in these months recovered and returned to the ranks. Fortunately the Portuguese were less prone to disease, being accustomed to the climate and the endemic ailments, so that their sick rate was only about 70 per cent that of the British, despite all the privations they suffered from lack of supplies.[5]

The British government made up the casualties suffered at Albuera and Fuentes by sending some 5,000 reinforcements to the Peninsula, most of whom arrived during July; this restored the number of British rank and file fit for duty to just over 35,000 men, a figure around which it hovered for the rest of the year as subsequent reinforcements only just kept pace with the increasing number of sick. General Graham joined the army from Cadiz in early August, and Spencer went home – a change that was almost universally popular. Wellington treated his new second-in-command with great consideration, and Graham's previous hostility soon changed into admiration, so that the two men worked harmoniously, as well as efficiently, together; the only problem was Graham's health, especially the state of his eyes. Wellington's old friend Alexander Campbell left to take up a more lucrative command on Mauritius where he remained for the rest of the war, and Lowry Cole was forced home by illness at the end of the year, but fortunately returned in the middle of 1812. Almost no senior officer in the army, other than Wellington, served in the Peninsula for the whole five years from the spring of 1809 to the end of the war in 1814.[6]

Maintaining the army in the barren, thinly-populated uplands of northern Portugal around Almeida was not easy, especially as the land had been swept bare by the exactions of different armies over the previous three years. Wellington and his Commissaries General (first Robert Kennedy, then John Bissett) gave this a good deal of attention in the summer of 1811 as they replaced the ad hoc arrangements of 1810 with a more efficient system that was to serve the army well for much of the rest of the war. There was no shortage of supplies that could be obtained from Britain, or from North Africa, the Baltic or even North America. Over 800,000 barrels of flour were exported from America to the Peninsula in 1811, and the trade continued undiminished in 1812 and 1813 despite the outbreak of war between America and Britain.[7] Similarly almost half the forage corn consumed by the horses and mules of Wellington's army was imported, and no fewer than ninety-eight convoys of merchantmen, six of them containing over a hundred vessels, sailed to the Peninsula in 1811 alone, mostly from British ports. This vital logistical lifeline depended on the Royal Navy's command of the sea, which was never seriously threatened, even though individual ships were occasionally chased and captured by French privateers.[8]

The real difficulty lay in getting supplies from the coast to the army. The first stage was obvious: supplies should be taken by water as far as possible, and the Tagus, the Mondego and the Douro were all employed, with important commissariat stations established at the upper navigable limit of each. The final stage was also well established: most supplies would be carried to the divisions on the frontier by the mule-train, while the meat the soldiers ate would generally arrive on its own hooves. Wellington calculated that each mule could carry 200 pounds plus its own food, a further 30 pounds of corn. Ideally troops should be no more than three marches (twelve leagues, or rather more than forty miles) from their magazine, so that the mule-trains could make the return journey in six days. A single mule could carry enough biscuit to feed 33 men for six days, or rum for 100 men, rice for 200 men or corn for three horses with a little to spare.[9] The difficulty of bringing up feed for horses was obvious, and the commissariat regarded maintaining a single regiment of cavalry as comparable to feeding a whole division of infantry. The army needed more than 9,000 mules for the commissariat, and could not find enough to meet the demand, especially for Portuguese units, which Spanish muleteers would not deign to serve.[10]

This left an important middle stage between the river-heads and the forward magazines. In the past the army had relied on conscripting local bullock carts, along with their bullocks and owners, but this was both unpopular and inefficient, and evidently in 1811 there were insufficient carts to meet the demand. Wellington and Kennedy therefore decided to create a special force of 800 bullock carts specifically designed and made for the task, with bullocks and drivers permanently employed to operate them. They were to be organised into brigades of twenty-five carts, each brigade to have fifty-four bullocks, with eleven men and fourteen boys who would receive regular pay and rations. Two brigades would form a division, and be supervised by a commissariat clerk, while one officer of the commissariat would be responsible for 400 carts. Quarters were to be established at each stage along the road, between four and five leagues apart, with the route between Raiva on the Mondego and Celorico the first to be established.[11]

Even when all this was in place and working smoothly many supplies were obtained locally or brought in by private contractors. When the army began moving forward it frequently outmarched the mule-trains following in its wake and had to depend on what the commissaries could find near its route, but that was generally fresh country where supplies could be requisitioned. Wellington's logistical arrangements were neither simple nor one-dimensional; it took a complicated supply chain to transform grain grown in America, or Sweden, or Algiers, to the biscuit that was issued to British and Portuguese soldiers camped in the little villages near Almeida, and in the end it only worked because Britain could pay each step of the way, not with ready money, but with credit which in turn depended on the abundance and quality of her exports.

Wellington's operations against Ciudad Rodrigo in 1811 were hampered by the absence of a siege train of heavy artillery to batter a breach in its walls. In May Wellington ordered the train, which had long been on board ship in Lisbon harbour, to sail to Oporto, and when the army returned north from Elvas he gave the word for it to be carried upriver as far as Lamego. It required 194 boats to carry the guns, their equipment, and ammunition, up the Douro; while to haul it overland from Lamego to Villa da Ponte needed no fewer than 4,170 pairs of oxen. Nearly 1,500 Portuguese militia were mobilised to improve the road and guard the guns, and the whole laborious enterprise was managed, between bouts of recurrent fever, by the hard-working, careful Alexander Dickson, who had already become Wellington's favourite gunner.[12] At the same time the defences of Almeida were repaired, and towards the close of the year the siege train was moved forward to it, only twenty miles from Ciudad Rodrigo, under the pretext that the guns were intended to re-arm the Portuguese fortress.

Other preparations were also being made to besiege Ciudad Rodrigo early in the new year. Captain Burgoyne of the Royal Engineers set about training 200 men from the regiments of the Third Division as sappers, for the Engineers had no rank and file, and the Royal Military Artificers were skilled craftsmen with little experience of working under fire. In mid-December orders were given for several divisions to set about making gabions (large baskets to be filled with earth) and fascines (bundles of light wood, used in earthworks) which alerted the troops to the probability of a siege – a prospect that aroused little enthusiasm after the failures before Badajoz. Finally the Royal Staff Corps constructed a trestle bridge over the Agueda a few miles downstream (north-west) of Ciudad Rodrigo.

Wellington issued orders for the siege on New Year's Day 1812, but its preliminary stages were delayed by a winter storm. Burgoyne wrote in his journal on 4 January that the weather was 'terrible, snow on the ground, and rain and sleet falling, with a high wind'; five men of the Third Division died that day 'from the inclemency of the weather, and the badness of the roads', so it is not really surprising that the army's muleteers and carters took two days to cover ten miles.[13] Wellington was testy with impatience at the delay, but the weather improved and the lost time was soon made up.

On 7 January Wellington made a close reconnaissance of Ciudad Rodrigo with his engineers and staff. They decided to follow the same line of attack used by the French in 1810, approaching the fortress from the north-west, and taking full advantage of two hills, the Greater and Lesser Teson, which overlooked the defences at a range of approximately 600 and 180 yards respectively.[14] A disadvantage of the plan was that the French were expecting to be attacked from this direction and had most of their heavy guns mounted to oppose it, but the practical advantages given by the lie of the land more than outweighed this consideration, while there was the added hope that the section of wall battered and then repaired by the French might not be as strong as the original stonework.[15]

The Light Division and Pack's brigade invested the fortress on 8 January and that night Colonel Colborne of the 52nd stormed a small redoubt that the French had constructed on the Greater Teson. The fighting was over almost as soon as it had begun, with the allies suffering around twenty-five casualties while the French had three killed, a dozen wounded and fifty unwounded prisoners.[16] As soon as the redoubt was taken a working party of 1,000 soldiers began constructing the First Parallel – a trench some 600 yards long with a rampart that faced toward the fortress, and which followed the line, still clearly visible, of the old French works. A communication trench to the rear was also begun, while the reverse slope of the hill afforded considerable protection. The night's work went well, and although the French kept up a heavy fire, and the range was not particularly long, there were only another twenty or thirty casualties. Altogether it was a most auspicious opening to the siege; a more cautious methodical approach would have required five days to batter the redoubt into submission and probably proved more costly in lives as well as time.[17]

At noon on the following day the Light Division was replaced by the First and marched back to their comfortable cantonments at El Bodon. The next day the Fourth Division took its turn, then the Third, which was followed by the Light Division again. This meant that while the men had a long march to and from the fortress, and twenty-four hours of hard duty when they got there, they had two days and three full nights in their own quarters to recover from each day of duty. The arrangement was not perfect – the men generally had to ford the icy Agueda and grumbled a good deal – but it reflects Wellington's concern at undertaking such an operation in midwinter.[18] Fortunately the weather improved greatly and remained good for the rest of the siege, being dry, fine and with only a light frost. The nights however were long and bitterly cold; the men hated the work; and the engineers found that nothing worked quite as smoothly as in their textbooks.

On 13 January, after consulting the chief engineer, Richard Fletcher, Wellington decided to attempt to breach the fortress from the First Parallel. If this succeeded it would save several days, and Wellington was anxious that Marmont and Dorsenne might be able to intervene if he allowed the engineers to take their time.[19] That night the siege guns, thirty-four iron 24-pounders with barrels nine feet long, and four iron 18-pounders, were moved forward to occupy the batteries. The guns opened fire on the following afternoon, but the short winter day was over before they could settle to their work. On 15 January the batteries resumed their fire and the effect of their shot was soon obvious as the repaired wall began to crumble. There were around 130 British and 300 Portuguese gunners, and Alexander Dickson was delighted with their performance praising their zeal and activity and boasting proudly: 'Never was better practice made.'[20]

The artillery continued firing for another three days; a new battery was established and a second point in the wall chosen as a target where a new, smaller breach soon opened. On the afternoon of 19 January Wellington made a careful reconnaissance of both breaches and agreed with the engineers that they were 'practicable'; storming troops might be able to scramble and clamber up the mound of rubble, which was what remained of the wall, and so enter the town. Sitting in the forward trenches, he prepared detailed instructions for the assault that evening. The plan was complicated with several diversionary and subsidiary attacks. The principal assault on the main breach was to be made by Mackinnon's brigade of the Third Division; this would be led by 180 sappers carrying large hay bags which were to be thrown into the ditch to enable the troops to descend the counterscarp. They would be followed by Lieutenant Mackie of the 88th at the head of the advanced storming party, or 'forlorn hope', then Major Manners of the 74th with 500 volunteers, and then the rest of the brigade. The lesser breach would be attacked by the Light Division in similar fashion with Lieutenant Gurwood of the 52nd heading the forlorn hope and Major George Napier commanding 300 volunteers. Three companies of the 95th would clear the ditch between the two breaches while the reserves would detach parties to keep up a heavy fire on the French defences.[21]

The assault began just before seven o'clock in the evening and generally went according to Wellington's plan. Burgoyne stated that the hay bags brought up by the sappers 'were found extremely serviceable' in breaking the twelve-foot drop of the counterscarp, while the breach itself was 'steep, but the footing excellent'. The leading allied troops to reach the summit were swept away by fire from each flank and from buildings beyond, while many of those who followed were killed when shells and bags of powder left scattered by the French around the breach exploded. But fresh troops continued to press forward. The inside of the breach was impassable: a sheer drop of sixteen feet with a *chevaux de frise* and other fearsome obstacles at its foot. The only way forward was along the walls on either side of the breach but the French had cut broad deep gaps to isolate the breach in each direction and mounted two heavy guns to fire canister at short range. In the narrow space losses were heavy, but the desperate assailants scrambled across the cuts and drove the French gunners and infantry from their post. At the moment of success a French mine exploded killing a number of men including General Mackinnon.[22]

The Light Division encountered much less resistance at the lesser breach. Its attack began a little after that of the Third Division and was further delayed when the leading troops mistook a ravelin for a bastion. This led to a press of men at the foot of the breach and heavy casualties in the space of a few minutes before the breach was carried. Gurwood and George Napier were both wounded as was Colborne, commanding the 52nd, and Craufurd, who was directing the assault from the foot of the breach.

With the fall of both breaches the French fled to the Plaza Mayor where the garrison assembled in order to surrender. General Barrié, who had chosen to direct his defence of the breaches from a safe distance, yielded his sword without a struggle; indeed, it is possible that he surrendered more than once as several British officers claimed the privilege of taking him prisoner, though the credit at the time was given to the intrepid Lieutenant Gurwood.[23]

The successful stormers, exhilarated with triumph and relief at having survived the ordeal, ran amok, searching for plunder and drink. They roamed the town completely out of control, firing wildly into the air, breaking into stores and private homes and threatening officers who attempted to restrain them. Some accounts suggest that isolated pockets of French soldiers who attempted to surrender were killed on the spot, while others talk of houses set on fire and many casualties suffered through indiscriminate firing. A young officer of the 43rd wrote: 'If I had not seen it, I never could have supposed that British soldiers would become so wild and furious. It was quite alarming to meet groups of them in the streets, flushed as they were with drink, and desperate in mischief.'[24] And a soldier of the 95th vividly describes the confusion tinged with hysteria as small parties of men wandered the unknown dark streets, firing at any light and often at other parties, looking for drink and for plunder.[25] With such chaos it is almost impossible to determine the scale of the anarchy, but most accounts suggest that there were few outrages of the worst sort – rapes and murders of civilians. Certainly order was quickly restored in the morning, with the victorious troops leaving the town in high good humour, 'some of whom were dressed in Frenchmen's coats, some in white breeches, and huge jack-boots, some with cocked hats and queues; most of their swords were fixed on the rifles, and stuck full of hams, tongues, and loaves of bread, and not a few were carrying bird-cages'. The Fifth Division formed on the side of the road, presented arms and cheered, while Wellington, in a story that surely grew in the telling, demanded to know 'Who the devil are those fellows?', to be answered that they were his elite Light Division.[26]

Given Wellington's constant concern to protect the civilian population from the depredations of his soldiers it is significant that he made no criticism of the disorder following the storm of Ciudad Rodrigo, apparently regarding some disorder and plunder as inevitable when a fortress was stormed. Instead he thanked the soldiers in warm terms for 'the brilliant result of their labours and gallantry', and remitted the flogging ordered by a court martial of two soldiers of the 88th, in consideration of the distinguished part played by the regiment in the storm.[27]

The army was delighted with the success, which went a large way towards extinguishing memories of the failures at Badajoz. Altogether it suffered just over 1,100 casualties, half in the siege and half in the storm. The entire garrison of almost 2,000 men was taken prisoner apart from those killed in the course of the siege. The most senior British casualty in the siege was Robert Craufurd who died after four days of great pain, and was buried with full honours in the breach on 26 January attended by the Light Division, Wellington, Castaños and many other senior officers and staff.[28]

The government in London greeted the news of the capture of Ciudad Rodrigo with delight; the Tower guns were fired, an *Extraordinary Gazette* was published, and Perceval had the inspired idea of associating the first act of the unrestricted regency with the government's most effective policy and a national triumph, by suggesting that the Prince make Wellington an earl. The Prince greeted this with enthusiasm; Lord Wellesley could not help approving; and when a message from the Prince was sent to Parliament asking that it grant Wellington £2,000 per annum to maintain the honour, the Opposition was forced to grit its teeth and make a show of patriotic enthusiasm, with only the lone voice of Sir Francis Burdett playing to his own constituency by opposing the grant.[29]

In private the Opposition was far from enthusiastic. Lord Grey, writing to one of his military advisers, had been puzzled by Wellington's initial advance on Ciudad Rodrigo: 'What can be the meaning of that operation? He surely cannot have any serious expectation of taking the place.'[30] And when news came that Wellington had indeed taken it, Grey wrote to General Graham: 'I confess I had thought the undertaking a very hazardous one, and without any real prospect of advantage from its success, as to balance the loss which would probably have attended its failure. I am still inclined to fear that it will do little to restore the cause of Spain, which seems to me absolutely hopeless.' But then, perhaps remembering that he was writing to a soldier who had risked his life in the siege, he added: 'It is at all events highly creditable to have taken the Place.'[31] Like other addictions, the Opposition's passion for gloom-laden prophecies proved almost impossible to break, although past humiliations had taught them to indulge it behind closed doors and to abstain in public.

The Opposition had some excuse for feeling jaundiced in February 1812, for it was becoming obvious that the Prince had no intention of dismissing Perceval and calling them to office. Although the Prince alluded to the war in the Peninsula in explaining his decision, it was far less significant than political lethargy and cowardice. His ties to the Whigs had been weakening for years, and he had become accustomed to Perceval and his colleagues; it was easier to do nothing than to instigate a change, even though his 'betrayal' of his old friends inevitably caused much bitterness and limited his room to manoeuvre in the future.

Lord Wellesley made a pitch for power at this time, hoping to give the Prince a third, more palatable choice. His patience with his fellow ministers was exhausted, with differences of temperament as much as policy becoming unendurable. He continued to advocate a much bolder, more extravagant policy in the Peninsula, and taking large numbers of Spanish troops into British pay. (Wellington had considerable doubts about this idea, and the limited experiments of this type had proved expensive and not very successful.)[32]

However, Lord Wellesley found no support among his colleagues, and the Prince refused to back him. He resigned and went into opposition with Canning, while Perceval replaced him with Castlereagh at the Foreign Office, and brought Sidmouth and his supporters into the government, making it a little more conservative, but also more stable and efficient. Perceval's position was greatly strengthened by the Prince's commitment to him, and it seemed likely that his refashioned government would last for years provided the war continued to go well.

Wellington was inclined to scoff at his brother's ambition to form a ministry independent of either of the great parties, telling Charles Arbuthnot: 'It would not answer for one day.'[33] But he regretted the resignation and wrote sympathetically to Lord Wellesley: 'In truth the republic of a cabinet is but little suited to any man of taste or of large views.' He went on to give virtual endorsement to Wellesley's main criticism of Perceval's administration:

> I believe that the government are not aware of the difficulties in which I am constantly involved from defects and deficiencies of all descriptions; nor of the shifts to which I am obliged to have recourse to get on at all. I am not a competent judge of the resources of the British empire, but I am convinced that if Great Britain had carried on the war in the Peninsula with the same generosity, not to say profusion of supply, with which other wars have been supported, matters would now have been in a very different state.[34]

This was not very loyal to Perceval and the other ministers who had given unqualified support to Wellington in the face of constant opposition, and who had defied frequent dire warnings of national exhaustion to send him as many reinforcements and as much money as they could find; but Wellington had never been convinced that their best was good enough. Whether deliberate or not, his letter (which could be shown to others) offered tacit encouragement to Lord Wellesley to set himself up in opposition to the ministry as a champion of greater efforts being made in the Peninsula.

CHAPTER TWENTY-SEVEN

BADAJOZ

(February–April 1812)

WELLINGTON'S SUCCESS AT Ciudad Rodrigo took Marmont completely by surprise. He was dining with Dorsenne at Valladolid on the evening of 14 January when he learnt that the allies had crossed the Agueda and broken ground before the fortress. The two French generals at once set about collecting their forces, and were confident that they would be able to relieve the beleaguered garrison in early February. But it was only a week later, before Marmont had even reached Salamanca, that he was told the fortress had fallen. Wellington had seized the initiative and opened the northern route into Spain, and Marmont had been unable to do anything to stop him.

The French had grown complacent in the second half of 1811, taking Wellington's relative inactivity during that period as a sign that they had contained his threat, and managed to brush aside the lessons that they should have learnt from Masséna's defeat. Napoleon's attention had turned to the east coast of Spain where Suchet had launched a major offensive against Valencia. In October 1811 he ordered Marmont to detach troops to support Suchet, and in the middle of December he rearranged his armies in Spain, increasing the responsibilities of the Army of Portugal, but not giving it matching resources.[1]

The fall of Valencia was a major blow to the regular Spanish armies, but it also increased the territory that the French had to occupy, spreading their troops more thinly at a time when Napoleon was beginning to withdraw forces from Spain to take part in the looming war with Russia, and when the regular flow of recruits needed to keep regiments in the Peninsula up to strength was slowing to a trickle. But there were still 320,000 French soldiers in the Peninsula at the beginning of 1812 – more than enough to hold Wellington on the Portuguese frontier and control large parts of Spain, but not enough to overrun the whole country or to suppress the guerrillas. Napoleon would have been wiser to abandon some outlying provinces and hold the rest more securely, rather than encourage fresh 'conquests', which proved far more troublesome after they had been conquered than before.

After capturing Ciudad Rodrigo, Wellington turned his attention back to Badajoz, scene of the abortive allied siege in April and May of the previous year. This time he would take personal charge of the operation, closely supervising the work of his engineers rather than delegating the task to Beresford. But first it was necessary to bring forward the heavy artillery needed to breach the walls of the fortress, for there would be no attempt to make do with the old and worn-out guns at Elvas, whose deficiencies had been so clearly shown in the earlier sieges. Practical problems, however, caused inescapable delays. The fine weather which had lasted throughout the siege of Ciudad Rodrigo broke on 29 January, and was followed by nine days of heavy rain causing the rivers to flood and bridges to be swept away or made impassable. Worse still, the draught oxen with the army were too weak to drag the heavy siege guns over 200 miles of bad roads in winter, and it would have been just as difficult to get the guns back to the Douro and send them south by sea. Some lighter guns (24-pounder howitzers) and other equipment made the overland journey, but for the battering guns Wellington relied on a fresh train of sixteen 24-pounders which had recently arrived in Lisbon from England. He tried to supplement these by borrowing guns from the navy, but Admiral Berkeley, while professing great eagerness to help, sent only some old Russian guns taken from Siniavin's squadron in 1808 which were virtually useless.[2]

Wellington delayed his departure from Freneda for as long as possible, not leaving until 6 March and arriving at Elvas on 11 March when preparations for the siege of Badajoz were almost complete. He knew that news of his arrival would soon reach Soult and Marmont and would alert them to the likelihood of an attack on Badajoz far more convincingly than the often confused and uncertain stories of troop movements. He concentrated almost the entire allied army in Estremadura. The actual siege of Badajoz was to be undertaken by the Third, Fourth and Light Divisions, joined later by the Fifth Division, while Graham and Hill each commanded powerful covering forces, watching for the approach of Soult and Marmont respectively. Wellington was prepared to fight the combined French army; there would be no repetition of the tame withdrawal of 1811 unless Soult and Marmont brought far more men into the field than Wellington believed they could muster.[3]

On 15 March the Guadiana was bridged some ten miles below Badajoz. This was the narrowest suitable part of the river, but the stream was still 120 yards wide, and the new bridge was vulnerable to any sudden rise in the river. The fortress was invested on 16 and 17 March, and a detailed reconnaissance undertaken which revealed that it had been considerably strengthened since the earlier sieges and that there was no easy line of attack. There was no thought of a repetition of the attack on Fort San Cristobal and Wellington made clear that he wished to attack the fortress from the south, as Soult had done thirteen months previously. Fletcher opposed this plan, arguing that such an attack would require vastly more resources than were available: thirty more siege guns and mortars, five or six times the number of gabions and no less than twenty times the amount of available timber; and then even so that it was likely to fail for want of trained miners and sappers.[4] Instead the engineers proposed an attack on the south-east front, including Fort Picurina. The chief attraction of this approach was that the main wall was not properly screened, and could be breached by batteries firing from the hill on which Fort Picurina stood.[5] Wellington gave way, but he was not very happy with his engineers, while they grumbled that yet again they were being asked to undertake an operation with insufficient means.[6]

While the investment was being completed many of the town's inhabitants left, carrying their possessions with them, and even driving flocks of sheep and goats. The French were happy to let them go; their loyalty was at the least doubtful and their presence might complicate the defence. It is likely that Philippon used the opportunity to send out messengers to Drouet and Soult with news of his plight.[7] The French governor had a garrison of some 5,000 men and food for six or seven weeks, but ammunition was rather short.

Late on the afternoon of 17 March a thunderstorm broke with heavy rain and high wind continuing all night. Fortunately the besieging troops had already established their camps, but the weather cannot have done much for their spirits. That night a working party of 1,800 men, protected by a guard of 2,000 men, broke ground on a gentle height some 250 yards in front of Fort Picurina, establishing a first parallel some 600 yards long with four extensive communications trenches zigzagging their way to the rear. Major-General Colville, who commanded a brigade in the Third Division, wrote home that 'General Picton has a nominal superintendence, but his Lordship is himself on the ground and when that is the case little is done in the way of direction but by himself'. Over the course of the siege Wellington paid repeated visits to the trenches and was fortunate to escape unharmed when a French shell burst in a battery he was visiting on 1 April.[8]

On 19 March the French made a sortie with around 1,000 infantry and 40 cavalry attacking suddenly at midday and causing a great deal of confusion and some damage before they were driven back, taking with them several hundred tools that they had captured. Colonel Fletcher was wounded in the sortie, a musket shot striking his purse and driving a dollar coin into his groin.[9] Wellington might have taken the opportunity to replace him, but instead visited Fletcher at his tent each morning to consult him over the progress of the siege – an arrangement that was both personally considerate, and which gave Wellington a much freer hand in directing the siege as he wished.

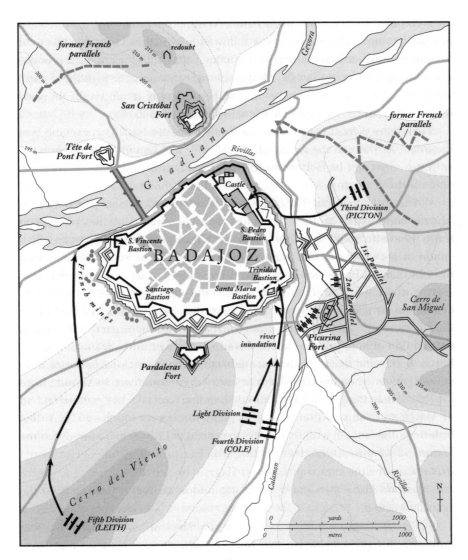

19 The siege of Badajoz, 16 March–6 April 1812.

Work on the first parallel and associated batteries continued for a week proceeding more slowly due to heavy rain. On 22 March the pontoon bridge was swept away by the rising river; eleven of the pontoons sunk at their anchors, although the rest of the equipment was saved.[10] With no means of retreat and his supply line broken it was an anxious time for Wellington, but fortunately there was as yet little sign of movement from Marmont or Soult.[11]

The rain finally stopped on the afternoon of 24 March and six batteries in the first parallel were completed. That night the guns, ten 24-pounders, eleven

18-pounders, and seven iron howitzers, were dragged into place, being brought forward along one of the roads into Badajoz that had been preserved for this purpose, rather than through the trenches. Fortunately the French fire, which had been heavy during the day, was light and sporadic that night, and there were few casualties.[12] At half past ten on the morning of 25 March the guns opened fire, some on Fort Picurina, the others on Badajoz itself, but all directed at the defences rather than battering the main wall. That evening Fort Picurina was stormed at a cost of more than 300 casualties including 19 officers, although observers on both sides felt that the defence might have been more determined.[13]

With Picurina in allied hands, work on the second parallel pressed ahead despite heavy fire from the fortress. On the night of 26 March work began on three new batteries designed to hold twenty guns and three howitzers which would be used to breach the walls. Wellington was impressed by the efforts of his men, telling Liverpool: 'It is impossible that I can do justice to this zeal, activity, and indefatigable labour of the officers and soldiers, with which these operations have been carried on in the most unfavourable weather.' The fall of Picurina and the location of these batteries made clear to the garrison the point destined for attack, and they set to work to strengthen their defences there as much as possible before the battering began.[14] The breaching batteries were completed on the night of 30 March and armed, some of the guns coming from the batteries in the first parallel, others from the reserve. They opened fire on 31 March making good practice, although the walls were tough and the visible results at the end of the first day were meagre. Charles Cocks described Wellington's tactics in the siege in his journal:

> Lord Wellington's principle in besieging is to open one or more breaches, according to the strength of the garrison, as soon as possible. They should be sufficiently near [each other] to enable the attacking columns, in case of success, to communicate shortly after entering, and yet should be so far [apart] that the troops defending one breach cannot see what passes at the other. To enable his troops to advance the assault he directs all the fire he has over and above the breaching batteries [on] those defences which flank the points to be breached, disregarding that part of the enemy's fire which only bears on the trenches or the batteries.
>
> . . . By this system, although the enemy's fire may be superior on the whole, yet ours is superior in the most critical points. It perhaps occasions a few more daily casualties and the artillery are usually averse to it for men naturally wish to fire at whatever annoys them but it saves means and it saves time and, in the end, to save time is to save men . . .[15]

The allied operation against Badajoz had been permitted to take its course throughout March with little or no interference from the French other than the defence made by the garrison. Soult had learnt of the concentration of allied forces at Elvas on 11 March, but it was not until the end of the month that he was ready to leave Seville with a mere 13,000 men to join Drouet's 12,000 facing Graham. He relied on Marmont repeating his march of the previous year; with luck the Army of Portugal might put 30,000 into the field, which would give the French an army of around 55,000, although it is probable that Wellington would still have given battle rather than abandon the siege.[16] Marmont had indeed been intending to march south as soon as the allies threatened Badajoz when, around the end of February, he received explicit orders from Napoleon that he should concentrate his army at Salamanca and assume an offensive posture which would, the emperor assured him, prevent Wellington from attacking Badajoz.[17] Later letters went even further: 'If Wellington were to march on Badajoz you have a sure, prompt, and triumphant means of bringing him back – that of marching on Rodrigo and Almeida.'[18] Faced with such direct orders, and much criticism of his previous operations, Marmont had no choice but to obey, even though he had no siege train with which to threaten Ciudad Rodrigo or Almeida, and no confidence that any advance into Portugal would do any good. In fact his movements caused Wellington considerable puzzlement and some anxiety – the repairs of Ciudad Rodrigo had not been pushed forward after it was handed over to a Spanish garrison, and it was also said to be short of supplies – but were still much less of a worry than if he had combined with Soult. So long as there was hope of gaining Badajoz Wellington would persist with the siege and leave Ciudad Rodrigo and Almeida to look after themselves as best they could.

Without the threat of Soult and Marmont intervening, the siege could proceed at a pace determined by Wellington. The breaching batteries continued their fire throughout the first days of April, and the walls began to crumble. According to Benjamin D'Urban there was some thought of making the assault as early as 4 April, but the breaches were not judged to be quite practicable.[19] The battering continued on the morning of 5 April and Wellington made a close personal reconnaissance from the most advanced point of the trenches, giving orders that the assault should be made that evening; but when subsequent observation by the engineers reported that the main breach had been prepared for obstinate resistance, he countermanded the order in the late afternoon, 'to the astonishment and disappointment of everyone'.[20] Battering on 6 April created a third breach which, it was hoped, would turn the flank of the interior defences of the two existing breaches. Soon after four o'clock Wellington inspected the work and ordered that the storm should go ahead that evening and in the meantime that all the guns be turned on the defences.[21]

Wellington was under no illusion that the fortress would fall easily or that casualties would be light. According to the rules of classical siegecraft the guns of the fortress should have been overwhelmed at the outset, then a second and a third parallel established, pushing the batteries right onto the glacis where they could destroy the walls and inner defences at very short range, while the counterscarp was mined and blown in. If this was accomplished the garrison was in no position to stand an assault and by convention was expected to surrender. However Wellington and his engineers both judged that the army was incapable of executing all these steps – mainly because of the lack of a corps of specialist sappers and miners, but also because the engineers and artillery officers had so little previous experience of conducting sieges. This left no alternative but to rely on the raw courage of his infantry to overcome all obstacles, or to avoid sieges altogether, which would prevent him advancing into Spain. The losses at Ciudad Rodrigo had not been excessive, and while Badajoz would certainly prove more costly Wellington believed that 'we had brought matters to that state where we could do no more, and it was necessary to storm or raise the siege'.[22]

The assault was originally intended to begin at half past seven, soon after dark, but this had to be changed until ten o'clock as some of the arrangements could not be made in time. The delay was most unfortunate, giving the French time to strengthen their defences under cover of dark. Given the postponement from the previous day it should not have been necessary. Just as at Ciudad Rodrigo the plan of attack was complicated with several subsidiary attacks as well as the main assault on the breaches. The operation began at about twenty to ten with the assault of the lunette of San Roque – an outwork lying between the castle and the breaches. The post was carried quite easily and an attempt was made to drain the Rivillias brook, though this had little effect until much later in the night, and the inundation greatly hampered the stormers of the main breaches. Soon after the attack on San Roque began Picton led the Third Division forward in an attempt to escalade the castle. Their advance was soon discovered and they came under heavy fire. Picton was wounded, as was Kempt who took over the command, and the attack went astray, being made on the wall of the fortress between two bastions which produced a deadly crossfire on the exposed assailants. With great difficulty five ladders were got forward against the wall, but the defence was resolute, and the few men who managed to climb to the top alive were immediately killed. After many fresh attempts had been repulsed the men of the Third Division fell back to some cover. Their attack had failed.

The assault on the main breaches was entrusted to the Fourth and Light Divisions. They advanced and were received in ominous silence as occasional fireballs illuminated the scene. The French knew they were coming, but waited until the leading troops were crowded together in the ditch before opening fire. They then ignited a train of shells and powder bags that had been carefully prepared; the resulting explosion killed most of the first wave of stormers, and set on fire a large amount of inflammable rubbish the French had piled into the ditch. One officer wrote soon afterwards: 'If hell is as bad as that ditch was, it is a worse place than I took it for.'[23] Nonetheless more troops pressed forward and the assault was renewed. Amid the horror there was confusion and little sense of direction or order with the strongest points attacked again and again while the new breach – the most promising of the three – was neglected. Brave men clambered up the breach and some even reached the summit, but once there could go no further for the French had blocked their path with formidable obstacles – tree trunks and giant wooden beams in which sword blades had been forced – while the whole was constantly swept with musketry and artillery fire. For nearly two hours the attack continued. Time and time again an officer or soldier from the ranks would collect a party of men in the ditch and make another rush on the breach only for the leaders, and many of their followers, to be mown down by the French who, secure and suffering almost no casualties, taunted them from a few dozen yards away. The soldiers were so confident in themselves that they could not believe that perseverance and courage would not bring success, but having sustained appalling casualties at last they gave way. As one officer wrote: 'I do not believe it was *possible* to carry them [the breaches]. Our brave fellows reached the top a hundred times, and were hurled down in sections by the most tremendous showers of shot, shell, grenades and large stones.'[24] The assault on the breaches had failed.

Wellington watched the storm from some open ground opposite the main breach. Colin Campbell and possibly other members of the staff joined the stormers, and did all they could without success.[25] It was soon apparent that the attack was in difficulty. James McGrigor, the Inspector General of Hospitals, placed himself near the headquarters, and records the scene:

Soon after our arrival, an officer came up with an unfavourable report of the assault, announcing that Colonel Macleod and several officers were killed, with heaps of men, who choked the approach to the breach … Another officer came up with a still more unfavourable report, that no progress was being made, and that he feared none could be made; for almost all the officers were killed, and none left to lead on the men, of whom a great many had fallen. At this moment I cast my eye on the countenance of Lord Wellington, lit up by the glare of the torch held by Lord March; I shall never forget it to the last moment of my existence; and I could even now sketch it. The jaw had fallen, and the face was of unusual length, while the torchlight gave his countenance a lurid aspect; but still, the expression of the face was firm.[26]

With the failure of the main assault the only hope of success lay in the subsidiary attacks, intended primarily as diversions, but which might establish a decisive lodgement in the fortress. Picton's men had rallied and caught their breath in a sheltered spot near the castle's walls. The second brigade of the division advanced while the French, their attention absorbed by the fighting at the breaches, paid little attention. Colonel Ridge of the 5th led his men forward, this time choosing the low point in the wall of the castle which had been missed in the first attack. The British seem to have had only two ladders at this point, and could not have succeeded against serious resistance, but the French guard was distracted, and in a few minutes Ridge and half a company of the 5th had surmounted the wall with almost no opposition. As more men steadily climbed the ladders the leading troops spread out along the walls and down inside the castle. They soon encountered some French infantry and there was an exchange of fire in which Ridge was mortally wounded. But Philippon had concentrated all his best troops and officers at the breaches and the garrison of the castle gave way before the men of the 5th, so that it was not long before it was securely held by the Third Division. However, Picton's men were unable to do more for some time. There were few exits from the castle and French reserves were soon in position to defeat any attempt to push through them into the town, while it was a slow business to send whole regiments up the ladders into the castle to accumulate enough men to force the defence. Nonetheless the fall of the castle made the town untenable, and if it could be held through the night Philippon would have had little choice but to surrender in the morning. But long before that the success of the Fifth Division had placed the town as well as the castle in the hand of the allies, and put an end to French resistance.[27]

Wellington had originally intended that the Fifth Division should only make a demonstration on the western side of Badajoz, but Leith had pressed hard for some ladders and received permission to push his attack home if the prospect seemed promising. However it was after eleven o'clock when the ladders reached his men, who then had to make a long approach march in order to come upon the fortress close to the Guadiana on the opposite side of the town to the castle. Consequently it was almost midnight when their attack got underway, but the garrison on this front had not relaxed their vigil and the leading British troops were met with heavy fire. Despite losses they made their way over the ditch and up the wall and established a foothold on the ramparts. When enough men had been collected Major-General Walker led them along the wall, capturing three bastions in succession before he was wounded and his men broke in panic believing that a mine was about to explode. The French pursued them, but Leith had a reserve in hand and the tide of fortune soon swung back in favour of the allies. The Fifth Division now advanced through the town in two columns, its bugles sounding the advance as it marched to take the breaches from behind. When Leith's calls were answered by Picton's men in the castle, the French abandoned the struggle and fled, with Philippon and some of his men taking refuge in San Cristobal.[28]

The scenes of looting, rape and plunder that followed were far more prolonged and brutal than at Ciudad Rodrigo. Soldiers sought release from the hardships of the siege and the horrors of the storm by shedding all ties of discipline, order and decency, and wreaking their vengeance on enemy soldiers and the civilian population. It was not only the 'few bad men' in any regiment who went wild, but the great majority, including many men who, in other circumstances, were steady, reliable and humane. Nor were their acts always unpremeditated. William Lawrence of the 40th was a good soldier who became a sergeant and wrote an attractive autobiography, but he admits that he and two comrades, who knew the town well from their residence there in 1809, planned to rob a rich silversmith's shop in the chaos after the storm.[29] Many men, and some officers, believed that they were entitled to pillage the town; self-justifying rumours swept through the ranks that Wellington had approved the sack and that the inhabitants were French sympathisers who deserved little mercy.[30] But other officers risked their lives trying to restore order or keep their men in their ranks, and it is said that some regiments remained under control at least until the garrison had been removed the following morning.[31] Civilians fled the town when they could. Two young sisters found refuge in the camp of the Light Division, where the fourteen-year-old Juana Maria de los Dolores de Leon encountered the twenty-four-year-old Captain Harry Smith; one of the great romantic stories of the Peninsular War was born amidst scenes of squalor and desolation.[32]

Wellington was extremely angry that the inevitable disorder following the storm did not cease the following morning.[33] In his first General Order he thanked his men for 'the uncommon gallantry displayed last night', but a few hours later he declared that 'it is now full time that the plunder of Badajoz should cease', and ordered that an officer and six steady NCOs should be sent from each regiment into the town to collect their stragglers, while the Provost Marshal was instructed to 'execute any man he may find in the act of plunder'. Even then the disorder did not end, and at eleven o'clock at night on 8 April, forty-nine hours after the storm had begun, he issued a new General Order that told its own tale: the roll was to be called every hour in all the camps around Badajoz, and General Power's Portuguese brigade, the new garrison, was censured because 'instead of being a protection to the people, [they] plunder them more than those who stormed the town'. The gates of the town and the breaches in the walls were to be guarded 'to prevent soldiers from entering the town, or from quitting it with bundles of any description'. These measures, combined with simple exhaustion, saw order gradually restored to the streets of Badajoz, although it is unlikely that many of its inhabitants viewed its 'liberation' with much joy or its 'liberators' with much affection. Still, even the highest estimate of civilian deaths in the sack of Badajoz is fewer than 100, and many towns in the Peninsula, and elsewhere, fared much worse from the ravages of war.[34]

The siege of Badajoz cost the allied army 4,670 casualties – losses that equalled those suffered at Albuera and Talavera, and were far greater than any other action in the war thus far.[35] Of these, a little under 1,000 fell in the siege, and 3,713 on the night of 6–7 April in the storm. Officers suffered particularly heavily in the storm with 62 killed and 251 wounded, or more than one officer casualty for every eleven men. Generals Picton, Walker, Colville, Kempt, Bowes and Harvey were all wounded, as was Wellington's young brother-in-law Hercules Pakenham.

Pakenham's experiences were not untypical. He was an Assistant Adjutant-General on the staff of the Third Division. When he was halfway up one of the ladders he was hit by a musket ball ricocheting off the wall and knocked off, although not wounded or otherwise much hurt. Getting back on his feet he climbed again, this time reaching the parapet, where he collected a group of soldiers and led them forward. They drove back a French party but were then attacked by a larger enemy group and a tussle ensued at very short range, in which Pakenham was hit: 'The ball struck the sword arm between elbow and wrist, passed along the wrist and through it slanting, came out in the palm of the hand and took off the top of a finger.' He fell and lost consciousness for a time. When he awoke he found that he had received a second wound: 'A bullet had entered his groin, split his bone and stuck in the cleft.' He was found and carried to a spot where his wounds could be dressed. Some days later, seeing signs of gangrene, the surgeons prepared to amputate his arm, but a medical amateur thought that with care it might be saved: ' "Well, I may as well have it tried, though I do not seem to have much chance of living in any case." The quack anointed it with what he called "Unguentum Anglicum", which with exquisite torture burnt off all the moribund flesh and cleaned the wound.' The hand was saved though it and the wrist were greatly shrunken and always cold, yet Pakenham could use it to carve, prune trees, shoot, and hold a whip. The hip wound remained open for the rest of his life and gave him great pain, although he could walk and ride as well as most men, and lived until 1850. Compared to many wounded officers and most wounded men he was fortunate in the care and attention he received, but his example is a useful reminder that the pain and suffering of war often persisted long after the last shots were fired.[36]

Pakenham was just one of many officers who were wounded or killed at Badajoz whom Wellington knew personally, liked and admired. Like any officer who had seen much active service, Wellington had long since accepted that officers and men under his command, including some he counted as friends, would fall in battle, but the losses at Badajoz were particularly heavy and fell disproportionately on the most gallant and daring officers and men. He was greatly affected when he saw the casualty returns. Picton wrote on 9 April:

> This is allowed to be the most brilliant achievement which has taken place in the Peninsula during the War; but it has been most dearly Purchased by many valuable Lives: but military reputation is not to be purchased without blood, and ambition has nothing to do with Humanity. *Yet our Chief, when I waited upon him next morning, shed as copious a torrent of Tears as any woman could have done on the occasion, and appeared most profoundly affected by our loss.*[37]

Ten years later Wellington confirmed the story, telling the Arbuthnots that when Picton came to congratulate him on the success, 'I assure you I actually could not help crying. I bit my lips, did everything I could to stop myself for I was ashamed he should see it, but I could not; he so little entered into my feelings that he said, "Good God, what is the matter?" '[38]

   This feeling underlay a private letter that Wellington wrote to accompany his official despatch to Lord Liverpool. In it, he argued in the strongest terms for the creation of a regular corps of sappers and miners, so that in future fortresses could be taken relying more on science and less on raw courage. In so doing he reveals a measure of the personal toll that the operation had taken on him: 'My dispatches of this date will convey the account of the capture of Badajoz which afford as strong an instance of the gallantry of our troops as has ever been displayed. But I anxiously hope that I shall never again be the instrument of putting them to such a test as that to which they were put last night . . . When I ordered the assault I was certain that I should lose our best Officers and Men. It is a cruel situation for any person to be placed in.'[39]

CHAPTER TWENTY-EIGHT

SALAMANCA
(April–July 1812)

A ROUND FIVE O'CLOCK on the afternoon of 11 May 1812 the Prime Minister, Spencer Perceval, arrived at the Houses of Parliament to take part in the evening's debate on the Orders-in-Council. He left his cloak and stick with an attendant and climbed the stairs to the lobby of the old House of Commons where a tall, large-boned stranger, John Bellingham, pressed a pistol to his chest and shot him through the heart. Perceval collapsed with the cry, 'I am murdered, murdered', gave two heavy groans and died. Bellingham quietly sat on a bench by the wall, making no attempt to escape or commit any further violence. Investigation soon established that he had acted alone, not from political motives, but from an irrationally exaggerated sense of his private grievances; the government had refused to compensate him for the imprisonment and losses he had suffered when he got into debt in Russia. He was tried at the Old Bailey on 15 May and his extended, cogent account of his grievances convinced the jury that he was sufficiently rational to be held accountable for his actions. He was convicted and executed on the morning of 18 May.[1]

Perceval's death triggered a political crisis. An attempt by the surviving ministers to carry on under Liverpool was defeated in the Commons on 21 May by a vote of 174 to 170. The Prince Regent then invited Lord Wellesley to form an administration, but Wellesley found that neither the outgoing ministers nor the Opposition were willing to support him. The Prince then turned to his old friend Lord Moira, who managed to cobble together an extremely weak ministry dominated by Canning and relying heavily on the tacit support of Liverpool and other members of Perceval's government. However this ministry fell apart before it could take office, and the Prince turned back to Liverpool, appointing him Prime Minister on 8 June. The negotiations created considerable ill feeling, but they proved to the world that the only choices were Liverpool or the Opposition; it was not possible to reunite all the splinters of the old Pittite party.

Nonetheless Liverpool tried hard to bring Canning back into office, offering to make him Foreign Secretary; but, in the most disastrous misjudgement of his career, Canning declined unless he was also made Leader of the House. Liverpool also repeatedly offered William Wellesley-Pole the War Department, but Pole discovered a new sense of loyalty to Lord Wellesley and refused. Both men soon regretted their folly, but probably assumed at the time that Liverpool's ministry was too weak to survive for long. Castlereagh remained at the Foreign Office and, without Perceval, became the government's chief spokesman in the Commons, where his tortured language attracted much ridicule, but his coolness, courage and determination began to be better appreciated. Sidmouth moved to the Home Office, and the genial, capable Lord Bathurst took Liverpool's place at the War Department. The new ministry comfortably won a vote of confidence 289 to 184 on 11 June, but it was still regarded as weak and vulnerable, especially in the Commons.[2]

Wellington learnt of Perceval's assassination towards the end of May while the army was in quarters on the Portuguese frontier.[3] He was shocked, and doubted whether Liverpool could hope to carry on the government without significant recruits:

You have undertaken a most gigantic task, and I don't know how you will get through it. When I was in office matters were not very successfully carried on in the House of Commons when Mr Canning, Lord Castlereagh, and Mr Perceval were on the Treasury Bench, and to all appearance at least acted well together. I should think that you won't have the assistance of both the survivors of poor Perceval; and you will scarcely be able to get on in the House of Commons with only one of them.

However, there is nothing like trying; and I can only assure your lordship that I shall be happy if I can be of any use to you in any way.[4]

His candid obituary of Perceval, in a confidential letter to Pole written a few weeks later, was neither flattering nor generous: 'Mr Perceval was a very honest Man, whose views were rather limited by professional habits & those acquired by long practice in His House; and I think he did not take a sufficiently enlarged view of our situation here; nor does Lord Liverpool.'[5] Nonetheless Wellington greatly regretted Pole's decision not to take office in Liverpool's administration and expressed the point forcefully to both Pole and Liverpool. He did not believe that Lord Wellesley had any hope of success in forming an administration independent of the two main parties and sympathised with the ministers in their refusal to serve under him. As for fraternal ties, he discounted them with some impatience:

The Sentiments of affection between brothers which are to induce them to espouse the same Political party are or ought to be reciprocal; and it is but fair to observe that he [Lord Wellesley] placed himself in the situation of a Personal Enemy of the Govt. of which you . . . form a Part. It does not follow that if you had continued with the Govt. you and he would have been worse friends; if that were the case I should have a worse opinion of domestic politicks and their professors than I now entertain.[6]

Nor did the great questions of policy count for much in his eyes at this juncture:

As for public principles on this question, they have nothing to do with it. I see that Lord Liverpool is about to enter upon that fatal measure the Catholic Emancipation as it is called; and as for the Orders in Council and American matters I believe that all parties excepting Mr Brougham and Mr Baring would act alike. In respect to the War in this country it would certainly get on better, if we were better supplied with money.[7]

Writing to Liverpool at the end of June Wellington acknowledged that he had expected the crisis to end with the Opposition in office, and that he still thought the ministry dangerously weak in the Commons. He added: 'I am much annoyed at the breach which prevails between your Govt. and Lord Wellesley, and particularly that Pole is no longer in Office. But I am perfectly satisfied with the arrangement which has been made for filling the War Department; and I am convinced that I shall derive as much satisfaction from my correspondence with Lord Bathurst as I have with Lord Castlereagh and yourself.'[8] And he followed this with a civil letter to Lord Bathurst assuring him that 'the arrangement by which you have been placed at the head of the War Department is perfectly satisfactory to me.'[9]

Pole complained that some government supporters were using these letters to claim that Wellington favoured the existing ministers and even *preferred* Bathurst to him at the War Department. Wellington replied that it was obvious that the letters had been written after Pole had repeatedly declined office and that:

The conduct of both Lord Liverpool and Lord Bathurst was to say no more of it civil both to you and to me; and if I had not expressed the approbation and satisfaction which I really felt at the arrangement for the War Department you having declined to accept it, and had not stated my intention to act confidentially with Lord Bathurst as I had before with Lord Castlereagh and Lord Liverpool, I should have behaved very uncivilly, and should have taken the field as a Partizan, very much to my own discredit, and without being of much use to any body.[10]

Essentially, Wellington's view was not very different from that of the Commons: he would have liked to see a strong government with a secure majority in Parliament that would prosecute the war with vigour, finding the money and the men he needed for his operations, and provide protection from ignominy if they went wrong. (But also, less plausibly, a government that would continue to give him a free hand in the actual conduct of his campaigns.) He would have liked to see all the scattered fragments of Pitt's friends reunited in a ministry that would include not just Castlereagh and Sidmouth, but Canning, Lord Wellesley and William Wellesley-Pole. However, the negotiations of May and June showed that the obstacles to this were insuperable, and – again as in the Commons – Wellington preferred Liverpool's weak ministry to the Opposition.

Throughout June during the first half of the Salamanca campaign Wellington acted with the knowledge that there was no settled government in England, and the belief that the next administration might well be formed by the Opposition which had for so long been critical of his operations. Even in July, when he knew that Liverpool was back in office, he also knew that the government was not strong and probably could not survive the shock of a setback in the Peninsula. But Wellington was determined not to become actively involved in domestic politics and made it quietly plain that 'his object is to serve his country, whatever be the party in power; and he would continue to serve, with equal zeal, under the Grenvilles and the Greys, for whom he has certainly no personal partiality'. Privately he told an old friend on 18 June: 'I always detested home politics, and late occurrences have not given me relish for them.'[11]

After the fall of Badajoz Wellington was tempted by the idea of an immediate offensive against Soult, driving him back into Andalusia and forcing him to fight at a disadvantage. Spring was the best time of the year for operations in southern Spain, before the overwhelming summer heat, and the army was at its healthiest. But Marmont was threatening Ciudad Rodrigo and Almeida and might go even further, menacing Oporto or marching south across the allies' lines of communication if Wellington disappeared into Andalusia. He therefore left Hill with 14,000 men to cover his southern flank and took the rest of the army north, forcing Marmont to retire hastily to Salamanca.

Wellington allowed his men to rest for six weeks in their familiar quarters near the frontier, although he did not immediately give up the idea of returning south. He had always regarded the liberation of Andalusia and the relief of Cadiz as his first objective in Spain after capturing the frontier fortresses, because it would release resources that could be used to rebuild the Spanish armies, and because of the importance attached to Cadiz in England. However by late May he had decided that the moment for striking at Soult had passed and that he should direct his efforts to the defeat of Marmont. The reason was simple: if he marched south Marmont would now be able to follow him with a considerable part of the Army of Portugal or, alternatively, would be able to besiege Ciudad Rodrigo and Almeida with the prospect of success, for a fresh siege train was well advanced on the road from France. On the other hand experience suggested that Soult was much less likely to lend support to Marmont if the latter was attacked – indeed, he was much less able to do so.

Wellington was encouraged by reports of imminent war between France and Russia and felt some guarded optimism as to the result, telling Bathurst: 'If the Emperor of Russia had any resources and is prudent, and his Russians will really fight, Buonaparte will not succeed.'[12] In any case it meant that the French armies could expect few reinforcements, creating a more favourable strategic position than at any time since 1809. Nonetheless there were still more than 300,000 French troops in the Peninsula, and if they concentrated against Wellington he would have no choice but to retreat, just has he had done after Talavera.

If Wellington was to have a free hand against Marmont it was important to distract the other French generals. Wellington asked Ballesteros to take the field in Andalusia, which he did, only for his army to be defeated, although not destroyed, at Bornos in June. On the other side of Spain, Castaños promised to advance from his base in Galicia and besiege Astorga and so threaten Marmont from the north-west. However his advance was delayed, and Wellington distracted Marmont from him, rather than the other way round. At the same time Wellington ordered General Silveira with four regiments of Portuguese militia and a brigade of Portuguese dragoons under D'Urban to blockade the French garrison of Zamora on the Duero.

Far more significant than these diversions were two operations that were not conceived by Wellington but which he embraced with enthusiasm. The first was a proposal from the Admiralty to send a squadron of frigates and small vessels, supported by a single ship of the line, with a couple of battalions of marines, to operate off the north coast of Spain during the summer, harassing the French and lending support to the guerrillas. The expedition, commanded by Sir Home Popham, arrived off the coast in the middle of June and was an unqualified success.[13]

The other diversion was a landing on the east coast of Spain by British troops based in Sicily, together with some Sicilian and Spanish troops. The idea was proposed in late January by Lord William Bentinck, the British commander in Sicily, at a time when his habitual preoccupation with Italian affairs had temporarily faded. He soon lost interest in the scheme, reducing the size of the expedition and giving its command to a subordinate (Lieutenant-General Frederick Maitland), but curiously this did not matter. Rumours about the expedition abounded, greatly exaggerating its strength, and Suchet was genuinely alarmed as well as being provided with a perfect excuse to decline weakening his army in any way. It was almost an anticlimax when Maitland finally arrived off the Spanish coast at the end of July and landed at Alicante, where his arrival made up for the crippling defeat suffered by the Army of Murcia at Castalla on 21 July.[14]

Wellington began his advance on 13 June. He had an army of around 50,000 men, not including the sick or Hill's detachment in Estremadura, which had now grown to almost 18,000 men. The number of sick had fallen from 15,700 in late April to just under 14,000 a month later, and the army was strengthened by reinforcements from home, both drafts of recruits for regiments already serving in the Peninsula, and new regiments. A powerful brigade of heavy cavalry under Major-General Le Marchant had arrived in 1811 and had distinguished itself at Villagarcia in April, where it broke Drouet's cavalry in a well-conducted operation. It had been joined by a brigade of the heavy dragoons of the King's German Legion, so that for the first time in the war the allies had a clear superiority of cavalry over the French. But infantry formed the great bulk and real strength of the army; there were now seven full divisions, plus two independent Portuguese brigades and Carlos de España's small Spanish division.[15] The army was now thoroughly seasoned and experienced, full of confidence in itself and in its commander. Yet it had never won a full-scale battle of manoeuvre or attacked in the open field (except Ney's rearguard in 1811), and Wellington had a lingering fear that his men might get carried away by their impetuosity in attack, leaving them disordered and vulnerable to an enemy counter-attack.[16]

On 16 June the leading allied troops encountered the first French outposts only a few miles west of Salamanca. Marmont's army was still widely dispersed, and he withdrew, leaving 800 men occupying three fortified convents in the ancient city to delay the allies. Wellington entered Salamanca amid scenes of wild celebration on 17 June and soon found that the convents represented a more formidable problem than he had anticipated. The siege train had not accompanied the army, and he had only four 18-pounder guns and ordinary field artillery with him. The result was that time and lives were lost for want of resources only three months after Wellington's passionate reaction to the sacrifices at Badajoz. The forts were finally taken on 27 June at a cost of 99 men killed and 331 wounded, many of them falling in an unsuccessful assault on 23 June.[17]

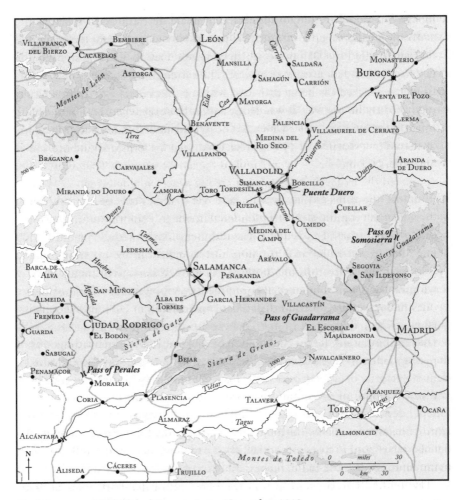

20 Salamanca, Madrid and Burgos, June–November 1812.

While the Sixth Division undertook the siege of the forts the rest of the army forded the Tormes and camped beyond Salamanca. The forts gained Marmont the time he needed to collect most of his army, but created a different problem: he could not simply abandon the garrison to its fate without disgusting his men and inviting rebuke from Napoleon. He therefore advanced on 20 June even though he had only five divisions in hand, some 25,000 men (two other divisions were approaching). Wellington suspended the siege of the forts and occupied a strong position at San Cristobal just outside the town. There was some skirmishing that afternoon and Wellington was heard to remark: 'Damned tempting! I have a great mind to attack 'em.'[18] But the day was drawing on and he preferred to wait until morning in the expectation that Marmont would then attack him. This Marmont declined to do, and 21 June passed with nothing more than some trifling skirmishing. Wellington's failure to attack led to considerable murmuring in the allied army, and a sense that he had missed a golden opportunity to defeat the French. The most likely explanations of his unwonted caution are that in the event of defeat he had an awkward retreat with a city and a river close to his rear; that he preferred to fight a defensive action; and that he may have been inhibited by the uncertain state of British politics where the Whigs might already have taken office. Yet none of these comes close to justifying a decision that he was soon to regret.[19]

Over the next few days Marmont attempted to out-manoeuvre Wellington and relieve the garrisons of the forts without bringing on a battle. In the process he ran considerable risks without achieving his objective or seriously discommoding the allies. When the forts fell he retreated rapidly but in good order to the Duero some forty miles to the north. Here he was joined by Bonnet on 7 July with his division from the Asturias, but Marmont's hopes of help from Caffarelli and the Army of the North were dashed due to the activity of Popham and the Spanish guerrillas. An appeal to King Joseph seemed also to have fallen on deaf ears.

Wellington pursued Marmont with enthusiasm and at first was confident of his ability to force the line of the Duero, but the river was full, and the French occupied formidable defensive posts guarding all the crossings the allies could discover. A stalemate ensued which lasted a fortnight, much to Wellington's frustration. It was at this point that Picton and Graham were both forced to go home; Picton's Badajoz wound had broken open, and Graham's eyes were so badly infected that he was at risk of going blind. At Picton's suggestion the Third Division was entrusted to Edward Pakenham, while Lowry Cole rejoined the army and the command of the Fourth Division. Wellington, who was never good at delegating, now complained of overwork. On 29 June he wrote to Pole:

I was never so fagged. My Gallant Officers will kill me. In the course of [the] fortnight that we were before Salamanca I don't believe I have been in bed, or rather laying down, altogether 48 hours – I am always on foot at 1 in the morning, and can't go to Rest till 9 at night . . . If I detach one of them he is not satisfied unless I go to him, or send the whole Army, and I am obliged to superintend every operation of the troops. However I hold out well.[20]

Marmont broke the impasse and took the initiative in the middle of July, wrong-footing Wellington and forcing the allied army to fall back and concentrate on the little River Guarena on 18 July. There was some fighting and at one point Wellington and his staff were caught up in a cavalry melee. According to John Cooke of the 43rd:

The Earl of Wellington was in the thick of it, and escaped with difficulty. His straight sword drawn, he also crossed the ford at full speed, smiling. I did not see his lordship when the charge first took place. When he passed us, he had none of this staff near him; he was quite alone, with a ravine in his rear.[21]

To Captain Kincard of the Rifles, however, 'The Duke himself did not look more than half pleased'.[22] Despite this flurry of action – probably lasting only a few minutes – the allies accomplished their withdrawal to the Guarena with little confusion or real danger, greatly helped by the superiority of their cavalry.

Marmont declined to attack Wellington's position on the Guarena, but was well pleased with the success of his manoeuvres. On 19 July he allowed his men to rest through the morning and heat of noon before marching south in the late afternoon. Wellington followed suit and the two armies marched in parallel, separated by barely a mile of open ground throughout 20 July. This was not easy; at such close quarters it would need only a trifling mistake – a gap opening between two divisions, confusion in passing some petty obstacle – to invite an immediate and devastating attack. The professional competence of both armies at all levels was thoroughly tested by the march and many British officers expressed their delight at the 'beautiful' sight of 100,000 men manoeuvring so close together without accident. By the evening of 20 July Wellington was almost back at the position of San Cristobal outside Salamanca, while Marmont in a late spurt pushed forward until his vanguard reached the fords of Huerta ten miles east of the city. On the following day the French army crossed the Tormes and occupied the castle at Alba de Tormes which guarded a bridge over the river fifteen miles south of Huerta. (Carlos de España had evacuated the castle's small garrison, but failed to inform Wellington that he had done so.) Wellington occupied San Cristobal as long as there was any hope that Marmont would attack him there, and then gradually shifted his army south across the river leaving the Third Division and D'Urban's Portuguese dragoons on the northern side. That night the allied troops were drenched by a heavy thunderstorm, and several dozen horses, mostly from Le Marchant's brigade, broke loose and galloped through the encampment causing much confusion and some injuries.

Wellington woke on the morning of 22 July to the knowledge that his campaign was on the brink of failure. Marmont had succeeded in manoeuvring him back from the Duero to the Tormes, and if the pattern continued the allies would be forced to abandon Salamanca and withdraw towards Portugal, not beaten but out-generalled, by an opponent whose army was a little weaker than their own. On the previous evening Wellington had learnt that Marmont would soon be joined by a brigade of cavalry sent by Caffarelli which had already reached the Duero. It would be a humiliating end to a campaign that

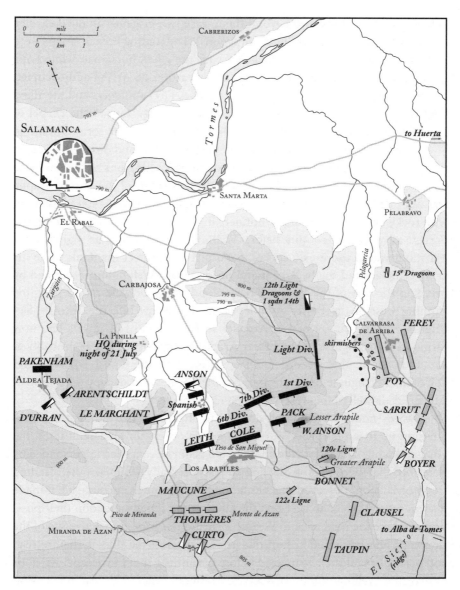

21 The battle of Salamanca, 22 July 1812. (All troop positions approximate, many conjectural.)

had promised so much, and it seems likely that Wellington faced the day determined to let no opportunity slip to reverse the tide of fortune.

Early that morning, British troops of Cole's Fourth Division occupied a steep isolated hill, known as the Lesser Arapile, some four miles south of the Tormes. To their north Pack's Portuguese brigade and the Seventh Division held a line of low hills, and beyond them were two brigades of allied cavalry (those of V. Alten and Bock's heavy dragoons). The leading French troops were further east; Boyer's dragoons bickered with the allied horsemen while Foy's infantry advanced through the village of Calvarrasa de Arriba and occupied the line of formidable west-facing bluffs beyond. Foy's *voltiguers* and the allied light infantry were soon skirmishing, contesting possession of the chapel of Nuestra Señora de la Peña, but not drawing their reserves into serious fighting.

Marmont brought Ferey's division up to support Foy and directed his other troops further south and west to continue turning Wellington's right flank as he had done on previous days. Nine hundred yards south of the Lesser Arapile was another isolated height, the Greater Arapile, some 300–400 yards long with rocky ends and steep sides. Bonnet's division, which was now leading the French advance, seized this before Wellington recognised its significance. Marmont would use it as a secure, fixed pivot to protect his flank while his army came around the back of it and headed west. Wellington responded by bringing the rest of the Fourth Division and Pack's brigade into a new line running west of the Lesser Arapile, occupying a low hill, the Teso de San Miguel, and the village of Los Arapiles in front (south) of it. His line now formed a right angle with the Lesser Arapile in the corner. It was probably at about this time that he ordered Pakenham with the Third Division and D'Urban's Portuguese dragoons to cross the Tormes and occupy a position at Aldea Tejada well to the west of the rest of the army.[23]

Towards midday Wellington decided to attack. He had brought the First Division up to support the Fourth and issued orders for an assault upon the Greater Arapile. But before the attack could begin he cancelled it, persuaded by Beresford that there were strong French reserves ready to support their leading troops. Marmont observed this hesitation and was much encouraged; it made it seem more likely than ever that the allies would quietly abandon their position and take the road back to Portugal. He did not want to risk the fate of the campaign on a battle, but he hoped to press and harass the allies in their retreat, and perhaps maul their rearguard before permitting them to escape. An hour or two after Wellington's aborted attack, Marmont ordered his leading division (now that of Maucune) onto the higher ground south of the village of Los Arapiles known as the Monte de Azan. Here the French established a powerful battery which commenced a noisy, if not particularly lethal bombardment of the allied lines. Maucune also pushed his light infantry forward towards the village, leading to some lively skirmishing, proving to be too aggressive for Marmont, who ordered him to break off his action and shift his men further south and east. At this point the left wing of the French army comprised Maucune's division with Curto's light cavalry and Thomières's division in support and, much further back, the divisions of Clausel and Taupin. There was a worrying gap between Maucune's right and Bonnet's men around the Greater Arapile, while the open ground of the Monte de Azan gave little protection. But then Thomières's division, instead of halting behind and in support of Maucune, overtook him and advanced further west along the Monte de Azan. This proved a fatal mistake; the French left was already dangerously isolated from the rest of the army, now it was overextended and vulnerable to attack as well.

Marmont recognised the problem immediately and ordered his reserves to move west as quickly as possible; Sarrut and Ferey would move from the right wing to the centre, while Taupin and Clausel, who had been marching through the broken country south of the Greater Arapile, were urged forward to support the left as soon as they could get their men into order. Marmont himself would take command on the left and ensure that no further mistakes were made, but just as he turned to mount his horse he was badly wounded by a shell from one of the British guns firing from the Lesser Arapile.[24] The command should have passed to Clausel, but he could not be found (he too had been slightly wounded in a separate incident and was having his heel dressed), and Bonnet, the next in line, had scarcely assumed the command before he was hit in the thigh.

The story has often been told of how Wellington was eating his lunch when he saw the French left extend its position, recognised his opportunity and resolved to attack all in a moment. His own version was recorded by Charles Greville many years later: '"I got up", he said, "and was looking over a wall round the farm-yard, just such a wall as that" (pointing to a low stone wall bounding the covert), "and I saw the movement of the French left through my glass. 'By God', said I, 'that will do, and I'll attack them directly.' I had moved up the Sixth [*sic*: Third] Division through Salamanca, which the French were not aware of, and I ordered them to attack, and the whole line to advance."'[25] This rather obscures the fact that Wellington had been anxiously looking for a reasonable chance to attack all day, and had carefully deployed his army so that it would be ready to move if the opening came. Having decided to attack he galloped to the far right wing of the army, outpacing the young men of his staff on the way, and issued his orders to D'Urban and Pakenham. In essence his plan was simple: Pakenham would advance south until he was level with the end of the Monte de Azan then wheel to the east catching the French in the flank and rolling them up. At the same time the Fifth Division (Leith) and Fourth Division (Cole) would advance frontally supported by the cavalry of Le Marchant and Anson, and with the Sixth and Seventh Divisions as well as Bradford's Portuguese and España's Spaniards well-placed in reserve. D'Urban's dragoons and the light cavalry of Arentschildt's brigade would cover Pakenham's outer flank. The overextended French left would be hit by two-thirds of the allied army attacking from two directions at once.

The early stages of the allied attack went perfectly according to Wellington's plan. Pakenham's advance was partly concealed by the ground, and when he arrived at the end of the Monte de Azan he found only part of Thomières's division facing him, and that in some disorder. D'Urban's dragoons had already broken the leading French battalion, while the strongest regiment in the division (1e Ligne, 3 battalions, 1,700 men) seems to have been kept farther back as a link with Maucune. The leading brigade of British infantry, under Colonel Wallace, wheeled into line and advanced steadily up the sharp slope in the face of heavy French fire, with the remaining allied troops pressed forward behind them. When the range closed Pakenham gave the signal and his men cheered loudly and charged forward, the French turning and fleeing before them. A few squadrons of Curto's cavalry attempted to charge the exposed southern flank of the line and did some damage to the 1/5th in the second brigade, but were soon driven off, while Arentschildt's horsemen put the rest of the brigade to flight. The only danger for the allies was that Wallace's men were overexcited by their success and pursued too recklessly, although the remaining two brigades of the division were kept in good order.[26]

Leith's division had to wait until Pakenham's men were in position before beginning its advance, and the troops grew impatient under steady French artillery fire. Wellington had ridden up to Leith from the right of the army and, giving his orders 'in a clear, concise, and spirited manner', instructed him to advance in two lines, with most of his British infantry in the first line, and the remainder and his Portuguese brigade in the second. Leith's ADC recalled that 'there was no appearance of contemplating a doubtful result; all he directed was as to time and formation, and his instructions concluded with commands that the enemy should be overthrown, and driven from the field'.[27] The 6,700 men of the Fifth Division advanced across a mile or more of open ground to the Monte de Azan, each of its two lines some 900 yards long, maintaining a steady pace and good order despite obstacles and the French fire. Maucune withdrew his men behind the skyline and formed them, it seems, in two lines of columns or squares, with artillery in the intervals between them. When the Fifth Division crested the rise there was a brief but heavy exchange of fire, in which Leith and two of his ADCs fell wounded, before the British infantry charged and the French fled. The French second line was also engaged and broken but not without effort; the Fifth Division suffered 650 casualties in the course of the day, almost all of them in this attack on Maucune.

The destruction of the French left wing was completed by the most brilliant British cavalry charge of the war. Major-General Le Marchant had advanced with his brigade of heavy dragoons in the gap between Leith and Pakenham; and by the time he arrived on the Monte de Azan he was able to follow in

Wallace's wake. The leading brigade of the Third Division was beginning to feel the need of assistance, for its advance was checked by the appearance of the 1e Ligne, and the other regiments of Thomières's division had begun to rally. Le Marchant could not have dreamt of a better opportunity; his men charged out of the westering sun, obscured by the dust and smoke of battle into the still confused and disordered ranks of the 62e and 101e Ligne, inflicting heavy casualties and driving most of the survivors to surrender to Wallace's infantry. (The 62e lost 868 casualties including prisoners, or 77 per cent of its strength; the 101st lost 1,186, or 82 per cent). The left-hand regiment in Le Marchant's brigade (probably the 5th Dragoon Guards) went on to crash into the exposed flank of Maucune's second line just as it had been broken by Leith's infantry, adding to the casualties suffered by the 66e and 15e Ligne. The remaining two regiments (3rd, 4th Dragoons) swept forward, disordered but full of impetus, and soon encountered the leading regiment of Taupin's division which they broke and destroyed. (French sources state that only two battalions of this regiment were on the field and that at the end of the day they could muster no more than 47 officers and men out of about 1,000.)[28] After this the charge dissolved into complete disorder as the whole of the Monte de Azan was covered with parties of fleeing French and pursuing dragoons. Some French units seem to have withdrawn in good order; the 1e Ligne did not suffer heavily, and the other brigade of Curto's light cavalry scarcely figures in any account of the battle but must have been on this part of the field. The other two regiments of Taupin's division were also unbroken, and it was probably in leading a charge against one of these that General Le Marchant was killed. His brigade suffered very little for its glory: 108 casualties or barely one-tenth of its strength, although by the end of the charge, horses and men were utterly spent – nothing more could be expected of them that day.[29]

The fighting in the centre was less one-sided. Cole's Fourth Division advanced to the left (east) of Leith's division, and probably a little later. It had rather a wide front to cover and had already detached one of its two British brigades to hold the Lesser Arapile, so that it formed with the three battalions of the Fusilier brigade on the right and the four Portuguese battalions of Stubbs's brigade to their left, in a single two-deep line, with caçadores and other light infantry providing the usual screen of skirmishers. At first they encountered no resistance for they were advancing into the gap between Maucune and the Greater Arapile; but as they pushed forward Cole became anxious that he was leaving Bonnet's whole division unscathed behind his left flank, and detached some of his Portuguese troops to try to guard against this threat. At this point the southern side of the Monte de Azan is marked by another rise in the ground, and it was probably here that Cole's men encountered Clausel's division. A firefight seems to have broken out between the Fusiliers and the 50e and the 59e Ligne and to have lasted some time before the French fell back. The second brigade of Clausel's division then charged forward, and the allies, already in some disorder from the firefight, broke before them. An officer in the Fusilier brigade describes what happened:

> When [the French were] about 30 paces distant our men began to waver, being still firing & not properly formed. The Ensigns advanced two paces in front & planted the colours on the edge of the hill & Officers stept out to encourage the men to meet them. They stopt with an apparent determination to stand firm, the enemy continued to advance at a steady pace & when quite close the Fuzileers gave way.[30]

At the same moment Bonnet's infantry sallied forth from behind the Greater Arapile overwhelming the men of Stubbs's brigade. Philip Bainbrigge, a staff officer, was on the scene and recalled that 'they . . . gave way like a wave of the sea; I can compare it to nothing else'. Colonel De Lancey, the acting Quartermaster-General, 'said to me "For God's sake bring up the 6th Division as fast as possible," then dashed in amongst the Portuguese, seized the colour of one of the regiments and endeavoured to rally them. I galloped off to the rear; as to restoring order and reinforcing the regiment it required some time and the work of regimental officers'.[31]

The collapse of Cole's division was made worse by the repulse of an extremely gallant but unwise attack on the Greater Arapile by Pack's brigade. The circumstances leading to this attack are not clear – whether Wellington gave the orders for it, or whether it was undertaken on Pack's own initiative to distract Bonnet from Cole's vulnerable flank. The Portuguese infantry showed good spirit in their advance but as they approached the summit they were out of breath and in disorder so that the three battalions of the 120e Ligne had no difficulty sending them reeling back. Pack's brigade seems to have lost some 470 casualties, or 18 per cent of its strength, during the battle and the greater majority of these would have occurred in the attack.[32]

The defeat of Pack and Cole was not as serious as it appeared to officers on the spot such as Colonel De Lancey and Philip Bainbrigge, for Wellington had ample reserves well placed to fill the gap in his line. The Sixth Division was already advancing behind Cole, while the First Division was ready to support the troops holding the Lesser Arapile. Beresford took personal command of the strong Portuguese brigade in the Fifth Division wheeling it east so that it protected Leith's flank and faced Clausel. Although the French had three regiments of Boyer's dragoons on the spot they proved unable to exploit their advantage beyond breaking a weak battalion at the end of the Sixth Division's line: the 2/53rd, which was cut up and lost a colour. Bonnet's infantry clashed with the main body of the Sixth Division and there was evidently heavy fighting although the details are sketchy. At about the same time Clausel's division was also engaged again and broken, possibly by the Fourth Division after it had rallied. (It is very difficult to reconcile the sources for this part of the battle.)[33]

More than half the French army had now been broken and the battle was clearly lost. All that remained was to salvage as much from the wreck as was possible by checking the allied pursuit until the long July evening drew to its close. This unenviable task fell principally on Ferey's division which occupied a long low ridge facing north-west less than a mile to the south of the Greater Arapile. Here it was assailed in the waning light by the already weary men of the Sixth Division, and a prolonged and bloody firefight followed before it was finally driven from the position. The Sixth Division was thus engaged against at least two separate opponents (Bonnet then Ferey), and it lost much more heavily than any other division in the allied army (1,803 casualties, or very nearly one-third of its strength). Despite its success there was a sense that it had not been well handled by Henry Clinton, its commander, and Andrew Leith Hay made the interesting comment that 'the 6th [Division] suffered very much having been halted when advanced about half way – which is a system that never will answer, the only way is to get at them at once with the Bayonet, that they can never stand, but as to firing they will do that as long as you like, and fire much better than we do'.[34]

The broken country south and east of the battlefield and the gathering dark concealed the French line of retreat (south-east towards Alba de Tormes) and Wellington, still unaware that Carlos de España had withdrawn the garrison from the castle at Alba de Tormes, directed his pursuit north-east towards the fords at Huerta. He joined the Light Division as it advanced against Foy's rear-guard, and one of its officers recalled: 'The Duke of Wellington was within fifty yards of the front, when the enemy's lines commenced firing. I thought he was exposing himself unnecessarily, the more so as I heard he had put every division into action that day.' William Napier, who was commanding the 43rd Light Infantry, takes up the story: 'After dusk . . . the Duke rode up *alone* behind my regiment, and I joined him; he was giving me some orders when a ball passed through his left holster, and struck his thigh; he put his hand to the place, and his countenance changed for an instant, but only for an instant; and to my eager inquiry if he was hurt, he replied, sharply, "No!" and went on with his orders.' Fortunately it was a spent bullet and Wellington was not hurt, although there was evidently some criticism of him in military circles at home for exposing himself excessively. When he learnt of this he replied: '"I assure you, it is not the case; but there are situations you know, and Salamanca is one, where a commander in chief must show himself and act in person."' The fact that he was not seriously wounded or killed in the course of his long career suggests that he was not reckless, but also that he was lucky, carefully balancing the need to see what was happening and be seen by his men with the risk of being incapacitated.[35]

The pursuit was resumed at first light on the following day, and Bock's brigade of the heavy dragoons of the King's German Legion achieved a notable triumph when it broke a regularly formed square of Foy's infantry at Garcia Hernandez. Foy's division lost more than 1,000 casualties in the engagement (including unwounded prisoners) while Bock's dragoons suffered 127 men killed, wounded and missing.

Salamanca was the greatest French defeat in open battle since the dark days of 1799, and the greatest British victory on land in a hundred years. Marmont's army was utterly routed with the loss of more than one-quarter of its men (13,500 casualties including those at Garcia Hernandez). The allied army suffered 5,220 casualties including 694 killed. A remarkable number of senior officers were among the casualties on both sides: Marmont and Bonnet were seriously wounded, Clausel slightly, Ferey and Thomières mortally. Le Marchant was killed and Beresford, Cotton, Leith and Cole were all seriously wounded, although Cotton's wound was accidentally inflicted by an allied sentry after the fighting was over. This meant that Henry Clinton was left the most senior officer after Wellington, although Rowland Hill could have joined the army in a few days from Estremadura if Wellington had been incapacitated.

Salamanca was the greatest triumph Wellington had yet achieved and in many ways it was the most accomplished and skilful of all his battles. The placement and handling of his troops was superb, while he deserves credit for forging them into an army capable of executing such an attack with so few mistakes. Despite the disappointment of being forced back from the Duero his spirit was not cowed, and he was able to recognise and seize the opportunity when it arose. Salamanca should forever have silenced the notion that he was a cautious or defensive general who preferred Fabian warfare to a decisive encounter on the battlefield. It also proved that his army was just as reliable in attack as in defence, and that the undoubted élan and enthusiasm of the men did not overcome their discipline. After the battle Fitzroy Somerset wrote home a well-deserved tribute to his commander: 'You will perceive by Lord Wellington's dispatch that he was fully as anxious as the Youngest *fireater* in the Army to avail himself of any favourable opportunity to attack the French and that when He did engage them, he displayed that coolness & ability for which he has always been so distinguished.'[36] Somerset was a biased judge, but General Foy was no less generous in his praise:

> The battle of Salamanca is the most masterly, the most considerable . . . and the most important in its results, battle that the English have gained in

modern times. It raises Wellington almost to the height of the Duke of Marlborough. Previously one recognized his prudence, his choice of positions, his ability in using them; at Salamanca he showed himself a great and able manoeuvrer; he kept his dispositions hidden almost all day; he watched our movements in order to determine his own; he fought in oblique order; it was like one of Frederick the Great's battles.[37]

First reports of the battle reached London at the beginning of August in a message from Sir Home Popham. John Wilson Croker, the Secretary to the Admiralty, recalled:

I myself passed a few painful hours when a blundering telegraphic despatch announced the battle of Salamanca as *won by the French* and '*Wellington killed*'. This was a Sunday in August 1812. Parliament was up – no minister in town – nobody at the Admiralty but my single self; and *there* I was for four cruel hours, sitting on a corner of the Admiralty garden-wall watching the slow telegraph and as Homer says 'eating my own heart'. They were the most painful hours I ever passed, and I had the tremendous secret all to myself – first because I had no one to tell it to, and secondly that it was not tellable to anyone, in the confused and imperfect state in which it was coming up.[38]

The mistake was corrected that afternoon, but newspapers on the following day could only report the bald fact that the battle had been fought and won, and the anxious public had to wait another fortnight until, on Sunday 16 August, Wellington's ADC Lord Clinton arrived in London in a chaise bedecked in laurel, carrying the captured French eagles and flags, and the official despatch giving full details of the victory. An excited crowd assembled outside Lord Bathurst's house in Mansfield Street and the tidings soon spread. Showing more feeling than dignity Lady Wellington ran to Lord Bathurst's from her house in Harley Street to hear the news, and on being told that her husband was safe she nearly fainted.[39] The following night the capital was illuminated and jubilant crowds filled the streets. Lord Wellesley ventured out to enjoy the scene and was recognised and cheered wherever he went, basking for the moment in the reflected glory of his younger brother. Wilder members of the mob showed the fickleness of their support by breaking the (unilluminated) windows of their erstwhile hero, Sir Francis Burdett.[40]

The Opposition was astonished by the news. Lord Grey reluctantly acknowledged that 'it must have been quite decisive, and it does certainly open a prospect of more favourable consequences both in Spain and in the North than could a few months ago have been reasonably looked for'. However, he could not resist adding: 'I suppose there is no bounds to the exultation of the Prince and his Ministers. The former I have no doubt, has by this time nearly convinced himself that he won the battle in person.' Lord Auckland could barely conceal his chagrin: 'Marmont's unaccountable folly has given a fortunate brilliancy to Lord Wellington's campaign, which was leading to a lame and impotent conclusion.' But Lady Bessborough expressed what must have been a common feeling among supporters of the Opposition when she wrote that 'the only reason I wish to have friends in office is that I might once in my life be allowed to rejoice in our successes, and not always be damp'd by doubts and buts and ifs etc'.[41]

The ministers felt no inhibitions about celebrating the victory. The Archbishop of Canterbury prepared a special prayer of thanks to be read in every church in Britain and Ireland,[42] and Liverpool took advantage of the news to call an election in October. The harvest was good, the Luddite disturbances had faded away, and the whole mood of the country was much more contented than it had been in May when Perceval was assassinated. The election took place with the usual scenes of cheerful drunkenness and festive disorder, and the ministry consolidated its support in Parliament while several leading members of the Opposition lost their seats. This did not ensure the ministry's survival – parliamentary majorities were made and lost at least as much in the Commons as on the hustings at this time – but it augured well for the new session beginning late in the year.

Liverpool congratulated Wellington upon 'the most decided as well as brilliant victory which has for centuries crowned the British arms, and which, whilst it reflects the highest lustre upon every individual who was engaged in it, redounds so peculiarly to the credit of the Commander, by whose foresight, decision and science those operations were conducted which have led to a result of such incalculable importance'.[43] After some discussion the ministers decided to elevate Wellington another step in the peerage, so that after only six months as an earl he was made a marquess. The honour would be sustained by a grant of £100,000, although Mulgrave argued that £150,000 would be more appropriate, as Nelson had been given £100,000 when he had been made an earl. Liverpool, himself an earl, acknowledged that 'an income of nine or ten thousand is after all a poor support for a marquess', but decided that it was not a time for extravagance. Lord Wellesley, judging his brother's wishes by his own, strongly urged the augmentation of Wellington's arms by the inclusion of a French eagle. Bathurst disliked the idea, feeling that eagles had become all too common in recent years (even Villiers had one!), and proposed instead the inclusion of the Union Jack – an honour enjoyed by no previous subject.[44] However, a suggestion that Wellington be made a Field Marshal was successfully resisted by the Horse Guards with the argument that it would only revive the jealousy previously felt towards Wellington in the senior ranks of the army at home. Torrens, who deployed this argument with apparent sincerity, redeemed himself by successfully pressing for an addition to Wellington's pay of £5,000 p.a. ('table money') to cover the expenses of maintaining his headquarters.

No one was more delighted by the victory than Wellington himself. He told Pole: 'I never saw an Army get such a beating in so short a time. I am afraid to state the extent of the Enemy's loss; it is said to be between 17,000 & 20,000 Men . . . What havoc in little more than 4 hours!' And he added: 'The people of Salamanca swear my Mother is a Saint; & the daughter of a Saint, to which circumstance I owe all my good fortune!! Pray tell her this. The Marhattas discovered that she was a Marhatta!'[45] He was very pleased with the grant of table money, for his expenses had risen sharply with his entry to Spain and he had actually written to Bathurst for some such allowance – the letter crossing with the news that his need had been anticipated.[46] He thanked the ministers for the other rewards, declaring that 'they are far beyond my hopes, and I can show my gratitude for them only by continuing to serve His Royal Highness with the same zeal and devotion which have already acquired for me such substantial proofs of His Royal Highness's favour'.[47] According to Tom Sydenham, a confidential friend visiting headquarters, he was rather less pleased, allegedly remarking: '"What the devil is the use of making me a Marquess?"', shuddering at the thought of the addition of a French Eagle to his arms, and hinting wistfully that 'a more distinguished and appropriate compliment to him as a military man' would have been promotion to the rank of Field Marshal.[48] But such regrets were fleeting, for his attention was firmly fixed on the campaign ahead.

CHAPTER TWENTY-NINE

MADRID AND BURGOS
(July–November 1812)

WHEN WELLINGTON AWOKE on 23 July, the morning after Salamanca, it was to a bright hopeful new world. Most of the problems that had preoccupied him twenty-four hours before had disappeared, and in their place was a grand vista of almost limitless potential. Instead of an ignominious retreat back to the Portuguese frontier he had the freedom to choose the line on which he would advance, confident in the knowledge that there was not a French army within 200 miles that would dare to oppose him. But it was important not to become intoxicated by success, for the underlying balance of forces in the Peninsula had been tilted by his victory, not completely overturned. There were still well over 250,000 French troops in the Peninsula, and while Marmont's army had been knocked out of action for a time, there remained three French armies (those of Soult, Suchet and Caffarelli's Army of the North) each at least as strong as Wellington's army, together with Joseph's much weaker Army of the Centre. The task that faced Wellington was to exploit the advantage he had gained without forcing the French generals to abandon their local concerns and concentrate against him, and the further he advanced the more difficult this would become. Even in the first flush of victory he recognised this problem, and in an otherwise exultant letter to William Wellesley-Pole he admitted: 'I must still expect that they will collect upon me in all directions; and I suspect that I shall have another battle to fight yet before I have done with this campaign.' Nonetheless the mood at headquarters was buoyant and Alexander Gordon assured his brother: 'If we are able to give one more blow to Marmont's Army before they are joined by anything, the Enemy must positively abandon both Valencia & the South of Spain to collect an Army superior to Lord Wellington.'[1]

For a week after Salamanca Wellington pursued Marmont's army as it fled first east and then north to its base at Valladolid and beyond. The first day of this pursuit saw the destruction of Foy's rearguard at Garcia Hernandez, but after that there was little contact and no serious fighting between the armies, for the French out-marched the allies. The pursuit has been criticised for lacking urgency and dash, but it is unlikely that Wellington would have gained much by pressing his men forward by forced marches in the midsummer heat. Indeed he was astonished by the rapidity of the French movements and, accepting that there was no hope of catching them, allowed most of his men to rest on 25 July with only the light cavalry and guerrillas attempting to keep up the pace. The French crossed the Duero on the night of 27 July and Clausel at once set about evacuating the stores, magazines and hospitals of Valladolid. The allied advanced guard crossed the river two days later, but Wellington left the main part of his army to the south, while he and his staff entered Valladolid on 30 July to a rapturous reception.

Wellington now had to choose between marching north and driving Clausel further back, beyond Burgos, to the Ebro; or south, over the Guadarramas to Madrid. If he went north he might add to the damage already done to the morale and organisation of the Army of Portugal and take Burgos unprepared, and so secure his northern flank when he turned south. But there were risks with this course: Burgos might not fall easily, and his siege train was far away in Almeida; also Caffarelli would be unable to ignore an allied advance into the heart of his territory and would be bound to concentrate his army against Wellington. Therefore there was the danger that advancing north would not prove a simple, easily limited operation, but would extend for some time when Wellington would be needed elsewhere, for it seemed probable that the defeat of Marmont and the subsequent allied advance would force Soult to abandon Andalusia and come north to re-establish his communications with France. If Soult moved quickly he might join Joseph at Madrid and use it as a base of operations in a campaign against Wellington who would be taken at a disadvantage if he was still involved in operations around Burgos or on the Ebro. There was much less danger of being caught between two fires if Wellington turned south, drove Joseph from Madrid (beating him in the process if possible) and fought the decisive battle with Soult as he emerged from Andalusia, before he could receive any reinforcements from Joseph or Suchet. If the battle went well – and after Salamanca there was a common assumption in the allied camp that a battle on anything like equal terms would go well – Soult's army would be trapped with the allies blocking his natural line of retreat. It seemed highly unlikely that Caffarelli or Clausel would pose a significant threat to the allied rear if Wellington did not advance beyond Valladolid and left a reasonable flank guard behind the Duero, at least until the autumn. Over and above these purely military considerations was the knowledge of the political impact that the fall of Madrid would have throughout the Peninsula, in Britain, France and across Europe including in Russia. It would provide the final, undeniable proof that Napoleon's attempt to conquer Spain was no closer to success in August 1812 than it had been four years before after Bailen, and that all the blood and treasure he had devoted to it had achieved nothing.

After some hesitation, in the face of an almost impossible decision, Wellington chose to march on Madrid. He left Henry Clinton with the battle-scarred Sixth Division and five newly arrived regiments from home, amounting in all to about 7,000 infantry cantoned around Cuellar south of the Duero. Anson's brigade of light cavalry provided a screen along the river, while the Spanish General Santocildes hurried forward with rather more than 3,000 men[2] and occupied Valladolid on 6 August. The rest of the allied army crossed the Guadarramas on 7 and 8 August. A young officer in the Light Division recalled the excitement of that march: '"Is this the road to Madrid?" many exclaimed. "Are we really going to the capital of Spain, the centre of romance?" My mind was filled with all sorts of illusions and anticipations of pleasure. My rest was disturbed, my dreams were of Madrid. Every day's march was counted and every object brought something new; I made up my mind to dance every night when I arrived.'[3]

In Madrid, King Joseph's court, its dependents, and several thousand ordinary Spanish civilians who felt that their ties to the Bonapartist regime would not bear 'patriotic' scrutiny, packed up their goods and families and prepared to leave. On the night of 9 August the vast convoy set out heading south towards Aranjuez. Against professional advice Joseph left a garrison in the Retiro, and this may have ensured that there was no breakdown of authority in the city before the allies arrived.

On 12 August 1812 the allied army entered Madrid, Wellington riding at the head of the column with Carlos de España on his right hand and Julian Sanchez on his left, followed by his generals and all their staff.[4] Madrid had seen little of the horrors of war after the Dos de Mayo, the event that had provided the spark for the initial uprising four years earlier, although there had been privation and hardship the previous winter.[5] The allies were astonished at the warmth of the welcome they received. Alexander Gordon wrote home on 16 August: 'It is impossible to conceive the way in which we are fêted by the People; they are absolutely quite mad for joy. They look up to Lord Wellington as a God and call him the Saviour of their Country: thousands of people when he is in public come to embrace him, and are too happy to kiss his hands, knees or hem of his garment.' Captain Kincaid of the Rifles explains: 'I believe that the prevailing opinion was that *we* should be considered as the intruders. It was, therefore, a matter of the most unexpected exultation . . . to find ourselves hailed as liberators, with the most joyous acclamations, by surrounding multitudes, who continued their rejoicings for three successive days.' And Charles Cocks told his sister: 'I was never kissed by so many pretty girls in a day in all my life, or expect to be again.' Food, flowers, wine, lemonade and sweetmeats were pressed on the soldiers as they marched into the city and the festivities lasted far into the night as the town was illuminated and crowds filled the streets.[6]

The outer walls of the Retiro were stormed without much difficulty and the garrison surrendered on the following day (14 August). As well as 1,800 prisoners Wellington captured vast quantities of stores in the Retiro including shoes and uniforms, most of which could be used by allied troops, and ammunition and weapons including almost 200 heavy guns. There were also two eagles: those of the 51e Ligne and 13e Dragoons which were sent home as a symbol of the triumph.[7] Unfortunately the capture was marred by an outbreak of looting as the soldiers, stretching the precedent established by Ciudad Rodrigo and Badajoz, felt they had a right to plunder and did so quite brazenly. Hearing of the disorder Wellington immediately intervened in person, seizing some looters and placing all the officers on guard under arrest for not preventing it. The strength and sincerity of his disgust for such behaviour is obvious, but the incident reflected poorly on the state of discipline in the army.[8]

The new constitution was proclaimed with great ceremony and Carlos de España was appointed governor of the city.[9] A grand bullfight was held, provoking a predictable range of reactions from British officers who attended. Alexander Gordon preferred to spend his leisure hours studying the paintings left in the royal palaces, although he provoked the scorn of his brother (a noted connoisseur) by admiring the works of Mengs as well as those of Titian, Guido and Correggio. He was tempted to buy a good Murillo or two for £50 or £100 on his brother's behalf, but was not quite sure his brother would approve and could not venture such a sum from his own small income.[10] Wellington sat for Goya, which resulted in a striking chalk sketch and two portraits in oils, one half-length (see plate 53), the other equestrian, which do not fit comfortably with other contemporary images of Wellington. He enjoyed the society of the Duchess de San Carlos, and also found time to visit 'some ladies of Joseph's party', going incognito as a commissary of the Fourth Division. One of these 'ladies' recognised him a few days later when he was riding with his staff in the Prado, but any embarrassment was fleeting.[11]

As always, most of Wellington's time was spent in work as he considered his next step and kept up with all the routine business of the army. This burden had fallen particularly heavily on him in recent months as both Charles Stewart and George Murray had gone home, the first temporarily, the latter to take up an appointment in Ireland.[12] The loss of the efficient and dependable Murray was a real blow, made worse by Wellington's suspicion that it had been orchestrated as part of a manoeuvre to allow Colonel James Willoughby Gordon, the Duke of York's favourite, to succeed him.[13] Still Wellington welcomed Gordon cordially when he joined the army at the beginning of August and made a determined effort to see if his talents could be put to effective use. Gordon for his part frankly admired Wellington, writing home from Madrid:

> Our great leader is undoubtedly a very superior man – you cannot discuss business with him without very soon being sensible of it, and he has every noble quality to attach military men to him – brave, candid, liberal, decisive, and just – he has a great knowledge of the affairs and ways of men & a considerable penetration into their designs – perhaps he acts in person when he might often much better direct, but this he knows and he does so because his experience has shown him that he cannot safely depute.
>
> Our Officers are very bad indeed: they will march up to a cannon's mouth (that's something and in battle no small matter) but they have not much intelligence or much knowledge, and they are dreadfully nervous upon all that regards what is called personal responsibility.[14]

The idea that Wellington should be relieved of some of the burden of routine work by delegating more had considerable appeal, especially at this time, and it led him to give some encouragement when Gordon floated a scheme to create a chief of staff, a position previously unknown to the British army. However the proposal aroused immediate and furious opposition in the Horse Guards, with the Duke of York resenting his protégé's presumption and ambition, and Torrens arguing that in most cases a chief of staff would soon usurp the authority of the general in nominal command of the army.[15] Gordon's position was further weakened when Wellington discovered that he was not only writing confidentially to the Duke of York and to Lord Grey, but that the contents of these letters were finding their way into the *Morning Chronicle*.[16] It appears that Gordon was naïve rather than sinister – he was not an active Whig, but he was accustomed to being on confidential terms with Grey and Whitbread and wished them to understand more about the war in the Peninsula. It is unlikely that he anticipated that his letters could be used in attacks upon the government, and while some of his remarks were incautious he became more discreet when the military situation became less favourable.[17] There were no generally accepted precepts on the ethics of officers writing home with confidential information: Charles Stewart had written equally freely to Castlereagh whether the latter was in office or not; Alexander Gordon (no relation to Willoughby) revealed the thinking behind Wellington's plans to Lord Aberdeen almost every week without sacrificing Wellington's confidence; and senior officers throughout the army had not hesitated to express their views freely at any time in the war. Willoughby Gordon merely posed the question more sharply than others because his position as Quartermaster-General (let alone chief of staff) gave him access to so much confidential information, and because he was sending it straight to one of the leaders of the opposition who, directly or indirectly, passed it on to the press.

It is possible that Gordon might have retained his position if he had proved efficient, but he did not. On 25 August Alexander Gordon wrote to his brother Charles in Ireland: 'Tell G[eorge] M[urray] that Everybody wishes him back here, that Gordon knows nothing about the matter, is quite a child out of his Office, and I think altogether a damned heavy fellow.'[18] Other officers at headquarters soon came to the same conclusion, while the autumn campaign was marred by problems unknown to previous operations due to ineffective staff work.[19] Wellington gave Gordon time to become accustomed to his task, but by the end of October he had made his mind, as he made clear in a brutally frank letter to Torrens: 'I don't agree with you because you think he has some Talents; whereas I am quite certain that he has none, excepting those of Clerk at his Desk. I was never so much deceived in my opinion of any Man. He is no more fit to be QMG of the Army than he is to be King of England. De Lancey, who is the Idlest fellow I ever saw, did the business much better.'[20]

The awkwardness of arranging Gordon's recall was avoided when he developed a bad case of piles and had to return home for an operation at the end of the year. Once assured that he was going, Wellington begged Torrens to spare Gordon's feelings as far as possible; this was managed so well that Gordon retained the impression that Wellington would be disappointed that he would be unable to return to the army! Torrens also ensured that George Murray resumed his former post and Wellington welcomed him back with a heightened appreciation of his talents, and placed much more confidence in him in 1813–14 than in previous campaigns.[21] Nonetheless the moral of the whole affair for Wellington was surely to reinforce his belief that attempting to delegate to others was more trouble than it was worth, and that the best way to ensure a job well done was to do it himself.

Wellington remained at Madrid for three weeks and the army benefitted from the rest. Nonetheless the number of men in hospital actually rose as the usual summer illnesses took their toll. On 25 July, there were 17,033 British rank and file in hospital including all the Salamanca wounded; a month later this had risen to 20,108 and it fell only marginally over the following month. In other words more British soldiers fell ill during July–August than were wounded in the battle.[22] These losses always fell heavily on troops who had just arrived in the Peninsula and had yet to become accustomed to the rigours of campaigning, the demands of the climate and the endemic diseases. According to the regimental history a draft of 16 officers and 200 men for the 43rd Foot, an excellent regiment, part of the Light Division, landed at Lisbon. Of these only six officers, two sergeants and eighteen men reached the regiment in Madrid on 22 August; all the rest had fallen ill and been unable to continue the march, and many had died.[23] This was, admittedly, an extreme example, but it helps to show why Wellington's fighting force showed no appreciable increase despite the thousands of reinforcements sent out to the Peninsula in the summer and autumn of 1812.

Wellington stayed in Madrid for so long because he was unsure of his next step. He considered advancing into Andalusia to bring Soult to battle, but was deterred by the heat of summer and the long vulnerable line of communication he would have behind him. He also toyed with the idea of marching into Valencia driving Joseph before him and joining hands with the expedition from Sicily which had landed at Alicante on 7 August. However this would certainly stir Suchet into action when he might otherwise ignore Wellington, and it would also create an overly long supply line. The defeat of Soult had to be Wellington's primary purpose and with it the liberation of Andalusia. Soult did not receive reliable news of Salamanca until 12 August and at once began to evacuate his viceroyalty. He lifted the siege of Cadiz and left Seville on 26 August heading for Cordova where he waited for some days for Drouet to join him. By late August it was clear that it would be some weeks before he would be able to advance on Madrid, and Wellington turned his attention back to the north where Clausel had had the audacity to advance on Valladolid.[24]

After its defeat at Salamanca and retreat over the Duero the Army of Portugal had been in a woeful state. Clausel had to adopt ruthless measures to restore order and discipline, including having fifty soldiers shot.[25] The strong medicine worked and within a fortnight the army was again capable of taking the field, although still very shaky and not to be trusted in battle. Clausel advanced, not to challenge Wellington, but to rescue the small French garrisons at Toro, Zamora and Astorga which were now far behind allied lines and besieged or blockaded by Spanish and Portuguese troops. He was too late for Astorga which had fallen on 18 August but relieved the garrisons of Toro and Zamora – a small success which lifted the morale of his army.

Wellington left Madrid on 1 September leaving behind some of his best troops including the Light, Third and Fourth Divisions, evidently wishing to rest them so that they would be fresh for the decisive battle against Soult. A much more serious and inexplicable mistake was Wellington's failure to bring forward a siege train, either from Almeida or the guns he had captured in the Retiro. Evidently he did not set off with the intention of capturing Burgos as his primary objective, but it was obvious that it might form part of the campaign and the experience of the Salamanca forts showed the dangers of relying on improvised expedients. No mistake in Wellington's entire military career was as wilful or as inexcusable as his failure to ensure that he had sufficient means to undertake the siege of Burgos.[26]

Wellington advanced across the Duero on 6 September with some 28,000 men. Clausel fell back before him and Wellington did not press him hard, with Alexander Gordon telling his brother: 'It is not our object at present to fight them, unless obliged to it, but by manoeuvres if possible to force them behind the Ebro.'[27] On the night of 17 September Clausel retreated through Burgos and fell back to the north-east towards Briviesca and Pancorbo on the main highway to France, but still well south of the Ebro.

The ancient castle of Burgos rises sheer from the midst of the town on an outcrop of rock 200 feet high. During the four years of its occupation by the French its defences had been strengthened and modernised, but it was not a first-class fortress and it could not have resisted an attack with a proper siege train for much more than a week.[28] It was held by an excellent garrison of some 2,000 men of the Army of the North under General Dubreton, most of whom had to camp in the open for there was little accommodation, and water was scarce although there was plenty of food. A high-angle bombardment with mortars would have made life intolerable for the garrison, and there were no civilians in the castle to be considered, but Wellington had no mortars with him. He carefully reconnoitred the castle on the 18 September and was surprised by its strength, admitting to Maitland: 'I doubt however that I have the means to take the Castle, which is very strong.'[29] Even now it would have not been too late to send for heavy guns from Almeida or Madrid, but Wellington did not think he had time; he expected to have to march south again to face Soult at the end of the month or in early October. The only guns available, apart from field pieces, were the three iron 18-pounders and five 24-pounder howitzers of Dickson's reserve battery, with just five Engineer officers supported by ten temporary assistants and eight Royal Military Artificers 'who knew nothing that could make them useful, but who certainly behaved with spirit'.[30] To undertake the siege with such obviously inadequate means was to invite disaster, and was most untypical of Wellington. Years later he admitted that it had been an error and suggested that he had been misled by his experience of capturing even more formidable hill forts in India, although at the time he may have been more influenced by the enthusiasm and assurance of John Burgoyne, who was filling Fletcher's place, and who was confident that he could take the castle with the means available.[31]

The castle was invested on 19 September but progress proved difficult and costly because the French artillery completely overpowered that of the besiegers. On the night of 22 September an unsuccessful attempt was made to escalade the outer walls on the western side. There was some criticism that the troops, particularly the Portuguese, had not shown much determination, and Burgoyne was unhappy that Wellington had employed only small storming parties. Wellington's argument was that small parties suffered fewer casualties and that there was no point having hundreds of men milling around at the foot of the walls – an easy prey to enemy fire – when only a few could attempt to climb the ladders at a time. Clearly the losses suffered by the Fourth and Light Divisions at the breaches of Badajoz were still all too fresh in his mind. Burgoyne however felt that 'large bodies encourage one another, and carry with them the confidence of success; because we had but ten or twelve ladders to storm the castle of Badajoz, and therefore not more than forty or fifty men could mount at once, I am convinced it was only carried by the whole 3rd Division being there, and the emulation between the officers of the different regiments to get their men to mount; and although we lost 600 or 700 men, it caused success, which eventually always saves men'. Despite this disagreement, and all the other problems that arose during the siege, Wellington and Burgoyne remained on excellent terms and worked well together.[32]

After the failure of the escalade on 22 September the allies concentrated their efforts on tunnelling under the walls. This was hard work for inexperienced and inexpert troops and it was made more difficult by the poor quality of the tools available.[33] The three 18-pounders were established in a breaching battery, but provoked such a torrent of fire from the French that they had to be withdrawn after two of the guns were damaged – one having been hit no fewer than eleven times.[34] Sir Home Popham sent forty barrels of powder from the Biscay coast and was eager to send guns as well, but Wellington discouraged him until it was too late.[35]

As well as lack of equipment the siege was increasingly hampered by the troops' poor morale and lack of energy, which was in turn exacerbated by the heavy rain that began to fall in early October.[36] Burgoyne complained particularly of the Portuguese infantry who did little work in the trenches and held back in the attempts at storming. Wellington provides some confirmation for this, writing to Beresford on 5 October: 'Something or other has made a terrible alteration in the troops for the worse. They have lately, in several instances, behaved very ill; and whether it be owing to the nature of the service, or their want of pay, I can't tell; but they are not at all in the style they were.' He thought that the decline was due to 'misery' of both officers and soldiers due to the long arrears of their pay and urged Beresford to press the Portuguese government to give this the highest priority.[37] But it is clear that the siege itself was having a bad effect on the morale of the whole army, not just the Portuguese troops. Alexander Gordon, whose commission was in the Scots Guards, told his brother Charles: 'The fact of it is, *entre nous*, the troops have not behaved so well as they ought in the attacks, and our friends in the Guards are not altogether very stout.'[38]

The outer wall was finally taken on 4 October and Wellington told Hill: 'This is altogether the most difficult job I have ever had in hand, with such trifling means. God send that they may give me a little more time.'[39] As the casualty lists grew, the psychological, if not the strategic, significance of Burgos increased, and it came to be seen as the key to the whole campaign. It was thought that if the allies could take Burgos, they could hold the line of the River Arlanzon through the autumn and winter while Wellington returned to Madrid to face Soult. This was probably over-optimistic, but the balance of forces was tilting heavily against the allies, and there was no better solution to the problem they faced.[40]

Any confidence created by the success on 4 October was lost when subsequent days brought no progress, and the mood darkened further when Charles Cocks was killed in a French sortie on 8 October. His death was keenly felt throughout the army for his fame had spread far beyond headquarters and the units in which he served. Wellington was moved and upset by the news. Frederick Ponsonby recalled him coming into the room the following morning, walking silently about then leaving, saying nothing more than 'Cocks was killed last night'; and Tom Sydenham, Lord Wellesley's old adherent who had known Wellington since their days in India together, said that he had never seen him so much affected. Of all the promising young officers in the army (apart from some of those on his personal staff) Cocks was Wellington's favourite protégé, for he combined intelligence, courage, enterprise and an unflagging enthusiasm for his profession. He had served as a regimental officer in both the cavalry and, more recently, the infantry, and had been employed on a number of occasions to observe enemy movements well in advance of the army, his reports proving to be both reliable and useful. Wellington, Cotton, Pack, Anson, the whole of their staff and all the officers of the 16th Light Dragoons and the 79th Foot (the regiments in which Cocks had served) attended the funeral, and Wellington told Lord Somers, Cocks's father, in words which were not lightly chosen:

> Your son fell, as he had lived, in the zealous and gallant discharge of his duty. He had already distinguished himself in the course of the operations of the attack of the castle of Burgos to such a degree as to induce me to recommend him for promotion; and I assure your Lordship that if Providence had spared him to you, he possessed acquirements, and was endowed with qualities, to become one of the greatest ornaments of his profession, and to continue an honour to his family, and an advantage to his country.[41]

The siege limped on. An assault on the night of 18 October was repulsed; again small storming parties were used, which kept casualties down to around 200. Wellington paid warm tribute to the courage of the troops employed in the attempt – the Guards and the King's German Legion – making it clear that they were not to blame for the failure. At the same time, writing of the siege as a whole, he praised the work of Burgoyne, Dickson and Lieutenant-Colonel Robe (who commanded the artillery) and, more surprisingly, expressed satisfaction with the conduct of all the officers and troops employed in the siege. This last was not entirely sincere, and he later could not resist the temptation to tell Liverpool that the operation would have succeeded if he had not left his best troops, the Third, Fourth and Light Divisions, at Madrid – but that was grossly unfair: he had set his men an impossible task, and if they showed any lack of spirit it may well have been because they recognised that they had little chance of success.[42] The whole operation has attracted considerable criticism and, while some of this is certainly justified, and some more debatable, the essential fact is that Wellington should never have left himself so short of means; at the very least he should have summoned a proper siege train as soon as he had reconnoitred the fortress. The combination of lack of foresight and poor judgement was most untypical. The army suffered over 2,000 casualties in the siege, its morale deteriorated greatly, and the French armies were left undisturbed to prepare their counter-offensive. It was the worst mistake of Wellington's military career.[43]

The siege of Burgos was raised on 21 October. Reports from deserters that the garrison's food was running short might have tempted Wellington to carry on for another few days, but the French armies in both the north and south had at last stirred into action and could not be ignored. Soult had met Joseph, Jourdan and Suchet in early October and they had decided that the Armies of the South and Centre would make a coordinated advance on Madrid, while Suchet remained in Valencia and protected their rear. Soult was able to leave his sick and dependents in security and when the two French armies advanced in the middle of October they had about 60,000 men,[44] compared to about 43,000 allied troops under Hill. The rains that had made life miserable in the trenches at Burgos had not fallen in central Spain so the rivers were fordable in many places, and Ballesteros had not responded to Wellington's request that he move to threaten Soult's flank and rear. In the north the Army of Portugal (now commanded by Souham) had been reinforced so that it amounted to some 45,000 men, and had been joined by Caffarelli with a further 10,000.[45] Caffarelli and Souham believed that Wellington had around 60,000 men at Burgos (the true figure was below 35,000), and they knew that their men could not face the British with confidence, but they pushed forward with care. The allied army withdrew on the night of 21 October, some of the troops crossing the bridge of Burgos under the guns of the castle without disaster. A long night-march ensured a clean break and a good head-start, but it also meant that the men were tired and jaded from the outset of the retreat.[46]

Over the next few days Wellington's army retreated to the Duero. A sharp rearguard action at Venta del Pozo on 23 October went badly; the spirit of the troops was not good, and one British officer wrote that the allied cavalry were '*cowed*'.[47] Wellington was shaken on 27 October when for the first time he had the opportunity of observing the full strength of the French forces facing him. That night he wrote to Hill: 'The enemy are infinitely superior to us in cavalry, and from what I saw today, very superior in infantry. We must retire, therefore, and the Duero is no barrier for us. If we go, and we cannot hold our ground beyond the Duero, your situation will become delicate. We certainly cannot stand against the numbers at present opposed to us in any situation.'[48] This meant that the army would have to retire at least as far as Salamanca and hope to hold the line of the Tormes, having first secured its junction with Hill.

Hill was still far to the south, but had begun his retreat. On 30 October the stores in the Retiro were destroyed and Madrid abandoned, to the despair of many of its citizens who had made their allegiances obvious and who feared punishment if the French returned. On 2 November Hill crossed the Guadarramas and marched west towards Alba de Tormes. Wellington had not been pressed by the French and remained near Ruedo until 6 November when he withdrew south-west to Salamanca. By 8 November the allied army had been reunited and occupied a line running from the heights of San Cristobal just outside Salamanca along the river to Alba de Tormes some fifteen miles to the south. Wellington was relieved, feeling that he had '"got clear, in a handsome manner, of the worst scrape that I ever was in"'.[49] The French pursuit of both halves of the allied army was markedly cautious, even timid; despite their great superiority of numbers there was no eagerness to force an engagement. The allied cavalry may have been '*cowed*' but the French generals were plainly intimidated.

Outriders from the Army of the Centre made contact with Souham's advanced posts near Medina del Campo on 7 November and the French armies soon united. Caffarelli had already returned to the north where the guerrillas of Navarre and Biscay were sweeping through the mountain country in a formidable insurrection. Detachments were also made to occupy Madrid and a few other posts, but the combined armies still amounted to about 90,000 men, including 11,000 cavalry, compared to less than 70,000 allied troops with only 3,500 cavalry.

The French commanders reconnoitred Wellington's position around San Cristobal and agreed that it was too strong for a frontal attack. Instead Soult turned its southern flank, crossing the Tormes on the night of 14 November. Wellington responded by occupying his old position south of Salamanca, but this time including the Greater Arapile. A fierce storm broke in the night with heavy driving rain which placed Soult in some difficulty, for the Tormes would soon rise and threaten to cut off his retreat. Wellington was willing to fight a defensive battle but he would not risk an attack when his cavalry was so heavily outnumbered. Soult would not risk an attack, and did not really want to fight at all, but unlike Marmont four months previously he was cautious and careful. He spent the morning consolidating his position and in the afternoon began edging round the allied flank. Wellington watched for a time, but knew in his heart that the grey November day would not see a repeat of the triumph of July, and gave the order to retreat.[50]

The allies withdrew in an ill humour while Soult shepherded them on their way rather than pursuing them with vigour. The four days' march that followed was marked by atrocious weather and a failure of the commissariat, which meant that most of the troops went at least two days without regular supplies and some received none at all. Discipline frequently collapsed under the strain and thousands of men fell out of the ranks, some with exhaustion, some in search of food. Hundreds died of cold and hunger, while almost all were miserable and foul tempered. On 17 November the French cavalry harassed the retreating columns, cutting off many stragglers and capturing Edward Paget who had only recently rejoined the army. That afternoon the Light Division was involved in a sharp rearguard action as it waited to cross the River Huebra at San Muñoz. Soult then called off the chase; his men were also suffering from the weather and the allies were clearly on their way back to the Portuguese frontier where they belonged. On the following day, 18 November, three generals, William Stewart, Dalhousie and, probably, Clinton, defied Wellington's orders and chose their own line of march – an act of insubordination unheard of in the army in the Peninsula, although one that may have reflected doubt about the competence of the quartermaster (J.W. Gordon) rather than lack of faith in Wellington. The result was a lengthy delay and the sharp rebuke: 'You see, gentleman, I know my own business best.'[51] The next day, 19 November, the army trudged to Ciudad Rodrigo where food, guarded by sentries with fixed bayonets to prevent a rush, was distributed to the men.[52] Thomas Henry Browne, of the Adjutant-General's department, describes how he had scarcely arrived and got comfortable than he was sent for by Wellington himself and ordered to retrace the last miles of the march to help bring in stragglers. At that moment his feelings towards his commander were anything but kind, but he appropriated a dozen empty waggons, a doctor, a party of soldiers and some supplies and set out. When dawn came they were some miles on the road to Salamanca and found themselves amid scenes of desolation and horror. With the supplies in the waggons Browne was able to put many exhausted soldiers back on their feet, while he carried more than a hundred men back with him to Ciudad Rodrigo. Despite his own weariness he records that 'I was deeply thankful that I had been sent out on the duty which I was performing & thus made the instrument of saving many lives'.[53]

When the retreat was over and the army settled back into their accustomed winter quarters along the frontier, Lowry Cole wrote home that it had been 'by far the severest lesson I ever experienced in my military career, and I believe the severest any British troops have experienced this war – Sir John Moore's retreat excepted'.[54] But in Wellington's eyes the army had badly failed an important test. The last stage of the retreat had been unpleasant, but it had only lasted four days, the marches had not been particularly long, the country was flat, and while the weather was bad it was not really extreme – snow or ice or intolerable heat would have been worse. The French pursuit had not been much of a threat nor the local civilian population hostile. The hardships of the campaign were real, but they did not excuse the wholesale collapse of discipline that affected much of the army. On 28 November he issued a circular letter to officers commanding divisions and brigades censuring the conduct of the army in sweeping terms and laying the blame squarely at the feet of the regimental officers whose neglect permitted, even encouraged, their men to misbehave.[55] Inevitably this order became public and it aroused deep and lasting resentment in the army, especially among officers who believed that their unit at least had emerged with credit from the ordeal, but who found themselves all subject to the same opprobrium.[56] As in other cases the sharpness of Wellington's pen did his reputation more harm than much harsher actions would have done; no one condemned Clausel for shooting fifty soldiers for misconduct after the retreat from Salamanca, yet even his admirers struggle to excuse Wellington's order.[57] Earlier in the year Wellington had chosen to overlook serious outbreaks of indiscipline; the sack of Ciudad Rodrigo and Badajoz, the looting which followed the fall of the Retiro, and the poor performance of the troops before Burgos, had led only to the punishment of a few individuals. Possibly the retreat from Salamanca was the last straw and Wellington's patience snapped, or he felt that with some months in cantonments ahead of them his generals would have time to deal with the problem. Alternatively he may have acted because the problem affected the majority of the army rather than a small section; but it seems likely that it was the spectre of Sir John Moore's retreat to Coruña that convinced him that he could not allow the poor conduct of the army to pass unnoticed. Ever since his return to the Peninsula in 1809 he had been concerned that in adversity the army might dissolve in his hands, and on the road from Burgos to Salamanca, and even more from Salamanca to Ciudad Rodrigo, he had seen signs that this was beginning to happen. No lasting damage had been done except the loss of soldiers on the retreat – those who reached Ciudad Rodrigo were soon as well fed and obedient as ever – but Wellington could not allow a precedent to be set that would entitle soldiers and their officers to believe that misconduct was the natural and acceptable consequence of adversity.

And so the high hopes aroused by the victory of Salamanca came to nothing, and the campaign of 1812 ended on a sour note with the allied army back on the frontier of Portugal. To the weary officers and jaded men it seemed that of all they had accomplished, only the capture of Ciudad Rodrigo and Badajoz remained. But a broader perspective reveals the falseness of this view. It was not just that the siege of Cadiz had been raised and the whole of Andalusia liberated, although that had been Wellington's principal objective; the whole structure of French rule in Spain had been shaken to pieces and all the world had seen that it was no more than a sham. Spanish supporters of the intrusive King could no longer delude themselves that the invincible French army would surely triumph in the end, while Napoleon's admirers from Bayonne to Berlin had been forced to realise that the Spanish war was not going well. In theory, if Napoleon had triumphed in Russia, he might have followed the precedent of 1809 and poured another 100,000 conscripts across the Pyrenees to force the allies back onto the defensive. But 1812 was not 1809; three years, tens of thousands of lives and countless treasure had been spent in the attempt to win the war in Spain, and to repeat the attempt would cost Napoleon dearly in support at home and abroad. The time had come when persevering leadership and determination appeared indistinguishable from obstinacy and folly.

Ultimately, Wellington's campaigns in 1812 achieved all that it was reasonable to hope for given the balance of forces in the Peninsula. With skill and better luck he might perhaps have wintered on the Duero, or even forced the French back to the Ebro and kept them there, but the odds were always against it. There were simply too many French troops in Spain, they were too resilient and their generals were too competent. To have achieved more Wellington would probably have had to defeat Soult before he could unite with Joseph, and possibly gone on to fight another major battle against Joseph and Suchet. Even if victorious, the cost of such a sustained series of operations would have been high, and the speed of French recovery meant that even a defeated army was not out of the reckoning for long. As it was, the French had collected such a numerical superiority by late October that it is unlikely the allies could have maintained their position in either the north or the south even if Burgos had been captured. At another time Wellington might possibly have used his central position after retreating across the Duero and uniting with Hill to bring a superior force against first Soult, then Souham, and so defeat his enemies in detail. But whatever the theoretical attractions of such a Napoleonic manoeuvre, November 1812 was not the time to attempt it, for the army was too tired and worn to undertake the rapid marches and succession of hard fights needed to bring it to fruition, or to exploit any victory it gained. Here, as almost everywhere other than Burgos, Wellington was coolly realistic – refusing to put future prospects at risk for a slim hope of avoiding an unpleasant retreat. The allied army emerged intact from the campaign of 1812, and with an overwhelming psychological ascendancy over the French. This, as much as any territorial gain, was Wellington's achievement, and it laid the foundations for the triumph of 1813.

CHAPTER THIRTY

LIFE AT HEADQUARTERS

HEADQUARTERS OF THE army remained at Freneda from 24 November 1812 until 22 May 1813, although Wellington himself was absent for six weeks from mid-December to late January visiting Cadiz and Lisbon for talks with the Spanish and Portuguese governments. It was not unusual for the army to spend long periods in winter quarters, nor for headquarters to remain in one place for months at a time, but it is striking that Wellington chose to keep his station so near the front even when there was no likelihood of active operations. Another commander might have preferred to base himself further back, at Guarda, Coimbra or even Lisbon, arguing that the bulk of his duties in these months revolved around correspondence with civil authorities and thus greater ease of communication with the governments in Lisbon, Cadiz and London was more important than his constant attendance upon the troops. Wellington would have none of this; he knew that his presence in the midst of the army was good for morale, that it discouraged his senior commanders from seeking to go home on leave as soon as the campaigning season was over, and that it kept him in touch with his network of correspondents in Spain. Above all it signalled that the duties of an officer did not stop with leading his men into battle; that as much care and attention to their welfare and discipline was required when the army was in cantonments as when it was in the field; and that these duties took precedence over the officer's personal comfort and convenience.

Life at Freneda was far from luxurious. In March 1813 Mr Larpent, the Deputy Judge Advocate to the forces in the Peninsula, described his quarters in a letter home:

Freneda is a village much in decay, very dirty; in the streets are immense masses of stones, and holes, and dung all about, houses like a farm kitchen, with this difference that there are the stables underneath ... I am now in a distinct building like a granary, with the stables below ... in which are my animals of all sorts, servants and all. The kitchen is a miserable shed, not water-tight, where the woman of the house and three children live quite separate. The building I occupy has one opening with a wooden door besides the entrance-door, and at the end, about eight feet wide by sixteen long, was boarded off by an officer last year. In this I sleep, eat, drink, write, &c, and live altogether, as it has a fireplace in the corner built by the same officer. The fireplace is so contrived, however, as to let more smoke into the room than up the chimney, and of course my eyes suffer, and all I have looks yellow and smells of smoke.[1]

Nonetheless, Larpent considered himself fortunate to have secured quarters in Freneda at all. The village was too small to house all the departments attached to headquarters, and some were forced to take up residence in other nearby villages where they may have had better housing, but felt cut off and out of the way of news, society and fresh supplies. James McGrigor, who spent the winter with half a dozen officers of his medical staff at Castello Bom three miles north of Freneda, complained that the little village, which had once held 150 or 200 inhabitants, now had only 20 or 30, the rest having died or fled to safer quarters. Of the survivors there were only two with whom the British officers felt they could associate and 'neither of them had their minds much cultivated'. The priest was a pious, good man of mild gentle manners who lived very simply and who was often invited to dine with McGrigor. The *juiz de faro* or magistrate was a rough, coarse man, though very good natured. Finding that he had a hard head some of McGrigor's party decided to test his limits and plied him with bottle after bottle of port wine. When this produced little effect they introduced him to Scotch whisky 'which he called "*nuevo*", praising it much; but without betraying any symptoms of intoxication, and when the party broke up, he showed but little inclination to take his departure'.[2] The charms of such a situation might easily be exhausted in less than six months.

Wellington naturally occupied the best quarters in Freneda, but this was still no more than a modest house next to the church, with living space on the first floor and stables and store rooms below. There was a dining room that could sit twelve with comfort and rather more with a little crowding, although grand entertainments to celebrate special occasions were either held in a marquee erected in Freneda (such as the dinner on the second anniversary of Albuera), or held in Ciudad Rodrigo (the fête and ball for Lowry Cole's investiture as a Knight of the Bath).[3] Some of Wellington's staff managed to make themselves quite comfortable. The young Prince of Orange, who had become one of Wellington's ADCs in 1811, had a house of his own; while Alexander Gordon took up residence in a small chapel, 'hung it with red baize, fitted up the altar as his dressing-table, put up an iron stove and made it one of the best quarters here'.[4] Even so, Gordon told his brother in November 1812, 'I am heartily sick of the War, and dread the idea of our Winter quarters at Freneda. I wish I had some excuse to go home'.[5]

The Portuguese winter in this high country on the Spanish border is cold, and few windows had glass. Before December had even begun Larpent observed: 'All the Sierras are white with snow. I found Lord Wellington's secretaries sitting with candles at twelve o'clock in the day, in order to stop their holes and windows with curtains, and burning charcoal fires'.[6] Supplies were at first rather scarce, and although this problem was soon overcome, additional comforts remained expensive and difficult to procure. Wellington's table was well supplied, but most of the officers attached to headquarters would dine with the commander only occasionally, and had to make their own arrangements to supplement their rations. Sutlers soon appeared at Freneda, but their prices were high and not all their goods suited British palates. 'There were hard Dutch pineapple cheeses so salt as to be scarcely eatable, & so hard that the teeth would with difficulty penetrate into a slice, the price of which was a dollar a pound. Dutch butter too was of pretty nearly the same quality & dearness. This Suttlers [sic] however had Tea, sugar, & Tobacco, & sometimes tolerable cigars, which were in great demand. They grew enormously rich & saucy as every sort of protection was afforded them & no bounds put to their extravagant charges'.[7]

Altogether the headquarters amounted to some 400 men or possibly a few more if all the Portuguese boys and Spanish muleteers are included. Of these about one-third belonged to Wellington's personal household: his military secretary (Fitzroy Somerset), a dozen aides-de-camp, two Spanish liaison officers (O'Lawlor and Alava), a Portuguese interpreter and about 100 servants, orderly dragoons and muleteers. The departments of the army – the Adjutant-General, Quartermaster-General, artillery, engineers, medical, commissary, paymaster and others – all had relatively small staffs at headquarters, not more than a handful of officers and some clerks, but the need for servants, grooms and orderlies swelled the total numbers. Beresford headed an almost equally large headquarters of the Portuguese army, for his responsibilities included not just the Portuguese troops in the field, but the whole military force of the country. He was in and around Lisbon during the winter of 1812–13 receiving treatment for his slow-healing Salamanca wound, but for much of the war he and the Portuguese headquarters were close to Wellington. On the march the baggage train of the two headquarters might extend for several miles if forced to advance along a narrow road, yet Wellington had taken pains to devolve as much administrative work as possible down to his divisions.[8]

Wellington did not always choose dilapidated buildings in small villages for his headquarters. In Madrid he resided in the Royal Palace and he frequently stayed in substantial houses as good as he would have had in England. He spent almost four months at Badajoz in the autumn of 1809 and more than three weeks in a gentleman's residence at Pero Negro in October–November 1810,[9] but more often than not the headquarters staff had to make the best of quarters like those at Freneda. In May 1810 Charles Stewart wrote to Castlereagh from Celorico: 'You can conceive of nothing more *triste* and desolating than this miserable village, or rather abominable mudhole.'[10]

Such discomforts were only to be expected when the army was on campaign, but May 1810, like the winter of 1812–13, was a period of inaction without the movement, excitement and interest of active operations to distract thoughts from petty miseries. Not that campaigning was always uncomfortable, least of all for the staff; most soldiers who survived the war went home with fond memories of a good bivouac in a picturesque location at the end of a day's march when everything had gone well. Still, life on campaign was generally rough and sometimes simply miserable. On the night before Salamanca, Thomas Henry Browne and the other officers of the Adjutant-General's staff were congratulating themselves on having found a comfortable billet before the thunderstorm broke, when they were turfed out into the rain by Stapleton Cotton and his staff.[11] Such a forthright exercise of the privileges of rank was by no means uncommon, and the Adjutant-General's department was peculiarly vulnerable at this time because Charles Stewart, its regular head, had gone home on leave, and Edward Pakenham, who would normally have replaced him, was commanding the Third Division. The senior officer present was John Waters, a mere lieutenant-colonel.[12]

However even the most senior officers could be vulnerable to mundane domestic disasters. One night in July 1813 the chimney of Wellington's quarters caught fire and, being partly made of wood, the flames seemed likely to spread. The Commander of the Forces was observed 'out in the rain with his hat off, and a silk handkerchief over his head, giving directions', and the operation succeeded, a wet blanket being forced down the chimney and the fire extinguished.[13] Then there was an unfortunate incident during the retreat from Burgos, recorded by Charles Whitman of the Royal Horse Artillery:

The troops went into the village to procure wood, and after unroofing several houses, they came to the house where Earl Wellington stopt (not knowing it was his quarters) and began very deliberately to unroof the house: My Lord hearing the noise came out, and perceiving what they were about, begged of them to go to some other place, for Gods sake to let him have the roof for one night, and shortly after seeing his head servant, a black man, on top of the house getting wood, called to him by his name, and said what are you about 'O nothing Master, My Lord, only getting a piece of wood to cook dinner with.['] He had on one of his Lordships old cock'd hats, with the feather round it, in the meantime the Prince of Orange came up to his Lordship, and seeing the black with my Lord's hat on, exclaimed by God, we have got a black general at last, at which his Lordship and attendant laughed heartily.[14]

The officers of headquarters usually slept in requisitioned houses but sometimes camped, especially in summer. Larpent records one such occasion during the advance to Vitoria in June 1813 where he was given quarters in 'a wretched dirty hole ... I have no place but a dirty passage to put up my bed in; I have a table and chair, but am surrounded by baskets, hampers, tubs, boxes, sheepskins, dirt, etc. Cobwebs and dirt are dropping upon me continually'. Larpent goes on to describe the scene: 'Lord Wellington and Marshal Beresford are walking up and down the street, and the Military Secretary is writing under a wall, upon his knees, whilst his servants are pitching his tent. In a little field where General Alava is about to encamp, there were just now the Military Secretary, Colonel Scovell, the Commander of the Police Corps, Fitzclarence, General Alava, the Spanish Aide-de-Camp, Colonel Waters, the Prince of Orange, and your humble servant, all lying upon the ground together, round a cold ham and bread, some brandy, and a bottle of champagne. And no bad fare either you will say. The Prince and Lord Fitzroy, like two boys, were playing together all the time.'[15]

When in settled quarters Wellington's habits were fairly consistent. He rose early – six o'clock in summer according to one account – and worked on his papers until taking breakfast at nine. Then he would see the heads of department: the Quartermaster-General, the Adjutant-General, the chief commissary, medical officer, deputy judge advocate and so on, which would often take until mid-afternoon. If there was time he might then go for a ride. The dinner hour varied: half past three by one account, five o'clock by another, and half past seven by a third, although this was probably an early supper with some other meal punctuating the long interval from breakfast. It was an era when fashionable mealtimes were changing in Britain, but it is not clear whether Wellington's changes reflect this or simpler considerations, such as whether he would take his exercise riding before dinner or walking after it. Finally he would retire for the night, sometimes spending another couple of hours writing before going to bed.[16]

Early in the war Wellington told Mr Villiers that 'excepting upon very important occasions, I write my dispatches without making a draft'.[17] He would retain the original, while a fair copy made by his military secretary (or one of the ADCs) would be sent home, or to whomever it was addressed. However his official accounts of battles and other important letters were worked over with considerable care, both to ensure their accuracy and so as not to overlook the part played by any of the troops.[18] As was the custom, he sent home both official despatches, which were documents of record and were often published, and 'private' letters to the Secretary of State, which might include unconfirmed reports and speculation about possible enemy movements and future operations. He was scrupulously honest in reporting the casualties suffered by his own army, but his estimates of those suffered by the enemy in the early campaigns were rather overgenerous, which led to some public debate in 1810, after which he generally avoided giving any figures (although he would still occasionally hazard an estimate – usually much too high – in purely private letters home, such as those to his brother William).[19] Commenting on the draft of a Portuguese proclamation he urged that it should be 'in plain language, without bombast, and . . . above all short'.[20] His own despatches were not always short – he wrote a vast amount, more than 2 million words in five years in the Peninsula, while busy with much else – but his style was remarkably direct, vigorous and devoid of pomp, while retaining enough formality to mark his letters as official documents. (His truly private letters were looser, and more colourful in expression, but quite clearly from the same pen.)

The sailing of the weekly packet from Lisbon to England gave his work a natural rhythm, although the structure was not rigid; the packet could be delayed, or news sent separately if it was particularly urgent or important. Each week he would usually write an official despatch to the Secretary of State, a 'private' letter and often several other letters dealing with specific subjects. He wrote frequently to the British ministers in Lisbon and Cadiz, to Hill and to Beresford, and also to Graham when he was in the Peninsula. There would be other letters over the course of the week: to other subordinates in the army, to Spanish generals and to correspondents in occupied Spain; to officials at home such as Colonel Torrens at the Horse Guards or to the Secretary of the Treasury; to the admiral stationed at Lisbon or in the Channel, or to the British commander in Sicily. All these letters, it seems, were originally written in his own hand for he rarely if ever gave dictation. More routine official business, such as an application for promotion, was dealt with by the military secretary, who might consult Wellington for his decision in cases of difficulty.

Wellington generally slept on a portable camp bed covered in Russian leather with a pillow of the same material. On campaign, if he thought it likely that he would be roused during the night, 'he used to lie down on this bedstead in his clothes, with his boots near him, ready to put on, & his cloak thrown round him. His horse, & that of his orderly dragoon were always ready saddled and ordering himself to be called upon the least alarm from the advance, & with a lamp near him, he would shut himself up for the night. In case of anything occurring before day-light, to make him think his presence was necessary at the Outposts, he would ride off, without having a single Aid[e] de

Camp called, taking with him only his Orderly Dragoon. Nothing could exceed his habits of watchfulness & activity.'[21]

When the army was in cantonments, and sometimes even on campaign, Wellington varied his routine by hunting (two or three times a week during the winter at Freneda) or, less frequently, shooting. According to Larpent: 'Lord Wellington has a good stud of about eight hunters; he rides hard, and only wants a good gallop, but I understand knows nothing of the sport, though very fond of it in his own way.'[22] Still, Fitzroy Somerset, who can hardly have been ignorant of the finer points of hunting, declared that 'we have occasionally some very quick and pretty Runs & it is certainly worth our while to keep up the Pack'. To this end he asked his brother, the Duke of Beaufort, to send them some hounds as reinforcements: 'About twenty or twenty one inches high & to have a good deal of bone. I should not think their being noisy will signify much, but I should like you to give us some Clever ones for the sake of your reputation.'[23] Beaufort obliged and the hounds reached Freneda before the end of March, much to Somerset's satisfaction.[24] According to one British officer the appearance of the hounds caused a sensation during the army's advance through Spain in June 1813: 'The women and children and girls, many of whom were very handsome, ranged themselves in front of their houses, with very joyous faces. Their delight was greatly heightened at the sight of his Lordship's fox hounds trudging beside us. The huntsman was close in our rear, but could not control the dogs, as they pressed forward in this narrow road, noticing individuals in the ranks as they passed. The natives had never before seen a pack of hounds, and the old women and their children actually screamed with delight.'[25]

George Murray claimed that on hunting days he could get almost anything done: 'Lord Wellington stands whip in hand ready to start, and soon despatches all business. Some of the Generals, Lord Wellington observed one day, used to come and hunt and then get on business, and get him to answer things in a hasty way, which he did not intend, but which they acted upon. "Oh, d____ them," said he, "I won't speak to them again when we are hunting." '[26] But Charles Colville ruefully records an occasion at the end of 1811 when he rode over to headquarters on business only to find Wellington in the stables and unwilling to discuss anything except his horses and hounds.[27]

When hunting, at least on one occasion in 1814, Wellington wore 'the Salisbury hunt coat, sky blue and black cape'.[28] According to Larpent: 'He is remarkably neat, and most particular in his dress, considering his situation. He is well made, knows it, and is willing to set off to the best what nature has bestowed. In short, like every other great man, present or past, almost without exception, he is vain. He cuts the skirts of his own coats shorter, to make them look smarter: and only a short time since I found him discussing the cut of his half-boots, and suggesting alterations to his servant.'[29] Estimates of his height range from 5ft 7in to 5ft 10in, with most being around 5ft 9in, and Kincaid tells us that he was delighted to overhear a fashionable officer of the Guards describe him as a 'beau'.[30] His usual dress was plain to the point of austerity: a simple grey frock coat or great coat, a round or cocked hat, white waistcoat, grey pantaloons and a white neckerchief, with sometimes an oilskin cape or a short white cloak from a captured French dragoon.[31] He generally wore 'a straight regulation Sword, with a plain black belt',[32] although portraits painted during the war show him with a more elaborate sabre in a richly ornamented scabbard. When mounted he carried one pistol, using the other saddle holster for writing materials, with a valise holding a few clothes and a plain dark blue shabraque over the saddle.[33]

Sir John Hope, writing home in October 1813, saw little sign of vanity: 'Lord W himself is not particularly ostentatious in his living, though I fancy it is quite proper. He is certainly not so in his dress, for he wears nothing but a common grey frock-coat not only so threadbare but so thin you could see light through it, grey pantaloons and half-boots, a white stock without sash or sword; and in this way he has been in all his actions. The only military dress he seems to wear is the feathered general's hat with the British Spanish and Portuguese cockades. His animation and activity are wonderful, for he is not only almost always in movement but he appears to write a great deal. He is certainly a very uncommon man.'[34] Yet even Hope could not resist imitating his commander's attire in one respect, asking his wife a few weeks later to 'order a hat for me from Oliphant [in] Cockspur Street. I wish it to be covered with oiled silk and the feathers, not much stuck over the sides, but very low, and instead of being the high, semi-circular shape they generally make their hats, I beg that you will order it very low, broad and flat, so as to cover the face and eyes well. This, you must know, is called the Wellington Cut in the Army, and probably all the London hatters know it already, and it is certainly most convenient.'[35]

Although his usual attire was plain, Wellington was happy to dress up for special occasions. In May 1813 he wore his full dress uniform as Colonel of the Blues for a grand review of the Household Cavalry 'and looked very well in it'.[36] And he marked the anniversaries of battles and other events in style, even if this meant some inconvenience. For example, when the fête and ball to mark Lowry Cole's investiture as a Knight of the Bath was held at Ciudad Rodrigo, Wellington rode the seventeen miles from Freneda in time to dress for dinner, danced, stayed to supper and left at half past three in the morning to ride back to headquarters, getting there by six and having a few hours sleep before returning to business. Of all his staff only Alexander Gordon accompanied him on the return ride, and he borrowed a fresh horse, leaving his own to follow later. Unsurprisingly Wellington was a little jaded as a result of his exertion, but he prided himself on being the most active man of the party.[37] Such celebrations helped to relieve the tedium of months in quarters and ensured that past triumphs were not forgotten, but by the end of 1813 Larpent was tired of them: 'I own, however, that I prefer his smaller parties when fewer grandees are there, and Lord Wellington talks more and we drink less. A great party is almost always stupid, unless there is good singing or good speechifying; and I have now seen all the lions likely to be there.'[38]

When George Eastlake, a civilian, accompanied Admiral Martin on his visit to headquarters at Lesaca in September 1813, he noted that their host greeted them surrounded by a score of aides-de-camp and other officers; 'His carriage and air are very dignified, and I thought he looked most noble when he received us, which he did in the most gracious manner.'[39] Wellington sat at the centre of one side of the table and generally nominated who should occupy the two places to his left and two to his right, leaving the remainder to be seated by Colin Campbell who, as Commandant of Headquarters, also presided at dinner in Wellington's absence. The Prince of Orange usually sat on Wellington's right, although when Eastlake was there the place of honour was taken by Admiral Martin, with General Hay sitting on Wellington's left.[40] 'The dinner was served on plate', Eastlake records, 'and the cooking excellent, though I cannot praise the size of the mutton, which I only saw, and the flavour of the beef, which I tasted. The sweet things appeared to be excellent, the stewed peaches delicious. The wines were port, claret, Madeira and country wine, the last light and very good. Lord Wellington carries himself with much dignity at table and is treated with profound respect when addressed. Indeed it seems impossible to take a liberty with him. He drank wine with no one and I learnt that this was his habit.'[41] According to one story, Wellington himself told a newly arrived staff officer: 'Cole gives the best dinners in the army; Hill the next best; mine are no great things; Beresford's and Picton's are very bad indeed!'[42] But in December 1813 Larpent remarked: 'Lord Wellington's table is now very good in every respect; and I think his aides-de-camp will be ill with excess, who have this daily fare (unless there is a move) especially if the roads remain too bad for exercise.'[43]

Conversation at dinner varied according to Wellington's mood. Thomas Henry Browne recalled: 'The cheerfulness or gloom of our Commander's table depended much on news which he received from England, or reports from the different divisions of the army. I have dined there at times, when scarce any one dare[d to] open his mouth except to take in his dinner, & at other times when the conversation was constant & general, & Ld Wellington himself the most playful of the party.'[44] Other accounts suggest that silence and gloom were unusual and that the conversation was usually kept light, or at least that it avoided the current state of the war in the Peninsula. A Guards officer wrote that 'at table [Wellington] seldom spoke of military matters, and never of passing events in Portugal; the news of the day from England, the amusements or social state of Lisbon, or allusions to foreign countries, most frequently formed the topics of his conversations'.[45] Larpent says that Wellington was well-informed and curious about legal appointments and similar official gossip, and confirms that he frequently talked of the state of British politics as if he was completely detached from them.[46]

The meal would be completed by dessert which on the occasion of Eastlake's visit consisted of 'apple, peaches and some fine walnuts . . . put down without removing the cloth'. 'At about a quarter before six', just over two hours after the meal had begun, '[Wellington] said, "Canning, order coffee", and Colonel Canning left the room for the purpose, there being no bells in Spain. Some very good coffee was served in dragon china basons, and so soon as we had partaken of it Lord Wellington rose and everybody instantly did the same. He said, "Admiral, will you walk?" and Admiral Martin and he left the room and we all dispersed'.[47]

Occasionally the dinner was enlivened with music. There was a young Spaniard called Fuentes at Freneda in 1812–13 who 'played the guitar prettily & sang droll songs to it', and who sometimes performed for Wellington, generally lifting the spirits of the company if they were dull.[48] Some of the songs were written in praise of Wellington's achievements, but this did not abash him; indeed he gave every sign of enjoying them.[49] Private parties of small groups of officers gathered to sing glees or play music, but we have no record of Wellington joining in on such occasions, despite his youthful love of music, even as a listener.[50]

According to Thomas Henry Browne, 'We never gamed nor do I remember to have seen a single pack of cards at Head Quarters'.[51] Wagers were certainly laid on occasion, both on public events, and, inevitably, on such things as horses, but there was remarkably little gambling. Wellington made William Warre promise to give up taking snuff, and disliked smoking; no 'seagars' were smoked at his table, although they were becoming increasingly popular in the army.[52] When the officers of the Light Division put on a production of Sheridan's The Rivals in the winter of 1812–13 Wellington intervened to ensure that it took place in a barn rather than a church to avoid offending the local priest, but also rode twelve miles over bad roads on a winter afternoon to attend the performance with many of the headquarters staff. At a critical moment one of the actors forgot his lines and things looked awkward, but Wellington 'rose up and began clapping his hands and crying Bravo!' The actor's confidence was restored and the production went on to a triumphant success. Recording the occasion in his private journal Captain Jonathan Leach of the 95th Rifles reflected:

This is the sort of man to be at the head of an Army. Whether in the field near the enemy or in winter quarters during the temporary inactivity of his Army he is all alive and up to anything. He gives no trouble to us whatever and knows perfectly well that the more the officers and soldiers enjoy themselves during winter, the more heartily they will embark in operations of the following campaign.[53]

Lack of female society was one of the principal deficiencies of headquarters. There were a few women servants (laundresses and the like); at least one redoubtable woman sutler;[54] a few 'ladies of a certain description';[55] and some-times the intrepid wife of a British or Portuguese officer – but her presence simply drew attention to the predominance of men.[56] When headquarters stopped at a large town or city the chance to converse, flirt and dance – if nothing more – with young ladies was welcomed with enthusiasm, but over five years of war such occasions were relatively few and brief, and the officers of Wellington's staff longed for leave in England. Most of Wellington's ADCs were sent home at least once, often carrying despatches announcing a victory – an honour that brought with it an automatic promotion. Wellington was unusual in staying the whole course of the war from April 1809 to April 1814 without interruption, except for occasional brief working visits to Lisbon or Cadiz.[57]

The army loved to gossip and it was not a prudish age, but there are very few references to Wellington's amours in these years, and those that do appear are not particularly convincing. There was the 'Spanish Girl' who, according to Charles Stewart, joined headquarters in the middle of 1809, but who was 'sent packing' when her presence attracted gossip and ridicule (see Chapter 20). 'Since which', Stewart wrote in 1811, 'I really believe nothing but his Employment and Fox Hunting have occupied all his Affections and all his wants'.[58] Wellington may have visited 'Joseph's ladies' when in Madrid, and possibly taken similar opportunities in Cadiz or in Lisbon, but he was remarkably discreet in the later years of the Peninsular War. Possibly he took warning from the damage Lord Wellesley's affairs did to his reputation, although if he did then the lesson was lost by the time he reached Paris in 1814. More probably there was simply no opportunity to conduct an affair with the sort of well-informed, sophisticated woman who appealed to him while campaigning or in winter quarters.

Wellington strongly supported the work of chaplains in the army and pressed the Horse Guards to improve their terms of service so as to attract more and better men.[59] He regularly attended church parade although he is said to have told one chaplain: 'Briscal[l], say as much as you like in five-and-twenty minutes, I shall not stay longer.'[60] Yet in January 1813 Larpent noted: 'There has been no chaplain here these eight or nine months, or any notice taken in any manner of Sunday! It used to be, I hear, a very regular and imposing thing to attend divine service performed out of doors with hats off, but the people must now think that we have no religion at all, as almost every public business goes on nearly the same as on ordinary days. The English soldiers, however, keep it as a holiday, though the Portuguese will many of them work, particularly after three o'clock.'[61]

There were no official war artists in the Peninsula, but in the autumn of 1813 Thomas Heaphy, a successful painter in watercolours, visited the army in Spain on a private venture, apparently with the encouragement of John Fremantle, one of Wellington's ADCs. Wellington sat for his portrait, and Heaphy also made many small studies of individual officers which he included in a grand – and badly overcrowded – painting of Wellington giving orders in battle, which was subsequently engraved (see plate 66). But while the visit was evidently a great success, both financially and artistically, Heaphy's welcome at headquarters wore a little thin, with even Fremantle declaring that he was 'universally observed to be the most impudent dog alive'.[62]

Wellington's domestic staff in October 1813 consisted of Bonduc and Smily (probably a butler and valet, although this is not specified), three footmen, two grooms, three cooks, three assistants, one Italian, one goat boy, three carmen, two huntsmen, six bâtmen (that is, men in charge of mules, not personal attendants) and three women. Also forming part of the establishment were a number of orderlies, a dozen Portuguese dragoons and about twenty mulet-eers.[63] In addition, each of the dozen or so ADCs had his own personal serv-ants (usually three or four, although the Prince of Orange had eight including two ADCs or companions of his own).[64] We know very little about these serv-ants. The orderly dragoon most often in attendance on Wellington in the field was Henry Beckersfield of the 1st Hussars, King's German Legion.[65] One of the cooks was the twenty-six-year-old James Thornton who had been engaged by Colin Campbell in London in 1811. Forty years later Thornton was interviewed by Lord Frederick Fitzclarence, his then employer, and his answers preserve some interesting details, but they do not convey much of the sense of daily life as experienced 'below stairs' at headquarters.[66] A passing comment by Mr Larpent is more revealing, although probably overstated: 'There is an shocking set of servants at headquarters; idle, drunken English servants and soldiers, almost all bad, and the Portuguese are almost every day running off with something or other from their masters and others.'[67]

At the head of Wellington's official 'family' was Colin Campbell, who held the ill-defined position of headquarters commandant. He was in charge of all the practical arrangements needed to make life tolerable, whether on the march or in quarters. These included supervising the servants, managing the move-ment of the luggage, allocating quarters, presiding at dinner in Wellington's absence, and superintending both the cellar and the stables (both of which were sizeable: Wellington alone had fifteen horses, and a single large dinner might lead to the consumption of a great deal of wine).

Fitzroy Somerset, the military secretary, was universally liked and admired for his good humour, perfect manners, courage and efficiency. In December 1813 Larpent commented that he 'gets through a great amount of business with little assistance, and always quite in public, almost in a common coffee or lounging room, in the midst of talking, noise, joking and confusion.'[68] The senior ADCs who had been with Wellington since 1809 were Alexander Gordon, Charles Fox Canning and Ulysses Burgh. Many of those who joined later did not stay for long, or left little trace, but the most important subsequent appointments were John Fremantle, a political connection of the Marquess of Buckingham;[69] Lord March, the Duke of Richmond's son; Lord Worcester, son of the Duke of Beaufort and Fitzroy Somerset's nephew; and the Hereditary Prince of Orange.

As ADCs all these young men were expected to make themselves useful in any way they could, but it seems that some were habitually chosen for particular tasks. For example, Alexander Gordon was often sent under a flag of truce to the French army to take a letter from Wellington to the enemy commander and at the same time pick up whatever news or intelligence he could.[70] This he did with considerable ability and became well known and liked in the French army. The role of the other ADCs is less clear, although there is a tantalising glimpse in a letter from Dr Hume to Sir Thomas Graham written in April 1813: 'All the staff are quite well at present . . . Gordon has gone to Béjar to a wedding but returns on Sunday. Lord Fitzroy and Burgh the steady labouring Military Secretaries, and March as usual going about amusing himself. He is growing very stout and has no ague this spring.'[71] Another letter written a few months later describes March and Fremantle as well as Somerset and Burgh as 'military scratchaways' and indicates that in their absence other officers attached to headquarters were being pressed into service to deal with urgent business.[72]

All these officers were young. Alexander Gordon turned twenty-seven in 1813 and felt that he was growing old. Fitzroy Somerset was only twenty-four when the year began; Worcester came of age on 5 February 1813 and the Prince of Orange not until December 1813. Colin Campbell was a decade older (he turned thirty-seven in 1813), while Wellington himself celebrated his forty-fourth birthday at the beginning of May. Campbell was also set apart from the others by his modest family background; the other ADCs were either aristocratic or at least well connected, for such appointments were highly sought and were a means of repaying favours and pleasing friends. This has sometimes led to the assumption that Wellington's ADCs were no more than young men of good family, brave no doubt, but probably brainless. The publication of Alexander Gordon's letters however has shown that he, at least, took his soldiering extremely seriously, and that he had an intelligent independent understanding of the strategic problems facing Wellington, and well-considered opinions of his own. The letters also show that Wellington discussed his plans much more freely with his staff than had been assumed, and that he was sometimes influenced by their views. There may have been moments of youthful high spirits and even the occasional drunken frolic,[73] but the prevailing atmosphere was of hard work, ambition and serious professionalism.

As in most armies there was some tension in relations between the headquarters staff and ordinary line officers. George Napier records that 'some' of the ADCs 'had not the most polite or conciliatory manners when a dinner was given at headquarters to *regimental* officers', although he hastens to exempt Lord March, Fitzroy Somerset and Colonel Burgh from his censure, and to observe 'I never saw any officers of Wellington's personal staff who were not ever ready to be of use to the sick and wounded, and to exert themselves in every way to make them comfortable and show them every real kindness'.[74] Another officer of the Light Division, Jonathan Leach, was sufficiently liberal to allow that there were 'many excellent fellows' who had *not* been spoilt by being given a staff appointment, but still, the recollection of the contemptuous glances bestowed on the poor half-starved horses belonging to infantry officers from 'young aides-du-camp . . . as they rode along the flanks of the columns on well fed, pampered chargers', still rankled years later.[75]

But if some of the ADCs were snobs, or just naturally rude, no one questioned their courage in action. In January 1812 Fitzroy Somerset, Lord March and the Prince of Orange entered Ciudad Rodrigo together through the main breach, the Prince taking off his sash to bind up George Napier's wounded arm.[76] Although Wellington was annoyed at this unauthorised escapade, Fitzroy Somerset again pushed forward into the firing line at Badajoz. The proper duties of ADCs in action – whether rallying troops, delivering messages, or finding out what was going on – necessarily exposed them to enemy fire, while in a melee their first duty was to protect their general at whatever risk to themselves. After Sorauren in July 1813 Larpent noted: 'Lord Wellington's staff were never so roughly handled. The Prince of Orange who was sent to thank one regiment by Lord Wellington, was very much exposed while executing this order. His horse was shot under him, and he was grazed in the sash'.[77]

The Prince's position on the staff was at first slightly awkward. He joined headquarters in the summer of 1811 as a very young man with no practical military experience, but with claims for consideration not just as the heir to the exiled Stadtholder of the Netherlands, but also as the prospective husband of Princess Charlotte, the heir to the British throne. As if this was not enough to arouse resentment, Wellington showed him marked favour and praised his services at El Bodon in his despatch. However the Prince showed himself willing, obliging and brave, tolerated his unflattering nickname of 'Slender Billy', and came to be accepted by his fellow ADCs.[78]

There were also two Spanish liaison officers at headquarters: Major-General D. José O'Lawlor and Major-General D. Miguel Ricardo de Alava. O'Lawlor had been attached to Wellington since the Talavera campaign and Alava had joined his headquarters in May 1810 although he was already a familiar figure. The few references to O'Lawlor in the sources tell us little, other than that his secretary absconded with quite a large sum of money in November 1813.[79] Alava is mentioned much more often. He has the rare, possibly unique distinction of having fought at both Trafalgar and Waterloo; fortunately his naval service left no resentment and he was a warm Anglophile, while he was always popular with the British. Henry Wellesley described him as 'one of the best Spaniards I have seen', while Wellington responded to the news of his appointment in 1810: 'I should be very glad, at any time, to see Alava, who is a very good fellow.' Larpent thought him clever, and noted in June 1813 that he was 'in high spirits, thinks all going on well, and is beginning to ask one or two to dine with him at his mansion near Vittoria, where his estates lie. He only begs that he may have a guard to preserve his green forage from our soldiers.'[80] After the war Alava's liberal views led to his imprisonment and exile, and he took refuge in England where Wellington greeted him warmly, introduced him into society, and gave him a home.[81]

All these officers belonged to Wellington's household, but they were outnumbered roughly two-to-one by staff officers and other men belonging to public departments attached to headquarters. Wellington had little say in the selection and appointment of these staff officers, although in the later years of the war the authorities at home usually took his wishes into account in filling the most senior positions. The original staff was selected entirely by the departments at home and even George Murray, the Quartermaster-General, was not consulted in the choice of his subordinates.[82] Thereafter most positions were filled by selection and promotion of officers within the army in the Peninsula, although the authorities in London retained the final say and did not scruple occasionally to impose a choice of their own. The officers of the staff and particularly the heads of departments owed a dual loyalty: to the commander of the army in which they were serving, but also to their superiors at home to whom they answered, and on whom they depended for their professional advancement. The problems that this could cause are obvious and were demonstrated in some other British expeditions of the period, but Wellington's authority as commander of the army was universally accepted, and even in the dark days of late 1809 when most of his subordinates could see no prospect of success, there was no attempt to cabal against him.

Staff officers came from a wide variety of social backgrounds ranging from aristocrats such as Charles Stewart and Edward Pakenham – and George Fitzclarence, the grandson of George III – to John Elley, whose father kept an eating house, and who joined the army as a private and rose to become a lieutenant-general and a KCB.[83] On any particular day, there would be a number of officers attending headquarters either because they had just arrived in the Peninsula, or because they had other business to transact. There might also be one or more civilian visitors from Britain, usually wealthy well-connected young men who fancied seeing a little of the war without the commitment of joining the army. For example in April and May 1813 the twenty-one-year-old Lord John Russell, the future Whig prime minister, spent over a month at headquarters, which was already overcrowded, visiting his brother, Lord William. Wellington treated such guests well, knowing that they could influence opinion at home, but he privately admitted that they were a nuisance, and that it was impossible to keep them out of danger.[84]

Most of the work done by the staff at headquarters was routine, bureaucratic and extremely tedious. The ceaseless preparation, collation and checking of a multitude of different returns was a sore trial to the patience of a young man of whatever rank who had looked to active service to bring adventure, romance and excitement. The growth of the size of the army ensured that attempts to streamline procedures did not lessen the actual burden at headquarters, although the arrival of three small portable printing presses in the middle of 1812 must have been a godsend.[85]

No one grumbled more at the dullness of the work than Charles Stewart, who would have much preferred the command of a brigade of cavalry. It was all very well for Castlereagh to argue that at headquarters he knew all that was going on and that he had the chance of learning the art of generalship at the elbow of a master, but the day-to-day reality was of endless pernickety paperwork.[86] Edward Pakenham agreed, describing the Adjutant-General's job as 'this insignificant Clerking business', and hankering to return 'into the Line of a Soldier by commanding a Brigade'.[87] It was unfortunate that two such natural fire-eaters as Stewart and Pakenham should have found themselves at the head of a staff department whose duties were so little to their taste. Wellington helped Pakenham get the field command in which he distinguished himself in 1812, and while Stewart would have been an uncomfortable subordinate for Payne or Cotton, it may be wondered if he would really have been any worse than some of the other officers, such as Erskine and Slade, who commanded the army's cavalry brigades.

Stewart did not blame Wellington for the tedium of his duties, explaining to Castlereagh that the problem lay deeper in the organisation of the British army: 'I think both the situations of adj[utan]t-gen[era]l and q[uarte]r-m[aste] r-gen[era]l are not understood in our army, nor is the business conducted through them in such a manner as to render the offices as interesting or as important as they are in most of the other armies in Europe.'[88] Even so it is likely that Wellington's style of doing business exacerbated the problem. Delegating little of importance to others, he sometimes cut corners and ignored organisational distinctions, leading to subsequent confusion. Even as great an admirer as Henry Torrens, who had first-hand experience of working with him in 1808 as military secretary, noted – probably with some exaggeration – that Wellington 'always employed whoever happened to be next to him to execute any business of any Depart[ment] and hence has originated the confusion in the communication of Orders and in the Conduct of the Departments which you so impressively describe'. Ironically Torrens felt that much of the blame for the problem lay with Stewart: 'I know the Adj[utant] General's Department has never been filled as it ought.' And: 'It rests with an Adjutant-General to prevent, or if it exists, to rectify such confusion.'[89] This may be a little unfair on Stewart – it is hard to imagine any staff officer forcing Wellington to work in a way which suited them – but by 1812 the concentration of decision-making at the top was creating an excessive burden and Wellington was feeling the strain. The attempt to solve it by the creation of a chief of staff in the person of Willoughby Gordon failed, but when George Murray returned to the army in 1813 Wellington entrusted him with much more responsibility than in previous campaigns, so that his position in fact, if not in name, was very little short of that of a chief of staff.[90]

When the army was in cantonments Wellington dealt with his staff mainly though his morning interviews with the heads of departments. Larpent was very impressed with his efficiency but found him rather intimidating: 'I like [Wellington] much in business affairs. He is very ready, and decisive, and civil, though some complain a little of him at times, and are much afraid of him. Going up with my charges and papers for instructions, I feel something like a boy going to school.'[91] And again: 'Lord Wellington reads and looks into every-thing. He hunts almost every other day, and then makes up for it with great diligence and instant decision on the intermediate days.' He had a quick eye and spotted even a 'wrong casting up of numbers' in a single column of a large return.[92] He had a relish for detail, even if he liked to grumble about his work-load. At the beginning of 1814 Larpent noted: 'I have . . . such an accumulation of business for Lord Wellington that I shall be almost fearful of seeing him – five Courts-martial, one of about ninety pages, another eighty. He always complains, and yet I think he likes to read these cases, and know himself exactly what is going on.'[93] Just occasionally the burden grew too heavy. When Wellington returned after five days away from headquarters he was 'quite overwhelmed' by the backlog of papers, and when Larpent 'went in with a great bundle to add to them, he put his hands before his eyes and said, "Put them on that table; and do not say anything about them now, or let me look at them at all" '.[94]

Wellington's knowledge of military affairs and command of the business of the army was formidable, even on technical matters. 'He thinks and acts quite for himself', Larpent noted after a few months; '*with* me, if he thinks I am right, but not otherwise. I have not, however, found what Captain _____ told me I should find, that Lord Wellington immediately determines against anything that is suggested to him. On the contrary, I think he is reasonable enough, only often a little hasty in ordering trials, when an acquittal must be the consequence.'[95] He would also sometimes be impatient when presented with difficulties, and ruthlessly cut through a problem when more patience might have unravelled it.[96] Observing this Larpent concluded: 'A man to thrive here must have his wits about him, and not see or feel difficulties, or start them, to go on smoothly.' He illustrated this with a story of the pursuit of the French after the battle of Vitoria: 'Lord Wellington saw a column of French making a stand as if to halt for the night. "Now, Dickson," said he, "if we had but some artillery up." "They are close by, my Lord." And in ten minutes, from a hill on the right, Lieutenant-Colonel Rose's [*sic*: Ross's] light division guns began bang – bang – bang! and away went the French ... I fear if there had been a General [commanding the artillery rather than Dickson], that we should have had, instead of this, a report of the bad state of the roads, and the impossibility of moving guns.'[97]

Larpent's most serious criticism of Wellington was that he could be severe, and that he 'never attends to individual hardships, but to the general good'. The instance that provoked the comment was the case of a doctor who, contrary to regulations, had a soldier servant from a regiment other than his own. The Deputy Judge Advocate would have been inclined to ignore the offence given the doctor's good character, but Wellington insisted that the doctor be tried for his flagrant violation of regulations. Larpent was not surprised at his intransigence: 'As many abuses go on at depots in the rear, every time [Wellington] discovers an instance he is inexorable in trying to punish [it], especially when he finds it out himself, as he did this in another trial of the same poor Doctor, by some of the evidence.'[98] Taken in isolation Wellington's insistence on enforcing the regulations can appear harsh, but these regulations were intended to check a real problem: the steadily growing proportion of the army serving in comfortable niches in the rear, rather than in the regiments in the front line. Where there was no such wider interest involved, or where it could be best served by compromise, Wellington was happy to be flexible. For example, a commissary who burnt a house down in Spain was allowed to escape trial, instead paying generous compensation to the owners – an arrangement devised by Larpent as the best outcome for the poor Spaniards, and approved by

Wellington even though it came at a moment when he was intent on punishing examples of misconduct committed on the retreat from Burgos.[99]

The prevailing spirit and ethos at headquarters was described by Larpent in December 1813: 'From Lord Wellington downwards, there is mighty little [humbug here]. Everyone works hard, and does his business. The substance and not the form is attended to; in dress, and in many other respects, I think almost too little so. The maxim, however, of our Chief is, "Let everyone do his duty well, and never let me hear of any difficulties about anything;" and that is all he cares about.'[100] There was remarkably little pomp or formality at headquarters – far less than was demanded by a French marshal in Spain. A corporal's guard was often all that was required to do the duty at headquarters,[101] and visitors were often astonished at the lack of outward show. One young commissary recalled the disappointment of his first impression when he arrived, expecting to see all 'the flower of the army . . . collected around the hero who commands it – gallant men and stately steeds, in short all the pomp and circumstance of war', and instead found: 'the veriest piece of still-life, not to be quite dead, that I ever saw. In the market-place were some half dozen Spanish women, sitting in a row, selling eggs and cabbages, and half a dozen soldiers in their undress were the buyers; now and then an officer in a plain blue coat would cross the plaza, on foot or on horse-back; and this was all which met the eye'.[102]

Although Eastlake was struck by the natural dignity of Wellington's manner at dinner there are many stories that show him in a more relaxed and very human light. He did not think it beneath him to take a kindly interest in the jackass belonging to Captain Burgoyne of the Royal Engineers which he had once had the pleasure of driving before him when it had strayed from its owner.[103] In winter quarters he would walk in the plaza after dinner talking to whoever approached or – according to one recollection – 'leading by the hand a little Spanish girl, some five or six years old, and humming a short tune or dry whistle, and occasionally purchasing little sweets, at the child's request, from the *paysannes* of the stalls'.[104] When the news arrived of Sir John Murray's victory at Castalla, 'he came running into the Military Secretary's room, where I was yesterday, to communicate this, saying "Murray has beaten Suchet, Fitzroy" '.[105] And on the frequent occasions when he was amused, he did not smile gently, but broke into a loud whooping laugh.[106]

But despite this lack of formality and relaxed attitude to inessentials, life was not easy for Wellington's ADCs and staff. He was an exacting master with a sharp tongue and ready scorn for those who failed to meet his standards, and he could be curiously tactless and uncaring of the feelings of others. When James McGrigor arrived at headquarters in 1812 Wellington 'received me most kindly', recalled their earlier meeting in Bombay, and then 'in the midst of a large party assembled in the dining room . . . asked if I had met my old regiment the 88th, or Connaught Rangers, on my route. On my replying that I had not, he laughingly said, "I hope from your long living with them, you have not contracted any of their leading propensities; for I hang and shoot more of your old friends for murders, robberies, &c than I do of all the rest of the army." The laughter of the whole party was loud'. Realising that this was hardly comfortable for McGrigor, Wellington tried to repair the damage by praising the undoubted gallantry of the 88th and the awkwardness passed, but it was no way to set a newcomer at ease, let alone win their devotion.[107]

McGrigor went on to establish a good working relationship with Wellington, but he records in his memoirs two occasions on which he was sharply reprimanded for acting on his own initiative, even though the steps he had taken were beneficial. On the other hand, he also records Wellington's praise on discovering that during the siege of Burgos McGrigor had been steadily sending the sick and wounded to the rear, so that when the retreat began the army was not encumbered by full hospitals. Just before the campaign of 1813 opened McGrigor had a long interview with Wellington in which they went over all the arrangements for the medical side of the army's operations. In the course of this McGrigor made several proposals which Wellington rejected. That night: 'When in bed, I received by an orderly dragoon a letter on two sheets of foolscap paper, giving in detail and in his own handwriting his lordship's reasons for dissenting from me. I was not a little surprised at his sending me any explanation, for his decision on any point was final, and it was my duty merely to carry his orders into execution. Again, this letter of such extraordinary length was written at a time when other business, the most important, was on his mind, previous to his moving the whole army against the enemy and opening the campaign.'[108] As Wellington said, 'I like to convince people rather than stand on mere authority',[109] and he was more interested in the medical arrangements for the army, than in smoothing McGrigor's introduction to the staff.

Captain Brotherton claimed that Wellington's staff and ADCs were frightened of him, and there is enough evidence to suggest that there is at least some truth in the remark.[110] Charles Stewart complained: 'Lord Wn's temper ... is more uneven than I had ever imagined or indeed witnessed until recently. One is obliged, therefore, to study him and no longer give way to the unreserved communication that is so delightful, and of course so interesting.'[111] However this was written at the beginning of September 1810 when Wellington was under intense pressure, and when Stewart's freely expressed doubts of the outcome of the campaign would have been enough to try anyone's patience. More significant may be the fact that George Scovell's journal, kept through many campaigns when he was serving at headquarters, contains not a single word of affection towards his chief.[112] Still, Scovell was not an intimate; he was an officer on the staff, not a member of the inner household.

Colin Campbell, however, had tied his fortunes more closely to Wellington than anyone, and ought to have been entitled, by virtue of his long friendship, to feel that he could take his troubles to his chief without hesitation. Yet in 1810 Campbell confided to Torrens that he found his duties at headquarters irksome, and felt that Wellington was indifferent to his services. The strangest thing about this complaint was that it was written at the very time that Wellington was engaged in a protracted struggle with the Horse Guards – indeed, with Torrens – to keep Campbell in the Peninsula, despite Campbell's appointment to a position at Malta, this appointment having been made as the only way of securing Campbell's promotion in response to hard lobbying from Wellington. No one could have had fewer grounds for thinking Wellington unappreciative than Campbell, but evidently there was something in Wellington's manner in day-to-day dealings with him which left that impression. Torrens urged Campbell to explain to Wellington that he disliked his duties ('I am certain he would see the case in the liberal point of view He does every other subject') but it is remarkable that such reassurance was necessary.[113]

Alexander Gordon had received many signs of Wellington's confidence and favour since joining his household just before Talavera, and he admired his chief enormously. Yet this admiration was tinged with bitterness, which occasionally broke through into his letters home. 'You ask me how I am with him, I assure you I have every reason to be flattered with my situation, and have vanity enough to believe that no young man ever had more to say to him than myself, and believe I am the only one in his family who has never had an ill-natured word from him; and I assure you in the field and in action I have the greatest possible cause for satisfaction in the manner in which he treats me. However enough of this. He is a man without a *heart* and enough of myself.' And again, a few months later: 'You do not know Lord Wellington's private Character. He has no idea of gratitude, favour, or affection, and cares not for anyone however much he may owe him or find him useful.'[114]

Such comments do not, of course, represent a balanced or rounded account of Wellington's character, but the fact that they could be written at all by one of his inner circle of trusted aides, shows that he failed to inspire the personal dedication, loyalty and affection that many generals received from their staff. The reasons for this are not entirely clear – some commanders with well-earnt reputations for explosive tempers and coarse language were still beloved by their ADCs, while Napoleon's rages and abuse of his staff were legendary – but it is likely that Wellington's sharp tongue was at least in part to blame. And there is no doubt that he could be a bully. One well-known example followed a foolish attempt by Charles Stewart to assert his supposed rights as Adjutant-General to question prisoners and, when this was ignored, to refuse to arrange for the feeding and escort of the captured men, on the pretext that they had been completely taken out of his hands. Wellington would not tolerate such pretensions and a stormy interview followed in which he threatened to send Stewart home in disgrace, and finally obtained a tearful apology and a promise not to make such trouble again. All this was probably necessary for the smooth functioning of the army, but what makes the story ugly is that Wellington told it with apparent satisfaction to a mutual friend years later.[115]

Then there is Wellington's treatment of Colonel Fisher, the commander of the Royal Artillery in the spring of 1813. Fisher was an able man and popular with the corps, but he lacked confidence and was easily flustered in his interviews with Wellington. After one such occasion Wellington remarked: '"I took care to let him feel that I thought him very stupid."' Upon which George Murray commented aside: '"That must have been by telling him so in plain terms, I have no doubt."'[116] After several such snubs Fisher resigned. One of his subordinates wrote angrily: 'Fisher who has done the Corps more good in four months than his predecessors could contrive in four years & who promised to represent & command us as ably as we could desire, is another sacrifice to [Wellington's] abominable intemperance & disregard of all consideration of feeling, &c. &c.'[117] But it was not unreasonable for Wellington to feel that a man who could not hold his head in conversation would be unlikely to do so in the heat of battle, and that if Fisher was unable to answer questions on the location of the artillery when the army was stationary in cantonments, he would not be capable of managing it on a long and demanding campaign.[118] Wellington had no power to dismiss Fisher, but by virtually forcing him to resign, and then ordering other senior artillery officers to remain at Lisbon, he ensured that the command went to Alexander Dickson, who had proved his nerve and mettle over many previous campaigns. It was a flagrant breach of the spirit of seniority, and harsh on Fisher personally, but it was undoubtedly the best result for the army as a whole.

Not all Wellington's bullying, however, could be justified on such utilitarian grounds, and the knowledge that such behaviour was possible must have helped create a tense atmosphere at headquarters. Sometimes his criticism was plainly unreasonable. In February 1814, when the weather was delaying operations, Larpent noted: 'This is the worst part of the business, for though the elements alone may be to blame, still Lord Wellington, if his plans are thwarted, will be in a rage with _____. He banishes the terms difficulty, impossibility, and responsibility from his vocabulary.'[119] A newly arrived officer noted that Wellington 'swears like a trooper at anything that does not please him', and on one occasion in 1813, when extremely annoyed, he is said to have 'raved like a madman ... [and used] every ungentlemanly and vile epithet that ever disgraced Billingsgate', although this only comes to us second-hand and is probably a little exaggerated.[120]

The fundamental problem seems to have been that Wellington did not make his staff feel valued. When McGrigor first arrived, 'his lordship dwelt on the little support he received from some of the heads of departments, whom he freely named, saying he had to do their duties as well as command the army'.[121] According to Torrens, Wellington frequently remarked: 'I care not who I have, provided He can write, for I do everything myself'.[122] Such remarks were unlikely to inspire devotion or build a sense of loyalty and common purpose. Nor were they much consolation for young men of good families for the hardships and privations they were enduring in the uplands of Portugal; and the recollection of them did not help the staff to forget the sharpness of their chief's most recent rebuke.

But if Wellington could make his disapprobation bitingly clear, he could also praise. In early February 1813 Larpent recorded: 'Lord Wellington is much more easy with me, and seems to trust me more. Yesterday I was pleased when he said, "If your friends knew what was going on here, they would think you had no sinecure. And how do you suppose I was plagued when I had to do it nearly all myself?"'[123] He was handsome in his public commendation of his staff in his despatches, even when things had gone wrong, as at Burgos; and he accepted McGrigor's suggestion to establish a precedent by noticing the good work of the doctors in the aftermath of the storming of Badajoz.[124] When his subordinates achieved independent success (such as Hill's at Arroyo dos Molinos) he was generous in both his public and private commendations; and on Alexander Gordon's return to the army in July 1810 he noted that he had been 'very warmly received by Lord Wellington'.[125]

Wellington could also be very kind. When Charles Stewart received the news of his wife's death and was so prostrated with grief that he could not ride, Wellington not only lent him his carriage, but rode with him for the day and tried to comfort him.[126] McGrigor too was lent the carriage when he had been kicked by a horse and was unable to ride during the retreat from Burgos, and Wellington 'came most kindly to make inquiry for me'.[127] When Mr Larpent was taken prisoner by the French in 1813 Wellington went to great trouble to secure his release, and greeted him with friendly warmth on his return.[128] He was much affected when the officers of his household, or others in whom he took a particular interest, were killed or wounded. Lord March was badly wounded at Orthez in 1814 and not expected to live. That night 'as Dr Hare was sitting dozing in a chair opposite Lord March's bed, who had fallen asleep, the door of the room gently opened and a figure in a white cloak and military hat walked up to the bed, drew the curtains quietly aside, looked steadily for a few seconds on the pale countenance before him, then leaned over, stooped his head, and pressed his lips on the forehead of Lord March, heaved a deep sigh, and turned to leave the room, when the doctor, who had anxiously watched every movement, beheld the countenance of *Wellington*! his cheeks wet with tears'.[129] This was the private man who pasted a watercolour of his two young sons to the lid of his dressing case (see plate 32), and who bought three beautifully made Castilian peasant dresses for his nieces to wear at masquerades.[130] For most of the time, however, it was kept carefully hidden, even from his closest staff.

It was probably this emotional reticence that kept Wellington's staff at a distance and prevented their admiration turning to love. It has also contributed to an image of him as cold, reserved and haughty which is only partly borne out by the evidence. He was certainly not a man who stood on his dignity, who relied on old-fashioned formality, or who put an undue emphasis on social or military rank. Far from being aloof, imperturbable or Olympian he was quick to laugh and volatile in his spirits which were seldom, if ever, hard to read. He was impatient, irritable and sharp-tongued, and lacked the charm or warmth of manner to make up for this and so win the affection of those around him. In the end, this probably mattered more in his later career in politics than when he was commanding an army. In Cabinet, in Parliament and in the country, he did not attract the intense emotional loyalty that is a key facet of at least one type of leadership. He did not fit the mould of a great hero in the age of Romanticism, and many of his officers and even his personal staff found no difficulty coming out in opposition to him later in life. This gave him some pain, but for Britain as a whole, it was no bad thing. One Napoleon was enough for any generation.

CHAPTER THIRTY-ONE

VITORIA
(December 1812–June 1813)

T HE DISAPPOINTMENT FELT in the allied camp after the retreat from Burgos was soon allayed by news of the failure of Napoleon's invasion of Russia and the almost complete destruction of his army. This meant, at the very least, that there would be no flood of French reinforcements crossing the Pyrenees to recover the provinces lost in 1812, and it might have much more sweeping repercussions. Napoleon might have been wise to cut his losses in Spain completely, but he was unwilling to make such an admission of weakness (which would certainly have emboldened his enemies and alarmed his allies), and instead only withdrew 20,000 picked men from the Peninsula, leaving almost 200,000 men in Spain.[1]

Wellington's army was now the main allied force in the Peninsula, but he could only hope to take the offensive in the new year if the Spanish regulars and guerrillas continued to absorb the attention of many, even most, of the French forces south of the Pyrenees. There was the prospect of greater, more coordinated cooperation than ever before. The previous September the Cortes, filled with enthusiasm for the victory of Salamanca and the lifting of the siege of Cadiz, had offered Wellington the command of the Spanish armies. It would not prove easy, for many patriotic Spaniards resented the idea that in a war against foreign domination they should yield the command of their armies to a foreigner, while Wellington had long believed that the Spanish armies could only be made more efficient with thorough reform and much greater resources. He needed to discuss the extent and limits of his authority with the Spanish government, and after a couple of weeks at Freneda he set out on the long ride south.

Wellington arrived at Cadiz at midday on 24 December 1812 and remained until 10 January 1813. He was greeted by large, enthusiastic crowds, illuminations, the roar of cannon, reviews and the opportunity to address the Cortes. One British observer in the city was impressed by his 'dignified deportment and sun-burnt visage', but was disappointed to see him wearing the Spanish costume as Duque de Ciudad Rodrigo rather than the plain uniform of an English general.[2]

Wellington's negotiations with the Spanish government were relatively successful. Most of what he wanted caused them some pain; for example, he suggested reducing the number of Spanish armies and removing many senior officers and their large staffs in order to free resources for the soldiers in the ranks. But the senior officers who lost their places usually had good political connections in Cadiz – which was how they had been appointed in the first place – and naturally were not pleased. Even worse, Wellington wanted to subordinate civil authorities to the military in order to mobilise the resources of the country to support the army. His concerns were purely pragmatic, but the issue was one of fundamental principle for the Spanish *liberales* who dominated the government, and although a compromise was devised at the time, the issue continued to be a source of friction. Wellington received assurances that senior appointments and troop movements would only be made through him and with his approval, and the Spanish government pledged to devote 90 per cent of its revenue to the war. While not quite everything he wanted, this was as much as Wellington could reasonably expect to achieve and he left Cadiz well satisfied, though aware that many pitfalls would lie ahead.[3]

While Wellington spent the next four months quietly at Freneda the strategic balance tilted in his favour. In central Europe the Russians continued their advance, Prussia rose against the French and the vanguard of the Swedish army landed at Stralsund. So rapid was the collapse of French power in the early spring that advanced allied units reached Hamburg before the end of March, although this proved too ambitious; Napoleon collected a fresh army and took the field in April winning two indecisive, hard-fought victories at Lützen and Bautzen in May, before accepting Austrian proposals for an armistice and peace talks. The prospect of peace negotiations filled the British with dismay – their interests, and those of Spain, Portugal and Sicily, would cheerfully be sacrificed by Metternich to achieve the settlement he desired – but neither Napoleon nor the Russians and Prussians had any real interest in a compromise peace. The armistice lasted until the middle of August but it did nothing to lessen Napoleon's need for troops in central Europe.[4]

In northern Spain, particularly in Navarre and Biscay, the insurrection triggered by the withdrawal of the Army of the North to face Wellington at Burgos proved almost impossible to suppress. The guerrillas were by now highly organised, experienced and disciplined, with arms and equipment supplied by the British, excellent intelligence and new-found confidence. The main highway from Paris to Madrid was cut for weeks at a time, while civilians who had previously cooperated with the French suddenly discovered their patriotism as they observed the way the wind was blowing.

On his return from Russia Napoleon turned his attention briefly to Spain, instructing Joseph to shift his capital from Madrid to Valladolid and abandon La Mancha altogether. Soult was recalled, but Joseph's authority was immediately undermined by direct interference from Napoleon. In March his general instruction that priority be given to the suppression of the northern insurrection was transformed into orders that most of the Army of Portugal be sent to assist the Army of the North in the task. This completely disarranged Joseph's plans (he had intended to employ the Army of the South for the task) and left him with only 60,000 men to face Wellington. Napoleon had decided, presumably on the basis of British press reports, that the allied army had been crippled by the Burgos campaign and remained a negligible force even six months later.[5] Clarke, Napoleon's Minister for War, wrote to Joseph in early June that:

> There was no reason to fear that [Wellington] would take the offensive: his remoteness, his lack of transport, his constant and timid caution in all operations out of the ordinary line, all announced that we had complete liberty to act as suited us best, without worry or inconvenience. I may add that the ill feeling between English and Spaniards, the voyage of Lord Wellington to Cadiz, the changes in his army, of which many regiments have been sent back to England, were all favourable circumstances allowing us to carry out fearlessly every movement that the Emperor's orders might dictate.[6]

This was a remarkable misjudgement, suggesting wishful thinking rather than cool analysis. In fact the allied army had benefitted greatly from its six months in cantonments. In late November 1812 there had been almost 21,000 British rank and file listed as sick; by late May 1813 this had fallen to only 9,605, the lowest figure since April 1811 and the lowest it would be for the rest of the war. At the same time the number of British rank and file fit for service rose from 33,121 in November to 47,927 in May 1813, which again was a peak that would not be surpassed. Obviously a large part of this increase came from sick men who recovered and returned to the ranks, but the army also received important reinforcements during the winter and spring including a brigade of the Household Cavalry, the Hussar brigade, six battalions of infantry and numerous drafts sent out to regiments already serving in the Peninsula. On 5 May Wellington told Bathurst: 'I never saw the British army so healthy or so strong . . . We have gained in strength 25,000 men since we went into cantonments in the beginning of December, and infinitely more in efficiency.'[7] When the campaign opened in the middle of May Wellington's army amounted to some 77,000 men, British and Portuguese, all ranks, and was supported by about 20,000 Spaniards (8,000 from Estremadura acting with the right wing,

12,000 from Galicia with the left), so that the total allied army was barely short of 100,000 men.[8]

In making his plans for a new campaign in the spring of 1813 Wellington faced the same fundamental problem as in previous years. He commanded an army of 100,000 men, but the French still had almost 200,000 men in Spain, and if he was not careful, any advance he made would simply compel them to evacuate territory and concentrate their armies until they had an overwhelming superiority of force, leaving him no choice but to retreat back to the safety of Portugal. This was where the Spanish armies made one of their greatest contributions to Wellington's success. They had a strong force on the East Coast of Spain in Catalonia and Murcia where they could act in conjunction with the Anglo-Sicilian force based at Alicante. Their task was simply to keep Suchet busy, so that he would have an excuse not to detach troops to assist Joseph in resisting Wellington. Their actual operations were not particularly successful. Wellington instructed Sir John Murray to descend by sea upon Tarragona and besiege it; Murray landed safely and was well supported by the Spanish armies, but lost his nerve and abandoned the siege, his heavy guns, and his allies in a shameful panic for which he was subsequently court-martialled (though acquitted). Fortunately Lord William Bentinck arrived on 18 June, superseded Murray, and took the expedition back to Alicante. Its failure was humiliating but not costly either in lives or strategically, for Suchet was kept busy and paid no attention to Wellington's operations until after Vitoria.[9]

This still left Wellington to face the 90,000 men of the Armies of the Centre, South and Portugal, backed by the 40,000 men of the Army of the North. If Wellington advanced along the most obvious route from Salamanca to Valladolid and Burgos, or if he came from the south through Madrid, the French would be able to delay his advance through a succession of rearguard actions, until they had collected enough troops to face him if not on the Duero, then at Burgos, or even on the Ebro. Wellington planned to avoid this by throwing the main part of his army across the Douro while still in Portugal, pushing through the rugged, difficult ground of Tras os Montes before the French were aware that his men had left their cantonments, and then advancing rapidly across the great plain of northern Leon and Old Castile, turning the flank of each defensive line before the French could even occupy it. At some point the opportunity would come to fight a decisive battle, and the allied army would be fully concentrated while the French would still be reeling in confusion. Like most good military plans, the outline was simple; the difficulties lay in the practical problems of implementation and in adjusting to the enemy's reactions.[10]

As winter turned to spring the allied army began to prepare for the coming campaign. The troops were sent on long marches in full gear, recruits were drilled, field days held, and musketry practised; the Sixth Division alone used some 10,000

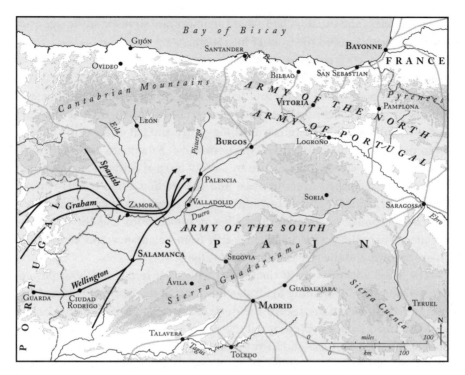

22 The Vitoria campaign, June 1813.

rounds of ball cartridge.[11] Fresh shoes, uniforms and other equipment were issued, including new light tin kettles to replace the large old iron cauldrons which had been infuriatingly slow to boil. For the first time in the war most of the British infantry were issued with tents, although their Portuguese comrades still slept under the stars. To lessen the weight the men carried on the march their greatcoats were put into store, but bill-hooks were issued at the rate of one for every six men and were much prized for cutting firewood.[12] By the end of March the men were bored with life in cantonments and looked forward with some eagerness to the resumption of active operations.[13] General Graham returned to command the left wing of the army, Picton came back to the Third Division and George Murray resumed his position as Quartermaster-General to universal satisfaction.

The army began to move on 13 May, but the first week and more was devoted to preliminary marches, concentrating divisions, and moving them across the Douro deep inside Portugal. These marches were not easy. Although the roads and tracks of Tras os Montes had been carefully surveyed by the reconnaissance officers of the Quartermaster-General's department, and Murray had arranged the routes the different units would take with his customary efficiency, it was not long before the men in the ranks began to appreciate why the region had hitherto been regarded as impassable for large forces. Nonetheless there were no major delays and the allies had gained an important strategic advantage even before the army crossed the frontier into Spain.[14]

Wellington left Freneda on 22 May. He advanced with the right wing of the army, under Rowland Hill, on Salamanca. This suggested to the French that this was the main allied thrust and led them to discount the significance of reports of movements north of the Duero. Hill's wing halted for a few days around Salamanca while Graham with the centre and left of the army pressed on to the Esla. Wellington left Hill in command at Salamanca and rode north to join Graham, crossing the Douro by a small ferry at Miranda.[15] A pontoon bridge was established over the Esla, and the leading allied troops entered Zamora. On 2 June the Hussar brigade broke two regiments of French dragoons in a sharp combat at Morales. The allies occupied Toro and the army was reunited when Hill's wing marched north from Salamanca and crossed the Duero at fords and the roughly repaired bridge of Toro.

The allied advance caught the French with their forces widely dispersed; one division was still holding Madrid, while most of the Army of Portugal was committed to operations against the northern insurgents. Although Marshal Jourdan urged King Joseph to recall the Army of Portugal on 30 May, Joseph doubted that he had the authority to do so, and limited himself to writing letters to Clausel (now in command of the Army of the North) and to Clarke in Paris, begging them to send it back as quickly as possible. He had already ordered the evacuation of Madrid, but without the Army of Portugal he was much too weak to make a stand near Valladolid as he had originally intended. There was no real choice but to retreat as slowly as possible in the hope that the Army of Portugal and perhaps even the Army of the North would join, and that together they would be able to check Wellington's advance.

Wellington concentrated his army on 3 June expecting the French to perhaps offer battle near Valladolid. When he found that they had retreated he advanced in four columns, all keeping to the north of the Duero. Only a few light troops actually followed the French maintaining contact. The advance was now heading north-east and on 10 June Wellington wrote to the British agent at Coruña asking him to direct the numerous laden cargo ships in the port eastwards to Santander, and if the French still had a garrison there, to wait offshore until it was withdrawn. This took full advantage of Britain's command of the sea to shift the army's supply base from Lisbon and Oporto to a port which, when he wrote, was still ahead of the army but which it was rapidly approaching. As well as supplies these ships carried a siege train that Wellington had ordered from England in February. At that time it had seemed likely that a sustained advance would lead to another siege of Burgos, but in the event the army was advancing well to the west of the fortress, and Wellington could afford to mask it with some Spanish troops and press on.[16]

Joseph hoped to halt his retreat at Burgos, but he was disappointed. Only a single division of the Army of Portugal was waiting there for him and only one more was in touch; the rest were far away, deep in the mountains, preoccupied with the hunt for elusive guerrillas. Worse still, the defences of Burgos were in disarray. Work had begun during the winter to strengthen them, but had not been completed, leaving them much weaker than before, and the magazines were severely depleted.[17] Nothing conveys the complete demoralisation and inefficiency of the French in Spain in 1813 better than this, for after 1812 no one could have been unaware of the importance of Burgos or the need for any repairs to be completed before the campaigning season began. Joseph ordered the retreat to continue to the Ebro and that the defences of Burgos be razed. The news that Burgos had been abandoned and destroyed was greeted with joy and relief in the ranks of the allied army and back in England, where the prospect of a second siege had been viewed with dismay.[18]

The French now placed their hopes on making a stand on the Ebro, but even before they were fully in position Wellington's army had curled around their flank, advancing on difficult hill paths and mountain tracks, and crossing the great river far upstream from the main highway. These marches would not have been possible at any other season of the year or against any serious resistance, but they were unopposed by the French, who had been in occupation of the region for the last five years, and did not believe that an army could cross the terrain.

Finding their flank turned the French abandoned the line of the Ebro and retreated to Vitoria where they hoped to cover the withdrawal of the vast convoys of baggage, loot and civilians which had preceded the army up the highway. By the evening of 19 June the whole French army had crossed the Zadorra and was camped on the small undulating plain around Vitoria. Joseph and Jourdan determined to wait here for at least a couple of days in the hope that Clausel might yet join them; this was the last chance of a junction, for any further retreat would mean that they were marching directly away from him. It was also the last chance to make a stand to defend the Bonaparte Kingdom of Spain and avoid the ignominy of abandoning the whole country without a fight. Then there were the wretched convoys that had collected around Vitoria rather than press on towards France. One large convoy was sent off on 20 June; another, even larger, at first light on the following day; but even so, a vast accumulation of vehicles, camp followers and civilians remained whose march would be covered if the French army could maintain its position for another two or three days. The French did not want to fight and had very little hope of victory, but felt that they had to try to maintain their position by offering battle, whatever the consequences.[19]

The French army did not even have a particularly good position to defend at Vitoria. The little town lay towards the eastern end of an undulating plain with narrow defiles at each end through which the Royal Highway passed. The River Zadorra snaked its way across the plain; occasionally fordable and with many bridges, it provided an obvious line of defence, especially against any attempt to turn the French position from the north. As Wellington had been pressing around the French right flank throughout the entire campaign this would seem to have been an obvious danger, especially as it would allow the allies to cut the French line of retreat; yet inexplicably Joseph and Jourdan took little account of it in their initial deployment, as if the only possible line of attack was straight up the highway from the south-west. Even worse, none of the bridges over the Zadorra was broken, and some were left virtually unguarded. The French army was deployed in three successive lines across the plain. First was the Army of the South under Gazan, some 25,000 men in four divisions of infantry, just where the plain began to open out from the Gorge of Puebla. Gazan's right rested on the Zadorra, his left on the village of Subijana, although he had troops beyond it holding the Heights of Puebla that defined the southern border of the battlefield. A mile-and-a-half or two miles behind (that is, north-east of) the Army of the South, lay the Army of the Centre, two divisions of infantry and a powerful force of artillery – rather more than 10,000 men in all. A third line, another couple of miles to the rear although still some way in front of the town of Vitoria, consisted of the three divisions of the Army of Portugal, the King's remaining Spanish troops, and a large force of cavalry which could be of little use in the mostly broken country. Maucune's division of the Army of Portugal was sent off as an escort to the convoy that marched early on 21 June, leaving only two divisions to take part in the battle. In total the French army amounted to approximately 57,000 men when the fighting began compared to 75,000 allies.[20]

The allies were not in a position to attack on 20 June or even early the next day, but Wellington resolved that if the French did not retreat he would attack them as soon as he could, and he spent 20 June reconnoitring their position and making his plans. The allied army would approach the battlefield in four columns. On the right Hill would advance up the main highway with some 20,000 men including the Second and Portuguese Divisions and Morillo's Spanish Division. On his left would be a column including the Fourth and Light Divisions which would take byways over the hills and approach the battlefield from the west around the village of Nanclares. It would then have to cross the Zadorra, unlike Hill who would have done so before reaching the battlefield. Wellington accompanied this column in the opening phase of the battle, and directed its movements in person. The third column, including the Third and Seventh Divisions, and commanded by Lord Dalhousie, would advance from the north-west. Finally, Graham's column, rather detached from the others, would also approach from the north-west, but well to the

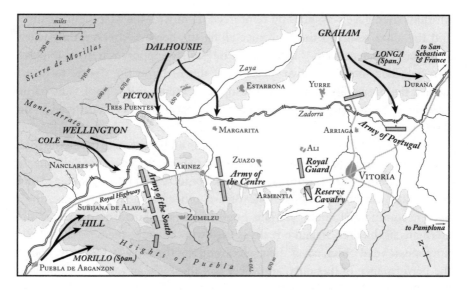

23 The battle of Vitoria, 21 June 1813. (All troop positions approximate, many conjectural.)

east of Dalhousie, striking at the French flank and rear behind the town of Vitoria. Wellington seems to have intended that Hill and Cole would begin the battle and fix the French by their frontal attack, while Dalhousie and Graham, attacking a little later, would turn the French flank and cut off their retreat. However his orders were not as clear as usual and are capable of several interpretations.[21]

On the night before the battle the French became concerned by reports of troop movements beyond their right flank, and Sarrut's division of the Army of Portugal was shifted from reserve to the north, across the Zadorra, to guard the flank – a move that placed it in the path of Graham's advance. Lamartinière's division and the cavalry of the Army of Portugal followed early on 21 June, although they did not cross the river. This left very few infantry (nothing more than the King's own Spanish Guards) in the third line in the centre by the time the serious fighting started. On the other side, Wellington's confidence was increased by a patriotic innkeeper who arrived in the morning with the news that Clausel's army was still many miles from the battlefield and could not arrive until 22 June at the earliest.[22]

The fighting began at the south-western edge of the battlefield as Hill's column led the allied advance. Hill sent part of Morillo's division onto the Heights of Puebla which overlooked the highway. The Spanish infantry drove in the French picquets and advanced rapidly until Gazan, alarmed at the risk of his flank being turned, committed Maransin's brigade to a counter-attack.

Morillo's men gave way, but Hill reinforced them with the 71st Light Infantry and the allies resumed their advance along the heights, checked only when Marshal Jourdan ordered Villatte's entire division to support Maransin. Jourdan also detached one of the two divisions of the Army of the Centre to guard against the possibility of a wider turning movement on this flank. The battle had barely begun and already the French reserves had been scattered in all directions.

The rest of Hill's column advanced along the highway and between the road and the heights. Here they were checked just beyond the village of Subijana de Alava and, rather than pushing their attack home, settled into a prolonged and costly skirmish at long range. One British officer who was present, Moyle Sherer, commented ruefully: 'The English do not skirmish so well as the Germans or the French; and it really is hard work to make them preserve their proper extended order, cover themselves, and not throw away their fire; and in the performance of this duty, an officer is, I think, far more exposed than in line fighting.'[23] Altogether the three battalions of O'Callaghan's brigade lost 490 casualties, or about one-fifth of their strength.[24]

With Hill's attack attracting the attention of the French, the next development should have been the advance of the Fourth Division over the bridges of Nanclares, and the Light Division on their left. The troops were in position and Wellington was on the spot to order them forward, but there was a delay. This was probably caused by reports that Dalhousie's column further to the left was running late. It brought an unexpected advantage when a Spanish civilian informed Wellington that to the left of the Light Division, beyond a sharp bend in the river and hidden by high ground, lay an unguarded bridge. Wellington quickly moved Kempt's brigade of the Light Division to exploit this opportunity, and the infantry were consolidating their position across the Zadorra when the third allied column burst onto the scene.

This column, under the overall command of Lord Dalhousie, was led by the Third Division. Picton's men were in position quite early in the day, but two of the three brigades of the Seventh Division, marching behind them, took a wrong turning and were much delayed. Picton was resentful enough at having been subordinated to a relative newcomer like Dalhousie, and he grew extremely impatient as he watched the battle begin without him. According to George Head, the commissary attached to the Third Division: 'Picton at last grew outrageous in the apprehension of losing a share of the conflict.'[25] H.B. Robinson, Picton's first biographer, takes up the tale:

> It was near noon, and the men were getting discontented, for the centre had not yet been engaged; Picton's blood was boiling, and his stick fell with rapid strokes upon the mane of his horse; he was riding backwards and forwards,

looking in every direction for the arrival of an aid-de-camp, until at length a staff officer galloped up from Lord Wellington. He was looking for the seventh division, under Lord Dalhousie, which had not yet arrived at its post, having had to move over some difficult ground. The aid-de-camp, riding up at speed, suddenly checked his horse and demanded of the general whether he had seen Lord Dalhousie. Picton was disappointed; he expected now at last that he might move; and, in a voice which did not gain softness from his feelings, he answered in a sharp tone, 'No, sir! I have not seen his lordship; but have you any orders for me, sir?' – 'None,' replied the aid-de-camp. – 'Then pray, sir,' continued the irritated general, 'what are the orders you *do* bring?' – 'Why,' answered the officer, 'that as soon as Lord Dalhousie, with the seventh division, shall commence an attack upon that bridge,' (pointing to the one on the left,) 'the fourth and [Light Divisions] are to support him.' Picton could not understand the idea of any other division fighting in his front; and, drawing himself up to his full height, he said to the astonished aid-de-camp with some passion, 'You may tell Lord Wellington from me, sir, that the third division under my command shall in less than ten minutes attack the bridge and carry it, and the fourth and [Light] divisions may support if they choose.' Having thus expressed his intention, he turned from the aid-de-camp, and put himself at the head of his soldiers, who were quickly in motion towards the bridge; encouraging them with the bland appellation of 'Come on, ye rascals! – come on, ye fighting villains!'[26]

Unfortunately there is no independent confirmation of the story; but while the details have probably been embellished, the essence may well be true. Commanding such subordinates was no easy task.

The Third Division charged over the Mendoza bridge in the face of fierce but short-lived resistance. The two leading brigades pressed forward towards Arinez in the centre of the French line where they overcame stiff opposition. Wellington was on the spot and, finding that the allied infantry were becoming disordered, made them pause, catch their breath and dress their ranks before pressing forwards again.[27] Meanwhile, closer to the river, Colville's brigade of the Third Division and Grant's brigade of the Seventh were engaged in a separate combat for the villages of Margarita and Crispijana. Some of the hottest fighting of the day took place here; Colville's four battalions suffered 548 casualties, and Grant's smaller brigade lost 334 before the French were broken.[28] After the battle Colville wrote home:

His Lordship, I am told, had a good view of us at one time and expressed much anxiety on account of the preponderating numbers against us. He was just, I am told, sending orders for something to be done, when he observed his wish was anticipated. He was as usual, I understand, here, there, and everywhere, and as he never minds how heavy the fire if he wants to have a nearer view of things, his numerous escapes are as extraordinary as they are fortunate for the army under him.[29]

Picton's attack had broken Leval's division and torn a hole in the French line. They fell back hoping to make a fresh stand closer to Vitoria in the position originally occupied by the Army of Portugal, and where there was a powerful battery occupying a commanding sweep of ground. The fire of these guns was not unchallenged; Alexander Dickson had already collected most of the British batteries from the centre and right of the army and employed them to some effect in support of the attack on the Arinez position. Now he pushed them forward again and engaged the French guns in the hottest artillery duel of the war in the Peninsula, with more than seventy guns employed on each side. But Joseph and Jourdan had no infantry left in reserve to support the artillery, and as the allied infantry pressed forward the French gunners soon began to waver and fall back. George Bingham was commanding a battalion in the Fourth Division: 'It was all confusion and smoke . . . [when] Lord Wellington rode up with all his staff; as he passed the battalion which was halted, he desired us to move on: I asked "In column or line?", never shall I forget the animation of his countenance "Any how, but get on" was the reply.'[30]

Wellington had intended that Graham should cross the Zadorra and cut the main highway behind (north-east of) Vitoria, and had indicated that his role was to encircle the French army rather than join in the main fighting. However, that was before the French had shifted the two divisions of the Army of Portugal to hold the line of the Zadorra. Graham's force was still much stronger than the French, but he overestimated their strength and advanced with some caution, while the French infantry held their ground well. The allies only succeeded in forcing the line of the Zadorra when Longa's Spanish division crossed at Gamarra Menor upstream of the French position and advanced down the highway. Even then it is puzzling that Graham did not do more to exploit this success. Indeed his whole conduct has been so sharply criticised by historians that it is worth noting that Wellington not only praised it highly in his official despatch, but remarked with evident enthusiasm to one of Graham's staff: '"You have had hard work on the other side; By God! Graham hit it admirably!"'[31]

As the French in the centre gave way, the troops on each flank were forced to retreat, and soon lost their cohesion and discipline as the allied advance became a pursuit. The Hussar brigade now came forward and, if they had been handled with more skill, might have struck a telling blow, but part of their force was misdirected into the town of Vitoria, while most of the rest attacked a superior force of French cavalry and was driven back. Nonetheless their presence added to the confusion and growing panic in the French army.[32]

By now the French generals had given up the battle as lost and looked only to salvage something from the wreckage. Even this would not be easy for there was no hope of forcing their way past Graham's men on the main highway, and the only alternative was a bad country road heading east to Salvatierra and Pamplona. This was not really suitable for anything more than a light force, while the French army was still encumbered with a vast mass of wheeled transport and civilian carriages parked near Vitoria. The drivers and their passengers soon panicked and in no time the road was blocked and impassable, although troops on foot or horseback could skirt around the obstacles. It is said that fleeing French soldiers and camp followers began the looting, but the allies joined in with enthusiasm as soon as they arrived upon the scene, as the plunder which the French had taken five years to accumulate found new owners. Edward Costello of the 95th describes how 'I observed a small but exceedingly heavy portmanteau that was carried by a Spanish muleteer in the French service. He was in the act of conveying it towards the town, and as I thought I contributed more towards its capture, I made him lay it down – not, indeed, before I was compelled to give him a few whacks of my rifle in the ribs. My comrades had gone in another direction, so that I had no one to claim a portion of my booty, which on inspection I found to consist of several small bags filled with gold and silver in doubloons and dollars. Although I never knew exactly the amount, I should think it not less than £1,000'.[33] Nor was it only the other ranks who took part in the pillaging. Thomas Henry Browne of the Adjutant-General's department had been wounded while leading a squadron of Hussars in pursuit of the French and was being helped to the rear by a sergeant when they came upon the scene. ' "Ah! your Honor, if you were but well enough, just to be able to sit on your Horse for a minute, & remain quiet, what a tight Day this would be for me – by the Power, it would be my making for ever." "Why my Lad, I owe you no trifle for this Horse on which I sit, & I care not if I remain a minute or two whilst you help yourself, as so many others are doing." ' The sergeant was so grateful, and the plunder so abundant, that he not only helped himself but filled Browne's pockets as well before finding him good quarters in the town of Vitoria. Having seen Browne settled the sergeant returned to have a second bite of the cherry and when he came back, just as the sun was rising, 'he laid on my bed a Watch, Chain & some Seals, a Spying glass & a writing Desk, an inkstand which had evidently formed part of a writing-case, & several Necklaces and Trinkets. "Much good & long life to your Honor, & keep the things for I've got as many as I can carry, but how the Devil I am to carry my dollars I can hardly even think of." ' In addition to these objects Browne found that his coat contained 470 dollars, or almost £120, which more than consoled him for the wound that only kept him in bed for ten days.[34]

Wellington was particularly annoyed at the prominent part in the plundering taken by the Hussars, especially the 18th, at a time when they should have been pressing the pursuit of the French. A carriage belonging to the French general staff had been captured and a sergeant and some men of the 18th had been ordered to guard it, but left their post to join in the pillaging and important papers were lost in the confusion.[35] Worse still was the story told that night by General Gazan's wife, who had been taken prisoner and who had been invited to dine at headquarters. She said 'that if it had not been for a private hussar, an officer of hussars would have plunder'd [her] of everything. That after she had delivered up her husband's sword to him and likewise a beautiful double barrell'd gun, he took by force off her finger a ring. Lord Wellington was in a great rage'.[36] This was by no means the only accusation made against the officers of the Hussars, and accounts from inside the 18th leave no doubt that many of them were well founded, with its commander privately admitting that it was 'in a shocking state'.[37] Colonel Colquhoun Grant, the brigadier, had mishandled his men in action and set them a poor example afterwards; rumour had it that Mrs Grant would soon be sporting some new jewels and lace dresses acquired in the plunder.[38] Wellington warned the regiment that if they misbehaved again he would take their horses from them and send them home in disgrace, and he transferred them to V. Alten's brigade so that they could learn their duty from the KGL Hussars; and replaced Grant in command of the 10th and 15th Hussars with Lord Edward Somerset – despite Grant being known to be a favourite of the Prince Regent.[39]

Amongst all the plunder and baggage was the entire impedimenta of the army: 151 guns, 415 caissons, 100 artillery waggons and vast quantities of other stores. However only one flag was taken (a disused battalion fanion), and no more than 2,000 prisoners. Altogether the French army lost just over 8,000 men killed, wounded or captured in the battle, while the allies had suffered over 5,000 casualties: 3,672 British, 921 Portuguese and 552 Spanish. The French army had been completely broken in a one-sided battle where the allies never appeared in the slightest danger of defeat. Charles Colville declared that it was 'perhaps the finest thing ever done by a British Allied Army', while Duncan Robertson of the 88th wrote home that 'the Victory was certainly the greatest that Lord Wellington gained'. Some later critics have been less generous in their praise, with Sir John Fortescue even concluding that 'the results of the day were very far from satisfactory'.[40] They argue that Wellington should have been able to encircle the French completely, cutting off their retreat to Pamplona as well as the main highway to Bayonne, and forcing them to flee in scattered parties over the hills or to surrender. This would certainly have been the best possible result of the battle for the allies, but very few battles result in the complete destruction of one side, and it seems rather unreasonable to declare that anything less than perfection was not 'satisfactory'. Vitoria was certainly not the most skilful of Wellington's victories; with a significantly larger army he defeated a poorly led and demoralised enemy. But it must be remembered that it was only due to his ability, energy and daring that the French were outnumbered and demoralised. For if Foy, Clausel and all the detached troops on both sides had been collected at Vitoria, the French would have had at least 30,000 more men than the allies. The victory reaped the reward of a brilliant campaign which showed that Wellington was a far abler strategist than even his friends had supposed.

The reaction in England followed a familiar pattern with the ministers and their supporters leading the public celebrations, while the Opposition privately grumbled about 'the drunken and inflamed enthusiasm of London', and the 'feverish ignorance which John Bull is so apt to display'.[41] The Prince Regent was especially pleased, and held a grand celebratory fête (organised by William Wellesley-Pole) for more than 1,000 guests at Vauxhall Gardens a month after the battle. His fancy had been taken by the capture of Jourdan's baton as a marshal of France, and he wrote to Wellington: 'You have sent me, among the trophies of your unrivalled fame, the staff of a French Marshal, and I send you in return that of England.' Unfortunately it turned out that there *was* no baton for field marshals in the British army, and it took some time for one to be designed and made, so that it was not until 1822 that Wellington, and the other field marshals in the British service, could receive their staff of office.[42] However the promotion was gazetted immediately and was backdated to the day of the battle, with Torrens perceptively commenting that 'this is the reward which I think he [Wellington] will truly appreciate'.[43] There was some grumbling among senior officers at the promotion, but the Duke of York now supported it warmly, and it opened the way for generals such as Lord Paget, the Duke of Richmond and Sir John Hope, who had previously been senior to Wellington, to serve under him. Hope and Richmond immediately wrote to the Horse Guards proffering their services, and when Graham's eyes again forced him to come home in the autumn, Hope took his place.[44]

King Joseph also lost all his private baggage at Vitoria. His silver chamber pot became the regimental souvenir of the 14th Light Dragoons and, with a little inflation, gave them the nickname 'The Emperor's Chambermaids'. There was also a large trunk or 'imperial' containing a mass of prints, drawings and pictures. Wellington had a quick look at them, then sent them home for safe-keeping. He was surprised to be told some months later that they included some fine works, including paintings by Titian, Velázquez and Murillo, probably from the royal collection. He offered to return them, but King Ferdinand waived the gesture aside and made a gift of them; they can be seen today in Apsley House in London.[45]

After Vitoria the French army fled, in great confusion and disorder, towards Pamplona some sixty miles to the east. Wellington pursued, but the French had a long start and moved rapidly, so that the allied advance guard only caught up with them on 24 June, and harassed them sufficiently to force them to abandon the only two pieces of artillery they had managed to carry from the battlefield. That evening the French sheltered behind the strong fortress of Pamplona, and on the following day continued the retreat, with part of the army marching up the Baztan valley and the rest heading north-east through the Roncesvalles Pass into France. Wellington left Hill to blockade Pamplona and shepherd the French over the mountains while he turned south in a vain effort to intercept Clausel who was retreating down the Ebro to join Suchet.

Early in the pursuit Wellington detached Graham with the left wing of the army to chase Foy out of the Biscay provinces. Foy withdrew dexterously, leaving a strong garrison at San Sebastian and a smaller one at Santoña, while checking Graham's advance in a sharp engagement at Tolosa on 25 June. There was some confusion and counter-marching when Graham was first detached, and Wellington, exasperated to see orders he had personally given disobeyed, placed Captain Norman Ramsay of the Horse Artillery under arrest. Ramsay had a good excuse and Wellington released him three weeks later without charge, following representations from Graham, Frederick Ponsonby and others. The affair was of no great importance, but it added to the existing resentment in the artillery towards Wellington, and became greatly magnified by some later writers who claimed that it left Ramsay broken-hearted – and caused his death at Waterloo two years later.[46]

By the end of June the campaign was over and the allied army, which only six weeks before had been behind the Portuguese frontier, now looked down into France from the heights of the Pyrenees. Only north-eastern Spain (Suchet's command of Catalonia, Aragon and Valencia) and a few garrisons (notably Pamplona and San Sebastian) remained of the Bonaparte Kingdom of Spain. Joseph's dream was over, and at the beginning of July Napoleon deprived him of his command and confined him to his estate at Montfontaine, in disgrace and a virtual prisoner.

It is possible that Wellington missed an opportunity to make his triumph even greater. He could have put the main effort of his pursuit into advancing up the highway into France and pressed on, across the Bidassoa, to Bayonne, some twenty miles beyond. By all accounts the defences of Bayonne were much neglected, so that it was in no state to resist an attack at the beginning of July 1813. If it had fallen Wellington would at a stroke have turned the line of the Pyrenees, and deprived the French of the principal depot which supplied their army for the next six months, and there was no suitable alternative closer than Toulouse or Bordeaux. The fall of Bayonne would have magnified the shock caused by the news of Vitoria, across Europe and especially in France. Against this there is the fact that if Bayonne did not fall to an immediate attack the army might have been dangerously overextended with one flank resting at Logroño on the Ebro and the other 100 mountainous miles away at Bayonne. Memories of Burgos the previous year did not lead to confidence that even a neglected fortress would fall easily, while Wellington may also have felt that a precipitate advance to Bayonne might provoke an uncomfortably strong reaction from Napoleon. There is no evidence in fact that he considered such a move so it remains in the speculative world of might-have-beens. The opportunity, if it ever existed, was fleeting, and it would not be until the end of the year that the allied army would actually invest Bayonne, time which the French employed in greatly strengthening its defences.[47]

Throughout the first part of the long march to Vitoria the allied army had been well supplied, but when the troops left the plains of Old Castile and headed into the mountains, rations became more irregular; many of the soldiers who fought at Vitoria were hungry and had empty haversacks. The battle was the climax of the campaign and the soldiers were tense with the sense of occasion, and when it was over they relaxed – a universal phenomenon made much more potent by the plundering of the French baggage. Edward Costello expresses the feelings of many men when he writes that with his new-found wealth, 'to tell the truth, I was not now over-anxious to go much to the front, as I began to look on my life as of some value'.[48] Then came more than a week of long marches on bad mountain roads with irregular supplies and not much prospect of more fighting to keep the men in the ranks. As a result the effective strength of the army fell sharply, while it left in its wake a disorderly trail of stragglers who committed dreadful crimes and harrassed the local population. On 2 July Wellington told Bathurst that more than 4,000 soldiers, British and Portuguese, had left the ranks since the battle in addition to the casualties and those left as regular detachments.[49] Ever since Wellington had first taken command of the army in the spring of 1809 he had feared that its discipline would dissolve under stress. There had been signs of this in the march south from Oporto in 1809 and on the retreat from Burgos in 1812, but it was especially mortifying to see the pattern repeated in an army which, only two months before, had been in such superb order. Wellington's pen, as so often, carried him away:

We have lost more men in the pursuit than the enemy have; and have never in any one day made more than an ordinary march.

This is the consequence of the state of discipline of the British army. We may gain the greatest victories; but we shall do no good until we shall so far

alter the system, as to force all ranks to perform their duty. The new regiments are, as usual, the worst of all. The 18th [Hussars] are a disgrace to the
name of a soldier, in action as well as elsewhere; and I propose to draft their
horses from them, and to send the men to England, if I can't get the better of
them in any other manner.[50]

That was on 29 June and on 2 July he went even further: 'It is quite impossible
for me or any other man to command a British army under the existing
system. We have in the service the scum of the earth as common soldiers; and
of late years we have been doing everything in our power, both by law and
by publications, to relax the discipline by which alone such men can be kept
in order.'[51]

Even Wellington's most ardent champions wince at 'the scum of the earth'.
At the very least it was ungracious to pin such a label on the men whose courage
and fortitude underlay all his achievements, and who went unrewarded while
he rose from being an insignificant sprig of the aristocracy to fame, wealth
and universal acclaim. The actual phrase is not original; it is an echo of St Paul
(1 Corinthians 4:13) and was applied to British soldiers by Sir Walter Raleigh
as early as 1617.[52] Wellington first used it in 1800, writing about Indian inter-
preters who abused their position to exploit the local population, and again in
1809 when discussing the blackmailers and swindlers associated with Mary
Anne Clarke.[53] However having once applied it to the men of his army he
repeated it on several occasions in the late 1820s and early 1830s, mostly,
although not exclusively, in private conversations, although he was then referring specifically to recruits.[54] He was not alone in his view: a memorandum
prepared for the Home Office in 1794 described Irish recruits of the day as 'the
refuse of mankind' and there is ample evidence to justify the phrase; while a
century later the Irish nationalist Ernie O'Malley had no hesitation in declaring
that only 'scapegoats, those in debt or in trouble over a girl had joined the
ranks'.[55]

But it raises a broader question: is the expression simply an example of bad
taste, of Wellington's unusually sharp turn of phrase getting him into trouble
again, or does it fairly reflect his attitude to the rank and file of his army? There
is no clear-cut answer. Certainly Wellington believed that even when regimental officers were assiduous in attending to their troops, their authority
needed to be supported by the threat of severe punishment; flogging, he
thought, was an essential bastion of the British army as it was constituted in
1813. Indeed his later uses of the 'scum of the earth' phrase were in the context
of a debate over the abolition of flogging which, he maintained, could only be
safely accomplished if combined with the introduction of conscription on the
French model, ensuring that a genuine cross-section of society served in the

ranks. Experience disproved this argument: flogging was gradually phased out over half a century until it was finally abolished in 1881 without the army falling apart, or the class of recruit being much improved; while the behaviour of French troops in Portugal and Spain does not support the idea that conscription would reduce the ill treatment of the civilian population.[56] However, it is doubtful that such an innovation could have been introduced in wartime, in the midst of active operations, and these doubts are increased by the discovery that even the 95th Rifles, an elite unit trained by Sir John Moore himself on the most enlightened principles, had considerable recourse to the lash during its service in the Peninsula. (Veterans of the regiment and military reformers alike concealed this after the war.)[57]

Wellington did not regard flogging as a panacea. The passage in which he describes the soldiers as scum continues:

> The officers of the lower ranks will not perform the duty required of them for the purpose of keeping their soldiers in order; and it is next to impossible to punish any officer for neglects of this description. As to the non-commissioned officers, as I have repeatedly stated, they are as bad as the men, and too near them, in point of pay and situation, by the regulations of late years, for us to expect them to do anything to keep the men in order.[58]

In other words Wellington did not blame the men for the disorders so much as the officers and NCOs whose care and attention to duty was needed to keep the men in check. This is a consistent theme right through the war, but he never had the power to solve the underlying problem completely. He recognised that NCOs were underpaid and strongly urged the government to reward them better, for many good soldiers were reluctant to accept promotion because the rewards did not compensate for the added responsibility.[59] He also recommended that provision be made for the families of married men who joined the army, in the hope that this would produce a better quality of recruit.[60] But neither of these proposals was fully adopted, although a few steps in the right direction were taken.

This failure is a reminder that Wellington's power was limited; he was the commander of the army in the field, not the Commander-in-Chief, and he had no control, and surprisingly little influence, over the organisation, pay, rules and regulations of the army as a whole. Nor was he generally able to interfere in the internal affairs of the regiments under his command; he could recommend a few officers for promotion, but he could not remove an incompetent or tyrannical colonel, who might be ruining a good regiment, unless his conduct had become notorious, and even then only with difficulty. Officers who neglected their duty frequently escaped punishment, and Wellington repeatedly complained of the reluctance of General Courts-Martial to punish even those who were flagrantly guilty.

Wellington had to make the best of the army he was given, and after four years of constant attention and effort he had raised the British (and Portuguese) army to an unprecedented level of skill and efficiency. It was a hard-won achievement and he was all too conscious how quickly the gains he had made could be lost. Probably he overreacted to the disorder after Vitoria, but if so, it was understandable. As for his attitude to his troops, he understood just what they were capable of, both the heroism in combat and the rapes and murders that might follow, and he knew that for their own sake, and for the sake of the hapless civilian population who had already suffered from the ravages of war, he needed to maintain their discipline. He was a cool cynical realist, who had been watching British soldiers on campaign for twenty years, and who had few illusions about the romance and glory of war.

CHAPTER THIRTY-TWO

THE PYRENEES
(July–September 1813)

HAVING SWEPT FROM the frontier of Portugal to the Pyrenees in a few short weeks, Wellington needed to consolidate his gains to ensure that there would be no repeat of the dashed hopes and miserable retreats that had put an end to his previous offensives in 1809 and 1812. The strategic environment in 1813 was much more favourable than in those years; the allied army was stronger and the French weaker, while Napoleon was threatened by a powerful coalition in central Europe, which would probably prevent him sending reinforcements south. Nonetheless Wellington's success in driving the French out of most of Spain (Suchet continued to occupy Catalonia and part of Valencia) meant that their forces were no longer dispersed across the country and could be concentrated against him. Thus, for most of the three months following Vitoria Wellington stood on the defensive, covering the siege of San Sebastian and the blockade of Pamplona. This gave him a forty-mile front to defend from the mouth of the Bidassoa on the coast to the mountain passes of the Maya and Roncesvalles further east, with only poor roads for lateral communication. And this in turn forced Wellington to rely more than usual upon his subordinates, with some unhappy results.

The news of Vitoria came at a bad time for Napoleon, in the midst of an armistice when he was trying to bully and intimidate Austria from joining the allies, and perhaps even to make a separate peace with Russia, Prussia and Sweden, his continental enemies. Although the defeat did nothing to directly affect the balance of forces in Germany, it undermined the prestige of the French army and heightened the sense that Napoleon was at last vulnerable. His best move might have been to release Ferdinand without conditions and withdraw Suchet's army, in the hope that this would disrupt the alliance between Britain, Portugal and Spain, and possibly open the door for a general settlement which would have left Napoleonic France the predominant power in western and central Europe. But Napoleon was only ever comfortable negotiating from a position of overwhelming strength, and he feared that any sign of weakness would simply encourage his enemies. He could not spare any reinforcements, but he sent Soult to take command of the army with orders to resume the offensive, restore the dignity of French arms, and move the seat of the war back into Spain.[1]

Soult reached Bayonne on 11 July and acted quickly to revitalise the army's organisation and restore its morale. He abolished the now embarrassing titles ('Army of Portugal', 'Army of the South'), uniting the whole force into a single army without any formal corps structure, although in practice the divisions

24 The battles of the Pyrenees, July–August 1813.

were grouped into four informal corps under Clausel, D'Erlon, Reille and Villatte. Altogether he had nearly 120,000 men under his command, but this included the garrisons of San Sebastian, Pamplona and Santoña (around 8,000 men, all behind the allied lines), a force of half-trained conscripts at Bayonne (between 5,000 and 6,000 men), the garrisons of Bayonne and St Jean Pied de Port (on the French side of the Roncesvalles Pass), and thousands of sick and wounded. This left a field force of only 85,000 men, and some of these really belonged to the garrison of Bayonne. Soult had remarkable success in restoring the spirits of the troops by way of shameless flattery, and by attributing all the misfortunes that had occurred to them to the gross incompetence of Joseph and Jourdan. The soldiers, who had recovered from the first shock of their defeat and who were baffled and ashamed at having retreated so far so rapidly, were eager to accept this explanation; and while Soult was never a particularly popular commander, his long record of service and undoubted competence inspired confidence. The French army began the new campaign in a surprisingly good mood, but its morale was brittle.[2]

Meanwhile the allies were undertaking the siege of San Sebastian. Wellington left the conduct of the operation largely to General Graham and the engineers. They proposed that rather than proceeding regularly by battering the strong landward defences on the isthmus, they would launch an attack across the tidal estuary of the River Urumea. The great advantage of this scheme was that the walls facing the estuary were comparatively weak and that a successful attack on them would lead straight into the heart of the town. The disadvantage was that the troops making the assault would have to cross hundreds of yards of open ground with difficult footing at a time determined by the tide, and therefore easily predicted by the French. Still, the Duke of Berwick had succeeded in this operation when he captured San Sebastian in 1719, and after reconnoitring the fortress on 12 July Wellington approved the proposed line of attack.

The battering train had already arrived at the little port of Pasajes a few miles along the coast, and preliminary operations began on 14 July, with the principal batteries opening fire on 20 July. This was contrary to Wellington's advice, for he feared that it would give the French time to establish interior defences, but he did not insist on getting his own way, deferring to the judgement of the men on the spot.[3] As Wellington expected, the town wall was easily breached, a large section falling on 23 July creating a gap fifty yards wide. Preparations were made to storm the fortress at daybreak on 24 July, but were then postponed until the following day, as parts of the town were in flames and it was feared that this might prevent allied troops advancing beyond the breach. The attack was then set for three o'clock in the morning of 25 July, well before dawn, notwithstanding Wellington's advice that it be made in daylight.[4] As a result the troops had great difficulty finding their way across the estuary and advanced without enthusiasm or dash. The fire of the defenders had not been subdued and their resistance was fierce, while it was said that General Oswald, commanding the Fifth Division, demoralised his troops by his lack of confidence.[5] Eventually the assault was abandoned; it had cost 571 casualties, of whom 330 were in the leading regiment, the Royal Scots. The result justified Mr Larpent's gloomy comment, made two days before, that 'things do not appear to go on well, unless Lord Wellington or General Murray are on the spot'.[6]

Wellington was not at San Sebastian to watch the storm. He had ridden over from headquarters at Lesaca on 23 July to examine progress, but clearly wished to give Graham the credit of the anticipated success. Besides, San Sebastian was at the extreme end of the allied line, more than forty miles from Roncesvalles, and he had been receiving ominous reports of French troop movements in the mountains. Mr Larpent noted that he was 'fidgetty' while waiting for news, and joined the other headquarters officers in the churchyard in the morning where they could hear the distant rumble of artillery. At eleven o'clock Colonel Burgh arrived with the news that the attack had failed, and Wellington immediately rode over to assess the setback and decide what should be done next.[7] Having given directions that the siege should be continued, he headed back to Lesaca only to be met on the road with the news that the French army had taken the offensive and that there had been hard fighting in the mountain passes, the result being still unknown. The disappointment of the failure of the siege was all the greater for being unexpected, while Wellington's anxiety over Soult's attack was heightened by his distance from the scene of action and sense that much would happen before he could reach the point of danger.[8]

Soult had not felt strong enough to march directly to the relief of San Sebastian, for the allies would certainly be prepared for an attack on the Bidassoa. Instead he decided to attack the other end of the allied line, and advance through the Roncesvalles and Maya passes to Pamplona, and then cut through the allied flank and rear. It was a bold, adventurous plan which would yield great dividends if it succeeded, but which was full of risk, quite apart from the chance that San Sebastian might fall before it could be relieved. Although Wellington was inclined to believe that the reports of French movements in the mountains were a diversion, he had issued fresh instructions to General Cole on 24 July, ordering that his position at Roncesvalles should be maintained 'to the utmost'.[9]

This order reached Cole at nine o'clock in the morning on 25 July when his position had already been under attack for several hours.[10] Soult had divided his army, with Clausel and Reille advancing on the Roncesvalles road, while D'Erlon attacked the Maya Pass. There were obvious disadvantages in such a division, but it was simply impractical to march more than 60,000 men along a single mountain road. An anonymous warning ensured that the allies were not taken by surprise, and the French could only advance on a narrow front, so that their great superiority of numbers counted for little. An attempt to turn the allied position was checked by Cole's reserves, and by five o'clock that afternoon, when fog descended, the allied infantry remained in control of the pass and had not suffered more than a few hundred casualties. Nonetheless Cole gave the order to retreat in the night. It seems that he was unnerved by the strength of the French force facing him, and was concerned about his flanks, but it is difficult to reconcile his decision with Wellington's instructions, especially as, by the end of the day, he had almost 13,000 men in hand, and the likelihood of the Third Division under Picton arriving on the following day. Above all, it was his duty to delay the French advance for as long as possible and so gain time for Wellington to concentrate his forces, and there was nowhere further back where he could hope to make a stand with as good a prospect of success as at the pass. Yet his decision to retreat drew little contemporary criticism, with Wellington blaming him much more for failing to keep him informed about what was happening than for the withdrawal.[11]

Further west, at Maya, the fighting was much more severe than at Roncesvalles, and the result more decisive. The pass was securely held by Cameron's brigade of the Second Division with four Portuguese guns dug in where they could command the main road. However a subsidiary track was left to a picquet of some eighty men, which was soon overrun, and the allied reserves arrived too late to repair the damage. By the time William Stewart, the divisional commander, reached the scene at about two o'clock, the fight was clearly hopeless and he could do no more than organise a withdrawal to a fresh position. The four Portuguese guns had to be abandoned, to the great annoyance of Wellington who blamed Stewart personally for their loss (the exact circumstances were much disputed).[12] The allies had lost almost 1,500 casualties including more than 300 prisoners, and the French had suffered even more, perhaps over 2,000 casualties. Given the relatively small number of men actually engaged it is clear that there was no lack of determination on either side.

The loss of the passes at Roncesvalles and Maya created a serious problem for Wellington. If the French pushed forward rapidly they would be able to unite their army at Pamplona before he could collect his own forces to oppose them; this would not simply raise the blockade and liberate the French garrison, it would expose the whole allied army to the risk of defeat in detail. The position was greatly compounded by Cole's culpable failure to keep his chief informed of his movements, so that while Wellington knew that there had been fighting at Roncesvalles he did not know its outcome, nor even with certainty that this was the main attack of the French. When the campaign was over Wellington told Lord Liverpool that 'there is nothing I dislike so much as these extended operations, which I cannot direct myself', while to his brother William, he wrote: 'You will perceive that my Generals are *Gallant Officers* in every sense of the word . . .'[13]

Fortunately for the allies neither French column pushed on with any urgency on 26 July. D'Erlon had been shaken by the resistance he had encountered at Maya and worried that his right flank would be exposed if he advanced. He ignored Soult's instructions, which stressed the need for rapid movements, and cautiously felt his way forward some six miles to Elizonda, making no effort to press the allied retreat. The main army also moved slowly with no excuse except the difficulties of the road and the persistence of fog in the morning. Nevertheless they picked up many prisoners; the allied troops, already tired and disheartened, had found their long march through the night exhausting and many had fallen out of the ranks. Picton joined Cole at Viscarret, but accepted Cole's assessment of the situation and ordered that the retreat continue. Neither general grasped the obvious importance of gaining time by giving ground slowly and forcing the French to deploy before they withdrew. Indeed, Cole was so unnerved that he was already considering which road he should take assuming that he was forced back beyond Pamplona![14] There was some skirmishing on the afternoon of 26 July, but the French did not have enough troops forward to press an attack, and Picton ordered the weary allies to make another night march to the rear. This took them to Sorauren, just outside Pamplona – the last position on the road on which a stand could be made.

It was not until the evening of 26 July that Wellington learned of Cole's abandonment of the Roncesvalles Pass more than twenty-four hours earlier. He at once ordered Picton to halt the French at Zubiri, promising that he would be there by mid-afternoon and that reinforcements were already on their way.[15] These orders arrived too late – Picton had decided to abandon Zubiri before they were even written – but they may have strengthened his resolve to fight rather than abandon Sorauren. Wellington slept that night at Almandoz on the road from Maya to Sorauren and Pamplona. He had been up since before four in the morning and had ridden many miles through the mountains as he pieced fragments of news into a coherent picture and adjusted his orders accordingly. The problem was now fairly clear: could he bring up enough men to the position at Sorauren before Soult overwhelmed Picton and Cole; and could Hill keep D'Erlon in check in the meantime?

Picton originally intended to fight on a long high ridge, the Heights of San Cristobal, about a mile and a half from the ramparts of Pamplona; but Cole persuaded him to allow the Fourth Division to occupy the high steep hill of Oricain a mile further north which separated the village of Sorauren and the road to Maya on one side, from the village of Zabaldica and the road to Roncesvalles on the other. This placed the Fourth Division, with Campbell's

Portuguese, a couple of Spanish battalions and Byng's brigade of the Second Division, well in advance of the main position, held by Morillo and O'Donnell's Spanish infantry and the Third Division. Four brigades of cavalry arrived in time to cover the outer, or eastern flank, although they were not seriously engaged.[16]

The French advance guard reached the allied position on the morning of 27 July, but their army stretched back along many miles of mountain roads, and Soult refused to attack until he had his army in hand, for the slopes of Oricain hill were almost as formidable as those of Busaco.

Wellington rose at sunrise and rode south over the Col de Velate on the road to Pamplona. At Ostiz, a few miles north of Sorauren, he found General Long, who told him that Picton had abandoned the Zubiri position and fallen back to Pamplona. This meant that the road he was on would soon be cut by the French, and that the reinforcements would have to be sent by a less direct route. Leaving Murray and the bulk of the headquarters staff to organise this, Wellington galloped on with only a handful of attendants. He reached Sorauren at eleven o'clock, as the French were approaching the village. There was just enough time to dismount and write a short note to Murray confirming that Picton's men were still in position and clarifying the route to be taken by the other divisions. Taking this, Fitzroy Somerset sped back the way they had come, while Wellington galloped out of the village, across the face of the advancing French and up the Oricain hill to join the army. Fifteen minutes later and Somerset would have had to take a much longer route, delaying the orders by several hours, while Wellington would have had to cross the river further south, closer to Pamplona.[17]

Wellington's arrival was greeted with delight by the soldiers. James Mill of the 40th wrote that 'cheers upon cheers were vehemently raised along the whole line, which were only lulled to quiet by the joyous conviction that all would yet go well'. George Bingham confirms the point in a letter to a friend: 'In the course of the day Lord Wellington made his appearance, which acted like magic on us all. You know falling back before an enemy is not very exhilarating; we had in the plentitude of our wisdom, criticized the position; it had in our eyes, every fault a position could have. A few short words from him reassured us, and we were convinced from that moment, a better could not have been selected between the Pyrenees and the Ebro.'[18]

The morning of 28 July was fine and bright. It was the fourth anniversary of Talavera and the allied soldiers decorated their caps with box, the only shrub they could find.[19] The previous evening Soult had decided that he had no choice but to take the bull by the horns and employ five of his six divisions in a converging attack on the Oricain hill. However, his men were still not in position and the whole morning was spent shuffling them into place. Wellington watched these movements carefully from his command post on the summit of the hill and began to doubt if the French would attack at all. The Sixth Division was near at hand and Wellington ordered it to advance towards Sorauren. This seems to have brought on the battle, as Clausel pushed Conroux's division forward to check them, while the other four French divisions scrambled up the steep hill. Wellington called the fighting that followed 'fair *bludgeon* work' as the French made attack after attack, trying by weight of numbers to overcome the self-confidence of the British and Portuguese infantry and the natural strength of the position. The French fought with great determination and at one point the allied line wavered, but Wellington restored the position with his reserves. By the end of the day the French had been repulsed at all points. In his official despatch Wellington wrote with unusual warmth: 'The gallant 4th division, which had so frequently been distinguished in this army, surpassed their former good conduct. Every regiment charged with the bayonet, and the 40th, 7th, 20th, and 23rd, four different times. Their officers set them the example, and Major Gen. Ross had two horses shot under him. The Portuguese troops likewise behaved admirably.' Altogether the allies suffered 2,652 casualties, while Soult's losses were probably between 3,000–4,000 (we have figures for total French losses over the campaign as a whole, but not for each day).[20]

Wellington and his staff were greatly exposed during the fighting, as the best command post was close to the front and in the line of fire. Alexander Gordon was wounded in the arm while rallying a Spanish battalion late in the action; the Prince of Orange had his horse killed under him, and many of the other staff were slightly hit. Captain Charles Forrest of the Buffs records that at the end of the day, 'Lord Wellington passed along on his return to Villalba about dusk, and was cheered by Every Batt[alio]n as he passed with the most enthusiastic huzzahs, how gratifying a conclusion to such a day – never did [a] Commr in Chief enjoy so fully the Confidence of his Troops, for none so well deserved it'.[21]

Soult almost gave up the campaign after the defeat, but his hopes revived when D'Erlon established contact the following morning. A renewed attack on the allied position would clearly be futile, but he decided to shift the line of his advance sharply to the north-west, with D'Erlon's men leading, in an attempt to cut between Wellington and Graham and so relieve San Sebastian. This was an extremely ambitious plan – far too ambitious for an army that was now demoralised by its defeat, and which had lost the advantage of surprise.

The first steps in Soult's new plan were to disengage the troops facing Wellington, and march to join D'Erlon who would push Hill aside at Lizaso and so open the road to Ernani or Tolosa. To achieve this, Soult ordered his army to withdraw silently during the night of 29–30 July, marching in the dark across the face of the allied army which was in places less than half a mile away.

Wellington was not a man to be caught napping, and it is astonishing that a general of Soult's experience should have thought that these orders were practical. Daylight found the French army in considerable confusion. Clausel had got two of his divisions safely onto the road north, but the rest of the army was strung out, mostly on the heights facing Oricain, but with Conroux's division still in Sorauren, and Foy a little farther to the east. Wellington's men had been under arms since well before dawn and he had returned to his post on the summit of the hill. Hugh Gough, of the 87th, observed: 'Early the third morning, the Marquis came up to our hill. I was standing with Thos. Picton, who with Sir Stapleton Cotton, Generals Colville and Ponsonby, was with us the whole time. He appeared in the most wonderful good spirits, and shook Sir Thos. (who by the bye he has not been hitherto on good terms with) most heartily by the hand.'[22]

Overnight the Fourth and Sixth Divisions had, with great labour, carried their batteries up onto the hill. These now opened fire on the French at relatively short range (about 500 yards) causing some panic and disorder, for their fire came as a complete surprise. Wellington then ordered a general attack along the whole line. Byng's brigade and the Sixth Division converged on Sorauren and eventually surrounded it. One of Conroux's brigades escaped but the others, and Maucune's whole division, were almost destroyed, and 1,700 prisoners were taken. Cole pressed the French front while Picton advanced rapidly on the right, but there was less fighting here simply because the French gave way with little resistance. Foy became separated from the rest of the army and eventually retreated on the Roncesvalles road, escaping from the campaign quite lightly. On the other flank, Dalhousie passed well to the west of Sorauren and fell upon Clausel's two leading divisions on the road halfway to Ostiz. This led to a scrambling fight on very difficult ground in which the French were chiefly concerned with making their escape, although a few units put up some resistance before both divisions dissolved in flight. The rapid collapse of the French army at the second battle of Sorauren owes much to the loss of morale it had suffered by its defeat on 28 July, but Soult had also placed it in a hopeless position in which the best troops in the world could scarcely have escaped disaster.[23]

While Soult's divisions were being beaten one after another, a separate action was being fought four or five miles to the north-west, where D'Erlon was attacking Hill. Here the French carried the day, although not without hard fighting, and not very decisively. Hill's men were driven back, out of their position, and the road west was opened, but they were not broken. Given the defeat of the main army the success was meaningless, although failure would have made the now inevitable retreat much more difficult.

Soult's attempt to continue the offensive was defeated before it had properly begun. He had more luck, or showed more skill, in managing his subsequent retreat, and escaped the danger of being cut off and surrounded which he had created for himself. There were a number of partial combats over the next few days, including an attack by Barnes's brigade of the Seventh Division which particularly impressed Wellington. He told Bathurst: 'We had some desperate fighting in these mountains, and I have never known the troops behave so well. In the battle of the 28th we had hard fighting, and in my life I never saw such an attack as was made by Gen. Barnes' brigade, in the 7th division, upon the enemy above Echalar yesterday.'[24]

Wellington himself had a narrow escape early on 2 August. He had pushed forward close to the enemy in his reconnaissance, escorted by half a company of the 43rd, when the French attempted to cut him off, and only escaped thanks to the alertness and activity of a young sergeant.[25] This incident, which came so soon after his brush with the French at Sorauren and the heavy fire and casualties among those serving him on Oricain hill, made him reflect, and he told his brother William: 'I escaped as usual unhurt, and I begin to believe that the finger of God is upon me.'[26]

At one point on 1 August, Wellington considered extending the campaign into France by pushing Hill's division over the Maya Pass, and around Soult's flank and onto his rear. He abandoned the plan when he found that Hill was not as far advanced as he thought. Soult's army was in no condition to resist an allied offensive, although Bayonne was now defensible and well garrisoned. Yet there were good reasons for Wellington not to push forward. His army was weary and short of supplies after eight days of marching through the mountains. If the soldiers had advanced into France, they would certainly have plundered the countryside; and now there was no important objective nearby that could be gained by a limited advance. Also, San Sebastian and Pamplona remained to be taken, while in Germany the armistice between Napoleon and the allies remained in place, and might yet lead to serious peace negotiations. Thus, on 3 August, Wellington ordered a halt to active operations and distributed the army back to their defensive positions.[27]

Despite some uneasy moments at the outset, the campaign had been a resounding success. The allied army had lost some 7,000 casualties – more than half of them in the Second and Fourth Divisions. The difficult task of holding a long line with poor lateral communications had been accomplished thanks to Wellington's skill and foresight, and the remarkable fighting quality and confidence of his men. Soult had done as much as it was reasonable to expect with an army inferior in numbers and in spirit. His initial plan was excellent and its execution was no more flawed than most military operations, but his refusal to accept defeat after 28 July and his second plan were simple folly. The defeat cost his army 12,563 casualties including over 2,700 prisoners, while many thousands more men left the ranks before the campaign was over but rejoined within a few days. Wellington was justifiably proud of his success. He told Pole that the operations were 'infinitely more difficult' than at Vitoria, and 'I believe the best I have yet carried on'.[28] Observers noted that he was in high spirits and particularly pleased with his troops,[29] although he was less satisfied with his subordinates, complaining with some justice: 'All the beatings we have given the French have not given our generals confidence in themselves and in the exertions of their troops. They are really heroes when I am on the spot to direct them, but when I am obliged to quit them they are children.'[30]

The siege of San Sebastian was suspended during Soult's offensive and the breaching batteries did not resume fire until 26 August when fresh guns and ammunition arrived from England. The garrison made good use of this time to strengthen its interior defences, especially around the breach facing the estuary. Rather surprisingly, the ordnance officers remained committed to the line of attack across the river rather than along the isthmus, and Wellington and Graham accepted their advice.

Wellington had some doubts whether the Fifth Division could be trusted to complete the siege, for its senior officers talked openly of their lack of confidence in the engineers and the impossibility of success. Such talk was fatal to any operation and Wellington considered bringing in another division to undertake the storm, even though this would publicly disgrace the Fifth.[31] However, on 29 August General Leith returned to the army having recovered from his Salamanca wound, replacing Oswald, and Wellington partly relented. The Fifth Division would undertake the storm but it would be 'assisted' by 750 volunteers from the First, Fourth and Light Divisions. Remarkably there was an overwhelming response to the call for volunteers with officers and men competing fiercely for the doubtful pleasure of repeating the horrors of Ciudad Rodrigo, Badajoz and Burgos.[32] The besieging troops deeply resented the insult, and Leith, who was in charge of the attack, determined to keep the volunteers well back as a reserve, but Wellington had succeeded in pricking the pride of the Fifth Division and inspiring it with fresh determination. It would be needed.

The assault began at eleven o'clock on the morning of 31 August, an hour before low tide. There would be no repetition of the stumbling in the dark of the first attempt, and the conflict was watched by a large crowd of spectators, both military and civilian, positioned on a nearby hillside, cheering and groaning as events unfolded. The storming troops reached the foot of the breach relatively easily, but found it hard to climb, and at its summit were confronted with a sheer drop of twenty feet while coming under heavy fire. The only possible way forward was from the ends of the breach where it joined the main wall, but the French had made elaborate precautions to defend these narrow passages. Leith commanded the operation from the sand near the foot of the breach, with Fletcher on one side and Oswald on the other. Wave after wave of troops was sent forward and advanced with resolute courage, only to be checked by the sheer impossibility of getting beyond the breach. Failure seemed almost inevitable until Graham, watching from the batteries, ordered the artillery to resume fire, even though this would cause some British casualties, from shots falling short as well as among the wounded men lying on the breach. For twenty minutes the batteries roared forth, inflicting heavy casualties on the French who dared not leave their posts, knowing that a renewed assault would soon follow.

This brief interval gave the allied troops a chance to recover their nerve and collect themselves for a final effort, and now they knew the problem that faced them. The guns fell silent, the stormers rushed forward, concentrating their efforts at the traverses at each end of the breach and, with hard fighting, and the loss of many men, carried them. A few minutes more and the resistance was crumbling as allied troops began to find their way down from the walls and into the town. They found many of the streets blocked with barricades, but Rey's plans for a protracted defence of the town failed as his men were too exhausted, confused, and had suffered too much for an immediate effort. Many found their way back to the castle, others surrendered, while isolated pockets continued fighting for more than an hour. The castle continued to resist until it was bombarded into submission on 8 September.

In the midst of the chaos following the storm, allied troops, free of all bounds of discipline, roamed the streets looking for plunder. Leith and Oswald had been wounded and Fletcher killed, leaving General Hay in command, and his attempts to check the disorder were ineffectual. San Sebastian was sacked, although there is some doubt as to whether the troops were as badly behaved as at Badajoz; most of the tales of rape and murder came from those who were not present at the scene, and a frank report of the provost of the Fifth Division suggests that while there was much pillaging, other excesses were largely avoided. Whatever the truth of this, the unfortunate inhabitants still suffered terribly, for fire swept through the town destroying most of it before the end of the day.[33]

The second siege of San Sebastian cost the allied army more than 2,300 casualties, and of the 1,500 men in the leading brigade, 332 were killed and 530 were wounded, including its commander. More than 750 prisoners were taken on the day of the storm, and another 1,000 when Rey and the castle surrendered. Although smaller in scale than the losses at Badajoz, many of the same criticisms can be made as of the earlier operation: too much was left to the raw courage of the troops, and the plan of attack was undoubtedly at fault. The ultimate responsibility for this rests, of course, with Wellington, but he was poorly served by the technical advisers whose opinion he had accepted. None of the old excuses apply at San Sebastian; there was plenty of equipment and ammunition, a strong force of sappers and miners, and no need to hurry the operation. Neither Wellington nor Graham interfered much in the detail of the conduct of the siege, and there was nothing preventing Fletcher and the engineers proceeding slowly and methodically according to the rules of their craft. They chose not to do so, and Wellington accepted their decision, but their own historian, Sir John Jones, has no hesitation in admitting that this 'caused an easy and certain operation of eighteen or twenty days to extend through a space of sixty days, and to cost the besiegers 3,500 officers and men killed, wounded or made prisoners [including casualties in the first siege]'.[34]

As Leith's men were struggling in the breach of San Sebastian, Soult made a forlorn attempt to relieve the beleaguered fortress. A frontal attack across the Bidassoa was repulsed at San Marcial by General Freyre with three divisions of the Army of Galicia in one of the few Spanish victories in open battle of the war. At the same time an attempt to turn the allied flank led to heavy fighting with the Fourth Division before the French withdrew and made their escape across the flooded river, forcing their way past a detachment of the 95th Rifles which was holding the bridge at Vera. The relative ease with which these attacks were repulsed stands in marked contrast to the fighting in late July, and signals the decline of Soult's army, which no longer had the strength or confidence to mount a serious offensive.

Throughout these operations Wellington was engaged in a series of acrimonious disputes with the British, Portuguese and Spanish governments which rumbled on for the rest of the year, achieving little. His relations with the ministers in London were made more difficult by a dispute with the Admiralty. As early as the beginning of July he had complained that the navy was not doing enough to protect his communications from French, and especially American, privateers, while its failure to blockade San Sebastian attracted his ire. Wellington was accustomed to being treated with deferential courtesy by the ministers in London; Castlereagh, Liverpool and Bathurst had all shown great patience in the face of his frequent and often intemperate grumbling. But the Admiralty was not so easily intimidated, having a fine sense of its own importance, and no great opinion of the foot-soldiers whose exploits had cast its own more important achievements somewhat into the shade in recent years. Wellington's complaints received extremely stiff responses from Lord Melville, which were supplemented by letters from J.W. Croker, the Secretary to the Admiralty, and then sent to the War Department which passed them on to Wellington.[35] Astonished and outraged at such treatment, Wellington wrote to Bathurst, who kept an admirably straight face while replying, unhelpfully:

You must not read Croker's compositions as you would those of any other official person. He has a talent for writing sharply & with great facility. When this is coupled together, it is a great misfortune in an Official person. His style is often what it should not be, when he addresses himself to Departments, at least *I* have often found it so, but I have not taken any Notice of it, for I know he does not mean anything by it – And as for you, you are the God of his Idolatory.[36]

Wellington either failed to see, or refused to acknowledge, how these words might be applied to himself, and complained to his brother William: 'I have heard nothing more . . . about the Admiralty; excepting that Lord Bathurst has told me that Mr Croker is in the habit of writing Impertinent letters and that I ought not to mind them!!'[37]

He was also annoyed by Liverpool's refusal to assist Gerald Wellesley's clerical career, or to find a suitable office for William, who had separated himself from Canning and Lord Wellesley and was eager to rejoin the government. He took offence when Liverpool and Bathurst tentatively suggested transferring his army to northern Europe, even though it was plain that they were determined to defer to his judgement, and only raised the possibility because he was evidently reluctant to advance across the Pyrenees. Finally a short-lived but serious recurrence of the old problem of a shortage of specie at the end of the year provoked him to complain to William that 'the Govt are tired of me and my operations; & wish both to the Devil'. And even, 'I am almost at open War with the Ministers upon every point; and I am quite certain they would get rid of me, if they could or dared'.[38] This was simply absurd; Liverpool and Bathurst were wholehearted in their support for Wellington and his operations, and his other correspondence suggests that he was not really this disillusioned with the government in London. Fortunately a fresh supply of specie soon arrived, and Wellington's ill humour quickly dissipated. Nonetheless it is striking that at a time when his operations were prospering, and when he was receiving almost unanimous political support at home, he should still have felt discontented and alienated from the politicians who had consistently supported him, and with whom he would continue to work closely for many years. Wellington was never the most patient of men, and he was always inclined to vent his grievances in the most inflammatory language, but it is possible that by the autumn of 1813 he was beginning to tire, having been on active service in the Peninsula for four-and-a-half years.

Wellington's relations with the Portuguese government were also difficult in 1813, although their low point came sooner, in the middle of the year. The departure of the allied army led to financial problems in Portugal, yet with the seat of the war removed far from Lisbon, it seemed less urgent. Wellington privately railed against the 'ingratitude' of the Portuguese authorities and expressed the hope 'that we have seen the last of Portugal', but he was generous in publicly acknowledging the role played by the country's troops in his victories, both at Vitoria and in the battles of the Pyrenees. He told Liverpool that they were 'now the *fighting cocks* of the army' and attributed their excellent performance not to their British officers, but to the fact that the Portuguese government was at last paying and feeding them properly.[39]

Relations with the Spanish government were even more difficult, and Wellington as Commander-in-Chief was more closely involved in the detail of negotiations. The fundamental problem was the complete difference of perspective: Wellington was only really interested in the immediate practical needs of the army at the front; whereas the politicians at Cadiz were engaged in a fierce ideological struggle over the nature of post-war Spain – a struggle in which both *liberales* and conservatives (*serviles*) were willing to play on popular xenophobia and resentment at British interference. The tightly enclosed world of Cadiz was remote from the experiences of the rest of the country, thus increasing the detachment of the politicians from reality. This led not only to a great deal of friction in correspondence with Wellington, but also to a low priority being given to the logistical support of the army. In the summer of 1813 the Spanish army had 160,000 men under arms, but only a third of them were at the front (including forces on the east coast), and they were kept chronically short of pay and supplies.[40]

At the end of August Wellington was so frustrated that he threatened to resign as Commander-in-Chief if the Spanish government did not abide by its agreement with him. Rather to his surprise the Spanish authorities chose to construe this as an actual resignation, but declined either to accept or reject it until a new Cortes was assembled. This period of limbo lasted for months, during which time Wellington continued to act as Commander-in-Chief but was unable to do much to improve the logistical support of the Spanish armies. It was not until the end of November that the Cortes voted narrowly to accept Wellington's terms for retaining command of the army, against the wishes of the Spanish government.[41]

The sack of San Sebastian caused great ill feeling in Spain, especially in Cadiz where the press took it up as a *cause célèbre*, alleging that Wellington had given deliberate orders for the destruction of the town because of its prominence in maritime trade between France and Spain.[42] This canard naturally incensed Wellington who was most unusual in his concern for the local civilian population. He protested vigorously and was eventually mollified by an official statement on the affair, but by then the damage had been done. The newspapers had moved on to an even more unlikely story: that Castaños had offered Wellington the Spanish crown provided he became a Catholic, and Wellington had accepted! This piece of fancy was first floated in an Irish newspaper and was only one of many similar stories printed about Wellington in these years.[43] As for San Sebastian, General Graham expressed the unpalatable truth when he wrote: 'I am quite sure that if Dover were in the hands of the French, and were to be taken by storm by a British army, the cellars and shops of the inhabitants would suffer as those of San Sebastian did.'[44]

Wellington's experiences dealing with the Spanish government in 1812–14 left him with little sympathy for the dominant *liberales*. He had always been sceptical of their much-vaunted constitution, and was astonished at their folly in attacking the Church which was playing a central role in mobilising resistance to the French across the country. He was left with the abiding impression that the *liberales* represented only a small section of society and had little in common with the great majority of their countrymen. This was probably a little overstated, for liberal ideas had a currency outside Cadiz, but it was not an unreasonable conclusion given the behaviour of the *liberale* politicians and press in these years. It was also a conclusion that fitted comfortably with Wellington's own outlook, his dislike of abstract political theorising and his opposition to the British radicals who shared many ideas with the Spanish *liberales*.

Nonetheless, despite all the friction and disputes, Wellington and the Spanish government continued to work together for the common cause, and the alliance proved immensely successful, first in absorbing Napoleon's attacks in 1808–11, and then in turning the tide of the war against him. Neither party could have succeeded without the other, and even when their arguments were most heated, they never quite forgot it.

CHAPTER THIRTY-THREE

CROSSING THE FRONTIER
(September–December 1813)

T HE FALL OF San Sebastian and the defeat of the French army at San Marcial and Vera opened the road into France. Autumn had scarcely begun and Wellington's troops were fresh and well supplied. Officers in the army talked of a grand offensive, advancing into France as far as Bordeaux or Toulouse before winter forced the army into cantonments – hopes which were a fair reflection of the actual balance of forces in the Pyrenees.[1] But Wellington was most reluctant to contemplate a significant invasion of France. His correspondence reveals several explanations for this restraint. He was worried that his army would plunder the countryside and abuse the local population, and that this might trigger a popular uprising in which the allies were the occupying power, reversing the situation in Spain. Many Portuguese and Spanish soldiers had personal grounds for seeking revenge, while the British had so long regarded the French as enemies that it would take time to convince the soldiers that the French civilians must be treated with respect. Already one British soldier had been arrested for rape who 'says he thought it was France, and that there it was all regular'.[2] A month after the fall of San Sebastian, William Napier wrote home to his wife:

> The plains of France lie before us, cultivated, enclosed, rich and beautiful beyond description. The Spaniards, Portuguese, and I am sorry to say the British, are exulting in the thought of robbing and murdering the unfortunate possessors of what they see before them. Lord Wellington says *they shall not do it* . . . The cause of our country may justify our killing our enemies in battle, but it cannot justify our being even *spectators* of the merciless acts of a licentious army; and well I know there is no cruelty hell can devise that this army is not capable of and anxious to inflict upon the wretched people below us.[3]

Larpent reported that Wellington was 'highly angry' at the plundering, stating that 'if officers will not obey orders, and take care that those under them do so also, they must go home, for he will not command them here; so many of our officers seem to think they have nothing to do but to fight'.[4] In the wake of the same incident Wellington himself wrote to a subordinate: 'If we were five times stronger than we are, we could not venture to enter France, if we cannot prevent our soldiers from plundering'.[5]

Strenuous efforts over several months eventually drove the lesson home: the soldiers of Wellington's army learnt that they were no more at liberty to misbehave in France than in Spain or England, and the regimental officers discovered that turning a blind eye to such misconduct would bring wrath down from on high. When the army did eventually advance into the interior of France the inhabitants were astonished to be paid for their goods, and treated far better by their enemies than by Soult's army. As a result there was little popular hostility to the invaders in southern France and official attempts to organise resistance, or even non-cooperation, fell flat. This could not have been achieved if Wellington had allowed the army to advance rapidly in the autumn of 1813. There would not have been time for the troops – or indeed the local inhabitants – to learn the rules, while the rigours of active campaigning would have created the excuse and the opportunity for many more abuses.[6]

There was another aspect to the problem. Wellington feared that the Spanish army would plunder the countryside not just from revenge and mischief but from sheer necessity. On 19 September Wellington wrote to Bathurst: 'The superiority of numbers which I can take into France will consist in about 25,000 Spaniards, neither paid nor fed, and who must plunder, and will set the whole country against us'.[7] He pressed the Spanish government hard to do more to provide for their troops, but with little effect, other than adding to the tension in his relations with Cadiz.[8] As a temporary measure he gave them some supplies from the British commissariat, but that was unsustainable. When the army did cross the frontier Spanish officers proved unable or unwilling to prevent their men from plundering. Wellington tried the expedient of keeping them under arms all day but this failed to bring a lasting improvement, and so, rather than risk alienating the French population, Wellington sent most of his Spanish troops back into Spain, quartering them on their own countrymen. It was an extraordinary move which proves both the sincerity of Wellington's commitment, as well as the comfortable superiority that his army enjoyed which made it a practical possibility. It is highly unlikely that any other general of his day would have done as much.[9]

A second, less compelling reason advanced by Wellington for his reluctance to invade France, was his fear that Suchet might defeat Bentinck and drive him back down the coast before turning against Wellington's exposed flank and rear.[10] This was not very plausible. It was far more likely that if Wellington pressed deep into France Suchet would evacuate his positions in Catalonia, leaving garrisons in Barcelona and a few other places, and bring his disposable force to assist Soult. That would be an unwelcome development, but Suchet did not have enough men left to tip the balance of forces against Wellington, especially as he would have to leave a force behind to guard the frontier at Rousillon.

Wellington's third reason was much more substantial. This related to the state of the war in central Europe, and the danger that the continental powers might be defeated or make a separate peace, leaving Britain to continue the war with only the support of Spain and Portugal. So long as the Russians, Prussians and Austrians were fighting Napoleon in eastern Germany, around Dresden, Leipzig and Berlin, Wellington could feel that his position on the French frontier was sufficiently advanced, and that if he pushed much further forward he might be left dangerously exposed. This idea appeared in his letters as early as July and recurred frequently. For example, on 18 October he told Bathurst:

> I am very doubtful indeed about the advantage of moving any farther forward here at present. I see that Buonaparte was still at Dresden on the 28th; and unless I could fight a general action with Soult, and gain a complete victory, which the nature of the country would scarcely admit of, I should do but little good to the allies; should hardly be able to winter in France; and, in retiring, should probably incur some loss and inconvenience.[11]

The downbeat tone of this letter reflects Wellington's consistently pessimistic view of the prospects of allied success. In August he wrote that it 'appears to me that Buonaparte has the allies, including Austria, exactly in the state in which he would wish to have them',[12] and he feared that Napoleon would use an extension of the armistice to transfer troops from Germany to reinforce Soult.[13] But it was a one-sided view; he did not consider how his actions might have improved the position of the allies in Germany, where the news that Wellington's army was advancing through Gascony would surely have weakened Napoleon's diplomatic position and demoralised his soldiers while heartening the allies. As a rule Wellington was only interested in how their success or failure might affect him. Even in late November, when the scale and consequences of Napoleon's defeat at Leipzig were clear, he urged Bathurst not to be overconfident: 'I recommend to your Lordship to make peace with [Napoleon] if you can acquire all the objects which you have a right to expect. All the powers of Europe require peace possibly more than France.'[14] And this despite finding no popular support for Napoleon and great war-weariness in the part of France he had occupied.

Underlying this pessimism were the dashed hopes of the last twenty years. So many powerful coalitions had been formed against France only to come crashing to defeat that it seemed almost unbelievable that Napoleon's empire, which had looked so strong little more than a year previously, could really be overthrown. For years Lord Liverpool had been mocked by the Whigs for his youthful advocacy of a 'march on Paris' – could such a strategy now become a practical possibility against Napoleon?[15] The last time allied troops had threatened the French capital was in 1792 when Brunswick's cautious advance had been halted at Valmy; it had triggered the worst excesses of Revolution, and created the monstrous 'nation in arms' that Europe had been struggling to contain ever since. Wellington had no wish to risk rousing a regalvanised French patriotism, especially while it was possible that a negotiated peace might be made acceptable to all parties without the need for an invasion of France. Mr Larpent expressed this view on 21 October when he wrote in his journal: 'I have still great doubts of the policy of entering France at all. The French now suffer severely, and grumble against their own government. Invasion may stir up the strong vanity of a Frenchman, and make him forget his grievances, in order to revenge himself on those who insult his native soil.'[16]

It is not clear if these arguments were the only reason Wellington was reluctant to invade France. But there is a sense in his letters that he seized gratefully upon them to justify his existing preference, rather than reluctantly abandoning his private wish for a speedy advance for the sake of the wider cause. He admitted to Bathurst 'that I feel a great disinclination to enter the French territory',[17] while he commented on the request for detailed maps of France: 'I wish I may not require them; but it is as well to have them at all events.'[18] A Napoleon or a Nelson would have been eager to carry the war onto enemy soil and treat the French as they had for so long treated others. But Wellington was never blind to the misery of war; he felt no hostility to the French people, although he loathed and despised Napoleon's regime; and he may have felt that the character of the war would change when operations moved from the liberation of Spain to the invasion of France.

Thus, Wellington looked to more limited objectives in the autumn of 1813 – modest advances that would keep Soult busy, accustom his army to being on French territory, and satisfy the allies that Britain was not inactive. He explained to Bathurst on 19 September:

> I see that . . . the Allies are very anxious that we should enter France, and that our government have promised that we should, *as soon as the enemy should be finally expelled from Spain*; and I think I ought, and will bend a little to the views of the Allies, if it can be done with safety to the army, notwithstanding that I acknowledge I should prefer to turn my attention to Catalonia, as soon as I shall have secured this frontier.[19]

Even so, four weeks of autumn passed after the surrender of the castle of San Sebastian before Wellington was ready to order his army forward across the

Bidassoa – a delay caused, or justified, by the slow movements of the pontoon train and the need to wait for the best tides.[20]

Soult used this unexpected but most welcome respite to construct a series of earthworks and field fortifications along the whole length of his line. Wellington examined the French position with care. He learnt from the local population that the broad estuary of the Bidassoa was passable at low tide, and that Soult had few troops guarding the further bank. He gave orders for the Fifth Division to ford the river with the help of Spanish guides, turning the French flank, while the rest of Graham's men advanced from San Marcial. Further inland, in the centre of the allied line, the Light Division and the Spanish infantry would endeavour to drive the French from the dominating heights of the Grande Rhune; while the right wing of the army would content itself with demonstrations, designed to distract Soult's attention without risking many casualties. The attack would be made on the morning of 7 October.

The Fifth Division had no difficulty with the fords and achieved complete surprise. Frederick Robinson, whose brigade was closest to the sea, describes what happened:

> At half past seven, it being then low water, the signal was made; when to my great surprise my Guide, who was full as tall as myself told me the water would be up to our chins at least – However the Peer [Wellington] had ordered us to cross and therefore *there could be no* impediments; To prevent the chance of drowning, or being exposed to severe fire from the enemy, I dismounted and placing myself with the Guide a little in front of the Brigade, gave the word to advance The men holding their arms and ammunition over their heads; sacrificing cheerfully Three days provisions which they had in their Haversacks rather than injure the ammunition, and with hearty cheering we greeted the French shore. The event justified the judgement of our sagacious Chief, for the French were taken so completely by surprise, that we were safely landed and formed before a single shot was fired, & those that did oppose us were soon dispersed by the Light Infantry.[21]

The First Division and the Spanish infantry encountered more resistance but soon drove the French from their positions, and Reille's reserves arrived too late to do more than cover the retreat. Neither side lost heavily, the allies suffering only about 400 casualties and the French scarcely more. Wellington forbade any pursuit.[22]

There was rather more bloodshed in the centre, although the forces engaged were relatively small. The French works on the Grande Rhune were formidable but they were assailed with skill and élan by the Light Division, while Giron's Spanish divisions kept Clausel's men busy on the flank. George Hennell commented that if the French had 'fought as French troops *have* fought, & as they *ought* to have fought, we should have lost a great number if not had been repulsed'.[23]

The passage of the Bidassoa was one of the most perfectly successful of all Wellington's battles. It makes a matching pair with the passage of the Douro at Oporto four-and-a-half-years earlier, with careful planning taking the place of the rapid seizure of a fleeting opportunity. The only technical criticism that can be made is that Wellington made no attempt to exploit his advantage, or press the French in their retreat. He might, without risk, have advanced across the Nivelle to the gates of Bayonne, but his aims were strictly limited. The allied army lost some 1,600 casualties, almost half of them Spanish, mostly in Giron's divisions which fought for hours on the slopes of the Rhune. Wellington made a point of praising their conduct in his despatch: 'It gives me singular satisfaction to report the good conduct of the officers and troops of the army of reserve of Andalusia . . . The attack made by the battalion of Las Ordenes, under the command of Col Hore, yesterday, was made in as good order and with as much spirit as any that I have seen made by any troops; and I was much satisfied with the spirit and discipline of the whole of this corps.'[24] French losses were probably not much heavier than those of the allies, but the defeat strengthened their sense of inferiority and damaged Soult's standing in the army, which was already thrumming with rumours that he had been recalled to Germany and replaced by Suchet.[25]

The Bidassoa was Graham's last action under Wellington's command. The strain of the siege of San Sebastian had so worn him down that he was unable to preside over the surrender of the garrison, and at sixty-five he had begun to feel that he was too old for active campaigning. He had warned Wellington as early as 15 August that he would soon have to resign, and the British government had selected Sir John Hope, Graham's cousin and friend, to succeed him.[26] Wellington was delighted with the choice, telling Bathurst: 'I am quite certain that he is the ablest man in the army.' And while Graham's departure was regretted for the loss of his generosity and warmth of character, few thought that the army's efficiency would suffer from the change.[27] Hope arrived on 6 October and Graham handed the command of the left wing to him at noon the next day, when the fighting was over.[28] He returned to London where he reluctantly yielded to pressure from the British government to take command of a motley force being sent to Holland to assist an uprising against the French. It proved a troublesome command including a minor disaster at Bergen-op-Zoom, but it did little to tarnish Graham's reputation as one of the ablest and most attractive of Wellington's subordinates.

The rest of October passed quietly as the French busily constructed earthworks along their new line on the Nivelle, and Wellington waited for decisive news from Germany. The garrison of Pamplona, which as rumour had it was on half-rations even in August, was finally forced by hunger to surrender on the last day of October. While less obviously heroic than that of San Sebastian, it too had held out for longer than Wellington had expected. But its surrender was more of an inconvenience than a threat; the argument that Wellington could not advance further into France until it had fallen is unconvincing. The fortress was securely masked by Spanish troops, while an advance which drove the French from St Jean de Pied du Port (on their side of the Roncesvalles Pass) would reduce the danger of its being relieved, and hence its strategic significance.[29]

The weather in October proved cold and wet, and the troops grumbled about the inadequacy of their tents and the discomfort of not being in quarters without the activity and variety of active campaigning.[30] In the middle of the month Wellington was still reluctant to advance any further, but on 30 October he was cheered by the news that Bavaria had joined the allies, 'so that I should think that there is already an end to the Confederation of the Rhine, and that Buonaparte must withdraw from the Elbe.'[31] Ten days later rumours reached him 'that the French have sustained a terrible defeat in Germany', with Larpent recording the details: 'Bony is beaten back to the Rhine, with the loss of three divisions cut off by blowing up a bridge too soon, &c.'[32] This was Leipzig, the greatest battle of the age involving more than half a million men over three days, resulting in Napoleon's complete defeat and the destruction of his army.

The news could not have reached the Pyrenees at a better moment, for Wellington was about to launch another attack and it encouraged the allied soldiers while disheartening the French. Soult had constructed a thick belt of earthworks and small forts all along his line on both the south and north banks of the Nivelle, wherever the ground was most commanding. To some extent these works were a poor-man's Lines of Torres Vedras, although far less time, effort and thought had gone into them and the ground was less favourable; the entire position was overlooked by the Grande Rhune. The other crucial difference was that Wellington had manned his Lines with Portuguese militia and other second-tier troops, holding his field army back in reserve, whereas Soult was forced to disperse his army into the works. By incorporating large numbers of conscripts he had almost 60,000 infantry in the front line (not counting the garrison of Bayonne and some other detached forces), but his men were dispirited and expected to be beaten.[33]

Wellington had more than 80,000 infantry ready for the attack. He had issued his orders a day or two before the battle while examining the French positions from the top of the Grande Rhune. Harry Smith gives us a rare glimpse of the plans being made:

The Duke was lying down, and begun a very earnest conversation. General
Alten, Kempt, Colborne, I, and other staff-officers were preparing to leave the
Duke, when he says, 'Oh, lie still'. After he had conversed for some time with
Sir G. Murray, Murray took out of his sabretache his writing materials, and
began to write a plan of attack for the whole army. When it was finished, so
clearly had he understood the Duke, I don't think he erased one word. He
says, 'My lord, is this your desire?' It was one of the most interesting scenes I
have ever witnessed. As Murray read the Duke's eye was directed with his
telescope to the spot in question. He never asked Sir G. Murray one question,
but the muscles of his face evinced lines of the deepest thought. When Sir
G. Murray had finished, the Duke smiled and said, 'Ah, Murray, this will put
us in possession of the fellows' lines. Shall we be ready tomorrow?' 'I fear not,
my lord, but next day.'[34]

Wellington decided to hold back his left, while making the main attack in the
centre and centre-right. The Light Division would storm the Petite Rhune, the
formidable ridge north of the Grande Rhune, while the Third and Sixth
Divisions would make a converging attack on the bridge of Amotz, and, on the
right, Hill's men would take the Finodetta ridge. Larpent dined at headquarters
the night before the battle and noted that Wellington 'was all gaiety and spirits;
and only said on leaving the room "Remember! At four in the morning."'[35]

Dawn on 10 November brought a cold clear day with excellent visibility. Just
after six o'clock three British guns fired, giving the signal for the attack to begin.
The 43rd Light Infantry, supported by the 17th Portuguese Line, assailed the
western end of the Petite Rhune with great impetuosity, while Colborne's
brigade of the Light Division took a wider turn and was soon in the French
rear. The French abandoned their strong position and fled.

To the right of the Light Division the allies swept forward with equal ease.
The advanced French positions around Sare were bombarded, and the Fourth
Division advanced with scaling ladders to tackle the small forts, but they were
not needed, for the French gave way without waiting for the allies to close.[36]
The Third Division, under Charles Colville, broke through the *abatis* and the
94th stormed the bridge of Amotz. Colville told his brother-in-law, the Rev.
Roger Frankland:

The day was one of the luckiest that ever came out of the heaven . . . Success
was so general and everything went on so swimmingly, that I think it was
altogether the most animating and (shall I say it to a parson?) agreeable day
of the kind I was ever engaged in: the loss not being in any comparison to the
difficulties overcome . . .[37]

Even so there was some fierce fighting in this part of the battlefield and the Third Division lost over 500 casualties, although the result was never in doubt.

Hill's attack on the right flank was equally successful. There might have been more serious fighting on the allied right if Foy had come forward to assist D'Erlon, but instead he attempted to turn the flank of the whole allied army with an advance through the Maya Pass. He soon ran into difficulties, for Hill had left a Spanish brigade to guard the pass which fought an excellent delaying action. Foy eventually forced the position but could then accomplish nothing more than the capture of some of the baggage of the Sixth Division, before realising the need to withdraw the way he had come. The affair did nothing to lessen his reputation for pursuing a course of his own, while leaving his colleagues in trouble.

The result of the battle was a complete and comprehensive allied victory, which made plain the difference in quality between the two armies. The French suffered 4,351 casualties, and were forced to abandon many heavy guns, mostly in the redoubts south of St Jean de Luz, while allied losses were approximately 3,250 (one-quarter of them Spanish).

In England this latest triumph made Queen Charlotte 'almost drunk with joy'.[38] Her enthusiasm is not surprising for it arrived at an intoxicating moment hot on the heels of reports of an uprising against the French in Holland, and followed within hours by news of the surrender of Marshal St Cyr at Dresden with 16,000 men. The Tower guns were fired twice in one day for two victories hundreds of miles apart.[39] Not even Lord Grenville's habitual despondency could withstand such a cascade of good tidings, and the spirit that had made him one of the leading opponents of a compromise peace in the 1790s revived, as he finally saw afresh the possibility of restoring the balance of power in Europe.[40] John Rous, a young officer in the Guards, had not even been born when the war broke out in 1793, but he too put the news into a wider perspective: 'If Perceval or Pitt had been alive now, they would almost have died for joy at the present state of affairs.'[41] For the first time in almost a generation, sober men dared to hope not just for peace, but for victory.

Wellington was content with his success and had no intention of pursuing further operations immediately. The weather was bad, with heavy rains reducing the roads to mud and making movement difficult. In any case he felt no enthusiasm for the siege of Bayonne, which was the obvious next step in an advance. So he put his army into cantonments and waited for news from Germany. Would Leipzig open the way for a negotiated peace with Napoleon? Would the allies put their army in winter quarters, giving Napoleon time to raise and organise yet another army; or would they attempt to cross the Rhine and invade France in the middle of winter? Without knowing more of the allied plans he could not cooperate with them.[42] Bathurst was dismayed when he learnt that Wellington intended to rest on his oars, for the most recent despatches from the Continent indicated that the allies had no intention of halting their advance, even temporarily, at the Rhine, although the Austrians continued to look for a negotiated peace. He therefore wrote to Wellington:

> Of the military expediency of continuing, your Lordship must be the best judge; but politically speaking, I must say we are all here most anxious that it should not be understood you have concluded your operations, knowing the prejudicial effect it will have upon our Allies. If it were to induce them to close the campaign, it is much to be apprehended that we should not be able to persuade them again to open it the next year.

And even if it did no more than allow Napoleon to transfer men from Soult's army to oppose the allies, it would be most unfortunate.[43] Wellington took the hint and declared that he had never intended to halt for long, and then moved on to the more familiar and congenial ground of grumbling about the government's failure to keep him supplied with enough cash to pay the army regularly.[44]

In fact his planned advance was modest: to push forward a few miles to the outskirts of Bayonne and to gain control of the south bank of the Adour in the hope of cutting off its main supply line, and so to force Soult to quit the town with his field army. Wellington did not intend to besiege Bayonne at this stage, or to attempt to cross the Adour. Even so the operation was not without difficulty, for the River Nive ran north into the Adour at Bayonne and Wellington would be forced to divide his army between the two sides of the Nive, with uncertain communications between them.

Soult's first idea, after being driven from the Nivelle, was to make a fresh stand on the Nive, but he soon found that the ground was unsuitable, and decided to keep only a light force on the river and the bulk of his army back in Bayonne. He would then be able to concentrate all his men against one part or the other of the allied army and have some hope of gaining a significant advantage. Wellington was aware of this danger, but felt that his army had gained such a psychological superiority over the French that he could afford to take liberties, even though he had sent most of his Spanish troops to the rear. The result proved him right, but not before much hard fighting, and more anxious moments than he had experienced since the battles of the Pyrenees.[45]

The allies crossed the Nive on 9 December. The operation was well planned and encountered little opposition. Soult decided to concentrate his whole army, except the garrison of Bayonne, west of the Nive on 10 December and attempt to cut through Wellington's centre. The attack would be led by Clausel, who would be supported by D'Erlon, while Reille made a secondary attack against

Hope. The initial French onslaught was made with some skill and dash, and the picquets of the Light Division had to fall back at full speed, even so losing more than fifty prisoners. The main body of the Light Division checked the French advance at Arcangues, and Clausel's attack stalled. However, on the allied left Reille's attack against Hope had more success. Again the allied outposts were taken by surprise, and Hope's reserves were much farther back; there was some panic among the allied troops, but the French were unable to exploit their advantage and by the middle of the afternoon the position was stabilised. Hope had lost about 1,500 casualties including some 400 prisoners.

That night three battalions of Nassau and Frankfort troops quit Soult's army *en masse*. News of Leipzig had reached them some time before, and they no longer felt any allegiance to Napoleon. Wellington had responded to discreet enquiries with assurances that they would not be treated as prisoners of war, but would be shipped home to Germany. Their defection forced Soult and Suchet to disarm the few German and Spanish troops who remained with them, and no doubt caused uneasy reflections on the speed with which their master's empire was unravelling.[46]

Both generals expected the other to take the initiative on the following day. Wellington anticipated that Soult would shift his forces across the Nive and attack Hill and the allied right, while Soult thought Wellington would launch a general attack. Neither did so, although a foggy morning meant that it took some time for this to become apparent, and there was some inconsequential but costly fighting on the allied left, in which Hope's outlying troops again lost quite heavily.

The next day, 12 December, passed quietly. Soult had now made up his mind to attack Hill, but delayed to give his men time to rest and because of bad weather. That night the French army again crossed the Nive to the eastern bank. Wellington had taken precautions to maintain his communications with Hill, building a new bridge at Villafranque and keeping two divisions ready to send across it whenever the need arose. But on the afternoon of 12 December the Nive rose sharply following heavy rain in the mountains and the new bridge was broken. This left only the old bridge at Ustaritz, which added ten miles to the march of any reserves sent to reinforce Hill. The new bridge was repaired by noon on 13 December, but much could happen even on one morning of a December day, and for some hours at least Hill was effectively isolated.

Hill's 14,000 men occupied an extensive position, more than three miles long, with the Nive on his left and the Adour on his right. Soult's best chance of success lay not in subtlety but in a fierce frontal attack on the centre of Hill's position, for he had an overwhelming numerical advantage, but only for a few hours. Abbé's division, which led the French attack, fought well, but made only slow progress in the face of tenacious resistance from Ashworth's Portuguese infantry. The allied artillery played a crucial role supporting the infantry, but even so William Stewart, commanding the Second Division, was forced to feed his reserves piecemeal into the struggle before the tide of battle turned decisively in the allies' favour.

Wellington arrived in the middle of the day having crossed by the repaired new bridge, telling Hill 'the day is your own',[47] and directing him to complete the victory. By then there was no doubt of the result, for the Sixth Division was close at hand and the Third was crossing the Nive behind Wellington, but there was still some hard fighting before the French were driven back to Bayonne. Altogether Hill's corps had suffered 1,775 casualties at the battle of St Pierre (as this action on 13 December was called), while the French had probably lost well over 3,000 casualties. It was the heaviest disproportion of casualties over the five days of the battles of the Nive. The grand total of allied casualties was approximately 5,000 while the French suffered about 6,000. Late on the afternoon of 13 December, as he was riding back to headquarters, Wellington told General Kempt: 'I have often seen the French licked but I never knew them get such a hell of a licking as Hill has given them.'[48] He granted the honour of taking his despatch, recounting all the battles of the Nive, to Rowland Hill's brother and ADC Clement Hill.

Sir John Hope had been wounded on 11 December while steadying his men, and Larpent commented that he was not the only senior officer to be in danger: 'Lord Wellington himself was foremost in trying to rally the Portuguese, etc; both he and his staff were much exposed, and had not often, as I hear, been in a warmer fire.'[49] Edward Pakenham had a horse shot under him, Frederick Robinson was seriously wounded, and two of Stapleton Cotton's ADCs who were present as amateurs were hit.[50] Nevertheless Wellington disapproved of senior officers exposing themselves recklessly, and wrote to Torrens praising Hope's worth, but wishing that his friends would warn him against placing himself among the sharpshooters without taking cover; as a result, he noted, his hat and coat were shot through in many places 'besides the wound in his leg', and it 'will not answer'. Torrens agreed and suggested to Hope's brother Alexander that a warning was in order, but, as Wellington said, it was 'a delicate subject'.[51]

Over the next few days Wellington established his position on the Adour, although he found that he could impede but not completely prevent the passage of vessels carrying supplies down the river. Nonetheless Soult gradually shifted his troops out of the town, fearing that if Wellington crossed the Adour his whole army might be trapped inside and eventually forced to surrender. Wellington was receiving more details of the allied success in Germany, the revolt in Holland and the plan to push across the Rhine. His soldiers were

generally behaving well and were received without hostility by the local population, while murmurs in favour of the Bourbons reached him ever more
frequently. As a result, Wellington's reluctance to advance into the interior of
France dwindled; by late December he sounded quite enthusiastic at the prospect when replying to a letter from Bathurst in which the minister had hinted
that more resources might be sent to Holland if he was unable or unwilling to
take the offensive in southern France. 'I beg you will assure the Russian
Ambassador that there is nothing that I can do with the force under my
command to forward the general interests that I will not do. I am already
farther advanced on the French territory than any of the allied powers; and I
believe I am better prepared than any of them to take advantage of any opportunities which may offer of annoying the enemy.' If he had money to feed and
pay the Spanish army he could take Bayonne and advance to the Garonne,
which would put far more pressure on Napoleon than besieging fortresses in
Holland; and 'if I am right in believing that there is a strong Bourbon party in
France, and that that party is the preponderating one in the south of France,
what mischief must our army do him in the position I have supposed, and what
sacrifices would he not make to get rid of us?' Practical problems remained,
notably the heavy winter rains which made military movements simply impossible. But the game was changing rapidly; Spain had been liberated and the
contest now was over the future shape and government of France. Wellington's
army was still a long way from Paris but it would play an important part in
shaping the momentous events of the next few months. And, after an autumn
of uncertainty, Wellington now saw the way ahead.[52]

CHAPTER THIRTY-FOUR

TOULOUSE AND THE END OF THE WAR
(January–April 1814)

NAPOLEON RETURNED TO Paris on 9 November 1813, three weeks after his disastrous defeat at Leipzig. A day later Wellington was to launch his attack on Soult's positions around the Nivelle but Napoleon's attention was elsewhere; for he knew that the critical point in the war would be in north-eastern, not south-western, France. Little remained of the army he had led in Germany, but he did not despair; if the allies waited until the spring to cross the Rhine he would have five or six months to turn the reluctant conscripts who were already being rounded up across France into soldiers. Still, to make an effective army he needed a leavening of experienced officers, NCOs and soldiers to teach the young boys how to survive the rigours of life on campaign. Inevitably his eye turned to his armies in the Pyrenees and Catalonia. Soult and Suchet still had 100,000 men, including a high proportion of seasoned veterans. With these men at his disposal Napoleon felt he could defy the allies and defend France against any invasion.

Napoleon, in any case, hoped to put an end to the war on his southern flank by negotiating the Treaty of Valençay (11 December 1813) with the captive Prince Ferdinand, promising to release him as soon as this was ratified by the Spanish government. Wellington was quite alarmed by the implications of this, and told Bathurst that he could not guess how the Cortes would react.[1] The Spanish government however showed no interest in Napoleon's peace terms and, while welcoming the prospect of Ferdinand's release, pointed to an old decree of the Cortes, declaring that any treaty signed by him in captivity would be considered as being made under duress, and thus void. Napoleon released Ferdinand in March, but the concession was far too grudging and too late to do any good, and Spain remained firmly in the war until the end.

As it was, Napoleon did not wait for the result of his diplomatic manoeuvre before withdrawing troops from his southern armies. On 10 January he ordered Soult to send half his cavalry to Orleans at once, with 10,000 infantry to follow soon after, and most of the rest of the army to march as soon as Wellington's army had abandoned its positions. Soult reported that he could see no sign of the allies withdrawing, but he nonetheless despatched 3,000 dragoons and eighteen guns on 16 January, followed by two full divisions of infantry and their batteries on 21 January. With the casualties suffered at the Nive and the loss of his German, Italian and Spanish troops, Soult's army was reduced by about one-third, to barely 60,000 men including garrisons. As Wellington had some 67,000 British and Portuguese, and large Spanish reserves to draw upon as well, there could no longer be any pretence that Soult was fighting on even terms (although, if anything, it is surprising that Napoleon did not demand even larger drafts).[2]

The first six weeks of 1814 passed quietly on the Garonne. The 'live and let live' policy long practised between the outposts of the two armies now reached its highest point, and some of the best stories of peaceful fraternisation date from this period. There is the tale of the British and French sentries both in their places a hundred yards or so apart, while the rest of each picquet happily caroused together in a ruined house midway between. Credulity strains a little at this, though it may have happened, but the long bow of exaggeration surely lies behind the story of a single Irish sentry carrying *two* muskets, his own and that of his French opposite number, who had gone to the rear to get them each a bottle of brandy.[3] More sober witnesses, though, leave no doubt about the tolerance and lack of animosity between the armies at this time, and the care taken at all levels to avoid the pointless loss of lives.

Wellington's operations were suspended because the heavy winter rain had turned the roads into quagmires. In late January Mr Larpent noted that 'our snow has ended in torrents of cold rain again; the roads, almost more impassable, if that be possible, than they were before'. And again on 4 February: 'Still rain, rain, rain all night. All yesterday, all the night before, and still continuing. Oh! that we had your frost instead; all things would have been very different.'[4] Yet the army remained surprisingly healthy with the number of sick falling from 15,394 British rank and file on 25 December, to 14,144 on 25 January and 12,972 on 25 February.[5]

Shortage of cash was as great a problem as the rain. Some specie had arrived in the middle of December but not enough to give any lasting relief and, as usual, Wellington did not suffer in silence. 'We are overwhelmed with debts', he told Lord Bathurst, 'and I can scarcely stir out of my house on account of the public creditors waiting to demand payment of what is due to them'. Some of the muleteers were now owed no less than twenty-six months' pay, and Wellington had been forced to give them some bills on the British treasury to satisfy their most urgent needs. (Wellington knew that the bills would be sold at once at an enormous discount, and that this would make it more difficult for the army to purchase coin locally.)[6] Help was offered from an unexpected quarter when M. Babesat, a French banker at Bayonne, appeared at Wellington's headquarters at the end of December. Ostensibly his purpose was to settle the accounts of some British officers taken prisoner, to whom he had lent money, but his real aim was to organise the importation of a large quantity (twenty ships' cargo) of colonial produce into Bordeaux in defiance of Napoleon's Continental System. In exchange he offered to provide the allied army with any supplies it needed, even cash. Wellington accepted the proposition with enthusiasm, but Bathurst strongly disapproved, and it is not clear that anything ever came of the scheme.[7] Wellington's problem was solved by the arrival of £100,000 in cash in the middle of January, followed by £400,000 on 3 February shipped from England.[8] A further £300,000 over the following weeks ensured that there would be no recurrence of the shortage.[9]

On 11 January, reacting to Wellington's complaints, the ministers had commissioned Nathan Meyer Rothschild to purchase up to £600,000 in French and foreign coin in the Low Countries and Germany to be shipped direct from Holland to Wellington's army. Rothschild's agents found the task more difficult than he had expected and the first consignment of money did not sail until March, so that Wellington only benefitted from it in the closing weeks of the war and subsequently, in paying off the army's debts. It was a useful contribution, but less significant than some later versions of the story suggest, as the crisis had already been overcome by the supplies raised in England by the government.[10] The resolution of the crisis went a long way towards soothing Wellington's irritation with the ministers, and in early April Wellington wrote to Colonel Bunbury, the Under-Secretary of State for War: 'I beg that you will tell Lord Bathurst that I am very much obliged to his lordship for the care he takes to supply us with money.'[11] The abundance of ready money with which to pay for supplies, and Wellington's care to maintain discipline and prevent plundering, both played a vital role in reconciling the French population to the presence of allied soldiers in their midst, and helped ensure that the country remained tranquil and that official attempts to raise a popular insurrection went unheeded.[12]

When the *Désirée* reached Pasajes with the £400,000, Wellington informed the government that 'I shall begin to move as soon as we can get up the money, by which time I hope that the rain will have ceased a little'.[13] His determination to resume active operations whatever the practical difficulties was encouraged by news of the progress of the allied armies in eastern France. Wellington already knew that the allies intended to press forward across the Rhine without waiting for the spring, but he was not confident of their success, and made it clear that in his view they would have been wiser to use the winter to consolidate their position, reduce the French-held fortresses in their rear (and so make available the blockading forces), and negotiate with Napoleon. He did not think Napoleon wanted peace, but felt that the pressure of opinion in France might compel him to accept it. If the negotiations failed, the allies would have no choice but to undertake the invasion of France and might as well bring forward the Bourbons. But it is clear that Wellington felt the campaign would be difficult and full of risk. The allies, he warned Bathurst, 'must not expect battles of Leipsic [*sic*] every day; and that which experience shows them is, that they ought, above all things, to avoid any great military disaster'.[14]

However, the *Désirée* brought news that the allied advance had been unexpectedly rapid, encountering so little resistance that Bathurst believed the campaign would have been decided, or Napoleon would have been forced to make peace, in a matter of weeks – by the end of February or the beginning of March.[15] And although Bathurst did not say so, Wellington could not help but feel that there would be something ignominious about remaining quietly on the Adour while the allied armies advanced from the Rhine to the gates of Paris and decided the fate of Europe.

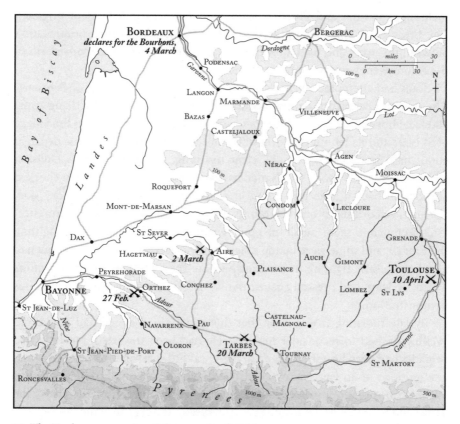

25 The Toulouse campaign, February–April 1814.

Wellington commenced his campaign on 12 February, greatly assisted by a week of fine weather which improved the roads. Soult still had most of his army south of the Adour, and Wellington drove these away from Bayonne, advancing east. There was some fighting, notably at Garris on 15 February, and by 18 February the French had been forced back to the River Saison. The first phase of the campaign was over.

The next step was the passage of the Adour by the left wing of the army under Sir John Hope. This was accomplished in an extremely bold operation between 23 and 26 February, when a pontoon bridge was constructed using local fishing boats downstream of Bayonne, almost under the nose of its substantial garrison. On 27 February the allies completed the investment of Bayonne, although Wellington did not convert this into a siege. The experience of San Sebastian and earlier sieges had left the army and its commander with little enthusiasm for the task, while Wellington must have dreaded the effect on French public opinion if the town was stormed and sacked. For the moment at least he was content to 'contain' the garrison, although the blockading force absorbed an uncomfortably large part of his army (well over 20,000 men including the First and Fifth Divisions and Aylmer's independent brigade). The bridge remained secure and was the principal line of communication between the army and its main supply depot at Pasajes, for the roads north of the Adour were better than those to the south.[16]

Soult had attempted to check the allied advance at Orthez on 27 February. The French occupied a strong position: a curving range of hills rising some 300 feet above the River Gave de Pau, with its right wing resting on the village of St Boes and its left on the town of Orthez and the river. The battle began at about half past eight on a cold, clear morning, when the Fourth Division advanced against St Boes. Cole's men had some success, but were then checked and driven back a little way before the fight descended into desultory skirmishing. According to one veteran in the Fusiliers, his comrades were interested as much in securing all the poultry and wine in the village as in fighting the French, and some were taking a swig of wine between each shot. There had also been a little fighting in the centre where the light companies of Picton's Third Division had pressed against the French skirmishing line in a vigorous demonstration.[17]

By late morning it was clear that the initial allied attack had failed and Wellington had to reconsider his plan. He had been thwarted, but only two brigades had been heavily engaged so there was little reason for alarm, although assumptions of an easy victory had been given a sharp jolt. Accepting this, Wellington ordered a general attack by the centre and left of the army; the Third and Sixth Divisions would press forward in the centre, while the Seventh Division would replace the Fourth on the left and make a new attempt to carry

St Boes, with the Light Division ready to assist either attack as required. Two hours of hard fighting followed. William Brown of the 45th, in Brisbane's brigade of the Third Division, recalled: 'The bullets flew as thick as hail, thirteen men of my company alone fell within a few yards of me on the brow of the hill. Notwithstanding we pressed on, and the enemy after dreadful carnage gave way, and left us in possession of a ditch, which we held till the brigade came up in line. We then gave three cheers, charged the enemy's light troops, and drove them from another ditch.' Brisbane himself declared that 'this was one of the severest actions that we had with that army', while John Keane, who commanded the other British brigade in the Third Division wrote: 'For two hours it was furious. The ground certainly was well contested. Crapaud truly fought to endeavour to restore his lost honour.'[18] Eventually Foy's troops facing Brisbane's attack crumbled and gave way – disheartened when Foy was wounded, according to some accounts – and this in turn exposed the flank of Darmagnac's division, forcing it to withdraw, although in good order, to a position in the rear already occupied by the French reserves.[19]

On the left, Major-General Walker, commanding the Seventh Division in Dalhousie's absence, made careful preparations for his attack on St Boes, and carried the village with little difficulty, for Taupin's troops were exhausted by their long fight in the morning. Walker's advance beyond the village was assisted by the intervention of Colborne's brigade of the Light Division, which ensured that Napier would regard this as the truly critical part of the battle, even though the casualty figures plainly reveal that the Third and Fourth Divisions bore the brunt of the fighting. (The Third Division lost 808 casualties; the Fourth Division 599; the Seventh Division 371; and the Light only 162.)[20]

By mid-afternoon the battle had been won and the French were falling back. Altogether Soult's army lost some 4,000 men in the battle including 1,350 prisoners compared to 2,164 allied casualties of whom 519 were Portuguese.[21] Late in the battle Wellington was hit in the thigh and slightly wounded by a spent bullet. Alexander Gordon described the wound as 'a contusion from a musket ball. He is however doing very well and it has not as yet [3 March] prevented his going out on horseback'. Larpent agreed, although he was concerned rather than reassured by Wellington's subsequent activity: 'Lord Wellington's [wound] was a bad bruise, and skin was broken: I fear his riding so much since has rather made it of more consequence, but hope the two days' halt will put him in the right way again, as all our prospects here would vanish with that man.'[22] Yet even on 6 March Wellington had not fully recovered, although he remained determined to make light of the wound. Larpent 'walked down to the bridge with Lord Wellington . . . and found him limp a little, and he said he was in rather more pain than usual, but it was nothing'. Already Wellington had made a good story of the incident, saying at dinner that 'he was laughing at

General Alava having had a knock, and telling him it was all nonsense, and that he was not hurt, when he received this blow, and a worse one, in the same place himself. Alava said it was to punish him for laughing at him.'[23] He does not seem to have mentioned being hit in any of his correspondence, even in his private letters home to Kitty, although it was naïve to think that the myriad letter-writers in the army would show similar restraint.[24] It was the worst wound he was to suffer in all his years of soldiering; indeed it was the only occasion on which he could properly be described as having been hurt, although he had been hit before at least once, at Salamanca, and had numerous narrow escapes.

There was a complete break between the two armies following Orthez, as the French sought to put as much distance between them and the allies as possible, and retreated first north-east then north to St Sever on the Adour. Soult's men, who had defended their positions so well in the battle, now left the ranks in their thousands. Many of them were recent conscripts from southern France, and it was easy for them to slip away and go home – all the more so if this was behind the allied army, for Wellington made it plain that he had no quarrel with them provided they went quietly about their private business. British officers were relieved by the friendly reception they encountered in their advance, having dreaded the thought of marching through a sullen hostile country. Beresford noted: 'It is not easy to describe the good will we are every-where received with, and the efforts of the inhabitants to be useful to us even against their own army. No one has ever exaggerated the detestation in which Bonaparte & his Government are held by the people of every description save some of the principal Functionaries, Civil and Military.' Major Jenkinson of the artillery provided part of the explanation: 'The enormities and depredations committed by the French army are equal to any they were ever guilty of in Spain and Portugal, and they retire with the just curses and execrations of their countrymen, who hail us in every town and villages as their deliverers.'[25] This ill treatment of their own countrymen was shocking enough to an officer accustomed to Wellington's constant concern for protecting the local popula-tion, but it is easy to see how French civilians, unaccustomed to the ravages of war, resented the demands of Soult's ill-supplied men; and how in turn the army resented the friendly reception accorded to the allies. Once the rift devel-oped it widened rapidly and helped undermine support for Napoleon's regime throughout south-western France.

Wellington's men did not behave perfectly, and he railed against the soldiers' misconduct and the regimental officers' neglect which he blamed for it; but the local population had no difficulty in appreciating the difference between an army which regarded its pillaging and plunder as normal, and one in which complaints of misconduct were rigorously pursued, the offenders flogged, and compensation paid to the victims. The result, as Mr Larpent noted on

11 March, was that the rear of the army was as safe as it had ever been in Spain or Portugal, and that small detachments and single officers travelled in almost complete security. 'If the country people had been like the Spaniards and against us, what we are doing now would have been out of the question. Half our army, by straggling about, would have been knocked on the head. We have, fortunately, just now plenty of money, and pay for everything; and the English are in the highest repute.'[26]

Soult faced an important choice at St Sever: retreat north to Bordeaux, or east to Toulouse? If he continued marching north he would probably have to fall back all the way to Bordeaux before making a stand, for the country in between was too poor to sustain an army for long. Bordeaux was the greatest city in south-west France and an important Atlantic port, but it was not a fortress, and retreating upon it would simply deliver it to the allies. However, Toulouse was a major arsenal and military depot and Soult would feel its loss keenly. He therefore chose a third option and marched south-east from St Sever back towards the Pyrenees, hoping to draw Wellington after him. This was a bold, clever move, though not without the risk of Wellington cutting off the French retreat and driving them into the mountains. On the other hand there was the slender hope that Suchet would respond to Soult's appeals that he bring his small remaining field force to join him and so repair some of the damage done at Orthez. However, Suchet preferred to remain independent, replying to Soult's letters with a plausible explanation for why he could do nothing and elaborating proposals of his own; and Wellington refused to follow Soult back to the mountains.[27]

Wellington entered St Sever on 1 March and remained for eight days, recovering from his wound and waiting for fresh units to come up from the rear. He had already summoned his cavalry from its green pastures in the Ebro valley and Freyre's two best Spanish divisions from Bayonne, replacing them with O'Donnell's Andalusian Reserve. The British commissariat would have to feed the Spanish troops if they were not to drive the country into insurrection, but the money from England and the readiness of French civilians to sell to the allies, made this manageable.[28]

While halted at St Sever Wellington considered the state of the war as a whole, not just his campaign against Soult. The latest reports from the allies in eastern France were, as usual, confused and full of contradictions, but it was clear that they had suffered setbacks and that hopes of an easy march on Paris had been too optimistic. Peace talks had begun at Châtillon on 5 February but there was no sign that they had made any progress, and officers in Soult's army evidently believed that they had been broken off.[29] Meanwhile the advance from Bayonne to St Sever had revealed a complete lack of popular support for Napoleon's government and a general willingness to embrace the Bourbons if their return meant peace. However, royalist sentiment was checked by the knowledge that the allies continued to negotiate with Napoleon, while the allies in turn doubted if there was much support for the Bourbons when it was not openly expressed.[30]

Wellington was acutely aware of this dilemma. His attitude was ambivalent, as he confided to Bathurst in August 1813 that 'my own opinion is, that the interests of the House of Bourbon and of all Europe are the same, viz, in some manner or other, to get the better and rid of Buonaparte'. Yet he thought that if Napoleon was contained within France he would soon fall, unable to maintain the cost of his government and army without foreign plunder; and as late as January 1814 he continued to favour the attempt to negotiate peace.[31] Bathurst was equally conscious of the difficulty of the issue and had been unable to give any simple guidance in 1813. There was the risk that an invasion of France would unite the country if it did not seek to appeal to at least one section of French society, while an attempt to impose the Bourbons would be disastrous if they lacked a solid foundation of domestic support. Moreover any such attempt would be very unpopular with the opposition in Britain, and would need the support of the continental powers which was not then forthcoming. Bathwest had concluded that it was too soon to think of bringing forward the Bourbons, although, as he told Wellington, 'I entirely agree with you in thinking that there can be no security for Europe as long as Buonaparte is on the throne of France. But it is a great question whether his downfall should not grow out of defeat, rather than being attempted by a formal attack'.[32]

If the British government had been acting alone it would have been more open in its encouragement of the Bourbons, but the ministers placed their highest priority on preserving the unity of the alliance against Napoleon, and Castlereagh strongly discouraged any open gesture of support.[33] The Emperor Alexander of Russia was contemptuous of the Bourbons, while the Austrians still hoped to preserve a humbled Napoleon as a counterweight to Russia in central and eastern Europe.[34]

In early February 1814 the Duc d'Angoulême, nephew of the putative Louis XVIII, arrived in southern France. Wellington received him with due deference although few British observers were impressed with his person or manner.[35] For the rest of the month he stayed quietly in the background receiving visits from local notables and gradually making contact with sympathisers in the interior. His presence was an important encouragement to royalists, but probably not as important as Wellington's advance to St Sever and the victory at Orthez.

On 4 March, at St Sever, Wellington received two emissaries on a secret mission from Comte Lynch, the governor of Bordeaux, who revealed that he and other leading inhabitants favoured the Bourbons, and were willing to commit themselves to the royalist cause if the allies occupied the city, which had only a small garrison. This was the catalyst Wellington needed. The attitude of the population as he advanced had convinced him that there was little support for Napoleon's regime, and that the great obstacle preventing a royalist uprising was the fear of a negotiated peace. He wrote to Lord Liverpool that 'any declaration from us [in favour of the Bourbons] would, I am convinced, raise such a flame in the country as would soon spread from one end of it to the other, and would infallibly overturn him [Napoleon]'. And: 'I cannot discover the policy of not hitting one's enemy as hard as one can, and in the most vulnerable place. I am certain that he would not so act by us, if he had the opportunity. He would certainly overturn the British authority in Ireland if it was in his power.'[36]

Three days later, on 7 March, Wellington took the plunge and sent Beresford with the Fourth and Seventh Divisions and Vivian's light cavalry brigade to occupy Bordeaux. Yet even now he was scrupulously careful not to do anything that would commit the British government to support the Bourbons, continuing to warn the royalists that the peace talks at Châtillon had not been broken off, and that if Napoleon accepted the allied terms Britain would have to make peace. Beresford was instructed to take possession of the city in the name of the allies, not for Louis XVIII, although if the civic authorities chose to proclaim a restoration of the old family he was not to interfere.[37]

The leading allied troops reached the outskirts of Bordeaux early on 12 March and were received with considerable enthusiasm. Comte Lynch managed a fine theatrical scene, casting off his *legion d'honneur* and putting a white cockade on his hat, while a carefully primed crowd followed suit, and the Bourbon flag was hoisted aloft. Beresford was carefully discreet in his reply. The duc d'Angoulême arrived a few hours later and issued a proclamation stating that the allies supported the restoration of the Bourbons and had resolved not to make peace with Napoleon. Wellington was furious and responded with a stinging rebuke threatening to publicly contradict the claim and so undermine their support, but the die was cast and the timing actually proved perfect.[38]

The news of the events at Bordeaux created great excitement in London and revealed widespread discontent with the idea of a negotiated peace. Liverpool warned Castlereagh that 'we should never be forgiven if we made peace with Buonaparte under these circumstances, unless forced to it by the Allies'.[39] The government even considered the possibility of continuing the war with only the support of Portugal, Spain and the French royalists if the continental powers insisted on making peace with Napoleon.[40] Slow communications meant that the news had less of an impact on the allies. Napoleon had not accepted the allied terms by the time they expired on 10 March, and did not suddenly change his mind even when Metternich kept the Congress open until 19 March. Only a dramatic reversal of the fortunes of war could have saved him then, and when the news of Bordeaux finally reached the allied ministers on 26 March they were already moving towards open support for the Bourbons.[41] In Paris the news was a strong indication to doubters and waverers that the Bourbons were the frontrunners in the race to succeed Napoleon, and this proved important, for at the critical moment most of the allied ministers were isolated at Dijon leaving Emperor Alexander the dominant figure, and he had to be guided towards the cause of Louis XVIII by Talleyrand.[42]

Back in southern France the war continued. Wellington recalled Beresford and the Fourth Division from Bordeaux, but left Dalhousie and the Seventh to hold the city. Soult had to fall back hastily to prevent Beresford cutting him off from Toulouse, and there were sharp rearguard actions at Vic-Bigorre on 19 March and Tarbes the day after.[43]

Soult's army reached Toulouse on 24 March, weary, despondent, short of equipment and in terrible condition. But the city contained a great depot of military stores and in a few days the army had been rested, re-equipped and revitalised. Soult set his men, and the civilian population, to work improving the defences of the city – much against the will of the inhabitants who had no wish to be caught up in a battle, and who were strongly inclined to support the Bourbons. Wellington arrived in front of Toulouse on 27 March, but had to cross the Garonne, swollen by recent rain, before he could enter the city or advance any further. He misled Soult into thinking that the crossing would occur below the city while the bridge was actually to be laid at Portet, five miles upstream, on the night of 27 March. However when the engineers set to work they discovered that the river was 159 yards wide at this point – 26 yards too wide for their pontoons – and the attempt was abandoned. George Napier remembered: 'Lord Wellington was furious. I never saw him in such a rage, and no wonder', yet the chief engineer could reply that he had warned Wellington months before that the pontoon train was inadequate to cross a really broad river.[44] Some of the responsibility may well have rested with Wellington who had become increasingly impatient of difficulties and inclined to cut corners, but the readiness of the engineers simply to abandon the attempt stands in sharp contrast to the success of Hope's crossing of the Adour, and the long record of the Staff Corps in improvising good bridges out of whatever materials lay to hand. Nor is it easy to understand why the width of the river had not been calculated before the attempt was made, especially as there were no French picquets on the opposite bank. Altogether the affair shows that even at this late stage in the war some parts of the allied army were not as efficient as their scientific training and professional pride might suggest.

A crossing at Portet would have enabled the army to approach Toulouse from the south, where it was relatively open, rather than from the north, where it had formidable natural and man-made defences. But after almost a week searching for a way forward Wellington was forced to look downstream of the city, to a site near Grenade. According to Larpent: 'Lord Wellington himself with two other officers went to the spot also to reconnoitre with his own eyes. Concealing his General's hat with an oil-skin, he got into conversation with the French *vidette*, dismounted, got down to the water-side, looked all about him, saw all he wished, and came away. I think this was risking too much; but no French soldier would have any idea of the commander of the allied forces going about thus with two attendants.'[45]

Work on the bridge began at dawn on 4 April and four hours later it was successfully completed – the river was narrower here although the current was strong. The left wing of the allied army – the Fourth, Sixth and Third Divisions, and three brigades of cavalry, all under Beresford's command – began crossing and took up a strong defensive position. But that evening the river rose alarmingly and the bridge had to be withdrawn. Wellington was naturally anxious and crossed the Garonne in a small boat to inspect Beresford's position, and ordered the construction of a battery that would provide some flanking fire in the event of an attack. When he crossed the river he found a scene that spoke volumes about the confidence of the British troops at this time, as Captain T. Edwardes Tucker, Picton's aide-de-camp, recorded in his diary: 'General [Picton] and his Staff [were] busy cooking lemon cream, notwithstanding Marshall Soult had 30,000 men in front.'[46] Three full days passed before the bridge could be relaid, during which time Beresford's force was isolated. British officers were astonished that the French did not fall upon the detachment with their whole army, but Soult had tried that trick at St Pierre, and had no wish to repeat the experiment. He knew that the poor troops who made up the bulk of his army were incapable of complicated manoeuvres or of sustaining an attack, but might defend a strong position with courage and tenacity, as they had done at Orthez, so he busily built redoubts and earthworks to cover the approaches to Toulouse and equipped them with heavy guns from its arsenal.

Advancing on Toulouse from the north Wellington faced a formidable tactical problem, for in front of the old walls of the city lay the great royal canal and its few bridges were extremely well guarded. The canal curved around the eastern side of the city as well, but here it was of less assistance to Soult for beyond it lay the Heights of Calvinet (Mont Rave) which overlooked Toulouse and made its defences untenable. Recognising this, Soult constructed a number of earthworks at the northern end of the heights, collectively if misleadingly known as 'the Great Redoubt', and other works further south along the ridge line. Any approach from the east was made much more difficult by the River

Ers which ran almost due north to the east of the Heights. The intervening ground, which was more than a mile wide at its northern end and less than half that to the south, was waterlogged and boggy. To the west of the city lay the Garonne, and the open southern approach to the city could not be reached, even by a wide turning movement, because the ground beyond the River Ers was too difficult.

On 7 April news reached the army that Napoleon had been defeated at Arcis-sur-Aube, and that he was attempting to manoeuvre against the rear of the Russian, Prussian and Austrian army. That evening a fresh report arrived that the Bourbons had been proclaimed at Paris, and that the Emperor of Austria had declared that the house of Napoleon had ceased to reign. However it was by no means clear that this, even if true (and the reports were unconfirmed), would mean an end to the war, for Napoleon might well fall back on Lyon where Augerau commanded an army, or even seek refuge with Soult. Only a couple of days earlier Wellington had said that if the allies entered Paris and proclaimed the Bourbons, 'he should not then despair of seeing Bonaparte a grand Guerrilla chief on a large scale, fighting about for his existence, which he had never expected to happen in his lifetime'. Until such reports were confirmed, it was too soon for Soult or Wellington to think of suspending their operations.[47]

Wellington carefully examined the French positions on 9 April, decided that there was no alternative to a direct assault, and issued his orders for an attack early the following morning, 10 April 1814 (this was Easter Sunday and, coincidentally, Wellington's eighth wedding anniversary). Hill, Picton and Alten would demonstrate against the western and northern fronts of the city in the hope of distracting Soult, but would not press their attacks home. The real blow would be struck by the left wing of the army where Beresford would lead the Fourth and Sixth Divisions south in the gap between the River Ers and the Heights of Calvinet, before wheeling sharply right to attack the French positions on the ridge from the east. This was a hazardous manoeuvre, for Beresford's men would expose their flank to the French throughout their march south, but Wellington was confident that his veteran infantry had the discipline and coolness to execute it, while the days when the French army could exploit such an opportunity were long gone.

Freyre's Spanish divisions linked Beresford to the rest of the army. Their first task was to capture an outlying French position – some detached high ground well to the north of the main Heights of Calvinet known as La Pujade. From here they would, in due course, advance against the Great Redoubt at the northern end of the Heights, although not until Beresford was in place to assail the eastern face of the Heights further south.

Skirmishing began at first light along the western and northern fronts, but Soult was not deceived, and by the middle of the day had shifted his reserves to

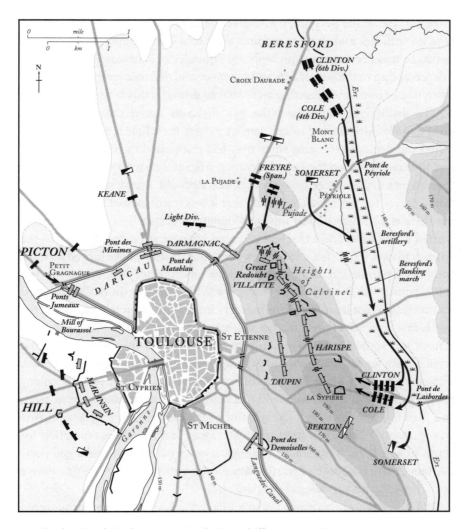

26 The battle of Toulouse, 10 April 1814. (All troop positions approximate, many conjectural.)

the critical point. In the centre Freyre's infantry carried La Pujade without difficulty and a strong battery of Portuguese artillery (including four 18-pounders from the army's reserve) took up their post on the hill and opened fire on the Great Redoubt. At the same time Beresford's column began its long march south through the mud. According to Charles Crowe of the 3/27th in the Fourth Division, 'our Division advanced in open column of Brigades over the morass, so soft that every general and field officer was compelled to march and have his horse led over'.[48] James Mill of the 40th agreed: 'The way was long and narrow for the numbers, and the difficulties of the defile greatly enhanced by reason too of the deep miry nature of the ground. You can easily conceive how we suffered, and in what manner their shot levelled and devastated our ranks. To this fire there was no reply, no rejoinder of a similar kind from our side, excepting in the way of a shout of menace and defiance from the regiment when one or more men together were striken down by this severe fire.'[49]

The artillery accompanying the two divisions found the soggy ground exceptionally difficult, and rather than let it delay the whole column, Beresford halted and deployed the guns when they had just passed the Great Redoubt so that they could fire on the French position from the east. Soon afterwards the Spanish infantry advanced to attack the Great Redoubt. British historians always blame Freyre for this advance, stating that it was unauthorised and premature, but there is no suggestion of this in Wellington's despatch or his other letters written at the time; and as he had taken up his post at La Pujade close to the Spanish troops, it is difficult to see how they could possibly have moved forward without his permission. If one of Wellington's subordinates disobeyed his orders at this point it was Beresford, not Freyre, for in his report on the battle Beresford acknowledges that he received fresh orders from Wellington to attack from the north-east rather than press further south, but that he chose to disregard them. 'I need not apologize to your Lordship for having put in practice your first arrangement for the attack, instead of going up the hill, as subsequently directed, from the village of Mont Blanc, as on arriving at this place I saw the enemy posted precisely in the manner you had made your first arrangement to meet; and therefore I followed but the spirit of your order in reverting to your first arrangements.'[50] Success washes most sins away, and for all his reputation for being an autocratic commander Wellington never believed in prolonged post-mortems; there is no sign of recrimination or resentment towards either Freyre or Beresford in his surviving correspondence.

Whatever the explanation, Freyre's infantry advanced in an unsupported assault against the Great Redoubt around eleven o'clock in the morning. According to one observer 'they crossed the valley with great bravery, under a most galling and severe fire of cannon and musketry', while another recorded that 'the troops marched in good order . . . and showed great spirit, the General and all his Staff being at their head'.[51] Mr Larpent was in the rear at the time and gleaned his account of what happened from talk at headquarters: 'If General Fre[y]re had been as skilful as brave, and the officers better, they would prob-ably have succeeded in their object, which certainly happened to be the most arduous duty of the day. They arrived on a sort of smooth glacis under the French works, subject to a fire admitted to be more severe than any since Albuera. Decision and skill and rapidity were then required. The men were kept too long in this fire – they broke – and then ran like sheep.'[52] However the more common view was that an unsupported attack could not have succeeded no matter how good the troops or how skilful their officers – an opinion neatly expressed by Colborne who said that he would have been sorry to have had to do it with *two* Light Divisions![53] Nonetheless there is a hint of relish in some British accounts of the flight of the Spanish infantry, even though the great majority of them rallied behind La Pujade and were even able to come forward and make a second attack a few hours later.[54]

With Freyre's failure, allied hopes of victory rested squarely on Beresford's column. Soult could see the danger and shifted Taupin's division south from its place in reserve behind the Great Redoubt, so that it kept pace with the allied advance while remaining well below the skyline. This southern part of the Heights was defended by Harispe's strong division but many of the redoubts and earthworks here were unfinished or had yet to be armed with artillery, for the approach was so difficult that it had seemed an unlikely point of attack. At last Beresford gave the order to wheel west; his men had left the Great Redoubt more than a mile behind them and faced a slightly lower, more accessible, but still difficult hillside. The Fourth Division, which had led the advance, was on the southern, or left-hand side of the attack, the Sixth Division to their right on the inside flank and apparently a little further back, while Somerset's cavalry covered the outer flank. Each division advanced on a front of one brigade, in line, and behind the usual screen of light infantry. They were still well short of the summit of the Heights when Taupin's division burst upon them. Possibly Taupin tried to avenge countless French defeats earlier in the war by catching the British breathless and disordered as they changed formation and struggled uphill. If so, his ploy failed and he paid for it with his life. The leading allied infantry were in good order and undaunted by the sudden attack, and it was Taupin's infantry which broke and fled, carrying away Harispe's nearest battalions with it. Beresford's victorious men were able to occupy the summit of the heights without further fighting, although they came under heavy artillery fire.[55]

A lull in the battle followed as the French reorganised their defences and Beresford ordered his batteries to join him on the Heights. Wellington also now joined Beresford, after helping to rally the Spanish troops near La Pujade, and decided that it was more important to drive the French from the northern part of the Heights than to attempt an attack on the bridges over the canal which still lay between the Fourth and Sixth Divisions and the city. Once the whole of the Heights was securely in allied hands Toulouse would be indefensible, and Soult would have to abandon it or risk being trapped and forced to capitulate.[56]

The last phase of the battle therefore consisted of a drive north along the crest of the Heights towards the Great Redoubt by the Sixth Division, while the Spanish infantry made a renewed attack from the opposite side. This led to the heaviest and most confused fighting of the day. At first the leading brigade of the Sixth Division swept all before it, carrying several strong works that lay in its path, although not without suffering severe casualties. Captain Malcolm, of the 42nd Highlanders, recalled:

> Amidst the clouds of smoke in which they were curtained, the whole line of redoubts would every now and then start into view amidst the wild and frightful blaze, and then vanish again into utter darkness. Our men were mown down by sections. I saw six of the company to which I belonged fall together, as if swept away by the discharge of one gun, and the whole ground over which we rushed, was covered with the dead.[57]

Harispe then launched a powerful counter-attack and drove the allies back, only for this to falter when the Portuguese brigade of the Sixth Division entered the fray. Again the French fell back but Soult threw in his final reserve – some battalions of Darmagnac's division – and regained the upper hand until Lambert's brigade intervened and a stalemate of exhaustion was accepted by both sides.

The battle ended with the French retaining control of the northern end of the Heights of Calvinet but with Beresford securely established further south. Soult recognised that his position was untenable; he withdrew his troops from the Great Redoubt that evening, and abandoned Toulouse late the following day, unmolested by the allies who were still recovering from the fighting and replenishing their ammunition.

The allied army lost 4,558 casualties at Toulouse of which 2,103 were British, 1,922 Spanish and 533 Portuguese. By far the heaviest losses were in the Sixth Division (1,520 casualties from 5,693 men present: 27 per cent) and Freyre's two divisions (most or all the 1,922 Spanish casualties from 7,916 men: 24 per cent). The French suffered less, 3,236 casualties, which is not surprising given the nature of the fighting and the lack of any pursuit. After the war some French soldiers and writers tried to claim Toulouse as a victory, which is hardly defensible given Soult's evacuation of the Heights that night and the city a day later. It makes more sense to say that Wellington's victory was incomplete – but then that is true of most victories.[58]

Wellington's boldness in conceiving of Beresford's march was remarkable, but the execution of the plan was marred by the lack of coordination between the Spanish and British attacks. And there were other flaws: the decision to entrust the attack on the Great Redoubt to Freyre's men is hard to justify; and Wellington left too many men with Hill so that he was short of strength at the decisive point (it would have been useful if another division could have followed Beresford's column well behind the Fourth and Sixth to help exploit their gains). Yet the tactical problem *was* extremely difficult and Wellington came up with a solution that was by no means obvious and which worked. At its root, though, it was a soldiers' battle won by sheer courage and dogged determination, rather than any tactical brilliance or fine manoeuvres. This was not because of any lack of skill on Wellington's part; it was inherent in the nature of the problem, for the defences covering most of the front were almost as formidable as those of a regular fortress. As usual, some mistakes were made by both sides in the course of the battle, but even with the advantage of hindsight it is difficult to improve upon the broad outline of Wellington's plan of attack.

The inhabitants of Toulouse were immensely pleased to see the departure of Soult's army. For more than a fortnight they had dreaded being caught up in a battle or a siege, and at first light on 12 April they sent messages to Wellington inviting him to enter the city and expressing their willingness to pledge allegiance to Louis XVIII. A British officer who ventured into the city by himself describes the crowds of 'men, women, and children, crying, "*Vivent les Anglais!*" "*Vivent nos Libérateurs!*" – all were full of joy, and in passing through the streets, all were asking, "*Où est Wellington; où est ce héros?*" '[59] Another officer records that at nine o'clock 'Lord W. entered at the head of the cavalry, all the National guards who had been the day before arrayed against us now lined the streets with the Mayor etc etc received us with open arms all wearing the white cockade. Whilst the inhabitants in thousands rent the air with cries of Long live the English, the King, and down with Bonaparte ... The windows crowded with women clapping and shouting, waving handkerchiefs etc etc and absolutely shedding tears of joy'.[60] There was an official reception, speeches were made and all over the city symbols of Napoleon's empire were cast down and the white cockade was brought forth.

Paris had been occupied by the allies on 31 March, and on 4 April Napoleon had attempted to abdicate in favour of his son. This was rejected and on 6 April he abdicated unconditionally. The news reached Toulouse in the late afternoon of 12 April when Colonel Frederick Ponsonby arrived with unofficial information, which was confirmed a few hours later. Lord Broughton describes the moment that Ponsonby passed on the momentous news to Wellington:

When [Ponsonby] arrived he found Wellington pulling on his boots in his shirt. He had entered Toulouse an hour.

'I have extraordinary news for you.'

'Ay, I thought so. I knew we should have peace; I've long expected it.'

'No; Napoleon has abdicated.'

'How abdicated? Ay, 'tis time indeed. You say so, upon my honour! Hurrah!' said Wellington, turning round on his heel and snapping his fingers.[61]

At dinner Wellington gave the toast 'Louis XVIII' and when this had been drunk Alava 'got up, and with great warmth gave Lord Wellington's health, as the *Liberator del' Espagna!* Everyone jumped up, and there was a sort of general exclamation from all the foreigners, French, Spanish, Portuguese, Germans, and all – *El Liberator d' Espagna! Liberator de Portugal! Le Libérateur de la France! Le Libérateur de l'Europe!* And this was followed, not by a regular three times three, but by a cheering all in confusion for nearly ten minutes! Lord Wellington bowed, confused, and immediately called for coffee. He must have been not a little gratified with what had passed'.[62]

Wellington then went to the theatre where an already excited crowd greeted the news of Napoleon's abdication, the restoration of the Bourbons and, above all, peace, with a tumult of joy. A hastily arranged ball was held at the prefecture where Wellington was staying, so that Mr Larpent concludes his description of the festivities: 'You will now, I think, guess what we felt, and what a species of trance we were in.'[63] Another officer ends his summary of the news from Paris: 'Although all these things are true, I can nevertheless scarcely believe their reality.'[64] The long war, which had lasted with scarcely a pause for more than twenty years, was over.

It was almost exactly five years since Wellington had landed at Lisbon and taken command of the British army. At that time, only a few months after Coruña, Napoleon's empire was at its height and the tide of French conquest appeared inexorable. Wellington had seized the initiative, driving Soult from Oporto and threatening Madrid before being forced to withdraw in the face of an unexpected concentration of French forces. He then, with remarkable foresight and determination, devised and implemented a comprehensive plan for the defence of Portugal against the inevitable French invasion, holding his nerve when even the best of his subordinates could see no hope of success. When Masséna finally retreated, Wellington pursued and, after several unsuccessful attempts, captured the border fortresses, and then crushed Marmont's army at Salamanca. This opened the road to Madrid, revealed to the world the hollowness of the Bonaparte Kingdom of Spain, and led to the liberation of Andalusia. Wellington's subsequent advance to Burgos, and the withdrawal of French garrisons to oppose him, stimulated a widespread insurrection across the whole of northern Spain, which in turn created the strategic opportunity which he exploited so skilfully in the Vitoria campaign. Wellington's soldiers were the first allied forces to cross the frontier into France in the closing campaigns of the war, and their presence deprived Napoleon of the veteran cadres he needed to rebuild his armies after the catastrophic defeat at Leipzig in late 1813. If Wellington's role was less obvious in the final months of the war it was largely because Paris is much closer to the Rhine than to the Pyrenees, but the proclamation of the Bourbons at Bordeaux helped to ensure that there would be no last-minute peace with Napoleon.

Wellington does not deserve all the credit for the allied success in the Peninsula. The opportunity was created by Napoleon's disastrous intervention in Spain, while his insistence that 'war must pay for war' encouraged popular resistance and led to fresh 'conquests' (such as Andalusia and Valencia) which were never really pacified, and which deprived the French of the men and resources needed to consolidate their hold on the parts of the country they had already overrun, or to face Wellington's army. Napoleon's more specific interventions were also generally counterproductive, and he grossly under-estimated Wellington and his army, even after the campaigns of 1812.

Wellington's campaigns were only possible because of the determination of the Spanish and Portuguese peoples not to submit to the French no matter how hopeless the cause appeared. Their resistance took different forms according to circumstances – sometimes regular armies fighting pitched battles, sometimes towns and fortresses enduring prolonged and bloody sieges, and sometimes the much-celebrated guerrillas – but whatever the form the result was that no part of Spain or Portugal was ever really secure in French hands, and that as soon as they withdrew their garrisons from one province to use elsewhere, it immediately erupted into revolt.

The French and Spanish created the environment within which Wellington operated; the Portuguese did more, providing him with a secure base and almost half his army, while placing themselves almost without reservation in his hands. Neither the Anglo-Portuguese nor the Anglo-Spanish alliance was without friction; at times Wellington might have been more tactful, just as at times the Spanish and Portuguese governments might have been more cooperative and conciliatory. But despite superficial tensions, both alliances remained solid foundations for Wellington's operations.

The most fundamental contribution that Wellington personally made to the success of the allies in the Peninsula was his insight that close cooperation between Britain and Portugal could create an army that would be large and powerful enough to play a central role in the war. He first raised this idea at the very outset of his campaigns, as his army began to disembark in Mondego Bay at the beginning of August 1808, and refined it in a memorandum which he prepared before he was sent back to Portugal in the following spring. These early ideas evolved significantly with experience, and their successful implementation was the result of the close collaboration between Wellington and Beresford, who did more than any other individual to assist Wellington in the Peninsula.

The British government played an equally vital role, and ministers deserve great credit for perceiving Wellington's ability and then maintaining faith in him despite the controversy over Cintra. In late 1809 and 1810 Perceval's weak government persisted in its commitment to Wellington and the defence of Portugal, despite the weight of opinion at home and from senior officers in the army, which predicted that the campaign would end in a costly and dangerous evacuation. Ministers endured Wellington's egotistical and unreasonable grumbling for years, responding with kindness and infinite patience while concentrating all their resources on the war in the Peninsula. They stoutly defended him when things went badly, for example the disappointing conclusion to the Talavera campaign and the retreat from Burgos, and celebrated his achievements with great enthusiasm and generosity, whisking him up the ranks of the peerage and promoting him to Field Marshal among many other honours.

But when every allowance has been made for the contribution of others, Wellington remains the central, indispensable, animating figure in explaining the allied success in the Peninsula. He understood the underlying dynamics of the war more clearly than anyone else, and, almost uniquely, he was never intimidated by the French. He worked constantly at improving the quality of his army, nurturing its confidence, educating its officers in the practicalities of campaigning, and insisting that they attend to their troops in order to maintain discipline, and to protect the local civilian population, whether Portuguese, Spanish or French, from marauders and abuse. He pressed the British government remorselessly whenever the army ran short of ready money, knowing that cash would make the soldiers behave better and encourage the local population to cooperate in feeding the army. And he went to great pains to ensure that the army was as well supplied as possible, especially during the long months it spent in winter quarters in the poor uplands of northern Portugal.

In the first campaigns, in 1808 and 1809, Wellington displayed remarkable confidence, taking the fight to the French with unhesitating aggression and forcing them to respond on his terms. Talavera made him more cautious; the French fought with more determination than he expected, and while it was a clear victory, there had been a moment when the battle hung in the balance. The defeat of Austria changed the strategic situation for the worse, forcing Wellington onto the defensive, and he was unsure how the new Portuguese army would perform in battle. Busaco resolved some of these doubts, while Masséna's refusal to attack at Torres Vedras gave the entire allied army confidence. Fuentes de Oñoro and El Bodon showed that the allied infantry could manoeuvre and retreat under great pressure without losing its nerve, while Albuera demonstrated its extraordinary fighting qualities. Nonetheless Wellington was still anxious that the troops might not have the discipline and composure to maintain their order in an offensive battle in open country, and he was uncharacteristically hesitant in the face of Marmont's manoeuvres until, on the afternoon of 22 July 1812, he seized a slight opening and in a few hours gained the greatest triumph of his career at Salamanca. The psychological advantage gained at Salamanca was retained for the rest of the war; even during the retreat from Burgos the French generals were plainly intimidated, while in 1813 Joseph and Jourdan were half-beaten before the campaign had even begun. Soult briefly revived the spirit of the army when he took command, but as the fighting in the Pyrenees and the south of France continued, the difference in quality between the two armies became ever more obvious, culminating in Wellington's extraordinarily bold tactics at Toulouse.

Wellington's tactical ability was remarkable. In the course of the Peninsular War he fought more than a dozen major battles without suffering a single defeat. While some operations, such as the passages of the Bidassoa and the Nivelle, were meticulously planned, most were either spontaneous (for instance, the crossing of the Douro at Oporto, or Salamanca, where he rapidly seized a fleeting opportunity and threw his army into action) or defensive, where he defied the enemy to drive him from a position of his choice (as at Talavera or Busaco). The greatest tactical mistake he made was probably at Fuentes de Oñoro, where he overextended his right wing in an attempt to cover his lines of communication, but he was able to retrieve the error without any significant harm being done, thanks to the discipline and confidence of the troops, and his own skill. Otherwise his handling of troops in battle was masterly, both in his initial deployment of the army and in the placement and control of reserves once battle was underway. He was careful with the lives of his men and abhorred useless fighting, but was quite prepared to incur heavy casualties when the objective warranted it.

Some credit for the remarkable success of the British army in the Peninsula belongs to the Duke of York and all the other officers who had laboured for many years to reform and improve it. They developed its tactical doctrine, demanded that its officers take their profession seriously, and fostered its fighting spirit. But the cream of the British army they created was severely damaged in the Coruña campaign and at Walcheren, and in his early campaigns (after 1808) Wellington's army had a large proportion of second tier units. This gradually changed, and even the poorest units which remained under his command soon improved to the point where he was most reluctant to part with them, even in exchange for two- or three-times their number of fresh-faced men.

Much more credit belongs to the officers and men themselves – the soldiers who marched and fought under Wellington, camping under the stars or in the rain, tramping endless miles in poor-quality shoes with a heavy pack on their shoulders, prey to dysentery, malaria and countless other diseases, enduring a hard life with only occasional moments of excitement or glory. Wellington had no illusions about these men, but despite the sharpness of his criticisms when they misbehaved he was proud of them, describing the army in 1813 as 'the most complete machine for its numbers now existing in Europe', while many years later he declared: 'I could have done anything with that army: it was in such splendid order.'[65] The troops responded with trust and admiration as the joyous reaction to Wellington's arrival at Sorauren makes clear.

Wellington gave few of his subordinates much discretion; his whole approach was ill-suited to delegation, and many of the attempts he made proved unsuccessful. The most obvious exception to this generalisation was Rowland Hill, whose operations in Estremadura repeatedly proved his quiet competence and complete dependability. Sir Thomas Graham and Sir John Hope were also capable of acting in a larger role, although each had their foibles and both made mistakes in the campaigns of 1813–14. Beresford's work with the Portuguese army was invaluable, but Albuera showed that he was unsuited to an independent command. Stapleton Cotton commanded the cavalry to Wellington's satisfaction, partly because he did not display too much enterprise or initiative; and George Murray was invaluable as Quartermaster-General, playing a particularly important role in the closing campaigns when the size of the army and its distribution over a broad front meant that Wellington was less able to attend to everything in person. But any of these, even Beresford, could have been replaced without any great change in the course of affairs. Wellington, by contrast, was quite simply irreplaceable – the essential ingredient of victory.

From the day he took command of the army in Portugal in April 1809 to the day that news of Napoleon's abdication reached him, Wellington took the weight of responsibility for success or failure squarely on his shoulders. A politically controversial figure at home, conducting a campaign that lacked bipartisan support, and with a weak government that would be unable to protect him in the event of failure, he would be held responsible for any defeat whether he was really to blame or not. Never one to suffer in silence he complained vehemently and indiscreetly at the difficulty of the position in which he was placed, but it is clear that he relished the responsibility and had no wish to have it lessened by instructions that would limit his discretion. Throughout the Peninsular War he displayed a remarkable confidence and self-sufficiency that sustained him through every difficulty. Whatever the problem, he was confident that he was better able to devise a solution than anyone else, and while he often discussed the state of the war with his personal staff and consulted Murray, there was never any suggestion that he looked to anyone for advice.

This confidence can be traced back to his earliest days in India when he did not hesitate to write lengthy memoranda on the internal government of Bengal or to advise his brother on questions of war and peace with Mysore. If, as seems likely, there was a touch of bravado about the early essays into unfamiliar territory, experience, especially of his independent command at Seringapatam, soon filled the gap. By the time of the Maratha War he was the ablest, best-informed and most accomplished officer to command a British army in the India for a generation or more. He understood the underlying dynamics of warfare in India, just as he would later understand those in the Peninsula, and his success was due to skill and expertise, not patronage or luck.

The combination of Wellington's self-confidence, the weight of responsibility on him, and years at the head of an army did not encourage modesty or self-effacement. While never pompous or so obviously vain as his eldest brother, he could be egotistical, inconsiderate to others and susceptible to some sorts of flattery. But he could also be very kind, had an unexpectedly sentimental side that he kept private, and retained a simplicity of manner that marked his complete lack of pretension. He was quick to laugh and, when not overwhelmed with business, relished life with enormous enthusiasm, being full of energy and with a strong sense of fun. An acquaintance who met him a few months after the end of the war, for the first time in years, was delighted to find that he remained as bright, open and ready to converse as he had ever been, with none of the pride and reserve that too often came with worldly success.[66] His powers of concentration were prodigious, his taste for detail very nearly insatiable, and his judgement astute and penetrating. He was always intensely practical, having little interest in abstract theories or principles, but he combined this with a remarkably broad vision; from his arrival in India onwards, if not before, he was never just a soldier, and always appreciated the wider context of military operations.

Wellington began his career searching for a modest level of success: financial independence and a secure place in the world. He achieved this and more in India, but discovered a taste and capacity for business – particularly, but not only, the business of soldiering – which left him eager to test himself in a more demanding arena. He did not go to Portugal for the sake of honours, money or even the acclaim of his peers; patriotism and a sense of duty were more important, but still secondary considerations. He went because he knew that he was very good at what he did and he enjoyed doing it. He had discovered his vocation and was determined to pursue it; and he pursued it so successfully that in 1814 he helped bring the war to a triumphant conclusion. He did not know what he would do next, but he was experienced in diplomacy, politics and civil administration, and he was ready for any role that would keep him busy and near the centre of affairs. It would take more than the defeat of Napoleon to stop him.

Epilogue

———⟫●⟪———

ARLY ON THE morning of 23 June 1814 His Majesty's sloop *Rosario* sailed into Dover Roads and fired a salute. Within minutes the yards of all the ships in the harbour were manned and their guns returned the salute. As Wellington came ashore the batteries of Dover Castle added their voice to the clamour, while on the pier heads an eager crowd gave three cheers. Despite the early hour more than 5,000 people were assembled to welcome the hero home, with more arriving every minute, and no sooner had he set foot on shore than he was lifted high and carried to the Ship Inn.[1]

It was almost six years since Wellington's previous homecoming, when he had been met with hisses and abuse from the crowd, and execration in the press for his role in the Convention of Cintra. The contrast could hardly have been greater or the acclamation louder or more general. The Prince Regent, on the advice of his ministers, had made Wellington a Duke, so that he had risen through every step of the peerage, with each step commemorating a separate triumph. When the government asked Parliament for a grant of £300,000 to support the honour it encountered opposition of an unexpected kind. Whitbread declared that 'there was no man so wicked, so stupid, or so envious, as to venture to detract from the glory of the Duke of Wellington', while George Ponsonby, the leader of the Whigs in the Commons, went further and proposed that the new grant be raised to £400,000, which was passed unanimously.[2]

Wellington's popularity in the summer of 1814 was immense and almost universal. His old enemies at the radical-dominated Corporation of the City of London gave him a splendid dinner at the Guildhall, while large crowds continued to cheer him at every opportunity. He was formally thanked by both Houses of Parliament, and carried the Sword of State at the national service of thanksgiving at St Paul's Cathedral. The Prince Regent held a superb fête in his honour in the gardens of Carlton House and, with the worldly shrewdness characteristic of universities, Oxford spotted the coming man and awarded him an honorary degree.

When Wellington visited the Salisburys at Hatfield, he was presented with the freedom of the boroughs of Hertford and St Albans, and was the guest of honour at a dinner for 120 people. After the meal, while the party took the evening air on the lawns, he shook hands with many of the immense crowd that had assembled beyond the palings, amid cheers and blessings and cries that he was 'the glory of England'. On another occasion, when his carriage was delayed, his arms were 'almost pulled off in the eagerness of the people to shake hands with him!' Far from being annoyed or disdainful of this attention, he treated it with great good humour and even a degree of relish, remarking on one occasion to Lady Shelley when the crowd parted to let them through: 'It's a fine thing to be a great man, is it not?'[3]

The season for celebrations did not last more than a few weeks before Wellington left England again to embark on the next stage of his career. He would never be quite as popular again until his death, almost forty years later, united the nation in mourning. He was just forty-five in the summer of 1814, and some of his greatest triumphs and most divisive controversies lay ahead of him, but already he had achieved a unique place in British and European affairs. The second half of his life would be as challenging, demanding and interesting as the long road which had led from Dublin Castle to victory in the Peninsula and a dukedom.

ONLINE COMMENTARY

O VER THE THREE decades I have been working on Wellington and subjects closely related to his life I have made many interesting discoveries which, for reasons of space, can only be touched on briefly in this biography. In the past, such material would have remained stashed away in my personal files, or at best trickled into the public realm via obscure scholarly articles and conference papers largely inaccessible to general readers, while future biographers and historians would have wasted many hours pointlessly following the same lines of inquiry.

I am pleased, therefore, that this material is now freely available on the biography's website:

www.lifeofwellington.co.uk

This self-contained Commentary is an additional resource for readers who are interested in following up details and digressions originating within the published text. The Commentary is extensive – about the same length as the main narrative – and consists of further descriptions of events, often from obscure or unpublished sources, deeper explanations of when and why my account differs from the established narratives and biographies, and the somewhat sobering chronicle of the red herrings and dead-ends thrown up by my research.

Most of the entries are short – just a paragraph or two – but they add significantly to the main narrative at almost every point of Wellington's life, sketching the character and careers of his friends, family, rivals and colleagues, testing the veracity of many old anecdotes, and including many first-hand glimpses of Wellington by contemporaries that could not be included in the book. For example, the battle of Assaye – Wellington's least understood and explored victory – gains further pages of Commentary which go through all the significant primary sources for the battle, and collate and compare the existing evidence for each point. This does not amount to a full study of the battle, of course, but it gives interested readers a much more detailed account of what happened and a clearer understanding of the difficulties of reconstructing the events of the day, and, indeed, of any battle.

The Commentary is not intended to replace the notes, which appear in their usual place and form. Neither should it distract readers from their pleasure in the main text; thus, there are no indicators in the book as to which points are discussed in the Commentary. Rather, I hope, the Commentary adds a third layer to historical writing: a parallel text that elaborates, elucidates and entertains, and whose electronic form makes it easy to search and explore.

Digest and Chronology of Wellington's Life and Career to 1814

⟶━●━⟵

(compiled with the assistance of Ron McGuigan and Howie Muir)

Birth date: Probably on or before 28 April 1769, although he always celebrated his birthday on 1 May.

Parents: The third surviving son of Garret Wesley (1735–81), 1st Earl of Mornington in the Irish peerage and his wife the Hon. Anne Hill (1742–1831), daughter of 1st Viscount Dungannon.

Education: Diocesan School Trim, Ireland, until the age of seven when he moved to London with his parents and attended Brown's Seminary, King's Road, Chelsea. Eton, 1781–84. Private tutor, Henry Michell, at Brighton, 1784. Private tutor, Louis Foubert, 1785. Royal Academy of Equitation at Angers, 1786–87. Returned to England, November 1787.

Marriage and children: On 10 April 1806 he was married to the Hon. Catherine Sarah Dorothea Pakenham (? January 1772–24 April 1831), daughter of 2nd Baron Longford. (He had proposed and had been rejected in 1792 and again more decisively in 1794, after which there was no further contact until shortly before their marriage.) They had two sons, Arthur Richard, later 2nd Duke of Wellington (3 February 1807–13 August 1884) and Charles (16 January 1808–9 October 1858).

Illegitimate children may have included: a son (probably Robert William Dixon, born 1793) by Mrs Dickson, his landlady in Dublin in the 1790s; and Arthur Freese, who was born at Seringapatam in July 1802. There is no proof of the paternity of either.

Commissions in the army:

Ensign, 73rd Foot	7 March 1787
Lieutenant, 76th Foot	25 December 1787
Lieutenant, 41st Foot	23 January 1788
Lieutenant, 12th Light Dragoons	25 June 1789
Captain, 58th Foot	30 June 1791
Captain, 18th Light Dragoons	31 October 1792
Major, 33rd Foot	30 April 1793
Lieutenant-Colonel, 33rd Foot	30 September 1793
Brevet Colonel in the army	3 May 1796
Brigadier-General in Egypt (never activated)	17 July 1801
Major-General	29 April 1802
Lieutenant-General	25 April 1808
Local rank of General in Spain and Portugal	31 July 1811
Field Marshal	21 June 1813
Colonel, 33rd Foot (to 1812)	30 January 1806
Colonel, Royal Horse Guards (to 22 January 1827)	1 January 1813

Colonel, Rifle Brigade	19 February 1820–*d*
Colonel, Grenadier Guards	22 January 1827–*d*
Commander-in-Chief	22 January–5 May 1827
	27 August 1827–14 February 1828
	15 August 1842–*d*

Honours:
(dates follow those given in the *Complete Peerage*)

KB	28 August 1804
Viscount Wellington	4 September 1809
Earl of Wellington	28 February 1812
Marquess of Wellington	3 October 1812
KG	4 March 1813
Duke of Wellington	11 May 1814
GCB	2 January 1815
GCH	22 March 1816

Foreign honours (to 1814):
(dates follow those given in the *Complete Peerage*)

Conde do Vimeiro and Knight Grand Cross of the Order of the Tower and the Sword of Portugal	October 1811
Duque de Ciudad Rodrigo and Grandee of Spain	January 1812
Order of St Ferdinand (Spain)	April 1812
Order of the Golden Fleece from Spain	August 1812
Marquez de Torres Vedras in the peerage of Portugal	September 1812
Duque da Vitória in the peerage of Portugal	December 1812
Grand Cross of the Imperial Military Order of Maria Teresa (Austria)	March 1814
Grand Cross of the Imperial Russian Military Order of St George	March 1814
Grand Cross of the Royal Prussian Military Order of the Black Eagle	March 1814
Grand Cross of the Royal Swedish Military Order of the Sword	March 1814

Arms:
Quarterly, 1st and 4th: Gules, a cross argent in each quarter five plates in saltire (Wellesley); 2nd and 3rd: Or, a lion rampant gules, ducally collared, gold (Cowley); in the centre chief point, an escutcheon of augmentation charged with the Union badge
Crest: Out of a ducal coronet or, a demi-lion rampant gules, holding in the paws of a forked pennon agent flowing the sinister, charged with the cross of St George, and the ends gules
Supporters: Two lions gules, gorged with eastern coronets and chained or
Motto: *Virtutis fortuna comes* (Fortune the companion of valour)

Prize money, pensions and other sums granted to him:
For his services in India:
£4,000 from the EIC for services as commissioner in the settlement of Mysore
£5,000 prize money from Seringapatam
£25,000 prize money from the Maratha War

For the Copenhagen expedition of 1807: £1,700 prize money

For the Peninsular War: £50,000 prize money

For the Waterloo campaign: He was entitled to £61,000 but took only £20,000,
   giving the rest to the Treasury

Pension of £2,000 p.a. to support his peerage	February 1810
A further £2,000 p.a. on being elevated to an Earldom	February 1812
Grant of £100,000 for the purchase of an estate in Britain	December 1812
Estate of Soto de Roma in Granada granted by the Spanish Regency	July 1813
Grant of a further £400,000 by Parliament for the purchase of an estate	June 1814

Political offices (to 1814):

MP for seat of Trim in Irish Parliament	1790–97
MP for Rye in the House of Commons	1 April 1806–1806 election
MP for Mitchell in the House of Commons	15 January 1807–1807 election
MP for Newport, Isle of Wight,	1807 election–4 April 1809
Privy Councillor	8 April 1807
Privy Councillor (Ireland)	28 April 1807
A lord of the Treasury of Ireland	May 1807–April 1809
Chief Secretary to the Lord Lieutenant of Ireland	April 1807–April 1809

Chronology

c. 28 April or 1 May 1769	Born
1776	Moves to England
1781–84	Attends Eton
1786–87	Royal Academy of Equitation at Angers
7 March 1787	First commission in the army
November 1787	Returns to England
1788–96	ADC to the Lord Lieutenant of Ireland (probably not during Lord Fitzwilliam's tenure, December 1794–March 1795)
1790–97	MP for Trim in the Irish Parliament
30 September 1793	Lieutenant-Colonel, 33rd Foot
June 1794–February 1795	Campaign in the Low Countries
November 1795–January 1796	Attempts to sail to West Indies thwarted by gales
June 1796	Sails for India
17 February 1797	Lands at Fort William (Calcutta), Bengal
August–November 1797	Abortive expedition to Penang
January–April 1798	Private tour to Madras
May 1798	Returns to Bengal; Mornington arrives in Bengal; changes spelling of surname from Wesley to Wellesley following his brother's lead
August 1798	Sails for Madras with the 33rd
February–May 1799	Advance to and siege of Seringapatam; it is stormed on 4 May
May 1799	Appointed Governor of Seringapatam and commander of British forces in Mysore
May–September 1800	Campaign against Dhoondiah Waugh
December 1800–April 1801	Prepares force for expedition to Egypt; superseded by Baird at Bombay
29 April 1802	Promoted Major-General
March–April 1803	March to Poona and restoration of the Peshwa

August–December 1803	Maratha War
23 September	Battle of Assaye
29 November	Battle of Argaum
15 December	Storming of Gawilghur
17 December	Peace signed with Raja of Berar
30 December	Peace signed with Sindia
24 June 1804	Resigns command in the Deccan
August–November 1804	In Bengal
10 March 1805	Sails from Madras for England
10 September 1805	Arrives in England
December 1805–February 1806	Expedition to northern Germany
1 April 1806	Elected to British House of Commons as MP for Rye
10 April 1806	Marries Kitty Pakenham
3 February 1807	Birth of eldest son, Arthur Richard Wellesley
8 April 1807	Made a Privy Councillor
April 1807–April 1809	Chief Secretary for Ireland
July–September 1807	Copenhagen expedition
29 August	Action at Kioge
7 September	Copenhagen capitulates
16 January 1808	Birth of second son, Charles Wellesley
25 April 1808	Promoted Lieutenant-General
July–September 1808	Expedition to Portugal
14 June	Appointed to command expedition
12 July	Sails from Cork
1–5 August	Army lands at Mondego Bay
17 August	Combat of Roliça
21 August	Battle of Vimeiro; AW is superseded by Burrard
22 August	Dalrymple takes command of army; suspension of arms signed by AW
31 August	Convention of Cintra signed by Dalrymple
20 September	AW sails from Lisbon
4 October	Lands at Plymouth
14 November–22 December 1808	Court of Inquiry into the Convention of Cintra
15 February 1809	Beresford appointed to command the Portuguese army
7 March 1809	AW's 'Memorandum on the Defence of Portugal'
26 March 1809	Cabinet decides to send AW back to Portugal
15 April 1809	Sails from Portsmouth
22 April 1809	Lands in Lisbon
27 April 1809	Takes command of the army in Portugal
29 April 1809	Commission as Marshal-General of Portuguese army
12 May 1809	Battle of Oporto
27–28 July 1809	Battle of Talavera
4 September 1809	Created Viscount Wellington
24 July 1810	Action at the Coa
27 September 1810	Battle of Busaco
10 October 1810	Occupies the lines of Torres Vedras
14 November 1810	French retreat to Santarem
5 March 1811	French begin their retreat from Portugal
3 April 1811	Action at Sabugal
3 and 5 May 1811	Battle of Fuentes de Oñoro
11 May 1811	Fall of Almeida; Brennier and part of the garrison escape

4–15 May 1811	First siege of Badajoz
16 May 1811	Battle of Albuera
19 May–10 June 1811	Second siege of Badajoz
25 September 1811	Action at El Bodon
8–19 January 1812	Siege of Ciudad Rodrigo
19 January 1812	Storming of Ciudad Rodrigo
16 March–6 April 1812	Third siege of Badajoz
6 April 1812	Storming of Badajoz
22 July 1812	Battle of Salamanca
12 August 1812	AW enters Madrid
22 September 1812	Cortes votes to give Wellington the command of the Spanish Armies
19 September–22 October 1812	Siege of Burgos
22 October–21 November 1812	Retreat to Portuguese frontier
4 March 1813	Made a Knight of the Garter
13 May 1813	Advance into Spain begins
21 June 1813	Battle of Vitoria; promoted Field Marshal (backdated from 3 July)
12–27 July 1813	First siege of San Sebastian
25 July–2 August 1813	Battles of the Pyrenees
28 July	First battle of Sorauren
24–31 August 1813	Second siege of San Sebastian
31 August 1813	Storming of San Sebastian
8 September 1813	Castle of San Sebastian capitulates
31 August 1813	Battle of San Marcial
7 October 1813	Battle of Bidassoa
31 October 1813	Pamplona surrenders
10 November 1813	Battle of Nivelle
9–13 December 1813	Battles of the Nive
27 February 1814	Battle of Orthez
12 March 1814	Bordeaux declares for the Bourbons
31 March 1814	Allies enter Paris
6 April 1814	Abdication of Napoleon
10 April 1814	Battle of Toulouse
18 April 1814	Armistice agreed ending the Peninsular War
11 May 1814	Created Duke of Wellington (gazetted 3 May 1814)
23 June 1814	Wellington arrives in England

ENDNOTES

Abbreviations

AW:	Arthur Wellesley
Complete Peerage:	*The Complete Peerage* by G.E.C[ockayne], 2nd edn, 12 vols. (1910–59; printed in microprint edition in 8 vols. by Sutton Publishing, 2000)
DNB:	*The Dictionary of National Biography*, ed. Leslie Stephen, 22 vols. (Smith Elder, 1885–1900)
Fortescue:	Hon. J.W. Fortescue, *A History of the British Army*, 13 vols. in 20 (London, Macmillan, 1898–1930)
General Orders:	Wellington, *General Orders. Spain and Portugal*, 4 vols. 1809–12 (London, printed by authority by T. Egerton, 1811–13)
HW:	Henry Wellesley
Longford:	Elizabeth Longford, *Wellington. The Years of the Sword* (London, Weidenfeld and Nicolson, 1969)
Maratha War Papers:	*The Maratha War Papers of Arthur Wellesley, January to December 1803*, ed. Anthony S. Bennell (London, Army Record Society, vol. 14, 1998)
ODNB:	*The Oxford Dictionary of National Biography*, ed. H.C.G. Matthew and Brian Harrison (Oxford University Press, online edition, 2004–present)
Oman:	Sir Charles Oman, *A History of the Peninsular War*, 7 vols. (Oxford, Clarendon Press, 1902–30)
Parliamentary Debates:	*The Parliamentary Debates from the Year 1803 to the Present Time*, published under the superintendence of T.C. Hansard
PRO:	The Public Record Office (now The National Archives)
Proceedings:	*Proceedings upon the Inquiry Relative to the Armistice and Convention, &c made and Concluded in Portugal* in *Parliamentary Papers* (1809), vol. 12
PRONI:	The Public Record Office of Northern Ireland
WD:	*The Dispatches of Field Marshal the Duke of Wellington*, ed. [John] Gurwood, 8 vols. (London, Parker, Furnivall and Parker, 1844)
WND:	Wellington, *Despatches, Correspondence, and Memoranda of Field Marshal Arthur Duke of Wellington, K.G.*, ed. his son, the Duke of Wellington, 'in continuation of the former series', 8 vols. (London, John Murray, 1857–80) [Known as *Wellington New Despatches*, and cover the years 1819–32]
WO:	War Office (War Office Papers in the Public Record Office, including papers from the Secretary of State for War and the Colonies)
WP:	Wellington Papers in the Special Collections of the Hartley Library, University of Southampton
WSD:	Wellington, *Supplementary Despatches, Correspondence and Memoranda of Field Marshal Arthur, Duke of Wellington, K.G.*, ed. his son, the Duke of Wellington, 15 vols. (London, John Murray, 1858–72) [Vol. 5 containing the Irish correspondence of 1807–09 carries the title *Civil Correspondence and Memoranda of Field Marshal . . .*]

1 An Unsettled Childhood (1769–88)

1. Philip Guedalla, *The Duke* (1931), p. 480, for Lord Mornington's attestation to the Office of Arms; Anne, Countess Mornington gave James Cuthbertson the same date in a letter dated London, 6 April 1815 printed in *Notes and Queries*, 7th series, vol. 11 (January 1891), pp. 34–5; Harriet Arbuthnot, *The Journal of Mrs Arbuthnot 1820–1832* (1950), vol. 2, p. 185, is one of a number of references to Wellington celebrating his birthday on 1 May; and this is also the date given by Colonel Gurwood in the chronology at the head of the 8-vol. 'enlarged' edition of Wellington, *The Dispatches of Field Marshal the Duke of Wellington* (1844), vol. 1, p. xiii (henceforth cited as *WD*). See also Francis L. Clarke and William Dunlap, *The Life of the Most Noble Arthur, Marquis and Earl of Wellington* . . . (1814), p. 28 – an early Life which gives quite extensive details of Wellington's family background, evidently supplied by a member of the family.

   The entry in the baptismal register is quoted in John Murray, *Wellington. The Place and Date of His Birth Ascertained and Demonstrated*, 2nd edn (1852), p. 9, and has been verified by Susan Hood, assistant archivist at the RCB Library, Dublin, where the register is now held (email of 2 September 2002).

   Murray's pamphlet also cites the announcement of Wellington's birth (without giving an exact date) in *The Dublin Mercury, Pue's Occurrences, The Public Register or Freeman's Journal, The Dublin Gazette* and '*Exshaw's Gentleman's Magazine*' whose correct title is *The Gentleman's and London Magazine and Monthly Chronologer* published in Dublin by Sarah and John Exshaw. There is a substantial discussion of this, heavily based on Murray's research but with some additional material, in Guedalla, *The Duke*, pp. 479–80.

   In November 2011, at my request, Dr Deidre Bryan of Bradan Research Service checked the original issues of several of these papers in Trinity College Dublin and confirmed the entries in *The Gentleman's and London Magazine, The Dublin Mercury* and *Pue's Occurrences*.

   Curiously there is similar uncertainty around the exact date of Marlborough's birth.

2. Garret's name is sometimes spelt Garrett. On the family background see: C.C. Ellison, 'Dangan, Mornington and the Wellesleys', *Riocht na Midhe (Records of the Meath Archaeological and Historical Society)*, vol. 3 (1967), pp. 316–24.

3. This is the form it is given in the *The Complete Peerage* by G.E. C[ockayne], 2nd edn (1910–59) although *History of the Irish Parliament 1692–1800* by E.M. Johnston-Liik (2002), vol. 6, p. 520, spells it Viscount Wesley.

4. Longford, *Wellington. The Years of the Sword* (1969; henceforward cited simply as Longford), p. 14, says that AW told Gleig that he was 'a dreamy, idle and shy lad', but G.R. Gleig, *The Life of Arthur, Duke of Wellington* (1911), p. 3, does not put the phrase in quotation marks or imply that it came directly from Wellington. The anecdotes about AW's childhood are most accessibly collected together in Longford, pp. 13–15.

5. Henry to Arthur Wellesley, 'Private', 19 May 1801, WP 1/78.

6. Longford, pp. 15–17.

7. See the *Complete Peerage* for flogging; Hatherton Journal, 26 June 1844, recording the conversation of Robert 'Bobus' Smith, in Staffordshire Record Office D260/m/f/5/26/30 f 8–9.

8. Lord Glenbervie, *The Diaries of Sylvester Douglas (Lord Glenbervie)* (1928; henceforth cited as Glenbervie, *Diaries*), vol. 2, pp. 226–7, 9 May 1817.

9. Gleig, *Life of Wellington*, p. 4.

10. Longford, p. 18.

11. Gleig, *Life of Wellington*, p. 5. Gleig and sources following him give the name as 'Goubert' but this is corrected to Foubert in Henri Bernard, *Le Duc de Wellington et la Belgique* (1973), pp. 32–3.

12. Gleig, *Life of Wellington*, pp. 5–6.

13. Glenbervie, *Diaries*, vol. 2, pp. 226–7.

14. 'I vow to God . . .' from Sir Herbert Maxwell, *The Life of Wellington and the Restoration of the Martial Power of Great Britain* (1900), vol. 1, p. 4, who does not give the source of Katherine Wellesley-Pole's remark; Katherine had married William on 17 May 1784, and so was a member of the family at the time. 'Food for powder' (an echo of Shakespeare, *Henry IV Part 1*, Act 4 scene 2) is quoted, again without source, in A. Brialmont and G.R. Gleig, *History of the Life of Arthur Duke of Wellington* (1858), vol. 1, p. 6.

15. Gleig, *Life of Wellington*, p. 5.

16. Mornington to Rutland, 8 December 1785, *Historical Manuscripts Commission Report on the Manuscripts of the Duke of Rutland* (henceforth cited as *HMC Rutland*) (1888–1905), vol. 3, p. 266.

17. Mornington to Rutland, 8 December 1785, 7 November 1786, 16 January and 8 March 1787, *HMC Rutland*, vol. 3, pp. 266, 354–5, 364–5, 377. J.L. Pimlott, 'The Administration of the British Army, 1783–1793' (1975), pp. 15–16, on surplus of deserving officers.

18. Francis, 1st Earl of Ellesmere, *Personal Reminiscences of the Duke of Wellington* (1904), p. 102n, and Thomas Raikes, *A Portion of the Journal of Thomas Raikes* (1856), vol. 4, p. 302, 6 October 1843, both record Mackenzie's recollections in very similar terms, although only Raikes preserves Vick's name. There is an obituary of Mackenzie in the *United Service Journal* (March 1854), pp. 314–15.

19. Philip Henry, 5th Earl Stanhope, *Notes of Conversations with the Duke of Wellington* (1888), pp. 164–7, 26 September 1839.

20. Lady Shelley, *The Diary of Frances Lady Shelley* (1913), vol. 1, pp. 119–20, July 1815.

21. Longford, pp. 21, 24 for Lady Mornington's reaction. Longford misdates AW's return to 1786, but see Mornington to Buckingham, 4 November 1787, in the Duke of Buckingham and Chandos, *Memoirs of the Court and Cabinets of George III* (1853), vol. 1, pp. 333–4. The Ladies of Llangollen were Lady Eleanor Butler and Sarah Ponsonby who fled their families and the possibility of unwanted marriages to set up house together near Llangollen in north Wales in 1778. They became quite famous and received many visitors as their eccentricity came to be celebrated.

22. Mornington to Rutland, London, 8 March 1787, *HMC Rutland*, p. 377, announces that Sir G. Yonge has given AW an ensigncy in a regiment now in India, and that Mornington intends to apply for long leave to ensure that AW need not join the regiment. Mornington to Grenville, 27 October 1787, *Historical Manuscripts Commission Report on the Manuscripts of J.B. Fortescue preserved at Dropmore* (henceforth cited as *HMC Dropmore*) (1892–1927), vol. 1, pp. 286–7 (Grenville's role; Yonge's terms; Mornington's delight); Buckingham to Mornington, November 1787, Buckingham, *Memoirs of the Court and Cabinets*, vol. 1, p. 335.

23. Lady Mornington to the Ladies of Llangollen, 26 November and 17 December 1787, in Guedalla, *The Duke*, p. 28.

24. Diary of Lady Eleanor Butler, 27 January 1788, in Ladies of Langollen, *The Hamwood Papers of the Ladies of Llangollen and Caroline Hamilton* (1930), p. 72.

2 Coming of Age in Ireland (1788–93)

1. Quote from James J. Sack, *The Grenvillites, 1801–1829* (1979), p. 5; see also John Beckett, *The Rise and Fall of the Grenvilles* (1994), p. 84.

2. See Arbuthnot, *Journal*, vol. 1, pp. 260, 26 September 1823.

3. *Parliamentary Portraits* (1795), vol. 1, p. 20, quoted in *Complete Peerage*, vol. 12, p. 578n.

4. Malone to Earl of Charlemont, 7 November 1794, quoted in *Complete Peerage*, vol. 12, p. 578n.

5. *Complete Peerage*, vol. 12, p. 578n; Lord Burghersh, *Correspondence of Lord Burghersh* (1912), p. 1.

6. Buckingham to Grenville, 9 January 1791, *HMC Dropmore*, vol. 2, pp. 10–11.

7. A. Aspinall 'The Cabinet Council, 1783–1835' (1952), pp. 190–1.

8. Quoted in R.G. Thorne, ed., *The History of Parliament* (1986), vol. 4, p. 208.

9. Arthur Wesley to William Fremantle (in Bath), 1 September 1789, Fremantle Papers, Centre for Buckinghamshire Studies D/FR/54/1/4.

10. *Parliamentary Debates*, vol. 12, col. 925, 21 February 1809; Thorne, *History of Parliament*, vol. 4, pp. 679–80; Pimlott, 'Administration', pp. 66–9 describes the dispute over his promotion and concludes that the King behaved badly, motivated by dislike of Buckingham.

11. The 'Town Bull of Dublin' comes from Rowland Hill's recollections, quoting General O'Hara at Gibraltar in 1800, as quoted in Gordon L. Teffeteller, *The Surpriser. The Life of Rowland, Lord Hill* (1983), p. 22. Other biographical sources on Cradock include the *ODNB*; *Complete Peerage*; George IV, *Correspondence of George, Prince of Wales* (1963–71), vol. 5, p. 465, vol. 6, pp. 190–1, vol. 8, pp. 133–4; and George Jackson, *The Diaries and Letters of Sir George Jackson* (1872), vol. 2, p. 391. I can find no evidence to support the claim made in the *ODNB* that Wellington was responsible for securing Cradock's peerage in 1819, and it is more likely that this recognised his very old, close friendship with the Prince Regent.

12. Melisina Trench, *The Remains of the Late Mrs Richard Trench* (1862), pp. 13 (Dangan) and 361–2 (Arthur Wesley).

13. Ibid., p. 406.

14. Ibid., pp. 405–6.

15. Thorne, *History of Parliament*, vol. 3, pp. 835–9; *Parliamentary Debates*, 25 January 1809, vol. 12, col. 150; Sack, *Grenvillites*, pp. 44–5; see also Ann Parry, ed., *The Admirals Fremantle* (1971) for family background and pp. 15–136 for the letters of T.F. Fremantle – the brother of W.H. Fremantle.

16. W.H. Fremantle to Sir Arthur Wellesley, 31 March 1809 and reply (same day), and AW to Fremantle, 25 August 1809, Fremantle Papers, Centre for Buckinghamshire Studies D/FR/47/11/6, 5, 4. There was some delay in John Fremantle's appointment due to AW's need to clarify recent changes to the regulations affecting staff officers. His letters home are published as John Fremantle, *Wellington's Voice. The Candid Letters of Lieutenant-Colonel John Fremantle, Coldstream Guards, 1808–1821* (2012).

17. A. Aspinall 'The Old House of Commons and its Members', pt. 5, *Parliamentary Affairs*, vol. 15, p. 38; Thorne, *History of Parliament*, vol. 5, pp. 582–3.

18. Hon. Lionel A. Tollemache, *Old and Odd Memories* (1908), p. 237; on Lady Aldborough see Glenbervie, *Diaries*, vol. 1, pp. 38–9 and vol. 2, p. 264.

19. Shelley, *Diary*, vol. 2, pp. 401–2; Ellison, 'Dangan, Mornington and the Wellesleys', p. 325.

20. T.M. Brisbane, *Reminiscences of General Sir Thomas Makdougall Brisbane* (1860), p. 31.

21. W.F.P. Napier, *The Life and Opinions of General Sir Charles James Napier G.C.B.* (1857), vol. 1, p. 52.

22. Sir Jonah Barrington, *Personal Sketches and Recollections of his Own Times* (1876), p. 170; Brialmont in Brialmont and Gleig, *History of the Life*, vol. 1, p. 11. In 1830 Barrington was deprived of his office of judge in the Court of Admiralty for repeated peculation of funds held by the court. He died in exile in 1834: see the entry on him in the *ODNB*.

23. Trench, *Remains*, pp. 297, 361.

24. Cradock to Fremantle, 10 July 1789; AW to Fremantle, 4 August 1789: both in Fremantle, *Wellington's Voice*, pp. 1–3. The original of AW's letter is in the Fremantle Papers, Centre for Buckinghamshire Studies D/FR/54/1/102. I must thank Charles Fremantle for drawing this letter to my attention prior to the publication of *Wellington's Voice*. The Alborough's family name was Stratford, so it is quite possible that AW was infatuated with one of her connections.

25. *The Times*, 2 August 1791; Longford, p. 27 tells the story of the bawdy-house, but it cannot be found in either of the sources she cites, so its origins and value are obscure.

26. *The Times*, 25 September 1789; Longford, p. 26.

27. Guedalla, *The Duke*, pp. 29–30, 54. Longford, p. 42 gives the figure as £955 14s 8 1/2d; for his dislike of debt see Gleig, *Life*, p. 8, though the claim made there that he avoided it is plainly untrue.

28. Quoted in Norman Gash, *Mr Secretary Peel* (1961), pp. 124–5; Elers tells a rather confused story which probably relates to this: George Elers, *Memoirs of George Elers* (1903), pp. 56–7.

29. Inspection Report, WO 27/68; G.L. Cole, *Memoirs of Sir Lowry Cole* (1934), p. 5 for the University of Stuttgart; I.E.A Dolby, ed., 'The Duke of Wellington's Services' (1872), pp. 212–13 cites muster-books of the regiment for the statement that Wesley and Cole were both in Major Villettis's troop.

30. Brisbane, *Reminiscences*, p. 8. In 1828 Wellington told Anglesey, 'I did know Lord Castlemaine very well, having been quartered at Athlone in his neighbourhood. But have not seen him for years …' (Wellington to Anglesey, 28 September 1828: Wellington, *Despatches, Correspondence, and Memoranda …* (1854; henceforth *WND*), vol. 5, pp. 91–2.

31. AW to Lt.-Col. Anstruther, 8 June 1807, Wellington, *Supplementary Despatches …* (1852–72; henceforth *WSD*), vol. 5, pp. 74–5; Clarence to Wellington, 27 April 1814, *WSD*, vol. 9, p. 42; Lt.-Col. Russell Gurney, *History of the Northamptonshire Regiment, 1742–1934* (1935), p. 80; Dolby, 'The Duke of Wellington's Services', p. 213.

32. Longford, pp. 22–3, usefully disproves the tale that Croker published despite Wellington's denial. Why anyone would *want* to weigh the private, rather than simply his kit, is unclear; but it is unlikely that any soldier, let alone a Highlander, would take kindly to such conduct.

33. Brisbane, *Reminiscences*, p. 8. It is not clear what Brisbane means by 'division' in this context.

34. J.A. Houlding, *Fit for Service. The Training of the British Army, 1715–1795* (1981), pp. 242–7. Brisbane's account contains many small inaccuracies, but it does link Wesley's knowledge of

drill to the introduction of Dundas's regulations, and Houlding's work provides the context that makes Brisbane's claim plausible.

35. Mornington may not have received full payment from Captain Burrowes for Dangan; on the other hand, he received £15,000 in compensation for his electoral interest at Trim when the Act of Union abolished the seat in 1801 (Johnston-Liik, *History of the Irish Parliament*, vol. 2, p. 306).

36. There is some interesting material on the Wellesley family finances in Lord Gerald Wellesley, ed., 'Some Letters of the Mornington Family', *County Kildare Archaeological Society Journal* (1935–45), vol. 12, pp. 30–40; see also Peter J. Jupp, *The First Duke of Wellington in an Irish Context* (1997), pp. 6–9; Ellison, 'Dangan, Mornington and the Wellesleys', pp. 324, 327; Iris Butler, *The Eldest Brother. The Marquess Wellesley* (1973), p. 36; and Constantia Maxwell, *Dublin under the Georges (1714–1830)* (1936), p. 77 (for the sale of Mornington House). However the subject still needs further investigation. From this it appears that the younger children may have received as little as £106 p.a. each – Lady Mornington mentions 115 Irish pounds (approximately £106 sterling) – and certainly not more than £250 p.a. each (interest on £20,000 at 5 per cent divided between four – based on the figures given by the agent in Wellesley, 'Some Letters', p. 36).

37. AW to Mornington, Camp near Grave, 19 September 1794, BL Add Ms 37,308 f 15.

38. *HMC Dropmore*, vol. 1, pp. 287–8.

39. Guedalla, *The Duke*, pp. 31–2.

40. Quoted in ibid., p. 31.

41. AW to Mornington, 20 March 1790, quoted in ibid., pp. 31–2.

42. Johnston-Liik, *History of the Irish Parliament*, vol. 6, p. 526 for William; Namier and Brooke, *The History of Parliament, 1760–1790* (1964), vol. 1, p. 97, and Thorne, *History of Parliament*, vol. 1, pp. 278–9 for the situation in England and numbers and examples of underage MPs in the British Parliament.

43. Ellison, 'Dangan, Mornington and the Wellesleys', p. 326; Gleig, *Life*, p. 2; Noel E. French, ed., *Wellington. His Irish Connections* (1992), p. 16.

44. Wellington, *The Speeches of the Duke of Wellington in Parliament* (1854), vol. 1, pp. 1–2.

45. E.M. Johnston, *Great Britain and Ireland 1760–1800*, pp. 242–3: 'implicit obedience in political matters was expected from the Lord Lieutenant's aides-de-camp'.

46. Thomas Bartlett, *The Fall and Rise of the Irish Nation* (1992), pp. 45–65 esp. 46–8 (rise of Catholic merchants) and 65; and R.B. McDowell, 'Ireland in 1800', in *New History of Ireland* (1976–2005), vol. 4, pp. 657–64, 671–3.

47. Bartlett, *Fall and Rise*, pp. 57–9, 70–2, 83–9; see also J.R. Western, 'Roman Catholics holding Military Commissions in 1798' (1955), pp. 428–32.

48. Bartlett, *Fall and Rise*, pp. 92–105, and p. 72.

49. Ibid., pp. 72, 121–45; R.B. McDowell, *Ireland in the Age of Imperialism and Revolution* (1979), pp. 390–401. For Pitt's lack of sympathy for the Irish Protestants see Glenbervie, *Diaries*, vol. 1, pp. 35–6.

50. Bartlett, *Fall and Rise*, p. 157.

51. Ibid., pp. 146–73; McDowell, *Ireland in the Age*, pp. 404–21; on pp. 418–19 McDowell argues that the immediate effect of the measures was quite limited, but they proved their significance over the next generation. Daniel O'Connell was among the first group of Catholic lawyers admitted to the bar under its provisions: Oliver MacDonagh, *The Herediary Bondsman Daniel O'Connell* (1988), pp. 29, 31.

52. Wellington, *Speeches*, vol. 1, pp. 3–4. R.B. McDowell praises this as 'a sensible speech' in *Ireland in the Age*, p. 416. In 1829, in the midst of the crisis over Catholic Emancipation, Wellington referred to 'the mistake made by the Irish Parliament in 1793'. However, this was writing privately to the Duke of Rutland, and may not have been his fully considered opinion. (Wellington to Rutland, 7 February 1829, *WND*, vol. 5, p. 491.)

53. It is, of course, notoriously hard to prove a negative – that they were *not* close friends – but H. Montgomery Hyde's thorough study of Castlereagh's life to 1801 has no evidence of a connection between them other than the single, well-known story told by Jonah Barrington, while allusions to Castlereagh in Wesley's letters written in India are neither frequent nor particularly flattering; for example, Arthur Wellesley to Lord Wellesley, 15 March 1804, *WSD*, vol. 4, pp. 355–60 (passage quoted below, pp. 153–4). H.M. Hyde, *The Rise of Castlereagh* (1933), pp. 98, 108; Barrington, *Personal Sketches and Recollections*, p. 170. On Castlereagh's

love of music see Johnston-Liik, *History of the Irish Parliament*, vol. 6, pp. 347–51, and Wendy Hinde, *Castlereagh* (1981), p. 106.

3 Love and War (1792–96)

1. Buckingham to Grenville, 6 May 1789, *HMC Dropmore*, vol. 1, p. 466. Kitty was the third child in the family until one of her elder sisters, Mary, died in July 1789.
2. Joan Wilson, *A Soldier's Wife. Wellington's Marriage* (1987), p. 6; Longford, p. 28.
3. Kitty's account, told to her niece Catherine Hamilton, and quoted in Wilson, *A Soldier's Wife*, p. 11.
4. In April 1793 AW borrowed 1,200 Irish pounds (approximately £1,100 sterling) from Capt. Stapleton to purchase his majority in the 33rd, Richard standing as guarantor, and the rest of the purchase price coming from the sale of AW's troop in the 18th Light Dragoons. (The fact that he could sell it implies that he had purchased it.) This is based on a bundle of letters from AW and from Mornington's agent John Page, now at Stratfield Saye, copies of which were kindly supplied to me by Jane Branfield, the archivist there, in an email of 27 April 2013.
5. Wilson, *A Soldier's Wife*, pp. 11–15.
6. Wellington, *A Selection from the Private Correspondence of the First Duke of Wellington* (1952), pp. 1–2; see also Wilson, *A Soldier's Wife*, p. 14. The letter is undated, and headed only 'Barracks. Tuesday'. It was probably written in May 1794 just before AW and the 33rd sailed to join Moira's expedition (see below).
7. This is implied in the letters of 1801–02 printed in Wellington, *Selection from the Private Correspondence*, pp. 3–6, and quoted below in Chapter 11.
8. Wilson, *A Soldier's Wife*, p. 14 quoting Catherine Hamilton.
9. AW to Mornington, quoted in Maxwell, *Life of Wellington*, vol. 1, p. 8.
10. Quoted in Brereton and Savory, *The History of the Duke of Wellington's Regiment (West Riding) 1702-1992* (1993), p. 91; see also Michael Duffy, *Soldiers, Sugar and Seapower. The British Expeditions to the West Indies and the War Against Revolutionary France* (1987), pp. 134–5.
11. Quoted in R.N.W. Thomas, 'Wellington in the Low Countries, 1794–1795' (1989), p. 29.
12. Sir Henry Bunbury, *Narrative of some Passages in the Great War with France* (1927), pp. 217–18.
13. There is no good history of Britain's role in the War of the First Coalition, but high-level strategy is well covered in John Ehrman, *The Younger Pitt. The Reluctant Transition* (1983) [vol. 2], and Duffy's *Soldiers, Sugar and Seapower*.
14. On the background to Moira's expedition see Ehrman, *Younger Pitt. The Reluctant Transition*, pp. 322–5, 331, 343. See also Moira to the Prince of Wales, 25 June 1794, in George IV, *Correspondence*, vol. 2, pp. 437–8.
15. Moira to the Prince of Wales, 25 and 26 June 1794, ibid., vol. 2, pp. 437–8; Thomas, 'Wellington in the Low Countries', p. 15 which includes the quote from Vyse to Dundas, 2 July 1794.
16. Duke of York to the Prince of Wales, 11 July 1794, in George IV, *Correspondence*, vol. 2, p. 444; AW to Lindsay in Thomas, 'Wellington in the Low Countries', pp. 17–18 and reply, 2 August 1794, WP 1/3; Craig quoted in Sir Neil Cantlie, *A History of the Army Medical Department* (1974), vol. 1, p. 219.
17. Quotes from an 'Officer of the Guards' in Thomas, 'Wellington in the Low Countries', p. 18; York's thanks: AW to Mornington, 19 September 1794, in ibid., p. 18. One of the Guards officers present was the twenty-two-year-old George Murray, who would serve Wellington so ably as Quartermaster-General in the Peninsula.
18. Cantlie, *History of the Army Medical Department*, vol. 1, p. 221.
19. Lord Cathcart quoted in C.T. Atkinson, 'Gleanings from the Cathcart Mss Pt IV The Netherlands, 1794–1795' (1951), p. 148.
20. Thomas, 'Wellington in the Low Countries', p. 29, quoting comments by the Duke of York and Colonel Craig.
21. Ibid., pp. 26–8. These figures for the number of men who died each month were much higher than in the summer months when it had usually been under twenty.
22. AW to Lt Col Mackenzie, 7 December 1794, BL Add Ms 46,703 f 234.
23. AW to Sir Chichester Fortescue, Ysendoom, 20 December 1794, *WSD*, vol. 13, pp. 1–2; the same letter is printed with minor variations in Thomas (Fortescue), Lord Clermont, *A History of the Family of Fortescue in all its Branches* (1880), pp. 204–5. Lord Paget also comments on

the fraternisation and good relations between the British and French armies: Marquess of Anglesey, *One Leg. The Life and Letters of Henry William Paget* (1963), p. 47.

24. Stanhope, *Notes of Conversations,* p. 182, 12 October 1839.

25. Gleig, *Life,* p. 12; see also Ellesmere, *Personal Reminiscences,* p. 161.

26. See Dorothy George, *English Political Caricature* (1959), vol. 2, pp. 5–9.

27. Ehrman, *Younger Pitt. The Reluctant Transition,* vol. 2, pp. 374–5; J.W. Fortescue, *A History of the British Army* [henceforth cited simply as fortescue] (1899–1930), vol. 4, p. 315; Simon Schama, *Patriots and Liberators* (1977), pp. 182–3 and 672n127 for Dutch discontent with York, a factor in his removal which has often been overlooked.

28. Maj.-Gen. David Dundas to the Prince of Wales, 27 September and 24 December 1794, in George IV, *Correspondence,* vol. 2, pp. 463, 526–7. For more on British misconduct leading to Dutch hostility see Schama, *Patriots and Liberators,* pp. 176, 184 and 672n133, and 187–8.

29. [? – unnamed officer] to Cornwallis, 11 November 1794, in Charles Ross, *Correspondence of Charles, First Marquis Cornwallis* (1859), vol. 2, p. 274.

30. For the Dutch background see Schama, *Patriots and Liberators,* pp. 163–92 and esp. 182–3.

31. Dundas to Harcourt, 6 January 1795, quoted in Thomas, 'Wellington in the Low Countries', pp. 21–2.

32. De Ros manuscript quoted in Maxwell, *Life of Wellington,* vol. 1, p. 14. According to Schama, *Patriots and Liberators,* p. 176, Utrecht was a hotbed of discontent.

33. Cantlie, *History of the Army Medical Department,* vol. 1, p. 219.

34. William Harness, *Trusty and Well-Beloved. The Letters Home of William Harness, an Officer of George the Third* (1957), p. 67; Fortescue, vol. 4, pt. 1, pp. 320 and 322 (includes the quote from Wallmoden).

35. AW to Mackenzie, 17 February 1795, quoted in Thomas, 'Wellington in the Low Countries', pp. 23–4.

36. Thomas, 'Wellington in the Low Countries', p. 24. AW was not the only officer to consider asking for leave: Lord Paget contemplated doing so in December and again in January. See Anglesey, *One Leg,* pp. 48, 50.

37. Thomas, 'Wellington in the Low Countries', p. 24 for the further fighting, and for the arrival in Harwich; Guedalla, *The Duke,* p. 47 for the date of embarkation; Brereton and Savory, *History,* p. 95 for the losses in the campaign.

38. This paragraph is highly speculative, based on scraps of circumstantial evidence – hence the many qualifying phrases ('may have', etc.). However, the fact that Wesley contemplated leaving the army is not in doubt – see below.

39. Abercromby had family ties to Henry Dundas, which were important in his advancement. Nonetheless his political views were distinctly liberal, as were those of his followers. See Duffy, *Soldiers, Sugar and Seapower,* pp. 163–5, and Piers Mackesy, *British Victory in Egypt 1801* (1995), pp. 7–8, but the whole subject needs further work. Napier's father was a Scottish peer, but he was born in London and grew up in Ireland; Colborne was English.

40. Quoted in Thorne, *History of Parliament,* vol. 4, pp. 881–2, which is also the source for the other biographical material in this paragraph and the earlier quote ('very pleasing and gentlemanly in his manners').

41. Mornington (as quoted in Guedalla, *The Duke,* p. 49) calls it Secretary at War, but no such post existed.

42. Guedalla, *The Duke,* pp. 50–51; this was probably the speech given in Wellington, *Speeches,* vol. 1, p. 4 under the date of 13 March 1794. As AW only reached England at the end of the first week of March after eight months' arduous campaigning, and as he saw Camden in London at that time, it is most unlikely – although not impossible – that he was in Dublin on 13 March. In his letter of 25 June 1795 to Camden (printed in Brialmont and Gleig, *History,* vol. 1, pp. 22–3) he says he 'accompanied' Camden to Ireland; and Camden did not reach Dublin until 31 March.

43. AW to Camden, 25 June 1795, printed in Brialmont and Gleig, *History,* vol. 1, pp. 22–3.

44. Camden to AW, 15 September 1795, WP 1/5.

45. On recruiting see Brereton and Savory, *History,* p. 95, and Duffy, *Soldiers, Sugar and Seapower,* pp. 170–4; on AW's illness, Guedalla, *The Duke,* p. 52, and Longford, pp. 40–41; on his illness in 1804–05 see below.

46. Duffy, *Soldiers, Sugar and Seapower,* pp. 202–9 for a full account of 'Christian's gales'.

47. Wilson, *A Soldier's Wife,* pp. 20–1.

48. Camden to AW, Dublin Castle, 5 June, 1796, WP 1/3.
49. Thorne, *History of Parliament*, vol. 5, p. 504.
50. Quoted in Lord Gerald Wellesley and John Steegman, *The Iconography of the First Duke of Wellington* (1935), p. 22. On Hoppner see the entry by John Wilson in Jane Turner, ed., *The Dictionary of Art* (c. 1996), vol. 14, pp. 753–5.
51. These portraits are all reproduced in black and white in Henry Wellesley, *The Diary and Correspondence of Henry Wellesley, First Lord Cowley, 1790–1846* ([1930]); see also Butler, *The Eldest Brother*, opp. pp. 96 and 97.
52. Wellesley, *Diary of Henry Wellesley*, pp. 22–30.
53. Lord Glenbervie to Mornington, 29 July 1799, Richard, Marquess Wellesley, *The Wellesley Papers* (1914), vol. 1, p. 107.
54. Glenbervie, *Diaries*, vol. 2, p. 131.

4 Arrival in India (1796–98)

1. *London Gazette*, 14 May 1796, p. 460; Gurwood's chronology in *WD*, vol. 3, p. xiii. The strange arrangement whereby many generals were also proprietary colonels of regiments reflected the fact that generals were only paid when they were actually employed. Being 'given a regiment' did not come automatically, but was a valuable piece of patronage bestowed by the Horse Guards and the King.
2. William R. O'Byrne, *A Naval Biographical Dictionary* (1990, reprint of 1849 1st edn), vol. 2, p. 714 says that AW sailed on the *Fox*, and secondary sources endlessly repeat the phrase that he sailed 'on a fast frigate', although as it sailed with a convoy its speed was irrelevant. Elers, *Memoirs*, p. 58 states that he sailed on the *Princess Charlotte*, but he is referring specifically to the voyage from the Cape to India, and as the *Fox* was destined for Madras not Calcutta, AW may have changed ships at the Cape.
3. Elers, *Memoirs*, pp. 51–2.
4. Guedalla, *The Duke*, pp. 54–65 has a bravura discussion of Wesley's library, based on the bookseller's bill, but is too bold in assuming that Wesley personally selected the books and that he read them; cf Sir James Mackintosh, *Memoirs of the Life of Sir James Mackintosh* (1835), vol. 1, p. 206.
5. Elers, *Memoirs*, p. 88 but cf Combermere quoted in Chapter 6 below.
6. Elers, *Memoirs*, pp. 55–6. Elers may have slightly underestimated Wesley's height: see Muriel Wellesley, *Wellington in Civil Life* (nd [1939]), pp. 39–40n; Longford, p. 100, and Norman Gash, in his entry on Wellington in the *ODNB*, both say that Wellington was 5 feet 9 inches.
7. Elers, *Memoirs*, pp. 55, 46–7.
8. Quote from AW to General Cunninghame, Fort William, 9 March 1797, WP 1/6; Elers says that the 12th reached Madras on 9 January after 'about two months' and kept passage with the 33rd most of the way, so they sailed together probably in the first half of November. The date of 17 February comes from Brereton and Savory, *History*, p. 96.
9. Cornwallis to Shore, 10 June 1796, Ross, *Cornwallis Correspondence*, vol. 2, p. 305; also in Lord Teignmouth, *Memoir of Life and Correspondence of John, Lord Teignmouth* by his son Charles Shore (1843), vol. 1, pp. 423–4.
10. Quoted in Guedalla, *The Duke*, p. 75.
11. Lord Teignmouth [Charles Shore], *Reminiscences of Many Years* (1878), vol. 2, p. 144; first quote also in Teignmouth, *Memoir*, vol. 1, p. 425.
12. Hobart to AW, 11 January 1797, WP 1/3; AW to Mornington, 12 July 1797, WP 1/6.
13. Thorne, *History of Parliament*, vol. 5, pp. 91–2 gives a good character sketch.
14. William Hickey, *Memoirs of William Hickey* (1925), vol. 4, p. 155.
15. Hickey, *Memoirs*, vol. 4, pp. 160–1; for AW's opinion of St Leger see AW to Mornington, 17 April 1797, WP 1/6.
16. AW to Mornington, 12 July 1797, *WSD*, vol. 1, pp. 12–17. The manuscript of this letter, with several important passages suppressed in the published version, is in WP 1/6.
17. AW to Mornington, 17 April and 20 May 1797, WP 1/6, partially printed in *WSD*, vol. 1, pp. 4–8.
18. AW to Sir John Shore, 23 June, 1 July and 6 August 1797; Shore to AW, 8 August 1797, *WSD*, vol. 1, pp. 9–12, 22–3n.

19. 'Memorandum on the Expedition Against the Spanish Islands' by AW, n.d. Teignmouth, *Memoir*, vol. 1, pp. 509–12 (and reprinted in *WSD*, vol. 1, pp. 4–5). William Henry Springer, 'The Military Apprenticeship of Arthur Wellesley in India, 1797–1805' (1966), pp. 39–40 prints Hobart's letter objecting to the idea of an attack on Batavia in passing.

20. 'Regimental Orders for on Board Ship' by AW, July 1797, *WSD*, vol. 1, pp. 19–24; Springer, 'Military Apprenticeship', p. 41n for the War Office regulations upon which these orders were modelled.

21. Hickey, *Memoirs*, vol. 4, pp. 171–2.

22. Elers, *Memoirs*, pp. 69–70; Memoranda by AW in *WSD*, vol. 1, pp. 24–34, 34–9.

23. Quoted in C. Northcote Parkinson, *War in Eastern Seas 1793–1815* (1954), p. 118.

24. Ibid., pp. 40–3, 117–19, 138–9.

25. Hickey, *Memoirs*, vol. 4, p. 190.

26. AW to John Page of Dundalk, 10 September 1797, WP 1/6.

27. AW to Gen. Cunninghame, 22 June 1797, WP 1/6, explains Norcott's problem; J. Taylor to AW, 18 March 1798, WP 1/7 offering to pay half the £600; Captain Keating to AW, 22 November 1797, WP 1/3, Norcott to AW, 13 December 1797, WP 1/3 and many other related letters in this file.

28. Details of Norcott's career from John A. Hall, *The Biographical Dictionary of British Officers Killed and Wounded, 1808–1814* (1998), pp. 439–41. In 1816 Wellington recommended Norcott's claims to the attention of the Horse Guards and the Commander-in-Chief: see Torrens to Wellington, 29 February 1816, *WSD*, vol. 11, pp. 310–11.

29. Wellington, 'Colonel Wellesley's Standing Orders to the Thirty-Third Regiment, 1798' (1972), pp. 65–77.

30. Quote from AW to Mr Adamson, nd, WP 3/1/1, pp. 16–17; the later memoranda referred to are in *WSD*, vol. 1, pp. 55–67, 70–6.

31. Captain Robert W. Eastwick, *A Master Mariner. Being the Life and Adventures of Captain Robert W. Eastwick* (1891), pp. 120–1.

32. Ibid., pp. 122–4.

5 Mornington and the Indian Scene

1. Franklin and Mary Wickwire, *Cornwallis. The Imperial Years* (1980), pp. 151–3, 162.

2. Denys M. Forrest, *Tiger of Mysore. The Life and Death of Tipu Sultan* (1970), pp. 222–35.

3. P.E. Roberts, *History of British India under the Company and the Crown* (1921), pp. 145–60.

4. *Royal Military Chronicle*, vol. 1, no. 1 (November 1810), p. 7, 'Life of Lord Wellington' and ibid. (December 1810), pp. 96, 144–6; see also Giles Hunt, ed., *Mehitabel Canning. A Redoubtable Woman* (2001), p. 185 for another example of the association between wealth from India and 'oppression and chicanery'.

5. Extracts from the Act (24 Geo. III, c. 25) are conveniently printed in P.J. Marshall, *Problems of Empire. Britain and India 1757–1813* (1968), pp. 131–6, 167–70, the passage quoted being on p. 167.

6. P.J. Marshall, *The Impeachment of Warren Hastings* (1965), pp. xvi–xvii is good on the hostility to British intervention in India at this time.

7. P.J. Marshall, '"Cornwallis Triumphant": War in India and the British Public in the Late Eighteenth Century' (1992), p. 67 and *passim*.

8. See, for example, Dundas to Mornington, 16 June, 13 August and 29 December 1798, in *Two Views of British India. The Private Correspondence of Mr Dundas and Lord Wellesley*, ed. Edward Ingram (1970), pp. 46–51, 64, 116–18; C.H. Philips, *The East India Company 1784–1834* (1961), pp. 70, 80, 91; and Raymond Callahan, *The East India Company and Army Reform* (1962) *passim* and esp. pp. 127–8 which shows that this neglect pre-dated the war.

9. Memorandum of 4 July 1841 quoted in Richard A. Brashares, 'The Political Career of Marquess Wellesley in England and Ireland' (1968), p. 90.

10. Mornington to Dundas, 23 February 1798, in Ingram, ed., *Two Views of British India*, pp. 16–28, quote on p. 18.

11. S.P. Sen, *The French in India* (1958), pp. 510–16, 540–2, which is based on substantial research in the French archives.

12. Tipu's hostility is acknowledged – and applauded – even in the highly sympathetic studies of B. Sheik Ali and Kate Brittlebank: B. Sheik Ali, *Tipu Sultan. A Study in Diplomacy*

and Confrontation (1982), *passim*; Kate Brittlebank, *Tipu Sultan's Search for Legitimacy. Islam and Kingship in a Hindu Domain* (1997), p. 27. Ali (p. 279) states that the expulsion of the British was 'the ruling passion of [Tipu's] life'.

13. On Tipu's contacts with Zeman Shah see Ali, *Tipu Sultan*, pp. 291–7 and Forrest, *Tiger of Mysore*, p. 243.

14. C.K.A. Antonova, 'Tipu Sultan and the French: Hitherto Unpublished Documents in the Leningrad Institute of History' (1963), pp. 72–88; R.P. Gates, 'Tipu Sultan of Mysore and the Revolutionary Governments of France, 1793–1799' (1964), pp. 7–19. There is a convenient summary in Forrest, *Tiger of Mysore*, pp. 241–3.

15. Mornington to Dundas, 28 February 1798, in Ingram, ed., *Two Views of British India*, pp. 28–43, quote on p. 36. On Mornington and the threat posed by Zeman Shah see also *Indian Record Series*, vol. 18, pp. 39–45 (Introduction).

16. Hickey, *Memoirs*, vol. 4, p. 200.

17. Mornington to Grenville, 17 November 1798, *HMC Dropmore*, vol. 4, pp. 381–7 esp. 383; Mornington to Dundas, 1 October 1798, in Ingram, ed., *Two Views of British India*, pp. 67–86 esp. 83; Hickey, *Memoirs*, vol. 4, pp. 235–6 (on Mornington and the C-in-C).

18. Forrest, *Tiger of Mysore*, pp. 248–56; Gates, 'Tipu Sultan of Mysore,' p. 15.

19. Forrest, *Tiger of Mysore*, pp. 260–1 establishes the sequence of events, and shows that Mornington had decided against war before he received objections from Madras. AW's 'Draft Observation upon Mornington's Minute of 28 June 1798', *WSD*, vol. 1, pp. 52–5 argues against the general policy of war against Tipu. For Mornington's opinion of Clarke, see Mornington to Dundas, 1st October 1798, in Ingram, ed., *Two Views of British India*, pp. 67–86, esp. 71, 79–80 and 85.

20. Mark Wilks, *Historical Sketches of the South of India* (1930–32; first published 1810–17), vol. 2, pp. 660–2 gives details of the force (see also S.R. Lushington, *The Life and Services of General Lord Harris*, 2nd edn, 1845, p. 143); Mornington to Dundas, 11 October 1798, in Ingram, ed., *Two Views of British India*, pp. 90–100 esp. 92–3 on negotiations with Hyderabad and obstruction at Madras.

21. Malcolm to Harris, 21 and 22 October 1798, Lushington, *Life of Harris*, pp. 167–71; Sir John Kaye, *The Life and Correspondence of Major-General Sir John Malcolm* (1856), vol. 1, pp. 72–9.

22. Dundas to Mornington, 18 March 1799 (praise for the success at Hyderabad); Mornington to Dundas, 23 February 1798 (refers to Dundas's warning), in Ingram, ed., *Two Views of British India*, pp. 125–30, 16–28. Harris to Mornington, 29 October 1798, Lushington, *Life of Harris*, pp. 164–5 (praise for the success).

23. A.B. Rodger, *The War of the Second Coalition* (1964), pp. 15–30 esp. 16–17; Sen, *French in India*, pp. 555–9; Edward Ingram, *Commitment to Empire. Prophecies of the Great Game in Asia, 1797–1800* (1981), pp. 38–61 esp. 47–9, 52, 59; John Ehrman, *The Younger Pitt. The Consuming Struggle* (1996) [vol. 3], p. 148.

24. Naval squadron: Ingram, *Commitment to Empire*, pp. 52–3, 293–6; troops: Fortescue, vol. 4, pt. 2, pp. 719–20; bullion: Philips, *East India Company*, pp. 105–6 although Ingram suggests a rather lower figure, op. cit., pp. 81, 99–100.

6 Seringapatam (1798–99)

1. Unfortunately this letter does not appear to have survived, but its contents are referred to in AW to Campbell, draft, 20 May 1798, WP 3/1/1, pp. 11–13.

2. These memoranda are printed in *WSD*, vol. 1, pp. 55–83.

3. AW to Mornington, 12 and 27 July 1797, *WSD*, vol. 1, pp. 12–17 esp. 16, 17–19. In the first letter AW complains that he has not heard from England since he left over a year earlier; but in the second he acknowledges the arrival of letters from Mornington written in March. Guedalla, *The Duke*, pp. 74, 76 and Longford, pp. 50–1 make more of this sense of neglect than I think is warranted by the evidence.

4. Longford, p. 54. Until his father died Mornington had borne the courtesy title of Viscount Wellesley (spelled thus), which may explain his decision to adopt the archaic spelling. Guedalla, *The Duke*, p. 14.

5. Butler, *The Eldest Brother*, pp. 96, 142.

6. The phrase is Guedalla's: *The Duke*, p. 80.

7. Extract of Mornington to Sir C. Fortescue, 1 May 1797, *WSD*, vol. 13, p. 3; Mornington to Bathurst, 25 July 1797, Wellesley, *Wellesley Papers*, vol. 1, pp. 37–8.
8. AW to Mornington, 27 July 1797, *WSD*, vol. 1, pp. 17–19.
9. AW to Henry Wellesley, 23 September 1798, *WSD*, vol. 1, pp. 93–6.
10. AW to Mornington, 11 October 1798, WP 1/8.
11. AW to Mornington, 15 September 1798, *WSD*, vol. 1, pp. 85–8.
12. See Parkinson, *War in Eastern Seas*, p. 56 for the Cornwallis precedent.
13. Thorne, *History of Parliament*, vol. 3, p. 453. Mornington was equally puzzled by his motives: Butler, *The Eldest Brother*, p. 179.
14. AW to Mornington, 15 September 1798, *WSD*, vol. 1, pp. 85–8.
15. Ibid.
16. AW to Mornington, 21 October 1798, *WSD*, vol. 1, pp. 110–12; AW to HW, 23 October 1798, WP 3/1/3, pp. 20–2; and AW to Mornington, 27 February 1799, WP 1/11. (These last two letters are printed in *WSD*, vol. 1, pp. 117–18, 195–200 with Harris's name suppressed.)
17. AW to Mornington, 25 September 1798, WP 1/8, printed with deletions in *WSD*, vol. 1, pp. 96–7.
18. AW to HW, 19 October 1798, WP 1/8, printed with deletions in *WSD*, vol. 1, pp. 108–10.
19. AW to HW, 12 October 1798, WP 1/8, printed with deletions in *WSD*, vol. 1, pp. 106–7.
20. AW to HW, 7, 12 and 19 October and 26 November 1798, WP 1/8, printed with deletions in *WSD*, vol. 1, pp. 104–10, 133–5.
21. Sepoys were Indian soldiers serving in the army of the East India Company, disciplined and trained to fight along European lines and with British officers. The term is also sometimes used to describe similar troops raised by Indian rulers and officered by European mercenaries.
22. AW to HW, draft, 23 October 1798, WP 3/1/3, pp. 20–2, printed with Harris's name suppressed in *WSD*, vol. 1, pp. 117–18.
23. AW to HW, 24 October 1798, *WSD*, vol. 1, pp. 118–19.
24. AW to HW, 31 October 1798, *WSD*, vol. 1, pp. 125–6.
25. Shee to AW, [20] and 22 March 1799, WP 1/9 (two letters); AW to Shee, 21 March 1799, printed in *WSD*, vol. 1, pp. 202–3 with Shee's name suppressed. On Aston's fatal duel see *WSD*, vol. 1, pp. 160–5, 169; and Elers, *Memoirs*, pp. 81–9.
26. AW to Harris, 27 December 1798, *WD*, vol. 1, p. 23.
27. Combermere, *Memoirs and Correspondence of Field Marshal Viscount Combermere . . .* (1866), vol. 1, pp. 75–6; Gash, *Mr Secretary Peel*, p. 254.
28. AW to HW, 14 December 1798, *WSD*, vol. 1, pp. 139–40.
29. 'Memorandum on Bazaars', 20 December 1798, *WSD*, vol. 1, pp. 143–6.
30. AW to Lt.-Col. Richardson, 20 January 1799, WP 1/10, printed in *WSD*, vol. 1, pp. 180–1 with name suppressed; reply printed p. 181n and original in WP 1/9. Richardson was also the QMG at Madras and in Harris's army: an extremely important staff position.
31. Stevenson to AW, 25 January 1799, WP 1/9.
32. AW to HW, 2 January 1799, *WSD*, vol. 1, pp. 152–9; see also AW to Mornington, 21 October 1798, *WSD*, vol. 1, pp. 110–12.
33. Mornington to Dundas, 12 January 1799, in Ingram, ed., *Two Views of British India*, pp. 119–21.
34. Mornington's draft instructions to Doveton are printed in *WSD*, vol. 1, pp. 152n–158n.
35. Wilks, *Historical Sketches*, vol. 2, pp. 683–6; Forrest, *Tiger of Mysore*, pp. 270–5; Ali, *Tipu Sultan*, p. 316.
36. Lushington, *Life of Harris*, pp. 175–8.
37. Harris to Mornington, 2 February 1799, Lushington, *Life of Harris*, p. 181.
38. AW to Mornington, 27 February 1799, *WSD*, vol. 1, pp. 195–200 esp. p. 199.
39. AW to HW, 7 January 1799, WP 1/10, printed in *WSD*, vol. 1, pp. 166–7 with names suppressed.
40. AW to Mornington, 4 February 1799, *WSD*, vol. 1, pp. 191–3.
41. AW to Mornington, 29 January 1799, *WSD*, vol. 1, p. 187; Mornington to AW, 7 February 1799, WP 1/9.
42. AW to HW, 4 December 1798, *WSD*, vol. 1, pp. 138–9; Lushington, *Life of Harris*, p. 192.
43. Lushington, *Life of Harris*, pp. 294–8; [Theodore Hook], *The Life of General, the Right Honourable Sir David Baird* (1832), vol. 1, pp. 174–5 but his quotations are shown to be inaccurate by Lushington. Harris told Baird that Wellesley's appointment was made at the request

of Meer Allum, the Nizam's commander, but there is no other evidence for this, and it seems unlikely that an ally would attempt to specify such a point.

44. Typescript of a letter from Lt Patrick Brown, 1/1st Regiment Native Infantry to his father, Camp at Hyderabad, 20 February 1800, NAM Ms 6810–46.

45. 'Draft description of our march to Major-General St Leger', *WSD*, vol. 1, pp. 203–5. Of the bullocks, only about 60,000 were in the public service of Harris's army – still 20,000 more than Wellesley had thought would be needed: see above.

46. Quoted in Major H.M. Vibart, *The Military: History of the Madras Engineers and Pioneers* (1881), vol. 1, p. 295.

47. On the role played by Indian bankers and finance see Rajat Kanta Ray, 'Indian Society and the Establishment of British Supremacy, 1765–1818' (1998), pp. 517–18.

48. It is printed in Richard, Marquess Wellesley, *The Despatches, Minutes and Correspondence of the Marquess Wellesley* . . . (1836–40), vol. 1, pp. 453–4.

49. Letter from Lt. Patrick Brown to his father, 20 February 1800, NAM 6810–46.

50. AW to Mornington, 5 April 1799, *WSD*, vol. 1, p. 208.

51. Captain John Malcolm, 'An Abstract of the present State of Tippoo Sultaun', 16 July 1798, printed in Wellesley, *Despatches, Minutes*, vol. 1, pp. 651–60.

52. Harris to Robinson, 26 February 1799, Lushington, *Life of Harris*, p. 188; AW to Mornington, 5 April 1799, *WSD*, vol. 1, p. 208; Forrest, *Tiger of Mysore*, p. 277; see also Wilks, *Historical Sketches*, vol. 2, pp. 712–13.

53. AW to Mornington, 5 April 1799, *WSD*, vol. 1, p. 208.

54. Lushington, *Life of Harris*, pp. 193–4.

55. AW to Mornington, 25 March 1799, *WSD*, vol. 1, p. 206, cf AW to Mornington, 16 February 1799, *WSD*, vol. 1, pp. 193–5.

56. Captain John Malcolm, 'Journal of the Mysore Campaign', entries for 18, 22 March 1799, BL Add Ms 13,664 f 31.

57. Quoted in Lushington, *Life of Harris*, p. 200.

58. This account is based mainly on Captain Colin Mackenzie, 'Journal of Remarks and Observations made on the March from Hyderabad to Seringapatam and during the Mysore Campaign along with the Subsidiary Forces serving with the Nizam in 1798 and 1799', BL Add Ms 13,663 f 53–8 (27 March 1799); and Lushington, *Life of Harris*, pp. 200–4 for Harris and the main army.

59. Quoted in Vibart, *History of the Madras Engineers*, vol. 1, p. 297.

60. Fortescue, vol. 4, pt. 2, p. 732.

61. This was the explanation current among his former officers in Mysore a few years later. Dr Francis Buchanan, *A Journey from Madras through the Countries of Mysore, Canara, and Malabar* . . . (1807), vol. 3, pp. 423–4.

62. Harris's diary quoted in Lushington, *Life of Harris*, p. 207; AW to Mornington, 5 April 1799, *WSD*, vol. 1, pp. 206–9.

63. Malcolm, 'Journal', 1 and 2 April 1799, BL Add Ms 13,664 f 41–3.

64. Buchanan, *Journey from Madras*, vol. 1, pp. 62, 77.

65. Mackenzie, 'Journal', BL Add Ms 13,663 f 69, cf Lt Nuthall's impressions, quoted in Forrest, *Tiger of Mysore*, p. 282n.

66. Harris's General Order, printed in Lushington, *Life of Harris*, p. 209; AW to Mornington, 5 April 1799, *WSD*, vol. 1, pp. 206–9.

67. On Baird's attack see Lushington, *Life of Harris*, pp. 210–11; Hook, *Life of Baird*, vol. 2, pp. 189–90.

68. AW to Harris, 5 April 1799, *WD*, vol. 1, p. 23; Colin Mackenzie describes the reconnaissance, although as he says it was from the left of the picquets in front of the army, as much as 2,000 yards from the tope, it is generous to describe it as a 'reconnaissance': Mackenzie, 'Journal', BL Add Ms 13,663 f 71. Harris's diary, as quoted by Lushington, *Life of Harris*, p. 210 certainly suggests overconfidence.

69. Chetwood's account quoted in Albert Lee, *History of the 33rd Foot, Duke of Wellington's Regiment* (1922), pp. 167–8. It is not clear when this was written, but Chetwood died in 1805, so it cannot have been more than a few years after the event. Mackenzie, 'Journal', BL Add Ms 13,663 f 72–5 confirms this account and adds many details.

70. Figures for these casualties vary widely, including the number captured and later executed by Tipu. Those given are based on McGrigor as quoted in Brereton and Savory, *History*,

p. 100, and Forrest, *Tiger of Mysore*, p. 226 for those captured and executed. For AW being hit, see AW to Mornington, 18 April 1799, *WSD*, vol. 1, p. 209.

71. Both quotes from Harris's journal are printed in Lushington, *Life of Harris*, p. 214.
72. Rowley quoted in Vibart, *History of the Madras Engineers*, vol. 1, p. 300; [J. Blakiston], *Twelve Years' Military Adventure in three Quarters of the Globe . . .* (1829), vol. 1, p. 81.
73. [Richard] Bayly, *Diary of Colonel Bayly, 12th Regiment, 1796–1830* (1896), p. 88; though called a 'Diary', internal evidence makes clear that this was written decades after the events described.
74. Elers, *Memoirs*, pp. 100–1; C.H. Philips, *The Young Wellington in India* (1973), p. 18.
75. See Lushington, *Life of Harris*, pp. 215–18; Hook, *Life of Baird*, vol. 1, pp. 191–2 for the operation of the following morning.
76. Malcolm, 'Journal', 13 April 1799, BL Add Ms 13,664 f 49.
77. Lushington, *Life of Harris*, p. 229; Wilks, *Historical Sketches*, vol. 2, pp. 725–6n tells the story of the peculation and its long protracted sequel; AW to Mornington, 18 April 1799, *WSD*, vol. 1, pp. 209–10.
78. Lushington, *Life of Harris*, p. 229 quoting Harris's journal for 16 April.
79. Vibart, *History of the Madras Engineers*, vol. 1, pp. 305–6, 310; Lushington, *Life of Harris*, p. 230.
80. Vibart, *History of the Madras Engineers*, vol. 1, p. 309.
81. Ibid., pp. 311–12; Lushington, *Life of Harris*, pp. 230–5.
82. Vibart, *History of the Madras Engineers*, vol. 1, pp. 305–16 gives the most detailed and reliable account of the siege.
83. Lt Patrick Brown to his father, 20 February 1800, NAM Ms 6810–46.
84. Elers, *Memoirs*, p. 99.
85. Figures from Fortescue, vol. 4, pt. 2, p. 744n.
86. Lt.-Col. L.B. Oatts, *Proud Heritage. The Story of the Highland Light Infantry* (1952–63), vol. 2, p. 67.
87. Mornington to Harris, 7 July 1799; Lushington, *Life of Harris*, p. 320.
88. Elers, *Memoirs*, p. 103; Charles C.F. Greville, *The Greville Memoirs* (1888), vol. 1, p. 64, 24 December 1822, while confused, appears to confirm that the events at Seringapatam contributed to York's hostility towards Wellington.

7 The Mysore Years (1799–1802)

1. Forrest, *Tiger of Mysore*, p. 298.
2. AW to Harris, 5 May 1799, *WD*, vol. 1, pp. 27–8; see also the other letters of this date in ibid., pp. 26–7, and AW to Mornington, 8 May 1799, *WSD*, vol. 1, pp. 212–17.
3. AW to Harris, 10 am, 5 May 1799, *WD*, vol. 1, pp. 26–7; there is a graphic description of the destruction of the tigers by Major Price, one of the prize agents, quoted in Forrest, *Tiger of Mysore*, p. 216.
4. James Welsh, *Military Reminiscences* (1830), vol. 1, pp. 148–9; Forrest, *Tiger of Mysore*, plate 2b.
5. AW to Mornington, 19 August 1799, *WSD*, vol. 1, p. 290.
6. *WSD*, vol. 1, pp. 242–7, 223n for AW's share; Elers, *Memoirs*, p. 99; Harris to Mornington, 27 June 1799, Lushington, *Life of Harris*, p. 317.
7. Figures on prize money from *WSD*, vol. 1, p. 223; see Lushington, *Life of Harris*, pp. 330–6, 339 for Harris's court battle etc.
8. Mornington to AW, 30 May 1799, WP 1/13, printed in *WSD*, vol. 1, pp. 236–9n with an important paragraph suppressed.
9. AW to Mornington, 23 May, 2 and 3 June 1799, *WSD*, vol. 1, pp. 219–22, 234–5, 236–42.
10. Mornington to AW, 10 June 1799, WP 1/16, passage deleted in *WSD*, vol. 1, pp. 242–4n; see also Mornington to Dundas, 29 April 1800, Ingram, ed., *Two Views of British India*, pp. 257–61.
11. P.E. Roberts, *India Under Wellesley* (1929), pp. 69–76; see also Mornington to AW, 6 June 1800, WP 1/67.
12. A.S. Bennell, 'Wellesley's Settlement of Mysore, 1799' (1952), pp. 124–32 *passim*; Roberts, *India Under Wellesley*, pp. 63–9; Wilks, *Historical Sketches*, vol. 2, pp. 773–4, a note by the editor on the later history of Mysore.
13. Forrest, *Tiger of Mysore*, pp. 328–33.

14. AW to Mornington, 23 June 1799, WP 1/17, printed, but with an important paragraph suppressed, in *WSD*, vol. 1, pp. 250–1.
15. AW to Mornington, 8 May 1799, *WSD*, vol. 1, pp. 212–17.
16. AW to Mornington, Seringapatam, 24 July 1799, and AW to Lt.-Col. Doveton, Seringapatam, 24 December 1799, *WSD*, vol. 1, pp. 277–8, 419–21.
17. AW, 'Instructions for Captain Malcolm …' (incl. additional instructions for Capt. Campbell), 27 August 1799; AW to Malcolm, 10 September 1799, *WD*, vol. 1 pp. 31–2, 32–4; AW to Lt.-Col. Dalrymple, 11 September 1799, *WSD*, vol. 1, p. 321; AW to Close, 2 October 1800, *WD*, vol. 1 pp. 200–3 on the treatment of civilians. See also instructions to AW from Agnew (writing on behalf of Harris), 24 August 1799, *WSD*, vol. 1, pp. 294–6n. Captain Malcolm was not the Captain John Malcolm who was returning to Hyderabad with Meer Allum, but an officer in the Bengal army.
18. AW to Col Sherbrooke, 29 August 1799, *WSD*, vol. 1, pp. 299–300.
19. AW to Uhthoff, 19 November 1799, *WSD*, vol. 1, pp. 390–2; see also AW to Maj. Macaulay, 1 October 1799, ibid., pp. 344–5 on the devastation caused, and AW to Uhthoff, 12 October 1799, ibid., pp. 358–9 on the return of prisoners.
20. AW to Lt.-Col. Agnew, 21 November 1799, *WSD*, vol. 1, pp. 392–3.
21. AW to Sherbrooke, 15 October 1799, in A. Patchett Martin, *Life and Letters of the Right Honourable Robert Lowe, Viscount Sherbrooke …* (1893), vol. 2, pp. 545–6.
22. AW to Harris, 4 December 1799, *WD*, vol. 1, p. 40.
23. AW to Webbe, 2 December 1799, *WSD*, vol. 1, p. 403; AW to Trevor, 20 February 1800, *WD*, vol. 1, p. 69.
24. AW to Maj.-Gen. Sydenham, 16 January 1800, *WSD*, vol. 1, pp. 432–6; AW to Close, 3 February 1800, *WD*, vol. 1, pp. 60–2.
25. AW to the Adjutant-General, 18 February 1800, *WSD*, vol. 1, pp. 451–5.
26. AW to the Secretary of Government, 20 March 1800, *WD*, vol. 2, pp. 1568–9. There is an interesting discussion of this incident which places it in a much wider context in D. George Boyce, 'From Assaye to the *Assaye*: Reflections on British Government, Force, and Moral Authority in India' (1999), pp. 643–8 esp. 648–9.
27. On Dhoondiah's background see G.S. Sardesai, *New History of the Marathas'* ([1958]), vol. 3 p. 361.
28. On AW's campaign against Dhoondiah Waugh see Huw J. Davies, 'Wellington's First Command: The Political and Military Campaign Against Dhoondiah Vagh, February–September 1800' (2010); Fortescue, vol. 4, pt. 2, pp. 753–9; and Randolph G.S. Cooper, 'New Light on Arthur Wellesley's Command-Apprenticeship in India: The Dhoondiah Waugh Campaign of 1800 Reconsidered' (1990), pp. 81–7.
29. Webbe to AW, 24 May 1799, *WD*, vol. 1, pp. 104–5n.
30. Mornington to AW, 13 May 1800, *WD*, vol. 1, pp. 103–4n, copy in WP 1/67 marked 'Most Private and Secret'.
31. AW to Webbe and Lord Clive, 29 May 1800, *WD*, vol. 1, pp. 103–4, 104–5 (two letters).
32. AW to Close, 11 July 1800, *WD*, vol. 1, p. 141.
33. AW to Close, 16 July 1800, *WD*, vol. 1, pp. 143–4.
34. AW to Close, 8 and 17 August 1800, *WD*, vol. 1, pp. 161–2, 167.
35. J. Colebrooke to ?, 10 September 1800, BL OIOC Ms Eur B 401. It is interesting to note the details of this account differ from those given by AW who says that all four regiments of cavalry were formed in a single line: AW to the Adjutant-General, 10 September 1800, *WD*, vol. 1, pp. 177–9.
36. AW to Mornington, 29 May 1800, *WD*, vol. 1, pp. 105–7. On Salabut Khan see note by Gurwood in ibid., p. 178n and AW to Purneah, 2 March 1805, *WD*, vol. 2, pp. 1437–8.
37. Lord Wellesley to AW, 'Private & Secret', 5 November 1800, WP 1/58; AW to Clive, 21 November 1800, *WSD*, vol. 1, p. 275 (his initial annoyance).
38. Parkinson, *War in Eastern Seas*, pp. 156–9. When AW met Mr Stokes in Bombay he came to share the admiral's doubts about him and the projected attack: AW to HW, 26 May 1801, *WSD*, vol. 2, pp. 407–11. AW had warned Mornington of the independence of the British admiral as early as 1797: AW to Mornington, 20 May 1797, ibid., vol. 1, pp. 6–8.
39. Hook, *Life of Baird*, vol. 1, pp. 253–8, Lord Wellesley to AW, 7 January 1801, *WSD*, vol. 2, pp. 323–4n; see also Braithwaite to AW, 10 May 1801, *WSD*, vol. 2, pp. 387–90n.
40. AW to Mornington, 23 June 1799, *WSD*, vol. 1, pp. 250–1.

41. Dundas to Lord Wellesley, 6 October 1800, WP 1/67.
42. AW to Capt. Pulteney Malcolm, 7 February 1801, WP 3/2/16, p. 22; Capt. P. Malcolm to AW, 7 February 1801, *WSD*, vol. 2, p. 337n; AW to Admiral Rainier, 14 February 1801, WP 3/2/16, p. 23; AW to [Frederick North], 18 February 1801, *WD*, vol. 1, pp. 236–7; Frederick North to AW, 17 and 20 February 1801, WP 1/71 (two letters). W.A.C. Halliwell, 'The Passage to Bombay, 1801' (1996), pp. 103, 109–11, and Jac Weller, *Wellington in India* (1972), pp. 108–9, both stress the magnitude of the responsibility which AW took upon himself in acting on Dundas's orders; but these instructions were so explicit and forthright, and time was so pressing, that the responsibility for *not* acting upon them would have been even greater.
43. AW to HW, Bombay, 25 March 1801, *WD*, vol. 1, pp. 242–3.
44. AW to Col. Champagné, Bombay, 11 April 1801, WP 3/2/16 – printed with this passage deleted in *WD*, vol. 1, pp. 251–2; see also Stanhope, *Notes of Conversations*, 16 October 1837, p. 103, and Longford, p. 75n. AW to Close, Bombay, 11 April 1801, *WD*, vol. 1, p. 251 ('*laudable*' quote).
45. Mackesy, *British Victory in Egypt*, pp. 199–201.
46. AW to HW, 23 March 1801, *WD*, vol. 1, pp. 241–2 (all the quotes); see also same to same, 31 March 1801, ibid., pp. 244–5, and AW to Lord Wellesley, 16 April 1801, *WSD*, vol. 2, pp. 362–5, and letters of 21, 22, 25 and 31 March, which have not survived, but which are referred to in HW to AW, 22 April 1801, *WSD*, vol. 2, pp. 364–5n.
47. HW to AW, 'Private', 18 May 1801, WP 1/78; the letter of 18 April referred to is probably that printed in *WSD*, vol. 2, pp. 362–5 under the date of 16 April.
48. Elers, *Memoirs*, p. 116.
49. AW to HW, 26 May 1801, *WSD*, vol. 2, pp. 407–11.
50. Ibid.
51. AW to HW, 26 May, 8 July (the quote) and 10 October 1801, *WSD*, vol. 2, pp. 407–11, 501–3, 570–5.
52. Elers, *Memoirs*, p. 122. Elers says that AW missed out by only five or six places, but in fact he was at least twenty below the cut-off point.
53. Dogs: GO, 24 July 1802, *WD*, vol. 1, p. 290n; corruption: AW to Clive, 23 October 1801, *WSD*, vol. 2, p. 592; protection for civilians: GOs, 6 September 1802 and 22 July 1801, *WD*, vol. 1, pp. 291 and 268; refuses to let court-martial minimise offence: AW to Close, 11 and 12 June 1801, and to the Commander-in-Chief, Madras, 12 June 1801, all in *WD*, vol. 1, pp. 258–60.
54. AW to the Deputy Adjutant-General, 19 March 1802, *WSD*, vol. 3, pp. 115–16; AW to Major Elliott, 15 May 1802, ibid., pp. 184–6; Brereton and Savory, *History*, pp. 104–5.
55. AW to Webbe, 4 October 1801, WP 1/98; private information from Ron McGuigan based on the *Army List* and the *London Gazette* which corrects the account in Brereton and Savory, *History*, p. 105.
56. John Keay, *The Great Arc. The Dramatic Tale of how India was Mapped and Everest was Named* (2000), pp. 23–4; Matthew H. Edney, *Mapping an Empire. The Geographical Construction of British India, 1765–1843* (1997), p. 157; W.C. Mackenzie, *Colonel Colin Mackenzie, 1st Surveyor-General of India* (1952), pp. 78–84.
57. AW to Lt.-Col. Robertson, 12 June 1801, *WSD*, vol. 2, pp. 438–9.
58. Elers, *Memoirs*, pp. 124, 120–1.
59. AW to HW, 8 July 1801, *WSD*, vol. 2, pp. 501–3.
60. Elers, *Memoirs*, pp. 122–4.
61. Ibid., p. 144.
62. Ibid., p. 126. Isabella Freese had been born in 1784 and had been married at the age of sixteen: John Orrok, *Letters of Captain John Orrok* (2008), p. 64. It is possible that the relationship was platonic (just as Harriet Arbuthnot was generally, although almost certainly wrongly, supposed to be Wellington's mistress many years later), but there seems little reason to question the obvious interpretation of Elers's account.
63. Elers, *Memoirs*, pp. 125–6; Longford, p. 102, and Longford, *Wellington. Pillar of State* (1972), p. 82. The dates are compatible with Arthur Wellesley being the father of Arthur Freese, although, of course, this can neither be proven nor disproven. The whole story of the aunt who died may have been a polite fiction, but it may also have been true.
64. Longford, pp. 102, 103; Orrok, *Letters*, p. 70. The Duke of Wellington now has no fewer than three portraits of Isabella Freese, although it is possible that one or two of these may

have come to the family later (information from Jane Branfield, archivist at Stratfield Saye, 15 September 2012).

65. *Don Juan*, Canto I, stanza 63; Longford, pp. 100–1.
66. AW to Capt Wilks, 14 June 1801, *WSD*, vol. 2, pp. 443–4.
67. AW to Major Macaulay, 22 December 1801, *WSD*, vol. 3, pp. 14–16.
68. AW to Webbe, 22 March 1802, *WSD*, vol. 3, pp. 119–20. The Preliminaries of the Peace of Amiens were signed on 1 October 1801; the full treaty on 25 March 1802.
69. *WSD*, vol. 3, pp. 36–8n; Roberts, *India Under Wellesley*, p. 178. Pagodas were worth approximately 8s meaning that AW's table allowance was reduced from about £240 to £160 per month.
70. AW to HW, 10 October 1801, and AW to Close, 10 October 1801, *WSD*, vol. 2, pp. 570–5, 575–7.

8 The Restoration of the Peshwa (1802–03)

1. See J.G. Duff, *A History of the Marathas* (1826), vol. 2, pp. 320–7 for the Gwaikar of Baroda and his negotiations with the British.
2. Sardesai, *New History of the Marathas*, vol. 3, pp. 333–7; Duff, *History of the Marathas*, vol. 2, pp. 273–4.
3. Duff, *History of the Marathas*, vol. 2, pp. 281–4, 295–300.
4. Ibid.
5. Sardesai, *New History of the Marathas*, vol. 3, p. 356.
6. Ibid.
7. Sindia and Baji Rao agreed to cooperate with the British in the campaign against Dhoondiah, who was a nuisance to everyone. The Peshwa told the southern lords, or jagirdars, to cooperate with Wellesley, and Sindia offered the support of one of his brigades in Poona, although Dhoondiah was defeated before it could take the field. Col Palmer to AW, Poona, 1 September 1800; Robert Sutherland to Capt Brownrigg (two senior officers in Sindia's army), 28 August 1800, both in WP 1/53.
8. Lord Wellesley to Clive, 23 August 1800, Wellesley, *Despatches, Minutes*, vol. 2, pp. 367–70; Clive to AW, 9 September 1800, WP 1/53; AW to Close, 12 September 1800, *WD*, vol. 1, p. 184.
9. AW to Close, 27 September 1800, *WD*, vol. 1, pp. 197–8.
10. AW to Munro, 20 August 1800, *WD* vol. 1, pp. 168–70.
11. Kirkpatrick to AW, 'Private', 28 October 1800; T. Sydenham to AW, 'Private', 29 October 1800, both WP 1/57; see also T. Sydenham to AW, 7 November 1800, *WSD*, vol. 2, pp. 268–71n.
12. Close to AW, 8 October 1800, WP 1/56.
13. AW to Close, 2 October 1800, *WD*, vol. 1, pp. 200–3.
14. AW to Close, 12 November 1800, WP 3/2/15, pp. 28ff, printed in *WSD*, vol. 2, pp. 257–8 with the names of Kirkpatrick and Sydenham suppressed.
15. AW to Kirkpatrick, 10 November 1800, *WSD*, vol. 2, pp. 254–6 – there is a draft of this letter in WP 3/2/15, pp. 23–6.
16. Sardesai, *New History of the Marathas*, vol. 3, pp. 363–7; Pratul Chandra Gupta, *Baji Rao II and the East India Company, 1796–1818* (1964), pp. 27–8.
17. Sardesai, *New History of the Marathas*, vol. 3, pp. 369–73; Pranjal Kumar Bhattacharyya, *British Residents at Poona, 1786–1818* (1984), pp. 178–9; Duff, *History of the Marathas*, vol. 2, pp. 312–13.
18. Sardesai, *New History of the Marathas*, vol. 3, p. 371.
19. Ibid., pp. 373–4; Bhattacharyya, *British Residents at Poona*, pp. 179–81; Gupta, *Baji Rao II*, pp. 37–9.
20. Sardesai, *New History of the Marathas*, vol. 3, p. 379 says that Holkar could have captured Baji Rao, but refrained from doing so; however this is contradicted by Bhattacharyya, *British Residents at Poona*, p. 182 and A.S. Bennell, *The Making of Arthur Wellesley* (1997), pp. 10, 18.
21. Bennell, *Making of Arthur Wellesley*, pp. 10–15, 18.
22. Ibid., pp. 16–26.
23. Webbe to AW, 9 November 1802, and same to same, 10 November 1802, *WSD*, vol. 3, p. 381n and WP 1/128.

24. AW to Webbe, 12 November 1802, *WSD*, vol. 3, pp. 381–2.

25. Webbe to AW, 16 November 1802, WP 1/128.

26. AW to Stuart, 1 December 1802, *WSD*, vol. 3, pp. 442–3; Webbe to AW, 24 November 1802, WP 1/129; letters from Stuart to AW of 19, 22, 23, 27 and 30 November 1802 in WP 1/129.

27. AW to Webbe, 1 December 1802, *WSD*, vol. 3, pp. 444–5; Webbe to AW, 7 December 1802 and Stuart to AW, 7 December 1802, both in WP 1/131; AW to Malcolm, 11 December 1802, *WD*, vol. 1, pp. 316–17 (also in *WSD*, vol. 3, pp. 460–1).

28. 'Memorandum upon Operations in Marhatta Territory', [September 1801], *WD*, vol. 1, pp. 295–300.

29. AW to Close, 22 February 1803, *WD*, vol. 1, pp. 333–4.

30. AW to Stuart, 2 December 1802, WP 1/133; this letter is partly printed, incl. the passage quoted, in *WSD*, vol. 3, pp. 445–6.

31. AW to Stuart, 27 November 1802, *WSD*, vol. 3, pp. 431–6.

32. Stuart to AW, 30 November 1802, WP 1/129; a copy of Goklah's application (translated into English) is in WP 1/130; AW to Stuart, 2 December 1802, WP 1/133; same to same, 4 December 1802, *WD*, vol. 1, pp. 311–13; Stuart to AW, 7 December 1802, WP 1/131 (saying that he will refer Goklah's application to Lord Clive); Webbe to AW, 7 December 1802, WP 1/131.

33. Webbe to AW, 25 October 1802, WP 1/126.

34. Webbe to AW, 28 December 1802, WP 1/132; AW to Webbe, 1 January 1803, *WSD*, vol. 3, pp. 507–10; Webbe to AW, 11 December 1802, WP 1/131; Stuart to AW, 20 December 1802, WP 1/132.

35. Stuart to AW, 13 January 1803, enclosing extract of instructions from Stuart to Baird, 11 January 1803, WP 1/135; AW to Baird, 26 January 1803 (two letters), *WSD*, vol. 3, pp. 557–60, 560–1.

36. 'Memorandum upon the draught bullocks with the Army' by AW, 15 February 1803, *WSD*, vol. 4, pp. 1–6; Stuart to AW, 17 February 1803, WP 3/3/86 f 25–6; AW to Close, 22 February 1803, *WD*, vol. 1, pp. 333–4.

37. Malcolm to AW, 'Private', 7 December 1802, and Webbe to AW, 11 December 1802, both in WP 1/131; Webbe to AW, 19 December 1802, and enclosure: copy of Webbe to Close, 19 December 1802, WP 1/132; Lord Wellesley to Clive, 'Private', 7 January 1803, Wellesley, *Despatches, Minutes*, vol. 3, pp. 27–8; B. Sydenham to AW, 'Private', 14 January 1803, WP 3/3/5 f 2–6.

38. Lord Wellesley to Clive, 'Secret – Official', 2 February 1803, Wellesley, *Despatches, Minutes*, vol. 3, pp. 41–5.

39. Webbe mentions both the state of affairs at home and the probability of renewed war with France as factors that convinced him that Lord Wellesley's policy was correct. Webbe to AW, 10 March 1803, WP 3/3/93 f 6; see also Stuart to AW, 3 May 1803, in Wellington, *The Maratha War Papers of Arthur Wellesley, January to December 1803* (1998), pp. 78–9 on the French.

40. AW to Stuart, 3 March 1803, *WD*, vol. 1, p. 338.

41. Stuart to AW, 3 March 1803, WP 3/3/87 f 49–50 partly printed in Wellington, *Maratha War Papers*, p. 32.

42. AW to Malcolm, 11 December 1802, *WD*, vol. 1, pp. 316–17.

43. Stuart to AW, nd [c. 24 March 1803], in Wellington, *Maratha War Papers*, pp. 39–40; Webbe to AW, 10 March 1803, WP 3/3/93 f 6 admits that the orders were 'such as not to be very acceptable to the General himself'.

44. Stuart to AW, 10 March 1803, in Wellington, *Maratha War Papers*, pp. 35–6; Hook, *Life of Baird*, vol. 2, pp. 80–1; see also Harness, *Trusty and Well-Beloved*, p. 175.

45. Return in *WD*, vol. 1, p. 343n. The artillery consisted of four iron 12-pounders, two brass 12-pounders, sixteen 6-pounders, four galloper 6-pounders, 'besides the guns attached to the cavalry' (probably four 3-pounders) giving a total of, probably, thirty guns: ibid., p. 343n. See also Weller, *Wellington in India*, pp. 140–2.

46. [Blakiston], *Twelve Years' Military Adventure*, vol. 1, p. 84; AW to Lord Wellesley, 2 November 1803 and 9 March 1804, *WD*, vol. 2, pp. 825–6 and 1087–90; see also AW to Close, 3 July 1800, *WSD*, vol. 2, pp. 47–8.

47. Stuart to AW, 9 March 1803, *WD*, vol. 1, pp. 345–7.

48. Webbe to AW, 10 March 1803, WP 3/3/93 f 6.

49. General Order, 11 March 1803, *WD*, vol. 1, p. 349n.

50. [Blakiston], *Twelve Years' Military Adventure*, vol. 1, p. 97; Harness, *Trusty and Well-Beloved*, p. 179. One hundred degrees Fahrenheit is approximately 37.8 degrees Celsius.
51. Harness, *Trusty and Well-Beloved*, pp. 175–6.
52. Maxwell, *Life of Wellington*, vol. 1, pp. 72–3, quoting the De Ros manuscript of conversations with Wellington, 1836–40.
53. [Blakiston], *Twelve Years' Military Adventure*, vol. 1, pp. 102–6, quote on p. 106.
54. AW to Close, 16 March 1803, *WD*, vol. 1, pp. 357–9.
55. AW to Stuart, 29 March 1803, *WD*, vol. 1, pp. 369–71; AW to Close, 16 April 1803, ibid., p. 399; see also Close to AW, 9 April 1803, Wellington, *Maratha War Papers*, pp. 43–4.
56. Close to AW, 15 March 1803, Wellington, *Maratha War Papers*, pp. 37–8.
57. AW to Stuart, 20 March 1803, *WD*, vol. 1, pp. 361–3; see also Clive to Stuart, 7 March 1803, ibid., p. 342 on Malcolm's position and Kaye, *Life of Malcolm*, vol. 1, pp. 212–13.
58. Bennell, *Making of Arthur Wellesley*, pp. 32–4, 44–9.
59. AW to Stevenson, 28 April 1803, *WD*, vol. 1, pp. 416–17; Close to AW, 2 April 1803, Wellington, *Maratha War Papers*, pp. 42–3.
60. AW to Close, 23 March 1803, *WD*, vol. 1, pp. 364–5 asking for an overture to Holkar; Close to AW, 9 April 1803, Wellington, *Maratha War Papers*, pp. 43–4 on the Peshwa's demands for money; AW to Close, 11 and 23 April 1803, *WD*, vol. 1, pp. 388–90 and 408, on the Peshwa's refusal to conciliate his own jagirdars; Close to AW, 27 and 29 April 1803, Wellington, *Maratha War Papers*, pp. 69–70, 71–2 on the difficulty of dealing with the Peshwa.
61. AW to Close, 11 April 1803, *WD*, vol. 1, pp. 388–90.
62. AW to Col Stevenson, 23 April 1803, *WD*, vol. 1, pp. 407–8; see also Close to AW, 9 April 1803, Wellington, *Maratha War Papers* pp. 43–4; AW to the Governor-General, 15 April 1803, *WD*, vol. 1, pp. 396–9, and AW to Close, 16 April 1803, ibid., p. 399.
63. Close to AW, 21 April 1803, Wellington, *Maratha War Papers*, pp. 53–4 (plundered to last rag); same to same, 17 April 1803, ibid., p. 51 (Mir Khan); AW to Close, 20 April 1803 and to Kirkpatrick, 20 April 1803, *WD*, vol. 1, p. 403 (both the forced march); cf Weller, *Wellington in India*, p. 145, which claims that AW marched sixty miles in thirty-two hours.
64. AW to Stuart, 21 April 1803, *WD*, vol. 1, pp. 403–4.
65. AW to the Governor-General, 21 April 1803, *WD*, vol. 1, pp. 404–6; AW to Close, 25 April 1803, *WD*, vol. 1, pp. 410–11; Close to AW, 30 April 1803, Wellington, *Maratha War Papers*, pp. 73–4; Close to AW, 23 June 1803, ibid., pp. 136–7; AW to Amrit Rao, 16 July 1803, *WD*, vol. 1, pp. 557–8. There is a good account of the negotiations with Amrit Rao, and of his later life, in Gupta, *Baji Rao II*, pp. 72–4.
66. Close to AW, 27 April 1803, Wellington, *Maratha War Papers*, pp. 69–70; see also, same to same, 29 April 1803, ibid., pp. 71–2.
67. Edmonstone to Close, 7 May 1803, ibid., pp. 99–100.

9 The Maratha War (1803)

1. On the ambitions of the Raja of Berar see AW to Close, 14 July 1803, and AW to Malcolm, 6 September 1803, *WD*, vol. 1, pp. 552–4, 684–5; and Close to the Governor-General, 25 June 1803, and Collins to AW, 26 July 1803, Wellington, *Maratha War Papers*, pp. 140, 185.
2. For an account of the negotiations see Bennell, *Making of Arthur Wellesley*, pp. 32–4, 47–67 and the related correspondence printed in *WSD*, vol. 4, and Wellington, *Maratha War Papers*.
3. 'Memorandum upon Operations in Marhatta Territory' by AW, [September 1801], *WD*, vol. 1, pp. 295–301. See also J.N.L. Baker, 'Some Geographical Factors in the Campaigns of Assaye and Argaon' (1929), p. 45n which points out that this observation had already been made by Rennell in his account of the campaigns of 1790 and 1791.
4. J. Pemble, 'Resources and Techniques in the Second Maratha War, 1803' (1976), pp. 375–403 contains much excellent material, although I do not find his overarching argument convincing. See also G.J. Bryant, 'Indigenous Mercenaries in the Service of European Imperialists: The Case of the Sepoys in the Early British Indian Army, 1750–1800' (2000), pp. 1–28 for a good account of the improvements in the Company's army in the late eighteenth century.
5. See below, pp. 130–1. Maratha figures based on Collins to AW, 25 July 1803, *WD*, vol. 1, p. 586n. Collins does not give a figure for the Maratha artillerymen, which adds to the already considerable uncertainty inherent in these figures. The figure of almost 40,000 operating

under Wellesley and Stevenson includes 16,000 Hyderabad troops, which is almost certainly a substantial overestimation.

6. AW's worries about his cattle and supplies began in early June and lasted until early July, and fill many letters. See, for example, AW to Close, 9, 18, 19 and 26 June 1803 in *WD*, vol. 1, pp. 493–4, 507–8, 510–11, 530–1. For his consequent loss of confidence see his letters to Close of 8, 18 and 25 June 1803 in ibid., pp. 490–2, 507–8 and 527–9. Some authorities have rather misunderstood the implicit criticism of Lord Wellesley's policy contained in these letters, by not connecting it to the logistical problems which were unnerving AW.

7. Memorandum by Malcolm, 30 June 1803, Wellington, *Maratha War Papers*, pp. 150–1 regards Baji Rao's flight and a settlement with Amrit Rao as no bad thing. Close to AW, 24 June 1803, ibid., p. 138 expresses his extreme irritation with Baji Rao. Lord Wellesley to AW, 27 June 1803, quoted in Bennell, *Making of Arthur Wellesley*, p. 95, considers employing Amrit Rao as head of the Peshwa's government, but warns against letting Baji Rao escape; and this is reinforced in Shawe to Malcolm, 'Most Secret and Private', 29 July 1803, WP 3/3/5 f 39 – see also loc. cit. f 42–50 for instructions on what to do if Baji Rao does manage to escape.

8. AW to the Governor-General, 10 May and 4 June 1803, *WD*, vol. 1, pp. 438, 481–3; Lord Wellesley to AW, 26 and 27 June 1803, Wellesley, *Despatches, Minutes*, vol. 3, pp. 149–53, 153–8; Bennell, *Making of Arthur Wellesley*, pp. 60–1; Enid M. Fuhr, 'Strategy and Diplomacy in British India under Marquis Wellesley' (1994), p. 16; W.M. Torrens, *The Marquess Wellesley. Architect of Empire* (1880), pp. 277–8. It is clear from Torrens that the alleged constitutional impropriety related to Lord Wellesley's neglect of his council, rather than the actual delegation of powers to Arthur Wellesley; and that the same criticism could have been made with equal force if Lord Wellesley had been on the spot and acted in person. Most of AW's letters to Collins are printed in *WSD*, vol. 4.

9. AW to Sindia, 6 August 1803, *WD*, vol. 1, pp. 616–17.

10. On the changes to the army see Weller, *Wellington in India*, pp. 152, 167; on the strength, see *WD*, vol. 1, pp. 631n and 725n; AW's praise for the Mysore light cavalry is in AW to Lake, 29 July 1803, *WD*, vol. 1, pp. 594–5; see also AW to the Governor-General, 9 March 1804, *WD*, vol. 2, pp. 1087–90.

11. *WD*, vol. 1, pp. 631n; AW to Stuart, 8 September 1803, ibid., pp. 692–3.

12. AW to Close, 30 June 1803, AW to Stevenson, 18 July 1803, and AW to Stuart, 30 July 1803, *WD*, vol. 1, pp. 536–7, 563–4, 597–9 all make this point.

13. Collins to AW, 25 July 1803, *WD*, vol. 1, p. 586n.

14. Stuart to the Governor-General, 8 August 1803, *WD*, vol. 1, pp. 629–30n.

15. AW to the Governor-General, 24 July 1803, *WD*, vol. 1, pp. 572–6; see also AW to Lake, 29 July 1803, ibid., pp. 594–5.

16. Proclamation, camp near Ahmednuggar, 7 August 1803, *WD*, vol. 1, p. 624.

17. Quoted in Maj. H. Davidson, *History and Services of the 78th Highlanders* (1901), vol. 1, p. 50n.

18. Capt. James Fraser to Dr A. Mackenzie, 'Camp before Amednugur', 10 August 1803, printed in Davidson, *History and Services of the 78th Highlanders*, pp. 146–7.

19. Welsh, *Military Reminiscences*, vol. 1, p. 164.

20. [Blakiston], *Twelve Years' Military Adventure*, vol. 1, pp. 140–1; see also Welsh, *Military Reminiscences*, vol. 1, p. 164, and AW's General Order, 12 August 1803, *WD*, vol. 1, p. 627n.

21. The *ODNB* gives most of the biographical details; S.G.P. Ward, *Wellington's Headquarters* (1957), pp. 38, 158; Wellington to Shawe, 6 March 1805, *WD*, vol. 2, pp. 1446–7 recommends Campbell. This Colin Campbell should not be confused with his younger namesake, later Lord Clyde, who ended his active career in India.

22. Sir T.E. Colebrooke, *Life of the Honourable Mountstart Elphinstone* (1884), vol. 1, pp. 1–7. Elphinstone turned twenty-four on 6 October 1803.

23. Elphinstone to Edward Strachey, 15 November 1803, Colebrooke, *Life of Elphinstone*, vol. 1, pp. 84–5.

24. Elphinstone to Strachey, 22–23 August 1803, Colebrooke, *Life of Elphinstone*, vol. 1, pp. 52–3.

25. [Blakiston], *Twelve Years' Military Adventure*, vol. 1, pp. 144–5.

26. AW to Stevenson, 17 and 20 August 1803, *WD*, vol. 1, pp. 640, 646.

27. See Brig. K.G. Pitre, *Second Anglo-Maratha War, 1802–1805* (1990), pp. 75–6 for an excellent discussion of why it 'would have been logistically and strategically impossible to conduct this campaign with a single force'.

28. Letter from Colin Campbell describing the battle printed in *WSD*, vol. 4, pp. 184–7n; 'Memorandum on the Battle of Assye [*sic*]' by AW, nd, *WD*, vol. 1, pp. 728–30; letter from Elphinstone, dated 27 September 1803, in Colebrooke, *Life of Elphinstone*, vol. 1, p. 65. The 'Kaitna' should properly be spelt 'Kailna', but the former seems too well established to change. It is also sometimes given as the 'Kistna' but this is quite a different river, many miles to the south.
29. 'Memorandum on the Battle of Assye [*sic*]' by AW, nd, *WD*, vol. 1, pp. 728–30.
30. Fortescue, vol. 5, p. 24n: this is a higher figure than the '5,000 and odd' which AW told Elphinstone (Colebrooke, *Life of Elphinstone*, vol. 1, p. 69) or the even lower figures sometimes given; but Fortescue's calculations appear well founded and convincing.
31. Pitre, *Second Anglo-Maratha War*, p. 61; Randolf G.S. Cooper, 'Wellington and the Marathas in 1803' (1989), pp. 35, 37–8.
32. Colebrooke, *Life of Elphinstone*, vol. 1, p. 87.
33. Letter from Colin Campbell describing the battle printed in *WSD*, vol. 4, pp. 184–7n; Campbell does not mention being wounded in this letter, and makes clear that he did not leave the field.
34. [Blakiston], *Twelve Years' Military Adventure*, vol. 1, pp. 163–4.
35. Elphinstone to Strachey, 14 October 1803, Colebrooke, *Life of Elphinstone*, vol. 1, p. 80; see also 'Memorandum on the Battle of Assye [*sic*]' by AW, nd, *WD*, vol. 1, pp. 728–30 and AW to Munro, 1 November 1803, ibid., vol. 2, pp. 820–3.
36. Oatts, *Proud Heritage*, vol. 2, p. 93.
37. It is odd, but apparently correct, that Campbell's relations were in the 74th, while he had been in the 78th before joining AW's staff. Oatts, *Proud Heritage*, vol. 2, p. 96 for casualties.
38. Maxwell's charge is one of the harder incidents of the day to reconstruct. This account is based on an anonymous eyewitness account in BL OIOC Eur B 401, and a letter from an unknown cavalry officer printed in Wellington, *Maratha War Papers*, p. 288. See also Col. John Biddulph, *The Nineteenth and their Times* ... (1899), pp. 142–3, map and caption in Colebrooke, *Life of Elphinstone*, vol. 1, pp. 69–71 and also ibid., pp. 67–8.
39. Campbell in *WSD*, vol. 4, pp. 184–7; [Blakiston], *Twelve Years' Military Adventure*, vol. 1, pp. 165–5; Davidson, *History and Services of the 78th Highlanders*, vol. 1, pp. 55–6; see also Colebrooke, *Life of Elphinstone*, vol. 1, p. 67.
40. [Blakiston], *Twelve Years' Military Adventure*, vol. 1, p. 167.
41. AW to HW, 3 October 1803 (the quote); AW to Major Malcolm, 26 September 1803, *WD*, vol. 1, pp. 755, 731; Kaye, *Life of Malcolm*, vol. 1, p. 233n.
42. Biddulph, *The Nineteenth and their Times*, p. 145 quoting a manuscript note in the India Office Library.
43. Elphinstone to Strachey, 27 September 1803, Colebrooke, *Life of Elphinstone*, vol. 1, p. 68.
44. Rogers, *Reminiscences and Table-talk of Samuel Rogers*, 2–3 October 1824, pp. 251–2.
45. I have followed Fortescue and other authorities in preferring the casualty return printed in Wellesley, *Despatches, Minutes*, vol. 3, p. 669 and, in greater detail, in Major William Thorn, *Memoir of the War in India conducted by General Lord Lake ... and Major-General Sir Arthur Wellesley ...* (1818), p. 280, rather than that printed in *WD*, vol. 1, p. 725n which gives a much higher total (2,057 casualties in all). There are significant discrepancies in detail between the two returns which make them difficult or impossible to reconcile. The return in Wellesley, *Despatches, Minutes*, and Thorn gains credibility by naming all the British officers it lists as killed or wounded; Thorn, indeed, gives a highly detailed, and apparently official, breakdown of the losses for each individual unit. For the losses of the 74th see Oatts, *Proud Heritage*, vol. 2, p. 96; for those of the 78th see Davidson, *History and Services of the 78th Highlanders*, vol. 1, p. 58; for the 19th Light Dragoons, Biddulph, *The Nineteenth and their Times*, p. 144.
46. AW to Malcolm, 28 September 1803, *WD*, vol. 1, p. 739.
47. Ibid.
48. [Blakiston], *Twelve Years' Military Adventure*, vol. 1, p. 175; AW to Stuart, 29 September 1803, *WD*, vol. 1, pp. 740–1 gives the numbers of guns and standards taken.
49. Letter from Colin Campbell describing the battle printed in *WSD*, vol. 4, pp. 184–7n.
50. Elphinstone to John Adam, nd, Colebrooke, *Life of Elphinstone*, vol. 1, pp. 71–2.
51. [Blakiston], *Twelve Years' Military Adventure*, vol. 1, pp. 164–5.
52. Elphinstone to Strachey, 9 October 1803, Colebrooke, *Life of Elphinstone*, vol. 1, p. 76. Elphinstone says that two regiments of Native Cavalry misbehaved, and Biddulph, *The Nineteenth and their Times*, p. 145, agrees; but Biddulph says that the 4th Native Cavalry

performed well, supporting the 19th Light Dragoons, while Elphinstone and the anonymous memorandum in BL OIOC Eur B 401 both say that the 7th Native Cavalry accompanied Wellesley and the 78th when they moved to retake the guns in the final stage of the battle. The most likely explanation is that either Biddulph or Elphinstone has mistaken the number of the regiment, but it is possible that two of the three regiments of Madras cavalry played their part in the battle. However it should be noted that Major R.J. Huddlestone commanded the 7th Native Cavalry – see Weller, *Wellington in India*, p. 205n.

53. AW to Malcolm, 26 September 1803, *WD*, vol. 1, p. 731; AW to the governor of Bombay, 27 September 1803, *WD*, vol. 1, pp. 735–6; General Order, 29 September 1803, *WD*, vol. 1, p. 740n; unpublished diary of Jasper Nicolls quoted in Davidson, *History and Services of the 78th Highlanders*, p. 60n on the wine.

54. Stevenson to AW, 19 and 21 October 1803, Wellington, *Maratha War Papers*, pp. 339–40, 342–4; AW to Malcolm, 22 October 1803, *WD*, vol. 1, p. 799.

55. Welsh, *Military Reminiscences*, vol. 1, pp. 185–8; AW to the Governor-General, 11 and 24 November 1803, *WD*, vol. 2, pp. 853–8, 884–8; AW to Shawe, 23 November 1803, ibid., pp. 879–81; the terms of the armistice are printed in ibid., p. 878n.

56. AW to Close, 6 December 1803, *WD*, vol. 2, pp. 902–3; [Blakiston], *Twelve Years' Military Adventure*, vol. 1, pp. 187–8; Harness, *Trusty and Well-Beloved*, p. 184.

57. AW to the Governor-General, 30 November 1803, *WD*, vol. 2, pp. 892–5; see also same to same, 21 January 1804, ibid., pp. 991–2.

58. Welsh, *Military Reminiscences*, vol. 1, pp. 189–92; [Blakiston], *Twelve Years' Military Adventure*, vol. 1, p. 206.

59. [Blakiston], *Twelve Years' Military Adventure*, vol. 1, pp. 198–9.

60. Ibid., pp. 199–201.

61. Ibid., pp. 202–3.

62. Ibid., pp. 203–4; Welsh, *Military Reminiscences*, vol. 1, pp. 191–2.

63. This is according to the return printed in *WD*, vol. 2, p. 895n; however Fortescue, vol. 5, p. 40, gives a figure of 361 casualties, adding two European soldiers to the 'missing' without comment or explanation. Thorn, *Memoir of the War in India*, p. 302 gives a total of 346 'men killed and wounded'.

64. [Blakiston], *Twelve Years' Military Adventure*, vol. 1, p. 205.

65. Heights given in a manuscript note by S.G.P. Ward in his copy of *WD*, vol. 2, p. 913, now in the Special Collections of Southampton University Library.

66. Welsh, *Military Reminiscences*, vol. 1, p. 196.

67. Stanhope, *Notes of Conversations*, p. 57, 8 May 1834.

68. [Blakiston], *Twelve Years' Military Adventure*, vol. 1, pp. 228–30. For confirmation see letter from unknown officer dated 16 December 1803 printed in Wellington, *Maratha War Papers*, pp. 410–12; Welsh, *Military Reminiscences*, vol. 1, p. 197; Colebrooke, *Life of Elphinstone*, vol. 1, p. 106; and even AW to the Governor-General, 15 December 1803, *WD*, vol. 2, pp. 913–6 where he says 'Vast numbers of [the garrison] were killed, particularly at the different gates'. Weller's attempts to minimise the incident (*Wellington in India*, pp. 225–6) are unconvincing.

69. [Blakiston], *Twelve Years' Military Adventure*, vol. 1, pp. 234–5.

70. There is a detailed record of the negotiations printed in *WSD*, vol. 4, pp. 221–63. The quote about Sindia and the French is on p. 245 and the references to a defensive alliance against Holkar are in ibid., pp. 267–72. The actual treaty is in ibid., pp. 264–7. Berar stated that he never employed European officers: ibid., p. 279. Bennell, *Making of Arthur Wellesley*, pp. 105–13 has a good account and discussion of the peace-making, and (on p. 112) points out the irony of AW insisting that Sindia keep his promise to Holkar.

71. The negotiations with the Raja of Berar are recorded in *WSD*, vol. 4, pp. 274–85, and the final treaty is printed in ibid., pp. 285–7.

72. AW to Malcolm, 11 February 1804, *WD*, vol. 2, pp. 1043–4. See below for more on this.

73. AW to the Governor-General, 9 January 1804, *WD*, vol. 2, pp. 954–7; rate of exchange given in *WD*, vol. 1, p. xxviii.

74. Lord Wellesley to AW, 27 October 1803, *WSD*, vol. 4, pp. 187–8; AW to the Governor-General, 17 December 1803, *WD*, vol. 2, pp. 916–19.

75. AW to the Governor-General, 30 December 1803, *WD*, vol. 2, pp. 933–8; see also AW's memo for Malcolm, 7 January 1804 and AW to Stuart, 11 January 1804 in ibid., pp. 945–52, 960–3 for the wider picture. These issues are discussed further in the next chapter.

10 Farewell to India (1804–05)

1. AW to the Governor-General, 5 February 1804, and AW to Stuart, 5 February 1804, *WD*, vol. 2, pp. 1022–4 and 1024. Welsh, *Military Reminiscences*, vol. 1, pp. 203–7 adds many details.
2. AW to Kirkpatrick, 16 January 1804; AW to the Governor-General, 19 January 1804; and AW to Shawe, 14 and 26 January 1804, *WD*, vol. 2, pp. 977–8, 986, 968–70 and 1004–6.
3. Memorandum for Major Malcolm [by AW], 7 January 1804, *WD*, vol. 2, pp. 945–52; see also Bennell, *Making of Arthur Wellesley*, pp. 114–45.
4. Kaye, *Life of Malcolm*, vol. 1, pp. 245–8; Bennell, *Making of Arthur Wellesley*, pp. 114–18, 132.
5. AW to Shawe, 14 January 1804, *WD*, vol. 2, pp. 968–70.
6. AW to Malcolm, 24 January 1804, WP 3/3/71, printed with important deletions, including the passage quoted, in *WD*, vol. 2, p. 998; and AW to Malcolm, 29 January 1804, *WD*, vol. 2, pp. 1011–12.
7. AW to Malcolm, 11 February 1804, *WD*, vol. 2, pp. 1043–4.
8. AW to Malcolm, 17 March 1804, *WD*, vol. 2, pp. 1104–7.
9. AW to Malcolm, 30 March and 13 April 1804, *WD*, vol. 2, pp. 1126 and 1143–4.
10. Lord Wellesley to AW, 27 June 1803, Wellington, *Maratha War Papers*, pp. 169–70.
11. Shawe to AW, 20 April 1804, WP 3/3/5 f 257–62; Shawe to Malcolm, nd, 22 April, and 1 May 1804, in Kaye, *Life of Malcolm*, vol. 1, pp. 271–2, 273–4, 275–6. See also Shawe to AW, 7 May 1804, WP 3/3/5 f 301–4.
12. Lord Wellesley to AW, 'Private & Confidential', 6 January 1804, WP 1/151 enclosing HW to Lord Wellesley, London, 31 August, 8 and 9 September 1803, WP 1/148 and 1/151.
13. AW to Lord Wellesley, 31 January 1804, *WSD*, vol. 4, pp. 334–8.
14. Shawe to AW, 16 March 1804, WP 3/3/5 f 279–84.
15. Shawe to Malcolm, 1 May 1804, Kaye, *Life of Malcolm*, vol. 1, pp. 275–6.
16. AW to Malcolm, 20 April 1802, *WD*, vol. 1, pp. 284–5.
17. AW to Webbe, 15 July 1802, *WSD*, vol. 3, pp. 234–5.
18. AW to Lord Wellesley, Bombay, 15 March 1804, *WSD*, vol. 4, pp. 355–60. The letter from Castlereagh is untraced.
19. AW to Stevenson, 11 and 7 February 1804, *WD*, vol. 2, pp. 1042–3, 1031; AW to Lake, Bombay, 23 April 1804, *WD*, vol. 2, pp. 1153–4.
20. AW to Shawe, 8 June 1804, *WD*, vol. 2, pp. 1219–20; for the news of AW's appointment to the staff, see Shawe to AW, 7 and 25 May 1804, WP 3/3/5 f 301–4 and WP 1/151 respectively.
21. Shawe to AW, Calcutta, 25 May 1804, WP 1/151; Lord Wellesley to AW, 'Private & Confidential', 6 January 1804, WP 1/151.
22. AW to Shawe, 7 March 1804, *WD*, vol. 2, pp. 1078–9; AW to Stuart, 14 February 1804, ibid., pp. 1045–9 (the Peshwa's personal hatred).
23. *WD*, vol. 2, pp. 1078–9.
24. There is a good account of the lighter side of these months in Bombay – the celebrations and socialising (even the shopping) – in Guedalla, *The Duke*, pp. 111–13.
25. AW to Jeswant Rao Holkar, 5 January 1804, *WD*, vol. 2, pp. 940–1.
26. AW to Lord Wellesley, 31 January 1804, *WSD*, vol. 4, pp. 334–8. For his belief that hostilities would be avoided see, for example, AW to Col. Murray, 13 April 1804, *WD*, vol. 2, pp. 1142–3, and AW to Webbe, 20 April 1804, *WSD*, vol. 4, pp. 373–4. See Bennell, *Making of Arthur Wellesley*, pp. 147–52, and Fuhr, 'Strategy and Diplomacy', pp. 230–5 for discussions of the origins of the war. Fuhr argues that Lake deliberately provoked the war, contrary to Lord Wellesley's wishes.
27. AW to Malcolm, 20 April 1804, *WD*, vol. 2, pp. 1150–1.
28. AW to the Governor-General, 21 January 1804, *WD*, vol. 2, pp. 990–1.
29. Compare AW to Duncan, 7 January 1804, *WSD*, vol 4, pp. 312–13 with AW to Shawe, 12 December 1803, WP 3/3/6 f 58–9 (printed, with the relevant passage suppressed, in *WD*, vol. 2, pp. 905–7); and AW to Malcolm, 26 January 1804, *WD*, vol. 2, pp. 1002–3 with AW to Lord Wellesley, 21 January 1804, WP 1/152 (printed, with the relevant passage suppressed, in *WD*, vol. 2, pp. 991–2); and AW to Shawe, 15 April 1804, *WD*, vol. 2, p. 1145.
30. AW to Stuart, 11 January 1804, *WD*, vol. 2, pp. 960–3; AW to Murray, 3 April 1804, ibid., pp. 1128–9.
31. AW to Webbe, Bombay, 20 April 1804, *WSD*, vol. 4, pp. 373–4.
32. AW to Lake, 27 May 1804, *WD*, vol. 2, pp. 1200–1.

33. Lord Wellesley to Lake, 'Most Secret and Confidential', 25 May 1804 with enclosure of the same date, sent to Lake, AW and the governors of Madras and Bombay, Wellesley, *Despatches, Minutes*, vol. 4, pp. 67–71.

34. AW to Webbe, 23 May 1804, *WSD*, vol. 4, pp. 390–2; AW to Shawe, 4 June 1804, *WD*, vol. 2, pp. 1214–5.

35. AW to Graham, 11 April and 5 May 1804, *WD*, vol. 2, pp. 1140–1, 1164.

36. AW to Henry Wellesley, 13 May 1804, *WSD*, vol. 4, pp. 383–6.

37. AW to the Governor-General, 2 May 1804, and AW to Shawe, 1 June 1804, *WD*, vol. 2, pp. 1162–3, 1210–1.

38. AW to Col Murray, 22 May 1804, *WD*, vol. 2, p. 1193. Murray's operations are discussed in detail in Bennell, 'Failure by Deputy: Arthur Wellesley and Colonel Murray in 1804' (1999), pp. 69–84.

39. AW to Shawe, 14 January 1804, and to Malcolm, 20 March 1805, *WD*, vol. 2, pp. 968–70, 1454–5; AW to Symons, 21 July 1804, *WSD*, vol. 4, pp. 456–7.

40. AW to Webbe, 29 May 1804, *WSD*, vol. 4, pp. 405–6.

41. AW to Stuart, 1 and 2 August 1804, *WD*, vol. 2, pp. 1291, 1292–3.

42. *Calcutta Gazette*, 16 August 1804, Wellesley, *Despatches, Minutes*, vol. 4, pp. 671–2. Barclay is spelt 'Berkeley' in the *Gazette*.

43. AW to Webbe, 5 and 20 June 1804, *WSD*, vol. 4, pp. 416–7, 441.

44. Quoted in Kaye, *Life of Malcolm*, vol. 1, pp. 288–9n, no date given.

45. Hickey, *Memoirs*, vol. 4, p. 304; Wellesley and Steegmann, *Iconography*, pp. 20–2 and plate 5.

46. D.D. Khanna, *Monson's Retreat in Anglo-Maratha War (1803–1805)* (1981), *passim*; Fortescue, vol. 5, pp. 80–8.

47. AW to Close, Fort William, 4 September 1804, *WD*, vol. 2, pp. 1301–2.

48. AW to Malcolm, 14 September 1804, Kaye, *Life of Malcolm*, vol. 1, pp. 291–3.

49. AW to Shawe, 20 November 1804, *WD*, vol. 2, pp. 1359–62; Governor-General to AW, 9 November 1804, *ibid.*, p. 1356n; the memoranda are printed in *ibid.*, pp. 1316–57.

50. AW to Shawe, 8 December 1804, *WD*, vol. 2, p. 1370; on Webbe's death see same to same, 24 November and 5 December 1804, *ibid.*, pp. 1365–6, 1369; on the state of affairs in Madras see AW to Shawe, 24 November 1804, *ibid.*, pp. 1365–6.

51. AW to Shawe, 11 December 1804, *WD*, vol. 2, pp. 1371–2; Malcolm to Shawe, 4 February 1805, Kaye, *Life of Malcolm*, vol. 1, pp. 298–300; AW to Malcolm, St Helena, 3 July 1805, *WD*, vol. 2, pp. 1456–8.

52. Fortescue, vol. 5, pp. 92–137 gives a detailed account of operations and is generally admiring of Lake; cf Fuhr, 'Strategy and Diplomacy', pp. 273–5 who is highly critical of Lake's whole conduct of the war and questions the motives for his attack on Bhurtpore.

53. AW to Shawe, 19 December 1804, *WD*, vol. 2, pp. 1379–80; see also same to same, 11 December 1804, *ibid.*, pp. 1371–2.

54. Malcolm to Shawe, 4 February 1805, Kaye, *Life of Malcolm*, vol. 1, pp. 298–300; AW to Shawe, 4 January 1805, *WD*, vol. 2, pp. 1389–91; AW to Malcolm, 17 February 1805, *ibid.*, p. 1426.

55. AW to Cradock, 15 January 1805, WP 1/160, printed with some alterations in *WSD*, vol. 4, pp. 483–4; Cradock's advice is inferred from this reply and from Lord Wellesley to AW, 'Private', 30 January 1805, WP 1/158, and Lt Benjamin Sydenham to AW, 'Private', Fort William, 7 December 1804, WP 1/151.

56. AW to Cradock, 15 January 1805, WP 1/160, printed with some alterations in the passage quoted (e.g. the word 'poverty' is suppressed) in *WSD*, vol. 4, pp. 483–4.

57. Elers, *Memoirs*, pp. 165–6; AW to Lord Wellesley, 27 February 1805, *WSD*, vol. 4, pp. 496–8; Lord Wellesley to AW, 22 May 1805, WP 1/158.

58. AW to the Secretary of the Military Board in Madras, 16 February 1805, *WSD*, vol. 4, p. 489 (the elephants); AW to Col. Gore, 2 March 1805, *ibid.*, p. 501 (the 33rd); AW to Shawe, 6 March 1805, *WD*, vol. 2, pp. 1446–7 (his staff); AW to Purneah, 2 March 1805, *ibid.*, pp. 1437–8; AW to Malcolm, 26 February 1805, *ibid.*, pp. 1435–6.

59. Colebooke, *Life of Elphinstone*, vol. 1, pp. 81–2; AW to Malcolm, 14 September 1804, Kaye, *Life of Malcolm*, vol. 1, pp. 291–3.

60. Not very ambitious: *WD*, vol. 2, pp. 1389–91; cares little for money: *WSD*, vol. 2, pp. 409–10n; less for comfort: *WSD*, vol. 4, pp. 486–7; sensitive to criticism: Colebooke, *Life of Elphinstone*, vol. 1, pp. 86–7; remarkably conscientious: *ibid.*, vol. 1, p. 77.

61. AW to Malcolm, 3 July 1805, *WSD*, vol. 4, pp. 509–12.

11 Return to England (September 1805–March 1807)

1. *The Times*, 12 September and 16 August 1805.
2. See, for example, *The Times*, 30 and 31 March and 2 April 1804.
3. For an example of the reports of Monson's failure see [Frances] Calvert, *An Irish Beauty under the Regency* (1911), p. 50, 18 August 1805.
4. For a favourable view of AW, see B. Sydenham to AW, 'Private', 7 December 1804, WP 1/151; for an unfavourable view, see Elers, *Memoirs*, p. 103, Greville, *The Greville Memoirs*, vol. 1, p. 64; see above, p. 87. For opinion of military reputation gained in India, see George Rose, *The Diaries and Correspondence of the Right Hon. George Rose* (1860), vol. 2, p. 180.
5. The 'Horse Guards' refers to the Commander-in-Chief and other senior officers who, with their staff, administered the British army from their offices overlooking Horse Guards Parade. The most important officers other than the Commander-in-Chief were the Adjutant-General, the Quartermaster-General and the military secretary to the Commander-in-Chief (the last being a more junior, but still highly influential officer).
6. The King to Pitt, 26 August 1804, Philip Henry Stanhope, *Life of the Right Honourable William Pitt* (1879), vol. 3, p. 438.
7. Baird's force had sailed on 31 August: Fortescue, vol. 5, p. 306. The draft instructions are printed in Lord Castlereagh *Correspondence, Despatches, and other Papers of Viscount Castlereagh* (1848–53), vol. 6, pp. 146–7, and dated 10 September 1805, but Castlereagh to the King, 12 September 1805, George III, *The Later Correspondence of George III* (1962–70), vol. 4, p. 356, submits them to the King for approval after the Cabinet meeting of that day. *The Times*, 14 September 1805, reports that AW was at the Foreign Office when the Cabinet met.
8. John Wilson Croker, *The Croker Papers* (1884), 1 October 1834, vol. 2, pp. 233–4; see also W.M. Parker, 'A Visit to the Duke of Wellington' (1944), pp. 80–1, and Oliver Warner, 'Wellington Meets Nelson' (1968), pp. 125–8; but cf Edgar Vincent, *Nelson. Love and Fame* (2003) pp. 556–7.
9. Wilson, *A Soldier's Wife*, p. 65.
10. Gerald Wellesley to Lord Wellesley, 24 May 1804, Wellesley, *Wellesley Papers*, vol. 1, p. 172.
11. Anne, Countess of Mornington, to her son, Lord Wellesley, 3 February 1804, Wellesley, *Diary and Correspondence of Henry Wellesley*, pp. 14–15.
12. Glenbervie, *Diaries*, vol. 1, p. 363, entry for 12 February 1804.
13. Thorne, *History of Parliament*, vol. 5, pp. 511–15 for William Wellesley-Pole, and vol. 4, pp. 847–49 for his son. S.T. Bindoff, E.F. Malcolm Smith and C.K. Webster, *British Diplomatic Representatives, 1789–1852* (1934), p. 166 says that Arbuthnot reached Constantinople in June 1805.
14. Lady Burghersh, *Correspondence of Lady Burghersh with the Duke of Wellington* (1903), p. 2.
15. Arbuthnot, *Journal*, 27 June 1822, vol. 1, pp. 168–9.
16. Colonel Beresford to AW, nd, *c.* 1801, Wellington, *Private Correspondence*, pp. 2–3; Wilson, *A Soldier's Wife*, pp. 38, 44–6.
17. Quoted in Wilson, *A Soldier's Wife*, pp. 59–60.
18. John Rosselli, *Lord William Bentinck and the British Occupation of Sicily 1811–1814* (1956), pp. 56–66 for some excellent material on Lady William Bentinck and Olivia Sparrow. AW's usual attitude can be guessed from AW to Josiah Webbe, 29 May 1804, WSD, vol. 4, pp. 405–6.
19. Kitty Pakenham to Olivia Sparrow, 8 October 1805, quoted in Wilson, *A Soldier's Wife*, pp. 69–70.
20. Ibid.
21. Quoted in Wilson, *A Soldier's Wife*, pp. 71–2, cf Wellington, *Private Correspondence*, p. 9.
22. Calvert, *An Irish Beauty*, p. 167.
23. AW to Lord Wellesley, 21 December 1805, WSD, vol. 4, pp. 533–41.
24. Ibid.; see also S.G.P. Ward, *Wellington* (1963), pp. 51–2 for some very suggestive comments.
25. W. [?] Dundas to AW, War Office, 27 November 1805, WP 1/159.
26. *The Times*, 12 February 1806, reported the arrival at Yarmouth of the brigades of Wellesley, Sherbrooke, Dundas and Hill, which suggests that they had arrived by about 10 February.
27. AW to Malcolm, 25 February 1807, WD, vol. 3 pp. 1–2; on AW's feeling for the 33rd see Brereton and Savory, *History*, pp. 108–9; and on his resentment at not being given a colonelcy: AW to Lord Wellesley, 21 December 1805, WSD, vol. 4, pp. 533–41.

28. Lady Bessborough to Granville Leveson Gower, 15 January 1806, Granville Leveson Gower, *Private Correspondence of Granville Leveson Gower* (1916), vol. 2, p. 159; see also same to same, 5 January 1805, ibid., vol. 2, p. 4, and Tom Grenville to Lord Grenville, 7 January 1805, *HMC Dropmore*, vol. 7, pp. 249–50.

29. Lord Wellesley to Grenville, 23 January 1806, Wellesley, *Wellesley Papers*, vol. 1, p. 198, also printed in *HMC Dropmore*, vol. 7, p. 332.

30. Lord Wellesley to Grenville, 25 [26 ?] January 1806, *HMC Dropmore*, vol. 7, p. 341.

31. Brashares 'Political Career of the Marquess Wellesley', pp. 136–7, 140; Lord Wellesley to Grenville, 25 and 25 [26?] January 1806, *HMC Dropmore*, vol. 7, pp. 336–7, 341; Fox to Windham, 25 December 1804, William Windham, *The Windham Papers* (1913), vol. 2, p. 246.

32. Shawe to Scott, 3 March 1804, David Scott, *The Correspondence of David Scott, Director and Chairman of the East India Company* (1951), vol. 2, pp. 436–8; Hickey, *Memoirs*, vol. 4, pp. 284–8; Thorne, *History of Parliament*, vol. 4, pp. 733–5.

33. AW to Malcolm, 31 July 1806, *WD*, vol. 3, pp. 2–3; same to same, 26 June 1813, Kaye, *Life of Malcolm*, vol. 2, p. 91. See also AW to Lord Wellesley, 21 December 1805, *WSD*, vol. 4, pp. 533–41.

34. *The Times*, 21 March 1806; Charles Abbot, Lord Colchester, *The Diary and Correspondence of Charles Abbot* (1861), vol. 2, pp. 46–7; Elers, *Memoirs*, pp. 204–5.

35. AW to Lord Wellesley, 3 October 1806, BL Add Ms 37,415 f 19–20; A. Aspinall, *Politics and the Press c. 1780–1850* (1949), p. 74 for Peter Stuart and the *Oracle*, pp. 88, 205 for Henry Redhead Yorke (on whom see also *DNB*). Other details from the excellent account of Wellesley's defence in Brashares, 'Political Career of the Marquess Wellesley', pp. 143–6.

36. Brashares, 'Political Career of the Marquess Wellesley', pp. 143–6; Philips, *East India Company*, p. 147. The figure of £30,000 is given in the introduction to *WSD*, vol. 5, p. v, and accepted by Brashares.

37. Philips, *East India Company*, p. 146; A.T. Embree, *Charles Grant and the British Rule in India* (1962), pp. 217–18; Brashares, 'Political Career of the Marquess Wellesley', pp. 141–3, 147.

38. Brashares, 'Political Career of the Marquess Wellesley', pp. 149–52.

39. AW to Malcolm, 25 February 1806, *WD*, vol. 3, pp. 1–2.

40. Castlereagh to AW, nd, *WSD*, vol. 5, p. iii–v.

41. The itemised bill is printed in Guedalla, *The Duke*, p. 129; Thorne, *History of Parliament*, vol. 4, pp. 358–9 (Lamb), and vol. 2, pp. 471–3 (Rye, which is listed as one of the Cinque Ports, separately from the counties), and vol. 5, pp. 503–4 (AW).

42. Thorne, *History of Parliament*, vol. 1, pp. 306–8.

43. On Craufurd and Windham see Thorne, *History of Parliament*, vol. 3, pp. 522–4; on Cotton and Newcastle see letters from Newcastle to Bathurst and replies 22–28 August in Earl Bathurst, *Historical Manuscripts Commission. Report on the Manuscripts of Earl Bathurst* (1923) (henceforth cited as *HMC Bathurst*), pp. 202–5; description of the Beresford family from Brian Jenkins, *Henry Goulburn 1784–1856. A Political Biography* (1996), p. 177.

44. AW to Malcolm, 31 July 1806, *WD*, vol. 3, pp. 2–3.

45. AW to Malcolm, 26 June 1813, Kaye, *Life of Malcolm*, vol. 2, p. 91.

46. J.W. Ward, *Letters to 'Ivy' from the first Earl of Dudley* (1905), nd, pp. 56–7.

47. Wilson, *A Soldier's Wife*, pp. 75–6.

48. The story is first told more than fifty years later, third-hand, in Shelley, *Diary*, vol. 2, p. 407.

49. Wilson, *A Soldier's Wife*, pp. 83–6 incl. Queen Charlotte, and a detailed account of a grand society party.

50. Wellington, *Speeches*, prints only eight speeches but twenty-seven are given in *Parliamentary Debates*, vols. 6–7, and although many of these are very brief, he spoke on at least nineteen days between 18 April and 18 July 1806. Thorne, *History of Parliament*, and Wellington, *Speeches*, both wrongly say that his first speech was on 22 April but cf *Parliamentary Debates*, vol. 6, col. 797.

51. See *Parliamentary Debates* for the full evidence and Brashares, 'Political Career of the Marquess Wellesley', pp. 154–9.

52. Lord Wellesley to Grenville, 13 and 17 June 1806, and reply 17 June, *HMC Dropmore*, vol. 8, pp. 186–7, 191–2; Brashares, 'Political Career of the Marquess Wellesley', p. 160.

53. Brashares, 'Political Career of the Marquess Wellesley', pp. 161–3. Unfortunately *Parliamentary Debates* prints very little of the evidence given.

54. *Parliamentary Debates*, vol. 7, col. 925–38; Temple to Lord Grenville, nd [6 July 1806], and Temple to Lord Wellesley, 'Private', 5 July 1806, *HMC Dropmore*, vol. 8, pp. 221, 222–3; Canning to his wife, 5 July 1806, cited in Thorne, *History of Parliament*, vol. 5, p. 354; Brashares, 'Political Career of the Marquess Wellesley', pp. 164–6.

55. *WD*, vol. 3, p. 1n. Gurwood does not identify the old friend of Wellington's who evidently told him this story, and while we have no reason to doubt its accuracy, it should be remembered that it is first recorded many years later and second-hand, although it is clear that the Duke approved it or else it would not have appeared so prominently in the *Dispatches*.

56. AW to Col J.W. Gordon, 10 June 1806, BL Add Ms 49,481 f 2–3.

57. Windham to Grenville and reply, 25 and 26 May 1806, *HMC Dropmore*, vol. 8, pp. 156–7, 159.

58. Grenville to Windham, 23 September 1806, *HMC Dropmore*, vol. 8, p. 353.

59. Unfortunately neither the letter nor the plan survives, and they have to be reconstructed from letters written about them; see AW to Lord Wellesley, 2 October 1806, Add Ms 37, 415 f 17–18, and Grenville to Buckingham, 3 October 1806, Buckingham, *Memoirs of the Court and Cabinets*, vol. 4, pp. 79–80. Other details emerge from AW's response cited below.

60. AW to Grenville, 21 November 1806, and 'Memorandum for Collecting Troops', 20 November 1806, *HMC Dropmore*, vol. 9, pp. 485–7: the memorandum is also printed in *WSD*, vol. 6, pp. 45–7.

61. Memorandum by AW, 20 November 1806, *HMC Dropmore*, vol. 9 (also in *WSD*, vol. 6, pp. 54–5); see also a memorandum 'On the Attack on Mexico from the Eastern Side' by William Jacob in Castlereagh, *Correspondence*, vol. 7, pp. 293–302.

62. Brashares, 'Political Career of the Marquess Wellesley', pp. 138 and 144n; Henry Wellesley to Lord Wellesley, 21 September 1806, BL Add Ms 37,415 f 236–7.

63. Grenville to W. Elliot, 7 November 1806, W. Elliot to Grenville, 'Private', 23 November 1806, *HMC Dropmore*, vol. 8, pp. 429–30, 439–40; Thorne, *History of Parliament*, vol. 2, p. 682.

64. Lord Wellesley to Grenville, 'Private', 25 November 1806, *HMC Dropmore*, vol. 8, pp. 442–3; Thorne, *History of Parliament*, vol. 5, p. 504, vol. 2, pp. 73–4 and vol. 4, pp. 166–70. AW appears to have paid £1,500 of the £4,000; the rest presumably coming from Lord Wellesley: AW to Lord Wellesley, nd and enclosure, BL Add Ms 37,415 f 36, 38.

65. Brashares, 'Political Career of the Marquess Wellesley', pp. 168–70; AW to Lord Wellesley, 22 October 1806, BL Add Ms 37,415 f 21–2.

66. Thorne, *History of Parliament*, vol. 5, pp. 733–5; George Spater, *William Cobbett. The Poor Man's Friend* (1982), vol. 1, pp. 179–82; Francis Horner, *The Horner Papers* (1994), p. 434. Col. Merrick Shawe to AW, 16 April 1808, *WSD*, vol. 5, p. v gives details of Paull's suicide.

67. Wilson, *A Soldier's Wife*, p. 90.

68. Ibid., p. 87, and Longford, p. 124, both print a particularly dry letter of 6 December 1806, but its tone may have been due to a passing disagreement or simply haste. Other letters are more personal, although still far from sentimental or intimate.

69. AW to Grenville, 17 February 1807, enclosing memorandum 15 February 1807, *HMC Dropmore*, vol. 9, pp. 40–4 (a slightly different version of the memorandum is printed in *WSD*, vol. 6, pp. 56–61); Windham, *Diary*, p. 467.

70. Windham, *Diary*, pp. 467–9, and Fortescue, vol. 5, p. 388, but cf contrary gossip recorded by Palmerston, *The Letters of the third Viscount Palmerston to Laurence and Elizabeth Sulivan, 1804–1863* (1979), p. 96, letter of 8 December 1807.

71. Tom Grenville to Buckingham, 21 July 1806, Buckingham, *Memoirs of the Court and Cabinets*, vol. 4, pp. 51–3; AW to Col J.W. Gordon, 10 June 1806, Ward Papers, University of Southampton, Ms 300/3/1.

72. Lord Wellesley to Grenville, 'Private', 21 February 1807, enclosing AW to Lord Wellesley, 21 February 1807, both in *HMC Dropmore*, vol. 9, pp. 51–2.

12 Chief Secretary for Ireland (1807)

1. Lord Wellesley to Richard Wellesley II, 2 May 1807, Carver Papers 34, University of Southampton.

2. Quoted in Thorne, *History of Parliament*, vol. 5, p. 512.

3. Mulgrave to Richmond, 4 October 1809, Richmond Papers, National Library of Ireland Mss. 59 no. 186; on Pole's unconciliatory manners see Richmond to Bathurst, 21 February 1811, *HMC Bathurst*, p. 155, where Richmond also praises Pole's efficiency.

4. Francis Jackson to George Jackson, 7 May 1810, George Jackson, *The Bath Archives* (1873), vol. 1, p. 115.

5. Thorne, *History of Parliament*, vol. 5, pp. 506–7.

6. Portland to the King, 'Wednesday night', 25 March 1807, George III, *Later Correspondence*, vol. 4, pp. 542–4.

7. AW to Lord Wellesley, London, 27 March 1807, BL Add Ms 37,415 f 39–40.

8. This supposition is supported by the presence of a copy of this letter among Lord Grenville's papers (*HMC Dropmore*, vol. 9, pp. 128–9) and of a letter from Grenville to Lord Wellesley, 29 March 1807, in which he expresses 'deep regret' at Arthur Wellesley's decision, but accompanied with 'every possible good wish for his honour and happiness, in whatever situation he may be' (ibid., p. 129).

9. AW to Buckingham, London, 8 July 1807, Buckingham, *Memoirs of the Court and Cabinets*, vol. 4, pp. 194–5.

10. AW to Sir J. Moore, Lumiar, 17 September 1808, Sir John Moore, *Diary of Sir John Moore* (1904), vol. 2, pp. 262–4.

11. AW to Olivia Sparrow, 8 November 1805, quoted in Wilson, *A Soldier's Wife*, p. 73.

12. Wilson, *A Soldier's Wife*, p. 101.

13. Portland to the King, 31 March 1807, George III, *Later Correspondence*, vol. 4, pp. 549–50.

14. On the role and duties of the Chief Secretary for Ireland see R.B. McDowell, *The Irish Administration, 1801–1914* (1964), pp. 56–8, 71–5, and Edward Brynn, *Crown and Castle. British Rule in Ireland, 1800–1830* (1978), pp. 47–56. For the Irish government see McDowell op. cit., *passim* esp. pp. 2–4. And for an excellent short account of AW's tenure see McDowell, 'Wellington and Ireland' (1952), pp. 214–17, and Michael Roberts, *The Whig Party, 1807–1812* (1965, first published 1939), pp. 35–9. Strangely there is no PhD devoted entirely to AW as Chief Secretary, but see the relevant chapters of Karen Robson, 'The Workings of Political Patronage, 1807–1865' (1997) and Karen Piggott, 'Wellington, Ireland and the Catholic Question, 1807–1827' (1990). Gash, *Mr Secretary Peel*, pp. 96–236 provides a richly informative point of comparison.

15. Mr Nevill to AW, 28 March 1807, WP 1/166/7.

16. Wellesley and Richmond received almost forty applications for peerages: either a new title or elevation in the Irish or UK peerages for existing peers. Yet the only new creation they made was that of Thomas Manners-Sutton who was made Lord Manners when appointed Lord Chancellor of Ireland in 1807. This example, albeits extreme, gives some idea of the general excess of demand compared to supply. Robson, 'Workings of Political Patronage', p. 85.

17. On this whole question see Robson, 'Workings of Political Patronage', Chapters 2 and 3, and her articles 'Military Patronage for Political Purposes: The Case of Sir Arthur Wellesley as Chief Secretary for Ireland' (1996) and 'What Every "Official" Man Seeks – Patronage and the Management of Parliament: The Experience of Two Chief Secretaries for Ireland, 1802–1809' (1999); also Robert Shipkey, 'Problems of Irish Patronage during the Chief Secretaryship of Robert Peel, 1812–1816' (1967), pp. 41–56.

18. AW to Richmond, 2 April 1809, *WSD*, vol. 5, pp. 633–5; Robson, 'Workings of Political Patronage', p. 91.

19. Richmond to H. Spencer, 29 October 1807, quoted in Robson, 'Workings of Political Patronage', p. 50.

20. *Memorandum by AW, nd [1809]*, printed in A. Aspinall and E. Anthony Smith, eds., *English Historical Documents* (1999), pp. 265–71.

21. AW to Lady Anne Smith, Dublin Castle, 10 June 1807, *WSD*, vol. 5, p. 82; Anne, Countess of Mornington to AW, 22 May 1807, WP 1/168/40/1.

22. Memorandum by AW, nd [1809], printed in Aspinall and Smith, eds., *English Historical Documents*, p. 270.

23. AW to Richmond, 5 July 1807, *WSD*, vol. 5, p. 107.

24. Robson, 'Workings of Political Patronage', p. 53.

25. Hawkesbury to AW, 6 May 1807, WP 1/166/83. See also Gash, *Mr Secretary Peel*, p. 141 for Peel's view that the episcopal bench was already 'rather overstocked with men of birth'.

26. For example, see AW to Charles Long, Dublin Castle, 28 April 1807, *WSD*, vol. 5, pp. 17–18.

27. AW to Hawkesbury, Dublin Castle, 18 May 1807, *WSD*, vol. 5, pp. 52–3.

28. See the excellent analysis of the election in Thorne, *History of Parliament*, vol. 1, p. 192.

29. AW to Hawkesbury, 9 May 1807, *WSD*, vol. 5, pp. 41–2; Hawkesbury to AW, 'Private', 14 May 1807, WP 1/166/40; Thorne, *History of Parliament*, vol. 3, p. 534; Myron F. Brightfield, *John Wilson Croker* (1940), pp. 25–6.

30. Henry Wellesley to AW, 2 May 1807, WP 1/166/63; Thorne, *History of Parliament*, vol. 5, p. 505 and vol. 2, pp. 185–6 (for Newport), 661–2 (for Tralee) and 371–4 (Ipswich); and Castlereagh to AW, 25 April 1807, *WSD*, vol. 5, p. 22.

31. For example see AW to Maurice Fitzgerald, the Knight of Kerry, 30 March 1807, and AW to Denis Browne, 22 May 1807, *WSD*, vol. 5, pp. 1 and 426.

32. AW to Castlereagh, 19 May 1807, *WSD*, vol. 5, p. 55; Thorne, *History of Parliament*, vol. 3, p. 221. On this whole question see an important article: Peter J. Jupp, 'Irish Parliamentary Elections and the Influence of the Catholic Vote, 1801–1820' (1967), pp. 183–96 esp. 187–9.

33. AW to Hawkesbury, Dublin Castle, 3 June 1807, *WSD*, vol. 5, pp. 72–3.

34. Lt.-Col. J.W. Gordon to AW, 'Private', 6 June 1807, WP 1/170/29.

35. Memorandum by AW, 26 April 1807, enclosed in AW to Hawkesbury, 27 April 1807, *WSD*, vol. 5, pp. 14–16.

36. AW to Hawkesbury, Dublin Castle, 19 April 1807, *WSD*, vol. 5, pp. 7–8.

37. AW to Brigade-Major Beevor, Dublin Castle, 1 June 1807, *WSD*, vol. 5, p. 71; and, for the clergy, AW to Robert Fowler, Archdeacon of Dublin, Dublin Castle, 21 April 1807, ibid., pp. 9–10.

38. Memorandum by AW, 26 April 1807, enclosed in AW to Hawkesbury, 27 April 1807, *WSD*, vol. 5, pp. 14–16; AW to Hawkesbury, 8 January 1808, ibid., pp. 292–3; for the quarrels inside the Catholic party see Oliver MacDonagh, *The Hereditary Bondsman Daniel O'Connell* (1988), p. 97–9, and Roberts, *Whig Party*, pp. 34–58.

39. AW to Charles Long, 'Private', Dublin Castle, 17 May 1807, WP 1/167/99.

40. AW to Hawkesbury, 7 May 1807, *WSD*, vol. 5, pp. 28–36, quotes on pp. 29 and 33.

41. F.S. Larpent, *The Private Journal of Judge Advocate Larpent* (2000), p. 75, 16 March 1813.

42. James Trail to AW, 16 July 1807, enclosed in AW to Hawkesbury, 19 July 1807, *WSD*, vol. 5, pp. 119–21.

43. AW to Hawkesbury, 19 July 1807, *WSD*, vol. 5, p. 119; Marianne Elliott, *Partners in Revolution. The United Irishmen and France* (1982), pp. 342–4.

44. Memorandum [by AW ?] enclosed in AW to Hawkesbury, 3 April 1808, *WSD*, vol. 5, pp. 395–7.

45. AW to Hawkesbury, 7 May 1807, *WSD*, vol. 5, pp. 28–36.

46. AW to Richmond, 15 July 1807, *WSD*, vol. 5, pp. 112–13, and AW to Hawkesbury, 7 May 1807, ibid., pp. 28–36 esp. 34–5 for attitudes to the Irish militia. There is an excellent discussion of AW's plans for the defence of Ireland in J.E. Cookson, *The British Armed Nation, 1793–1815* (1997), Chapter 2. See also Ross, *Cornwallis Correspondence*, vol. 3, pp. 297ff for an interesting comparison.

47. *The Jockey Club* (1792) quoted in the *Complete Peerage* entry for Harrington; Lt.-Col. R. Bourke to Lt.-Col. J.G. Le Marchant, Limerick, 3 June 1808, Ward Papers 300/8/2 citing Le Marchant Mss 5a. See also *Royal Military Calendar* (1820), vol. 1, pp. 319–24 and *DNB* (under Stanhope).

48. AW to Harrington, 1 June 1807, *WSD*, vol. 5, pp. 68–9; Harrington to AW, 27 May 1807, WP 1/168/70; and – for their easy cooperation – same to same, 'Private', 25 October 1807, WP 1/175/66 and Lt.-Col. H.M. Gordon to AW, 'Private', 21 July 1807, WP 1/173/96.

49. AW to Hawkesbury and reply, 9 and 12 November 1807, *WSD*, vol. 5, pp. 175–7.

50. AW to Trail, 27 June 1807, *WSD*, vol. 5, pp. 94–6. At this time Grey was still Viscount Howick, but I have changed this to the more familiar form to avoid confusion. This was the debate on the Lord Commissioner's speech and it ranged over the whole spectrum of the government's policies, but Howick, Whitbread and Newport all raised the issue of Mr Grogan, the latter two concentrating on it. *Parliamentary Debates*, vol. 9 (1807), cols. 623 (Howick), 656–7 (Whitbread), 657 (AW) and 657 (Newport).

51. AW to Foster, 2 July 1807, *WSD*, vol. 5, p. 105.

52. Stanhope, *Notes of Conversations*, pp. 152–3, 20 September 1839; Lady Bessborough to Granville Leveson Gower, 1 August [1807], Leveson Gower, *Private Correspondence*, vol. 2, pp. 270–1; Thorne, *History of Parliament*, vol. 5, pp. 157–8. *Parliamentary Debates*, vol. 9,

(1807), cols. 751–2, 909–26, 969–71 (for Sheridan's opposition) – this does not record the exchange, but the record is incomplete as reporters were excluded from some to the debates. Horner to John Allen, 19 August 1807, Leonard Horner, *Memoirs and Correspondence of Francis Horner* (1843), vol. 1, pp. 407–8; Henry Grattan, *Memoirs of the Life and Times of the Rt Hon Henry Grattan* (1849), vol. 5, pp. 363, 364–5; Roberts, *Whig Party*, pp. 35–6.

13 Copenhagen (July–September 1807)

1. Capt B. Sydenham to AW, 29 May 1807, WP 1/168/83.
2. AW to Castlereagh, 1 June 1807, *WSD*, vol. 5, pp. 66–7.
3. See above, p. 184.
4. Castlereagh to AW, 'Private', London, 26 May and 7 June 1807, WP 1/168/63 and 1/170/32.
5. Castlereagh to AW, 'Private', 7 June 1807, WP 1/170/32; Fortescue, vol. 6, pp. 57–8 for the figure of over 30,000 men. See Christopher D. Hall, *British Strategy in the Napoleonic War 1803–1815* (1992), p. 154 for the shortage of transport ships.
6. Canning to Richmond, 'Private', 16 August 1807, Canning Papers 39, West Yorkshire Archive Service, Leeds.
7. For the background to the Copenhagen expedition see A.N. Ryan, 'The Causes of the British Attack on Copenhagen in 1807' (1953), pp. 37–53. The view that Denmark was becoming increasingly pro-French and hostile to Britain even in 1806 may have been mistaken, but it was held by the Grenville as well as the Portland governments. On the reports of 10 July: see Ryan, 'Causes of the British Attack', p. 49; on those of 12 July, Lady Bessborough to Granville Leveson Gower, in Leveson Gower, *Private Correspondence*, vol. 2, p. 261. Mulgrave to the King, and reply, 14 July 1807, George III, *Later Correspondence*, vol. 4, p. 604. Fresh intelligence arriving daily: e.g. Canning to the King, 15 July 1807, ibid., p. 604. Castlereagh to the King, 17 July and reply 18 July, ibid., pp. 606–7; Portland to the King, 19 July, ibid., pp. 607–8; Canning to Granville Leveson Gower, 18 September 1807, PRO 30/29 9/1 f 202–3 (for Canning's role in the inception of the expedition). Thomas Munch-Petersen's excellent study *Defying Napoleon. How Britain Bombarded Copenhagen and Seized the Danish Fleet in 1807* (2007) was published after this chapter was written and provides the best and most accessible account of the subject.
8. Charles Chambers, 'The Bombardment of Copenhagen, 1807: The Journal of Surgeon Charles Chambers of H.M. Fireship Prometheus' (1927), pp. 374, 380.
9. AW to Richmond, 'Private & Confidential', 24 July 1807, WP 1/174/12, printed *WSD*, vol. 5, pp. 125–6.
10. AW to Richmond, 'Private & Confidential', 24 July 1807, WP 1/174/12, printed in *WSD*, vol. 5, pp. 125–6; Richmond to AW, 27 July 1807, ibid., pp. 126–7; AW to Trail, 27 July 1807, ibid., pp. 129–30.
11. AW to Hawkesbury, 'On board the *Prometheus*', 5 and 7 August 1807, *WSD*, vol. 6, pp. 1–2 (two letters).
12. T.H. Browne, *The Napoleonic War Journal of Captain Thomas Henry Browne, 1807–1816* (1987), pp. 48–9.
13. A.N. Ryan, 'The Navy at Copenhagen in 1807' (1953), pp. 205, 208; Thomas Munch-Petersen, 'Lord Cathcart, Sir Arthur Wellesley and the British Attack on Copenhagen' (1999), pp. 107–8; A.N. Ryan, 'The Copenhagen Expedition, 1807' (1951), pp. 170–5 describes Danish efforts to get their ships ready for sea.
14. Murray quoted in Munch-Petersen, 'Lord Cathcart', p. 115; see also Francis Jackson to George Jackson, 15 August 1807, Jackson, *Diaries and Letters*, vol. 2, pp. 194–8.
15. AW to Hawkesbury, 14, 21 and 28 August 1807, *WSD*, vol. 6 pp. 2–3, 3–5, and *WD*, vol. 3, pp. 8–10.
16. AW to Hawkesbury, 21 and 28 August 1807, *WSD*, vol. 6, pp. 3–5 and *WD*, vol. 3, pp. 8–10; Francis Jackson to George Jackson, 16 August 1807, Jackson, *Diaries and Letters*, vol. 2, pp. 198–202.
17. Richard Howarth to his father, nd [September 1807], *HMC Kenyon*, vol. 4, pp. 560–1; see also AW to Cathcart, 27 August 1807, *WSD*, vol. 6, pp. 7–8, and AW to Cathcart, 19 [*sic:* 29] August 1807, *WD*, vol. 3, pp. 7–8, and Fortescue, vol. 6, pp. 70–2.
18. AW to Cathcart, 19 [*sic:* 29] August 1807, *WD*, vol. 3, pp. 7–8. Losses of 95th from Col. Willoughby Verner, *History and Campaigns of the Rifle Brigade 1800–1813* (1912–19), vol. 1, p. 125 – the missing men came from 2/95th and were probably not lost in the action. Losses

of the 92nd from Lt. Col. C. Greenhill, Gardyne, *The Life of a Regiment. The History of the Gordon Highlanders from its Formation in 1794 to 1816* (1929), vol. 1, p. 131.

19. Browne, *Napoleonic War Journal*, p. 53; AW to Cathcart, 10.30 pm 29 August and noon 30 August 1807, *WSD*, vol. 6, pp. 10–11, 11 for release of captured officers on parole.

20. Francis Jackson to Mrs Jackson, HMS *Prince of Wales*, 1 September 1807, Jackson, *Diaries and Letters*, vol. 2, pp. 206–9.

21. See Lady Bessborough to Granville Leveson Gower, 10 September 1808, Leveson Gower, *Private Correspondence*, vol. 2, p. 328 for an example of how this impression lingered.

22. AW to Hawkesbury, 21 August 1807, *WSD*, vol. 6, pp. 3–5; see also AW to Hawkesbury, 28 August 1807, *WD*, vol. 3, pp. 8–10.

23. Gardyne, *Life of a Regiment*, vol. 1, p. 130 quotes AW's order and gives supporting evidence. Lt.-Col. Beckwith to Brig-Gen R. Stewart, 30 August 1807, and to Major-Gen Sir A. Wellesley, 31 August 1807, WP 1/175/10 and 11; AW to the Countess of Holstein, 1 September 1807, *WSD*, vol. 6, pp. 13–14.

24. Major John Pine-Coffin to Lt.-Col. J.G. Le Marchant, Bath, 9 November 1807, Ward Papers 300/2/6 quoting Le Marchant Mss 12a.

25. Lt.-Col. J. Leach, *Rough Sketches of the Life of an Old Soldier* (1986; reprint of 1831 edn), pp. 34, 37; Gardyne, *Life of a Regiment*, vol. 1, pp. 133–4; and William Surtees, *Twenty-five Years in the Rifle Brigade* (1973; first published 1833), pp. 70–1.

26. Major John Macdonald to Sir John Hope, Head Quarters, nd [September 1807], Ward Papers 300/2/6 citing Linlithgow Mss 6 f 1–20.

27. Major John Pine-Coffin to Lt.-Col. J.G. Le Marchant, Bath, 9 November 1807, Ward Papers 300/2/6 quoting Le Marchant Mss 12a.

28. Ryan, 'Copenhagen Expedition', pp. 152–7. On Cathcart's reluctance see: George Jackson to Mrs Jackson, 14 September 1807, Jackson, *Diaries and Letters*, vol. 2, p. 211; and also Gomm to his sister Sophia, 7 September 1807, W.M. Gomm, *Letters and Journals of Field Marshal Sir William Maynard Gomm … 1799–1815* (1881), pp. 84–7.

29. George Jackson to Mrs Jackson, 14 September 1807, Jackson, *Diaries and Letters*, vol. 2, pp. 209–14.

30. Quoted in Ryan, 'Copenhagen Expedition', p. 160.

31. Munch-Petersen, *Defying Napoleon*, p. 200; Browne, *Napoleonic War Journal*, p. 61.

32. Ward Papers 300/8/2 quoting 'Murray Gartshore's Notes' TD 178 XI; Ryan, 'Copenhagen Expedition', p. 166 for Danish concern that British troops be excluded as far as possible from the town. Wellesley, Murray and Popham were, of course, acting within instructions determined by Cathcart and Gambier who decided the terms that would be demanded.

33. AW to Hawkesbury, 8 September 1807, *WD*, vol. 3, pp. 10–11; the articles of the capitulation are printed in *WSD*, vol. 6, pp. 23–4.

34. AW to William Wellesley-Pole, Braesenborg, 15 September 1807, in Wellington, 'Some Letters of the Duke of Wellington to his brother William Wellesley-Pole' (1948), pp. 1–4. In the same letter he writes of 'this cursed capitulation'.

35. AW to Cathcart, 14 September 1807, *WSD*, vol. 6, pp. 24–5.

36. Canning to Granville Leveson Gower, 5 November 1807, PRO 30/29 8/4 f 466–70; George Jackson's diary, 1 October 1807, Jackson, *Diaries and Letters*, vol. 2, pp. 221–2; AW to Cathcart, 1 October 1807, and AW to Castlereagh, 1 October 1807, *WSD*, vol. 6, pp. 26–7, 28–9. AW reached London on the night of 30 September: Georgiana, Lady Chatterton, *Memorials Personal and Historical of Admiral Lord Gambier* (1861), vol. 2, p. 70.

37. Castlereagh to Cathcart, 27 August 1807, Ryan, 'Documents Relating to the Copenhagen Operation 1807' (1984), pp. 318–20, instructs him to send home the 'Light Brigade' under AW for another service. Castlereagh to the King, 27 August 1807, George III, *Later Correspondence*, vol. 4, pp. 620–1 shows that this service was the defence of Lisbon. Castlereagh to Hawkesbury, 1 October 1807, Castlereagh, *Correspondence*, vol. 6, pp. 188–9 refers to wanting Wellesley 'for Flushing'.

38. The King is quoted in Canning to Mrs Canning, 26 August 1807, George III, *Later Correspondence*, vol. 4, p. 607n; Wilberforce in *Parliamentary Debates*, vol. 10, cols. 1288–9; Lady Bessborough to Granville Leveson Gower, 19 September 1807, Leveson Gower, *Private Correspondence*, vol. 2, pp. 284–5.

39. Freer, 'Letters from the Peninsula: The Freer family correspondence, 1807–1814' (1953), p. 50, 10 September 1807. William James, *The Naval History of Great Britain from the*

Declaration of War by France in 1793 to the Accession of George IV (1902; first published 1822–24), vol. 4 p. 208 gives the combined losses of army and navy as 56 officers and men killed, 179 wounded and 25 missing, or 260 in all. See also Fortescue, vol. 6, p. 73. The army lost 211 of the 260 casualties.

40. Canning to Richmond, 'Private', 16 August 1807, Canning Papers 39.
41. Canning to Rose, 'Private', London, 22 September 1807, Rose Papers, BL Add Ms 42,773 f 194–5.
42. Hawkesbury quoted in Cookson, *The British Armed Nation*, p. 53; Littlehales in ibid., p. 38n.

14 Dublin and Westminster (October 1807–July 1808)

1. Castlereagh to Emily, Lady Castlereagh, 3 [?] October [1800 ?], Blickling Hall Papers, MC3/291, vol. 2, Norfolk Record Office, Norwich.
2. AW to Kitty, London, 25 July 1807, Wellington, *Private Correspondence*, pp. 12–13.
3. AW to Richmond, 1 February 1808, *WSD*, vol. 5, pp. 317–18; see also same to same, 24 July 1807 and 4 June 1808, ibid., pp. 125–6 and 443–4.
4. The letters from Denmark are quoted in Wilson, *A Soldier's Wife*, pp. 100, 103–4.
5. Ibid., p. 107.
6. Their father had died in 1805: ibid., p. 169.
7. Ibid., pp. 105–6.
8. Gash, *Mr Secretary Peel*, p. 101; Wilson, *A Soldier's Wife*, p. 105.
9. Richmond to AW, 5 January 1808, WP 1/187/34; Georgiana, Lady de Ros, 'Personal Recollections of the Great Duke of Wellington' (1889), p. 37.
10. AW to Richmond, Dublin Castle, 25 December 1807, National Library of Ireland Mss 58, no. 12, copy in WP 1/181/44.
11. Thorne, *History of Parliament*, vol. 5, pp. 409–10; Glenbervie, *Diaries*, vol. 1, pp. 35–6; AW to Trail, 27 July 1807 and 12 July 1808, *WSD*, vol. 5, pp. 129–30, 472.
12. Littlehales to AW, 20 July 1807, WP 1/173/90; reply 25 July 1807, *WSD*, vol. 5, pp. 128–9; AW to Richmond, 15 March 1809, *WSD*, vol. 5, pp. 607–8.
13. J.M. Robinson, *The Wyatts. An Architectural Dynasty* (1979), pp. 93–7; AW to Hawkesbury, 4 July 1808, *WSD*, vol. 5, pp. 465–6.
14. Hawkesbury to AW, 23 December 1807, *WSD*, vol. 5, pp. 256–7. For the alarmists see Lord Auckland to Grenville, 28 November 1807 and Buckingham to Grenville, 3 January 1808, *HMC Dropmore*, vol. 9, pp. 152–3, 164–6; and Richmond to Hawkesbury, 9 December 1807, BL Loan Ms 72 vol. 16 f 114–16.
15. Hawkesbury to AW, 'Private', 22 October 1807, WP 1/175/58. For evidence of Chatham's deficiencies at the Ordnance during the invasion scare of 1803–05 see S.G.P. Ward, 'Defence Works in Britain, 1803–1805' (1949), pp. 18–37.
16. AW to Hawkesbury, London, 31 January 1808 and 13 November 1807, *WSD*, vol. 5, pp. 314–15 and 180–2; and AW to Castlereagh, 9 December 1807, ibid., pp. 217–20.
17. AW to Richmond, 1 October 1807, *WSD*, vol. 5, pp. 136–7.
18. AW to Trail, 24 March 1808, *WSD*, vol. 5, pp. 382–4, WP 1/195/72; for problems caused by the turnover of troops see AW to Hawkesbury, 9 November 1807, *WSD*, vol. 5, pp. 175–6.
19. AW to Hawkesbury, 22 April 1808, *WSD*, vol. 5, p. 403.
20. Abbot, *Diary*, vol. 2, pp. 137–8; *Parliamentary Debates*, vol. 10, cols. 190–4; Wellington, *Speeches*, vol. 1, pp. 37–9; AW to Hawkesbury, 31 January 1808 (quoted), and to Richmond, 1 February 1808, *WSD*, vol. 5, pp. 314–15, 317–18.
21. Hawkesbury to AW, 'Private', 29 December 1807, WP 1/179/137; AW to Trail, 1 February 1808, *WSD*, vol. 5, pp. 316–17; Aspinall, 'The Old House of Commons and its Members', pt 3, pp. 308–11. AW had sent out a summons on 24 January – Wyatt to Trail, 24 January 1808, WP 1/189/117 – but relaxed it by 1 February.
22. AW to Richmond, 27 February 1808, *WSD*, vol. 5, p. 353.
23. AW to Lord Manners, 13 March 1808, *WSD*, vol. 5, pp. 364–5.
24. AW to Richmond, 12 May 1808, *WSD*, vol. 5, p. 419; *Parliamentary Debates*, vol. 11, cols. 89–99, 121–8, 145–57 – col. 155 (a taunt from Windham) shows that Canning *was* present at one point but declined to join the debate to defend the government. Canning to Richmond quoted in George III, *Later Correspondence*, vol. 5, pp. 74n–75n; Perceval to the King, [11 May 1808], ibid., pp. 73–5; Abbot, *Diary*, vol. 2, p. 149.

25. Perceval to the King, [26 May 1808], George III, *Later Correspondence*, vol. 5, pp. 80–1&n; AW to Richmond, 26 May 1808, *WSD*, vol. 5, p. 441.
26. Brashares, 'Political Career of Marquess Wellesley', pp. 195–8; Thorne, *History of Parliament*, vol. 5, pp. 421–2; Palmerston to Sulivan, 23 March 1808, Palmerston, *Letters*, p. 100 (which gives a good account of the March debates).
27. *Parliamentary Debates*, vol. 10, cols. 792–3 (Lake); Wellington, *Speeches*, vol. 1, p. 46.
28. William Clinton, Diary, 17 October 1807, vol. 46, p. 151, noted in Ward Papers 300/3/1. Clinton's hostility to Wellesley gives the story added weight. On Murray and Anstruther see S.G.P. Ward, 'General Sir George Murray' (1980), pp. 193–6. On AW's talks with Anstruther see AW to Harrington, 14 October 1807, *WSD*, vol. 5, pp. 136–7.
29. India: AW to R. Dundas, 20 April 1808, *WSD*, vol. 4, pp. 592–601, and related material printed there as notes. Sweden: Lt.-Col. G. Murray to AW, Dublin, 14 March 1808, WP 1/193/53; AW to Murray, 19 March and 8 April 1808, *WSD*, vol. 5, pp. 375–6, 399–400.
30. Stanhope, *Notes of Conversations*, 2 November 1835, p. 69; AW, memorandum [on Spanish America], *WSD*, vol. 6, pp. 61–6; W.S. Robertson, *The Life of Miranda* (1969; first published 1929), vol. 2, pp. 9–12.
31. Portland to the King and reply, 21 and 22 April 1808, George III, *Later Correspondence*, vol. 5, pp. 67–9; Castlereagh to Portland, 'Secret', Stanmore [22 April 1808], Portland Papers, University of Nottingham, PwF 8583. Memoranda by AW, nd, *WSD*, vol. 6, pp. 74–7, 80–2.
32. Memorandum by AW, 1 June 1808, *WSD*, vol. 6, pp. 68–70; Castlereagh to the King, 1 June 1808, George III, *Later Correspondence*, vol. 5, p. 82.
33. AW to Richmond and reply, 4 and 8 June 1808, and AW to Richmond, 14 June, *WSD*, vol. 5, pp. 443–4, 444–5, 453.
34. *The Times*, 9 June 1808; *Morning Chronicle* of 15 June 1808 quoted in Roberts, *Whig Party*, p. 119; Cobbett's *Political Register* of 2 July 1808 quoted in Joseph Farington, *The Farington Diary* (1922–28), vol. 5, p. 84.
35. Rory Muir, *Britain and the Defeat of Napoleon, 1807–1815* (1996), pp. 37–41; A.D. Harvey, *Britain in the Early Nineteenth Century* (1978), p. 212.
36. *Parliamentary Debates*, vol. 11, cols. 890–1.
37. The Duke of York to AW, 14 June 1808, *WD*, vol. 3, pp. 16–17n; Anstruther to AW, 28 June 1808, WP 1/205; letterbooks: Ward, *Wellington's Headquarters*, p. 163; Castlereagh instructions to Dyer, Roche and Patrick, 19 June 1808, Castlereagh, *Correspondence*, vol. 6, pp. 371–3; Castlereagh to Lt.-Col. Browne, 21 June 1808, *Parliamentary Papers* (1809), vol. 2, p. 7; De Ros, 'Personal Recollections', pp. 48–9 (the Prayer Book); Barrington, *Personal Sketches*, p. 172.
38. Canning to the King, 26 June 1808, George III, *Later Correspondence*, vol. 5, p. 90; Castlereagh to AW, 30 June 1808, *WD*, vol. 3, pp. 19n–20n.
39. Castlereagh to AW, 30 June 1808, *WD*, vol. 3, pp. 19n–20n.
40. Castlereagh to AW, 'Private', 30 June 1808, WP 1/205.
41. Cotton to William Wellesley-Pole, 'Secret', 12 June 1808, PRO WO 1/237 f 89–90; Mulgrave to the King, 9 pm, 30 June 1808, George III, *Later Correspondence*, vol. 5, p. 93.
42. Castlereagh to AW, 30 June 1808, *WD*, vol. 3, p. 21n.

15 Vimeiro and Cintra (July–September 1808)

1. Gomm to his sister Sophia, 11 June 1808, Gomm, *Letters and Journals*, p. 97; Warre to his mother, 27 June 1808, William Warre, *Letters from the Peninsula, 1808–1812* (1999), p. 8.
2. Clinton, Diary, London, Sunday, 3 July 1808, vol. 47, p. 50, Ward Papers 300/7/1, p. 50; Lady Hester Stanhope to George Rose, 13 September 1809, Rose, *Diaries and Correspondence*, vol. 2, p. 343. See also T. Graham to R. Graham, Lisbon, 20 September 1809, [Robert Graham], *Historical Manuscripts Commssion. Supplementary Report on the Manuscripts of Robert Graham Esq of Fintry* (1942; henceforth cited as *HMC Graham of Fintry*), pp. 149–50.
3. Ward, *Wellington's Headquarters*, p. 61; William Napier to his wife, 15 December 1812, H.A. Bruce, *Life of General Sir William Napier* (1864), vol. 1, pp. 124–5.
4. *Annual Biography and Obituary* (1817–29), vol. 13, p. 62.
5. Ibid., p. 58 (for time at school – see also *DNB*); Lady Anne Barnard to Col Andrew Barnard, 11 July 1813, *Barnard Letters, 1778–1824* (1928), p. 226.
6. AW to Castlereagh, 21 July 1808, *WD*, vol. 3, pp. 31–4; see also another letter of same date, ibid., pp. 28–31.

7. Diary of Harriot Slessor in Oporto, quoted in Alethea Hayter, *The Backbone. Diaries of a Military Family in the Napoleonic Wars* (1983), p. 178.

8. AW to Castlereagh, 25 and 26 July 1808, *WD*, vol. 3, pp. 36–7, 38–9.

9. AW to Spencer, 26 July 1808; AW to Castlereagh, and AW to Richmond, both 1 August 1808, *WD*, vol. 3, pp. 37, 42–6, 46.

10. Castlereagh to the King, 14 July 1808, George III, *Later Correspondence*, vol. 5, pp. 103–4; Castlereagh to Dalrymple, 15 July 1808, *Parliamentary Papers* (1809), vol. 11, no. 22, p. 18; Muir, *Britain and the Defeat of Napoleon*, pp. 46–7.

11. Castlereagh to AW, 15 July 1808, *WD*, vol. 3, p. 26n; same to same, 15 July 1808, Castlereagh, *Correspondence*, vol. 6, p. 385.

12. Castlereagh to Dalrymple, 15 July 1808, *WD*, vol. 3, p. 27n.

13. AW to Castlereagh, HMS *Donegal*, 1 August 1808, *WD*, vol. 3, pp. 46–7. Pole's letter does not survive, but AW refers to it, and to verbal explanations from Lord Burghersh, who brought out the news.

14. AW to Castlereagh, 1 August 1808, *WD*, vol. 3, pp. 46–7.

15. Capt Pulteney Malcolm's evidence to the Cintra Inquiry, *Proceedings upon the Inquiry Relative to the Armistice and Convention, &c made and Concluded in Portugal* in *Parliamentary Papers* (1809) (henceforth cited as *Proceedings*), p. 36, and H.N. Shore, 'The Navy in the Peninsular War' (1912–14), pt. 5, 'Naval Operations during Sir A. Wellesley's First Campaign', vol. 47, pp. 153–6.

16. Quoted in Geike, *Life of Sir Roderick I. Murchison*, vol. 1, p. 25.

17. [Benjamin] Harris, *Recollections of Rifleman Harris as told to Henry Curling* (1970), pp. 13–14.

18. GO, 31 July 1808, *WD*, vol. 3, pp. 43–44n.

19. AW to Lt.-Col. [J.W.] Gordon, Leiria, 11 August 1808, *WD*, vol. 3, pp. 69–70. See also a most interesting letter from Roderick Murchison to his uncle, printed in Geike's *Life of Murchison*, vol. 1, pp. 27–8 describing the aftermath of landing and praising AW's General Order.

20. AW to Hawkesbury, London, 13 June 1808, *WSD*, vol. 6, p. 83 and further letters in ibid., pp. 83–7.

21. Capt. Francis Duncan, *History of the Royal Artillery* (1872), vol. 2, pp. 197–202 prints Robe's letters and the Board's replies – the horses were the most serious, but not the only, example of the inefficiency of the Ordnance.

22. Thorne, *History of Parliament*, vol. 3, pp. 741–2; *Royal Military Calendar*, vol. 2, pp. 256–67; Ward, *Wellington's Headquarters*, p. 33 (where he quotes from Torrens's letter to the Duke of York explaining why Ferguson was offered a command at Cadiz); Thomas Creevey, *The Creevey Papers* (1923), pp. 105–6, 109.

23. Samuel Laing, *Autobiography of Samuel Laing of Papdale 1780–1868* (2000), p. 113; Harris, *Recollections*, p. 14; Murchison to his uncle, Vimeira, 23 August 1808, quoted in Geike, *Life of Murchison*, vol. 1, p. 27.

24. AW to Castlereagh, 16 August 1808, *WD*, vol. 3, pp. 77–80, 80 (two letters); Sir Charles Oman, *A History of the Peninsular War* (1902–30; henceforth cited simply as Oman), vol. 1, p. 233, vol. 2, pp. 232–3.

25. AW told the Cintra Inquiry that the Portuguese had sent him 1,000 regular infantry, 400 light troops and 250 cavalry: *Proceedings*, p. 27 (in *WD*, vol. 3, p. 141).

26. Charles Leslie, *Military Journal of Colonel Leslie* (1887), p. 40.

27. Col Wilkie in W.H. Maxwell, ed., *Peninsular Sketches by Actors on the Scene* (2002; first published 1844), vol. 1, pp. 8–9.

28. Murchison to his uncle, Vimeira, 23 August 1808, printed in Geike, *Life of Murchison*, vol. 1, pp. 26–35, quote on p. 28, cf Oman, p. 234n citing Portuguese accounts that only forty-one of the *garde de police* joined the army.

29. Verner, *Rifle Brigade*, vol. 1, p. 144 citing manuscript Journal of Maj.-Gen. J Cox; AW to Capt Bligh Alcobaca, 14 August 1808, *WD*, vol. 3, p. 76 (French commissaries); Anon., *A Soldier of the 71st. The Journal of a Soldier in the Highland Light Infantry, 1806–1815* (1975), p. 15 (French corpse).

30. Verner, *Rifle Brigade*, vol. 1, pp. 145–7 gives the best account of the skirmish.

31. AW to Burrard, 8 August 1808, *WD*, vol. 3, pp. 57–61; AW to Col J.W. Gordon, 11 August 1808, ibid., pp. 69–70.

32. Oman, vol. 1, p. 216.

33. Col. George Thomas Landmann, *Recollections of My Military Life* (1854), vol. 2, pp. 126–8.
34. Loison had reached Santarem on 13 August but paused there for two days and on 16 August camped between Alcontre and Cercal barely halfway to Roliça. He left a Hanoverian battalion in garrison at Santarem probably to guard his sick.
35. This differs from the standard account in Oman (vol. 1, pp. 237–8), Fortescue (vol. 6, p. 211) and other authorities, but is based on a close study of the evidence, much of which was published after Oman and Fortescue wrote their accounts: see especially AW to William Wellesley-Pole, 19 August 1808, Wellington, 'Letters to Pole', pp. 4–5, and John M. Wynyard, 'From Vimeiro to Corunna: An Eyewitness Account' (1969) pp. 35–6. On Browne see *Royal Military Calendar*, vol. 4, pp. 186–7. See also Landmann, *Recollections*, vol. 2, pp. 138–40, and the contemporary map published in John Joseph Stockdale, *A Narrative of the Campaign which preceded the Convention of Cintra* (1809), which agrees with this interpretation. This map is closely based on and prepared by the QMG's office from a sketch by Lieutenant-Colonel Browne, a copy of which is in the Holworthy Collection, CKS-U929, in the Centre for Kentish Studies, Maidstone.
36. Major H. Everard, *History of Thos. Farrington's Regiment subsequently designated the 29th (Worecestershire) Foot* (1891), p. 279.
37. Landmann, *Recollections*, vol. 2, pp. 137–8.
38. For example Oman, vol. 1, p. 238, Fortescue, vol. 6, pp. 211–13, Michael Glover, *Britannia Sickens. Sir Arthur Wellesley and the Convention of Cintra* (1979), p. 82.
39. AW to William Wellesley-Pole, 19 August 1808, Wellington, 'Letters to Pole', pp. 4–5. Napier's account supports this (*History*, vol. 1, p. 130: bk. 2, ch. 4). See also Thomas Gell to his brother Robert, 22 August 1808, Gell Papers, Derbyshire Record Office D3287/Box 1040/1, and Leslie, *Military Journal*, pp. 44–5 although their evidence is ambiguous and, as junior officers, it is based on partial information.
40. Leslie, *Military Journal*, pp. 42–3; see also Thomas Gell to his father, 19 August 1808, Gell Papers, Derbyshire Record Office D3287/Box 1040/1.
41. AW told the Cintra Inquiry that a captured French officer told him that Delaborde only gave battle in the belief that Loison was close by and would join him around one o'clock, and this seems plausible: *Proceedings*, p. 27 (*WD*, vol. 3, p. 141). See Wynyard, 'From Vimeiro to Corunna', p. 35 for the success of the 5th.
42. Return printed in *Proceedings*, pp. 162–3.
43. Oman, vol. 1, pp. 239–40; General M. Foy, *History of the War in the Peninsula, under Napoleon* (1827), vol. 2, pp. 505–6. French casualties at Roliça: Foy, *History*, vol. 2, p. 505 says that Delaborde's force amounted to fewer than 2,500 men and (p. 506) that it lost one-quarter of its strength: hence 600 casualties. The same figure is given in *Victoires, Conquêtes, Désastres, Revers et Guerres Civiles des Francais, de 1792 a 1815* (1818–25), vol. 18, p. 101. The British captured three guns.
44. AW to Castlereagh, 18 August 1808, *WD*, vol. 3, p. 85.
45. Laing, *Autobiography*, p. 113; Colborne to Mr Bargus, Camp near Veimira [*sic*], 3 September 1808, G.C. Moore Smith, *The Life of John Colborne, Field-Marshal Lord Seaton* (1903), p. 84.
46. AW to Burrard, Lavos, 8 August 1808, *WD*, vol. 3, pp. 57–61.
47. AW to Burrard, 8 August 1808, *WD*, vol. 3, pp. 57–61; Burrard's Narrative at the Cintra Inquiry, *Proceedings*, pp. 85–6; AW's comments on it, ibid., pp. 103–4, and Torrens's evidence, ibid., p. 102; Moore, *Diary*, vol. 2, pp. 253–5.
48. For example by Oman, vol. 1, pp. 242–4, and Fortescue, vol. 6, p. 217.
49. Anon., *Soldier of the 71st*, p. 16.
50. Harris, *Recollections*, p. 24, Anon., *Soldier of the 71st*, p. 17.
51. Fortescue, vol. 6, p. 223.
52. AW to Burrard, 21 August 1808, *WD*, vol. 3, pp. 90–2; Foy, *History*, vol. 2, pp. 516–19. Curiously each attributes the first move to the open flank to the other army.
53. Anstruther's Journal quoted in an anonymous review by George Murray of Napier's *History of the War in the Peninsula* in *Quarterly Review*, vol. 56 (April 1836), pp. 198–9; see also Colonel Walker's account, which gives much greater credit to his regiment, the 50th, in Col A.E. Fyler, *History of the 50th or (Queen's Own) Regiment* (1895), pp. 105–6, and Wynyard, 'From Vimeiro to Corunna', p. 36.
54. Casualty figures from *London Gazette*, 3 September 1808. Strength of 20th Light Dragoons from Oman, vol. 1, pp. 250–1n. Verner, *Rifle Brigade*, vol. 1, p. 166 cites battalion records in

stating that the four companies of 2/95th lost 34 casualties this day whereas the official return lists only 24. This is a most surprising discrepancy more than the official figure of the whole campaign.

55. See Torrens's evidence to the Cintra Inquiry, *Proceedings*, p. 103, and many other accounts.

56. As is often the case in describing battles, apparently simple statements of the line on which troops advanced and where a clash occurred involves a good deal of conjecture and uncertainty.

57. Murchison to his uncle, 23 August 1808, in Geike, *Life of Murchison*, vol. 1, pp. 32–4. It is noticeable how in this and many other first-hand accounts, the authors greatly exaggerate the number of enemy they faced.

58. AW to Col [J.W.] Gordon, London, 1 March 1809, *WSD*, vol. 6, p. 201; Warre, *Letters from the Peninsula*, p. 23; Robert Southey, *History of the Peninsular War* (1837), vol. 1, pp. 562–3: the Highland Society voted Mackay a gold medal.

59. Murchison's later recollection in Geike, *Life of Murchison*, vol. 1, p. 35.

60. Lt.-Gen. Laurence Shadwell, *The Life of Colin Campbell, Lord Clyde* (1861), vol. 1, pp. 4–5.

61. Anon., *Soldier of the 71st*, p. 18.

62. Harris, *Recollections*, p. 28.

63. For further discussion of this see Rory Muir, *Tactics and the Experience of Battle in the Age of Napoleon* (1998), pp. 200–3 and 186–9.

64. Torrens's evidence, *Proceedings*, p. 103.

65. Southey, *History*, vol. 1, p. 562; Teffeteller, *The Surpriser*, p. 37 quoting Hill's epitome; Wellesley, *Diary and Correspondence of Henry Wellesley*, p. 46; Ross-Lewin, *With 'The Thirty-Second' in the Peninsular and other Campaigns* (1904; reprinted 2000), p. 112. For Henry Clinton's possible interference at this crucial moment see Tom Grenville to Lord Grenville, 8 November 1808, *HMC Dropmore*, vol. 9, pp. 239–41, and Willaim Windham, *The Diary of the Right Hon. William Windham 1784–1810* (1866), p. 481, 15 October 1808. The more cutting version comes from Moyle Sherer, *Recollections of the Peninsula* (1996; first published 1824), p. 30.

66. [George Murray], review of Napier's *History of the War in the Peninsula* (1836), p. 200, Fortescue, vol. 6, p. 234.

67. Warre, *Letters from the Peninsula*, p. 19.

68. Harris, *Recollections*, pp. 37–40.

69. Return printed in the *London Gazette*, 3 September 1808, corrected to include officers named as wounded but not included in table; see the Commentary for a discussion of the difficulties with this figure.

70. AW to Castlereagh, 22 August 1808, *WD*, vol. 3, p. 95. Writing to Richmond on 27 August, AW increased his estimate of French losses to not fewer than 4,000 men: ibid., pp. 102–3.

71. Foy, *History*, vol. 1, p. 524; Oman, vol. 1, p. 262; Fortescue, vol. 6, p. 234.

72. Return of ordnance captured on 21 August in Cintra, *Proceedings*, p. 167: this lists the guns as one 6-pounder, four 4-pounders, two 3-pounders and six 5½-inch howitzers – generally lighter and more disparate than one would expect.

73. AW to William Wellesley-Pole, 22 August 1808, Wellington, 'Letters to Pole', pp. 5–6.

74. Dalrymple's Narrative, *Proceedings*, pp. 39–40.

75. AW to William Wellesley-Pole, 24 August 1808, Wellington, 'Letters to Pole', pp. 6–7. See also Torrens's evidence to the Cintra Inquiry, *Proceedings*, pp. 64–5, also in *WD*, vol. 3, p. 160. Torrens identifies the officer as Murray.

76. Dalrymple's Narrative, *Proceedings*, pp. 39–42.

77. Hulot quoted in Oman, vol. 1, p. 267; this whole paragraph is based on Oman, vol. 1, pp. 266–7. See also Foy, *History*, vol. 2, pp. 525–8.

78. Oman, vol. 1, pp. 268–70, terms of the Suspension in *WD*, vol. 3, p. 96.

79. AW at Cintra Inquiry, *Proceedings*, pp. 5–7.

80. AW expressed his views freely: this emerges from *Proceedings*, pp. 16, 40–1, 57–8 59, 67. Dalrymple told the Cintra Inquiry that Burrard did not, and AW did, take an active part in the discussions, but that both approved the result apart from AW's reservation over the duration of the Armistice. *Proceedings*, p. 67.

81. AW to Castlereagh, 23 August 1808, Castlereagh, *Correspondence*, vol. 6, pp. 410–12. Col. Torrens gave evidence to the Cintra Inquiry that AW had expressed his reservations about the armistice early on 23 August, mentioning especially the Russians and the duration of the suspension of arms. *Proceedings*, p. 63 (*WD*, vol. 3, pp. 159–60).

82. AW to William Wellesley-Pole, 24–26 August, Wellington, 'Letters to Pole', pp. 6–8.
83. AW to Castlereagh, 23 August 1808, Castlereagh, *Correspondence*, vol. 1, pp. 410–12.
84. AW to William Wellesley-Pole, 25–26 August 1808, Wellington, 'Letters to Pole', pp. 6–8.
85. Moore, *Diary*, vol. 2, pp. 257–8.
86. AW to William Wellesley-Pole, 16 September 1808, Wellington, 'Letters to Pole', pp. 9–11.
87. AW to Capt. P. Malcolm, 29 August 1808, *WD*, vol. 3, pp. 103–4. *Proceedings*, pp. 62–3 cf 68–9: for example, AW argued that the French be required to evacuate Lisbon and wait on the south bank of the Tagus until they could be transported back to France, thus opening the harbour to British shipping and facilitating preparations for the march of the British army into Spain.
88. AW to William Wellesley-Pole, 16 September 1808, Wellington, 'Letters to Pole', pp. 9–11.
89. AW to Dalrymple, Lumiar, 17 September 1808, *WD*, vol. 3, p. 124.
90. AW to Moore, 17 September 1808, *WD*, vol. 3, pp. 123–4; Moore, *Diary*, vol. 2, pp. 262–6; see also Charles Stewart to Castlereagh, 17–18 September 1808, PRONI D3030/P/213/1 for some shrewd comments on AW and Moore.
91. *WD*, vol. 3, pp. 110–11.
92. Paget quoted in Anglesey, *One-Leg*, p. 67. Hope: Hope to Mrs Hope, nr Sintra, 3 September 1808, Linlithgow Mss Box 19 f 105 in Ward Papers Ms 300/2/6. Moore: see above.
93. Laing, *Autobiography*, pp. 120–1.

16 The Cintra Inquiry (September–December 1808)

1. Ross-Lewin, *With 'The Thirty-Second'*, p. 123.
2. Auckland to Grenville, 'Private', 4 and 7 August 1808, *HMC Dropmore*, vol. 9, pp. 210–12, 212–13.
3. Hawkesbury to Canning, 11 August 1808, Canning Papers 69; Edward Cooke to Sir Charles Stewart, 10 August 1808, PRONI D3030/AA/1; Castlereagh to Stewart, 10 August 1808, PRONI D3030/Q2/2/49.
4. Auckland to Grenville, 13 August 1808, *HMC Dropmore*, vol. 9, p. 213; Lady Bessborough to Lord Granville Leveson Gower, 22 August [1808], Leveson Gower, *Private Correspondence*, vol. 2, pp. 320–2; Grey to Col. J.W. Gordon, 19 August 1808, BL Add Ms 49,477 f 18–19.
5. Glover, *Britannia Sickens*, pp. 158–61, and Palmerston to Lady Malmesbury, 11 August 1808, Palmerston Papers, University of Southampton, BR 22(i)/1.
6. Castlereagh to AW, 4 September 1808, *WSD*, vol. 6, p. 125; Hawkesbury to Richmond, 'Private', 7 September 1808, BL Add Ms 38, 320 f 66–8.
7. Cobbett quoted in Spater, *William Cobbett*, vol. 1, p. 212; Lord Granville Leveson Gower to Lady Bessborough, 3 September 1808, Leveson Gower, *Private Correspondence*, vol. 2, p. 326; Duke of York to Col J.W. Gordon, nd [1 September 1808], BL Add Ms 49,472 f 136.
8. *Morning Chronicle*, quoted in Glover, *Britannia Sickens*, p. 164; *The Times* in Wendy Hinde, *George Canning* (1973), p. 201; Dorothy M. George and Frederick George Stephens, *Catalogue of Political and Personal Satires … in the British Museum* (1978; first published 1870–1954), vol. 8, p. 671, no. 11024.
9. Lord Wellesley to Richard Wellesley II, 7 September 1808, Carver Papers 34, University of Southampton.
10. Lord Wellesley to Hyacinthe Wellesley, 5 September 1808, quoted in Butler, *The Eldest Brother*, p. 396.
11. Portland to Lord Wellesley, 'Private and Confidential', 7 September 1808, Wellesley, *Wellesley Papers*, vol. 1, pp. 240–1.
12. AW to William Wellesley-Pole, 16 September 1808, Wellington, 'Letters to Pole', pp. 9–11. This letter replies to one from Pole of 4 September, which most unfortunately does not appear to have survived. The date of Portland's letter cited above shows that when Pole wrote, the proposed peerage was still being considered.
13. J.W. Gordon to Sir John Moore, 'Secret', Horse Guards, 5 September 1808, BL Add Ms 49,512A f 24–6; see also Calvert, *An Irish Beauty*, pp. 109–10 for Gen. Calvert's view.
14. The King to Canning, 4 September 1808, George III, *Later Correspondence*, vol. 5, p. 121; Portland to Castlereagh, 4 September 1808, and Castlereagh to Stewart, 4 September 1808, Castlereagh, *Correspondence*, vol. 6, pp. 423–4, 421–3; J.W. Gordon to Moore, 'Secret', Horse Guards, 5 September 1808, BL Add Ms 49,512A f 24–6.
15. Palmerston to Miss Temple, Killarney, 24 September 1808, Palmerston Papers BR 24/1.

16. William Napier to his mother, 1 October [1808], in Bruce, *Life of Napier*, vol. 1, p. 63 cf Napier, *History*, vol. 1, pp. 171–2; *Lady Stanhope's Letter-Bag*, vol. 1, p. 164, quoted in Muriel Wellesley, *The Man Wellington* (1937), p. 152; Auckland to Grenville, 29 September 1808, *HMC Dropmore*, vol. 9, p. 220.

17. Farington, *Diary*, vol. 5, p. 100, 19 September 1808; *The Times*, 16 September 1808.

18. Canning to Perceval, 'Private', Sat[urday] morn[ing], 17 September 1808, Canning Papers 32/1.

19. Castlereagh to Canning, 'Private', Sun[day] Even[ing], [18] September 1808, Canning Papers 34.

20. Hawkesbury to Canning, 'Private', 18 September 1808, Canning Papers 69; Portland to Canning, 'Private', 18 September 1808, Canning Papers 33A.

21. Canning to Castlereagh, 'Private and Secret', 17 September 1808, Canning Papers 32/3.

22. Castlereagh to Perceval, nd [18 September 1808], Perceval Papers, House of Lords Records Office, 8/VII/6.

23. Castlereagh to AW, 26 September 1808, Castlereagh, *Correspondence*, vol. 6, pp. 453–4.

24. Castlereagh to the King, and reply, 21 and 22 September 1808, George III, *Later Correspondence*, vol. 5, p. 127; Castlereagh to Dalrymple, 21 September 1808, Castlereagh, *Correspondence*, vol. 6, pp. 447–8.

25. Lord Wellesley to Richard Wellesley II, 13 October 1808, Carver Papers 34, University of Southampton.

26. Lord Wellesley to Temple, 20 September 1808, Buckingham, *Memoirs of the Court and Cabinets*, vol. 4, pp. 258–9.

27. [Mr Dardis] to the Marquis of Buckingham, nd, ibid., pp. 253–5.

28. AW to Castlereagh, 23 August 1808, *WSD*, vol. 6, pp. 122–5. AW's letter to Pole went slightly further: 'Sir Hew has agreed to a suspension of hostilities which he made me sign.' AW to William Wellesley-Pole, 24 August 1808, Wellington, 'Letters to Pole', pp. 6–8.

29. Aspinall, *Politics and the Press*, p. 266; Lady Bessborough to Granville Leveson Gower, 28 September 1808, Leveson Gower, *Private Correspondence*, vol. 2, pp. 330–1. Lady Bessborough says that Richmond showed his guests letters from AW and quotes bits from them which do not resemble any of his letters which have survived; it is quite possible that she embroidered her account which was simply written to amuse a friend.

30. *The Times*, 29 September 1808.

31. Samuel Whitbread to Mr Creevey, 25 September 1808; Cobbett to Lord Folkestone, 9 October 1808, both in Creevey, *Creevey Papers*, pp 89–90.

32. Lady Mornington to Lord Wellesley, London, 8 October 1808, BL Add Ms 37,416 f 100–101; AW to Lord Wellesley, London, 5 October 1808, BL Add Ms 31,415 f 47, printed in Wellington, *Wellington at War, 1794–1815. A Selection of his Wartime Letters* (1961), p. 150.

33. AW to Castlereagh, London, 6 October 1808, *WD*, vol. 3, pp. 126–8.

34. AW to Barclay, 28 October 1808; AW to Croker, 23 October 1808; AW to ___, 25 October 1808; AW to ___, 3 November 1808: all *WD*, vol. 3, pp. 131–3; George III, *Later Correspondence*, vol. 5, p. 139n quotes Robert Ward on Stockdale offering to publish anything of AW's.

35. AW to Castlereagh, Lisbon, 14 October 1809, *WSD*, vol. 6, pp. 401–3.

36. Buckingham to Grenville, 25 November 1808, *HMC Dropmore*, vol. 9, pp. 244–5; Grenville to Buckingham, 25 November 1808, and Temple to Buckingham, 4 November 1808, both Buckingham, *Memoirs of the Court and Cabinets*, vol. 4, pp. 280–2, 273–5.

37. Duke of York to J.W. Gordon, 18 September and 16 October 1808, BL Add Ms 49,472 f 139–40, 143–4.

38. George, *BM Catalogue of Satires*, vol. 8, nos. 11034, 11035, 11042, 11043, 11046 and 11047.

39. *The Times*, 20 and 29 October and 4 November 1808; Spater, *William Cobbett*, vol. 1, pp. 212–14.

40. *The Times*, 3 November 1808; AW to Spencer, Dublin Castle, 22 October 1808, *WD*, vol. 3, pp. 130–1; for an example of bitterness slipping out see AW to Lt.-Gen. St John, Dublin Castle, 30 October 1808, *WSD*, vol. 6, pp. 180–1, name supplied by Chris Woolgar in email of 28 April 2008.

41. The offending paragraphs and the lawyer's opinion are among the Wellesley papers in BL Add Ms 37,309 f 259–61.

42. AW to Castlereagh, London, 14 November 1808, *WD*, vol. 3, pp. 133–4; William Wellesley-Pole to AW with postscript by Lord Wellesley, 19 and 27 October 1808, *WSD*, vol. 6, pp. 164–5, 170–4; see also same to same, 26 October, Raglan Papers, Gwent Record Office,

Wellington B no. 90, and AW's reply to the first letter, 23 October 1808, Raglan Papers, Wellington A no. 7.

43. AW to Moore, London, 8 October 1808, *WSD*, vol. 6, pp. 150–1; AW to J.W. Gordon, Dublin Castle, 21 October 1808, *WD*, vol. 3, p. 129 (see also same to same, 15 October 1808, ibid., p. 129); Duke of York to J.W. Gordon, 5 November 1808, BL Add Ms 49,472 f 155–156.

44. Thorne, *History of Parliament*, vol. 4, pp. 679–80.

45. *Royal Military Calendar*, vol. 1, pp. 374–5; *Complete Peerage*, vol. 10, pp. 427–8; George III, *Later Correspondence*, vol. 5, pp. 537–8&n.

46. Two letters from the Duke of York to J.W. Gordon, both 28 October 1808, BL Add Ms 49, 472, f 152, 153 make clear that the selection of officers was made by the Duke in consultation with the King but without reference to the ministers.

47. *Proceedings*, pp. 16–17; *The Times*, 23 November 1808.

48. *Proceedings*, pp. 38–40.

49. Ibid., pp. 54–5.

50. AW to Richmond, 23 November 1808, *WD*, vol. 3, p. 179; for the bystander's remark see Arbuthnot, *Journal*, vol. 1, p. 233, 11 May 1823.

51. *Proceedings*, pp. 73–81.

52. *The Times*, 29 November 1808.

53. *Proceedings*, pp. 84–9.

54. Ibid., pp. 93–5.

55. Arbuthnot, *Journal*, vol. 1, p. 234, 11 May 1823; *Proceedings*, pp. 96–7.

56. *The Times*, 14 December 1808. See also Walter Scott to George Ellis, 23 December 1808, *The Letters of Sir Walter Scott* (1932–37), vol. 2, pp. 139–41.

57. *The Times*, 29 September 1808 (quoted above), 15 and 24 December 1808.

58. *Proceedings*, pp. 111–21; Duke of York to Sir David Dundas, 25 December 1808, in ibid., pp. 121–2.

59. *Proceedings*, pp. 122–4. Moira's opinion is also printed in Oman, vol. 1, pp. 628–30.

60. AW to Burghersh, Dublin Castle, 11 January 1809, *WD*, vol. 3, p. 180; see also AW to Williams, 9 January 1809, *WSD*, vol. 5, pp. 524–5; AW to Castlereagh, 9 January 1809, Castlereagh, *Correspondence*, vol. 7, p. 25.

61. The declaration is in *Annual Register*, 1808, pp. 281–2; see related letters Castlereagh to King and reply, 17 and 18 January 1809, George III, *Later Correspondence*, vol. 5, p. 167, and Castlereagh to Duke of York, 18 January 1809, Castlereagh, *Correspondence*, vol. 7, p. 20.

17 Politics, Scandal and Wellesley's Return to Portugal (January–April 1809)

1. *Parliamentary Debates*, vol. 12, cols. 106–13.

2. Ibid., cols. 145–58; Perceval to the King, 25 January 1809, George III, *Later Correspondence*, vol. 5, pp. 176–8.

3. *Parliamentary Debates*, vol. 12, cols. 312–13; *The Times*, 3 February 1809; Whitbread had already raised the question on 20 January, asking Castlereagh if AW was still in possession of the office: *Parliamentary Debates*, vol. 12, col. 93.

4. *Parliamentary Debates*, vol. 12, cols. 366–71; *The Times*, 7 February 1809; Wellington, *Speeches*, vol. 1, pp. 51–3.

5. *The Times*, 22 February 1809; *Parliamentary Debates*, vol. 12, cols. 897–917 (quotes taken from the version in *The Times*; that in *Parliamentary Debates* is a shade less enthusiastic in its praise of Wellesley).

6. *Parliamentary Debates*, vol. 12, p. 925; *The Times*, 22 February 1809; Thorne, *History of Parliament*, vol. 4, pp. 679–80.

7. *The Times*, 22 February 1809; *Parliamentary Debates*, vol. 12, cols. 925–8. On Tarleton see Thorne, *History of Parliament*, vol. 5, pp. 332–6.

8. *The Times*, 22 February 1809; *Parliamentary Debates*, vol. 12, cols. 928–36; Wellington, *Speeches*, vol. 1, pp. 57–65 gives the fullest version. Fremantle quoted by Aspinall in George III, *Later Correspondence*, vol. 5, p. 207n.

9. *The Times*, 22 February 1809; *Parliamentary Debates*, vol. 12, cols. 936–59; quotes from *The Times*.

10. *History of Parliament*, vol. 5, pp. 485–90 (on Wardle). There is a good account of the campaign against the Duke of York in Harvey, *Britain in the Early Nineteenth Century*, pp. 233–47.

Philip Harling, 'The Duke of York Affair (1809) and the Complexities of Wartime Patriotism' (1996), pp. 963–84 is disappointing. A full study of the Duke's role in the improvement of the British army, and of the public controversy of 1809, is still needed.

11. *Parliamentary Debates*, vol. 12, cols. 188–90; Wellington, *Speeches*, vol. 1, pp. 47–9; AW to Richmond, 1 February 1809, *WSD*, vol. 5, pp. 553–4.

12. Denis Gray, *Spencer Perceval. The Evangelical Prime Minister* (1963), p. 196 quoting Wilberforce, *Life*, vol. 3, p. 402.

13. AW to Richmond, 12 February 1809, *WSD*, vol. 5, pp. 566–7; *Parliamentary Debates*, vol. 12, cols. 544–5 and 563.

14. Gray, *Perceval*, p. 198; George, *English Political Caricature*, vol. 2, p. 116; Perceval to the King, 14 February 1809, George III, *Later Correspondence*, vol. 5, pp. 194–5.

15. AW to Richmond, 17 and 19 February, 12 March 1809, *WSD*, vol. 5, pp. 574–5, 578–9, 604–5 (re Harrington); see also Perceval to the King, 17 February 1809, George III, *Later Correspondence*, vol. 5, pp. 197–9. In Perceval's account the allegation involved £40,000 not £70,000 and he was probably taking more care to be accurate than Wellesley; but Perceval's conclusion 'that this case did not make any bad impression on the House' was clearly too optimistic. See also Lady Salisbury's diary for 22 December 1833 when Wellington told her that he believed that the Duke of York must have been aware of Mrs Clarke's activities; however this was not necessarily his view at the time: Carola Oman, *The Gascoyne Heiress. The Life and Diaries of Frances Mary Gascoyne-Cecil* (1968), p. 99.

16. Gray, *Perceval*, pp. 203–4; the King to Portland, 18 March 1809, George III, *Later Correspondence*, vol. 5, p. 237; AW to Richmond, 22 March 1809, *WSD*, vol. 5, p. 614.

17. Quoted in Harvey, *Britain in the Early Nineteenth Century*, p. 244.

18. 'I have no small talk and Peel has no manners' – Wellington's account of the Tories' disadvantage in dealing with the young Queen Victoria can only be traced back to G.W.E. Russell's *Collections and Recollections* (*c.* 1903), vol. 1, p. 142; however, a slightly different form of the quote appeared in the press as early as 1841: see, for example, the *Bristol Mercury*, 22 May 1841, where it is attributed to the *Weekly Chronicle*.

19. Arbuthnot, *Journal*, vol. 1, p. 378, entry for 19 February 1825. Harriette Wilson, *The Memoirs of Harriette Wilson written by Herself* (1909; first published 1825), vol. 1, pp. 55–65, 81–4, 163, 203–5, 253 (the hammering on the door scene is pp. 203–5; the ratcatcher remark is on p. 65). There is a good modern biography of Harriette Wilson: Frances Wilson, *The Courtesan's Revenge. Harriette Wilson, the Woman who Blackmailed the King* (2003). See also Aspinall, 'The Old House of Commons and its Members', pt. 5, *Parliamentary Affairs*, vol. 15, pp. 15–38, which prints some of her blackmailing letters to Brougham and sheds light on the sexual morals of MPs of the period. Regrettably there is no good evidence that Wellington ever told Harriette Wilson, or her publisher, to 'publish and be damned', let alone that he dashed this across a blackmailing letter in flaming red ink. See Longford, pp. 166–8; Norman Gash, *Wellington Anecdotes. A Critical Survey* (1992), pp. 8–9; and Wilson, *Courtesan's Revenge*, pp. 224–5.

20. There are excellent accounts of this affair, with copious quotations from the primary sources, in Anglesey, *One-Leg*, pp. 89–104, 109–12 (quote from Caroline, Duchess of Argyll is on p. 111), and Robert Pearman, *The Cadogans at War, 1783–1864. The Third Earl Cadogan and His Family* (1990), pp. 101–14. The suggestion that the affair prevented Lord Paget from commanding the cavalry of Wellington's army in the Peninsula is misplaced. Paget was the senior officer and could not serve under Wellington until Wellington was promoted above him by being made a Field Marshal in 1813 (or, much more debatably, when Wellington was given local rank of general in 1811). Nor did Wellington believe that Paget was suited to the cautious role he wanted the cavalry to play (Wellington to Liverpool, 27 August 1811, WP 1/339, passage deleted from the printed version of this letter).

21. Villiers to Canning, 'Private', 26 December 1808, and 'Private and Confidential', 3 January 1809, Canning Papers 48/12 and 13 (quote from second letter).

22. Portland to Canning, 'Private & Confidential', 31 December 1808, Canning Papers 33/A/3; Canning to Villiers, 'Private', 28 January 1809, Canning Papers 48/4; Duke of York to Col J.W. Gordon, 27 January 1809, BL Add Ms 49,473 f 3; Beresford quoted in Michael Glover, *Wellington's Army in the Peninsula, 1808–1814* (1977), p. 121. [Castlereagh] to Beresford, 15 February 1809, PRO WO1/239, pp. 1–5. For more on the evolution of British policy towards Portugal in late 1808 and early 1809 see Muir, *Britain and the Defeat of Napoleon*, pp. 79–87.

23. *Pace* Oman, vol. 2, p. 217.

24. Four British majors and twenty captains gave up their commissions in British regiments to join the Portuguese army (as colonels and lieutenant-colonels respectively), while being promoted one step (to lieutenant-colonels and majors) in their non-regimental rank in the British army. More than 300 other British officers joined the Portuguese army during the course of the war, while retaining their existing rank in the British army and their commissions in their regiments. A number of sergeants and a few other ranks were also employed to help train the Portuguese. Glover, *Wellington's Army*, p. 123, and information from Ron McGuigan.

25. Circulars to the Cabinet by Canning, 10 and 24 February 1809. Canning Papers 41 and 41A: quote from the second circular; Canning to Villiers, 'Private & Confidential', 28 February 1809, Canning Papers 48/5.

26. There is little evidence for this, but see Castlereagh to the King, 1 October 1809, George III, *Later Correspondence*, vol. 5, pp. 378–81, and Castlereagh's instructions to Cradock of 28 January and 27 February 1809, PRO WO 1/232, pp. 287–91, and Castlereagh, *Correspondence*, vol. 7, pp. 37–9, which are much more pessimistic than Canning's letters to Villiers of the same time.

27. Castlereagh to Cradock, 27 February 1809, Castlereagh, *Correspondence*, vol. 7, pp. 37–9; Fortescue, vol. 7, pp. 120–1, for Sherbrooke's force. Sherbrooke reached Lisbon on 12 March: ibid., p. 123.

28. Canning to Villiers, 'Private & Confidential', 28 February 1809, Canning Papers 48/5; Stewart to Castlereagh, Cintra, 21 October 1809, PRONI D3030/P/233.

29. Memorandum on the Defence of Portugal, 7 March 1809, *WD*, vol. 3, pp. 181–3; AW to Castlereagh, 1 August 1808, ibid., pp. 46–7.

30. AW to Richmond, 12 and 22 March 1809, *WSD*, vol. 5, pp. 604–5, 614.

31. Canning to Portland, 'Private & Secret', 21 March 1809, Canning Papers 33/A/5.

32. Castlereagh to the King and reply, 26 and 27 March 1809, George III, *Later Correspondence*, vol. 5, pp. 246–7.

33. Castlereagh to AW, draft, 2 and 3 April 1809, Castlereagh, *Correspondence*, vol. 7, pp. 47, 49–50 (both also in *WSD*, vol. 6, pp. 210–13).

34. AW to Richmond, 28 March 1809, *WD*, vol. 3, p. 184; AW to Sir Charles Saxton, 25 and 28 March 1809, *WSD*, vol. 5, pp. 619, 627.

35. AW to Richmond, London, 7 April 1809, *WSD*, vol. 5, p. 643.

36. Castlereagh to Cradock, 30 March 1809 (two letters), Castlereagh, *Correspondence*, vol. 7, pp. 44–6; Castlereagh to AW, 11 and 13 April 1809, ibid., pp. 56–7, 58–9; Stewart to Castlereagh, 21 October 1809, PRONI D/3030/P/233.

37. The best version of the story is in [George Fitzclarence, Earl of Munster], 'An Account of the British Campaign of 1809', vol. 1, no. 5 (May 1829), pp. 526–7; see also Longford, p. 176. John Sweetman, *Raglan. From the Peninsula to the Crimea* (1993), p. 26 quotes the logs of the captain and the master (both in the PRO) to discredit the story.

18 Oporto (April–May 1809)

1. Prints in shops: Robert Semple quoted in Ian Robertson, *Wellington at War in the Peninsula, 1808–1814. An Overview and Guide* (2000), p. 75; illuminations: Dickson diary, 27 April 1809, Alexander Dickson, *The Dickson Manuscripts* (1987–91; reprint of original 1905–08), vol. 1, p. 16; Portuguese request for AW: Villiers to Canning, 'Private', Lisbon, 26 December 1808, Canning Papers 48/12.

2. [?] to Leven, Lisbon, 13 April 1809, Scottish Record Office, Melville Papers, GD 26/9/534; see also Capt Bowles to Lord Fitzharris, Coimbra, 3 May 1809, in James Harris, Earl of Malmesbury, ed., *A Series of Letters of the first Earl of Malmesbury, His Family and Friends* (1870), vol. 2, pp. 93–5; Leslie, *Military Journal*, p. 103; and diary of Maj.-Gen. J.R. Mackenzie, BL Add Ms 39,201, entry for 25 April 1809, courtesy of John Brewster.

3. For Villiers pressing the government for reinforcements, see Villiers to AW, 11 May 1809, WP1/259, and Canning to Villiers, 'Private and Confidential', 19 May 1809, Canning Papers 48/6, and Villiers to Canning, 'Private and Confidential', 5 June 1809, Canning Papers 48/17; for Wellesley's regret at his decision to retire, see Wellington to Beresford, Badajoz, 5 October 1809, *WD*, vol. 3, p. 535; see also the entry on Villiers in Thorne, *History of Parliament*, vol. 5, pp. 454–7.

4. Creevey to Miss Ord, 24 August [1827], Creevey, *Creevey Papers*, pp. 468–9 (this letter also contains the details of Beresford's parentage).

5. For more on this see Chapter 21 below.

6. A return in *WSD*, vol. 13, p. 317 which shows over 24,000 rank and file available on 1 May; add one-eighth for officers and NCOs for a total of 27,000 all ranks; see also Fortescue, vol. 7, p. 145.

7. AW to Castlereagh, 24 April 1809, *WD*, vol. 3, pp. 189–90, Castlereagh to Dundas, 28 April 1809, and Castlereagh to AW, 13 and 22 May 1809, Castlereagh, *Correspondence*, vol. 7, pp. 60–1, 61–2, 69–70.

8. Cotton to AW, 28 January 1808, WP 1/188/65.

9. Wellington to Torrens, 7 September 1812, *WD*, vol. 6, pp. 55–6, cf Fortescue, vol. 7, p. 161.

10. *Royal Military Calendar*, vol. 2, pp. 406–10; *Annual Obituary*, vol. 10, pp. 411–13; AW to A. Campbell, 7 November 1803, 4 September 1809, 14 February 1810, *WD*, vol. 2, pp. 842–3, *WD*, vol. 3, p. 473, 734; Hall, *Biographical Dictionary*, pp. 102–4; Miles Nightingall, 'The Nightingall Letters: Letters from Major-General Miles Nightingall in Portugal, February to June 1811' (1973), p. 151 (contemporary resentment of a senior officer while Campbell commanded a brigade). See also p. 426 below on the escape of the garrison of Almeida.

11. Wellington to J. Murray (Commissary General), Lisbon, 19 October 1809, *WD*, vol. 3, pp. 553–4; Wellington to Liverpool, 1 June 1810, *WD*, vol. 4, pp. 99–100; Wellington to Payne, 28 May 1810, ibid., pp. 91–2. A.L.F. Schaumann, *On the Road with Wellington. The Diary of a War Commissary-General in the English Army* (1925), pp. 167–8 gives a commissary's views of Payne.

12. AW to Frere, Lisbon, 24 May 1809, *WD*, vol. 3, pp. 187–9.

13. AW to Castlereagh, Coimbra, 7 May 1809, *WD*, vol. 3, pp. 219–20. For more on this see pp. 319–20 below.

14. AW to Frere, Lisbon, 24 April 1809, *WD*, vol. 3, pp. 187–9; see also AW to Richmond, 14 April 1809, ibid., pp. 185–6 where he estimates Soult's force at only 15,000 men.

15. AW to Frere and to Cuesta, both 29 April 1809, *WD*, vol. 3, pp. 197; 197–8.

16. See Mackenzie's diary, 29 April 1809, BL Add Ms 39,201, courtesy of John Brewster.

17. AW to Castlereagh, 27 April 1809 (two letters), *WD*, vol. 3, pp. 192–3, 193–4 (quote in second letter).

18. See AW to Sherbrooke, Leiria, 30 April 1809, *WD*, vol. 3, p. 200.

19. Many British witnesses describe the reception: see esp. Capt. G. Bowles to Lord Fitzharris, Oporto, 25 May 1809, Malmesbury, *Letters*, vol. 2, p. 98; Captain William Stothert, *A Narrative of the Principal Events of the Campaigns of 1809, 1810 & 1811 in Spain and Portugal* (1997; reprint of 1812 edn), p. 26; John Aitchison, *An Ensign in the Peninsular War. The Letters of John Aitchison* (1981), p. 38; and [Col. Peter Hawker], *Journal of a Regimental Officer during the Recent Campaign in Portugal and Spain under Lord Viscount Wellington* (1981; first published 1810), pp. 43–4.

20. [Thomas Bunbury], *Reminiscences of a Veteran* (1861), vol. 1, p. 29.

21. J.S. Cooper, *Rough Notes of Seven Campaigns, 1809–1815* (1996; first published 1869), pp. 6–7.

22. Many memoirs give evidence of Protestant feeling in the army and aversion to Catholics, for example Charles Boutflower, *Journal of an Army Surgeon during the Peninsular War* (1997; first published 1912), *passim*, but esp. pp. 38–9, and the anonymous *Memoirs of a Sergeant late in the Forty-Third Light Infantry Regiment, previously to and during the Peninsula War; including an Account of his Conversion from Popery to the Protestant Religion* (1998; first published 1835). However there were also many Catholic soldiers in the army, who may well have appreciated these gestures of official respect to their Church.

23. Oman, vol. 2, pp. 318–21, Fortescue, vol. 7, p. 154; Samuel E. Vichness, 'Marshal of Portugal: The Military Career of William Carr Beresford, 1785–1814' (1976), pp. 176–8.

24. Ward, 'General Sir George Murray', *passim*; Murray's letters to Maj.-Gen. Alexander Hope in the Hope of Luffness Papers in the Scottish Record Office. Charles Stewart's letters to Castlereagh are in the Public Record Office of Northern Ireland and formed a major source for his *Narrative of the Peninsular War* (this was after he changed his name and inherited his father's title, so that it appears in library catalogues as written by Charles William Vane, Marquess of Londonderry). George Fitzclarence's 'An Account of the British Campaign of 1809' was published anonymously in a series of articles in the *United Service Journal*

beginning with vol. 1, no. 5 (May 1829). When his father came to the throne as King William IV in 1830, Fitzclarence was created Earl of Munster.

25. AW to Beresford, 7 and 11 May 1809, *WD*, vol. 3, pp. 216–18, 225.
26. Cocks to his father, Coimbra, 6 May 1809, Julia V. Page, *Intelligence Officer in the Peninsula. Letters and Diaries of Maj. the Hon. Edward Charles Cocks, 1786–1812* (1976), p. 25; Aitchison to his father, Coimbra, 5 May 1809, Aitchison, *Ensign in the Peninsular War*, p. 39.
27. Oman, vol. 2, pp. 324, 331. The strength of Lorge's force is uncertain, but probably no more than 1,500 men.
28. William Tomkinson, *The Diary of a Cavalry Officer in the Peninsular War and Waterloo Campaign* (1895), p. 7; see also Hawker, *Journal*, p. 51.
29. Oman, vol. 2, pp. 331–4.
30. Dickson, Diary, 12 May 1809, in Dickson, *Dickson Manuscripts*, vol. 1, p. 20. Murray's force consisted of the KGL light infantry, one line battalion, a squadron of the 14th Light Dragoons and two guns.
31. Dickson, Diary, 12 May 1809, in Dickson, *Dickson Manuscripts*, vol. 1, p. 20.
32. Oman, vol. 2, pp. 333–5; Fortescue, vol. 7, pp. 158–9.
33. Unfortunately Foy's journal, which would probably have shed valuable light on the French side of the campaign, has been lost; and the account of Girod de l'Ain's biography of him is brief and unhelpful. Maurice Girod de l'Ain, *Vie Militaire du Général Foy* (1900), pp. 80–2.
34. Oman, vol. 2, pp. 335–8.
35. Calvert, *An Irish Beauty*, p. 136.
36. Oman, vol. 2, pp. 338–41.
37. Ibid., p. 340 and Fortescue, vol. 7, pp. 161–2 are both critical of Murray; N. Ludlow Beamish, *History of the King's German Legion* (1832–37), vol. 1, pp. 196–7 states that the KGL light infantry *did* skirmish with the French. But the question really depends on how completely disordered the French were and the exact position of the troops involved – details which are not given in the surviving evidence.
38. Figures from Charles William Vane Londonderry, *Narrative of the Peninsular War* (1829), Appendix 3.
39. French officer casualties from A. Martinien, *Tableaux par corps et par batailles des Officiers Tués et Blessés pendant les Guerres de l'Empire (1805–1815)*, made much easier to use by Marcus Stein's work arranging them chronologically (at www.napoleon-online.de). Oman, vol. 2, pp. 341–2 and 361 discusses French losses.
40. Burgoyne's diary, quoted in George Wrottesley, *Life and Correspondence of Field Marshal Sir John Burgoyne* (1873), vol. 1, p. 41, records that this bridge was completed at 8 pm on the day after the action; see Hawker, *Journal*, p. 59 for other details.
41. Oman, vol. 2, pp. 343–66; S.G.P. Ward, 'Milgapey, May, 1809, A Peninsular War Puzzle in Geography' (1952), pp. 148–55; Mark Urban, *The Man Who Broke Napoleon's Codes. The Story of George Scovell* (2001), pp. 37–49; Vichness, 'Marshal of Portugal', pp. 178–87.
42. AW to Villiers, 17 and 19 May 1809, and to Castlereagh, 18 May 1809, *WD*, vol. 3, pp. 238–41.
43. AW to Castlereagh, Montalegre, 18 May 1809, *WD*, vol. 3, pp. 239–41.
44. Captain G. Bowles to Lord Fitzharris, Oporto, 25 May 1809, Malmesbury, *Letters*, vol. 2, pp. 98–110.
45. Quoted in Duncan, *History of the Royal Artillery*, vol. 2, p. 245.
46. AW to Villiers, Ruiaves, 17 May 1809, *WD*, vol. 3, pp. 238–9.
47. Oman, vol. 2, pp. 360–1.
48. AW to Villiers, 17 May, and to Frere, 20 May, *WD*, vol. 3, pp. 238–9, 244.
49. Moira to Sir Charles Hastings, 25 March [1809] (written before Arthur Wellesley was appointed and probably in response to the despatch of Hill's reinforcement, but the underlying scepticism and disapproval are just as applicable, as is shown by Moira's later letters), Hastings, *Historical Manuscripts Commission. Report on the Manuscripts of the Late Reginald Rawdon Hastings Esq ...* (1934–37; henceforth cited as *HMC Hastings*), vol. 3, p. 271; Auckland to Grenville, [14 April 1809], *HMC Dropmore*, vol. 9, pp. 302–3.
50. Moore's opinion: Moore to Castlereagh, 25 November 1808, James Moore, *A Narrative of the Campaign of the British Army in Spain, commanded by his Excellency Lieut.-General Sir John Moore* (1809), pp. 265–6, and is discussed Fortescue, vol. 7, pp. 126–8, and Oman, vol. 2, p. 286. Roberts, *Whig Party*, pp. 141–2; Wellington to Liverpool, 2 April 1810, *WD*, vol. 3, pp. 809–12.

51. Grey to Grenville, 25 May 1809, *HMC Dropmore*, vol. 9, p. 308; this was also the line taken by the *Morning Chronicle* on 26 May 1809 when it dismissed Oporto as nothing more than a skirmish with the French rearguard. On the general point see Roberts, *Whig Party*, pp. 133–71, and E.A. Smith, *Lord Grey 1764–1845* (1990), p. 172.
52. Castlereagh to Charles Stewart, 31 May [1809], PRONI D 3030/Q2/2, p. 70; Castlereagh to George III, 25 May 1809, George III, *Later Correspondence*, vol. 5, p. 284.
53. Castlereagh to AW, 26 May 1809, Castlereagh, *Correspondence*, vol. 7, pp. 73–4; Castlereagh to the King, 25 May 1809, and reply 26 May, George III, *Later Correspondence*, vol. 5, pp. 284–5.
54. AW to William Wellesley-Pole, 1 July 1809, Wellington, 'Letters to Pole' pp. 13–15.
55. AW to Ferguson, 22 June, Ferguson to Whitbread, 21 July, Whitbread to AW, 30 July, and reply 4 September 1809, AW to Whitbread, 4 September 1809, all in Creevey, *Creevey Papers*, pp. 101–5. Whitbread's remarks were contained in his speech on the Vote of Credit on 31 May 1809, *Parliamentary Debates*, vol. 14, cols. 810–19. The report in *Parliamentary Debates* is based on newspaper reports, but it includes the phrases Wellesley found objectionable (see esp. col. 816).

19 Talavera (June–August 1809)

1. Muir, *Britain and the Defeat of Napoleon*, pp. 81–2, 85–7; John M. Sherwig, *Guineas and Gunpowder. British Foreign Aid in the Wars with France, 1793–1815* (1969), pp. 207–15; Castlereagh to Stewart, 31 July 1809, PRONI D 3030 /Q2/2, pp. 70–5.
2. Gordon C. Bond, *The Grand Expedition. The British Invasion of Holland in 1809* (1979), *passim*; Fortescue, vol. 7, pp. 49–96 (figure of 11,000 sick on 1 February 1810 from ibid., p. 91n); Carl Christie, 'The Royal Navy and the Walcheren Expedition of 1809' (1981), pp. 190–200; Wellington to Liverpool, 11 September 1811, and 20 March 1812, *WD*, vol. 5, pp. 270 and 554 on the lasting effect on the men's health; Liverpool to Wellington, 26 June 1810, *WSD*, vol. 6, pp. 547–8 on the determination to concentrate efforts on the Peninsula.
3. *The Times*, 25 May 1809.
4. Canning to Frere, 'Private', 19 April 1809, Canning Papers 45.
5. Castlereagh to Charles Stewart, 'Private', 31 July [1809], PRONI D 3030/Q 2/2, pp. 70–5.
6. Castlereagh to AW, draft, 25 May 1809, Castlereagh, *Correspondence*, vol. 7, p. 71.
7. There is no letter at the time recording the King's view, but see his letter to Castlereagh of 3 October 1809, George III, *Later Correspondence*, vol. 5, pp. 387–8.
8. Oman, vol. 2, pp. 625–7 shows that the French army in Spain on 1 February 1809 had a gross strength of 288,551 men (possibly not including officers) so it would not have been fewer than 250,000 gross four months later and was probably more. Almost 194,000 were present and fit for duty in February, a figure unlikely to have changed very much. For Mortier see ibid., pp. 410–11.
9. AW to Villiers, Abrantes, 11 July 1809, *WD*, vol. 3, pp. 287–8; AW to Lt.-Col. Carroll, 19 June 1809, *WSD*, vol. 6, pp. 289–90; AW to Lt.-Col. Bourke, 21 June 1809, *WD*, vol. 3, pp. 310–11.
10. General Order, 29 May 1809, *WD*, vol. 3, p. 258.
11. AW to Castlereagh, 30 June 1809, and to Beresford, 27 June 1809, *WD*, vol. 3, pp. 334–5 and 327–8.
12. AW told Castlereagh on 27 June that including Craufurd he would have 20,000 rank and file infantry and 3,000 rank and file cavalry: to which must be added one-eighth for officers and a further allowance for artillery (AW to Castlereagh, 27 June 1809, *WD*, vol. 3, pp. 329–30). The figure of 25,000 men includes the reinforcements which reached the army before the battle of Talavera (i.e. 1/48th, 1/61st).
13. AW to Castlereagh, 30 June 1809, *WD*, vol. 3, pp. 334–5.
14. AW to Castlereagh, 15 July 1809 (2 letters), *WD*, vol. 3, pp. 358–9, 359; AW to William Wellesley-Pole, 15 July 1809, Wellington, 'Letters to Pole' p. 15.
15. See Charles Stewart to Castlereagh, Abrantes, 27 June 1809, PRONI D 3030/P/224: 'halting here has given us all the spleen' and 'I think Whitbread and Tarleton have put us not a little out of sorts'. AW to Huskisson, Coimbra, 30 May 1809, and AW to Castlereagh, 11 and 22 June 1809, *WD*, vol. 3, pp. 261–2, 289, 318
16. AW to Villiers, 31 May and 19 July 1809, *WD*, vol. 3, pp. 262–3 and 364; see also his letter to Huskisson, 28 June 1809, ibid., pp. 331–2. It is worth noting that AW's most violent complaints were generally – but not exclusively – in letters to Villiers which were less at risk of being intercepted than those going to England. This also shows that he thoroughly trusted Villiers.

17. Castlereagh to AW, draft, 11 July 1809, Castlereagh, *Correspondence*, vol. 7, pp. 95–6.
18. Oman, vol. 2, pp. 458–60.
19. Hawker, *Journal*, p. 83: 'Sir J___ B___' in text but the identification with Banks is fairly obvious.
20. There is an excellent first-hand description of the meeting in Londonderry, *Narrative of the Peninsular War*, vol. 1, pp. 381–7; AW to Frere, 13 July 1809, *WD*, vol. 3, pp. 353–4; see also Oman, vol. 2, pp. 470–3.
21. AW to Frere, Abrantes, 12 June 1809, *WD*, vol. 3, p. 291; also Canning to Frere, 'Private', 19 April 1809, Canning Papers 45/12. Oman, vol. 2, pp. 463–7. It is clear that the impulse for this came, not from the British government, nor from Wellesley, but from Frere and, possibly, some of his Spanish friends in Seville.
22. AW to Castlereagh, 15 July 1809, *WD*, vol. 3, pp. 358–9.
23. AW to General O'Donoju, Plasencia, 16 July 1809, *WD*, vol. 3, p. 360 and Oman, vol. 2, pp. 484–6; see also AW to Frere, 16 July 1809, and AW to Junta of Plasencia, 18 July, ibid., pp. 361, 363.
24. *WD*, vol. 3, p. 362. There is a fascinating description of the construction of a bridge over the Tietar by the Royal Staff Corps in Lt.-Col. F.S. Garwood, 'The Royal Staff Corps, 1800–1837' (1943), pp. 83–4.
25. Stothert, *Narrative*, p. 77.
26. [Fitzclarence], 'An Account of the British Campaign of 1809', pp. 672–3; Aitchison, *Ensign in the Peninsular War*, p. 52; see also the lively account of the day's events in Schaumann, *On the Road with Wellington*, pp. 168–70.
27. Oman, vol. 2, pp. 489–90; Londonderry, *Narrative of the Peninsular War*, vol. 1, pp. 393–6; S. Whittingham, *A Memoir of the Services of Lieutenant-General Sir Samuel Ford Whittingham* (1868), p. 95.
28. AW to Frere, 24 July 1809, *WD*, vol. 3, pp. 366–7.
29. Ibid., pp. 367–8; see also AW to William Wellesley-Pole, 25 July 1809, Wellington, 'Letters to Pole', pp. 16–17.
30. AW to Frere, 13 and 24 July 1809, *WD*, vol. 3, pp. 353–4, 367–8.
31. AW to Frere, 24 July 1809, *WD*, vol. 3, pp. 367–8.
32. Ibid., pp. 366–7.
33. For examples see Carss, letter of 25 July 1809, in S.H.F. Johnston, ed., 'The 2/53rd in Peninsular War: Contemporary Letters from an Officer of the Regiment [Captain John Carss]' (1948), p. 5; Bingham to his mother, 26 July 1809, Gareth Glover, ed., *Wellington's Lieutenant, Napoleon's Gaoler. The Peninsula and St Helena Diaries and Letters of Sir George Ridout Bingham 1809–1821* (2004), p. 44; Hill to his sister, 25 July 1809, in Edwin Sidney, *The Life of Lord Hill* (1845), pp. 105–6; Aitchison to his father, 10 and 25 July 1809, Aitchison, *Ensign in the Peninsular War*, pp. 50 and 53; and Hawker, *Journal*, p. 93.
34. Oman, vol. 2, pp. 460–2, 496–8.
35. Londonderry, *Narrative of the Peninsular War*, vol. 2, pp. 404–5.
36. Ibid., pp. 404–5; Fitzclarence, 'An Account of the British Campaign of 1809', p. 4. Oman, vol. 2, pp. 503–6; Fortescue, vol. 7, pp. 226–8; however neither takes account of the fact that Donkin's brigade was engaged in the evening fighting and so both attribute all the losses on 27 July to the combat at Casa de Salinas.
37. See description of battlefield in Oman, vol. 2, pp. 507–12, 557–8, and Fortescue, vol. 7, pp. 223–6, and the sketch map by Lt. Unger, King's German Legion artillery, in Maj.-Gen. B.P. Hughes, *Firepower. Weapons Effectiveness on the Battlefield* (1974), pp. 140–1.
38. Oman, vol. 2, pp. 512–14 and General Orders of 12 and 21 August 1809, Wellington, *General Orders. Spain and Portugal, April 27th to December 28th 1809* (1811), pp. 126, 131–2, and 27 August, ibid., p. 137 makes clear the presence of British among those fleeing.
39. Oman, vol. 2, pp. 513–14; Whittingham, *Memoir*, p. 98.
40. Hill's 1827 memorandum on the battle in Sidney, *Life of Hill*, p. 111; Everard, *History of Thos. Farrington's Regiment*, pp. 301–3; I am grateful to Howie Muir for bringing this point to my attention.
41. Donkin to R. Brownrigg, 'Private', Talavera, 29 July 1809, Hope of Luffness Papers, GD 364/1/1193.
42. Oman, vol. 2, p. 649.

43. The French return in Oman, vol. 2, pp. 652–3 gives a fair basis for estimates, although we cannot be sure which casualties were suffered on 27 July and which on the following day. Over the two days Ruffin's division lost a total of 1,632 casualties.

44. Oman, vol. 2, pp. 515–16, 519; Fortescue, vol. 7, pp. 230, 235; Napier, *History*, vol. 2, pp. 179–80.

45. Fitzclarence, 'An Account of the British Campaign of 1809', p. 4.

46. Ibid., p. 9.

47. Ibid., p. 9.

48. The British army began the campaign with about 25,000 men; it had around 23,000 at Plasencia; make allowances for losses on 27 July and some wastage since Plasencia gives a total of approximately 22,000 at Talavera.

49. George Murray to Alexander Hope, 'Private', Talavera, 31 July 1809, Hope of Luffness Papers, GD 364/1/1193; casualty figures from Oman, vol. 2, pp. 650–1.

50. Donkin to Brownrigg, 'Private', Talavera, 29 July 1809, Hope of Luffness Papers, GD 364/1/1193.

51. Beamish, *History of the King's German Legion*, vol. 1, p. 210.

52. Oman, vol. 2, p. 652: the 24e Ligne lost 567 casualties, and the 96e Ligne 606, both over the entire battle. The 9e Léger was not, apparently seriously engaged in the morning fight, but probably still suffered a few casualties.

53. Fitzclarence, 'An Account of the British Campaign of 1809', p. 11.

54. Oman, vol. 2, pp. 527–9; cf Fortescue, vol. 7, p. 243n.

55. Oman, vol. 2, p. 532; Andrew Leith Hay, *A Narrative of the Peninsular War* (1831), vol. 1, p. 155.

56. For example, see Aitchison to his father, Belem, 14 September 1809, Aitchison, *Ensign in the Peninsular War*, p. 57.

57. Carss, letter of 16 August 1809, in Johnston, ed., 'The 2/53rd in Peninsular War', pp. 5–6.

58. Information supplied by Charles Esdaile (in an email of 14 September 2004), based on General Eguia's evidence. British sources provide a good deal of support for this, although the sequence of events is confused, see Whittingham, *Memoir*, p. 99 (recollections rather than a contemporary letter); Leslie, *Military Journal*, p. 170; Bingham to Tryon, 1 August 1809, Glover, ed., *Wellington's Lieutenant, Napoleon's Gaoler*, p. 48, and Oman, vol. 2, pp. 535–6.

59. Stothert, *Narrative*, pp. 90–1.

60. Cocks to his father, 30 July 1809, Page, *Intelligence Officer in the Peninsula*, p. 37.

61. Sebastiani quoted in Malmesbury, *Letters*, vol. 2, p. 129.

62. British strength figures based on comparison between those given by Oman, vol. 2, pp. 645–6 (which exclude officers) and those in Londonderry, *Narrative of the Peninsular War*, Appendix 4 (which relate to 15 July – almost a fortnight before the battle and so are only approximate). Allowance has been made for losses on 27 July.

63. Anonymous, 'Battle of the Talavera de la Reyna', *WSD*, vol. 13, pp. 340–3. See also Frederick Ponsonby to Lady Duncannon, 3 September 1809, Earl of Bessborough and A. Aspinall, eds., *Lady Bessborough and her Family Circle* (1941), pp. 188–9, and *The Times*, 23 August 1809, for other first-hand accounts of the charge.

64. Beamish, *History of the King's German Legion*, vol. 1, pp. 216–7; Sir Rufane Donkin to Lt.-Gen. Napier, London, 24 May 1830, published in *United States Journal* (1830), pt. 2, pp. 96–8; Cocks, letter of 30 July 1809, in Page, *Intelligence Officer in the Peninsula*, p. 37; Stothert, *Narrative*, p. 89; AW to William Wellesley-Pole, 1 August 1809, Wellington, 'Letters to Pole', pp. 17–18; George Murray to Maj.-Gen. Alexander Hope, Talavera, 31 July 1809, Hope of Luffness Papers, GD 364/1/1193.

65. Oman, vol. 2, pp. 555–6, 649–53.

66. See his letters to Beresford and the Duke of Richmond, both 29 July 1809, *WD*, vol. 3, pp. 379–80.

67. Oman, vol. 2, pp. 574–7.

68. Fortescue, vol. 7, pp. 266–8; Oman, vol. 2, pp. 572–3.

69. See Fortescue, vol. 7, pp. 270–1 for some interesting comments on British accusations that Cuesta 'abandoned' their wounded and p. 268 for the differing views of Cuesta and O'Donoju.

70. Castlereagh to Stewart, 'Private', 5 August 1809, PRONI D 3030/Q2/2, pp. 76–7.

71. Palmerston to Miss Temple, 14 August 1809, and Lady Malmesbury to Palmerston, 17 August 1809, Palmerston Papers, University of Southampton, BR 24/1 and GC/MA/179.

72. *Gentleman's Magazine*, August 1809, p. 772.
73. Brightfield, *John Wilson Croker*, pp. 267–70.
74. William Wellesley-Pole to AW, [Private], 22 August 1809, Raglan Papers, Wellington B no. 93.
75. William Wellesley-Pole to AW, 22 August 1809, Raglan Papers, Wellington A no. 93, 1809; AW to Pole, 13 September 1809, Wellington, 'Letters to Pole', pp. 23–4.
76. Tom Grenville to Lord Grenville, 15 August 1809, *HMC Dropmore*, vol. 9, p. 313.
77. Calvert, *An Irish Beauty*, 15 and 28 August 1809, pp. 138–9, 141.
78. Duke of York to Col J.W. Gordon, [Private], 14 August 1809, BL Add Ms 49,473 f 20; the King to Portland, 16 August 1809, George III, *Later Correspondence*, vol. 5 p. 324.
79. Graham to Robert Graham of Fintry, 27 September 1809, *HMC Graham of Fintry*, pp. 58–9 (a 'street man' was evidently a term for a male prostitute). See also Charles Napier's comments in June 1810, Napier, *Life of Charles Napier and Opinions*, vol. 1, pp. 126–7. Like Graham, Charles Napier was a protégé and great admirer of Moore.
80. Clinton, Diary, vol. 48, 6 September 1809, Ward Papers 300/7/1, p. 54.
81. Roberts, *Whig Party*, p. 140.

20 Misery on the Guadiana (August–December 1809)

1. Cooper, *Rough Notes*, p. 28; see also Stothert, *Narrative*, pp. 102–5.
2. AW to Lord Wellesley, [Private], Deleytosa, 8 August 1809, *WD*, vol. 3, pp. 404–5; GO, 9 August 1809, Wellington, *General Orders. Spain and Portugal*, 1809, pp. 122–4. (Although for the sake of simplicity AW referred to as Wellington in the text, he had yet to receive his title when this General Order and the letter to his brother were written.)
3. Anon, 'Biographical Sketch of G.J. Guthrie, Esq. F.R.S.', *The Lancet*, 1850, vol. 1, p. 729; G.A. Kempthorne, 'The Medical Department of Wellington's Army, 1809–1814' (1930), p. 138.
4. AW to Villiers, 12 August 1809, *WD*, vol. 3, pp. 414–15.
5. AW to Lord Wellesley, [Private], Deleytosa, *WD*, vol. 3, pp. 404–5.
6. AW to Eguia and to Lord Wellesley, 18 and 24 August and 1 September 1809, *WD*, vol. 3, pp. 427, 427–9, 445–8, 464–8; Lord Wellesley to AW, Seville, 22 and 30 August 1809, Richard, Marquess Wellesley, *The Despatches and Correspondence of the Marquess Wellesley, K.G. during His Lordship's Mission to Spain as Ambassador Extraordinary to the Supreme Junta in 1809* (1838), pp. 60–3, 87–91; and Lord Wellesley to AW, 29 August 1809, *WSD*, vol. 6, p. 337.
7. Castlereagh's letter of 4 August does not appear to have survived and its contents must be deduced from AW's reply: AW to Castlereagh, 25 August 1809, *WD*, vol. 3, pp. 449–54; see also Castlereagh to AW, 12 August 1809, Castlereagh, *Correspondence*, pp. 102–3. Extract of Canning to Lord Wellesley, 12 August 1809, *WSD*, vol. 6, pp. 350–3.
8. Canning to AW, 'Private', 27 August 1809, and Canning to Lord Wellesley, 'Private and Confidential', 12 August 1809, Canning Papers 46A and 34.
9. AW to Castlereagh, 25 August 1809, *WD*, vol. 3, pp. 449–54, quote on p. 451.
10. Ibid., pp. 449–54.
11. Ibid., pp. 449–54.
12. Wellington to William Wellesley-Pole, 22 October 1809, Wellington, 'Letters to Pole', pp. 26–7.
13. Wellington to Buckingham, Badajoz, 16 November 1809, *WSD*, vol. 13, pp. 369–71.
14. Liverpool to Wellington, 1 November 1809, *WSD*, vol. 6, p. 421.
15. Wellington to Liverpool, Badajoz, 28 November 1809, *WD*, vol. 3, pp. 610–11.
16. Liverpool to Wellington, 1 November 1809, *WSD*, vol. 6, p. 421; see also his letter of 20 October, ibid., pp. 412–13.
17. Alexander Gordon to Aberdeen, Lisbon, 19 October 1809, in Alexander Gordon, *At Wellington's Right Hand. The Letters of Lieutenant-Colonel Sir Alexander Gordon, 1808–1815* (2003), p. 62.
18. Memorandum for Lieutenant Colonel Fletcher, Lisbon, 20 October 1809, *WD*, vol. 3, pp. 556–60.
19. Wellington to Liverpool, 14 November 1809, *WD*, vol. 3, pp. 583–8 (two letters). Wellington's figures for the additional cost of keeping the army in Portugal were decidedly optimistic, and took no account of the fact that soldiers in Britain, unlike those in Portugal or Spain, could be paid in paper currency, which would not place any burden on the exchange, and much of which would return to the Treasury after circulating through the economy.
20. Wellington to Liverpool, Badajoz, 28 November 1809, *WD*, vol. 3, pp. 610–11.

21. Liverpool to Wellington, 15 December 1809, *WSD*, vol. 6, p. 441– full text in BL Add Ms 38,244 f 112–18.
22. Charles Stewart to Castlereagh, [21 December 1809], PRONI D 3030/P/3, and Liverpool to Wellington, 26 June 1810, *WSD*, vol. 6, pp. 547–8.
23. Lieutenant William Swabey, *Diary of Campaigns in the Peninsula for the Years 1811, 12 and 13* (1984) p. 182, 4 March 1813.
24. The Light Brigade had a field day on 23 September – Mark Urban, *Rifles* (2003), p. 37, and a review by Wellington on 18 November, Verner, *Rifle Brigade*, vol. 2, p. 81.
25. Sherer, *Recollections*, pp. 73–4.
26. *The Monthly Magazine*, vol. 28, no. 191 (1 November 1809), p. 353, quoted in 'The British Army, Wellington and Moore: Some Aspects of Service in the Peninsular War' by Philip Haythornwaite (1999), p. 93.
27. Lady Sarah Napier to Lady Susan O'Brien, 25 October 1809, S. Lennox, *The Life and Letters of Lady Sarah Lennox, 1745–1826* (1901), vol. 2, p. 229.
28. Charles Stewart to Frances, Lady Londonderry, 18 December 1811, PRONI D 3030/Q 3.
29. Wellesley and Steegman, *Iconography*, p. 40 and plate 9.
30. Ellesmere, *Personal Reminiscences*, pp. 89–90.
31. Quoted in Urban, *Rifles*, p. 27 which gives a good account of the hostility between Craufurd and the officers of the 95th including its CO Sidney Beckwith. See also Major George Simmons, *A British Rifleman. The Journals and Correspondence of Major George Simmons ...* (1899), pp. 26–7.
32. Bingham to his mother, 5 January 1810, in Glover, ed., *Wellington's Lieutenant, Napoleon's Gaoler*, p. 78; George Napier, *Passages in the Early Military Life of General Sir George T. Napier* (1884), p. 182.
33. Return, 25 July 1809, ibid., p. 481.
34. Return printed in ibid., p. 420.
35. 'Return of Casualties which have taken place in the British Army serving in Spain and Portugal, between 31st March 1809 and 24th December 1809', *Papers Relating to Spain and Portugal* in *Parliamentary Papers* (1810), no. 1.
36. Cooper, *Rough Notes*, pp. 149–50.
37. Wellington to the Commander-in-Chief, Badajoz, 16 November, *WD*, vol. 3, p. 592; Wellington to Liverpool, 29 November and 7 December 1809, *WD*, vol. 3, pp. 611 and 627, and Cantlie, *History of the Army Medical Department*, vol. 1, p. 318.
38. Memorandum by Wellington, 11 October 1809, *WD*, vol. 3, pp. 544–7.
39. Wellington to Villiers, 20 September 1809, *WD*, vol. 3, p. 510; cf AW to William Wellesley-Pole, Truxillo, 21 August 1809, Raglan Papers, Wellington A no. 18.
40. Moyle Sherer, *Military Memoirs of Wellington*, vol. 1, p. 265, quoted in Wellesley, *The Man Wellington*, p. 180.
41. Warre, *Letters from the Peninsula*, pp. 45–7; Boutflower, *Journal of an Army Surgeon*, pp. 16–17, 27 October 1809.
42. Stewart to Castlereagh, Merida, 24 August 1809, PRONI D 3030/P/229; Murray to Alex Hope, 'Private', 6 and 31 December 1809, Hope of Luffness Papers GD 364/1/1197; Hill to his sister, 10 October and 10 November 1809, BL Add Ms 35,061 f 17–18, 19–20. The second of these letters is printed in full in Sidney's *Life of Hill*, pp. 116–18.

21 Preparing for the Storm (December 1809–June 1810)

1. Wellington to Liverpool, Badajoz, 7 December 1809, *WD*, vol. 3, pp. 628–9.
2. Aitchison to his father, Coimbra, 26 December 1809, Aitchison, *Ensign in the Peninsular War*, p. 75.
3. Wellington to Admiral Berkeley, 7 April 1810, and to Liverpool, 26 April 1810, *WD*, vol. 4, pp. 7–8, *WSD*, vol. 6, p. 516; Cantlie, *History of the Army Medical Department*, vol. 1, Appendix A, p. 504.
4. Johnston, ed., 'The 2nd/53rd in the Peninsular War', p. 9 (letter of 6 May 1810); Lowry Cole to Lady Grantham, 28 February 1810, G.L. Cole, *Memoirs of Sir Lowry Cole* (1934), p. 60; Sir Benjamin D'Urban, *The Peninsular Journal of Major-General Sir Benjamin D'Urban ... 1808–1817* (1930), p. 96, 2–10 April 1810; see also Page, *Intelligence Officer in the Peninsula*, pp. 87–9.

5. 'Confidential Memorandum' for General Leite [by Wellington], 28 February 1810, *WD*, vol. 3, pp. 753–4.
6. For memories of Loison's behaviour see Burgoyne's journal for 20 February 1810, in Wrottesley's *Life of Burgoyne*, vol. 1, p. 68.
7. Vichness, 'Marshal of Portugal', pp. 137–54; Napier, *History*, vol. 6, pp. 254–6 on the negotiations with Regency; Beresford to Wellington, 4 January 1811, *WSD*, vol. 7, pp. 38–40.
8. Vichness, 'Marshal of Portugal', pp. 156–7, 226–8, 276.
9. Wellington to Beresford, 15 September 1809, Wellington to Villiers, 24 September 1809, *WD*, vol. 3, pp. 502–3, 519–20; Villiers to Wellington, 2 October 1809, *WSD*, vol. 6, pp. 383–4; Wellington to Liverpool, 14 November 1809, *WD*, vol. 3, pp. 583–6; Liverpool to Wellington, 15 December 1809, *WSD*, vol. 6, pp. 438–41; Vichness, 'Marshal of Portugal', pp. 281–3 for new pay scales.
10. Vichness, 'Marshal of Portugal', pp. 161–4, 240–4.
11. Ibid., pp. 284–6.
12. All these examples from ibid., pp. 258–9.
13. Ibid., p. 266.
14. Ibid., pp. 269–73. Beresford's plan would require 179 British officers, whereas he had 84 in October 1809 and 107 in May 1810. The protracted dispute over whether the officers receive one or two steps of promotion, and the widespread expectation that the British would soon evacuate Portugal, both discouraged officers from joining the Portuguese service.
15. D'Urban, *Journal*, p. 77.
16. Vichness, 'Marshal of Portugal', p. 291n.
17. Wellington to Liverpool, Coimbra, 4 January 1810, *WD*, vol. 3, pp. 675–6; Alexander Gordon to Aberdeen, 13 December and 3 January 1810, Gordon, *At Wellington's Right Hand*, pp. 75–7, 79–81; see also Burgoyne, *Journal*, 5 January 1810, Wrottesley, *Life of Burgoyne*, vol. 1, p. 65.
18. A further six battalions of caçadores were raised in 1811; otherwise this remained the official strength of the Portuguese army throughout the war: S.G.P. Ward, 'The Portuguese Infantry Brigades 1809–1814' (1975), p. 103.
19. Wellington to Liverpool, 21 February 1810, *WD*, vol. 3, pp. 741–3; Wellington to Beresford, 27 February 1810, *WSD*, vol. 6, pp. 488–9.
20. General Order, 22 February 1810, *WD*, vol. 3, p. 744n.
21. Vichness, 'Marshal of Portugal', pp. 326–8.
22. Ibid., pp. 329–32.
23. Ibid., pp. 338–41; Oman, vol. 2, pp. 544–7.
24. Wellington to Forjaz, 24 April 1812, *WD*, vol. 5, p. 609; John Grehan, *The Lines of Torres Vedras* (2000), pp. 33–4; Donald D. Horward, *Napoleon and Iberia. The Twin Sieges of Ciudad Rodrigo and Almeida, 1810* (1984), pp. 28–9.
25. Oman, vol. 3, p. 420 is good on the development of the plans subsequent to Wellington's initial memorandum.
26. Mulcaster to Burgoyne, 2 January 1810, in Wrottesley, *Life of Burgoyne*, vol. 1, pp. 64–5.
27. D'Urban, *Journal*, p. 88. There is a good description of the Lines in Grehan's *Lines of Torres Vedras*, pp. 44–67, though J.T. Jones's Memoranda remains the indispensable primary source in Sir John T. Jones, *Journals of the Sieges carried on by the Army under the Duke of Wellington in Spain* (1846; reprinted 1998), vol. 3. See also *WSD*, vol. 6, pp. 538–47.
28. Philip J. Haythornthwaite, *The Armies of Wellington* (1994), p. 239.
29. Jones, *Journal of the Sieges*, vol. 3, p. 13.
30. Ibid., pp. 19–20; Oman, vol. 3, pp. 425–6.
31. Alexander Gordon to Aberdeen, 14 February 1810, Gordon, *At Wellington's Right Hand*, pp. 83–5; Capt John Squire to Lt.-Col. Henry Bunbury, Under Secretary for War and the Colonies, 27 May 1810, BL Add Ms 63,106 f 3–4, courtesy of Mark Thompson. Two other engineers, Captain George Ross and Captain Henry Goldfinch, were equally sceptical: see their comments quoted in Grehan, *Lines of Torres Vedras*, pp. 65 and 67.
32. On Stuart's work in Portugal see Mildred L. Fryman, 'Charles Stuart and the "Common Cause": The Anglo-Portuguese Alliance, 1810–1814' (1974), *passim*, and pp. 163–4 for his visit to Thomar. The description of him is from [David Roberts], *The Military Adventures of Johnny Newcome* (1904; first published 1816), pp. 133–4.
33. I cannot find a contemporary account of this meeting, which seems to have taken place about 8 February before Stuart's arrival. The only sources for it are Wellington's later comments,

Wellington to the Prince Regent of Portugal, 30 November 1810, and to Charles Stuart 18 January 1811, *WD*, vol. 4, pp. 439–42 and 529–32.

34. Wellington to William Wellesley-Pole, 4 January 1810, Wellington, 'Letters to Pole' p. 30; Wellington to Villiers, 2 January 1810, *WD*, vol. 3, pp. 670–1.

35. Wellington to William Wellesley-Pole, 9 May 1810, Wellington, 'Letters to Pole' pp. 33–4.

36. Memorandum by [Colonel Meyrick Shawe], January 1814, WP 1/445, printed with extensive and important silent deletions in *WSD*, vol. 7, pp. 257–88. Written as an apologia in 1814 by a close friend and confidant, this needs to be treated with care, but it reveals more of Wellesley's extraordinary vanity and contempt for his colleagues – as well as his views on policy questions – than any document composed while Wellesley remained in office. See also William Wellesley-Pole to Wellington, 5 April 1810, Raglan Papers, Wellington B no. 102 on the suspicions his conduct produced in his colleagues.

37. Wellington to William Wellesley-Pole, Viseu, 6 April 1810, Wellington, 'Letters to Pole', pp. 31–2.

38. Memorandum [by Colonel Meyrick Shawe], January 1814, WP 1/445 gives the best statement of Wellesley's proposals.

39. [Huskisson's memorandum on the War], 13 August 1809, Huskisson Papers, BL Add Ms 37,416 f 355–68. See Muir, *Britain and the Defeat of Napoleon*, pp. 110–13 for a larger discussion of the problem.

40. Perceval to Wellesley, nd [January 1810], BL Add Ms 37,295 f 227.

41. Wellington's disagreement with Lord Wellesley's ideas for greater British involvement in Spain is implicit in all the strategic discussions Wellington had with the ministers in 1809 and 1810. See in particular Wellington to Liverpool, 1 March and 30 May 1810, *WD*, vol. 3, pp. 759–62, *WD*, vol. 4, p. 98.

42. *Parliamentary Debates*, vol. 15, cols. 130–54 (Lords), 277–302, 440–7; vol. 16, pp. 14**– 11****; see also comments on the debates in the Commons printed in George III, *Later Correspondence*, vol. 5, pp. 504, 516 and 539; Creevey, *Creevey Papers*, pp. 126–7 on the restraint imposed by Buckingham and Temple on radical criticism of Wellington; and Roberts, *Whig Party*, pp. 139–44 on the Opposition's attitude to the war in 1810.

43. Wellington to Admiral Berkeley, 22 January 1810, *WD*, vol. 3, pp. 689–90.

44. Extract of Liverpool to Wellington, 15 December 1809, *WSD*, vol. 6, p. 441: full text in BL Add Ms 38,244 f 112–18.

45. Wellington to Liverpool, 16 and 23 May 1810, *WD*, vol. 4, pp. 72–3, 87.

46. Sherwig, *Guineas and Gunpowder*, p. 232n.

47. Wellington to Liverpool, 31 January 1810, *WD*, vol. 3, pp. 719–22.

48. Liverpool to Wellington, 13 March 1810, *WSD*, vol. 6, pp. 493–4. The manuscript in BL Add Ms 38,325 f 27–31 is marked 'Private & Confidential'.

49. Wellington to William Wellesley-Pole, 9 May 1810, 'Letters to Pole' pp. 33–4; Wellington to Liverpool, 2 April 1810, *WD*, vol. 3, pp. 809–12.

50. Wellington to Liverpool, 2 April 1810, *WD*, vol. 3, pp. 809–12.

51. Liverpool to Wellington, nd [April 1810], *WSD*, vol. 6, p. 517.

52. Liverpool to Wellington, 24 April 1810, PRO WO 6/50, pp. 61–8.

53. Wellington to Liverpool, 'Private and Confidential', 21 December 1809, BL Loan Ms 72 vol. 20 f 36 printed with a number of deletions in *WD*, vol. 3, pp. 659–60; Liverpool to Wellington[?], April 1810, *WSD*, vol. 6, p. 517; Wellington to Liverpool, 23 May 1810, *WD*, vol. 4, p. 87. Payne was recalled because he was senior to Spencer and so would have succeeded to the command if anything happened to Wellington, until Graham could arrive from Cadiz.

54. Wellington to William Wellesley-Pole, 5 September 1810, Raglan Papers, Wellington A no. 34 (passage suppressed in version of the letter published in *WSD* but partly quoted in Oman, vol. 4, p. 552n and Fortescue, vol. 7, p. 499). For the high opinion in which Spencer was held at the time of his appointment see Liverpool to Wellington, 4 May 1810, *WSD*, vol. 6, pp. 520–1 and Charles Stewart to Castlereagh, 30 May 1810, PRONI D 3030/P/9. Wellington approved of Spencer's appointment: Wellington to Liverpool, 23 May 1810, *WD*, vol. 4, p. 87.

55. Stanhope, *Notes of Conversations*, 2 November 1835, pp. 68–9.

56. Leith Hay, *Narrative of the Peninsular War*, p. 241; Sir George Head, *Memoirs of an Assistant Commissary-General* (1840), pp. 291–5.

57. Cornet Francis Hall, 'Recollections in Portugal and Spain during 1811 and 1812' (1912), p. 1407; Oatts, *Proud Heritage*, vol. 2, pp. 132–3 for his kindness to a soldier of the 74th.

58. Favourable opinions: Hercules Pakenham to Lord Longford, in E. Pakenham, *Pakenham Letters, 1800 to 1815* (1914), p. 123; John Colville, *The Portrait of a General* (1980), pp. 24, 40, 101–2; Head, *Memoirs of an Assistant Commissary-General*, pp. 291–5. Hostile comments: Harry Smith, *The Autobiography of Sir Harry Smith* (1910), pp. 47, 163 for Light Division, and William Grattan, *Adventures with the Connaught Rangers, 1809–1814* (2003), *passim*.
59. Picton to [Mr Flanagan?], 20 February 1810, Sir T. Picton, 'Some Unpublished Letters of Sir Thomas Picton', vol. 12 (1927), pp. 141–2.
60. Ibid., pp. 141–2.
61. Picton to [Mr Flanagan?], 7 May 1810, ibid., pp. 146–7.

22 Busaco (July–September 1810)

1. Napoleon to Berthier, 29 May 1810, Napoleon, *The Confidential Correspondence of Napoleon Bonaparte with his Brother Joseph* (1856), vol. 2, pp. 123–5.
2. Horward, *Napoleon and Iberia*, p. 120.
3. Wellington to Herasti, 7 May, 6 June, 19 June 1810, *WD*, vol. 4, pp. 55, 105, 125. See also Wellington to Liverpool, 27 October 1810, ibid., pp. 365–7 where Wellington strongly defended himself against accusations of having betrayed Herasti or broken his word to help him. For the argument against intervening see Wellington to Henry Wellesley and to Liverpool, both 20 June 1810, ibid., pp. 130–1, 132–3.
4. Jean Jacques Pelet, *The French Campaign in Portugal, 1810–1811* (1973), p. 61.
5. Horward, *Napoleon and Iberia*, pp. 80–186 is the definitive modern account; and figures for French casualties come from p. 182; those for the Spanish from Oman, vol. 3, p. 253.
6. Wellington to Craufurd, 8 pm, 22 July 1810, *WD*, vol. 4, p. 179.
7. William Napier in Bruce, *Life of Napier*, vol. 1, p. 54; Charles Napier in Urban, *Rifles*, p. 57 for the antithesis between Craufurd and his men.
8. Oman, vol. 3, pp. 257–66; Fortescue, vol. 7, pp. 477–84; Horward, *Napoleon and Iberia*, pp. 202–24; Verner, *History and Campaigns of the Rifle Brigade*, vol. 2, pp. 120–32; Urban, *Rifles*, pp. 55–65.
9. Alexander H. Craufurd, *General Craufurd and His Light Division* (1987; first published 1891), pp. 149–50, 154; Verner, *History and Campaigns of the Rifle Brigade*, vol. 2, pp. 131–2.
10. George Murray to Alex Hope, 25 July 1810, Hope of Luffness Papers, GD 361/1/1197; see also Alexander Gordon to Aberdeen, 24 July 1810, in Gordon, *At Wellington's Right Hand*, pp. 98–100.
11. Wellington to Beresford, 29 July 1810, *WD*, vol. 4, pp. 192–3.
12. Oman, vol. 3, p. 514.
13. Ibid., pp. 267–77; Wellington to Charles Stewart, 31 August 1810, *WD*, vol. 4, p. 252; Terms of Capitulation printed in *WD*, vol. 4, p. 257.
14. Charles Stewart to Castlereagh, 4 September 1810, PRONI D3030/P/22, cf his earlier letter of 11 July praising the fortress (loc. cit. no. 14); Alexander Gordon to Lord Aberdeen, 29 August 1810, Gordon, *At Wellington's Right* Hand, pp. 109–10; Lady Bessborough to Granville Leveson Gower, 19 September 1810, Leveson Gower, *Private Correspondence*, vol. 2, pp. 366–7 inc. Tierney's views.
15. Auckland to Grenville, 2 October 1810, *HMC Dropmore*, vol. 10, pp. 52–3; Gordon to Grey, 12 October 1810, Earl Grey Papers, Durham University Library GRE/B19/55; Richard Ryder to Harrowby, 29 September 1810, Harrowby Papers, vol. V f 23–27.
16. Charles Stewart to Castlereagh, 4 September 1810, PRONI D3030/P/22.
17. AW to Charles Stuart, 11 September 1810, *WD*, vol. 4, pp. 273–5.
18. Quoted in Oman, vol. 3, pp. 352–3.
19. Proclamation to the People of Portugal, 4 August 1810, *WD*, vol. 4, p. 208; see also Wellington to Cotton, 6½ pm, 11 August 1810, ibid., p. 223, for an example of enforcing this policy.
20. Maj.-Gen. Henry Mackinnon, *A Journal of the Campaign in Portugal and Spain* (1999; first published 1812), p. 63; Pelet, *French Campaign in Portugal* confirms this.
21. Schaumann, *On the Road with Wellington*, p. 242; also Page, *Intelligence Officer in the Peninsula*, p. 80 for a good description.
22. Oman, vol. 3, pp. 341–2; Wellington to Masséna, 9 and 24 September 1810, *WD*, vol. 4, pp. 267–8, 297–8; Pelet, *French Campaign in Portugal*, p. 155.

23. Wellington to Charles Stuart, 18 September 1810, *WD*, vol. 4, pp. 289–90.

24. Wellington to Cotton, 9½ pm, 21 September 1810, *WD*, vol. 4, p. 294.

25. Boutflower, *Journal of an Army Surgeon*, p. 59; Tomkinson, *Diary of a Cavalry Officer*, p. 42; see also Page, *Intelligence Officer in the Peninsula*, p. 81, and Gomm, *Letters and Journals*, p. 181.

26. The interpretation of Wellington's reasons for fighting at Busaco given here differs from that which I put forward in *Britain and the Defeat of Napoleon*, p. 131. This is not based on new evidence, but on subsequent consideration of existing evidence.

27. Lt.-Col. Bathurst to Beresford, 7 pm, 19 September 1810, Wellington to Cotton, 9½ pm, 21 September 1810, *WD*, vol. 4, pp. 291, 294. Robertson, *Wellington at War*, p. 136 identifies the road as the modern N334–1 cf Jac Weller, *On Wellington. The Duke and his Art of War* (1998), pp. 55–8. Murray to Cotton, 24 September 1810, Combermere, *Memoirs*, vol. 1, pp. 158–9 asks him to send a patrol discreetly along the road. Cocks observed the French march along the road later and records that 'the road was so bad that the whole of the French cavalry led their horses down the hill'. Cocks, Journal, 29 September 1810, Page, *Intelligence Officer in the Peninsula*, p. 82.

28. Sherer, *Recollections of the Peninsula*, p. 108.

29. Oman, vol. 3, p. 361.

30. Ibid., pp. 362–4; C.T. Atkinson, 'A Swiss Officer in Wellington's Army' (1957), p. 74 for Cole's move.

31. Oman, vol. 3, pp. 368–9; Lt.-Col. G.L. Chambers, *Bussaco* (1994; first published 1910), p. 184; Donald D. Horward, *The Battle of Bussaco. Masséna vs. Wellington* (1965), pp. 70–2. See Pelet, *French Campaign in Portugal*, pp. 175–7 for a defence of Masséna's decision.

32. Masséna's orders are printed in Oman, vol. 3, p. 549. See Pelet, *French Campaign in Portugal*, p. 176 for some interesting comments.

33. Oatts, *Proud Heritage*, vol. 2, pp. 135–6, 140 drawing on Trench's letter; Picton to Wellington, 10 November 1810, *WSD*, vol. 6, pp. 633–5.

34. Lemonnier-Delafosse quoted in Horward, *Battle of Bussaco*, p. 99.

35. Wellington to Liverpool, 30 September 1810, *WD*, vol. 4, pp. 304–8. There is a vivid account of the role played by the 88th in this fighting in Grattan's *Adventures with the Connaught Rangers*, pp. 33–5.

36. Leith's report enclosed in Leith to Wellington, 10 November 1810, *WSD*, vol. 6, pp. 635–9; Gomm to Major Henry Gomm, 1 November 1810, Gomm, *Letters and Journals*, pp. 189–91; see also Andrew Leith Hay to his father, 27 September 1810, Scottish Record Office GD 225/1041 24–7. Foy was reluctant to make this attack and had no confidence that it would succeed: Girod de l'Ain, *Vie Militaire du General Foy*, p. 103 cf Horward, *Battle of Bussaco*, p. 105. Leith's role in the battle was the subject of much controversy in the nineteenth century, but a consensus emerged from the work of Chambers, Fortescue and to a lesser extent Oman, which has gained wide acceptance.

37. Unpublished letter quoted in Urban, *Rifles*, p. 78.

38. George Napier, *Passages in the Early Military Life*, p. 142; see also W.F.P. Napier's *History*, vol. 3, pp. 26–7.

39. Horward, *Battle of Bussaco*, pp. 173–5; See Muir, *Tactics and the Experience of Battle*, pp. 60–1, 91–4 for further discussion of Loison's attack.

40. Oman, vol. 3, p. 382; Pelet, *French Campaign in Portugal*, pp. 182–3; Sherer, *Recollections of the Peninsula*, p. 108 (the fraternisation).

41. Sherer, *Recollections of the Peninsula*, p. 110.

42. Atkinson, 'A Swiss Officer in Wellington's Army', p. 74: the text is a very close paraphrase of Atkinson's words, themselves a paraphrase of Roverea.

43. Schaumann, *On the Road with Wellington*, p. 249.

44. Cocks to Capt John Somers Cocks, 5 October 1810, Page, *Intelligence Officer in the Peninsula*, p. 84.

45. Horward, *Battle of Bussaco*, p. 173: this figure, based on the official returns, is not quite complete; total French losses were probably in the region of 4,600–5,000 or a little more: see Oman, vol. 3, pp. 552–5, 385.

46. Ibid., pp. 550–1.

47. Scovell's diary for 28 September 1810, PRO WO 37/7, pp. 49–51 gives a most interesting account of how he observed the French march and estimated their strength.

48. See Trant's account of his march in his 1828 letter to Londonderry printed in Londonderry's *Narrative of the Peninsular War*, vol. 2, pp. 302–11.
49. Alexander Gordon to Aberdeen, 27 September 1810, Gordon, *At Wellington's Right Hand*, p. 115; Wellington to Liverpool, 30 September 1810, *WD*, vol. 4, pp. 304–8.
50. Lt. Rice Jones, *An Engineer Officer under Wellington* (1986), p. 73 – diary for 27 September 1810; Colborne to his sister, 29 September 1810, in Moore Smith, *Life of Colborne*, p. 141; Cocks to Hon John Somers Cocks, 5 October 1810, Page, *Intelligence Officer in the Peninsula*, pp. 84–5. See also Boutflower, *Journal of an Army Surgeon*, pp 60–1.
51. Charles Stewart to Castlereagh, 30 September 1810, PRONI D 3030/P/23.
52. Wellington to William Wellesley-Pole, 4 October 1810, *WSD*, vol. 6, pp. 606–7.
53. Elizabeth Lady Holland, *The Journal of Elizabeth, Lady Holland* (1908), vol. 2, p. 264.
54. Grey to Col J.W. Gordon, 15 October 1810, BL Add Ms 49,477 f 101–2.
55. Auckland to Grenville, 16 October 1810, Tom Grenville to Grenville, 17 October 1810, *HMC Dropmore*, vol. 10, pp. 54, 55–6.
56. Quoted in Auckland to Grenville, 16 October 1810, *HMC Dropmore*, vol. 10, p. 54.
57. Liverpool to Wellington, 17 October 1810, *WSD*, vol. 6, p. 618.
58. Edward Cooke to Charles Stewart, 13 September [*sic*: October] 1810, PRONI D 3030/AA/17.

23 Torres Vedras (October 1810–February 1811)

1. Oman, vol. 3, pp. 400–3. Pelet, *French Campaign in Portugal*, pp. 199–200.
2. Boutflower, *Journal of an Army Surgeon*, p. 62, entry for 1 October written on 9 October 1810.
3. F.A. De La Fuente, 'Dom Miguel Pereira Forjaz: His Early Career and Role in the Mobilization and Defense of Portugal during the Peninsular War, 1807–1814' (1980), pp. 331–4; Pelet, *French Campaign in Portugal*, p. 256 says that most of the mills had been made inoperable. For examples of Wellington's complaints see Wellington to Admiral Berkeley, 16 October 1810, and to Liverpool, 27 October 1810, *WD*, vol. 4, pp. 334–5, 362–3.
4. Wellington to Henry Wellesley, Leiria, 3 October 1810, *WD*, vol. 4, p. 313; Alexander Gordon to Lord Aberdeen, 13 October 1810, Gordon, *At Wellington's Right Hand*, pp. 118–19; Charles Stewart to Castlereagh, 13 October 1810, PRONI D 3030/P/26.
5. Pelet, *French Campaign in Portugal*, p. 199.
6. Ibid., p. 205.
7. Ibid., p. 224. See Gordon, *At Wellington's Right Hand*, p. 154 for a different example of this axiom.
8. Horward in Pelet, *French Campaign in Portugal*, p. 207 cf Oman, vol. 3, pp. 411–12, Trant to Beresford, Coimbra, 7 October 1810, *WD*, vol. 4, pp. 345–6.
9. Masséna to Ney, 16 October 1810, quoted by Horward in Pelet, *French Campaign in Portugal*, pp. 232n and 241–2n.
10. Wellington to Henry Wellesley, 21 October 1810, *WD*, vol. 4, p. 349; Oman, vol. 3, p. 445 (for the opinions of Junot, Ney and Reynier).
11. Pelet, *French Campaign in Portugal*, p. 242.
12. Masséna to Berthier, 29 October 1810, quoted by the editor in Pelet, *French Campaign in Portugal*, pp. 448–9.
13. James Stanhope, *Eyewitness to the Peninsular War and the Battle of Waterloo. The Letters and Journals of Lieutenant Colonel the Honourable James Stanhope, 1803 to 1825* (2010), p. 84 in a journal entry for 23 June 1812 recalling the incident. Fortescue, vol. 7, p. 547n quotes the passage with minor variations of punctuation, and makes Wellington say 'the last army England has here, we must …' Charles Stewart to Castlereagh, 3 November 1810, PRONI D 3030/P/31; Wellington to Liverpool, 1 December 1810, *WD*, vol. 4, pp. 444–6. See also same to same, 27 October and 3 November, *WD*, vol. 4, pp. 368–9, 388–91 and his letter to William Wellesley-Pole of 4 October 1810 when he mentions 'the croakers about useless battles', *WSD*, vol. 6, pp. 606–7.
14. Pelet, *French Campaign in Portugal*, p. 255.
15. Oman, vol. 3, p. 447: no news from Masséna's army reached Almeida between 18 September and 15 November. For Napoleon's concern at this silence see Napoleon to Berthier, 3 and 9 November 1810, *Confidential Correspondence*, vol. 2, pp. 154–5, 156.
16. Masséna to Berthier, 29 October 1810, quoted by the editor in Pelet, *French Campaign in Portugal*, p. 260n.

17. Wellington to Charles Stuart, 7 September 1810, *WD*, vol. 4, pp. 263–4; De La Fuente, 'Forjaz', pp. 131–7.
18. Wellington to Liverpool, 13 September 1810, *WD*, vol. 4, pp. 227–9, see also Wellington to Beresford, 8 September 1810, *WD*, vol. 4, p. 266.
19. Wellington to Charles Stuart, 6 October 1810, *WD*, vol. 4, pp. 319–20; Stuart to Wellington, 5 (three letters) and 6 October 1810, WP 1/316.
20. Admiral Berkeley to Lord Bathurst, 10–14 October 1810, *HMC Bathurst*, pp. 150–1.
21. Sidney, *Life of Hill*, pp. 148–9 quoting letter home of Lt Clement Hill, Rowland Hill's brother, and ADC, dated 27 October 1810.
22. Wellington to Charles Stuart, 15 June 1810, *WD*, vol. 4, pp. 121–2; Warre, *Letters from the Peninsula*, 20 June 1810, p. 84.
23. Colville, *Portrait of a General*, pp. 22, 37.
24. Charles Stuart to Wellington, 10 October 1810, WP 1/316.
25. Wellington to Charles Stuart, 29 October, and to Liverpool, 27 October 1810, *WD*, vol. 4, pp. 375–6, 363–4. Aberdeen to Alexander Gordon, 9 April 1811, Gordon, *At Wellington's Right Hand*, pp. 188–91.
26. Wellington to T. Rowcroft, Cartaxo, 11 January 1811, *WD*, vol. 4, pp. 514–15.
27. *The Times*, 24 October 1810; Harrowby to Lady Harrowby, 10 and 12 November 1810, Harrowby Papers vol. LVII f 291–4, 295–6.
28. Ryder to Harrowby, 25 October 1810, Harrowby Papers vol. V f 59–61.
29. Grenville to Grey, 1 November 1810, *HMC Dropmore*, vol. 10, pp. 61–2.
30. Gray, *Perceval*, pp. 403–7; Aspinall in George IV, *Correspondence*, pp. 63–5.
31. Wellington to Torrens, 11 December 1810, *WD*, vol. 4, p. 456.
32. Wellington to Henry Wellesley, Cartaxo, 31 December 1810, *WSD*, vol. 7, pp. 11–12; for an example of Wellington's gloomy view of politics see Wellington to Beresford, 10 January 1811, *WD*, vol. 4, p. 52.
33. Wellington to William Wellesley-Pole, 11 January 1811, Raglan Papers, Wellington A no. 39, printed with extensive silent deletions in *WSD*, vol. 7, pp. 40–4.
34. Muir, *Britain and the Defeat of Napoleon*, pp. 110–13 (re finance); Sir David Dundas to Liverpool, 8 June 1810, PRO WO 25/3224 (unfoliated); same to same, 30 December 1810, BL Add Ms 38,378 f 106–7; figures of strength and sick based on the General Monthly Returns, WO 17/2465.
35. See Wellington's letters to Charles Arbuthnot, 5 October 1810, *WSD*, vol. 6, pp. 611–12; to William Wellesley-Pole, 15 December 1810, *WSD*, vol. 7, pp. 4–5; and to Beresford, 10 January 1811, *WD*, vol. 4, p. 52.
36. Roberts, *Whig Party*, pp. 363–71; Aspinall in George IV, *Correspondence*, vol. 7 pp. 124–38; Abbott, *Diary*, vol. 2, pp. 316–18. The Prince to Perceval, 4 February 1811, George IV, *Correspondence*, vol. 7, pp. 200–1.
37. First reports of the King's illness reached Portugal by the middle of November and caused some concern (Charles Stewart to Castlereagh, 16–21 and 24 November 1810, PRONI D 3030/P/32–33). But it was only on 8 December that letters dated mid-November reached the army (Alexander Gordon to Aberdeen, 8 December 1810, Gordon, *At Wellington's Right Hand*, p. 133; Cooke to Stewart, 18 November 1810, is receipted 8 December, PRONI D 3030/AA/19). Wellington's letters seem to have been particularly slow in coming to hand: he only replied to Pole's letter of 27 October on 8 December (*WSD*, vol. 7, pp. 1–2) and on 11 December complained to Torrens that he had received nothing since 31 October (*WD*, vol. 4, p. 456).
38. Pelet, *French Campaign in Portugal*, p. 282.
39. Ibid., p. 348, also pp. 334, 346–7.
40. Foy to Masséna, 4 December 1810, quoted by Horward in Pelet, *French Campaign in Portugal*, p. 323n; see also Oman, vol. 3, p. 457.
41. Muir, *Britain and the Defeat of Napoleon*, pp. 181–4, and Girod de l'Ain, *Vie Militaire du General Foy*, pp. 122–3.
42. Wellington to Liverpool, 16 February 1811, *WD*, vol. 4, pp. 605–6; WO 17/2465 and 2467 for figures.
43. Wellington to Torrens, 28 January 1811, *WD*, vol. 4, pp. 560–2.
44. Wellington to Bathurst, 20 April 1813, *WD*, vol. 4, p. 434; Leach Ms Journal quoted in Urban, *Rifles*, p. 202; Verner, *History and Campaigns of the Rifle Brigade*, vol. 2, p. 393; Leach, *Rough Sketches*, pp. 262, 323–4.

45. Liverpool to Wellington, 17 January 1811, *WSD*, vol. 7, pp. 45–6 on the order to sail; T.H. McGuffie, ed., *Peninsular Cavalry General (1811–1813). The Correspondence of Lieutenant-General Robert Ballard Long* (1951), pp. 59, 51 details of their progress. For Wellington's early doubts about Badajoz's resistance see Wellington to Henry Wellesley, 3 and 10 February 1811, *WD*, vol. 4, pp. 577, 593; and for his sudden confidence, Wellington to Beresford, 12 February, and to Henry Wellesley, 17 February 1811, ibid., pp. 594–5, 607.

24 The Pursuit of Masséna (February–April 1811)

1. Wellington to Beresford, 6 am, 4 March, and noon, 5 March 1811, *WD*, vol. 4, pp. 650, 651–2, 652; Alexander Gordon to Aberdeen, 6 March 1811, Gordon, *At Wellington's Right Hand*, p. 168 – they knew that the French were about to make a move but 'we could not determine whether it was one of advance or retreat'.
2. Wellington to Beresford, 5 am, 6 March 1811, *WD*, vol. 4, p. 655.
3. Hall, 'Recollections in Portugal and Spain', p. 1402.
4. Wellington to Liverpool, 14 March 1811, *WD*, vol. 4, pp. 661–70.
5. R.B. Long to his brother C.B. Long, 17 March 1811, in McGuffie, ed., *Peninsular Cavalry General*, pp. 63–4. See also George Simmons to his parents, 26 March 1811, Simmons, *A British Rifleman*, p. 152.
6. Verner, *History and Campaigns of the Rifle Brigade*, vol. 2, pp. 238–42, Fortescue, vol. 8, pp. 83–6, Oman, vol. 4, pp. 155–9, and Simmons, *A British Rifleman*, p. 155.
7. Simmons, *A British Rifleman*, p. 145, Verner, *History and Campaigns of the Rifle Brigade*, vol. 2, pp. 238, 240.
8. Wellington to Liverpool, 16 March 1811, *WD*, vol. 4, pp. 676–8.
9. Wellington to Charles Stuart, 31 March 1811, *WD*, vol. 4, p. 715 cf same to same, 30 March, ibid., pp. 712–13.
10. Head, *Memoirs of an Assistant Commissary-General*, pp. 246–7.
11. Picton to Flanagan, 11 April 1811, Picton, 'Some Unpublished Letters', p. 162.
12. A.E. Clark-Kennedy, *Attack the Colour! The Royal Dragoons in the Peninsula and at Waterloo* (nd [1975]), pp. 34–5.
13. GAO 16 March 1811, *General Orders*, 1811, pp. 55–9, printed in part in *WD*, vol. 4, p. 671n.
14. GO 17 March 1811, *General Orders*, 1811, pp. 59–70, in *WD*, vol. 4, pp. 678–9.
15. GO 18 March 1811, *General Orders*, 1811, pp. 60–1, *WD*, vol. 4, p. 678.
16. GO 20 March 1811, *General Orders*, 1811, also in *WD*, vol. 4, p. 681n.
17. Oman, vol. 4, pp. 38–61.
18. Wellington to Beresford, 2 pm, 27 March 1811, *WD*, vol. 4, pp. 704–5.
19. Wellington to Beresford, 4 April 1810, *WD*, vol. 4, pp. 722–4; Wellington to Liverpool, 23 March 1811, *WD*, vol. 4, pp. 693–4.
20. For example, Rice Jones to his father, 14 April 1811, Jones, *An Engineer Officer*, pp. 96–7; and George Scovell to J.G. Le Marchant, quoted in Urban, *Rifles*, p. 102.
21. Alexander Gordon to Aberdeen, 25 March 1811, Gordon, *At Wellington's Right Hand*, p. 179. Two weeks later Wellington put the French losses even higher, at 45,000 men, although his estimate included sick and wounded (Wellington to Liverpool, 9 April 1811, *WD*, vol. 4, pp. 735–6).
22. Oman, vol. 3, pp. 540–3, vol. 4, pp. 13–14.
23. *Examiner*, no. 166, 3 March 1811, p. 137.
24. Scott to Southey, 10 April [1811], Scott, *Letters*, vol. 2, pp. 473–6.
25. *Parliamentary Debates*, vol. 19, cols. 394–5.
26. For a contemporary comment on Grey's speech see Aberdeen to Alexander Gordon, 30 April 1811, Gordon, *At Wellington's Right Hand*, p. 195.
27. *Parliamentary Debates*, vol. 19, p. 776.
28. Ibid., May 1811, p. 782. Whitbread went further, writing to Wellington to announce and explain his change of views – see Wellington's reply, 23 May 1811, *WD*, vol. 5, pp. 43–4.
29. T. Grenville to Lord Grenville, 4 May 1811, *HMC Dropmore*, vol. 10, pp. 131–3.
30. Wellington to Liverpool, 7 May 1811, *WD*, vol. 4, pp. 787–90.
31. Liverpool to Wellington, 'Private', 30 May 1811, BL Add Ms 38,325 f 115–19 – with another copy in Add Ms 59,772 f 19–23. A draft of these instructions, including many cautious

qualifications crossed out, is in BL Loan Ms 72 vol. 21 f 63–4, and a version of this with the qualifications is printed in *WSD*, vol. 7, pp. 144–5, dated 29 May 1811. The shorter instructions without the qualifications is in WO 6/50, pp. 223–4: it is dated 30 May 1811.

25 Fuentes de Oñoro (April–June 1811)

1. Wellington's letters of 18 April 1811 are in *WD*, vol. 4, pp. 755–9.
2. Responsibility for the failure at Campo Mayor was much debated at the time and subsequently, and it is not clear whether the blame should rest on Beresford, his subordinate Charles Long, or the indiscipline of the cavalry. For a good modern account see Mark S. Thompson, *The Fatal Hill. The Campaign in Southern Spain in 1811* (2002), pp. 63–76. On the problems facing the engineers bridging the Guadiana see Sir Howard Douglas, *An Essay on the Principles and Construction of Military Bridges and the Passage of Rivers* ... (1853), pp. 278–9.
3. Wellington to Liverpool, Nisa, 18 April, and Villar Formoso, 7 May 1811, *WD*, vol. 4, pp. 759, 787–90.
4. Wellington to Beresford, Elvas, 8 am, 21 April 1811, *WD*, vol. 4, pp. 760–1.
5. Jones, *Journals of the Sieges*, vol. 1, pp. 12–13. It is important to note that both these calculations begin from the day that trenches could be opened, not from when the deliberations occurred.
6. Ibid., pp. 12–15. The best secondary account of the siege is in Mark Thompson, 'The Rise of the Scientific Soldier as seen through the Performance of the Corps of Royal Engineers during the Early Nineteenth Century' (2009), pp. 125–44.
7. Memorandum to Marshal Beresford, Elvas, 23 April 1811, *WD*, vol. 4, pp. 763–5.
8. Memorandum to the Officers in Command of Corps in Estremadura, Elvas, 23 April 1811, *WD*, vol. 4, pp. 766–7. Wellington to Castaños, 13 May, and to Henry Wellesley, 22 May 1811, *WD*, vol. 5, pp. 8, 30.
9. Oman, vol. 4, pp. 299–305.
10. Charles Stewart to Castlereagh, 1 May 1811, PRONI D 3030/P/237.
11. Napier, *History*, vol. 3 (Bk XIII, ch. 5), p. 148 claims that Loison attacked the village without Masséna's orders but this is refuted by Oman, vol. 4, p. 313 citing Masséna's own despatch.
12. Anon., *Soldier of the 71st*, pp. 60–1. See also Joseph Donaldson, *Recollections of the Eventful Life of a Soldier* (2000), pp. 123–5 for another excellent account of this fighting.
13. Oman, vol. 4, pp. 313–13, 622, 630.
14. These details from Duncan Cameron to Alan Cameron, 4 June 1811, Loraine Maclean, *Indomitable Colonel* (1986), pp. 231–2, and Anon., *Soldier of the 71st*, p. 62. Oman, vol. 4, p. 345, and Fortescue, vol. 8, p. 159, say that there was some fighting in the village on 4 June, but this is contradicted, not just by these two accounts, but also by Scovell, Alexander Gordon and Ingilby, all written at the time.
15. For example Cocks in Page, *Intelligence Officer in the Peninsula*, p. 103 cf p. 108 where he calls it manoeuvring.
16. Cocks, Journal, 4 May 1811, in Page, *Intelligence Officer in the Peninsula*, p. 103.
17. Oman, vol. 4, pp. 316, 329.
18. To be more specific: we do not know the exact location of any of Masséna's units, or the convoy of supplies intended for Almeida, nor do we know the quality of the crossroads leading south, or the impression Masséna had of the nature of the country – he may have believed that the ground around Poco Velho was too wooded and marshy for the passage of a larger force; or he may have believed if he attempted to shift a larger portion of his army south it would become vulnerable to an allied counterattack. Marmont's fate at Salamanca springs to mind.
19. Napier, *History*, vol. 3 (Bk XII, ch. 5), p. 149 states that this extension of the flank was undertaken at 'Spencer's earnest suggestion' but I have seen no supporting evidence of this suggestion.
20. Hall, 'Recollections in Portugal and Spain', pp. 1539–41. Hall's account is largely confirmed by that of Captain Thomas Brotherton, printed in Sir Thomas Brotherton, *A Hawk at War. The Peninsular War Reminiscences of General Sir Thomas Brotherton* (1986), pp. 39–40.
21. Wellington to Liverpool, 8 May 1811, *WD*, vol. 4, pp. 794–8.
22. Oman, vol. 4, pp. 341, 623–4 – the tables at the back of the volume aggregate all the Portuguese losses, but some figures are given in the text. Craufurd had returned to the army on 4 May.

23. A point made by Napier, *History*, vol. 3 (Bk XII, ch. 5), p. 155 and Fitzclarence in Maxwell, *Peninsular Sketches*, vol. 1, pp. 195–6.

24. Oman, vol. 4, pp. 622–4, 630.

25. Wellington to William Wellesley-Pole, 2 July 1811, *WSD*, vol. 7, pp. 175–7; Page, *Intelligence Officer in the Peninsula*, p. 104.

26. Scovell, Diary, PRO WO 37/7 opp. p. 39.

27. Simmons to his parents, 18 May 1811, Simmons, *A British Rifleman*, p. 183.

28. Alexander Gordon to Lord Aberdeen, 5 May ('*perfect*') and 8 May 1811, Gordon, *At Wellington's Right Hand*, pp. 201, 202.

29. Oman, vol. 4, p. 350.

30. Wellington to Liverpool, 15 May 1811; Wellington to Beresford, 12 May 1811, *WD*, vol. 5, pp. 20–2, 6.

31. Fitzroy Somerset to the Duke of Beaufort, 14 May 1811, Badminton Muniments, FmM 4/1/6/12; Alexander Gordon to Aberdeen, Villar Formoso, 15 May 1811, Gordon, *At Wellington's Right Hand*, pp. 203–6.

32. Wellington to Maj.-Gen. Alex. Campbell, Villar Formoso, 15 May 1811, *WD*, vol. 5, pp. 14–17 (Cochrane's name is suppressed in printed version, but is in the original in WP 1/332).

33. General Order, 1 September 1811, *General Orders*, 1811, pp. 173–6. Before the court-martial, Wellington had written a long, and quite sympathetic private letter to Cochrane urging him to withdraw the offensive letter to Campbell, but without success. It is not difficult to imagine the mixture of hurt and irritation felt by all parties to the dispute. Wellington to _____, 18 August 1811, *WD*, vol. 5, pp. 223–5.

34. Maj. T. Downman, 'Diary of Major Thomas Downman, Royal Horse Artillery, in the Peninsula' (1926), entry of 11 July 1811, p. 186. Downman had a recent grievance with Wellington over the promotion of two of his subordinates: see Adjutant-General to Major Downman, 24 May 1811, *WD*, vol. 5, p. 47.

35. Although he did do so many years later when asked about the affair by Stanhope; but by then his memory of the detail of the incident had faded, and he was speaking casually, and would have been most annoyed if he had known that a record was being kept of his conversation. Stanhope, *Notes of Conversations*, 31 October 1836, p. 89. But cf Browne, *Napoleonic War Journal*, pp. 142–3 where Browne comments: 'It is hard indeed if a General commanding, cannot at his discretion, use terms of censure or of praise, on actions which may have caused him disappointment or gratification, in military arrangements. Officers of superior rank were included in the same disapprobation with Lieut. Col. Bevan [*sic*], and yet they bore it calmly, and in a very few weeks nothing more was thought of the affair.'

36. Bevan's last letter is printed in full in Archie Hunter, *Wellington's Scapegoat. The Tragedy of Lieutenant-Colonel Charles Bevan* (2003), pp. 176–7; on Bevan's bouts of depression see ibid., pp. 97–8, 133.

37. Wellington to Maj.-Gen. Alex. Campbell, Villar Formoso, 15 May 1811, *WD*, vol. 5, pp. 14–17.

38. Compare his account of his meeting with Nelson, on p. 184 above, and comments on Napoleon quoted later in this chapter.

39. Wellington to Major Ridewood, Villar Maior, 6 April 1811, *WD*, vol. 4, p. 726.

40. Colville, *Portrait of a General*, pp. 64–5.

41. Wellington to Alan Cameron, 15 May 1811, Maclean, *Indomitable Colonel*, pp. 240–1 (pp. 236–43 prints much related material including Wellington's letter of 8 May, pp. 236–7); Wellington's letter of 15 May is also in *WD*, vol. 5, p. 17.

42. Dickson to Maj.-Gen. MacLeod, Elvas, 29 May 1811, Dickson, *Dickson Manuscripts*, vol. 3, p. 394.

43. Oman, vol. 4, p. 389 takes this line but Fortescue dismisses it (vol. 8, pp. 203, 212) and Thompson (*Fatal Hill*, p. 140), although less emphatic, is inclined to agree with Fortescue. Contemporaries believed that Beresford ordered a retreat.

44. Cooper, *Rough Notes*, p. 63.

45. Quote from Stanhope, *Notes of Conversations*, p. 90 (31 October 1836), see also Wellington to Pole, 2 July 1811, *WSD*, vol. 7, pp. 175–7 and C.M. Woolgar, 'Writing the Despatch: Wellington and Official Communication' (1999), pp. 12–16. The rewritten despatch is printed in *WD*, vol. 5, pp. 36–9n.

46. Wellington to Beresford, Elvas, 4½ pm, 19 May 1811, *WD*, vol. 5, p. 25.

47. Wellington to Liverpool, 15 May 1811, *WD*, vol. 5, pp. 20–2.

48. Wellington to Pole, 15 May 1811, *WSD*, vol. 1, pp. 123–5. See also Alexander Gordon to Aberdeen, 15 May 1811, Gordon, *At Wellington's Right Hand*, pp. 203–5.

49. On Wellington's self-reliance and his attitude to it, see also Wellington to Villiers, 25 May 1811, *WD*, vol. 5, pp. 48–9.

50. Wellington to Liverpool, 23 May 1811, *WD*, vol. 5, pp. 42–3.

51. Wellington to Charles Arbuthnot, Elvas, 28 May 1811, Charles Arbuthnot, *The Correspondence of Charles Arbuthnot* (1941), pp. 6–7; similar views appear in Wellington to Liverpool, Elvas, 23 May 1811, *WD*, vol. 5, pp. 42–3.

52. Wellington to Liverpool, Elvas, 18 June 1811, *WD*, vol. 5, pp. 104–5.

53. Wellington to Henry Wellesley, Elvas, 29 May 1811, *WD*, vol. 5, pp. 57–8.

54. Wellington to Picton, 1 pm, 3 June 1811, *WD*, vol. 5, p. 67.

55. Fletcher to Wellington, ¾ 5 pm, 3 June 1811, *WSD*, vol. 7, p. 151.

56. Fletcher's reports to Wellington are printed in *WSD*, vol. 7, pp. 151–4, 157–81, Wellington to Fletcher, ¼ before 8, 4 June 1811, *WD*, vol. 5, pp. 69–70.

57. Oman, vol. 4, p. 429.

58. Wellington to Liverpool, 13 June 1811, *WD*, vol. 5, p. 94.

59. Alexander Gordon to Aberdeen, 13 June 1811, Gordon, *At Wellington's Right Hand*, pp. 221–3.

60. Burgoyne to Squire, 1 September 1811, Wrottesley, *Life of Burgoyne*, vol. 1, pp. 135–6.

61. Wellington to Liverpool, 13 June 1811, *WD*, vol. 5, pp. 88–94.

62. *The Times*, 22 and 29 May 1811; *Examiner*, no. 178, 26 May 1811, pp. 327–8.

63. S.T. Coleridge, *The Collected Works of Samuel Taylor Coleridge*, vol. 3, *Essays on His Times in The Morning Post and The Courier*, published in 3 vols. (1978), vol. 2, 4 June 1811 and 22 May 1811, pp. 180, 157–8.

64. *Parliamentary Debates*, vol. 20, cols. 511–17, 519–32.

65. Grey to Grenville, 4 June 1811, Auckland to Grenville, 5 June 1811, *HMC Dropmore*, vol. 10, pp. 144–5, 146–7. See also Roberts, *Whig Party*, pp. 152–5.

66. Torrens to Taylor, 28 March 1811, W03/599, pp. 112–14 cited in Ward Papers 300/3/4.

67. *The Times*, 27, 26 and 30 May 1811. Even Coleridge in the *Courier* denounced the reappointment of the Duke, although the article was suppressed on orders from the Treasury. Coleridge, op. cit., vol. 3, part 3, pp. 220–3, *Examiner*, 2 June 1811, pp. 387–8.

68. See Pakenham, *Pakenham Letters*, p. 92, Gomm, *Letters and Journals*, pp. 203, 227. Fortescue, vol. 8, p. 281 declares that the reappointment restored efficiency at the Horse Guards and gave unbounded satisfaction to the Army.

69. Wellington to Torrens, 20 June 1811, *WSD*, vol. 7, p. 163.

70. Wellington to Liverpool, 25 June 1811, *WD*, vol. 5, pp. 115–16.

26 Ciudad Rodrigo (July 1811–January 1812)

1. Colville, *Portrait of a General*, pp. 69–71; Boutflower, *Journal of an Army Surgeon*, p. 114; Oman, vol. 4, pp. 562–71, Fortescue, vol. 8, pp. 260–3.

2. Typically for every hundred British soldiers fit and present for duty in the ranks there would be another thirty, forty or even fifty who were sick and a further ten or twenty 'on command' – detached on other duties, convalescents returning to their units, or otherwise absent. See returns in WO17/2467 and 2468.

3. Wellington to Liverpool, 2 October 1811, *WD*, vol. 5, pp. 300–1.

4. 'Return of Casualties of the Army under the Command of His Excellency General Lord Viscount Wellington ... from 29th April, 1809 to the 15th December, 1811, inclusive', *WSD*, vol. 7, p. 249.

5. Cantlie, *History of the Army Medical Department*, vol. 1, p. 334. The morning state of 23 July 1811 in WP 1/336 does not quite confirm Cantlie's figure, showing that 25.3 per cent of total British rank and file were sick compared with 20.6 per cent of Portuguese; still, the Portuguese were clearly healthier.

6. Beresford is the only senior British officer in the army other than Wellington who served throughout the war in the Peninsula, from 1809–14, and he had an extended period of recuperation near Lisbon after he was prostrated by the mental strain of commanding at Albuera; and was out of action for some months after he was wounded at Salamanca.

7. W.F. Galpin, 'The American Grain Trade to the Spanish Peninsula 1810–1814' (1922), p. 25n.

8. T.M.O. Redgrave, 'Wellington's Logistical Arrangements in the Peninsular War, 1809–1814' (1979), p. 100 (forage corn); Christopher D. Hall, 'Royal Navy and the Peninsular War' (1993), p. 404 – see also Christopher D. Hall, *Wellington's Navy. Seapower and the Peninsular War, 1807–1814* (2004), *passim*, and Tina M. McLauchlan, 'Wellington's Supply System during the Peninsular War, 1809–1814' (1997), *passim*.

9. Memorandum for the Commissary General, 20 November 1811, *WD*, vol. 5, pp. 371–3.

10. Fortescue, vol. 8, pp. 343–4.

11. Memorandum for the Commissary General, 20 November 1811, *WD*, vol. 5, pp. 370–1.

12. Wellington to Major General Howorth, 14 May 1811, memorandum for Cols Framington, Fletcher and Mr Kennedy, 19 July 1811, *WD*, vol. 5, pp. 9–10, 168–9; Dickson, *Dickson Manuscripts*, vol. 3, pp. 417–65 (number of bullocks given on p. 456 cf Jones, *Journals of the Sieges*, vol. 1, p. 364 which gives a rather lower figure, but still almost 5,000 bullocks).

13. Jones, *Journals of the Sieges*, vol. 1, p. 91; Burgoyne's journal in Wrottesley, *Life of Burgoyne*, pp. 153–4; Wellington to Liverpool, 7 January 1812, *WD*, vol. 5, pp. 461–2.

14. Jones, *Journals of the Sieges*, vol. 1, p. 97.

15. Cocks in Page, *Intelligence Officer in the Peninsula*, p. 162; Jones, *Journals of the Sieges*, vol. 1, pp. 95–100.

16. Oman, vol. 5, pp. 167–8, Moore Smith, *Life of Colborne*, pp. 166–71. Colborne's report, and Craufurd's, are printed in *WD*, vol. 5, p. 463n.

17. Burgoyne in Wrottesley, *Life of Burgoyne*, p. 156, Jones, *Journals of the Sieges*, vol. 1, pp. 105–6.

18. Instructions to General Officers, 1 January 1812, *WD*, vol. 5, pp. 450–1; Wrottesley, *Life of Burgoyne*, vol. 1, p. 156; Colville, *Portrait of a General*, p. 82; Col. Willoughby Verner, ed., 'The Diary of a Private Soldier in the Peninsular War [John Timewell, 43rd]' (1897), p. 5.

19. Wellington to Liverpool, 15 January 1812, *WD*, vol. 5, pp. 468–9.

20. Dickson to DAG, 29 January 1812, in Duncan, *History of the Royal Artillery*, vol. 2, p. 315.

21. Arrangements for the assault of Ciudad Rodrigo, 19 January 1812, *WD*, vol. 5, pp. 470–2.

22. Oman, vol. 5, pp. 177–83; Fortescue, vol. 8, pp. 358–63; Jones, *Journals of the Sieges*, vol. 1, pp. 127–31.

23. There was a bitter controversy over this, or rather several controversies, although all the overwhelming weight of contemporary evidence supports Gurwood's claim: see C.H. Dudley Ward, *A Romance of the Nineteenth Century* (1923), pp. 78–81; Smith, *Autobiography*, p. 58; Bruce, *Life of Napier*, vol. 1, pp. 81–6; Oman, vol. 5, pp. 589–90; Jones, *An Engineer Officer*, p. 124.

24. Quote from Lt John Cooke, *A True Soldier Gentleman. The Memoirs of Lt. John Cooke, 1791–1813* (2000), p. 108; see also Captain Sir John Kincaid, *Adventures in the Rifle Brigade and Random Shots from a Rifleman* (1981), p. 56, T. Dyneley, *Letters written by Lieut.-General Thomas Dyneley C.B., R.A., while on Active Service between the years 1806 and 1815* (1984; first published 1896), pp. 16–17.

25. Edward Costello, *The Peninsular and Waterloo Campaigns* (1967), p. 79–81.

26. Kincaid, *Adventures in the Rifle Brigade*, p. 59 ('bird-cages'); Costello, *Peninsular and Waterloo Campaigns*, pp. 82–3.

27. GO, 22 January 1812, *General Orders*, 1812, pp. 18, 19–21, also *WD*, vol. 5, p. 484.

28. Verner, *History and Campaigns of the Rifle Brigade*, vol. 2, pp. 352–5.

29. Perceval to Col McMahon, 18 February 1812, George IV, *The Letters of King George IV 1812–1830* (1938), vol. 1, p. 20; Perceval to Wellington, 10 February 1812, BL Add Ms 37,296 f 187–8; Perceval to Lord Wellesley, 7 February 1812, Wellesley, *Wellesley Papers*, vol. 2, pp. 70–1, *Parliamentary Debates*, vol. 21, cols. 842, 855–9, 869–83 (cols. 873–6 for Burdett).

30. Grey to Col J.W. Gordon, 28 January 1812, BL Add Ms 49,477 f 164–5.

31. Grey to Graham, 6 February 1812, Lynedoch Papers, National Library of Scotland Ms 3610 f 24–6.

32. Compare Wellington to Liverpool, 2 February 1811, *WD*, vol. 4, p. 575, and Wellington to Henry Wellesley, 29 August 1811, *WD*, vol. 5, pp. 247–8, with Henry Wellesley to Wellington, 9 May 1811 and 28 October 1811, *WSD*, vol. 7, pp. 122–3, and FO 72/114 f 83–87. On the Anglo-Spanish corps established by Whittingham and Roche see Bathurst to Wellington, 23 November 1812 and enclosure, WP 1/353; and also Bathurst to Wellington, 3 February 1813, WP 1/366, Sir J. Murray to Wellington, 28 May 1813, WP 1/369.

33. Wellington to Arbuthnot, 31 December 1811, *WSD*, vol. 7, pp. 250–1.

34. Wellington to Lord Wellesley, 20 March 1812, *WSD*, vol. 7, pp. 307–8.

27 Badajoz (February–April 1812)

1. Oman, vol. 5, pp. 188–91.
2. There is much confusion and uncertainty over the origin and movement of the various siege guns, but comparing Wellington's memorandum of 26 January 1812 (*WD*, vol. 5, pp. 485–6) with Dickson to Macleod, 29 January 1812, Dickson, *Dickson Manuscripts*, vol. 4, pp. 530–1, and Jones, *Journals of the Sieges*, vol. 1, p. 472, it seems clear that the original idea of moving the heavy guns back down the Douro was abandoned. For Berkeley's contribution see Jones, *Journals of the Sieges*, vol. 1, p. 145.
3. Wellington to Henry Wellesley, Elvas, 14 March 1812, *WD*, vol. 5, p. 550.
4. Jones, *Journals of the Sieges*, vol. 1, pp. 376–7.
5. Ibid., p. 153.
6. Ibid., p. 377.
7. Wrottesley, *Life of Burgoyne*, vol. 1, p. 169.
8. Colville, *Portrait of a General*, p. 92; Page, *Intelligence Officer in the Peninsula*, p. 223.
9. Jones, *Journals of the Sieges*, vol. 1, p. 162n.
10. Ibid., pp. 168–9 cf Wellington to Graham, 11 am, 24 March 1812, *WD*, vol. 5, pp. 557–8; Page, *Intelligence Officer in the Peninsula*, p. 233.
11. See Wellington to Graham, 11 am, 24 March 1812, *WD*, vol. 5, pp. 557–8, and Wellington to Maj.-Gen. Victor Alten, 26 March 1812, WP 1/346, printed in *WD*, vol. 5, pp. 560–1 with Alten's name suppressed.
12. Jones, *Journals of the Sieges*, vol. 1, p. 171; Wrottesley, *Life of Burgoyne*, vol. 1, pp. 172–3, Page, *Intelligence Officer in the Peninsula*, p. 226.
13. Wrottesley, *Life of Burgoyne*, vol. 1, p. 174, Fortescue, vol. 8, pp. 387–90 including Philippon's censure of the garrison. See also Colville, *Portrait of a General*, pp. 92–3 and Page, *Intelligence Officer in the Peninsula*, pp. 229–30.
14. Wellington to Liverpool, 27 March 1812, *WD*, vol. 5, pp. 560–1; Jones, *Journals of the Sieges*, vol. 1, p. 179.
15. Cocks in Page, *Intelligence Officer in the Peninsula*, p. 231.
16. Oman, vol. 5, p. 272 gives the numbers.
17. Ibid., pp. 205–6.
18. Berthier to Marmont, 21 February 1812, quoted in Oman, vol. 5, pp. 209–10.
19. D'Urban, *Peninsular War Journal*, pp. 247–8.
20. Quote from Wrottesley, *Life of Burgoyne*, vol. 1, p. 174; other information from Jones, *Journals of the Sieges*, vol. 1, pp. 192–3, see also D'Urban, *Peninsular War Journal*, p. 248.
21. Jones, *Journals of the Sieges*, vol. 1, p. 195.
22. Wellington to G. Murray, 28 May 1812, *WD*, vol. 5, p. 677.
23. H.N. Shore, 'Letters from the Peninsula during 1812–13–14' (1916), pp. 93–4.
24. Shore, 'Letters from the Peninsula', pp. 93–4; see also Cooke, *True Soldier Gentleman*, p. 125.
25. Torrens to Lt.-Col. C. Campbell, 27 April 1812, WO 3/602, pp. 49–52 comments on Campbell's role at the breach, but Campbell's letter which would give more details is untraced.
26. Sir James McGrigor, *Autobiography and Services of Sir James McGrigor* (1861), p. 273; see also Sergeant William Lawrence, *The Autobiography of Sergeant William Lawrence* (1886), pp. 113–14.
27. This follows Fortescue, vol. 8, pp. 400–2, 408–9 but no interpretation of the role of the Third Division can reconcile all the discrepancies in the sources.
28. Gomm to his brother Henry, 15 April 1812, Gomm, *Letters and Journals*, pp. 260–3.
29. Their plan failed: both the other men were killed, and Lawrence himself was wounded without entering the town, so the silver they sought turned to lead, Lawrence, *Autobiography*, p. 111. See also Costello, *Peninsular and Waterloo Campaigns*, pp. 96–9 for a vivid picture of the sack by a soldier who took part in it.
30. William Bragge, *Peninsular Portrait 1811–1814. The Letters of Captain William Bragge Third (King's Own) Dragoons* (1963), p. 51 believed that the soldiers 'richly deserved the Liberty of plundering the Town'. Verner, 'Diary of a Private Soldier', p. 6 for the belief that Wellington permitted the plunder. Tomkinson, *Diary of a Cavalry officer*, p. 146 on the feeling that the inhabitants were pro-French. See also Kincaid, *Adventures in the Rifle Brigade*, pp. 69 and 233 but cf Cooke, *True Soldier Gentleman*, p. 119.

31. Douglas, *Douglas's Tale of the Peninsula*, pp. 37–9; Kincaid, *Adventures in the Rifle Brigade*, pp. 67–9, 282–3.
32. See Kincaid, *Adventures in the Rifle Brigade*, pp. 286–9 and Harry Smith's own *Autobiography*, pp. 68–72 for the official version of the story which formed the basis of Georgette Heyer's novel *The Spanish Bride* (1940).
33. Stanhope, *Eyewitness*, p. 78.
34. Wellington, *General Orders*, 1812, pp. 52–4; estimate of deaths, Tomkinson, *Diary of a Cavalry Officer*, p. 146 says that the town's inhabitants claimed that 85 inhabitants had been killed, while he believed that the true figure was 32. Neither Esdaile nor Lovett give any figures. It is worth contrasting Wellington's General Orders with the letter in which the French General Bugeaud told his sister how much the nuns and old women of Lerida enjoyed being raped by French grenadiers – T.R. Bugeaud, *Memoirs of Marshal Bugeaud* (1884), vol. 1, p. 71.
35. Oman gives total Anglo-Portuguese losses at Albuera as 4,548 and British loss at Talavera as 5,365.
36. John Hamilton, *Sixty Years' Experience as an Irish Landlord ...* ([1894]), pp. 14–16; details of pension from Hall, *Biographical Dictionary*, p. 457–8. Hamilton was Pakenham's nephew and ward.
37. Picton to Flanagan, 9 April 1812, Picton, 'Some Unpublished Letters', pt. 2, pp. 11–12.
38. Arbuthnot, *Journal*, vol. 1 p. 143, 12 February 1822. See also Edward Pakenham to Lord Longford, Lisbon, 27 April 1812, Pakenham, *Pakenham Letters*, pp. 151–2: 'Wellington has been affected in the extreme.' However Pakenham was not present at Badajoz: he only left London to return to the Peninsula on 14 April (ibid., p. 148).
39. Wellington to Liverpool, 7 April 1812, Wellington, 'A Missing Letter from the Duke of Wellington' (1889), p. 537. Liverpool was able to reply that the Ordnance Department had been working on establishing a corps of Sappers and Miners since late 1811 and that the first company, trained by Captain Pasley, had already sailed for Lisbon: Liverpool to Wellington, 'Private', 28 April, BL Add Ms 38,326 f 30–1. See also T.W.J. Connolly, *History of the Royal Sappers and Miners* (1857), vol. 1, pp. 182–9.

28 Salamanca (April–July 1812)

1. Gray, *Spencer Perceval*, pp. 455–62.
2. No single secondary source gives a full account of the political negotiations of mid-1812. Michael Roberts's 'The Ministerial Crisis of May–June 1812' (1936), pp. 466–87 and his *Whig Party*, pp. 382–405, are excellent, but naturally concentrate on the Opposition. For the point of view of the ministers, Lords Wellesley and Moira and Canning, Roberts's work needs to be supplemented by other sources including George IV, *Letters* (with invaluable notes by Aspinall), Thorne, *History of Parliament*, Wellesley, *Wellesley Papers*, HMC Hastings and letters printed in biographies of Eldon, Sidmouth and others, as well as unpublished sources.
3. The first reference seems to be a postscript to his letter to Graham of 28 May, WD, vol. 5, p. 675. See also Major Currie to Sir R. Hill, 28 May 1812, Sidney, *Life of Hill*, pp. 198–9.
4. Wellington to Liverpool, Fuente Guinaldo, 9 June 1812, WSD, vol. 7, p. 343.
5. Wellington to William Wellesley-Pole, 29 June 1812, Raglan Papers, Wellington A no. 47.
6. Ibid.
7. Ibid.
8. Wellington to Liverpool, [Private], 29 June 1812, BL Loan Ms 72 vol. 21 f 187–8.
9. Wellington to Bathurst, 4 July 1812, WD, vol. 5, p. 733.
10. Wellington to William Wellesley-Pole, Madrid, 27 August 1812, Raglan Papers, Wellington A no. 50.
11. Extract of a letter from T. Sydenham to B. Sydenham, Torquemada, 13 September 1812, WSD, vol. 7, pp. 423–4; Wellington to Lt.-Gen. A. Campbell, Salamanca, 18 June 1812, WD, vol. 5, p. 712.
12. Wellington to Bathurst, 25 July 1812, WD, vol. 5, p. 761; earlier Wellington had been misled by inaccurate press reports into believing that the war had begun in April: Wellington to Graham, 25 April 1812, WD, vol. 5, p. 612. The likelihood of a war in the north was an open secret.
13. There is much useful information on Popham's operations in Admiral Lord Keith, *The Keith Papers* (1927–55), vol. 3, pp. 259–89, and in Hugh Popham, *A Damned Cunning Fellow. The Eventful Life of Rear-Admiral Sir Home Popham* (1991), pp. 197–211.

14. John Rosselli, *Lord William Bentinck and the British Occupation of Sicily 1811–1814* (1956), pp. 53–5; Oman, vol. 5, pp. 341–8, 571–2.

15. Numbers of sick: WO 17/2469. Reinforcements: 'Return of the Corps and Detachments of Cavalry and Infantry embarked for the Peninsula between 1st January 1812 and the Present Period', Adjutant-General's office, 27 November 1812, PRONI D3030/3387 – this does not include artillery or sappers; details of the King's German Army dragoons from 'Return of Regiments arrived in Peninsula in year ending 15 December 1812', WP 1/359. Seven divisions with Wellington; nine including Hill's corps.

16. See discussion of this point in Rory Muir, *Salamanca 1812* (2001), pp. 38–9 and sources cited there.

17. Wrottesley, *Life of Burgoyne*, vol. 1, pp. 190–4; Robert Garvett, 'A Subaltern in the Peninsular War: Letters of Robert Garrett 1811–1813' (1934), pp. 8–10 (two letters describing the operation). Jones, *Journal of the Sieges*, vol. 1, pp. 243–67; Oman, vol. 5, pp. 360–4, 370–2, 375–9.

18. James Stanhope's journal as quoted in Fortescue, vol. 8, p. 462; in Stanhope, *Eyewitness*, p. 82 the last word is given as 'um' which seems less plausible than Fortescue's reading.

19. That he expected a Whig government to emerge from the political crisis is clear from Wellington to Liverpool, 29 June 1812, BL Loan Ms 72 vol. 21 f 187–8. Stanhope, *Eyewitness*, pp. 82–3 suggests other reasons why Wellington did not attack and mentions the regret this provoked in the army.

20. Wellington to William Wellesley-Pole, 29 June 1812, Raglan Papers, Wellington A no. 47. It is possible that '1 in the morning' should read '4 in the morning', but the numeral does look like a '1' and the army did commence its march very early in the day when on campaign.

21. Cooke, *True Soldier Gentleman*, p. 138.

22. Kincaid, *Adventures in the Rifle Brigade*, p. 78.

23. For a full account of the battle of Salamanca and the problems posed by the sources, see Muir, *Salamanca, passim.*

24. The timing of Marmont's wound and his intentions for the French left at that point are among the most important but intractable problems in determining what happened in the battle, and this is only one of several possible interpretations – see Muir, *Salamanca*, pp. 65–7, 78–81 for a discussion.

25. Greville, *Memoirs*, vol. 4, p. 40.

26. Muir, *Salamanca*, pp. 84–104.

27. Leith Hay, *Narrative of the Peninsular War*, p. 257.

28. Jean Sarramon, *La Bataille des Arapiles* (1978), p. 223.

29. Much of this account of le Marchant's charge – who charged whom and when – is based on fragmentary evidence capable of other interpretations. See Muir, *Salamanca*, pp. 124–45 for a full discussion.

30. Anonymous letter from an officer of the Fusilier Brigade, 27 July 1812, NAM 6807–333.

31. Sir Philip Bainbrigge, 'The Staff at Salamanca' (1878), pp. 73–4.

32. Muir, *Salamanca*, pp. 165–75.

33. Ibid., pp. 151–64.

34. Andrew Leith Hay to his father, 2 August 1812, Leith Hay Papers, National Archives of Scotland, GD 225 Box 34/26; see Muir, *Salamanca*, pp. 186–7 for other sources making the same point.

35. Anon., 'Sketch of the Battle of Salamanca', *United Service Journal*, vol. 1, no. 1 (1829), p. 294, reprinted in Maxwell, *Peninsular Sketches*, vol. 1, pp. 345–7; Napier's account quoted in Bruce, *Life of Napier*, vol. 1, pp. 101–2. For the criticism for exposing himself recklessly, and his response, see Stanhope, *Eyewitness*, p. 90.

36. Fitzroy Somerset to the Duke of Beaufort, 26 July 1812, Badminton Muniments FmM 4/1/8/16.

37. Girod de l'Ain, *Vie Militaire du Général Foy*, pp. 177–8 quoting in Foy's journal written at the time.

38. Croker to Lord Hardwicke, 17 November 1854, Croker Papers, Box 14, Special Collections Library, Duke University – my thanks to Dr C.I. Hamilton for sending me this quote (email 26 September 2001).

39. *The Times*, 17 August 1812.

40. *The Times*, 19 August; Frederick Robinson to Catherine Harris, 20 August 1812, Cole, *Memoirs of Sir Lowry Cole*, p. 92.

41. Lord Grey to Grenville, 19 August 1812, *HMC Dropmore*, vol. 10, pp. 291–2; Auckland to Grenville, 25 August 1812, ibid., pp. 293–4; Lady Bessborough to Granville Leveson Gower, 7 September [1812], Leveson Gower, *Private Correspondence*, vol. 2, p. 454.
42. Sidmouth to the Prince Regent, 21 August 1812, George IV, *Letters*, vol. 1, p. 131.
43. Liverpool to Wellington, 19 August 1812, *WSD*, vol. 7, pp. 401–2.
44. Bathurst to the Prince Regent, 21 August 1812, *HMC Bathurst*, pp. 201–2; Bathurst to Wellington, 22 August 1812, *WSD*, vol. 7, pp. 406–8.
45. Wellington to William Wellesley-Pole, 25 July 1812, Raglan Papers, Wellington A no. 49.
46. Wellington to Bathurst, 24 August 1812 and 7 September, *WD*, vol. 6, pp. 41–2 and 58.
47. Wellington to Liverpool, 7 September 1812, *WD*, vol. 6, p. 58.
48. T. Sydenham to Sir H. Wellesley, Head Quarters, 12 September 1812, *WSD*, vol. 7, pp. 419–23.

29 Madrid and Burgos (July–November 1812)

1. Wellington to William Wellesley-Pole, 25 July 1812, Raglan Papers, Wellington A no. 49; Alexander Gordon to Aberdeen, 26 July 1812, Gordon, *At Wellington's Right Hand*, p. 303.
2. Oman, vol. 6, p. 6 says over 3,000 bayonets i.e. rank and file, so around 3,400 all ranks.
3. Cooke, *True Soldier Gentleman*, p. 151.
4. Henry Hough, 'The Journal of Second Lieutenant Henry Hough, Royal Artillery, 1812–1813' (1916), pp. 22–3.
5. Fortescue, vol. 8, p. 444.
6. Alexander Gordon to Lord Aberdeen, 16 August 1812, Gordon, *At Wellington's Right Hand*, pp. 312–13; Kincaid, *Adventures in the Rifle Brigade*, pp. 86–7; Cocks in Page, *Intelligence Officer in the Peninsula*, p. 191; Private William Wheeler, *Letters of Private Wheeler* (1951), pp. 90–1; see also Browne, *Napoleonic War Journal*, pp. 176–7 and Lt.-Col. A.F. Mockler-Ferryman, *The Life of a Regimental Officer during the Great War, 1793–1815* (1913), p. 213.
7. Wellington to Bathurst, Madrid, 15 August 1812, *WD*, vol. 5, pp. 26–8. For some reason Oman, vol. 5, pp. 516–17 gives these as the 51st Line and 12th Léger but Wellington's statement is confirmed by Pierre Charrié, *Drapeaux et Etendards de la Révolution et de l'Empire* (1982).
8. Colonel J.W. Gordon to the Duke of York, 'Confidential and Secret', 'Copy [to Lord Grey]', Madrid, 16 August 1812, Grey Papers, Durham University Library, GRE/B19/117; General Orders, 15 August 1812, *General Orders*, 1812, pp. 141–2; cf Douglas, *Douglas's Tale of the Peninsula*, p. 50.
9. See Boutflower, *Journal of an Army Surgeon*, p. 155.
10. Alexander Gordon to Aberdeen, 25 August 1812, Gordon, *At Wellington's Right Hand*, pp. 313–15.
11. Longford, pp. 360–1; Oman, *Gasgoyne Heiress*, Lady Salisbury's diary for 9 November 1835, p. 182.
12. Curiously it was Murray, not Stewart, who ultimately returned to the army in 1813, but when they left, and throughout 1812, Murray's departure was officially permanent, and Stewart's only temporary.
13. Wellington to Torrens, Nisa, 22 January 1813, WP 1/365 (printed with relevant passage deleted in *WD*, vol. 6, pp. 243–4.
14. J.W. Gordon to Lord Grey, Madrid, 25 August 1812, Grey Papers, Durham University Library, GRE/B19/118.
15. It is clear that Wellington gave the idea of the appointment of a chief of staff some encouragement even before Gordon reached the army: see Torrens to C. Campbell, 'Private and Confidential', 24 June 1812, WO 3/602, pp. 224–31; Torrens to Wellington, 'Private', 6 August 1812, WO 3/602, pp. 355–60; Wellington to Torrens, 27 August 1812, *WD*, vol. 6, p. 44; Bathurst to Wellington, 'Private', 9 September 1812, WP 1/350; Torrens to Wellington, 'Secret and Confidential', 29 September 1812, WO 3/603, pp. 126–33.
16. Wellington to Bathurst, 23 September 1812, *WSD*, vol. 7, pp. 427–8; Gordon's name is suppressed but there is no doubt of his identity. Wellington knew that he intended to write to Lord Grey and felt that he could make no objection to this, but the publication of confidential information in the newspapers was clearly unacceptable.
17. Gordon's letters to Grey are in the Grey Papers, Durham University Library GRE/B19/112–34. Many are simply copies of his letters to the Duke of York, frequently marked 'Confidential & Secret' and 'Copy' – a conjunction which evidently did not strike him as incongruous. He

repeatedly asks that the letters not be shown to anyone except Whitbread, and even begs the Duke of York not to make Gordon's views known to any of the ministers in whose 'truth and honesty' he had no faith! (J.W. Gordon to Duke of York, 'Confidential & Secret', 'Copy [to Lord Grey]', Madrid, 24 August 1812, Grey Papers, Durham University Library, GRE/B19/119.) This restriction was not honoured by his friends, and it was naïve to suppose that it would be. As well as the incriminating paragraphs in the *Morning Chronicle* see Creevey to Mrs Creevey, 19 October [1812], Creevey, *Creevey Papers*, pp. 171–2.

18. Alexander Gordon to Charles Gordon, Madrid, 25 August 1812, Gordon, *At Wellington's Right Hand*, pp. 307–8.

19. Fortescue, vol. 8, p. 611 and sources cited there. However S.G.P. Ward, in his excellent article on Gordon, has argued that most of the problems for which Gordon was blamed were probably beyond his control. S.G.P. Ward, 'General Sir Willoughby Gordon' (1953), pp. 58–63 esp. p. 52n.

20. Wellington to Torrens, Rueda, 31 October 1812, WP 1/351.

21. Torrens to Wellington, 'Private', 30 December 1812, 13 January 1813, 16 February 1813, WO 3/604, pp. 18–23, 60–2, 135–8.

22. WO 17/2470; Cantlie, *History of the Army Medical Department*, vol. 1, p. 349.

23. Sir Richard Levinge, *Historical Records of the Forty-Third Regiment* (1868), pp. 170–1.

24. The evolution of Wellington's plans at this time are best seen in the letters of Alexander Gordon and J.W. Gordon: Alexander Gordon to Lord Aberdeen, 16, 25 and 30 August 1812, Gordon, *At Wellington's Right Hand*, pp. 312–17. J.W. Gordon to Duke of York, 'Confidential & Secret', 'Copy [to Lord Grey]', 16 August 1812, and J.W. Gordon to Lord Grey, 25 August 1812, Grey Papers, Durham University Library, GRE/B19/117–118. J.W. Gordon to Duke of York, 24 August 1812, no. 119. But see also Wellington to Bathurst, 18 August (two letters) and 30 August, *WD*, vol. 6, pp. 33–4, 35–6, 48–9.

25. Oman, vol. 6, p. 7. This is confirmed by Jeffrey Graceffo, 'Making of a Marshal: Bertrand Clausel takes Command of the Army of Portugal, 1812' (2005), p. 49 citing Clausel to Clarke, 18 August 1812, in the French archives.

26. Oman, vol. 6, pp. 24–6, 49–51; Fortescue, vol. 8, pp. 583–4 agree in condemning this mistake.

27. Alexander Gordon to Aberdeen, 21 September 1812, Gordon, *At Wellington's Right Hand*, pp. 320–3.

28. Wrottesley, *Life of Burgoyne*, vol. 1, p. 230; Dickson, *Dickson Manuscripts*, vol. 4, pp. 768–9; Whitworth Porter, *History of the Corps of Royal Engineers* (1889), vol. 1, p. 330.

29. Wellington to Maitland, 20 September 1812, *WD*, vol. 6, pp. 79–80; see J.W. Gordon to Duke of York, 'Secret and Confidential', 20 September 1812, Grey Papers, Durham University Library GRE/B19/124 for the reconnaissance.

30. Wrottesley, *Life of Burgoyne*, vol. 1, p. 230; Oman, vol. 6, pp. 21–4.

31. Ellesmere, *Personal Reminiscences*, p. 146; Wrottesley, *Life of Burgoyne*, vol. 1, pp. 230–1, 236.

32. Wrottesley, *Life of Burgoyne*, vol. 1, pp. 235–7.

33. Ibid., p. 230.

34. Dickson, *Dickson Manuscripts*, vol. 4, p. 750.

35. Oman, vol. 6, pp. 39–40; Popham, *Damned Cunning Fellow*, pp. 206–8.

36. Dickson, *Dickson Manuscripts*, vol. 4, p. 751 refers to the night of 2–3 October being tempestuous with very heavy rain; Hough, 'Journal', p. 31 wrote on 6 October 'We had rain all this day', while Jones, *Journals of the Sieges*, vol. 1, p. 311 wrote of the night of 7 October, 'the rains now became exceedingly heavy ...'

37. Wrottesley, *Life of Burgoyne*, vol. 1, pp. 231–2; Wellington to Beresford, 5 October 1812, *WD*, vol. 6, pp. 104–5; see also Dickson, *Dickson Manuscripts*, vol. 4, p. 753, and Porter, *History of the Royal Engineers*, vol. 1, p. 322 quoting Jones, *Military Autobiography*.

38. Alexander Gordon to Charles Gordon, 3 October [1812], Gordon, *At Wellington's Right Hand*, pp. 325–6.

39. Wellington to Hill, 5 October 1812, *WD*, vol. 6, p. 104.

40. Alexander Gordon to Aberdeen, 5 October 1812, Gordon, *At Wellington's Right Hand*, pp. 326–7.

41. Wellington to Lord Somers, 11 October 1812, *WD*, vol. 6, p. 115. See also Ponsonby in Samuel Rogers, *Reminiscences and Table-talk of Samuel Rogers* (1903), p. 240; Tom Sydenham to Sir Henry Wellesley, 16 October, *WSD*, vol. 7, pp. 458–60; Tomkinson, *Diary of a Cavalry Officer*, p. 210, Wellington to Beresford, 9 October 1812, *WD*, vol. 6, p. 111.

42. Wellington to Lord Bathurst, 26 October 1812, *WD*, vol. 6, pp. 133–7; Wellington to Liverpool, 23 November 1812, *WD*, vol. 6, p. 174.

43. Fortescue, vol. 8, pp. 583–8 makes many criticisms of the actual conduct of the siege; see also Oman, vol. 6, pp. 49–51, 741, and Porter, *History of the Royal Engineers*, vol. 1, pp. 318–30. The sources quoted by Porter and Dickson, *Dickson Manuscripts*, vol. 4, esp. pp. 750–1 make it clear that Wellington was very closely involved in the day-to-day conduct of the siege.

44. Oman, vol. 6, p. 90; Fortescue, vol. 8, p. 593.

45. Fortescue, vol. 8, pp. 594–5; cf Oman, vol. 6, pp. 54–5 gives slightly lower figures.

46. Fortescue, vol. 8, pp. 592–7; Oman, vol. 6, pp. 54–5, 64–8.

47. Alexander Gordon to Aberdeen, 28 October 1812, Gordon, *At Wellington's Right Hand*, pp. 332–6. On Venta del Pozo see also Sir Charles Oman, 'A Dragoon of the Legion' (1913), pp. 299–301, and William Smith, 'Journal of Captain William Smith, 11 Light Dragoons during the Peninsular War' (1915), p. 176. The effect on the morale of the allied cavalry is confirmed by Stanhope, *Eyewitness*, p. 96

48. Wellington to Hill, 9 pm, 27 October 1812, *WD*, vol. 6, pp. 137–8. See also Col. J.W. Gordon to Duke of York, 'Most Secret and Confidential', 'Copy [to Lord Grey]', 28 October 1812, Grey Papers, Durham University Library GRE/B19/132.

49. Wellington to Charles Stuart, 31 October 1812, *WD*, vol. 6, p. 141.

50. Oman, vol. 6, pp. 131–7; Fortescue, vol. 8, pp. 614–16; see also Alexander Gordon to Aberdeen, 19 November 1812, Gordon, *At Wellington's Right Hand*, pp. 338–41, and Col. J.W. Gordon to the Duke of York, 'Confidential and Secret', 'Copy[to Lord Grey]', 19 November 1812, Grey Papers, Durham University Library GRE/B19/134, both of which shed some light on the movements around Salamanca.

51. Oman, vol. 6, p. 152; Wellington to Torrens, 6 December 1812, WP 1/355 (printed with names suppressed in *WSD*, vol. 7, pp. 494–5).

52. Leach, *Rough Sketches*, p. 296.

53. Browne, *Napoleonic War Journal*, pp. 195–8.

54. Cole to Lady Grantham, 13 December 1812, Cole, *Memoirs of Sir Lowry Cole*, pp. 88–9.

55. 'To Officers commanding Divisions and Brigades', 28 November 1812, *WD*, vol. 6, pp. 180–2. See also Wellington to Bathurst, 19 November 1812, WP 1/351.

56. For example, Sherer, *Recollections of the Peninsula*, pp. 223–5; Kincaid, *Adventures with the Rifle Brigade*, pp. 96–8; Leach, *Rough Sketches*, p. 298; Grattan, *Adventures in the Connaught Rangers*, pp. 306–7; T.H. McGuffie, 'The Bingham Manuscripts' (1948), pp. 108–9; Napier, *History*, vol. 4, pp. 403–5.

57. Oman, vol. 6, pp. 156–61; Fortescue, vol. 8, pp. 621–3.

30 Life at Headquarters

1. Larpent, *Private Journal*, 6 March 1813, pp. 68–9.

2. McGrigor, *Autobiography and Services*, pp. 317–19.

3. Larpent, *Private Journal*, 17 May and 15 March 1813, pp. 115–16, 71–4 respectively.

4. Ibid., 4 April 1813, p. 81; John Green, *A Soldier's Life, 1806–1815* (1973); first published 1827 p. 132 for the Prince of Orange's house.

5. Alexander Gordon to Charles Gordon, 20 November 1813, Gordon, *At Wellington's Right Hand* p. 343.

6. Larpent, *Private Journal*, 26 November 1812, p. 28.

7. Browne, *Napoleonic War Journal*, p. 200.

8. Ward, *Wellington's Headquarters*, pp. 56–8, 194–7; Vichness, 'Marshal of Portugal', p. 473 for Beresford's presence at Lisbon.

9. See photographs of the house at Pero Negro in Warre, *Letters from the Peninsula*, opp. p. 104.

10. Stewart to Castlereagh, 30 May 1810, PRONI D 3030/P/9.

11. Browne, *Napoleonic War Journal*, pp. 165–6.

12. For similar exercises of the privileges of rank see Smith, *Autobiography*, p. 82; and Captain A. Gordon, *The Corunna Campaign. Journal of a Cavalry Officer* (1990), pp. 188–9.

13. Larpent, *Private Journal*, 9 July 1813, p. 183.

14. Charles Whitman, 'Journal of the Campaigns in the Peninsula', NAM-8408-37, pp. 66–7. Every effort has been made to trace the copyright owner of this unpublished account to obtain permission to quote it, but without success. I have been unable to trace any other

reference to the black servant mentioned in this quote, and do not know whether the obvious idea that he had accompanied Wellington home from India, has any foundation.

15. Larpent, *Private Journal*, 14 June 1813, p. 148.
16. Tomkinson, *Diary of a Cavalry Officer*, p. 108; Browne, *Napoleonic War Journal*, pp. 200–1; George Eastlake, 'Mr Eastlake's Visit to Spain in 1813' (1992), pp. 76–8; Sir Augustus Simon Frazer, *The Letters of Colonel Sir Augustus Simon Frazer, K.C.B. commanding the Royal Horse Artillery in the army under the Duke of Wellington* (2001), pp. 107–8; Larpent, *Private Journal*, 21 April and 19 May 1813, pp. 93 and 149–50, and 14 January 1814, p. 358 all give details.
17. AW to Villiers, 2 May 1809, *WD*, vol. 3, pp. 203–4.
18. Woolgar, 'Writing the Despatch', pp. 1–25 esp. 7–9.
19. For example, Wellington to William Wellesley-Pole, 25 July 1812, Raglan Papers, Wellington A no. 49 where he states that the French loss at Salamanca 'is said to be' between 17,000 and 20,000 men, well above the actual figure.
20. Wellington to Charles Stuart, 13 May 1810, *WD*, vol. 4, p. 65.
21. Browne, *Napoleonic War Journal*, pp. 155–6 cf p. 201.
22. Larpent, *Private Journal*, 26 January 1813, pp. 48–9.
23. Fitzroy Somerset to the Duke of Beaufort, Freneda, 10 February 1813, Badminton Muniments, FmM 4/9/1.
24. Fitzroy Somerset to the Duke of Beaufort, Freneda, 31 March 1813, Badminton Muniments, FmM 4/9/3.
25. Charles Crowe, *An Eloquent Soldier. The Peninsular War Journals of Lieutenant Charles Crowe of the Innisillings, 1812–1814* (2011), 7 June 1813, p. 85.
26. Larpent, *Private Journal*, 24 April 1813, p. 96.
27. Colville, *Portrait of a General*, p. 78.
28. Larpent, *Private Journal*, 14 January 1814, p. 357.
29. Ibid., 22 February 1814, p. 403.
30. Elers, *Memoirs*, pp. 65–6 says 5ft 7in; sources quoted in Wellesley, *The Man Wellington*, pp. 211–12 suggest the slightly taller figure cf note by J.E.E., 'The Duke of Wellington's Height' (1951), p. 182; Kincaid, *Adventures in the Rifle Brigade*, p. 248.
31. Antony Brett-James, *Life in Wellington's Army* (1972), pp. 78–9.
32. AW to William Wellesley-Pole, 22 May 1809, Wellington, 'Letters to Pole', pp. 12–13.
33. Major G. Tylden, 'The First Duke of Wellington as a Horseman' (1965), p. 70.
34. Sir John Hope to his wife, Camp in Hendaye, 17 October 1813, Linlithgow Papers, Box 20 f 17–18, quoted in Ward Papers, University of Southampton, Ms 300/3/7.
35. Sir John Hope to his wife, Guéthary, 24 November 1813, Linlithgow Papers, Box 20 f 42, quoted in Ward Papers, University of Southampton, Ms 300/3/11. See also Webb-Carter, 'Cockades worn by the Duke of Wellington', p. 106 and illustration.
36. Larpent, *Private Journal*, 10 May 1813, p. 112.
37. Ibid., 15 March 1813, pp. 70–4.
38. Ibid., 21 December 1813, p. 335.
39. Eastlake, 'Mr Eastlake's Visit to Spain', p. 75.
40. Ibid., p. 75; Larpent, *Private Journal*, 5 May 1813, p. 104; McGrigor, *Autobiography and Services*, p. 303.
41. Eastlake, 'Mr Eastlake's Visit to Spain', p. 76.
42. Quoted in Brett-James, *Life in Wellington's Army*, p. 125. The earliest version of this story that I have been able to trace is in J.W. Cole, *Memoirs of British Generals distinguished during the Peninsular War* (1856).
43. Larpent, *Private Journal*, 5 December 1813, p. 312.
44. Browne, *Napoleonic War Journal*, p. 155.
45. [John Stepney Cowell], *Leaves from the Diary of an Officer of the Guards* (1994), pp. 36–7.
46. Larpent, *Private Journal*, 26 November 1813, and 8 November 1812, pp. 306 and 31.
47. Eastlake, 'Mr Eastlake's Visit to Spain', p. 76; see also Browne, *Napoleonic War Journal*, pp. 155–6.
48. Browne, *Napoleonic War Journal*, p. 180.
49. Larpent, *Private Journal*, 22 February 1813, p. 60.
50. Ibid., 23 January 1813 p. 47.
51. Browne, *Napoleonic War Journal*, p. 202.

52. Warre, *Letters from the Peninsula*, 15 May 1810, p. 79; Eastlake, 'Mr Eastlake's Visit to Spain', p. 82; Norman Gash, *Robert Surtees and Early Victorian Society* (1993), p. 314.

53. Quoted in Urban, *Rifles*, p. 202; see also Browne, *Napoleonic War Journal*, pp. 204–5, Verner, *History and Campaigns of the Rifle Brigade*, vol. 2, p. 436, and Leach, *Rough Sketches*, pp. 298–9.

54. Browne, *Napoleonic War Journal*, p. 200.

55. Larpent, *Private Journal*, 26 November 1812, p. 28.

56. Ibid., 21 April 1813 p. 93.

57. All the ADCs who came out with Wellington in 1809 or who joined him soon after were sent home with despatches. Some staff officers such as George Scovell remained in the Peninsula from 1809 to 1814 but Scovell's wife joined him, and he had at least one spell of leave with her in Lisbon. Some regimental officers and many rank and file would also have served the full five years, although the fact that, as officers gained seniority, they were occasionally interchanged between the different battalions of the same regiment, would have reduced the number serving continuously in the Peninsula.

58. Stewart to Frances, Lady Londonderry, 18 December 1811, PRONI D 3030/Q3.

59. Wellington to Lt.-Gen. Calvert, 6 February 1811, *WD*, vol. 4, pp. 584–5.

60. [Cowell], *Leaves from the Diary*, p. 36.

61. Larpent, *Private Journal*, 23 January 1813, p. 47.

62. John Fremantle to his uncle, W.H. Fremantle, Vera, 8 November 1813, Fremantle, *Wellington's Voice*, pp. 162–3; see also Fremantle's letters of 22 July, 24 August, 20 September, 4 and 18 October and 5 December, ibid., pp. 148–9, 153–60, 165, and also the entry on Heaphy in the *ODNB*.

63. Ward, *Wellington's Headquarters*, pp. 194 and 58 (for bâtmen).

64. These were Baron de Constant and H.A. Johnson – see Browne, *Napoleonic War Journal*, p. 202. Some of Johnson's letters home have survived and been published as H. A. Johnson, 'Letters from Headquarters, 1812–1813' (1965), pp. 92–104.

65. Ward, *Wellington*, p. 90. In 1808 and 1809 it was Thomas Doe of the 20th Light Dragoons who Wellington recommended for a place in the police in 1821. He only left Wellington because his regiment was sent to Sicily: Fitzroy Somerset to Henry Hobhouse, 8 June 1821, WP 1/671/6.

66. James Thornton, *Your Obedient Servant. Cook to the Duke of Wellington* (1985), *passim*.

67. Larpent, *Private Journal*, 23 January 1813, p. 46 cf 1 May 1813, p. 100.

68. Ibid., 2 December 1813 p. 309.

69. According to the *Royal Military Calendar*, vol. 5, p. 23, Fremantle acted as Wellington's ADC 'and private secretary', while Thornton, *Your Obedient Servant*, p. 58 says that he acted as Commandant when Campbell was absent. He was sent home with the Vitoria despatch and Jourdan's captured baton. According to his letters in *Wellington's Voice*, Fremantle worked primarily as an assistant to Fitzroy Somerset, and was formally appointed assistant military secretary in October 1813.

70. Gordon says this explicitly in his letter to Aberdeen of 19 October 1809, Gordon, *At Wellington's Right Hand*, p. 60.

71. Hume to Graham, 24 April 1813, Lynedoch Papers, quoted in Ward Papers, University of Southampton 300/3/1.

72. Johnson, 'Letters from Headquarters', p. 101. See also Fremantle's letters in *Wellington's Voice* for some glimpses of the inevitable quarrels and rivalries among the ADCs.

73. An unsavoury incident of this kind is described in Larpent, *Private Journal*, 12 April 1813, p. 89, but such outbreaks seem to have been rare.

74. Napier, *Passages in the Early Military Life*, pp. 135–6.

75. Leach, *Rough Sketches*, pp. 225–6; see also [Roberts], *The Military Adventures of Johnny Newcome*, p. 161.

76. Napier, *Passages in the Early Military Life*, p. 218.

77. Larpent, *Private Journal*, 3 August 1813, p. 208.

78. Ibid., 12 April 1813, p 88. The original 'Slender Billy' was William Heberfield, a disreputable character well known to the boys of Westminster School, who was hanged in 1811 for passing forged bank notes: Earl of Albemarle, *Fifty Years of My Life by George Thomas, Earl of Albermarle* (1876), vol. 1, pp. 324–6. Larpent, *Private Journal*, 11 January 1814, p. 354 on the Prince's answering to the name without rancour.

79. Ibid., 5 November 1813 p. 290.

80. Ibid., 7 February and 12 June 1813, pp. 53 and 145; Henry Wellesley to Wellington, Cadiz, 18 May 1810, *WSD*, vol. 6, pp. 523–5; Wellington to Henry Wellesley, 11 May 1810, *WD*,

vol. 4, p. 61. See also [Cowell], *Leaves from the Diary*, pp. 41–3, and Leith Hay, *Narrative of the Peninsular War*, vol. 2, p. 88.

81. Arbuthnot, *Journal*, vol. 1, pp. 335, 358.

82. G. Murray to Alex Hope, 'Private', 31 December 1809, Hope of Luffness Papers, Scottish Record Office GD 364/1/1197.

83. Ward, *Wellington's Headquarters*, pp. 62–3; *ODNB*.

84. Larpent, *Private Journal*, 15 May 1813, p. 114 mentions Lord John Russell's visit and the overcrowding. Biographies of Russell also mention it, but without giving details. Lord William Russell had been Graham's ADC. The date of his appointment to Wellington's staff is uncertain, but he was given the honour of taking home the despatch announcing the victory of Toulouse. For Wellington's attitude to such visitors see Wellington to Buckingham, 7 December 1810, *WSD*, vol. 13, pp. 526–7.

85. Ward, *Wellington's Headquarters*, p. 89.

86. Charles Stewart to Castlereagh, 24 August 1809, PRONI D 3030/P/229.

87. Pakenham to Lord Longford, 22 May 1811, Pakenham, *Pakenham Letters*, pp. 96–7. See also Stewart to Castlereagh, 17 April 1811, PRONI D 3030/P/39 which mentions Pakenham's discontent with his work.

88. Charles Stewart to Castlereagh, 24 August 1809, PRONI D 3030/P/229.

89. Torrens to Col. J.W. Gordon, 'Secret', 10 September 1812, WO 3/603, pp. 59–66.

90. Ward, *Wellington's Headquarters*, pp. 157–8; Larpent, *Private Journal*, 23 July 1813, p. 199.

91. Larpent, *Private Journal*, 31 December 1812, p. 35.

92. Ibid., 7 February 1813, p. 52.

93. Ibid., 5 January 1814, p. 344.

94. Ibid., 9 January 1814, p. 349.

95. Ibid., 12 February 1813, p. 57.

96. For an example see ibid., 18 February 1814, p. 397.

97. Ibid., 31 October 1813, p. 288. For another example of Dickson's ability to overcome obstacles with little notice see ibid., 10 February 1814, p. 386.

98. Larpent, *Private Journal*, 10 February 1814, p. 386; see also ibid., 5 December 1813, p. 313 for another example of Wellington's perceived harshness.

99. Ibid., 12 and 22 February 1813, pp. 54 and 59.

100. Ibid., 21 December 1813, p. 334.

101. Grattan, *Adventures with the Connaught Rangers*, p. 50.

102. [E.W. Buckham], *Personal Narrative of Adventures in the Peninsula … by an Officer late in the Staff Corps Regiment of Cavalry* (1995; first published 1827), pp. 43–4.

103. Wrottesley, *Life of Burgoyne*, vol. 1, p. 69.

104. Costello, *Peninsular and Waterloo Campaigns*, pp. 116–17.

105. Larpent, *Private Journal*, 1 May 1813, p. 100.

106. Samuel Rogers, *Reminiscences and Table-talk*, p. 250.

107. McGrigor, *Autobiography and Services*, p. 259.

108. Ibid., p. 329.

109. Croker, *Croker Papers*, 1826, vol. 1, p. 346.

110. Brotherton, *A Hawk at War*, pp. 19–20. See also Frazer, *Letters*, p. 107 (19 May 1813) for a similar comment in a more limited context; Louis C. Jackson, 'One of Wellington's Staff Officers: Lt.-Gen. William Staveley' (1935), p. 162 gives another example from 1815; and Ellesmere, *Personal Reminiscences*, p. 65 for a similar story from well after the war, though involving some of the same individuals.

111. Stewart to Castlereagh, 4 September 1810, PRONI D 3030/P/22.

112. Urban, *The Man Who Broke Napoleon's Codes*, p. 48.

113. Torrens to Campbell, 'Private', 19 December 1810, WO 3/598, pp. 272–3; see also same to the same, 'Private & Confidential', 11 December 1810, loc. cit. pp. 248–50. Wellington's letters urging Campbell's promotion include Wellington to Torrens, 4 January and 18 February 1810, *WD*, vol. 3, pp. 675, 737; and the issue (both the promotion and the need for him to go to Malta) appears repeatedly in Torrens's letters to Wellington throughout 1810 and into 1811 including those of 22 January 1810, WO 3/595, pp. 382–5, 7 March 1810, WO 3/596, pp. 325–7, and 13 February 1811, WO 3/597, pp. 4–6.

114. Alexander Gordon to Lord Aberdeen, 30 May and 27 November 1811, Gordon, *At Wellington's Right Hand*, pp. 210, 268.

115. Croker, *Croker Papers*, 1826, vol. 1, p. 346.

116. Larpent, *Private Journal*, 24 April 1813, p. 96.
117. Capt. R.M. Cairnes to Maj.-Gen. Cuppage, 11 June 1813, Dickson, *Dickson Manuscripts*, vol. 5, pp. 902–6; Col Fisher to Wellington, 5 May 1813, WP 1/369; see also Dickson to Maj.-Gen. Macleod, 25 May 1813, Dickson, *Dickson Manuscripts*, vol. 5, pp. 890–2.
118. See Fisher to Lt.-Col. W. Robe, 3 November 1812, Dickson, *Dickson Manuscripts*, pp. 781–2 which shows that Fisher probably lacked the confidence to cope with the strains of command, even if Wellington had been more supportive.
119. Larpent, *Private Journal*, 18 February 1814, p. 394.
120. George Woodberry quoted in *Charging Against Napoleon. Diaries and Letters of Three Hussars* by Eric Hunt (2001), p. 80; Swabey, *Diary of Campaigns in the Peninsula*, 22 July 1813, p. 211 (for 'Billingsgate'). Swabey says that his informant was Col Frazer, whose detailed account of the incident in his letters does not mention Wellington swearing (Frazer, *Letters*, pp. 185–9).
121. McGrigor, *Autobiography*, p. 261.
122. Torrens to Col. J.W. Gordon, 'Secret', 10 September 1812, WO 3/603, pp. 59–66.
123. Larpent, *Private Journal*, 7 February 1813, p. 52.
124. See above, p. 488, for Burgos; McGrigor, *Autobiography and Services*, p. 278 for the doctors at Badajoz.
125. Alexander Gordon to Lord Aberdeen, 4 July 1810, Gordon, *At Wellington's Right Hand*, p. 90 (see also p. 291 for similar comment on his return to headquarters in July 1812 after another absence); Wellington to Hill, 7 and 8 November 1811 (two letters), *WD*, vol. 5, pp. 357–9.
126. Thornton, *Your Obedient Servant*, pp. 115–17.
127. McGrigor, *Autobiography and Services*, p. 315.
128. Larpent, *Private Journal*, 7 October 1813, p. 264.
129. Napier, *Passages in the Early Military Life*, pp. 246–7. In 1811 when Lord March had been sick, Wellington sent Campbell to him every day to take him little luxuries and enquire as to his progress. [Lord William Pitt–Lennox], *Memoir of Charles George Gordon, Fifth Duke of Richmond* (1862), p. 26.
130. The watercolour of Wellington's sons is reproduced with explanation in Wilson, *A Soldier's Wife* (plates between pp. 82 and 83); the dresses: Larpent, *Private Journal*, 12 April 1813, p. 89.

31 Vitoria (December 1812–June 1813)

1. Oman, vol. 6, pp. 244–6; Napier, vol. 5, p. 430.
2. G.L. Chesterton, *Peace, War and Adventure. An Autobiographical Memoir* (1853), vol. 1, pp. 30–1.
3. Wellington to Hill, 14 January 1813; Wellington to Bathurst, 27 January 1813, *WD*, vol. 6, pp. 241, 255–7; Alexander Gordon to Aberdeen, 27 January 1813, Gordon, *At Wellington's Right Hand*, pp. 362–3; Charles J. Esdaile, *The Duke of Wellington and the Command of the Spanish Armies, 1812–1814* (1990), pp. 85–107.
4. See Muir, *Britain and the Defeat of Napoleon*, chs. 14 and 16 for more on this.
5. Oman, vol. 6, pp. 242–51.
6. Quoted in ibid., p. 251.
7. Wellington to Bathurst, Freneda, 5 May 1812, *WD*, vol. 6, pp. 467–70; figures on sick etc. from WO 17/2470–2472: monthly returns dated 25th of each month. The 25,000 mentioned by Wellington probably includes Portuguese, otherwise it is hard to reconcile with the figures from the returns.
8. Fortescue, vol. 9, pp. 130–1.
9. Oman, vol. 6, pp. 488–522.
10. Wellington to Bathurst, 11 May 1813, *WD*, vol. 6, pp. 479–80. As well as the discussion in Oman (vol. 6, pp. 301–5) and Fortescue (vol. 9, pp. 128–32) see Huw Davies, 'Wellington's Use of Deception Tactics in the Peninsular War' (2006), pp. 723–50.
11. R.E.R. Robinson, *The Bloody Eleventh. History of the Devonshire Regiment* (1988–95), vol. 1, p. 446; Crowe, *Eloquent Soldier*, p. 61; Urban, *Rifles*, pp. 207–8.
12. Oman, vol. 6, pp. 236–7; Crowe, *Eloquent Soldier*, pp. 61–2.
13. Wheeler, *Letters*, p. 108; Glover, *Wellington's Lieutenant, Napoleon's Gaoler*, p. 187; cf Crowe, *Eloquent Soldier*, p. 72.

14. See Tomkinson, *Diary*, p. 232, and Gomm, *Letters and Journals*, pp. 299–300 for the difficulties of the march.
15. Not, as some secondary accounts state, in a basket running on a cable between two cliffs. Swabey, *Diary*, p. 191 explicitly states that Wellington crossed by the ferry, and this is supported by Frazer, *Letters*, pp. 127–8 and Larpent, *Private Journal*, 3 June 1813, p. 129. The story of Wellington crossing in a basket began with a speculative remark by Southey, and was then repeated until it was treated as an established fact, without considering how Wellington's horses, and those of his staff, were to use such means.
16. Wellington to Lt.-Col. R. Bourke, 10 June 1813, *WD*, vol. 6, p. 521; Oman, vol. 6, pp. 348–50.
17. Oman, vol. 6, p. 355.
18. Ibid., pp. 357–9; Head, *Memoirs of an Assistant Commissary-General*, pp. 295–7; Larpent, *Private Journal*, 14 June 1813, p. 147; Bathurst to Wellington, 2 July 1813, *WSD*, vol. 8, pp. 46–7.
19. Oman, vol. 6, pp. 387–8, 398.
20. Ibid., pp. 386–94, 754–6.
21. Instructions for the Movements of the Army on 21 June, 20 June 1813, *WD*, vol. 6, pp. 536–8n; QMG to Graham, 20 June 1813, *WD*, vol. 6, p. 538n and two sets of additional instructions to Graham issued during 21 June, ibid., p. 538n. The main instructions are also printed in a slightly expanded form in the *Memoir to Accompany an Atlas* [by George Murray] (1841), pp. 98–100: this version is a little more explicit, but both are capable of several interpretations. Oman, vol. 6, pp. 395–7, 447 argues that Wellington envisaged a double-envelopment, with Hill's corps turning the French left flank. I can see little evidence for this in the instructions, and think it unlikely that, if this had been Wellington's purpose, he would have commenced the action with Hill's attack which inevitably attracted French reserves to that side.
22. Croker, *Croker Papers*, vol. 2, p. 232, 24 March 1834; Oman, vol. 6, pp. 393–4.
23. Sherer, *Recollections of the Peninsula*, p. 238.
24. Oman, vol. 6, p. 758.
25. Head, *Memoirs of an Assistant Commissary-General*, vol. 2, p. 297.
26. H.B. Robinson, *Memoirs of Lieutenant-General Sir Thomas Picton* (2nd edn, 1836), vol. 2, pp. 208–10. The printed text refers to the Sixth Division, which was not present at the battle, instead of the Light Division.
27. See Wellington to Picton, 'Private', 16 July 1813, WP 1/373, printed with suppressions in *WD*, vol. 6, pp. 598–9, and Robertson, letter of 23 June 1813, Capt Duncan Robertson, 'Buenos Aires and Vitoria' (2002), pp. 353–4.
28. Colville, *Portrait of a General*, p. 119 prints his official report to Picton; Oman, vol. 6, pp. 758–9 for casualty statistics. One brigade of the Light Division also joined in this part of the action, leading to claims that its role was decisive: see Smith, *Autobiography*, pp. 97–8; however this is hard to believe given that this brigade suffered only 32 casualties.
29. Colville, *Portrait of the General*, p. 120.
30. Glover, *Wellington's Lieutenant, Napoleon's Gaoler*, p. 197; for the artillery duel see Swabey, *Diary*, p. 201, and Dickson's account in *Dickson Manuscripts*, vol. 5, pp. 916–17.
31. For critical historians see Oman, vol. 6, pp. 447–9 and Fortescue, vol. 9, pp. 189–90. Wellington's remark comes from James Stanhope's journal: Stanhope, *Eyewitness*, p. 117; see also Antony Brett-James, *General Graham, Lord Lynedoch* (1959), p. 269.
32. Hunt, *Charging Against Napoleon*, pp. 101–5; Browne, *Napoleonic War Journal*, pp. 214–16.
33. Costello, *Peninsular and Waterloo Campaigns*, p. 127.
34. Browne, *Napoleonic War Journal*, pp. 216–18.
35. Tomkinson, *Diary*, p. 252.
36. Hunt, *Charging Against Napoleon*, p. 114 quoting George Woodberry who writes 'Madam Guizl', but it seems reasonable to assume that she was the Countess de Gazan mentioned in many British accounts of the battle (see esp. Larpent, *Private Journal*, pp. 160–1). She was escorted back to the French army as soon as operations permitted.
37. James Hughes quoted in Hunt, *Charging Against Napoleon*, p. 109; see also ibid., pp. 110, 118.
38. Bragge, *Peninsular Portrait*, p. 116.
39. Hunt, *Charging Against Napoleon*, pp. 110, 114; Bragge, *Peninsular Portrait*, p. 114.
40. Fortescue, vol. 9, p. 189; Colville, *Portrait of a General*, p. 119; Robertson, 'Buenos Aires and Vitoria', p. 353.
41. T. Grenville to Lord Grenville, nd [July 1813], *HMC Dropmore*, vol. 10, p. 348.

42. Prince Regent to Wellington, 3 July 1813, *WD*, vol. 6, p. 600n; A.S. White, 'Field Marshal's Baton' (1949), pp. 92–3.
43. Torrens to Lt.-Col. C. Campbell, 3 July 1813, WO 3/605, pp. 38–9.
44. Grumbling is reported by Lady Anne Barnard to Col. Andrew Barnard, 11 July 1813, Barnard, *Barnard Letters*, p. 224; on the Duke of York see Torrens to Lt.-Col. C. Campbell, 3 July 1813, WO 3/605, pp. 38–9; Torrens to Wellington, 21 July 1813 and enclosures, *WSD*, vol. 8, pp. 95–7, Richmond's letter was actually written in September 1812, but it is clear that he renewed the offer: see Bathurst to Wellington, 9 September 1813, *WSD*, vol. 8, p. 246 which also covers Hope's appointment.
45. Wellington to Henry Wellesley, 16 March 1814, *WD*, vol. 7, p. 375; see Susan Jenkins, 'The "Spanish Gift" at Apsley House' (2007), pp. 112–27 for a full account.
46. Frazer, *Letters*, pp. 185–9; Swabey, *Diary*, pp. 210–11; Ponsonby to Wellington, 13 July 1813, WP 1/372. The incident is not mentioned by Napier or in other early histories of the war, but was given inflated treatment by Duncan, *History of the Royal Artillery*, vol. 2, pp. 357–60 who treats Ramsay as a martyred saint. His lead was followed by Fortescue (vol. 9, pp. 199–200) and Oman (vol. 6, pp. 456–8), but there is little evidence in first-hand sources that the affair made much impression, even at the time, outside the artillery.
47. See Napier, *History*, vol. 5, p. 137 (Bk 20, end of ch. 8) who says that this point was raised by French critics and some British officers. Oman, vol. 7, pp. 232–3 says that Bayonne's defences had been neglected until after Vitoria. See also Larpent, *Private Journal*, 7 October 1813, p. 266.
48. Costello, *Peninsular and Waterloo Campaigns*, p. 129 cf Kincaid, *Adventures in the Rifle Brigade*, p. 113.
49. Wellington to Bathurst, 2 July 1813, *WD*, vol. 6, pp. 575–6.
50. Wellington to Bathurst, 29 June 1813, WP 1/370 printed in *WD*, vol. 6, pp. 558–9 with the name of the regiment suppressed.
51. Wellington to Bathurst, 2 July 1813, *WD*, vol. 6, pp. 575–6.
52. Raleigh's *Apology*, p. 26, in the 1829 edition of his works edited by Oldys and Birch.
53. AW to Lt.-Col. Close, 2 October 1800, *WD*, vol. 1, pp. 200–3, a letter in which he also denounces two British officers for using, and not paying, forced labour. AW to Richmond, 12 February 1809, *WSD*, vol. 5, pp. 566–7.
54. Memorandum of 22 April 1829, *WND*, vol. 5, pp. 592–7; Stanhope, *Notes on Conversations*, pp. 14 and 18.
55. The 1794 memorandum quoted in Bartlett 'Indiscipline and Disaffection', pp. 189–90; O'Malley quoted in Peter Karsten, 'Irish Soldiers in the British Army, 1792–1922: Suborned or Subordinate?' (1983), p. 37.
56. J.R. Dinwiddy, 'The Early Nineteenth-Century Campaign against Flogging in the Army' (1992), pp. 125–48.
57. Urban, *Rifles*, pp. 284, 287 and *passim*.
58. Wellington to Bathurst, 2 July 1813, *WD*, vol. 6, pp. 575–6.
59. Wellington to Liverpool, 10 June 1812, *WD*, vol. 5, pp. 704–6; Wheeler, *Letters*, p. 109; Lawrence, *Autobiography*, pp. 125–6.
60. Wellington to Torrens, 28 January 1811, *WD*, vol. 4, pp. 560–2; see also Wellington to Bathurst, 24 September 1813, *WD*, vol. 7, pp. 21–2.

32 The Pyrenees (July–September 1813)

1. Oman, vol. 6, pp. 546–52; Maj.-Gen. F.C. Beatson, *With Wellington in the Pyrenees, being an Account of the Operations between the Allied Army and the French from July 25 to August 2, 1813* (1993; first published 1914), pp. 4–5.
2. Oman, vol. 6, pp. 587–98.
3. Wellington to Graham, 19 July 1813, *WD*, vol. 6, pp. 606–7; Larpent, *Private Journal*, 23 July 1813, p. 199.
4. Wellington to Graham, 2 pm, 20 July 1813, *WD*, vol. 6, p. 611; Fortescue, vol. 9, p. 229; Dickson, *Dickson Manuscripts*, vol. 5, p. 971.
5. Hew Ross to Sir Hew Dalrymple, 31 October 1813, Ross, *Memoir of Sir Hew Dalrymple Ross*, p. 50; Wellington to Bathurst, 23 August 1813, WP 1/375, passage deleted from the version of this letter printed in *WD*, vol. 6, pp. 706–7.

6. Larpent, *Private Journal*, 23 July 1813, p. 199.

7. Ibid., 25 July 1813, p. 200; Oman, vol. 6, pp. 584–5.

8. Wellington to Graham, 25 July 1813, *WD*, vol. 6, pp. 624–6; Browne, *Napoleonic War Journal*, p. 226 comments on his disappointment and silence at dinner.

9. The Quartermaster-General to Cole, 24 July 1813, *WSD*, vol. 8, p. 114; see also same to same, 23 July, ibid., pp. 112–13.

10. Cole to Murray, 27 July 1813, *WSD*, vol. 8, pp. 124–5. This letter is evidently misdated, probably by Cole who admits that he was exhausted.

11. Larpent, *Private Journal*, 24 August 1813, p. 242 for Wellington's complaints.

12. Wellington to Bathurst, 23 August 1813, WP 1/375 (printed with many deletions in *WD*, vol. 6, pp. 706–7) and Wellington to W. Stewart, 13 September 1813, WP 1/377 (*WD*, vol. 6, p. 757 with deletions) cf Dickson, *Dickson Manuscripts*, vol. 5, p. 1022.

13. Wellington to Liverpool, 4 August 1813, WP 1/375, printed with names deleted in *WD*, vol. 6, pp. 649–50; Wellington to William Wellesley-Pole, 3 August 1813, Raglan Papers, Wellington A no. 56.

14. Cole to the QMG, 27 July 1813 [should be 26 July], and Picton to Wellington, 26 July 1813, *WSD*, vol. 8, pp. 124–5, 121–2; Oman, vol. 6, pp. 645–54.

15. QMG to Picton, 26 July 1813, *WD*, vol. 6, p. 630n.

16. Oman, vol. 6, pp. 654–7.

17. Larpent, *Private Journal*, 24 August 1813, p. 242; Wellington to Graham, 10.30 am, 28 July 1813, *WD*, vol. 6, pp. 630–3; Sweetman, *Raglan*, p. 42. There is little evidence to support the statement that Wellington was left 'alone' when Somerset rode off. Napier (*History*, vol. 5, p. 226) states that Somerset was 'the only staff officer who had kept up with him' but no witness confirms this, and even if it is true it does not mean Wellington was without any attendants.

18. Bingham to Mansel, 3 August 1813, Glover, *Wellington's Lieutenant, Napoleon's Gaoler*, p. 207; James Mill to his father, 5 August 1813, Major James Mill, 'Service in Ireland, the Peninsula, New Orleans and at Waterloo' (June 1870), p. 216.

19. Glover, *Wellington's Lieutenant, Napoleon's Gaoler*, p. 208.

20. Wellington to Bathurst, 1 August 1813, *WD*, vol. 6, p. 640; see Cole's delight in Wellington's praise, Cole, *Memoirs of Sir Lowry Cole*, pp. 98–9; Oman, vol. 6, pp. 667–80, 769–70, 773.

21. Quoted in Andrew Uffindell, *The National Army Museum Book of Wellington's Armies* (2003), p. 230; Barnard, *Barnard Letters*, 4 August 1813, p. 230 on Wellington and his staff being in danger.

22. R.S. Rait, *The Life and Campaigns of Hugh, first Viscount Gough, Field Marshal* (1903), vol. 1 p. 115.

23. Oman, vol. 6, pp. 691–700, see also Capt Forrest in Uffindell, *National Army Museum Book of Wellington's Armies*, pp. 230–1.

24. Wellington to Bathurst, 3 August 1813, *WD*, vol. 6, pp. 645–6.

25. Napier, *History*, vol. 5, p. 248 (Bk XXI, ch. 5).

26. Wellington to William Wellesley-Pole, 3 August 1813, Raglan Papers, Wellington A no. 56.

27. Oman, vol. 6, pp. 729–31.

28. Wellington to William Wellesley-Pole, 18 August 1813, Raglan Papers, Wellington A no. 57.

29. George Hennell, *A Gentleman Volunteer. The Letters of George Hennell from the Peninsular War, 1812–1813* (1979), 4 August 1813, p. 117.

30. Quoted in Oman, vol. 6, p. 623, and Fortescue, vol. 9, pp. 255–6 without a reference. All attempts to locate the origin of this quotation have failed, but it sounds authentic.

31. Wellington to Graham, 23 and 27 August 1813, WP 1/375 (printed with deletions in *WD*, vol. 6, pp. 704–6, 714–15; Wellington to Bathurst, 23 August 1813, WP 1/375 printed with the relevant paragraph omitted in *WD*, vol. 6, pp. 706–7. It is evident from these letters that General Graham communicated his concern at the mood of the Fifth Division to Wellington; and that Wellington already had a poor opinion of General Oswald.

32. Larpent, *Private Journal*, 29 August 1813, p. 248 cf Eastlake, 'Mr Eastlake's Visit to Spain', pp. 85–6; Costello, *Peninsular and Waterloo Campaigns*, p. 133; Hennell, *Gentleman Volunteer*, pp. 123–4. See also Douglas, *Douglas's Tale*, pp. 81–2 for another ranker's view, albeit from the Fifth Division.

33. Oman, vol. 7, pp. 23–4; [Andrew Leith Hay], *Memoirs of the Late Lieutenant-General Sir James Leith* (1817), pp. 143–50; Gomm, *Letters and Journals*, p. 319; Wrottesley, *Life of Burgoyne*, vol. 1, pp. 279–81; 'Statement by Assistant Provost Marshal Edward Williams', *WSD*, vol. 8, p. 314.

34. Jones, *Journals of the Sieges*, vol. 2, p. 96.
35. Melville to Wellington, 28 July and 3 September 1813, *WSD*, vol. 8, pp. 144–7, 223–6; Croker to Bunbury, 2 September 1813, enclosed in Bathurst to Wellington, 7 September 1813, WP 1/376. Also Lord Keith to Croker, 27 August 1813; Croker to Bunbury, 31 August 1813, both enclosed.
36. Bathurst to Wellington, 9 October 1813, WP 1/378.
37. Wellington to William Wellesley-Pole, 2 December 1813, Raglan Papers, Wellington A no. 66.
38. Wellington to William Wellesley-Pole, 24 September, 2 December 1813, 9 January 1813 [*sic* 1814], Raglan Papers, Wellington A nos. 65–7 (both quotes from the last of these letters). On the strategic discussions compare Muir, *Britain and the Defeat of Napoleon*, pp. 262–3 with Oman, vol. 6, pp. 558–61.
39. Wellington to Liverpool, 25 July 1813, *WD*, vol. 6, pp. 627–8; Wellington to Charles Stewart, 20 July 1813, ibid., pp. 616–17.
40. Oman, vol. 6, p. 560, vol. 7, pp. 112–14; Wellington to Liverpool, 25 July 1813, *WD*, vol. 6, pp. 627–8.
41. Wellington to Minister of War, Cadiz, 30 August 1813, *WD*, vol. 6, pp. 719–25, Wellington to Bathurst, 5 October 1813, *WD*, vol. 7, p. 42, Wellington to Henry Wellesley, 23 October 1813, *WD*, vol. 7, pp. 77–8, Henry Wellesley to Wellington, 2 November 1813, *WSD*, vol. 8, pp. 334–5; Henry Wellesley to Wellington, 1 December 1813, *WSD*, vol. 8, pp. 405–7; Esdaile, *Wellington and the Command of the Spanish Armies*, pp. 143–58.
42. Esdaile, *Wellington and the Command of the Spanish Armies*, pp. 155–6.
43. Wellington to Henry Wellesley, 9, 11 and 16 October, 6 and 19 November, *WD*, vol. 7, pp. 46–9, 55, 65–6, 116, 149–50.
44. Graham to Wellington, London, 9 October 1813, *WSD*, vol. 8, pp. 301–2. This letter is misdated; Graham was still in Spain on 9 October; the correct date should probably be 9 November.

33 Crossing the Frontier (September–December 1813)

1. For example, Dalhousie to Cairnes, 3 August 1814, Dickson, *Dickson Manuscripts*, vol. 5, pp. 1019–20; Rous to his father, 18 July 1813, John Rous, *A Guards Officer in the Peninsula. The Peninsula War Letters of John Rous, Coldstream Guards, 1812–1814* (1992), pp. 68–70; cf Wellington to Bathurst, 8 August 1813, *WD*, vol. 6, pp. 663–5.
2. Larpent, *Private Journal*, 22 July 1813, vol. 2, p. 5 of first edition (3 vols., 1853) – this passage omitted from the one-volume edition. See also Wellington to Bentinck, 20 July 1813, Wellington to Bathurst, 19 September 1813, and Wellington to Hope, 8 October 1813, *WD*, vol. 6, pp. 614–15, vol. 7, p. 10, 44–5, and Kincaid, *Adventures in the Rifle Brigade*, pp. 127–8.
3. William Napier to his wife, 8 October 1813, Bruce, *Life of Napier*, vol. 1, pp. 154–5.
4. Larpent, *Private Journal*, 9 October 1813, p. 275, see also GO, 8 October 1813, *WD*, vol. 7, p. 45n.
5. Wellington to Hope, 8 October 1813, *WD*, vol. 7, pp. 44–5.
6. Compare Rous, *A Guards Officer in the Peninsula*, p. 79 (6 October 1813) with his letter of 27 November (ibid., p. 90), and Gomm, *Letters and Journals*, p. 328 (2 December), Sidney, *Life of Hill*, p. 265 (27 November), Carss in Johnston, 'The 2/53rd in the Peninsular War', p. 17 (29 December 1813), and Smith, *Autobiography*, pp. 165–6 (1814). Wellington to Bathurst, 21 November 1813, *WD*, vol. 7, pp. 151–3.
7. Wellington to Bathurst, 19 September 1813, *WD*, vol. 7, p. 10; see also Wellington to Bathurst, 21 November 1813, *WD*, vol. 7, pp. 151–3.
8. For example, Wellington to the Minister of War at Cadiz, 3 September 1813, *WD*, vol. 7, p. 734.
9. Oman, vol. 7, pp. 216–18, Wellington to Freyre, 14 November 1813 and 24 December 1813, *WD*, vol. 7, pp. 137–8, 221–3, Wellington to Bathurst, 21 November 1813, *WD*, vol. 7, pp. 151–3.
10. Wellington to Bathurst, 19 September 1813, *WD*, vol. 7, p. 10.
11. Wellington to Bathurst, 18 October 1813, *WD*, vol. 7, pp. 71–2.
12. Wellington to Bathurst, 14 August 1813, *WD*, vol. 6, pp. 680–2.
13. Wellington to Bathurst, 18 August 1813, *WD*, vol. 6, p. 690.
14. Wellington to Bathurst, 21 November 1813, *WD*, vol. 7, pp. 151–3.
15. Norman Gash, *Lord Liverpool* (1984), pp. 24–5, 72.

16. Wellington to Bathurst, 8 August 1813, *WD*, vol. 6, pp. 663–5, Larpent, *Private Journal*, 21 October 1813, p. 281.

17. Wellington to Bathurst, 19 September 1813, *WD*, vol. 7, p. 10.

18. Wellington to Bunbury, 19 September 1813, *WD*, vol. 7, pp. 8–9.

19. Wellington to Bathurst, 19 September 1813, *WD*, vol. 7, p. 10.

20. Ibid., p. 10, Oman, vol. 7, p. 114.

21. Robinson's letter of 9 October 1813, in Sir F.P. Robinson, 'A Peninsular Brigadier: Letters of Major-General Sir F.P. Robinson, K.C.B. dealing with the Campaign of 1813' (1956), p. 169.

22. Oman, vol. 7, pp. 119–27.

23. Hennell's letter of 13 October 1813, in Hennell, *Gentleman Volunteer*, p. 135; Oman, vol. 7, pp. 127–33.

24. Wellington to Bathurst, 9 October 1813, *WD*, vol. 7, pp. 49–51.

25. Larpent, *Private Journal*, 7 October 1813, pp. 269, 271; Frazer, *Letters*, p. 293; Ross, *Memoir of Sir Hew Dalrymple Ross*, pp. 49, 50.

26. Graham to Wellington, 15 August 1813, *WSD*, vol. 8, pp. 191–2; Brett-James, *General Graham*, pp. 282–4; Frazer, *Letters*, p. 309.

27. Wellington to Bathurst, 25 September 1813, *WD*, vol. 7, pp. 22–3; Rous, *A Guards Officer in the Peninsula*, p. 79; Pakenham, *Pakenham Letters*, p. 223 (11 September, where Edward Pakenham is very critical of Graham's conduct of the siege of San Sebastian; and pp. 228–9, 26 September where he welcomes reports of Hope's appointment).

28. Alex M. Delavoye, *Life of Thomas Graham, Lord Lynedoch* (1880), pp. 681–2 prints the order.

29. Nonetheless Wellington repeatedly used Pamplona as an excuse for not advancing further into France in the autumn of 1813, e.g. Wellington to Graham, 6 October 1813, and to Bathurst, 18 October 1813, *WD*, vol. 7, pp. 43, 71–2.

30. For example, Leach, *Rough Sketches*, pp. 344–5; Head, *Memoirs of an Assistant Commissary-General*, p. 321.

31. Wellington to Beresford, 30 October 1813, *WD*, vol. 7, p. 96.

32. Wellington to Hope, 9 November 1813, *WD*, vol. 7, pp. 122–3; Larpent, *Private Journal*, 9 November 1813, first edition, vol. 2, p. 154 – the one-volume edition prints 'Bony' as 'Bonaparte', p. 295.

33. Oman, vol. 7, pp. 159–64. Oman is very critical of Soult's reliance on field fortifications, but It is hard to see that he had any better alternative.

34. Smith, *Autobiography*, pp. 142–3.

35. Larpent, *Private Journal*, 10 November 1813, p. 296.

36. Glover, *Wellington's Lieutenant, Napoleon's Gaoler*, p. 225; Carss in Johnston, 'The 2/53rd in the Peninsular War', pp. 16–17.

37. Colville, *Portrait of a General*, p. 147. The Third Division lost 518 casualties in all: 81 killed, 421 wounded and 14 missing – it had two British and one Portuguese brigades but the losses were heavily concentrated in the leading British brigade. Oman, vol. 7, pp. 541, 544.

38. Queen Charlotte to Prince Regent, 25 November 1813, George IV, *Letters*, vol. 1, pp. 331–2.

39. T. Grenville to Grenville, nd, *HMC Dropmore*, vol. 10, p. 360.

40. Grenville to Grey, 24 November 1813, *HMC Dropmore*, vol. 10, pp. 360–3; Peter J. Jupp, *Lord Grenville 1759–1834* (1985), pp. 441–2.

41. Rous, *A Guards Officer in the Peninsula*, p. 91.

42. Wellington to Bathurst, 21 November 1813, *WD*, vol. 7, pp. 151–3.

43. Bathurst to Wellington, 24 November 1813, *WSD*, vol. 8, pp. 401–2.

44. Wellington to Bathurst, 8 December 1813, *WD*, vol. 7, p. 189.

45. Oman, vol. 7, pp. 221–4.

46. Larpent, *Private Journal*, pp. 319–20; Wellington to William Clinton, 11 December 1813, *WD*, vol. 7, pp. 190–1; Frazer, *Letters*, pp. 364–9.

47. Sidney, *Life of Hill*, p. 267.

48. Hennell, *A Gentleman Volunteer*, p. 155.

49. Larpent, *Private Journal*, 11 December 1813, p. 317.

50. Ibid., pp. 320–1.

51. Wellington to Torrens, 15 December 1813, *WD*, vol. 7, p. 203, Torrens to Wellington, 5 January 1814, *WSD*, vol. 8, pp. 482–3.

52. Wellington to Bathurst, 21 December 1813, *WD*, vol. 7, pp. 213–16.

34 Toulouse and the End of the War (January–April 1814)

1. Wellington to Bathurst, 10 January 1814, *WD*, vol. 7, pp. 252–4.
2. Oman, vol. 7, pp. 308–12; cf Maj.-Gen. F.C. Beatson, *Wellington. The Crossing of the Gaves and the Battle of Orthez* (1994), pp. 202–5. Napoleon also made large demands on Suchet's forces at the same time.
3. Bell quoted in Oman, vol. 7, pp. 294–7. Oman also expresses some scepticism about this story. See also, Philip J. Haythornthwaite, '"Carrying On the War as It Should Be": Fraternization' (1998), pp. 115–30. For an example described at the time, rather than in later memoirs, see letter quoted in Claud Vivian, *Richard Hussey Vivian, First Baron Vivian. A Memoir* (1897), pp. 184–6.
4. Larpent, *Private Journal*, 29 January and 4 February 1814, first edition, vol. 2, pp. 270, 282.
5. WO 17/2474–5.
6. Wellington to Bathurst, 21 December 1813, *WD*, vol. 7, pp. 213–16.
7. Wellington to Bathurst, 1 January 1814, Wellington to Bunbury, 4 February 1814, *WD*, vol. 7, pp. 237, 302–3; Bathurst to Wellington, 21 January 1814, *WSD*, vol. 8, pp. 531–2. See also Larpent, *Private Journal*, 26 December 1813, vol. 2, pp. 215–16. The name of the banker is not printed in the *Dispatches* and is hard to decipher in the manuscript in WP 1/395: I read it as Babesat, Oman (vol. 7, p. 286) thinks it should be Batbedat.
8. Wellington to Bathurst, 16 January 1814, *WD*, vol. 7, pp. 270–1, Bathurst to Wellington 20 January 1814, *WSD*, vol. 8, pp. 524–5; Wellington to Bunbury, 4 February 1814, *WD*, vol. 7, pp. 302–3.
9. Edward Herries, *Memoir of the Public Life of the Right Hon. John Charles Herries* (1880), vol. 1, p. 79.
10. The best account is in Herbert H. Kaplan, *Nathan Meyer Rothschild and the Creation of a Dynasty. The Critical Years 1806–1816* (2006), pp. 73–4, 81–9; see also Lord Rothschild, *The Shadow of a Great Man* (1982), pp. 19–22, and Richard Davis, *The English Rothschilds* (1983), pp. 29–31 who shows that Nathan Rothschild himself probably contributed to the legend that the bank played a large role in financing Wellington's campaigns.
11. Wellington to Bunbury, 1 April 1814, *WD*, vol. 7, pp. 407–8.
12. See Larpent, *Private Journal*, first edition, vol. 3, pp. 44–5, 11 March 1814, on this – also below.
13. Wellington to Bunbury, 4 February 1814, *WD*, vol. 7, pp. 302–3.
14. Wellington to Bathurst, 10 January 1814, *WD*, vol. 7, pp. 252–4.
15. Bathurst to Wellington, 21 January 1814, *WSD*, vol. 7, pp. 532–3.
16. Oman, vol. 7, pp. 330–40, 381.
17. Cooper, *Rough Notes*, pp. 110–11; Oman, vol. 7, pp. 357–60.
18. Brown quoted in Ian Robertson, *Wellington Invades France. The Final Phase of the Peninsular War, 1813–1814* (2003), p. 208; Brisbane, *Reminiscences*, pp. 25–6; Keane, letter of 17 March 1814, in Colville, *Portrait of a General*, pp. 169–70. *Crapaud* (toad) was a slang term for the French, Jean Crapaud being the equivalent of John Bull.
19. Oman, vol. 7, pp. 360–4.
20. Napier, *History*, vol. 6, pp. 106–7; Oman, vol. 7, pp. 361, 366, 552–5.
21. Oman, vol. 7, pp. 372–3 cf Beatson, *Wellington. The Crossing of the Gaves*, p. 253, and Fortescue, vol. 9, pp. 513–14 for slightly different figures.
22. Alexander Gordon to Lady Alicia Gordon, 3 March [1814], Gordon, *At Wellington's Right Hand*, p. 398; Larpent, *Private Journal*, 5 March 1814, first edition, vol. 3, p. 37.
23. Larpent, *Private Journal*, 7 March 1814, first edition, vol. 3, p. 41.
24. Maria Edgeworth to Mrs Ruxton, Dublin, March 1814, Maria Edgeworth, *The Life and Letters of Maria Edgeworth* (1894), vol. 1, p. 222; Wilson, *A Soldier's Wife*, p. 155 quoting letter from Lady Wellington to John Malcolm.
25. Beresford to Lady Anne Beresford, 2 March 1814, Biblioteca de Artes, Gulbenkian Foundation, Lisbon, Beresford Papers BC 919; Jenkinson to Frazer, 4 March [1814], Frazer, *Letters*, p. 430.
26. Larpent, *Private Journal*, 11 March 1814, first edition, vol. 3, pp. 44–5; for Wellington's anger see Wellington to Torrens, 8 March 1814, WP 1/406 printed in *WSD*, vol. 8, pp. 626–8 with some names deleted.
27. Oman, vol. 7, pp. 377–9, see also pp. 499–500 for Suchet.
28. Ibid., pp. 319, 380–2.

29. Larpent, *Private Journal*, 26 February 1814, first edition, vol. 3, p. 18.
30. Beresford to Lady Anne Beresford, 2 March 1814, Beresford Papers BC 919; Picton to Flanagan, 4 March 1814, Picton, 'Unpublished Letters', pt. 2, p. 22.
31. Wellington to Bathurst, 8 August 1813, *WD*, vol. 6, pp. 663–5; Wellington to Bathurst, 10 January 1814, *WD*, vol. 7, pp. 252–4.
32. Bathurst to Wellington, 9 September 1813, *WSD*, vol. 8, p. 245.
33. Castlereagh to Liverpool, 30 and 31 December 1813, in C.K. Webster, ed., *British Diplomacy 1813–15. Select Documents* (1921), pp. 128–31.
34. Muir, *Britain and the Defeat of Napoleon*, pp. 311–19; Castlereagh to Liverpool, 'Most Secret', 22 January 1814, *WSD*, vol. 8, pp. 534–5.
35. Larpent, *Private Journal*, first edition, vol. 2, p. 288.
36. Wellington to Liverpool, 4 March 1814, *WD*, vol. 7, p. 345; see also Oman, vol. 7, pp. 389–94.
37. Wellington to Beresford, 7 March 1814, *WD*, vol. 7, pp. 352–5.
38. Wellington to Angoulême, 16 and 29 March 1814, *WD*, vol. 7, pp. 376–7, 399–401; Beresford to Wellington, Bordeaux, 12 March 1814, *WD*, vol. 7, p. 369n. See also Vivian, *Richard Hussey Vivian*, pp. 215–18, and Frazer, *Letters*, pp. 449–51 (letter from Major Jenkinson, 20 March 1814) – both give good first-hand accounts of the reception at Bordeaux. And also Guillaume de Bertier de Sauvigny, *The Bourbon Restoration* (1966), pp. 24–8.
39. Liverpool to Castlereagh, 22 March 1814, in C.K. Webster, *The Foreign Policy of Castlereagh, 1812–1814* (1931), pp. 529–30; see also Bathurst to Castlereagh, 22 March 1814, in Webster, *British Diplomacy*, pp. 171–2.
40. Liverpool to Wellington, 24 March 1814, Bathurst to Wellington, 29 March 1814, *WSD*, vol. 8, pp. 680–2, 702–3.
41. Webster, *Foreign Policy of Castlereagh*, p. 243.
42. The news of Bordeaux was known in Paris by 18 March: Sauvigny, *Bourbon Restoration*, p. 28. See also Barbara Norman, *Napoleon and Talleyrand. The Last Two Weeks* (1976), pp. 80–1 and, for the hesitations and uncertainty surrounding the restoration, *passim*, esp. pp. 246–8.
43. Oman, vol. 7, pp. 434–50.
44. Napier, *Passages in the Early Military Life*, p. 254; Larpent, *Private Journal*, 28 March, first edition, vol. 3, pp. 92–3; Robert Burnham, 'British Bridging Operations in the Peninsula', in *Inside Wellington's Peninsular Army* by Rory Muir et al (2006), p. 267.
45. Larpent, *Private Journal*, 6 April 1814, first edition, vol. 3, p. 121.
46. Capt T.E. Tucker, 'Captain T. Edwardes Tucker's Diary' (1924), 6 April 1814, p. 112.
47. Larpent, *Private Journal*, 5 and 7 April 1814, first edition, vol. 3, pp. 113, 122, 123.
48. Martin Cassidy, *Marching with Wellington 1808–1815* (2003), pp. 109–10.
49. James Mill to his father, nd April [1814], in Major James Mill, 'Service in Ireland, the Peninsula, New Orleans and at Waterloo' (1870), p. 558.
50. Beresford to Wellington, 13 April 1814, *WSD*, vol. 8, pp. 739–41; British historians including even Oman, vol. 7, pp. 475–6, and Fortescue, vol. 10, p. 82.
51. First quote from Frazer, letter of 13 April 1814, *Letters*, p. 471; the second from Wellington to Bathurst, 12 April 1814, *WD*, vol. 7, p. 425–31, quote on p. 427.
52. Larpent, *Private Journal*, 13 April 1814, first edition, vol. 3, p. 141.
53. Moore Smith, *Life of Colborne*, pp. 204–5.
54. For example George Napier, *Passages in the Early Military Life*, pp. 257–8; Moore Smith, *Life of Colborne*, p. 205.
55. Oman, vol. 7, pp. 478–81; Fortescue, vol. 10, pp. 84–6.
56. Oman, vol. 7, pp. 485–7; Fortescue, vol. 10, pp. 86–9; Beresford to Wellington, 13 April 1814, *WSD*, vol. 8, pp. 739–41, and Frazer, *Letters*, p. 473 both mention Wellington's movements. See Hunt, *Charging Against Napoleon*, p. 211, and Frazer, *Letters*, p. 472 for his personal role in rallying the Spanish infantry.
57. 'Reminiscences of a Campaign in the Pyrenees and South of France' by John Malcolm, in *Memorials of the Late War*, Constable's Miscellany (1828), vol. 1, p. 296.
58. See, for example, Stanhope, *Notes of Conversations*, 5 November 1840, p. 246.
59. Frazer, *Letters*, p. 460.
60. Arthur Kennedy in Hunt, *Charging Against Napoleon*, p. 212.
61. Broughton, *Recollections of a Long Life*, vol. 1, pp. 189–90, journal entry dated 17 December 1814 recounting Ponsonby's account of the scene.
62. Larpent, *Private Journal*, 13 April 1814, first edition, vol. 3, pp. 138–9.

63. Ibid., 13 April 1814, p. 140.

64. Frazer, *Letters*, 13 April 1814, p. 469.

65. Wellington to Bathurst, 21 November 1813, *WD*, vol. 7, pp. 151–3; Oman, *Gascoyne Heiress*, p. 266 quoting Lady Salisbury's diary for 6 January 1838. See also Creevey, *Creevey Papers*, pp. 228, 237.

66. J.W. Ward to Miss Berry, Paris, 11 May 1814, *Extracts from the Journals and Correspondence of Miss Berry ... 1783 to 1852* (1865), vol. 3, p. 16.

Epilogue

1. *Annual Register*, 1814, 'Chronicle', p. 55, entry for 28 [*sic*] June 1814.

2. *Parliamentary Debates*, vol. 27, cols. 825–32.

3. Shelley, *Diary*, vol. 1, pp. 70–1; Calvert, *An Irish Beauty*, pp. 233–4 for Hatfield.

BIBLIOGRAPHY

Wellington is once said to have complained that he had been 'much exposed to authors', and over the last 200 years he has been the subject of innumerable books, articles and even films, television programmes and websites. No history of Britain or Europe in the first half of the nineteenth century can avoid mentioning him, although his shadow does not hang as heavy over the period as that of Napoleon. And, like Napoleon, his reputation has evolved in interesting and revealing ways, reflecting the broader beliefs of each generation as attitudes towards the army, empire, and the certitudes of the mid-Victorian liberal political establishment, have changed.

Anyone studying Wellington's life is fortunate that so much of his correspondence has been preserved and published. The first edition of his *Dispatches* appeared between 1834 and 1839 in thirteen volumes, and was reissued in an enlarged edition in eight volumes in 1844 (the edition cited here as *WD*). These *Dispatches* print Wellington's official and semi-official letters during his military career from 1799 to 1815, together with a meagre handful of earlier letters from 1794, and some later letters and papers on military subjects. After Wellington's death a further fifteen volumes of *Supplementary Despatches* (*WSD*) were edited by the 2nd Duke, covering a slightly extended period (from his arrival in India in 1797 to the end of the Army of Occupation of France in 1818), and including a volume devoted to his correspondence as Chief Secretary for Ireland. Unlike the *Dispatches*, the *Supplementary Despatches* included large numbers of letters Wellington received as well as those he wrote. The 2nd Duke also edited a further series of eight volumes covering his father's correspondence from 1819 to 1832, colloquially referred to here and elsewhere as *Wellington New Despatches* (*WND*), which again includes letters received as well as those sent. In 1975 and 1986 the Historical Manuscripts Commission produced two further volumes which take the sequence down to 1835, but the last years of Wellington's life remain relatively poorly documented. The 7th Duke edited two volumes of Wellington's private correspondence with family and friends (although inevitably many of these letters discuss public affairs); Professor C.K. Webster published a selection of important letters from Wellington to his brother William Wellesley-Pole in the *Camden Miscellany* in 1948; and Wellington's letters to a number of individuals have been separately published (for example, his correspondence with his niece Lady Burghersh; with Miss J[enkins] and with Mrs Jones of Pantglas) which show unexpected sides to his character. More recently Anthony Bennell has edited a volume of Wellington's correspondence of 1803 relating to the Maratha War, which includes much new material. Gurwood (the editor of the original *Dispatches*) published a two-volume collection of the Duke's parliamentary speeches in 1854. Altogether there are more than forty volumes devoted exclusively to Wellington's correspondence and speeches, while many other letters are printed in the published correspondence of his contemporaries. There are also the diaries, letters and reminiscences of his friends and colleagues, some of which are works of the greatest importance for different periods of his life (and these are discussed in more detail below).

Lying behind this published correspondence is the even more extensive collection of manuscript material now held by the archives department of the University of Southampton. This contains some 100,000 items (mostly individual letters), while the University also holds a number of important subsidiary collections, both of manuscripts and books, including contemporaries associated with Wellington during his lifetime, and later writers who have been interested in him and his period (including the books and notes of S.G.P. Ward). A highly detailed calendar of Wellington correspondence has been prepared for the years 1807–08 and 1819–32 and this is freely available online. Visitors to the archives can consult the manuscripts and benefit from the expert advice of Professor Christopher Woolgar and his helpful and knowledgeable staff.

Some of the Duke's private papers (chiefly relating to the second half of his life) remain at Stratfield Saye. There is a rich and important collection of his correspondence with his brother William in the Raglan Papers in the Gwent Record Office (some of these were published in *WSD*, others by Professor Webster, but there remain letters of great interest and importance that have never been printed). And a volume of Colonel Gurwood's papers in the British Library contains copies of many important letters from Wellington to various correspondents which were partially or wholly omitted from the published *Dispatches*. There are many other collections of unpublished papers which include correspondence from or about Wellington, and it has not been possible to consult them all; indeed it would take more than a long lifetime to read everything that is available relating to Wellington's long life.

The best writing on Wellington has seldom been in the form of biographies. The breadth of his career has acted as a deterrent; historians whose primary interest is in military history have been put off by the politics and *vice versa*. The fullest, most comprehensive biography is that by Elizabeth Longford, published over forty years ago. Longford was an extremely skilled writer who knew how to make Wellington's life interesting to a very broad market. Her writing is light and unremittingly amusing, avoiding any serious analysis or detailed discussion of the problems facing Wellington, and sadly the result is to trivialise him by leaving the reader with the recollection of a fund of good anecdotes, but no real understanding of the substance of Wellington's achievements. Philip Guedalla's *The Duke* (1931) is urbane and stylish, but affects to regard British India, military operations and parliamentary politics with sophisticated disdain; and there is little left of Wellington's life if these subjects are dismissed as inherently boring. Sir Herbert Maxwell's two-volume *The Life of Wellington and the Restoration of the Martial Power of Great Britain* (1899) is equally the work of its time: conventional, patriotic and shallow. Its limitations are revealed sharply by a comparison with the contemporaneous works of Sir Charles Oman and Sir John Fortescue which, unlike Maxwell, remain models of deep research and detailed authoritative historical narrative.

A number of biographies have been published since Longford, but none pretends to break much new ground or to re-examine Wellington's life in great depth. The works by Corrigan, James, Holmes, Roberts, Delaforce, Hibbert, Wellesley, Snow and others have each found a slightly different audience, appealing to different tastes reflecting their author's style as much as their arguments. Far more significant is Neville Thompson's *Wellington After Waterloo* (1986) which addresses the part of Wellington's career that is most often neglected. Thompson understands the period well, and his work displays sound judgement and solid research, although he does not have the space to explore fully some aspects of the subject. Huw J. Davies's *Wellington's Wars. The Making of a Military Genius* (2012) only appeared after this volume was complete. Any comparison will reveal that we differ greatly in our interpretation of the evidence, our conclusions and our view of Wellington, but Davies's arguments are stimulating, provocative and based on substantial research.

There is little fresh material relating to Wellington's youth, and the same sources have been used and re-used by successive biographers with the occasional fresh discovery added to the common stock (for example, his illegitimate son), while some old favourites are shown to be baseless and are discarded (for example, the remark falsely attributed to Wellington that the battle of Waterloo was won on the playing fields of Eton). The family background is best covered in Ellison's article 'Dangan, Mornington and the Wellesleys (1967)', while the uncertainty surrounding the date and place of Wellington's birth was ably set out in John Murray's 1852 pamphlet, which has been heavily drawn upon, directly or indirectly, by all subsequent biographers. The details of his youth and education were collected by early biographers, notably G.R. Gleig, while later sources add some useful fragments. We know the succession of his military commissions from the official announcements in the *London Gazette*, but not how much time he actually spent with any of these regiments. Equally we have only glimpses of him as an ADC at Dublin Castle, and his intellectual development is a mystery; he emerges in India almost fully formed. His record as an Irish MP can by found in E.M. Johnston-Liik's invaluable *History of the Irish Parliament* (2002) and there are many excellent secondary works on the Irish background which will be discussed below. Wellington's relations with Kitty Pakenham are explored most fully in Joan Wilson's *A Soldier's Wife. Wellington's Marriage* (1987) which benefits greatly from the author's unrivalled command of the relevant unpublished material (she was the archivist at Stratfield Saye), something which more than compensates for the popular tone of the work. And Wellington's baptism of fire in the Low Countries in 1794–95 is particularly well covered in an excellent article by R.N.W. Thomas (1989).

Wellington's Indian correspondence fills two volumes of the *Dispatches* and four of the *Supplementary Despatches*, but there are many occasions on which these printed letters have been silently edited to remove sharp, indiscreet or personal remarks, making it well worth the effort to check the original manuscripts at Southampton. There are also a significant number of important letters which have not been published at all; the manuscripts for the Indian years are noticeably more rewarding than those for the Peninsular War. A further important source of Wellington's correspondence is *The Maratha War Papers of Arthur Wellesley* ably edited by Anthony Bennell and published by the Army Record Society in 1998, which includes both published and unpublished material and which is an essential source for the events of 1803.

Material on the broader strategic context can be garnered from the five volumes of Lord Wellesley's Indian despatches, although only the most dedicated or foolhardy student would attempt to read these in their entirety. Far more accessible and useful is Edward Ingram's excellent *Two Views of British India* (1970), an edition of the private correspondence between Lord Wellesley and Henry Dundas, the minister in London responsible both for India and for overall British strategy in the war, until he left office in 1801. There is also important material in Lord Grenville's correspondence (*HMC Dropmore*) and Castlereagh's correspondence.

The only published secondary work which covers the whole of Wellington's time in India is Jac Weller's *Wellington in India* (1972). Unfortunately this is unscholarly, simplistic in its analysis and overly partisan in its arguments. There is also an unpublished thesis by Springer, which is quite useful on Wellington's first year in India, but lacks the depth to compete with other accounts of later events. Anthony Bennell's monograph on Wellington and the Maratha War (*The Making of Arthur Wellesley*, 1997) is well researched, thoughtful and interesting. Randolf Cooper's study of the Maratha War and his articles are more quirky, and some of his arguments are more stimulating than convincing, but like Bennell's work, this is serious scholarship which deserves to be treated with respect. There is no comparable study of the Seringapatam campaign, but Denys Forrest's *Tiger of Mysore* (1970) gives a good introduction to the subject. There are more specialist works on Tipu by B. Sheik Ali and Kate Brittlebank; on the campaign against Dhoondiah Waugh by Huw Davies and Randolf Cooper; on the supersession at Bombay by W.A.C. Halliwell.

The Maratha War has attracted much more attention. Sardesai's *New History of the Marathas* ([1958]) is essential for the background, without which the complex dynamics of Maratha politics that created the opportunity for British intervention cannot be understood. This can be supplemented by Bhattacharyya's study of the British Residents at Poona, and Gupta's *Baji Rao and the East India Company* (1964), works which help to avoid the impression that the Indians were passive subjects to British actions rather than equally active players in a complex web of competing interests. The military background – the nature of the armies and the underlying factors that influenced the course of the campaign – is discussed in important articles by Pemble and Bryant as well as Cooper, who gives much new information and an interesting perspective on Sindia's 'regular brigades'. While drawing on material from all these accounts, my own conclusions differ considerably from theirs.

Published primary sources, often Victorian biographies which print considerable amounts of correspondence or extracts from their subject's diaries, enormously enrich the picture. Of particular importance for Wellington's Indian years are Lushington's *Life of Harris* (1845), Kaye's *Life of Malcolm* (1856), Colebrooke's *Life of Elphinstone* (1884) and, to a lesser extent, Gleig's *Life of Munro* (1830). Memoirs by regimental officers also add a great deal, especially those by George Elers (for his many lively reminiscences about Wellington), John Blakiston and James Welsh (both for the Maratha War). Other first-hand material is more scrappy: for 1799, particular mention must be made of the unpublished journals kept by Colin Mackenzie and John Malcolm in the British Library; the typescript of an unpublished letter of Lieutenant Patrick Brown of the 1st Madras Native Infantry in the National Army Museum; extracts of accounts written by Charles Macgrigor and John Chetwood published in the histories of the 33rd Regiment; and the wonderfully colourful and rewarding diary of Ensign Rowley of the Madras Engineers. There is a good letter about Conaghul in the Oriental and India Office Collection of the British Library. For 1803 there is an excellent letter from Colin Campbell describing Assaye printed in *WSD*, an anonymous account of the battle in the British

Library, and good material in *The Maratha War Papers*. Regimental histories often print extracts from letters or diaries of officers or men: both Lee's history, and Brereton and Savory's works on the 33rd are useful for 1799; while for the Maratha War, Davidson's *History and Services of the 78th Highlanders* (1901) and Biddulph's history of the 19th Light Dragoons deserve mention.

Two invaluable sources which I could only consult with considerable difficulty in overseas libraries when I was writing these chapters, but which are now freely available online, are Wilson's *History of the Madras Army* (1882–89, vols. 2 and 3) and Vibart's *Military History of the Madras Engineers and Pioneers* (1881). Both are immense troves of military data, much of it available nowhere else, but not very readable. Much more accessible are the relevant chapters of Fortescue's *History of the British Army* (1899–1930, vol. 4 pt 2 for Seringapatam; vol. 5 for the Maratha War), although they are not quite as good as the later volumes on the Peninsular War.

Stepping back to examine the wider context brings Lord Wellesley into focus. Iris Butler's *The Eldest Brother* (1973) fleshes out his personality and private life very fully, while showing less interest in his policies. John Severn's *Architects of Empire* (2007) is more scholarly in its approach, and much more sympathetic to Lord Wellesley than to his younger siblings. P.E. Roberts's *India Under Wellesley* (1929) is full of praise for the Governor-General, even on occasions when it does not seem warranted; while Edward Ingram's books and articles seem to veer in the opposite direction, although supported by very extensive research. Enid Fuhr's thesis is well worth reading, although some of her arguments seem strained; while C.N. Parkinson's *War in Eastern Seas* (1954) gives a refreshingly different perspective by concentrating on naval operations and considerations. British grand strategy in the world as a whole is best understood by works such as John Ehrman's life of Pitt, and Piers Mackesy's studies of the War of the Second Coalition, rather than works which have a primary focus on India, for, as Lord Wellesley discovered to his chagrin, Indian affairs were overshadowed by the war closer to home. The reaction of the East India Company to Lord Wellesley's policies, and the Company's relations with the British government, are well described in the works by Embree, Philips and Roberts (*The History of British India* [1921] as well as *India Under Wellesley*). Finally the social world of British India is vividly portrayed in the memoirs of William Hickey and William Dalrymple's *White Mughals* (2002).

Biographers of Wellington often skate over the years between his return from India and the beginnings of the Peninsular War, well aware that some readers – especially those whose primary interest lies in military history – will be impatient to get on to the Peninsular War. Yet there are good reasons to linger, for these years established Wellington's place in the political world and in the public consciousness, and played a crucial role in how he was perceived by his contemporaries as well as the direction his career would take. Hurrying over them encourages the mistaken idea of Wellington as a non-political soldier. This is what makes his role in the defence of his brother's policies and conduct in India so interesting; however, it has never received the detailed scrutiny that it deserves, and the best secondary account is in the unpublished thesis by Brashares. There is, however, an abundance of primary source material both published in correspondence and the newspapers, and in unpublished correspondence. Wellington's private and family life are rather better covered in the existing biographies, with Joan Wilson's *A Soldier's Wife* the essential work despite its obvious flaws. Neither the expedition of late 1805 to the Weser, nor Wellington's role advising the ministers on planned expeditions to Spanish America, have ever received detailed scrutiny, although there is ample primary source material, especially for the latter where vol. 6 of the *Supplementary Despatches* is particularly important. Otherwise there is little apart from Fortescue's *History of the British Army*.

Fortunately there are excellent secondary sources on Ireland in the early nineteenth century including Thomas Bartlett's impressive and engaging *Fall and Rise of the Irish Nation* (1926); vol. 5 of the *New History of Ireland* edited by T.W. Moody, F.X. Martin and F.J. Bryne; R.B. Macdowell's *The Irish Administration* (1964); and Edward Brynn's useful if sometimes frustrating *Crown and Castle* (1978). Surprisingly there has been no thesis devoted to Wellington's role as Chief Secretary but Karen Robson's important study 'The Workings of Political Patronage, 1807–1865' (1997) uses Wellington and Palmerston as its principal examples. There is also R.B. McDowell's brief but excellent article on 'Wellington and Ireland' (1952). Wellington's own correspondence is printed in vol. 5 of the *Supplementary Despatches* and a very detailed and useful calendar of the manuscripts at Southampton is available online – a wonderful resource.

A.N. Ryan's thesis and many subsequent articles are invaluable for the Copenhagen expedition, and they have now been joined by Thomas Munch-Petersen's *Defying Napoleon* (2007) which provides an excellent overview and introduction: well researched and readable. S.G.P. Ward uncovered some fascinating details of the discontent with Cathcart's leadership in the British army, and these can be seen in his beautifully arranged and organised papers, now held by the archives in Southampton. Ward was an indefatigable scholar whose published work mostly appeared in articles in the *Journal of the Society for Army Historical Research (JSAHR)*, but he knew far more than he was ever able to publish, and his notes have been invaluable in showing how Wellington was viewed by other officers in these years, ranging from Anstruther's admiration to the distrust of the Clinton brothers.

There is a vast literature on the Peninsular War, much of it hugely enjoyable to read. The preeminent works are undoubtedly Sir Charles Oman's *A History of the Peninsular War* (7 vols., 1902–30), Sir William Napier's *History of the War in the Peninsula and the South of France* (6 vols., first published 1828–40), and the relevant portions of vols. 6–9 of Sir John Fortescue's *A History of the British Army* (13 vols. in 20, 1899–1930). Each has its particular strengths and weaknesses, but they are outstanding works of scholarship which have weathered the passage of time remarkably well. There are many other general histories of the war: of the earlier works Londonderry's *Narrative* (1829) is still worth consulting; while by far the best modern history is Charles Esdaile's *The Peninsular War. A New History* (2002).

The broader strategic context of the war and Wellington's relations with the government in London are explored in my *Britain and the Defeat of Napoleon, 1807–1815* (1996), the first half of which is largely based on my thesis on 'The British Government and the Peninsular War, 1808 to June 1811' (where there was space to explore some topics at greater length). Christopher Hall's *British Strategy in the Napoleonic War, 1803–1814* (1992) covers some of this ground, but is generally best on the years before 1808; while Joshua Moon's *Wellington's Two-Front War* (2011) is disappointing. Sherwig's *Guineas and Gunpowder* (1969) is excellent on British subsidies and other foreign aid during the wars with France; Webster's *Foreign Policy of Castlereagh* (1931) is essential for relating Wellington's campaigns in the closing years of the war to Britain's evolving war aims; and Schroeder's outstanding *Transformation of European Politics* (1994) is a most intelligent and stimulating account of international relations based on immense learning.

Within the Peninsula, Esdaile's monograph on Wellington and the command of the Spanish armies is a model of tightly-focussed scholarship, while his many other works on the guerrillas and the war in Spain challenge longstanding assumptions and are essential to understanding the context in which Wellington operated. Unfortunately there is no full study of the Anglo-Portuguese alliance that was the keystone of Wellington's success, but three excellent unpublished theses by Vichness, Fryman and De La Fuente are full of valuable information and go a long way towards filling the gap. Nonetheless Portuguese voices and perspectives remain lamentably scarce among our sources, which makes it very difficult to correct the natural bias of our British sources.

There are a number of good studies shedding light on the British army in the Peninsula, although no single work covers all the ground. The books on Wellington's army by Oman, Michael Glover and Philip Haythornthwaite are all useful and complementary; broader studies by Houlding, Richard Glover, Linch, Cookson, Keith Bartlett, and Burnham and McGuigan, fill in much of the background; although much work remains to be done on how the remarkable improvement of the army from 1793 to 1808 was achieved, and on the internal politics of the higher ranks of the army. Michael Glover's *Wellington as Military Commander* (1968) also deserves mention as a good overview including many interesting details. S.G.P. Ward's monograph *Wellington's Headquarters* (1957) is invaluable for understanding how Wellington worked; while Professor Christopher Woolgar's two articles add a fresh dimension to the subject, revealing how much an original manuscript can reveal to a trained eye. Antony Brett-James's *Life in Wellington's Army* (1972) remains one of the best and most enjoyable books on the Peninsular War, while Edward Coss makes an important attempt to rehabilitate the reputation of Wellington's rank and file, but pushes a good argument rather too far. Other topics are explored in several useful collections of essays including those edited by Paddy Griffith and Ian Fletcher, and *Inside Wellington's Peninsular Army* by Muir, Burnham, Muir and McGuigan (2006) – this last contains a particularly significant article by Howie Muir which breaks new ground in understanding the mechanics of how the army formed and operated on the battlefield.

The importance of sickness in determining the effective strength of the army can be traced in the general monthly returns in WO 17, while the medical history of the army is capably explored in Cantlie's *History of the Army Medical Department* (1974), Howard's *Wellington's Doctors* (2002), Kempthorne's three-part article, Crumplin's life of Guthrie, Blanco's life of McGrigor, and, of course, McGrigor's autobiography. Two important articles by Hodge and Greenwood underline the significance of disease as by far the leading cause of mortality for British soldiers of the period.

The logistical framework supporting Wellington's operations – often the subject of crude and misleading generalisations – is best explored in an unpublished thesis by T.M.O. Redgrave, and by S.G.P. Ward in *Wellington's Headquarters* and in his entertaining article 'The Peninsular Commissary' (1997). Galpin's article on the American grain trade to the Peninsula is revealing, while Christopher Hall's study of the role of the Royal Navy in supporting Wellington's operations is much needed and most useful.

Regimental histories often contain useful primary source material, sometimes with significance beyond the individual regiment (Donald E. Graves's work on the Royal Welch Fusiliers, R.E.R. Robinson's on the 11th, and Carole Divall's on the 30th, all spring to mind). Not surprisingly the 95th Rifles have received more than their fair share of attention, with Verner's exemplary two-volume history being supplemented by David Gates's study of *The British Light Infantry Arm* (1987) and Mark Urban's *Rifles* (2003) – a work whose populist style conceals substantial research and which raises some fresh and significant questions. Beamish remains invaluable on the history of the King's German Legion, while the role of the Engineers has been explored in an excellent thesis by Mark Thompson. Unfortunately Duncan's *History of the Royal Artillery* (1872) is both disappointing and dated; it is surprising that it has not yet been superseded despite an abundance of published and unpublished (much of it in WO 55) raw material.

There have been a number of studies of individual campaigns, varying widely in merit. Neither Michael Glover's *Britannia Sickens* (1979) nor Richard Schneer's article fully fathom the events of 1808, although both broaden the picture depicted by Oman and Fortescue. Donald D. Horward's works on Masséna's invasion of Portugal in 1810–11 add greatly to our understanding, especially of the French command and its difficulties; while Chambers's account of Bussaco is still useful. My own study of Salamanca endeavours to explore the gaps and contradictions in the evidence concerning this single day's fighting, and so discover the limits of what we could know about the battle. As I write, Carole Divall's study of the retreat from Burgos has been announced but not yet published. Ian Robertson weaves a rich tapestry from a wide selection of first-hand accounts of the war in a fairly traditional framework in his *A Commanding Presence* (2008), and has also made a more detailed study of the last phase of the war. And Major-General F.C. Beatson wrote three highly-detailed monographs on aspects of the campaigns of 1813–14 which remain rewarding. Several primary sources deserve mention here as well: Fitzclarence's articles on the campaign of 1809; Burghersh's memoir of Wellington's early campaigns; and above all Jones's account of the sieges undertaken by the army, are works of enduring significance. Finally, after years of relying on the maps in Oman and Fortescue, we have recently been given two good atlases of the Peninsular War, by Robertson and Lipscombe, while those who wish to go further can consult the astonishingly rich collection of old maps reproduced in the magnificent Spanish publication *Cartograpfía de la Guerra de la Independencia* (2008).

Biographies of Wellington's subordinates are often useful and interesting. S.G.P. Ward's article on Sir George Murray is excellent, and heightens our sense of loss that his full biography, long contemplated, was never written. Antony Brett-James tells Graham's story with a sure touch (there are useful primary sources for Graham in the earlier biography by Delavoye and in *HMC Graham of Fintry*). There is a modern life of Hill by Teffeteller, and an old one by Sidney that is useful for the original letters that it prints. Picton has received more attention with two modern biographies (by Myatt and Havard), an early one by Robinson, and, best of all, the publication of some fascinating letters in the *West Wales Historical Records*. The *Memoirs of Sir Lowry Cole* (1934) is a later compilation with some letters of interest from Cole; while the study of Craufurd by his descendent is worthwhile, but gives only a partial picture of that difficult officer.

Biographical details for more junior officers can be discovered in a variety of reference works including the five volumes of the *Royal Military Calendar* (which covers officers still alive and in the army in 1820, holding the rank of major or above). The *Army List* is comprehensive, but limited; Dalton's *Waterloo Roll Call* (1978) is often interesting if the subject was present at Waterloo. Hall's *Biographical Dictionary of British Officers Killed and Wounded, 1808–1814* (1998) includes much good material; while Challis's roll call (available online through the Napoleon Series) gives only the barest bones, but is comprehensive. Many officers are included in the *Oxford Dictionary of National Biography*, including some who made their name in other fields; while the *History of Parliament*'s volumes on *The House of Commons, 1790–1820* and *1820–1832* (edited by R.G. Thorne and D.R. Fisher respectively) are an invaluable source for the surprising number of officers who served as MPs. (The connection between politics and the army is a subject which I have explored in an article in *Wellington Studies IV*.)

Biographies of more junior officers, often incorporating valuable primary source material (letters, diaries and the like) include Julia Page on Charles Cocks (exceptionally useful); Mark Urban on George Scovell; G.C. Moore Smith on Colborne; H.A. Bruce on William Napier (whose letters home are as fine as any part of his *History*); R.H. Thoumine on Le Marchant (including some good background on the 'scientific soldiers' in the army); Michael Crumplin on Guthrie; and John Colville on his ancestor Sir Charles Colville. Wrottesley's *Life and Correspondence of Field Marshal Sir John Burgoyne* (1873) and Gomm's *Letters and Journals* (1881) contain fascinating material.

The most revealing letters, diaries and memoirs about Wellington in the Peninsula are probably Larpent's *Private Journal* (2000; reprint of 1854 third edition) and the letters home of Alexander Gordon. Larpent is full of vivid vignettes of life at headquarters and Wellington at work, but only covers the last part of the war (from late 1812). Gordon joined Wellington's staff just before Talavera and remained on it until Waterloo, but his surviving letters tail off after Vitoria. His letters are full of insight into Wellington's strategic thinking, and show that he was much more willing to confide his plans to his immediate staff than had been assumed. There are also excellent unpublished letters from Charles Stewart and George Murray, Wellington's two most senior staff officers (in the Public Record Office of Northern Ireland, and the Hope of Luffness papers in the National Records of Scotland, respectively). However, Fitzroy Somerset's letters home (at Badminton House) are comparatively disappointing; pleasant and entertaining, but too discreet. John Fremantle's letters add some human touches to our knowledge of Wellington's ADCs, but leave us unsatisfied; he could have told us so much more. There is some excellent material in McGrigor's *Autobiography* (1861) and in the letters of Sir Augustus Frazer; while Mr Eastlake's account of his visit to Spain adds some amusing colour and shows how the headquarters struck an intelligent outsider. The recent publication of James Stanhope's letters and journals, edited by Gareth Glover, finally gives us the context for the tantalising fragments quoted by Fortescue, and adds an important new voice to the record.

Less immediately relevant to Wellington, but still a vital source for the understanding of the campaigns in the Peninsula, are the mass of letters and diaries of other officers that have been published in the last 200 years (the first, even while the war was in progress). There are far too many to list them all, even in the bibliography, but a few can be mentioned here. The *Dickson Manuscripts* (1987–91; first published 1905–08) and D'Urban's *Peninsular Journal* (1930) are not the most appealing for casual readers, but contain invaluable information for the serious researcher. William Warre served on Beresford's staff and his letters home are delightful and full of interest. Uffindell's collection of previously unpublished sources from the National Army Museum is full of good fresh material. For the rest, any selection will be arbitrary and personal, but some favourites include (in alphabetical order) Aitchison, Bell, Bingham, Boutflower, Carss, Crowe, Dyneley, Hawker, Head, Kincaid, Leslie, (Rice) Jones, Schauman, Sherer, Simmons, Swabey and Tomkinson. These were all officers, but there are a number of good voices from the ranks, although unfortunately (if understandably) all written years after the war: Cooper, Costello, Douglas, Harris, Lawrence and the anonymous Soldier of the 71st are all excellent, entertaining and revealing. There is a comprehensive listing of all these first-hand accounts by Bob Burnham in Muir et al, *Inside Wellington's Peninsular Army* (pp. 275–303), which is usefully arranged by unit, making it easy to see who may have been present at any particular engagement or incident. The success of military memoirs as a literary genre after the war was not immediate or certain; the story of their reception is told in a strikingly original study by Neil Ramsey, *The Military Memoir and Romantic Literary Culture, 1780–1835* (2011) which sheds much light on changing attitudes to the army, to the war, and to Wellington in Britain after 1815. But that is a subject that belongs in the second volume of this biography.

Since I began work on this biography in 1999 the internet and enterprises such as Google Books and Internet Archive have transformed historical research. Books and journals which, in the past, were particularly obscure and inaccessible, available only in a handful of overseas libraries, are now freely available to anyone with a computer. *The Times Digital Archive* and *Nineteenth-Century British Library Newspapers* have put an end to the misery of scanning ancient newspapers on microfilm, while the British Museum's Collection Database makes crisp colour images of all the wonderful political caricatures listed in Dorothy George's invaluable *Catalogue* instantly available. Through the University of Adelaide website I can read the great majority of academic journals, old and current, without leaving my desk. The Napoleon Series Discussion Forum brings experts and enthusiasts from around the world together to share their interest and knowledge with courtesy and good humour. And there is the detailed calendar of Wellington's correspondence for 1807–08 and 1819–32 freely available through the University of Southampton, while many other archives have less comprehensive but still useful records of their holdings available online. All these new tools will soon be taken for granted, but the essential requirement of serious scholarship will remain the same: time. Time to read widely and to reflect upon what has been read; time to pursue ideas which are just as likely to prove red herrings as revelations; and time to write and rewrite. No historian ever has enough time to pursue every idea and track down every source. Some compromise is inevitable, but good work cannot be rushed.

MANUSCRIPTS

University of Southampton

Ms 61 Wellington Papers: WP 1 The main sequence of Wellington's correspondence (incoming and outgoing) arranged in folders in chronological sequence from 1790: WP 1–412, 1790–April 1814, and a few later documents individually cited in the notes; WP 2/7 Wellington's correspondence from 1833–34 including letters to Gurwood about the publication of some passages in his Indian correspondence; WP 3 Indian letter books: copies and original letters from Wellington in India

Ms 62 Palmerston Papers: Palmerston's correspondence, 1808–14

Ms 63 Carver Papers: Papers of Marquess Wellesley and his son Richard Wellesley II

Ms 69 Collins Papers: Papers of Wellington's servant, Christopher Collins, including a few letters from Wellington, 1807–52

Ms 296 Pack and Reynell Papers: Correspondence of Sir Denis Pack, including letters to Sir T. Reynell, during the Peninsular War

Ms 300 Peninsular War Papers of S.G.P. Ward: Ward's meticulous notes on many aspects of British military history during the Napoleonic Wars, especially the career of Sir George Murray, with many extracts from a wide variety of unpublished sources

Ms 308 Malcolm Papers: Correspondence between Sir John Malcolm and Wellington, 1801–16

Gwent Record Office

Raglan Papers: Confidential letters between Wellington and his brother William Wellesley-Pole, 1807–17, some of which were partly printed in *WSD* and some others were published by Sir Charles Webster in *Camden Miscellany*, vol. 18, 1948; but many remain partly or completely unpublished: Wellington A 1–89 Letters from Wellington to Pole; Wellington B 90–129 Copies of Pole's letters

Badminton Muniments, Badminton House, Gloucestershire

Fitzroy Somerset's letters home to his brother and sister-in-law the Duke and Duchess of Beaufort, 1808–13: FmM 4/1/4/1–5; 4/1/4/6; 4/1/4/11; 4/1/6/12–13; 4/1/8/16–17 and 4/9/1–20

Stratfield Saye

A bundle of letters from AW and from Mornington's agent John Page, 1793, concerning a loan to AW from Capt Stapleton (copies kindly supplied via email by Jane Branfield, the archivist)

British Library

Bathurst Papers: Loan Ms 57 vols. 3, 6, 7

Broughton Papers: BL Add Ms 56,552 including notes of a conversation with Sir Colin Campbell (in 1828) giving details of AW's passage to Portugal in 1809

Col. Sir Henry Bunbury Papers: BL Add Ms 63,106 Letters from Capt John Squire RE (transcripts of these important letters sent to me by Dr Mark Thompson); Bunbury was Liverpool's Under-Secretary for War

Don Papers: BL Add Ms 46,703; 43,706 (re 1794–95 campaign in the Low Countries)

Col. J.W. Gordon Papers: BL Add Ms 49,472–73; 49,476–77; 49,480–82; 49,484–85; 49,488; 49,512A Correspondence with the Duke of York, government ministers, opposition politicians and leading officers in the army (including Wellington) by the military secretary to the Commander-in-Chief

Gurwood Papers: BL Add Ms 38,522 (includes copies of some important unpublished letters from Wellington)

Herries Papers: BL Add Ms 57,367–68 Correspondence with Liverpool and Wellington incl. about specie

Lt.-Gen. Sir Rowland Hill Papers: BL Add Ms 35,061 Letters home to his family

Huskisson Papers: 38,738 Includes letters from Col J.W. Gordon, Canning, Arbuthnot and others

Liverpool Papers: BL Add Ms 38,244; 38,246; 38,249; 38,320; 38,325; 38,326 (letter book to Wellington); 38,362–63; 38,378; 59,772 and Loan Ms 72 vols. 16, 20, and 21

Lt Edward McArthur, 39th Regiment: BL Add Ms 44,022 Journal 1813–14 including account of Vitoria

Captain Colin Mackenzie's 'Journal of Remarks and Observations made on the March from Hyderabad to Seringapatam and during the Mysore Campaign along with the Subsidiary Forces serving with the Nizam in 1798 and 1799': BL Add Ms 13,663

Major-General John Randoll Mackenzie: BL Add Ms 39,188; 39,201; 40,722 Diary and correspondence in Portugal in 1809 (transcripts sent to me by John Brewster)

Captain John Malcolm's 'Journal of the Mysore Campaign': BL Add Ms 13,664

Sir John Moore Papers: BL Add Ms 57,544 Comments on Vimeiro and Cintra

Robert Peel Papers: BL Add Ms 40,232–33 Correspondence 1813–14 including several letters from Lord March; BL Add Ms 40,221 Memorandum by AW on the interests and claims of Irish MPs on the Irish government

Col C.W. Pasley Papers: BL Add Ms 41,962 Comments on the Copenhagen expedition and AW's reputation in the army

George Rose Papers: BL Add Ms 42,773 Letter from Canning commenting on the effects of the Copenhagen expedition

Wellington Papers: BL Add Ms 64,131 Mostly relating to the Peninsular War and mostly published

Wellesley Papers: BL Add Ms 13,724; 13,778; 13,806; 37,283–84; 37,286–88; 37,292–96; 37, 308–10; 37,314–15; 37,415–16

Windham Papers: BL Add Ms 37,842; 37,852; 37,906 Secretary for War and the Colonies in the Ministry of All the Talents, and subsequently an influential member of the Opposition, including a few letters from AW

Oriental and India Office Collection (OIOC): Eur Mss B 276 Letter from an officer in the Seringapatam Campaign; Eur Mss B 401 Letter from J. Colebrooke describing Conaghul and anonymous letter about Assaye; Eur Mss F 175/7 Journal of Jasper Nicholls, September–November 1803

Biblioteca de Artes, Gulbenkian Foundation, Lisbon

Beresford Papers: BC 919 Typescript of Beresford's letters to Lady Anne Beresford, 1809–14

The National Archives (formerly The Public Record Office), Kew

Foreign Office Papers: FO 63 Portugal: FO 63/74–78, 88, 93–94, 105; FO 72 Spain: FO 72/60, 71, 93, 108, 111, 114, 127, 128, 132, 142

War Office Papers: WO 1 In Letters: WO 1/226, 232, 234, 237, 239, 240, 244, 276; WO 3 Private Correspondence of Henry Torrens as Military Secretary to the Commander-in-Chief, 1809–14: WO 3/595–607; WO 6 Out Letters from the Secretary of State: WO 6/29, 34, 36, 49–51, 185, 205; WO 17 General Monthly Returns: WO 17/2464–5, 2467–76 Spain and Portugal 1808–14; WO 25/3224–5 Establishment of the British Army and Means of Recruiting, 1809–11, 1813–15; WO 27/63, 68 Irish Inspection Reports 1788–90; WO 37/7 Diary of George Scovell; MFQ 1/448/2 Sketch of the Action at Talavera by Lt.-Col. Richard Fletcher R.E.; MFQ1/448/3 Drawing of the passage of the Douro by Henry Sturgeon

Leveson Gower Papers: 30/29 8/4 and 9/1 Letters from George Canning, 1807

Public Record Office of Northern Ireland (PRONI)

Castlereagh Papers: D 3030/AA/1–25 Letters from Edward Cooke to Charles Stewart, 1808–14; D 3030/P/1–40, 205–39 Letters from Charles Stewart to Castlereagh, 1808–11; D 3030/Q2/2

Bound volume of typescript copies of letters, mostly from Castlereagh to Charles Stewart; D 3030/Q3 Further bound volume of typescript copies of letters; D3030/3387 'Return of the Corps and Detachments of Cavalry and Infantry embarked for the Peninsula between 1st January 1812 and the Present Period', Adjutant General's Office, 27 November 1812

National Army Museum, Chelsea, London

NAM 1966–08–32–1 Photocopy of a letter from AW, 1795 to Army Agents re 33rd's loss of accou-trements in the retreat; NAM Ms 6810–46 Typescript of a letter from Lt Patrick Brown, 1/1st Regiment Native Infantry to his father, Camp at Hyderabad, 20 February 1800; NAM 1963–08–11–1 Nicolls Papers: Manuscript order book of Sir Arthur Wellesley's orders, February 1803 to June 1804; NAM 2006–03–47 Typescript copy of journal of Assistant-Surgeon William Mathew Brookes, 87th Regiment, 1809–10; NAM 6807–333 Anonymous letter from an officer of the Fusilier brigade, 27 July 1812; NAM 8408–37 Charles Whitman, 'Journal of the Campaigns in the Peninsula'; NAM 1974–07/142 Letter from Henry Cadogan on the storming of Badajoz; NAM 2002–05–03 Letters home of the Rev. Samuel Briscall, 1810–15; NAM 1999–06–149 Letters of William Staveley from the Peninsula; NAM 2006–04–15 Letters associated with Benjamin Sydenham and Lord Wellesley

National Records of Scotland (formerly the Scottish Record Office), Edinburgh

Hope of Luffness Papers: GD 364/1/1175 Melville to Sir David Dundas on state of the war, 1808; GD 364/1/1181 Letters re the Peninsula, late 1808; GD 364/1/1193 Letters from officers (mostly G. Murray) in the Peninsula to Alexander Hope 1809; GD 364/1/1196 Letters from George Murray in the Peninsula (to Brownrigg), 1810; GD 364/1/1197 Letters from Murray and others, 1809–10; GD 364/1/1200 Alexander Hope's correspondence, 1810; GD 364/1/1224 Letters from officers in the Peninsula, 1811–12
Leith Hay Papers: GD 225 Box 34/26 Leith Hay's letters home, 1809–12; GD 225/1041–44 Andrew Leith Hay letters to his father
Melville Papers: GD 26/9/534 Letter from an unknown officer in the army, Lisbon, 13 April 1809

National Library of Scotland, Edinburgh

Lynedoch Papers: NLS Ms 3610 Correspondence, 1812
Marshall Papers: NLS Ms 15,371 Typed narrative, including many letters, of the services of the sons of William Marshall, 1790–1815
Murray Papers: Adv Ms 46.1.12 Baltic 1807–08; Adv Ms 46.3.6 General Orders, Portugal, 1808; Adv Ms 46.2.15, vol. 38, 1812

National Library of Ireland, Dublin

Papers of the fourth Duke of Richmond: Mss 58–61, 1807–15

West Yorkshire Archive Service, Leeds

Canning Papers: Bundles 32, 33A, 34, 39, 41, 41A, 45, 46A, 48 and 69

University of Nottingham Library, Nottingham

Papers of the Duke of Portland as Prime Minister, 1807–09: PwF 8582–84
Papers of Lord William Bentinck: PwJc 5–7, 27, 112

House of Lords Record Office, Westminster

Papers of Spencer Perceval, belonging to D.C.L. Holland Esq.: Microfilm copy reels 7–10, Bundles I, II, VII, XIV, XXI, XXII, C

Sandon Hall, Stafford

Papers of Lord Harrowby: Vols. V and LVII

Staffordshire Record Office, Stafford

Hatherton Journal, 26 June 1844: D260/m/f/5/26/30

Centre for Buckinghamshire Studies, Aylesbury

Fremantle Papers: D 192/12/21 Copy of AW to Cooke, Vimeira, 22 August 1808; D/FR/47 and 54 Some early letters of AW in Dublin, and some later correspondence with W.H. Fremantle

Derbyshire Record Office

Letters of Captain Thomas Gell, 29th Foot: D3287/Box 1040/1

Durham University Library, Durham

Earl Grey Papers: Letters of Col J.W. Gordon to Lord Grey, GRE/B19/1–138, 1807–13

Norfolk Record Office, Norwich

Blickling Hall Papers: Castlereagh Private Correspondence, MC3/291, vol. 2 (a private letter from Castlereagh to his wife *c.* 1800 cited in Chapter 14)

Duke University, North Carolina

Croker Papers: Box 14 Croker to Lord Hardwicke 17 November 1854 (my thanks to Dr C.I. Hamilton for sending me a transcript of this letter)

NEWSPAPERS

The Bristol Mercury, 22 May 1841; *Examiner*, 1811; *Gentleman's Magazine*; *London Gazette*, 1787–93, 1796, 1808–10; *Morning Chronicle*, 1809; *Royal Military Chronicle*, 1810–13; *The Times*, 1789–1814

BOOKS AND ARTICLES

Abbot, Charles, Lord Colchester, *The Diary and Correspondence of Charles Abbot, Lord Colchester* ed. his son, Charles, Lord Colchester, 3 vols. (London, John Murray, 1861)

Aitchison, John, *An Ensign in the Peninsular War. The Letters of John Aitchison*, ed. W.F.K. Thompson (London, Michael Joseph, 1981)

Albemarle, Earl of, *Fifty Years of My Life by George Thomas, Earl of Albermarle*, 2 vols. (London, Macmillan, 1876)

Aldington, Richard, *Wellington* (London, Heinemann, 1946)

Alexander, Don W., *Rod of Iron. French Counterinsurgency Policy in Aragon During the Peninsular War* (Wilmington, Scholarly Resources, 1985)

Alexander, Sir James, *Life of Field Marshal, His Grace the Duke of Wellington*, 2 vols. (London, Colburn, 1839–40)

Ali, B. Sheik, *Tipu Sultan. A Study in Diplomacy and Confrontation* (Mysore, Geetha Book House, 1982)

Anglesey, Marquess of, *One-Leg. The Life and Letters of Henry William Paget, first Marquess of Anglesey (1768–1854)* (London, Jonathan Cape, 1963)

Annual Biography and Obituary, vols. 1–13 (London, Longman, Hurst, Rees, Orme and Brown, 1817–29)

Annual Register, or A View of the History, Politics, and Literature for the Year . . . (published annually)

Anonymous, 'The Battle of Busaco' *United Service Journal,* vol. 16, no. 190 (September 1844) pp. 89–101

Anonymous, *Memoirs of a Sergeant late in the Forty-Third Light Infantry Regiment, previously to and during the Peninsula War; including an Account of his Conversion from Popery to the Protestant Religion* (Cambridge, Trotman, 1998; first published 1835)

Anonymous, 'The 29th Regiment at Roliça', *United Service Journal* (November 1830), pp. 745–9

Anstruther, Journal, quoted in an anonymous review by George Murray of Napier's *History of the War in the Peninsula, Quarterly Review*, vol. 56 (April 1836)

Antonova, C.K.A., 'Tipu Sultan and the French: Hitherto Unpublished Documents in the Leningrad Institute of History', *Central Asian Review*, vol. 11 (1963), pp. 72–88

Arbuthnot, Charles, *The Correspondence of Charles Arbuthnot*, ed. A. Aspinall (London, Royal Historical Society, 1941; Camden 3rd series, vol. 65)

Arbuthnot, Harriet, *The Journal of Mrs Arbuthnot 1820–1832*, ed. Francis Bamford and the Duke of Wellington, 2 vols. (London, Macmillan, 1950)

Archer, Mildred, *Tippoo's Tiger* (London, HMSO, 1959)

Army List: A List of all the Officers of the Army and Royal Marines on full and half pay (published annually by the War Office)

Armytage, Mrs, 'The Ladies of Llangollen: Fragmentary Recollections of Lady Eleanor Butler and Miss Ponsonby', *Belgravia. A London Magazine*, vol. 72 (May–August 1890), pp. 136–55, 248–64

Arnold, James R., 'A Reappraisal of Column versus Line in the Napoleonic Wars', *JSAHR*, vol. 60, no. 244 (Winter 1982), pp. 196–208

Aspinall, A., 'The Cabinet Council, 1783–1835', *Proceedings of the British Academy*, vol. 38 (1952), pp. 145–252

——, 'The Irish "Proclamation" Fund, 1800–1846', *English Historical Review*, vol. 56 (1941), pp. 265–80

——, 'The Old House of Commons and its Members (*c.* 1783–1832)', *Parliamentary Affairs*, vols. 14–15 (1960–62)

——, *Politics and the Press* c. *1780–1850* (London, Home and Van Thal, 1949)

Aspinall, A. and E. Anthony Smith, *English Historical Documents*, vol. XI, *1783–1832* (London, Eyre and Spottiswoode, 1969)

Atkinson, C.T., 'The "Battalions of Detachments" at Talavera', *JSAHR*, vol. 15 (1936), pp. 32–8

——, 'The Composition and Organisation of the British Forces in the Peninsula, 1808–1814', *English Historical Review*, vol. 17 (1902), pp. 110–33, 416

——, 'Gleanings from the Cathcart Mss Pt IV The Netherlands, 1794–1795', *JSAHR*, vol. 29, no. 120 (Winter 1951), pp. 144–57

——, 'A Swiss Officer in Wellington's Army', *JSAHR*, vol. 35 (June 1957), pp. 71–8

Bainbrigge, Sir Philip, 'The Staff at Salamanca', *United Service Journal* (January 1878), pp. 72–5

Baker, J.N.L., 'Some Geographical Factors in the Campaigns of Assaye and Argaon', *Army Quarterly*, vol. 17 (1929), pp. 45–53

Barnard, Sir Andrew, *Barnard Letters, 1778–1824*, ed. Anthony Powell (London, Duckworth, 1928)

Barrington, Sir Jonah, *Personal Sketches and Recollections of his Own Times* (Glasgow and London, Cameron and Ferguson, 1876)

Bartlett, Keith J., 'The Development of the British Army during the Wars with France, 1793–1815' (unpublished PhD thesis, University of Durham, 1997)

Bartlett, Thomas, *The Fall and Rise of the Irish Nation. The Catholic Question, 1690–1830* (Dublin, Gill and Macmillan, 1992)

——, 'Indiscipline and Disaffection in the French and Irish Armies during the Revolutionary Period', in *Ireland and the French Revolution*, ed. Hugh Gough and David Dickson (Dublin, Irish Academic Press, 1990)

Bathurst, Earl. *Historical Manuscripts Commission. Report on the Manuscripts of Earl Bathurst preserved at Cirencester Park* (London, HMSO, 1923) [cited as *HMC Bathurst*]

Bayly, [Richard], *Diary of Colonel Bayly, 12th Regiment, 1796–1830* (London, Army and Navy Co-operative Society, 1896)

Beamish, N. Ludlow, *History of the King's German Legion*, 2 vols. (London, Boone, 1832–37)

Beatson, Alexander, *A View of the Origin and Conduct of the War with Tippoo Sultaun* ... (London, Nicol, 1800)

Beatson, Maj.-Gen. F.C., *Wellington. The Bidassoa and Nivelle* (London, Tom Donovan, 1995; first published 1931)

——, *Wellington. The Crossing of the Gaves and the Battle of Orthez* (London, Tom Donovan, 1994; first published 1925)

——, *With Wellington in the Pyrenees, being an Account of the Operations between the Allied Army and the French from July 25 to August 2, 1813* (London, Tom Donovan, 1993; first published 1914)

Beckett, J.C., *The Making of Modern Ireland, 1603–1923* (London, Faber and Faber, 1967)

Beckett, J.V., *The Rise and Fall of the Grenvilles. The Dukes of Buckingham and Chandos, 1710–1921* (Manchester University Press, 1994)

Bell, Sir George, *Soldier's Glory* (London, G. Bell and Sons, 1956)

Bennell, A.S., 'The Anglo-Maratha War of 1803–1805', *JSAHR*, vol. 65 (1985), pp. 144–61

——, 'Arthur Wellesley as Political Agent, 1803', *Journal of the Royal Asiatic Society*, vol. 119 (1987), pp. 272–88

——, 'Factors in the Marquis Wellesley's Failure against Holkar', *School of Oriental and African Studies Bulletin*, vol. 28 (1965), pp. 553–81

——, 'Failure by Deputy: Arthur Wellesley and Colonel Murray in 1804', *Wellington Studies II* (1999), pp. 69–84

——, *The Making of Arthur Wellesley* (Hyderabad, Orient Longman, 1997)

——, 'Wellesley's Settlement of Mysore, 1799', *Journal of the Royal Asiatic Society* (October 1952), pp. 124–32

Berkeley, Alison D., *New Lights on the Peninsular War* (Lisbon, British Historical Society of Portugal, 1991)

Bernard, Henri, *Le Duc de Wellington et la Belgique* (Brussels, La Renaissance du Livre, 1973)

Berry, Miss, *Extracts from the Journals and Correspondence of Miss Berry . . . 1783 to 1852*, ed. Lady Theresa Lewis, 3 vols. (London, Longmans, 1865)

Bessborough, Earl of and A. Aspinall, eds., *Lady Bessborough and her Family Circle* (London, John Murray, 1941)

Bew, John, *Castlereagh. Enlightenment, War and Tyranny* (London, Quercus, 2011)

Bhattacharyya, Pranjal Kumar, *British Residents at Poona, 1786–1818* (Calcutta, Progressive Publishers, 1984)

Biddulph, Col. John, *The Nineteenth and their Times . . .* (London, John Murray, 1899)

Bidwell, Shelford, *Swords for Hire. European Mercenaries in Eighteenth-Century India* (London, John Murray, 1971)

Bindoff, S.T., E.F. Malcolm Smith and C.K. Webster, *British Diplomatic Representatives, 1789–1852* (London, Royal Historical Society, 1934; Camden 3rd series, vol. 50)

Bingham: see Glover

Blackstock, Allan, 'The Union and the Military, 1801–1830', *Transactions of the Royal Historical Society*, 6th series, vol. 10 (2000), pp. 329–51

Blakeney, Robert, *A Boy in the Peninsular War. The Services, Adventures and Experiences of Robert Blakeney . . . An Autobiography* (London, John Murray, 1899)

[Blakiston, J.], *Twelve Years' Military Adventure in three Quarters of the Globe . . .*, 2 vols. (London, Henry Colburn, 1829)

Blanco, Richard L., *Wellington's Surgeon General. Sir James McGrigor* (Durham, NC, Duke University Press, 1974)

Bond, Gordon C., *The Grand Expedition. The British Invasion of Holland in 1809* (Athens, GA, University of Georgia Press, 1979)

Bourne, Kenneth, *Palmerston. The Early Years, 1784–1841* (London, Allen Lane, 1982)

Boutflower, Charles, *Journal of an Army Surgeon during the Peninsular War* (Staplehurst, Spellmount, 1997; first published 1912)

Boyce, D. George, 'From Assaye to the *Assaye*: Reflections on British Government, Force, and Moral Authority in India', *Journal of Military History*, vol. 63, no. 3 (July 1999), pp. 643–68

Boydell, Brian, 'Music, 1790–1850', in *New History of Ireland*, ed. T.W. Moody et al, 9 vols. (Oxford, Clarendon Press, 1976–2005)

Bragge, William, *Peninsular Portrait 1811–1814. The Letters of Captain William Bragge Third (King's Own) Dragoons*, ed. S.A.C. Cassels (London, Oxford University Press, 1963)

Braham, Allan, 'Goya's Equestrian Portrait of the Duke of Wellington', *Burlington Magazine*, vol. 108 (December 1966), pp. 618–21

——, 'Goya's Portrait of the Duke of Wellington in the National Gallery', *Burlington Magazine*, vol. 108 (December 1966), pp. 78–83

Brashares, Richard A., 'The Political Career of Marquess Wellesley in England and Ireland' (unpublished PhD thesis, Duke University, 1968)

Brereton, J.M. and A.C. Savory, *The History of the Duke of Wellington's Regiment (West Riding) 1702–1992* (Halifax, Duke of Wellington's Regiment, 1993)

Brett-James, Antony, *General Graham, Lord Lynedoch* (New York, St Martin's Press, 1959)

——, *Life in Wellington's Army* (London, George Allen and Unwin, 1972)

——, 'Wellington in his Wartime Letters', *History Today* (August 1959), pp. 552–9

Brialmont, A. and G.R. Gleig, *History of the Life of Arthur Duke of Wellington,* 4 vols. (London, Longman, Brown, Green, Longmans and Roberts, 1858)

Brightfield, Myron F., *John Wilson Croker* (London, George Allen and Unwin, 1940)

Brisbane, T.M., *Reminiscences of General Sir Thomas Makdougall Brisbane* (Edinburgh, printed for private circulation, Thomas Constable, 1860)

Brittlebank, Kate, *Tipu Sultan's Search for Legitimacy. Islam and Kingship in a Hindu Domain* (Delhi, Oxford University Press, 1997)

——, 'The White Raja of Srirangapattana: Was Arthur Wellesley Tipu Sultan's True Successor?', *South Asia: Journal of South Asian Studies,* vol. 26, no. 1 (2003), pp. 23–35

Brotherton, Sir Thomas, *A Hawk at War. The Peninsular War Reminiscences of General Sir Thomas Brotherton, CB,* ed. Bryan Perrett (Chippenham, Picton Publishing, 1986)

Brougham, Henry, *The Life and Times of Henry, Lord Brougham, written by himself,* 3 vols. (New York, Harper and Brothers, 1872)

Broughton, Lord, *Recollections of a Long Lifetime by Lord Braghton,* ed. his daughter Lady Dorchester, 6 vols. (London, John Murway, 1910)

Browne, T.H., *The Napoleonic War Journal of Captain Thomas Henry Browne, 1807–1816,* ed. Roger Norman Buckley (London, Bodley Head for the Army Records Society, vol. 3, 1987)

Bruce, Anthony, *A Bibliography of the British Army, 1660–1914* (London, Saur, 1985)

Bruce, H.A., *Life of General Sir William Napier,* 2 vols. (London, John Murray, 1864)

Bryant, G.J., 'Indigenous Mercenaries in the Service of European Imperialists: The Case of the Sepoys in the Early British Indian Army, 1750–1800', *War in History,* vol. 7, no. 1 (January 2000), pp. 1–28

Brynn, Edward, *Crown and Castle. British Rule in Ireland, 1800–1830* (Toronto, Macmillan of Canada, 1978)

Buchanan, Dr Francis, *A Journey from Madras through the Countries of Mysore, Canara, and Malabar . . .,* 3 vols. (London, Cadell and Davies, 1807)

[Buckham, E.W.], *Personal Narrative of Adventures in the Peninsula . . . by an Officer late in the Staff Corps Regiment of Cavalry* (Cambridge, Trotman, 1995; first published 1827)

Buckingham and Chandos, Duke of, *Memoirs of the Court and Cabinets of George III,* 4 vols. (London, Hurst and Blackett, 1853)

——, *Memoirs of the Court of England during the Regency, 1811–1820,* 2 vols. (London, Hurst and Blackett, 1856)

Bugeaud, T.R., *Memoirs of Marshal Bugeaud,* 2 vols. (London, Hurst and Blackett, 1884)

Bunbury, Sir Henry, *Narrative of Some Passages in the Great War with France (1799–1810)* (London, Peter Davies, 1927)

[Bunbury, Thomas], *Reminiscences of a Veteran,* 3 vols. (London, Charles J. Skeet, 1861)

Burghersh, Lady (Priscilla Fane, née Wellesley-Pole), *Correspondence of Lady Burghersh with the Duke of Wellington,* ed. her daughter Lady Rose Weigall (London, John Murray, 1903)

Burghersh, Lord, *Correspondence of Lord Burghersh, afterwards eleventh Earl of Westmorland, 1808–1840,* ed. his granddaughter Rachel Weigall (London, John Murray, 1912)

[Burghersh, Lord], *Memoir of the Early Campaigns of the Duke of Wellington in Portugal and Spain* (London, John Murray, 1820)

Burke, Sir Bernard, *The Rise of Great Families* (London, Longmans, Green and Co., 1873)

Burnham, Robert, 'British Bridging Operations in the Peninsula', in *Inside Wellington's Peninsular Army* by Rory Muir, Robert Burnham, Howie Muir and Ron McGuigan (Barnsley, Pen and Sword, 2006)

Burnham, Robert and Ron McGuigan, *The British Army Against Napoleon. Facts, Lists and Trivia 1805–1815* (Barnsley, Frontline, 2010)

Burton, R.G., 'The Field of Assaye', *United Service Journal,* vol. 45 (1912), pp. 297–302

——, *Wellington's Campaigns in India* (Calcutta, Govt. Printing, 1908; reprinted 2008)

Butler, Iris, *The Eldest Brother. The Marquess Wellesley* (London, Hodder and Stoughton, 1973)

Callahan, Raymond, *The East India Company and Army Reform* (Harvard Historical Monographs, no. 67, 1962)

Calvert, the Hon. [Frances] Mrs, *An Irish Beauty under the Regency compiled from 'Mes Souvenirs' – the Unpublished Journals of the Hon. Mrs Calvert, 1789–1822,* ed. Mrs Warrenne Blake (London, John Lane The Bodley Head, 1911)

Campbell, Lt. A., 'The Seringapatam Letter [from Lt A. Campbell, 74th Highlanders, 20 June 1799]', *Journal of the Royal Highland Fusiliers*, vol. 6 (June 1969), p. 80

Canning, M., *Mehitabel Canning. A Redoubtable Woman. Family Letters*, ed. Giles Hunt (Royston, Rooster Books, 2001)

Cantlie, Sir Neil, *A History of the Army Medical Department*, 2 vols. (Edinburgh and London, Churchill Livingstone, 1974)

Carnegie, Nicholas, George and Thomas, *The Mahratta Wars, 1797–1805. Letters from the Front by three brothers Nicholas, George and Thomas Carnegie of Charleton, Montrose*, ed. A.A. Cormack (Peterculter, A.A. Cormack, 1971)

Carss: see Johnston

Cartograpfía de la Guerra de la Independencia (Madrid, Ministerio de Defensa and Ollero y Ramos Editiores, 2008)

Cassidy, Martin, *Marching with Wellington 1808–1815* (Barnsley, Leo Cooper, 2003) [including much material from the diary of Charles Crowe, 1813–15]

Castlereagh, Lord, *Correspondence, Despatches, and other Papers of Viscount Castlereagh, Second Marquess of Londonderry*, ed. his brother Charles William Vane, Marquess of Londonderry, 12 vols. (London, William Shoberl, 1848–53).

Cathcart: see Atkinson

Challis, Capt L.S., 'British Officers Serving in the Portuguese Army, 1809–1814', *JSAHR*, vol. 27, no. 110 (1949), pp. 50–60

——, *Peninsula Roll Call*, available online through the Napoleon Series website: www.napoleon-series.org/research/biographies/GreatBritain/Challis/c_ChallisIntro.html

Chambers, Charles, 'The Bombardment of Copenhagen, 1807: The Journal of Surgeon Charles Chambers of H.M. Fireship Prometheus', *Naval Miscellany*, vol. 3 (Navy Record Society, vol. 63, 1928), pp. 365–466

Chambers, Lt.-Col. G.L., *Bussaco* (East Felling, Worley, 1994; first published 1910)

Chandler, David, *The Campaigns of Napoleon* (New York, Macmillan, 1974)

Charrié, Pierre, *Drapeaux et Etendards de la Révolution et de l'Empire* (Paris, Copernic, 1982)

Chatterton, Georgiana, Lady, *Memorials Personal and Historical of Admiral Lord Gambier*, 2 vols. (London, Hurst and Blackett, 1861)

Chesterton, G.L., *Peace, War and Adventure. An Autobiographical Memoir . . .*, 2 vols. (London, Longman, Brown, Green and Longmans, 1853)

Christie, Carl, 'The Royal Navy and the Walcheren Expedition of 1809', in *New Aspects of Naval History*, ed. Craig L Symonds (Annapolis, Naval Institute Press, 1981), pp. 190–200

Cintra Inquiry: see under *Proceedings . . .*

Clarke, Francis L. and William Dunlap, *The Life of the Most Noble Arthur, Marquis and Earl of Wellington . . .* (New York, Van Winkle and Wiley, 1814)

Clark-Kennedy, A.E., *Attack the Colour! The Royal Dragoons in the Peninsula and at Waterloo* (London, Research Publishing, 1975)

Clermont, Thomas (Fortescue), Lord, *A History of the Family of Fortescue in all its Branches* (London, Ellis and White, 1880)

Cleveland, Duchess of, *The Life and Letters of Lady Hester Stanhope* (London, John Murray, 1914)

Colchester: see Abbot

Cole, G.L., *Memoirs of Sir Lowry Cole*, ed. Maud Lowry Cole and Stephen Gwynn (London, Macmillan, 1934)

Cole, J.W., *Memoirs of British Generals distinguished during the Peninsular War*, 2 vols. (London 1856)

Colebrooke, Sir T.E., *Life of the Honourable Mountstuart Elphinstone*, 2 vols. (London, John Murray, 1884)

Coleridge, S.T., *The Collected Works of Samuel Taylor Coleridge*, vol. 3, *Essays on His Times in The Morning Post and The Courier*, ed. David V. Endman, 3 vols. (London, Routledge and Kegan Paul, 1978)

Colley, Linda, *Britons. Forging the Nation, 1707–1837* (New Haven and London, Yale University Press, 1992)

Collins, Bruce, 'Siege Warfare in the Age of Wellington', *Wellington Studies IV* (2008), pp. 22–53

——, *War and Empire. The Expansion of Britain, 1790–1830* (Harlow, Longman, 2010)

Colville, John, *The Portrait of a General* (Salisbury, Michael Russell, 1980)

Combermere, [Stapleton Cotton], Lord, *Memoirs and Correspondence of Field Marshal Viscount Combermere . . .*, by Mary, Viscountess Combermere and Capt. W. Knollys, 2 vols. (London, Hurst and Blackett, 1866)

The Complete Peerage by G.E.C[ockayne], 2nd edn, 12 vols. (1910–59; printed in microprint edition in 8 vols., Sutton Publishing, 2000)

Compton, Herbert, *A Particular Account of the European Military Adventurers of Hindustan from 1784 to 1803* (London, T. Fisher Unwin, 1893)

Connelly, Owen, *Napoleon's Satellite Kingdoms* (New York, Free Press, 1969)

Connolly, T.W.J., *History of the Royal Sappers and Miners*, 2 vols. (London, Longmans, Brown, Green, Longmans and Roberts, 1857)

Cooke, Lt John, *A True Soldier Gentleman. The Memoirs of Lt. John Cooke, 1791–1813*, ed. Eileen Hathaway (Swanage, Shinglepicker, 2000)

Cookson, J.E., *The British Armed Nation, 1793–1815* (Oxford, Clarendon Press, 1997)

Cooper, J.S., *Rough Notes of Seven Campaigns, 1809–1815* (Staplehurst, Spellmount, 1996; first published 1869)

Cooper, Randolf G.S., *The Anglo-Maratha Campaigns and the Contest for India. The Struggle for Control of the South Asian Military Economy* (Cambridge University Press, 2003)

——, 'New Light on Arthur Wellesley's Command-Apprenticeship in India: The Dhoondiah Waugh Campaign of 1800 Reconsidered', in Alan J. Guy, *The Road to Waterloo* (London, National Army Museum, 1990), pp. 81–7

——, 'Wellington and the Marathas in 1803', *International History Review*, vol. 11 (February 1989), pp. 31–8

Cornwallis: see Ross

Corrigan, Gordon, *Wellington. A Military Life* (London and New York, Hambledon and London, 2001)

Coss, Edward J., *All for the King's Shilling. The British Soldier under Wellington, 1808–1814* (Norman, OK, University of Oklahoma Press, 2010)

Costello, Edward, *The Peninsular and Waterloo Campaigns*, ed. Antony Brett-James (London, Longmans, Green, 1967)

[Cowell, John Stepney], *Leaves from the Diary of an Officer of the Guards* (Cambridge, Ken Trotman, 1994; first published 1854)

Craufurd, Alexander H., *General Craufurd and His Light Division* (Cambridge, Ken Trotman, 1987; first published 1891)

Crawford, Capt. A., *Reminiscences of a Naval Officer. A Quarter-Deck View of the War against Napoleon* (London, Chatham, 1999)

Creevey, Thomas, *The Creevey Papers. A Selection from the Correspondence and Diaries of the late Thomas Creevey, MP*, ed. Sir Herbert Maxwell (London, John Murray, 1923)

Croker, John Wilson, *The Croker Papers. The Correspondence and Diaries of the late Right Honourable John Wilson Croker*, ed. Louis J. Jennings, 3 vols. (London, John Murray, 1884)

Crowe, Charles, *An Eloquent Soldier. The Peninsular War Journals of Lieutenant Charles Crowe of the Innisillings, 1812–1814*, ed. Gareth Glover (Barnsley, Frontline, 2011)

Crowe, Charles: see also Cassidy, Martin

Crowe, K., 'Thomas Burns Catherwood and the Medical Department of Wellington's Army', *Medical History*, vol. 20, no. 1 (January 1976), pp. 22–40

Crumplin, Michael, *Guthrie's War. A Surgeon of the Peninsula and Waterloo* (Barnsley, Pen and Sword, 2010)

Dalrymple, Sir Hew, *Memoir written by General Sir Hew Dalrymple, Bart . . .* (London, Boone, 1830)

Dalrymple, William, *White Mughals. Love and Betrayal in Eighteenth-Century India* (London, HarperCollins, 2002)

Dalton, Charles, *The Waterloo Roll Call* (London, Arms and Armour, 1978)

Daly, Gavin, 'A Dirty, Indolent, Priest-Ridden City: British Soldiers in Lisbon during the Peninsular War, 1808–1813', *History*, vol. 94, no. 316 (2009), pp. 461–82

Davidson, Maj. H., *History and Services of the 78th Highlanders (Ross-shire Buffs)* (Edinburgh and London, W. and A.K. Johnston, 1901)

Davies, Godfrey, *Wellington and His Army* (Oxford, Blackwell, 1954)

Davies, Huw J 'Integration of Strategic and Operational Intelligence during the Peninsular War', *Intelligence and National Security*, vol. 21, no. 2 (April 2006), pp. 202–23

——, 'Naval Intelligence Support to the British Army in the Peninsular War', *JSAHR*, vol. 86 (2008), pp. 34–56

——, 'Secret Intelligence in the Peninsular War: The Case Study of El Bodon 25 September 1811', *Archives*, vol. 30 (April 2005), pp. 47–59

——, 'Wellington's First Command: The Political and Military Campaign Against Dhoondiah Vagh, February-September 1800', *Modern Asian Studies*, vol. 44 (2010), pp. 1081–113

——, 'Wellington's Use of Deception Tactics in the Peninsular War', *Journal of Strategic Studies*, vol. 29 (August 2006), pp. 723–50

——, *Wellington's Wars. The Making of a Military Genius* (New Haven and London, Yale University Press, 2012)

Davis, Richard, *The English Rothschilds* (London, Collins, 1983)

Delaforce, Patrick, *Wellington the Beau* (Moreton-in-Marsh, Windrush, 1990)

De La Fuente, Francisco Arturo, 'Dom Miguel Pereira Forjaz: His Early Career and Role in the Mobilization and Defense of Portugal during the Peninsular War, 1807–1814' (unpublished PhD thesis, Florida State University, 1980)

Delaney, Mary, *The Autobiography and Correspondence of Mary Grenville, Mrs Delaney*, ed. Lady Llanover, 3 vols. (London, Richard Bentley, 1861)

Delavoye, Alex M., *Life of Thomas Graham, Lord Lynedoch* (London, Richardson and Marchant Singer, 1880)

De Ros, Georgiana, Lady, 'Personal Recollections of the Great Duke of Wellington', *Murray's Magazine* (January and February 1889), pp. 37–53, 193–201

De Toy, Brian M., 'Wellington's Admiral: The Life and Career of George Berkeley, 1753–1818' (unpublished PhD thesis, Florida State University, 1997)

Dickinson, H.T., ed., *Britain and the French Revolution, 1789–1815* (Basingstoke, Macmillan, 1989)

Dickson, Alexander, *The Dickson Manuscripts*, ed. Major John H. Leslie, 5 vols. (Ken Trotman, Cambridge, 1987–91; reprint of original in 2 vols., 1905–08)

Dinwiddy, J.R., 'The Early Nineteenth-Century Campaign against Flogging in the Army', in Dinwiddy, *Radicalism and Reform in Britain, 1780–1850* (London, Hambledon, 1992)

Divall, Carole, *Inside the Regiment. The Officers and Men of the 30th Regiment During the Revolutionary and Napoleonic Wars* (Barnsley, Pen and Sword, 2011)

——, *Redcoats Against Napoleon. The 30th Regiment during the Revolutionary and Napoleonic Wars* (Barnsley, Pen and Sword, 2009)

DNB: The Dictionary of National Biography, ed. Leslie Stephen, 22 vols. (London, Smith, Elder and Co., 1885–1900)

Dolby, I.E.A., ed., 'The Duke of Wellington's Services', in *The Journal of the Household Brigade* (1872), pp. 212–13

Donaldson, Joseph, *Recollections of the Eventful Life of a Soldier* (Staplehurst, Spellmount, 2000)

Donkin, Sir Rufane, Letter to Lt.-Gen. Napier, London, 24 May 1830, in *United Service Journal* (1830), pt. 2, pp. 96–8

Douglas, Sir Howard, *An Essay on the Principles and Construction of Military Bridges and the Passage of Rivers . . .* (London, John Murray, 1853)

Douglas, John, *Douglas's Tale of the Peninsula and Waterloo*, ed. Stanley Monick (London, Leo Cooper, 1997)

Downman, Maj. T., 'Diary of Major Thomas Downman, Royal Horse Artillery, in the Peninsula', *JSAHR*, vol. 5 (October 1926)

Dropmore: Historical Manuscripts Commission. Report on the Manuscripts of J.B. Fortescue preserved at Dropmore, 10 vols. (London, HMSO, 1892–1927) [cited as *HMC Dropmore*]

Du Cann, Edward, *The Duke of Wellington and his Political Career after Waterloo – the Caricaturists' View* (Woodbridge, Antique Collectors' Club, 2000)

Duff, J.G., *A History of the Marathas*, 3 vols. (London, Longmans, Rees, Orme, Brown and Green, 1826)

Duffy, Michael, *Soldiers, Sugar and Seapower. The British Expeditions to the West Indies and the War Against Revolutionary France* (Oxford, Clarendon Press, 1987)

——, 'World-wide War and British Expansion, 1793–1815', in *The Oxford History of the British Empire*, vol. 2, *The Eighteenth Century*, ed. P.J. Marshall (Oxford University Press, 1998)

Duncan, Capt. Francis, *History of the Royal Regiment of Artillery*, 2 vols. (London, John Murray, 1872)

Dunne-Lynch, Nicholas, 'Humour and Defiance: Irish Troops and their Humour in the Peninsular War', *JSAHR*, vol. 85 (2007), pp. 62–78

D'Urban, Sir Benjamin, *The Peninsular Journal of Major-General Sir Benjamin D'Urban ... 1808–1817*, ed. I.J. Rousseau (London, Longmans, 1930)

Dutton, Geoffrey and David Elder, *Colonel William Light – Founder of a City* (Melbourne University Press, 1991)

Dyneley, T., *Letters written by Lieut.-General Thomas Dyneley C.B., R.A., while on Active Service between the years 1806 and 1815*, ed. Col. F.A. Whinyates (London, Ken Trotman, 1984; first published 1896)

E., J.E., 'The Duke of Wellington's Height', in *JSAHR*, vol. 29, no. 120 (Winter 1951), p. 182

Eastlake, George, 'Mr Eastlake's visit to Spain in 1813', ed. S.G.P. Ward, *JSAHR*, vol. 70 (Summer 1992), pp. 71–86

Eastwick, Capt. Robert W., *A Master Mariner. Being the Life and Adventures of Captain Robert W. Eastwick*, ed. Herbert Compton (London, T. Fisher Unwin, 1891)

Edgeworth, Maria, *The Life and Letters of Maria Edgeworth*, ed. Augustus Hare, 2 vols. (London, Edward Arnold, 1894)

——, *Maria Edgeworth. Letters from England, 1813–1844*, ed. Christina Colvin (Oxford, Clarendon Press, 1971)

Edney, Matthew H., *Mapping an Empire. The Geographical Construction of British India, 1765–1843* (University of Chicago Press, 1997)

Edwards, Peter, *Talavera. Wellington's Early Peninsula Victories* (Marlborough, Crowood, 2005)

Ehrman, John, *The Younger Pitt. The Reluctant Transition* [vol. 2] (London, Constable, 1983)

——, *The Younger Pitt. The Consuming Struggle* [vol. 3] (London, Constable, 1996)

Elers, George, *Memoirs of George Elers*, ed. Lord Monson and George Leveson Gower (London, William Heinemann, 1903)

Eliot, William G., *A Treatise on the Defence of Portugal* ... (London, Egerton, 1811)

Ellesmere, Francis, 1st Earl of, *Personal Reminiscences of the Duke of Wellington* (London, John Murray, 1904)

Elliott, Marianne, *Partners in Revolution. The United Irishmen and France* (New Haven and London, Yale University Press, 1982)

Ellis, J.D., 'Promotion with the Ranks of the British Army: A Study of the Non-Commissioned Officers of the 28th (North Gloucestershire) Regiment of Foot at Waterloo', *JSAHR*, vol. 81 (2003), pp. 216–27

Ellison, C.C., 'Dangan, Mornington and the Wellesleys: Notes on the Rise and Fall of a Great Meath Estate', *Riocht na Midhe (Records of the Meath Archaelogical and Historical Society)*, vol. 3 (1967)

Embree, A.T., *Charles Grant and British Rule in India* (London, George Allen and Unwin, 1962)

Emsley, Clive, *British Society and the French Wars, 1793–1815* (London and Basingstoke, Macmillan, 1979)

Esdaile, Charles J., *The Duke of Wellington and the Command of the Spanish Armies, 1812–1814* (Basingstoke, Macmillan, 1990)

——, *Fighting Napoleon. Guerrillas, Bandits and Adventures in Spain, 1808–1814* (New Haven and London, Yale University Press, 2004)

——, *The Peninsular War. A New History* (London, Allen Lane, 2002)

——, *Spain in the Liberal Age. From Constitution to Civil War, 1808–1939* (Oxford, Blackwell, 2000)

——, *The Spanish Army in the Peninsular War* (Manchester University Press, 1988)

Everard, Maj. H., *History of Thos. Farrington's Regiment subsequently designated the 29th (Worecestershire) Foot* (Worcester, Littlebury and Co., 1891)

Fane: see Burghersh

Farington, Joseph, *The Farington Diary*, ed. James Grieg, 8 vols. (London, Hutchinson, 1922–28)

Fenton, Capt. T.C., 'The Peninsular and Waterloo Letters of Captain Thomas Charles Fenton', *JSAHR*, vol. 53 (Winter 1975), pp. 210–31

Ferguson, Niall, *The House of Rothschild*, vol. 1, *Money's Prophets, 1798–1848* (New York, Penguin, 1999)

Fergusson, William, 'Observations on the Venereal Disease in Portugal, as affecting the Constitutions of the British Soldiery and Natives', *Medico-Chirugical Transactions*, vol. 4 (1813), pp. 1–16

Fisher, D.R., ed., *The History of Parliament. The House of Commons, 1820–1832*, 7 vols. (Cambridge University Press for the History of Parliament Trust, 2009)

[Fitzclarence, George, Earl of Munster], 'An Account of the British Campaign of 1809', *United Service Journal*, vol. 1, no. 5 (May 1829), pp. 521–31; no. 6 (June 1829), pp. 660–73; no. 7 (July 1829), pp. 1–12; no. 8 (August 1829), pp. 144–53

Fletcher, Ian, *Galloping at Everything. The British Cavalry in the Peninsular War and at Waterloo, 1808–1815. A Reappraisal* (Staplehurst, Spellmount, 1999)

——, ed., *The Peninsular War. Aspects of the Struggle for the Iberian Peninsula* (Staplehurst, Spellmount, 1998)

——, *Wellington's Regiments* (Staplehurst, Spellmount, 1994)

Forrest, Alan, *Napoleon's Men. The Soldiers of the Revolution and Empire* (London and New York, Hambledon and London, 2002)

Forrest, Denys M., *Tiger of Mysore. The Life and Death of Tipu Sultan* (London, Chatto and Windus, 1970)

Fortescue, J.W., *The County Lieutenancies and the Army, 1803–1814* (London, Macmillan, 1909)

——, *A History of the British Army*, 13 vols. in 20 (London, Macmillan, 1899–1930)

——, *Wellington* (London, Ernest Benn, 1960; first published 1925)

Foy, Gen. M., *History of the War in the Peninsula, under Napoleon*, 2 vols. (London, Treuttel and Würtz, 1827)

Franklin, Robert, *Lord Stuart de Rothesay. The Life and Times of Lord Stuart de Rothesay of Highcliffe Castle, 1779–1845* (Upton-upon-Severn, Images, 1993)

Frazer, Sir Augustus Simon, *The Letters of Colonel Sir Augustus Simon Frazer, K.C.B. commanding the Royal Horse Artillery in the army under the Duke of Wellington*, ed. Edward Sabine (Uckfield, Naval and Military Press, 2001; first published 1859)

Freer, 'Letters from the Peninsula: The Freer Family Correspondence, 1807–1814', ed. Norman Scarfe, *Transactions of the Leicestershire Archaeological Society*, vol. 29 (1953)

Fremantle, Lt.-Col. John, *Wellington's Voice. The Candid Letters of Lieutenant-Colonel John Fremantle, Coldstream Guards, 1808–1821*, ed. Gareth Glover (Barnsley, Frontline Books 2012)

French, Noel E., ed., *Wellington. His Irish Connections* (Trim, Meath Heritage Centre, 1992)

Fryer, Mary Beacock, *'Our Young Soldier'. Lieutenant Francis Simcoe* (Toronto and Oxford, Dundurn Press, 1999)

Fryman, Mildred L., 'Charles Stuart and the "Common Cause": The Anglo-Portuguese Alliance, 1810–1814' (unpublished PhD thesis, Florida State University, 1974)

Fuhr, Enid M., 'Strategy and Diplomacy in British India under Marquis Wellesley: The Second Maratha War, 1802–1806' (PhD thesis, Simon Fraser University, 1994)

Fyler, Colonel A.E., *History of the 50th or (Queen's Own) Regiment* (London, Chapman and Hall, 1895)

Galpin, W.F., 'The American Grain Trade to the Spanish Peninsula 1810–1814', *American Historical Review*, vol. 28 (1922), pp. 24–44

Gardyne, Lt.-Col. C. Greenhill, *The Life of a Regiment. The History of the Gordon Highlanders from its Formation in 1794 to 1816*, 2 vols. (London, Medici Society, 1929; reprinted Naval and Military Press, nd)

Garrett, Robert, 'A Subaltern in the Peninsular War: Letters of Robert Garrett 1811–1813', ed. A.S. White, *JSAHR*, vol. 13 (1934), pp. 3–22.

Garwood, Lt.-Col. F.S., 'The Royal Staff Corps, 1800–1837', *Royal Engineers Journal*, vol. 57 (1943), pp. 81–96, 247–60

Gash, Norman, *Lord Liverpool* (London, Weidenfeld and Nicolson, 1984)

——, *Mr Secretary Peel. The Life of Sir Robert Peel to 1830* (London, Longmans and Co., 1961)

——, *Robert Surtees and Early Victorian Society* (Oxford, Clarendon Press, 1993)

——, *Wellington Anecdotes. A Critical Survey* (4th Wellington Lecture, University of Southampton, 1992)

——, ed., *Wellington. Studies in the Military and Political Career of the First Duke of Wellington* (Manchester University Press, 1990)

Gates, David, *The British Light Infantry Arm c.1790–1815* (London, Batsford, 1987)

——, *The Spanish Ulcer. A History of the Peninsular War* (London, Allen and Unwin, 1986)

Gates, R.P., 'Tipu Sultan of Mysore and the Revolutionary Governments of France, 1793–1799', *Bengal: Past and Present*, vol. 83 (1964), pp. 7–19

Geike, Archibald, *Life of Sir Roderick I. Murchison*, 2 vols. (London, John Murray, 1875)

General Orders: see under Wellington

George III, *The Later Correspondence of George III*, ed. A. Aspinall, 5 vols. (Cambridge University Press, 1962–70)

George IV, *Correspondence of George, Prince of Wales 1770–1812*, ed. A. Aspinall, 8 vols. (London, Cassell, 1963–71)

——, *The Letters of King George IV 1812–1830*, ed. A. Aspinall, 3 vols. (Cambridge University Press, 1938)

George, M. Dorothy, *English Political Caricature. A Study of Opinion and Propaganda*, 2 vols. (Oxford, Clarendon Press, 1959)

George, M. Dorothy and Frederick George Stephens, *Catalogue of Political and Personal Satires preserved in the Department of Prints and Drawings in the British Museum*, 11 vols. (London, British Museum Publications, 1978; first published 1870–1954)

Gibson, H., 'The Duke of Wellington' [letter from Countess of Mornington concerning the date of his birth], *Notes & Queries*, 7th series (10 January 1891), pp. 34–5

Girod de l'Ain, Mauricer, *Vie Militaire du Général Foy* (Paris, Plon, 1900)

Gleig, G.R., *The Life of Arthur, Duke of Wellington* (London, Dent, 1911) [a popular condensation of Brialmont and Gleig, but contains some new (and even contradictory) information added by Gleig]

——, *The Life of Major-General Sir Thomas Munro . . .*, 3 vols. (London, Colburn and Bentley, 1830)

——, *The Subaltern. A Chronicle of the Peninsular War* (Barnsley, Leo Cooper, 2001)

Glenbervie, Sylvester Douglas, Lord, *The Diaries of Sylvester Douglas (Lord Glenbervie)*, ed. Francis Bickley, 2 vols. (London, Constable, 1928)

Glover, Gareth, *From Corunna to Waterloo. The Letters and Journals of Two Napoleonic Hussars, 1801–1816* (London, Greenhill, 2007)

——, ed., *Wellington's Lieutenant, Napoleon's Gaoler. The Peninsula and St Helena Diaries and Letters of Sir George Ridout Bingham 1809–1821* (Barnsley, Pen and Sword, 2004)

Glover, Michael, *Britannia Sickens. Sir Arthur Wellesley and the Convention of Cintra* (London, Leo Cooper, 1979)

——, ' "An Excellent Young Man": The Rev. Samuel Briscall, 1788–1848', *History Today*, vol. 18, no. 8 (1968), pp. 578–84

——, *Legacy of Glory. The Bonaparte Kingdom of Spain* (New York, Scribners, 1971)

——, 'Misconduct at St Pierre, 13 December 1813', *JSAHR*, vol. 55, no. 223 (Autumn 1977), pp. 186–7

——, 'Purchase, Patronage and Promotion in the Army at the time of the Peninsular War', *Army Quarterly*, vol. 103 (1972–73), pp. 211–15, 355–62

——, *A Very Slippery Fellow. The Life of Sir Robert Wilson, 1777–1849* (Oxford University Press, 1978)

——, *Wellington as Military Commander* (London, Batsford, 1968)

——, *Wellington's Army in the Peninsula, 1808–1814* (Newton Abbot, David and Charles, 1977)

——, *Wellington's Peninsular Victories* (London, Batsford, 1963)

——, 'Writing News and Keeping Coffee-Houses', *History Today*, vol. 27, no. 7 (July 1977), pp. 452–8

Glover, Richard, *Peninsular Preparation. The Reform of the British Army, 1795–1809* (Cambridge University Press, 1963)

Gomm, W.M., *Letters and Journals of Field Marshal Sir William Maynard Gomm . . . 1799 to 1815*, ed. Francis Culling Carr-Gomm (London, John Murray, 1881)

Gontaut, Duchesse de, *Memoirs of the Duchesse de Gontaut*, 2 vols. (London, Chatto and Windus, 1894)

Goodbehere, Lt Edmund, 'The Letters of Lieutenant Edmund Goodbehere, 18th Madras N.I. 1803–1809', ed. S.G.P. Ward, *JSAHR*, vol. 57, no. 229 (Spring 1979), pp. 3–19

Gordon, Alexander, *At Wellington's Right Hand. The Letters of Lieutenant-Colonel Sir Alexander Gordon, 1808–1815*, ed. Rory Muir (Thrupp, Sutton Publishing for the Army Records Society, 2003)

Gordon, Capt. Alexander, *The Corunna Campaign. Journal of a Cavalry Officer* (Felling, Worley, 1990)

Gordon, Stewart, *The Marathas, 1600–1818*, New Cambridge History of India, vol. 2, pt. 4 (Cambridge University Press, 1993)

Gower: see Leveson Gower

Graceffo, Jeffrey, 'Making of a Marshal: Bertrand Clausel takes Command of the Army of Portugal, 1812' (MSc thesis, Florida State University, 2005)

[Graham, Robert], *Historical Manuscripts Commission. Supplementary Report on the Manuscripts of Robert Graham Esq of Fintry*, ed. C.T. Atkinson (London, HMSO, 1942) [cited as *HMC Graham of Fintry*]

Grattan, Henry, *Memoirs of the Life and Times of the Rt Hon Henry Grattan*, by his son Henry Grattan, 5 vols. (London, Henry Colburn, 1849)

Grattan, William, *Adventures with the Connaught Rangers, 1809–1814* (London, Greenhill, 2003)

Graves, Donald E., *Dragon Rampant. The Royal Welch Fusiliers at War, 1793–1815* (London, Frontline, 2010)

——, *Fix Bayonets! A Royal Welch Fusilier at War, 1796–1815* (Toronto, Robin Brass, 2006)

Gray, Denis, *Spencer Perceval. The Evangelical Prime Minister* (Manchester University Press, 1963)

Green, John, *A Soldier's Life, 1806–1815* (Wakefield, EP Publishing, 1973; first published 1827 as *The Vicissitudes of a Soldier's Life*)

Greenwood, Maj., 'British Loss of Life in the Wars of 1794–1815 and in 1914–1918', *Journal of the Royal Statistical Society*, vol. 105 (1942), pp. 1–16

Gregory, Desmond, *No Ordinary General. Lt General Sir Henry Bunbury (1778–1860), The Best Soldier Historian* (Madison, NJ, Fairleigh Dickinson University Press, 1999)

Grehan, John, *The Lines of Torres Vedras* (Staplehurst, Spellmount, 2000)

Greville, Charles C.F., *The Greville Memoirs. A Journal of the Reigns of King George IV, King William IV and Queen Victoria*, ed. Henry Reeve, 8 vols. (London, Longmans, Green and Co., 1888)

Griffith, Paddy, *Forward into Battle* (2nd edn, Swindon, Crowood Press, 1990)

——, ed., *A History of the Peninsular War*, vol. 9, *Modern Studies of the War in Spain and Portugal, 1808–1814* (London, Greenhill, 1999)

——, ed., *Wellington Commander. The Iron Duke's Generalship* (Chichester, Antony Bird, nd [1985])

Grocott, Terence, *Shipwrecks of the Revolutionary and Napoleonic Eras* (Caxton Editions, 2002)

Guedalla, Philip, *The Duke* (London, Hodder and Stoughton, 1931)

Gupta, Pratul Chandra, *Baji Rao II and the East India Company, 1796–1818* (Bombay, Allied Publishers, 1964)

Gurney, Lt.-Col. Russell, *History of the Northamptonshire Regiment, 1742–1934* (Aldershot, Gale and Polden, 1935)

Guthrie, G.J., 'Biographical Sketch of G.J. Guthrie, Esq. F.R.S.', *The Lancet*, vol. 1 (1850), pp. 726–38.

Guy, Alan, ed., *The Road to Waterloo* (London, National Army Museum, 1990)

Haley, Arthur H., *Our Davy. General Sir David Baird, K.B. 1757–1829* (Liverpool, Bullfinch, nd [c. 1991]

Hall, Capt. Basil, *Voyages and Travels of Captain Basil Hall, RN* (London, Nelson, 1895)

Hall, Christopher D., *British Strategy in the Napoleonic War 1803–1815* (Manchester University Press, 1992)

——, 'Royal Navy and the Peninsular War', *Mariner's Mirror*, vol. 79, no. 4 (1993), pp. 403–18

——, *Wellington's Navy. Seapower and the Peninsular War, 1807–1814* (London, Chatham, 2004)

Hall, Cornet Francis, 'Recollections in Portugal and Spain during 1811 and 1812', *Journal of the Royal United Services Institution*, vols. 56–7: (October 1912), pp. 1389–1408; (November 1912), pp. 1535–46; (December 1912), pp. 1735–9; (October 1913), pp. 1319–34

Hall, I.S., 'John Robert Hume Personal Physician to the First Duke of Wellington', *Journal of the Royal College of Surgeons of Edinburgh*, vol. 25, no. 4 (July 1980), pp. 219–32

Hall, John A., *The Biographical Dictionary of British Officers Killed and Wounded, 1808–1814* (published as vol. 8 of the 1998 reprint of Oman's *History of the Peninsular War*)

Halliday, Andrew, *Observations on the Present State of the Portuguese Army . . .* (London, John Murray, 1811)

Halliwell, W.A.C., 'Lord Wellesley's Confrontation with the Maratha "Empire"' (unpublished PhD thesis, University of Southampton, 1999)

——, 'The Passage to Bombay, 1801', *Wellington Studies I* (1996), pp. 91–114

——, 'Peace Negotiations with Sindhia and the Raja of Berar', *Wellington Studies II* (1999), pp. 48–68

Hamilton, C.I. 'John Wilson Croker: Patronage and Clientage at the Admiralty, 1809–1857' *Historical Journal*, vol. 43 (2000), pp. 49–77

Hamilton, John, *Sixty Years' Experience as an Irish Landlord* . . . (London, Digby, Long and Co., [1894])

Harling, Philip, 'The Duke of York Affair (1809) and the Complexities of Wartime Patriotism', *Historical Journal*, vol. 39 (December 1996), pp. 963–84

Harness, William, *Trusty and Well-Beloved. The Letters Home of William Harness, an Officer of George the Third*, ed. Caroline M. Duncan-Jones (London, SPCK, 1957)

Harrington, Peter, *British Artists and War. The Face of Battle in Paintings and Prints, 1700–1914* (London, Greenhill, 1993)

Harris, [Benjamin], *Recollections of Rifleman Harris as told to Henry Curling*, ed. Christopher Hibbert (Hampden, Archon Books, 1970) [Hibbert says 'John' but research by Eileen Hathaway has established that the author's name was Benjamin: see her edition entitled *A Dorset Rifleman*]

Harvey, A.D., *Britain in the Early Nineteenth Century* (London, Batsford, 1978)

——, *Collision of Empires. Britain in Three World Wars, 1793–1945* (London, Hambledon, 1992)

Hastings, Reginald Rawdon, *Historical Manuscripts Commission. Report on the Manuscripts of the Late Reginald Rawdon Hastings Esq., of the Manor House, Ashby de la Zouch*, ed. Francis Bickley, 4 vols. (London, HMSO, 1934–37) [cited as *HMC Hastings*]

Hatherton, Lord, 'Extracts from Lord Hatherton's Diary' [Edward Littleton], ed. A. Aspinall, *Parliamentary Affairs*, vol. 17 (1964), pp. 15–22, 134–41, 254–68, 373–88

Havard, Robert, *Wellington's Welsh General. A Life of Sir Thomas Picton* (London, Aurum, 1996)

[Hawker, Col. Peter], *Journal of a Regimental Officer during the Recent Campaign in Portugal and Spain under Lord Viscount Wellington* (London, Trotman, 1981; first published 1810)

Hay: see Leith Hay

Hayman, Sir Peter, *Soult. Napoleon's Maligned Marshal* (London, Arms and Armour, 1990)

Hayter, Alethea, *The Backbone. Diaries of a Military Family in the Napoleonic Wars* (Edinburgh, Pentland Press, 1983)

Haythornthwaite, Philip J., *The Armies of Wellington* (London, Arms and Armour, 1994)

——, 'The British Army, Wellington and Moore: Some Aspects of Service in the Peninsular War', in *A History of the Peninsular War*, vol. 9, *Modern Studies of the War in Spain and Portugal, 1808–1814*, ed. Paddy Griffith (London, Greenhill, 1999)

——, ' "Carrying On the War as It Should Be": Fraternization', in *The Peninsular War. Aspects of the Struggle for the Iberian Peninsula*, ed. Ian Fletcher (Staplehurst, Spellmount, 1998)

Head, Sir George, *Memoirs of an Assistant Commissary-General*, published in his *Home Tour through the Manufacturing Districts* . . . (London, John Murray, 1840)

Heathcote, Ralph, *Ralph Heathcote. Letters of a Young Diplomatist and Soldier during the time of Napoleon*, ed. Countess Gröben (London, John Lane, 1907)

Heathcote, T.A., *The Military in British India. The Development of British Land Forces in South Asia, 1600–1947* (Manchester University Press, 1995)

Hennell, George, *A Gentleman Volunteer. The Letters of George Hennell from the Peninsular War, 1812–1813*, ed. Michael Glover (London, Heinemann, 1979)

Herries, Edward, *Memoir of the Public Life of the Right Hon. John Charles Herries*, 2 vols. (London, John Murray, 1880)

Hibbert, Christopher, *Wellington. A Personal History* (London, HarperCollins, 1997)

Hickey, William, *Memoirs of William Hickey*, ed. Alfred Spencer, 4 vols. (London, Hurst and Blackett, 1925)

Hinde, Wendy, *Castlereagh* (London, Collins, 1981)

——, *George Canning* (London, Collins, 1973)

Hodge, William Barwick, 'On the Mortality Arising from Military Operations', *Quarterly Journal of the Statistical Society*, vol. 19 (September 1856), pp. 219–71

Holland, Elizabeth, *The Journal of Elizabeth, Lady Holland*, ed. the Earl of Ilchester, 2 vols. (London, Longmans, Green, 1908)

Holmberg, Tom, 'Monson's Retreat: India, 1804', available online through the Napoleon Series website: www.napoleon-series.org/military/battles/c_monson.html

Holmes, Richard, *Wellington. The Iron Duke* (London, HarperCollins, 2002)

[Hook, Theodore], *The Life of General, the Right Honourable Sir David Baird, Bart.*, 2 vols. (London, Richard Bentley, 1832)

Horner, Francis, *The Horner Papers. Selections from the Letters and Miscellaneous Writings of Francis Horner, MP 1795–1817*, ed. Kenneth Bourne and William Banks Taylor (Edinburgh University Press, 1994)

Horner, Leonard, *Memoirs and Correspondence of Francis Horner, MP*, 2 vols. (London, John Murray, 1843)

Horward, Donald D., *The Battle of Bussaco. Masséna vs. Wellington* (Tallahassee, Florida State University, 1965)

——, 'The French Invasion of Portugal, 1810–1811' (unpublished PhD thesis, University of Minnesota, 1962)

——, *The French Revolution and Napoleon Collection at Florida State University. A Bibliographical Guide* (Tallahassee, Friends of Florida State University, 1973)

——, *Napoleon and Iberia. The Twin Sieges of Ciudad Rodrigo and Almeida, 1810* (Tallahassee, University Presses of Florida, 1984)

Hough, Henry, 'The Journal of Second Lieutenant Henry Hough, Royal Artillery, 1812–1813', prepared by Major J.H. Leslie, *Journal of the Royal United Services Institution*, vol. 61, no. 444 (1916), pp. 1–43

Houlding, J.A., *Fit for Service. The Training of the British Army, 1715–1795* (Oxford, Clarendon Press, 1981)

Howard, Martin, *Wellington's Doctors. The British Army Medical Services in the Napoleonic Wars* (Staplehurst, Spellmount, 2002)

Howard, Michael, ed., *Wellingtonian Studies* (Aldershot, privately printed, 1959)

Hughes, Maj.-Gen. B.P., *Firepower. Weapons Effectiveness on the Battlefield, 1630–1850* (London, Arms and Armour, 1974)

Hunt, Eric, *Charging Against Napoleon. Diaries and Letters of Three Hussars* (Barnsley, Leo Cooper, 2001)

Hunt, Giles, *The Duel. Castlereagh, Canning and Deadly Cabinet Rivalry* (London, I.B. Tauris, 2008)

Hunter, Archie, *Wellington's Scapegoat. The Tragedy of Lieutenant-Colonel Charles Bevan* (Barnsley, Leo Cooper, 2003)

Hyde, H.M., *The Rise of Castlereagh* (London, Macmillan, 1933)

Hyden, John S., 'The Sources, Organization and Uses of Intelligence in the Anglo-Portuguese Army, 1808–1814', *JSAHR*, vol. 62 (1984), pp. 92–104, 169–75

Hylton, Lord, *The Paget Brothers, 1790–1840* (London, John Murray, 1918)

Indian Record Series Fort William (India House Correspondence): vol. 18, *Foreign Political and Secret, 1796–1800* (Delhi, National Archives of India, 1974), pp. 35–8 (intro. by Rev. Father H. Heras); vol. 21, *Military Series*, ed. Sita Ram Kohli (Government of India for National Archives, 1969)

Ingilby, Lt. W.B., 'Diary of Lieutenant Ingilby, R.A. in the Peninsular War and during the Waterloo Campaign', ed. Major E.A. Lambert, *Minutes of the Proceedings of the Royal Artillery Institution*, vol. 20 (1893), pp. 241–62, 315–23

Inglis, Brian, 'Sir Arthur Wellesley and the Irish Press, 1807–1809', *Hermathena*, vol. 83 (1954), pp. 17–29

Ingram, Edward, *Commitment to Empire. Prophecies of the Great Game in Asia, 1797–1800* (Oxford, Clarendon Press, 1981)

——, *Empire-Building and Empire-Builders. Twelve Studies* (London, Cass, 1995)

——, 'A Further Confidential Letter from Wellesley to Dundas', *Journal of Indian History*, vol. 50 (1972), pp. 15–20

——, 'The Rules of the Game: A Commentary on the Defence of British India, 1798–1829', *Journal of Imperial and Commonwealth History*, vol. 3 (January 1975), pp. 257–79

——, ed., *Two Views of British India. The Private Correspondence of Mr Dundas and Lord Wellesley* (Bath, Adams and Dart, 1970)

Innes, Roderick, *The Life of Roderick Innes, lately of H.M. Seventy-eight Regiment* (Stonehaven, Alexander Clark, 1844)

Intercepted Letters. Letters Intercepted on board the Admiral Aplin captured by the French; and inserted by the French Government in the Moniteur (London, Wilson, 1804)

International History Review, vol. 11, no. 1 (February 1989), special issue on 'Wellington at War'

Jackson, George, *The Bath Archives. A Further Selection from the Diaries and Letters of Sir George Jackson, K.C.H. from 1809 to 1816*, ed. Lady Jackson, 2 vols. (London, Richard Bentley, 1873)

——, *The Diaries and Letters of Sir George Jackson, K.C.H. from the Peace of Amiens to the Battle of Talavera*, ed. Lady Jackson, 2 vols. (London, Richard Bentley, 1872)

Jackson, Louis C., 'One of Wellington's Staff Officers: Lt.-Gen. William Staveley', *JSAHR*, vol. 14 (1935), pp. 155–65

James, Lawrence, *The Iron Duke. A Military Biography of Wellington* (London, Weidenfeld and Nicolson, 1992)

James, William, *The Naval History of Great Britain from the Declaration of War by France in 1793 to the Accession of George IV*, 6 vols. (London, Macmillan, 1902; first published 1822–24)

Jenkins, Brian, *Henry Goulburn 1784–1856. A Political Biography* (Montreal and Kingston, McGill-Queen's University Press, 1996)

Jenkins, Susan, 'The "Spanish Gift" at Apsley House', *English Heritage Historical Review*, vol. 2 (2007), pp. 112–27

Johnson, H.A., 'Letters from Headquarters, 1812–1813', ed. Michael Glover, *JSAHR*, vol. 43 (June 1965), pp. 92–104

Johnston, E.M., *Great Britain and Ireland 1760–1800. A Study in Political Administration* (Edinburgh, Oliver and Boyd for the University of St Andrews, 1963)

Johnston, S.H.F., ed., 'The 2/53rd in Peninsular War: Contemporary Letters from an Officer of the Regiment [Captain John Carss]', *JSAHR*, vol. 26, no. 105 (Spring 1948), pp. 2–17

Johnston-Liik, E.M. *History of the Irish Parliament, 1692–1800*, 6 vols. (Belfast, Ulster Historical Foundation, 2002)

Jomini, Baron de, *The Art of War* (Westport, Greenwood, 1971)

Jones, Edward B., 'Henry Dundas, India, and the British Reactions to Bonaparte's Invasion of Egypt, 1798–1801', *Proceedings of South Carolina Historical Association* (1973), pp. 41–57

Jones, Sir John T., *Journals of the Sieges carried on by the Army under the Duke of Wellington in Spain*, 3 vols. (London, Weale, 1846; reprinted Cambridge, Ken Trotman, 1998)

Jones, Lt. Rice, *An Engineer Officer under Wellington*, ed. H.V. Shore (Cambridge, Ken Trotman, 1986)

Jupp, Peter J., *The First Duke of Wellington in an Irish Context* (9th Wellington Lecture, University of Southampton, 1997)

——, *The Governing of Britain, 1688–1848. The Executive, Parliament and the People* (Abingdon, Routledge, 2006)

——, 'Irish Parliamentary Elections and the Influence of the Catholic Vote, 1801–1820', *Historical Journal*, vol. 10 (1967), pp. 183–96

——, 'The Landed Elite and Political Authority in Britain, ca 1760–1850', *Journal of British Studies*, vol. 29 (January 1990), pp. 53–79

——, *Lord Grenville 1759–1834* (Oxford, Clarendon Press, 1985)

——, 'Pictorial Images of the first Duke of Wellington', in *Avenues to the Past. Essays Presented to Sir Charles Brett on his 75th Year*, ed. Terence Reeves-Smyth and Richard Oram (Belfast, Ulster Architectural Heritage Society, 2003)

Kanter, Douglas, 'Robert Peel and the Waning of the "Influence of the Crown" in Ireland, 1812–1818', *New Hibernia Review*, vol. 5, no. 2 (Summer 2001), pp. 54–71

Kaplan, Herbert H., *Nathan Meyer Rothschild and the Creation of a Dynasty. The Critical Years 1806–1816* (Stanford University Press, 2006)

Karsten, Peter, 'Irish Soldiers in the British Army, 1792–1922: Suborned or Subordinate?' *Journal of Social History*, vol. 17 (1983), pp. 31–64

Kaufmann, W., *British Policy and the Independence of Latin America, 1804–1828* (New Haven, Yale University Press, 1951)

Kaye, Sir John, *The Life and Correspondence of Major-General Sir John Malcolm . . .*, 2 vols. (London, Smith Elder, 1856)

Keay, John, *The Great Arc. The Dramatic Tale of how India was Mapped and Everest was Named* (London, HarperCollins, 2000)

Keegan, John, *The Face of Battle* (New York, Viking, 1976)

——, *The Mask of Command* (London, Cape, 1987)

Keith, Adm. Lord, *The Keith Papers*, ed. W.G. Perrin and Christopher Lloyd, 3 vols. (London, Navy Records Society, 1927–55)

Kempthorne, G.A., 'The Medical Department of Wellington's Army, 1809–1814', *Journal of the Royal Army Medical Corps*, vol. 54 (1930), pp. 65–72, 131–46, 213–20

Kent, Conrad, *Estampas de la Guerra de la Independencia en la Provincia de Salamanca* (Salamanca, Instituto de las Indentidades, 2010)

Kenyon, Lord, *Historical Manuscripts Commission. Report on the Manuscripts of Lord Kenyon* (London, HMSO, 1894)

Khanna, D.D., *Monson's Retreat in Anglo-Maratha War (1803–1805)*, Defence Studies Papers, no. 5 (University of Allahabad, 1981)

——, 'Supply System of Wellington's Army in India', *Journal of the United Service Institution of India*, vol. 94 (1964), pp. 195–9

Kincaid, Capt. Sir John, *Adventures in the Rifle Brigade and Random Shots from a Rifleman* (Glasgow, Richard Drew, 1981)

Knight, George D., 'Lord Liverpool and the Peninsular War, 1809–1812' (unpublished PhD thesis, Florida State University, 1976)

Laing: Historical Manuscripts Commission. Report on the Laing Manuscripts, 2 vols. (London, HMSO, 1914–25)

Laing, Samuel, *Autobiography of Samuel Laing of Papdale, 1780–1868*, ed. and suppl. by R.P. Fereday (Kirkwall, Orkney, Bellavista Publications, 2000)

Landmann, Col. George Thomas, *Recollections of My Military Life*, 2 vols. (London, Hurst and Blackett, 1854)

Landsheit, Norbert and G.R. Gleig, *The Hussar. A German Cavalryman in British Service throughout the Napoleonic Wars* (Leonaur, 2008)

Larpent, F.S., *The Private Journal of F.S. Larpent, Esq. Judge Advocate General of the British Forces in the Peninsula attached to the Headquarters of Lord Wellington during the Peninsular War from 1812 to its Close*, 3 vols. (1st edn, London, Richard Bentley, 1853) [This edition includes some passages omitted from later reprints]

——, *The Private Journal of Judge Advocate Larpent attached to the Headquarters of Lord Wellington during the Peninsular War from 1812 to its Close* (Staplehurst, Spellmount, 2000; reprint of the 3rd edn, 1854) [Except when specified, this edition is that cited in the notes]

Lawrence, Sgt William Lawrence, *The Autobiography of Sergeant William Lawrence, a Hero of the Peninsular and Waterloo Campaigns*, ed. George Nugent Bankes (London, Sampson Low, Marston, Searle and Rivington, 1886)

Leach, Lt.-Col. J., *Rough Sketches of the Life of an Old Soldier* (Cambridge, Ken Trotman, 1986; reprint of 1831 edn)

Leaves from the Diary of an Officer of the Guards: see under [Cowell, John Stepney]

Lee, Albert, *History of the Thirty-third Foot, Duke of Wellington's Regiment* (Norwich, Jarrold and Sons, 1922)

Leith Hay, Andrew, *A Narrative of the Peninsular War*, 2 vols. (Edinburgh, Daniel Lizars, 1831)

[Leith Hay, Andrew], *Memoirs of the Late Lieutenant-General Sir James Leith* (Barbados, privately printed, 1817)

Le Marchant, Denis, *Memoirs of the late Major-General Le Marchant, 1766–1812* (Staplehurst, Spellmount, 1997)

Lennox, S., *The Life and Letters of Lady Sarah Lennox, 1745–1826*, ed. the Countess of Ilchester and Lord Stavordale, 2 vols. (London, John Murray, 1901)

Leslie, Charles, *Military Journal of Colonel Leslie, K.H. of Balquhain . . . 1807–1832* (Aberdeen University Press, 1887)

Leslie, Maj. J.H., 'Some Remarks concerning the Royal Artillery at the Battle of Talavera July 27–28 1809', *Journal of the Royal Artillery*, vol. 34 (1907–08), pp. 503–8

L'Estrange, Sir George, *Recollections of Sir George B. L'Estrange* (London, Sampson Low, Marston, Low and Searle, nd [c. 1874])

Leveson Gower, Lord Granville, *Lord Granville Leveson Gower (First Earl Granville) Private Correspondence 1781 to 1821*, ed. Castalia Countess Granville, 2 vols. (London, John Murray, 1916)

Levey, Michael, *Sir Thomas Lawrence* (New Haven and London, Yale University Press, 2005)

Levinge, Sir Richard, *Historical Records of the Forty-Third Regiment* (London, W. Clowes, 1868)

Linch, Kevin, *Britain and Wellington's Army. Recruitment, Society and Tradition, 1807–1815* (Basingstoke, Palgrave Macmillan, 2011)

Lipscombe, Nick, *The Peninsular War Atlas* (Botley, Osprey, 2010)

Llangollen, Ladies of, *The Hamwood Papers of the Ladies of Llangollen and Caroline Hamilton*, ed. G.H. Bell (London, Macmillan, 1930)

Londonderry, Charles William Vane [formerly Charles Stewart], Marquess of, *Narrative of the Peninsular War*, 2 vols. (London, Colburn, 1829)

Longford, Elizabeth, *Wellington. The Years of the Sword* (London, Weidenfeld and Nicolson, 1969) [cited as Longford]

——, *Wellington. Pillar of State* (London, Weidenfeld and Nicolson, 1972)

Lord, Douglas, 'Sequeira: A Neglected Portuguese Painter', *Burlington Magazine*, vol. 74, no. 433 (April 1939), pp. 153–63

Lovett, Gabriel H., *Napoleon and the Birth of Modern Spain*, 2 vols. (New York University Press, 1965)

Lushington, S.R., *The Life and Services of General Lord Harris* (2nd edn, London, Parker, 1845)

Lynch, John, 'British Policy and Spanish America, 1783–1808', *Journal of Latin American Studies* vol. 1 (1969), pp. 1–28

MacDonagh, Oliver, *The Hereditary Bondsman Daniel O'Connell* (London, Weidenfeld and Nicolson, 1988)

Macdonell, A.G., *Napoleon and His Marshals* (London, Macmillan, 1934)

McDowell, R.B., *Ireland in the Age of Imperialism and Revolution, 1760–1801* (Oxford, Clarendon Press, 1979)

——, 'Ireland in 1800', in *New History of Ireland* ed. T.W. Moody et al, 9 vols. (Oxford, Clarendon Press, 1976–2005)

——, *The Irish Administration, 1801–1914* (London, Routledge and Kegan Paul, 1964)

——, 'Wellington and Ireland', *The Irish Sword*, vol. 1 (1952), pp. 214–17

McGrigor, Sir James, *Autobiography and Services of Sir James McGrigor* (London, Longman, Green, Longman and Roberts, 1861)

——, 'Sketch of the Medical History of the British Armies in the Peninsula of Spain and Portugal during the late Campaigns', *Transactions of the Medico-Chirugical Society*, vol. 6 (1815), pp. 381–489

McGuffie, T.H., 'The Bingham Manuscripts', *JSAHR*, vol. 26, no. 107 (1948), pp. 106–11

——, 'The Bingham Papers and the Peninsular War', *Army Quarterly*, vols. 58, 59 and 61: (April 1949), pp. 124–8; (July 1949), pp. 254–6; (October 1949), pp. 126–8, (October 1951), pp. 125–8

——, ed., *Peninsular Cavalry General (1811–1813). The Correspondence of Lieutenant-General Robert Ballard Long* (London, Harrap, 1951)

——, 'The Significance of Military Rank in the British Army between 1790 and 1820', *Bulletin of the Institute of Historical Research*, vol. 30 (1957), pp. 207–24

[Mackenzie, A.], Obituary of General Sir Alexander Mackenzie, *United Service Journal* (March 1854), pp. 314–15

Mackenzie, W.C., *Colonel Colin Mackenzie, 1st Surveyor-General of India* (Edinburgh, Chambers, 1952)

Mackesy, Piers, *British Victory in Egypt 1801. The End of Napoleon's Conquest* (London and New York, Routledge, 1995)

——, *Statesmen at War. The Strategy of Overthrow, 1798–1799* (New York, Longman, 1974)

——, *The War in the Mediterranean, 1803–1810* (Westport, Greenwood, 1981)

——, *War Without Victory. The Downfall of Pitt, 1799–1802* (Oxford, Clarendon Press, 1984)

Mackie, William, 'The Battle of Busaco and the Third Division', *United Service Journal*, vol. 9 (March 1837), pp. 366–79

Mackinnon, Maj.-Gen. Henry, *A Journal of the Campaign in Portugal and Spain* (1812; repr. with Malcolm's *Reminiscences* as *Two Peninsular War Journals*, Cambridge, Ken Trotman, 1999)

Mackintosh, Sir James, *Memoirs of the Life of Sir James Mackintosh*, ed. his son Robert James Mackintosh, 2 vols. (London, Moxon, 1835)

McLauchlan, Tina M., 'Wellington's Supply System during the Peninsular War, 1809–1814' (unpublished MA thesis, McGill University, 1997)

Maclean, Loraine, of Dochgarroch, *Indomitable Colonel* (London, Shepheard-Walwyn, 1986)

Madden, C.D., 'The Diary of Charles Dudley Madden, Lieutenant 4th Dragoons, Peninsular War, 1809–1811', *Journal of the Royal United Services Institution*, vol. 58 (March and April 1914), pp. 334–58 and 501–26

Madrid, Museo Municipal, *La Alianza de dos monarquias. Wellington en España* (Fundación Hispano-Británica, 1988) [Exhibition catalogue]

Malcolm, John, *The Political History of India, 1784–1823*, 2 vols. (New Delhi, Associated Publishing, 1970; first published 1826)

[Malcolm, John], review of *An Historical Account of the Rise and Progress of the Bengal Native Infantry, Quarterly Review*, vol. 18, no. 36 (May 1818), pp. 385–423

Malmesbury, James Harris, Earl of, ed., *A Series of Letters of the first Earl of Malmesbury, His Family and Friends*, 2 vols. (London, Richard Bentley, 1870)

Marbot, Baron de, *Memoirs of Baron de Marbot*, 2 vols. (London, Longmans, Green, 1892)

Marmont, Marshal A.L.F.V. de, *The Spirit of Military Institutions* (Westport, Greenwood, 1974)

Marshall, P.J., '"Cornwallis Triumphant": War in India and the British Public in the Late Eighteenth Century', in *War, Strategy and International Politics. Essays in Honour of Sir Michael Howard*, ed. Lawrence Freedman, Paul Hayes and Robert O'Neill (Oxford, Clarendon Press, 1992)

——, *The Impeachment of Warren Hastings* (London, Oxford University Press, 1965)

——, *Problems of Empire. Britain and India 1757–1813* (London, George Allen and Unwin, 1968)

Marshall-Cornwall, James, *Marshal Massena* (Oxford University Press, 1965)

The Martial Achievements of Great Britain and Her Allies from 1799 to 1815 (London, James Jenkins, [1815], repr. Cambridge, Ken Trotman, 2008) [A colour-plate book of contemporary illustrations of battles and military scenes, many by William Heath]

Martin, A. Patchett, *Life and Letters of the Right Honourable Robert Lowe, Viscount Sherbrooke . . .* (including a 'Memoir of Sir John Coape Sherbrooke, GCB'), 2 vols. (London, Longmans, Green and Co., 1893)

Martinien, A., *Tableaux par corps et par batailles des Officiers Tués et Blessés pendant les Guerres de l'Empire (1805–1815)* (Paris, Éditions Militaires Européennes, nd)

Maurice, J.F., 'Assaye and Wellington', *Cornhill Magazine*, vol. 73 (3rd series, September 1896), pp. 291–304

Maxwell, Constantia, *Dublin under the Georges, 1714–1830* (London, Harrap, 1936)

Maxwell, Sir Herbert, *The Life of Wellington and the Restoration of the Martial Power of Great Britain*, 2 vols. (4th edn, London, Sampson Low, Marston and Co., 1900)

Maxwell, W.H., *Life of Field Marshal His Grace the Duke of Wellington*, 3 vols. (London, Baily, 1839)

——, ed., *Peninsular Sketches by Actors on the Scene*, 2 vols. (Uckfield, Naval and Military Press, 2002; first published 1844)

Memorials of the Late War, 2 vols., *Constable's Miscellany* vols. 27–28 (Edinburgh, Constable, 1828)

Meyer, Jack A., 'Wellington's Generalship: A Study of His Peninsular Campaigns' (unpublished PhD thesis, University of South Carolina, 1984)

Mill, Maj. James, 'Service in Ireland, the Peninsula, New Orleans and at Waterloo', *United Service Magazine* (April–September 1870), pp. 43–51, 70–80, 210–20, 390–9, 493–503 and 550–9

Millar, C.M.H., 'The Dismissal of Colonel Duncan Macdonald of the 57th Regiment', *JSAHR*, vol. 60, no. 242 (Summer 1982), pp. 71–7

Mills, John, *For King and Country. The Letters and Diaries of John Mills, Coldstream Guards, 1811–1814*, ed. Ian Fletcher (Staplehurst, Spellmount, 1995)

Mockler-Ferryman, Lt.-Col. A.F., *The Life of a Regimental Officer during the Great War, 1793–1815* (Edinburgh, Blackwood, 1913)

Moody, T.W., F.X. Martin and F.J. Byrne, eds., *A New History of Ireland*, 9 vols. (Oxford, Clarendon Press, 1976–2005)

Moon, Joshua, *Wellington's Two-Front War. The Peninsular Campaigns at Home and Abroad, 1808–1814* (Norman, OK, University of Oklahoma Press, 2011)

Moore, James, *A Narrative of the Campaign of the British Army in Spain, commanded by his Excellency Lieut.-General Sir John Moore* (London, Joseph Johnson, 1809)

Moore, Sir John, *Diary of Sir John Moore*, ed. Maj.-Gen. Sir J.F. Maurice, 2 vols. (London, Edward Arnold, 1904)

Moore Smith, G.C., *The Life of John Colborne, Field-Marshal Lord Seaton* (New York, Dutton, 1903)

Moorsom, W.S., *Historical Record of the Fifty-Second Regiment . . .* (London, Bentley, 1860)

Morecroft, Eleanor N., '"For the British Soldier is Keenly Sensitive to Honour": Military Heroism and British Identities in the Works of William Napier' (unpublished PhD thesis, University of Queensland, 2011)

Muir, Rory, *Britain and the Defeat of Napoleon, 1807–1815* (New Haven and London, Yale University Press, 1996)

——, 'The British Government and the Peninsular War, 1808 to June 1811' (unpublished PhD thesis, University of Adelaide, 1988)

——, 'Politics and the Peninsular Army', *Wellington Studies IV* (2008), pp. 72–93

——, *Salamanca 1812* (New Haven and London, Yale University Press, 2001)

——, *Tactics and the Experience of Battle in the Age of Napoleon* (New Haven and London, Yale University Press, 1998)

Muir, Rory, Robert Burnham, Howie Muir and Ron McGuigan, *Inside Wellington's Peninsular Army* (Barnsley, Pen and Sword, 2006)

Muir, Rory and Charles Esdaile, 'Strategic Planning in a Time of Small Government: The Wars against Revolutionary and Napoleonic France, 1793–1815', *Wellington Studies I* (1996), pp. 1–90

Mullett, C.F., 'British Schemes Against Spanish America in 1806', *Hispanic American Historical Review*, vol. 27 (May 1947), pp. 269–78

Munch-Petersen, Thomas, *Defying Napoleon. How Britain Bombarded Copenhagen and Seized the Danish Fleet in 1807* (Stroud, Sutton, 2007)

——, 'Lord Cathcart, Sir Arthur Wellesley and the British Attack on Copenhagen', *Wellington Studies II* (1999), pp. 104–22

[Murray, George], *Memoir to Accompany an Atlas* (London, James Wyld, 1841)

——, review of Napier's *History of the War in the Peninsula*, *Quarterly Review*, vol. 56 (April 1836), pp. 131–207

Murray, John, *Wellington. The Place and Date of His Birth Ascertained and Demonstrated* (2nd edn, Dublin, for the author, 1852)

Murray, Thomas, *Where was Wellington Born?* (1993) [A 16pp pamphlet not to be confused with the more substantial work of John Murray, cited above]

Myatt, Frederick, *Peninsular General. Sir Thomas Picton, 1758–1815* (London, David and Charles, 1980)

Nair, U.B., 'Wellington and the Pyche Rajah', *East & West*, vol. 4 (1905), pp. 420–36, 551–63

Namier, Sir Lewis and John Brooke, *The History of Parliament. The House of Commons, 1760–1790*, 3 vols. (HMSO for the History of Parliament Trust, 1964)

Napier, George, *Passages in the Early Military Life of General Sir George T. Napier* (London, John Murray, 1884)

Napier, Priscilla, *The Sword Dance. Lady Sarah Lennox and the Napiers* (London, Michael Joseph, 1971)

Napier, Sir W.F.P., *History of the War in the Peninsula and the South of France, from the Year 1807 to the Year 1814*, 6 vols. (London, Thomas and Wiliam Boone, 1853)

——, 'Letters from Colonel William Napier to Sir John Colborne', ed. Prof. Moore Smith, *English Historical Review*, vol. 18 (1903), pp. 725–53

——, *The Life and Opinions of General Sir Charles James Napier G.C.B.*, 4 vols. (London, John Murray, 1857)

Napoleon, *The Confidential Correspondence of Napoleon Bonaparte with his Brother Joseph*, 2 vols. (New York, Appleton, 1856)

Neale, Adam, *Letters from Portugal and Spain; comprising an account of the Operations of the Armies under their Excellencies Sir Arthur Wellesley and Sir John Moore* . . . (London, Richard Phillips, 1809)

Newitt, Malyn and Martin Robson, eds., *Lord Beresford and British Intervention in Portugal, 1807–1820* (Lisbon, Imprensa de Ciências Sociais, 2004)

Nightingall, Miles, 'The Nightingall Letters: Letters from Major-General Miles Nightingall in Portugal, February to June 1811', ed. Michael Glover, *JSAHR*, vol. 51 (Autumn 1973)

Norman, Barbara, *Napoleon and Talleyrand. The Last Two Weeks* (New York, Stein and Day, 1976)

Nosworthy, Brent, *Battle Tactics of Napoleon and his Enemies* (London, Constable, 1995)

Notes and Queries, 7th series, vol. 11 (January 1891), pp. 34–5

Oatts, Lt.-Col. L.B., *Proud Heritage. The Story of the Highland Light Infantry*, 4 vols. (London, Nelson, 1952–63)

O'Byrne, William R., *A Naval Biographical Dictionary*, 2 vols. (Polstead, Hayward, 1990; reprint of 1849 first edn)

ODNB: The Oxford Dictionary of National Biography, ed. H.C.G. Mathew and Brian Harrison (Oxford University Press, online edn, 2004–)

Oman, Carola, *The Gascoyne Heiress. The Life and Diaries of Frances Mary Gascoyne-Cecil, 1802–1839* (London, Hodder and Stoughton, 1968)

Oman, Sir Charles, 'A Dragoon of the Legion', *Blackwoods Magazine*, vol. 193 (March 1913), pp. 299–301

——, *A History of the Peninsular War*, 7 vols. (Oxford, Clarendon Press, 1902–30)

——, *Studies in the Napoleonic Wars* (London, Methuen, 1929)

——, *Wellington's Army, 1809–1814* (London, Edward Arnold, 1913)

O'Neil, J.J. et al, 'Family Records and the Duke', *Times Literary Supplement* (1, 8, 15, 22 and 29 September, and 6 October 1921), pp. 564, 580, 596, 612, 628, 644 [Correspondents advancing pet theories and some new evidence]

Orrok, John, *Letters of Captain John Orrok*, ed. Alison McBrayne (Leicester, Matador, 2008)

Page, Julia V., *Intelligence Officer in the Peninsula. Letters and Diaries of Maj. the Hon. Edward Charles Cocks, 1786–1812* (Staplehurst, Spellmount, 1976)

Pakenham, Edward, *Pakenham Letters, 1800 to 1815* (London, privately printed, Bumpus, 1914)

Pakenham, Eliza, *Soldier, Sailor. An Intimate Portrait of an Irish Family* (London, Weidenfeld and Nicolson, 2007)

Palmerston, Henry John Temple, Viscount, *The Letters of the third Viscount Palmerston to Laurence and Elizabeth Sulivan, 1804–1863*, ed. Kenneth Bourne (London, Royal Historical Society, 1979; Camden 4th series, vol. 23)

Parker, C.S., *Sir Robert Peel . . . 1788–1827* (London, John Murray, 1891)

Parker, W.M., 'A Visit to the Duke of Wellington', *Blackwood's Magazine*, vol. 256 (August 1944), pp. 77–82

Parkinson, C. Northcote, *War in Eastern Seas 1793–1815* (London, George Allen and Unwin, 1954)

The Parliamentary Debates from the Year 1803 to the Present time, published under the superintendence of T.C. Hansard

Parliamentary Papers (1809): *Papers Relating to the Army employed in Spain and Portugal* (Session 19 January to 21 June 1809), vol. XI

Parliamentary Papers (1810): *Papers Relating to Spain and Portugal* ordered by the House of Commons to be printed, 4 May 1810, no. 1, being pt. L of vol. XV, 'Discussions with Foreign Powers'

Parry, Ann, ed., *The Admirals Fremantle* (London, Chatto and Windus, 1971)

Partridge, Michael S., *The Duke of Wellington, 1769–1852. A Bibliography* (Westport, Meckler, 1990)

Pearce, Robert R., *Memoirs and Correspondence of the Most Noble Marquess Wellesley*, 3 vols. (London, Richard Bentley, 1846)

Pearman, Robert, *The Cadogans at War, 1783–1864. The Third Earl Cadogan and His Family* (London, Haggerston Press, 1990)

Pears, Iain, 'The Gentleman and the Hero: Wellington and Napoleon in the Nineteenth Century', in *Myths of the English*, ed. Roy Porter (Cambridge, Polity, 1993)

Peaty, John, 'Architect of Victory: The Reforms of the Duke of York', *JSAHR*, vol. 84 (2006), pp. 339–84

Peers, Douglas, 'Between Mars and Mammon: The East India Company and Efforts to Reform its Army, 1796–1832', *Historical Journal*, vol. 33 (1990), pp. 385–401

Pelet, Jean Jacques, *The French Campaign in Portugal, 1810–1811*, ed. and trans. Donald D. Horward (Minneapolis, University of Minnesota Press, 1973)

Pemble, J., 'Resources and Techniques in the Second Maratha War, 1803', *Historical Journal* (June 1976), pp. 375–403

Percival, Victor, *The Duke of Wellington. A Pictorial Survey of his Life (1769–1852)* (London, HMSO, 1969)

Personal Narrative: see Buckham

Philips, C.H., *The East India Company 1784–1834* (Manchester University Press, 1961)

——, *The Young Wellington in India*, Creighton Lectures in History (London, Athlone Press, 1973)

Picton, Sir T., 'Some Unpublished Letters of Sir Thomas Picton', ed. E. Edwards, *West Wales Historical Records*, vol. 12 (1927), pp. 133–62, vol. 13 (1928), pp. 1–32

Piggott, Karen, 'Wellington, Ireland and the Catholic Question, 1807–1827' (unpublished PhD thesis, University of Southampton, 1990)

Pimlott, J.L., 'The Administration of the British Army, 1783–1793' (unpublished PhD thesis, Leicester University, 1975)

—, 'The Raising of Four Regiments for India, 1787–1788', *JSAHR*, vol. 52 (1974), pp. 68–88

Piozzi, Hester Lynch, *The Piozzi Letters. Correspondence of Hester Lynch Piozzi, 1784–1821*, ed. E.A. and L.D. Bloom (Newark, University of Delaware Press, 1996)

Pitre, Brig. K.G., *Second Anglo-Maratha War, 1802–1805 (A Study in Military History)* (Poona, Dastane Ramchandra and Co., 1990)

[Pitt-Lennox, Lord William], *Memoir of Charles George Gordon, Fifth Duke of Richmond* (London, Chapman and Hall, 1862)

—, *Three Years with the Duke, or Wellington in Private Life* (London, Saunders and Otley, 1853)

Plumer Ward, Robert, *Memoirs of the Political and Literary Life of Robert Plumer Ward*, ed. E. Phipps, 2 vols. (London, John Murray, 1850)

Popham, Hugh, *A Damned Cunning Fellow. The Eventful Life of Rear-Admiral Sir Home Popham* (Tywardreath, Old Ferry Press, 1991)

Porter, Whitworth, *History of the Corps of Royal Engineers*, 2 vols. (London, Longmans, Green, 1889)

Proceedings upon the Inquiry Relative to the Armistice and Convention, &c made and Concluded in Portugal in *Parliamentary Papers*, vol. 12 (1809) [cited as *Proceedings*]

Raikes, Thomas, *A Portion of the Journal of Thomas Raikes*, 4 vols. (London, Longman, Brown, Green and Longmans, 1856)

Rait, R.S., *The Life and Campaigns of Hugh, first Viscount Gough, Field Marshal*, 2 vols. (London, Constable, 1903)

Ramsey, Neil, *The Military Memoir and Romantic Literary Culture, 1780–1835* (Farnham, Ashgate, 2011)

Ray, Rajat Kanta, 'Indian Society and the Establishment of British Supremacy, 1765–1818', in *The Oxford History of the British Empire*, vol. 2, *The Eighteenth Century*, ed. P.J. Marshall (Oxford University Press, 1998)

Redgrave, T.M.O., 'Wellington's Logistical Arrangements in the Peninsular War, 1809–1814' (unpublished PhD thesis, King's College, University of London, 1979)

Riley, J.P., *Napoleon and the World War of 1813. Lessons in Coalition Warfighting* (London, Frank Cass, 2000)

Roberts, Andrew, *Napoleon and Wellington* (London, Weidenfeld and Nicolson, 2001)

[Roberts, David], *The Military Adventures of Johnny Newcome* (London, Methuen, 1904; first published 1816)

Roberts, Frederick, Lord, *The Rise of Wellington* (London, Sampson Low, Marston, 1902)

Roberts, Greg, 'The Forgotten Brother [William Wellesley-Pole]' (unpublished MA thesis, Queen Mary, University of London, nd)

Roberts, Michael, 'The Ministerial Crisis of May–June 1812', *English Historical Review*, vol. 51 (1936), pp. 466–87

—, *The Whig Party, 1807–1812* (London, Frank Cass, 1965; first published 1939)

Roberts, P.E., *History of British India under the Company and the Crown* (Oxford University Press, 1921)

—, *India Under Wellesley* (London, G. Bell and Sons, 1929)

Robertson, Capt. Duncan, 'Buenos Aires and Vitoria', ed. James Irvine Roberton, *JSAHR*, vol. 80, no. 323 (Autumn 2002), pp. 346–55

Robertson, Ian, *An Atlas of the Peninsular War* (New Haven and London, Yale University Press, 2010)

—, *A Commanding Presence. Wellington in the Peninsula, 1808–1814. Logistics, Strategy, Survival* (Stroud, Spellmount, 2008)

—, *Wellington Invades France. The Final Phase of the Peninsular War, 1813–1814* (London, Greenhill, 2003)

—, *Wellington at War in the Peninsula, 1808–1814. An Overview and Guide* (Barnsley, Leo Cooper, 2000)

Robertson, James, *Narrative of a Secret Mission to the Danish Islands in 1808* (London, Longman, Green, Longman, Roberts and Green, 1863)

Robertson, W.S., *The Life of Miranda*, 2 vols. (New York, Cooper Square, 1969; first published 1929)

Robinson, Sir F.P., 'A Peninsular Brigadier: Letters of Major-General Sir F.P. Robinson, K.C.B. dealing with the Campaign of 1813', ed. C.T. Atkinson, *JSAHR*, vol. 34, no. 140 (December 1956), pp. 153–70

Robinson, H.B., *Memoirs of Lieutenant-General Sir Thomas Picton*, 2 vols. (2nd edn, London, Richard Bentley, 1836)

Robinson, J.M., *The Wyatts. An Architectural Dynasty* (Oxford University Press, 1979)

Robinson, R.E.R., *The Bloody Eleventh. History of the Devonshire Regiment*, vol. 1 (1685–1815), 3 vols. (Exeter, Devonshire and Dorset Regiment, 1988–95)

Robson, Karen, 'Military Patronage for Political Purposes: The Case of Sir Arthur Wellesley as Chief Secretary for Ireland', *Wellington Studies I* (1996), pp. 115–38

——, 'What Every "Official" Man Seeks – Patronage and the Management of Parliament: The Experience of Two Chief Secretaries for Ireland, 1802–1809', *Wellington Studies II* (1999), pp. 87–103

——, 'The Workings of Political Patronage, 1807–1865: Case Studies of the first Duke of Wellington and the third Viscount Palmerston' (unpublished MPhil thesis, University of Southampton, 1997)

Robson, Martin, 'British Intervention in Portugal, 1793–1808', *Historical Research*, vol. 76 (2003), pp. 93–107

Rodger, A.B., *The War of the Second Coalition* (Oxford University Press, 1964)

Rodger, N.A.M., *The Command of the Ocean. A Naval History of Britain, 1649–1815* (London, Allen Lane, 2004)

Rogers, Samuel, *Reminiscences and Table-talk of Samuel Rogers*, ed. G.H. Powell (London, Brinley Johnson, 1903)

Rose, George, *The Diaries and Correspondence of the Right Hon. George Rose*, ed. Rev. Leveson Vernon Harcort, 2 vols. (London, Richard Bentley, 1860)

Ross, Charles, *Correspondence of Charles, First Marquis Cornwallis*, 3 vols. (London, John Murray, 1859)

Ross, H.D., *Memoir of Field Marshal Sir Hew Dalrymple Ross R.H.A.* (Woolwich, Royal Artillery Institution, 1871)

Rosselli, John, *Lord William Bentinck and the British Occupation of Sicily 1811–1814* (Cambridge University Press, 1956)

——, *Lord William Bentinck. The Making of a Liberal Imperialist* (Chatto and Windus for Sussex University Press, 1974)

Ross-Lewin, Harry, *With 'The Thirty-Second' in the Peninsular and other Campaigns*, ed. John Wardell (Dublin, Hodges, Figgis and Co., 1904; reprinted Cambridge, Ken Trotman, 2000)

Rothenberg, Gunther E., *The Art of Warfare in the Age of Napoleon* (London, Batsford, 1977)

Rothschild, Lord, *The Shadow of a Great Man* (London, privately printed, 1982)

Rous, John, *A Guards Officer in the Peninsula. The Peninsula War Letters of John Rous, Coldstream Guards, 1812–1814*, ed. Ian Fletcher (Staplehurst, Spellmount, 1992)

Rowley, Ensign G., 'Journal of the Siege of Seringapatam', *Reports, Correspondence and Original Papers . . . of the Corps of Engineers, Madras Presidency*, vol. 4 (1856), pp. 119–30 [also quoted extensively in Vibart]

Royal Military Calendar, 5 vols. (3rd edn, London, Egerton, 1820)

Russell, George W.E. *Collections and Recollections*, 2 vols. (London, Nelson, nd *c*.1903)

Rutland, Duke of, *Historical Manuscripts Commission Report on the Manuscripts of the Duke of Rutland*, 4 vols. (London, HMSO, 1888–1905)

Ryan, A.N., 'The Causes of the British Attack on Copenhagen in 1807', *English Historical Review*, vol. 68 (1953), pp. 37–53

——, 'The Copenhagen Expedition, 1807' (unpublished MA thesis, University of Liverpool, 1951)

——, 'Documents Relating to the Copenhagen Operation, 1807', ed. N.A.M. Rodger, *Naval Miscellany*, vol. 5 (London, Allen and Unwin for the Naval Records Society, vol. 125, 1984)

——, 'The Navy at Copenhagen in 1807', *Mariner's Mirror*, vol. 39 (1953), pp. 201–10

Rydjord, John, 'British Mediation between Spain and Her Colonies, 1811–1813', *Hispanic American Historical Review*, vol. 21 (February 1941), pp. 29–50

Sack, James J., *From Jacobite to Conservative. Reaction and Orthodoxy in Britain, c. 1760–1832* (Cambridge University Press, 1993)

——, *The Grenvillites, 1801–1829. Party Politics and Factionalism in the Age of Pitt and Liverpool* (Urbana, University of Illinois Press, 1979)

Sandes, Lt.-Col. E.W.C., *The Military Engineer in India*, 2 vols. (Chatham, Institution of Royal Engineers, 1933–35)

Sardesai, G.S., *New History of the Marathas*, 3 vols. (Bombay, Dhawale for Phoenix Publications, [1958])

Sarkar, Sir Jadunath, *The Fall of the Mughal Empire*, 4 vols. (Calcutta, M.C. Sarkar and Sons, 1949–52, reprinted 1972)

Sarramon, Jean, *La Bataille des Arapiles* (Toulouse, Université de Toulouse, 1978)

Sauvigny, Guillaume de Bertier de, *The Bourbon Restoration* (Philadelphia, University of Pennsylvania Press, 1966)

Schama, Simon, *Patriots and Liberators. Revolution in the Netherlands, 1780–1813* (London, Collins, 1977)

Schaumann, A.L.F., *On the Road with Wellington. The Diary of a War Commissary-General in the English Army*, ed. and trans. Anthony M. Ludovici (New York, Knopf, 1925)

Schneer, Richard M., 'Arthur Wellesley and the Cintra Convention: A New Look at an Old Puzzle', *Journal of British Studies*, vol. 19, no. 2 (Spring 1980), pp. 93–119

Schneidman, J.L., 'The Proposed Invasion of India by Russia and France in 1801', *Journal of Indian History*, vol. 35 (1957), pp. 167–77

Schroeder, Paul W., *The Transformation of European Politics, 1763–1848* (Oxford, Clarendon Press, 1994)

Scott, David, *The Correspondence of David Scott, Director and Chairman of the East India Company . . . 1787–1805*, 2 vols. (London, Royal Historical Society, 1951, Camden 3rd series, vol. 76)

Scott, Sir Walter, *The Letters of Sir Walter Scott, 1787–1832*, ed. H.J.C. Grierson, 12 vols. (London, Constable, 1932–37)

Semmel, Stuart, *Napoleon and the British* (New Haven and London, Yale University Press, 2004)

Sen, S.P., *The French in India* (Calcutta, Mukhopadhyay, 1958)

Severn, John, *Architects of Empire. The Duke of Wellington and his Brothers* (Norman, OK, University of Oklahoma Press, 2007)

——, *A Wellesley Affair. Richard Marquis Wellesley and the Conduct of Anglo-Spanish Diplomacy, 1809–1812* (Tallahassee, University Presses of Florida, 1981)

Shadwell, Lt.-Gen. Laurence, *The Life of Colin Campbell, Lord Clyde*, 2 vols. (Edinburgh, Blackwood, 1861)

Shelley, Frances, Lady, *The Diary of Frances Lady Shelley*, ed. Richard Edgcumbe, 2 vols. (New York, Scribners, 1913)

Sherer, Moyle, *Recollections of the Peninsula* (Staplehurst, Spellmount, 1996; first published 1824)

Sherwig, John M., *Guineas and Gunpowder. British Foreign Aid in the Wars with France, 1793–1815* (Cambridge, MA, Harvard University Press, 1969)

Shields, Nancy K., ed., *Birds of Passage. Henrietta Clive's Travels in South India, 1798–1801* (London, Eland, 2009)

Shipkey, Robert, 'Problems of Irish Patronage during the Chief Secretaryship of Robert Peel, 1812–1816', *Historical Journal*, vol. 10 (1967), pp. 41–56

Shore, H.N., 'Letters from the Peninsula during 1812–1813–1814', *Journal of the Royal United Services Institution*, vol. 61 (February 1916), pp. 91–140

——, 'The Navy in the Peninsular War', 15 parts in *United Service Magazine* (new series 1912–14)

Sidney, Edwin, *The Life of Lord Hill* (London, John Murray, 1845)

Silvestre, José de S., 'Busaco in 1810: Extracts from the Diary of a Carmelite Friar', *Gentleman's Magazine*, vol. 275, no. 1953 (July–December 1893), pp. 281–93

Simmons, Maj. George, *A British Rifleman. The Journals and Correspondence of Major George Simmons . . .*, ed. Lt.-Col. Willoughby Verner (London, A&C Black, 1899)

Smart, William, *Economic Annals of the Nineteenth Century*, 2 vols. (London, Macmillan, 1910–17)

Smith, Charles Hamilton, *Costumes of the British Army*, reprinted as *Wellington's Army. The Uniforms of the British Soldier, 1812–1815* with text by Philip J. Haythornthwaite (London, Greenhill, 2002)

Smith, E.A., *George IV* (New Haven and London, Yale University Press, 1999)

——, *Lord Grey 1764–1845* (Oxford, Clarendon Press, 1990)

Smith, Harry, *The Autobiography of Sir Harry Smith*, ed. G.C. Moore Smith (London, John Murray, 1910)

Smith, William, 'Journal of Captain William Smith, 11 Light Dragoons during the Peninsular War', *Journal of the Royal United Services Institution*, vol. 60 (August 1915), pp. 165–76

Snow, Peter, *To War with Wellington. From the Peninsula to Waterloo* (London, John Murray, 2010)

A Soldier of the 71st. The Journal of a Soldier in the Highland Light Infantry, 1806–1815, ed. Christopher Hibbert (London, Leo Cooper, 1975) [According to a note by Victor Sutcliffe, the bulk of the work is probably based on the experiences of Private James Todd, edited and written up by Thomas Howell. Sutcliffe cites an article by Jones in the *Bulletin of the Military Historical Society* (May 1992) describing an inscription by Howell in a copy of the work in the library of the Royal Highland Fusiliers.]

Southey, Robert, *History of the Peninsular War*, 6 vols. (new edn, London, John Murray, 1837)

Spater, George, *William Cobbett. The Poor Man's Friend*, 2 vols. (Cambridge University Press, 1982)

Spear, Percival, *A History of India*, vol. 2 (Harmondsworth, Penguin, 1977)

Spence, Peter, *The Birth of Romantic Radicalism. War, Popular Politics and English Radical Reformism, 1800–1815* (Aldershot, Scolar Press, 1996)

Springer, William Henry, 'The Military Apprenticeship of Arthur Wellesley in India, 1797–1805' (unpublished PhD thesis, Yale University, 1966)

Srivastava, B.B., 'Aftermath of the Treaty of Seringapatam (1792) in Anglo-Mysore Relations', *Quarterly Review of Historical Studies*, vol. 17 (1977–78), pp. 231–43

——, *Sir John Shore's Policy towards the Indian States* (Allahabad, Chugh Publications, 1981)

Stanhope, James, *Eyewitness to the Peninsular War and the Battle of Waterloo. The Letters and Journals of Lieutenant Colonel the Honourable James Stanhope, 1803 to 1825*, ed. Gareth Glover (Barnsley, Pen and Sword, 2010)

Stanhope, Philip Henry, 5th Earl, *Life of the Right Honourable William Pitt*, 3 vols. (London, John Murray, 1879)

——, *Notes of Conversations with the Duke of Wellington* (2nd edn, London, John Murray, 1888)

Stanley, Maria, 'Letters from Maria Josepha Lady Stanley to her father, Lord Sheffield', ed. Lord Stanley of Alderley, *History Today*, vol. 4 (1954), pp. 628–37

Stewart, William, *Cumloden Papers* (Edinburgh, privately printed, 1871)

Stockdale, John Joseph, *A Narrative of the Campaign which preceded the Convention of Cintra* (London, Stockdale, 1809)

Stocqueler, J.H., *The Life of Field Marshal the Duke of Wellington*, 2 vols. (London, Ingram, Cooke and Co., 1852)

Stothert, Captain William, *A Narrative of the Principal Events of the Campaigns of 1809, 1810 & 1811 in Spain and Portugal* (London, 1812, repr. Cambridge, Ken Trotman, 1997)

Strong, J.W., 'Russia's Plans for an Invasion of India in 1801', *Canadian Slavonic Papers*, vol. 7 (1965), pp. 114–26

Stronge, Susan, *Tipu's Tigers* (London, V&A Publishing, 2009)

Stuart Wortley, Mrs Edward, *Highcliffe and the Stuarts* (London, John Murray, 1927)

Surtees, William, *Twenty-five Years in the Rifle Brigade* (London, Frederick Muller, 1973; first published 1833)

Sutcliffe, Victor, *The Sandler Collection. An Annotated Bibliography of Books Relating to the Military History of the French Revolution and Empire . . .* (Cambridge, Ken Trotman, 1996)

Swabey, Lt William, *Diary of Campaigns in the Peninsula for the Years 1811, 12 and 13*, ed. Col F.A. Whinyates (London, Ken Trotman, 1984)

Sweetman, John, *Raglan. From the Peninsula to the Crimea* (London, Arms and Armour, 1993)

Swinton, J.R., *A Sketch of the Life of Georgiana, Lady de Ros . . .* (London, John Murray, 1893)

Teffeteller, Gordon L., *The Surpriser. The Life of Rowland, Lord Hill* (Newark, University of Delaware Press, 1983)

Teignmouth, [Charles Shore, Lord], *Reminiscences of Many Years*, 2 vols. (Edinburgh, David Douglas, 1878)

Teignmouth, Lord, *Memoir of Life and Correspondence of John, Lord Teignmouth*, by his son Charles Shore, Lord Teignmouth, 2 vols. (London, Hatchard, 1843)

Thiébault, D., *Memoirs of Baron Thiébault*, 2 vols. (London, Smith Elder, 1892)

Thomas, R.N.W., 'Wellington in the Low Countries, 1794–1795', *International History Review*, vol. 11, no. 1 (February 1989), pp. 14–30

Thompson, Edward and G.T. Garratt, *Rise and Fulfilment of British Rule in India* (London, Macmillan, 1935; repr. AMS, 1971)

Thompson, F.M.L., *English Landed Society in the Nineteenth Century* (London, Routledge, 1963)

Thompson, Mark S., *The Fatal Hill. The Campaign in Southern Spain in 1811* (Chapelgarth, Mark Thompson Publishing, 2002)

——, 'The Rise of the Scientific Soldier as Seen through the Performance of the Corps of Royal Engineers during the Early Nineteenth Century' (unpublished PhD thesis, University of Sunderland, 2009)

Thompson, Neville, *Earl Bathurst and the British Empire* (Barnsley, Leo Cooper, 1999)

——, 'The Unpredictable Rise of the Duke of Wellington', *Historian*, no. 64 (Winter 1999), pp. 4–8

——, *Wellington After Waterloo* (London, Routledge and Kegan Paul, 1986)

Thorn, Maj. William, *Memoir of the War in India conducted by General Lord Lake . . . and Major-General Sir Arthur Wellesley . . .* (London, Egerton, 1818)

Thorne, R.G., ed., *The History of Parliament. The House of Commons, 1790–1820*, 5 vols. (Secker and Warburg for the History of Parliament Trust, 1986)

Thornton, James, *Your Obedient Servant. Cook to the Duke of Wellington* (Exeter, Webb and Bower, 1985)

Thornton, L.H., *Light and Shade in Bygone India* (London, John Murray, 1927)

Thoumine, R.H., *Scientific Soldier. The Life of General Le Marchant, 1766–1812* (London, Oxford University Press, 1968)

Tollemache, Hon. Lionel A., *Old and Odd Memories* (London, Edward Arnold, 1908)

Tomkinson, William, *The Diary of a Cavalry Officer in the Peninsular War and Waterloo Campaign*, ed. James Tomkinson (London, Swan Sonnenschein, 1895)

Tone, John Lawrence, *The Fatal Knot. The Guerrilla War in Navarre and the Defeat of Napoleon in Spain* (Chapel Hill, University of North Carolina Press, 1994)

Torrens, W.M., *The Marquess Wellesley. Architect of Empire. An Historic Portrait* (London, Chatto and Windus, 1880)

Trench, Melisina, *The Remains of the Late Mrs Richard Trench, being selections from Her Journals, Letters and other Papers*, ed. her son, the Dean of Westminster (London, Parker, Son and Bourn, 1862)

Tucker, Capt T.E., 'Captain T. Edwardes Tucker's Diary [ADC to Picton, 1813–1814]', *West Wales Historical Record*, vol. 10 (1924), pp. 87–114

Turner, Jane, *The Dictionary of Art*, 34 vols. (New York, Grove, *c* 1996)

Tylden, Maj. G., 'The First Duke of Wellington as a Horseman', *JSAHR*, vol. 43, no. 174 (June 1965), pp. 67–72

Uffindell, Andrew, *The National Army Museum Book of Wellington's Armies* (London, Sidgwick and Jackson, 2003)

Urban, Mark, *The Man Who Broke Napoleon's Codes. The Story of George Scovell* (London, Faber and Faber, 2001)

——, *Rifles* (London, Faber and Faber, 2003)

Vann, J.A., 'Habsburgh Policy and the Austrian War of 1809', *Central European History*, vol. 7 (December 1974), pp. 291–310

Verner, Col. Willoughby, ed., 'The Diary of a Private Soldier in the Peninsular War [John Timewell, 43rd]', *Macmillan's Magazine*, vol. 77 (November 1897), pp. 1–10

——, *History and Campaigns of the Rifle Brigade, 1800–1813*, 2 vols. (London, J. Bale, Sons and Danielsson, 1912–19)

Vibart, Maj. H.M., *The Military History of the Madras Engineers and Pioneers*, 2 vols. (London, W.H. Allen, 1881)

Vichness, Samuel E., 'Lord Wellington and the Francisco de Mello Affair', *JSAHR*, vol. 53 (Spring 1975), pp. 22–5

——, 'Marshal of Portugal: The Military Career of William Carr Beresford, 1785–1814' (unpublished PhD thesis, Florida State University, 1976)

Victoires, Conquêtes, Désastres, Revers et Guerres Civiles des Francais, de 1792 a 1815 'par une société de militaries et de gens de lettres', ed. Charles Beauvais de Preau, 30 vols. (Paris, Panckoucke, 1818–25)

Vincent, Edgar, *Nelson. Love and Fame* (New Haven and London, Yale University Press, 2003)

Vivian, Claud, *Richard Hussey Vivian, First Baron Vivian. A Memoir* (London, Ibister, 1897)

Walker, Richard, *Regency Portraits*, 2 vols. (London, National Portrait Gallery, 1985)

Walpole, Spencer, *The Life of the Rt Hon Spencer Perceval . . .*, 2 vols. (London, Hurst and Blackett, 1874)

Ward, C.H. Dudley, *A Romance of the Nineteenth Century* (London, John Murray, 1923)

Ward, J.W., *Letters to 'Ivy' from the first Earl of Dudley*, ed. S.H. Romilly (London, Longmans, Green, and Co., 1905)

Ward, S.G.P., 'Brenier's Escape from Almeida, 1811', *JSAHR*, vol. 35 (Spring 1957), pp. 23–35

——, 'Defence Works in Britain, 1803–1805', *JSAHR*, vol. 27, no. 109 (Spring 1949), pp. 18–37

——, 'General Sir George Murray', *JSAHR*, vol. 58, no. 236 (Winter 1980), pp. 191–208

——, 'General Sir Willoughby Gordon', *JSAHR*, vol. 31, no. 126 (Summer 1953), pp. 58–63

——, 'Milgapey, May, 1809, A Peninsular War Puzzle in Geography', *JSAHR*, vol. 30, no. 124 (Winter 1952), pp. 148–55

——, 'The Peninsular Commissary', *JSAHR*, vol. 75 (Winter 1997), pp. 230–9

——, 'The Portuguese Infantry Brigades, 1809–1814', *JSAHR*, vol. 53 (Summer 1975), pp. 103–12

——, *Wellington* (London, B.T. Batsford, 1963)

——, *Wellington's Headquarters. A Study of the Administrative Problems in the Peninsula, 1809–1814* (London, Oxford University Press, 1957)

Warner, Oliver, 'Wellington Meets Nelson', *History Today*, vol. 18 (1968), pp. 125–8

Warre, William, *Letters from the Peninsula, 1808–1812* (Staplehurst, Spellmount, 1999)

Webb, E.A.H., *History of the 12th (the Suffolk) Regiment, 1685–1913* (London, Spottiswoode, 1914)

Webb-Carter, B.W., 'Cockades Worn by the Duke of Wellington', *JSAHR*, vol. 43, no. 174 (June 1965), p. 106

——, 'Lieutenant-Colonel the Honourable Arthur Wesley, 33rd Regiment', *JSAHR*, vol. 37, no. 152 (December 1959), pp. 143–4

Webber, William, *With the Guns in the Peninsula. The Peninsula War Journal of Captain William Webber, Royal Artillery* (London, Greenhill, 1991)

Webster, C.K., ed., *British Diplomacy 1813–1815. Select Documents* (London, G. Bell and Sons, 1921)

——, *The Foreign Policy of Castlereagh, 1812–1814* (London, G. Bell and Sons, 1931)

Weller, Jac, *On Wellington. The Duke and his Art of War*, ed. Andrew Uffindell (London, Greenhill, 1998)

——, *Wellington in India* (London, Longman, 1972)

Wellesley, Lord Gerald, 'Some Letters of the Mornington Family', *County Kildare Archaeological Society Journal* (1935–45), vol. 12, pp. 30–52

Wellesley, Lord Gerald and John Steegmann, *The Iconography of the First Duke of Wellington* (London, J.M. Dent and Sons, 1935)

Wellesley, Henry, *The Diary and Correspondence of Henry Wellesley, First Lord Cowley, 1790–1846* ed. the Hon. F.A. Wellesley (London, Hutchinson and Co., [1930])

Wellesley, Jane, *Wellington. A Journey Through my Family* (London, Weidenfeld and Nicolson, 2008)

Wellesley, Muriel, *The Man Wellington* (London, Constable, 1937)

——, *Wellington in Civil Life* (London, Constable, nd [1939])

Wellesley, Richard, Marquess, *The Despatches and Correspondence of the Marquess Wellesley, K.G. during His Lordship's Mission to Spain as Ambassador Extraordinary to the Supreme Junta in 1809*, ed. Montgomery Martin (London, John Murray, 1838)

——, *The Despatches, Minutes and Correspondence of the Marquess Wellesley, K.G. during his Administration in India*, ed. Montgomery Martin, 5 vols. (London, W.H. Allen, 1836–40)

——, *The Wellesley Papers* 'by the editor of "The Windham Papers"', 2 vols. (London, Herbert Jenkins, 1914)

[Wellesley, Richard, Marquess], *Notes Relative to the Late Transactions in the Marhatta Empire* (London, Stockdale, 1804)

Wellington, Arthur Wellesley, 1st Duke of, 'Colonel Wellesley's Standing Orders to the Thirty-Third Regiment, 1798', ed. Brig. B.W. Webb-Carter, *JSAHR*, vol. 50, no. 202 (Summer 1972), pp. 65–77

——, *Despatches, Correspondence, and Memoranda of Field Marshal Arthur Duke of Wellington, K.G.*, ed. his son, the Duke of Wellington 'in continuation of the former series', 8 vols. (London, John Murray, 1857–80 [Known as *Wellington New Despatches* or *WND* these vols. cover 1819–32]

——, *The Dispatches of Field Marshal the Duke of Wellington*, ed. [John] Gurwood, 8 vols. (London, Parker, Furnivall and Parker, 1844) [cited as *WD*]

——, *The General Orders of Field Marshal the Duke of Wellington, K.G ...* ed. Col. Gurwood (London, Clowes, 1837) [This selection from the General Orders is arranged by subject]

——, *General Orders. Spain and Portugal*, 4 vols., 1809–12 (London, printed by authority by T. Egerton, 1811–13)

——, *The Maratha War Papers of Arthur Wellesley, January to December 1803*, ed. Anthony S. Bennell (London, Army Record Society, vol. 14, 1998)

——, 'A Missing Letter from the Duke of Wellington', ed. C. Leeson Prince, *The Athenaeum*, no. 3209 (27 April 1889), p. 537

——, *The Mysore Letters and Dispatches of the Duke of Wellington* (Bangalore, Mysore Government Press, 1862)

——, 'The Newly Discovered Autograph Letters of Wellington', ed. H.N. Sinha, *Bengal Past & Present*, vol. 39, pt. 2 (April–June 1930), pp. 91–9

——, *A Selection from the Despatches, Memoranda, and other Papers relating to India of . . . the Duke of Wellington*, ed. Sidney J. Owen (Oxford, Clarendon Press, 1880)

——, *A Selection from the Private Correspondence of the First Duke of Wellington*, ed. the Duke of Wellington (printed by the Dropmore Press for the Roxburghe Club, 1952)

——, 'Some Letters of the Duke of Wellington to his brother William Wellesley-Pole', ed. Prof. Sir Charles Webster (London, Royal Historical Society, 1948, Camden 3rd series, vol. 79)

——, *The Speeches of the Duke of Wellington in Parliament*, coll. and arr. Col. [John] Gurwood, 2 vols. (London, John Murray, 1854)

——, *Supplementary Despatches, Correspondence and Memoranda of Field Marshal Arthur, Duke of Wellington, K.G.*, ed. his son the Duke of Wellington, 15 vols. (London, John Murray, 1858–72) [cited as *WSD*; vol. 5 containing the Irish correspondence of 1807–09 carries the title *Civil Correspondence and Memoranda of Field Marshal . . .*]

——, 'Unpublished Letters of Wellington, July-August 1812', ed. I.J. Rousseau, *Cambridge Historical Journal*, vol. 3, pt. 1 (1929), pp. 96–101

——, *Wellington at War, 1794–1815. A Selection of his Wartime Letters*, ed. Antony Brett-James (London, Macmillan, 1961)

Wellington Lectures, University of Southampton, vols. 1–23 (1989–2011)

Welsh, James, *Military Reminiscences*, 2 vols. (London, Smith, Elder and Co, 1830)

Western, J.R., 'Roman Catholics Holding Military Commissions in 1798', *English Historical Review*, vol. 70 (July 1955), pp. 428–32

Wheatley, Edmund, *The Wheatley Diary. A Journal and Sketchbook kept during the Peninsular War and Waterloo Campaign*, ed. Christopher Hibbert (London, Longmans, 1964)

Wheeler, Private William, *Letters of Private Wheeler*, ed. B.H. Liddell Hart (London, Michael Joseph, 1951)

White, A.A., *A Bibliography of Regimental Histories of the British Army* (Darlington, Naval and Military Press, 1992)

White, A.S., 'Field Marshal's Baton', *JSAHR*, vol. 27, no. 110 (1949), pp. 92–3

Whittingham, S., *A Memoir of the Services of Lieutenant-General Sir Samuel Ford Whittingham* (London, Longman, Green, 1868)

Wickwire, Franklin and Mary Wickwire, *Cornwallis. The Imperial Years* (Chapel Hill, University of North Carolina Press, 1980)

Wilkin, Walter H., *The Life of Sir David Baird* (London, G. Allen, 1912)

Wilks, Mark, *Historical Sketches of the South of India*, 2 vols. (Mysore, Government Branch Press, 1930–32; first published 1810–17)

Willis, Clive, 'Colonel George Lake and the Battle of Roliça', *Portuguese Studies*, vol. 12 (1996), pp. 68–77

Wilson, Frances, *The Courtesan's Revenge. Harriette Wilson, the Woman who Blackmailed the King* (London, Faber and Faber, 2003)

Wilson, Harriette, *The Memoirs of Harriette Wilson written by Herself*, 2 vols. (London, Eveleigh Nash, 1909; first published 1825)

Wilson, Joan, *A Soldier's Wife. Wellington's Marriage* (London, Weidenfeld and Nicolson, 1987)

Wilson, W.J., *History of the Madras Army*, 5 vols. (Madras, Government Press, 1882–89)

Windham, William, *The Diary of the Right Hon. William Windham 1784 to 1810*, ed. Mrs Henry Baring (London, Longmans, Green, and Co., 1866)

——, *The Windham Papers*, 2 vols. (London, Herbert Jenkins, 1913)

Wood, Capt. George, *The Subaltern. A Narrative* (Cambridge, Ken Trotman, 1986)

Woolgar, C.M., *Wellington, His Papers and the Nineteenth-Century Revolution in Communication* (Inaugural Lecture as Professor of History and Archival Studies, University of Southampton, 2009)

——, ed., *Wellington Studies*, vols. I–IV (Hartley Institute, University of Southampton, 1996–2008)

——, 'Wellington's *Dispatches* and their editor, Colonel Gurwood', *Wellington Studies I* (1996), pp. 189–210

——, 'Writing the Despatch: Wellington and Official Communication', *Wellington Studies II* (1999), pp. 1–25

Wrottesley, George, *Life and Correspondence of Field Marshal Sir John Burgoyne*, 2 vols. (London, Bentley, 1873)

Wyld: see Murray, George

Wynyard, John M., 'From Vimeiro to Corunna: An Eyewitness Account', ed. S.G.P. Ward, *Journal of the Royal United Services Institution*, vol. 114 (December 1969), pp. 33–42

Yapp, M.E., *Strategies of British India. Britain, Iran and Afghanistan, 1798–1850* (Oxford, Clarendon Press, 1980)

Yonge, Charles D., *The Life and Administration of Robert Banks, Second Earl of Liverpool*, 3 vols. (London, Macmillan, 1868)

——, *The Life of Field Marshal Arthur, Duke of Wellington*, 2 vols. (London, Chapman and Hall, 1860)

INDEX

Individuals are listed under the name or title most relevant to the period covered by this volume (for example, Lord Castlereagh under Castlereagh rather than Stewart or Londonderry).

Abbot, Charles (later Lord Colchester) 178, 226
Abercromby, Lt-Gen. Sir Ralph 33, 37, 38, 40, 98, 176, 180
Aberdeen, Lord 296, 482
Acland, Brig. Wroth Palmer 237, 249, 253, 262, 278
Addington, Henry (Lord Sidmouth) 104, 117, 153, 178, 192, 283, 372, 445, 459
Adour, passage of 570
Ahmednuggar 111, 132–3, 158–9
Aitchison, Ensign John 308–10
Alava, Maj.-Gen. M.R. de 495, 497, 507, 572, 584
Albuera, battle of 429–30
Aldborough, Lady 17
Alexander I, Emperor 103, 210, 218, 574, 576
Alicante, expedition to 463, 520
Almeida 244, 380–1, 399, 412, 417, 418, 425, 440
Almonacid, battle of 346
Alten, Maj.-Gen. Charles 180, 405, 578
Alten, Maj.-Gen. Victor 180, 530
Amiens, Peace of 104, 118
Amrit Rao 107, 111, 112, 123, 124–5, 128, 131
Anstruther, Lt.-Col. Robert 37–8, 228, 237, 249, 251–3, 262
Antrim, Co., patronage in 195
Angoulême, Duc d' 574
Arbuthnot, Charles 172, 445, 457
Arbuthnot, Harriet 290, 457
Argaum, battle of 144–6
Argenton, Capt. 305–6
Arentschildt, Lt.-Col. F. von 469–70
Argyll, Duke of 290–1

Army, British
  Duke of York's reforms 34–5
  patronage networks 37–8, 175–6
  in the Maratha War 119–20, 127–8, 130, 136
  officers in Parliament 180
  in 1808 (AW's) 240–1
  in 1809 (AW's) 302–3, 307–8, 322, 345–6, 355–6
  in 1810–11 (Wellington's) 402, 405
  sickness in 1811 437
  reinforcements 437–8
  supply system 438–9
  in Salamanca campaign 463
  poor performance at Burgos and after 485–6, 488–9
  in 1813 519–20
  misconduct after Vitoria 533
  see also Regiments of the British Army
Army, French
  resilience 315, 418, 492
  at Talavera 333, 339
  losses in Masséna's invasion of Portugal 413
Army, Maratha 127–8, 131, 137–8, 141, 145
Army, Portuguese
  AW's proposal for Britain to rebuild 238–9
  in 1808 243
  British officers serve in 292–3, 362
  in Oporto campaign 307–8, 310
  revival 1809–10 362–6
  at the Coa 379
  performance at Busaco 392
  inefficiency of its commissariat 409
  at Burgos 486
Army, Spanish
  at Talavera 333, 336, 339
  Wellington given command of 517–8

role in Vitoria campaign 519–20
at battle of Vitoria 525–6
at San Marcial 549
problems in 1813 551, 554
in Spain 554
performance at the Bidassoa 558
Freyre's divisions brought into France 573
Freyre's attack at Toulouse 580–2
Armytage, John 8–9
Arroyo dos Molinos, combat of 437, 515
Assaye, campaign and battle of 132–6,
    136–41, 141–3, 169
Aston, Col. H.H. 46, 54, 69, 140
Auckland, Lord 264–5, 268, 315, 380, 393,
    433, 476
Austerlitz, battle of 176, 339
Austria, war of 1809 318–9

Baccelar, Gen. Manuel 391
Badajoz
    French siege of (1811) 405–6, 411
    British sieges of (1811) 416–8, 429,
        431–2
    British siege of (1812) 447–57
Bagwell, John 198
Bainbrigge, Capt. Philip 472
Baird, Maj.-Gen. David 74, 81, 89,
    296
    at the storm of Seringapatam 85–6
    superseded by AW 87
    supersedes AW at Bombay 97–8
    hopes for role in Maratha campaign 116–7,
        119
    expedition to the Cape of Good
        Hope 170
    wounded at Coruña 292
Baji Rao II see Peshwa
Ballesteros, Gen. F. 462, 488
Bankes, Henry 288
Barclay, Capt. Robert 101, 160, 273
Barlow, Sir George 152
Barnard, Lady Anne 235
Barnes, Maj.-Gen. Edward 546
Barrington, Jonah 18, 232
Bassein, Treaty of 112
Bathurst, Lord 178, 459–60, 475–6, 549–50,
    562, 567–8, 574
Bayly, Lt. Richard 83
Bayonne 532–3, 570
Beckwith, Lt-Col. S. 215
Bellingham, James 458
Bentinck, Lady William 173
Bentinck, Lt.-Gen. Lord William 160, 180,
    188, 462–3, 520, 554
Berar, the Bhonsle Raja of 106, 111, 122, 124,
    126–30, 131, 141, 143–4, 144–6,
    147–9
Beresford, Col. Marcus 172

Beresford, Lt.-Gen. and Marshal, Sir William
        Carr 180, 185, 188, 382, 497, Plate 39
    given command of the Portuguese army
        292–3, 302
    character 302
    relations with AW 302
    in the Oporto campaign 308, 314
    revives the Portuguese army (1809–10) 362–6
    Busaco 385
    Torres Vedras 399
    takes command of detached corps in
        Alentejo 405
    in Estremadura 411–12, 416–8
    at Albuera 429–30
    subsequent breakdown 430
    at Salamanca 468, 472, 474
    his headquarters 495, 501
    warm welcome by French people 572
    at Bordeaux 575
    the advance on Toulouse 576–7
    at Toulouse 578–83
    importance of his role 585, 588
Berkeley, Adm. George 400, 447
Berkeley, Lt.-Col. George 296
Bessborough, Lady 177, 219, 380, 476
Bevan, Lt.-Col. Charles 426–7
Bhurtpore 163
Bidassoa, passage of the 557–8
Bingham, Lt.-Col. George 355, 528, 543
Bissett, John (Commissary-General) 438
Bistnapah Pundit 120, 166
Blake, Gen. J. 418
Blakiston, Capt. John 82–3, 122, 133, 139, 141,
    142, 144, 146–7
Bligh, Thomas, MP 198
Blunt, Rev. 50–1
Boigne, Benoit de 106
Bonaparte see Napoleon; Joseph
Bourbons, restoration to the French throne
    565, 573–6, 578
Bordeaux 573–6
Bourke, Lt.-Col. Richard 205
Boutflower, Charles 356–7, 384
Bowles, Capt. George 314
Boxtel, combat of 33
Braithwaite, Maj.-Gen. John 49
Brennier, Gen. A.F. 251–2, 254, 425, 434
Brisbane, Maj.-Gen. T.M. 20, 571
Briscall, Rev. Samuel 503
Brotherton, Capt. Thomas 512
Brougham, Henry 460
Broughton, Lord 583
Brown, Lt. Patrick 74, 76, 85
Brown, Pte. William 571
Browne, Lt.-Col. Samuel 232, 245–6
Browne, Lt. Thomas Henry 490, 496, 501–2,
    529–30
Buchanan, Dr Francis 79

Buckingham, Marquess of
  relations with AW 38, 175, 191, 350
  AW serves as his ADC 11–13
  Lord Lieutenant of Ireland 12–13, 20
  AW visits in England 14
  on Catholics 23–4
  attends dinner in support of Lord
      Wellesley 178
  and the Convention of Cintra 273
  Wellington renews connection 350
Buckinghamshire, Earl of see Hobart
Bullum, Raja of 93, 101
Bunbury, Henry, Col. and Under-Secretary
      for War 30, 568
Bunbury, Lt. Ralph 244
Burdett, Sir Francis 370, 444, 475
Burgh, Lt.-Col. Ulysses 392, 505–6, 540
Burghersh, John Fane, Lord 14, 279
Burgos 479, 485–8, 492, 523
Burgoyne, Maj. John 367, 440, 442, 485–6,
      488, 511
Burrard, Lt.-Gen. Sir Harry 212, 237, 249–50
  refuses AW's advice to advance 255–7
  and the suspension of arms 258–60
  evidence to Cintra Inquiry 279
  later life 281
Busaco, battle of 384–91
Byng, Lt.-Col. John 29, 543, 545

Cadiz 359, 365, 374, 492, 517–18
Cadogan, Lt.-Col. Henry 296, 419
Caffarelli, Gen. M. 465–6, 478–9, 488–9
Calvert, Frances 343
Camden, Lord 38–9, 175, 178
Cameron, Brig. Alan 322, 329, 338, 428–9
Cameron, Lt.-Col. Phillips 424, 428–9
Campbell, Maj.-Gen. Alexander 303, 329, 336,
      354, 405, 416, 426, 438
Campbell, Lt.-Col. Colin 133–4, 138, 139, 142,
      160, 164, 211, 234, 265, 303, 453
  role as Commandant of Headquarters 501,
      504–5
  relations with Wellington 513
Campbell, Ensign Colin (later Lord Clyde)
      254–5
Campbell, Maj.-Gen. Dugald 119, 131
Campo Mayor 416
canals 203
Canning, Lt.-Col. Charles Fox 296, 502, 505
Canning, George 183, 189, 192, 199, 372, 414
  and Copenhagen expedition 211, 219–20
  and Catholic Question 227
  and the Spanish uprising 231
  and Convention of Cintra 268, 269, 273
  commitment to defend Portugal with AW
      in command 292–5
  praises AW 319
  queries strategy after Talavera 347–8

resignation and duel with Castlereagh 348
does not return to office (1812) 458–9
caricatures 1, 265, 274, 287
Carss, Lt. John 336, 360
Castaños, Gen. X. 418, 443, 462, 551
Castenschiold, Gen. 214
Castle Coote, Lord 196
Castlereagh, Lord Plate 37
  and AW in Ireland 25
  and India 153, 154, 170, 175, 178
  advises AW to accept seat in Commons 179
  in Portland's government 189, 190, 195
  and the Catholic Question 199, 227
  and the Copenhagen expedition 208–10,
      219
  marriage 221
  and expedition to Latin America 229–30
  and AW's campaign in Portugal (1808)
      232–3, 237–8, 240
  and Cintra 260–1, 264–5, 267, 269–70,
      283–5
  reluctance to supersede Cradock 293
  instructions to AW 295–7
  tepid praise for Oporto 316
  warm praise for AW 320, 342
  strategy after Talavera 347–8
  resignation and duel with Canning 348
  subsequent career 372, 445, 459
  and restoration of the Bourbons 574
Cathcart, Lt.-Gen. Lord 211–19
Catholic Question 22–5, 188, 198–9, 199–200,
      226–7, 203, 227
Chambers, Charles 211
Charlotte, Princess 506
Charlotte, Queen 182, 561
Chatham, Lt.-Gen. Lord 224–5, 232–3, 237,
      262, 273, 285, 318–19, 320, 370
Chetwood, Capt. John 81
Chief Secretary for Ireland
  AW appointed (1807) 190–3
  use of patronage 193–6
  and 1807 election 196–9
  and the Catholic Question 199–201
  and disaffection 201–2, 225
  Ireland's underlying problems 202–4
  and the defence of Ireland 204–6, 219–20,
      224
  in Parliament 206–7, 225–7
  pay and residences 222–3
  AW criticised for holding office while
      serving abroad 284
  AW resigns 296
Christian, Rear-Adm. Sir Hugh 40
Cintra, Convention of
  suspension of arms 258–60
  final Convention 261
  popular reaction against 1, 264,
      267–9, 274

controversy over AW's involvement 1, 269–74
  Inquiry 1–2, 15, 276–9, 280
  effect on public opinion 278–80, 282
  debates in Parliament 284–6
Ciudad Rodrigo, sieges and blockade of
    377–8, 436, 439–45
Clarence, Duke of (William IV) 20, 308
Clarke, Lt.-Gen. Sir Alured 63, 67–8
Clarke, Mary Anne 241, 286–9, 534
Clausel, Gen. B. 469, 474
  after Salamanca 479, 484–5, 491
  and Vitoria campaign 522–3, 525, 531–2
  in the battles of the Pyrenees 539–41,
    544–5
  battles of the Nive 562–3
Clinton, Capt. Robert, Lord 475
Clinton, Maj.-Gen. Henry 180, 228, 249, 256,
    258, 473–4, 480, 490
Clinton, Maj.-Gen. William 180, 228, 234, 344
Clive, Edward, Lord (governor of Madras) 67,
    69, 94, 99, 104, 113, 118, 119,
    120, 192
Close, Lt.-Col. Barry 99, 108, 162
  character 68, 100, 104–5
  role in Seringapatam campaign 72, 86
  AW's admiration for 99–100, 104–5, 163
  appointed Resident at Poona 104–5
  and Maratha affairs (1800) 109
  negotiates Treaty of Bassein 111–12
  role in implementing Lord Wellesley's
    policy 122–3
  difficulties with the Peshwa 123–5, 128–9
  the path to war 128–9
Coa, combat of the 378–9
Cobbett, William 231, 265, 272, 275, 350, 434
Cochrane, Lt.-Col. Basil 426–7
Cocks, Maj. Charles 308, 337, 339, 390, 450,
    480–1, 487
Coffin see Pine Coffin
Colborne, Lt.-Col. John 38, 248, 429, 440,
    560, 581
Cole, Maj.-Gen. G. Lowry 20, 172, 180, 354,
    438, 465, 474, 491, 501, 525, Plate 47
  character 355
  opinion of Wellington 360
  at Albuera 430
  investiture with KB 494, 500
  and battles of the Pyrenees 540–2, 545
Coleridge, Samuel Taylor 434
Collier, Capt. Sir George 297
Collins, Lt.-Col. John 123, 129, 131, 135
Collins, Wilkie 85
Colville, Maj.-Gen. Charles 405, 428, 436, 448,
    456, 499, 527–8, 530, 545, 560
commissariat 409–10, 438–9
Common Council of the City of London 344,
    370, 590
Conaghul 95–6

Convention of Cintra see Cintra
Cooke, Edward 264, 393
Cooke, Lt. John 465–6
Cooper, Cpl. John S. 306–7, 346, 355–6
Copenhagen expedition 208–20
Cornwallis, Lord 29, 38, 45, 47, 57, 60, 67,
    170, 175, 176, 195
Coruña
  AW lands at (1808) 235
  battle of 283
Costa see Neves Costa
Costello, Pte. Edward 529, 533
Cotton, Adm. Sir Charles 233, 236, 260
Cotton, Lt.-Gen. Sir Stapleton 70, 180, 303,
    374, 405, 412, 474, 496, 508,
    545, 588
The Courier 393, 434
Cox, Brig. William 380
Cradock, Lt.-Gen. Sir John 15, 18, 163–4, 188,
    292–7
Craig, Lt.-Gen. Sir James 32
Craig, Gen. Peter 277, 280
Craufurd, Brig. Robert 180, 340, 405, 412,
    Plate 46
  character 354
  action at the Coa 378–9
  at Busaco 389–90
  mortally wounded at Ciudad Rodrigo
    442–3
Creevey, Thomas 227, 302, 350
Croker, John Wilson 197, 273, 342–3, 475,
    549–50
Crowe, Lt. Charles 579
Cuesta, Gen. G. 304–5, 321, 324–8, 331,
    334–5, 339
Cruickshank, George 274
Culling, see Smith, Charles Culling

Dalhousie, Lt.-Gen. Lord 490, 524, 526–7,
    545, 576
Dalrymple, Lt.-Gen. Sir Hew 237–8, 257–61,
    267–8, 270, 277, 281, Plate 25
Dardis, William 270
Delaborde, Brig. 244–8, 312
De Lancey, Capt. William 48, 472, 483
D'Erlon see Drouet
Dhoondiah Waugh 93–6
Dickson, Lt.-Col. Alexander 429, 432, 439–41,
    485, 488, 510, 514, 528
Dickson, Mrs 19
Diomed (AW's horse) 140
Donegal, Lord 195
Donkin, Lt.-Col. Rufane 329, 332, 334, 339
Dorsenne, Gen. J. 436, 446
Dos de Mayo and the Spanish uprising 230–1
Douglas, Lt.-Col. James 364
Downman, Maj. Thomas 426–7, 429
Drogheda, Lord 196

Drouet, Gen., Count d'Erlon 404, 431, 451, 463, 484, 540–2, 544–5, 561–3
Dubreton, Gen. J.-L. 485
Duigenan, Dr 200, 227
Duncan, Jonathan 154, 157
Dundas, Gen. Sir David 20, 34, 35, 38, 176, 235, 276, 280, 288, 296, 402, 434
Dundas, Henry (Lord Melville) 31, 60, 64, 104, 192–3
Dundas, Robert Saunders (Lord Melville) 193, 228, 549
Dungannon, Lady (AW's maternal grandmother) 6, 8
D'Urban, Benjamin 360, 362, 364, 368, 451, 462, 469–70

East India Company 59, 60, 104, 117, 153, 178–9, 182–3, 188
Eastlake, George 501–2, 511
Eastwick, Capt. 54
Edgeworth, Maria 27
Edmonstone, Neil 125, 152
El Bodon, combat at 436–7, 507
Elder, Lt.-Col. 364, 379
Eldon, Lord 199, 287
elections
 1806 186–7
 1807 196–9, 206
Elers, Capt. George 89, 99
 recollections of voyage to India 45–6
 Penang expedition 51
 on Sultanpettah Tope affair 83
 on sack of Seringapatam 86
 on the Duke of York and General Harris 87
 description of life at Seringapatam 101–2
Elley, Lt.-Col. John 508
Elliot, Maj. Walter 101
Elphinstone, Mountstuart 134, 140, 147, 166
Erskine, Lt.-Gen. Sir William 405, 508
España, Gen. Carlos de 463, 466, 473, 480–1
The Examiner 413, 434–5

famine of 1804 in the Deccan 151, 157–9
Fane, Brig. Henry 251, 253
Fane see Westmorland
Farington, Joseph 268
Ferdinand VII, King of Spain 229, 231, 531, 537, 566
Ferguson, Maj.-Gen. Ronald 241, 245, 253, 262, 278–9, 316–17
Fingall, Lord 198, 199, 200
Fisher, Lt.-Col. George 514
Fitzclarence, Lt. George 308, 332–3, 335, 497, 508
Fletcher, Lt.-Col. Richard 367–8, 417, 432, 441, 447–8, 548–9
Floyd, Maj.-Gen. John 70, 74
Folkestone, Lord 227, 272, 274–5, 283, 287, 350

Forrest, Capt. Charles 544
Fortescue, Sir John (historian) 36, 78, 247, 257, 530, 677
Fox, Charles James 134, 175, 177, 179, 183, 186
Foy, Gen. M. 257, 311, 387–8, 398–9, 468, 474–5, 531–2, 545, 561, 571
France, civilians welcome Wellington's army 572
Francis, Philip 60
Freese, Arthur 102, 222
Freese, Isabella 102–3, 165, 172, Plate 14
Freese, Capt. John 102
Freire, Gen. Bernadino 243
Fremantle, John 16, 504–5
Fremantle, W.H. 16, 18, 283, 286
Frere, John Hookham 325, 327
Freyre, Gen. Manuel 549, 573, 578–82
Friedland, battle of 210, 339
Fuentes de Oñoro, battle of 418–25

Gaikwar of Baroda, Anud Rao, the 106–7
Gambier, Adm. James 217, 219
Garcia Hernandez 474, 478
Garrow, William 178
Gawilghur, fortress of 144, 146–7
Gazan, Gen. H. 524–5
Gazan, Mde. 530
Gebora, battle of 406
Geldermalsen, action at 35
Gentleman's Magazine 342
George III, King 11, 15, 34, 177, 188–9, 343, 393, 402–3
 dislikes Lord Wellesley 42, 169
 does not favour AW 169–70
 and Copenhagen expedition 210, 219
 approves intervention in Latin America 230
 vetoes attempt to remove Moore from his command 237
 reaction to Convention of Cintra 267
 approves recall of Dalrymple 270
 appoints Dundas C-in-C 288
 and Portugal 295, 316, 320
George, Prince of Wales (Prince Regent; later George IV) 15, 31, 46, 223, 276, 402–3, 434, 444–5, 458, 531, 590
Giffard, John 200
Gillray, James 274, Plate 7
Gleig, Rev. G.R. 7, 8
Godoy, Manuel de 229
Gohud, Rana of 149, 152–4, 157
Goklah (Maratha lord) 95, 110, 116, 122, 130
Gomm, Maj. William, 234
Gordon, Lt.-Col. Alexander 296, 365, 369, 380, 382, 392, 413, 424, 432, 478, 500
 at Torres Vedras 395
 and escape of garrison of Almeida 426
 with Wellington at Madrid 480–1

letters to Aberdeen 482
and Col. J.W. Gordon 482, 483
at Burgos 486
quarters at Freneda 494–5
duties as ADC 505
and strategic problems 506
wounded at Sorauren 544
on Wellington's wound at Orthez 571
Gordon, Lt.-Col. H.M. 206
Gordon, Col. James Willoughby 194, 267, 380,
481–3, 490, 509
Gore, Col. Arthur 101
Gough, Maj. Hugh 545
Gower *see* Leveson Gower
Goya, Francisco 230, 481, *Plate 53*
Graham, Maj. James George 158–9
Graham, Lt.-Gen. Sir Thomas 37, 180, 374,
437–8, 447, 465, 531–2, 558, 588
hostility to Wellington (1809) 343–4
in Vitoria campaign 521–2, 524–5, 528
siege of San Sebastian 539–40, 547–9, 552
Grant, Lt-Col. C. 530
Grattan, Henry 21, 25, 38, 206, 227
Grenville, Lord George 414
Grenville, Thomas (Tom) 186, 343, 392–3
Grenville, William, Lord 9, 12, 14, 24, 38, 42,
175, 177, 188–9, 348, 561
helps bring AW into Parliament 179
and expedition to Latin America 185–6
praise of AW 185
becomes a stern critic of AW 191, 273, 316,
401–2, 414
Greville, Charles 469
Grey, Charles, Lord 186, 206, 265, 316, 348,
392, 414, 434, 444, 475–6, 482
Grijo, action at 310
guerrillas, Spanish 359, 422, 446, 462, 465,
479, 489, 518, 585
Gurwood Lt. John 184, 442, 673–4
Guthrie, Dr George James 346
Gwalior 149, 152–4, 157

Haider Ali, Sultan of Mysore 57
Hall, Cornet Francis 422–3
Hamilton, Lord Archibald 227
Hamilton, John 222
Hamilton, Maj.-Gen. John 366, 431
Hardwicke, Lord 192
Harness, Lt.-Col. William 36, 120, 121
Harrington, Lord 205–6, 224, 288, 295
Harris, Rifleman Benjamin 239–41, 251,
255–7
Harris, Lt.-Gen. George 54, 62, 89, 91, 92,
175–6, *Plate 8*
and preparations for war with Mysore 67–9
relations with AW 67, 72–3
plan of campaign 71–2
and Seringapatam 75–86

appoints AW to command in
Seringapatam 87
Harrowby, Lord 192, 283, 401
Hastings, Warren 59–60, 177–8
Hatfield 187, 591
Hawker, Capt. Peter 325
Hawkesbury *see* Liverpool, Lord
Hawkins, Sir Christopher 186
Hay, Maj.-Gen. Andrew 421, 501, 548
Head, George 409, 526
Heaphy, Thomas 504, *Plates 65 and 66*
Heathfield, Gen. Lord, 277, 280
Hennell, Lt. George 557–8
Herasti, Gen. A. 378, 411
Hertford, Lord 195, 223
Hickey, William 48, 50–51, 52, 62, 161,
177, 223
Hill, Lt.-Gen. Sir Rowland 180, 251, 295, 303,
312, 385, 405, 431, 436, 447, 474,
489, 501, 522, 532, 578, 561
ability 241, 588
at Talavera 331, 333–4
sees no hope in the Peninsula 357, 374
victory at Arroyo dos Molinos 437, 515
battle of Vitoria 524–6
battles of the Pyrenees 542, 544–6
at the Nive 563–4
Hobart, Robert (Lord Buckinghamshire)
14–15, 16, 24, 47–8, 49, 51, 54, 68,
175, 283
Holkar, Jaswant Rao
campaigns against the Peshwa 110–12
and restoration of the Peshwa 114–25
avoids war with the British 126–7
position after defeat of Sindia and Berar
148–9, 151
war with British (1804) 156–9, 161–3
Holkar, Vitoji 110, 111, 116
Holland, Elizabeth, Lady 392
Holland, Lord 186
Home, Robert 161, 164
Hood, Cdre Samuel 169–70
Hope, Lt.-Gen. Alexander 37, 180, 564
Hope, Lt.-Gen. Charles 180
Hope, Lt.-Gen. John 37, 180, 237, 262–3, 500,
531, 563, 570, 588
replaces Graham as Wellington's
second-in-command 558
wounded at the Nive 564
Hoppner, John (artist) 40–1, *Plates 9 and 17*
Horner, Francis 206
House, Mr 410
Howarth, Richard 214
Howick *see* Grey
Howorth, Brig. Edward 315
Huddleston, Maj. Robert 143
Hunt, Leigh 413
Huskisson, William 190, 371

Hyderabad, in restoration of Peshwa and
       Maratha War 120, 123, 125, 128, 130
   see also Nizam

Imaz, Gen. J. 411
Insurrection Bill (1807) 206, 225
Ireland
   AW's attitude to 21, 191–2
   in the 1790s 22–5
   AW appointed Chief Secretary 190–1
   underlying problems of 199–204, 225
   AW and the defence of 204–6, 224
   and Copenhagen expedition 210, 219–20

Jackson, Francis 213, 214, 216
Jackson, George 216–7
Jena-Auerstädt, battles of 186
Jenkinson, Maj. George 572
Jones, Capt. J.T. 368, 549
Joseph, King of Spain 230, 264, 480, 488, 519
   and Talavera campaign 321, 327–8, 333,
       340, 346
   overruns Andalusia 358–9
   in Vitoria campaign 522–8
   disgraced by Napoleon 532
Jourdan, Marshal 328, 488, 522–4, 526,
       528, 531
Junot, Gen. A. 1, 224, 232–3, Plate 21
   estimates of his army 233, 235–6, 244
   difficulties of his position 244–5
   advances from Lisbon 250
   Vimeiro 251–7
   Convention of Cintra 258–61
   role in Masséna's invasion of Portugal
       (1810–11) 377, 387, 397

Keane, Maj.-Gen. John 571
Kellermann, Gen. F.E. 252, 258–60, 270,
       272, 277
Kennedy, Robert (Commissary-General) 409,
       438–9
Kent, Edward, Duke of 286
Khan, Soubahdar Kawder Nawez 160
Kharda, battle of 57, 109
Kincaid, Capt. John 466, 480, 500
Kioge, action at 214–5
Kirkpatrick, Capt. James 63, 108, 122
Kirkpatrick, Maj. William 61
Koorg, Raja of 72, 164

Lacerda, Col. Antonio de Lemo Pereira de 362
Laing, Ensign Samuel 241, 248, 263
Lake, Lt.-Col. George 247–8
Lake, Lt.-Gen. Gerard 127, 131, 144, 147, 153,
       155, 180
   and the war with Holkar (1804)
       156–9, 161–3
   granted a peerage 164, 169

Lamb, Thomas Davis 179–80
Lambton, Lt. William 81, 101
Landmann, Capt. George Thomas 245
Larpent, Francis Seymour 559–60, 567,
       580, 584
   at Freneda 493–4
   life at headquarters 495, 497, 501, 503–4,
       511
   on Wellington 499, 502, 509–11, 514, 515,
       540, 553–4, 571
   praises Fitzroy Somerset 505
   on Wellington's ADCs 506
   on Alava 507
   on France 556, 572–3
   Wellington much exposed at the Nive 564
   on Wellington's wound at Orthez 571
   on the Garonne 577
   The last harvest or British Threshers makeing
       French Crops 265, Plate 27
Lauderdale, Lord 179
Lawrence, Sgt. William 455
Leach, Capt. Jonathan 354, 389, 502, 506
Leipzig, battle of 559, 563
Leith, Maj.-Gen. James 180, 385, 388, 454,
       470, 474, 547–8
Leith Hay, Lt. Andrew 473
Le Marchant, Maj.-Gen. John Gaspard 180,
       215, 463, 470–1, 474
Lemonnier-Delafosse, Capt. 388
Lennox, Lady Sarah 353
Lennox see Richmond, 4th Duke of
Leon, Juana Maria de los Dolores de 455
Leslie, Lt. Charles, 247–8
Leveson Gower, Lord Granville 265
Light Brigade 212, 303, 322, 340, 354
Lines of Torres Vedras 351, 366–9, 396–7
Lisbon
   strategic significance (1808) 244
   Wellington visits (Oct. 1809) 351, 367;
       (Feb. 1810) 369
Littlehales, Sir Edward 193, 220, 223
Liverpool, Lord 189, 195, 199, 220, 224,
       264–5, 283, 289, 393, 414–15, 476,
       556, 575
   offers AW position as Chief Secretary for
       Ireland 190
   blocks Gerald Wellesley's mitre 196, 550
   and AW's threat to resign (1807) 208–9
   and AW's involvement in Cintra 269
   becomes Secretary of State for War and the
       Colonies 349
   relations with Wellington 350–2, 372–4,
       402–3, 415, 549–50
   becomes Prime Minister 458–9
   praise for Salamanca 476
Llangollen, Ladies of 10–11, 194, 232
Loison, Gen. 244
Long, Charles 211

Long, Maj.-Gen. Robert Ballard 408, 543
Longford, Lord and Lady (Kitty's parents) 27–8
Louis XVIII, King 574–6, 583–4
Lowther, Lord 193
Lynch, Comte 574–5

Macdonald, Maj. John 216
MacDonnel, Lt.-Col. J.W. 364
McGrigor, James 453, 494, 511–12, 515
Mackenzie of Fairbairn, Gen. Sir Alexander 10
Mackenzie, Capt. Colin 79, 81, 101
Mackenzie, Maj.-Gen. John Randoll 303–5, 329, 331, 337
Mackinnon, Brig. Henry 383–4, 442
Mackintosh, Sir James 46
McNaghten, Edmond Alexander, MP 195
Madrid 479–80, 480, 489
Maitland, Lt.-Gen. Frederick 463, 485
Malartic (governor of Mauritius) 62, 64
Malavelly, action at 77–9
Malcolm, John 45, 64, 74, 83, 120, 134, 141, 147, 160–2, 166, 303
    joins AW in the advance on Poona 122
    AW confides in 128
    negotiates alliance with Sindia 151
    and interpretation of peace treaties 152–4
    AW's admiration for 163
    AW leaves 164–6
    later correspondence with AW 178, 179, 181
Malcolm, Capt. John 582
Malcolm, Capt. Pulteney (RN) 45, 97, 234
Malmesbury, Lady 342
Malmesbury, Lord 193
Manila expedition 49–52
Maratha Confederation 57
    and Tipu's defeat 91–2, 107
    cooperate against Dhoondiah Waugh 94–5
    internal conflicts 106–12
    British intervention to restore the Peshwa 112–25
    Maratha lands after war 149–50, 157–9
Maratha War (1803)
    the path to war 126–9
    contending armies 127–8, 130, 131, 141
    Assaye campaign 132–6
    battle of Assaye 136–41
    battle of Argaum 144–6
    siege of Gawilghur 146–7
    peace negotiations 147–9
March, Capt. Charles Gordon Lennox, Lord 505–6, 515
Marmont, Marshal A.F.L.V. *Plate 49*
    replaces Masséna 433
    relieves Ciudad Rodrigo 436
    hears of fall of Ciudad Rodrigo 446

and siege of Badajoz 451
and Salamanca 461, 464–75
badly wounded 469, 474
Martin, Adm. Thomas Byam 501–2
Masséna, Marshal André *Plate 48*
    instructions for the invasion of Portugal 377–8
    capture of Ciudad Rodrigo and Almeida 378–80
    advance to Busaco 382–4
    refuses to recognise the ordenanza 384
    battle of Busaco 387–90
    advances to Torres Vedras 395–6
    refuses to attack the Lines or retreat 396–9
    and regency crisis in London 403–4
    withdraws to Santarem 404–5
    retreats from Portugal 407–13
    advances to relieve Almeida 418
    Fuentes de Oñoro 419–25
    replaced by Marmont 433
Mauritius, proposed expedition to 96–7
Maxwell, Lt.-Col. Patrick 139–40, 143
Maya, combat of 541
Maynooth College 200, 227
Medina del Rio Seco, battle of 235–6, 264
Meer Allum 74, 79, 87, 88
Melville *see* Dundas, Henry; Dundas, Robert Saunders
Metternich, Prince Clemens von 518, 576
Mexico, proposed expedition to 185–6, 187–8, 229
Michell, Rev. Henry 8
militia, Portuguese 361
Mill, Lt. James 543, 579–80
Miranda, Francisco de 229–30
Mitchell (Cornwall), AW elected MP for 186
Moira, Lord 31, 38, 276, 280–1, 283, 315, 328, 458
Monson, Col. William 158, 161–2, 169
Montresor, Lt.-Col. 75–6
The Moonstone (Collins) 85
Moore, Lord Henry 196
Moore, Lt.-Gen. Sir John 37, 169, 180, 232, 491, 535
    AW implicitly compared to 228, 234, 263
    sent to Portugal 237
    corps not used to block French retreat 250, 258, 277, 279
    praises AW's conduct of campaign 261, 263
    AW wants him to command the army 262
    campaign in Spain 278
    death at Coruña 283
    says that Portugal is indefensible 316, 373
Mosinho, Manoel de Brito 362
The Morning Chronicle 230, 265, 275, 482
Mornington, Lady, Anne Wesley (AW's mother) 6–11, 171, 195, 272, 477, *Plate 3*

Mornington, Lord, Garret Wesley (AW's father) 5–7
Mornington, Lord, Richard Wellesley (AW's brother) *see* Wellesley, Richard
Morillo, Gen. Pablo 524–6, 543
Mughal Empire 59
Mulcaster, Capt. E.R. 367–8
Mulgrave, Lord 180, 189–90, 194, 210, 283, 476
Munkaiseer, action at 150
Munro, Thomas 108
Murat, Marshal 229
Murchison, Ensign Roderick 239, 241, 243, 253–4
Murray, Maj.-Gen. George 481, 483, 499, 514, 521, 543, 560
    character and ability 307–8
    at Copenhagen 212, 218
    admires AW 228
    AW recommends to Castlereagh 229
    and the campaign of 1808 and Cintra 237, 249, 256, 258, 261
    as QMG of AW's army 307–8, 382 507
    at Talavera 334, 339
    no hope of defending Portugal 357, 374
    importance in final campaigns 509, 540, 588
Mysore 90, 99–100, 120, 130, 159–60
    see also Tipu Sultan

Nana Phadnavis 107
Napier, Lt.-Col. Charles 38
Napier, Lt.-Col. George 355, 442, 506, 576
Napier, Maj. William 18, 235, 268, 378–9, 473, 553, 571, 677
Napoleon 103, *Plate 23*
    expedition to Egypt 64
    style of his *Bulletins* 121, 427
    victory at Austerlitz 176
    defeats Prussia 186
    victory at Friedland 210
    attacks Portugal 224
    intervenes in Spain 229–30
    defeats Spanish armies 278
    1809 war with Austria 318
    and French armies in Spain in 1809 320, 328
    reinforces armies in the Peninsula 358
    plans for the conquest of Portugal 377
    orders Masséna to maintain his position 404
    his armies in Spain overstretched 404–5, 446
    Wellington's opinion of 431
    fails to recognise threat posed by Wellington 446
    and siege of Badajoz 451
    consequences of his invasion of Russia 517

1813 campaigns in Germany 518, 555
    does not think Wellington will take offensive 519
    refuses to cut his losses in Spain 537–8
    defeat at Leipzig 555, 559
    unpopularity of his government 572–4
    refuses allied terms at Châtillon 575–6
    defeated at Arcis-sur-Aube 578
    abdication 583
    mistakes in Spain and Portugal 585
Navy, Royal 438, 549
Nelson, Adm. Lord 71, 103, 170, 212, 256, 427, 476
Neves Costa, Maj. José Maria das 367
Nevill, Mr 193
Newcastle, Duke of 180
Newport, Isle of Wight, AW elected MP for 198
newspapers *see* press; under individual titles
Ney, Marshal M. 305, 320, 325, 328, 340–1, 377
    attacks Craufurd on the Coa 378–9
    at Busaco 387–90
    and the Lines of Torres Vedras 396–7
Nicolls, Capt. Jasper 132
Nicolls, Lt.-Gen. Oliver 276, 280
Nive, battles of the 562–4
Nivelle, battle of the 559–61
Nizam of Hyderabad, the (Asaf Jah II, Nizam-ul-Mulk) 57, 61, 127, 135, 150
    and French officered corps of sepoys 57, 61, 63–4
    army takes part in Seringapatam campaign 73–4, 75, 76
    cooperates against Dhoondiah Waugh 94 94, 127, 135, 150
Norcott, Capt. Amos (33rd) 52–3
North, Frederick (governor of Ceylon) 97
Nugent, Lt.-Gen. George 15, 276, 280, 285

Obidos, skirmish at 244
O'Connell, Daniel 25
O'Lawlor, Maj.-Gen. J. 495, 507
Olivenza 406
O'Malley, Ernie 534
Oman, Sir Charles (historian) 247, 257, 677
O'Neill, John, MP 195
O'Neill, Lord 195
Oporto
    AW visits (1808) 236
    campaign (1809) 305–15
Oracle 178–9
Orange, William, Hereditary Prince of 494, 497, 501, 504, 506–7, 544
Orange Order 200
ordenanza 361, 368, 384
Orrok, John 103

Orrok, Lt.-Col. William 138, 142, 143, 166
Orthez, battle of 515, 570–2
Ostend, expedition to 31
Oswald, Maj.-Gen. John 540, 547–8

Pack, Lt.-Col. Denis 425
Page, John 19
Paget, Lt-Gen. Edward 180, 304, 307, 311–12, 490
Paget, Henry William, Lord 263, 291–2, 531
paintings captured at Vitoria 531–2
Pakenham, Catherine (Kitty) see Wellesley, Catherine
Pakenham, Maj.-Gen Edward 180, 181, 465, 469–70, 496, 508, 564
Pakenham, Henry 222
Pakenham, Capt. Hercules 244, 456
Palmer, Col. William 108, 111
Palmerston, Lord 198, 267–8, 342
patronage
    in the army 37–8, 175–6
    in the government of Ireland 193–6, 197
Paull, James 177–9, 182–3, 187, 227
Payne, Maj.-Gen. William 304, 307, 322, 338, 508
Peel, Robert 19, 70, 223, 296
Pelet, Maj. J.J. 378, 396–7, 404
Pellegrini, Domenico 354, Plate 35
Pembroke, Lt.-Gen. Lord 276, 280
Penang expedition 49–52
Perceval, Spencer 183, 189, 199, 200, 206, 227, 276, 286, 289, 345, 371, 393, 402, 414, 444, 445
    becomes Prime Minister 349
    assassinated 458
    Wellington's opinion of 459
Pereira de Lacerda, Col. Antonio de Lemo 362
Peshwa (Baji Rao II, Maratha Prince)
    and Tipu's defeat 91–2
    and internal conflicts within Maratha Confederacy 106–12
    signs Treaty of Bassein 112
    proves a difficult ally 123–5, 128–9, 156
    weakness of his authority 149
Petty, Lord Henry 284–5
Peymann, Maj.-Gen. Heinrich 214, 216–17
Philippon, Gen. A. 448, 454
Picton, Maj.-Gen. Thomas 180, 465, 501, 521, 577–8, Plate 45
    character 375
    view of Wellington 375–6
    Busaco 385, 387
    praises commissaries 409
    at Badajoz 448, 452, 456–7
    battle of Vitoria 526–7
    battles of the Pyrenees 542, 545
Pine Coffin, Maj. 215–16

Piron (commander of sepoys in Hyderabad) 63, 64
Pitt, William 9, 23, 24, 30, 34, 103–4, 175, 177, 199
    his 1784 India Bill 59, 109–10
    appoints Mornington Governor-General of Bengal 60
Pittite party, nature of 191
Pole Wellesley, William see Wellesley-Pole, William
polygars, campaigns against 93, 101
Pondicherry 118
Ponsonby, Lt.-Col. Frederick 487, 532, 545, 583
Ponsonby, George 414, 590
Popham, Cdre Sir Home 185, 218, 462, 475, 486
Portland, Duke of 209–10, 266–7, 269, 287, 348
    becomes Prime Minister 188, 189
    and AW's appointment as Chief Secretary for Ireland 190
    high opinion of AW 292
Portugal
    1807 occupation by the French 224
    uprising against the French 233, 235–6
    AW proposes that Britain rebuild Portuguese army 238–9
    Portuguese troops join AW's army 243
    appeals to Britain for assistance 292–3
    AW's memorandum on its defence 294
    idea that it was indefensible 316, 373
    AW discusses future of commitment to, after Talavera 347–8, 351–2
    Wellington's plans for the defence of 360–9
    compared to Spain 359
    civilian population and the French invasion of 1810–11 383–4, 394–5, 400, 407–8
    strains in alliance 399–401
    foundation of British strategy in the Peninsula 415
    1813 disputes with Portuguese government 550–1
    role in the allied victory 585
    see also Army, Portuguese
    press 400, 435, 551–2
        AW's views of 178–9, 226
        and the campaign of 1808 and Cintra 1–2, 265, 268, 270–2, 278
public opinion
    and India 59–60, 64
    and Seringapatam 89–90
    AW's reputation in 1805 169–70
    Lord Wellesley's campaign to defend his reputation 178–9
    and Copenhagen expedition 214–5, 219
    enthusiasm about Spanish uprising 230–1, 264
    and news of Vimeiro 265–7

and Convention of Cintra 1, 264, 267–8,
    271–2, 274, 281–2
and the Mary Anne Clarke affair 287–8
and Oporto 315–7
and the Talavera campaign 342–4
and Busaco 392–3
awaits decisive battle 401–2
and news of Masséna's retreat 413–14
views of subsequent operations 433–5
and Salamanca 475
Purneah (minister of Mysore) 90, 99,
    104, 164, 166, *Plate 14*
Pyche Raja 93, 96, 101
Pyrenees, battles of the
    Roncesvalles 540–1
    Maya 541
    first Sorauren 542–4
    second Sorauren 544–5

Rainier, Adm. Peter 51, 94, 96, 97, 165, 169
Raleigh, Sir Walter 534
Ramsay, Capt. Norman 532
Rao *see* Amrit Rao; Baji Rao II; Gaikwar of
    Baroda
Raymond (French officer in Hyderabad)
    61, 63
regency crisis 402–3
Regiments of the British Army
    5th Dragoon Guards 471
    3rd Dragoons 471
    4th Dragoons 471
    10th Hussars 530
    12th Light Dragoons 10, 19–20
    14th Light Dragoons 313, 422, 531
    15th Hussars 530
    16th Light Dragoons 487
    18th Hussars 530
    19th Light Dragoons 95, 119, 139–41
    20th Light Dragoons 240, 252–3
    23rd Light Dragoons 322, 338
    25th Light Dragoons 70, 95
    Guards 303, 314, 322, 329, 336–8, 423, 486
    1st Regiment (Royal Scots) 540
    3rd Regiment (the Buffs) 176, 306, 311, 332
    4th Regiment 426
    5th Regiment 248, 454, 470
    7th Regiment (Fusiliers) 306, 430, 544
    8th Regiment 176
    9th Regiment 248, 388
    12th Regiment 45–7, 51, 81
    20th Regiment 544
    23rd Regiment 544
    24th Regiment 337, 419, 424
    27th Regiment 579
    29th Regiment 247–8, 254, 332
    31st Regiment 329
    33rd Regiment
        AW takes command 29–30

campaign in Low Countries 31–7
intended for West Indies 39–40
AW's regulations for shipboard
    routine 50
social life of officers in Bengal 48–9, 52
AW's standing orders 53
sent to Madras (1798) 66
AW keeps careful eye on 69
unites with the Nizam's army 74
at Malavelly 78
at Sultanpettah Tope 81–2
AW promoted out of the regiment 100
no part in the restoration of the
    Peshwa 120
AW leaves 164
AW appointed Colonel 176
34th Regiment 353, 385
36th Regiment 176, 233, 239, 253–4, 426
38th Regiment 410
40th Regiment 322, 356, 544, 579–80
41st Regiment 10
42nd Regiment 582
43rd Regiment 212, 252–3, 303, 379,
    389–90, 410, 443, 483–4, 546, 560
45th Regiment 233, 329, 388, 571
48th Regiment 312, 322. 332, 337
50th Regiment 252
52nd Regiment 212, 252, 303, 378, 389–90,
    410, 427, 440, 442
53rd Regiment 360
58th Regiment 11, 20
60th Regiment (5th battalion) 329
61st Regiment 322
66th Regiment 312
71st Regiment 254, 419–21, 424, 526
73rd Regiment 10
74th Regiment
    at Seringapatam 84
    and restoration of the Peshwa 120
    at Assaye 138–9, 141, 143
    at Busaco 387–8
    at Fuentes de Oñoro 424
    at Ciudad Rodrigo 442
76th Regiment 10
78th Regiment 130, 132–3, 138–41
79th Regiment 419, 424, 428, 487
82nd Regiment 253
85th Regiment 422–3
86th Regiment 45
87th Regiment 329, 332
88th Regiment 329, 332, 375
    at Busaco 388
    at Fuentes de Oñoro 424
    at Ciudad Rodrigo 442–3
    Wellington's opinion of 512
92nd Regiment 212, 214
94th Regiment (or Scotch Brigade) 120,
    130, 560

95th Rifles 53, 212, 214, 215, 303, 378, 389, 410, 442–3, 535, 549
97th Regiment 252
King's German Legion
   1st Hussars 322, 338, 410
   5th Line Battalion 334
   6th Line Battalion 214
   7th Line Battalion 332
   Chasseurs Brittaniques 423
Reynier, Gen. J. 377, 382, 387–8, 397
Richmond, 4th Duke of 16, 194, 195, 288, 295, *Plate 15*
   relations with AW 192, 207, 211, 221, 223, 224
   as Lord Lieutenant 192, 196, 199, 219–20, 223, 226–7
   excessive hospitality 223
   defends AW over Cintra 271
   offers to serve under Wellington 531
Ridewood, Maj. Henry 427–8
The Rivals (Sheridan) 502
Robe, Lt.-Col. William 240–1, 488
Roberts, Lt.-Col. George 63
Robertson, Capt. Duncan 530
Robinson, Maj.-Gen. Frederick 557, 564
Robinson, H.B. 526–7
Rogers, Samuel 140
Rolica, combat of 1, 245–9
Romana, Marquis de la 231, 397
Romilly, Samuel 223
Roncesvalles, combat of 540–1
Rosslyn, Lt.-Gen. Lord 215
Rothschild, Nathan Meyer 568
Rous, Ensign John 561
Rovera, Maj. Alexander de 390
Rowley, Ensign George 75, 78, 82
Russell, Lord John 508
Russell, Maj. Lord William 508
Ruxton, Mr 17
Ryder, Richard 192, 276, 380, 401
Rye, AW elected MP for 180

Sabugal, combat of 412
Salabut Khan 96, 164
Salamanca, campaign and battle of 461–75
Salisbury, Lady 187, 591
Salmond, Capt. 183
Sanchez, Julian 422, 480
San Marcial, battle of 549
San Sebastian 532, 539–40, 547–9, 551–2
Saxton, Sir Charles 271, 275
Schaumann, Augustus 384, 390
Scott, Walter 413–14
Scovell, Lt.-Col. George 391, 424, 497, 512
'scum of the earth' 533–6
Sebastiani, Gen. H. 321, 324–8, 336–8
Sedaseer, action at 75–6
Seringapatam, siege and storm of 79–85, 89

Shawe, Col. Merrick (or Meyrick) 152–6, 166
Shawe, Col. Robert 81
Shee, Maj. John 69, 100–101
Sherbrooke, Maj.-Gen. John Coape 69, 84, 91–2, 101, 180, 374
   under AW in the 33rd 29–30
   sent to Portugal 293
   in Oporto campaign 303, 307
   in Talavera campaign 322, 328–9, 335–8
Sherer, Lt. Moyle 353, 385, 390, 526
Sheridan, Richard Brinsley 206, 502
Shore, Sir John 47, 50, 55, 57, 60, 62, 107, 183
sickness in the army in the Peninsula 322, 345–6, 355–6, 359, 402, 405, 437, 463, 483, 519, 567
Sidmouth *see* Addington
Silveira, Lt.-Gen. Francisco (Conde de Amarante) 308, 310, 313
Simmons, Lt. George 424
Sindia, Daulat Rao
   and internal conflicts in Maratha Confederacy 106–12
   British intervention to restore the Peshwa 122–4
   the path to war 126–30
   his army 131
   Assaye campaign 135–6
   effects of Assaye 141, 143–4
   peace overtures 144
   peace terms 147–9, 152–3
   and subsidiary alliance 148, 150, 153
   role in 1804 war with Holkar 157
Siniavin, Adm. 224, 244, 259–60, 447
Smith, Anne Culling (AW's sister) 6, 21, 41, 171, 195
Smith, Charles Culling (husband of AW's sister Anne) 6, 171
Smith, Capt. Harry 455, 559
Somers, Lord 487
Somerset, Lt.-Col. Lord Edward 530, 581
Somerset, Lt.-Col. Lord Fitzroy 234–5, 239, 426, 474, 495, 497, 499, 505, 506, 543
Sorauren
   first battle of 542–4
   second battle of 544–5
Souham, Gen. J. 488–9
Soult, Marshal *Plate 22*
   and Oporto campaign 305–15
   and Talavera campaign 325, 328, 335, 340–1
   besieges Badajoz 405–6, 411
   attempts to relieve Badajoz 417–8, 429–30, 433
   at Albuera 429–30
   and British siege of Badajoz (1812) 451
   and Wellington's plans after Salamanca 478–80, 484
   advances against Wellington 488–90

recalled by Napoleon 519
takes command of the Army of
    Spain 538–9
battles of the Pyrenees 540–7
final attempt to relieve San Sebastian 549
on the Bidassoa 557–8
on the Nivelle 559–61
battles of the Nive 562–4
Napoleon withdraws many of his
    troops 566–7
at Orthez 570–2, 573
at Toulouse 576–82
Sousa Coutinho, Chevalier de 267
Sousa, José Antonio ('the Principal') 399
Spain
    Napoleon deposes royal family 229–30
    insurrection against the French 230–2
    AW condemns conduct of Spanish
        government 348
    continuing Spanish resistance 359
    Wellington given command of Spanish
        armies 517–18
    insurrection against the French 518–9
    Wellington's disputes with the Spanish
        government 551–2
    refuses separate peace with Napoleon 566
    role in the allied victory 585
Sparrow, Olivia 172, 173, 191
specie, shortages of 318, 322–4, 371–3, 415,
    550, 567–8
Spencer, Lt-Gen. Sir Brent 180, 230, 232, 236,
    240–1, 246, 253, 382, 438
    and Cintra Inquiry 278–9
    returns to Portugal as second-in-command
        374–5
Stanhope, Capt. Fitzroy 211, 234, 315
Stanhope, Lady Hester 234
Stanhope, Lt-Col. James 398
Stevenson, Col. James 155
    commands contingent from Hyderabad
        120, 123, 125, 128, 130
    Assaye campaign 135–6
    captures Burhampore and Asseerghur 143
    at Argaum 144–6
    at Gawilghur 146–7
Stewart, Maj.-Gen. Sir Charles (later Lord
    Londonderry) 180, 267, 294, 313,
    398, 418, 481–2, 496, Plate 38
    character 308
    and Wellington 381–2, 512, 513–14, 515
    on a young woman at headquarters 353–4
    pessimistic 357, 374, 380
    and Busaco 392, 395
    tedium of paperwork 508–9
Stewart, Lt-Col. John 248
Stewart, Brig. Richard 232, 334
Stewart, Maj.-Gen. William 490, 541, 564
St George, Melisina (later Trench) 16

St George, Lt-Col. Richard 15–16
St Leger, Maj.-Gen. John 48, 49, 50
St Vincent, Adm. Lord 275
Stokes, Mr 96–7
Stothert, Capt. William 326, 337, 339
Stretford, Mrs 18
Stuart, Lt-Gen. Sir Charles 232
Stuart, Charles (diplomat) 235, 369,
    384, 399–400, Plate 40
Stuart, Lt-Gen. James, 72, 113, 114, 116,
    118–19, 120, 122, 131, 160
Stuart, Peter 178
Suchet, Marshal L.G. 305, 320, 463, 488, 520,
    532, 537, 554–5, 563, 566, 573
Sultanpettah Tope 80–3
Swettenham, Ann Maria 18
Sydenham, Benjamin 163, 208
Sydenham, Thomas 108, 477, 487

Talavera, campaign of 320–42
Talleyrand-Périgord, Charles-Maurice de,
    Prince 576
Tarleton, Gen. Banastre 285, 414
Taupin, Gen. E.C. 468–9, 471, 571, 581
Temple, Lord (later 1st Duke of
    Buckingham and Chandos) 13,
    179, 183, 273–4
33rd Regiment see under Regiments of the
    British Army
Thornton, James 504
'Threshers' 199
Tierney, George 188, 380
Tilsit 210
The Times 169
    support for Spanish uprising 230, 265
    on Cintra 1, 268, 271, 278
    opinion of AW 279–80
    on Portugal (1810) 401
    on Fuentes de Oñoro and Albuera 434
    on reappointment of the Duke of
        York 435
Tipu, Sultan of Mysore 51, 57–9, 85–6,
    88, 90, 383, Plate 10
    hostility to the British 61
    overtures to the French 61–3
    and outbreak of war 71
    and the campaign 75–9
    and siege of Seringapatam 79–85
Tomkinson, Capt. William 310, 384
Torrens, Lt-Col. Henry 235, 278, 476–7,
    482–3, 509, 513, 515, 531, 564
Torres Vedras, Lines of see Lines of Torres
    Vedras
Toulouse, battle of 576–83
Trail, James 193, 201, 211, 223, 233, 262
Trant, Lt-Col. Nicholas 243, 245, 364, 385,
    391, 396, 408
Trench, Lt-Col. Richard 387

Trim, AW as MP for, in the Irish Parliament 21–2

Tucker, Capt. T. Edwardes 577

United States, grain exports from 438

Valençay, Treaty of 566
Vellore mutiny 90, 188
Venegas, Gen. F. 321, 324–5, 328, 335, 340, 346
Venezuela, proposed expedition to 187–8
Venta del Pozo, combat of 489
Vera, combat of 549
Victor, Marshal 304–5, 321, 324–42
Villiers, J.C. 292, 301–2, 369, 476, 497
Vimeiro, battle of 1, 251–7, 265–6
Vitoria, campaign and battle of 520–9

Wagram, battle of 318, 340
Walcheren expedition 318–9, 437
Wallace, Thomas, MP 179, 227
Wallace, Lt.-Col. William 120, 134, 156, 162
Ward, J.W. 181
Wardle, Gwyllym 286, 288
Warre, Capt. William 234, 256, 356, 502
Waterford, Marquess of 180
Waters, Lt.-Col. John 311, 496–7
Waugh, Dhoondiah 93–6
Webbe, Josiah 68, 94, 99, 104, 112–13, 116, 119, 160
  and intervention to restore the Peshwa 117, 120–1, 123
  illness and death 162–3
Wellesley, Anne (AW's sister) see Smith, Anne Culling
Wellesley, Arthur, 1st Duke of Wellington
  family and private life
    birth and background 5–10, 15–26, 597
    Wellesley name 65
    appearance 11, 18, 46, 54, 70, 99, 101, 291, 499–500, 501, 511, 517–18
    health 31–2, 39, 98, 155, 163, 166, 356, 416, 418
    recreations 8, 10, 20, 25, 28, 29, 46, 48, 52, 54, 101–2, 122, 140, 170–1, 187, 223, 290, 354, 499, 501–2, 505
    social life 15–26, 48, 52, 90, 101–2, 103, 192, 503, 221–3
    amours 18, 19, 27–8, 102–3, 290–1, 353–4, 481, 503
    marriage 172–5, 181, 187, 221–2, 230, 289–90
    children 19, 102–3, 187, 205–6, 222, 511, 516
    money 19, 21, 26, 52, 89, 104, 164, 176, 181, 222, 343, 444, 476, 477, 590
    religious views 307, 503–4
    makes will (1807) 192

  portraits 40–1, 161, 354, 481, 504, *Plates 1, 5, 9, 16, 17, 18, 31, 35, 53, 63, 65 and 66*
  public career
    junior officer and ADC 9–11, 13–14, 19–20, 28
    MP in Irish Parliament 21–5, 199
    lack of independence 25–8
    in Low Countries 31–7
    seeks civilian office 37–9, 40
    in Bengal and Penang 45–53
    the war with Tipu 63, 70–87
    commands in Mysore 87–93, 99–103, 159–60
    determination to protect civilian population 91, 100
    campaign against Dhoondiah Waugh 93–6
    Mauritius expedition and supercession by Baird 94, 96–99, 153
    opposes intervention in Maratha affairs 108–110
    and restoration of the Peshwa 112–25
    and Maratha War 129–53
      battle of Assaye 136–43
    leaves India 153, 155, 162–4
    meets Nelson 170
    defends Richard's conduct in India 175, 178–9, 182–4, 227
    elected MP at Westminster 179–81, 186, 198
    as a parliamentarian 206–7, 228
    importance of political connections 2, 12, 16, 37–8, 175–6, 180–1, 219, 292–5
    expedition to Latin America 185–6, 187–8, 229–30
    as Chief Secretary for Ireland 190–207, 219–27, 284, 296
    and Copenhagen expedition 208–19
    expedition to Portugal (1808) 232–63
      Roliça 245–9
      Vimiero 251–7
    Convention of Cintra 1–2, 181, 258–60, 264, 269–86
    Cabinet debates sending him back to Portugal (1809) 292–6
    Oporto campaign 305–15
    Talavera campaign 319–42
    plans for the defence of Portugal 360–9
    Busaco campaign 378–93
    at Torres Vedras 397–403
    pursues the French as they retreat from Portugal 407–13
    battle of Fuentes de Oñoro 418–25
    relations with his army 425–9
    does not go home throughout the war 438, 503

siege of Ciudad Rodrigo 439–45
siege of Badajoz 447–57
Salamanca campaign 461–75
enters Madrid 480–1
siege of Burgos 485–8
retreat from Burgos 488–91
life on campaign 494–7, 500–2, 504
working methods 497–8, 509
lack of formality and outward show 511
relations with his staff 511–16
given command of the Spanish armies
        517–18
Vitoria campaign 520–9
fury at subsequent misconduct of troops
        530, 533–6
battles of the Pyrenees 540–7
reluctance to invade France 553–6,
        561, 565
passage of the Bidassoa 557–8
battle of the Nivelle 559–61
battles of the Nive 562–4
and the Bourbon cause 565, 569, 573–6
battle of Orthez 570–2
battle of Toulouse 578–83
reaction to Napoleon's abdication 583
character
    ability to absorb information 46
    ambition 98, 100, 155, 162, 166, 185,
        191, 207–9, 426–7, 513
    grumbling and use of exaggerated
        language 128, 322–3, 372–3,
        402–3, 550
    slides into despair when thwarted
        128, 257
    vanity 156, 166, 499–500, 502
    strong sense of duty 162, 184–5, 208–9
    pride 266–7
    burden of responsibility 357, 429
    sarcasm, sharpness and ill-temper
        381–2, 491, 511–4, 533
    physical toughness and stamina 416,
        500–1
    lack of humbug 511
    emotional reticence 516
characteristics as a general
    lessons learnt in the Low Countries
        34, 37
    concern for logistics 70, 92–3, 94, 97,
        114, 128, 322–3
    skill in cooperating with allies 87,
        96, 165
    determination to protect civilian
        population 91, 121, 132, 165,
        215–16, 240, 321–2, 346, 383, 410,
        530, 536, 553–4, 572–3
    favours 'light and quick' operations 93,
        114–6
    unremitting aggression 94, 132, 135

style of his General Orders 121, 427
cool and collected in battle 142, 255
his boldness 313
reluctance to delegate 379, 412, 430–1,
        465, 481, 483, 509, 512, 537,
        539–42, 547, 588
ability as a strategist 531
opinions and beliefs
    the Ancien Régime 10
    Ireland 21–5, 191–2, 201, 225
    India and Indians 49
    British expansion in India (1800) 108–110
    political justice and aggressive wars
        109–10
    the subsidiary system 150
    political superiors 154–5, 218
    the power of the press 178–9, 272
    Pittites 179, 191, 349–50
    party politics 191, 349–50, 461
    flogging in the army 228, 534–5
    horror of revolution 229
    Perceval and government 349–50, 445,
        459, 461
    Napoleon's regime 431
    Lord Wellesley's resignation 445
    Catholic Emancipation 460
    Spanish liberales 552
sayings and anecdotes attrib. to or about
        Wellington 2, 9, 20, 184, 191,
        208–9, 256, 348, 382, 392, 431, 542,
        489, 490, 512, 546, 551, 588
    'playing fields of Eton' 7–8
    'grown d_____d ugly' 181
    'publish and be damned' 290
    'scum of the earth' 533–6
honours and rewards 89, 156, 262
    KB 164, 169
    appointed Colonel of the 33rd 176
    Thanked in Parliament 225–6, 283, 371,
        414
    elevated to the peerage 343
    made an Earl 444
    made a Marquess 476
    arms augmented by the Union Jack 476
    promoted Field Marshal after Vitoria 531
    made a Duke 590
Wellesley, Arthur Richard (AW's son) 187,
        Plate 32
Wellesley, Catherine (Kitty, Duchess of
        Wellington) Plate 6
    AW's courtship 27–8
    illness (1795–96) 40
    marriage to AW 172–5, 181, 187, 221–2,
        289–90
    and Queen Charlotte 182
    children 187, 222
    does something she regrets 222, 289–90
    on news of Salamanca 475

Wellesley, Charles (AW's second son) 222,
    Plate 32
Wellesley, Gerald (AW's younger brother) 6,
    21, 41, 171, 181, 196, 550
Wellesley, Henry (later Lord Cowley, AW's
    youngest brother) 6–7, 21, 41, 104,
    153, 187, 507
  and relations between Richard and
    Arthur 66, 99
  marries Lady Charlotte Cadogan 171
  accused of murder by James Paull 182
  Secretary to the Treasury 190, 197–8
  collapse of his marriage 291–2
  sent as Ambassador to Cadiz rather than
    Lisbon 369
Wellesley, Hyacinthe (Richard's wife)
    41–2, 266
Wellesley, Richard, Lord Mornington,
    Marquess Wellesley (AW's eldest
    brother) 6–9, 41–2, 161, Plate 4
  assists AW's early career 10–11, 14, 38–9
  always short of money 19, 21
  sells Irish estates 21
  brings AW into Irish Parliament 21
  appointed Governor-General of Bengal 55,
    56, 59, 60
  his approach to India 60–2
  and war with Tipu 63, 70–1
  disbands French corps in Hyderabad 63–4
  relations with AW in Bengal 65–7
  praises AW's role at Madras 71
  dispute with army over prize money 89
  anguish over Irish marquessate 90
  proposes expedition to Batavia 94
  proposed expedition to Mauritius 96–7
  gives Baird command of the force at
    Trincomalee 97
  damage to relations with AW 98–9
  position weakened by Pitt's resignation 104,
    117, 153
  policy towards the Maratha Confederacy
    61, 107–8, 112, 117, 125, 126
  and peace terms negotiated by AW 149–53
  urged to go home 153–4
  and war with Holkar 156
  return to England 176–7
  defends against James Paull 177–9, 182–4,
    187, 227
  declines the Foreign Office 189
  presses for a command for AW in
    Copenhagen expedition 208
  and news of Vimeiro 266
  presses for AW to be granted a peerage
    (1808) 266
  defends AW over Cintra 270
  fury at attacks in Morning Chronicle 275
  as Ambassador to Spain 347
  becomes Foreign Secretary 348, 350

  expects to dominate Perceval's government
    348–9, 370
  alienated and inefficient as a minister
    370–1
  failed bid for power 444–5, 458
  and news of Salamanca 475–6
Wellesley-Pole, Katherine (William's wife) 41
Wellesley-Pole, Priscilla (AW's niece)
    14, 172
Wellesley-Pole, William (AW's elder brother;
    later Lord Maryborough) 6, 41,
    171–2, 175, 183, 187, 238, 261, 349,
    531, 550, Plate 29
  inherits Pole estates 21
  defends AW's probity in Parliament 59
  as Secretary to the Admiralty 189–90
  claims on Irish patronage 196
  AW's letters to 247, 257, 260, 266, 349–50,
    370, 373, 392, 402–3, 424, 431,
    477–8, 498, 542, 546, 547, 550
  defends AW over Cintra 270–1, 275, 286
  chooses AW's titles 343
  assures Welington of government's
    support 403
  declines the War Department 459–61
Wellesley-Pole, William (AW's nephew; later
    Pole-Tylney-Long-Wellesley, 4th
    Earl of Mornington) 172, 234
Welsh, Capt. James 132, 145
Weser expedition 176
Wesley, Anne (AW's mother) see Mornington,
    Lady, Anne Wesley
Wesley, Garret (AW's father) see Mornington,
    Lord, Garret Wesley
West, Capt. Francis (AW's ADC) 101, 102
Westmorland, John Fane, Lord 13–14, 24,
    175, 198
Whitbread, Samuel 206, 272, 283–4, 286,
    316–17, 350, 414, 482, 590
Whitelocke, Lt-Gen. John 1–2, 188, 229, 234,
    235, 268
Whitlock the second or another tarnish of
    British valor 274, Plate 28
Whitman, Charles 496–7
Wilberforce, William 219, 287, 289
Williams, Charles 265, 274
Williams, Robert 16–17
Wilson, Harriette 290–1, Plate 30
Windham, William 180, 185, 187, 188,
    286, 354
Worcester, Capt. Henry, Lord 505
Wyatt, Benjamin Dean 223–4
Wynn, Charles Williams 288–9

York, Duke of 16, 176, 188, 199, 206, 209, 235,
    237, 241, 262, 265, 343, 434, 482,
    531, 587, Plate 26
  commands in the Low Countries 31–4

appointed C-in-C 34–5
prejudiced against AW 87, 169, 176, 228
possibly cuckolded by AW's
     brother-in-law 171
assures AW regarding political
     office 190, 209
and Cintra 273, 276, 280

and the Mary Anne Clarke affair 286–9
  selects Beresford for Portugal 292
Yorke, Charles 192
Yorke, Henry Redhead 178

Zeman Shah of Afghanistan 61–2
Zouche, Lady de la 17